INTERIOR DESIGN

by

Stephanie A. Clemons, Ph.D., FASID, FIDEC
Colorado State University
Fort Collins, Colorado

Publisher
The Goodheart-Willcox Company, Inc.
Tinley Park, Illinois
www.g-w.com

Manufactured in the United States of America.

Hardcover ISBN: 978-1-61960-242-7
Softcover ISBN: 978-1-63126-504-4

1 2 3 4 5 6 7 8 9 10 — 17 — 20 19 18 17 16 15

Cover Image: ©Judy Davis/Hoachlander Davis Photography/Designed by ForrestPerkins

About the Author

Dr. Stephanie Clemons, Ph.D., FASID, FIDEC, has been a professor of interior design for over 25 years at Colorado State University (CSU). She has been the recipient of both the *Outstanding Teacher* and *Advisor* awards from her college, *Best Teacher* award from the Alumni Association, the *University Distinguished Teaching Scholar* award (2014), and the *Board of Governors Undergraduate Excellence in Teaching* award (2015) from the campus. For the last 15 years, her research focus has involved working with high school interior design instructors.

Within the profession, Dr. Clemons has served in numerous leadership positions including President of both the Interior Design Educators Council (IDEC) and the IDEC Foundation. In addition, Dr. Clemons has been Chair of the *Journal of Interior Design* and Chair, *K-12 Network*. She is currently serving as *Chair* of the National Board of Directors for the *American Society of Interior Designers (ASID).* Dr. Clemons was awarded the *Fellow Award* from both IDEC and ASID in recognition of her contributions to their organizations and the field of interior design.

Dr. Clemons has also cochaired the development of high school interior design standards for the state of Colorado, codeveloped teaching modules for high school interior design teachers (see the IDEC website), served as one of the developers for the *AAFCS Pre-Professional Assessment and Certification* for *Interior Design Fundamentals Assessment and Credential*, authored 4HCC interior design lesson plans, served on a subcommittee for revisions to the national Housing and Interior standards, participated in textbook adoption processes, coauthored the *STAR Event Interior Design Competition Scenario* for high school interior design students for four years, and offered many workshops for interior design instructors in a three-state radius. Dr. Clemons offers an online residential interior certificate for high school interior design teachers through her institution.

Reviewers

The author and publisher are grateful to the following reviewers who provided valuable input to this edition.

Rebecca Amy
Interior Design Professional and FCS Teacher
Shawnee High School
Medford, NJ

Katey Armstrong
Instructor
West Aurora High School
Aurora, IL

Barbara J. Bush
National Board Certified Teacher
Family and Consumer Sciences Building Chair
Normal Community West High School
Normal, IL

Alexis Smith
Interior Design Instructor
Central High School
Omaha, NE

Joanne Grogan
Interior Design/FACS Instructor
Joe E. Newsome High School
Lithia, FL

Carrie Humphrys, EdS
Interior Design and Fashion Design Instructor
Viera High School
Interior Design Instructor
Eastern Florida State College
Cocoa, FL

Tanja Huffman
Lead Faculty, Interior Design
Spokane Falls Community College
Spokane, WA

Vicki LaBeau
Instructor/Consultant
East Valley High School
Yakima, WA

Kathleen Leddy
Career and Technology Teacher
Dubiski Career High School
Grand Prairie, TX

Connie Lutz
FACS Teacher
Shawnee Mission Northwest High School
Shawnee, KS

Lindsay Posillico
Family and Consumer Sciences Teacher
Gardner Edgerton High School
Gardner, KS

Sandra Reicis
Associate Professor of Interior Design
Art Department Chairperson
Villa Maria College
Buffalo, NY

Kristin Skorupa
FACS Teacher
Lincoln Northeast High School
Lincoln, NE

Malissa Sloan, M.A.
Interior Design Educator
Career and Technical Education Department Chair
Standley Lake High School
Westminster, CO

Contents in Brief

Contents

Unit 1

Unit 2

Features

DESIGNER PROFILE

CASE STUDY

DESIGNER MATH SKILLS

LINK TO HISTORY

STUDENT SPOTLIGHT

Captivating Illustrations Engage Learners

Images and illustrations convey important design information and details about creating functional, yet aesthetically pleasing, interiors

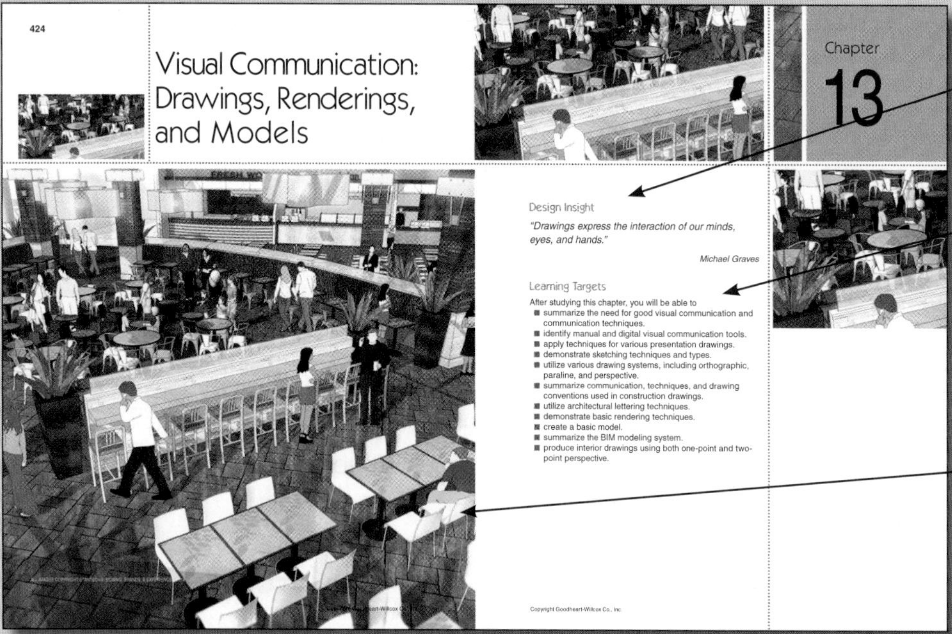

Inspiring quotes capture learner attention

Learning Targets focus students on key concepts and skills

Motivating chapter opening visuals focus on various aspects of interior design

Professional designers showcase their visual examples

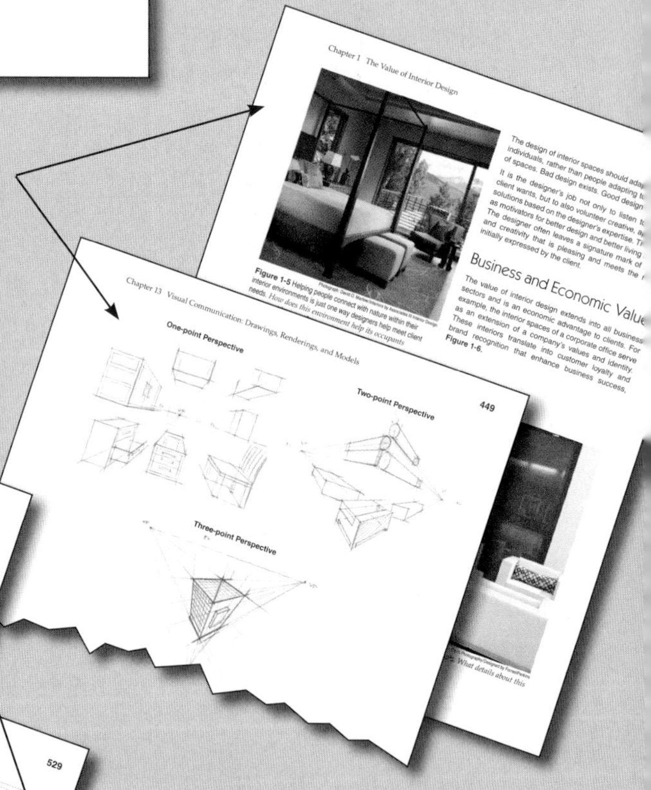

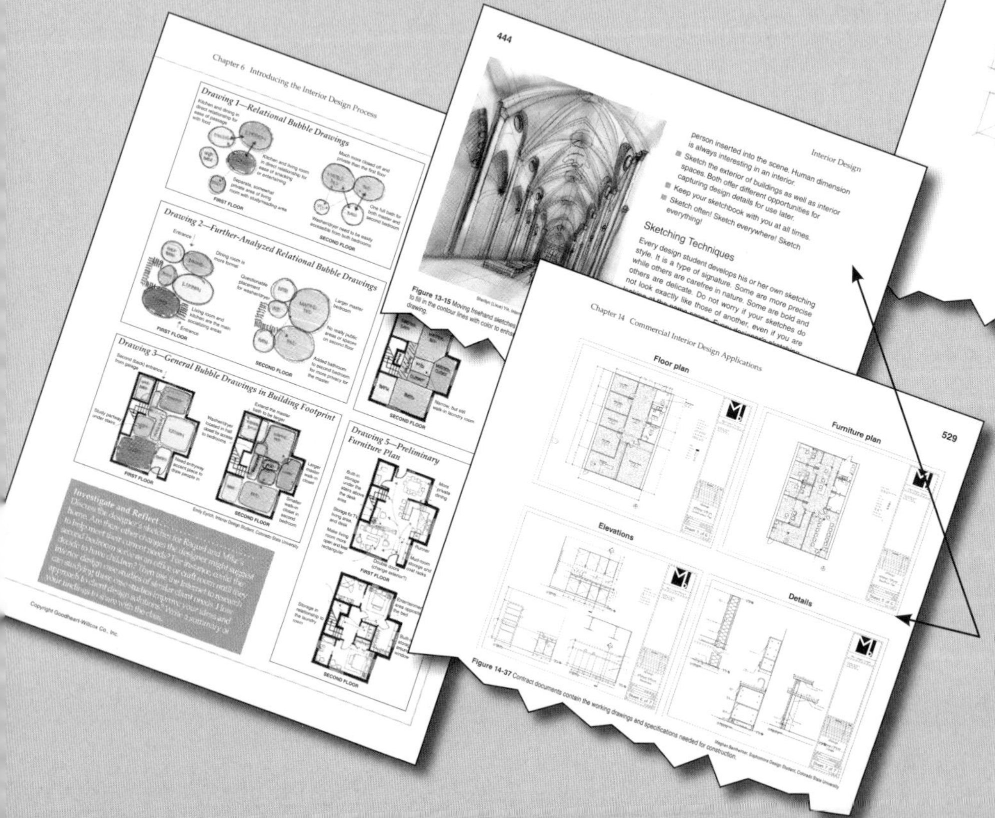

Student "designers in progress" demonstrate their skill development

Features Integrate Learning

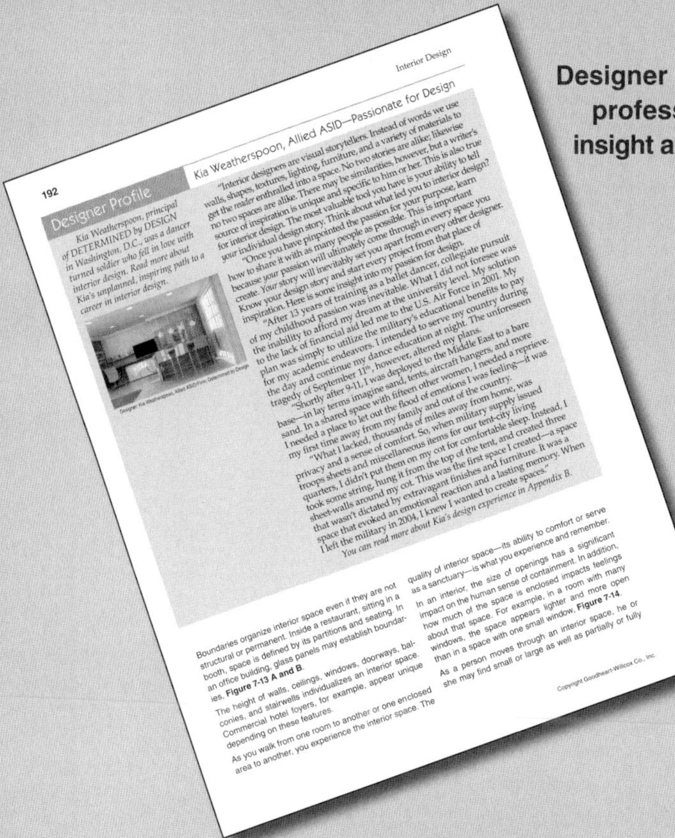

Designer Profile—Renowned professionals share job insight and relevant issues

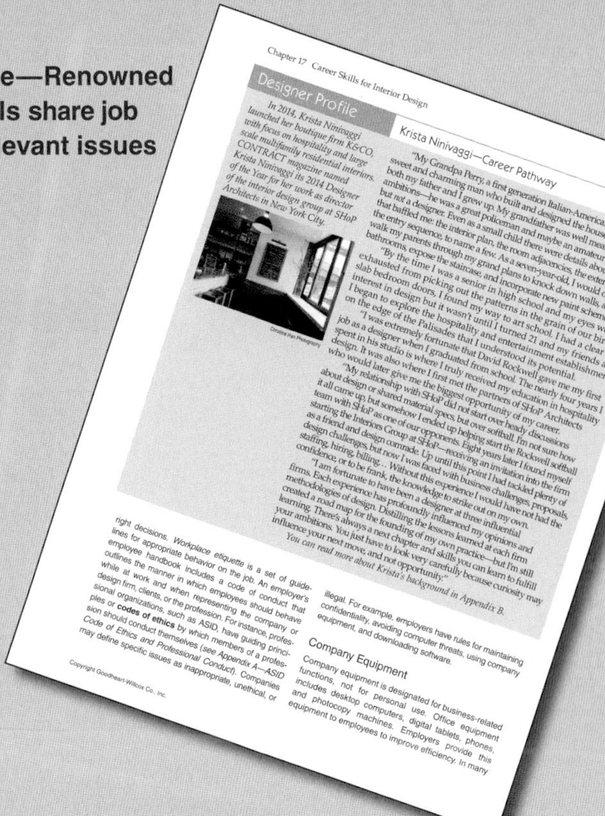

Case Study—Real-life examples focus on interior design issues and chapter concepts; include Investigate and Reflect follow-up questions and activities

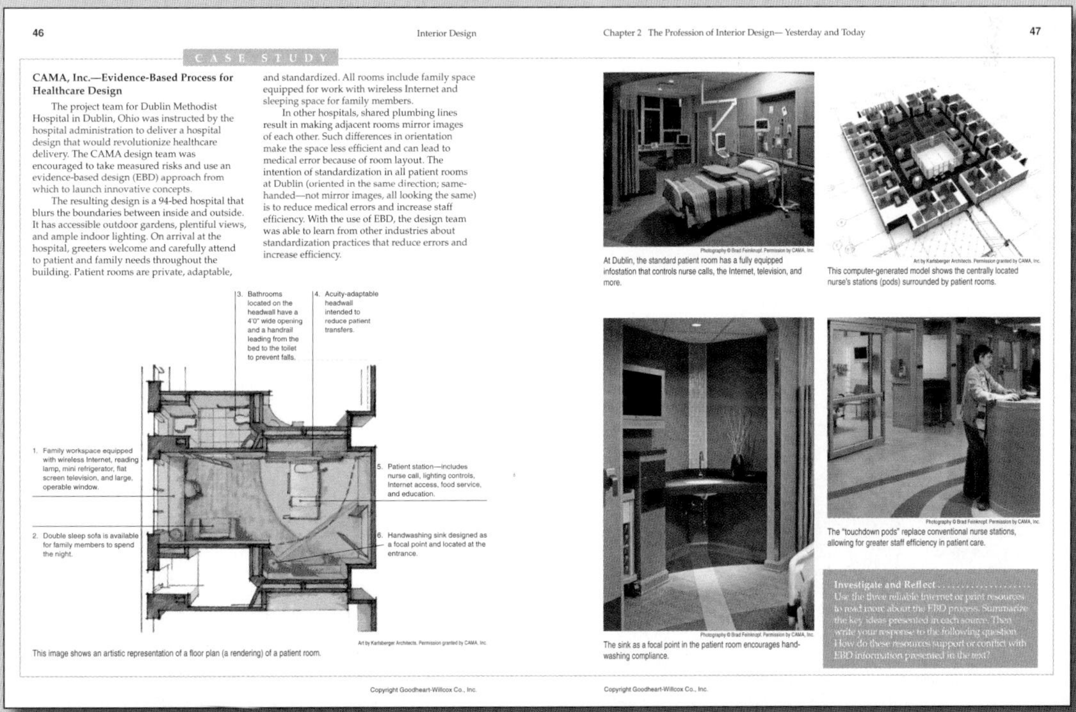

46 Interior Design

CASE STUDY

CAMA, Inc.—Evidence-Based Process for Healthcare Design

The project team for Dublin Methodist Hospital in Dublin, Ohio was instructed by the hospital administration to deliver a hospital design that would revolutionize healthcare delivery. The CAMA design team was encouraged to take measured risks and use an evidence-based design (EBD) approach from which to launch innovative concepts.

The resulting design is a 94-bed hospital that blurs the boundaries between inside and outside. It has accessible outdoor gardens, plentiful views, and ample indoor lighting. On arrival at the hospital, greeters welcome and carefully attend to patient and family needs throughout the building. Patient rooms are private, adaptable, and standardized. All rooms include family space equipped for work with wireless Internet and sleeping space for family members.

In other hospitals, shared plumbing lines result in making adjacent rooms mirror images of each other. Such differences in orientation make the space less efficient and can lead to medical error because of room layout. The intention of standardization in all patient rooms at Dublin (oriented in the same direction; same-handed—not mirror images, all looking the same) is to reduce medical errors and increase staff efficiency. With the use of EBD, the design team was able to learn from other industries about standardization practices that reduce errors and increase efficiency.

Chapter 2 The Profession of Interior Design—Yesterday and Today 47

At Dublin, the standard patient room has a fully equipped infostation that controls nurse calls, the Internet, television, and more.

This computer-generated model shows the centrally located nurse's stations (pods) surrounded by patient rooms.

This image shows an artistic representation of a floor plan (a rendering) of a patient room.

The sink as a focal point in the patient room encourages hand-washing compliance.

The "touchdown pods" replace conventional nurse stations, allowing for greater staff efficiency in patient care.

Investigate and Reflect

Use the three reliable Internet or print resources to read more about the EBD process. Summarize the key ideas presented in each source. Then write your response to the following question: How do these resources support or conflict with EBD information presented in the text?

Features Expand Knowledge

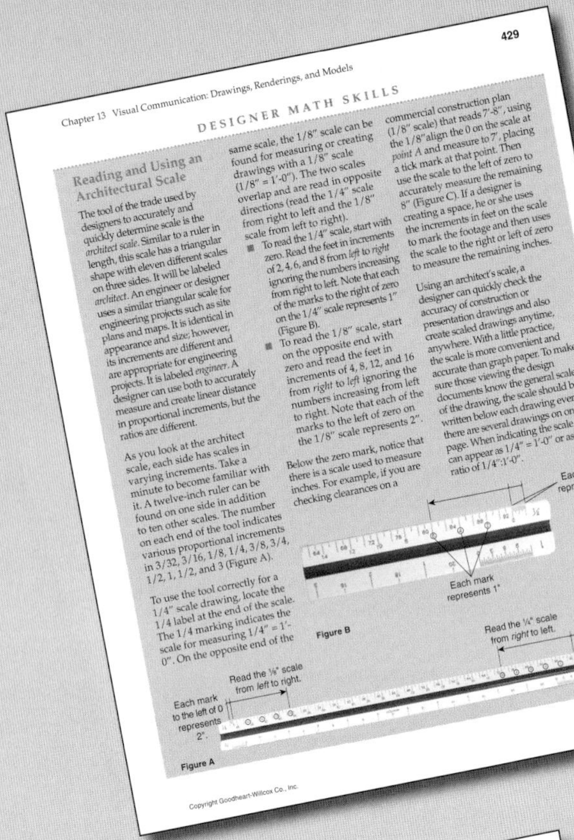

429

Chapter 13 Visual Communication: Drawings, Renderings, and Models

DESIGNER MATH SKILLS

Reading and Using an Architectural Scale

The tool of the trade used by designers to accurately and quickly determine scale is the *architect scale*. Similar to a ruler in length, this scale has a triangular shape with eleven different scales on three sides. It will be labeled *architect*. An engineer or designer uses a similar triangular scale for engineering projects such as site plans and maps. It is identical in appearance and size; however, its increments are different and are appropriate for engineering projects. It is labeled *engineer*. A designer can use both to accurately measure and create linear distance in proportional increments, but the ratios are different.

As you look at the architect scale, each side has scales in varying increments. Take a minute to become familiar with it. A twelve-inch ruler can be found on one side in addition to ten other scales. The number on each end of the tool indicates various proportional increments in 3/32, 3/16, 1/8, 1/4, 3/8, 3/4, 1/2, 1, 1 1/2, and 3 (Figure A).

To use the tool correctly for a 1/4" scale drawing, locate the 1/4 label at the end of the scale. The 1/4 marking indicates the scale for measuring 1/4" = 1'-0". On the opposite end of the same scale, the 1/8" scale can be found for measuring or creating drawings with a 1/8" scale (1/8" = 1'-0"). The two scales overlap and are read in opposite directions (read the 1/4" scale from right to left and the 1/8" scale from left to right).

- To read the 1/4" scale, start with zero. Read the feet in increments of 2, 4, 6, and 8 from *left to right* ignoring the numbers increasing from right to left. Note that each of the marks to the right of zero on the 1/4" scale represents 1" (Figure B).
- To read the 1/8" scale, start on the opposite end with zero and read the feet in increments of 4, 8, 12, and 16 from *right to left* ignoring the numbers increasing from left to right. Note that each of the marks to the left of zero on the 1/8" scale represents 2".

Below the zero mark, notice that there is a scale used to measure inches. For example, if you are checking clearances on a commercial construction plan (1/8" scale) that reads 7'-8", using the 1/8" align the 0 on the scale at *point A* and measure to 7', placing a tick mark at that point. Then use the scale to the left of zero to accurately measure the remaining 8" (Figure C). If a designer is creating a space, he or she uses the increments in feet on the scale to mark the footage and then uses the scale to the right or left of zero to measure the remaining inches.

Using an architect's scale, a designer can quickly check the accuracy of construction or presentation drawings and also create scaled drawings anytime, anywhere. With a little practice, the scale is more convenient and accurate than graph paper. To make sure those viewing the design documents know the general scale of the drawing, the scale should be written below each drawing even if there are several drawings on one page. When indicating the scale it can appear as 1/4" = 1'-0" or as a ratio of 1/4":1'-0".

Each mark represents 1"

Each mark represents 1"

Figure B

Read the ¼" scale from *right* to left.

Each mark to the right of 0 represents 1".

Read the ⅛" scale from *left* to right.

Each mark to the left of 0 represents 2".

Figure A

Copyright Goodheart-Willcox Co., Inc.

Designer Math Skills—Discuss math skills relating to chapter topics and interior design

Student Spotlight—Student "designers in progress" discuss their experiences

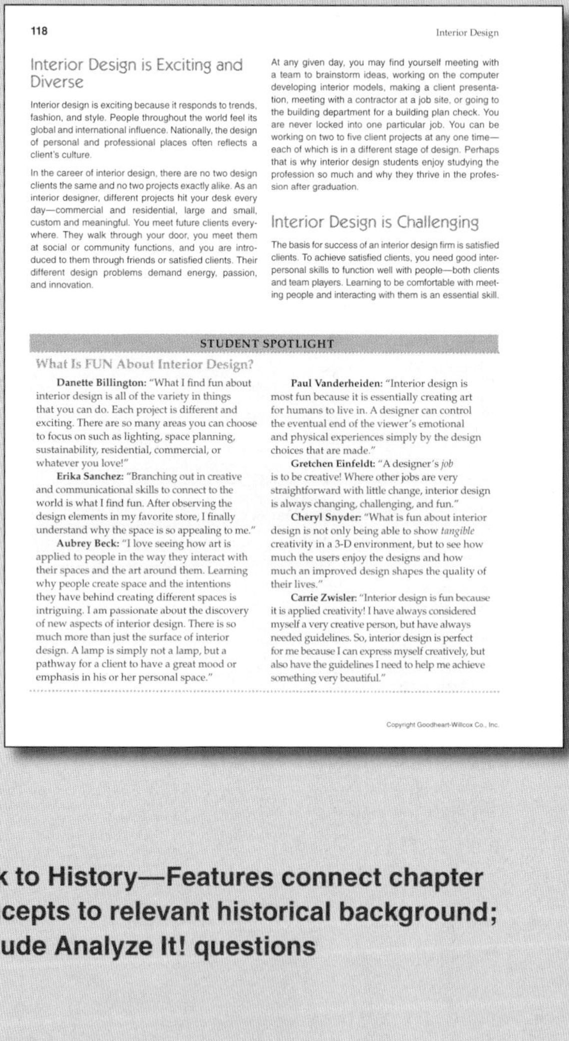

118 Interior Design

Interior Design is Exciting and Diverse

Interior design is exciting because it responds to trends, fashion, and style. People throughout the world feel its global and international influence. Nationally, the design of personal and professional places often reflects a client's culture.

In the career of interior design, there are no two design clients the same and no two projects exactly alike. As an interior designer, different projects hit your desk every day—commercial and residential, large and small, custom and meaningful. You meet future clients everywhere. They walk through your door, you meet them at social or community functions, and you are introduced to them through friends or satisfied clients. Their different design problems demand energy, passion, and innovation.

At any given day, you may find yourself meeting with a team to brainstorm ideas, working on the computer developing interior models, making a client presentation, meeting with a contractor at a job site, or going to the building department for a building plan check. You are never locked into one particular job. You can be working on two to five client projects at any one time—each of which is in a different stage of design. Perhaps that is why interior design students enjoy studying the profession so much and why they thrive in the profession after graduation.

Interior Design is Challenging

The basis for success of an interior design firm is satisfied clients. To achieve satisfied clients, you need good interpersonal skills to function well with people—both clients and team players. Learning to be comfortable with meeting people and interacting with them is an essential skill.

STUDENT SPOTLIGHT

What Is FUN About Interior Design?

Danette Billington: "What I find fun about interior design is all of the variety in things that you can do. Each project is different and exciting. There are so many areas you can choose to focus on such as lighting, space planning, sustainability, residential, commercial, or whatever you love!"

Erika Sanchez: "Branching out in creative and communicational skills to connect to the world is what I find fun. After observing the design elements in my favorite store, I finally understand why the space is so appealing to me."

Aubrey Beck: "I love seeing how art is applied to people in the way they interact with their spaces and the art around them. Learning why people create space and the intentions they have behind creating different spaces is intriguing. I am passionate about the discovery of new aspects of interior design. There is so much more than just the surface of interior design. A lamp is simply not a lamp, but a pathway for a client to have a great mood or emphasis in his or her personal space."

Paul Vanderheiden: "Interior design is most fun because it is essentially creating art for humans to live in. A designer can control the eventual end of the viewer's emotional and physical experiences simply by the design choices that are made."

Gretchen Einfeldt: "A designer's *job* is to be creative! Where other jobs are very straightforward with little change, interior design is always changing, challenging, and fun."

Cheryl Snyder: "What is fun about interior design is not only being able to show *tangible* creativity in a 3-D environment, but to see how much the users enjoy the designs and how much an improved design shapes the quality of their lives."

Carrie Zwisler: "Interior design is fun because it is applied creativity! I have always considered myself a very creative person, but have always needed guidelines. So, interior design is perfect for me because I can express myself creatively, but also have the guidelines I need to help me achieve something very beautiful."

Copyright Goodheart-Willcox Co., Inc.

65

Chapter 3 Interior Design Specialty Areas of Practice

Link to History

Evolution of the Work Environment

Historically, work in the office is the same as it is today: moving the product out the door, tasks to complete, socialization, formal meetings, and storage or access to files. The goal was to help the company or employer prosper. As cities grew larger, during such years as the Victorian era, central business districts developed that were solely devoted to business activities. Because telephones did not exist, closeness was important for making business communication fast and easy. Skyscrapers and passenger elevators were developed to squeeze more people and work into limited space. Offices inside tall buildings were strictly utilitarian with rows of small offices arranged along corridors so that every office would have access to windows for light and ventilation. Private offices existed and waiting rooms boasted glazed wooden partitions. The office as a social setting was lost as the manufacturing mentality of repetitive tasks entered the office.

Workplace philosophies changed dramatically in the 1950s. The Quickborner Team, from Germany, introduced the concept of *office landscape*. Office walls were replaced with screens or partitions, plants, or bookcases. In the 1960s, the use of office-system furniture seriously changed office design. To use panels and work surfaces, rather than desks, demanded the designer understand communication patterns within the organization. New specialists in space planning emerged and flexible workstations began to appear. Companies such as *Steelcase, Haworth, Knoll,* and *Herman Miller* led the way in developing open-office design strategies. These strategies enhance collaboration, develop workplace flexibility, and reconfigure physical space. Today, the office has returned to a place where socializing is important to generate new knowledge and collaboration, rather than encouraging specific repetitive tasks.

Analyze It!

Knowing a little history behind office design and current office trends, predict what you think the next generation of workspace will look like. What type of office environment would you like for the future?

A great deal of office design comes under the category of **tenant improvement work (TI)**, which involves the design and construction upgrades to a leased space. Often the lessor will pay for a small part of the upgrades to attract tenants; however, the majority of changes to the interior space are paid for by the tenant.

TI involves changes to the interior of a commercial property, such as a large office building, by its owner to accommodate the needs of a tenant, such as a law firm. The law firm hires an interior design firm for assistance in remodeling the tenant space. Changes generally involve floor and wall coverings, ceilings, partitions, air conditioning, fire protection, and security. The lessor (landlord) and the law firm (lessee) negotiate a portion of the TI costs which is usually documented in the lease agreement.

Businesses often lease building space rather than own their buildings outright. As different tenants, or businesses, move into the space, they sign a new lease and a relocation of interior walls or partitions occurs to reflect the new owner's business. In addition to a new space plan, TI addresses all existing and new furniture, fixtures, and equipment to meet the business needs. As businesses grow or possibly shrink, designers who specialize in TI can play a significant role in shaping future business success. **Figure 3-13**.

Haworth, Inc.

Figure 3-12 Furnishings that fit the human body well help increase worker productivity in the office environment.

Copyright Goodheart-Willcox Co., Inc.

Link to History—Features connect chapter concepts to relevant historical background; include Analyze It! questions

Abundant Activities and Assessments Maximize Success

Critical Analysis—Questions and activities promote higher-order critical analysis of key design issues

Think like a Designer—Application activities link core skills and instrumental design skills

Design Application—Project-related activities that help learners develop design skills

Portfolio Builder—Activities that help learners showcase their design-skill progress

G-W Integrated Learning Solution

The **G-W Integrated Learning Solution** offers easy-to-use resources for both interior design students and instructors. Digital and blended (print + digital) teaching and learning content can be accessed through any Internet-enabled devise such as a computer, smartphone, or tablet. From the following options, choose the ones that work best for you and your students.

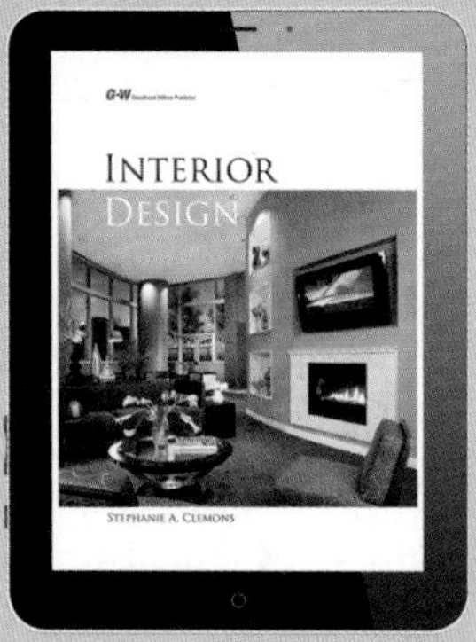

G-WLEARNING.com

The easy-to-navigate **G-W Learning Companion Website** for *Interior Design* offers students multiple opportunities to increase comprehension of key concepts and reinforce learning. The website complements chapters of the text and is available to students at no charge.

www.g-wlearning.com/interiordesign/

The **Online Learning Suite** for *Interior Design* is available as a classroom subscription. It combines the digital student text and online interior design projects in digital format.

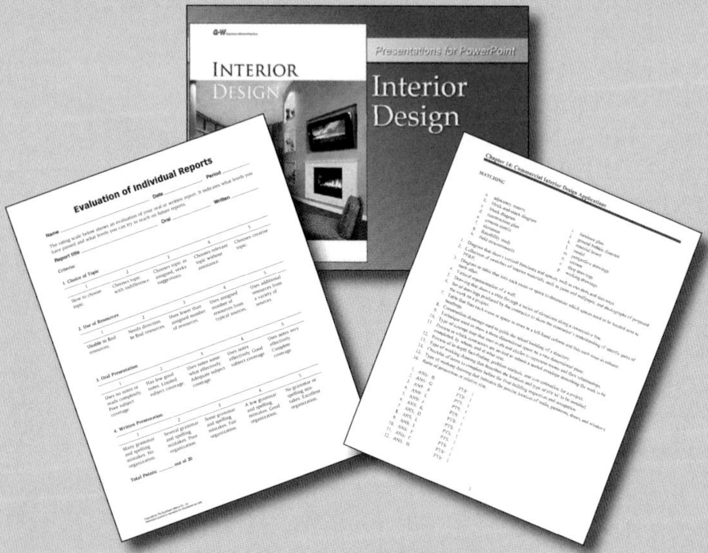

The **Online Instructor Resources** provide extensive support for interior design instructors. Available in one accessible location, support materials include *Instructor's Presentations for PowerPoint*®, *ExamView® Assessment Suite,* lesson plans, answer keys, and more! The Online Instructor Resources are available as a subscription and can be accessed at school or at home. These resources are also available on CDs.

Are you looking for a **Blended Solution**? G-W offers the Online Learning Suite bundled with the printed textbook in one easy-to-access package for school districts and instructors seeking a combination of print and digital tools. With this option, individual students and instructors have the flexibility of using solely print, solely digital, or a combination of print and digital versions of *Interior Design* educational materials to best meet their particular learning/teaching styles.

Introduction

The study of interior design is exhilarating! It is a field filled with creative excitement, innovative beauty, and dynamic design! As a profession, it is never static or predictable primarily because the focus is on *PEOPLE*!

- **Interior spaces can move us in profound ways.** Interior spaces can fill us with awe and wonder, enchant us by their delicacy and beauty, or overwhelm us with their magnificence and magnitude. Beyond their aesthetic and practical functions, beyond their sense of place, spaces have the potential to address our deepest human needs.
- **We do not just inhabit interior spaces; we interact with them.** Interior spaces, in turn, impact us. The ways design impacts the health and well-being of occupants, as well as the environment, is more important today than ever before.
- **According to the Environmental Protection Agency (EPA), we spend 93 percent of our time indoors.** This statistic includes the time we spend in our homes, schools, a favorite restaurant, or a doctor's office. Therefore, this textbook introduces us to the study of both *public* (commercial) and *private* (residential) interior spaces.
- **Interior design is a study of culture.** Interiors are a reflection of the people who inhabit them. While linguistics is the science of spoken languages, there are many unspoken languages in various cultures. These include the visual cues and profound messages contained in and communicated through interior places. The study and analysis of the messages visible, but not necessarily heard, in immediate environments will be part of what is covered in this textbook.
- **Interior design is a business.** Therefore, basic procedures, contracts, professional standards, ethics, and business models will be studied.
- **Interior design is an essential partner in the construction industry.** As a field of study, it is sometimes called "interior architecture." Therefore, technologies such as Revit, CAD, and industry standards are discussed as part of the profession.
- **Interior design is a science and an art.** Interior design is meaningful and purposeful.
- **Interior design is about YOU!** Interior design involves the ways you live, work, and play within the spaces you inhabit. Join us in the study of interior design! It will change your understanding of people, place, and life.

Stephanie A. Clemons

UNIT 1 Introduction to Interior Design

Haworth, Inc.

The Value of Interior Design

Photograph: David O. Marlow/Interiors by Associates III Interior Design

Chapter 1

Design Insight

"We shape the spaces that shape the human experience. This is what we do, what we create, what we give. It is how we earn our place at the human table. It is why our work is important to our clients, to our societies, and to ourselves. It is the difference we make and why we choose this noble profession."

International Federation of Interior Architects/Designers (IFI)
DFIE Interiors Declaration

Learning Targets

After studying this chapter, you will be able to
- interpret the definition of interior design.
- summarize the individual value of interior design.
- assess the value of interior design for the public.
- summarize the business and economic value of interior design, including local, national, and global value.
- explain the impact of culture and society on the value of interior design.

Introduction

Interior design is one of the most rewarding professions in which to work. It is also one of the most interesting to study. In an interview with *Metropolis Magazine*, Suzan Globus—past president of the *American Society of Interior Designers (ASID)*—defined interior design as the "...creation of environments that sustain and support human beings to live to the highest of their capabilities." This description begins to capture the creativity that is part of the process of design. It also captures the ability of well-designed spaces to shift people from a mundane, sometimes frustrating existence to a better life.

Interior Design Defined

Design, in general, is a way of making sense of things people see, interact with, or perceive in their environments. Through design, professionals try to make environments better, safer, healthier, more effective, and understandable.

When design moves into the **interior**—a space enclosed by walls, ceilings, and floors with such openings as windows and doors—it often reflects how people work and live in their spaces. An interior space, a volume within an enclosure, is a location where life takes place. These places often have unique characteristics depending on their function, the people living in or using them, and the construction of the building itself.

For the purpose of this text, the following definition captures the complexity of the interior design profession. **Interior design** is the creation of interior environments that support the function, aesthetics, and cultures of those who inhabit, live, and thrive in interior spaces. It enhances the well-being of people who live, work, and play in those interiors as well as protects their **health, safety, and well-being (HSW)**—a key responsibility of the interior design profession to produce designs that do not adversely impact the public.

The study of interior design involves a mixture of art, business, and psychology—sometimes with a different twist. Where art serves as an expression of personal emotions, interior design serves to capture and express someone else's taste, style, and needs. Where art claims its value in beauty and aesthetics alone, interior design is an applied, practical, and functional art that addresses serious human problems. Such problems include living well with chronic illness, as well as ordinary, everyday needs such as more storage in a bedroom. People often undervalue the artistic nature of interior design for the primary reason that it is difficult to measure beauty and its impact. Therefore, it is difficult to explain and sell to potential clients. It is much easier to applaud efficiencies and productivity than it is to sell aesthetics. It is the art of interior design, however, that ensures beauty in a space, and elicits the human response—often touching the human heart, **Figure 1-1**.

Interior design as a business is similar to such professional services as medicine or dentistry. When a client leaves the interior designer's office, however, often the product a client buys is **intangible** (abstract). It is a creative idea rather than an obvious product such as a set of clean teeth or new braces. Therefore, it is important for a successful designer to have a plan that ensures the business will be profitable and protective of those who purchase his or her design services. Good business organization and management are necessary for any design practitioner. All must be familiar with the basic principles of running a business.

The field of interior design is comprised of people—the clients you serve, the team members you work with, and the people who inhabit or use the spaces you design, **Figure 1-2**. Because of this, a foundational principle of interior design is an understanding of the psychology of human needs and emotions—from dreams and disabilities to frivolity and function.

Hornrock Properties Inc. builder of HighPointe at Woodbury Junction, Woodbury, NY/Builder Marketing Services in association with Michael Kehl Productions/Designer: Lita Dirks & Co.

Figure 1-1 The beauty of an interior space should capture and evoke human emotion. *What aspects of this interior capture your emotions? What is your response to this space?*

spotmatik/Shutterstock.com

Figure 1-2 Interior designers must understand the psychology of human needs and emotions. *From your perspective, what are this family's needs?*

Consider the needs of the client first. For instance, clients may ask you to design a series of spaces that they themselves cannot even envision, such as their dream homes. Others might ask you to design something you may never use yourself, such as a healthcare unit for those with disabilities. To solve both of these *client problems*, the designer must listen carefully to the client to understand and apply theories of human psychology and behavior to a given problem. Because each client problem is different, each day in the design world is different. This is why it is a fascinating profession to study and practice.

Another set of human needs to consider and for which to design, is those of the users visiting or living in a space. For the home of a multigenerational family, the designer may need to understand needs of a grandfather, mother, and children. For an unconventional yet stylish urban restaurant, the designer should consider all ages of those who may dine there.

Designers also work with another set of people—their design team. These experts may be peers, project managers, architects, engineers, construction managers, or furniture-manufacturer representatives. The team **collaborates,** or works jointly to solve pre-design or on-site issues and problems that arise. This fulfilling—yet challenging—part of the profession involves working smoothly with a variety of personalities, opinions, and communication styles. This is essential when working with and for people.

Those who practice interior design do so with the ability to envision something not yet built. It is the only profession specializing in the creation of interior places that addresses the following needs:

- rest and renewal (home)
- productivity and efficiency (home and work)
- entertainment, healing, education, and inspiration (home, work, and all other places)

Interior design has a great deal of overlap with other fields such as architecture, graphic design, landscape design, and social sciences (for example, environmental psychology). Interior design—at its best and simplest—is a practical art, a successful business, and an application of psychology to human needs.

The Compelling Value of Interior Design

The value of interior design is multidimensional and complex. By nature its value is hidden, unnoticed, and private—even when it is public. Only a limited number of people see any given interior, and they usually do not notice it when it works. The nation is evolving into more design awareness and appreciation of the relative beauty or ugliness of the built environment—hence the avid interest in design websites.

The value of interior design is often analyzed first on how well the spaces function for whom they are designed. For example, can the user accomplish the task he or she needs to perform in the kitchen, office, or hotel lobby? Does the user have to walk too many steps to move from one room to another? Can the user reach an object in an overhead cupboard?

> *"Interior design comprises a relatively small segment of the entire building industry, but its impact is enormous. From homes to hospitals, restaurants to retail stores, schools to state houses, interior design directs and influences the look, the feel, the quality and the functionality of the interior environments we move in every day."*
>
> *ASID State of the Industry Report, 2012*

People also perceive the value of interior design in terms of how they feel in a well-designed interior space—their comfort or the warmth in the space. They can discuss their responses to the aesthetics of the space and its beauty. Therefore, its value equates to feelings and emotions experienced in the interior space that previously were merely dreams. Interior design is the only profession dedicated to altering the way people perceive the immediate environment. In a way, interior design shapes spaces that reassure people they matter.

STUDENT SPOTLIGHT

Perspectives on the Value of Interior Design

Carrie Zwisler: "To me, the value of interior design is its ability to form environments and experiences that can both consciously and unconsciously change your life. Living in a well-designed environment can have a tremendous impact on your emotional, mental, and physical health—the same way living in a poorly designed environment can have an incredibly large negative impact. People often overlook interior design's ability to shape productive, healthy, positive, and beautiful environments."

Lauren Richards: "In the design world, possibilities are endless. Once a creative idea comes to mind, a designer can place that thought into a real-world application. The beauty of this concept is that *anything* can be an inspiration for a design. Anything: seen, unseen, felt, read, and heard can be translated and applied to a design. Specifically for interior design, I value the understanding that the design of a space has complete effect on the users. From the first initial idea, which was then manipulated into a physical structure, now impacts the user's human behavior in every aspect."

Jason Schleisman: "Interior design is something that shapes my everyday life in ways that I often take for granted. Actively conscious of them or not, influences created by design are present in all spaces I occupy whether at home, school, work, or elsewhere. From the utensils I use to eat with, to how I access my kitchen; from the way my desk is illuminated, to how I am guided from a building's entry to an office, interior design shapes the way I think, feel, and act. Because these influences, sometimes very subtle, have such an impact on my overall behavior, I find the power of design to be of tremendous value in fostering not only my own intangible personal well-being, but that of others, too. Sharing this power by creating spaces that enhance quality of life for others is something I find meaningful."

Discussion of the value of interior design focuses on the impact on public health, safety, and well-being when addressing laws, regulations, or the built environment. The **built environment** refers to manmade surroundings that provide the setting for human activity, from the largest civic buildings to the smallest personal place. The use of the health and safety language relates to laws regulating the licensing of professions that protect people, **Figure 1-3.**

The previous examples are just a few reasons why interior design may be of value to you as a career and why the public values it. The next section describes more. As you study the field and profession, record other reasons you discover. You will be amazed how many there are!

The Value of Interior Design to *You*

As you think about a career in interior design, it is important to examine the effects interior design has on *you.* Whether you realize it or not, the design of interior places wields great power and influence in your life. Interior places shape your behaviors, feelings, and perceptions just as they will for your future clients.

- **Behaviors (or actions).** The shape of a room, the available light you have to complete a homework assignment, or the location of dishes in a kitchen can all influence your behaviors and actions.
- **Feelings.** Your choices in color, connection with nature through window placement, and symbols of individuality that mark your personal territories all influence your feelings.
- **Perceptions.** Your perceptions involve your sensory awareness of environmental elements in your space. For instance, the textural surfaces on an object (rough or smooth), the comfort in furniture (soft or firm), or privacy to meditate (visual privacy to reflect) all influence your perceptions about a space.

The influence of interior design on your daily life is very real and significant. Moreover, you have the power to control the design of the interiors you occupy by the choices you make, by what you specify, or what you buy. As a future interior designer, you will deal with these realities as you work with clients and their spaces.

Boulder Community Hospital/LaCasse Photography

Figure 1-3 Protecting the health, safety, and well-being of the public is a prime focus of the interior design profession. *Predict what types of laws and regulations protect the public in this environment.*

A Creative Outlet

Many people enter the interior design field because it serves as an outlet for their creative ideas. They love to think differently and offer unique ideas to help others achieve their goals. They enjoy the challenge of doing something different—like nothing ever before. Part of the value of interior design involves the ability of professionals to creatively solve client problems.

Interior designers use their creativity daily. Newly-constructed buildings offer the chance to design new, innovative spaces for people who inhabit them. Similarly, the remodel of a commercial office space or the redesign of a master suite in a home both offer new problems to solve. Therefore, when you practice interior design, no two days on the job and no two clients are the same. As a practicing interior designer, you constantly face new challenges.

> *"Skillfully designed spaces can arouse in us a sense of purpose, or a sense of the profound."*
>
> *IFI DFIE Interiors Declaration*

A Fulfilling Career

Designers indicate many reasons for choosing an interior design career. For some, it is as simple as having a desire to help people. They might desire to work with residential clients who desire to build their dream homes. While for others, fulfillment comes as they help a client who has a physical impairment or disability better his or her current home to reflect changing needs. Still others desire an interior design career because of the number of people their appropriate design of a commercial space positively influences. Consider the number of people who enjoy a well-designed hospital or an elementary school that engages students through fun, yet functional learning spaces.

Others select interior design because they wish to reshape the physical environment—transforming an ordinary space to an extraordinary place. For instance, a coffee shop design may provide a reading nook for cozy privacy, or an interactive, lively place to meet and greet others. A library can be a social gathering place or a place that provokes contemplation and learning, **Figure 1-4**. Your desire to study design may be more

Conrado/Shutterstock.com

Nagel Photography/Shutterstock.com

Figure 1-4 A career in interior design gives you an opportunity to reshape interior environments to meet the needs of others, such as designing a coffee shop for meeting friends or a library for research and study.

about developing meaningful spaces that are good for the planet for the next generation than about the client.

Some choose interior design as a career because it can flex with lifestyle, age, and interests. When young, it can be a very fast-paced, energetic, exciting career that includes travel around the world. If a designer wants to start a family or remain state-side, he or she may wish to work specific hours and days in a large architectural firm. Still later, a designer may set up his or her own private firm that allows consultation with clients on specific projects that resonate with a personal value system.

Still others select interior design because of the variety of opportunities to work in both commercial and residential design with the same undergraduate degree. For example, as a professional you may work in the hospitality sector designing and managing the installation of relaxing spas in boutique hotels. After working for 15 years in that design specialty, you may desire a different challenge.

With the same interior design degree, you can move into the corporate office specialty with its different challenges and unique client needs. You may feel the rejuvenation of shifting into a different career, yet you do not need a different degree. Why not create functional, thought-provoking, and more meaningfully designed spaces that make an intellectual contribution to those exposed to them?

The Value of Interior Design to the Public

While having a creative outlet and fulfilling career is important to you, of equal or greater importance is what you bring the public, or your clients. The profession draws many designers because of its connection with *people*. The design of quality spaces begins with caring about the people who use the space and the desire to make their work or personal spaces function better. Understanding the personal value of interior design to the public along with how to best meet human needs through effective design, helps shape who you are as a designer.

> *“In the spaces that are important to us, we experience not only a sense of place, but a sense of who we are, and of what we can be.”*
>
> *IFI DFIE Interiors Declaration*

Personal Value

All interior places influence people at the individual level; therefore, they have personal value. People inhabit spaces and perceive them as more than shelter. In a way, they are a type of billboard on which visual

Designer Profile

Marc Herndon—The Value of Interior Design

Marc Herndon is an interior designer/project manager at Gensler in the Washington DC area and has practiced interior design for more than 13 years. Here is what Mark has to say about the value of interior design.

©Ron Pollard, courtesy of RNL

“As a practitioner, I have experienced first-hand the value interior design brings to the public. No matter where you are, be it the office, a café, a shopping mall, the library, or a hospital, you are surrounded by decisions made by an interior designer. *Interior design is about living.* It is an intimate, diverse discipline, and one that significantly influences behavior, streamlines efficiencies, protects occupants, and improves the human condition. It is a weighty responsibility and one that requires a great deal of preparation.”

You can read more about Marc’s background in Appendix B.

displays of pattern, color, and form express personalized statements. If designed accurately, these spaces reflect the preferences, styles, values, personalities, and behaviors of the users—a type of design thumbprint.

The conscious and deliberate design of interior spaces to meet people's needs and desires indicates their worth as individuals. It also indicates their perceived value to society.

Meeting Human Needs

There are many psychological, physical, and sociological human needs that the design of interior spaces should accommodate. Some of these include *territoriality, privacy,* the need for nature, and the desire for well-designed spaces. As designers meet these needs, the value of the profession becomes obvious.

> *"It is the nature of Humankind not only to use spaces, but to fill them with beauty and meaning. It is, after all, for Humanity, our ultimate client, that we design."*
>
> *IFI DFIE Interiors Declaration*

The Need for Personal Territory and Privacy

Quite simply, you witness **territoriality**—the need to control a fixed area by laying claim to it—when you see people put their names on books or other personal items. Such markers define territories and communicate ownership. Markers can be as subtle as leaving a book on a chair to reserve a classroom seat. Likewise, personal markers can be very obvious, such as a sign on a piece of land that reads "private property—keep out."

One of the major functions of territorial behavior for humans is acquiring and regulating privacy. **Privacy** is a process that involves both seeking human interaction and controlling it. People control access to themselves through selective distance or isolation.

Cultural background plays a role in regulating privacy. For example, people in Latin or Middle Eastern cultures often require less personal space during a conversation while those from Western cultures may need more personal space for comfort. Making eye contact in some cultures is a sign of honesty while in other cultures it may be a sign of disrespect or rudeness. Privacy is a complex human need involving several other important needs, including survival, physical/psychological health, self-identity, and emotional release.

Interior designers address these diverse human needs through multiple ways. These include offering people the ability to personally control their environments (such as changing the thermostat or opening windows) or to be alone with their thoughts. For example, spaces for solitude can be designed both into commercial and residential environments. Awareness of these human needs helps designers create spaces that can assist people in being more productive and feeling less stress.

The Need for Nature

A paradox exists that humans are a species that build, but then pay thousands of dollars to travel elsewhere, such as a cabin in a remote area, in order to vacation where people are not. Why is it important for many people to be near the security of human contact yet still have an innate desire to spend time outdoors?

The most recent Environmental Protection Agency (EPA) statistic indicates people spend 90 percent of their lives indoors and only two percent in nature. Many believe that humans suffer from nature deprivation. People have an inherent need for nature.

The ways interior designers create environments can help people reconnect with nature. For example, although workers may spend 90 percent of their time indoors, having a view to the outdoors and living green plants indoors helps meet the human need for nature. Creating interiors that support the protection of the environment and preserve natural areas also meet human needs and add value to the profession, **Figure 1-5**.

The Need for Good Design

The human need for good design often has low priority in people's lives, especially if it requires money they do not have. Humans are very good at adapting to situations and dilemmas—it is part of their survival instinct. People, however, yearn for and delight in well-designed spaces, objects, signage, food, fashion, and cars. If you think of a tool that works well, you may envision one that is ergonomically sensitive to your needs. Some examples include a well-designed toothbrush, keyboard, or chair. If you think of spaces that you want designed well, you may think of desired changes for your kitchen or workplace.

Photograph: David O. Marlow/Interiors by Associates III Interior Design

Figure 1-5 Helping people connect with nature within their interior environments is just one way designers help meet client needs. *How does this environment help its occupants connect with nature?*

The design of interior spaces should adapt to people as individuals, rather than people adapting to the designs of spaces. Bad design exists. Good design matters.

It is the designer's job not only to listen to what the client wants, but to also volunteer creative, appropriate solutions based on the designer's expertise. They serve as motivators for better design and better living spaces. The designer often leaves a signature mark of quality and creativity that is pleasing and meets the needs initially expressed by the client.

Business and Economic Value

The value of interior design extends into all business sectors and is an economic advantage to clients. For example, the interior spaces of a corporate office serve as an extension of a company's values and identity. These interiors translate into customer loyalty and brand recognition that enhance business success, **Figure 1-6.**

©Judy Davis/Hoachlander Davis Photography/Designed by ForrestPerkins

Figure 1-6 Building brand recognition is one way interior designers serve their commercial business clients. *What details about this space capture your interest in design?*

The business and economic value of interior design relates to its ability to attract customers. For example, a well-designed coffee shop interior attracts people to visit, spend money, and stay longer. Therefore, the design brings additional business to the restaurant, generating revenue and additional client base.

While many understand the value of quality interior spaces in the home, others are still learning how interior design brings concrete and measurable value to the workplace. A well designed space will maximize the use of real estate through the following:

- efficient space planning
- appropriate levels of natural and electric light
- incorporation of safe and appropriate designs and materials that protect human health and safety

For companies, this means increased employee satisfaction, productivity, and well-being. It can also decrease absenteeism. In addition, if you consider design through its cultural and global impact, it is a factor in economic development and cultural sustainability.

> *“The profession of interior design provides value to the stakeholders. It improves well-being as a factor of economic development. It provides strategic thought leadership resulting in multifaceted return on investment.”*
>
> *DFIE Declaration, IFI, 2011*

Local Value

Bad design has real economic consequences. In a recent study, Gensler—a well-known, world wide architectural and design firm—published a document entitled “U.S. Workplace Survey.” It explained that the effect of bad office design on lost worker productivity in the United States is estimated around $330 billion annually for just the industry groups that were sampled in the survey. Redesigning the offices with open-access workspaces significantly improved the decision-making process, group cohesion, and team effectiveness. This, in turn, had direct impact on the organization’s financial bottom line.

On a local level, organizations often view the hiring of an interior designer as an additional, unnecessary expense. Quite the contrary is true. Instead, professional interior designers can save their clients time and money while increasing efficiency and productivity in the workplace. This leads to a more successful bottom line for a business. For economic value, a professional designer may

- **Bring *design thinking* to your project. Design thinking** is an active practice that develops in the proper environment and causes you to look at the world with evolving potential and probable possibilities. It is a nonlinear problem-solving process that combines future thinking and analysis with creativity. Rather than a system of sequential steps, the ebb-and-flow (or back-and-forth layering) of design thinking allows interior designers to envision possibilities others cannot imagine and show how out-of-the-box alternatives can work.

  Interior designers bring that innovative, creative thinking to their projects to produce designs that can influence the home and workplace. Although interior designers have utilized design thinking in practice over many years, David Kelley of IDEO coined the phrase *design thinking*.
- **Save money by *doing it right* the first time.** Many times, people attempt to save money by completing design work themselves (for example, a home or small commercial project). In some cases, the scope of work is minimal, and a talented consumer can complete the work. For the more complex or technical work, hiring a professional can avoid costly design-decision mistakes.
- **Save time by completing the *legwork*.** Time is money. In both residential and commercial design, a professional designer has an accessible resource network to tap to save you *legwork* on tracking down the best resources for the scope of work to be completed.
- **Capitalize on what the client already owns.** There is a myth that interior designers want to toss out whatever the client owns and purchase all new items for the spaces. This is not true. Professional designers understand the importance of memory pieces that are important to residential clients. In addition, they appreciate that a corporate office workplace cannot afford to recycle all their furnishings and equipment when moving into a new space. Professional designers are skilled in reusing existing items in the design of new or existing spaces, **Figure 1-7**.

RM Ruwart Design/Rosalie M. Ruwart, ASID

Photographer: Kimberly Gavin/Andrea Schumacher Interiors

Figure 1-7 Reusing existing items that a client already owns is one way interior designers show they understand the importance of a client's possessions. *What is one memory piece you own that you would want an interior designer to work into a new design for your room? Why?*

- **Access design products, custom materials, reputable contractors, and craftspeople.** Professional interior designers have a network of quality resources for the client to access beyond the Internet and local retail stores. It is difficult to locate design products and reputable craftspeople to produce and install the design their clients prefer. The interior designer can offer references to ensure the client is pleased with the final result.
- **Manage and coordinate work, contractors, and job details.** Part of the interior designer's education and training involves project management. You learn how to schedule, coordinate, and facilitate the final design installation into a facility. Shortening the downtime for your client's business can save real dollars.
- **Enhance spaces that invite repeat business.** Many commercial interiors, if designed well, create an engaging atmosphere that invites people to visit the space again and again—bringing additional business to the owner. For example, a fun, community ice cream shop—designed well—may invite individuals to return again and again as a family tradition.

Good design offers improved health, safety, privacy, security, productivity, profitability, employee and customer satisfaction, and sustainability.

National Value

The downturn in the U.S. economy in 2008 was in part due to the overbuilding and overinflating of residential and commercial real estate—designed spaces and places. Many investors never thought such real estate would lose value. This led to a global real estate bubble resulting in a tremendous amount of vacant space. Another value of interior design involves rethinking possible uses for space the initial purpose of which no longer has market demand.

The use of interior designers in residential design and renovation projects clearly links to the economic conditions of the time. When the economy is good, more people are likely to use interior design services. Commercial real estate projects requiring interior design professionals, however, often occur regardless of current economic conditions. For example, the budget allocations for the building of a school or a remodeling project typically happen over a period of years. This makes such projects more affordable over time. An added economic advantage of such projects is that clients use these renovations to enhance their business images in the community.

Global Value

Presented as the creative industry of the twenty-first century, many perceive design as having a serious advantage over other industries for increasing the global economy. As developing nations struggle to compete with such traditional industries as manufacturing, creative industries—such as design—are becoming the *new* knowledge economy. The basis of a **knowledge economy** is on investing in such intangible assets as leadership, management, and human skills—such as the ability to design.

Gary Becker, a Nobel Laurette, indicated that ideas drive the economy. The transformation of IBM is an example of Becker's point. After selling its computer manufacturing divisions to China, IBM now licenses ideas and sells services. According to the *International Federation of Interior Architects/Designers (IFI) President's Update in 2011*, design is perceived as a skill needed to creatively address such world problems as expanding employment, stimulating urban regrowth, and improving quality of life.

The value of interior design is globally needed, yet universally misunderstood. Its perceived value varies in different parts of the world as illustrated by its growth in individual countries.

- In Africa, the profession of interior design is just beginning to receive recognition, and therefore holds minimal value at this time.
- In Europe, interior design is more often referred to as interior architecture and has a long-standing reputation and value.
- In China, interior design is a celebrated profession that is highly valued. Design is under the control of the local and national Chinese government rather than individuals.

In the United States, interior designers work in a variety of fields such as architecture. According to the *American Society of Interior Designers' (ASID) State of the Industry Report*, among employed designers, about 20 percent work in architectural firms. Gensler—a world-renown architecture and planning firm—claimed the top spot in a recent *Top 250 Architecture Firms* list, which ranks U.S. companies based on architectural revenue from the prior year. Gensler's growth in its $764 million in revenue was directly related to *global growth* according to Andy Cohen, Gensler's executive director. Recently, Gensler opened seven offices in burgeoning cities such as São Paulo and Bangkok. The global value of interior

Designer Profile

Christopher D. Martinez—Importance of Interior Design

Christopher D. Martinez has practiced design for several years in the Greater New York area at Poggenpohl, a German company specializing in high-end kitchens. Read about Christopher's view on the importance of interior design.

Margaret Mosiej, Owner and Principal, Poggenpohl Paramus, LLC

"As an emerging practitioner, I believe that interior design is of great importance primarily because of its ability to transcend what is physically seen. The context in which design exists goes deeper than that of surface level aesthetics, although this is a component. It affects the senses, the mind, and even the spirit. From the very heart is the need to change, impact, and improve. Interior design takes on this role; namely by empowering one who enters these spaces peace and affording them opportunities of improved health and welfare."

You can read more about Christopher's background in Appendix B.

design is highly regarded when firms that employ many designers, such as Gensler, are contracted to complete projects in other countries.

On behalf of their clients, interior designers specify interior materials, products, and furnishings from around the world. The *ASID State of the Industry Report* indicated that interior designers specify over $46 billion in products every year. Their influence and impact in other parts of the world is often clearly significant. For example, interior designers can diminish the demand for tropical woods and instead increase the use of rapidly renewable materials. Interior designers have direct influence on the planet by what products they use in interior spaces—a direct global value.

As part of the built-environment team, interior designers work closely with the construction industry. In the world, construction constitutes over 10 percent of the global **Gross World Product (GWP)**—the sum value of all final products and services produced worldwide in a given year. As indicated in a recent *IFI President's Update*, China alone, where many buildings and cities are under construction, is responsible for one-sixth of all construction activity due to its population growth. Entire cities in China are planned and built rather than evolving over time from small towns to large metropolitan areas. How Chinese design begins to accommodate all aspects of life for the Chinese people has, and will continue to have, global impact on design. As an example, the focus of China's government and national policy on design rather than manufacturing can be clearly seen in their product tags that read *designed in China* rather than *made in China*.

The *International Federation of Interior Architects/Designers (IFI)* is the global voice and authority for professional Interior Architects/Designers. In 110 countries, IFI represents 270,000 designers, educators, and industry stakeholders in the international design community. IFI holds an annual **congress**—a formal meeting of delegates—in various countries to discuss global objectives and initiatives for interior design.

In the fall of 2011, the IFI held a congress in Taiwan, Taipei. At this congress, they made public the *IFI Interiors Declaration* after holding worldwide focus groups about the global value of interior design. (A **focus group** is a small group of people who study a response to something, such as a product, to determine the response of a larger population.) This document defines the value, relevance, responsibility, culture, knowledge, business, and identity of interior architecture/interior design. The global economic value of interior design was enhanced through such marketability and visibility. Quotes from this document are threaded throughout this book to raise your awareness of agreed-on global philosophies related to interior design.

Cultural and Societal Value

Interior spaces are vessels, or containers, for materials and artifacts that communicate items of cultural value in an unspoken language within physical environments. What does this mean? In essence, it means that the objects and belongings you surround yourself with reflect who you are and who you want to become. They reflect the culture and society in which you live, learn, play, and dream. The rooms you design never cease to send messages. Perhaps Shashi Caan, previous IFI president said it best, "Our interiors are the repositories of our memories and the containers of our dreams, aspirations, wants, and needs. They are the reflections of us, our society, our culture, and our time." See **Figure 1-8**.

Photographer: Rhonda Grimberg/Interior Designer: Andrea Schumacher Interiors

Figure 1-8 Affirming cultural and social value is one way the interior designer helps clients. *What features in this image affirm cultural and social value?*

Cultural Value

As globalization brings cultural changes in the U.S. and throughout the world, interior designers are striving to understand the new design preferences and requirements of changing populations. For example, cultural differences in a home may be observed in the

- meaning and symbolism of color usage
- adjacency of private to public rooms
- placement of front entry doors
- location of the family altar
- amount of space needed to perform a kitchen task
- location of where individuals sleep
- preferred size of dining spaces

Both public and personal spaces should reflect the cultures of those using and living in such places. Sensitivity to various cultural needs is only one way of communicating societal value, **Figure 1-9**.

Societal Value

Design can be a powerful force and have significant social impact. Often, the phrase *socially responsible design* communicates the perception that designers have a responsibility to effect real change in the world through better design for all people. For example, are the materials or processes for manufacturing carpet good for the planet and therefore, future generations? The perception is that through good design, it is possible to address social, environmental, and economic issues. The societal value of interior design is both global and local.

> *"Great spaces are indispensable for great creative cultures. They encourage connections between people, ideas and entire fields of thought."*
>
> *IFI 2011*

Design is human centered. Designers must think of people in a holistic way. As a profession, interior design has a history of addressing issues relating to social responsibility such as sustainable design and design that meets the needs of all people, including those who have special needs. Interior designers are also designing for a growing population of people who view the world differently, including those who may have autism, traumatic brain injuries, and Alzheimer's disease. For example, the ideal workspace for those who have some level of autism or traumatic brain injury

romakoma/Shutterstock.com

©Stirling Elmendorf

Figure 1-9 Culture can impact dining space and furnishings.

is a distraction-free environment which eliminates background noise, activity, bright colors, and the flicker and hum of fluorescent lights. This is at odds with the trend today for collaborative workplaces.

Emerging more recently is the concept of *socially beneficial design*. This movement concerns

- the way problems and needs are defined
- how solutions are developed
- how those solutions are implemented

For example, suppose a rural downtown area is no longer attracting the community. Through a process, town leaders identify the problem and needs and address them through design. The community develops a new town center boasting a gathering space for different age groups that invites new life into the downtown. The goal is to avoid shallow design concepts and instead evoke societal change. Critical skills for socially beneficial design include the ability to prioritize and to be empathetic. With the help of designers, communities can address social issues of those who are homeless, who have fewer advantages, and those with physical limitations. This is one area in which the younger generation is going to change the world by caring.

Ethnic and Societal Identity

Interior design shapes spaces that reassure people of all cultures that they matter. Communal spaces in many countries reflect self, family values, gender, class, cultural heritage, and religious affiliations. The home may serve as a sacred space (religion), a small kitchen for personal space (gender), and a large place in which families eat together (social). The interior spaces that hold belongings—both group and individual—capture ethnic and social identity. Interior spaces foster kinship and familiarity because they encourage interaction and exchange of ideas. The conscious design of these spaces celebrates cultural diversity and, if acceptable, individuality, **Figure 1-10**.

The practice of interior design is a unique, ever-changing, fun, and innovative discipline. It is a business, an art, a study of people, a unique way of thinking, **Figure 1-11**. It involves intense problem-solving skills as well

Photographee.eu/Shutterstock.com

Figure 1-10 The design of a space that fosters kinship and familiarity helps provide comfort and reassurance to clients. *What social values does the design of this space affirm?*

Tyler Olson/Shutterstock.com

Figure 1-11 The practice of interior design offers the designer an opportunity to meet critical client needs in a unique, creative way.

as people skills. It involves business acumen as well as a graphic ability to communicate design by computer or hand sketching. The interior environment is composed of procedures, processes, and products. However, the critical element is the person who inhabits the space. This variety keeps design professionals engaged in the profession for many decades.

> *"As a creative enterprise, interior design and interior architecture are a mode of cultural production. They are place-makers that interpret, translate, and edit cultural capital. In a global world, interior design and interior architecture must play a role in facilitating the retention of cultural diversity."*
>
> *IFI Declaration, 2011*

Chapter 1 Review and Assess

Summary

- Interior design supports the function, aesthetics, and culture along with protecting the health, safety, and well-being of those who inhabit spaces.
- Interior design involves working with many people, including clients, team members, and people who inhabit designed spaces.
- As a valued profession, interior design is multidimensional and complex.
- Interior design has personal value to designers and clients and shapes behaviors, feelings, and perceptions about a space.
- A fulfilling career in interior design provides an opportunity to use creativity to meet the needs of others.
- The design of quality spaces begins with caring about people and the desire to make work and personal spaces function better.
- Understanding psychological, physical, and sociological needs of humans is important to designing spaces to meet such needs.
- Effectively designed spaces offer an economic advantage to clients and enhance customer loyalty and brand recognition.
- Interior design has local, national, and global value that impacts economies.
- Interior designers support cultural value by creating designs that reflect client cultures.
- Interior design is human-centered in recognizing the special needs of people and in shaping interior spaces that support cultural and ethnic identify.
- Interior design is socially responsible in addressing such issues as sustainable design and design for all.

Chapter Vocabulary

Write the definition of each of the following terms. Then write a sentence using each term in a design-related context.

built environment
collaborate
congress
design thinking
focus group
Gross World Product (GWP)
health, safety, and well-being (HSW)
intangible
interior
interior design
knowledge economy
privacy
territoriality

Review and Study

1. Summarize the definition of interior design in your own words.
2. How is interior design similar to and different from other professional services?
3. For what three needs is interior design the only profession to specialize in the creation of interior places to meet these needs?
4. What are three ways that make the value of interior design compelling?
5. What are three ways the value of interior design affects you?
6. Contrast the human needs of territoriality and privacy. Give a personal example of each.
7. How can interior designers help support peoples' need for nature and add value to the profession?
8. Name three ways that a well-designed space maximizes real estate and supports business and economic value.
9. On the local level, how can interior designers save their clients money while increasing efficiency and productivity in the workplace?
10. In contrast to residential design projects, why do commercial interior design projects often occur regardless of national economic conditions?
11. What is a *knowledge economy*?
12. Give an example showing how interior designers impact global value through product specification.
13. What is defined in the International Federation of Interior Architects/Designers (IFI)—Interiors Declaration?
14. Name three cultural differences in a home that designers should understand that may influence design preferences.
15. Contrast socially responsible design with socially beneficial design.

Critical Analysis

16. **Analyze.** Reread and analyze the *Design Insight* quotation at the beginning of the chapter. In your own words, write a summary of what this means to you regarding your potential career as an interior designer.
17. **Evaluate.** Evaluate the value of design in your community. Create a design chart including the following sections: *Public Value* (meeting human needs), *Economic Value*, and *Culture/Societal Value*. As you observe your community in the next 48 hours, note examples of how the value of design is evident in each of the areas. Discuss your findings with the class. What similarities and differences were noted by your classmates?
18. **Infer relationships.** The author states that "conscious and deliberate design of interior spaces to meet people's needs and desires indicates their worth as individuals." Infer how well-designed interiors support the worth and value of individuals in society. Cite the text and if necessary, additional reliable Internet or print resources to support your inferences.
19. **Analyze problems.** Think about social issues in your community. What are some societal issues that could be addressed through empathy, caring, and good design?
20. **Analyze meaning.** According to the author "the value of interior design is globally needed, yet universally misunderstood." What does the author mean by this statement? Discuss your responses in class. Cite the text and additional reliable Internet or print resources to support your analysis.
21. **Identity evidence.** Take an actual or virtual (Internet) field trip to two or more restaurants in your community. Study and analyze the cultural design in each restaurant. Demonstrate effective verbal skills by citing evidence that communicates a specific culture (for example, a cowboy hat versus Thai colors). To extend this activity, take pictures of various restaurants (with the owner's permission) that support your findings.

Think like a Designer

22. **Value video clip.** Use a digital camera and a school-approved video creation application to create a video about the value of interior design to the public and to clients. Share your video with the class or post it on a school-approved website or blog.
23. **Reading.** Go to the website for the International Federation of Interior Architects/Designers and click on the link for the *IFI Interiors Declaration*. Read the entire declaration. What does this declaration state about the value and relevance of interior design? What does it indicate about the role of interior design in culture and business? Discuss your findings in class.
24. **Cultural identification.** As a new acquaintance enters one of your spaces, ask him or her to describe the culture in which you live or who you are. Just as your clothing choices send a message, your interior spaces send one (or more), too. Write a summary regarding what you learned about how others perceive you and your culture.
25. **Writing.** Read the following statement from the *ASID State of Industry Report*: "While not all interiors are created by design professionals, interior design can, and does, contribute to addressing a wide range of social, economic, and health issues confronting our nation." Select one social, economic, or health issue confronting the nation, and write a paper that reflects how interior designers can assist in addressing or solving the problem. Use the text and additional Internet or print resources to support your reflection.
26. **Speaking.** Apply your oral communication skills clearly, concisely, and effectively to explain the difference between *socially responsible design* and *socially beneficial design*. Research examples of each to enhance your explanation of each type of design.
27. **Writing.** Use the text and additional reliable resources to write an essay on why interior design is "...a unique, ever-changing, fun, and innovative discipline." Share your essay with the class.

Design Application

28. **Field observation.** Raise your awareness of "behaviors, feelings, and perceptions" of interior spaces through observation. Visit both a commercial/public space (such as cell phone store) and a residential space (such as a kitchen) that you do not often use. Request permission of the owners to observe how people use the place and act in the space. In the commercial space, note the human behavior that is guided by entrances, displays, or service desks. How does the interior space planning and decoration in these spaces influence human choices and actions? Where were your feelings and perceptions about these spaces? Give an oral presentation to the class about what you observed regarding the influence of interior design.
29. **Portfolio builder.** When you apply for a job or community service or to a college, you may need to tell others about how you are qualified for this position. A portfolio is a selection of related materials that you collect and organize. These materials show your qualifications, skills, and talents. These materials may be in the form of certificates of achievement, written essays on a number of design-related issues, and a transcript of your school grades and courses.

    Two types of portfolios are commonly used: print portfolios and electronic portfolios (e-Portfolios).

    A. Use the Internet to search reliable sources for print portfolio and e-Portfolio. Read articles about each type. Then briefly describe each type in your own words.

    B. You will be creating a portfolio in this class. Write a paragraph describing which type of portfolio you prefer. What might be the benefit of creating both?
30. **Portfolio builder.** After reading the chapter, write your own definition of interior design. Save this definition in your portfolio for future reference.

The Profession of Interior Design—Yesterday and Today

Photograph: David O. Marlow/Interiors by Associates III Interior Design

Chapter 2

Design Insight

"We use space responsibly. We practice our profession with highest regard for engaging the world's economic and natural resources in a sustainable manner. We design for health, safety, well-being, and the needs for all."

IFI Design Frontiers: The Interiors Entity

Learning Targets

After studying this chapter, you will be able to

- identify misconceptions about the interior design profession.
- understand the historical roots of the interior design profession and its significance in today's world.
- understand the major components of a profession, specifically those of interior design.
- summarize career paths in the interior design profession.
- summarize the roles and responsibilities of today's interior design practitioner.
- contrast residential and commercial interior design in terms of demographics; trends in how the profession is changing in regard to security, safety, and sustainable design; global design; aging-in-place, inclusive, and universal design; evidence-based design; and technologies.

Introduction

Interior design, a licensed profession in over half of the United States, has grown rapidly in breadth and depth over the past 50 years. In the last decade alone, the popularity of design-focused television shows increased public exposure to the influence of creatively designing interior spaces. When *Trading Spaces* was cable's top-rated show, one of its 2003 episodes was the highest rated program ever on *The Learning Channel (TLC)* with 9.1 million viewers in one night.

There are benefits and drawbacks to this type of mainstream publicity for interior design. Although it is now commonplace to discuss aspects of interior spaces in everyday conversations, such as color and space, the public's perception has been somewhat misled in the portrayal of the profession by reality TV shows.

Interior Design Misconceptions

At the onset, the majority of viewers of design reality shows were teens. As they graduated from high school between 2000 and 2010, many of these teens chose interior design as a college major. Students flooded higher education interior design departments nationwide, creating unexpected faculty shortages. Many of these students had misconceptions about interior design.

The time and thought processes behind interior-design solutions were often left in the reality-TV editing room. This reinforced the misconception that *interior decoration* was *interior design*. As a result, more and more students arrived at college looking for classes that taught accessorizing and color mixing—commonly known as **interior decoration**—rather than space planning and the design process, or interior design. They were looking for a hobby rather than a profession, **Figure 2-1**.

Today, from the professional designer's viewpoint, the publicity from design-reality shows is more of a benefit than a deficit due to the increase in public awareness. However, the perception still exists that professional skills are easy to acquire. Many think design solutions can be quickly executed in 60 minutes or less—depending on the number of TV commercials. In addition, the focus in these shows still is on the designer rather than the client. These programs can trivialize and misrepresent the interior design professional's expertise, education, and skills.

In some ways, the interior design profession has not clarified this misconception. Too often, design-firm websites and design magazines show interiors as uninhabited beautiful spaces. Little is said about the client's design-related problems, how the problems

aruemar/Shutterstock.com

Figure 2-1 Many students who pursue an interior design major in college were influenced by design reality television. *What factors have influenced your decision to pursue a career in interior design?*

were solved, the time it took, the client's budget, and the design process the designers followed.

Understanding both the public myths and the inner workings of the profession is essential to developing into a successful future designer. To that end, this chapter discusses the evolution of the interior design profession in the United States. This includes the qualifications of interior design professionals; their primary roles, responsibilities, and functions; and how the field is changing. This chapter will bring into focus the full scope of services interior design professionals offer. In addition, you will learn about key events in the evolution of the interior design profession.

The Interior Design Profession in the United States

The field of interior design is complex. It involves multiple factors that impact people, society, and the world. It relates to the function of a space, the physical and psychological comfort of people, responsibility to the environment, as well as beauty and creativity.

> *“Our interiors are the repositories of our memories and the containers of our dreams, aspirations, wants, and needs. They are the reflections of us, our society or culture, and our time.”*
>
> *Shashi Caan, 2011 IFI Annual Council of Delegates*

Interior design is challenging on many levels because it involves working with people, places, and products. Designers work with the needs of a client and translate these needs into spaces that enhance human relationships and behavior. In addition, designers shape and finish the surfaces of these spaces. They select appropriate furnishings, fixtures, and equipment (FF & E), and accessorize the space—making it functional as well as beautiful. They modify space that impacts where people walk, work, and live.

Furniture, fixtures, and equipment (FF & E) refers to many objects used in residential and commercial interiors. *Furniture* can be anything from a chair and table to a file cabinet. *Fixtures* are those items that fasten to a wall and are a permanent part of the interior, such as a ceiling light. *Equipment* can be fixed or mobile and include objects or tools used in the everyday operation of the organization within their interior spaces, such as a bank safe (fixed) or a medical cart (mobile).

Designer Profile

Chelsea Lawrence—Healthcare Design

Chelsea Lawrence is an interior designer with Rowland + Broughton Architecture/Urban Design/Interior Design in Denver, Colorado.

SCI Design Group/Photographer: Michael McLane

"Designing for healthcare offers me the opportunity to design spaces that possess the power to literally help—or hinder—the healing process. Healthcare design professionals design and create facilities for healing, focusing on functionality and aesthetics along the way. It is critical for the patients, families, loved ones, doctors, medical-support staff, and every user involved that the design of the space promotes wellness, healing, and recovery. Additionally, healthcare design is a great example of the value a designer provides in terms of health, safety and welfare (HSW)—all critical elements to any design, but especially in a facility where immobility or incoherence may be a factor in an emergency situation.

"The variety of work and responsibilities I encounter as a designer is what I enjoy most. My job involves taking what I've learned from one project and bringing it into the next—with the realization that no two projects are the same. The creativity and knowledge it takes to solve new problems or challenges based on the specific application makes work enjoyable."

You can read more about Chelsea's design experience in Appendix B.

What Is a Profession?

Webster defines a **profession** as an occupation that requires specialized knowledge and in-depth academic education and training. When understanding any specific profession, it is helpful to know the characteristics common to all professions. Professions all require

- use of skills based on theoretical knowledge
- education and training in these skills
- competence of professionals verified by examinations
- a code of conduct to ensure professional integrity
- performance of a clearly defined service for the good of the public
- a professional association that organizes members and advances the profession
- an identified *body of knowledge*—concepts, terms, and activities that make up a profession

As you will see, the profession of interior design reflects all of these characteristics.

Beginnings of the Profession

The following passages highlight key events and organizations that shaped the interior design profession. This mini-history is a mere snapshot of important activities and people instrumental in the growth of the profession, **Figure 2-2**.

Interior Decoration and Elsie de Wolfe

In the United States, the phrase *interior design* did not commonly appear until after World War II. Before the twentieth century, *interior decoration* was completed by artisans (architects and sculptors), shopkeepers (upholsterers and painters), and craftspeople (furniture designers and carpenters) who were primarily men.

Elsie de Wolfe (1865–1950) generally receives credit for bringing professionalism to interior decoration in two major ways. First, she established herself as a supervising designer of other people's houses rather than an artisan doing so. Second, she made interior design and decorating a suitable occupation for women. The latter may have been influenced by an article published in 1895 in *The Outlook* magazine, authored by Candace Wheeler, titled "Interior Decoration as a Profession for Women."

George Grantham Bain Collection (Library of Congress)

Figure 2-2 Elsie de Wolfe was an early leader in the design field. *Which professional leaders have influenced you most?*

Elsie brought a stance of independence and social standing to interior design. She began her career in 1904 in New York City after receiving accolades about the successful decoration of her home.

Elsie's classic interiors reflected light colors (beige, ivory, gray, and white) and pastels against white backgrounds. This theme differed from the dark, stuffy, cluttered Victorian styles of the time. She removed many objects collected by her clients, creating spaces that reflected light, air, and comfort. Her clients were wealthy and well-known, which shaped the public's perception that decoration belonged to the upper class.

Elsie received her first commercial decorating commission in 1905 for the interior of the Colony Club. This was a new club for a women's organization in New York City. Elsie also wrote one of the first books about interior decoration, *The House in Good Taste* (1913), **Figure 2-3**. Other women published books soon after, clearly showing that women were moving

Images Courtesy of the University of Wisconsin Digital Collections

Figure 2-3 In her book, *The House in Good Taste*, Elsie de Wolfe featured her designs of many homes—creating spaces that reflected light, air, and comfort.

into the profession. Note that the beginnings of the interior design profession in the U.S. related to wealth, residential design, and women designers. These now outdated views still skew public perception today.

First Interior Design Courses

At the same time Elsie launched her career (1904), the *New York School of Applied and Fine Arts* (now the *Parsons School of Design*) began offering courses in interior decoration. The *New York School of Interior Design* followed thereafter in 1916.

After World War I, postwar prosperity trickled down to the middle class. This increased society's interest in and employment of the interior decoration professional—most of whom were women. These women used their good taste as a commodity to sell products and services to American housewives seeking self-expression in their homes. The interior decoration and design for commercial structures, however, was still completed primarily by men.

During the twentieth century, the middle class continued to develop its presence and identity. These people desired to live the American dream and a better way of life. To that end, they sought advice of such social superiors as well-known decorator of the time, Dorothy Draper (1888–1969). The middle class counted on Draper. Deemed a tastemaker because of her gender and class, she delivered decorating advice for their new homes in the suburbs via her regular column in the *Good Housekeeping* magazine.

Draper was well-known for her design of many commercial interiors, **Figure 2-4**. These included the restaurant at the *Metropolitan Museum of Art* in New

A From the archives of Dorothy Draper & Co., Inc. (New York)/The Carleton Varney Design Group

B Courtesy of The Greenbrier; Designed and styled by Dorothy Draper & Company.

Figure 2-4 Dorothy Draper, an early leader who was well-known for her commercial designs, was also counted on for advice by the emerging middle class of the time (A). *The Greenbrier Hotel* in West Virginia was one of Dorothy's commercial designs (B). Her influence remains today.

York and the *Greenbrier Hotel* in West Virginia. Public spaces were her favorite places to decorate. They were locations where everyone could experience great beauty. She was a very confident individual who designed not only museums and hotels, but also fabrics, staff uniforms, restaurants, theaters, department stores, private corporate offices, jet-plane interiors, automobiles, and packaging for cosmetics. In addition, she created residential designs for houses and apartments of prominent and wealthy society figures.

Furniture stores sprang up in department stores with the first one established by Nancy McClelland in 1913. Magazines, such as *House Beautiful* or *House and Garden*, showcased home furnishings displays and publicized the field. Furniture manufacturers flourished in places where craftspeople settled, such as Grand Rapids, Michigan and High Point, North Carolina. By 1914, a number of women decorators formed the *Decorators Club* of New York. In the late 1920s, increasing numbers enrolled in formal college courses. This encouraged the first textbooks and research citations to support the profession's publication needs. The profession began to move from decoration to interior design as it became more formalized. The expert was evolving from untrained decorator to educated professional.

First Professional Interior Design Organizations

An economic depression in the 1930s influenced the formation of the first nationwide professional organization for interior decoration. It arose from a need. The *Great Depression* discouraged the middle class from purchasing furniture in the U.S. Therefore, many furniture manufacturing centers began to close. The leaders of one of the Grand Rapids manufacturing centers decided to invite interior decorators from around the nation to

- develop a national professional organization
- listen to renowned architects and designers, such as Frank Lloyd Wright
- participate in the design of model room displays sponsored by furniture manufacturers

By the end of the conference, the *American Institute of Interior Decorators (AIID)* was founded in Chicago. In 1936, AIID relocated to New York City. This series of events enhanced the exposure of furniture manufacturers to interior decorators and designers. This may have helped prevent many manufacturers from going out of business.

In a 1931 statement, AIID defined the decorator as "… one who, by training and experience, was qualified to plan, design, and execute interiors and their furnishings and to supervise the various arts and crafts essential to their completion." About the same time, those who were acquiring additional design-related qualifications (such as education) sought to distinguish themselves from those who provided furnishings and other elements for the interiors. The emergence of the phrase *interior designer* was the result.

Interior Design Field Broadens and Specializes

After World War II, due to new building construction methods (such as skyscrapers), commercial design became an increasingly important part of the profession. Until then, office interiors were almost solely left to the office manager and the furniture supplier. As a result, the decorators of post-World War II had to rely on more than good taste to obtain clients and employment. These decorators now needed rigorous educational preparation to address client needs and move forward in the profession.

Changes in workplace philosophy created new furniture concepts such as *office landscape*. As practiced in Germany during the first half of the twentieth century, this was the embryo of **open-office planning**, **Figure 2-5**. These offices, rather than appearing in long rows with full-height walls, were designed in groupings with partitions to encourage more collaboration among workers. As companies embraced this planning philosophy, new specialists in space planning, lighting design, and acoustics became part of the profession. Additionally, specialties in the profession, such as healthcare design, began to emerge. In the residential sector, the construction of new homes created booming opportunities for professional designers.

First Interior Design Educator Organization

New branches of interior design organizations splintered from AIID and evolved. In 1957, the *National Society for Interior Designers (NSID)* was formed. Three years later, in 1961, the *American Institute of Decorators (AID)* became the *American Institute of Designers*. In the 1950s and early 1960s, discussions emerged regarding the

- need for additional educational training
- development of a testing procedure for professional qualifications
- licensing necessary for restricting practice for interior designers

Haworth, Inc.

Figure 2-5 This open-office landscape reflects a modern-day workplace philosophy. *Who were some of the early German leaders in the open-office planning movement?*

As the profession gained visibility, more full-time students enrolled in colleges, universities, and private art programs. This interest generated the need to hire more interior design educators. To support learning and collaborating, and to keep educators up to date in their profession, the *Interior Design Educators Council (IDEC)* was formed in 1968. Today, there are roughly 800 educators/members of IDEC. One of the great contributions that arose from IDEC was the publication of the only national scholarly journal for the profession—the *Journal of Interior Design*, **Figure 2-6**.

New Organizations for Residential and Commercial Interior Designers

In the late 1960s, the *Institute of Business Designers (IBD)* formed to meet the needs of commercial interior designers. Its origins emerged from professionals working in office furnishing dealerships. In 1975, the *American Society of Interior Designers (ASID)* was founded, **Figure 2-7A**. Its predecessor organizations were *The American Institute of Interior Design (AID)* and the *National Society of Interior Designers (NSID)*. In 1994, the *International Interior Design Association (IIDA)*, **Figure 2-7B,** was founded as the result of a merger of *IBD*, the *International Society of Interior Designers (ISID)*, and the *Council for Federal Interior Designers (CFID)*. Additional design-related professional organizations formed for such areas as lighting design, retail furniture, facility planning, and color marketing. See the websites for ASID and IIDA.

Accreditation of Interior Design Programs

The movement toward professionalism continued forward. In 1971, AID, NSID, and IDEC collaborated to develop the *Foundation for Interior Design Education Research (FIDER)*. The purpose of this organization was to facilitate, lead, and monitor accreditation efforts. Years later, FIDER was renamed the *Council for Interior Design Accreditation (CIDA)*. Currently in the U.S., CIDA accredits about 170 four-year interior-design education programs, **Figure 2-8 A**. **Accreditation** by CIDA means that an institution conforms with and maintains the professional standards required to prepare students for interior design practice. Strong accreditation standards help groom students for entry-level interior design positions.

American Society of Interior Designers

A

The International Interior Design Association

B

Figure 2-7 The *American Society of Interior Designers* is largest interior design professional organization (A).The *International Interior Design Association (IIDA)* (B) not only provides continuing education opportunities for its members, it also offers an environment for networking—both locally and globally.

Figure 2-6 As its mission, *IDEC* is dedicated to advancing interior design education, scholarship, and service. *Why do you think scholarship and service are intertwined with interior design education?*

Interior Design Educator's Council

A

Council for Interior Design Accreditation

B

Council for Interior Design Accreditation

Figure 2-8 Attending a CIDA-accredited college or university will help you become a responsible, well-informed, and skilled interior designer (A). *What are the CIDA standards that accredited schools must maintain?* Taking and passing the NCIDQ exam helps give proof to the public of your qualifications (B).

Professional Examination Developed

Just as lawyers must pass the bar exam, interior designers apply for and take the *NCIDQ Examination*, **Figure 2-8 B**. It is a rigorous, entry-level exam for interior design professionals. Interior designers may take the exam after meeting educational and work experience requirements. Continuous updates ensure the exam aligns with the expanding knowledge in the profession. Although interior designers must have a wide range of knowledge, the NCIDQ Examination tests only those aspects of the practice that impact the health, safety, and welfare of the public. Organized in 1974, CIDQ is located in Washington D.C.

Health, Safety, and Welfare (HSW) of the Public

The next three decades—1970s, 1980s, and 1990s—were marked with new pressures and responsibilities for interior designers. Tragic fires in public buildings encouraged new strict fire codes for commercial interiors and building structures. This meant that commercial designers had to address fire-safety issues, such as safe exiting strategies from a building.

Rapid increases in the size of business organizations created a need for new space-efficient furnishings and tightly designed spaces. Then and now, the largest expense for a business is employee wages. Therefore, the goal of increasing employee productivity created the need for comfortable and physically supportive furnishings to improve work output and reduce absenteeism.

The personal computer also strongly affected the workplace. As a result, designers had new problems to solve. Such emerging problems included glare from overhead lighting on computer screens, carpel tunnel syndrome from improper equipment placement, and storage issues for paper and electronic files.

Interior products that affect health increasingly concerned designers and manufacturers. Such products included chemicals from paints, furnishings, and building materials. Other environmental issues came to the forefront. Designers began rethinking the use of interior products that endanger natural materials such as tropical woods that could not rejuvenate for 100 years. During these decades, a movement toward healthier and environmentally friendly interiors, or *green interiors*, was set in motion that would shape the twenty-first century.

Green interiors are those that incorporate the use of products that are healthy for humans, save landfill space, and adhere to earth-friendly criteria of quality, sustainability, beauty, and time-tested performance. **Sustainability**, according to CIDQ, is a way of using resources that does not deplete them. It involves a method of practice or way of using materials that has minimal long-term effect on the environment.

The health and safety of individuals is partially based on their ability to safely access building interiors. For instance, if a person is temporarily using crutches and there is no elevator access in a multistory building, taking the stairs can be a safety hazard for the person. Therefore, the need for regulations regarding the safe access to buildings became a need.

In 1990, the passage of the *Americans with Disabilities Act (ADA)* by the U.S. Congress had a large impact on the design of interior spaces. In general, ADA concerns a wide-range of civil rights laws that prohibit discrimination based on an individual's limitations, **Figure 2-9**.

Goodluz/Shutterstock.com

Figure 2-9 The ADA law requires builders and building owners to meet guidelines for universal/inclusive design.

Title III—Public Accommodations (and Commercial Facilities) relates specifically to the access an individual has to lodging, recreation, transportation, education, dining, stores, and care providers. This means that all public spaces must be accessible to and accommodate people with disabilities. Interior designers of public spaces must adhere to the ADA in the design and planning of the interiors and in access to the exteriors of buildings.

First Title Registration for the Profession

In 1982, Alabama passed the first legislation for registration of the interior design profession. Those who wanted to call themselves *interior designers* (a title registration) had to acquire certain qualifications, such as passing the NCIDQ Examination, to use the title, *Interior Designer*. This *title act* protected the title and only restricted use of the title. No longer could a talented person acquire only a business card and sales tax license to claim to be an interior designer. This legislation, however, did not protect who could practice as an interior designer. Therefore, Alabama further expanded *title registration* to include legislation that restricted who could practice interior design in the state. This protected the public by allowing them to make informed decisions about the expertise of individuals from whom they purchase services to complete their jobs.

Recent determinations indicate that *interior designer* is too generic to protect as a title. Therefore, similar to registration for architects who practice in each state, legislation in Alabama and other states now limits the title to *Registered Interior Designer*. Although legislation defines and protects the profession, ultimately such legislation in individual states only passes to protect the public. The public needs to know the qualifications of experts whom they choose to hire.

Unified Voice for the Interior Design Profession

The end of the recession in the early 1990s created pressures for all those working in the building industry. Just as today, obtaining clients and producing revenues became everyday challenges. At the same time, the existence of too many interior design organizations fractured the *voice* of the profession.

In 1994, leaders of the interior design professional organizations met to discuss a merger to *unify* the profession under one organization. Several attempts have been made to merge ASID and IIDA. To this date, this goal has not been achieved due to their different membership missions and organizational goals, **Figure 2-10**.

The mid-1990s began a decade of economic prosperity in the U.S. New construction was at a peak—in both residential and commercial design—in response to mortgage incentives. This factor increased the need for professional interior designers. Similarly, membership in interior design professional organizations increased as attention turned to greening the built environment, both inside and out.

Body of Knowledge

In 2001, Denise A. Guerin and Caren S. Martin, while at the University of Minnesota, published the first interior design *Body of Knowledge (BOK)*. A **body of knowledge** is the foundation of any profession and includes the concepts, skills, and activities involved in carrying out such work. A growing amount of evidence supports the significant effect of interior design in the built environment. The BOK relates to the health, safety, and well-being (HSW) of the public. It has been broken into 65 knowledge areas and is periodically updated. The six major categories for these knowledge areas include

- human environment needs
- interior construction, codes, and regulations
- products and materials
- design theory and process
- communication
- professional practice

Primary Interior Design Organizations			
Organization	**Acronym**	**This is...**	**Use of Acronym**
American Society of Interior Designers	ASID	Largest interior design professional organization. Approximately 25,000 members consisting of both residential and commercial designers; industry and student members. Primarily an interior design practitioner organization.	ASID after name (for example, Jane or John Doe). ASID indicates Professional membership status in organization.
Council of Interior Design Accreditation	CIDA	Independent, nonprofit accrediting organization for interior design education programs at colleges and universities in the United States and Canada. More than 170 interior design programs are accredited by the Council.	Interior design programs at universities or colleges that are accredited by CIDA have voluntarily invited assessment of their programs. If accredited, programs meet the quality standards recognized by the profession.
Interior Design Continuing Education Council	IDCEC	Central organization that approves continuing education units (CEUs) for design professionals.	Use of *IDCEC Approved* logo indicates the continuing education course has been assessed as applicable to the profession and is a high-quality, lifelong learning activity for a practitioner.
Interior Design Educators Council	IDEC	Leading authority on interior design education; dedicated to the advancement of interior design education, scholarship, and service.	IDEC after name (for example, Jane Doe, IDEC) indicates *Professional* membership status in organization.
Interior Designers of Canada	IDC	The Interior Designers of Canada (IDC) is the national advocacy association for the interior design profession. IDC represents more than 5,500 members including fully qualified interior designers, intern members (who have yet to pass their exams), students, educators, and retired members.	IDC members can use the designation IDC after their provincial affiliation. As in Sally Brown, ARIDO, IDC *A Fellow IDC Member would use the designation FIDC.*
International Federation of Interior Architects/ Interior Designers	IFI	International organization that seeks to connect the global Interior Architecture/ Interior Design profession and community to identify and provide design solutions to global problems. Membership in IFI is by organization not individual.	IFI acronym is used in relation to an organization and is visible in countries around the world.
International Interior Design Association	IIDA	The International Interior Design Association (IIDA) is a professional networking and educational association with more than 13,000 members practicing worldwide in more than 50 countries.	IIDA after name (for example, Jane or John Doe, IIDA) indicates "Professional" membership status in organization.
Council for Interior Design Qualification	CIDQ	Independent, nonprofit organization of state and provincial credentialing bodies. Administers rigorous interior design examination.	NCIDQ logo is used with a certificate number (NCIDQ # 5508). Usage indicates that the designer passed all parts of the professional examination.

Figure 2-10 These organizations are dedicated to moving the interior design profession forward. The letter "F" before an acronym means "Fellow." This indicates the individual was recognized for significant contributions to the organization and the interior design profession.

Designer Profile — Denise A. Guerin and Caren S. Martin—Body of Knowledge

Denise A. Guerin, Ph.D., FIDEC, FASID, IIDA, is currently a Principal at InformeDesign, LLC and formerly a Morse-Alumni Distinguished Professor of Interior Design at the University of Minnesota. Caren S. Martin, Ph.D., CID, FASID, IDEC, is currently a Principal at InformeDesign, LLC and formerly an associate professor of interior design at the University of Minnesota. Read the following about Guerin and Martin's view on body of knowledge.

"A profession's *body of knowledge* tells people both inside and outside the profession exactly what it is that people who practice the profession know. Do you know what an attorney does... what a detective does? Sure, you have seen television shows that feature attorneys in courtrooms and detectives solving murders. These programs show only a glimpse into those professions and what these people *know* and *do*—and sometimes what is shown is inaccurate. The same can be true of what some reality-TV design-programming shows about the interior design profession.

"The *Interior Design Profession's Body of Knowledge (BOK)* provides you with full understanding of the broad range of knowledge possessed and applied by competent, well-qualified interior designers. The BOK removes the stereotypical view that people have of interior designers and replaces it with knowledge about a profession that designs the interior environments where people live, work, learn, and play. Interior designers are committed to people by keeping them safe, improving their quality of life, and providing beauty and comfort all through a sustainable approach. What interior designers know to meet their commitment is documented in their body of knowledge."

Guerin and Martin co-edited *The State of the Interior Design Profession (2010)*. They also co-authored three body of knowledge studies: The *Interior Design Profession's Body of Knowledge: Its Definition and Documentation, 2001 and 2005*, and *The Interior Design Profession's Body of Knowledge and its Relationship to Health, Safety, and Well-Being (2010)*. Together they created InformeDesign®, with Guerin serving as coordinator and Martin as director.

You can read more about Denise Guerin and Caren Martin in Appendix B.

Changes and Challenges

Interior design, both as a career and program of study, meets all characteristics common to any profession. Theoretical knowledge forms the basis of skills interior designers use in a practical way. Their education and training supports the skills needed for success in the field. Rigorous examination ensures their competency. Their professional organizations mandate designers conduct business for the public good and perform services with professional integrity.

Before the 1990s, interiors were much simpler in regard to functional planning. Technologies and practice areas had fewer categories and specialties. The twentieth century witnessed the profession's development into specializations such as healthcare design and office design. In turn, these specializations resulted in specialty areas of practice.

Today, in part due to recent reality-design shows and inconsistent legislation across the states, practitioners still face a public that does not distinguish very well between interior design and decoration. The public primarily thinks of the profession as related to home design. Rarely do they consider that commercial design also requires specialized skills to ensure the health, safety, and well-being of the public. These, and other challenges, continue to be addressed as the profession matures.

Professional Path: The Four E's

There are many ways to become a member of the interior design profession. Traditionally, becoming a professionally qualified interior designer involves obtaining a college degree. Once you graduate from college, you continue the career path by taking *Section 1 Interior Design Fundamentals Exam (IDFX)* of the interior design professional examination administered by the *Council for Interior Design Qualification (CIDQ)*. The NCIDQ Examination is the recognized professional interior design exam in North America. The NCIDQ Examination determines if you can design space that is safe, functional, accessible, sustainable, built on time, within budget, and code compliant. This exam does not assess aesthetics. Instead, it assesses all factors that relate to the health, safety and well-being of the public.

Section 1 of the exam—the IDFX—assesses your knowledge of design application, construction standards, and building systems. Section 2—the IDPX—assesses your knowledge of building systems, building codes, professional practice, and project coordination. The third section is a practicum that requires you to create solutions to given design problems. You must pass all sections of the exam to obtain your NCIDQ Certificate. Every state with interior design licensure requires practitioners to have passed the NCIDQ Examination.

Along the path to becoming a professional interior designer, you encounter a series of steps called the Four E's—*education*, *experience*, *examination*, and *continuing education*, **Figure 2-11**. Note that continuing education can take many forms. Once you have your college degree, you might take graduate courses, weekend workshops, or break-out sessions at a conference meeting of your professional association. It is your education, experience, and qualifications that set you apart as a designer. In contrast, an interior decorator requires no formal training.

Today's Roles and Functions

The roles and functions of the professional interior designer are ever-evolving. As the world becomes globally interconnected and technologically integrated, it becomes more important to understand the designer's responsibilities and scope of services now, as well as what the predictions are for the future of the profession.

Definition of Interior Design

As mentioned previously, today, many individuals use the terms *interior design* and *interior decoration* interchangeably. These two fields, however, differ in critical ways. Historically, *decoration* was valued for its artistic contributions and beautification of a space. Similarly, today, it relates to the selection and installation of furnishings and the adornment of space with interior materials that are typically applied to surfaces. While skilled decorators do extraordinary work in the United States, their primary work is aesthetics, not design, **Figure 2-12**.

In contrast according to CIDQ, **interior design** as a profession "is the art and science of understanding people's behavior to create functional spaces within a building." Understanding these behaviors helps the designer better meet human needs. Although decoration is part of what they do, designers primarily use their education and practice experience to develop design solutions to

- be functional
- enhance the quality of life
- protect the public
- reflect the culture of the people
- be aesthetically attractive

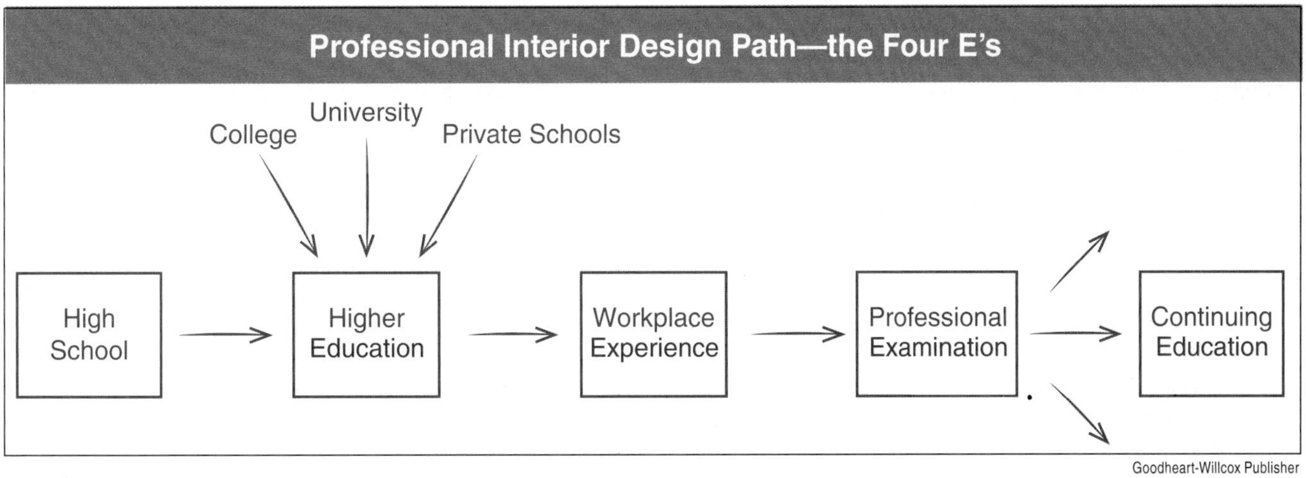

Figure 2-11 The Four E's is the typical path an interior designer takes to workplace success.

CandyBox images/Shutterstock.com

Figure 2-12 The primary work of decorators is aesthetics and enhancing beauty of a space.

According to the U.S. Department of Labor, Bureau of Labor Statistics, interior designers plan, design, and furnish interiors of residential, commercial, or industrial buildings that reflect client goals and needs. Their designs can enhance productivity, increase merchandise sales, develop an environment for healing, or improve a lifestyle.

Designers align their solutions with the building shell and are sensitive to developing designs to enhance *placemaking*. **Placemaking** is the ability to transform a space from simple habitation to one that holds meaning, reflects self-identity, and evokes the history of the individual or culture. Designers also improve the health, safety, and well-being (HSW) of the public by adhering to local and state codes and regulatory requirements. They encourage sustainability when working with their clients. To do so, they educate clients to make design decisions that will not adversely affect critical resources of the natural environment. Well designed interiors invite beauty into the spaces and support human interaction and personal relationships.

Today, ASID, IIDA, IDEC, and CIDA endorse the definition of a professional interior designer prepared by CIDQ. See **Figure 2-13** for an excerpt from the CIDQ website on the formal list of services a professional interior designer may offer.

Residential versus Commercial Design

There are two major categories of interior design practice: residential and commercial. **Residential design** involves designing the interiors of such primary or secondary dwellings as private homes (single-family), condominiums, apartments, town houses, and model homes. Residential design overlaps with many sectors of commercial design. This is because people want to feel *at home* in such facilities as resorts, healthcare facilities, and cruise ships. Therefore, an interior designer incorporates many aspects of residential design into commercial spaces.

Commercial design, or nonresidential design, involves all *other* interior spaces. It includes specialty areas of practice such as

- office design
- healthcare (hospitals, veterinary clinics, assisted-living facilities)
- hospitality (hotels, restaurants, health clubs/spas, museums)
- retail (boutiques, shopping malls)
- institutional (government offices, universities, places of worship)
- industrial (manufacturing facilities)
- transportation (airports, cruise ships, planes)

Recent studies of interior designers show that roughly two-thirds indicate their primary design practice is residential design. In contrast according to ASID, studies sampling architects, facility managers, and interior designers indicate that roughly 55 percent of their primary design practice is commercial. Many interior designers practice both residential and commercial design.

CIDQ—Services Performed by Interior Designers

According to the *Council for Interior Design Qualification (CIDQ)*, interior designers may

- Research and analyze the client's goals and requirements, including development of documents, drawings, and diagrams that outline those needs.
- Formulate preliminary space plans and two- and three-dimensional design concept studies and sketches that integrate the client's program needs. These are based on knowledge of the principles of interior design and theories of human behavior.
- Confirm that preliminary space plans and design concepts are safe, functional, aesthetically appropriate, and meet all public health, safety and welfare requirements, including code, accessibility, environmental, and sustainability guidelines.
- Select colors, materials, and finishes to appropriately convey the design concept and to meet socio-psychological, functional, maintenance, lifecycle performance, environmental, and safety requirements.
- Select and specify furniture, fixtures, equipment (FF & E) and millwork. This includes layout drawings, detailed product descriptions, and provision of contract documentation to facilitate pricing, procurement, and installation of furniture.
- Provide project-management services including preparation of project budgets and schedules.
- Prepare construction documents consisting of plans, elevations, details, and specifications to illustrate non-structural and/or non-seismic partitions layouts, power and communications locations; reflected ceiling plans and lighting designs; materials and conditions; and furniture layouts.
- Prepare construction documents to adhere to regional building and fire codes, municipal codes, and any other jurisdictional statutes, regulations and guidelines applicable to the interior space.
- Coordinate and collaborate with other allied design professionals who may be retained to provide consulting services. These include but are not limited to architects; structural, mechanical and electrical engineers; and various specialty consultants.
- Confirm that construction documents for non-structural and/or non-seismic construction are signed and sealed by the responsible interior designer, as applicable to jurisdictional requirements for filing with code enforcement officials.
- Administer contract documents, bids, and the negotiations as the client agent.
- Observe and report on the implementation of projects while in progress and upon completion, as a representative of and on behalf of the client; and conduct post-occupancy evaluation (POE) reports. POE's are conducted after a design is installed to assess how the newly designed interior spaces meet the intended goals.

Council for Interior Design Qualification (CIDQ)

Figure 2-13 Acquiring certification helps the public to know that you are capable of performing the services here to meet health, safety, and well-being (HSW) requirements.

"Both commercial and residential designs require the need to "balance well being with living well."

Jill Salisbury, Founder and chief designer of el: Furniture, Chicago, IL

There are many similarities in residential and commercial design, **Figure 2-14 A and B**. These include, but are not limited to, the skills you will use, the education you require, the business of maintaining a practice, and the code of ethics to follow.

Demographic Influences

In response to human needs and changing times, the roles and functions of today's interior designer are changing. New areas of practice continue to emerge (for example, eco-resort design) and new technologies continue to enhance communication with the client.

Tremendous changes impacted the interior design profession during the recession that began in 2008. No set of professionals was hit harder than those who worked in the built environment. Both the number of interior design firms and the number of practicing interior designers dwindled.

Warren Diggles Photography/Jon Rentfrow, Rentfrow Design, LLC

A

Photography by Fred Fuhrmeister/Design by RB+B Architects

B

Figure 2-14 Interior designers who practice residential design provide functionality, safety, and aesthetics for their client's homes (A). Commercial design involves the design of all other public spaces; however, many aspects of residential design influence some sectors of commercial design practice (B).

According to the *2010 U.S. Bureau of Labor Statistics* data and the *ASID 2012 State of the Industry Report*, there were about 41,000 employed interior designers in the U.S., down from 46,000 in 2009. Of these, 80 percent are women and 25 percent are 34 years of age or younger. In addition, seventy-five percent have a college degree.

The *2012 ASID Facts and Figures Report* indicated that among employed designers, 39 percent work in interior design firms while another 21 percent work in architecture or landscape architecture firms. The remaining 40 percent work in construction firms, government positions, home furnishings, furniture stores, and retail positions. The states with the highest published employment and wages for this profession are along the coastlines: California, Texas, New York, and Florida. See the U.S. Bureau of Labor Statistics website for specific information on wages.

More recently, the U.S. Bureau of Labor Statistics projects that by 2020 employment of interior designers will increase by almost 20 percent. Within specialty firms, the increase will be closer to 30 percent.

Nearly two-thirds of U.S. interior design firms are concentrated in ten states—California, Texas, Florida, New York, Illinois, Georgia, Ohio, North Carolina, Pennsylvania, and Washington. Note that these states also have some of the largest metropolitan areas. Only three of these states—North Carolina, Ohio, and Washington—do not have some form of interior design legislation.

Architects, builders, contractors, and designers have all struggled to reshape their scope of work to meet the expectations of today's consumer. This consumer is more educated on design options—demanding value for money spent, requesting shorter timelines to accomplish the work, and requiring integrated technologies in design solutions. As designers reshape their work, it reshapes the profession. In addition, the composition of teams that coordinate and collaborate in a built-environment project have continued to evolve, **Figure 2-15**.

wavebreakmedia/Shutterstock.com

Figure 2-15 Collaboration among design-team members is necessary to develop effective design solutions for the client. *What does collaboration mean to you?*

Trends—How Interior Design Is Changing

At the beginning of the twenty-first century, many trends began having a significant effect on the practice of interior design. This section outlines the leading trends to monitor as the profession continues to evolve.

Security and Safety Trends

The century began with real optimism. This changed with the September 11, 2001 terrorist attack on the United States. Security and safety took on new meaning that has a direct link to the design and use of interior spaces. Building owners and users felt insecure in their own offices and homes.

The *American Institute for Architects (AIA)* and professional interior design organizations held forums and conferences. They published documents to educate designers about security planning and design for an open society. Topics included understanding threats, building security technologies, biochemical and radiological protection, and emergency operations. How do you keep the occupants safe in the building? How do you keep them safe as they move through and leave the building? Safety and security are primary human needs that interior designers continue to address.

Sustainable Design Trends

Sustainable design and green design have had explosive interest in the United States. Sustainability protects the earth's resources. According to the United Nations, it is the ability to meet "...the needs of the present without compromising the ability of future generations to meet their own needs." Sustainability is based on the principles of ecology, human equity, and economy. Green design supports environmentally sound principles of construction, selection of materials, and energy use. This aligns with the CIDQ definition of sustainability described earlier in the chapter.

Supporting this trend was the development of the U.S. Green Building Council (USGBC) *Leadership in Energy and Environmental Design (LEED)* rating system in 2000. The **LEED rating system** ensures built environments are designed and built using strategies aimed at achieving high performance in key areas of human and environmental health. The voluntary use of this rating system has earned great success in raising the public awareness of the triple bottom line—people, planet, and profit.

Interior designers use this rating system to guide their designs specific to such areas as indoor air quality, lighting design, and specification of green products for both commercial and residential clients. The interest of the nation in these topics has made it essential for interior designers to understand the concepts and practices related to sustainable design. As a design professional, becoming LEED accredited is one qualification that holds national and international recognition, **Figure 2-16**.

Another concept related to sustainable interior design is *Cradle-to-Cradle*, or *C2C*, that emerged as a phrase with Walter Stahel in the 1970s. The concept of **C2C** is based on a simple theory that the planet has nonrenewable resources that cannot be consumed indefinitely. Therefore, according to C2C, all materials used in industrial or commercial processes should be recycled into new products at the end of their life. As architect William McDonough said, "...it is not about *doing without* but instead, about *doing it right*."

By embracing sustainable and green design, many interior designers are advancing a no-waste policy and taking on new responsibilities. They respect the needs of current and future generations. They accept the responsibility to be good stewards of the environment. As interior designers accept this social responsibility, they design ecologically sound, healthy interiors.

Since sustainability has become a mainstream trend, higher sustainability standards are under development. In addition, *resiliency* (an ability to recover easily) is now receiving attention. This interdisciplinary concept and movement refers to creating cities and communities that lessen or eliminate the impact of future shocks that arise from factors such as climate-change related disasters, energy costs, and/or environmental change.

Global Design Trends

The focus on sustainable design becomes even more intense when an interior designer works in the global marketplace. Globally, the world's population is projected to reach 9.1 billion by 2050, up from 6.9 billion today. The technology explosion has opened doors to Western ideals, lifestyle, and design. While is it

LEED® and the related logo is a trademark owned by the U.S. Green Building Council® and is used with permission.

Courtesy Eric Laignel Photography/Lighting Design by Clanton and Associates, Inc.

Figure 2-16 The U. S. Green Building Council's LEED program is the most highly recognized green-building program around the world.

flattering for others to have interest in Western design, it is a potential pitfall to impose such interior design and architecture styles and functions globally. Interior design professionals must be responsible in creating spaces that respond to the cultures of the place.

While work in the U.S. slows when the economy slows, other countries—such as China—have ever increasing demands for interior design services. Many U.S. interior design and architectural firms have satellite offices and design studios in international locations. Others compete for large- and small-scale international design projects from U.S. locations.

There are challenges in practicing design in other countries. Language barriers are sometimes the least of them. Communication—speaking the same *design* language—is another. Other barriers include

- different color meanings (for example, white in the U.S. is a color used in weddings and celebrations and in China it is the color of mourning)
- intellectual property rights (your idea and designs are not considered yours in some countries)
- difficulty of producing design work in unfamiliar cultures (For example, the painter or framer you work with in the U.S. will not be available to achieve the quality of work your design demands. Can you locate another expert in the country where your design is being installed?)

The benefits outweigh the challenges. Global design is increasing in response to population explosions in developing countries. Interior designers can make a positive difference in those areas of the world.

The global economy is a reality. Preparation of future interior design graduates to practice across international borders is critical to the continuing success and growth of the profession.

Trends in Design for All

As a population ages, physical limitations can increase. To meet these needs, as well as those of younger people with various health challenges, interior designers develop solutions based on strategies called *aging-in-place*, *inclusive*, and *universal design*.

Aging-in-Place

In 1900, there were three million Americans age 65 and older (1 in 25). By 2000, the numbers grew to 31 million (1 in 8). According to the U.S. Census projections, by 2050 there will be over 88 million people comprising the *baby boomers*—the generation born between 1946 and 1964 who are entering the retirement phase of their lives.

Baby boomers are motivated to stay active, healthy, and engaged participants of society, **Figure 2-17**. This market segment has a higher education level and more

Monkey Business Images/Shutterstock.com

Figure 2-17 Because baby boomers are choosing to remain longer in their own homes, they are more motivated to stay physically active. *Conduct an oral history interview with an older adult (or baby boomer) you know about their opinions on aging-in-place.*

discretionary income than the previous generation. One of their goals is **aging-in-place**—living longer and independently in their homes rather than moving to retirement facilities. Research indicates they will live longer and happier lives if they do. Therefore, this group places a high value on the functionality as well as the appearance of their homes.

The aging process can include fear of abandonment, dependency, and depression. Effective design solutions can discourage helplessness and becoming a burden on family members. The health, safety, and well-being (HSW) of older adults is a critical aspect of any design solution.

Commercial designers want to support baby boomers in every public building they enter. These include doctor's offices, hospitals, banks, fitness centers, food stores, and retail stores as well as retirement centers, and continuous care retirement communities (CCRC). It is projected that design work for this population in the U.S. will require approximately two decades.

Inclusive and Universal Design

Some designs are better designs for all individuals, regardless of age, ability, or physical stature. While a push button is helpful outside a building to provide access for those who use a wheelchair, that same button is helpful for a student with an armload of books. Likewise, a lever doorknob is helpful for a person with arthritis and it is also helpful in bringing independence to a small child who cannot turn a round knob. A design practitioner seeks better design ideas to enhance functionality and make spaces more comfortable for everyone. The solution is *inclusive design*, also known as *universal design*.

> *"People are only disabled when they can't do what they want to do. Universal design can be considered a type of orthopedic device which does more than accommodate disability. It actually eliminates disability by letting people do what they want to do."*
>
> *Cynthia Leibrock, MA, ASID, Hon. IIDA*

Inclusive design, a phrase often used in Europe and Canada, supports any individual by removing barriers and improving personal well-being (for example, increasing light levels to sharpen the vision of aging eyes).

Similarly, **universal design**, a phrase often used in the U.S. and developed by Ron Mace, is the "...design of products and environments to be usable by all people, to the greatest extent possible, without adaptation or specialized design." It is a user-friendly approach to design in the living environment. People of any

Designer Profile

Rosalyn Cama—Evidenced-Based Design

Rosalyn Cama, FASID, EDAC is President and Principal Interior Designer at the evidence-based planning and design firm CAMA, Inc., located in New Haven, Connecticut.

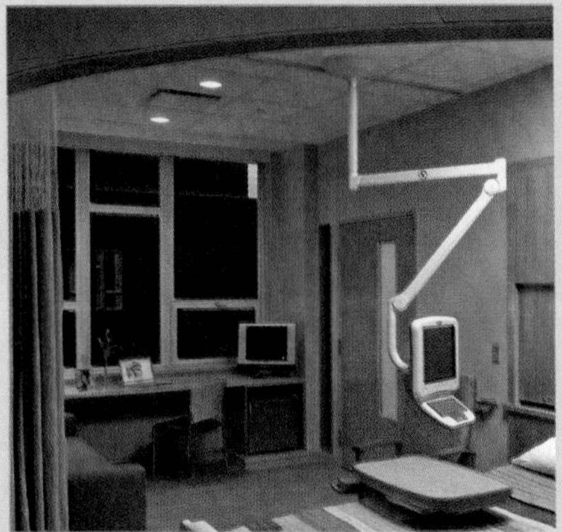

Photography © Brad Feinknopf. Permission by CAMA, Inc.

"Evidence-based design is the process of basing decisions about the built environment on credible research to achieve the best possible outcomes. What I like about this practice methodology is its ability to liberate the creative process from a trust-me model of decision-making to a show-me model that enables innovative solutions. In most design decision-making situations a designer presents the concept of a design after a lengthy investigative process with a client. If the creative solutions are based upon hunches and the expectation is that the client should trust the designer's skill in order to accept the solution, then there is a strong possibility that the concepts will be challenged and rejected. When the premise of the design solution is built from measured outcomes that are aligned with the client's goals then the proposed solution becomes that more likely to be approved. This process allows innovative solutions to be launched from a tried and true baseline of knowledge and encourages those who innovate to measure these new concepts and share their findings with others."

You can read more about Roz's design experience in Appendix B.

culture, age, size, weight, race, gender, and ability can experience an environment that promotes their health, safety, and well-being (HSW) today and in the future.

Evidence-Based Design Trends

Students perform better on tests—seven to 18 percent better—if their classrooms have large windows and skylights compared to those who sit in rooms with little view to the outside. Students who can hear their teacher's instructions also get higher grades. According to a Herman Miller study, the ability for students to move and adjust their furniture not only improved their learning but their class performance, too. They could more clearly understand the teacher (14 percent) and view the instructional materials (17 percent). These research results positively impact the design of classrooms and educational facilities.

Evidence-based design (EBD) is an approach to design that uses facts and professional judgment to develop informed design solutions for clients. In practice, its most frequent use is in the design of such healthcare facilities as clinics, hospitals, and surgical centers. EBD, however, is becoming more common in the design of schools, office spaces, hotels, museums, and residences, too!

While designers use EBD primarily for large, complex public facilities, they may also use it for a simple design task such as selecting fabric for a client's chair. In some cases, synthetic fibers can worsen a client's medical condition when he or she touches the upholstery fabric. EBD, supported by scientific research, assists the designer in specifying fabrics that do not interfere with a client's health or medical condition.

EBD links to sustainable and green design due to the need to collect evidence and data for a building or interior to achieve a LEED rating. The designer can use this data for the design of future facility projects.

Simply put, EBD is a process of seeking answers to design problems—and seeking them in a structured manner. As a growing trend and practice, this is one critical way interior designers can provide long-standing value and better informed design solutions for their clients.

Technology Trends

There are many technology trends that significantly impact the field of interior design. The Internet changes how businesses conduct their work. For example, familiar retailers increase sales and provide customer convenience by adding an online presence. In addition, online banking and online library lending offer flexibility to the consumer. As a result, interior designers are making necessary shifts in how they design these interior spaces for their clients.

These technology trends also force designers to change the way they do their work. For instance, some interior designers are completing designs for clients without ever meeting them or personally visiting the space. They perform all the work via the Internet.

The connectivity to clients and the world through digital devices has shaped how and when designers discuss and complete their work. The ability to work any place, anytime is real time, **Figure 2-18**.

LDprod/Shutterstock.com

Figure 2-18 Interior Designers use a variety of digital media to connect with clients.

CASE STUDY

CAMA, Inc.—Evidence-Based Process for Healthcare Design

The project team for Dublin Methodist Hospital in Dublin, Ohio was instructed by the hospital administration to deliver a hospital design that would revolutionize healthcare delivery. The CAMA design team was encouraged to take measured risks and use an evidence-based design (EBD) approach from which to launch innovative concepts.

The resulting design is a 94-bed hospital that blurs the boundaries between inside and outside. It has accessible outdoor gardens, plentiful views, and ample indoor lighting. On arrival at the hospital, greeters welcome and carefully attend to patient and family needs throughout the building. Patient rooms are private, adaptable, and standardized. All rooms include family space equipped for work with wireless Internet and sleeping space for family members.

In other hospitals, shared plumbing lines result in making adjacent rooms mirror images of each other. Such differences in orientation make the space less efficient and can lead to medical error because of room layout. The intention of standardization in all patient rooms at Dublin (oriented in the same direction; same-handed—not mirror images, all looking the same) is to reduce medical errors and increase staff efficiency. With the use of EBD, the design team was able to learn from other industries about standardization practices that reduce errors and increase efficiency.

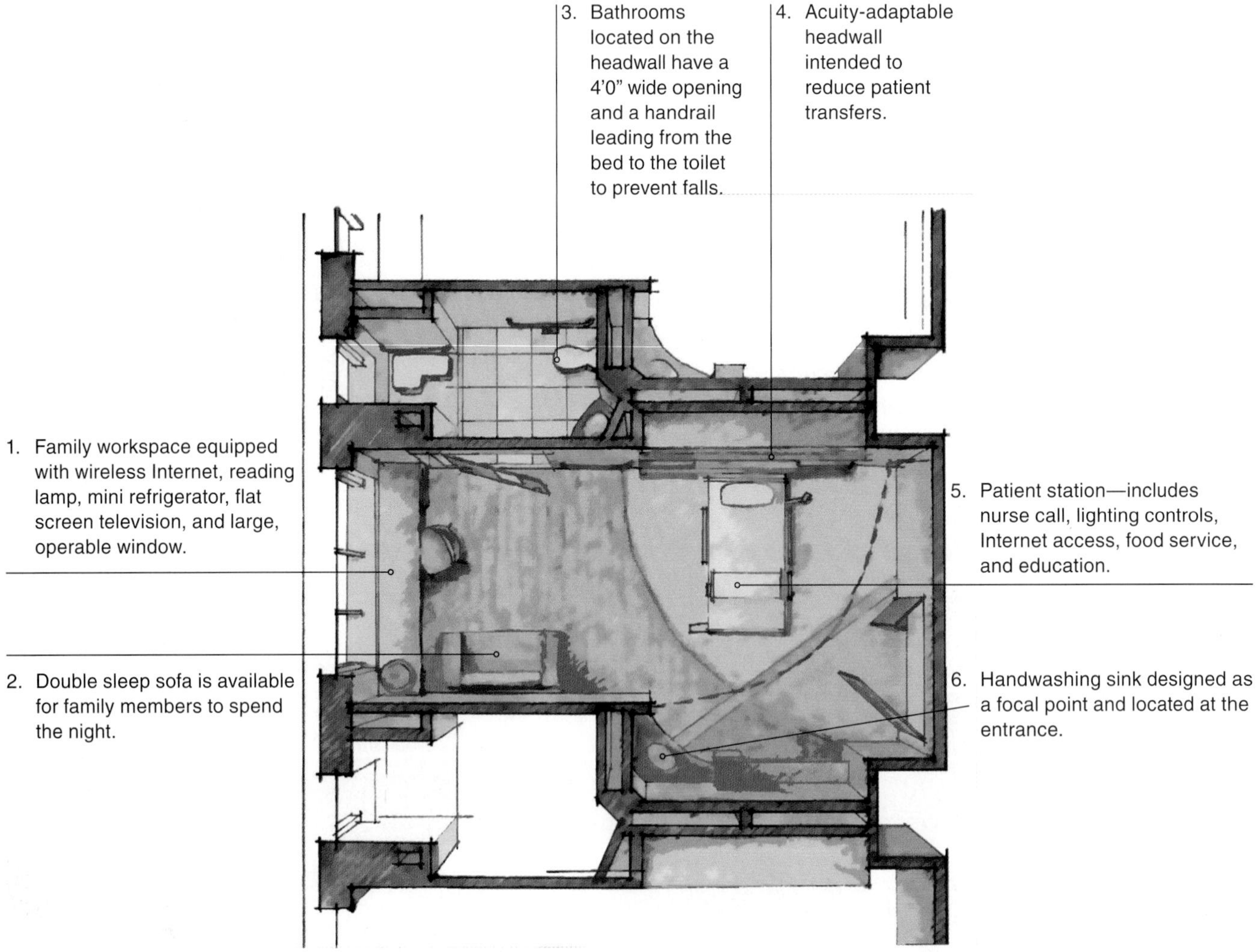

Art by Karlsberger Architects. Permission granted by CAMA, Inc.

This image shows an artistic representation of a floor plan (a rendering) of a patient room.

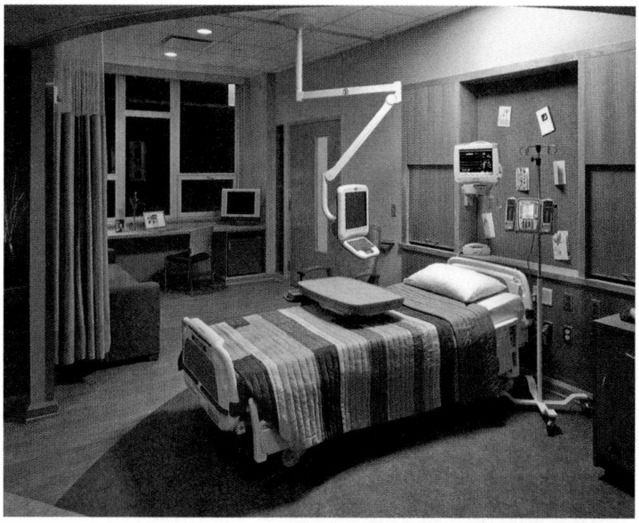

Photography © Brad Feinknopf. Permission by CAMA, Inc.

At Dublin, the standard patient room has a fully equipped infostation that controls nurse calls, the Internet, television, and more.

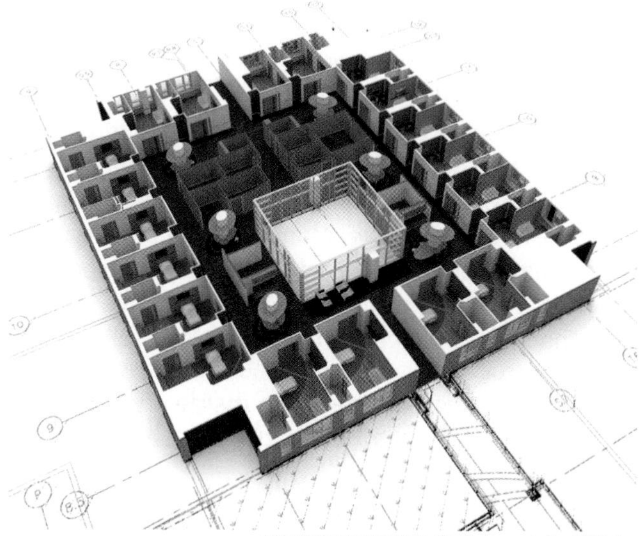

Art by Karlsberger Architects. Permission granted by CAMA, Inc.

This computer-generated model shows the centrally located nurse's stations (pods) surrounded by patient rooms.

Photography © Brad Feinknopf. Permission by CAMA, Inc.

The sink as a focal point in the patient room encourages hand-washing compliance.

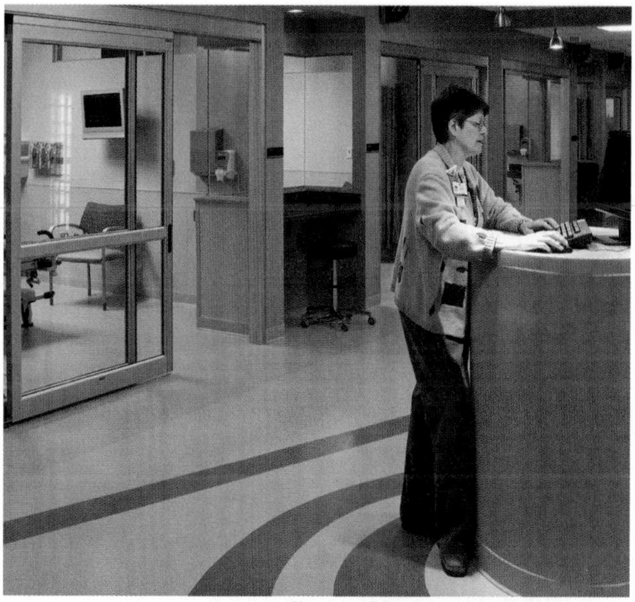

Photography © Brad Feinknopf. Permission by CAMA, Inc.

The "touchdown pods" replace conventional nurse stations, allowing for greater staff efficiency in patient care.

Investigate and Reflect . . . .

Use the three reliable Internet or print resources to read more about the EBD process. Summarize the key ideas presented in each source. Then write your response to the following question. How do these resources support or conflict with EBD information presented in the text?

Social networking affects the way designers connect with other designers, potential clients, and manufacturing representatives. Because referrals significantly affect the interior design business, social networking plays a critical role in marketing a designer's work and generating new clients. Through social collaboration technologies, a designer can impact the field by spreading design tips, contacts, and ideas to large volumes of people. Many of these people would never have benefited from traditional collaboration methods such as conferences. Mobile devices connect designers more quickly and accurately to clients and their referrals.

Imagery technologies, such as the standard video, combined with such new technologies as mobile computing is changing how the client perceives and views design solutions proposed by a practitioner. According to ASID, in the near future more than 25 percent of the content viewed in a day will be dominated by images, video, and audio. The written word will not be enough. Clients will demand more details of the design professional's proposed designs, such as that provided through pictures, **Figure 2-19**. To that end, new computer software and multimedia applications continue to improve the offering of enhanced three-dimensional modeling of interior spaces in real time.

Technologies that help interior design professionals accomplish their *work*—such as mobile computing and **cloud technology** used to store data, software applications, and design information—will also be important in the upcoming years. Lastly, technologies also related to building systems and lighting design will have significant effects on the design industry for many years to come.

Courtesy of Chelsea Lawrence

Figure 2-19 As clients demand more visual details about their design proposals from interior designers, the designers utilize various imagery technologies to enhance client presentations and understanding. *Analyze the benefits of how the interior designer is best using digital technology in this design. What features do you think would help the designer "sell" this design to the client?*

Chapter

2

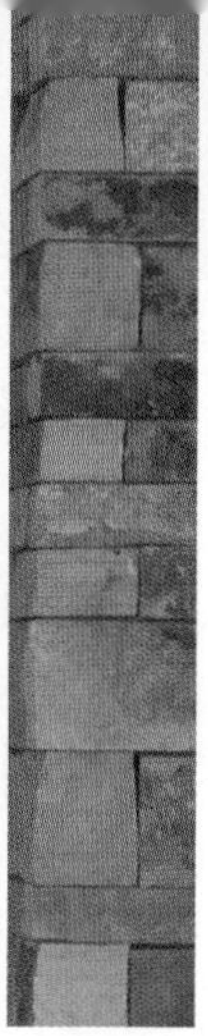

Review and Assess

Summary

- Interior design is a popular field, receiving much attention from design-related reality TV shows.
- Interior design professionals need to explain what they do and its value to the public.
- According to an *ASID* report, interior design comprises a relatively small segment of the entire building industry, but its impact is enormous.
- Interior design is a complex profession. The education is rigorous and time-consuming.
- Understanding the inner workings of the profession is essential to developing into an interior designer who is caring, sensitive, professional, and socially responsible.
- The economy impacts the profession of interior design—thriving during economic booms and reshaping itself in a slow economy.
- Interior design is more than the selection of materials, finishes, and colors to create a pleasing environment.
- Designers reflect the function and aesthetic needs in the placemaking of client's interiors. From homes to hospitals, restaurants to retail stores, and schools to capitol buildings—interior design influences the function, safety, and beauty of the interiors.
- Interior designers may practice residential or commercial design or both.
- Strong interior design trends include safety and security, sustainable and global design, resiliency, designing for all people, evidence-based design, and technology.

Chapter Vocabulary

Write the definition of each of the following terms. Then write a sentence using each term in a design-related context.

accreditation
aging-in-place
body of knowledge
C2C
cloud technology
commercial design
evidence-based design
furniture, fixtures, and equipment (FF & E)
green interiors
inclusive design
interior decoration
interior design
LEED rating system
open-office planning
placemaking
profession
residential design
sustainability
universal design

Review and Study

1. Name two misconceptions about the profession of interior design.
2. What is a profession? Cite three characteristics common to all professions.
3. Name three women who were instrumental in the early development of the interior design profession.
4. What circumstances surrounded the formation of the first professional organization for interior decoration?
5. What is meant by the term *accreditation*?
6. What aspects of interior design does the NCIDQ Examination assess?
7. Name three factors of the 1970s, 1980s, and 1990s that presented interior designers with new pressures and responsibilities.
8. What is meant by the term *body of knowledge*?
9. What are the *Four E's*?
10. Contrast *interior design* with *interior decoration*.
11. According to CIDQ, name six services that interior designers may perform.
12. What is the difference between residential design and commercial design?
13. What are two factors that support the trend of sustainable design?
14. What challenges do designers face when practicing in other countries?
15. What is meant by the terms *aging-in-place* and *universal design*?
16. What is evidence-based design (EBD)? Name two examples where an interior designer might use EBD.
17. Identify two ways technology trends influence the way an interior designer works.

Critical Analysis

18. **Analyze.** Analyze the quote at the beginning of this chapter. Write a justification indicating why an interior designer must be responsible for designing spaces that meet the health, safety, and well-being (HSW) needs for all people while using resources in a sustainable manner.
19. **Assess similarities and differences.** Watch an episode of a reality-TV design show that involves the design of interior space. Then review the text definition of an interior designer. Identify five similarities and five differences between what the design host does and what a professional interior designer offers to the public. Compile your list and discuss your responses with the class. Then review the website for *Careers in Interior Design* to view additional information about what a design professional offers to the public.
20. **Draw conclusions.** Based on information the author provides in the chapter, draw conclusions about the need for forming various interior design professional organizations. How did such organizations benefit designers then and now?
21. **Compare and contrast.** Create a T-chart—labeling the left column *Aging-in-place* and the right column *Universal Design*. Brainstorm design features for each and list them under the appropriate column. Compare and contrast your lists of design features. Which features might appear in *both* types of interiors? Discuss in class.
22. **Analyze and predict.** Tour the neighborhoods in your community and analyze the different types of residential and commercial buildings. Keep a tally of how many you see of each. Based on those numbers, predict the types of clients an interior designer might have in your area.
23. **Make inferences.** With teams of 10 classmates in 10 minutes, make a list of 10 inferences (based on the text) about roles and responsibilities of the interior designer might have on the job and how social media influences the way an interior designer does business. Write your inferences on a large sheet of paper. Each team should post its paper on the board. How are the inferences similar and different for each team? Do all inferences have value? Discuss in class.

Think like a Designer

24. **Writing.** With a team member, review the websites for the following interior design professional organizations in the U.S.: ASID, IDEC, IIDA, CIDQ, and CIDA. Develop a table listing each organization, its mission, and vision. Analyze the similarities and differences and how the work of each organization shapes the interior design profession. Then write a team summary on your findings.
25. **Reading.** Use the Internet to read about Victorian era interiors. Locate several photos of Victorian living spaces. Compare these photos to the design photos of Elsie de Wolfe in Figure 2-3. Identify three ways that Elsie's designs differ from those of the Victorian era. Write a summary of your findings to share with the class.
26. **Research.** Choose one or more of the following trends in interior design to research: safety and security, green design and sustainability, global design, or technology trends. Use the CIDQ or ASID websites to research further information about your chosen trend(s). Prepare and post a summary for your school-approved class blog page. Be sure to cite the source(s) of your research.
27. **Speaking.** To get a feel for how interior designers use *evidence-based design*, visit a retail store. Count how many people enter the store in 30 minutes. Note if each person turns right or left on entering to start shopping. Then note if high-priced items are in the path of the shopper. Analyze how you might change the store design given your new understanding of shopping behavior. Give an oral report explaining how your findings can become a piece of evidence for EBD.
28. **Career path.** Write your goal for your career in interior design. Then review the Four E's that people traditionally follow to become a professional interior designer. Look ahead five years in your life. Draw a diagram that illustrates the ideal path you might take to become a professional interior designer.
29. **Website review.** Visit the ASID and IIDA website. Select the section for *students*. Review the opportunities and resources these organizations offer to you as a design student. What new information did you learn about the profession from your web visit? Write a summary.

Design Application

30. **Designing for aging-in-place.** Suppose you have a relative, neighbor, or friend who is older and has difficulties functioning in the interior space of his or her home. You want to do something to help. Do the following to develop a plan:
    A. Use the Internet to locate images of interior design ideas that would enable this person to better function with daily living activities in his or her home.
    B. Create a digital slideshow. Include a slide or two that identifies the functional needs of this person.
    C. Present the societal need for better designed interiors by showcasing your slideshow on the class or school website.
31. **Technology for design.** Interior designers use a variety of technologies to communicate with clients and potential clients. Research various forms of technology designers use for design creation and communication. Use a school approved digital application to create a digital poster or blog page about such technologies to share on the class website or web page.
32. **Portfolio.** Visit the ASID website. Locate the link for your state and the designers in your area. Select two different professional designers in your state and look up their websites. Review their portfolios or award winning designs. Compare and contrast the different types of designs created and the website presentation. What ideas does this give you for your future portfolio? Save your notes in a portfolio folder on your computer.

Interior Design Specialty Areas of Practice

Photography © Pat Sudmeier/Architecture by Poss Architecture + Planning/Interiors by Associates III Interior Design

Chapter 3

Design Insight

"Thoughtfully designed spaces help us learn, reflect, imagine, discover, and create."

IFI DFIE Interiors Declaration

Learning Targets

After studying this chapter, you will be able to

- differentiate between commercial and residential interior design specialties.
- understand the residential interior design specialties in terms of creating a home and working with team members, time lines, and budgets.
- summarize residential design trends and their impact on interior design.
- identify characteristics of various sectors of commercial interior design including office, hospitality, healthcare, institutional, and retail design.
- summarize commercial interior design trends for office, hospitality, healthcare, institutional, and retail design.

Introduction

Within every profession there are specialty areas of practice. A dentist can specialize in orthodontics and a doctor can specialize in surgery. The career of interior design is no different. Both commercial and residential sectors of interior design practice have specialties that offer exciting opportunities that contribute to a thrilling and fulfilling lifetime career.

Exploring Interior Design Practice

As you explore the specialty practice of interior design practice, keep three things in mind.

- **Link between commercial and residential design.** There is a growing link between commercial and residential design. For instance, commercial specialties—such as hospitality and healthcare design—reflect the use of many design details that encourage beauty, warmth, and comfort as in residential settings. There is a growing need for designers to develop sensitivity to and knowledge of these design details to be successful in either area of practice.
- **Impact of global and local design.** It is important to *think global* and *design local* in both residential and commercial projects. Design decisions, such as the specification of interior materials impact tropical forests or finite resources in the world. Minimizing impact and developing environmental awareness is important in all design projects.
- **Practice in commercial and residential sectors.** According to the most recent *ASID State of the Industry* report, the majority of practicing interior designers in the United States work in *both* commercial and residential sectors. Many work on two or more types of design projects in a year. The most common specialty areas are residential and office design. In part this is due to business diversification.

Which specialty area would you find the most intriguing to study? Is there one that ignites your excitement and resonates with your personal values? Which would support the lifestyle you foresee in your future? Whatever your choice, you will be shaping space and human behavior in any specialty you select—a creative, exciting responsibility.

Commercial versus Residential Design

Commercial interior design involves the planning and design of primarily public spaces. In contrast, residential interior design focuses on private dwellings such as houses, apartments, and multiunit housing buildings, **Figure 3-1**. While a residential client is typically the primary occupant, commercial design clients are not often the end users such as with the design of a hospital. Residential clients are often more personally vested in the final design solution than commercial clients, who may never use the hospital in question.

Project Types—Residential and Commercial Specialties

Types of Residential Design	Types of Commercial Design
Single-family dwellings (primary or secondary homes; detached)	Offices
Town houses, apartments, duplexes, condominiums, and patio homes (attached)	Hospitality
Home remodels	Healthcare
Historic home restoration or preservation	Education
Model homes	Government
Private yachts and houseboats	Retail
Motor homes	Institutional

Figure 3-1 Residential and commercial interior design encompass many specialties.

A second major difference between commercial and residential design is the *project time line*. Completion dates for residential projects range between two months and 18 months, while commercial projects may run from six months to five years depending on the size and scope of the projects.

A third major difference is *budget*. Residential design projects are often much less expensive than commercial projects. The process to acquire funding for commercial projects may also be different. For example, if a new elementary school design is proposed, the community may have to pass a **levy**—a tax increase—to pay for the new facility.

Other differences between commercial and residential interior design projects exist. These include

- size of project
- project team members
- client-designer relationship
- building codes and **egress** (exit) issues
- fee structure for payment
- process for acquiring the project
- type of construction
- type of contract documents
- needs of the end user, universal design
- occupancy loads
- complexity of building systems
- signage and graphics
- interior finishes and furnishing standards
- post-occupancy evaluations

Residential designers work through the complexities and interpersonal relationships essential to the character of a home environment. Commercial designers work with large numbers of people and must have the ability to work with a multitude of complex details.

The size of any design project has great impact on who is part of your design team. For example, as a commercial designer, your project team often includes an architect, engineer, general contractor (GC), plumber, heating and air-conditioning (HVAC) expert, lighting designer, electrician, and many subcontractors, **Figure 3-2**. **Subcontractors** are individuals or firms—often specific tradespeople—who contract to perform all or part of the project's work. They may be experts in flooring, walls, furnishings, windows and doors, millwork, window treatments, ceilings, hardware. In addition, subcontractors may also work with audio, alarms, music, technologies, phones, noise control, and such safety features as smoke alarms and sprinkler systems. Both residential and commercial designers work closely with many vendors, contractors and other service providers, coordinating and orchestrating the entire design team.

Depending on the client, sometimes the interior designer is the lead project manager and sometimes the architect or general contractor takes the lead. In large architecture firms or design-build firms, interior designers may be on staff.

Both commercial and residential design specialties require the same education and many of the same design skills. Some of these include

- ability to work with all different types of people
- team skills and strong **work ethic**—a set of values that promote hard work and diligence (in other words, team members work hard for the team)
- creative-thinking and problem-solving skills
- verbal and nonverbal communication skills, including good oral and writing abilities
- research skills
- in-depth knowledge of products, materials, and finishes
- ability to visualize three-dimensional space, including space-planning abilities
- training to plan, schedule, execute, and manage the project

James Steidl/Shutterstock.com

Figure 3-2 Interior designers work with many contractors and subcontractors like this plumber.

Understanding some of the similarities and differences between residential and commercial design are important when the design process of each project type is discussed in later chapters.

Following are the major specialties within both residential and commercial design sectors. Each is very individual in its own way. For instance, space planning for offices may focus on functional cubicles. In contrast, space planning for a residence includes creating a functional kitchen. Office and residential design are respectively the most commonly practiced specialties in the nation. See if there are one or two specialties that appeal to you, **Figure 3-3**.

Residential Interior Design Specialties

Residential interior design involves the planning and design of private dwellings to reflect the client's tastes, preferences, and functional needs. A *client* may be an individual, two people, or a couple with children. This category of practice involves everything from small-scale bathroom remodels to large-scale, multiunit town houses. Residential design serves the individual and family rather than the general public.

As the second largest area of practice in the U.S., residential design has great influence on human behavior, personal interactions, and private relationships. Residential designers help clients make informed decisions about the design of personalized, physical home environments. These spaces nurture meaning, attachment, and capture the identity of the inhabitants.

Designer Areas of Specialization

Specializations	Percent of Business
Office	76%
Residential	52%
Hospitality	47%
Healthcare	41%
Education	41%
Government	37%
Retail	31%
Institution	25%
Other	7%

*Source: *ASID 2012 Scanning Report*

Figure 3-3 Office and residential design are the most commonly practiced interior design specialties. *Which specialties capture your interest most?*

When discussing single-unit dwellings, an expert designer uses psychology and knowledge of human behavior to assist the client in analyzing space and prioritizing both function and preferences for the home. For multiunit dwellings, such as a set of town houses, understanding of the client profile that might be attracted to the design of the town house and its location is critical. Residential design is a complex, and fulfilling, creative sector of interior design practice, **Figure 3-4**.

Creating a Home

What is a home? By definition, a home is the private living quarters of a person or family that is a personalized physical space and a social environment that nurtures attachment. A home should be a place where people rejuvenate. It should serve as a safe haven in the midst of hustle, bustle, and change.

Whether you are designing a new residence or remodeling an existing one, there are basic issues to address with the client. Interior designers understand that the interview process identifies how client preferences shift an empty space to a profound living place. The types of questions a designer often asks center around

- personalization of space
- personal and family needs
- functional places to support activities
- size, views, and building orientation
- budget and time line
- client *wants* if budget and time allow
- aesthetic considerations

Areas within Residential Design

- Vacation homes
- Manufactured homes
- Smart homes
- Universal design
- Sustainable, green, eco-design
- Kitchen and bath design
- Home offices
- Home-theater or media-room design
- Custom closet/storage design

Figure 3-4 Residential interior design is fulfilling and complex. *Which of these areas do you think requires the most creativity? Why?*

There are additional and important complex factors affecting the design of a client's dwelling. These factors—that change an impersonal container or *house* to a personalized *home*—are often interwoven and at times, difficult to identify. However, an interior designer must incorporate them into the space to create a **sense-of-place**—a personal experience in a place and how a person feels about it, and a **sense-of-self**—your personal identity or who you are as a person—for the client.

A home should reflect occupant personalities, offer beauty, meet needs, and function properly. The design should comply with building codes to provide client safety. In such a dwelling, people also receive inspiration, acceptance, love, and create memories that last a lifetime. Designing physical space with the psychological goals of achieving a quality space gives interior designers an extraordinary responsibility.

Often television programs and online websites show what characteristics make an ideal client home. However, what is ideal to one person may not be ideal to another.

According to expert Dr. Chad Gibbs at Colorado State University, there are four major categories that comprise attributes of *home*—personal, temporal, social, and physical. These categories, if addressed in the interior, result in an environment that meets client needs, life preferences, and dreams. See **Figure 3-5**.

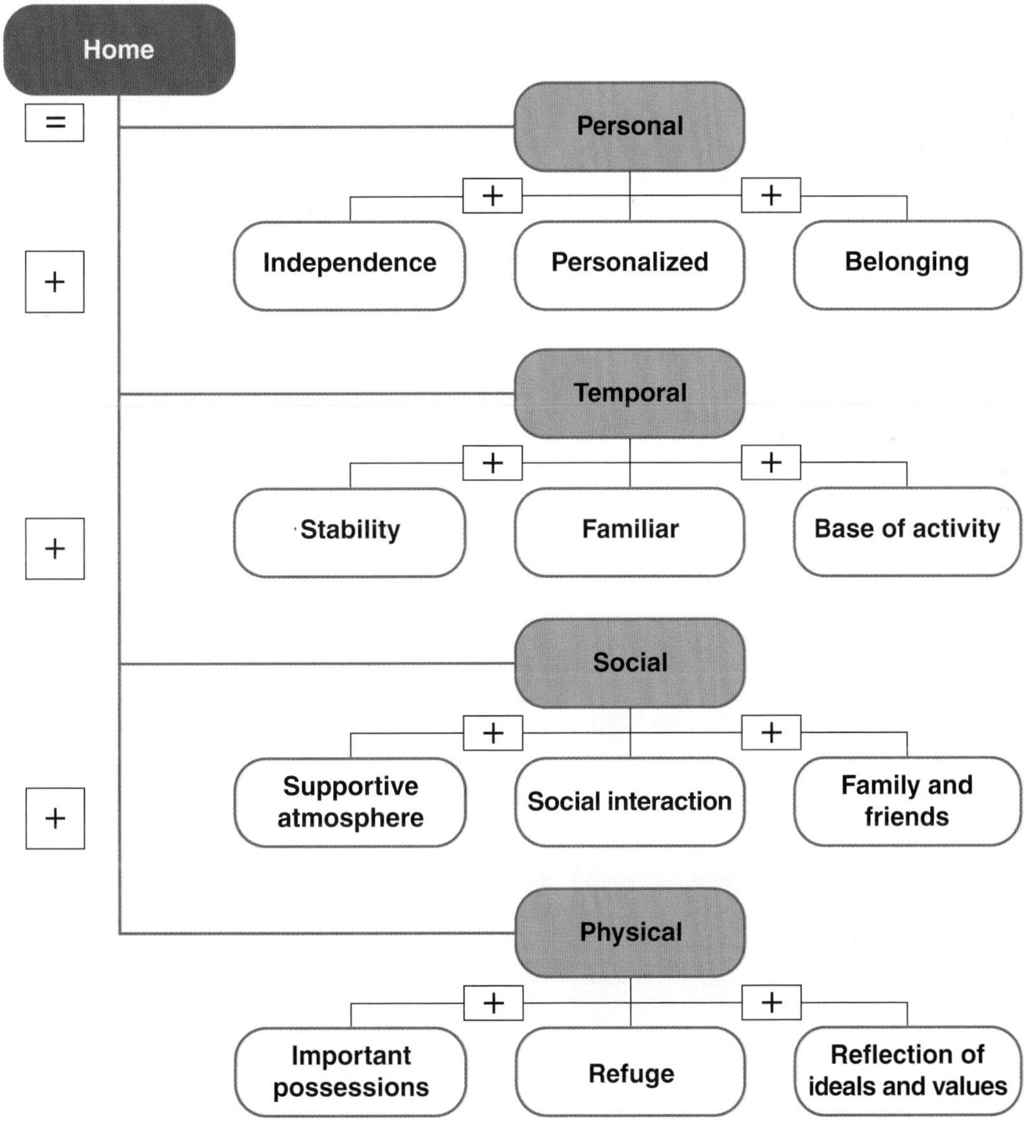

Courtesy of Chad W. Gibbs, Ph.D./Art by Goodheart-Willcox Publisher

Figure 3-5 Meeting these attributes of home results in an environment that satisfies client needs. *Discuss your views on how understanding these attributes of home can help an interior designer best meet client needs.*

Team Members, Time Lines, and Budgets

Team members on a residential project may include the architect, contractor, engineer, subcontractors, landscape designer, and lighting designer. A small-scale project, such as a bathroom, may take a couple months to complete. An entire residence may take anywhere from six months to several years to finish. Likewise, a client budget can range from a modest amount to millions. Therefore, it is important to realize that money does not equate to good design (a design that meets the client's needs for function and aesthetic preferences). A very large mansion may cost a great deal and still be poorly designed.

Some of the best projects on which an interior designer may work are those that offer the most impact on peoples' private lives at a fraction of the cost. For instance, when Hurricane Katrina hit New Orleans and displaced many families, new, well-designed, lower-cost houses with well-designed interiors were constructed. Although many think high-end residential design is an exciting and innovative career, the smaller, socially responsible projects are just as thrilling to design—or more so. A designer can achieve a quality residential design at many different **price points**—standard prices set by the designer, **Figures 3-6 A and B**.

Residential Trends

There are many residential interior design trends in the United States. The following includes a few from both the new construction and remodeling sectors. You will learn about others later in the text.

Living Large in Small Spaces

Many residential interior designers and real estate agents are indicating an increasing interest in smaller, well-designed homes. The larger homes in the United States are not as desirable to heat or maintain, nor do many people see such homes as attainable.

The average home in 1950 was about 983 square feet with 66 percent containing two or fewer bedrooms. In 1970, the average was about 1500 square feet. In 2011 the average new single family home was similar in size at 2480 square feet. In 2013, the U.S. Census Bureau reported that the average square footage for a new single-family house was 2598 square feet.

Many consumers no longer perceive a larger home to be a better home. This aligns with the national consciousness for sustainability, energy conservation, and the economy which drives design. In contrast to this notion, NAHB reported that homes which began construction in 2011 were larger than those in 2010 and more likely to have 4 or more bedrooms, at least

A Jupiterimages/Photos.com/Thinkstock

B Peter Rymwid Architectural Photography/Design: Lita Dirks & Co.

Figure 3-6 Quality residential interior design is achievable at many different price points. *Which of these images do you think reflects a lower to moderate price point, the kitchen/great room combination (A) or the living/dining room combination (B)? Which seems higher end, A or B? Which do you think creates the most personal satisfaction for the interior designer? Why?*

NAHB®
National Association of Home Builders

Image courtesy of NAHB

Figure 3-7 The members and employees of the *National Association of Home Builders (NAHB)* strive to improve housing affordability, availability, and choice.

three-car garages, and finished basements, **Figure 3-7**. This phenomenon occurred because of the economy. Only a certain segment of buyers could afford to build houses and when they did, they built them better-than-average.

One example of smaller and smarter is the number of *pocket neighborhoods* springing up across the nation. This lifestyle is a throwback to yesteryear in which everybody in the neighborhood knows all their neighbors. Research indicates that baby boomers or younger people from Generation Y particularly prefer the smaller, community-oriented cottage or bungalow homes that offer shops and medical facilities within walking distance. The interior spaces of these homes can appear spacious (with larger windows, for example) even with a smaller **building footprint**—the area a building structure takes up on a site as defined by its perimeter. Compact, functional design is necessary particularly for those boomers who are downsizing and living with less.

The concept of living large in small spaces is not just for pocket neighborhoods. This concept can be found in new 700-square-foot cabins in secluded areas, 2500-square-foot condominiums, and 1600-square-foot farmhouses in rural America. Quality design does not necessarily equate to quantity of space.

Remodeling versus Moving

With the recession of 2008, the residential building industry came to a standstill. With job losses and less available credit, many Americans chose to remain in their homes instead of moving. Although statistics indicate that Americans move on average every six years, this was not possible with a stagnating job market. The growing popularity of living a *green* lifestyle made it socially acceptable for people to refurbish, reuse, and conserve within their current interior spaces rather than moving. **Conspicuous nonconsumption**—the avoidance of lavish or wasteful spending for social prestige—became the trend.

As family budgets became tighter, resourceful interior designers helped clients repurpose and rethink how to use current spaces in multiple ways to maximize available square feet. Often this involved the placement of new *partition walls* (walls that divide space without bearing weight) and relocation of plumbing or electrical features. Designers helped clients choose new finishes and colors to refresh and revitalize the interior, boosting the morale of the client and family.

Residential remodeling has encouraged many designers to rethink the focus of their design practices toward such areas as home office design, and kitchen and bath design. Designers also expanded the breadth of their remodeling services by offering design solutions online to clients to avoid costly travel time and money. The continuing development of new technologies makes this relatively unexplored new line of services a bonus for clients. Remodeling design is a consistent sector of the residential design field—in both good and poor economic times.

Aging-in-Place

A recent study by the *National Conference of State Legislatures* and the *AARP Public Policy Institute* indicates that 90 percent of people over the age of 65 want to stay in their own homes for as long as possible, and 80 percent believe their current residence is where they will always live. Most baby boomers live in single-family units and own their homes. Many of them are interested in aging-in-place. Research indicates that remaining in your private home as you age increases lifespan and health.

Physical obstacles often exist in the homes of older adults. Such obstacles include too many stairs, narrow doorways, and obstructive doorknob design. Older adults hire designers who use universal design concepts to suggest changes to key functional areas such as kitchens, bathrooms, utility rooms, and front-entry areas. Interior designers have a unique opportunity to counsel this growing group of people and to assist them in remaining vital contributors to their communities, **Figure 3-8.**

Multigenerational Living

With more children returning home after college and more parents moving in with their adult children, multigenerational homes are increasing in popularity. In a recent study, NAHB indicates that multigenerational living has jumped 30 percent in the past few years. With this in mind, resourceful interior designers began assisting clients in remodeling basements and other parts of their houses to accommodate multiple generations living under one roof. Such design changes to interior spaces require space planning. **Space planning** is the analysis and design of interior spaces in response to occupancy needs. Space planning often requires the design and/or relocation of walls, partitions, and doorways to better meet the needs for the client or end users of the space.

Design: Cynthia Leibrock, MA, ASID, Hon. IIDA, EASY ACCESS TO HEALTH/Photography courtesy of Kohler

Figure 3-8 Designing functional areas to assist older adults with aging-in-place is a fulfilling goal for many interior designers.

Designer Profile — Cynthia Leibrock—Aging Beautifully

Cynthia Leibrock (MA, ASID, Hon. IIDA) is an award winning author, an international lecturer, and a designer with over 30 years of experience. She is the principal/founder of EASY ACCESS TO HEALTH, LLC. Consider Cynthia's mission to improve health, longevity, and life quality through the understanding of universal design as you read the following.

Design: Cynthia Leibrock, MA, ASID, Hon. IIDA, EASY ACCESS TO HEALTH, LLC/Photography courtesy of Kohler

"Imagine your home as a place for regeneration, a sanctuary for healing the wounds of the outside world. It is clean, not cluttered and unmanageable. It prevents disease and injury and restores you when the inevitable occurs. It regenerates you on a daily basis, supporting good sleep, encouraging exercise, making it fun to do healthy cooking.

"That's a lot to ask of a house, but it can be done. For the last six years my husband and I have been living with contractors to demonstrate regenerative design. We have integrated over 200 "Design Details for Health," the title of my last book. Most are illustrated on my *Aging Beautifully* website. About half of these ideas cost less than $50, but some are expensive. Check out the steam shower, bathtub inside a bathtub, magnetic induction wok, steam oven to seal in nutrients, and dual refrigeration to keep veggies fresh for weeks. Our exercise room is the most beautiful part of the house, not the basement. Notice the relaxing views, the clean lines, and the green design. You won't notice the grab bars, the gurney accessible bathroom, the ceiling track lift, or the accessible route through the house. It's there, but it's invisible...and we suddenly needed all of it.

"In the last few months my husband tore his Achilles tendon, and I had unexpected hip surgery. He was on a scooter and I was using a walker. The hospital was recommending a *rehab facility.* In other words, we were heading for a *nursing home.* Instead we headed for *our* home—a safe and comfortable place with a seat in the steam shower, recessed wool area rugs, and beautiful wood floors that are slip-resistant both wet and dry. After surgery we transferred from our car, wheeled into the accessible entry, pushed a button on the automatic door, and entered a space filled with healing natural light, beautiful views, soothing music, and so much more. This is a home for regeneration, our home for life."

You can read more about Cynthia's design experience in Appendix B.

Lock-off units—self-contained living quarters consisting of an apartment with a separate entrance attached to the home—are becoming popular, as well as two master suites on separate levels of the home. Universal design features such as wider hallways, elevators, and grab bars are also becoming the norm.

Sustainable and Green Design

Sustainable design is an environmental responsibility that considers the protection of the health and welfare of global ecosystems for current and future generations. It is a method of practice or use of materials that has minimal negative long-term effect on the environment. For instance, an ideal example of sustainable design is the client's use of an existing commercial building rather than constructing a new one. New construction and remodeling sectors are adopting **green-design practices**—those practices that protect people's health and welfare in the built environment. In practice, this involves the selection of healthful interior materials or the incorporation of more daylight into a hotel or home. The *National Association for Home Building (NAHB)* has an excellent program and checklist for eco-friendly and green construction of new homes. Likewise, the *United States Green Building Council (USGBC)* has moved into the residential building sector with a *LEED (Leadership in Energy and Environmental Design) for Homes Certification* to encourage architects and builders to design smarter and wiser. *REGREEN*—a partnership program between ASID and USGBC—is an excellent and constantly updateable set of resources, case studies, and tools for green-home remodeling projects in the United States.

Photography by Ben Tremper/Interiors by Associates III Interior Design

Figure 3-9 This residence meets LEED standards for sustainability and green design. Some of the green features include the native rock fireplace, Forest Stewardship Council approved lumber for floors, millwork, and cabinetry, and eco-lighting solutions. *How do consumers and interior designers benefit from using sustainable and green design practices?*

Eco-friendly residential interiors utilize energy-efficient practices. In addition, use of recyclable materials, vintage finds (reuse), and a smaller building footprint add to the sustainability of such interiors. In these houses, designers may use such local, natural materials as oak or maple woods and nontoxic paints, **Figure 3-9.** They also use **daylighting strategies**—those that harvest natural light to minimize the use of artificial lighting during the day.

Specialty Spaces

There are several specialty spaces in the home receiving extra attention. Based on reports from ASID, NAHB, and AIA, they include the following:

- **Home offices.** Such spaces are still the most popular special-function rooms. With the popularity of telecommuting—and with many workers catching up on work at home, and of the labor force working on a self-employed basis—home offices remain a priority.
- **Mud rooms/drop zones.** Spaces for backpacks, outerwear, or even personal electronics are becoming necessary in many homes.
- **Outdoor living areas.** As an extension of living space, outdoor living areas reflect the growing lifestyle informality of typical households. This trend cuts across all geographical areas—cold and warm.

Specialty spaces that are declining in popularity are media rooms/home theaters, exercise/fitness/sauna spaces, and interior greenhouses. In addition, many people replace their formal living rooms with flexible, informal spaces near the kitchen hub.

Residential designers are experts in working through the complexity of individual or family needs. They help clients prioritize the spaces in their most private dwelling—the home. These designers play a critical role in shaping successful interactions and increasing functionality of the home, reflecting human value.

Commercial Interior Design Specialties

Commercial interior design involves designing the use of public spaces. These places may be where you eat, work, play, recover health and heal from medical conditions, exercise, meditate, or enjoy life, **Figure 3-10**. According to the U.S. Department of Energy (DOE), commercial buildings consume 19 percent of the energy in the U.S. Therefore, the design of them is critical to conserving natural resources.

Of particular concern for commercial designers is the health and safety of the public. Because 75 percent of building codes relate to fire safety, the interior designer must focus on what might keep a group of people from exiting a building safely in case of fire. Awareness of the responsibility and liability of this project type and understanding of the public's needs are critical for the commercial designer. There are many commercial design specialty areas. The following includes the major ones in order of the most commonly practiced.

Corporate Design

Today, corporate office design is the largest interior design specialty, surpassing even residential design. Office design involves not only private offices for executive CEOs it also involves office systems for thousands of employees, such as those found in Google's corporate headquarters. The corporate-office design specialty spans work from a single room to entire high-rise office centers. This design focus is exciting, fast-paced, and technology driven, **Figure 3-11**.

Although technology continues to become a deeper part of peoples' lives, office design needs for employees are very basic—meeting space, furniture, and technology access. Spatial needs for the entire organization are greater. They include collaborative spaces and private offices, conference and training rooms, cafés, fitness centers, child care centers, and healthcare centers. In addition, the lobby areas play a critical role for customers and clients. They communicate the first corporate impression, ensures security, and directs visitors to specific locations within the facility.

Interior Designer: SCI Design Group/ Photographer: Michael McLane
A

RB+B Architects, Inc./Photography by Fred Fuhrmeister
B

Figure 3-10 The interior design of this physical therapy room is shaped by the need for health and safety (A). The design of this school library is engaging but also addresses the need for safety (B). *Discuss which design features address the health, safety, and well-being of the public.*

Types of Corporate Design

- Cafes and cafeterias
- Child care facilities
- Conference rooms (small and large)
- Office supply areas and workrooms
- Corporate or executive suites
- Fitness centers; locker rooms
- Gathering places
- Lobby areas
- Mailroom
- Office systems
- Private professional offices
- Restrooms
- Outdoor spaces

Haworth, Inc.

Figure 3-11 Corporate/office design involves meeting the interior needs of a vast array of employees. *Why do you think corporate/office design is technology driven?*

There are several important factors related to office design. They include

- **Work-flow patterns.** Understanding work-flow patterns within an organization is critical knowledge for the designer. Interior spaces must support the way the organization and its employees function best.
- **Communication needs.** Office design must enhance communication channels within the organization. In an increasingly complex and competitive world, where creativity and innovation are vital, office design is key. It must bring people, information, and space together in a way that helps them maximize individual performance. In addition, office design must streamline efficiencies and enhance workplace productivity.
- **Flexible office configurations.** The technologies of tomorrow promise to revolutionize how people collaborate, power their devices, and navigate the world. Change is constant. Therefore, the design of an office space must be flexible to address current and future needs. For example, historically a private, corner office was the reward that accompanied a promotion. Today, offices for employees may be open spaces without privacy doors or partition walls. The message this sends supports collaboration and open communication. Such configurations make workers more creative.
- **The office chair.** The chair is the most important piece of furniture in the office space. The chair supports the comfort of the user whose salary is the major expense for their organization. Chairs that properly fit the human body enhance productivity at work, **Figure 3-12**.
- **Powering up.** As the proliferation of mobile devices increases, the need for electricity explodes. Wi-Fi, Bluetooth, and wireless networks encourage more and more data to be sent wirelessly; thereby placing a demand for more power from batteries. Offices need to accommodate the increasingly constant need to recharge. The future offers options of recharging without outlets and cords.
- **Human preferences.** Designers must understand human behavior in public spaces. For example, strangers prefer not to touch each other when sitting in close proximity in public spaces. Chair arms, tables, plants, and lighting often serve as physical or perceptual dividers to enhance physical and visual privacy.

As technology drives change and a new generation enters the workplace, designers are responding to their needs. They are creating spaces that are flexible, anticipate technology, and reflect the current culture of collaboration.

Link to History

Evolution of the Work Environment

Historically, work in the office is the same as it is today: moving the product out the door, tasks to complete, socialization, formal meetings, and storage or access to files. The goal was to help the company or employer prosper. As cities grew larger, during such years as the Victorian era, central business districts developed that were solely devoted to business activities. Because telephones did not exist, closeness was important for making business communication fast and easy. Skyscrapers and passenger elevators were developed to squeeze more people and work into limited space. Offices inside tall buildings were strictly utilitarian with rows of small offices arranged along corridors so that every office would have access to windows for light and ventilation. Private offices existed and waiting rooms boasted glazed wooden partitions. The office as a social setting was lost as the manufacturing mentality of repetitive tasks entered the office.

Workplace philosophies changed dramatically in the 1950s. The Quickborner Team, from Germany, introduced the concept of *office landscape*. Office walls were replaced with screens or partitions, plants, or bookcases. In the 1960s, the use of office-system furniture seriously changed office design. To use panels and work surfaces, rather than desks, demanded the designer understand communication patterns within the organization. New specialists in space planning emerged and flexible workstations began to appear. Companies such as *Steelcase, Haworth, Knoll,* and *Herman Miller* led the way in developing open-office design strategies. These strategies enhance collaboration, develop workplace flexibility, and reconfigure physical space. Today, the office has returned to a place where socializing is important to generate new knowledge and collaboration, rather than encouraging specific repetitive tasks.

Analyze It!

Knowing a little history behind office design and current office trends, predict what you think the next generation of workspace will look like. What type of office environment would you like for the future?

A great deal of office design comes under the category of **tenant improvement work (TI)**, which involves the design and construction upgrades to a leased space. Often the lessor will pay for a small part of the upgrades to attract tenants; however, the majority of changes to the interior space are paid for by the tenant.

Haworth, Inc.

Figure 3-12 Furnishings that fit the human body well help increase worker productivity in the office environment.

TI involves changes to the interior of a commercial property, such as a large office building, by its owner to accommodate the needs of a tenant, such as a law firm. The law firm hires an interior design firm for assistance in remodeling the tenant space. Changes generally involve floor and wall coverings, ceilings, partitions, air conditioning, fire protection, and security. The lessor (landlord) and the law firm (lessee) negotiate a portion of the TI costs which is usually documented in the lease agreement.

Businesses often lease building space rather than own their buildings outright. As different tenants, or businesses, move into the space, they sign a new lease and a relocation of interior walls or partitions occurs to reflect the new owner's business. In addition to a new space plan, TI addresses all existing and new furniture, fixtures, and equipment to meet the business needs. As businesses grow or possibly shrink, designers who specialize in TI can play a significant role in shaping future business success. **Figure 3-13**.

© Ron Pollard, courtesy of RNL

Figure 3-13 For office design under the category of *tenant improvement work (TI),* the building owner accommodates the needs of a tenant.

Office design issues include

- traffic patterns and circulation needs
- workflow between departments and key individuals
- technology to support integration
- signage and **wayfinding**—use of signs and graphics to help individuals easily find their way when travelling through a building—particularly useful in large buildings
- enhancing employee productivity and innovative thinking

- acoustics and privacy issues
- territoriality and confidentiality
- equipment needs
- lighting and climate controls

Office Design Trends

Office design trends reflect how and where people work, who they work with, and the time of day they work. These trends are ever-changing due to increasing integration of technology and the demand for innovative thinking to solve future problems.

Anytime, Anywhere Work Environments

The emergence of new technologies in the workplace is changing the way people work and conduct business. Today, virtual work is not only possible, it is probable. This type of work is free from the requirements of physical spaces, such as a brick and mortar building, and is associated with high levels of team collaboration.

With so much job consolidation in the U.S., work roles are quickly changing. Connection is everything because people must be able to quickly and effectively produce their work. These new connection technologies allow the design professional to offer a quicker response to both team members and clients. For example, when a designer is on-site working with a subcontractor, he or she can take a digital picture of the existing cabinetry, draw a suggested revision on the digital table, and download it to the subcontractor and team members without changing locations. There is no need to return to the office to complete work. The designer conducts work and communication on-site, thereby allowing him or her to complete the client's project in a timely, less costly, and accurate manner.

In addition, global roles necessitate doing work at different times of the day due to time zones. Research indicates that 62 percent of employees regularly communicate with people in different time zones and geographic areas. Anytime, anywhere work environments are becoming a norm.

Younger Workers Desire Flexibility

Traditional ways of working in an office involve the nine-to-five job. As younger workers enter the workforce, the expectation is that they will be mobile. The rise of the mobile workforce allows companies to get work done faster and more efficiently. A recent study indicated that there are about 119 million mobile workers in the U.S. There is pressure, therefore, to create more flexible spaces with smaller budgets. There is also a need to design workspaces for a transient population and creating specific spaces that are welcoming for mobile workers.

Alternative Work Styles

Alternative work styles such as hotelling, telecommuting, and co-working are remaining popular. Hotelling began with consulting firms whose employees were gone for several days out of the week. Why provide an office for those who are rarely in the building? **Hotelling** is the ability for employees to check into an office space, similar to checking into a hotel, to use the space to conduct necessary business without having exclusive assignment to or ownership of it.

Telecommuters, also called *nomad workers*, are those who conduct work from anyplace but their business offices. Telecommuters often work from home. They may also use mobile telecommunication devices and set up their offices in cafés, hotel lobbies, or on airplanes, **Figure 3-14**.

Co-working involves multiple individuals who gather to work in a shared space to split costs for overhead.

iofoto/Shutterstock.com

Figure 3-14 Mobile telecommunication devices allow telecommuters to conduct their work from almost any location, including a hotel lobby such as this.

They share values and enjoy working around people and usually have different jobs—such as various young entrepreneurs.

The previous phrases describe creative ways of working from home, job sharing, office sharing, and sharing office expenses and in-house resources. Appropriate furniture, finishes, and equipment must support all types of work, even work done from vehicles. In addition, designers are still examining new ways to support social media in interior spaces. These often impact office work and, therefore, office design.

International/Global Work

Around the world, people collaboratively create information in a wide array of spaces. Although technology has made virtual work possible, the physical office space remains crucial. Such spaces foster trust, creativity, information-sharing, and communicating a company's identity.

Global markets have cultures colliding in the workplace. What are the attitudes, values, and beliefs of a specific culture? What makes one culture more prone to collaborate than another? Which cultures encourage informal discussions across an organization, and in contrast which cultures hold to a top-down hierarchy in communication? What type of business protocols should the designer understand? What type of communication styles are best used and should be supported in the interior? Understanding how cultural issues translate into the workplace affects the design of future, physical office spaces.

Smart Surfaces

A recent study indicates that the future of office spaces may be the surfaces themselves. Research of five-year-olds indicates that when handed a smartphone, their first impulse is to manipulate the screen directly rather than use any buttons. That future may be already here. New types of paint roll onto a variety of surfaces to allow electrical signals to run across the surface. This innovation promises to transform walls and floors into interactive tools. The headliners (the inside covering of the car roof) and panels inside cars have already become active-touch surfaces. Predictions indicated that touch technology will shift to types of flooring, too. Wires and cables allowing technology access often mar the beauty of an office design. The shift to innovative active-touch surfaces eliminates such problems.

Generational Collaboration

Not only is the design of the workplace changing, but so are the people in it. Baby boomers and those from generations X and Y are working together, bringing their values, goals, and communication approaches to the workplace. A study produced by the *Business and Professional Women's Foundation* indicates that by 2025, generation Y will account for 75 percent of the world's workforce. Employers are facing the difficult task of creating workspaces that can accommodate all generations. Clients are looking to designers to develop environments that attract and retain the best employees.

Link to History

Historical Roots of Hospitality Design

In early America, the inn or tavern served as a place of food, lodging, socialization, safety, and community gathering. The earliest hotels were established near county seats of government where travelers visited and needed lodging for one or more nights. They were also places of rendezvous for groups of people to meet.

The better inns offered a fireplace, benches and tables for eating or games, and private rooms. Often, the inns were places where local people gathered to collect information on crop prices, politics, battles, weather, and local news. As inns evolved, separate private rooms were offered to ladies to rest in—away from the hubbub of the inn. In colonial America, the majority of taverns were owned by women, particularly widows.

Critical business took place in many inns or taverns. Many early governments met in taverns. The First Continental Congress was formed in a tavern. The United States Postal Service can trace its origins to taverns and coffeehouses.

Analyze It!

Select three types of hotels or three types of restaurants. Analyze their differences in: clientele, food types, and interior design. Describe how they are similar and different? What features make furnishings, ceilings, walls, and floors unique? What makes each space appealing to customers?

The dynamics of the office environment have dramatically changed over the last few years and will continue to do so in the future.

Hospitality Design

The second largest commercial interior design specialty area is hospitality design. It is an exciting and creative specialty of the interior design profession and is widely diverse. There are many different types of hotels and motels in this industry. Each provides the guest with a different type of accommodation and experience, ranging from historic to modern and traditional to unique. They include

- bed-and-breakfast lodging
- boutique hotels
- convention centers
- destination hotels
- franchised hotels
- historic hotels
- motels
- resort and theme hotels

Today, the specialty area of hospitality design reflects its historical roots. The hospitality-design specialty has two major branches—lodging and food/beverage. The lodging branch includes the interior design of hotels, motels, spas, resorts, and bed-and-breakfast inns. These places offer a point of rendezvous, a place to relax and feel safe, and a location to purchase lodging and possibly food. The food and beverage branch includes fast-food or fine-dining establishments, cafés, coffee shops, cocktail lounges, and bars. Specially designed hospitality facilities are for those who

- travel for or transact business on-site
- attend educational events
- pursue relaxation, entertainment, or vacation
- enjoy a quiet meal during a hectic day

The interior design of these facilities often communicates a sense-of-place by using local or regional design characteristics. They are often visually and culturally unique.

Hotel Design and Trends

With global and regional travel, hotels are often a travel destination rather than just a place to sleep. Services hotels provide include lodging, dining, entertainment, office, relaxation—including spas, pools, mini golf, and other amenities, and such personal-care tasks as laundry and dry cleaning. Hotel design goals evolve around improving the guest experience.

Hotel sizes vary from quaint inns and bed-and-breakfast establishments to large destination hotels. Their interior designs range from very modern and chic like the *W Hotel* in New York City to a rustic lodge in Yellowstone National Park. Hotel design includes many different types of lodging, **Figure 3-15**.

Berni/Shutterstock.com

Figure 3-15 The goal of hotel design is to improve the guest experience.

Hospitality design employment is diverse. A hospitality designer may have his or her own firm and work in a local community, or travel around the country working for a specific hotel category, such as boutique hotels. Such designers may also be staff designers for one hotel franchise—employed to repeat a standard design in various cities of the world. Spaces designed in a lodging facility include the lobby, ballroom, meeting rooms, guest registration area, guest rooms, and offices. Common issues designers address in hotel design include

- customer service
- convenience
- guest safety
- quality amenities
- noise control
- privacy
- layered light levels and control
- signage, wayfinding, and hotel identity

A hospitality designer often comes up with very creative ideas. Travelers appreciate different, memorable experiences to relate to friends on their return home. Hence, design concepts should be strong, clearly developed, and consistent throughout the hotel.

Hotels are **mixed-use design facilities**—a phrase that describes those structures that combine elements of commercial and residential design spaces in the same facility. Guest rooms are the primary revenue-generating area of a lodging facility. They should feel like, or be better than your personal bedroom, yet be able to handle the wear, tear, and constant maintenance requirements for different guests every night. The furnishings should not be fragile, but sturdy, stylish, and easily maintained to meet the commercial grade standard.

Just as a foyer offers the first impression of a home, the hotel lobby makes a first impression on hotel guests. Any grand views or large architectural elements such as a fireplace—a common element in historic inns—serve as focal points of the interior, **Figure 3-16**. Custom details are critical in strategic areas of the hotel to achieve a unique and memorable experience for the guest.

Allegria Spa at the Park Hyatt Beaver Creek/Photography by Don Riddle/Interiors by Associates III Interior Design

Figure 3-16 Grand views and interesting architectural details, such as this fireplace, are interior design features critical to a quality guest experience. *What design features were the most attractive to you as a guest at a hotel?*

Depending on the hotel type and size, **amenities**—attractive features that hold value to guests—may differ. Many guests expect hotels to offer such amenities as suites, Internet access, refrigeration, spectacular views, spa-like bathrooms, fitness areas, pool areas, laundry facilities, and child care. In addition, multiple types of cafés, coffee shops, restaurants, meeting and convention rooms, cocktail lounges, gift shops, concierge services, and small-group areas for conversation are also requirements. In the right climate, indoor spaces flowing into outdoor spaces are also very desirable.

With the recession in 2008, the hospitality industry was hit hard. Fewer people could afford to travel and interior designers practicing in this specialty had very few new projects. With a good upswing in new work, many trends are emerging that enhance the guest experience.

Total Immersion

A flourishing hospitality trend is **immersion**—the use of local design elements to showcase a location's unique materials, cultures, and traditions to provide visitors with a memorable, flavorful experience. Hotels, resorts, and spa properties desire to reflect their physical locations in their design inspirations. The hospitality designer's goal is to create spaces that bring local people, the environment, and the taste and smell of place into the venue to enhance the guest's memory of place. Thoughtful use of colors, regional furniture, local tiles, textiles, and lighting all assist in achieving this goal.

The immersion concept extends beyond specific places or cultures. Designers are also asked to transport visitors to a previous era that evoke guest's memories and emotions of the time. If the design is successful, visitors feel they are experiencing another place or time, with a modern twist to ensure their comfort.

International hotel design also reflects local cultural in the aesthetics of hotels—giving them a feeling of calm and comfort that helps guests identify where they are located. Whether travelling across the world or across the country, guests expect to experience the destination's culture rather than sit in a hotel that looks exactly like the last one they visited that was a 12-hour flight away. This trend gives hospitality venues an edge in a competitive market.

This shift to reflecting local design and cultural immersion supports sustainability and local commerce. Instead of purchasing products from other countries, money is spent in the local community. This trend will continue in the future given the global and cultural appreciation within the U.S.

Repositioning of Boutique Hotels

Boutique hotels first appeared in 1981 with their luxury, independent experience, **Figure 3-17**. They focused on offering services in a comfortable, personal, and welcoming setting that was quite different from large hotels. Guests

Atiketta Sangasaeng/Shutterstock.com

Figure 3-17 Customers who choose a boutique hotel such as this are seeking something different than a cookie-cutter approach to hotel design. Note the unique use of bamboo throughout this room.

of boutique hotels are looking for something different than a *cookie-cutter approach* to hotel design. It is essential to give guests an experience they will remember fondly. Boutique hotels are particularly suited to conversions of historic or interesting buildings.

In recent years, boutique hotels have partnered with other hotel organizations to gain access to a larger customer base. This move has made them extremely competitive. The repositioning of boutique hotels includes

- forming partnerships to outsource food and beverage facilities to acclaimed chefs
- catering to the needs of guests in a variety of ways from serving locally sourced, seasonal food to allowing guests to control their energy usage
- offering technology that is at least as good as the guest would expect to have at home (*Note:* The technology must also fit comfortably if installed in heritage buildings, and not be obtrusive with its surroundings.)

Eco-Resorts

Although going green in a hotel has been a trend in recent years—such as reuse of bath towels to save water—ecotourism and eco-resorts take the guest experience to another level. **Ecotourism**—the practice of touring natural habitats in manner meant to minimize ecological impact—enhances economic opportunities for the host areas. An **eco-resort** supports quality, natural, and local living. These resorts do not have the air conditioning, pumped swimming pools, groomed lawns, and light pollution that are considered amenities at other hotels.

Eco-resort design takes the guest back to the basics. Facility managers encourage guests to bring along headlamps, torches, and car chargers for phone or camera batteries. Electricity these resorts use is from renewable energy sources (wind, solar, biogas, or water power). These accommodations tend to use less concrete and more natural products. The structures are made of wood, bamboo, or canvas. Other sustainable materials are used, but the whole point is that there is little between you and the natural environment that you paid to see and feel.

Restaurant Design

The specialty area of restaurant design is one of the most creative in the interior design profession. Under the umbrella of hospitality design, restaurant design includes any dining style from retro to elegant and any size project from small café to a large establishment seating 500 guests, **Figure 3-18**. Restaurant locations are often near hotels and other points of travel to market to guest needs.

Similar to other sectors of hospitality design, restaurant design requires a strong, innovative concept that reflects dining choices for the patron. Space-planning design and acoustical privacy are critical as guests eat, visit, or transact business. Such privacy requires physical or perceptual barriers. The designer can achieve these barriers through lighting, types of seating, panels, and partitions. Research indicates that a view to the outside—particularly in the morning or early afternoon—can enhance the dining experience. Outdoor patio dining is also popular in certain locales with pleasant weather conditions. It may not be the food that brings guests back, but the whole dining experience.

Two areas of restaurant design needing particular attention are the seating areas for guests and a place guests rarely see—the kitchen. Guest seating should accommodate different body types and age groups. Within the same dining space, restaurants generally offer tables with chairs, booths, and a combination. With older adults travelling more, restaurants must offer chairs with arms and hard seats to help individuals push off as they stand up. In addition, family friendly spaces and special amenities for children can also benefit and increase clientele.

Types of Restaurant Facilities

- Cafés
- Coffee shops
- Cultural dining
- Dinner theaters
- Fast food
- Fine dining
- Sandwich shops
- Novelty experiences (paddle boat)

Figure 3-18 As a specialty area under hospitality design, the design of restaurants includes many different dining experiences. *Which type of restaurant would you find most intriguing to design? Why?*

In the kitchen area, function, efficiency, and staff circulation are key factors designers must consider. How food is prepared, organized, served is an art as well as a basic restaurant function.

Color plays a key role in restaurant design because it impacts revenue generation. Bright, warm colors along with cool air can move people quickly through fast-food chains. Greater guest turnover ensures greater profit. Warm colors—such as red, yellow, and orange—increase food consumption and food sales, **Figure 3-19**. Drinks and desserts generate revenue in fine, elegant-dining establishments. The longer guests stay, the more they will spend. Therefore, use of cool, soft colors—such as blues, greens, and purples—in fine-dining restaurants encourages guests to sit back, relax, and experience the food and locale.

Designers may have chain restaurant projects. In such restaurants, guests expect standardization—the same cuisine, quality of service, and interior amenities. Identity and name recognition is critical for a chain restaurant. In contrast, one-of-a-kind restaurants often communicate the *place* and community to entice guests to try new or local food. The interiors of these restaurants communicate an experience as well as a unique memorable style. Restaurant design issues include

- sense of arrival
- seating
- lighting (natural and electric)
- color usage
- privacy (visual and acoustic)
- back-of the-house (kitchen)
- different guest ages and populations
- codes and life safety

Alexander Chaikin/Shutterstock.com

Figure 3-19 The use of certain colors in the design of a fine-dining restaurant can encourage guests to relax and take their time.

Entertainment and Recreation Design

Another area of hospitality design is entertainment and recreation design. The design of entertainment facilities is challenging and diverse. The facilities are often multifunctional spaces and include many specialties of interior design in one establishment, such as a baseball stadium. Interior spaces of a stadium often include offices, food services, lodging, restrooms, stadium boxes, locker rooms, and specialty entertainment.

People expect an entertainment and recreation location to be a place where they can leave their troubles behind, enjoy the moment, and create a life memory to share with others. Increasing use of technologies stimulate all human senses during the actual entertainment or recreation—animations, smells, and a cacophony of sounds, **Figure 3-20**. Custom details enhance the experience and often the design projects are unique. For the designer, there are often no cookie-cutter projects or previous examples to guide the design solution.

Similar to any commercial project, the entertainment and recreation designer works with a large team. To access the projects, travel is often required, making the job of finding dependable subcontractors a challenge. Entertainment and recreation design issues include

- strong, creative concepts
- custom details
- code compliance
- circulation and egress
- populations of varying ages
- signage and wayfinding

Types of Entertainment and Recreation Facilities

- All types of clubs, such as country clubs, yacht clubs, golf clubs, tennis clubs, and adjoining clubhouses
- Amusement parks
- Casinos
- Concert halls
- Nightclubs
- Resorts (ski, beach, and others)
- Spas
- Sports arenas
- Stadiums
- Theaters and auditoriums
- Theme parks

Allegria Spa at the Park Hyatt Beaver Creek/Photography by Don Riddle/Interiors by Associates III Interior Design

Figure 3-20 The interior design of entertainment and recreation facilities is challenging and diverse.

Healthcare Design

Throughout history, the places where the sick go for care and healing have evolved. Environments that promote healing began in the home. Later, religious workers took responsibility for those people in their communities who were ill. Hospitals began to emerge on the edges of villages or cities and populations often grew to surround them. Many were built around large, central courtyards with secondary courtyards adjoining specific hospital wards.

Currently, the United States is in the middle of a healthcare building boom that will shape the industry for another generation. According to the *ASID State of the Industry* report, it is the fourth largest interior design specialty area of practice, **Figure 3-21**.

Due to the life-saving and care-giving nature of this type of project, design practitioners in this specialty area often have subspecialties. Those who design long-term, continuous-care communities may have different client priorities and issues than those working on new hospital construction. However, all are concerned with designing interiors that enhance the patient's journey from illness or injury back to improved health. In addition to designing for patient wellness, the healthcare design practitioner strives to design beautiful, hopeful, and comforting places for the family support system. Additional goals include providing efficient workplaces for the hardworking medical staff.

Evidence-Based Design (EBD) Trend

There is not a specialty area of interior design more technical, life-changing, and steeped in critical details than the healthcare design industry. For that reason, interior

Types of Healthcare Facilities

Interior designers in the healthcare specialty may develop designs for

- Assisted living facilities
- Birthing centers
- Clinics
- Hospice centers
- Hospitals
- Long-term care facilities
- Medical and dental office
- Medical laboratories
- Mental health facilities
- Outpatient services/urgent care facilities
- Pediatric facilities
- Psychiatric facilities
- Rehabilitation
- Wellness centers

Figure 3-21 Interior designers who work in the healthcare design specialty utilize evidence-based design strategies to help generate design solutions.

designers use **evidence-based design (EBD)** strategies that originated in the healthcare industry. With EBD, strategic team members gather *quantitative* (statistics) and *qualitative* (patient interviews) information based on research goals. After analyzing the data, design-team members discuss outcomes prior to generating possible design solutions. Simply put, gathering EBD data provides the proper foundation for innovative design solutions. EBD is emerging as a trend across all specialty areas of interior design.

Additional Trends in Healthcare Design

Along with EBD, another trend in healthcare design is the introduction of hospitality design features. Healthcare facilities, like hotels, are integrating such homelike features as fireplaces, views of outdoor gardens, art, and beautiful textures and colors into lobbies, waiting areas, and patient rooms. Research indicates that such features soothe and accelerate recovery. Healthcare designers use these design features to transition the patient back to his or her home environment.

The increasing need for patient confidentiality is another trend. Others should never overhear or read a patient's personal information. The *Family Educational Rights and Privacy Act (FERPA)* legislation mandates the division of private conversation spaces for the general public. Interior designers are facing the challenge of dividing space without sacrificing the integrity of the design or the privacy of the public. As they balance the need for private areas, they must avoid generating feelings of confinement and isolation, particularly in stressful medical situations. Technologies continue to evolve, and are integrated, to ensure patient confidentiality.

As with all professions, yet another trend involves the increasing integration of technology systems into the everyday practice of healthcare to address the swift pace of meeting the public's needs. Whether you are in a doctor's office or a patient in a hospital, technology integration can literally save lives, **Figure 3-22**. New technologies include easily accessible digital patient records in the case of life-threatening allergic reactions, or technical equipment located in patient room cabinetry that can be easily accessible in an emergency. The interior design plans of such facilities must incorporate these technologies.

Lastly, an increasingly important healthcare design trend is addressing needs of the older adult population and those with obesity. Healthcare is one of the primary areas where people spend money and rarely consider such expenditures optional.

Healthcare for older adults is a significant and growing proportion of designed facilities such as clinics,

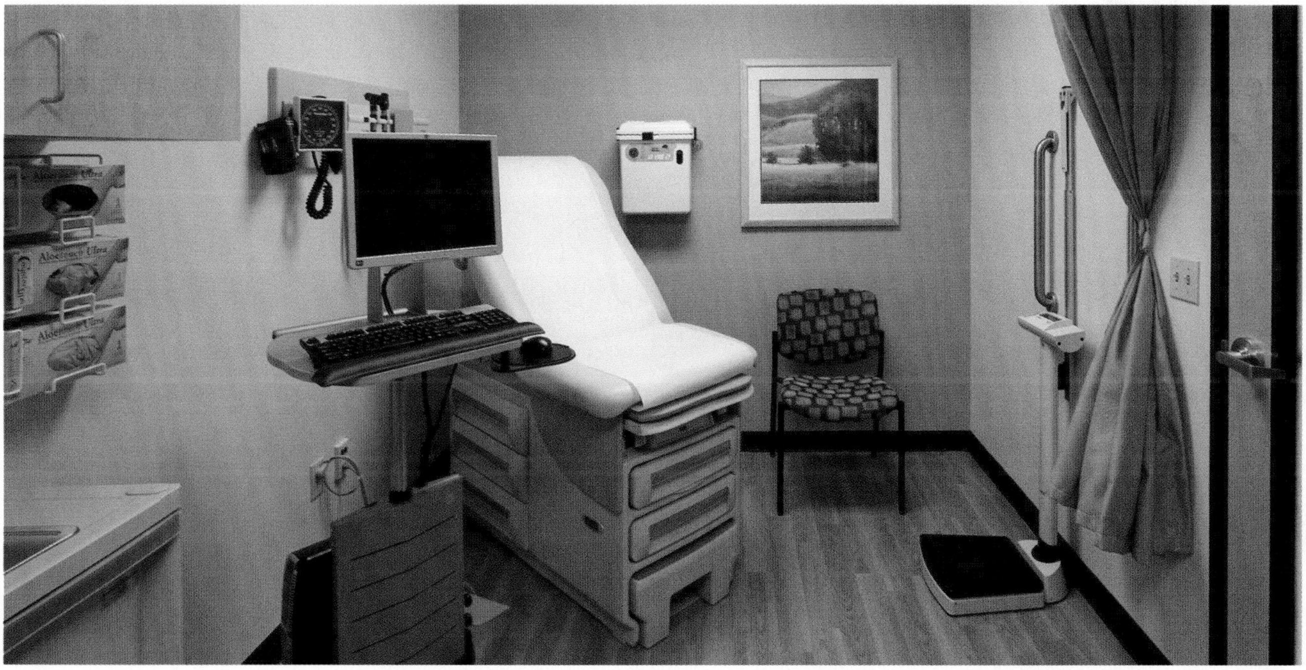

Courtesy of Boulder Community Hospital: LaCasse Photography

Figure 3-22 Designing space for an express clinic such as this is just one of the subspecialties of healthcare design.

outpatient facilities, extended care, and assisted care facilities. Additionally, the increasing numbers of people with obesity and other weight-related health problems have become one of the top three national concerns. Accommodations for this population in healthcare facilities must be designed into the facility. Weight and size impacts everything from the lobby furnishings to mechanistic support of hospital beds to new methods of patient maneuvering without loss of dignity to prevention of physical strain to the nursing staff.

Healthcare designers must work well with the medical community, staff, and general public. They need to know procedures that are offered to patients, understanding what each procedure is called and what it entails. These designers view the patient as a whole individual. They gain an understanding of human psychology, health, and wellness issues by taking related healthcare courses and shadowing healthcare workers. Healthcare designers can design within the codes and regulations that support the health, safety, and well-being of the public.

Many healthcare designers have passed the rigorous *National Council for Interior Design Qualification (NCIDQ)* exam and may be licensed in their states. They may also be certified by the *American Academy of Healthcare Interior Design (AAHID),* an advanced qualification specific to healthcare designers which requires a minimum of five years experience in healthcare design and NCIDQ certification.

Institutional Design

Institutional design involves public spaces that are funded from both private and public funds, but not privately owned, **Figure 3-23**. This interior design specialty includes such facilities as

- schools
- colleges and universities
- religious facilities
- recreational areas

Design: RB+B Architects, Inc./David Patterson Architectural + Interior Photography

Figure 3-23 The interior design of schools is often publically funded. *Identify ways in which quality interior design of school institutions benefits students and the public.*

- libraries
- museums
- banks, credit unions, and other financial institutions

According to the *Facility Planners and Architects (FP & A)* group reports, the educational, government, and institutional sectors are experiencing the most robust increase in new construction and renovation. Other than financial and religious institutions, most institutional projects involve public funding rather than private. This characteristic carries the responsibility of answering to the public for expenditures in the design and construction of buildings. Therefore, interior designers in this specialization often coordinate the design among groups with varied vested interests and perspectives. Typically, the four groups of stakeholders involved in institutional projects are the

- government or other entity responsible for the project
- employees working in the building
- public who receive services in the building
- taxpayers whose money is used to construct, remodel, and maintain the building

Institutional design projects are often long-term and technical in nature. Interior designers may work on a community college, town hall, or federal building all in the same community. Such designers have the benefit of a steady place of employment even in difficult economic times. Often, if budget constraints are in place for new construction, renovations of institutional buildings are always underway.

Educational Facility Design

One of the largest areas within the institutional design sector is education. It is where the fifth largest amount of commercial work is happening. Educational design may include

- staff and administration areas
- libraries
- elementary and secondary schools
- community colleges
- technical colleges and occupational learning centers
- colleges and universities

Today across America, millions of dollars are spent to update schools or build new ones based on healthful, green-building practices. Acoustics, energy efficiency, and smart classrooms with integrated and interactive learning technology dominate educational design trends. Home schooling and online learning dominate the alternative classroom delivery systems.

Educational facility design can encompass a single college classroom or a large research lab. The design of such centers focuses on how to enhance learning and what keeps students safe in that learning environment. It is a

Link to History

School Design

Historically in the United States, learning took place in the home between chores and crop harvests. Teachers travelled from town to town or taught in one-room school houses where multiple grades met together. At the turn of the 20th century, scholarly attention was turned to developing a standardized classroom design that featured a front-facing teacher's desk and lined-up rows of student desks flanked by two sets of windows. Standardized school designs, known as the *Common School Movement* popularized the notion of free schools paid for by local property taxes. Schools designed in the late nineteenth and early twentieth centuries were utilitarian, crowded, and impersonal. Only later was attention turned to proper lighting and ventilation of the classroom. University campuses, another sector of education design, were developed in colonial America as early as 1693, such as the College of William and Mary in Williamsburg, Virginia.

As noted in an AIA editorial, children, rather than tanks, bombs, or airplanes, were the greatest output from WW II. Seven million war babies entered first grade and $20 billion dollars were spent for new school construction to accommodate the demand.

Analyze It!

Use appropriate Internet sources to identify types of historical schools, current school types, and future school suggestions. Analyze similarities and differences of findings. How do they compare to your school?

CASE STUDY

Red Hawk Elementary School—RB+B Architects, Inc.

The design for Red Hawk Elementary stems from the desire to create a vibrant place for children to learn. The design approach to create this environment centers around a central space that is connected to all parts of school and allows for multiple ways of interaction amongst and between students and teachers.

As inspiration, the design team studied scenes of urban areas during street festivals. During these festivals, buildings on each side of the street frame the central space where multiple pavilions of different colors and shapes are set up. The most important aspect of this scene is the movement of people. Their ability to go in and out of the buildings and weave in and around the pavilions is a joyful part of experiencing the festival. This interaction and flexibility is carried through the school in creative spaces for students to learn and interact.

There are many elements in and around the building that allow the teachers and students to interact and learn from their surroundings, from the *Plains to Peak Eco-Trail* and the *Interpretive Wall* on the site, to the *Weather Funnel* and the *Mineral Garden* on the interior of the building.

The building also provides a number of passive elements that encourage better learning. The daylighting and views throughout the building keep its occupants connected to the outdoors. Displacement ventilation is used in the entire building to deliver air from the ground source heat pumps into the occupied zone of each space. All of these elements, along with many others have allowed us to achieve a *LEED Gold Certification* and a *Designed to Earn ENERGY STAR* award.

Investigate and Reflect . . . .
Take a walking tour of your school or a school nearby in your community. Identify positive and negative aspects about the design. How might these design items impact the school students and staff? To extend this activity, identify what you think the philosophy of design might be for the school. Compare the design of this school to another nearby school. Which do you think is the better-designed learning environment? Why? What sustainability features did each school use?

A Weather tunnel, indoor view

B Weather tunnel, outdoor view

C Daylighting, indoor view

D Exterior view, Red Hawk Elementary School

Design: RB+B Architects, Inc./Photography by Fred Fuhrmeister diverse specialty area of interior design and can demand knowledge of a variety of other specialty areas. For example, a university campus has lodging and food facilities, entertainment and recreation, places for reflection and studying, administrative offices, and healthcare.

For universities, the focus is on the design of general classrooms and residence halls for students. These spaces affect the success and retention of students. Research facilities, security of students, and retention of freshmen are also primary goals of university educational design. Universities often have an in-house interior designer to assist with remodeling of campus buildings.

Similar, but on a smaller scale, is the design of elementary and secondary schools. The preference is that such buildings should be designed from the inside out rather than the outside in. As places of learning, classrooms are the primary design spaces to consider. Classroom design today focuses on acoustics, smart technologies, green-design practices, supportive furniture (allowing for continual rearrangement to support learning activities), appropriate colors, and signage that reflect age group and teaching and learning styles. In addition, the security of the building is a critical focus.

Religious Institution Design

Another type of institutional design is in the religious sector. Designers who specialize in religious design find that each denomination or sect has different requirements for the space planning and design of the interiors. For some, the goal of the architecture is to lift peoples' eyes to the heavens. In others, it is to encourage humility or to provide serenity. Regardless of the goal, the interior designer must practice sensitivity to ceremony, privacy, sacred areas, and design details to enhance the reverence of the space and reflect the beliefs of the occupants.

Often religious ceremonies are held in certain areas of the building, necessitating custom furnishings, lighting, and interior materials. Light, color, and art often highlight key features within each area of a facility. Controlling natural light to avoid glare within a sacred space is a design issue. Acoustics are important to enhance hearing and the sound musical instruments produce.

The emergence of mega-facilities is a trend with which religious designers work. These very large facilities include integration of complex audiovisual technologies in the form of multiple screens, music and sound systems, lights, and color interplay. These structures also serve as community centers with adjoining schools, child care centers, and playgrounds. The facilities must also accommodate multipurpose rooms for food service for large groups. Circulation patterns and safe exit are important considerations.

Government Facility Design

The fifth largest specialty interior design practice is government design. Types of government facilities include

- federal, state, and city administrative buildings
- justice centers and courtrooms
- military training centers, officer clubs, family centers, and lodging
- prisons, juvenile detention centers, and correctional facilities
- research and scientific facilities
- museums

Link to History

Public Building Design

Most of the government buildings in the U.S. were constructed between 1900 and 1941, years of great progress in technology, civil planning, and America's emergence as a world leader in the western culture. The Chicago Exposition of 1893, with classical pavilions glowing with Thomas Edison's new lights, shaped the government's approach to dignified public building design. Federal buildings were classical in design and clad with white limestone or marble. In 1992, the design philosophy was honed further to reflect the belief that future federal buildings should be symbolic of what government is about, not just where public business is conducted.

Analyze It!

What were some of the first federal buildings in the U.S. and where were they located? How different are they from federal buildings in your state?

CASE STUDY

USGBC—A Model for Sustainable Design

The *Research Support Facility (RSF)* located on the campus of the U.S. Department of Energy's (DOE) National Renewable Energy Laboratory (NREL) has been certified LEED® Platinum for New Construction by the U.S. Green Building Council (USGBC). It is considered the first net-zero building in its league. A *net-zero building* is one that harvests the energy it needs on-site using various energy producing technologies, such as solar and wind. The annual result is that the building does not use fossil fuels to power the building.

©Ron Pollard, courtesy of RNL

Considered a sustainable product because it is harvested from dead trees that are still standing, interior designers have found creative ways to incorporate the beauty of *beetle-kill pine* into their designs.

At 222,000 square-feet, the RSF is a model for sustainable, high-performance building design. It reflects the best energy efficiency and environmental performance in a large-scale commercial office building. The interior of this building (housing 820 staff members) focused on material choices with low-health impact and reduced-resource consumption. Several highly visible, innovative local materials were incorporated into the project, including the use of reclaimed natural gas pipe as structural columns and *beetle kill pine* used as decorative wall elements throughout and as a multi-story feature wall in the lobby.

Investigate and Reflect

Use the Internet to locate net-zero commercial buildings in your city or state. What features make the structure a net-zero building? What materials were used in construction? Were the sources materials local? What energy-producing technologies does the building use? What would be the benefits to your city or state if more structures were net-zero buildings?

Government buildings are remodeled or constructed based on established standards, regulations, and codes at the federal, state, city, and local levels. Typically, a government designer works for the government as a facility planner and designer, or a private interior designer working under contract for the government. If a designer or design firm is not under contract with the government, he or she submits designs in response to a **request for proposal (RFP)** from the government entity. The bid proposal outlines identified government construction and design needs—as well as a deadline when all interested parties can submit proposals. This process encourages fair access to government projects and enables the government to explain expenditures to its citizens.

Above and beyond the typical public safety issues in commercial design, government buildings often have additional security issues that the designer must address during space planning. For example, a justice center used for court hearings or trials may have three different end users—judges, criminals, and victims. All these individuals need to be kept separate from each other until they meet in the appropriate space. Therefore, the designer must develop three different circulation patterns in the same building to ensure paths do not cross. These circulation patterns include three different sets of elevators, hallways, parking locations, and exit doors to ensure privacy and security. This example gives you just a little insight into the complexity of designing government facilities.

There is one major trend in government facility design today: high-performance buildings with energy-efficient interiors. The government desires to protect the environment and use renewable resources wisely. Government facility design focuses on creating successful high-performance buildings by applying an *integrated design process (IDP)* to the project during the stages of planning and design. An **integrated design process (IDP)** is the collaboration of all project team members early and often throughout the project's process of design to achieve a holistic design. It is known as the *whole building design* approach.

Financial Institution Design

Another area of institutional design is related to financial institutions. Financial institution design is radically changing as digital alternatives replace physical transactions. Video tellers and mobile banking are replacing traditional customer service via the bank teller. Dramatic statistics support this trend. By 2020, projections suggest that digital transactions will exceed 143 billion, whereas physical transactions will decrease to less than 10 billion in the same year.

How does this trend impact the interior design field? Instead of people coming to the banks, banks are going to the people. Physical buildings and branches are becoming smaller and with a more social focus. Rather than developing larger traditional banks, many banks have smaller **boutique banks** that use 500–1000 square feet of space in such prime locations as coffee shops, library lobbies, retail stores, or post offices. These spaces may also feature food bars, lounges in the lobby to access wireless Internet, and retail areas. As in other places, the digital world and social media is driving design.

With the face of banking changing, interior spaces must reflect a new social presence and new identity as the industries leap from reality to the virtual world. Although confidentiality remains important, the interior spaces should also appear socially inviting, trustworthy, and secure. Private bank offices now sport open, glass-paned cubicles. Technologies for banking practices and security have increased. Designers must accommodate these design needs when specifying the furnishings, fixtures, and equipment. Design issues for financial institutions include creating

- backup security systems
- layered lighting to create interest
- efficient customer service

Retail Design

As the seventh largest specialty area of interior design practice, retail design is a very diverse sector. The primary goal is to sell product. Therefore, the design of the interior must *visually market* the retailer's product. The retail design sector includes individual boutiques, large department stores, cell-phone stores, and entire shopping malls.

A retail store could be anything from a posh clothing store to a temporary *pop-up* retail shop with one-of-a-kind merchandise. The products these vendors sell can range from select specialty foods and franchise cell phones to seasonal costume products and unique clothing items, **Figure 3-24**.

Goals of Retail Design

Retail design has a number of goals that ultimately involve the development of a well-planned store layout that maximizes square footage with great visual appeal to increase sales. Customer traffic patterns can enhance purchase volume and increase profits. Research indicates that on entering a store, almost 90 percent of customers will circulate to the right. Retailers and designers can capitalize on this fact by displaying new products on these pathways to encourage consumers to buy.

Frequently, shopping does not involve making a purchase. For consumers, window-shopping has become a popular pastime. Visual merchandisers create *miniature worlds* for merchandise in an effort to attract the attention of consumers and draw them into the store. With the many choices available in retail shopping today, the design of the store must maximize the consumer experience to invite them in and to frequently return and make purchases. Retail design issues include

- configuring the store layout to enhance buying
- choosing types of fixtures and displays

Types of Retail Design Facilities

- Malls and shopping centers
- Department stores
- Specialty stores
- Gift shops
- Fitness centers
- Food courts
- Spas and salons
- Pop-up stores

Raywoo/Shutterstock.com

Figure 3-24 Retail design is a diverse sector of interior design practice. *What aspects of retail design do you find most interesting?*

- identifying lighting layers
- communicating image
- identifying security and prevention of shoplifting
- creating atmosphere and mood
- developing adequate storage
- increasing visibility and flexible merchandising
- identifying key customer service areas

Trends in Retail Design

There are a couple of trends that impact retail design today. One major trend is the increasing presence of online shopping. As a form of electronic commerce, an e-shop, e-store, webshop, or virtual store circumvents the need for in-store shopping. Its success relates to buyer convenience, limited time, travel costs, and increased selection, supposedly, at a reduced price.

The second trend, the pop-up retail shop, is becoming increasingly popular. Appearing in Los Angeles in the late 1990s, this is a type of temporary store that pops-up in various cities or locations to sell unique or seasonal products. A store that opens to sell Halloween goods in October is one example. It generates consumer excitement and serves as a popular tool for landlords who wish to lease short-term real estate in a down economy. Pop-up retail stores can revitalize neighborhoods and spread company identity without the normal expenses associated with long-term retail spaces.

These two trends impact retail interior design by increasing the demand to reshape the buyer's experience when they do enter a store, **Figure 3-25**. To stay abreast of other retail design trends or connect with retail designers, visit the *Retail Design Institute* website.

Interior Designer: SCI Design Group/Photographer: Michael McLane

Figure 3-25 Interior designers reshape the design of retail spaces to best visually market the retailer's product.

Chapter 3 Review and Assess

Summary

- There are many specialty areas of practice within the field of interior design.
- Residential design involves the planning and design of dwellings while commercial design involves the planning and design of primarily public spaces.
- Although there are many differences between residential and commercial interior design, both require the same education and some of the same skills.
- Residential design reflects the client's tastes, preferences, and functional needs in creating a home or dwelling.
- Trends in residential design include such specialty areas as well-designed smaller dwellings, remodeling, aging-in-place, multigenerational living, sustainability and green design, and specialty spaces.
- As with commercial design projects, residential design projects often involve a variety of team members, budget constraints, and varying time lines.
- The health, safety, and well-being (HSW) of the public is a particular concern to designers of public spaces.
- Specialty areas within commercial interior design include, but are not limited to, corporate/office, hospitality, healthcare, institutional, and retail design.
- Trends in commercial design specialties expand the designer's options for creative, fulfilling, meaningful work for a lifetime.

Chapter Vocabulary

For each of the following terms, identify a word or group of words that describes an attribute—or quality of the term. Discuss your descriptions with the class to increase understanding.

amenities
boutique bank
building footprint
conspicuous nonconsumption
co-working
daylighting strategies
eco-resort
ecotourism
egress
evidence-based design (EBD)
green-design practices
hotelling
immersion
integrated design process (IDP)
levy
lock-off unit
mixed-use design facilities
price point
request for proposal (RFP)
sense-of-place
sense-of-self
space planning
subcontractor
sustainable design
telecommuter
tenant improvement work (TI)
wayfinding
work ethic

Review and Study

1. What are three factors you should consider as you explore interior design specialties? Give a reason for each.
2. Name six differences between commercial and residential interior design projects.
3. What design skills are often the same for both commercial and residential design?
4. On what factors should a designer focus questions about a design project with a client?
5. Give an example showing why the amount of money spent on a residential design project does not always equate to good design.
6. How is a pocket neighborhood an example of living smaller and smarter?
7. Contrast aging-in-place with multigenerational living as related to interior design.
8. What is the difference between sustainable design and green-design practices?
9. Name two concerns of commercial interior designers.
10. What are six important factors that commercial interior designers must address related to corporate/office design?
11. What is tenant improvement (TI) and how can commercial interior designers influence it?
12. Name three office design issues of concern to commercial interior designers and their clients.
13. What are the common issues designers must address in hotel design?
14. To what does a *mixed-use facility* refer?
15. Why does color play a key role in restaurant design?
16. Name four issues interior designers must consider with restaurant design.
17. Why do healthcare designers use evidence-based design?
18. Explain one trend in healthcare design.
19. What types of facilities are included in the institutional design specialty? Which are most often privately funded?
20. What issues must the retail designer address in order to maximize consumer experiences and meet the retailer's goal of selling product?

Critical Analysis

21. **Analyze.** Reread and analyze the *Design Insight* quote at the beginning of this chapter. In your perception, how can working in one of the interior design specialties help you to 1) learn, 2) reflect, 3) imagine, 4) discover, and 5) create? Apply your written communication skills clearly, concisely, and effectively in writing a summary of your perception to share with the class. Discuss how your perception differs from those of your classmates.
22. **Analyze.** After reading the text information on *sense-of-self*, invite three friends to your home to look at and analyze your personal spaces. Ask them to describe your personality based on what you have hanging in your spaces. Have them view walls, accessories, color, and lighting and make a statement about each regarding your personality. Analyze the results. How do your friends' views on how your environment describes your personality compare to your personal view?
23. **Cause and effect.** What text evidence can you cite to illustrate the cause and effect relationship between use of *sustainable* and *green design practices* and failure of the designer to use such practices? How would failure to use these practices influence the health, safety, and well-being of the client? Discuss your evidence of the effects in class.
24. **Analyze.** Select one of the following office-design trends the author discusses in the text: anytime, anywhere work environments; younger workers desire flexibility; alternative work styles; international or global work; smart surfaces; or generational collaboration. Analyze the details the author sites are key to this trend. Then use the Internet to locate a photograph depicting this trend. Share your photograph with the class and relate the details that emphasize the trend.

Think like a Designer

25. **Reading.** Read and analyze Dr. Gibbs' four categories in Figure 3-5 that comprise the attributes of home. Then demonstrate your understanding by creating a digital word cloud using Dr. Gibbs' categories that enhance the meaning of *home*. Post your word cloud to the school-approved class website.
26. **Research.** Use reliable resources to locate floor plans for middle-income homes for the 1950s, 1970s, and 2000s. Analyze the homes for amount of living space, workspace, and sleeping space. Discuss how they are similar and different. What lifestyle differences do you think influenced the changes in floor plans?
27. **Writing.** Go to Cynthia Leibrock's website, *Aging Beautifully.* Click on the *Fellowships* tab and scroll until you reach the *Green Mountain Ranch: A Demonstration Project.* Then read and analyze the examples given about universal design and aging-in-place. Write a summary of the top 10 most important examples for an older person you know from your community. What evidence supports your examples?
28. **Speaking.** Evaluate multiple sources of information to research one of the following specialties areas in residential design: lock-off units, home offices, mud rooms or drop zones, and outdoor living areas. Draw conclusions about the key factors a designer must consider when developing designs for these spaces. Give an oral presentation to the class, identifying evidence to support your conclusions.
29. **Technology.** Visit a vendor website for office furnishings, such as *Steelcase, Herman Miller,* or *Knoll.* Use their planning features or design apps for room design to quickly and easily locate or develop a layout for your dream office in three dimensions (3-D). Make a printout of your room design and discuss the features with the class.
30. **Writing.** After reading about various interior design specialties, write a client description for both a residential and commercial specialty of your choice. Include client needs, functions for the space, and preferences. Put your description in a box along with those of other class members. Draw a different description out of the box. Write how you feel it should be designed based on the specialty description.

Design Application

31. **Commercial design plan.** Design and develop a plan for a pop-up retail shop.
    A. Give it a name.
    B. Determine its merchandise.
    C. Suggest a location and price points.
    D. List the needs and issues the designer should consider when developing a design plan.
    E. Manually sketch or use Internet images to communicate features of the final store design.
    F. Use presentation software or a school-approved web-based application to develop your plan and share it with the class.
32. **Residential design plan.** Presume you are a residential designer. Your interpersonal skills—your ability to listen, speak, and empathize—are a great asset in working with clients. Lilly is your latest client. She is an older adult that is choosing to age-in-place in her own home. Because she has osteoporosis and a few other health conditions, Lilly has engaged your services to help modify her home. Write a list of questions you would ask Lilly in order to best identify the needs she has and which areas of the home are most in need of remodeling? Locate digital photographs of options to show Lilly that might best meet her needs. Create a slideshow to show Lilly.
33. **Portfolio builder.** Before you begin collecting information for your portfolio, you should write an objective. Are you creating this portfolio for a job interview, a college application, or a volunteer position in your community? Writing an objective will help you focus on the task of creating appropriate documents and design projects to accomplish your goal.
    A. Decide which type of portfolio you are creating—employment, career, or application for college.
    B. Do research on how to write an objective. Your instructor can guide you.
    C. Write your objective to guide you through your portfolio project.

The Business of Interior Design

hxdbzxy/Shutterstock.com

Chapter 4

Design Insight

"One cannot achieve long term success in the profession of interior design without a complete understanding of the 'business' of design."

Michael Thomas, FASID, Design Collective Group

Learning Targets

After studying this chapter, you will be able to

- identify business trends that impact the business of interior design.
- summarize why referrals and personal contacts serve as a strategic business practice.
- identify major types of business structures used in the interior design profession.
- understand important business practices and procedures used in the interior design profession, especially those that protect the client and the designer or firm.
- understand the importance and impact of public policy on the business of interior design.
- analyze what a brand stands for and the business tools that work to best reach clients.
- understand why branding and market segmentation differentiate you from your competitors.
- summarize why ethics are critical to the interior design profession.
- summarize the differences between copyrights, trademarks, and patents.
- identify best practices for interior design businesses.

Introduction

The interior design profession is based on a common business model. Although the practice of interior design is highly creative and innovative, to remain in business the designer must

- follow appropriate business procedures
- implement sound financial practices
- engage in continuous business marketing and development
- utilize ethical practices and judgment

Whether you desire to run your own business or work for a large architectural or design firm, basic understanding of the business side of interior design is critical. It significantly affects how you work, the decisions you make, your credibility, the bottom line of the firm, and therefore *your* success!

Business Trends Affecting Interior Design

As the interior design profession continues to evolve, the ways of doing business also change. As indicated in the *ASID Environmental Scanning Report* (a report on forecasts, economic trends, and business strategies by noted design professionals), mobility is everywhere. By choice, people are flooded with data, influenced by blogs and tweets, and connected through social networking sites. The emerging new world links everyone through a mobile device with immediate, ongoing connectivity which people perceive as essential.

The benefits of mobility have direct effects on the business of interior design. A forecast report by *International Data Corporation* suggests that mobile working will increase due to higher productivity, lower employee turnover, and increasing morale. Key findings from this report indicate that the United States will remain a highly concentrated market for mobile workers. For interior design, that means the office can be anywhere in the world. Connections to clients can be in real time and communication with team members can be instantaneous, **Figure 4-1**.

Interior design work and new business opportunities are always available. Every remodel, move, or new construction project offers opportunities for new clients. Understanding the demographics and changing needs of your clients is an important business practice.

Importance of Personal Relationships

The success of a design firm directly relates to connections with people. People are the most important assets of your business. Although globally there are thousands of interior designers, once in the design profession you will feel that you are in a small community network. In this community, client trust and colleague support is critical to doing business. Your name is your reputation. In turn, your reputation is your key to credibility and business success.

The challenge today is to *own* the new, trend-conscious, educated consumers or clients—to meet or exceed their needs and dreams with a quality, value-driven design that is often described as "cheap, chic, and unique." Their buying power is one of personal choice. They want more involvement, personalization, and continuing education.

On the other end of the spectrum, the clients who desire quality, classic designs are an integral portion of any design-business client base. These clients are at all price points. They are not driven by value, but by intelligent enduring design. All smart business owners today are connecting with this range of consumers to build relationships, establish trust, and develop brand loyalty, **Figure 4-2.**

Supri Suharjoto/Shutterstock.com

Robert Kneschke/Shutterstock.com

Figure 4-1 Using technology to instantaneously connect with clients is an asset for interior design professionals. *What forms of technology do you think are most effective? Why?*

Stephen Coburn/Shutterstock.com

Figure 4-2 Strong designer-client relationships help the designer acquire client trust. *Discuss why trust is important in such relationships.*

Potential Client Trends

Clients today are multigenerational and global-oriented. For the first time, four generations of the same family are present in the workforce—you and your parents, grandparents, and great-grandparents. Research indicates that each of the four generations has different work expectations, management styles, technology skills, ethics, and values. As a design professional, you need to be very aware of these differences in working with your clients or team members.

Both current and future client trends are important for a design firm. In coming years, the *millennials* (those born between 1981 and 2000) will have more spending power than the *baby boomers* (those born between 1946 and 1964). The values that millennials hold indicate they like

- product customization
- invitations for involvement (for instance, serving on a board of directors)
- meaningful relationships with service providers

Research also indicates that young Americans are more transient, meaning they move more often. Rather than living in the same community and working at the same job until retirement, mentors recommend that new college graduates change jobs to avoid entrenchment in one firm and being locked into a particular way of doing business. As they move, Americans buy and sell their homes more frequently. They commute farther to work if they do not have remote access to work from home. Understanding this mobile behavior opens up opportunities for future clients and design projects. Tapping into such business and consumer trends puts interior design businesses in a better position to meet customer needs. Understanding these trends opens up new opportunities for design projects—at work, home, and play.

Positioning Yourself

Another tip to developing a successful design business is the importance of positioning yourself in the market. **Positioning** refers to actions the designer takes to create a certain image—as a recognizable brand of a service in the minds of their clients. How do you position yourself to be the designer of choice? What qualifications and education do you need to do the work desired by others? What **market niche**—or specialized market—can you fill that is not on the radar screen of others? Future planning—one year, five years, and ten years—is a deliberate, conscious goal-setting task to begin now.

One way to position yourself is to clearly determine trends impacting the design field. Watch both global and national trends—it is your business to do so either as an employee or as the employer. Read and listen to news relating to such things as fashion, lifestyles, economy, and political climate. Also look for developments in the family unit, ecological changes, scientific discoveries, and workplace changes. Eileen Jones, a senior designer for *Perkins + Will Branded Environments*, identifies several issues that affect the business of interior design. Some of these include

- **Advancement (speed) to market.** How fast can a new design product become available to the consumer?
- **Technology and communications.** What is the best way to effectively use technologies to enhance communication with people? See **Figure 4-3.**
- **Brand and market share.** Is the brand or logo of your firm recognized by the client or consumer? Is the work offered by your firm needed by the market?
- **Design awareness of the general public.** How knowledgeable is the general public about good design?

Many trends affect the field of interior design. Develop research skills as you position yourself and think about the work you want to do when you graduate.

NAN728/Shutterstock.com

Figure 4-3 As with other businesses, interior design practitioners must follow appropriate business principles and organizational practices. *Discuss what might happen to a design business when the designer prepares outstanding designs, but fails to use good business practices.*

Interior Design Businesses

Interior design, as a business entity, is a professional service for hire similar to law, medicine, and accounting. To ensure your doors stay open for business, you must follow best practices for organization and management.

The following passages will introduce different types of interior design business structures. Once you understand the business structures, it will be easier to understand the employment roles and the team members you might have. Finally, you will learn some best practices for an interior design professional.

Types of Business Structures

People create businesses to meet perceived needs in the community. There are many types of business organizational structures as well as legal formations. Each differs in financial and personal liability, and tax ramifications. Because laws and regulations differ from state to state, it is best to hire an attorney and an accountant to guide your decision making about business structure.

The typical types of business structures include sole proprietorships, partnerships (general and limited), corporations, and limited liability companies. Each has advantages and disadvantages.

Sole Proprietorship

Self-employment is common in the U.S. with many interior designers working in small firms of fewer than five employees. According to *ASID*, 80 percent of design practitioners work in small design firms of this size. Another 15 percent have between six and 20 employees with only five percent reporting more than 20 employees.

The simplest and least expensive type of business structure is a **sole proprietorship**—a structure in which the company and the owner are one entity. The proprietor performs many different duties in this type of business. He or she is the manager and owner, controls the business, handles assets, receives all profits, and is responsible for all losses. There is simplicity in forming this type of business due to the minimal steps in setting it up. These include

- select a business name and city/state and register it
- register the business with appropriate tax offices
- open a bank account in the business name
- develop credit and form relationships with showrooms and tradespeople
- print business cards and appropriate forms

The simplicity of forming the business, the minimal cost to establish one (about $500), and the benefit of keeping all the profits is attractive. The flip side of this type of business formation is that the owner is responsible for everything. This includes all start-up costs, debts, operation costs, and unlimited personal liabilities relating to potential losses and taxes.

If you decide to set up your business as a sole proprietorship, you can choose to use the word *company* as part of your business name. However, you cannot legally use the words *incorporated, limited,* or *corporation* as part of your business name. If you wish to sell your firm, it may be difficult because your reputation is tied to the business.

Various states in the U.S. require different qualifications for becoming a sole proprietor. For instance, Florida is a licensed interior design state. Therefore, your interior design license and your business must be in your legal licensed name, for example, *George Smith Interiors*.

A common recommendation for graduating design students is to work for several years for a design firm before opening their own interior design businesses. While you may make less money doing so, you will gain greater experience working with established interior designers and avoid costly mistakes.

Partnership

As the word implies, a **partnership** involves two or more people who carry on a business, **Figure 4-4**. They share in the vision, risks, workload, profits, losses, and stresses of the business. A *general partnership* holds all members, individually and as a group, liable for all debts and obligations incurred in the name of the firm. Likewise, all profits and losses are split by the partners. Each partner must include his or her share of the business income or losses on his or her tax return. *Note*: If you develop a partnership, it is critical to keep personal and business profits separate to avoid fines for not paying enough taxes.

If a partner leaves the firm or passes away, you can dissolve the business or develop it into a new partnership. New partners are not liable for debts incurred prior to entering the partnership.

Decide to set up a partnership as a business structure only if you know the individual(s) well. Make sure you understand their personalities and work ethic. Ask critical

Yuri Arcurs/Shutterstock.com

Figure 4-4 Partnerships involve two or more people in a business. *What are the pros and cons of a business partnership?*

questions, such as whether or not potential partners equally share in the work load? Before you form a partnership, determine legal powers that impact partnership disputes.

A *limited partner* may be a silent partner who invests in the business and who has no desire to handle the work. A limited partnership, as a business structure, must have at least one general partner. That individual assumes all the liability for losses. Creditors cannot touch a limited partner's personal assets if the design business fails.

Corporation

A **corporation** is a legal entity consisting of several individuals known as shareholders or stockholders. Shares of stock are issued and the *Articles of Incorporation* outline shareholder rights. The shareholders elect a board of directors to run the business.

The act of forming a corporation is called **incorporation**. The first act of incorporation is to develop a legal document called the **Articles of Incorporation**. This document includes such information as the

- name of incorporation and original incorporators
- purpose and nature of the business
- place of business to be incorporated
- board of directors' names
- number of shares and stakeholders' rights
- initial capital structure

A corporation is a separate entity distinct from individuals—legally and financially. Firms generally incorporate in states where they do business. State rules govern the formation of a corporation. If a corporation does business in other states or overseas, the corporation will likely need to obtain a *certificate of authority* or a *certificate of foreign business* from those states or countries. An interior design or architectural corporation is almost always a **closed corporation.** Its shares of stock are privately held and not traded on any public markets.

Many interior design firms use the corporation structure, **Figure 4-5**. This structure has limited liability for the founder, incorporators, and stockholders, protection for personal assets, and tax benefits. If an individual decides he or she no longer wishes to associate with the business, he or she can sell shares of stock back to the company or to others.

The disadvantages of the corporate business structure are many. For example, the initial costs of business formation can be great. A corporation requires a great deal of paperwork, such as tracking unemployment insurance and social security payments. If you are not on the board of directors, you will have a minimal voice in running the business. State and federal governments also impose more extensive regulations on your business.

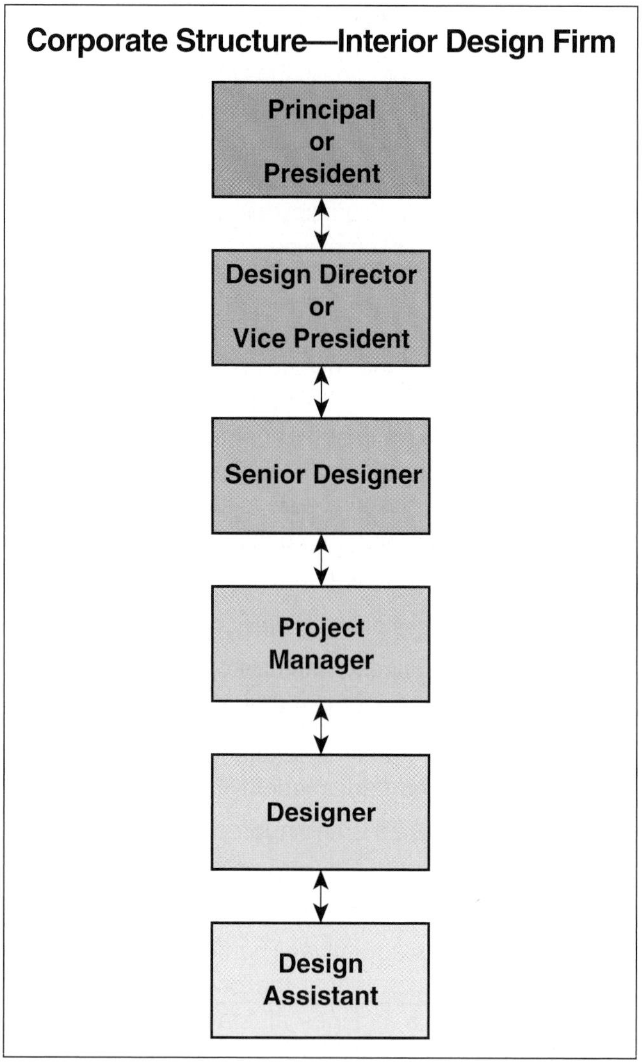

Goodheart-Willcox Publisher/Stephanie A. Clemons

Figure 4-5 Interior design corporations generally include these positions. Note the arrows indicate the ebb-and-flow relationships in the business.

Limited Liability Company (LLC)

A **limited liability company (LLC)** is a combination of a general partnership and a corporation. It is developed as a partnership but boasts the limited liability protection of a corporation. Depending on the state, setting up as LLC requires a minimum of one person, with no limit to the total number that may be involved. Investors are members. A member has no personal liability and his or her personal assets have protection in this business structure. The name of the company must contain the *LLC* or *LC* acronym in it.

The business will need to file **articles of organization** with the state. The articles of organization include the business name, address, the name of the members, and possibly the name and address of the person who is authorized to accept legal documents for the business. Many states also require the filing of an *operating agreement*. An operating agreement is a very important document that

- identifies the percentage of each member's ownership
- describes each member's responsibilities, duties, and powers
- explains how the business will distribute profits and losses
- describes how and when meetings are held
- identifies procedures for buying out or transferring interest when members leave

Many licensed professionals, such as lawyers, cannot form an LLC in their states. Similarly, interior design professionals may not be able to form an LLC in their states if a license is necessary to practice.

Business Roles in Interior Design

As an interior design professional, you may hold a number of positions at different levels in a design or architectural firm during your career, **Figure 4-6**. Your income will vary depending on the position you hold and your geographical location. For instance, average salaries for an entry-level interior design position are higher in Los Angeles than in Albuquerque. This is primarily because the cost of living is higher in California. Many design-related employers hire graduates with an interior design degree. These include

- interior design firms
- architectural firms
- designbuild firms
- lighting design firms
- furnishing or textile manufacturers
- research organizations
- in-house design departments within hotels, government agencies, restaurants, medical/health-care facilities, retail stores/shopping centers, and educational facilities

When you work for a studio-based design firm, some general titles or positions you may hold include

- **Principal designer or president.** Usually one of the owners or vested partners, the role of principal designer includes guiding the company vision, establishing initial client contacts, and spearheading marketing efforts.
- **Design director or vice president.** This individual is responsible for managing interior design professional staff and working closely with the *Principal*.
- **Senior interior designer.** The senior interior designer is usually the most experienced interior design professional in the field. He or she is the lead designer, often supervises other designers, and maintains critical client contact.

Huntstock.com/Shutterstock.com StockLite/Shutterstock.com

Figure 4-6 When beginning a career with an interior design firm, you generally work with experienced professionals.

- **Project manager.** This individual leads complex projects with other designers who report to him or her. A designer can be a senior designer and project manager simultaneously.
- **Designer or staff designer.** This individual works under supervision of senior designer or project manager. He or she often completes preliminary designs, completes computer-aided design (CAD), and compiles research and/or case studies that guide client's designs.
- **Design assistant or junior designer.** This is an entry-level position with responsibilities that include drafting, maintenance of the interior finish library, preparing interior finish boards, and gathering specifications for client's designs.

Many design-related firms also employ a variety of *specialists*. These individuals have very specific education and training and may include the following:

- **Computer-aided design (CAD) operator.** Working with a computer and design software, this individual often inputs and/or makes revisions to drawings that others design, **Figure 4-7**.
- **LEED specialist.** This specialist ensures every project acquires the points required for United States Green Building Council (USGBC)

Corepics VOF/Shutterstock.com

Ionia/Shutterstock.com

Courtesy of Chelsea Lawrence, Designer

Figure 4-7 A CAD operator generally takes the design drawings of others and refines them. For instance, the third image above began as a CAD design drawing and has had color added through rendering for a realistic quality.

Leadership in Energy and Environmental Design (LEED) certification.

- **Rendering specialist.** This individual produces perspective drawings that are enhanced with color, texture, and light to indicate suggested interior materials used in space.
- **Graphic design specialist.** This expert designs company graphics for business cards and company marketing materials.
- **Website specialist.** This individual manages company web page including graphics, content, and design.
- **Codes official.** This specialist evaluates design solutions to determine if they are in compliance with all local, state, and federal regulations.
- **Lighting designer (electric and daylighting).** As a specialist that understands integration of daylight and electric light within an interior space, he or she develops lighting strategies to highlight interior spaces.
- **ADA specialist.** This individual understands the laws pertaining to accessibility in commercial buildings under the Americans with Disabilities Act (ADA).

Your Design Team

Simply put, a client comes to an interior designer to solve one or more spatially-related problems. Sometimes the problems are easy—remodel a bathroom for someone who uses a wheelchair. At other times the problems are very complex—how to design spaces that enhance organizational recruitment and retention while addressing staff growth reflected in a building expansion. Whether the problems are easy or complex, the solution almost always requires a design team to complete the job. Therefore, team skills are one of the most valuable assets in today's workplace.

Solving a client problem often requires an inter disciplinary project team. This team should have diverse views and **collaborate**—work jointly together—effectively. If diverse expertise is not present in the team, the design solution or the execution of it may not be as strong or on target, **Figure 4-8**.

The client usually selects the designer or design firm to complete the project. Depending on the size and scope of the project, if the client comes to you first as the interior designer, you may recommend the rest of your team to the client. If a client selects the architect or builder first, the architect or builder influences whether you or your design firm are selected as designer of choice. Typical team members for a built-environment project include the following:

wavebreakmedia/Shutterstock.com

Figure 4-8 The ability to collaborate well in a team is an essential skill for an interior design practitioner. *Predict what types of problems may occur when effective collaboration is missing from a team.*

- interior designer
- structural engineer
- architect
- construction manager
- lighting specialist
- plumber
- electrician
- heating, ventilation, and air conditioning (HVAC) specialist
- code official
- landscape architect
- subcontractors

Interdisciplinary design teams may also include

- an anthropologist
- a workplace specialist
- an information technology (IT) expert
- an ergonomics expert

Whatever your team composition, strong leadership, clear communication, cooperation, and collaboration helps team members share the knowledge necessary for accomplishing their work. Collaboration eliminates single team members working independently away from the rest of the team. It also avoids the lack of project communication that results from such isolation.

Important Business Practices

To set up a business is easy. To stay in business, you must understand its procedures and practices. One simple concept is the importance of making more money than is spent. This is called *profitability*, **Figure 4-9**. Another concept is the importance of signed contracts—even among friends. This relates to common understanding and clear communication. A third is to avoid giving your design ideas away for free. This concept ensures your colleagues or clients value your expertise. Although these are elementary business practices, many very intelligent and talented designers have been innocently caught in dilemmas that result from ignoring them. Awareness of solid business practices is just as important as staying abreast of new design trends. Following are a few other important business practices.

Minerva Studio/Shutterstock.com

Figure 4-9 Profitability is important for a growing business.

Ethical Issues for Interior Designers

As a professional interior designer, your clients, team members, and the public will offer you a significant level of trust—both personal and financial. It is essential that you support this trust with competence, honesty, integrity, and objectivity.

A **code of ethics** combines best practices in business with moral principles to guide the interior design professional in simple, personal, or complex business relationships, **Figure 4-10**. Numerous professional organizations have formulated and published a code of ethics. The *ASID Code of Ethics and Professional Conduct* (Appendix A) breaks down the categories of ethical behavior for an interior designer as

- Responsibility to the public
- Responsibility to the client

travellight/Shutterstock.com

Figure 4-10 Ethical behavior is essential to all aspects of business. Read through the *ASID Code of Ethics and Professional Conduct* at the end of the text. *How do these principles relate to your personal code of ethics?*

- Responsibility to other interior designers and colleagues
- Responsibility to the profession
- Responsibility to the employer

What are some ethical dilemmas that may occur as a practicing interior designer? Here are just a few examples.

- **Stealing ideas.** One of the intangible, but greatest assets designers can offer is their creative ideas. Stealing another's idea and also claiming it as your own is unethical. It can even ruin your reputation and your business.
- **Deceptive statements about qualifications.** Making misleading or deceptive false statements regarding your professional qualifications or design capabilities is wrong. Clients trust in and depend on their designers to represent their credentials and abilities accurately when hiring them for a project.
- **Misleading clients.** Avoiding the disclosure of any financial interests that you may have with a project or service you are recommending to your client is unethical. You need to tell your client about any additional compensation you receive as a result of their purchase or project.

"Do business as though your mother is watching! Because she probably is along with your clients and potential clients!"

Michael Sutton, ASID Colorado Communications Director

- **Refusing to inform public officials.** Failing to provide information to public officials about any defect in a building that may endanger the health, safety, and well-being of the people who will use it is wrong. Recently, it was discovered that the roof rating on an elementary school was not appropriately specified. If it collapsed, it would cause harm to the children and teachers. If this information came to the interior designer, it would be his or her legal responsibility to inform the code officials. The interior designer could be sued if he or she did not do so.
- **Interfering with projects of others.** Interfering with another interior designer's existing contractual relationship with a client is unethical. After a contract is signed between a designer and a client, you should not try to entice the client to hire you instead.

CASE STUDY

Consequences of Misusing Social Media

Consider the following scenario: You graduate from college and get your first big job at a well-known design firm in an urban area. You announce your new job on a social media website. All your friends are excited for you. After six months, you realize the firm and job is not a good fit for your skill set and professional interests. You wait until the first year of employment is up before you start looking for another job. Using social media, you announce your decision to leave the firm. You express your dissatisfaction with the job and in particular, your current boss.

As an emerging designer, one of the biggest mistakes you can make is using social media to communicate dissatisfaction with a boss or previous place of employment. You do not want to leave an impression you regret or would like to change. As a professional interior designer, you commit to maintaining the highest standards of the profession and show honorable conduct in all personal and business dealings.

Investigate and Reflect

Examine the possibilities of the scenario above. Discuss the consequences you may face now and in the future as a result of posting this information on a social-media site. Then consider your own online image. To manage your online image, plug your name into one or more search engines to examine what is posted about you. What did you find? Was there anything you would not want a future employer to see? Why? Delete anything that concerns you within your control. Because you cannot control the flow of online information, be prepared to answer questions employers may ask.

Marketing, Brand, and Reputation

There are many ways to grow and enhance your design practice. A **best practice**, a method that shows superior results, is to develop a brand and market it strategically. Enhancing visibility and credibility of your firm will drive more work your direction and afford you a choice of better design projects.

Marketing

Whether you work for a large firm or own your design practice, marketing is critical to current and future business success. A **market assessment** identifies perceived needs in the community or overseas, the competition, and the demand for services based on economy, geographical locale, and resources available. Simplistically, it is getting your foot in the door to sell your services and design firm to the client. Roughly, it takes three to five percent of your *gross income* (income before taxes) to market your services.

Once a market assessment is conducted, often a target marketing strategy is used to identify one or more groups of potential customers. This group, with common characteristics such as age or design preferences, is sometimes called a **market segment**. A market segment is one that is more likely to utilize the services of the firm, thereby creating a market niche.

Before marketing the services of your firm, however, identify your *brand* and a *brand strategy*. A **brand strategy** helps to precisely identify your marketplace position and what is different about your services from others in the market, **Figure 4-11**. For example, does your design firm have international connections or use the Internet to provide consulting services? What unique skills and services does your firm offer to the client, such as an in-house lighting designer or LEED expert?

What Is Your Brand?

Before an interior designer markets the firm's services, it is important to identify the company brand. It is the company signature and its face or image projected to the world. It should be highly recognizable. The company brand represents your product, your services, and you!

Branding is an advertising process for creating a unique name and image for a product or service that attracts the public and loyal clients. A **brand** is more than a graphic or logo. It is your identity enveloped in a communication device that sets you apart from your competitors. Your brand should entice prospective clients to perceive you as the only one that can provide solutions to their problems. A brand should be clean, memorable, and recognizable among the multitude of other brands, **Figure 4-12**.

iQoncept/Shutterstock.com

Figure 4-11 Brand development and marketing an interior design business helps establish a firm's marketplace position. *What do you notice first about a company's brand? What does the brand tell you?*

Otter Products LLC DBA OtterBox

Figure 4-12 Examine the Otterbox brand. *What comes to mind when you see it? What does the Otterbox logo communicate?*

Understanding client needs and preferences prior to establishing your brand is essential. You want to create an awareness of your business in their mind. To be successful, your business and your brand should capture the market niche. A good brand

- clearly delivers the message of your product and/or services
- confirms your (or the firm's) credibility
- focuses on your market segment
- draws an emotional response from the potential client or viewer—creates a connection
- motivates the client to contract with your firm
- establishes and encourages client loyalty

Brand position—the image a brand has in the mind of a client—matters. In this global world, your brand is accessible from everywhere via a tremendous international platform that consists of web pages, blogs, tweets, and Facebook. Brand positioning is not just written, it is also word of mouth. How people talk about you, your firm, and your services is the best and most valuable means for marketing a brand. How you position your brand in the workplace determines your clientele. Questions to ask as you develop and position your brand might include

- Where do you want to compete? Who is your target market?
- Who are your clients? What are they saying about your work?
- What characteristics make your design services different?
- What is the current position of your work/firm in relation to the desired position?

Brand positioning evolves with ongoing research and conversation about the value you bring to the client. As part of the conversation, it is important to determine when you need to refresh your brand or undergo a brand makeover.

What Is Your Design Philosophy?

All people have personal philosophies that shape how they view the world and how they interpret events in their lives. There are many well-known familiar life philosophies used in daily conversations, such as "When life gives you lemons, make lemonade." One way to identify a personally held philosophy is to ask "If your life's philosophies could be summed up in a bumper sticker, what would it be?"

Similarly, there are philosophies related to design. The following are well-known quotes published by renowned architects/designers of the last generation.

- "When I am working on a problem, I never think about beauty. But when I have finished, if the solution is not beautiful, I know it is wrong." Buckminster Fuller. (Interpretation: A good design solution must include beauty.)
- "What *works* good is better than what *looks* good. Because what works good lasts." Ray Eames. (Interpretation: Function is more important than aesthetics.)
- "Less is more." Ludwig Mies Van Der Rohe. (Interpretation: Simplicity leads to good design.)
- "Form follows function." Louis Sullivan. (Interpretation: Function should drive the shape or form of the object or building.)

Designer Profile

Lisa Henry—Brand Image

Lisa Henry, FASID, LEED AP, is currently CEO of Greenway Group and was a former Director of Architecture and Design with Knoll. Read more about what Lisa has to say regarding brand image.

"Every type of design firm needs a clear brand image. The *Knoll* brand, recognized around the world, communicates what Knoll stands for and believes. The brand is a promise to clients. Knoll believes in the meaning of new materials, the emergence of new technologies, the purpose of new processes, and the value of applying new ideas based upon research. The Knoll brand stands for innovation which helps clients sustain their competitive edge. It stands for design leadership which ultimately enhances their environment; and for commitment to enduring value which promotes their long-term growth and success. In each company communication, whether it is delivered with graphics, pictures, verbal language or behavior, the Knoll brand promise is congruently delivered."

You can read more about Lisa's background and experience in Appendix B.

As you practice in the interior design field, your reflections and experiences evolve into a set of guiding principles that form your **design philosophy**. The foundation of these guiding principles is often a set of beliefs and values related to how you design. Your philosophy becomes real and evident in your client's design solutions.

Once developed, your design philosophy guides your approach to design. It also becomes a business marketing tool to use in conjunction with your brand. It should set you apart from other design practitioners and offer a vocabulary to describe your designs. It also gives your client words to describe why he or she selected you or your firm.

A design philosophy becomes particularly apparent when you interview practicing designers and they discuss why they designed the space(s) the way they did. Your design philosophy should always be evolving and in development. In this way, it remains timely and timeless.

Designers derive many rewards from inner standards of excellence and intrinsic satisfaction with the end result of their labors. They love to design—a passion often comes from within. Interior design, however, *is* a business. Practice it as such.

Develop a Portfolio

A **portfolio** is a visual sample of your design and communication abilities. It includes such items as photographs of finished interior spaces, floor-plan drawings, freehand sketches, or conceptual models, **Figure 4-13**. A

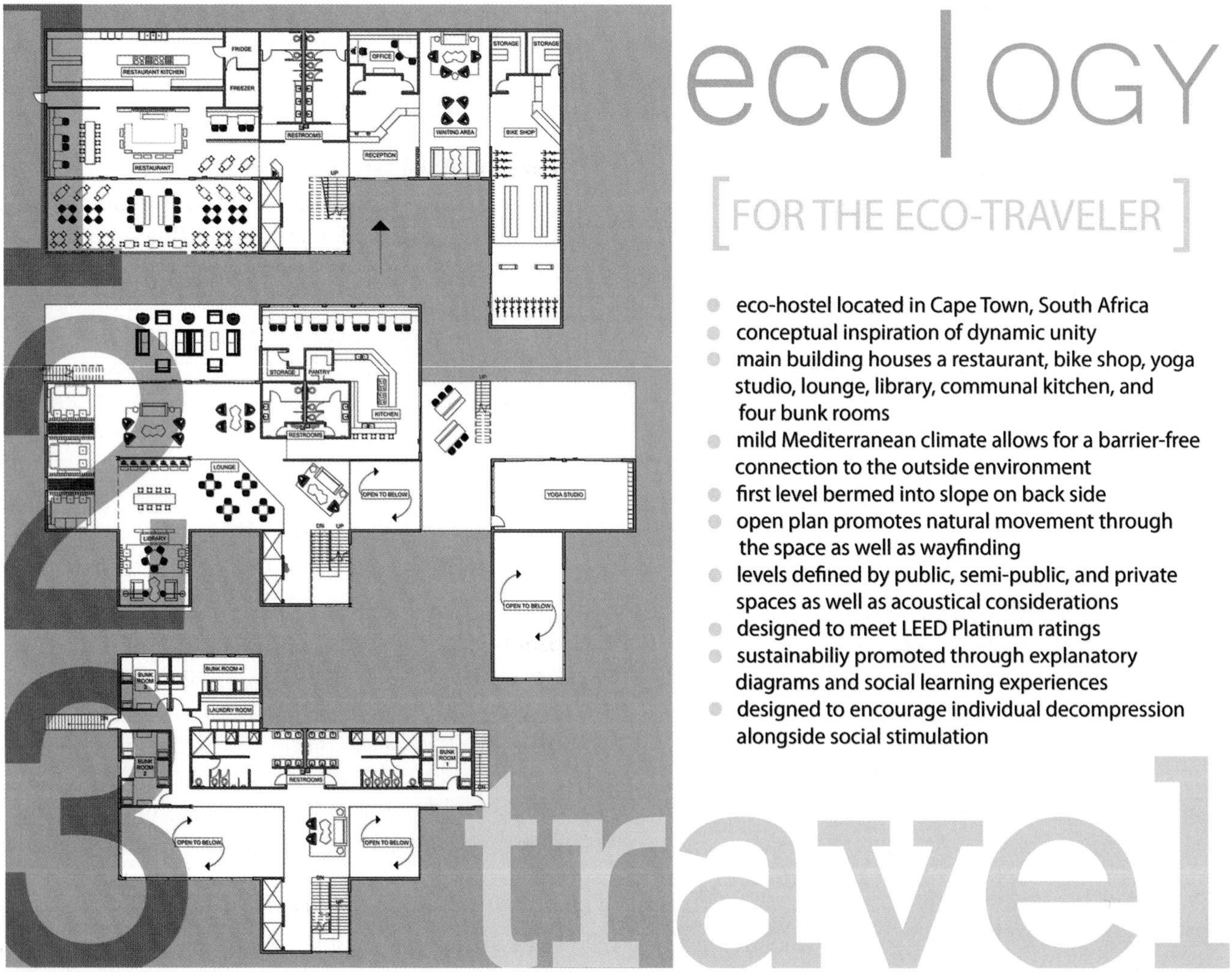

Courtesy of Carrie Zwisler

Figure 4-13 Showcase visual examples of your design capabilities in your portfolio. *What does this floor plan illustration tell you about the designer?*

portfolio is a fluid document that showcases your skills and requires frequent updating to best represent you and your work. Historically, designers carried their portfolios in large cases from place to place to show what or how they designed spaces. Today, many professionals publish their portfolios on individual web pages through the Internet. Ultimately, the portfolio is a reflection on and reflective of *you.*

Well-designed portfolios are a visual tool. They should be professional looking and unique. Your portfolio should

- feature your résumé and contact information
- showcase your best design and technology skills
- include work that illustrates your design thinking—capturing creativity and displaying innovative ideas as well as process
- be organized with good page composition
- be carefully sequenced with strong projects and/or skills at the beginning and end of the portfolio
- allow for easy navigation through pages if on a website
- be easily modified to allow the insertion of new designs or ability to delete others
- include explanatory documentation, such as the issue your design was addressing, or captions or bulleted explanations of the client priorities
- indicate awards received for your work

Optional items to include in your portfolio are

- a statement of your design philosophy
- examples of art or design related skills (such as sculpture or fine-art drawings), **Figure 4-14**

If an example in your portfolio work was a team project, clearly indicate the work you did on it and its significance to the project solution.

Conversely, there are a number of things that you should *not* include in your portfolio. These include

- photographs of yourself
- poor examples of your work or skills
- misspelled words, a font type that slants, or poor grammar

Portfolios are a strong marketing tool for you and/or the design firm. It can open doors to future opportunities *or* it can close doors if done poorly or haphazardly. It serves as proof of what you can do and what you have done. Keep it clean, organized, and professional.

The Importance and Impact of Public Policy on Interior Designers

The impact of public policy—whether legislative or regulatory—on interior design focuses on the *right* of an interior designer to adequately provide his or her services to a client(s) to increase consumer protections and uphold public safety. To achieve both, interior design laws must include certain education, experience, and examination requirements for persons interested in practicing in either commercial or residential spaces.

As of 2015, there are 27 states, the District of Columbia and US territory of Puerto Rico that have laws regulating the interior design profession. While each law is different, they all reinforce their shared fundamental and necessary purpose; to guarantee the legal right of any qualified interior designer to practice the profession of interior design. Therefore, it is imperative that an individual understand the differences between each type of law as well as the regulations that may result from them.

Understanding Interior Design Laws

A **title act** guarantees the right of an interior designer to use a certain title such as *licensed interior designer, registered interior designer,* or *certified interior designer.* These titles are the most commonly used, but they vary by state as does the process for obtaining permission to use them. Most states will require an individual to register his or her name with a state agency or board that has jurisdiction over interior designers. During this process an individual may be required to show proof of education, work experience, or other qualifications. In addition to professional recognition, some states with title acts extend the right for interior designers to sign and seal their own drawings without needing approval from an architect.

A **practice act** incorporates the professional recognition rights found in a title act, but goes further to strengthen individuals' right to practice interior design. These laws give qualified interior designers the right to not just sign and seal their drawings as only some states allow, but also to pull building permits. Guaranteeing interior designer's ownership over these services as well as professional recognition may be referred to as "full practice rights." *Full practice rights* mean an interior designer is not legally subservient to or dependent on another member of the design team, such as an architect, to execute their practices within the building envelope. Consequently, a practice act legally estab-

Courtesy of Carrie Zwisler

Figure 4-14 This fine-art illustration is just one type of art or design skill you can showcase in your portfolio.

lishes the independence of the interior designer next to others on a design team and in the built environment, **Figure 4-15**.

It is important to note that neither type of law or state restricts anyone from practicing interior design or referencing themselves as an interior designer. Final judgment on these issues came in 2011 from the United States Court of Appeals 11th Circuit in Locke vs. Shore. The court ruled in favor of a state establishing professional qualifications for interior designers to work in certain spaces, such as commercial and or residential.

Two qualification requirements many states use are formal interior design education and the successful passage of all sections of the *National Council for Interior Design Qualification (NCIDQ)* professional exam. Some states also require that individuals pass a state exam which assesses the individual's knowledge on codes and regulations specific to his or her state, such as in California. The court also ruled states could set qualifications for a person's use of professional recognition titles such as *registered* interior designer. The court, however, said the term *interior designer* alone could *not* be reserved by law, indicating any person may use it. Therefore, a state may have certain qualifications for an individual to use titles like *registered interior designer," certified interior designer,"* and *licensed interior designer,"* but an individual can always call themselves an "interior designer".

Understanding Interior Design Regulations

When a state legislature passes a *title* or *practice act*, most of the time this law will assign a regulatory agency within the executive branch to oversee the interior design profession. In some states, interior designers have their own board such as the Alabama State Board of Registration for Interior Design. Others will have a board that governs multiple built environment professionals like in Florida with the Florida Board of Architecture and Interior Design. Sometimes, interior designers may have difficulty finding which board regulates them because there may

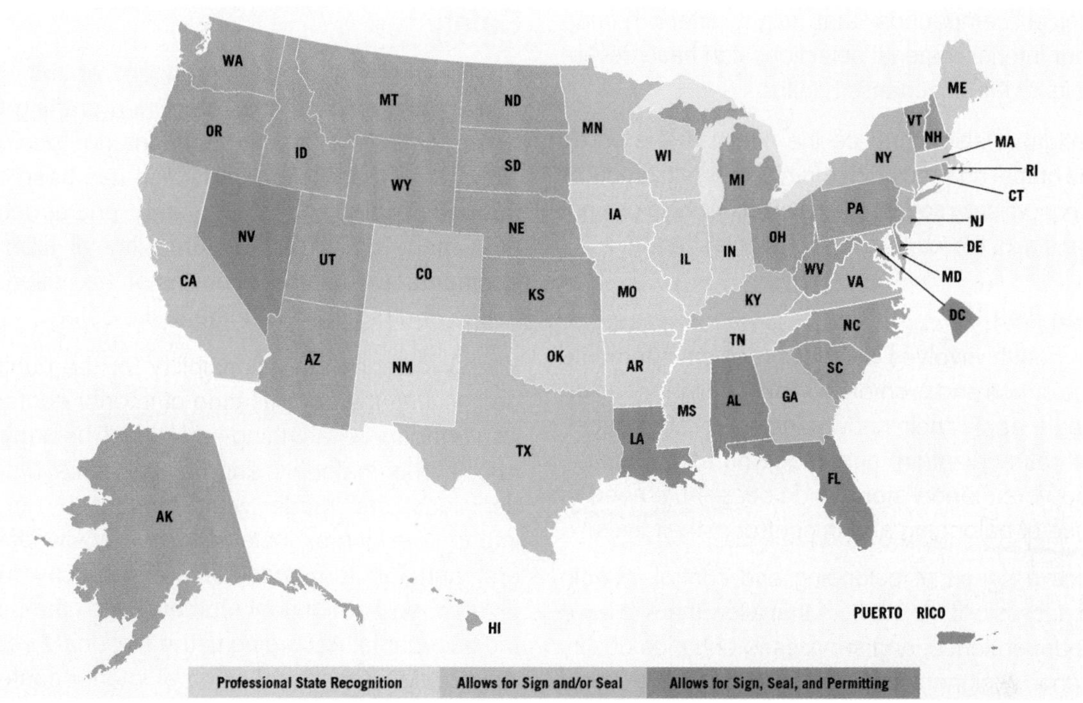

Used with permission from the American Society of Interior Designers, Inc. (ASID), ©2015

Figure 4-15 Currently, no state with a title act gives permitting rights to interior designers. However, numerous states with title acts do allow interior designers to sign and seal their own drawings. All states with practice acts guarantee interior designers the rights for sign and seal as well as permitting.

not be one or the name of the profession does not appear in the title of the entity. Many times the purpose of this regulatory body is to review built environment issues in order to release new policies that expand or dilute previously passed laws that affect interior designers.

Importance of Health, Safety, and Welfare (HSW)

Commercial and residential building owners increasingly are requesting the use of products and design techniques that will positively affect the health, safety, and welfare (HSW) of future occupants. The role of the interior designer to guarantee their HSW goals are met is vital. Consider a few of the ways interior designers impact the HSW of the public.

Health

There are a number of ways interior designers impact the health of the building occupants. These include physical and emotional health. Traditionally, protecting the public's health meant attending to disease prevention and nuisance control. The mandate of the twenty-first century is broader, encompassing emotional (mental) and physical health.

Physical Health

Developing a healthy interior environment is very important today when EPA statistics indicate that people spend more than 90 percent of their time inside. The sealing of windows in commercial buildings to enhance heating, ventilation, and air-conditioning (HVAC) efficiencies increases the chance for dirty air to be trapped, causing illnesses to occur. Such illnesses include

- **Sick building syndrome (SBS)**—a term used to describe acute health and discomfort effects that people experience after spending time in a building.
- **Building-related illness (BRI)**—a term used when symptoms of a diagnosable illness are identified and attributed directly to an airborne building contaminant.

In addition, with the development of new interior finishes and materials, pressure is on the interior designer to select those that consider issues of climate, moisture, and chemical compounds that might affect human health. Poor interior material selections can have devastating results to the occupant's health.

Interior designers also influence the health of the public through the proper specification of furnishings and products that are ergonomically sound. Such selections help prevent back or eye strain, thereby protecting people's health.

Emotional Health

Emotional health involves the design of environments that reduce stress and promote wellness. Interior design professionals apply their knowledge to create spaces that foster self-realization, encourage human potential, and develop hope and vision. To do so, people need to feel a sense of belonging and in control of their lives.

To enhance a sense of belonging and control, people also need accessibility to interiors that allow them to have careers, independence, and services to enhance quality of life. Interior designers must be knowledgeable about and use *Americans with Disabilities Act (ADA)* guidelines to provide interior spaces that are accessible and without barriers in all new or remodel design projects.

> *“It is not buildings that burn. It is the contents of the buildings that do.”*
>
> *Kevin Wilson, Fire Marshall, Poudre Fire Authority (PFA), retired, Fort Collins, Colorado*

Safety

Public safety is a major concern of the HSW triad that public officials consider when crafting legislation or regulations that affect the interior design profession. Often the public's protection has been addressed through building codes, fire safety, and structural integrity—many times the responsibility of architects and engineers. In fact, three-fourths of the national building codes and regulations relate to fire safety.

Interior designers' responsibility for the public's safety begins with the specification of interior content. *Interior content* can be anything—personal belongings, furniture, interior materials, and wall partitions. Many content decisions are made without input by professional interior designers. Instead, property owners, managers, and furniture manufacturers specify furnishings, fixtures, and equipment, sometimes to the detriment of the occupants. According to the *National Fire Protection Association*, proper selection of interior content primarily determines whether accidents become tragedies, **Figure 4-16**.

Currently a gap exists in the protection of the public. In the United States, regulations emphasize fire suppression and response rather than preventative measures that determine who can specify interior content in public buildings. Interior designers are in the process of educating legislators to pass interior design legislation to address this gap. Here is the dilemma.

Monkey Business Images/Shutterstock.com

Figure 4-16 Proper selection of interior materials and following building codes helps interior designers protect the safety of their clients.

With the design and construction of *new* buildings, existing regulations ensure the basic HSW of the public. Many licensed experts, such as engineers and code enforcement officials, visit the building site to inspect it to guarantee public safety. An interior designer will comply with the codes as part of the design team. Building code officials assess the designer's work and determine if it is safe. If it is not safe, the code officials will require changes. Interior design legislation is less important here due to checks and balances.

Extensive remodeling of *existing* buildings requires the acquisition of a building permit. Such remodeling often includes moving **load-bearing walls**—those walls that hold the roof up and support the structure. Regulations to protect the HSW of the public insist that inspections occur again to ensure the building is still structurally sound and the roof will not fall in. A building code official will assess any interior design work—such as specification of furnishings, fixtures, and equipment. Again, a check and balance is in place.

A gap in the protection of the HSW of the public comes with the remodeling or redesign of interiors, especially commercial interiors, with the movement of nonload-bearing walls such as half- or three-quarter height office partitions. **Nonload-bearing walls** shape space but do not support the structure. For example, a common office-design problem you may encounter is the request to move and redesign divisions or departments of an organization that are physically identified with office cubicles divided by panels.

When no load-bearing or nonload-bearing walls require movement, *no* regulations or inspections are required to reconfigure the offices. As a result, office cubicle panels may be too close for safe exit or may entirely block an exit route from a building. Anything that provides fuel for a fire near an exit or anything that blocks an exit hinders peoples' escape in the event of fire. Such occurrences were the findings from a 1988 fire in the *First Interstate Bank* of Los Angeles, California. This fire resulted in one fatality, 40 injuries, and lack of ability to use of a 62-story building for six months.

The public became very aware of the importance of interior contents after *The Station* fire in West Warwick, Rhode Island. In 2003, this fire killed 100 people and injured 200 others. The fire began in the nightclub from a band's fireworks display. The fire spread quickly through materials added to the space to soundproof the concert area. Over the life of the building, changes to the interior content profoundly affected life-safety performance. A number of people had severe consequences (prison time and fines) due to interior changes that resulted in these deaths and injuries.

Another gap in fire safety is in the regulation of *who* specifies interior materials and furnishings in interior spaces of large auditoriums, conference rooms, or assembly spaces. According to the *National Fire Protection Association (NFPA) (2009)*, interior finishes and furnishings in public assembly spaces (for 50 or more people) have more impact on the protection of life and property than any other issue except the actual fire-ignition source itself. In the last 25 or more years, many major fires at public venues were directly affected by interior finishes and furnishings, resulting in multiple injuries and deaths.

CASE STUDY

Occupant Safety and Aesthetics

An example of a fire hazard related to aesthetic modifications in wall coverings can be found in a local coffee shop. After the retail space was remodeled into a coffee shop, the final building inspection was completed and a certificate of occupancy granted. The shop opened for business, but the owner worried about the aesthetics of the space. A friend was hired to *decorate* the interior and hung burlap coffee bags on all the walls. A firefighter buying a morning coffee noted the fire hazard of the flammable wall coverings. The shop was shut down for a short time until the wall coverings were replaced. A professional interior designer would not have made the same mistake. He or she would know the fire codes that guide the selection of wall coverings and the flammability ratings of such.

Investigate and Reflect

Research and write a report on local and state fire codes related to interior textile use. As an alternative, research the significance and use of *ASTM E1537-12 Standard Text Method for Fire Testing of Upholstered Furniture.* What significance does this test hold for interior designers? Write a summary of your findings.

Welfare

Welfare, by definition, is the state of doing well, especially in respect to happiness, health, or prosperity. The welfare of people relates to enhancing the public's ability to do well in their interior spaces. Welfare, the third element in the HSW triad, is the most difficult and vague to define. Interior designers continue to profoundly affect work in this area. Within the realm of professional interior design, well-being includes

- using sustainable practices and environmentally friendly resources to protect the environment (using guidelines for environmental codes such as those of the U.S. Green Building Council)
- applying the current best practices in the areas of design, design theory, products, business, and ethics
- enhancing the comfort, privacy, pleasure, and satisfaction of the users within the space

Human outcomes of well-being include sense of identity, ability to adapt, place attachment, sense of security, and a feeling of refuge amidst stress. Interior designers use a process to systematically identify and solve problems that result in a sense of well-being (or welfare) for the user in their interior spaces.

Interior designers have few statistics to clearly show how interior design affects the HSW of the public. This is partly because few or no laws or regulations exist to protect the public when interior designer errors occur. The absence of such public policy means it is almost legally impossible to report violations except through a *civil* lawsuit against a professional in civil court. This is not the case in other professions. For example, the medical profession has malpractice cases that routinely provide industry-wide statistics on the affect of an individual's actions on the public. Lawsuits based on professional error are one way accurate statistics can be collected on a regular basis. Regardless, the overall point is this; the interior design profession must have a process, through either legislation or regulation, to help measure what they already know—their qualifications, skills, and actions are vital to upholding the HSW of the public in any type of structure.

Copyrights, Trademarks, and Patents

Interior designers, by the very nature of their work, create and develop many new ideas—and sometimes products—that have *intellectual property* rights. Understanding how to protect your design work is an important business practice.

Arcady/Shutterstock.com

Figure 4-17 Obtaining a copyright for your work provides protection for your designs. *How can failure to secure a copyright negatively impact a designer's business?*

For example, who owns the professional photographs of your interior design installation? *Answer:* The professional photographer owns the copyright to the photos unless an agreement is made ahead of time.

Copyrights

Copyright issues relate to the intellectual property evident in your publications, educational materials, drawings, and designs. A design *idea* can only be copyrighted if it is documented.

According to Webster, a **copyright** is the exclusive legal right to reproduce, publish, sell, or distribute the matter and form of something. A copyright protects your designs, ideas, and drawings during the design process. You have to begin copyrighting your work immediately. If you give your work to a client without indication of copyright, it becomes public domain and anyone can use it without any compensation to you—the author and creator of the work, **Figure 4-17**.

If a design firm employs you, the copyright of your work belongs to your employer under the concept of *work for hire*. Any design you create as part of your normal responsibilities during your work hours belongs to your employer.

When someone uses copyrighted materials created by another person, the user infringes on the author's copyright. Suppose you created a beautiful office design for a new client. You were diligent in obtaining copyright protection and noting it on your work. Your new client in her excitement about the design, began photocopying the work and passing it out to friends. Without your documented permission and without monetary compensation, this is an example of infringement of copyright.

On an international level, copyright issues are gathering attention because some designers are conducting design work overseas. In many countries, even if you provide documents, materials, or designs that have U.S. copyright protection, your protection against unauthorized use of your materials depends on the national laws of that particular country.

Some countries do not object to copying the materials for use elsewhere without any compensation to the author. For example, suppose a design instructor in the U.S. develops a continuing education course to use when teaching color theory to practicing designers. A professional from another country takes the course. Although clearly copyrighted, the foreign design professional then shares course materials with many designers in his or her country without compensation to the originator (the design instructor in the U.S.) of the course. Design professionals must handle the copyright situations in other countries with sensitivity and caution. Working with an expert who is familiar with foreign copyright laws can help.

Trademark

A **trademark**, another type of intellectual property, protects something very specific such as words, phrases, designs, or symbols. Your brand, logo, or *tagline*—a phrase that identifies your business—fall into this category. You must investigate your trademark to see if it is already registered by someone else. If not, you may file an application to do so. It is important to complete comprehensive searches of federal and state registrations and of common law unregistered trademarks. Attorneys commonly become part of the process of securing a trademark for your intellectual property. See the *United States Patent and Trademark Office (USPTO)* website for more information on trademarks.

An example of a trademark can be found on the website of ForrestPerkins, an internationally acclaimed interior design firm. With offices in Dallas, Washington D.C., and San Francisco, the firm is known for specializing in luxurious, custom details and high-quality design solutions for luxury hotels, resorts, and multi-residential projects worldwide. Such dedication to its specialty helped ForrestPerkins win an International Property Award for 2012 in the category of: Interior Design Apartment, USA with WestEnd25. ForrestPerkins' trademark can be seen on its website: Defining Luxury, **Figure 4-18**.

Patent

The third form of intellectual property, a **patent**, protects your unique or novel design or invention for a limited time (for example, an innovative, new desk chair with a unique mechanism). The *United States Patent and Trademark Office* is responsible for granting all patents in the U.S. A patent serves to exclude others from making, selling, or importing the *work* for the term of the patent, usually 20 years.

Photographer: Kenneth M Wyner/Designed by Forrest Perkins

FORRESTPERKINS
defining luxury®

Courtesy of ForrestPerkins

Figure 4-18 The trademark for ForrestPerkins—as shown here—can be found on their website. This trademark helps protect the intellectual property rights of ForrestPerkins.

An example of an innovative desk-chair patent is the *Leap Chair®* developed by Steelcase, Inc., **Figure 4-19**. Steelcase wanted to design and manufacture a chair that could enhance employee productivity through creating healthier ways to sit. After analyzing research conducted by 27 ergonomic scientists, they designed a chair that supports and moves with the body in new ways. In fact, the Leap Chair technology has 42 protected U.S. patents on one chair. What is the result for employers who began using this chair? Through an independent health and productivity study, those using the chair over a one-year period showed an 18 percent increase in employee productivity. Steelcase has since partnered with other industries to allow patented Leap technology to be used in cars and airplane

Leap® chair by Steelcase

Figure 4-19 A patent on the *Leap® Chair* design protects Steelcase and keeps others from using and profiting from its design. *Investigate the process for procuring a patent. Report your findings to the class.*

Establishing Fees and Payments

Do *not* give away your professional work, ideas, and designs. They have value! Similar to many professions, the fee and payment structure that interior designers use depends on the *scope of services* they contract to complete for the client.

Scope of services is the type and extent of design services the designer or design team completes for the client's design project which affects the associated fees.

DESIGNER MATH SKILLS

Determining Retail Markup

When considering profitability, a company owner or self-employed designer must determine how to price products for selling. *Markup* is a retail term for the amount by which price exceeds the cost. For example, suppose a design firm purchases a chair for $400 from the manufacturer, but then sells it to the customer for $700. There are two ways to express this type of pricing—by *dollar markup* or *markup percentage.*

- **Dollar markup.** To determine the dollar markup amount, you subtract the chair cost from the selling price.

  $700 (selling price) - $400 (cost) = $300 (dollar markup)

- **Markup percentage.** To determine the percentage markup, you divide the markup amount by the cost.

  $300 (the markup amount) ÷ $400 (cost) = 75% markup

If the markup percentage is already determined and the designer wants to establish the selling price, use the following steps:

1. **Convert** the markup percentage to a decimal. (0.75)
2. **Multiply** the cost by the markup percentage to get the dollar markup. ($400 × 0.75 = $300)
3. **Add** the dollar markup to the cost to determine the selling price. ($300 + $400 = $700).

Markup pricing is used in all areas of retail and varies depending on the specific industry. For instance, in the women's apparel industry the markup pricing can be 2.3%–2.5% or more while jewelry can be a triple (3%) markup. The book industry markup can range from 30–40% but online purchases can be as low as 20%. Shipping costs greatly impact today's cost of retail pricing.

Your scope of services may be the entire project, part of the project (such as concept only), working drawings, specifications, programming, or CAD work. Before taking on a new project, designers and their clients should determine and agree on the scope of services. As they develop the scope of work or services, interior designers should be fair and candid with their clients about their abilities, time line, and resources.

When determining fees and payment, evaluate the cost of doing business (for example, your overhead to keep your design studio open and insurances), and a reasonable profit for completing the work. Once the designer and client reach an agreement, designers serve as an advocate for their clients and anyone they have contracted with for the given project.

When completing a residential project, the designer and client agree on a fee or rate, both sign a contract, and the job may begin. This may be the case for smaller commercial projects as well.

For larger commercial projects, days and weeks of work by a design-firm team may go into developing a bid packet to submit as part of the *bid process*. In the **bid process**, a designer or architectural firm typically presents a packet with a conceptual design, a description of services the firm offers, and a statement of fees as in response to a *request for proposal (RFP)*. Once awarded the bid, the design firm can begin the work. If your bid is not accepted, you will write off the time spent as a loss. You will receive no payment. If the bid is accepted, the work begins.

There are many ways to charge for design services. Some common ones include the following:

- **Hourly fee**—a per hour dollar amount the designer charges for an hour of design services. The amount charged will depend on the expertise provided by the designer. For example a senior designer in the firm will charge more than a CAD operator.
- **Daily rate**—a flat-dollar amount quoted for one day of design work that the designer gives the client.
- **Flat fee (or fixed fee)**—a flat-dollar amount quoted for the total sum of the design services the designer provides the client. This is a risky way for a designer to charge because it is difficult to estimate the time it takes to complete a design project. It gives the client, however, a set amount to fit into his or her project budget.
- **Percentage fee**—a quoted dollar amount based on a percentage of the total project cost.
- **Consulting fee**—a fee negotiated between client and designer for provision of ideas and resources.

Scope creep occurs when a client adds project requirements onto the existing project demands that are not defined in the scope of work or services. If the client requests additional work after signing the initial contract, a contract revision should take place and a contract addendum should be signed by both parties. Scope creep, if allowed, dilutes the profitability of the project for the designer. For example, if your scope of services is to complete the design of an attorney's office and the client asks you to "throw in the design of the receptionist office, too," resulting in scope creep, negotiating a contract addendum will help you maintain project profitability. The designer uses an addendum for adding to or reducing the scope of services, clarifying ambiguities, and changing the quality of work.

Similarly, when a client requests a project change, the designer develops a **change order**—written instructions that modify a part of the project's design, such as changing the location of a window or door. The designer

DESIGNER MATH SKILLS

Calculating Area of a Space

Square footage is the total amount of *area* in a residential or a commercial environment. Ability to calculate area and, therefore, the amount of furniture, fixtures, and equipment that will fit in the space helps designers create *safe* spaces.

You can calculate the total area by adding together the square footage space from all rooms in the environment. The dimensions of each room will appear on the floor plan, or you can measure the length and width of each room. Note that closets and storage space do not count toward total square footages. To calculate square footage for each room or area, use the following formula:

$$\text{Area} = \text{Length} \times \text{Width}$$

To calculate the total square footage for a residence or commercial space, complete the calculation for each room and add them together.

and client must both sign the change order to ensure clear understanding of the expectations. Modifications to the scope of services and change orders become part of the project's contract documents.

Many times a client requests a quote before signing a contract. Someone—such as an employee of the firm—who knows the scope of services the designer will offer, the client budget, and the different fee structures available should develop the quote. There are many subtle distinctions and intricacies in developing a fee structure to ensure a business profit as well as a fair price. There is no standard interior design project.

Additional Best Practices for Business

The following includes a few additional best practices to use in an interior design business. These are best practices from a variety of interior design practitioners.

- **Specialize.** Avoid trying to be all things to all clients, but instead select a niche for your design work and become exceptional at performing it.
- **Get credentialed and certified.** Your qualifications go a long way for selling your knowledge, which leads to design credibility.
- **Sell innovative design solutions rather than products.** Custom products, such as furnishings, are now commonly available and discounted for the consumer.
- **Collaborate rather than partner.** A partnership is binding. Instead develop a team of professional associates, such as lighting designers or acoustic specialists.
- **Build relationships.** When you are busy with design projects, it is common to neglect the future. Remember to market even in the busy times. If the economy slows down, the firm will be able to weather the storm.

An interior design business has many goals including client satisfaction, an ethically and responsibly run firm, and a healthy bottom line. When those are achieved, you have success, **Figure 4-20**.

Yuri Arcurs/Shutterstock.com

Figure 4-20 Following best practices for an interior design business leads to business success and client/designer satisfaction.

Chapter 4

Review and Assess

Summary

- Understanding evolving business and consumer trends impacts ways interior designers do business and opens opportunities for design projects.
- Understanding client demographics and their changing needs is an essential business practice.
- Building strong relationships is critical to gaining client trust and a credible reputation.
- Careful positioning helps the designer to build a recognizable brand.
- Interior designs use typical business structures, each having advantages and disadvantages.
- The type of firm and geographic location influences the career positions a designer might hold.
- Interior designers may work with interdisciplinary teams to solve client problems for a project.
- Because clients, design-team members, and the public give the designer significant levels of trust, the designer must act ethically with competence, honesty, integrity, and objectivity.
- Developing a brand and marketing it strategically is critical to a designer's business success.
- A personal design philosophy guides the designer's approach to design and is also a marketing tool for the designer's brand.
- An effective portfolio showcases a designer's best work.
- Because interior designers impact the health, safety, and well-being (HSW) of the public, there is a strong need for legislation and regulation.
- Protecting design work using copyrights, trademarks, and patents is a critical business practice.
- Establishing fees and payments requires evaluation of the costs of doing business.
- Using best practices helps an interior design firm achieve a healthy bottom line and success.

Chapter Vocabulary

Read the text paragraphs that contain each of the following terms. Then write the definition of each term in your own words. Double-check your definitions by reading the text and using the text glossary.

Articles of Incorporation
articles of organization
best practice
bid process
branding
brand
brand position
brand strategy
change order
closed corporation
code of ethics
collaborate
copyright
corporation
design philosophy
incorporation
licensing
limited liability company (LLC)
load-bearing wall
market assessment
market niche
market segment
nonload-bearing wall
partnership
patent
portfolio
positioning
practice act
proprietorship
scope creep
scope of services
sole proprietorship
title act
trademark

Review and Study

1. List three trends that impact interior design businesses.
2. What is positioning? Give an example of an action a designer can take for better positioning.
3. How does a sole proprietorship differ from a partnership?
4. What is a corporation? Give an advantage and disadvantage of this structure.
5. Name the general titles or positions in a studio-based design firm.
6. List four types of specialists an interior design firm may hire.
7. What are three concepts or procedures a designer must understand to stay in business?
8. What are the categories of ethical behavior for an interior designer according to the *ASID Code of Ethics and Professional Conduct*?
9. What is a market assessment and how do designers use it?
10. Contrast brand, branding, and brand strategy.
11. What are the characteristics of a successful brand?
12. Describe the characteristics of interior design portfolio.
13. Contrast title acts and practice acts.
14. How do interior designers protect the physical and emotional health of clients?
15. What are the differences among copyright, trademark, and patent?
16. What is the *scope of services* and what does it include?
17. Name three common ways to charge for design services.
18. List five additional best practices that can help an interior designer have a successful design business.

Critical Analysis

19. **Analyze relationships.** List ten different types of personal and/or professional relationships a designer may have with individuals who work with them in the field. Analyze which ones would be most important to maintaining a successful business. Discuss why relationships are so important to a designer's success.
20. **Assess business structures.** Study the business structures used for design firms. Assess which business structure would have the most liability, be the most lucrative, and offer the most protection for you as an individual. Discuss your assessment in class.
21. **Assess brands.** Identify five interior design firms in your state and collect their company logos and/or brands. Line them up on one document. Then assess the portfolio design projects for all the firms. Next to each brand, briefly describe the firm's work. Does each firm's brand reflect its work? Why or why not?
22. **Predict consequences.** Suppose an interior designer posts in his or her electronic portfolio a completed design project that was not completed by him or her. Predict the consequences of the designer's behavior in this situation. How might this impact the designer's practice of interior design?
23. **Predict outcomes.** Why will limiting interior design legislation be a hot topic if the economy spirals downward? Use text and reliable Internet resources to provide evidence for your conclusions.

Think like a Designer

24. **Speaking and listening.** Analyze the *Design Insight* quote at the beginning of this chapter. Discuss with a classmate specific examples of why knowing the *business* of interior design will lead to success in the profession.
25. **Writing.** Explore and identify your personal design philosophy. Do the following:
    A. Research other designer's philosophies such as interior designers, architects, graphic designers, and artists. Capture their philosophies in a chart.

B. List your values, life philosophies, and beliefs. Using unique phrases and words, craft your personal philosophy and then your design philosophy.
C. Save your philosophy. Review it periodically throughout this course and at course completion.

26. **Reading.** Visit the ASID website to research which states in the U.S. have interior design legislation. Which states currently have legislation issues under discussion? Locate your state and read about the legislative policies in place for the practice of interior design. What education, experience, and examinations would you need in order to practice interior design in your state?
27. **Writing.** Visit three restaurants in your nearby community. Analyze the HSW for the occupants or users of the space. Are exits properly marked and accessible? Do the occupants seem comfortable? In your perception, are they healthy buildings to visit and use? Write a summary of your experiences to share with the class.
28. **Math practice.** Suppose a commercial client wants to remodel the employee cafeteria. The room dimensions are 45'-0" × 100'-0". What is the total area of the space you will have to work with?
29. **Math practice.** As a designer, a client accompanies you to the local design center to select fabric for window treatments. The design center is open to you and your clients to shop for products available only to industry. You explain that the tag price in the various shops is retail pricing and as the designer you receive a 50-percent discount. The client's cost, however, will be 25 percent above designer's cost resulting in the client paying 75 percent of the retail tag price. Your client has a successful shopping day and purchases the following:
    - 5 yards of fabric (tag price: $128/yard)
    - 1 ceiling light fixture for breakfast area (tag price: $900)
    - 1 couch (tag price: $1640)
    - 2 table lamps—matching (tag price: $220/ea)

    Create an itemized bill for your client for today's purchases showing the tag price, the designer's price, the price to the client, and the subtotal of the total purchase.

Design Application

30. **Develop a design.** A zany, trendy costume store is contracting with your firm to develop a new conceptual *look* for them in an urban center of your state.
    A. Describe the design firm you are working for and its business structure.
    B. Identify the scope of services for which you are being hired.
    C. Indicate fees you will charge for your designs. Remember the importance of being competitive with other local design fees.
    D. Develop a new "look" for the client's store. Use images to reflect the look of their new urban store.
    E. Determine the store's market segment. Design their brand.
    F. Make a client presentation. Include your research of similar stores, your concept using a montage of images, the written market segment you identified, and their new brand reflective of their store. Be sure to exhibit professionalism through dress, speech, and manners appropriate to the profession.
31. **Portfolio builder.** Develop your personal brand for your portfolio. Realize you will use it for several elements in your portfolio, including the cover and business cards. If desired, include a tagline and link it to your personal design philosophy. Save copies of items developed with your personal brand in your portfolio.
32. **Portfolio builder.** Save a copy of your design philosophy from activity 25 in your portfolio to review and update as needed.

Is Interior Design for You?

Design by: Lita Dirks & Co./Photography by: Brian Gassel Photography

Chapter 5

Design Insight

"Design is an emotional, aesthetic, and intellectual pursuit. Engage your passion. Satisfy your curiosity."

IIDA Home Website

Learning Targets

After studying this chapter, you will be able to

- summarize the diverse and complex skills necessary for a career in interior design.
- explain the education, experience, examinations, and continuing education necessary for a successful career in interior design.
- summarize the interior design areas of study that contribute to career success, including the studio environment, communication, and design thinking.
- identify the aspects of various credentials, qualifications, and preparation requirements in the field of interior design.
- summarize ways to develop career connections in interior design.
- determine why the field of interior design needs you and can benefit you.

Introduction

The array of employment opportunities is vast and the necessity to obtain an education to access these opportunities is increasing. Do you have a desire to do something creative, innovative, and meaningful in your career? What career choice might be fulfilling and enriching for you throughout your life? Could it be *interior design*?

Interior Design—the Career for You

Many people are attracted to the interior design profession because of the different clients they may work with and the different places to which they may travel. It is exciting to use your creativity to imagine how to design spaces—perhaps for a friend—as an artistic, stylish, or romantic interior in a New York City loft. It is also satisfying and fulfilling to assist aging individuals, such as the older adults in your life, your neighbors, or grandparents, to maintain their dignity and independence while remaining in their own homes.

Everyone has experienced the importance of good design. For instance, a great pair of designer shoes can go from being your favorite pair of shoes to dust collectors if they hurt your feet. Likewise, interior spaces can look good but function poorly. If you are interested in improving the world through good design, perhaps this is the career for you, **Figure 5-1**.

Investigate your interest in interior design by asking yourself the following questions:

- Do you notice things like light, color, and space?
- Do you have creative ideas?
- Do you like looking through architecture or interior magazines or watching reality design shows?

A Photography by Emily Minton Redfield; Design by Andrea Schumacher Interiors

B ©Ron Pollard, courtesy of RNL

Figure 5-1 The career of interior design offers diverse opportunities to meet client needs for aesthetically attractive and functional spaces as is evident in these images showing residential (A) and commercial design (B).

- Do you enjoy *watching people* and how they interact in stores or hotels?
- Do you like moving furniture around at home to reshape space?
- Does it bother you when something seems out of place or does not work like it should in an interior?
- Do you enjoy working with friends to help them visualize how their interior spaces can be rearranged?
- Are you interested in designing responsibly for the planet and helping others function better in their spaces?

The profession of interior design is not for everyone. However, if some of these questions describe your interests, then interior design may be the career for you.

One Degree—Many Options

The professional workplace has become increasingly specialized. If you go to school to become an endodontist, you will perform root canals all day long with minimal variation. In contrast, if you go into interior design, you can do many things with a single professional degree, from homes and apartment complexes to luxury resorts and hospitals. One degree opens a wide variety of career opportunities that meet today's needs.

According to the U.S. Bureau of Labor Statistics, there is an expected 19 percent increase in the need for interior designers by 2020. For those in a specialty area, such as kitchen or bath design, the expected job growth is as much as 27 percent during this time.

Skill Preparation for the Twenty-First Century

Success in the twenty-first century requires the development of essential skills such as critical thinking, creativity, problem solving, communication, and collaboration, **Figure 5-2**. You have learned many of these skills through such core academic subjects as English, math, history, and geography. Creativity and innovation are additional skills necessary to think and work creatively with others, and then follow through by implementing innovations. Interior design education helps you learn these skills as instructors guide you through the process of understanding a client problem and analyzing needs to the stage of creating something new or different for the client. The study of interior design prepares you to be successful at work and in life in the twenty-first century.

The career of interior design involves travel, meeting new people, budgeting, marketing, and teamwork. It is a career that encompasses design as well as human behavior, psychology, health, and wellness. As a service profession, it demands discipline and organization. The demand on the designer is equaled to or surpassed by interesting opportunities to solve problems for people that result from living and working indoors the majority of the day. Creativity and innovation are necessary when solving complex human problems.

takayuki/Shutterstock.com fcxphotography.com/Shutterstock.com

Figure 5-2 A career in interior design offers vast opportunities. *What captures your interest about the opportunities available for a career in interior design?*

Interior Design is Exciting and Diverse

Interior design is exciting because it responds to trends, fashion, and style. People throughout the world feel its global and international influence. Nationally, the design of personal and professional places often reflects a client's culture.

In the career of interior design, there are no two design clients the same and no two projects exactly alike. As an interior designer, different projects hit your desk every day—commercial and residential, large and small, custom and meaningful. You meet future clients everywhere. They walk through your door, you meet them at social or community functions, and you are introduced to them through friends or satisfied clients. Their different design problems demand energy, passion, and innovation.

At any given day, you may find yourself meeting with a team to brainstorm ideas, working on the computer developing interior models, making a client presentation, meeting with a contractor at a job site, or going to the building department for a building plan check. You are never locked into one particular job. You can be working on two to five client projects at any one time—each of which is in a different stage of design. Perhaps that is why interior design students enjoy studying the profession so much and why they thrive in the profession after graduation.

Interior Design is Challenging

The basis for success of an interior design firm is satisfied clients. To achieve satisfied clients, you need good interpersonal skills to function well with people—both clients and team players. Learning to be comfortable with meeting people and interacting with them is an essential skill.

STUDENT SPOTLIGHT

What Is FUN About Interior Design?

Danette Billington: "What I find fun about interior design is all of the variety in things that you can do. Each project is different and exciting. There are so many areas you can choose to focus on such as lighting, space planning, sustainability, residential, commercial, or whatever you love!"

Erika Sanchez: "Branching out in creative and communicational skills to connect to the world is what I find fun. After observing the design elements in my favorite store, I finally understand why the space is so appealing to me."

Aubrey Beck: "I love seeing how art is applied to people in the way they interact with their spaces and the art around them. Learning why people create space and the intentions they have behind creating different spaces is intriguing. I am passionate about the discovery of new aspects of interior design. There is so much more than just the surface of interior design. A lamp is simply not a lamp, but a pathway for a client to have a great mood or emphasis in his or her personal space."

Paul Vanderheiden: "Interior design is most fun because it is essentially creating art for humans to live in. A designer can control the eventual end of the viewer's emotional and physical experiences simply by the design choices that are made."

Gretchen Einfeldt: "A designer's *job* is to be creative! Where other jobs are very straightforward with little change, interior design is always changing, challenging, and fun."

Cheryl Snyder: "What is fun about interior design is not only being able to show *tangible* creativity in a 3-D environment, but to see how much the users enjoy the designs and how much an improved design shapes the quality of their lives."

Carrie Zwisler: "Interior design is fun because it is applied creativity! I have always considered myself a very creative person, but have always needed guidelines. So, interior design is perfect for me because I can express myself creatively, but also have the guidelines I need to help me achieve something very beautiful."

Becoming a good team leader and good team player is necessary for success.

It is challenging to understand the artistic and technical requirements to plan space as well as visually present the plan. Similarly, it is important to understand the structural requirements of the plans and building codes.

Although it seems contradictory, a designer—who is creative—must also have good time-management skills or the client's project will never see completion. In addition, because so many details go into a client's design, you need to develop good project-management skills because you will likely work on more than one project at a time. These are daily challenges for an interior designer.

Interior Design is Ethical, Sustainable, and Integrated

It is important to design sustainably and ethically. Interior designers work in concert with many different *systems*. They work with systems of nature; therefore, they owe allegiance to maintaining a healthy planet, **Figure 5-3**. A design should be enduring and beautiful, even as it is highly functional.

Designers work with building systems. They know that great projects result from a truly integrated design process in which every team member is part of the conversation every step of the way.

Interior designers understand the ethics of designing for those who do not have much and those who have plenty. All people deserve dignity and delight within their interior places.

mangostock/Shutterstock.com

Figure 5-3 As they work in concert with systems of nature, interior designers create designs with sustainability in mind.

Interior Design Involves Complex Problems

There are many complex problems in addressing client issues in their built environment (also known as *wicked problems* in the design world—those problems that go beyond reasonable or predictable limits). Some are heart-wrenching, such as working with an aging individual who must leave his or her home and move to a retirement facility. How do you design a new space to express comfort and meaning of home in this new space? Others are critical, such as designing a pediatric ward in a new hospital wing. How do you design spaces that take a child's mind off a medical procedure and make the experience educational, fun, and engaging?

Clients' complex problems may also relate to their preferences in their built environments, **Figure 5-4**. A few such real-life residential client preferences might include

- **Uncomplicated delight** (or undeniable or simple). Design a *green* sustainable house using **minimalist** (characterized by extreme sparseness and simplicity), clean-lined elements such as natural daylight, functional essentials, and simplistic beauty.
- **Sculpted spaces.** Design around magnificent views in the mountains. The owners have a robust sculpture collection both inside and outside. Start the interior design around their art. The client prefers a minimalist concept.
- **Acute, uncomfortable angles.** Family heirlooms must be incorporated into an awkward 1950s home on a narrow lot in the suburbs outside Chicago.
- **Southwest modern.** Clients come to you for a current, more modern expression of Santa Fe's historic downtown.
- **Unpretentious indecision.** Your client says, "I leave for work at an accounting firm at 8:00 a.m. I travel to work on a subway. My job has high stress. When I come home, I want to relax and de-stress. I have no preferences. Can you help?"

A Warren Diggles Photography/Jon Rentfrow, Rentfrow Design, LLC

B RM Ruwart Design/Rosalie M. Ruwart, ASID

Figure 5-4 The client who owns this kitchen is an artist who wanted her kitchen to have a simple, industrial look—including concrete floors, exposed Parallam® beams, and a load-bearing column wrapped with HVAC duct work (A). This university atrium offers students a place to relax between classes (B). *Discuss what complex problems each of the clients may have presented to the designer.*

Skills and Natural Strengths

A successful interior designer is human-centered, understands business, acts professionally at all times, and brings creative and innovative solutions to address client problems. A wide range of skills and education are necessary, whether you practice interior design or work in an **allied** (closely associated) field. Some of these skills are inherent in your personality, some you develop through formal education, and others emerge from your workplace experiences.

Because there are many different types of interior design positions in the profession, there is not one personality type necessary to achieve success in the field. In fact, design is about differences. The following are suggestions for useful traits and skills in the field. How many of these personality traits and natural strengths do you have?

- respect for others
- listening skills
- leadership skills
- integrity—firmly adhering to ethical values
- interest in people
- creative thoughts and ideas
- eye for design detail
- strong work ethic
- teamwork skills

Path to Becoming a Professional Interior Designer

No two roads to the interior design profession are the same. Everyone joins the profession at different points and times of their lives. Some students make the decision in high school, **Figure 5-5**. Other students find it after acquiring another degree. Read about Charisse Johnston's unconventional journey to an interior design career.

If you select interior design as your career early in your life, you will want to follow the *Four 4 E's*—education, experience, examination, and continuing education. It is your education, experience, and qualifications that set you apart as a designer.

Education

As you review college, university, or private school websites, one standard of excellence to look for in interior design programs is whether they are accredited. The *Council for Interior Design Accreditation (CIDA)* is an international organization that accredits three-to-five-year postsecondary interior design education programs in the United States and Canada. Working with many professionals, CIDA developed professional standards that evaluate interior design programs to prepare students for entry-level interior design practice.

auremar/Shutterstock.com michaeljung/Shutterstock.com Monkey Business Images/Shutterstock.com

Figure 5-5 The path to an interior design career is different for everyone. Many make the decision in high school.

Over its 40-year history, the CIDA has evaluated interior design programs of hundreds of colleges and universities throughout North America. It is important to note that not all programs seeking accreditation or re-accreditation are accepted. Although CIDA is not the only measure of quality for interior design education, it is a reliable indicator of standards met by the interior design programs.

There are several types of institutions—both public and private—you can attend to acquire the formal education necessary to be a qualified, professional interior designer, **Figure 5-6**. Many interior design programs are

Education and Degrees		
Institution Type	**Degree Earned**	**Years of School**
Community Colleges	Associate's Degree	2
Art and Design Schools	Associate's or Bachelor's degree	2, 3, or 4
Colleges and Universities	Bachelor's Degree	4
Colleges and Universities	Master's Degree	5 and/or 6

Figure 5-6 There are many educational options from which to choose on your pathway to a career in interior design. *Which educational degree best fits your career path?*

Designer Profile

Charrisse Johnston—An Unconventional Journey

Charrisse Johnston, ASID, LEED AP, Associate AIA, is a principal at Steinberg Architects in California and was formerly with Gensler—a global architecture, design, planning and consulting firm of 2500 or more professionals.

Ryan Gobuty, Gensler

"I was working in the financial-services industry (Wall Street) after acquiring a behavioral biology background when I quit my job and began a small business in Santa Monica. As I was growing my business, I received a postcard about UCLA Extension's Interior Design Program. I tried a night class and found a whole new world. I realized that interior design was an exciting profession that required artistic creativity, analytical skills, client management and business acumen—everything that interested me.

"My first job was with Gensler's Workplace Studio in Los Angeles, California. Recently, I made the move to our new Education practice where I am the sole designer. I now design spaces for both K–12 private schools and higher education facilities. I work with technical staff, architects, and project managers in various stages of design."

You can read more about Charrisse's experience in Appendix B.

located on the campuses of colleges, universities, and within schools of art. There are probably several in your state. All programs may elect to go through the rigorous, voluntary process of becoming accredited through the *Council for Interior Design Accreditation (CIDA)*.

Acceptance into Interior Design Programs

The competition for getting into many college interior design programs is significant. You may want to check to see if there is a **selective admissions process** to get into the major or a **selective advancement process**—such as a portfolio review—to move into sophomore, junior, or senior levels of the program. Because many colleges have a limited number of openings, not every student who applies to the major is accepted. Having a strong portfolio can give you a competitive edge when going through the college admissions or selective advancement process.

Degree Levels and Related Careers

An associate's or bachelor's degree is the beginning requirement to achieve professional status as an interior designer. An *associate's degree* in interior design will prepare you for employment in

- CAD work
- furniture or interior retail stores
- specialty areas in kitchen and bath design
- cabinet design
- sales and marketing
- specialized accessories showrooms
- interior finish showrooms (floor coverings)
- organizing stores (closet design)
- specialty residential spaces (media rooms, home offices)

A *bachelor's degree* in interior design will prepare you for employment in any entry-level interior design position. These include positions in firms of interior design, architecture, construction, or such related design firms as lighting design.

Once you acquire your degree, you can apply to take the *Interior Design Fundamentals Examination (IDFX) (Section 1)* available through the *Council for Interior Design Qualification (CIDQ)*. CIDQ is the organization that administers the professional interior design examination in North America. It is an independent corporation concerned with maintaining the standards of interior design practice.

The IDFX assesses the knowledge you gained during your education about such topics as building systems, construction standards, and design application, **Figure 5-7**. It is a multiple-choice exam of 100 questions.

Robert Kneschke/Shutterstock.com

Figure 5-7 After acquiring a college degree in interior design, you can apply to take the first section of the *Interior Design Fundamentals Examination* available through the CIDQ.

Experience

After earning your formal degree, the next step is to acquire entry-level work experience. You have two major options after graduation. The first involves serving a formal internship with an architecture or interior design firm. One such structured program is the *Interior Design Experience Program (IDEP)* available through the Council for Interior Design Qualification (CIDQ). IDEP is a monitored, documented experience program administered by the CIDQ to help entry-level professionals obtain a broad range of quality professional experience. The second involves going directly into the interior design field and acquiring an entry-level interior design position after graduation. The experience you gain as an entry-level interior designer in working with clients and colleagues further teaches you the language and business of the interior design profession.

Examination

After acquiring a maximum of two years experience in the interior design field, it is time to take the last two sections of the NCIDQ exam: *Section II—Interior Design Practicum Examination (IDPX)* and *Section III—Interior Design Practicum (PRAC)*. The NCIDQ exam is the recognized, qualifying examination for professional membership in many interior design organizations. It also serves as the primary exam for those in the United States that have licensing, certification, or other registration statutes. Because the requirements can change, see the CIDQ website for more information about the examination details.

The NCIDQ exam consists of two multiple-choice sections (IDFX and IDPX) and a design practicum problem (PRAC) that focuses on the health, safety, and welfare of the public. There are seven content areas tested in this examination including

- building systems
- codes
- construction standards
- contract administration
- design application
- professional practice
- project coordination

Continuing Education

After practicing in the interior design field you will want to continue learning by participating in continuing education learning opportunities. Continuing education strengthens interior design professionals by keeping them current in the field and competent in their work. The *Interior Design Continuing Education Council (IDCEC)* offers over 4,000 courses to design professionals, **Figure 5-8**. ASID, IDC, and IIDA—the practitioner organizations in North America—jointly administer IDCEC.

You can obtain **continuing education units (CEUs)**—optional courses offered by design or industry professionals to keep the design practitioner informed about trends, theories, and skills to remain competitive in the workforce by taking courses in person, online, or at conferences. IDCEC approves interior design related courses.

The IDCEC offers a centralized website to search all approved IDCEC continuing education units, report your

IDCEC
INTERIOR DESIGN
CONTINUING EDUCATION COUNCIL

Courtesy of the Interior Design Continuing Education Council

Figure 5-8 The *Interior Design Continuing Education Council* offers continuing education opportunities to interior design practitioners.

CEU credits to CIDQ, and to submit CEUs for approval. Each credentialing agency requires that interior designers take and report a certain number of CEUs each year.

Interior Design—College Level

Many students are interested in the difference between the study of interior design, architecture, and art. Students often explore all three majors, **Figure 5-9**.

Interior Design Areas of Study

Once you select interior design as a major, there are usually questions about the college courses you might take in an interior design program. The following gives you a glimpse into the areas of study and skills you need to develop for a successful career in interior design.

Studio Environment

The teaching of interior design is a very hands-on, experiential learning process. The traditional way of teaching students the *process of design* is still the one-on-one (teacher-to-student) collaborative partnership in a studio-based environment. Many students select the major for this reason.

Design students are passionate about experimenting and designing. They become engaged in the research, brainstorming, presenting, and reflecting about possible design solutions that are integral to the process of design. Perhaps this is why students often arrive engaged and enthusiastic to the studio classroom.

Interior design college courses prepare you to be successful as you begin your first entry-level design job. Although these courses may differ among four-year institutions, there are many similarities. These include design fundamentals, technology skills, space planning, building systems and codes, history of architecture and interiors, textiles and interior materials, professional practice, global and cultural design, and sustainable design practices.

Communication Skills

Good communication skills are the foundation of successful relationships, both personal and professional. Any accredited college interior design program will teach you to be proficient in three areas of communication—written, oral, and graphic. Communication is essential to inform, instruct, motivate, and persuade. These skills are necessary to clearly and accurately communicate with your clients and team members as you work through the process of design from concept to final installation of furnishings, fixtures, and equipment.

Art and Architecture versus Interior Design	
Art	**Architecture**
■ Art is the study of personal expression without parameters. ■ Some art-related majors consider a client, such as graphic design, and others do not. ■ Areas of study include art theory, art history, and use of different mediums for expression such as oil, watercolors, fibers, and sculpture. ■ Drawing classes and art history classes are often taken by art and interior design students.	■ Architecture is the study of the relationship between the building to the land or site and the design of the structure itself. ■ Areas of study include architecture theory and history, design foundation classes, and courses that relate to building load and wind shear. ■ Math is taken through the calculus level to perform proper calculations. ■ Interior design and architecture, students often take identical design foundation and architecture history classes.
Interior Design	
If students select interior design as a major rather than architecture, they often say they are interested in studying the relationship of *people to the interior* rather than *building to the site.* They want to study human behavior and how to meet peoples' needs within interior spaces.	

Figure 5-9 Careers in architecture, art, and interior design have many similarities. *How could you benefit from exploring the differences between architecture, art, and interior design?*

Do not discard the idea of interior design as your career of choice because you do not currently have these skills. You can learn and practice these skills before you leave the college campus. How well you use them after you graduate is a reflection of your professionalism.

Written Communication

Written communication is a primary skill on which others will judge your work, learning, and intellect—in college, in the workplace, and in the community. Writing expresses who you are and makes your thinking visible. Since it is portable, you may use it with social media, corresponding with clients and team members, and communicating project designs to others. Your written communication must clearly, concisely, and effectively explain and justify your design actions in a way that others can easily understand. As a professional, the expectation is to use appropriate grammar and avoid misspelling words in any document you produce.

Written skills help in the preparation of business-related documents, such as letters of agreement; contracts; specifying furnishings, fixtures, and equipment; as well as marketing, selling your designs, and working with public-relations initiatives.

Goodluz/Shutterstock.com

Figure 5-10 Using effective oral communication to express the details of a design concept is an essential workplace skill for designers in the twenty-first century.

Oral Communication

In the field of design, you will use oral communication skills (a type of verbal skill) to communicate your ideas, sell your designs, discuss project contracts, and direct design installations. In addition, you may have responsibilities for employee management and project management that necessitate effective oral skills, **Figure 5-10**.

Listening to and conveying information accurately is crucial. Effective listening is needed to decipher meaning, including knowledge, values, attitudes, and intentions. In addition, giving instructions and explanations clearly is essential. Your oral skills represent your way of thinking and your respect for the opinions of others.

Good oral skills are necessary in the interior design profession. Employers value them because they know that as you speak you are representing their organizations.

The ability to orally discuss your design ideas is a unique skill to this profession. Many clients cannot visualize designs in three-dimensions without vivid descriptions. Your ability to communicate a design verbally (painting an effective picture with words) in a clear and concise manner will help clients grasp the overarching concept. Designers also frequently use oral skills to give client presentations and work with team members. The ability to clearly and professionally communicate your ideas and design solutions is essential. In addition, critical-listening skills will ensure you understand the concerns of clients or team members and address them as the design is refined.

Along with oral skills, you will become—if you are not already—a *people watcher.* Most of the messages people send to one another are nonverbal. **Nonverbal communication** includes facial expressions, gestures, eye contact, posture, and tone of voice. The ability to understand and use nonverbal communication—or body language—is a powerful tool that can help you connect with others, express what you really mean, navigate challenging situations, and build better relationships. Both oral and nonverbal skills are vital in working with different clients and team members.

Graphic Communication

Excellent communication with graphics is crucial. Design professionals communicate with symbols on a daily basis. **Graphic communication** includes shapes, pictures, and lettering. In combination, graphics allow both the client and designer to understand the purpose of the communication.

The old adage "a picture is worth a thousand words" is appropriate in understanding the importance of good graphic communication skills in the design field. As a designer, one of the most difficult parts of your job is communicating design ideas to the client. The more accurate you are in visually communicating the design to the client, the less chance of misunderstandings later. Therefore, an interior designer uses many pictures and images to help the client visualize a design prior to its construction and installation.

Interior designers can communicate and produce their designs using manual and technological skills. The most valuable manual skill is freehand sketching. Designers frequently use sketching on a building site or at a conference table to quickly generate an idea or clear up a misunderstanding. Even though it is a manual skill, it is versatile and does not require more than a felt-tip pen and a paper napkin or digital tablet.

Computer-generated images and designs require various multimedia techniques. These can be created using digital tablets, personal computers, and such common software products as Adobe® Illustrator®, Photoshop®, Sketchup®, and Revit®. The easier it is for the client to grasp your design proposal, the more quickly he or she may buy it. Therefore, good graphic communication skills directly equate to business success, **Figure 5-11**. Designers often communicate design ideas using a combination of both manual and technology skills.

Denis Tabler/Shutterstock.com

Alexey Kashin/Shutterstock.com

sabri deniz kizil/Shutterstock.com

ANRIR/Shutterstock.com

Figure 5-11 Interior designers frequently use a combination of hand-sketching and various multimedia techniques to communicate design concepts to clients. *When might you use hand-sketching techniques versus multimedia techniques?*

Design Thinking

Problem-solving skills are valuable in any life pursuit, but design thinking is more than just creatively solving problems. *Design thinking* is an active practice that develops in the proper environment and causes you to look at the world as having potential and probable possibilities. It is not a predictable, linear way of thinking that moves you toward a problem solution. Instead it is the capacity to synthesize different types of information—looking at the mixture of different, often disconnected ideas in a new way. It is weighing and refining the creative, practical, and strategic possibilities against the given problem.

How do designers think when they work? How do they envision new ideas or visualize new spaces that do not yet exist? For interior design students, design thinking often begins with their evaluation of specific designed environments. For example, here are some questions students might ask.

- Why do some spaces—such as a school classroom—work better than others?
- How do people function within a certain type of office space in comparison to another type?
- How does one outdoor living space or reading alcove make you feel rather than another space?

Critical analysis and evaluation of human behavior and preferences is one part of design thinking—which is a desirable skill for the twenty-first century workforce. It is this type of thinking that encourages new thoughts, new skills, and new solutions to never-before-encountered problems.

A second way to develop design thinking is through the use of associations or analogies. It is a rigorous thought process that encourages participation from others. Thinking *outside the box* is a part of this process, **Figure 5-12**. Designers look for something new based on its similarity to what they already know. They then look for potential, parallel solutions for the problem at hand. Other techniques used in design thinking may include

- **reassembly**—chopping something up and rearranging it for a new purpose
- **inversion**—flipping something upside down or right-side out to interpret it a different way
- **sidewise**—twisting something 180 degrees to view it from a different angle

Interior designers encounter many *wicked problems*—those that are particularly sticky and tricky to unravel. They do so because they constantly work with new and difficult human issues within structural boundaries. Therefore, design thinking uses a collaborative process that brings different experts together to reflect, discuss, and research the problem. If design thinking is done poorly or not at all, the result is designed spaces that are ineffective, failed solutions that do not meet client needs.

Bryan Ooi/Shutterstock.com

Figure 5-12 Thinking outside the box is just one part of the rigorous thought process in design thinking.

Other Interior Design Areas of Study

In addition to communication skills and design thinking, typical subjects taught in foundation courses include

- freehand sketching and/or drawing
- manual and/or computer-aided drafting
- elements and principles of design, and the design process
- two- and three-dimensional compositions
- color theory
- construction materials
- furniture arrangement

Additional topics or classes for the interior design major include courses in construction methods, codes, textiles and interior materials, space planning studios (commercial and residential in nature), lighting design, color, building systems such as heating, ventilation and air conditioning (HVAC), history of interiors and furnishings, professional practice, business practices, and portfolio development.

Overarching topics integrated throughout the curriculum include global and cultural design, sustainable design, team building, idea-generation techniques such as brainstorming, and better design for all people. These are topics that cross all design subjects.

By the time design students graduate, they often understand whether they wish to practice in the residential or commercial design sector or both. These students then tailor their portfolios to that specific type of job for their interviews. There are several ways to determine your employment preferences including job- shadowing opportunities, internships, and interviews with professional designers. **Job shadowing** involves following a designer for a day or more while observing and recording what the job involves. Job-shadowing experiences may also involve interviewing the designer about his or her career.

Internships and Work Experience

Most colleges, universities, and private art schools recommend or require an internship as part of formal interior design education, **Figure 5-13**. An **internship** offers you the chance to investigate different areas of the interior design field, learn the culture of various firms, and perceive how your academic preparation corresponds to the practice of design. Internships are those you complete to receive academic credit. Some firms offer a small wage to the student for his or her time working at the firm. *Work experiences* are job opportunities that place students into different design-related organizations for which they receive no course credit. The majority of the time work-experience students receive payment for their work.

Many students participate in more than one job-shadowing experience, internship, or work experience prior to graduation. This helps them understand whether they want to work in a large or small interior design or architectural firm.

Even if you do not get credit for an internship experience, *do it*! Many times your internship connections will translate into a job when you graduate. Some firms even offer to pay part of your school tuition prior to graduation. In some ways, it is the best money you will spend during your formal education.

Study Abroad

Another recommended part of your formal education is to plan now to complete a study abroad experience. Design is global and international. Experiencing the diversity of living in another country and immersing yourself in another culture translates into an invaluable design experience. Your design philosophy and style often change as a result. This type of education will shape and define your work as you enter the design field.

Many colleges have institutional partnerships in other countries that allow you to study design in such places abroad as Florence, Italy; Copenhagen, Denmark; London, England; Dublin, Ireland; and Melbourne, Australia. These are usually semester-long experiences. You should register for college credit before you go overseas. Often the credits will waive other graduation requirements.

StockLite/Shutterstock.com Yuri Arcurs/Shutterstock.com

Figure 5-13 Internships and various work experiences offer prospective interior designers a chance for real-life exposure to enhance their educational experiences and hone their skills.

STUDENT SPOTLIGHT

Study Abroad

Kelly Witt, LEED Green Associate, interior design student: "My study abroad experience in Italy will forever impact the way I view the world and design. You cannot understand a culture until you have lived in it. Studying abroad offers life-changing experiences that open the mind and excite the soul."

Guadalupe Mendoza, interior design student: "It is the little things in life that make a difference in peoples' experiences; the way they think and define who they are as people. Once you submerge yourself into the culture of the country during your study abroad experience, you begin to realize it's the day-to-day experiences that teach you new things, not just about design but also about yourself."

David Walker, interior design student: "Studying abroad changed how I look at life. I met the most incredible people and saw the most beautiful sites the world has to offer. Exposure to those things opened my eyes to how amazing life can be, and how wonderful other cultures are. I treasure my time abroad more than any other experience I have had in college."

Preparing for the Interior Design Major

Many students question how to better prepare for the interior design major at the college level. There are suggested courses and competitions you might want to participate in as a student. The goal is to improve your transition into the interior design major.

A common competition at the high school level is the FCCLA Interior Design STAR Event. *STAR Events* (Students Taking Action with Recognition) are competitive events in which members are recognized for proficiency and achievement in chapter and individual projects, leadership skills, and career preparation. The Interior Design STAR Event offers individual skill development and application of learning through a different design scenario every year. If you participate, you do so representing your school at the state level. If you win at the state level, you can move on to the national level. The Interior Design STAR Event scenarios are either residential or commercial design and offer students a great experience in going through part of the process of design, **Figure 5-14 A and B**.

Courses to take while still in high school include any interior design courses, drafting, history, math, art, psychology, and economics. Such courses as marketing, business, personal finance, and any research-oriented classes are also important. Additional skills require courses in foreign languages and technology.

If you do take interior design related courses in high school, you can register and participate in the national American Association of Family and Consumer Sciences (AAFCS) *Pre-Professional Assessment and Certification (Pre-PAC) Interior Design Fundamentals* exam. Developed by leaders in the field of Interior Design, this assessment leads to a certificate that verifies your new knowledge of interior design. The exam assesses your knowledge of interior design career paths, design fundamentals, factors that influence design, design communications and skills development, interior design application and analysis, and professional practice. Many states have articulation agreements between specific high schools and nearby colleges that accept the successful completion of the AAFCS exam to waive college credit—similar to advance placement courses. See the AAFCS website and your instructor for more information, **Figure 5-14 C and D**.

There are a number of online interior design courses you can take prior to beginning your first semester in college. There are also certificates offered for these courses. These courses may help you determine if you would enjoy the interior design major before moving onto a college campus.

Not all education happens in the classroom. In addition to courses, look for any work or volunteer experiences in the design, construction, or architecture fields during your high school years. For example, volunteer with Habitat for Humanity, work part-time at a building materials supplier, or gain employment at a retail store where you work with people. Ask parents or friends about their contacts to the design and construction industry and then follow up by requesting a part-time job. Every type of work experience relates back to designing interior spaces. Such experiences serve as a reference when you begin to design.

Courtesy of Family, Career and Community Leaders of America (FCCLA)

Courtesy of the American Association of Family and Consumer Sciences (AAFCS)

Figure 5-14 Participation in student and professional organization events and assessments, such as FCCLA (A and B) and AAFCS (C and D), can help you prepare for a career in interior design.

Interior Designer Credentials and Qualifications

As you graduate and move into the interior design profession, it is important to add to your education and experience with certain credentials and qualifications.

Depending on the interior design specialty area you choose to practice in, there are different examinations. Once you pass the exam, the credentials indicate to the public the additional knowledge and skills you offer on a design project. Following are a few suggested credentials you may wish to acquire.

NCIDQ Certificate

As you know, achieving the *National Council of Interior Design Qualification (NCIDQ)* certificate requires at least six years of combined college-level interior design education and work experience in the field to qualify to take the exam. That means, if you graduate with an associate's degree, you need to work in the field as part of an established design firm for *four* years. If you graduate with a bachelor's degree, you will need to practice with an established design firm for *two* years to qualify to take the NCIDQ exam.

The NCIDQ assessment differs from a college exam. It is not a test of facts; rather it is an *application* of facts. It assesses your knowledge of the health, safety, and welfare (HSW) of the public.

LEED® Certification

The *U.S. Green Building Council (USGBC)* developed professional credentials and an exam to assess knowledge of green building practices and construction operations. This credential is known as *Leadership in Energy and Environmental Design (LEED®)* and is a registered trademark of the U.S. Green Building Council, **Figure 5-15**.

The *LEED Green Associate* exam assesses understanding of sustainable design language, rating systems, sustainability concepts, and the LEED rating systems. Prior to taking one of the other LEED Accredited Professional (AP) exams, an interior designer must pass the LEED Green Associate exam.

LEED AP exams are in specialized areas of green building and construction. Eligibility requirements include passage of the LEED Green Associate and documented professional experience on a LEED project in the previous three years. The following table lists the specialized exams with the corresponding acronyms a designer can use after successfully passing the exams, **Figure 5-16**.

Interior Design Healthcare Certification

If you move into the healthcare design specialization, many interior designers participate in the *American Academy of Healthcare Interior Designers (AAHID)* examination. Their organization is recognized by the healthcare industry as the certification board of choice in assessing and qualifying the knowledge, skills, and abilities of healthcare interior designers. Board Certified Healthcare Interior Design Certificate holders are distinguished and qualified by education, examination, and work experience to practice healthcare interior design, distinguished from other architects, designers, decorators, and interior designers, **Figure 5-17 A**.

Figure 5-15 Active members of the U.S. Green Building Council can use the USGBC Member Logo to promote their membership in the organization. According to the USGBC, "The LEED® green building certification program is the nationally accepted benchmark for the design, construction, and operation of green buildings."

LEED® Professional Credentials™	
Credential	**Affiliated Logo**
LEED Green Associate (LEED Green Associate)	LEED GREEN ASSOCIATE™
LEED AP Building Design + Construction (LEED AP BD+C)	LEED AP BD+C™
LEED AP Homes (LEED AP Homes)	LEED AP HOMES™
LEED AP Interior Design + Construction (LEED AP ID+C)	LEED AP ID+C™
LEED AP Neighborhood Development (LEED ND)	LEED AP ND™
LEED AP Operations + Maintenance (LEED AP O+M)	LEED AP O+M™

Figure 5-16 Many interior designers seek LEED credentials. According to the USGBC, "The LEED® Professional Credentials™ refers to the LEED AP credential, all LEED AP specialty credentials, and the LEED Green Associate credential. LEED Professional Credentials are earned through passing a LEED® Professional Exam™."

Kitchen and Bath Designer Certification

Available through *National Kitchen and Bath Association (NKBA)*, the Certified Kitchen Designers (CKD) and Certified Bath Designers (CBD) specialize in the design, planning, and execution of residential kitchens and bathrooms, and prove advanced knowledge of technical and personal communication skills required to succeed as a design specialist. Applicants must document a minimum of seven years of experience; three of which must be as full-time residential kitchen/bath designer.

The CKD and CBD design/practical exams are hand-drafted or CAD-design scenarios which must be completed within a six (6) hour time frame. These exams test practical skills in space planning, placement of fixtures, fitting knowledge, and basic presentation skills. The candidate is required to produce four (4) project documents: a floor plan, construction/mechanical plan, elevation plan, and complete an NKBA specifications form, **Figure 5-17 B**.

The Associate Kitchen and Bath Designer (AKBD) exam must be passed prior to taking the CKD or CBD exam. Applicants must supply documentation of a minimum of two years experience; minimum of one year in the kitchen/bath industry. Applicants must also earn a minimum of 30 hours of NKBA education or NKBA approved college coursework. The examination covers four major content categories: planning and design, construction and mechanical systems, business management, and products and materials.

Certified Aging-in-Place Specialist (CAPS)

This credential is available after passing an exam related to home modifications for aging in place, a segment of the residential remodeling industry. Certification is available through the *National Association of Home Building (NAHB)*. Requirements to take the exam include successfully passing two required CAPS courses and a course on Business Management for Building Professionals. The candidate must also sign a Code of Ethics.

Certified Green Building Professional (CGP)

This credential is available after passing an exam related to cost-effective green building, whether it relates to a new home, remodel, site development, or multifamily project. Two courses are required to qualify for this exam and a

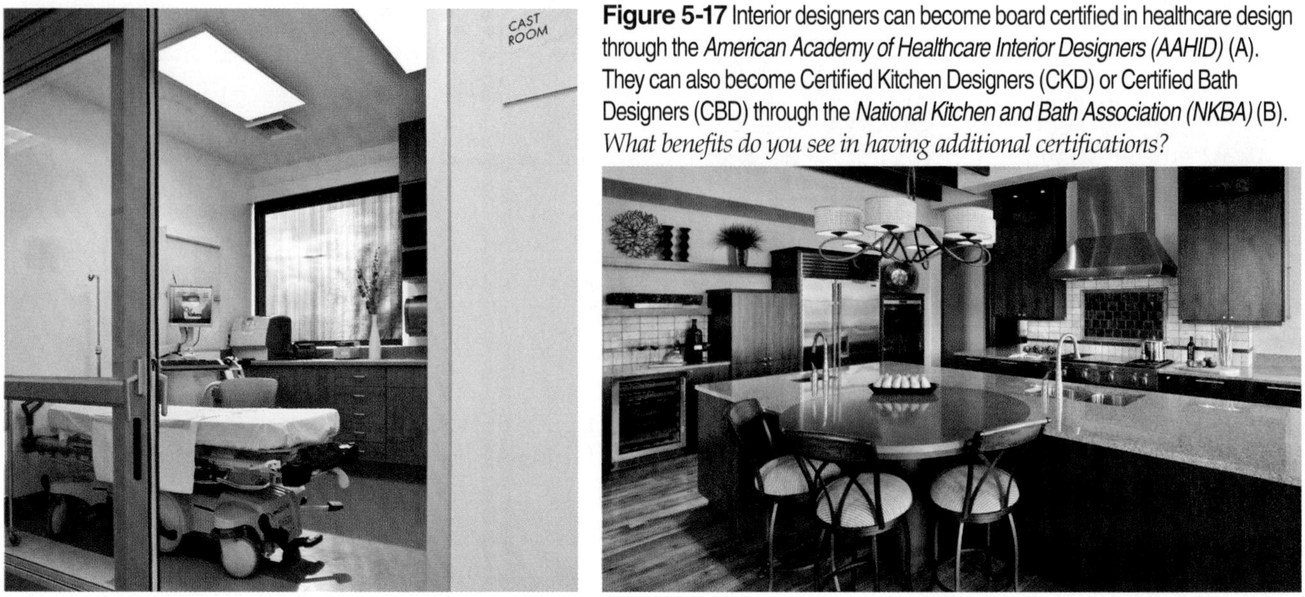

Figure 5-17 Interior designers can become board certified in healthcare design through the *American Academy of Healthcare Interior Designers (AAHID)* (A). They can also become Certified Kitchen Designers (CKD) or Certified Bath Designers (CBD) through the *National Kitchen and Bath Association (NKBA)* (B). *What benefits do you see in having additional certifications?*

A Interior Designer: SCI Design Group/Photographer: Michael McLane B Interior Designer: JJ Interiors /Photography: Ron Ruscio Photography

minimum of two years of building industry experience. Courses, exam, and certification are available through the *National Association of Home Building (NAHB)*.

State/Jurisdiction Licensed Designer

Depending on where you live, you have the option to become a registered interior designer in your state or jurisdiction. To ensure professionalism, competency, and quality services, some states and jurisdictions in the United States and Puerto Rico require their interior designers to take the *National Council for Interior Design Qualification (NCIDQ)* exam. Currently, 28 states and jurisdictions have some type of legislation to ensure quality interior design practice.

Developing Career Connections

Any professional you interview will tell you about the importance of making personal and professional connections to further your career. The benefits are significant.

Benefits of Professional Organization Membership

With social media dominant in peoples' lives, the benefits of personal relationships and networking are clear. Similarly, your membership in interior design-related associations is critical to establishing professional credibility and advancing your visibility.

Benefits of professional organization membership include

- **Enhanced credibility through standards recognition.** Professional organizations have different levels of membership. As you move through and up the organization, you will have an acronym or meaningful credential to place after your name that the public recognizes as a standard of excellence.
- **Access to valuable education.** Continuing education courses allow you to easily update your expertise and knowledge of rapidly changing technologies.
- **Connection to colleagues.** It is always fun to join a network of those who have similar interests and who can offer a pulse point of what is happening in the field.
- **Access to collated data specific to your field.** You will not have time to read or process all the information you need to do your job. Your professional associations summarize the data for you to use and put it in lay terms.
- **Opportunities for leadership and growth.** Leadership training and opportunities open windows for you and your firm. Professional organizations will use your volunteer time but in return will train you as a leader and spokesperson for the profession.
- **Connections to industry representatives and partners.** Professional associations offer opportunities to connect with additional team members who can be invaluable when conducting your work.

- **Enhanced visibility.** Professional associations offer you opportunities to be seen and recognized. Respect comes as you and your work become more visible and appreciated.
- **Referrals, referrals, referrals.** Your interior design work—residential or commercial—will significantly depend on referrals. Professional associations connect you to colleagues and clients, and therefore, future work. Get your business card in their hands or add them to your LinkedIn network and let them know you are interested in new projects. As another option, join one of their referral services where clients can be connected to you via the Internet, **Figure 5-18**.

Benefits of Student Membership

There are many professional interior design organizations you can join as a student before moving into the profession. Student memberships come with reduced dues.

If you join and attend professional functions, such as workshops, social events, or community service opportunities, you will be noticed and mentored! Professional designers know students are very busy—they will notice and appreciate you when you attend events.

No matter how you do it, get involved! Doors will open for you through your volunteer service and student involvement. Benefits of student membership include

- connections for future employment
- referrals for an internship
- real-world education
- stories and experiences that help you determine a career path
- life-changing moments through design experiences and discussions
- opportunities for leadership training
- leadership experiences for résumé building
- connections for job shadowing
- resources and materials for school projects
- access to design showrooms closed to public

Michal Kowalski/Shutterstock.com

Figure 5-18 The career connections you make through memberships in various professional organizations can lead to referrals and potential work. *Interview a professional interior designer about the benefits of belonging to his or her professional association.*

Designer Profile

Shirley Hammond—Becoming a Registered Interior Designer

Shirley E. Hammond, FASID, is a graduate of The University of Alabama with a B.S. and M.S. in interior design. She has 38 years of experience in residential and commercial projects and has promoted licensure legislation for more than 30 years.

Shirley E. Hammond, FASID, NCIDQ, RID, principal with Perceptive Designs, Decatur, AL

"Registration and licensure of a profession is about the health, safety, and welfare of the public. The primary value of interior design registration and licensure is the public's ability to rely upon the training and expertise of the registered professionals it hires. A secondary value, and important by-product of registration and licensure, is the resulting refinement and consistency of professional standards for education, testing, experience, and practice. Thus, a registered interior designer represents a *learned profession* with a distinct scope of practice and expertise. With the privilege of registration and licensure comes the responsibility of the registered interior designer to protect the health, safety, and welfare of his or her clientele."

You can learn more about Shirley's experience in Appendix B.

- opportunities to give back to the community through service projects
- invitations to professional events, tours, and education
- opportunities for scholarships
- access to student design competitions, **Figure 5-19**
- reduced fees to exhibits and events

Choosing Professional Organizations

Which professional organization should you join? There are many related to the interior design profession. Each organization has a different mission and vision, so take time to visit their websites. Here are some of the major interior design related organizations.

- **The American Society of Interior Designers (ASID).** ASID advances the profession, and communicates the impact of interior design to enhance the human experience.
- **The Interior Designers of Canada (IDC).** The vision of IDC is to provide access to the latest business tools, education, communications, and networking opportunities for its members.
- **Interior Design Educators Council (IDEC).** The mission of The Interior Design Educators Council, Inc. is the advancement of interior design education, scholarship, and service.
- **International Federation of Architects/ Designers (IFI).** IFI exists to expand—internationally and across all levels of society—the contribution of the Interior Architecture/ Design profession through the exchange and development of knowledge and experience in education, practice, and fellowship.
- **International Interior Design Association (IIDA).** IIDA strives to create a strong niche for the most talented and visionary interior design professionals, to elevate the profession to the level it warrants, and to lead the way for the next generation of interior design innovators.
- **International Association of Lighting Designers (IALD).** The mission of IALD is to create a better world through leadership and excellence in lighting design.
- **National Kitchen and Bath Association (NKBA).** The mission of the NKBA is to enhance member success and excellence, promote professionalism and ethical business practices, and provide leadership and direction for the kitchen and bath industry worldwide.
- **U.S. Green Building Council (USGBC).** The goal of USGBC is to transform the way buildings and communities are designed, built, and operated to enable an environmentally and socially responsible, healthy, and prosperous environment that improves the quality of life.
- **Network of Executive Women in Hospitality (NEWH).** NEWH is the premier networking resource for the hospitality industry, providing scholarships, education, leadership development, recognition of excellence, and business development opportunities.

Image provided by Lifetouch, courtesy of FCCLA.

Figure 5-19 Participating in an interior-design competitive event is a benefit of student membership in organizations.

The Field of Interior Design Needs You!

There is great need for your expertise, knowledge, and skills to solve the new problems that are arising in the interior environments where people live, work, and play. As you consider the interior design profession, realize that parents and friends may not understand the complexity, rigor, and intellectual proficiency needed to do well in the field. Educate them. Help them look around their interior spaces and imagine how they may function better and be more productive in a well-designed interior.

As you ponder a career in interior design, take time to examine your skills, career goals, and interests and whether they align with this creative but demanding field of study and practice. Personal and monetary rewards follow your passion for good design and quality work. Certainly there is enough variety within the profession to keep you vitally engaged, fulfilled, and successful for a lifetime.

Chapter 5 Review and Assess

Summary

- Interior design requires a range of diverse and complex skills.
- A career in interior design also involves travel, meeting people, and understanding human behavior, psychology, health, and wellness.
- Complex artistic and technical skills are necessary to plan space well and visually present plans to clients.
- Along with solving complex problems for clients, interior designers follow ethical and sustainability standards that benefit all people.
- A wide range of personality traits and natural strengths are needed for success in interior design. Some are inherent in your personality, and others you gain through formal education and work experiences.
- The pathway to a career in interior design involves the Four E's: education, experience, examination, and continuing education.
- The study of interior design is a very hands-on experiential process. It involves learning to communicate effectively and developing problem-solving skills to creatively solve client problems.
- Interior designers use design thinking to solve particularly complex client problems.
- Internships and study abroad help prospective interior designers learn about the workplace and experience the diversity of immersion in another culture—both of which can impact a person's design philosophy.
- After college graduation and moving into the interior design profession, it is important for designers to add to their education and experiences with certain credentials and qualifications.
- Membership in a professional interior design organization, both as a student and professional member, helps a designer establish professional credibility and advance visibility in the profession.
- Although the missions of professional organizations vary, all provide opportunities to advance education and network with other professionals.
- Examine your skills, career goals, and passion for interior environments to determine if interior design is the career for you.

Chapter Vocabulary

Write the definition of each of the following terms. Then write a sentence using each term in a design-related context.

allied
continuing education units (CEUs)
graphic communication
internship
inversion
job shadowing
minimalist
nonverbal communication
reassembly
selective admissions process
selective advancement process
sidewise

Review and Study

1. List at least five skills essential for success in the twenty-first century workplace and in interior design?
2. Explain how interior design is ethical, sustainable, and integrated.
3. Summarize a real-life example of a complex interior design problem.
4. What are four types of college degrees and institutions at which you can receive them that can lead to a career in interior design?
5. Why is it beneficial to choose an accredited college program?
6. Contrast the selective admissions process with the selective advancement process.
7. What are the seven content areas tested in the NCIDQ examination?
8. Describe the studio environment for studying interior design.
9. What are three types of communication skills with which interior designers must be proficient? Give an example showing the importance of each.
10. How can you benefit from an internship or other work experience related to interior design?
11. How does the NCIDQ exam differ from a college exam?
12. What are five benefits each for membership in a professional or student organization?

Critical Analysis

13. **Analyze.** Reread and analyze the *Design Insight* quote at the beginning of the chapter. Why is interior design is an emotional, aesthetic, and intellectual pursuit? How does it capture your passion? Write a paragraph summarizing your thoughts.
14. **Analyze data.** Research employment opportunities including internship, entrepreneurship, and preparation requirements for interior design. Use the Internet to compile and analyze real-time and projected market data such as the U.S. Bureau of Labor Statistics to investigate local and regional occupational opportunities and trends in interior design. Synthesize the data you collect and develop a graphic comparing occupations by educational requirements, job availability, salaries/wages, and benefits.
15. **Analyze evidence.** The text states that interior design deals with complex client problems in the built environment—those that are sticky and tricky to unravel. Describe an interior built environment you know of that is problematic for some reason. Analyze what issues make the problem complex for a client. Discuss how good interior design can make a difference.
16. **Identify attributes.** Think about your values, skills (such as problem solving and leadership), technology knowledge, interests, abilities, and personality traits. Offer one or two examples of how you use these attributes everyday.
17. **Draw conclusions.** Select three online or print interior design or shelter magazines. Read the magazines and analyze the illustrations or videos. Draw conclusions about what *wicked problems* the client might have brought to the designer. How do you think the designers use *design thinking* to solve client problems? How effective is the written, oral, and graphic communication in the designs? Cite text examples about the different design skills needed to develop the finished designs.
19. **Analyze reasoning.** Visit IDEC website to view the student-developed video clips showing why going into interior design is a good career choice. What evidence did the students give regarding why interior design is a good career choice? How were the students persuasive in their reasoning?

Think like a Designer

20. **Interest self-assessment.** Use the O*NET *Interest Profiler* self-assessment to help identify your interests in an interior-design related career.
21. **Skills self-assessment.** Use the O*NET *Skills Profiler* to create a list of your skills and match them to job types that use those skills. How do your skills compare to those needed for an interior design career? Write a summary.

22. **Writing.** Teamwork skills involve leadership and having common goals, collaboration, cooperation, and effective communication. Review the ASID website for ways interior designers use teamwork skills. Write a summary of your findings and identify ways you can build your teamwork skills.
23. **Reading.** Explore different interior design associate and bachelor degree programs in three states to research internships, entrepreneurship, and preparation requirements in the field of interior design. To do so, visit the online magazine *Plinth & Chintz*. Select "The Extras" on the left sidebar and then click on "Design Schools." After you explore the interior design programs on their websites, create a written list of questions for other students to use when exploring colleges or private schools.
24. **Speaking.** Use Internet resources to research two successful designers and read about their careers. Gather information about designers (for instance, their design positions, professional path, specialty areas of practice, and favorite projects, mentors they had). Give an illustrated oral report to the class about the designers you chose.
26. **Speaking/writing.** Visit the *Plinth & Chintz* online magazine. Select their "Design Speak" glossary. Learn ten new words or phrases related to the interior design profession. Find ways to integrate them into your conversation over the next two days. Did you use the words correctly? What conversations did using these terms generate? How did your nonverbal communication impact the experience? Write a paper describing your experiences.
27. **Speaking.** Select an interior designer to job shadow and interview from the local ASID or IIDA chapters or a local design firm. Follow the designer for a day or two and then interview the designer and ask the designer to tell his or her career story. How did the designer find the interior design profession? What was his or her journey from high school to present day? Did he or she attend a two-year or four-year program? Why does the designer enjoy the profession? What advice would the designer give to those exploring the profession? Give an oral report to the class of your findings.

Design Application

29. **Experiment with design.** Rearrange a personal space in your home. Use the following process:
    A. Take an inventory of what you have, what you want to repurpose in the future, and what you would want to buy. Take digital pictures of the space before you make any changes.
    B. Set goals for how you would like to use the space. Was your space just the way you liked it?
    C. Explore what changes (if any) may need to be made to color and light in the space. Identify specific needs.
    D. Invite family members to help you rearrange your space to meet the identified goals. Leave enough space in the room for you and others to move from one area to another.
    E. Organize your new space and critically analyze it. Take pictures of your new space.
    F. Reflect on how this process helped you understand issues and preferences a client may have that guide the design of the space. Use presentation software to create an illustrated oral report to share with the class.
30. **Portfolio builder.** Create a video clip promoting the interior design profession. Then post your video clip to the class web page or school website. Have your classmates evaluate your video by using the class discussion board. Save and maintain a copy of your slideshow in your project portfolio to help document interior design projects using a variety of multimedia techniques.
31. **Portfolio builder.** You will be creating both a print portfolio and an eportfolio in this class. Set up a folder for the electronic files that will be in the eportfolio.
    A. Save your documents on the school network or your flash drive.
    B. After you have decided the storage place, create a folder with your name and the title *Portfolio*. For instance, if your name is Emily Perez, your folder will be EPerezPortfolio.

UNIT 2 Design Fundamentals

©Ron Pollard, courtesy of RNL

Welborn Sullivan Meck & Tooley

Introducing the Interior Design Process

Allegria Spa at the Park Hyatt Beaver Creek/Photography by Don Riddle/Interiors by Associates III Interior Design

Chapter

6

Design Insight

"Design is a noun, a verb, and a problem-solving process."

John R. Berry, from Herman Miller—The Purpose of Design, *©2004*

Learning Targets

After studying this chapter, you will be able to

- differentiate between good and bad design.
- understand the aspects of creativity and innovation and their relationship to interior design.
- summarize the phases of the interior design process.

Introduction

As children, many love to construct, draw, build, and shape without restrictions. Some tinker with generic, fun forms—exploring imaginary creatures and environments. Others draw recognizable miniature house plans or develop intriguing structures with wooden blocks. To design is innate and when encouraged, teaches you *how* to look at and analyze your surroundings.

The term *design* has many meanings. For many, it relates to a pattern used on wallpaper, a fashion style worn by a model, or a drawing placed around a blog page. For others, it relates to beauty and art, the way a process unfolds, or how a marketing plan develops. According to Webster, design is to "Create, fashion, execute, or construct according to plan. It is the conversion of facts into ideas and of ideas into spaces and forms." Design is more than how something looks. It is a way of thinking, planning, and problem solving—based on an intended purpose or function—that often in interior design results from a collaborative team effort.

Design has many purposes. For example, the use of design can

- bridge the gap between objects and people
- increase the efficiency of a process
- save time and materials

For the interior designer, design is a problem-solving activity rather than a style. Interior design improves peoples' accommodations in a space and positively shapes behavior in the physical surroundings. At its best, a successfully designed interior can delight and inspire; continually drawing an individual back for another visit or for an extended period of time. At its worst, an unsuccessful interior design can adversely impact the health, safety, and well-being (HSW) of the public—something to avoid.

Good and Bad Design

Design is everywhere. In the *natural environment*, design is evident in solar systems, the human skeleton, and nature. You can discover it in an aspen grove, in wild animals, and roving insects, **Figure 6-1.** Those that study the human body find it well designed and incredibly intricate in its ability to function, heal, and survive.

Vaclav Volrab/Shutterstock.com

Figure 6-1 Design in the natural environment is evident in the dew drops on this blade of grass.

In the *built environment*, there are many designed objects beginning with the cell phone people pick up in the morning to the chairs and classrooms in which they learn.

Good design has an endless list of benefits, **Figure 6-2**. Depending on the application, design can

- facilitate functionality
- grab attention
- increase comfort
- simplify the complex
- communicate innovation
- enhance visibility
- create recall
- build brand awareness
- increase sales

Rafal Olechowski/Shutterstock.com

Figure 6-2 Good design improves function and positively shapes behavior. *What are some examples of good design in your school, neighborhood, or community?*

- prevent accidents
- increase handgrip
- increase functionality
- solve problems

What Is Good Design?

Good design is influenced by its environment—it does not exist in isolation. Often, good design is subtle and need not call attention to itself. What makes a design *good*? To be considered good, design should

- solve a problem
- function well
- integrate design elements and principles
- use appropriate materials for the specified application
- add beauty (be aesthetically successful)
- reflect meaning and intent
- respect impact on the environment

What factors do interior designers use to make sure their designs meet each of these criteria? The examples that follow illustrate how these criteria help develop an effective and successful design.

Solves a Problem

The need to solve a given user problem is the difference between design and art. For interior design, solving the problem is one of the major reasons clients hire a designer. If clients could solve their own problems, they most likely would not need your services. For example, a residential client may ask, "How do you incorporate a fireplace into an unusually angled wall?" In contrast, a commercial client may ask, "How do you design a lobby chair that is comfortable for both tall and short guests?"

If the designer does not solve the problem, the design fails. If the designer almost solves the problem, the design fails. If the designer solves the problem effectively, the solution is the product of good design.

When solving a certain problem, creativity and innovation are assets. Creativity, however, at the expense of good design often fails to solve a client's problem. For example, if you creatively design a new dinner plate but it lacks a horizontal surface, it does not solve the client's problem of where to place food. In an interior, if you design an innovative office chair, but it is not comfortable, employees will look for reasons to avoid using it, which can result in reduced productivity. Successfully solving the problem is an aspect of good design.

Functions Well

A successful design functions well. It implies a plan or conscious intent. Good design serves the needs and requirements of its user, your client. For example, when discussing an everyday chair, its primary function is to provide seating for the individual. Secondary needs may relate to maintenance or portability—such as the ability to move it easily or its ability to fit under a specific table height.

Function, or lack thereof, is one of the most noticeable criteria of good design. For example, if a stairwell or a kitchen floor plan does not function well, you will notice! If a product design, such as the wheels on a suitcase or fabric on a sofa does not function well, you will notice! Individuals often describe good design in terms of how well something functions—or does not function.

Sometimes how a person perceives functionality changes with age. **Figure 6-3** is an example of a contemporary tub design. For a 25-year-old person, this design may work well. It is aesthetically appealing, inspired by nature, and innovative in design. As this person ages to 65, this tub may be difficult to use. It may not provide enough support

Axor Starck Collection

Figure 6-3 Although attractive and functional for most people, this bath may not be functional for older adults or those with disabilities. *What changes would you suggest to meet the needs of an older adult you know?*

in the seat to enhance comfort or stability. The older adult could sit down but may not easily stand up to get out of the tub.

Integrates Design Elements and Principles

Design elements and principles are those tools and guidelines that provide a framework for designing an object or space. The wrong *scale*—a ratio of proportion or relative size—among objects in a room while fun in some places can have a devastating effect in others. Too many patterns can lead to visual chaos, or a lack of order. Too much sameness results in boredom and enhances the ordinary in peoples' lives. You will learn more about design elements and principles later in this text.

Uses Appropriate Materials and Applications

Most objects and furnishings in interior spaces are constructed of appropriate materials. If the appropriate material is not used, the function of the design suffers. If quality materials are not used, the product will not last. For example, a silk fabric is an exquisite, natural material to specify for in an interior. It rarely works, however, for a large commercial sofa located in a hotel lobby. With wear and tear from guest use, this fragile fabric would quickly rip and shred.

Is Aesthetically Beautiful

Simply put, a designed object or space should be beautiful. Beauty can be subtle, distinctive, or outrageous. If successful, you cannot add to or subtract from the object or composition without destroying the harmony of the whole. Beauty is complete.

When aesthetically successful, a design evokes an emotional response on many levels—visually and meaningfully. Often a person can verbalize the emotion a design evokes, but may not be able to explain how a designer achieved it.

Frequently, interior designers use design elements and principles to explain why an interior space or place is aesthetically unsuccessful. For example, a space or composition may appear chaotic without negative

CASE STUDY

Choosing Appropriate Textiles

In the 1960s, one of the fashion trends was the paper dress. One benefit of such a design was that if the hem of the skirt was too long for you, it could just be cut off. A second benefit was that if you were tired of the dress, it could just be thrown away. Can you imagine this product in geographical areas where rain, sleet, and hail would be encountered? The fashion trend did not last long.

Similarly, in interior design if you specify rayon for long draperies in a hotel lobby or specify it for a custom office chair, the fabric will not wear well. Rayon sags if placed in a vertical design application and natural sunlight will cause decay. Rayon on an office chair would rip with only a little use.

igor kisselev/Shutterstock.com

Investigate and Reflect

Use reliable Internet and print resources to further research the paper dress of the 1960s. Why do you think this fashion fad did not last? What might happen if the same sort of thinking was used with interior design? Discuss your reflections in class.

space between furnishings or rooms. Lacking texture, a space may be boring and without human interest.

Many people claim that "beauty is in the eye of the beholder." Decoratively, that may be true. If a designed object or space is not reflective of your personal style, however, it can still be aesthetically pleasing and perceived as good design because it is responsive to the problem at hand, **Figure 6-4.**

violetblue/Shutterstock.com

Figure 6-4 A design can be perceived as good even if it does not reflect your personal style.

Reflects Meaning and Intent

Design has both meaning and purpose. Otherwise, by its very definition it is *art.* Where both art and design emerge from a creative process, design has conscious purpose or intent. Design evolves from a perceived need. Through a process of research, brainstorming, and model building, the designer often discards the bad, leaving the *good.* This last criterion is the essence of good design in interior spaces.

When a client brings a problem, the designer helps him or her explore multiple options. Often the client has too many needs and must prioritize them. These are the *trade-offs,* or compromises. Once the client selects a final option, the designer carries out the plan up to and through installation. The completion of this process should reflect the meaning and intent of the need.

Good design—both man-made and natural—is pur-pose-ful. It is a joy to use a well-designed, man-made object and it is a gift to rest for a time in a natural environment such as a mountain refuge. People yearn for good design. They do not always know or recognize it even when it is in their hands, but they know they prefer it if given a choice, **Figure 6-5.**

Many assess design as good based on personal preferences. The standard phrase "I like it" is often a rationale for why people consider a design good. What people like and dislike, however, changes over time. For example, consider how your favorite music, movie, and food have changed since you were a child. Therefore, as you explain and defend your decisions about characteristics of *good design,* use research and case studies to support your design decisions. By doing so, you establish credibility and begin a great discussion about design.

Good design can increase efficiency, prevent accidents, and allow proper function. For people, it offers comfort, creates enjoyment, and relieves stress. Good design should be the expectation and certainly, with thought, is always achievable.

Respects the Environment

Good design respects planet, profits, and people. It offers the opportunity to address client needs while avoiding negative effects on the Earth. Good design reflects sensitivity to the environmental, economic, social, and cultural implications of what the design produces—both during and after the design is complete.

Sustainability applies to more than the environment. The designer's goal is to enhance the human experience and address the client's needs while doing no damage to civilization. Designers and manufacturers must continually make efforts to improve the sustainability of products and systems to consume less and diminish reliance on limited natural resources. Meeting current needs while preserving the environment for future generations is a major challenge of good design.

Is in the Details

Whether the design is an object or an interior, good design is about *details.* In interiors, capturing client-preferred details through active listening is important. The difference between *quality* and *mediocre* design involves skillfully incorporating beautifully designed architectural elements that enhance the design of the space and personalize the place.

Photographs in the Carol M. Highsmith Archive (public domain), Library of Congress, Prints and Photographs Division.

Figure 6-5 Designed by Frank Lloyd Wright, the well-known Guggenheim Museum is located in New York City. *What aspects of good design can you identify?*

Adriano Castelli/Shutterstock.com

Making time to carry out details related to completing the job in a timely manner is critical. Details take a mediocre design and turn it into a memorable—and often timeless—design, **Figure 6-6**. Make time and take time to pay attention to details. This trait will set you apart as a designer, offer enjoyment, and bring added success to your work and career.

What Is Bad Design?

Bad design exists. The number of poorly lit, inadequately ventilated, overly noisy, physically uncomfortable, and occupationally hazardous, residential or commercial spaces people inhabit indicate the gap in understanding good design. Many of these same spaces also *lack* the true beauty also characteristic of good design.

> *“Expect good; demand better; and inspire the best.”*
>
> *Stephanie A. Clemons*

John Wollwerth/Shutterstock.com

Figure 6-6 Creativity and innovation are highly valued skills and are evident in the design details of this crown molding.

Many perceive that bad design exists due to budget constraints. This is not so. Designers can achieve good design on a minimal budget. Conversely, poorly designed products and interiors can result even with a million dollar budget.

Design is poor if it does not function well for the user of the space. Think of a kitchen in which you have difficulty maneuvering or a bathroom in which nothing you need is in the right place. If the design of interior spaces is poor, the spaces will shape you (and your behavior) rather than you shaping the spaces.

Only through increased demand for well-designed places and spaces will better design evolve. The best way to control the proliferation of bad design is to avoid purchasing it.

Decide now to be an advocate of good design. Encourage and demand products and spaces with better design. Good design begins with creativity, innovation, and understanding the problem to be solved.

Creativity and Innovation Impact Good Design

Inherent in the development of good design—and well-designed interiors—is the generation of creative ideas in response to a given problem. The development of creative ideas is a critical skill needed by interior designers with the many client challenges involving function, culture, technologies, and safety.

> *“In our time there are many artists who go for novelty, and see their value and justification in novelty; but they are wrong—novelty is hardly ever important. What matters is always just the one thing: to penetrate to the very heart of a thing, and create it better.”*
>
> *Henri-Marie-Raymond de Toulouse-Lautrec*

Definitions of creativity are fuzzy and varied. Popular press often describes creativity as the development of a novel or whimsical idea. The *Encyclopedia of Creativity*, however, defines *creativity* as a “mental activity performed in situations where there is no prior correct solution or answer.” It is a complex process to develop and communicate a creative idea when there is no correct road map available for you to follow.

Historically, the definition of a creative person was someone who changed an aspect of a culture as opposed to someone who simply expressed an unusual thought or experience in a novel way. Such creative geniuses include Benjamin Franklin and Steve Jobs.

Creativity is highly prized in business sectors. *Innovation* is the process of introducing creative ideas to a firm or organization that can result in increasing product or service performance. The process of innovation involves extracting the value from a creative idea that has direct impact on the performance of the company or organization, and using it toward future success, **Figure 6-7**.

Innovation is an essential part of the interior design field. For example, many commercial establishments, such as retail stores, need interior spaces that support the generation of new ideas or increased business as well as spaces reflecting their up-to-date image that embraces innovation.

Conversations about creativity often focus on the creative person, the creative process, and the environment that promotes creativity.

Facts About Creativity and Innovation

- People are not born with creativity. It is enhanced through life experiences.
- Creativity is not a factor of intelligence.
- Everyone has creative ideas.
- Creativity is not restricted to the arts and design; it is essential in science, math, engineering, and technology (STEM).
- Creative people see things and circumstances in more than one way.
- People you meet often impact whether you feel comfortable expressing creative ideas. If they positively recognize your ideas, you continue to seek creative solutions.
- Innovative thinking in business is encouraged and rewarded.
- Demonstrating innovative thinking improves your prospects in the job market.
- Being an innovative thinker is personally rewarding.

Figure 6-7 Creativity is something you can learn through life experiences.

CASE STUDY

Bisociative Thinking and Creativity

Arthur Koestler, author of *The Act of Creation* coined the phrase *bisociation* to describe the means of joining unrelated, often conflicting, information in a new way. It is a method of *association* in which the brain engages when exposed to two ideas from different categories or disciplines that relate to a problem. This history of engineering and science is full of serendipitous discoveries, for which the bisociative process is the basis (for example, Newton's inspiration for the theory of gravitation, as well as the development of penicillin and aspartame.) Here are a few stories.

Spencer Silver was searching for a stronger adhesive. His college friend, Art Fry—who sang in a choir and was constantly annoyed when bookmarks fell out of his book of music—came up with an idea. By *associating* his problem with Silver's weak adhesive, Fry dreamed up the… Post-It® note.

Bette Nesmith Graham was a secretary in Dallas who sometimes made typing mistakes (this was before computers). In her spare time, she dreamed of being an artist. By *associating* the method oil painters used to cover their mistakes on their canvases to her typing problem, she invented the correction fluid, or "Wite-Out®" or "Liquid Paper®," still used today.

What do these two scenarios have in common? They both involve *bisociative thinking*, or combining *two* unrelated ideas into something new. Bisociative thinking generates creative ideas in the interior design and built environment worlds, too.

Investigate and Reflect
Use reliable Internet or print resources to locate other well-known examples of bisociative thinking. How do these examples combine unrelated ideas into something new? When have you used bisociative thinking (perhaps unknowingly)? Discuss your findings in class.

The Creative Person

The ability to be creative is inherent in every human being. Creative people have many common characteristics and are often described as

- courageous and daring—not to be confused with bold
- confident with a belief that their work has worth
- comfortable with chaos—willing to sort through disorganization
- divergent thinkers—having ability to brainstorm and avoid undue attachment to one idea while exploring many
- lateral thinkers—taking an idea from one discipline and applying it to another
- slow to judge—can consider multiple ideas different from their own before making a decision
- hard workers—retain vision and work toward it
- observant—continually taking notes and storing observed details for future use

Creative people often act on gut instinct, which is really a feeling based on the many experiences and thoughts on which they have deeply pondered over a period of time. Creative interior designers put extra time and effort into challenging themselves to purposely analyze a variety of possible solutions before they—with the client—decide on the best one to solve the problem at hand.

Creativity derives from inspiring objects, exciting trips, engaging places, and meeting thought-provoking people, **Figure 6-8**. Other sources of creative inspiration include observation and engagement with:

Sunny studio-Igor Yaruta/Shuttestock.com

Martin M303/Shutterstock.com

riaua/Shutterstock.com

Renata Sedmakova/Shutterstock.com

Figure 6-8 Many people, objects, and places can inspire creativity. *What inspires your creativity?*

- everyday objects
- conversations with diverse individuals
- textile weavings and natural materials
- observing a child at play
- human behavior
- photography at dusk
- living in or visiting other countries
- music and other arts
- education—development of new thoughts
- weather patterns and astronomy
- marbles scattered on the floor
- classic architecture
- light forming shade and shadows
- a garden alcove
- an honest thought
- a good book

Once a creative idea is developed, the implementation of it takes hard work. Perseverance is an attribute that allows a designer to continue with an idea that others may not be able to envision. Many creative ideas never make it to production or installation—and should not. Some creative ideas are terrible design. Remember, creativity is important—just not at the expense of good design.

The Creative Environment

Creative ideas develop in a culture that encourages discovery and experimentation—where wild ideas are invited and welcomed. Sometimes ideas flow freely; other times they do not.

A creative environment is one that promotes questions such as, "Why does this work?" "How could it work better?" "How could this space better impact human actions or behavior?" "How could this job be done differently and more efficiently?" Never stop asking questions!

Creativity is encouraged when

- an individual is accepted as a person of worth
- a person is free to think and feel what is deep inside him or her
- there is no worry of social disapproval and criticism as he or she explores ideas

From childhood forward, there may be people in your life that discourage creativity—the exploration of new ideas. These people may be teachers, parents, or even best friends. At other times, your own self-doubt or self-criticism gets in the way of creativity. Remaining confident of your creative abilities is critical during times of discouragement. Purposely surround yourself with people who thrive on asking questions rather than those who squash good ideas. You will be amazed how your ideas begin to flow, **Figure 6-9**.

The Creative Process

Creative ideas and creativity are often developed. The process is not mystical or magical. Rather it involves a type of *design thinking*. Remember, design thinking is a process of lateral, expansive, speculative thinking that often takes place in a collaborative team environment. It is an interwoven process of thinking and making.

Design Thinking

Every thinking, inquisitive individual can be a design thinker. To be such, you become a "question asker" rather than a "question answerer." Begin with simple questions such as "Why are things the way they are?" or "How can I make things better?" Design-thinking techniques can help jumpstart innovative solutions.

Design thinking is a way to stretch your thoughts and develop innovative possibilities that shape new designs. These ideas do not arise in a vacuum—rather both general knowledge and field-specific knowledge is needed. Here are seven actions you can use to further develop your design-thinking skills:

- identify the problem—THINK
- observe and gather information
- brainstorm
- sketch

Tips on Developing Creativity

- **Accept change—**realize it is an opportunity for new ideas.
- **Take risks—**challenge yourself.
- **Embrace failure—**do not let failure paralyze your progress. Failure is part of the process of learning.
- **Be a sponge—**be alert and absorb information and experiences around you.
- **Reward your curiosity—**give yourself the opportunity to explore new topics.

Figure 6-9 Remain confident in your creative abilities and seek ways to enhance your creativity.

- build models
- test, evaluate, and revise
- communicate—present designs

Identify the Problem—THINK

Problems can be big or small. Big problems can involve how to achieve world peace. Small problems can be as simple as solving how to make cheeseburgers less messy to eat. As you go through your day, listen to what people say about things that annoy them or things they wished worked better. There are many problems that have solutions that are less costly, smarter, efficient, or more fun. As you hear people talk about problems, record them. As you continue to think about these ideas in your mind, one day you may make a connection between one of them and develop a possible solution.

Observe and Gather Information

Once you have a problem you want to work on, capture it as a problem statement in one sentence. It should be broad and open-ended—not too specific. For example, "design a way for batteries to last longer" is much different than "design a pair of long-lasting batteries for an iPad." Then gather information from reputable sources. This is where evidence-based design (EBD) comes into the process. Research results are important to study and use to inform the design.

If research is not available, set up a research project by gathering a group of *experts* who use the *problem* product or related process. Listen carefully to what they say and watch what they do. These experts will inform your creative design solution.

Brainstorm

Bring together a multidisciplinary team to brainstorm ideas for possible solutions to the problem. The goal is to generate lots of ideas in a short period of time that lead to potentially innovative solutions. Some call brainstorming a type of *divergent thinking* because your thoughts avoid a linear path and instead branch out in all directions. See **Figure 6-10** for some do's and don'ts about brainstorming.

If you get stuck during a brainstorming session, try one of the following techniques. Crazy, wild ideas come from these strategies:

Brainstorming Do's and Don'ts

Do's

- Identify a facilitator
- Have warm-up exercises
- Have one conversation at a time
- Use plenty of sketches, mind-mapping or diagrams
- Practice active and empathetic listening
- Have fun!

Don'ts

- Prohibit critiquing and debate
- Don't let the "boss" speak first
- Don't insist everyone takes a turn
- Don't limit discussion to "expert" opinions
- Don't outlaw silly ideas or penalize those that bring them up
- Don't try to write everything down

leedsn/Shutterstock.com

Figure 6-10 Brainstorming is part of the creative process, yet requires following some guidelines. *How do you think brainstorming can benefit interior design?*

- *Transference*—application of an idea from one context to another
- *Rescaling*—interpreting and envisioning a different scale (such as larger or smaller) for an object or situation
- *Inversion*—flipping something upside down and looking at it from a new direction
- *Reassembly*—splicing something into puzzle pieces and rearranging them into a new design or viewing them from a new perspective
- *Bisociation*—a mental occurrence simultaneously associated with two habitually incomparable contexts

Once you are through brainstorming an abundance of ideas, you have to narrow down which ones you want to work on individually or as a group. Convergent thinking is part of this process. *Convergent thinking* is the ability to use logical and evaluative thinking to critique and narrow ideas to ones that best fit certain situations or set criteria.

Sketch

Some concepts and ideas are difficult to capture with words. Instead, sketch them! A sketch is a drawing made quickly—typically using a pencil or liquid-ink pen. Explore, doodle, draw, and play. You can do this when brainstorming or afterwards. Sketches need not be fancy or professional-looking. Rather, they are a quick way to make ideas visual and visible to others—bringing the ideas to life. Also, if one picture is overwhelming, use a storyboard technique or mind-map the idea. Designers make many quick sketches as they refine an idea. As Steven Keller said, "Your fingers and hands are the best digital tools." **Figure 6-11.**

Interior designers often use quick sketches to develop their ideas or communicate them to team members. These *process drawings* are helpful to understand the thoughts of the designer. Sketches can be completed on something as simple as a paper napkin or as sophisticated as special drawing paper.

Models

A **model** is an idea produced in three dimensions—an original prototype of your product or idea. Take some of your best ideas or sketches and use inexpensive materials to build models. Materials can be foam core, cardboard, clay, wire, canvas, paper, or a combination of all. If the group has several good ideas, divide into subgroups and invite each to build a prototype. Designers often use characteristics from each prototype in the final model.

Models used early in the creative steps capture how the designer sees the product or process. A designer often develops several subsequent prototypes that indicate color, materials, form, function, and textures.

Interior designers often make three-dimensional models of specific spaces or an entire set of spaces for their clients. Clients understand models much easier than a set of two-dimensional drawings.

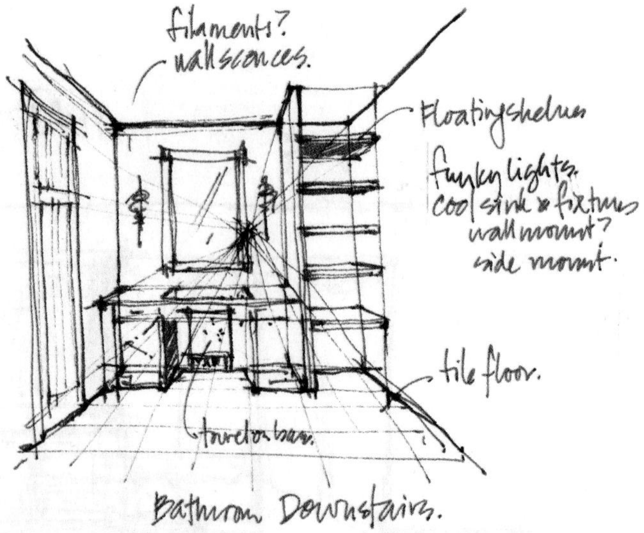

Image by Jacqui McFarland

Nadiia Gerbish/Shutterstock.com

Figure 6-11 Quick perspective sketches help interior designers communicate ideas.

Test, Evaluate, and Revise

Once you have a somewhat refined model, "take it on the road" so to speak to test the design. If possible, determine what works and what does not in a real-life setting. Ask the experts if the design is meeting their needs and solving the problem. Observe how they act, react, move, or avoid the prototypical model. Based on your evaluation of the users' reactions, revise your design. Continue to revise until you refine and complete the design.

Communicate—Present Designs

After developing, testing, refining, and revising your creative idea, it is time to move forward. Once you or your team reach a certain level of confidence, verbally present the idea to the client. Include some of the process drawings (for example, the sketches), material boards of products, and the three-dimensional models. Explain the

- identified problem
- how it was solved
- why people may want to use the product or process
- process you went through to arrive at the solution

Following the actions in design-thinking process offers a way for creative ideas in the brain—which are often hazy thoughts or feelings—to move from concept to installation and into reality. In addition to interior designers, many other design professionals and inventors—such as landscape designers, industrial designers, engineers, and architects—use design thinking.

Techniques for Enhancing Creativity

How do creative people come up with new ideas or imagine environments that do not yet exist? Here are several ways to enhance creativity that are common to the fields of design.

- **Analogies.** Many designers use analogies to look for something new based on what is already known or discovered. They do not start from scratch.

  For example, take two words or concepts that are not similar or associated like *cosmic* and *shoreline* or *appliance* and *landscape* and associate them. What comes to mind? Analogies help with the creation of a new visual and exploration of a new concept for the client, **Figure 6-12**.

- **Rule-breaking and assumption destruction.** Often, too often, people view or perceive a situation in a traditional manner. The rules have been set on how to act, think, or work in a certain environment. Creativity can involve throwing the rules out and destroying assumptions to begin fresh and anew. In a way, this is a type of thinking outside the box, but it is more than that. It is looking at a problem with new eyes without the influence of old traditions and rules.

  For interior designers, looking at spaces or structures with new eyes happens often when a client's need involves remodeling or redesigning. Too often a client cannot imagine his or her physical environment with a clean slate to envision a totally new solution to the problem.

- **Multiple-solution generation.** Generating multiple solutions through brainstorming requires placing any criticism on hold. Avoid listening to well-meaning words that often squelch new and innovative ideas. Instead, embrace the wacky, wild, and convoluted ideas others generate. Designers often use this process to avoid going with the first proposed solution. Good ideas come from many ideas.

  Similarly, many design students work hard to avoid accepting their first design solution to a problem.

wavebreakmedia/Shutterstock.com

Figure 6-12 Team members can use many techniques for generating creative ideas. *What techniques do you find most helpful and why?*

It is important to explore and discover a variety of design solutions before choosing the best one for a particular situation. As students explore different ideas, they stretch and challenge their minds.

- **Question ladder.** Another option for enhancing creativity is to use a question ladder to delve deeper into possible solutions. You can do this individually or in a group. Begin with simple questions about the problem, such as: What can be adapted? How could it be modified? Could it be magnified? What substitute could I use? How do I rearrange the parts? If I reverse the parts or flip them, what happens? What happens if I combine two suggestions?

  Then ladder the questions to take the analysis deeper. In other words, as you answer the questions, ask the next obvious one. Perhaps even use the simple question *why* to determine the idea's importance and significance. This creativity technique really moves you to new and deeper meanings.

The Creative Product

Many interior design manufacturers utilize creative and innovative skills when developing new products for interior spaces that enhance the health, safety, and well-being (HSW) of the client. It is often due to the vast amount of new products on the market that clients hire an interior designer. For example, it can be overwhelming to determine which cabinets to purchase for a kitchen or which office chairs to order for a large conference room in an office complex.

After the presentation of creative ideas, many manufacturers use a great deal of research to refine the design ideas. In fact, many world renowned furniture manufacturers, such as Steelcase, Haworth, Herman Miller, and Knoll have their own divisions of research within which to develop proprietary furniture designs. Once the designs are ready to market to the public, the manufacturers present them at large design tradeshows.

The largest tradeshow of its kind in North America is *The National Exposition of Contract Furnishings (NEOCON)*, which occurs in the Merchandise Mart in Chicago every June. The new creative products for both

CASE STUDY

Biomimicry—Nature as Inspiration for Creative Products and Processes

Interior designers often study people and human behavior in during the process of developing innovative and creative design solutions. However, designers also turn to nature and the natural environment for potential solutions.

Biomimicry, a word derived from meanings of *life* and *imitate* was a discipline first defined in 1974. It has recently reached national recognition through the work of a biologist, innovation consultant, and author of six books: Janine Benyus, a Montana native. Since her first book in 1997, *Biomimicry*, Janine has evolved the practice of sustainable businesses. See the *Biomimicry 3.8* website.

Janine Benyus offers a message to designers and inventors: look to nature—a competent universe—for solving design problems. Nature offers inspired designs that impact the built environment and therefore interior design.

Put your bisociative-thinking cap on for a minute. In nature, you will find inspired designs for making things waterproof, solar-powered, and repellant. For example, Janine has worked with national paint companies to develop a paint that dries in a pattern that enables simple rainwater to wash away dirt. Her inspiration: A self-cleaning leaf. Advocates of biomimicry believe that nature has solved many of the problems society faces today. The solutions just need to be rediscovered. Nature becomes the source of inspiration as a constructive model and mentor.

Investigate and Reflect

Use the Internet to visit the Biomimicry 3.8 website to read more about biomimicry. What does research show about biomimicry? How are educators using biomimicry? What are some ways you might use biomimicry as a future interior designer? Write an essay reflecting your thoughts.

residential and commercial design are unveiled in the 700 showrooms. Professional designers and architects journey from around the world to attend this tradeshow.

In addition to furnishings, many interior design products are inspired from nature. See the Case Study on page 154 to understand how nature is inspiring the creative development of new products that are not harmful to the planet.

You Are Creative!

Creativity is one of the most exciting parts of the design process. Express yourself with confidence. As you have creative ideas, do not keep them to yourselves. You will always have new ones that are sparked by new and different experiences. As you have new ideas, write them down. They may never come again!

The Phases of the Design Process

Interior designers are creative design thinkers. They use the design-thinking process to take a creative idea from their minds and make it visible to others. All designers use design thinking. Specific to the discipline, interior design practitioners use their design-thinking skills to create well-designed, interior spaces.

> *"The practitioner listens, observes, analyzes, improves and creates original ideas, visions, and spaces that have measurable value."*
>
> *DFIE IFI, 2011*

The **design process** is a method that interior designers use for organizing their work, guiding their actions, and finalizing their decisions when working with team members and clients. At its foundation, the process has a series of phases ranging from idea generation to the client's final evaluation of the design solution after installation. Although phases of the design process are presented in a linear fashion in this text, it is not unusual for a designer to revisit them several times as a client changes his or her mind or a design is further refined. Phases of the design process include

- Phase 1: Pre-Design
- Phase 2: Programming
- Phase 3: Schematic Design (SD)
- Phase 4: Design Development (DD)
- Phase 5: Contract Documents (CD)
- Phase 6: Contract Administration (CA)
- Phase 7: Move-in and Post-Occupancy Evaluation (POE)

Interior design does not exist in a state of isolation away from others who influence design. It is an integral part of any building construction or renovation project. The connections that come from working with professionals in related fields and disciplines *inform*—or guide and direct—good interior design. This is especially true of sustainable interior design. This integrated design process (IDP) is collaborative from two perspectives. First is the recognition that different building systems help make up any man-made structure. The second involves understanding how professionals responsible for different parts of the building system have important information to offer one another. As part of the design process, integrated design is becoming more and more the norm of doing business in the built environment.

Designer Profile

Penny Bonda—Sustainability and Integrated Design

Penny Bonda, FASID, LEED Fellow, works in the fields of environmental consulting and communications and is a prominent writer and lecturer. She is the founding chair of the US Green Building Council committee for LEED Commercial Interiors rating system.

"The most recent version of the LEED green building rating system added a new category of points for *integrated design*. This is an important recognition of the necessity to begin the design process with an analysis of the goals of the project by the interdisciplinary teams. Eliminating or even postponing this step may well result in missed synergies between design strategies, such as minimizing energy consumption by maximizing the use of natural light for interior spaces. Design—always a collaborative effort—is more so with the focus on sustainability."

You can read more about Penny's background in Appendix B.

Understanding the Process Flow

Depending on the size or scope of the client problem, the execution of the design process can be relatively simple or amazingly complex. The phases of the process are not distinct or permanently set. There is back-and-forth movement among the phases that frequently involves the interweaving and blending of ideas and decisions.

At times, designers revisit previous phases and call the end result a *redesign*, **Figures 6-13 A and B.** Redesigns are common because clients change their minds. A designer may revisit some phases of the design process two and three times before moving into the actual construction and installation of the project.

If a project is small, such as a guest bathroom remodel, the designer may not formally record or document all phases of the design process. If a project is large, it may involve many pages of documentation to capture its detail and complexity and clearly communicate the design to each team member and the client.

Realize that an interior-design practitioner may work on multiple design projects at the same time, each within different phases of the design process. For example, a commercial designer may have five to seven client projects that are in different phases. As a designer, you may work on only one phase of the design process, while other team members complete earlier or later phases on the same project.

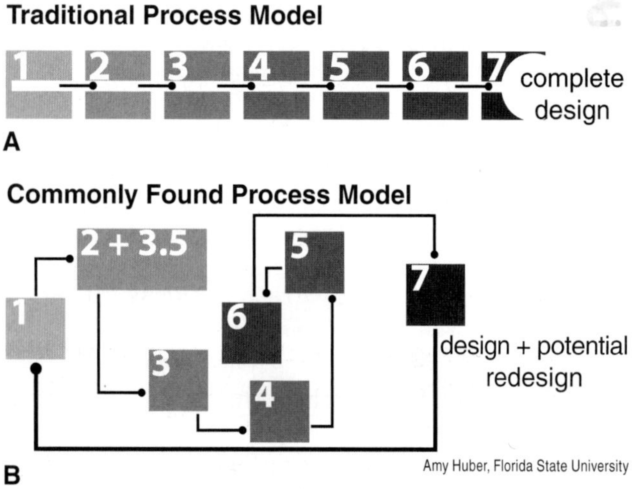

Amy Huber, Florida State University

Figure 6-13 The interior design process is complex and does not always move in a linear way. *Compare process models A and B. Why do you think the "Commonly Found in Practice Model" is more typical of the way interior designers work?*

Phase 1: Pre-Design

At the beginning of the design process, there are a number of Pre-Design tasks the designer practitioner may complete. For instance, the designer interviews the client and asks very specific questions to clearly understand the client's needs. If the skills of the designer match the needs of the client, the designer develops a *letter of agreement,* or contract, for retention of the designer's services on the part of the client. The initial written letter of agreement outlines the expectations of each party. It includes a shared project vision, confirms a design and documentation schedule, and outlines budget parameters. Both the client and designer sign the letter of agreement.

If a project is small, the client and designer may sign a simple letter of agreement. If a project is large, such as a new hotel design, the design and construction team—along with other team members—often meet together with the client to clearly understand the scope of project services and their overlapping roles, goals, and time lines before signing a contract (integrated design process). Understanding the scope of services for a larger project is critical in achieving a strong team approach.

Some Pre-Design tasks the designer or design team may complete to reach understanding about the scope of services the client requires include

- identification of the client's problem and scope of project
- identification of the scope of services necessary to develop a quality solution
- determination of whether to take on the project—whether it is a good fit between designer and client
- consideration of schedules and budgets—can the designer complete the project within the time frame and budget

Note the scope of services can change as the interior design project unfolds. At this time, the designer and client can revise the scope of services and the contract. Here is a sample client problem, **Figure 6-14**.

After all parties reach consensus on the scope of services and sign the agreement, the second phase of the design process begins. The following takes you through the remaining phases of the design process practitioners use in the development and installation of a client's project.

Sample Client Problem

- **Design problem:** The client identifies and clearly communicates that there is a lack of filing storage around his desk.
- **Issue:** Purchasing additional filing cabinets has not proven to be a good solution. In addition, the office is space-challenged.
- **Design solution:** A professional designer has the tools and the process to analyze the big picture and develop a good design solution.

trekandshoot/Shutterstock.com

Figure 6-14 Clients often have diverse design problems. *What questions might you ask this client to help solve this client's storage problem?*

Phase 2: Programming

During the Programming phase of the design process, the designer or design team more clearly identifies the client's design problem, current situation, and future needs.

The **client program** is a document that outlines the client project—functions, specific need requirements in each space, issues, and current status. When complete, the program is a checklist-type document that helps the designer understand the client's situation and needs, and ensures inclusion of every requirement in the final design solution.

Development of the program requires such skills as interviewing, observation, research, analysis, organizing, documenting data, and writing skills. Team members during this phase may include other designers, architects, project managers, or engineers (for example, mechanical, electrical, plumbing, structural experts). It may also include other specialists such as lighting designers or security-system designers.

The Programming phase involves fact-finding, client interviews, and an on-site analysis of the project. If a project is small, such as a medium-sized home, this phase of the design process may end with a client meeting to review the collection of information.

If a project is large, a detailed identification of the client problem may require the development of a feasibility study. A **feasibility study** involves in-depth fact-finding, analysis of the problem, and estimates of product and construction costs to solve the problem. It sounds like an easy task, but it really is not. Without clear and accurate identification of the problem, you may develop a great design solution that may not solve the client's problem. Think of a target with concentric circles. It is best to hit the bull's-eye rather than the surrounding areas to win the game. The same is true of meeting the client's design needs—it is very important to be on target.

Completion of the Programming phase may occur in one afternoon or it may take months depending on the size, scope, and type of the client project. By the end of the phase, the designer should fully understand the needs of the project in detail. The client should verify the program's accuracy before the designer proceeds to the Schematic Design phase.

Major tasks a designer completes in the Programming phase include

- identification of client preferences and resources
- discovery—researching and gathering key facts and information related to the client project
- inventory of existing furnishings, fixtures and equipment (or FF&E) for potential reuse
- analysis of data collected
- development of matrices and relational bubble diagrams
- summary and presentation information to the client

The following paragraphs describe each of these tasks in detail. Again, these tasks culminate in a written document and a checklist known as your *client program*. If printed, a program may be five pages in length or fill several three-ring binders. The length on the program depends on the size and complexity of the project, and the different representative groups who will use the finished interior.

Identification

The Programming phase begins with an in-depth client interview. Realize that the client may be more than one person. Therefore, make sure to include all decision-makers in the interview process.

Design preferences, determining space needs, and physical interrelationships between distinct spaces are discussion points. The goal of the interview is to understand the client's viewpoint, preferences, needs, and issues in relationship to the project.

Developing a client profile and the occupant or user requirements is part of the identification process. For commercial projects, you may conduct interviews with several stakeholders or users of the space to ensure you meet their concerns and needs, **Figure 6-15**.

The client interview also includes questions concerning the personal or organizational preferences, functions of spaces—current and future, and priorities to consider for the newly designed spaces. For a commercial project, the designer often completes a *desk audit*. A **desk audit** is the evaluation of a company's organization chart as well as policies and procedures that impact the design of the series of spaces. For a residential project, the interview includes questions relating to the family structure, such as extended family members that may be frequent visitors.

Client interviews may take only a couple hours if the project is small and of minimal difficulty. If the project is complex and large in scope, the interview process may take several days to months to complete.

In addition to client interviews, a second set of interviews may take place. Designers generally conduct these interviews with representative user groups. User groups could be staff, clients, customers, or even family members. This second set of interviews allows the designer to understand all perspectives that might impact the success of the design project. Here are some examples of interviews a designer may conduct.

- College admissions office: The designer may interview the director of admissions, representative staff members, parents, and students of several ages.
- Retail store: The designer will interview the owner of the store, staff members, and a representative group of shoppers (customers).
- Law office: The designer often interviews the owners of the firm as well as other attorneys, staff, and clients.

Monkey Business Images/Shutterstock.com

Figure 6-15 Interviewing clients, stakeholders, and end users helps the interior designer develop an accurate client profile.

Discovery—Information Gathering

Once the client and user group interviews are complete, the next step is to complete the discovery and information gathering process. This part of the design process helps you understand how others have solved similar client problems, and what research is available to ensure the final design solution is strong and on target.

The designer gathers information, data, and research from a variety of sources that pertain to the client problem. These include

- locale, building, site, and interior condition of the project
- research that could influence the design solution that leads to evidence-based design (EBD)
- aspects of human behavior that relate to the space
- site visits, field measurements, and case studies, **Figure 6-16**
- applicable building and life-safety codes

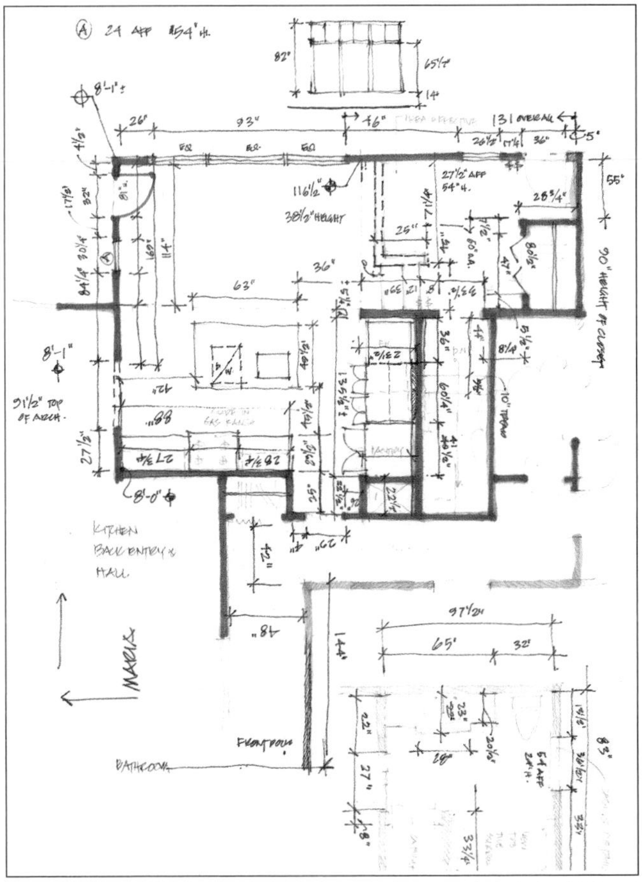

Image by Jacqui McFarland

Figure 6-16 Site measurements are an important part of data collection for interior design.

Interior designers often use the locale of the client's project as a source of inspiration for new design elements in the space. They gather this information to understand such issues as the culture, climate, and community of the building location or building site. For example, understanding the climate helps to select materials and finishes that are appropriate to the weather. The designer also studies design elements—such as lines, form or shapes—that appear in the surrounding natural or man-made structures. Understanding the community assists the designer in reflecting the *place*, or distinct characteristics of the location in the interior.

It is important to gather and study research related to the design project, especially for such complex projects as the re-design of an elementary school or retail store. To perform research, the designer may visit the project location. The data the designer collects helps him or her shape and support the final design solution. Two types of research interior designers often perform include

- **Qualitative research:** This is a type of research (such as a personal observation) that requires judgment and more than *yes* and *no* answers to determine how the existing structure and spaces shape human behavior.
- **Quantitative research:** This research that deals with facts and figures that can be numerically analyzed. For example, for the design of a retail store quantitative data might include analysis of diagrams measuring peak times consumers visit the store.

Another form of research involves *case studies*—real-life situations to examine or study to learn about something. For interior design, a case study is a similarly completed interior design project. You can view these projects online by looking in design firm portfolios or visiting places in person.

Visiting a similar project in person is a **site visit.** For example, if a college hires a design team to design a new collegiate admissions office, the team will often tour nearby newly completed offices. The team seeks advice from experts, project managers, and users of that project.

The goal of the information gathering during a site visit is to determine how a similar client problem has been solved. These interviews are very revealing and often prevent future mistakes. Data collection from a site visit often includes photos, field notes, critical measurements, production information, and personal observations. It is important for designers to summarize the helpful information from each case study when writing the program.

Other discovery tasks involve seeking and understanding building-code requirements and other life-safety issues inherent in the client's project. Client interviews are critical at this point. *Life-safety issues* relate to the health and safety of the building occupants, such as inclusion of safe egress from a building, smoke detectors and fire alarm systems, backup power and light systems, and fire extinguishers.

In regard to life-safety issues, it is best to seek additional information rather than jump into the process of design. For instance, you may need to seek additional evidence-based design (EBD) solutions. Available research and understanding others' solutions to similar problems helps shape and ensure your final design solution is strong and on target.

This part of the Programming phase is significant. Rather than developing a design off the top of your head, you develop a design with a foundation of research and gathered data. When you present potential design solutions to the client, you establish significant credibility if you can cite research studies, precedents, statistics, or consumer interviews that support your design. You are developing a design storyline that is easy to communicate and justify to others—whether it is a client, end user of the space, or community member financing the project. Your design will then be *defensible*.

Inventory

The inventory task in the Programming phase is a two-part process. The first is to understand the type and dimensions of the building structure and interior spaces *or* if new construction, parameters of the site and goals of the architect.

If the building exists, it is important to understand its condition—whether it is a client's house or commercial building. For example, a designer documents such existing conditions as the current floor plan. Sometimes the client can provide existing drawings of the building and interior for your use.

To verify accuracy of existing drawings, be sure to take field measurements. **Field measurements** are those the designer takes of room dimensions, windows, doors, placement of outlets, lighting, HVAC locations, and wall and flooring finishes. Often a designer will sketch the plans and details on-site and take photographs of existing conditions. The reason for taking field measurements is that often the plan filed with the building department may not reflect actual conditions because of changes made on-site, **Figure 6-17**.

If the building is a new construction, then an interior designer may be part of the design team that shapes the building structure and resulting interior spaces. An interior designer brings understanding and knowledge of the following to the project:

- human behavior
- effective circulation patterns and universal design elements to incorporate
- impact of door and window placement on the function of the space
- site orientation and its impact on gathering daylight and views in the space

Often, the team brings in the interior designer at the end of the project to complete the furniture and finishes package.

In the second part of the inventory process, if the client has existing furnishings, fixtures, and equipment (or FF&E) to reuse for either a residential or commercial project, the designer completes an inventory and categorizes these items for use in the new design. For a commercial design client, this can be quite an extensive part of the process. Clients, such as corporate office firms, may have an FF&E inventory database. Even if they do, the challenge for the designer is to help the client create an inventory of what the company wants to keep for its newly designed office and identify what to

Viktoriya/Shutterstock.com

Figure 6-17 Field measurements, along with site sketches and photos of existing conditions, helps the designer verify conditions that impact the project. *Practice your measuring skills by measuring rooms at home or school.*

sell, recycle, or donate. For a residential design client, the process is similar but on a smaller scale.

Analysis

The analysis part of Programming phase occurs as the designer reviews the client's functions and needs broken down by division (if commercial) or by room (if residential). The designer uses the client program (checklist) to understand and analyze the data to determine the following:

- functions to group together to increase efficiency
- spaces that need to be located near other spaces
- departments or divisions that need to be near each other to enhance communication
- spaces that need to be near a window or located near an exit
- offices that require acoustical or visual privacy

Before the *Schematic Design phase* begins, the des-igner analyzes the answers to these issues. Some of the tools a designer uses for such analysis include *adjacency* and *criteria matrixes,* and *relational bubble diagrams.*

Matrixes

On completion by the designer, a **matrix** is a concise visual summary that organizes the Program requirements. This summary allows the designer to extract and shape vast amounts of information from the Program and capture it concisely to enhance understanding. It is revealing to see the client's needs summarized succinctly. Analysis takes place as the designer reviews the matrix and perceives how client priorities impact the design solution.

There are two types of matrices. One is an *adjacency matrix* and the other is a *criteria matrix.* If the project is small enough, the designer can combine them into one matrix.

An **adjacency matrix** is a diagram or table that lists each room or space, **Figure 6-18 A**. The goal is to determine, with the Program at the foundation, which spaces need to be next to each other or who needs to be directly adjacent to another. This matrix allows the designer and client to look broadly at connections between different spaces in the project.

For a residential client, this analysis may result in locating a bathroom next to a bedroom. For a commercial office client, this analysis may result in locating an administrative assistant adjacent to a department head.

For a commercial project, these matrices depict the organizational structure, operational flow, and circulation patterns of the client project. To facilitate the creation of the adjacency matrix, the designer needs to request organizational structure diagrams from the business during the Programming phase.

A **criteria matrix** is a table that lists each room or space of the client's project in the rows of the left-hand column, and lists each issue—as prioritized by the client—as column headings. The goal of this matrix is to determine the client's specific needs and in what order they occur within each space.

Priorities the criteria matrix might include are square footage needs, daylight or views, acoustical or visual privacy, access to a business center, and security. For a residential client, this may result in the design of a master bedroom overlooking a garden view with acoustical privacy. For a commercial office client, this may result in

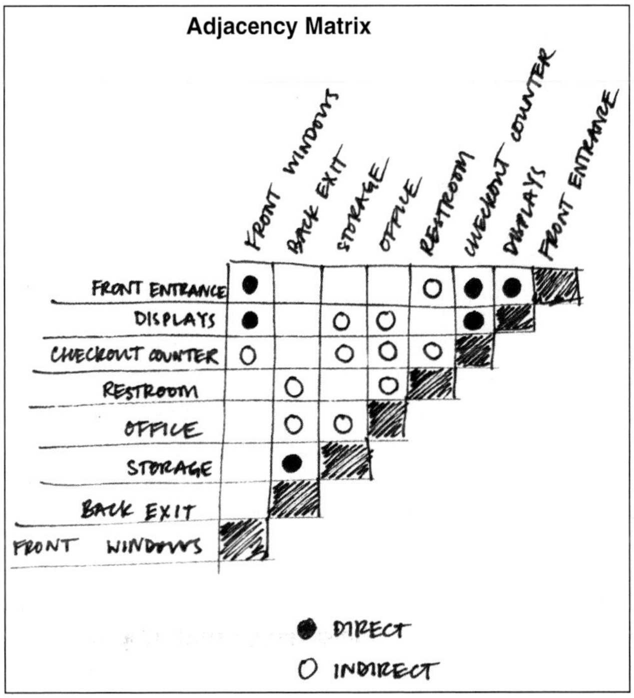

Courtesy of Sarah Ricci

Figure 6-18A Adjacency matrixes help interior designers take a broad look at the connections between spaces to develop a plan to meet client needs.

a reception space having 120 square feet, no visual or acoustical privacy, but with access to the business center. Answers resulting from the matrices directly impact the client's floor plan within a given structure.

Relational Bubble Diagrams

There are two types of bubble diagrams: *relational* and *general*. The designer completes the relational bubble diagrams first. As one type of concept map, the goal of a **relational bubble diagram** is to capture—in the form of a two-dimensional illustration—the priority relationships of spaces to each other as identified in the adjacency matrix, **Figure 6-18 B**. This diagram guides the bubble placement *without* the framework of the building footprint or floor plan. Analysis of how the bubbles, or spaces, relate to each other takes place. You will read about general bubble diagrams later in the chapter in the Schematic Design phase. Keep the following steps in mind when creating bubble diagrams, **Figure 6-19.**

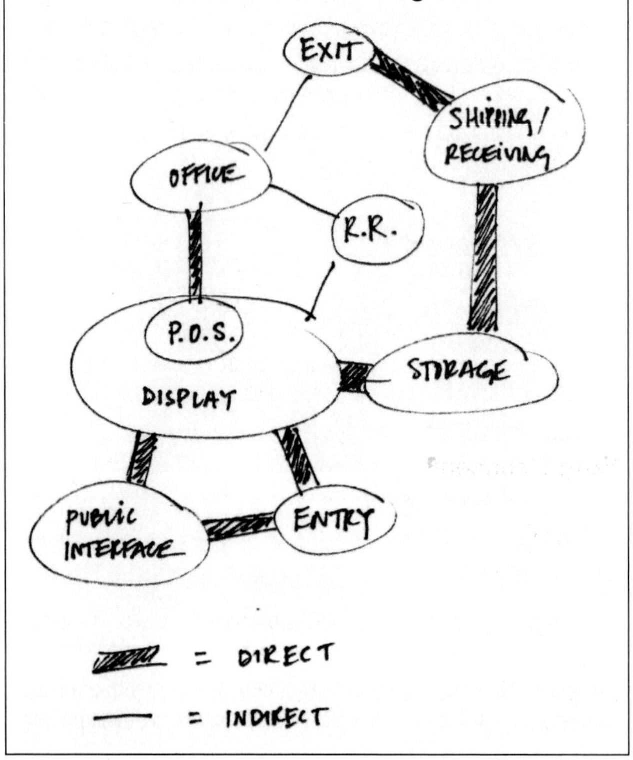

Courtesy of Sarah Ricci

Figure 6-18B Like adjacency matrixes, relational bubble diagrams help designers examine connection between spaces.

Summarize and Present

Once you finish the analysis tasks, you need to organize the Programming data into a written report for the client. By compiling this data, you and the client can visualize the project's existing and future needs.

The written client program qualifies and quantifies the client's or user's needs for a project and becomes a project checklist the designer or design team uses throughout the design process. It consists of the project summary and location, project goals, culture of the location or project, client or user demographics and needs, square footage recommendations for each space, and drawings for proposed layouts. The written program also includes any photos, site observation sketches or diagrams, and field measurements. The written program should be clear, concise, and effectively explain and justify the design actions in a convincing way that is easy for others to understand.

If there is too much information, as with many commercial projects, it is your job to condense the information into a manageable, accessible report. By the end of the Programming phase, the designer should be able to identify and state the client problem, list square footage needs for each space, and analyze the collection of data to develop an understanding of needs within each space.

Once complete, you present the written program to the client in an oral presentation. The client presentation helps determine if both parties are in agreement and understand the specifics of the project. A client's approval and *sign-off* on the program shows his or her agreement with the project. Once agreed on, the process moves forward to the *Schematic Design phase.*

Phase 3: Schematic Design (SD)

The Schematic Design (SD) phase is a brainstorming or "what-if" phase. It is the fun, creative and innovative part of the design process in which the designer or design team explores and generates multiple ideas and multiple-design solutions based on the client problem. They complete these activities before deciding on the best solution.

The designer communicates the brainstorming ideas that take shape with the use of **schematics**. These are

Steps in Using Bubble Diagrams

Write a list of these steps to use as reference when you are creating bubble diagrams. Keep a copy with your sketch pad or digital device.

1. Place the building shell drawing under tracing paper
2. Keep a list of the general functions or rooms needed nearby
3. List functions/spaces according to size—largest to smallest
4. Draw ovals to represent space locations, beginning with largest spaces first
5. Fill in remaining areas with smaller bubbles keeping in mind the organization chart and needs of each space as identified in the program—labeling spaces as you go through the process
6. Add short horizontal lines to indicate circulation patterns from space to space—use arrows to capture thoughts outside the plan perimeter
7. Use markers to add color to each bubble, keeping the bubble color consistent from one diagram to another
8. Analyze organization of the overall space with representative bubbles
9. List pros/cons along the plan margin as a reminder of plan advantages to discuss with team members or even the client
10. Repeat the process by changing the location of the largest bubbles

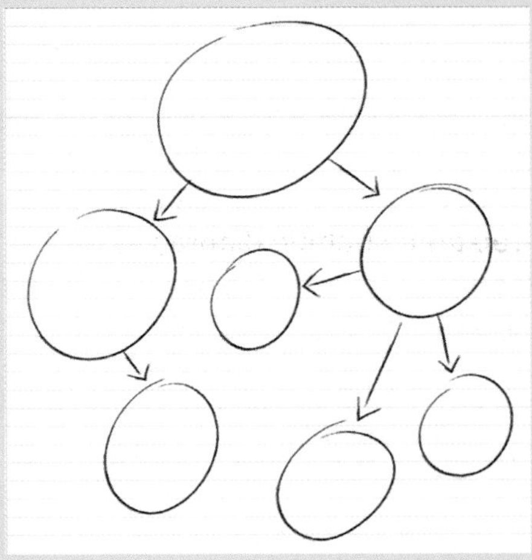

wongwean/Shutterstock.com

Figure 6-19 As you learn to create bubble diagrams, keep these steps handy to guide your work.

quick drawings that help the designer and client envision floor plans, circulation patterns, three-dimensional spaces, and more.

The Schematic Design phase can be an individual or collaborative process. It involves analyzing the merit of all worthwhile design ideas and their potential in addressing the client problem. This requires such skills such as creativity and innovation, open-mindedness, problem-solving, and teamwork.

The Schematic Design phase includes the following major tasks:

- **Concept development**—a process that guides future design decisions for the client's project
- **Preliminary space planning**—tasks to explore the layout of the physical space within the building shell
- **Drawings** (for example, sketches and elevations)—to explore the client's three-dimensional space(s) and the designer's proposed ideas
- **Furniture, fixtures and equipment (FF&E)**—proposed furnishings and equipment needed for spaces
- **Budget projection**—a preliminary budget proposal

By the end of the Schematic Design phase, the designer or design team will have explored multiple-design solutions that address the client's problem. The designer provides the client with enough information to be able to select a proposed solution based on the merit of the design and projected costs.

Concept Development

Concept theory suggests that a designer is more creative with ideas about interior space when he or she has an image of the mood or feeling of the space prior to engaging in the design and planning processes. A **design concept**—an abstract idea, thought, notion, or image—involves an imagery-evoking statement that describes the desired mood or feeling for the client's interior space(s).

A design concept also reflects the client's Programming needs and design intent of the project. It links the place and function of the space with the aesthetics and evoked mood. It is a creative statement and image that functions as a guideline for the remainder of all design decisions.

It is very important to finish the task of concept development before moving forward in the design process. Without a design concept, every other design decision lacks a target and measurement for determining success.

Communicating the Concept

Concept development is one of the most creative and innovative parts of the design process. A concept drives every decision throughout the design process to the final design solution. Therefore, a designer must find ways to clearly express the concept to the client and possibly the design team. A concept can be expressed as

- a word, metaphor, or descriptive phrase of a mental image
- an idea based on visual aesthetics or functional needs
- an idea that is measurable against the success of the final project

In addition to words (written or oral), the designer communicates the concept to the client or team members using

- inspiration or idea boards
- concept squares or models
- ideation—freehand sketches including perspectives

Throughout the entire design process, every decision made about the client's design—such as floor plan, furniture, and finishes—should focus on the concept, **Figure 6-20**. For example, if a decision about furnishing style needs to be made, the question to ask is: Will the style reflect and support the approved concept?

Concept versus Theme

There is a fine line between an interior *design concept* and an interior design *theme*. Both act as a framework for developing design solutions. While a concept deals with the basic planning of the space, and defines the relationship among different design elements (such as light, color, and shape), a *theme* is a framework that ties all spaces together.

Themes are not abstract, but are highly figurative and easily understood by the user. Themes most commonly apply to retail and hospitality design in which creating an *experience* is a goal. As healthcare design readily adopts hospitality comforts, themes are appearing in hospitals—particularly in pediatric wings. Common themes—such as a western theme or a beach theme—tend to use familiar images to make the space appear less clinical.

The advantage of a theme is its universal appeal. The advantage of a concept is that it is specific to the client and abstract enough to avoid locking the client into a specific look at the onset of the project.

A designer must visually communicate a concept for clients to understand it. Clients want and deserve to know the design direction of their projects. Reassurance results when clients can envision the mood or feeling of the overarching design. A clearly defined concept also keeps clients on course when other design ideas pop up during the course of the project's completion. Clients find it reassuring to have a concept that helps narrow the myriad possibilities of interior products on the market.

Concept Inspiration

Where do you look for concept ideas? In practice, when a design team accepts a new project, the team seeks creative concepts from such multiple sources of inspiration. Sources may include

- the clients' interview material (picking up on a phrase used)
- the project's location—urban city versus rural country
- historical precedents and case studies
- a new twist to a historic idea
- books, trade publications, architectural style magazines, or a story
- cultural resource centers or museums
- geometric designs
- natural designs of land or sea
- geographical anomalies, such as shifting earth plates
- beautiful objects, natural or man-made, such as the Rocky Mountains
- travel across or out of country
- inviting gardens
- fashion

Concept development can be dangerously time-consuming. There is always another exciting, new idea to explore. Without self-control, time is lost which hinders the project time line. The skills designers may use

Figure 6-20 Inspiration boards help the designer express the concept to the client and the design team. *What do the images on this inspiration board tell you about this client? Check your perceptions by reading the Case Study about Raquel and Mike Gonzalez on pages 168–169 of the text.*

during concept development include space planning, sketching, drawing three-dimensional (3-D) perspectives, renderings, and model-building, **Figure 6-21**.

Preliminary Space Plans

Preliminary space planning involves the analysis of the client program for needs and spatial relationships. Analyzing the various schematics, or drawings, helps the designer and client understand how the spaces interact within the building shell. Drawings and presentation boards include

- general bubble diagrams
- block diagrams
- block-and-stack diagrams
- preliminary drawings of interior elevations and building sections

Designers use a task of the Schematic Design phase to capture ideas about how to shape the interior spaces given the identified concept and client program. Though they can envision the space in three dimensions, designers must capture their creative ideas rapidly with simple, quickly executed *general bubble diagrams*.

A **general bubble diagram** is a type of concept-map that uses ovals and circles to represent rooms and their relationships. These diagrams depict overall **zones**—areas of space according to activity and function, relationships to other spaces, and sometimes potential locations. General bubble diagrams communicate the organization of space and functions *within* a building footprint. Each oval shape represents one space. The designer draws each shape in its location within the building—in proportionate size—and adds circulation between spaces, such as hallways.

Just like relational bubble diagrams the designer used in the Programming phase, general bubble diagrams allow the designer to quickly and creatively assess potential associations between spaces without the need to invest time in a complex plan that may not work. The goal is to explore as many options as possible in a short period of time. If the plan becomes too finite, too quickly the floor plan will be weak.

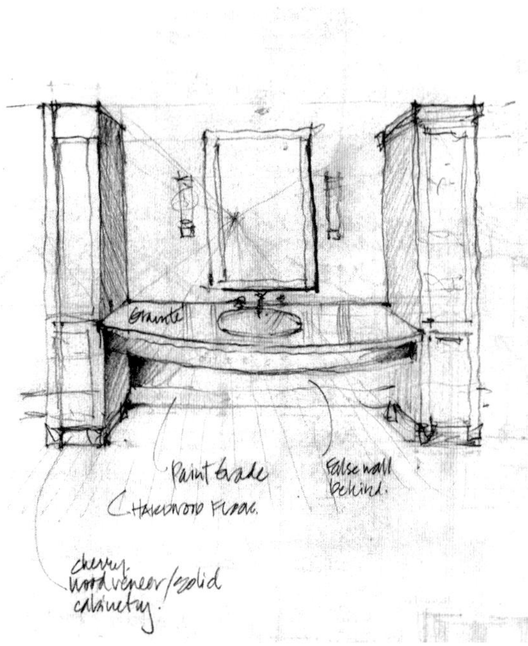

Image by Jacqui McFarland

Figure 6-21 Interior designers use multiple sources of inspiration to create design concepts and sketches. *What do you think are some sources of inspiration for this perspective sketch?*

The designer then rearranges the large spaces into several locations within the scaled building footprint to analyze location preferences. Similar to the game of chess, there are many different moves to make with the same game pieces. As a further step of organization, large design projects use zones to group together areas or spaces with similar activities or functions. For example, when designing a community justice center, a designer may create a zone specifically for the judges away from prisoners or the public.

Once the designer organizes the spaces into approximately scaled general bubble diagrams, overlays are used—typically tracing paper or a different computer layer—to *block* the spaces into rooms. These **block diagrams** refine the shapes of the bubbles into approximate room sizes with doorways and more clearly align the shapes and detail their locations within the building structure.

A designer may work with a multistory house or high-rise office complex. If so, he or she may develop and evaluate use of **block-and-stack diagrams**—or *stacking diagrams*, which show such vertical functions as elevators and stairways the designer must consider and place in the same location on each floor. The addition of doorways to the block-and-stack diagram illustrates flow and movement of people from one space to another.

As a designer, it is important to avoid becoming too invested with your first set of general bubble diagrams. Instead, due to the fluid nature of this type of drawing, this is the time to explore multiple ways to shape the space by moving different rooms or spaces around in the building footprint.

Designers know there are always trade-offs based on client priorities and preferences. It is important to develop multiple-design solutions for the client's problem. Therefore, designers develop, analyze, and refine multiple-bubble diagrams. After analysis of all plans, it is common to merge advantages and features from several possible plans into one strong, final plan for the client proposal. See the Case Study on pages 168–169 to see how such diagrams unfold.

Once the designer identifies the spaces in the building footprint, he or she roughly draws them to **scale**—a specific ratio between two sets of dimensions relative to the object drawn and its actual size. Then the designer adds furniture and equipment to the floor plan to determine whether each room or area needs more or less space. This diagram is called a **furniture plan**. Scale for commercial projects is typically 1/8" = 1'-0". Scale for residential projects is typically ¼" = 1'-0". Designers regularly use walls and furniture symbols to represent the rough amount of space needed.

Drawings

Clients may not always understand floor plans or furniture-plan proposals, but they often understand a quick sketch showing a perspective of their proposed space(s). A sketch is a rough drawing, often with some detail, that serves as a preliminary study of a given space. A **perspective drawing** is a technique designers use to show a three-dimensional space on a two-dimensional plane. These beginning perspective sketches explore the proposed ideas used in this phase to

- help the practitioner envision design ideas in proposed or given spaces
- assess client preferences of proposed design ideas

Designers also use preliminary perspective sketches to capture and communicate idea suggestions for such custom architectural details as a wall niches, or big ideas that show relationships between adjoining spaces.

Sketches may also be two-dimensional in nature. Designers sketch or draw floor plans and furniture arrangements by hand on paper or on a digital tablet. They can also sketch **elevations**—or vertical representations of walls in the space, or **sections**—slices through a series of elevations along a consecutive line.

The overarching goal of perspective drawings, floor plans, elevations, and sections is to assist the client in understanding the design of their spaces before construction begins and installation is complete. The clearer the communication and understanding between the designer and the client at this stage of the design process, the fewer misunderstandings in the future, **Figure 6-22.**

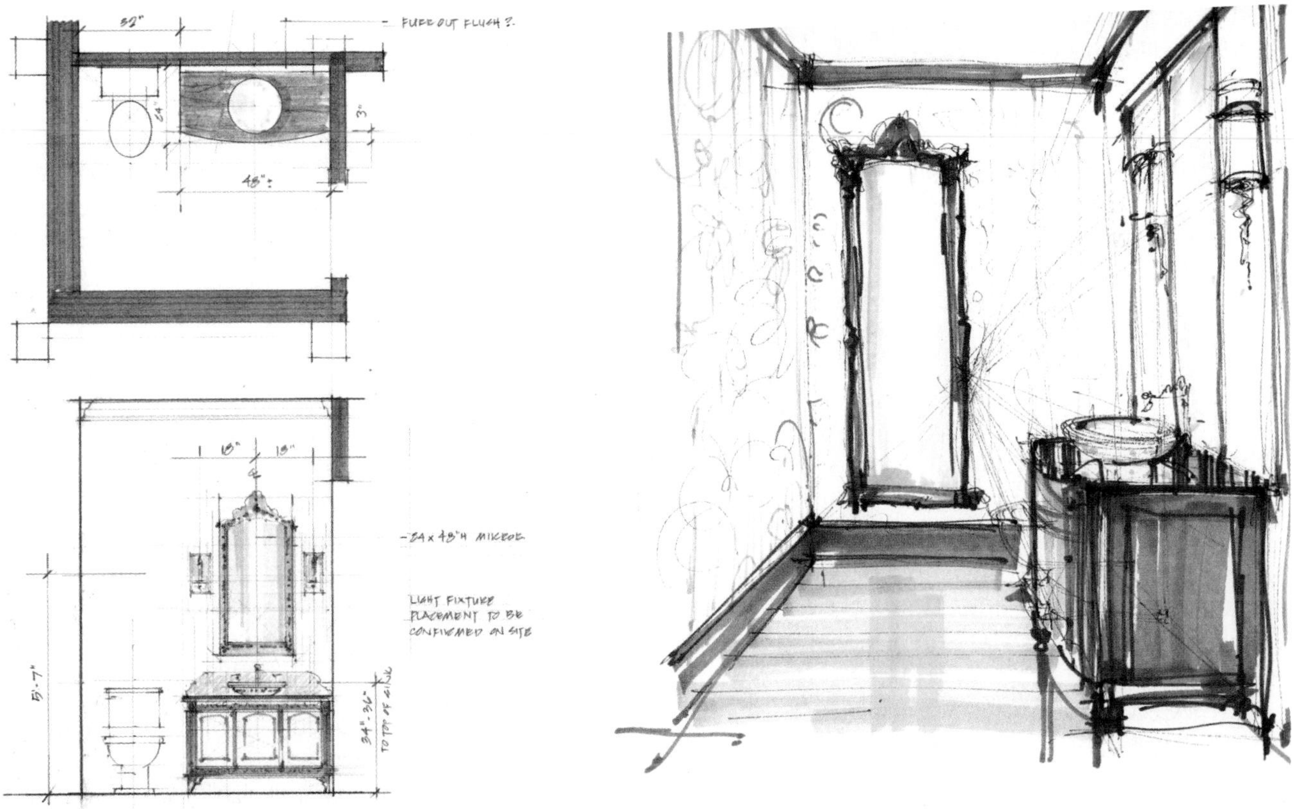

A B

Image by Jacqui McFarland

Figure 6-22 These elevation (A) and perspective (B) sketches help the interior designer clearly present the concept leading to fewer misunderstandings.

CASE STUDY

The Client Program Drives Design

During the Programming phase, the interior designer works with a potential client to develop the client program. As you recall, the client program outlines the client project—its functions, specific need requirements in each space, and client issues. Completion of this document helps the designer understand the client's situation and needs, and ensures all will be addressed in the final design solution.

The following is an example of a *preliminary* client program and initial sketches that a designer compiles after one or more interviews.

Client Program—Raquel and Mike Gonzalez

Executive Summary

An "Austinite" couple in their late 20s, Raquel and Mike Gonzalez are building their first home outside Austin, Texas. They work full time and are looking for a vibrant, youthful, organic environment to escape to when leaving their city-centered jobs. They are interested in beginning their family in the next couple years.

Scope of Services

Raquel and Mike desire design assistance with the conceptual development, space planning, and furniture arrangement of the new house. Their priorities include clever utilization of limited space and a strong connection to the outdoors.

Client Profile: Young Couple

Mike is a software engineer for a large engineering firm. His interests include golf, skiing, and biking. *Raquel* is a pharmaceutical sales consultant. Her interests include running, fashion, and world travel. Additional profile details include

- Active
- Outdoorsy
- Social
- Enjoy live music
- Have pets
- Possibility of children
- Commute from downtown Austin
- Enjoy going out at night

Community Summary

Callahan/Shutterstock.com

Austin, the capital of Texas, is located in south central Texas where the Colorado River crosses the Balcones Escarpment. It offers a chic city life surrounded by 14,000 square miles of Hill Country.

Austin is experiencing a population and cultural boom. This *Live Music Capital of the World®* plays to a diverse population of cultures including Hispanic, African-American, and Asian influences. The establishment of the University of Texas made Austin a regional center for higher education, as well as a hub for state government.

The Colorado River flows through the heart of the city, creating a series of sparkling lakes that stretch for more than 100 miles. Austin's climate is subtropical with prevailing southerly winds and an average of 300 days of sunshine each year. Summers are hot; winters are mild, with only occasional brief cold spells. Snow is rare.

Preferred Home Features

- Two-story house
- Green design features
- Large windows with deep sills
- Energy-efficient lighting
- Nine-foot and/or vaulted ceilings
- Efficient, clever, storage spaces including built-ins
- Loft

Required Spaces

- Kitchen/living/dining area; compact and efficient
- Two bedrooms minimum; master with walk-in closet
- Upstairs master bedroom preferred to capture view of nearby greenbelt area
- Laundry area
- One full and one-half bath (minimum)
- Study area
- Back door access to garage
- Central stairwell

Considerations

- Future needs of a small family
- Easily maintained interior materials
- Additional seating for guests

Drawing 1—Relational Bubble Drawings

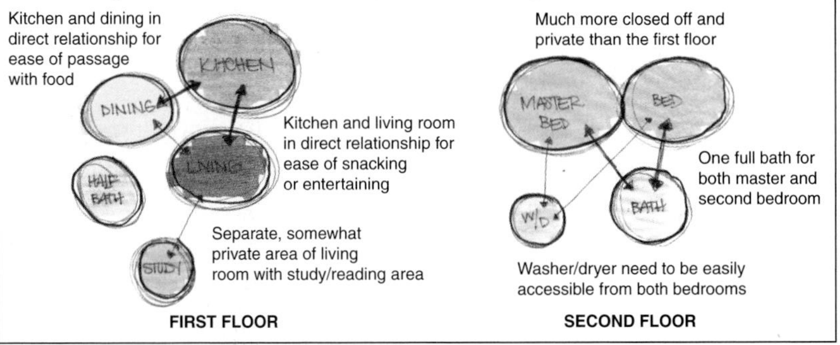

Drawing 2—Further-Analyzed Relational Bubble Drawings

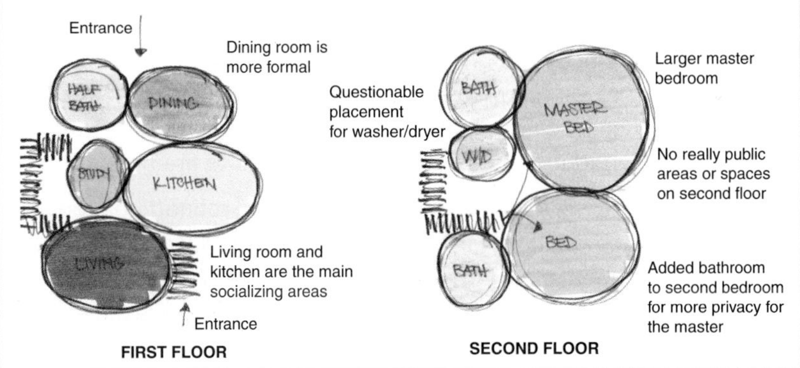

Drawing 3—General Bubble Drawings in Building Footprint

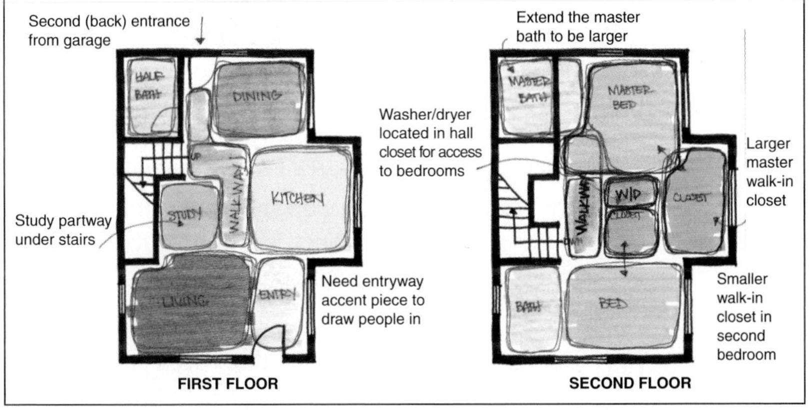

Emily Eyrich, Interior Design Student, Colorado State University

Drawing 4—Blocking in Building Footprint

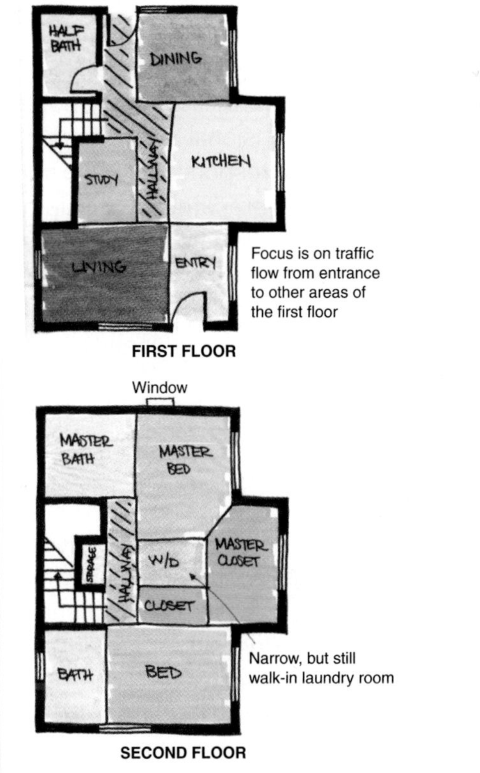

Drawing 5—Preliminary Furniture Plan

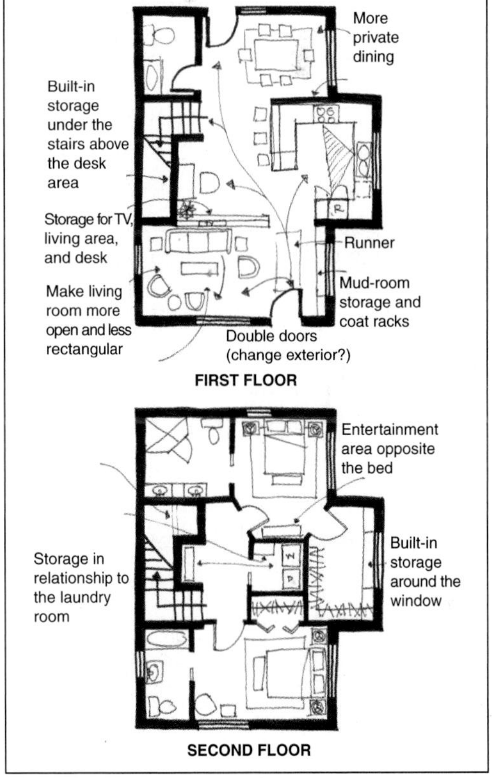

Investigate and Reflect

Discuss the designer's sketches for Raquel and Mike's home. Are there other changes the designer might suggest to help meet their current needs? For instance, could the second bedroom serve as an office or craft room until they decide to have children? Then use the Internet to research interior design case studies of similar client needs. How can studying these case studies improve your ideas and approach to client design solutions? Write a summary of your findings to share with the class.

Furniture, Fixtures, and Equipment (FF&E)

The designer uses **material boards** to communicate to the client proposed color palettes for the designed spaces. Again, where clients may not be able to envision a three-dimensional space from two-dimensional drawings, they do respond quickly to color preferences. Material boards—prepared by the interior designer—contain swatches of interior materials (for example, paint, wallpaper, window coverings, and flooring) as well as photographs of furniture proposed for the spaces based on the client's concept and program.

Budget Projection

The fifth task in the Schematic Design phase is the presentation to the client of the project costs based on the proposed design. This educated estimate lists the design fees, labor costs, and materials, and services of tradespeople. Respect for a client's budget is one of the surest ways to achieve client loyalty, satisfaction, and future referrals. By the end of this phase, the client should have a good idea of the concept, the proposed design solution, and how much it will cost.

Phase 4: Design Development (DD)

The Design Development (DD) phase is the refinement of designs and decisions the designer and client made in the Schematic Design phase. This, too, is a phase of critical analysis, problem solving, and creativity. Tasks to complete during this stage include

- floor plan revisions based on codes and laws
- revisions of furniture plans
- evaluation of building system details—mechanical, plumbing, electrical, and lighting plans
- refinement of interior material and furnishings
- development of interior architectural detailing
- refinement of the project budget
- client sign-offs and approval

All of these tasks include attention to sustainable-design strategies that may impact the revisions and final design. Skills the interior designer uses for this entire phase include space planning, furniture arrangement, computer skills using design-software programs, understanding construction documents, custom details, developing budgets, and using oral presentation skills.

Floor Plan

After approval of the floor-plan proposal in the Schematic Design phase, the designer now evaluates and refines the plan with the client's concept in mind. A key question might be: Are there elements of the concept reflected in the plan?

The designer and client also evaluate and refine the plans against local, regional, and national building codes. **Building codes** are regulations adopted by a community to govern the construction of buildings. Local governments enforce these standards to ensure the structural integrity of buildings and the safe evacuation of people in the event of fire. Such standards include hallway and doorway widths as well as size and height of windows from the finished floor. Seventy-five percent of the building codes relate to fire safety.

The proposed plans are also refined based on *Americans with Disabilities Act (ADA)* compliance. These standards significantly impact the remodel or new construction of commercial interiors. Public entities must comply with ADA regulations—as developed by the U.S. Department of Justice—that prohibit discrimination based on disability. Such strategies as building access and public restroom design influence refinements of space plans to meet ADA requirements.

After these tasks, the designer evaluates the plan against the Client Program. Questions to ask include: For a commercial project, are the departments or divisions that need to be next to each other placed as such? Are there enough offices or space for enough workstations planned into the design? For a residential project, is the family room next to the kitchen? Are there enough bedrooms?

Furniture Plan

The rough furniture plans from the Schematic Design phase are refined during this task. Multiple "what-if" scenarios take place to make sure the spaces are large or small enough to accommodate the furniture and equipment needs of the client. For instance, the designer may raise questions about the function of each space and the flow of human traffic from one space to another. The ability to envision each space in three dimensions is a critical skill at this point. The designer not only critically evaluates the shaping of space, but also analyzes the placement of furniture to ensure efficiency and comfort in the interior, **Figure 6-23**.

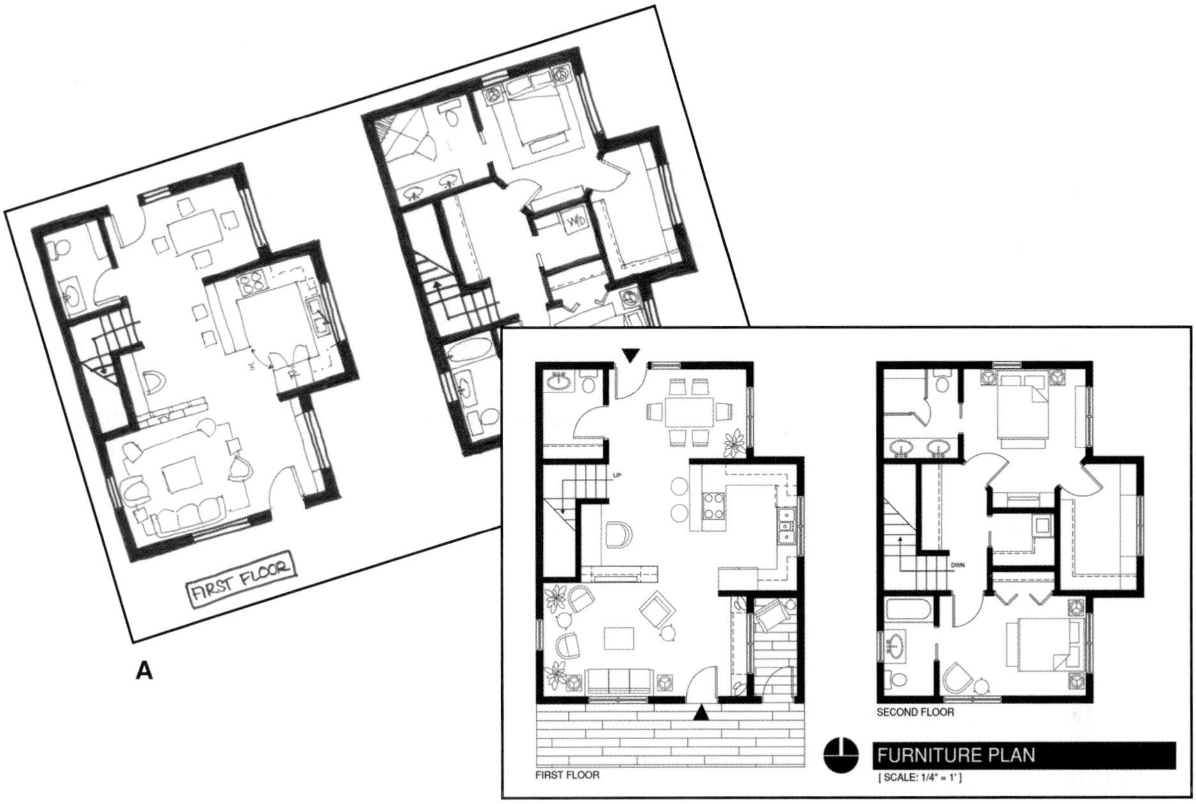

A

B

Emily Eyrich, Interior Design Student, Colorado State University

Figure 6-23 The rough furniture plan (A) from the Schematic Design phase is refined to meet the client needs during the Design Development phase (B). *How does this refined plan meet the Raquel and Mike Gonzalez's design preferences as outlined in the Case Study on pages 168–169?*

Evaluation of Building Systems

Interior designers do not design the mechanical, plumbing, and electrical systems of buildings but must know how the location of these systems directly influences the interior spaces. Therefore, designers critically analyze how the building systems impact the floor plan and furniture arrangements and make adjustments accordingly.

In particular, designers pay attention to the natural daylighting strategies and the lighting-design systems that influence the users' perception of interior space. Daylighting can cause glare that is avoidable through a variety of ways. Lighting designs can make or break the quality of an interior space. Designers pay attention to the color and location of light entering and existing in the spaces.

Refinement of FF&E

The basis for furnishings and interior materials selection is the client's concept. Interior materials include those that not only go on the walls, floors, and ceilings, but also those that designers select for the furnishings and equipment. Selections of colors, textures, and patterns come from the myriad of choices available. They must reflect the individual nature of the proposed design.

The designer also critically analyzes materials for maintenance and durability demands of the project. For a commercial interior, for example, the material choices for an office chair must meet certain industry standards to ensure durability and ease of maintenance.

The designer addresses sustainability issues during this task, too. For example, evaluating whether materials choices negatively affect indoor air quality or daylight strategies is one important task. Another is investigating whether wood flooring materials are from a renewable resource.

Development of Interior Architectural Details

After refining the floor plan, the designer explores, draws, and refines interior architectural details. Often, these are custom details that add interest and design to the spaces. These include such aesthetic elements as niches and soffits. At this time, the designer also creates designs for custom millwork for window and door moldings, bookcases, and baseboards. Such custom details should reflect the architecture of the building and the client's design concept, **Figure 6-24.**

Refinement of Projected Budget

As the designer refines the floor plan, furniture arrangement, and furnishings and materials selections, he or she adjusts and itemizes the proposed budget. For example, if furnishings selections are too expensive for the client budget, the designer locates similar but more budget-conscious replacements. The client's budget affects many of design ideas in this phase of comparisons and prioritization.

Client Approval and Sign-Offs

As with other phases of the design process, the designer makes a client presentation of the work to this point and acquires a sign-off of approval. If the client wants further changes, the designer makes revisions and additional presentations until reaching agreement with the client. All of these refinements lead to the development of construction documentations needed for Phase 5. Once the client approves the final design, the project moves forward into the final drawing and documentation phase of the design process.

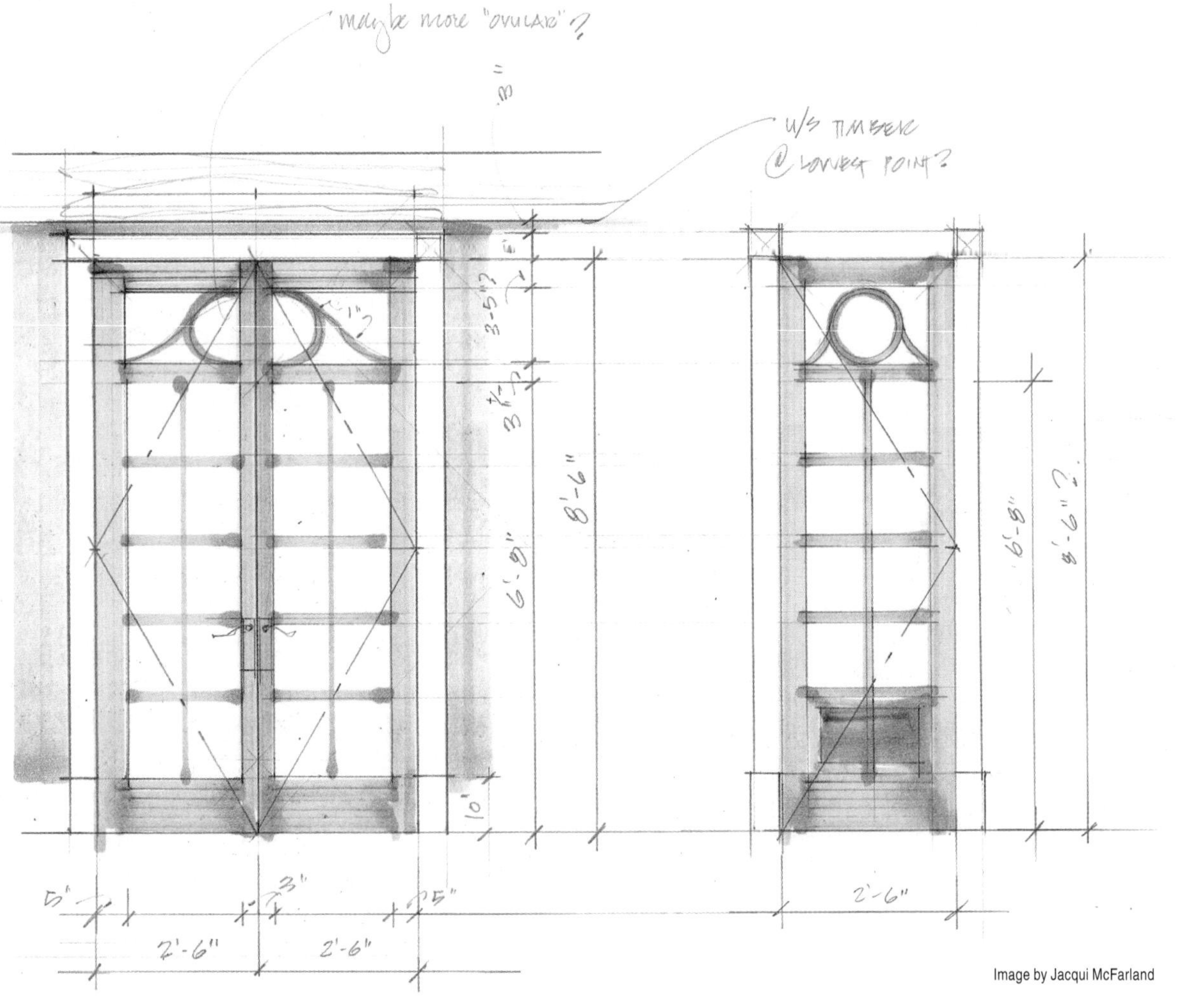

Image by Jacqui McFarland

Figure 6-24 This custom door detail shows the refinement of interior architectural details.

Phase 5: Contract Documents (CD)

The Contract Documents (CD) phase of the design process involves preparing formal, standards-driven documents for the construction and installation of the design. By the end of this phase, these documents become part of the legally binding agreement between client and designer regarding the proposal for building, installing, and executing the design plan. Refinement of budget continues through this phase. For a residential project, this phase may include writing purchase orders for furniture and fabrics.

Designers continue to use their organizational and budgetary skills, computer skills, ability to read working drawings, and professional communication skills that are critical for working with contractors and subcontractors. Although you may not prepare all documents during this phase, as the designer you need to understand the plans to ensure they accurately reflect the design concept.

Tasks the designer completes during Contract Documents include

- development of working drawings
- production of the specification book
- bidding, negotiating, and selecting a contractor
- acquiring client approvals and sign-offs

Working Drawings

Working drawings—or construction documents—are drawings that builders and tradespeople use to guide the building of a structure. Historically, these drawings were called *blueprints.* With computer design and drawing available today, use of blueprints is rare.

The goal of working drawings is to provide enough detail to clearly communicate to each tradesperson or subcontractor the work they are to do themselves and in relation to others on the team. Each trade has common sections in the plans that follow a specific order. Accurate labeling makes it easy to retrieve and understand the drawings, **Figure 6-25**. Working drawings include the

- **Title page** with name, project location, list of drawings enclosed, and general notes for the contractor to use during the construction process
- **Demolition plan** identifying existing areas of a building to demolish
- **Construction plan** indicating locations of walls, columns, partitions, doors, and windows with rooms and areas labeled in relation to each function, such as the kitchen—often with elevations and details that explain custom features related to the design
- **Furniture and equipment plans** that depict built-in cabinetry, furnishings, and equipment—often showing elevations and sections
- **Lighting plan,** which may also include drawings to show the location of architectural ceilings that interface with lighting fixtures and such other building systems as sprinklers and smoke detectors. (Lighting plans also include wall sconces and portable floor lamps.)
- **Mechanical plan** that describes the location and type of heating, ventilation, and air conditioning (HVAC) for installation in the building
- **Power and communications plan** that explains wiring information and the location for such technical systems as computers and security
- **Finish plan,** or a section of working drawings, that describe the type and location of materials to be installed on walls, windows, and floors
- **Door and window schedules** or tables that show the numbers, sizes, and locations for interior doors and windows

Many interior-design students who perform internships as well as entry-level interior designers assist in developing the working drawings using computers and specialized drawing and design software. People who are experts in their fields (electricians and plumbers) often prepare some of the working drawings. They generally use a standard document template and then send the drawings electronically for insertion into the set of working drawings. *Note*:

Denis Tabler/Shutterstock.com

Figure 6-25 Working drawings are construction documents that help guide builders and tradespeople in building the structure.

These working drawings are part of the building information management (BIM) system.

Specification Book

Working drawings offer a great deal of information to those who construct and install the client's design. There are many, many construction and design decisions that guide the quality of the work and selection of materials. Therefore, the designer or design team writes a specification book. The *spec book* contains the contract and noncontract documents for a particular client's project, **Figure 6-26**.

Specifications provide the precise written instructions that builders and tradespeople use to describe the appearance, performance, and construction methods for the building of the structure or interior. These specifications include manufacturer's brands, model numbers, and performance expectations. Drawings are notated, dimensioned, and properly cross-referenced with other drawings in the construction set. The quality and performance of items listed in the spec book relate directly to the quality and price of the finished building and interior.

Once the specifications book and working drawings are complete, the appropriate professionals (often the architects) *stamp* the drawings prior to the submission to the local government agency. The stamp or seal indicates the plans were developed by, or under the guidance of, an architect who holds licensure in the state. If the drawings are complete and appropriately communicated and located on-site, the government agency issues a **building permit**—authorization to construct the building in a specific location—for the client's project.

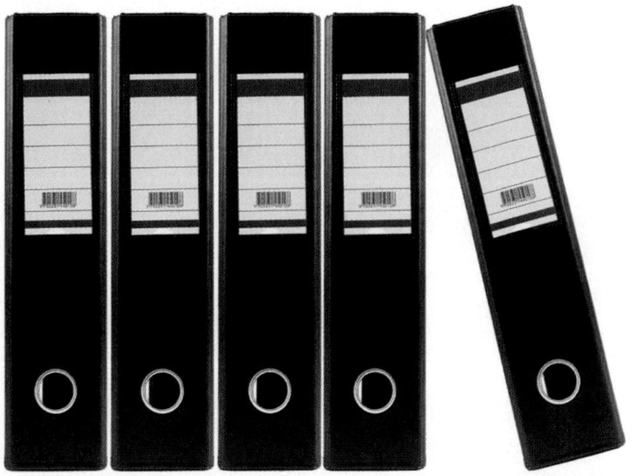

Kitch Bain/Shutterstock.com

Figure 6-26 The specification book (or books) provides the necessary instructions for implementing and completing a client's design project.

Bid Process and Selecting the Contractor

When the working drawings and specifications are complete, it is time to select the building contractor and subcontractors. If the client's project is large and complex, such as an educational institution, contractors participate in a **competitive bid process** in which each contractor submits a sealed envelope detailing the type of work to complete, by whom, and at what cost. This process begins with a *request for proposals (RFP)* including a list of specifications to a minimum of three firms. If the project is smaller, designers still advise their clients bid the work out to a variety of builders and subcontractors.

Client Approvals and Sign-Offs

After choosing a contractor and developing and refining all the documents, the designer puts them together as a set of contract documents. The client must approve these documents and sign off on them. If the client requests a change after signing these documents, the designer and contractor must develop and authorize any changes through a *change order*—a written order from the client directing the designer and contractor to modify a part of the project design, such as moving a window along a specific wall, **Figure 6-27**. All parties must sign the change order. Such modifications to the project become part of the contract documents and may include additional costs.

Phase 6: Contract Administration (CA)

The Contract Administration phase of the design process makes all the careful planning, analysis, and refinement worthwhile. The design comes to life! Along with having an eye for detail and knowledge of building systems, skills the designer uses during this phase include project management, administration skills, negotiation, teamwork, and collaboration with other professionals or subcontractors. Tasks the designer completes in this phase include

- scheduling and monitoring construction costs
- ensuring construction conforms with the contract documents and complies with building safety codes (the designer acts as a liaison with contractors and consultants throughout construction and reviews shop drawings and submissions from contractors)

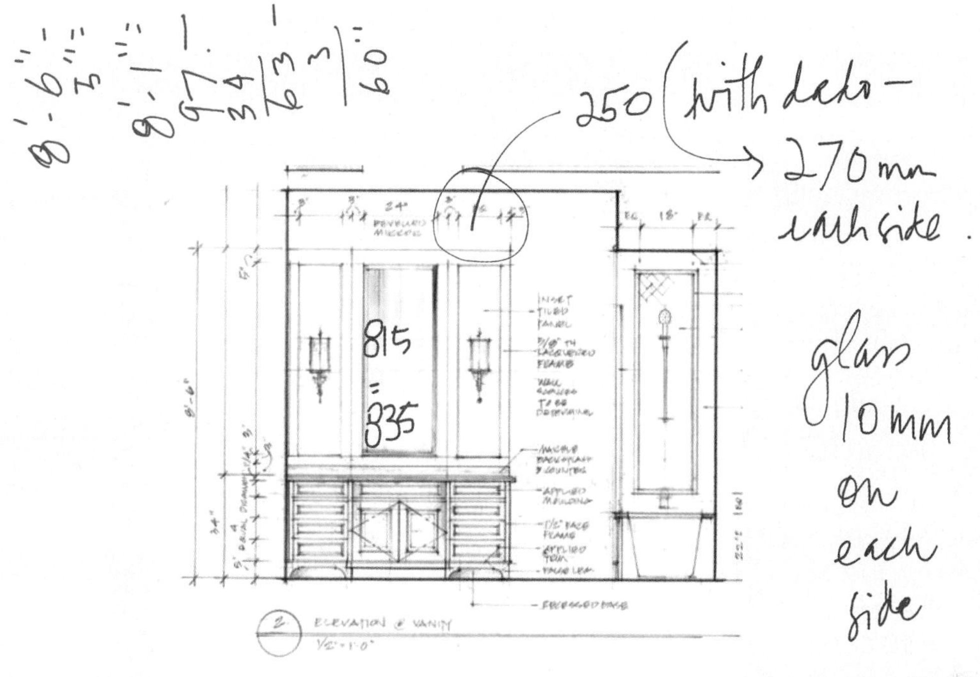

Image by Jacqui McFarland

Figure 6-27 The notes on this elevation drawing relate to a client change request. The designer then creates a written change order to modify the project.

- creating **punch lists**—checklists of items to complete before the final building inspection and client occupation—during and after construction
- monitoring final details—setting the client move-in date, installation of furniture, fixtures, and equipment (FF&E), and the client move

Scheduling and Monitoring Construction Costs

The contractor develops a time line for the project during this phase. Using the time line, the designer schedules the subcontractors and tradespeople one after the other according to current building practices.

The client's budget requires constant monitoring. Unexpected expenses may impact the estimates given in Phase 5. Therefore, negotiations continue through this phase to ensure the end product meets the client's budget.

Construction

Breaking ground and installing the foundation or beginning the demolition of a specific part of the building is always exciting. The designer and contractor ensure that construction conforms to contract documents and complies with building safety codes. The contractor is responsible for completion of the work and is liable for such, **Figure 6-28.**

auremar/Shutterstock.com

Figure 6-28 Because they are responsible for carrying out the design concept, interior designers meet regularly with the contractor and other personnel to observe progress and make needed corrections. *What results may occur if the designer fails to meet with contractors and other personnel?*

DESIGNER MATH SKILLS

Reading and Using a Tape Measure

When taking measurements, designers in the United States commonly use an American standard measuring tape versus a metric ruler. A trip to a hardware store will help you understand the numerous choices you have when selecting measuring tapes. They vary in information, clarity of numbers, flexibility, and durability. Select the measuring tape that helps you be the most accurate. Accuracy counts!

When learning to read a measuring tape (or ruler), the lines between the inch markers indicate *fractions*. Some measuring tapes label the fractions of an inch as $\frac{1}{8}$, $\frac{2}{8}$, $\frac{3}{8}$, $\frac{4}{8}$, $\frac{5}{8}$, $\frac{6}{8}$, $\frac{7}{8}$, while others provide only visual fraction marks. Since each inch is identical, you only need to learn how to read the fractions within one inch to read the rest of the measuring tape. Measurements can be "somewhat accurate" by rounding up for safe measure in certain instances. However, an interior designer must understand and utilize the $\frac{1}{16}$, $\frac{1}{8}$, $\frac{1}{4}$, $\frac{1}{2}$, inch markers exactly when ordering, cutting, and fitting materials. For example, if the stripes on wallpaper or the fabric on a chair do not match by $\frac{1}{4}$ inch, it is very noticeable! A granite countertop that is $\frac{1}{4}$ inch too wide can be costly to re-fabricate.

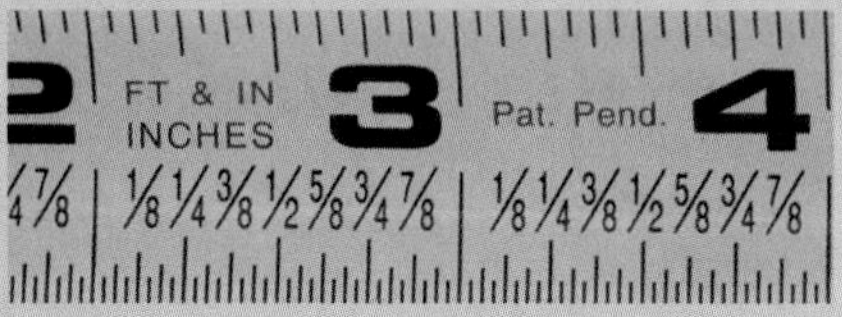

Theo Fitzhugh/Shutterstock.com

Looking at the ruler above, how many (red) lines are there between one inch and the next? The ruler has sixteen lines within one inch, allowing the designer to accurately measure to $\frac{1}{16}$ of an inch ($\frac{2}{16}$, $\frac{3}{16}$, $\frac{4}{16}$, $\frac{5}{16}$, and so forth). The eighth inch (blue) lines divide the inch into eight equal sections. The quarter divisions (green lines) indicate $\frac{1}{4}$ inch and black markers indicate $\frac{1}{2}$-inch and 1-inch divisions. Note: you would commonly refer to $\frac{2}{8}$" or $\frac{4}{16}$" as $\frac{1}{4}$ inch, while $\frac{4}{8}$ inch or $\frac{8}{16}$ inch indicates $\frac{1}{2}$ inch.

When writing measurements, you will write

- nine and three-eighths inches as 9 $\frac{3}{8}$"
- seven feet, four and one-half inches is written 7'-4 $\frac{1}{2}$"

auremar/Shutterstock.com

Interior designers serve as a liaison with contractors and consultants throughout construction process. They remain responsible for properly carrying the details related to their work. Therefore, designers regularly meet with the contractor and other responsible personnel. They routinely visit the building site to observe progress and share insights to correct anything overlooked in the design-related plans.

Designers review **shop drawings**—a set of drawings the contractor produces that show the contractor's understanding about the fabrication and installation of specific parts of the work on a project. For instance, shop drawings may show the manufacture and installation of an elevator, custom cabinetry, or ductwork for the heating and cooling system. Designers also order merchandise, such as flooring, wall and window treatments, and furnishings along with scheduling delivery and installation of such.

The interior designer is responsible for alleviating client anxiety. He or she ensures the project continues to move forward in a timely manner from the client's point of view.

Punch List

As the building or remodel moves to completion, the client, designer, and contractor develop a punch list.

A **punch list** may include something that still requires installation, repair, or replacement by the contractor prior to the client's move into the space. Punch-list items may include a simple carpet repair or the installation of a new window.

Phase 7: Move-In and Post-Occupancy Evaluation

The designer sets a move-in date for the client and uses this date to schedule proper delivery and placement of furnishings and equipment. For a large-scale commercial project, this can be a complex part of the design process.

There should be minimal disruption to your client's business to alleviate negative impact on their revenue generation. A business may only close a couple days to move hundreds of employees into a new space. This requires developing very detailed time lines. For a commercial remodel project, the designer makes every effort to minimize disruptions as construction and furniture installation takes place while work continues. Smaller residential projects require no less effort.

Clients often have existing furniture and equipment they wish to use in conjunction with new. Removal of these items from storage and their installation occurs simultaneously with the installation of new furnishings.

Assessing client satisfaction is one of the most often avoided or overlooked tasks in the design process. A designer is often busy with other client deadlines and moves on to his or her next project.

The end of the Move-In and Post-Occupancy Evaluation phase is when assessment of the client's or user's satisfaction occurs, **Figure 6-29**. If the client is not satisfied, an opportunity exists to make it right and preserve your good reputation. This is one of the most important tasks of this phase.

A **post-occupancy evaluation (POE)** is the systematic evaluation of the client's and user's opinions after project completion. During POE, the designer analyzes the client's original goals, identifies the problem, and compares them to the final design solution. Some questions the interior designer might ask include

- Were the client's intended goals and objectives satisfied?
- Was the client pleased and satisfied?

bikeriderlondon/Shutterstock.com

Figure 6-29 The Move-In and Post-Occupancy Evaluation gives both the client and designer an opportunity to evaluate the effectiveness of the final design. *How could failure to do this evaluation impact the client and the designer?*

- How could this information be used for a similar client problem in the future?

If a design uses sustainable strategies, the designer will file a checklist and documents with the United States Green Building Council (USGBC) to determine LEED rating. The evaluation of the design ensures the cycle is complete. The interior designer learns from each client's project what worked well and where to make potential improvements. This learning applies to future projects and helps ensure continuous improvement and future success.

The Process in Action

Understanding the differences between good and bad design is necessary as you begin your journey toward an interior design career. By learning the interior design process and practicing the various tasks involved in each phase, you will use your creativity as well as develop valuable career skills. **Figure 6-30** takes you on a visual tour through the design process from initial tasks to the final result. Remember, your goal as an interior designer is to meet the functional and aesthetic needs of your client's project.

The Process in Action

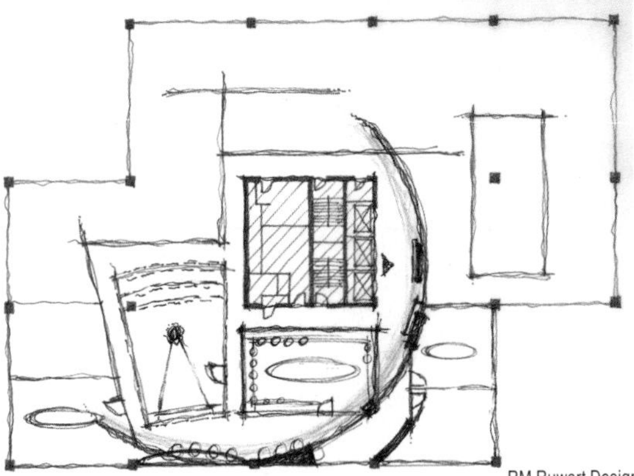

A General bubble diagram RM Ruwart Design, Rosalie M. Ruwart, ASID

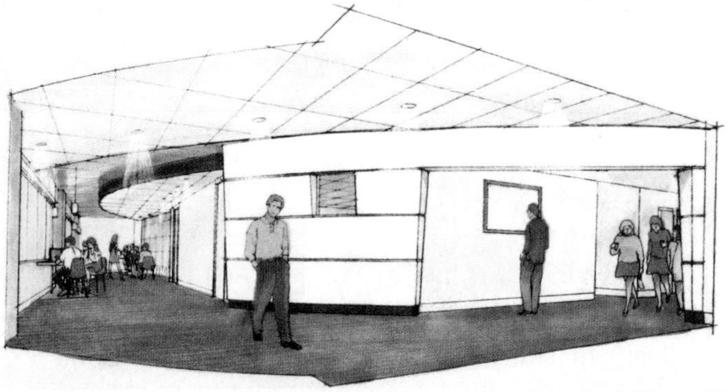

B Rendered perspective sketch RM Ruwart Design, Rosalie M. Ruwart, ASID

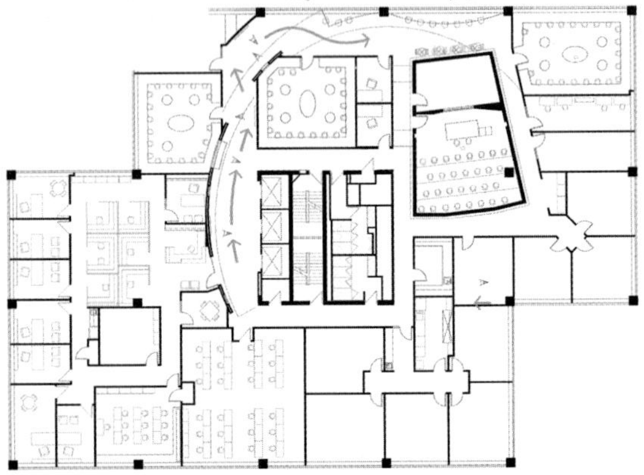

RM Ruwart Design, Rosalie M. Ruwart, ASID

C Furniture plan

D Final design RM Ruwart Design, Rosalie M. Ruwart, ASID/LaCasse Photography, Ed LaCasse

E Final design RM Ruwart Design, Rosalie M. Ruwart, ASID/LaCasse Photography, Ed LaCasse

Figure 6-30 From very initial sketches (A, B, and C) to the end result (D and E), the interior design process helps meet the functional and aesthetic needs of clients.

Chapter 6

Review and Assess

Summary

- Good design has endless benefits, but ultimately must be practical to meet client needs.
- Developing skills in creativity and innovation is critical for the interior design professional.
- Creative people find sources of inspiration through observation and engagement with their surroundings.
- A creative environment is one in which people feel acceptance and worth, and can think freely.
- Creativity and innovation are essential in developing products for interior spaces that promote the health, safety, and well-being (HSW) of clients.
- The design process is a method designers use to organize their work as they seek design solutions for clients.
- During the Pre-Design phase, the interior designer interviews the client to determine the client's problem, scope of the project, and whether the designer's skills match the client needs.
- The Programming phase involves fact-finding, client interviews, and on-site project analysis.
- During Schematic Design, the designer explores multiple solution ideas for the client's problem.
- During Design Development, the designer refines the designs and decisions made by the designer and client during the Schematic Design phase.
- During the Contract Documents phase, the designer prepares formal, standards-driven documents for the design construction and installation.
- As the design comes to life during Contract Administration, the designer manages all aspects of the project to ensure it meets the client's program.
- During the Move-In and Post-Occupancy Evaluation (POE) phase, the designer schedules the move-in date and systematically evaluates client satisfaction after project completion.

Chapter Vocabulary

Read the text passages that contain each of the following terms. Then write the definitions of each term in your own words. Double-check your definitions by rereading the text and using the text glossary.

adjacency matrix
block-and-stack diagram
block diagram
bubble diagram
building codes
building permit
client program
competitive bid process
criteria matrix
design concept
design process
desk audit
elevation
feasibility study
field measurements
furniture plan
general bubble diagrams
material board
matrix
model
perspective drawing
post-occupancy evaluation (POE)
punch lists
relational bubble diagram
scale
schematics
section
shop drawings
site visit
specifications
working drawings
zones

Review and Study

1. What are seven characteristics of a good design?
2. Give an example of poor design.
3. Contrast creativity and innovation.
4. List six sources of inspiration for a creative person.
5. What are the seven steps to design thinking?
6. Contrast convergent and divergent thinking. Give an example of when you might use each.
7. Name four techniques for enhancing creativity.
8. What are two ways the integrated design process (IDP) is collaborative?
9. What tasks occur during the Pre-Design phase?
10. List four major tasks that occur during the Programming phase of the design process.
11. What is the difference between an adjacency matrix and a criteria matrix?
12. How do relational bubble diagrams and bubble diagrams differ?
13. What are the five major tasks of the Schematic Design phase?
14. In addition to words, what other means does a designer use to express a concept to a client during the Schematic Design phase?
15. What is a furniture plan and how does a designer use it?
16. What tasks does a designer complete during Phase 4: Design Development?
17. What are working drawings?
18. How does the specifications book relate to the finished building and interior?
19. What must occur before construction and installation of the design begins?
20. What tasks must the designer complete during Phase 6: Contract Administration?

Critical Analysis

21. **Identify evidence.** Take a walking field trip around your neighborhood or community. Use the author's criteria for good and bad design to identify evidence of such in the buildings and structures you observe. Make a list of what you see and, if possible, take digital pictures. Discuss your list and photos in class.
22. **Analyze evidence.** Reread the passage on *The Creative Environment.* The author identifies several aspects that enhance creativity and several that do not. Think about these aspects in regard to your own environment. What qualities enhance or discourage creativity? How can you be intentional about maintaining an environment of creativity?
23. **Draw conclusions.** Review the tasks that occur during the Pre-Design phase. Draw conclusions about why each task is essential to client satisfaction with the final design. Discuss possible outcomes if the designer skips any Pre-Design tasks.
24. **Identify consequences.** The author states that post-occupancy evaluation is one of the most important and often overlooked tasks of Phase 7. Discuss the consequences for both the client and the designer for failure to complete this task.

Think like a Designer

25. **Writing.** Review the *Design Insight* quote at the beginning of the chapter. Based on the author's chapter content, write a summary expressing your interpretation of why and how design is a *noun*, *verb*, and a *problem-solving process*. Discuss your interpretation with the class.
26. **Creative thinking.** Examine the dwelling in which you live. Identify one design area you would like to change for better function and aesthetics. State your design issue as a question. Then choose one or more sources of inspiration to observe. Brainstorm a list of possible solution ideas and determine which options are realistic possibilities.
27. **Reading/writing.** Investigate a past or present design innovator. For instance, designers such as Mies van der Rohe, Michael Thonet, Charles and Ray Eames, Florence Knoll, and Marcel Breuer played significant roles in modern, innovative furniture design. Use Internet or print resources to read about this individual. Identify one or more of his or her design successes. Write a short summary of your findings to post to the class blog.

28. **Writing.** In teams, create client program for the following client who is remodeling the family kitchen. The family profile includes a parent (owner), three young teens, and a grandparent who uses a walker. Write a list of questions for an in-depth client interview for the Programming phase. Use the text and Internet resources. Be sure to include questions for each user. Discuss your team's questions with other teams for identifying client needs and preferences.
29. **Schematic design practice.** Suppose your new client wants to add a master bedroom suite during a home remodel. The suite is to include a sleeping area, sitting area, closet storage, and an en suite five-piece bath (toilet, double sinks, bathtub, and separate shower). Create a bubble diagram for this master suite.
30. **Design development practice.** Create a *final* material board for the bubble diagram you created in item 29. Choose interior materials samples for such finishes as paint, tile, flooring, counters, and window coverings. Add photos for fixtures and other materials. Arrange the material board to encourage client understanding.
31. **Math practice.** Using a measuring tape, accurately measure and record your measurements for the following:
    - height, width, and depth of a cell phone
    - dollar bill
    - height, width, and depth of a classroom chair
    - length and width of a rectangular classroom

Design Application

32. **Small-space design.** Suppose Alena, your latest client, just purchased two shipping containers and wants to convert them into a weekend getaway space. Alena has a limited budget, but desires the following spaces: sleeping areas—one for herself and one for a guest or two, bathroom, an efficiency kitchen with dining space, and a living area. Use your knowledge of interior design phases (theory) to complete Programming and Schematic Design tasks.
    A. Complete the following Programming tasks:
       - create a list of questions for your client interview
       - identify Alena's preferences and resources
       - research and gather key facts, including shipping container dimensions, measurements, and photos
       - analyze your data collection
       - create an adjacency matrix and bubble diagram to represent Alena's preferences and your ideas for the space
       - prepare a summary and present the information to Alena (the class)

    B. Complete the following Schematic Design tasks:
       - develop a concept to guide the design decisions for Alena's containers and create a way to clearly express the concept to her
       - create bubble and block diagrams by hand to explore the physical layout of the space within the shipping containers
       - draw a furniture plan to determine whether each room or area needs more space
       - create a material board with swatches of interior materials and photographs of furniture you propose for the spaces based on Alena's concept and program (or create a digital material board)
       - estimate the project costs and present your Schematic Design plans to Alena
33. **Portfolio builder.** Write a summary of your design thinking for the project in item 32. Include this summary, along with the products you created (print or digital) for the design in your traditional portfolio or e-portfolio.

The Elements and Principles of Interior Design

Warren Diggles Photography/Jon Rentfrow, Rentfrow Designs, LLC

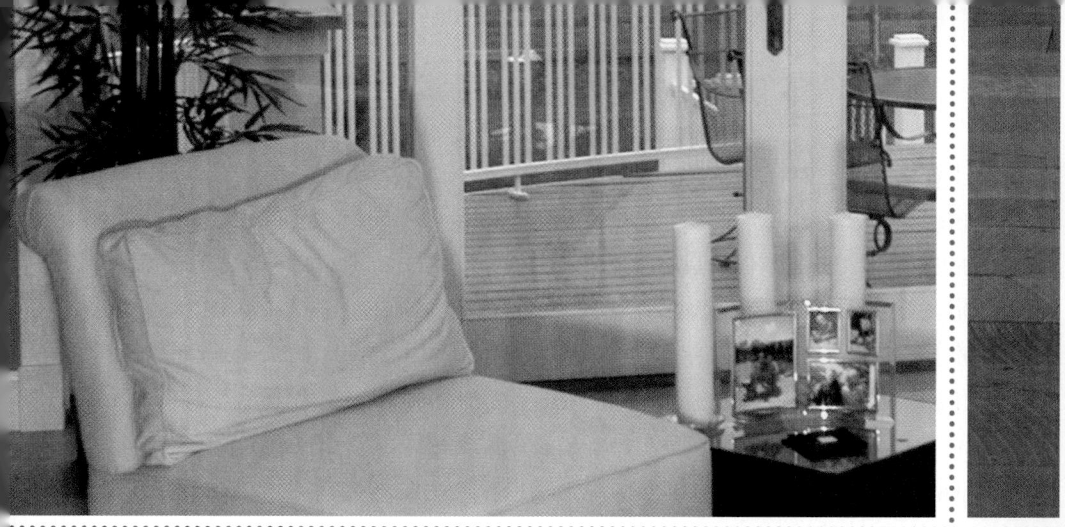

Chapter 7

Design Insight

"Thoughtfully designed spaces help us learn, reflect, imagine, discover, and create."

International Federation of Interior Architects/Designers (IFI), 2011

Learning Targets

After studying this chapter, you will be able to

- identify the vocabulary of the elements and principles of the design of interior spaces.
- analyze the elements and principles of design and their use in interior spaces.
- apply the elements and principles of design to interior spaces.

Introduction

There is something wonderful and exciting about the elements and principles of design. Perhaps it is because *how* you use them differentiates your interior spaces from other places. Possibly it is through the innovative use of them you express your creativity in an interior. When applied in a personal space, they express your individuality. When applied in a client's space, they are the tools and guidelines used to innovatively solve problems and reflect your client's preferences in design.

Design Tools and Guiding Rules

The elements and principles of design are the fundamental design vocabulary of the profession. They are the tools and guidelines designers use to create, discuss, and evaluate good design in aesthetic, but functional spaces.

The **elements** of interior design—line, shape, form, space, texture, pattern, color, and light—are the *tools* used to achieve the **principles** of interior design—guidelines that govern choices and actions designers take to achieve good design—including proportion, scale, focal point, balance, rhythm, and harmony. If used together properly, they produce a quality designed space. If used improperly, the space often appears ugly or chaotic. A sense of beauty and order are both essential components of a well-designed space.

To understand the relationship of elements to principles, consider two other artistic fields: music and culinary arts.

- To compose music, the proper combination of notes, dynamics, and tempo (elements of music) achieve harmony (principle of music). This combination results in a pleasing melody or tune.
- In culinary arts, the chef combines spices and ingredients (elements) according to a recipe or formula. With harmonious display (principle), these elements result in a beautifully presented and yummy-tasting dish.

As you walk into every space, begin to ask yourself, how does this space make me feel? How did the designer achieve this look? Focus on the *details* of *how* the elements and principles are used. Is the ceiling too high or too low to make you feel comfortable? Does the light add drama to the space or is it too dim to read a book? Does its shape and size please you? Is the wall color enchanting or do you find it depressing? Is there an intriguing alcove created by a volume of space? Is there a charm created by a mixture of specific textures? The way elements and principles of design are applied differentiate one space from another, **Figure 7-1**.

The world of interior design unfolds as you realize that the power of creating spaces begins with your proper use and application of the elements and principles. Before beginning your study of them, it is important to know several factors.

- Clients routinely expect interior designers to be creative on demand. At the same time, well-designed spaces require thoughtful consideration of client needs. Proper use of the elements and principles offers designers a systematic approach to more quickly achieve this goal.
- Good design rarely results from intuition or instinct, but from proper use of the design elements and principles.
- It is important to *observe* the application of the elements and principles of design in the spaces around you. Start now. As you study and analyze them, their use becomes second nature.
- The elements and principles of interior design are not used singly or in isolation. Different combinations create a unique space.
- The application of the elements and principles of design does not have the same exactness as physics or mathematics. A designer cannot neatly categorize and describe them. Instead, their flexibility allows the interior designer to creatively manipulate and interpret them, sometimes with great fancy or fun.

©Jim Roof Creative. Inc./Rabaut Design Associates

Figure 7-1 Quality interior design results from proper use of the elements and principles of design.

- The interior designer may use elements and principles of design in a conversation with experts in another discipline but with different meanings. For instance, architects use *primary elements and ordering principles* of architecture in which the elements and principles have different meanings. This may complicate communication with team members from other disciplines.

The elements and principles are the language of the profession. Similar to learning a foreign language, it is important to learn not only how to apply them but to speak the language accurately as you explain, defend, and evaluate designs to your client or the public. The elements and principles communicate design decisions—they become your vocabulary to explain your choices.

Elements of Interior Design

The elements of interior design are key tools in developing design plans for your clients. For this text, the elements of interior design include *line, shape, form, space (volume), texture, pattern, color,* and *light*.

Line

As the most basic element of design, a **line** connects two points, **Figure 7-2**. Lines serve as visual grammar throughout the world. Lines

- exist as a single dimension
- are greater in length than width
- can create order in a composition
- shift direction

Vlue/Shutterstock.com

Figure 7-2 Lines exist in a single dimension and connect two points.

- can be thick or thin, segmented or dashed
- can be straight or curved

Lines are directional. They can give the impression of movement in a space. A space generally uses a combination of lines, although it is not uncommon for one type of line to dominate an interior. There are four types of lines: horizontal, vertical, diagonal, and curved, **Figure 7-3**.

- **Horizontal lines.** Parallel to the horizon, the perceptions of horizontal lines include feelings of calmness, stability, solidness, restfulness, and security.
- **Vertical lines.** Perpendicular to the horizon, vertical lines communicate height, strength, and dignity. They are more formal than horizontal lines.
- **Diagonal lines.** Suggesting movement or action, diagonal lines are angled, jagged, or zigzag lines.
- **Curved lines.** Communicate movement but with a graceful feel, curved lines are wavy and flowing; gentle and sometimes delicate. Curved lines introduce a sense of whimsy or energy to a design. If curved lines are poorly constructed, overused, or used inconsistently, the space can look too busy, cluttered, or chaotic.

Within interiors, lines create movement and have the ability to direct the eye visually, moving a person around the room without taking a physical step. They can increase or decrease the impression of height, produce textures and patterns, and alter the physical dimension of the space.

Lines can draw attention to an architectural feature such as a fireplace and follow the contour of objects. In addition, lines convey emotions. For instance, delicate lines seem soothing and serene while bold, jagged lines suggest explosive energy. Lines can also create a sense of calm or a feeling of strength.

Use of horizontal lines alters the perception of space by visually expanding it. They direct the eye around a room rather than up into the volume of space. Therefore, they communicate informality, calmness, and serenity. They visually anchor a person in the space.

Indicative of earth's horizon, floors are the common horizontal line people see in interiors. Use of horizontal lines in contemporary spaces generates a minimalistic sleek style. An interior designer can add them with beams in a ceiling, a wall of short cabinets, low bookshelves, long pieces of built-in furniture, counters, or conference tables, **Figure 7-4 A and B**.

Too many horizontal lines can

- generate boredom due to lack of variety
- close in a space and develop a sense of foreboding
- enhance the feeling that the ceiling or roof is too low

Vertical lines lift the eye upward in a space. Their use is common in buildings such as Gothic cathedrals and other places of worship to inspire awe. In comparison to these vast spaces, the size of humans seems greatly diminished. Vertical lines make an interior ceiling appear higher, perceptually creating more volume. In an interior, vertical lines appear as columns, tall pieces of furniture, stairwell spindles, vertical louvers, and tall, graceful draperies, **Figure 7-5**.

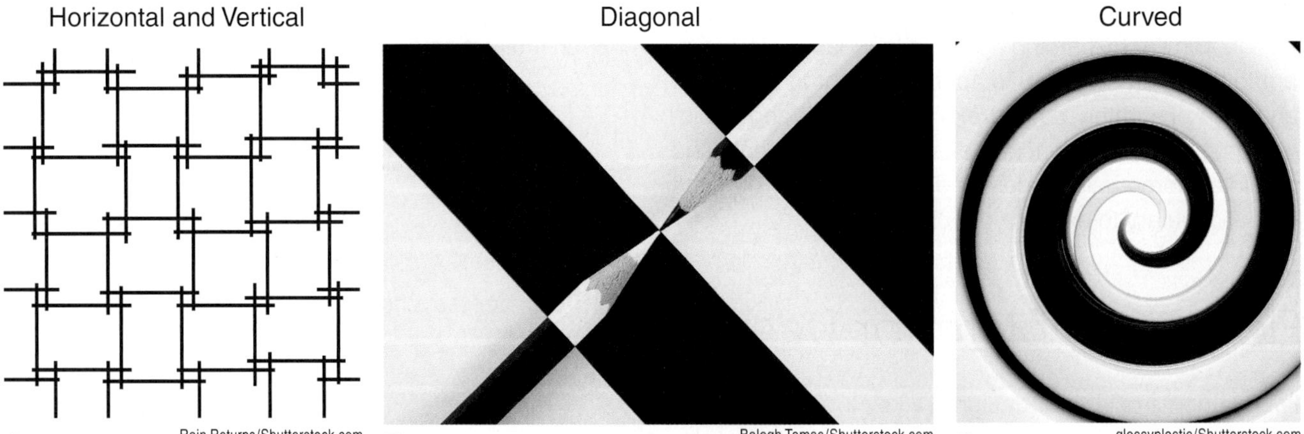

A Rain Returns/Shutterstock.com
B Balogh Tamas/Shutterstock.com
C glossyplastic/Shutterstock.com

Figure 7-3 Lines create movement in a space and visually direct the eye, and can be (A) horizontal and vertical, (B) diagonal, and (C) curved. *Discuss ways each type of line is used in the environments around you.*

A Designer: Aneka Jensen/Photography: Damon Searles Photography B Kuznetsov Alexey/Shutterstock.com

Figure 7-4 Vertical lines (A) direct the eye upward while horizontal lines (B) direct the eye around a space.

Builder: Woodmont Properties/Photographer: Fred Forbes/Designer: Lita Dirks + Co.

Figure 7-5 The vertical lines in this living room add height and dignity to this interior space.

Formal spaces often use vertical lines and generate a psychological impression of steadiness and strength as well as simplicity, height, and dignity. In residences, you will find vertical lines used in dining rooms, entryways, and living rooms. In commercial spaces, they often appear in lobbies, theaters, and entryways. Too many vertical lines can

- seem stiff or overly formal
- lack *grounding* in the space, or a place for the eye to comfortably land in the space
- take the eye up rather than around the room

Diagonal lines create drama and excitement in a space. They move the eye across an interior more quickly than any other type of line. Therefore, diagonal lines can camouflage awkward corners by moving the eye swiftly across the space. They attract attention and add a sense of energy. In interiors, uses for diagonal lines include staircases, vaulted ceilings, and contemporary furniture, **Figure 7-6**. In a space, too many diagonal lines can produce feelings of

- instability and too much motion
- unrest and overstimulation
- fatigue or restlessness

Curved lines replicate the sinuous lines of the human body and most objects found in nature. They can be organic and irregular or sturdy and fanciful. In interiors, you can see them in arches, drapery swags, room shapes, curved furniture, and domes. Curved lines

Builder: Woodmont Properties/Photographer: Fred Forbes/Designer: Lita Dirks & Co.

Figure 7-6 Diagonal lines create a feeling of movement. *How does the designer use diagonal lines in this space?*

provide relief and grace to horizontal or diagonal lines. Tight downward curves generate feelings of sadness while large upward curves suggest gentle relaxation. Too many curved lines

- become tiresome or too ornate
- make people feel seasick (perceptually)
- communicate instability and fussiness

A balanced use of line—as a design element—creates a feeling of comfort and cohesiveness in a space. In interior design practice, designers also use lines for such things as sketches and floor plans, **Figure 7-7**.

takito/Shutterstock.com

Figure 7-7 Interior designers use all types of lines in creating floor plans. *What types of lines can you identify on this plan?*

Shape

When the beginning and end points of any line meet, a **shape** is created. You can see shapes in nature and within interior spaces. Shapes

- are two dimensional
- are angular and sharp or curved and rounded
- become a pattern when repeated

There are several categories of shapes. Geometric shapes suggest order and regularity. They include circles, triangles, rectangles, and squares, **Figure 7-8**.

A ihor_seamless/Shutterstock.com B ihor_seamless/Shutterstock.com C SSylenko/Shutterstock.com; Iriana Shiyan/Shutterstock.com

Figure 7-8 Geometric shape is just one category of shape used in interior design. These shapes include (A) circles, (B) triangles, and (C) rectangles or squares.

- **Circles.** Symbolizing infinity, unity, continuity, femininity, safety, and protection, circles confine what is within them and keep other things out. Their use in design is less common; therefore, they attract attention. Use them sparingly for more impact.
- **Triangles.** Symbolizing stability, action, and masculinity, triangles give the feeling of dynamic energy.
- **Rectangles and squares.** Symbolizing solidity, order, formality, security, and equality, rectangle shapes are more pleasing to the eye than square ones. Most interior spaces are rectangular and, therefore, most construction materials support this shape. Squares are stable, serene, and represent the pure and rational. Repetitive use of square shapes is pleasing to the eye.

Organic, or shapes based on nature, are pleasing and suggest constancy, comfort, and spontaneity. More curved than angular, they are interestingly irregular in their design. Two organic or natural types of shapes include *amoeba-like curves* that are meandering and irregular, and *spirals* that symbolize creativity, expansion, and transformation (often found in such items as seashells).

In interiors, one shape may predominate, such as a square or rectangle. Using multiple types of shapes in the same room is ideal. Using only one shape in a room can produce monotony or boredom. Too many of both types of shapes create chaos and a lack of order that is difficult for the human brain to process. What is the result in either case? The person will leave the room.

Repeated use of identical shapes produces movement in a space and carries the eye around a room, **Figure 7-9**.

An interior designer can modify or enhance shapes by using elements such as light, color, and texture.

In interior design practice, there are many uses for shapes. These include

- company logos
- directional signage
- interior materials (patterned fabrics)
- furniture plans
- accessories (area rug)

pics721/Shutterstock.com

Figure 7-9 Using multiple shapes in a room is ideal. *What shapes can you identify in this image?*

Form

A **form** results from the combination of line, shape, and volume. Volume adds the third dimension to a shape, **Figure 7-10**. When a two-dimensional shape (square) moves into the third dimension, it becomes a form (cube).

Rectangular and square forms—which are most commonly used in interior design and architecture—appear as floors, beams, and columns that support the weight of a structure. You can also see them as dropped soffits and floating ceilings in a space, **Figure 7-11 A and B**.

Triangular shapes become forms known as pyramids and cones. They give a sense of visual stability. Circular forms (spheres and cylinders) often appear in domes, columns, or accessories. Every piece of furniture and three-dimensional accessory is a type of form.

Forms can be solids and voids. A *solid* is the object itself—a positive in the space—such as a column or piece of furniture. A *void* is a negative area or hollow space, such as a hallway or stairwell. These forms can have a powerful influence in the composition of a space.

Forms, solid or void, define space and need space. They shape space merely by their placement and presence in an interior. Interior designers use forms to direct the user within the space, thereby manipulating human behavior. For example, as you walk through an interior space, if a chair is near the entrance you will walk around it. Be aware of the responsibility and delight in shaping human behavior for good.

Forms are not always static or positioned in a space. You can move a chair or pull down a blind. In addition, the human body is an ever-moving form. As people enter a room, they reshape the space.

From early infancy, people see forms all around them in the three-dimensional world. They collect forms as personal belongings that describe who they are. When people place furnishings, accessories, and other types

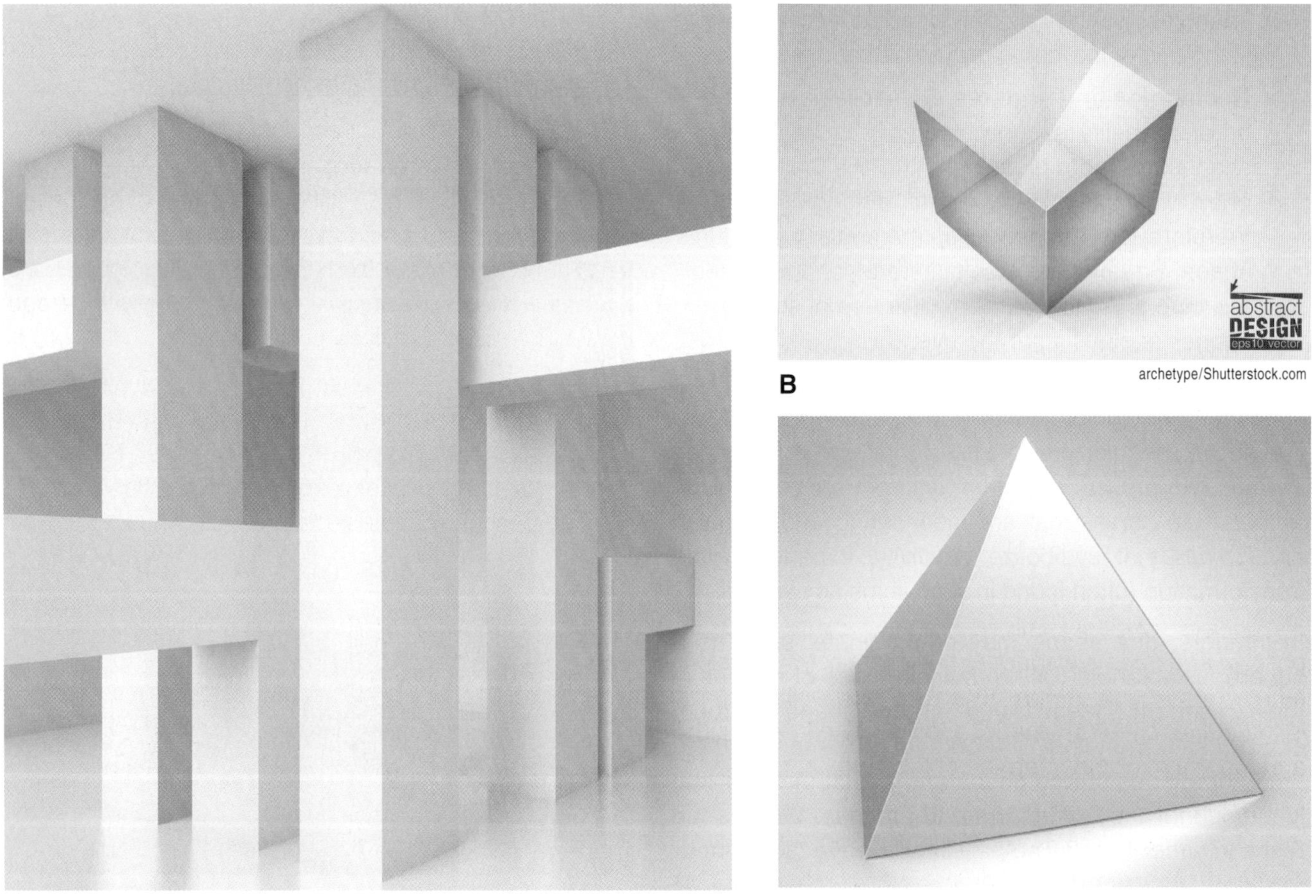

A Max Krasnov/Shutterstock.com

B archetype/Shutterstock.com

C ThreeArt/Shutterstock.com

Figure 7-10 Forms are three dimensional and include (A) rectangular forms, (B) cubes, and (C) pyramid forms.

Design by: Lita Dirks & Co./Photo by: Brian Gassel Photography

A

©Ron Pollard, courtesy of RNL

B

Figure 7-11 Interior designers may use several shapes in a space. *What shapes can you identify in these images (A and B)? How are the shapes used in these spaces?*

of forms in their private spaces, they communicate a sense of self and express their individuality.

Space planning involves moving forms, such as walls and partitions, within a space. When using forms in interiors,

- consider the height and width of forms in a space. For example, high-backed chairs visually divide a space.
- incorporate design details. Forms give a space identity, character, charm, and integrity.
- realize that forms indicate cultural differences. The details of a Chinese-inspired chair are different from an English Queen Anne chair.
- understand that forms change the mood and visual interest of any space.

Space

Space is boundless until boundaries shape it. Using positive and negative space is important in the development of any composition, **Figure 7-12**. Positive space is the actual object or image, and negative space is the area around and between the object and image.

In the built environment, a physical space is an area defined by some type of enclosure. Often, interior space is a three-dimensional volume comprised of walls, floors, and ceilings. Physical space is the area in which people live, contemplate, excel, and enjoy life. Interior space is limited and expensive due to building expense and taxes allocated to both commercial and residential buildings. Because of these factors, space should be maximized, well-planned, functional, and beautiful. Designing and manipulating interior space has its challenges. Each space has a different amount of enclosure, a different relationship to adjoining spaces, and a different set of user needs and preferences. People or corporations often hire interior designers for their ability to visualize and manipulate space creatively yet functionally.

Space is endless until it has definition. It can be simple and inexpensive to create a space. For instance, in the outdoors a simple blanket on the ground defines space. In contrast, in an interior an area rug on a floor defines space and achieves the same goal.

Jef Thompson/Shutterstock.com

Figure 7-12 Effective use of positive and negative space helps create interest in a space.

Designer Profile

Kia Weatherspoon, Allied ASID—Passionate for Design

Kia Weatherspoon, principal of DETERMINED by DESIGN in Washington, D.C., was a dancer turned soldier who fell in love with interior design. Read more about Kia's unplanned, inspiring path to a career in interior design.

Designer: Kia Weatherspoon, Allied ASID/Firm: Determined by Design

"Interior designers are visual storytellers. Instead of words we use walls, shapes, textures, lighting, furniture, and a variety of materials to get the *reader* enthralled into a space. No two stories are alike; likewise no two spaces are alike. There may be similarities, however, but a writer's source of inspiration is unique and specific to him or her. This is also true for interior design. The most valuable tool you have is your ability to tell *your* individual design story. Think about what led you to interior design?

"Once you have pinpointed the passion for your purpose, learn how to share it with as many people as possible. This is important because *your* passion will ultimately come through in every space you create. *Your* story will inevitably set you apart from every other designer. Know your design story and start every project from that place of inspiration. Here is some insight into my passion for design.

"After 13 years of training as a ballet dancer, collegiate pursuit of my childhood passion was inevitable. What I did not foresee was the inability to afford my dream at the university level. My solution to the lack of financial aid led me to the U.S. Air Force in 2001. My plan was simply to utilize the military's educational benefits to pay for my academic endeavors. I intended to serve my country during the day and continue my dance education at night. The unforeseen tragedy of September 11th, however, altered my plans.

"Shortly after 9-11, I was deployed to the Middle East to a bare base—in lay terms imagine sand, tents, aircraft hangers, and more sand. In a shared space with fifteen other women, I needed a reprieve. I needed a place to let out the flood of emotions I was feeling—it was my first time away from my family and out of the country.

"What I lacked, thousands of miles away from home, was privacy and a sense of comfort. So, when military supply issued troops sheets and miscellaneous items for our tent-city living quarters, I didn't put them on my cot for comfortable sleep. Instead, I took some string, hung it from the top of the tent, and created three sheet-walls around my cot. This was the first space I created—a space that wasn't dictated by extravagant finishes and furniture. It was a space that evoked an emotional reaction and a lasting memory. When I left the military in 2004, I knew I wanted to create spaces."

You can read more about Kia's design experience in Appendix B.

Boundaries organize interior space even if they are not structural or permanent. Inside a restaurant, sitting in a booth, space is defined by its partitions and seating. In an office building, glass panels may establish boundaries, **Figure 7-13 A and B**.

The height of walls, ceilings, windows, doorways, balconies, and stairwells individualizes an interior space. Commercial hotel foyers, for example, appear unique depending on these features.

As you walk from one room to another or one enclosed area to another, you experience the interior space. The quality of interior space—its ability to comfort or serve as a sanctuary—is what you experience and remember.

In an interior, the size of openings has a significant impact on the human sense of containment. In addition, how much of the space is enclosed impacts feelings about that space. For example, in a room with many windows, the space appears lighter and more open than in a space with one small window, **Figure 7-14**.

As a person moves through an interior space, he or she may find small or large as well as partially or fully

A

Dorian C. Shy/Shutterstock.com

Figure 7-13 Boundaries help shape a space. *How are boundaries created in the restaurant space (A) and the office space (B)?*

B

Haworth, Inc.

enclosed spaces. This makes investigating a home or commercial building exciting or, at times, bewildering.

Large and small spaces have an appeal to clients. Each has advantages and disadvantages.

Small spaces

- offer feelings of comfort and security
- become places for solitude that are personalized
- establish territory and ownership
- can be restricting or confining

Large spaces

- enhance a sense of freedom
- invite more people
- allow larger movements and actions
- offer flexibility for change
- can create feelings of insecurity

An interior designer can use many different architectural elements to define space without the use of four walls as physical boundaries. A designer can

- add a half-wall
- include columns
- add a step up or down
- mark boundaries on a floor (area rug)
- interlace different spaces together

Photograph: David O. Marlow/Interiors by Associates III Interior Design

Figure 7-14 The size of openings impacts the human sense of containment. *Describe how the interior designer creates a sense of openness in this space.*

- add windows
- drop the ceiling
- incorporate freestanding objects

Space can be real or perceived. For example, a three-dimensional computer model of an interior space is an example of an *illusionary space*—a space that does not yet exist. Interior designers often sell their clients on spaces they design with drawings of perceived space. Assisting a client to understand perceived space is a continual challenge for a designer, **Figure 7-15**.

Perceived, rather than physical, space involves the human senses—sight, hearing, touch, and smell. As you enter a space, your senses process information and send it to your brain. This results in a perceptual experience—either good or bad.

People experience or perceive space differently, **Figure 7-16**. In part, this relates to their physical dimensions, such as height or reach (human measurements), which allows them to move or operate within the space. It also depends on the health of their eyes when perceiving a color used in the space and on their cultural upbringing, such as how comfortable they feel when someone stands close to them in a public place.

Clearly, many factors impact your client's spatial experience. It is important to understand that a designer must not only know how to manipulate the physical space, but must also appreciate that people perceive and experience designed physical spaces differently.

Texture

Texture, as a surface characteristic, exists in all natural and built environments. It is the characteristic that invites people to explore an object or material through touch. It creates intriguing interest in a space or place. It evokes a human response such as warmth or pleasure and enhances a mood or feeling in an interior. Texture makes a space exciting and filled with life or cozy and moody. Discussion of texture falls into two categories—tactile and visual.

Tactile Texture

Tactile texture, or surface texture, is real—you can feel it through simple human touch, **Figure 7-17**. It communicates a great deal about a place. For instance, whether you are in a forest or a skyscraper, tactile textures

Photo by: E.L. imagery/Design by: Lita Dirks & Co.

Figure 7-15 The elements of design help create perceptions about a space. *What elements did the interior designer use to shape the perception you have about this dining room?*

Using Perception to Shape Space	
To make small, physical spaces look larger, consider use of	**To make large, physical spaces feel cozier, consider use of**
■ mirrors	■ medium- to larger-scaled patterns
■ continuity of color	■ dark or vivid colors to perceptually make walls advance
■ windows as connections to the outdoors	■ heavier- or larger-scaled furniture
■ fewer structural barriers	■ placement of area rugs to break up expanses of space
■ higher quality electric light or daylight	■ multiple furniture groupings
■ half-walls	■ lowered light fixtures
■ wider door openings to visually open a space	■ darker color paint on ceilings
■ low and minimal furniture	■ *wainscoting*—an interior wall treatment that covers the lower part of the wall to about four feet above the floor
■ built-in storage	■ *chair rails*—strips of wood on interior walls that are placed about four feet above the floor
■ vertical lines	

Figure 7-16 Interior designers use many different items to shape your perception of a space.

Reinhold Leitner/Shutterstock.com JoeyPhoto/Shutterstock.com krsmanovic/Shutterstock.com

Figure 7-17 Texture evokes many different human responses.

- bring character and visual interest to the space.
- become a maintenance factor. It is more difficult to clean a tactile texture than a visual texture. Similarly, visual textures may show fingerprints.
- impact light reflection and absorption and therefore modify color. For example, if light is trapped in a texture, the color of the material appears darker than if you see it on a smooth, reflective texture.
- absorb sound. Soft or rough textures absorb sound and hard, smooth textures reflect it. Sound bouncing around a room is irritating, such as in a kitchen when several people are talking.
- provide comfort or irritation to the human body depending on the selection of materials and construction (such as wool fabric).

Smooth textures, such as satin, shiny metal, and polished glass, give the perception of formality and sleekness in style. They can also communicate a cold and impersonal mood. In contrast, rough, coarse textures suggest informality and casual comfort. Course textures also communicate warmth and replicate features of nature. In interiors, you can see tactile texture on upholstery and in window treatments, in such flooring as acoustical tile, bricks, woods, metals, and stones, **Figure 7-18**. Tips for using texture in interiors include

- using tactile textures of different types in the same space to please the eye. For example, glass in contrast to a rough, deep-pile rug is a strong design statement.
- realizing distance changes the perception of texture. Close up, the surface quality may be rough, but far away it may appear smooth.
- adding more textures to spaces that reflect a neutral color palette, such as white, tan, or gray. With such colors, texture is necessary to generate the interest and variety that people prefer.
- understanding that high-gloss paint on walls makes them easier to clean but also highlights imperfections in the walls.
- noting that rough textures collect dirt and grime easily.

Photograph: David O. Marlow/Interiors by Associates III Interior Design

Figure 7-18 Identify the different tactile textures used in this space. *What feeling does each texture communicate?*

Refrain from using certain textures that are within reach of a small child. For example, because grass cloth is fragile and easily damaged, specifying it for a wall covering for a family with children is something a designer avoids.

Visual Texture

Visual texture is a perception—it is an illusion of physical texture. When the eye sees visual texture, the brain interprets it as three dimensional. In interiors, visual textures add excitement, interest, and can camouflage dirt, **Figure 7-19**. A person can see visual textures on printed fabric, wall coverings, glass panels, cabinet doors, and ceramic tiles. A combination of both tactile and visual textures in an interior is aesthetically pleasing.

Time can affect the look and feel of an object's texture. Repetitive human touch can enhance a texture, such as the way in which aging wood develops a **patina**—a surface appearance that grows beautiful with age. Many recycled materials show evidence of time and the wear-and-tear that indicates a previous application and place. People often celebrate and enjoy this type of texture in a new location.

The *feel* of a texture is important to the human body and human psyche. Sense of touch and the visual-

Kutlayev Dmitry/Shutterstock.com

Figure 7-19 Visual textures help create illusions in a space. *What illusions do the visual textures in this bathroom create?*

CASE STUDY

Textures in Zach and Bacon Elementary Schools, Fort Collins, Colorado

When selecting interior materials for an elementary school filled with active, inquisitive children, an interior designer must think of durability, maintenance, and flammability. Textures impact maintenance. Rough textures are more difficult to clean; however, smooth textures can become easily scratched.

The interior designer at RB + B Architects came up with a great solution for school walls: brushed steel within children's reach and paint above. The steel is easily cleaned, can be given an interesting texture, and is very durable. To create visual interest, the steel was corrugated and installed in Zach Elementary School.

A designer, however, cannot always predict how human behavior will interact with texture choices. At Zach Elementary, children quickly discovered that it was noisy and fun to run their pencils down the half walls of corrugated steel as they went to class or the lunchroom. In the next school RB + B designed, Bacon Elementary, the same material was used but with a smooth texture.

Photos provided by Poudre School District/Design by RB+B Architects

Zach Elementary School

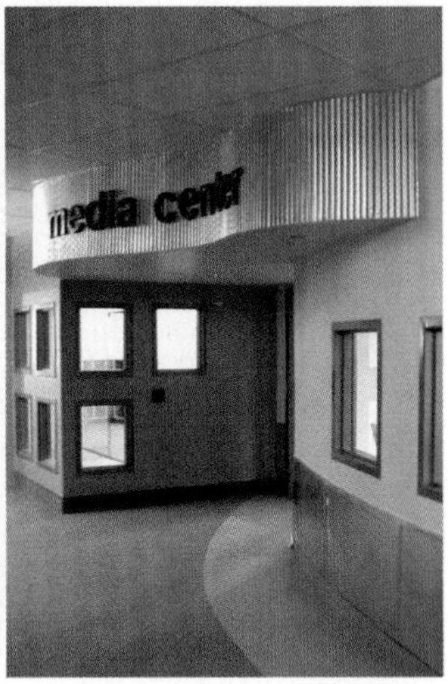

RB+B Architects

Bacon Elementary School

Investigate and Reflect

For one or two days, take a number of digital pictures of the textures you see in the various environments that surround you. What textures do you see and feel? How do these environmental textures appear to influence the behavior of yourself and others? Create an illustrated report of your findings and reflections.

textile experience are essential characteristics in interior design, reflecting the variety inherent in the natural world. If you are like other interior designers, the most difficult sign you will encounter is one that reads "do not touch." Designers appreciate the tactile feel of objects, materials, and fabrics, and so do their clients!

Pattern

Patterns are evident in nature, people's lives, and in built environments. In nature, patterns can camouflage or communicate danger. For example, the cuttlefish is a sea creature that can change its patterns—depending on its surroundings—to protect itself from predators. People are all familiar with patterns in their daily lives. They perceive patterns in their class schedules, life decisions, and organizational tools. Within the built environment, patterns can decorate surfaces, express a style, and create visual interest.

In interiors, **pattern** is the repetition of a specific motif (artistic design) in an orderly manner. Often used with texture, pattern relates to applied decoration and communicates culture and place. Patterns can be large or small scale.

There are two different ways to utilize pattern. *Surface or applied patterns* include the conscious repetition of a shape or motif, such as on fabrics or wall panels. *Structural patterns* involve the placement of a form in a repetitive design, such as with stone floor pavers. There are three different types of pattern motifs used in interior design: geometric, naturalistic, and abstract (see **Figure 7-20**).

In interiors, you can see patterns in fabric and upholstery used for furnishings and wall panels. Patterns are also visible as *recessed* or *relief designs*—designs that are carved into or bump out—in architectural elements or furniture motifs. Additionally, patterns are evident in carpet and ceramic tile designs, and with the use of pleasing repetition with the geometric arrangement of doors and drawers.

Using Pattern Motifs

Geometric patterns include stripes, checks, plaids, chevrons, or polka dots. Surface materials, such as fabric or carpet are common uses for these patterns.

New Line/Shutterstock.com

svkv/Shutterstock.com

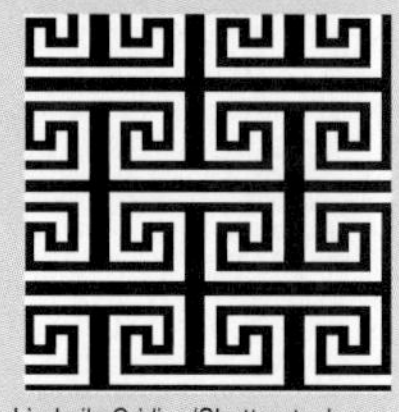
Liudmila Gridina/Shutterstock.com

Naturalistic patterns use designs in nature such as botanical images (leaves and flowers) or motifs of humans or animals. These patterns can be stylized—such as in paisley—or representational—as with scenes of people.

KhrobostovA/Shutterstock.com

Anna Davidyuk/Shutterstock.com

paranormal/Shutterstock.com

Abstract patterns utilize unique motifs that have no recognizable shapes or images. They can be whimsical, sophisticated, or casual.

Lukas Radavicius/Shutterstock.com

Betacam-SP/Shutterstock.com

Polina Katritch/Shutterstock.com

Figure 7-20 Patterns can create interest in the built environment. Use them with care.

An interior designer can easily change the appearance of patterns through color and size. For instance, changes in the pattern color can cause some parts of the pattern to advance while others appear to move to the background. Change the size of the pattern and it will look like a different design.

The size and dimensions of patterns is critical. Bold and large patterns can overwhelm an object or delicate piece of furniture. Use them sparingly and only for drama or impact. Likewise, small patterns, when viewed from a distance, become textures. Therefore, they are a good choice for an office chair or family-room sofa to hide wear-and-tear.

Patterns evoke a human response in both commercial and residential interiors, some of which are unpredictable. People perceive patterns differently depending on their demographic profile (for instance, their gender or the region in which they live) and personal or cultural experiences. The beauty of a pattern may also be perceived differently depending on personal taste, **Figure 7-21.**

Documentation exists tracing certain popular patterns to specific decades in U.S. history. Therefore, if you are completing a historical renovation or restoration, you need to be aware of the patterns communicating a particular time and place. For example, in the 1940s large, natural-floral patterns were used in fabrics, while in the 1960s metallic-vinyl fabrics and pop-art prints were common in fashion and interiors. When using patterns in interiors, understand they can

- make people more aware of a surface and enhance visual interest of an object
- convey a specific mood or theme (childlike, cheerful, or homey)
- communicate a period of time or style (country or traditional)
- give variety to a space (too many patterns used in same space, however, can give chaotic feel)
- camouflage awkward corners or disguise a boundary
- hide architectural defects through distraction (hiding cracked wall plaster with patterned wallpaper)
- make an object look larger or smaller
- add visual interest to a space if the room's patterns are not all the same size (same-size patterns fight for attention and conflict)
- add order to a space and interest to planes that are otherwise ignored, such as a ceiling

Placement of patterns in interiors can hinder or help the design. Patterns can overwhelm the architectural details of a space. Chaotic carpet patterns can become tripping hazards depending on the age of the client or user of the space. Patterns can also cause conflict in a room if styles are not compatible. For instance, country mini-prints often conflict with contemporary patterns.

Patterns need *breathing space*. If they are too close together in the same room, their impact, beauty, or drama is lost.

Figure 7-21 Repeated patterns in a space help bring order. *What patterns are used in this kitchen? How is pattern used in this bathroom?*

pics721/Shutterstock.com

Photograph: Emily Minton Redfield/Interior Designer: Andrea Schumacher Interiors

Color

Color is one of the most powerful, exciting, and life-shaping elements of design, **Figure 7-22.** Dependent on light, color can alter the shape and size of an object. Attraction and interest in color grows as people mature and develop personal preferences for colors in their interior spaces. These preferences become part of peoples' identities, communicating to others who they are and what they like.

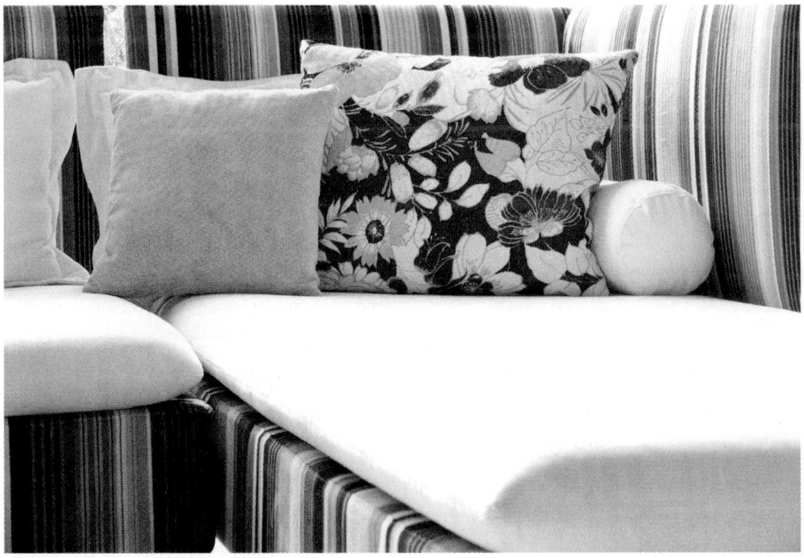

ponsulak/Shutterstock.com

A

B

Photograph: Rhonda Grimsberg/Interior Designer: Andrea Schumacher Interiors

Figure 7-22 Color can be used many different ways in a space. *How does color attract interest in this living space (A)? How does the designer use color to transform this interior (B)?*

Color can transform spaces. As an inexpensive element of design, most people can afford to change colors on a whim with a can of paint and a little expertise. That is what makes color fun and fascinating.

Color trends inspire conversations about how color impacts and modifies the world. That is influence and power in action! Because the study of color is complex, you will learn more about this element later.

Light

Light, both manufactured and natural, is an often overlooked and trivialized element of design. Other than providing illumination for good vision, how can light improve interiors? Why study light?

Like color, light is an exceptionally powerful element of design. Its quantity, quality, and color control peoples' behavior, mood, and ability to function on the most basic level, **Figure 7-23.** At its most exciting, people see light in majestic sunrises and sunsets. In its most basic use, people can see light as a bare bulb hanging from a rustic ceiling. Because the impact of light is great, you will learn more about it as you study color.

Principles of Interior Design

The elements of design are the tools designers use to achieve the principles of design. Principles of design are the guidelines that govern the choices and actions designers take to achieve good design. Creatively using design elements and principles differentiates your work from others. In the following, you will study how to achieve the principles of design in interior spaces through the appropriate use of the design elements. The principles of interior design are *proportion, scale, emphasis, balance, rhythm,* and *harmony.*

Alexander Chaikin/Shutterstock.com

Figure 7-23 Light can impact peoples' behavior and ability to function in a space.

Proportion

Proportion describes the relationship between a whole object and one of its parts. A *whole* can be one object, person, or an entire composition within a two-dimensional or three-dimensional space. Proportions describe internal relationships and are not dependent on a specific size or standard. Assessing proportion is a visual judgment. It is determined by looking at the composition, object, or person to see if the proportion is appropriate. People rarely notice proportion until something is *out* of proportion.

The human body is a great example of proportion, **Figure 7-24.** The body consists of many parts that make up the whole. Finger joints, hands, and arms have predictable mathematical relationships to each other and are part of the whole. The comparison of leg length to torso, waist to height, and shoulder width to body length are all ratio measurements of the body. When analyzing facial features, the eyes can appear set apart or close together; the ears big or small; and the mouth wide or tiny—all in comparison to other facial features.

Variances in proportion make people look different from one another. If part of the human body is out of proportion, it is very noticeable. For example, if a man wears a size 15 shoe and he is only five feet tall, his feet are out of proportion to the rest of his body (consider a clown). There are several different ways to compare proportions. These include

- height, width, and depth of one element within an object (or composition) to another
- size of one area to the size of another area
- amount of space between two or more elements within an object

Over time, rather than visually assessing proportion, individuals or groups—particularly ancient Greeks—developed *proportioning systems* to describe an ideal—a pleasing aesthetic within a composition. One such system, known as the *golden mean* closely relates to human body proportions. It is a mathematical system inspired by the pentagon shape evident in organic life and nature's patterns of order.

The golden mean involves a line that divides the parts of a whole into two unequal, yet visually harmonious parts. For example, on a wall that is eight feet high, the golden mean is somewhere between one-third and one-half way up the wall. It appears in everything from sunflowers, apple blossoms, and daisies in the plant world to spiral (nautilus) shells beneath the seas.

The **golden section** is a proportion in which the ratio of the whole to the larger part is the same as the ratio of the larger part to the smaller. It moves in progressions of 3 to 5 to 8 to 13 to 21. The Greeks used this proportioning system to design new structures, columns, and sculptures to be more visually pleasing. The Parthenon is a good example of the golden section.

After using the golden section, the Greeks found that if they followed the golden section too exactly the result would be uninteresting. In developing the golden section, the Greeks discovered that a rectangle was more visually pleasing than a square. This resulted in the **golden rectangle**—a rectangle with sides in the *golden ratio* of 1:1.618, **Figure 7-25**.

One of the unique properties of the golden rectangle is its ability to be divided innumerable times into a square and another golden rectangle, of which then can also be divided into a square and another golden rectangle, and so on. The Greeks were also the first to record that odd numbers were more visually pleasing than even numbers when grouped together. This rule is often used today in accessorizing spaces.

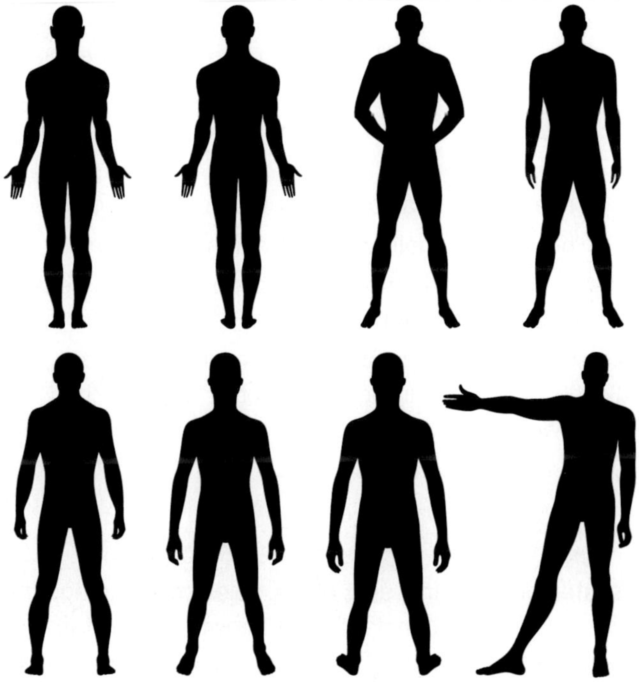

Anna Rassadnikova/Shutterstock.com

Figure 7-24 Proportion of the human body greatly impacts the design of a space. *Why do people rarely notice proportion until something is out of proportion?*

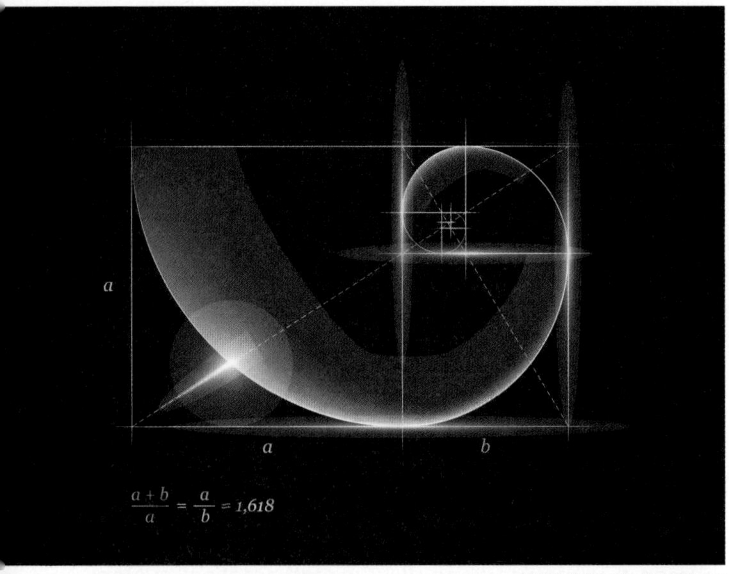

Victoria Kalinina/Shutterstock.com

Figure 7-25 Why is the proportion of the golden rectangle more visually pleasing?

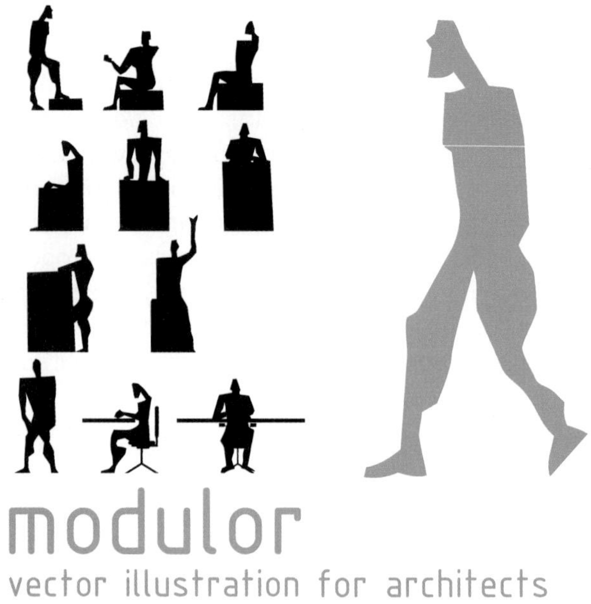

2j architecture/Shutterstock.com

Figure 7-26 Le Corbusier's Modular uses geometric ratios based on proportions of the human body in determining patterns for architectural design. *What aspects of your classroom or school design relate to this proportioning system?*

As a closely linked mathematical cousin to the golden mean, section, rectangle, and ratio, the most commonly taught proportioning system is the **Fibonacci Series** developed by a thirteenth century mathematician named Leonardo of Pisa, who was called *Fibonacci.* This proportioning system was comprised of a series of numbers that include 0,1,1,2,3,5,8,13,21,34. Note that each new number is the sum of the previous two. Evidence of his geometry can be found in such early structures as the Egyptian pyramids and Stonehenge.

Another well-known proportioning system is the twentieth century *Le Corbusier's Modulor,* **Figure 7-26**. The **Le Corbusier's Modulor** is a complex measuring system using geometric ratios based on proportions of the human body to determine patterns *of* and *for* architectural design. The height of the average man (different depending on nationality) was divided into ratios according to the golden section. Le Corbusier, an architect, then used these dimensions for creating heights of ceilings, counters, desks, tables, and chairs that fit the human body. His system studied the way the proportions of the human body were linked to pleasing architecture.

Rather than using a universal proportioning system, units of measurement for proportion can also be specific to today's interior spaces. For example, in the U.S., a unit size of the standard hospital bed influenced the size of entire hospitals. In Japan, traditional houses and rooms were influenced by the size of the tatami flooring mat (3 feet by 6 feet), originally a luxury item for nobility.

In interiors, designers use proportion when evaluating the

- floor plan length and width (golden-section dimensions result in easier furniture arrangements)
- relationship of an architectural element (fireplace) to the space as a whole
- relationship of a chair seat to the whole chair (Is it too wide?)
- relationship of a base to the tabletop (Is it too slim?)
- height of a chair rail to the height of the wall
- width of crown molding, baseboard, or door casing to a wall or room

An example of poor proportion in an interior would be to place a 4-foot by 8-foot island into a 10-foot by 12-foot kitchen. The island would be too big in relation to the room as a whole.

Scale

Scale refers to the size of an object or building relative to a known constant. The known constant is typically the human body. Students of design often confuse proportion and *scale*. One easy way to remember the difference is to understand that proportion is a comparison, or ratio, within *one* whole. In contrast, scale is the

DESIGNER MATH SKILLS

Golden Mean

Have you ever thought about how many rectangles there are in your daily life? Some examples include a cell phone, a debit card, a dollar bill, a textbook, and even a piece of notebook paper.

Calculating Ratios

Squares have sides of equal distance creating a 1:1 ratio. Rectangles have two unequal sides, but are more appealing and harmonious to the eye than squares.

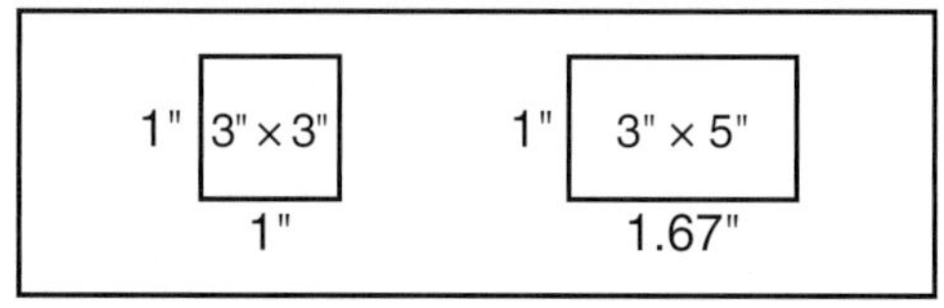

3 ÷ 3 = 1:1 ratio
5 ÷ 3= 1:1.66 ratio (round up to 1:1.67)

For example, a 5'-0" × 7'-0" area rug (1:1.4 ratio) is more appealing than a square 7'-0" × 7'-0" area rug (1:1 ratio).

How does a designer determine ratio? It is actually quite easy—just divide the larger number by the smaller number. A ratio can be written with a colon (:) or using the word *to* such 1:1 or 1 to 1 ratio. A 3" × 5" index card has a 1:1.66 (1:1.67 rounded up) or 1 to 1.67 ratio. Note that a 5" × 7" picture frame has the same ratio as the 5'-0" × 7'-0" rug.

Calculating Proportion Using the Golden Mean

Ratio defines *proportion*. For centuries a ratio called the *Golden Mean* (1:1.618) has been used for determining proportions. In interior design, you can use the Golden Mean to determine how high to hang pictures or wall accessories, the height of a chair rail, or where to place drapery tiebacks. To calculate the height to hang a picture, poster, or a shelf in a room with 9' (108") ceiling, you divide the ceiling height by the golden mean.

108" ÷ 1.618 = 66.74" (rounded up to 66.75" or 66 3/4").

The object is hung 66 ¾" up from the floor. To determine the height of a chair rail in the same room, you can measure down from the ceiling 66 ¾" (or 41 ¼" up from the floor). See the following example.

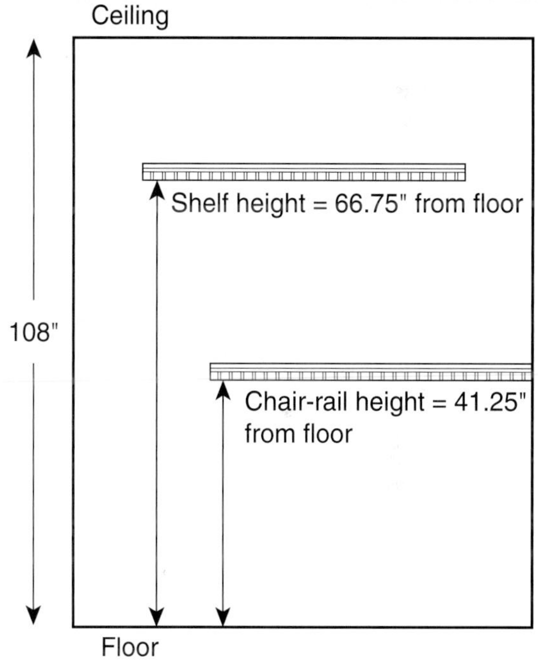

comparison of *two* wholes to each other. Here are some examples.

- **External and internal relationships.** Scale identifies external relationships—the size of human body to an object. Proportion describes internal relationships such as the size of ears on a human head.
- **Function and perceived beauty.** Scale in interiors often relates to the function of space. Proportion in interiors typically relates to perceived beauty within the composition.

People often reference scale in everyday language when discussing *small* scale or *large* scale objects. The human body, however, is not a static standard, **Figure 7-26**. It changes size, so there are a variety of scales with which to compare. For example, if you visit your childhood home after growing to your adult height, you will notice how much smaller the house is in comparison to you. A chair that accommodated your size then does not fit you now. Do you remember the childhood story *Goldilocks and the Three Bears*? Goldilocks tested out three differently sized chairs to find one that fit "just right." That story is an example of scale.

Bob Narod, Photographer/Design by: Lita Dirks + Co.

Figure 7-27 Scale is an important principle of design. *How does the scale of all items in this space relate to the function of the space?*

Visual scale is a comparison of one object to another as perceived with your eyes. When you compare the Empire State Building to a small rural town, the scale seems too large. A child's play table compared to a typical dining table seems small. Use of scale in furnishings, doorways, and windows alters a viewer's perception of a building or of an interior space.

Human scale, in contrast, is the perception people experience within a space. You may feel small in scale when you stand in your state's capital building rotunda. Another example is when the scale is too tight, such as with a small elevator. In this case, you may feel closed in—sometimes even feeling claustrophobic.

Extremes of scale can be surprising. The *Thorne Room Miniatures* is a well-known set of historical interior spaces developed to depict finishes and furnishings of a specific period. They are delightful to view in their modeled, miniature detail.

Entering a large palace can be surprising as well, but inspire different emotions. The fireplace in the grand hall can be two or three times the width and height of a standard residential fireplace and make the tallest person look small. Thus, unexpected use of scale often makes a design statement, **Figure 7-28**.

The wrong scale, while fun in some places, can have a devastating effect in some areas of design. Furniture size should fit the scale of the room. If it does not, the furniture can crowd a small room, making it look even smaller. In contrast, furniture that is too small in scale for a room appears even smaller in an oversized space.

The proportion example used earlier regarding a large island in a small kitchen applies here, too. While the large island was in the *wrong* proportion for the kitchen, the island was in *correct* scale. Note that a piece of furniture can be in the correct scale, but poorly proportioned for the room. One of the goals of good design and beauty is the selection of furnishings and fixtures that are in scale with one another and the whole of the interior space.

Furniture should also be in scale to other furniture around it. A small, delicate end table will appear more so if placed next to an overstuffed lounge chair. With this in mind, you can use different scales in the same interior space to achieve a design statement. Very large or very small furnishings can contrast with large-size works of art. In interiors, designers use scale to

- place the right-size furniture in a room. *Is king size bed too large for space?*
- determine if pattern motifs are appropriately sized for the object they cover.
- select the accessories. *Is the art piece too large for the fireplace surround?*

Photograph by: ©TaylorPhoto.com (Bill Taylor)/Design by: Lita Dirks & Co.

Figure 7-28 Scale can add drama to a space. *How is scale used unexpectedly in this living space?*

- determine if a chair is the appropriate size for the person using it.

In practice, designers use scale to draw floor plans. (In the U.S., the architectural standard for a floor plan is 1/4" = 1'-0" when drawing residences. When drawing commercial projects, the scale is 1/8" = 1'-0".) Designers also use scale to discuss client projects. Are they large-scale or small-scale? A large-scale commercial project can be 10,000 to 50,000 square feet. A small-scale residential project can be less than 2,000 square feet.

Focal Point or Emphasis

Focal point, or emphasis, is the creation of a dominant feature for a space or composition that is the first to demand your attention. In other words, focal point is the center of attention or activity to which the eye goes first when looking at a design. As a designer, you want to draw attention to a particular point of focus rather than a mass of details of equal importance. Designers use the terms *emphasis* and *focal point* interchangeably when discussing design.

Whenever people enter a room, their eyes and brains try to make sense of what they see. This goes back to primal needs of survival. People scan a space to look for threats and to understand their location. As part of that natural instinct, peoples' eyes naturally scan for a place to rest. This is the emphasis or focal point of a room. The human eye desires a pleasing object or scene to rest on. In a space, a focal point

- directs attention of the viewer
- provides a hierarchy for viewing
- can be consciously achieved layer upon layer
- unifies a space when elements work together

If a focal point does not exist in a room, it will be visually uninteresting and bland. A person often feels bored in this type of space and will likely leave the room. If a room has multiple focal points, it creates chaos and conflict for the viewer. The viewer thinks "What should I look at first?" Too much visual stimuli will also cause a person to leave the room.

The three levels of focal point or emphasis designers incorporate in an interior space include (see **Figure 7-29 A, B, and C**)

- **Dominant.** A breathtaking view, a massive fireplace, or architectural feature such as a large, built-in bookshelf can achieve this high level of dramatic emphasis.
- **Subdominant.** This level supports the dominant emphasis and is of secondary importance. For example, designers may use the subdominant level when centering large pieces of furniture on the fireplace.

A Photograph: Ron Ruscio/Interior Designer: Andrea Schumacher Interiors

B Rodenberg Photography/Shutterstock.com

C Photograph: Emily Minton Redfield/Interior Designer: Andrea Schumacher Interiors

Figure 7-29 Three levels of focal point (emphasis) include (A) dominant, (B) subdominant, and (C) subordinate.

- **Subordinate.** This level supports the subdominant level and has the least visual weight. Accessories that sit on tables, fireplace mantels, small furnishings, or bookshelves are examples of this level.

Determine the focal point *first* when incorporating it in interiors. Use an architectural or historical detail, such as a fireplace, to create a focal point, or consider an item that demands attention because of its large size in relationship to surrounding objects. Then add the other features to support it in the room. Remember, two or more focal points create chaos and do not offer a resting place for the eyes.

Balance

As a child, you learn to stand upright, walk, run, and ride a bike. As a teen or an adult, you may learn to rock climb, walk a beam, balance a tire, or use a scale in a science class. All of these activities require balance. **Balance** is the equilibrium of elements in a space. Two major categories of balance include

- *physical balance*—an actual weight of an object which depends on gravity and equilibrium
- *visual balance*—an illusion that relates to perceived relative weights of objects in space

In interiors, designers create visual weight or an illusion of balance. Rather than physically weighing furnishings and objects, designers create balance through a visual judgment. Every object in a space has a degree of lightness or heaviness. For example, light colors appear lighter in visual weight than dark colors. Similarly, transparent objects appear lighter than opaque objects. As objects or furnishings are designed into a space, the design professional creates visual balance.

Visual balance is a quality in a room that gives a feeling of equilibrium, stability, or steadiness. It is a distribution of visual weight that results in a comfortable atmosphere. If balance is not achieved, a sense of imbalance and discomfort results and causes the occupant to leave the room. There are three types of balance. They include

- symmetrical
- asymmetrical
- radial

Symmetrical Balance

Symmetrical balance is the arrangement of objects on both sides of a center point or line (either vertical axis or horizontal axis) that results in a mirror image. In nature, the human body reflects symmetrical balance on the vertical axis. In a reflected mountain scene in a nearby lake, you can view symmetrical balance on a horizontal axis. In architecture, you can find it in stately historical buildings such as state capitol buildings. In interiors, more formal spaces such as living rooms, historic parlors, and places of worship utilize symmetrical balance, **Figure 7-30 A**.

Symmetrical interiors are often exact *mirror* images that form when using identical elements on either side of the center point, or visual axis. Designers use symmetrical balance to emphasize a focal point such as a beautiful view outside a window.

People perceive symmetrical interiors as predicable, stable, dignified, and calm. For that reason, commercial interiors such as courtrooms, museums, hotel lobbies, and such large residences as private palaces use symmetrical balance. You can also see symmetrical balance in many formal historic interiors. Symmetrical balance is the simplest to achieve and the most obvious type of balance in a room.

You can achieve symmetrical balance in interiors by

- aligning a formal dining table with the same number of matching chairs across the table
- placing parallel matching loveseats in front of a hotel lobby fireplace
- using identical side chairs on either side of a foyer table

Asymmetrical Balance

Asymmetrical balance occurs when objects on both sides of the central visual axis are dissimilar yet appear to have identical visual weight. In nature you see this type of balance walking in a forest, in a flower garden, or in large rock formations. In interiors, you see asymmetrical balance in the majority of spaces, **Figure 7-30 B**. Asymmetrical interiors incorporate dissimilar furnishings and objects on either side of the center point that provide balance in visual weight.

People perceive asymmetrical interiors as more informal, flexible, creative, exciting, and vigorous. It is a subtle balance that requires more thought and imagination than symmetrical balance, and is more interesting to view over a longer period of time.

Use of asymmetrical balance in contemporary interiors provides a more spacious appearance. Interior furniture

Interior Design: Senger Design Group/Architect: HB&A/Photographer: Paul Kohlman Photography

Figure 7-30 A Symmetrical balance. *What elements create the symmetrical balance in this interior?*

Warren Diggles Photography/Jon Rentfrow, Rentfrow Design, LLC

Figure 7-30 B Asymmetrical balance. *How does the interior designer use asymmetrical balance in this space?*

arrangements, the arrangement of wall art over a sofa, or the placement of objects on a fireplace mantel may use asymmetrical balance. To achieve asymmetrical balance, you can

- use small areas of vibrant color (red) to balance larger areas of neutral (tan or gray) or cool colors (blue or green)
- use a larger area of gray to balance a smaller area of black
- balance flat, even surface textures with smaller areas of interesting textures
- balance a grouping of smaller objects with a large object

Radial Balance

Radial balance occurs when all elements radiate out from one center point in a circular fashion similar to spokes on a wheel. The petals of a daisy or the ripples that appear after throwing a rock into water are examples from nature. In interiors, radial balance is visible in a ceiling detail, in chairs circling a round table, and in curved stairwells. In commercial interiors, radial balance often appears in hotel or office lobbies, rosette windows in places of worship, and central areas of shopping malls around a water fountain, **Figure 7-30 C**.

Rhythm

The first thing that likely comes to mind when you hear the word *rhythm* is the beat of your favorite music. Music may be soothing, dramatic, or heart-thumping! Similarly, the principle of **rhythm** is a creative, repetitive blend of movement and visual form in a conscious, regular arrangement. It often attracts attention and always develops visual unity that enhances beauty within a space.

In nature, you can hear rhythm in the blowing wind, lapping of ocean waves, and the human heartbeat. In dance, you may see it as a sequence of repeated steps. Rhythmic design communicates with the brain. Once the brain recognizes a pattern or understandable rhythm in design, it relaxes as it then appreciates the final design. Hence, rhythm is important for human comfort in a space.

In interiors, achievement of rhythm often occurs by using repetitive elements of design, such as color, light, shape, and line, or structural forms such as exposed ceiling beams, columns, or windows. You can easily attain rhythm as color trails through adjoining spaces, in repeated shapes of furniture, or forms repetitively used in accessories.

One of the simplest forms of repetition is the use of color throughout a space in furnishings, pillows, and accesso-

Warren Diggles Photography/Jon Rentfrow, Rentfrow Design, LLC

Figure 7-30 C Radial balance. *How does radial balance enhance the beauty of this space?*

ries. For example, you can introduce a single color in an interior and repeat it in strategic places to move the eye around and through the space. In commercial spaces, designers also create rhythm with simple patterns using ceiling grids, colored floor tiles, or suspended light fixtures over a conference table, **Figure 7-31**.

pics721/Shutterstock.com

Figure 7-31 Rhythm is a repetitive blend of movement and visual form. *How is rhythm used in this space?*

Rhythm also includes the repetition of visual patterns in space. Like music, the spacing of visual patterns can be in regular and irregular intervals—such as the steady beat of a waltz or the stops and starts of rock music. It develops as the elements of design lead the eye (and mind) around the room or space. An underlying order, like meter in a poem, rhythm gives a space its rhyme and reason.

Here are four types of rhythm interior designers commonly use. See **Figure 7-32 A, B, C, and D**.

- **Alternation.** This type of rhythm uses a repeated pair of contrasting elements such as the dash and dot of Morse code. You can see it in such design elements as a parquet floor (a wood pattern laid two different, alternating ways) or a checkerboard floor (black and white color tiles). Alternation moves a viewer's eye around the room and adds variety and interest. Alternating warm (red, orange) and cool colors (blue, green) around the room also creates rhythm.
- **Progression.** Also known as *gradation*, progression is a gradual increase or decrease in size of a design element, typically as an identical form, color, or shape but in a different scale. For example, a designer may create this effect on a sofa table with a series of vases in a succession of increasing or decreasing sizes or as a series of small to large stacked boxes. You can also

A Photographer: Ron Ruscio/Interior Designer: Andrea Schumacher Interiors

B Kasia Bialasiewicz/Shutterstock.com

C Patrick McCall/Shutterstock.com

D pics721/Shutterstock.com

Figure 7-32 Interior designers typically use four types of rhythm—(A) alternation, (B) progression, (C) repetition, and (D) transition. *Discuss how each type of rhythm might be used in an interior space.*

observe progression when using one color, from dark to light, in a room.

- **Repetition.** As the simplest type of rhythm, it controls the eye movement by repeating a single element again and again. Typically, the elements are in similar size and length.
- **Transition.** This type of rhythm uses a line that carries the eye easily and without interruption from one point to another. An architectural element such as an arched window or doorway is an example.

To make your rhythmic pattern more interesting, you can vary the amount of space between an element's reoccurrence. This changes the pace of visual rhythm. It can move from graceful, calm, and regular to sharp, dramatic, and stimulating. As with music, the elements or notes do not change as the songwriter creates new tunes. Instead, it is the arrangement of the elements or notes that bring about original compositions.

Rhythm is a powerful principle of design. When used properly, it is a recurrence of successive elements in a pattern of repetition.

Harmony

Harmony is the combination of design elements and principles in an aesthetically pleasing or orderly whole. It is the hallmark of good design and results when all design elements—such as the architectural features and furnishings—work together in an interesting composition of belonging and relationship. To form a visual decision, designers often ask the following:

- Do these elements look like they belong together?
- Do adjacent colors, similar shapes, or related textures create an interesting visual connection throughout a space?
- Is there is a relationship between the design elements that relate to and reinforce a key concept developed for the space?

Harmony results with the correct application of the design principles. If elements and principles are unrelated or compete with each other, harmony does not exist, the design looks chaotic or boring, and it visually falls apart.

Harmony requires planning for a balance of unity and variety in a space. **Unity** is a set of conscious choices to tie the composition together, a sense of order, oneness, and uniformity. The elements have a sense of belonging to each other such as colors that mesh and complement each other or furnishings used from a similar period.

Unity in design is a concept that stems from **Gestalt theory**. This theory—related to visual perception and psychology—concerns how the human brain perceives and organizes visual information into categories or groups. The visual world is so complex that the mind tries to determine ways to cope with the confusion. It often seeks the simplest solution or meaning to a design it is viewing by organizing or grouping the information. Gestalt theory includes the following four harmonious concepts (see **Figure 7-33 A, B, C, and D**):

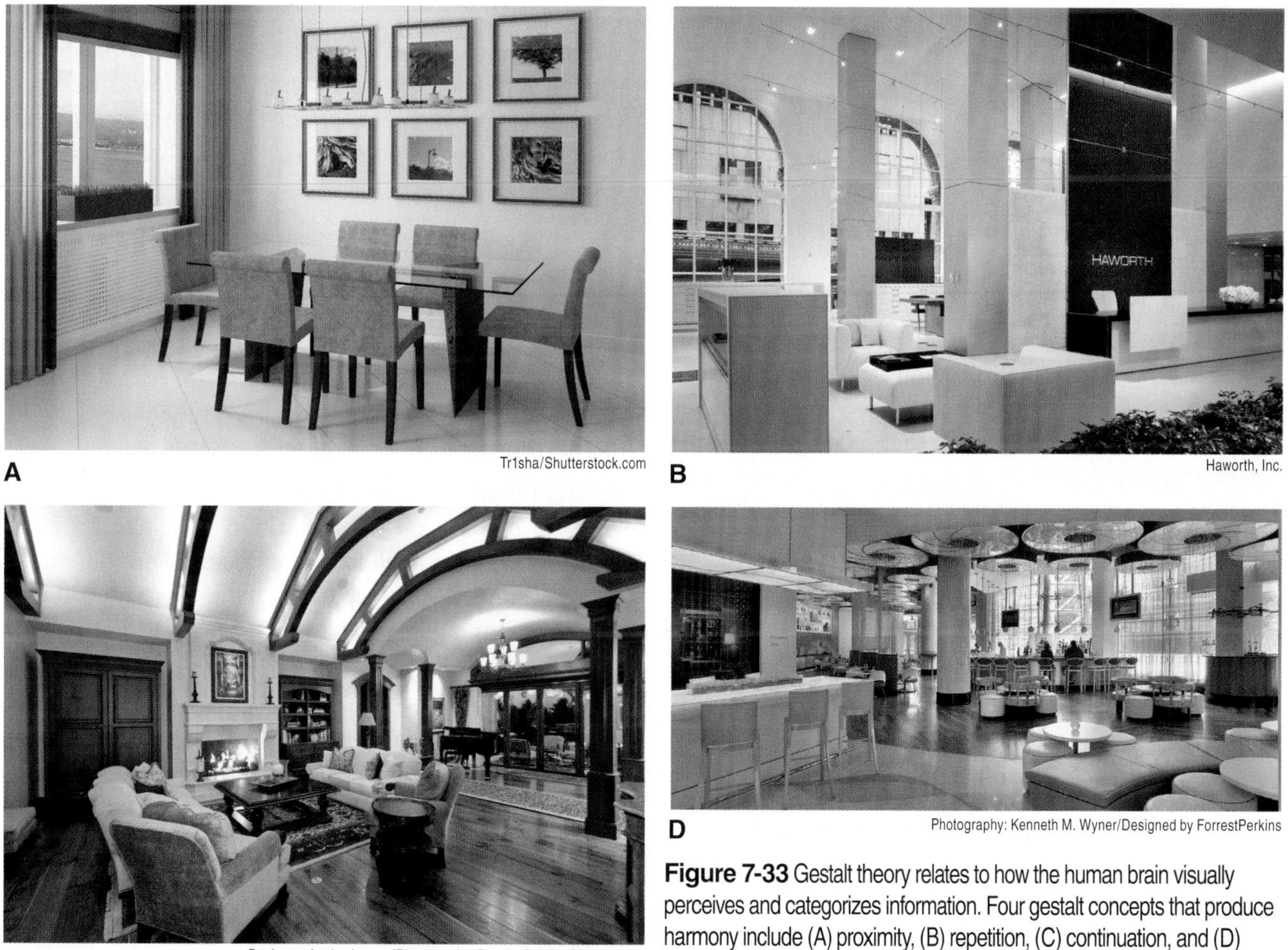

A Tr1sha/Shutterstock.com

B Haworth, Inc.

C Designer: Aneka Jensen/Photography: Damon Searles Photography

D Photography: Kenneth M. Wyner/Designed by ForrestPerkins

Figure 7-33 Gestalt theory relates to how the human brain visually perceives and categorizes information. Four gestalt concepts that produce harmony include (A) proximity, (B) repetition, (C) continuation, and (D) alignment. *Discuss design examples that support each concept.*

- **Proximity.** By organizing distinct elements into groups that are near each other, the designer uses the concept of proximity. Placing elements next to each other, such as accessories on a sofa table or pictures on a wall, develops a relationship between objects and is the easiest way to achieve unity.
- **Repetition** Repeating the same color, texture, pattern, or shape throughout a space or building creates harmony through unity. Repeating a geometric pattern, such as a square, is an example.
- **Continuation.** Used as a line or edge to transition from one form to another, continuation moves the eye through the visual composition or space. This is the most difficult way to achieve harmony.
- **Alignment.** Lining up forms or images to organize and create groups involves using alignment. For example, creating clusters of furniture around a focal point creates alignment.

Unity, coupled with variety, develops an interesting, cohesive design. **Variety** is the absence of monotony or sameness. Variety adds vitality, interest, and diversity to a design. It brings life to a room. In interiors, designers achieve variety in several ways, such as

- selecting different colors, furniture, or accessory styles
- creating interest by using materials of very different textures
- associating historic furniture pieces with contemporary items

Remember, variety without unity can create disorder and chaos. Unity alone is not boredom, but beauty. Lastly, the stronger the grouping, the stronger is the gestalt. Placing a grouping in order achieves unity and understanding of meaning in the design. If a client desires variety, the designer can reverse the same concept to form groups to add interest to the composition.

Understanding Gestalt theory helps you to control unity and variety, therefore achieving harmony. Gestalt allows you to control the order, arrangement, and design of a space based on client needs and preferences.

In the design of an interior space, harmonious use of the elements and principles creates **visual literacy**—the ability to interpret and derive meaning from the composition of images rather than words. Harmony results from practice. In general, designers achieve harmony when

- interior materials and furnishings blend with existing architectural features
- furniture is appropriate in scale and proportion to the space
- colors and textures are compatible with the design and style of furnishings
- floor coverings and window treatments assist in developing the style and concept
- accessories enhance and build on the existing design rather than introduce a new theme or style

The images and forms that fill an interior space express meaning. These images and forms guide the eye around the room often with a stop at the dominant element, such as a focal point. In combination, the human eye and brain continually gather meaning—visual literacy—from the composition in sight.

What gathered meanings are the viewers and users of your designed spaces perceiving? How a designer uses the elements and principles of design develops meaning within the space, and thereby achieves visual literacy.

The interior designer manipulates the elements and principles to create spaces that express the client's function and please the senses. How the elements and principles of design are used changes as new styles appear on the scene. However, they remain the design vocabulary of the profession and the tools and guidelines to achieve good design.

As a student of design, develop a toolbox of different ways to manipulate elements and principles to adapt and transform spaces to address new client needs. As you experiment, you will understand more how to see, feel, and use objects within a space.

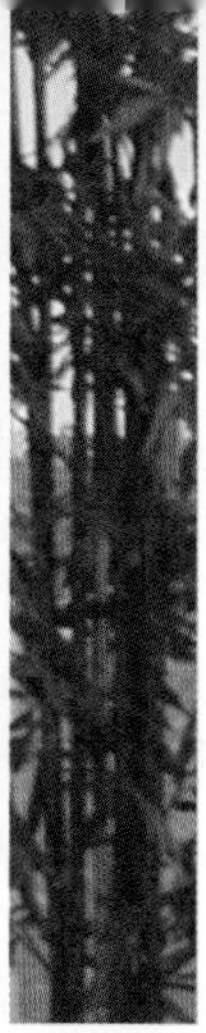

Chapter 7 Review and Assess

Summary

- The elements and principles of design are the fundamental design vocabulary of the interior design profession.
- The elements and principles can be used in other disciplines (such as architecture) but may have different meanings. Learning the design vocabulary of other disciplines is important
- The elements of design include line, shape, form, space, texture, pattern, color, and light.
- The principles of design are the guidelines that govern the choices and actions designers take to achieve good design. They include methods by which the elements of design are organized.
- The principles of design include proportion, scale, focal point (emphasis), balance, rhythm, and harmony.
- Visual literacy results from the harmonious, appropriate use of the elements and principles of design to meet client needs.
- The concepts of unity and variety together help designers achieve harmony in their designs.
- Interior designers manipulate the elements and principles of design to adapt and transform spaces that meet client needs for function and beauty.

Chapter Vocabulary

Create a three-column chart. In the left column, list the following terms. In the middle column, identify a word or group of words that you think describe an attribute of each term. As you read the chapter, write the definitions for each term in the right column.

asymmetrical balance
balance
elements
Fibonacci Series
focal point
form
Gestalt theory
golden rectangle
golden section
harmony
human scale
Le Corbusier's Modulor
line
patina
pattern
principles
proportion
radial balance
rhythm
scale
shape
symmetrical balance
tactile texture
unity
variety
visual literacy
visual scale
visual texture

Review and Study

1. What is the result if the elements and principles of design are used properly? improperly?
2. Name six factors you need to understand about the use of the elements and principles of design.
3. What are the four types of lines and what does each communicate?
4. Name four types of geometric shapes and identify what each symbolizes.

5. How do organic shapes differ from geometric shapes?
6. Name an example showing how form is used in interior design.
7. What is the difference between positive and negative space?
8. Contrast tactile texture with visual texture.
9. What are two different ways to utilize pattern?
10. What are the three types of pattern motifs used in interior design? Give an example of each.
11. Name five proportioning systems used in design ranging from ancient times to modern day.
12. List three ways interior designers use proportion.
13. Contrast visual scale with human scale.
14. How does focal point impact a person who walks into a room?
15. What are the differences among symmetrical, asymmetrical, and radial balance?
16. How does rhythm in design communicate with the brain?
17. What are the four concepts of unity in interior design that stem from the Gestalt theory?
18. List three factors that indicate a designer has achieved harmony.

Critical Analysis

19. **Compare and contrast.** Some design disciplines, such as architecture and interior design, have the same elements and principles in common. The elements and principles, however, may have different definitions. Use the text and Internet or print resources to compare and contrast the elements and principles of interior design with the *primary elements and ordering principles* of architecture. How are these two similar and different? Discuss how such factors complicate communication between team members from different disciplines who may be working on the same design project.
20. **Predict consequences.** Select two or more elements of design (such as shape and texture). Use each one as a predominant design characteristic of a given space. Based on what you have learned from chapter content, predict how the space would look different depending on which element was used. For example, describe how the visual appeal of the space would differ if you use shape versus texture.
21. **Identify textures.** Divide into four teams—A, B, C, D. Cooperate, contribute, and collaborate as group members to locate five items of different textures, put them into a paper bag, close up the bag, and label the bag with the team letter. Pass the bags around to each team. Team members should take turns reaching into the bags without looking to identify the mystery textures, keeping a list per team bag. After everyone has had a chance to feel the textures, each team should reveal the contents of its bag. How many classmates correctly identified the textures? Discuss how ability to identify textures can enhance textures chosen for interior design.
22. **Analyze evidence.** As the author states, visual literacy is the ability to interpret and derive meaning from a composition. Use the Internet or design magazines to locate several examples of well-designed rooms. Analyze the images for the principle of harmony. What evidence of unity and variety can you identify that contribute to harmony in these spaces? Along with a school-approved web-based application, use your images to create a digital poster about your findings. Be sure to add a credit line to your images.

Think like a Designer

23. **Writing.** Read the *Design Insight* quote at the beginning of the chapter. Use your written communication skills to clearly, concisely, and effectively write an essay explaining and justifying how you think that thoughtfully designed spaces help people learn, reflect, imagine, discover, and create.
24. **Speaking.** Use Internet or print resources to locate images of good and poor examples of each type of line discussed in the chapter: horizontal, vertical, diagonal, and curved. Share your images in an illustrated report to the class. Identify the type of line in each image and why it is used effectively or ineffectively.

25. **Manipulate space.** With your classmates, move classroom furniture to manipulate different behavior within the space. How did the change in *form* impact the class behavior in the space? Why?
26. **Digital photo essay.** For three to five days, use a digital camera (or phone camera) to take photos of spaces you encounter. The images can include indoor and outdoor spaces, and small and large spaces. Focus on features that help form boundaries of these spaces. Once you have your images, analyze them for ways that perception and physical boundaries were used to create the space. Which features enhance the quality of the space? Why? Then use presentation software to create a photo essay. Embed your comments about how perception and physical boundaries were used to create space. Share your photo essays with the class.
27. **Writing.** The author states that "color is one of the most powerful, exciting, and life-shaping elements of design." Write an essay that clearly, concisely, and effectively explains and justifies how your life experiences with color support the author's statement.
28. **Speaking.** Use the Internet or design magazines to locate one or more photos showing quality examples of focal point and balance in a room design. Evaluate the images. How do the images meet text guidelines for focal point, including the three levels of emphasis? Which type(s) of balance are used in the images? What elements or objects are used to achieve balance? Give an oral report to the class summarizing your evaluation.
29. **Rhythm video.** Find an interior space (commercial or residential) that displays rhythm. With permission from the owner or occupant, take a short video clip of the space. Locate a piece of music that captures the rhythm of the space/interior and merge it with the video. Present your video to the class. Discuss the features that show rhythm in the space.
30. **Math practice.** Review *Designer Math Skills* on page 203 and then complete the following. A designer staging a model home wants the window shades in the living room open. The windows are 36" h x 18" w.
    A. Sketch the window showing the height of the shade using a 1:1 ratio, and label thedimensions.
    B. Sketch another window showing the height of the opened shade to reflect the proportion created by using the 1:1.618 ratio. How high would you raise the shade?

Design Application

34. **Create a nature-inspired pattern.** Presume you have a client who desires a unique wallpaper design with a nature theme. Collect and study shapes and patterns from nature and translate them into a new wallpaper design for a client. Use the following process to design your wallpaper:
    A. Take 10 close-up digital photos of an element in nature. Download them to your computer and print them out.
    B. Place a 5-inch by 5-inch square of tracing paper over the image printouts. On the tracing paper, create an abstract drawing of each photorealistic image. Use lines and shapes that stylize the images within tracing paper squares.
    C. Select the best two of the 10 designs to replicate as a wallpaper sample.
    D. Refine the nature-inspired pattern designs you started in step B for use as the new wallpaper design. Once final, scan the designs into a computer and use a paint program to render or add color to the images. Print the final design. (You can also manually color the images with markers, water colors, or colored pencils, or a combination of the three. Then scan your rendered image into your computer and print it out.)
    E. Wrap the finished design around the outside of an empty 16-ounce food can.
    F. Write a client proposal for your design and identify key features that fit the client's design needs. Present the design to your client (the class).

    Source: Assignment inspired by Darrin Brooks, IDEC, Utah State University.
35. **Portfolio builder.** Save copies of your projects for items 27 and 29 in your digital portfolio for future use.
36. **Portfolio builder.** Take digital photographs of each step of the wallpaper project you create for item 34. Place printout of the photographs in your hard copy portfolio or save the digital images to your digital portfolio. Write a summary explaining your experiences with this project to keep with the images in your portfolio.

Color and Light

RM Ruwart Design, Rosalie M. Ruwart, ASID/David Patterson Photography

Chapter

8

Design Insight

"The power of color in interiors cannot be underestimated. Designers are able to shape space, communicate meaning, and support human behavior as well as create a significant first impression of a space with color."

Margaret Portillo, Ph.D., Professor and Chair, Department of Interior Design, University of Florida, Author of Color Planning for Interiors

Learning Targets

After studying this chapter, you will be able to

- summarize the importance of color and communicating color.
- utilize basic color theory.
- understand various color systems and color wheels used in interior design.
- demonstrate knowledge of the theory and use of color in interior design, including how to use color schemes and harmonies, and understanding aspects of the psychology of color, color preferences, and color trends and forecasting.
- understand the impact of multicultural and global use of color.
- summarize important factors regarding light in interiors, including daylight, electric light, color perception and light, and the categories of light.
- understand the vocabulary of light and its impact on color.
- identify types of lamp families, and their uses and applications in interior design.
- identify the major categories luminaires and types of lighting fixtures used in interior design.
- summarize how interior designers choose lighting effectively.

Introduction

Color feeds the soul and surrounds people in nature. It expresses personality and reflects mood. It may cause people to eat more or less, but it almost always influences what they buy such as cars, clothing, and food. Color is an exciting part of everyone's world.

Color is the first design element you notice in an interior space and the last you remember as you leave it. As a child, color names are some of the first words you utter. Color is an influential part of a person's life, **Figure 8-1.** How? Color can affect a person's emotions, energy level, and sense of order. It can make an interior space feel informal and masculine, unconventional, or cool and aloof. Color communicates your sense of self and personal tastes.

Color preferences often relate to a life experience. What are your preferences? What is your favorite color? What color do you dislike wearing? Can you trace it to a memory?

Using color effectively can pose challenges, but color is fun! It is a part of life. Experiment with it. Be creative with it! Realize the power of it!

catwalker/Shutterstock.com

Vitar Malyshchyts/Shutterstock.com

Figure 8-1 Color is the element of design that people most often notice first. *What are your color preferences? What do you think influences these preferences?*

The Importance of Color in Interiors

Color has an exciting, mood-changing impact on interior spaces. Just selecting a different wall color can change the mood and physical appearance of a space in a very dramatic way.

Of all the elements of interior design, color is the *most* exciting and powerful. Color can

- define space
- reflect personality
- communicate function
- influence moods
- illustrate trends
- indicate culture
- guide wayfinding
- enhance a focal point
- change the appearance of materials
- define formality or informality in a space
- change the apparent weight and size of furnishings and rooms

Interior design clients find color the easiest element to relate to and, therefore, something they often feel comfortable discussing with a designer. The simplest choices, however, can be overwhelming. For example, although paint is inexpensive and relatively easy to apply, clients often become anxious over the myriad of choices available in just one color family. The fear of picking the wrong color causes many to avoid picking one at all.

Selecting Color

When determining how to use color in a space, designers need to consider many factors. These factors influence how people perceive a color or how a color changes depending on its location in an interior space. Perhaps that is why selecting a color can seem so daunting to you or your clients. See **Figure 8-2** for factors that impact the appearance of color.

Determining placement of color can also be difficult. It is hard to know how much color to use, and where to use it. More confusing yet may be visualizing how the color will appear and shape the space after application, especially with ever-changing light and shadows. For these reasons, color can be unpredictable. Therefore, one challenge with selecting a color is acquiring the ability to predict and control the result of the color choice in an interior space.

Color Selection Factors

Light

- Orientation of the room to sunlight
- Amount of sunlight in space
- Color of electric light in the space

Client

- Client preferences and associations with color
- Age of client(s) using space(s); age of eyes

Space

- Location of color used in room—ceilings, walls, or flooring
- Adjoining colors
- Adjoining room colors
- Shadows cast
- Room size and ceiling height
- Amount of color to be used in space
- Texture of colored surface and reflectance level

Trends and Style

- Color trends in the country
- Colors available; longevity of trend
- Colors that reflect mood or style in space
- Colors reflective of historical context or period

World

- Location in the world; compare northern Canada to southern Cozumel
- Cultural associations and use of color

Figure 8-2 When choosing colors for clients, there are many factors interior designers must consider.

Due to its powerful impact, the selection and placement of color must be deliberate and purposeful. For example, the use of color in a healthcare facility can either assist in creating a healing environment or cause tripping hazards for aging individuals. Deliberate and purposeful selection of color necessitates accurate communication about color with clients to meet their needs and the requirements of the space.

Communicating About Color

Although color is very easy for clients to discuss, it is very difficult to accurately communicate. There are several reasons for this. The first relates to the physiology of the human eye. The eye perceives color differently, depending on its age. For example, the eyes of older adults have a yellowing to the cornea that changes how they perceive the same color you may be viewing. In addition, your client may have a color deficiency. You will learn more about how the eye functions and color deficiency later in this chapter.

Second, using words to describe a color can be tricky. The color you verbally describe to your client may bring up a different brain image from the one you are picturing because of your different reference point. For example, if you describe a wall color to your client as "sky blue," he or she may visualize a different sky color than you had in mind. This difference can be critical when using a color in a large interior space such as a bank.

Third, people never see color in isolation. Adjoining colors, surface textures, and surface size are other factors that impact colors people see. For this reason, interior designers develop a client's *color palette*, *color board*, or *color scheme* to indicate which colors will be next to others in specific spaces, or the relationships of colors in adjoining rooms. If a color is going into a critical area, such as a swanky hotel lobby or The Blue Room of the White House, the designer may even provide the client with a mock-up of the color with the final surface texture, **Figure 8-3**. Texture impacts color, too!

The larger the design project, the more complex the use of color becomes. For example, a hospital or large hotel lodge may include several building wings. These structures may use different colors to communicate to the guests their location in the building—a sense of place. With trim and baseboard paint colors, a hotel may have as many as 30 colors to specify in the building. In a hospital, it could involve over 80 colors. This adds to the complexity of completing the design project and accurate communication about color.

severija/Shutterstock.com

Photography: Kenneth M Wyner/Designed by ForrestPerkins

SCI design group

Figure 8-3 A color board shows relationships among colors from room to room and is critical to enhancing client understanding of the design concept.

Basic Color Theory

While selecting colors is very individual and fun, it is also a science. Knowledge of color theory and its use in interior design acts as a common reference point and vocabulary as you communicate about and experiment with color.

Color theory involves principles used to understand color relationships. A basic understanding of color theory helps you apply rules rather literally and come up with a conservative, but successful, use of color. Once you learn the basics, you can be more creative and bend the rules.

Eliks/Shutterstock.com

Figure 8-4 This illustration shows the range of *value* from light to dark for the color *red.*

Attributes of Color

To communicate color choices to a client, begin with the color vocabulary. The following paragraphs introduce attributes of color—the terms and definitions commonly used when discussing color and color theory. There are three attributes that define every color—*hue, value,* and *chroma.*

Hue

Hue is the pure name of a color. For example, the color *red* is the name of a hue. The **color wheel** is a diagram with an arrangement of spectrum colors in a continuous circle. It represents the basic colors (hues) and their relationships that are visible to the human eye.

Value

Value describes the lightness and darkness of a color. Lighter values, or **tints**, result from adding white to a hue. Pink is a tint of red. Darker values, or **shades**, result from adding black to a hue. Burgundy is a shade of red, **Figure 8-4.**

Chroma

Chroma, the saturation or intensity of a color, describes the brightness or dullness of a hue. Adding gray to a hue lowers its chroma or intensity, creating a **tone**. For instance, adding gray to the color red creates a dull red, or a tone of red. Note the color wheel shows all hues at full intensity and is the basic tool in understanding color.

Warm and Cool Colors

Other common color vocabulary words are *warm* and *cool*. **Warm colors** are those that perceptually appear to advance toward you in a space. They include such hues as red, orange, and yellow. **Cool colors** are those that perceptually recede from you in a space. They include such hues that as blue, green, and purple, **Figure 8-5.**

Because verbally describing a color is difficult, color theorists, scientists, and artists developed diagrams and models to illustrate color interactions. The following briefly discusses the visible color spectrum and the most commonly used theories and color systems in the design industry.

The Visible Color Spectrum

Between 1664 and 1666, Sir Isaac Newton, a physicist, developed the first color wheel consisting of primary and secondary colors as seen when colored light was refracted through a prism, **Figure 8-6**. This later became known as the *visible spectrum*. The **visible spectrum** is that portion of colored light within the electromagnetic spectrum that is visible to the human eye. Newton's work directly impacts interior spaces as it relates to the *additive color theory* and the way light impacts and modifies your perception of colored objects.

When light waves travel through a prism, they separate into the visible spectrum (or color spectrum). Similarly, a prism-like effect occurs when rain falls and light travels through a raindrop. Light **refracts**—or splits apart—

Phaitoon Sutunyawatchai/Shutterstock.com

A

Phaitoon Sutunyawatchai/Shutterstock.com

B

Figure 8-5 Warm colors appear to advance and cool colors appear to recede in a space. *Which colors would you select for a small room? large room?*

Andrea Danti/Shutterstock.com

Figure 8-6 When light travels through a prism, it refracts into the visible spectrum—the colors as they appear to the human eye.

and appears to the human eye as a rainbow. The larger the drops of rain, the brighter the rainbow will be and the more rainbows appear. You will learn more about how the visible spectrum functions later in the chapter in the discussion about lighting.

Additive Color

The *color* of light that strikes an object in an interior greatly impacts how the viewer perceives the object's color. Because of this factor, it is important to understand properties and characteristics of light.

Electric light mimics natural light in replicating the visible spectrum to produce *additive color*. The **additive color theory** describes color mixing with light. The primary colors for the additive color theory are *red*, *green*, and *blue*. Light secondary colors are yellow, cyan, and magenta. When present in equal amounts, the combination of the primary colors produces white light.

Interior designers count on white light in their interior spaces to accurately perceive the pigment colors of furnishings and fabric selections. In contrast, theater productions widely use additive color theory where the goal is to produce colored lights, not white light. Combining primary and secondary colors produces different-colored light waves for use in lighting dramatic and musical performances in auditoriums and theaters. Colored lights can change the appearance of costumes and the scenery.

Subtractive Color

All objects for use in interiors contain pigments. **Pigments**—substances that impart black, white, or a color to other materials—absorb certain parts of the light wave and reflect others. The part of the light wave that is reflected is the color you see. **Subtractive color theory** describes color mixing resulting from the use of the pigments *cyan* (blue), *magenta* (red), and *yellow*. When all light waves are absorbed, you see black, **Figure 8-7.**

The Color Wheel and Color Systems

Developed by printer and publisher Louis Prang in 1876, the most common color wheel taught in U.S. primary schools is based on Prang's theory. His color wheel, commonly called the *Prang Color Wheel*, is comprised of primary, secondary, and tertiary hues, **Figure 8-8**. His diagram is based on the mixing of pigment colors, such as tubes of paint, together. Prang's color diagram indicates that

- **Primary colors** are yellow, red, and blue.
- **Secondary colors** are formed by mixing two primary colors together. Secondary colors are green, orange, and purple.
- **Tertiary colors** (or intermediary) are formed by mixing a primary with a secondary color. The tertiary colors are yellow-green, blue-green, blue-violet, red-violet, red-orange, and yellow-orange.

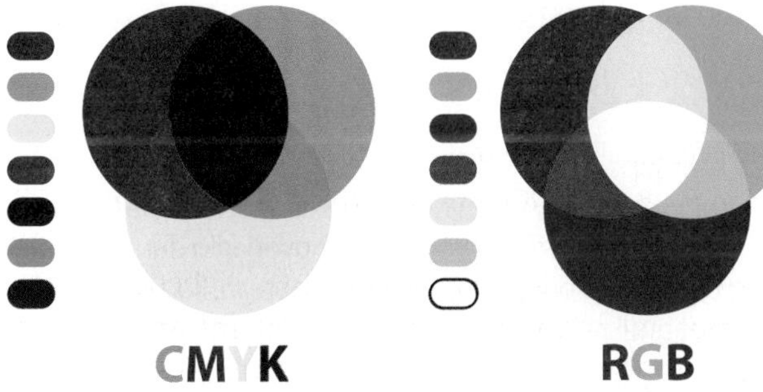

Claudiu Mihai Badea/Shutterstock.com

Figure 8-7 Mixing the pigments cyan (blue), magenta (red), and yellow result in black when all light waves are absorbed. When present in equal amounts, the combination of red, green, and blue colors produce white light.

Several other color systems influence the practice of interior design. These include such systems as the Munsell Color Tree, the Natural Colour System (NCS), Pantone, Albers Simultaneous Contrast, and the Itten Color Wheel, **Figure 8-9**.

Color Schemes

As you know, you never see color in isolation in an interior space. Colors always surround or bump into other colors. Some manufacturers, such as paint companies, offer color palette suggestions that may or may not work well together. In contrast with the questionable nature of some possible color schemes, there are color combinations that always provide beauty and harmonious relationships. These color scheme combinations, or *color harmonies*, offer a perfect balance of color relationships that do not overwork the eyes when viewing the space. The basis

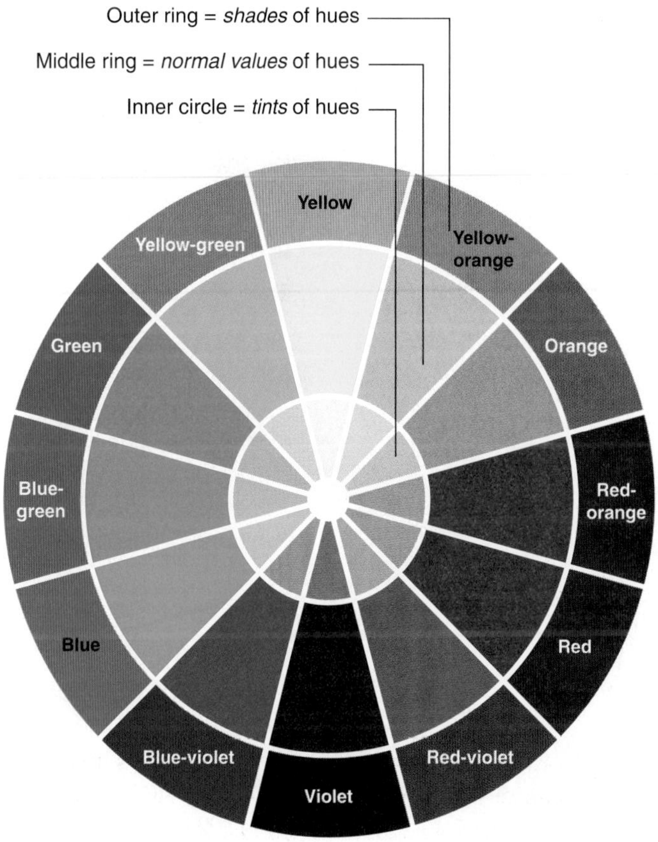

Goodheart-Willcox Publisher

Figure 8-8 The Prang Color Wheel is one of the most common color systems and is made up of primary, secondary, and tertiary hues.

<table>
<tr><th colspan="2">Other Influential Color Systems</th></tr>
<tr><th>Color System</th><th>Description</th></tr>
<tr><td>

Albert H. Munsell—The Munsell Color Tree

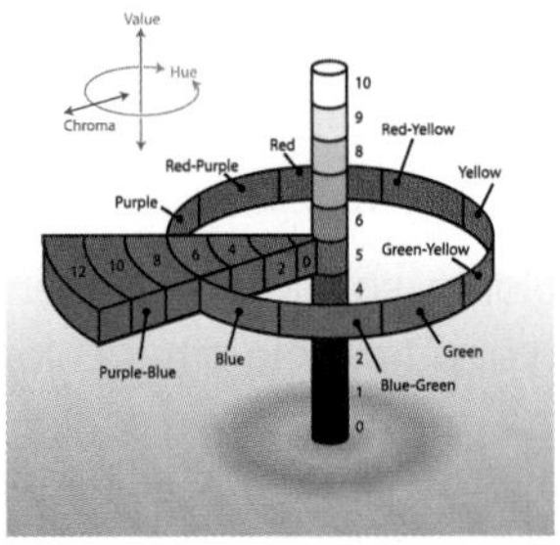

LOVEgraphic/Shutterstock.com

</td><td>

The most widely used color system—called a color tree—was developed by Albert Munsell and appeared in his book *A Color Notation* in 1905. His desire was to create a rational way to describe color using decimal notations rather than color names. His color tree has three dimensions of color: hue, value, and chroma (saturation). Values make up the center pole of his color model. His five primary (or principle) colors—red, yellow, green, blue, and purple—and his five intermediate colors—yellow-red, green-yellow, blue-green, purple-blue, and red-purple—radiate out and around the pole. Each hue is assigned a letter and numerical notation to indicate its logical placement on the color tree. The hues are: 5R (red), 5YR (yellow-red), 5Y (yellow), 5GY (green-yellow), 5G (green), 5 BG (blue-green), 5B (blue), 5PB (purple-blue), 5P (purple), 5RP (red-purple).

</td></tr>
<tr><td>

The Natural Colour System (NCS)

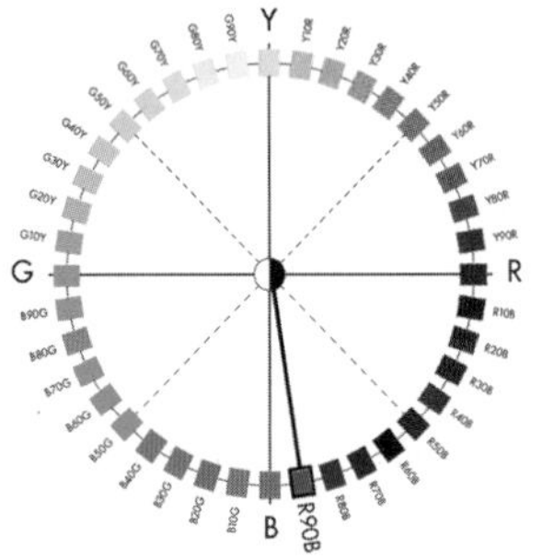

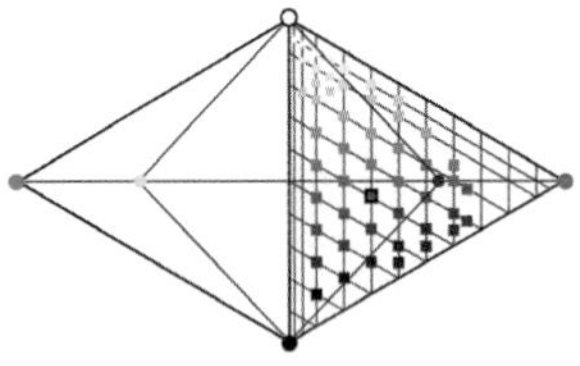

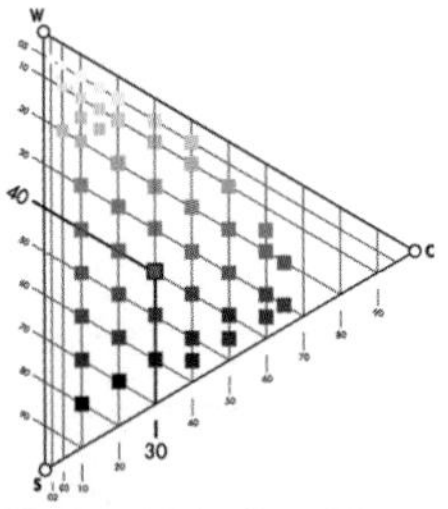

NCS—Natural Colour System®© is property of NCS Colour AB, Stockholm 2013. References to NCS®© in this publication are used with permission from NCS Colour AB.

</td><td>

NCS Colour AB, previously known as the Scandinavian Colour Institute, founded in 1945, is an organization working with color in research, education, design, architecture, marketing, and in industrial color management. Based on research about color and people's visual perception from more than 400 years, this organization researched, developed, and finally launched *The Natural Colour System (NCS)* in 1979. A group of psychologists, physicists, architects, and designers ran tens of thousands of experiments to come to the final conclusions about how people see color.

Hence, this color order system and the corresponding color notation model are entirely based on how humans see color. NCS makes use of the *opponent colour theory* and uses the same six elementary colors that the human brain understands as pure colors: blue, green, yellow, red, white, and black. These colors are placed into the following opponent pairs and positioned in a three-dimensional color space:

- white–black
- green–red
- yellow–blue

All other colors that humans can perceive are described in relation to the achromatic white and black, and one or two of the chromatic elementary colors. NCS provides a system in which designers and all people can communicate about color using a common color language. NCS is represented in more than 60 countries and is one of the most widely used international systems for color communication among designers. It is a national color standard in Sweden, Norway, Spain, and South Africa, and considered to be one of the few systems that can actually be considered a standard for everybody.

</td></tr>
<tr><td>

Pantone

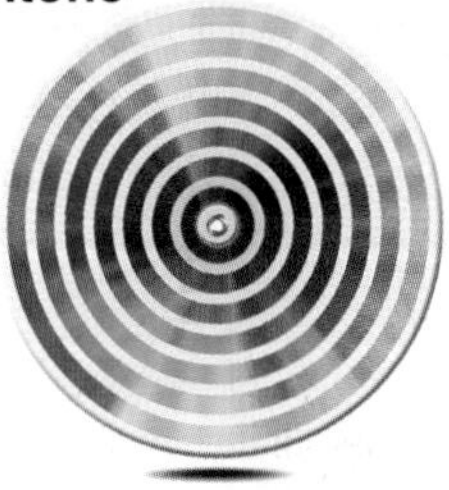

Alberto Masnovo/Shutterstock.com

</td><td>

Pantone, another color system, was developed originally for the graphic arts industry in 1963. It allowed designers to pick colors from a swatch book and receive *accurate* color-matching in their printed materials. Since then, Pantone has moved into such fields as fashion, home, interior, plastics, architecture, paint, and industrial design. Today, the *Pantone Matching System* is an international reference for selecting, specifying, and matching ink colors. For interior designers, Pantone is a color communication tool used for selecting and specifying color for textile manufacturing. Pantone also offers a forecasting tool that indicates seasonal color for the home furnishings industry. Forecasting of these color trends is based on consumer tastes, cycles, and current events.

</td></tr>
</table>

Figure 8-9

(Continued)

Other Influential Color Systems *(Continued)*	
Color System	**Description**
Joseph Albers—Simultaneous Contrast  BeatWalk/Shutterstock.com In the likeness of the Albers color square.	Albers was an artist and educator at the Bauhaus School of Design in Weimar, Germany. In 1933 with the closing of the Bauhaus School, he migrated to the United States to teach at Black Mountain College in North Carolina. His work investigates relationships, illusions, and interactions of color—the way one color impacts another in close proximity. Often a discussion point in interior design, *simultaneous contrast* relates to the contrast that occurs when colors placed side by side appear to change. This visual perception particularly intensifies when complementary colors of high saturation, or brightness, are contrasted. They appear to vibrate or *sing*. In addition, to simultaneous contrast, Albers was also fascinated by the illusion of transparency. Albers' best known work is *Homage to the Square*, an exploration of color interactions with flat-colored squares arranged concentrically. In 1963, he published *Interaction of Color*—his theories about color interactions. Before his death, he served as head of the Department of Design at Yale University. His work has direct bearing on color choices that interior designers make today since color is never seen in isolation.
Johannes Itten  elenabo/Shutterstock.com	A contemporary of Josef Albers, Swiss-born Itten also taught at the Bauhaus School of Design until 1922. An educator, painter, and textile designer, Itten developed the 12-pointed color star to explain contrast, most notably cold-warm combinations. Warm colors are associated with sun, heat, and dryness and make an interior space feel smaller. Cool colors communicate coolness, shadows, and humidity and visually expand an interior space. Among his many publications, *The Art of Color* describes the following ideas about color contrast: ■ contrast of hue ■ contrast of saturation ■ contrast of light and dark ■ contrast of complements Understanding of these contrasts allows a designer to use color to identify focal points or camouflage awkward corners of a space.

Figure 8-9 *(Continued)*

for these color combinations is the *red, yellow,* and *blue (RYB)* (Prang) pigment system.

There are six standard color scheme harmonies. They are monochromatic, analogous, complementary, split complementary, triadic, and tetrad color combinations. Although not one of the color harmonies, achromatic as a color-neutral scheme is also popular.

- **Monochromatic** schemes utilize one hue in multiple and different values and intensities. For example, a residential designer might choose several greens that range from soft green to dark green for use in a kitchen. Likewise, a commercial designer might select soft reds to dark reds for use in an upscale restaurant.

  Monochromatic is a very restful color combination because there are no contrasts in color. Textures, to add variety and interest, are very important in spaces that utilize this scheme. This is the easiest harmony to identify and create successfully.
- **Analogous** (uh-NAH-luh-gus) schemes include three to five adjacent hues next to each other on the color wheel. This harmony works well if people desire a calm, restful interior to relieve stress and anxiety. For example, green, green-blue, and blue might be used in a city-center aquarium. In contrast, red, red-orange, and orange might be used for a mall entrance. Analogous colors can feel very warm or very cool in a space, **Figure 8-10**.
- **Complementary** schemes utilize colors directly opposite each other on the color wheel for high contrast and visual interest. For example, blue and orange are complementary colors you see

Photographee.eu/Shutterstock.com

Figure 8-10 Analogous color schemes utilize hues adjacent to each other on the color wheel. *Take a walk in your community. Where do you observe the use of analogous schemes?*

poligonchik/iStock/Thinkstock

Figure 8-11 The complementary color scheme in this room offers high contrast. *When and where might you use complementary color schemes?*

in some football uniforms. This scheme usually includes one cool and one warm hue.

Colors opposite each other on the wheel, when next to each other, intensify each other and appear to vibrate (recall simultaneous contrast). This color scheme evokes feelings of strength and power, **Figure 8-11**. Such color harmonies are also consciously used for detergent packaging. See your supermarket detergent aisle.

- **Split-complementary** schemes consist of three colors—one main hue plus the two hues each adjacent to its complement. For example, blue, red-orange, and yellow-orange, or red-orange, green, and blue are split-complementary schemes, **Figure 8-12.** Although this scheme does not have the same bold contrast as the direct complement, it offers variety for the planning of interior color schemes. This color scheme might be fun for a hospital pediatric unit for children.
- **Triadic** and **Tetrad** scheme harmonies utilize either three or four colors respectively that are equally spaced along the color wheel, such as blues, greens, and blue-violets. Similar to complementary schemes, these harmonies offer contrast as well as color palettes that are predominately warm or cool. The use of green, yellow, and purple in a unique restaurant café is an example of the *triadic* scheme. A designer might use a fun tetrad color scheme in a school library.
- **Achromatic** (a-kruh-MA-tik) or *neutral* schemes possess no hue and are commonly comprised of such neutral colors as gray, ivory, beige, black, white, tan, and brown. For example, think about the design of a technology office utilizing black, gray, and white. Likewise, consider the design of a residence great room utilizing tans, ivory, and browns. To prevent boredom, using texture and/or pattern is important in these spaces, **Figure 8-13**.

Photographer: Don Riley/Interior Designer:Andrea Schumacher Interiors

Figure 8-12 The split-complementary hues offer variety when developing a client's color scheme.

MR. INTERIOR/Shutterstock.com

Figure 8-13 Small bursts of color add interest to the achromatic scheme in this kitchen. *In what other spaces might an achromatic scheme be effective?*

The Psychology of Color

By definition, **color psychology** is the study of how colors impact the moods, feelings, and behaviors of people. It includes the study of how color influences both individuals and groups.

Color impacts not only interiors, but people, too. When studying the topic of color, you also study how colors affect peoples' moods, productivity, and functions within the spaces. For example, colors in a home can make it feel exciting, upbeat, and joyful—or depressing, dreary, and dated. Similarly, colors in a work environment can enhance employee attitudes, increase productivity, or make people feel colder on an already cold day.

Color usage, association, and preference are all very personal—and should be. Each individual responds to it on a very personal level—physically and psychologically, **Figure 8-14**.

Color impacts brainwaves and emotions. Surrounding colors and colored lights have the ability to increase and decrease heart rate, blood pressure, respiratory rate, body temperature, and depression. As people spend more of their time indoors, the choice of colors placed on walls and floors plays a more important role.

For some people, the power of color can offer a healing environment, make them pay more for a car, wake them up easier in the morning, and minimize stress. If color has that much power over a person, it is necessary to understand and control its use in the immediate surroundings.

Color Preferences

Color preferences and associative learning are opinions shaped by life experiences. From childhood, you learned to associate red and green colors with actions taken at traffic lights. Your favorite toys, clothes you wore for special occasions, or special holiday symbols often evoke positive associations of specific colors. You may associate colors you do not like with your least favorite childhood babysitter, a traumatic event, or a school uniform you wore every day. Your preferences may also relate to your emotional response to color. These responses are not always predictable. One person may perceive a dark color as ominous and overbearing, while another may perceive it as warm and inviting.

Color Meanings and Associations in the United States		
Color	**Characteristics**	**Applications to Interiors**
Red	■ Considered exciting and stimulating; first color infants see after birth ■ *Physically*—increases blood pressure, respiratory rate, stimulates the adrenal glands (increasing strength and stamina), increases occupant fatigue, and increases appetite ■ *Emotionally*—refers to love, ambition, passion, danger, and courage ■ *Psychologically*—means fire, life, and strength	■ Uses include small, strategic amounts to direct attention and claim focal point in active environments—athletic and sports facilities, cosmetic areas, dining establishments, factory and industrial areas, fast-food restaurants, office areas, physical therapy facilities
Pink	■ Relates to delicate emotions, being indulged, sweetness, innocence, and females ■ *Physically*—weakens muscles and stimulates a sweet tooth ■ *Emotionally*—associated with gentleness, indulgence, and protectiveness ■ *Psychologically*—makes people feel calm, protected, warm, and nurtured	■ Uses include candy stores and cosmetics, and prisons and jails
Orange	■ Relates to boldness, cheer, activity, happiness, and endurance ■ *Physically*—decreases hostility and irritability, can be seen at a distance, encourages movement, can strengthen the immune system, and aid in digestion ■ *Emotionally*—decreases feelings of self-pity, low self-esteem, and unwillingness to forgive; helps release emotion ■ *Psychologically*—can denote danger, and is associated with store sales and low-priced items	■ Uses include informal home spaces, such as family rooms; and commercial spaces, such as cell phone stores—appealing to teens ■ Uses include such other areas as athletic and sports facilities, dancing establishments, healthcare environments, industrial/safety areas, shower and restroom areas, passageways and corridors, and office areas
Yellow	■ Encourages cheer, vigor, and radiates warmth ■ Advocates innovation, denotes a modern attitude, and encourages spontaneity ■ *Physically*—can increase irritability and hostility, can enhance concentration, can stimulate the brain which encourages alert and decisive behavior ■ *Emotionally*—bold yellow enhances self-confidence and encourages optimism; dull yellow can bring on fear; can cause an angry person to remain angry longer ■ *Psychologically*—associated with memory, clear thinking, discernment, decision making, and good judgment	■ Uses include schools to assist in memory retention, office designs to improve workplace attentiveness, creative environments, fast-food restaurants, healthcare areas, stairwells, industrial/safety areas, and recreational facilities
Green	■ Relates to wealth, refreshment, growth, and birth ■ *Physically*—offers balance and rejuvenation, encourages deeper and slower breathing, good for heart ■ *Emotionally*—renews the spirit, promotes security, and facilitates good judgment; helps balance emotions due to the connection with nature ■ *Psychologically*—brings feelings of relaxation, comfort, and calmness	■ Uses include residential and commercial buildings—conference facilities, courtrooms, spa areas, hospital operating rooms, libraries, study locations, theater waiting areas, and thoughtful activity areas

Figure 8-14 Understanding color meanings in the United States can help shape design decisions for the client. *(Continued)*

Color Meanings and Associations in the United States *(Continued)*		
Color	**Characteristics**	**Applications to Interiors**
Blue	■ Associated with serenity, loyalty, peacefulness, and sincerity; a favorite color of people in the U.S. ■ *Physically*—can lower blood pressure, slow respiratory rates, cool and relax a person, suppresses appetite—makes food look unappealing; and helps regulate sleep cycles ■ *Emotionally*—calms the spirit; combats tension ■ *Psychologically*—promotes thoughtfulness and introspection; perceptually cools a space that is warm in temperature	■ Uses to *avoid* include restaurants and school cafeterias ■ Uses include banks and financial institutions, conference and meeting rooms, detainment centers, law enforcement areas, libraries, prison cells, private offices, healthcare treatment rooms, diet centers, waiting rooms
Purple or Violet	■ Associated with royalty, quietness, and reverence, high ideals, beauty, and elegance ■ *Physically*—lowers blood pressure, relates to daydreaming, suppresses appetite and hunger and helps keep metabolism on track ■ *Emotionally*—allows meditation, cultivates dignity, invites surprise ■ *Psychologically*—relates to creativity especially in children, helps develop intuitive understanding, aids mental health because it helps balance the mind	■ Uses include places of worship, luxury hotels, entertainment environments, festive areas, gift shops, lecture halls, lobbies and entrances, magical environments, museums (nongallery), perfume and cosmetics areas, and spa facilities
White	■ Positive associations include brides, nurses, joy, birth, hope, innocence, and cleanliness ■ Negative associations include ghosts, death, icebergs, and sterility ■ *Physically*—brings no response in people ■ *Emotionally*—brings feelings of comfort and peace, but can also represent despair ■ *Psychologically*—too much exposure causes feelings of separation, coldness, and isolation	■ Uses include commercial interiors, high tech products, food centers, places, of worship, wedding centers, new residential interiors, modern designs (Note: use of white or off-white wall enhances the look of all colors; warm wood tones brings white spaces to life)
Black	■ Associated with evil, death, mystery, elegance, and dignity ■ *Physically*—relates to mourning ■ *Emotionally*—can invoke a range of feelings including shock, comfort, and protection; implies submission ■ *Psychologically*—can relate to power, intimidation, and aloofness	■ Adds sophistication to residential or commercial interiors ■ Uses include high-tech stores, courtrooms, and elegant restaurants
Brown	■ Associated with nature, safety, and comfort ■ *Physically*—can cause boredom ■ *Emotionally*—enhances feelings of reliability, stability, and tranquility ■ *Psychologically*—relates to sturdiness, reliability, credibility, and shrewdness	■ Uses include wood finishes and furniture, casual home interiors, lawyers' offices
Gray	■ Associated with independence and dignity ■ *Physically*—brings no response in people (similar to white) ■ *Emotionally*—can relate to indecision or lack of commitment ■ *Psychologically*—can represent separation, lack of involvement, and loneliness	■ Uses include products (to denote a long, useful life), an alternative in residential or commercial interiors to brown

Color preferences depend on different aspects of the environment and many variables impact these preferences. Some variables include

- geographical location
- ethnicity
- age and gender

In the United States, favorite colors in order of preference are blue, red, green, violet, orange, and yellow. Blue is still the first choice of Western cultures with the navy blue suit as the power suit of color. These color preferences do not hold true in other countries. For example, the Japanese people rank red as the favorite color.

Research also indicates that as people age color preferences change. Newborns prefer to look at high-contrast edges and patterns. Large black and white patterns present the highest possible contrast (100 percent) to the eye and thus are the most visible and attractive to babies. Recent studies at the University of California Berkeley show infants as young as two weeks of age have color vision and can distinguish a red object from a green one even when these objects are perfectly matched in brightness.

Children age seven to 10 prefer the color red. They seem to relate it to happiness. Later, children's color preferences change to blue. In general, children associate bright colors with happiness and dark colors with sadness.

Adults generally prefer more subdued colors and seem reluctant to use color because they know about its communication properties. As people age, a trend indicates a greater liking for hues of blue, green, and purple over red, orange, and yellow.

Gender also plays a role in color preferences. Boys often choose favorite colors based on their favorite sports teams. The color of their food is more important to them than how it tastes. Men also are more accepting of neutral hues such as black, white, and gray than women. Women are more likely than men to have a favorite color and generally prefer soft versus bright colors.

Color preferences are personally held opinions based on life experiences. They often impact client color choices. Designers must understand such preferences before selecting color palettes for an interior space.

Color Trends and Forecasting

One of the fascinating topics of color is the ever-changing color trends in fashion, interiors, and automotive industries. What influences color trends? A few factors include

- lifestyle and demographics
- social and economic activity
- political climate
- regional and historical differences
- fashion
- art and architecture
- film and television
- social media
- cross cultures

Manufacturers realize forecasts hold critical information that influences the success of their companies because they cannot afford to produce items that do not sell to the consumer. Therefore, color trends are predicted and protected. Color experts come from industries such as appliances, transportation (automotive), industrial design, interior design, cosmetics, and fashion design. They meet annually, from around the globe to forecast the next color palettes for use in future years. Their forecasts are often reliable and accurate, **Figure 8-15.**

As the world becomes smaller through communication technologies, cultural influences have a strong presence in the final decisions. It is the designer's job to understand color forecasting variables and to stay ahead of the color trends for their clients.

There are several national and international color-forecasting organizations that help interior designers stay up-to-date on color trends. Two major ones include the following:

Fedor Selivanov/Shutterstock.com

Figure 8-15 Color forecasters predict color trends that influence design in many industries.

- **Color Association of the United States (CAUS).** This panel of professionals is active in the fields of color styling, color research, marketing, and merchandising.
- **Color Marketing Group (CMG).** This is an international organization for color design professionals from all industries. Founded in 1962, it forecasts color trends nineteen months or more in advance for manufactured products and services.

These groups have a unique color language that describes such color trends as those coming "over the horizon" and those that have "reached consumer acceptance." New color palettes are kept very secret and guarded carefully until they are announced. No single industry receives preferential treatment to get a head start against their competitors.

Consumer preferences do not always shift with the predicted color trends. Colors labeled *passé* several years ago—such as mauve in the 1980s—may still show up after the introduction of new palettes. Clients and consumers still have personal preferences.

Interior designers watch fashion colors closely. Colors the fashion industry uses are often three years ahead of color predictions and popular use in interior spaces.

The Impact of Color on Behavior

Color impacts human behavior. According to the Color Marketing Group (CMG), color increases brand recognition by up to 80 percent, accelerates learning from 55 to 78 percent, and may be up to 85 percent of the reason people decide to buy an item or object.

Bright colors make a person move faster, while soft colors encourage rest and relaxation. Specific colors, such as red, generally increase the perception of time spent in a space. Color creates the sparkle—or the glittering distinction—that attracts the human eye and enhances first impressions.

Strong colors, such as pure red or yellow, can cause fatigue if viewed for extended periods of time. Certain stimuli, similar to a rock concert, can have negative impact on the body's energy level from overexposure. Eyestrain from overexposure to certain intense colors results in brain confusion and discomfort.

Placement of color can also prevent accidents and injuries in interior spaces. In a hospital, for instance, color can cue staff to quickly locate emergency equipment. In a distribution center, color can communicate toxins and poisons.

Color and Space

Color's compelling attraction is its ability to shape space and focus attention. It shapes space by camouflaging awkward corners, changing the perception of ceiling height (low or high), or causing a wall to feel as if it is advancing or receding (for example, dark versus light colors, bright versus dull colors). Color focuses people's attention by guiding what the eye looks at first when walking into an interior, **Figure 8-16.** A bright color over a fireplace focal point causes people to look at it immediately on entering the room.

©Judy Davis/Hoachlander Davis Photography/Designed by ForrestPerkins

Figure 8-16 Color helps guide the eyes of those who enter a room. *How does use of color focus your attention in this room?*

Link to History

20th Century Color Palettes in the United States

Historically, there are many of these influences that impact color palettes during specific decades. Although generalized in the following table, these color palettes show you how the color trends reflected specific eras of twentieth-century history in the United States.

Analyze It!

Use Internet or print resources to investigate one or more of the decades below. Locate illustrations of interior designs of the decade and analyze them against factors that influenced the color palettes. How are these factors evident in the room designs? Write an illustrated report of your analysis to share with the class.

Decade	Color Palettes and Influencing Factors
1920s	*Interior color palette:* primary colors, and black, white, and gray *Influencing factors:* This decade encompassed the Depression through the beginning of 1939. Color became subdued and reflected the economy, rationing of dyes, and the nation's war effort related to technology.
1930s	*Interior color palette:* softer all-white rooms with neutrals; some combinations of yellows, dark browns, and greens; peachy-pinks, corals, teals, and tans were also introduced *Influencing factors:* Memories of the Great Depression along with tragic losses from WWI; Wall Street crash; Franklin D. Roosevelt's *New Deal* introduced optimism; the golden age of the radio that introduced into homes the comedy of Jack Benny and heroes like Lone Ranger. People turned to movies for relief from problems and watched such well-known actresses as Shirley Temple.
1940s	*Interior color palette:* sharp reds, yellows, aqua with bright yellow, and crisp white; large variety of grays—dark to light, with dark brown, and black; nude, periwinkle, and a grayed purple also used. *Influencing factors:* The Japanese bombing of Pearl Harbor, WWII, baseball games, housing shortages, and GI bill of rights also greatly influenced color choices.
1950s	*Interior color palette:* salmon, sea foam, and hot pink *Influencing factors:* WWII was over and the world celebrated with color.
1960s	*Interior color palette:* chartreuse, hot pink, hot orange, red, white, black, and center-line yellow. *Influencing factors:* This decade was a mixture of civil rights demonstrations, the space age, go-go dancing, psychedelic drugs, and the Vietnam War. Colors appear warlike.
1970s	*Interior color palette:* earth tones, avocado greens, harvest gold, rust, and beige *Influencing factors:* This decade was about technological advances, Vietnam, Watergate, Roe vs. Wade, the Nixon resignation, NASA, and the energy crisis.
1980s	*Interior color palette*—first half of decade: mauve (pink/purple), plum, sea foam, slate-green, peach, and French blue; the second half of the decade saw the use of such jewel tones as fuchsia, violet, emerald, teal, cobalt, and coral; whitewash was big *Influencing factors:* This decade reflected corporate mergers, AIDS—a health focus, a bull market, and hunger for natural light.
1990s	*Interior color palette*—electric colors: primary colors, mustards, bronzes, coppers, earth reds, blazing oranges, clean blues, greens, and deep plums *Influencing factors:* This was known as the *Green Decade*. Ecology, the planet, and preservation became popular. It was also a decade of people spending money.
2000–2006	*Interior color palette:* traditional colors including deep and denim blues, hunter greens, reds, winter whites, golden yellows; some colors were quite bold and saturated; gray became the new black *Influencing factors:* America was seeking sense of connection to each other as well as past—linkage, heritage, and history. People's lives became more home-centered.
2007 and beyond	*Interior color palette:* toned-down colors for relaxation, bright yellow, and tribal colors from Africa and Native America *Influencing factors:* The last half of the decade was captured by an economic downturn. The U.S. no longer was a *throw-away* society. Conservatism, world travel, and diverse cultures, expand horizons but bring the global community to the home along with environmentally responsible living. For example, in 2009 Mimosa (golden yellow) was chosen as color of the year to embody hopefulness and reassurance in a climate of change.

Color forms a person's first impression of space and place. Contrasting color combinations can create excitement or cause distraction. Colors can enhance a feeling of spaciousness or develop a cozy feeling of comfort and sanctuary. Soft, blended uniform colors can expand a space. A warm color can cause a wall to perceptually advance while a cool color can cause it to recede or move away. Your first impression of a space may cause you to think *dreary* or *stunning* due to the color choices.

Color can enhance a view outside, and use of neutral colors will support a colorful focal point. Color can highlight beautiful, graceful architectural elements such as columns and arches. Color can direct traffic through such commercial spaces as retail shops, hotel lobbies, and hospital hallways. For instance, a hospital might use a different color floor tile to help direct people to the cafeteria or other areas of the hospital.

Color creates brand recognition such as store identification in retail spaces. Through color combinations, you recognize McDonalds®, Holiday Inn®, or an iPad®. Color choices can communicate danger in work areas, designate different storage areas in a child's bedroom, or identify parts of an assembly line.

When selecting color placement, consider texture used for furnishings and wall coverings. Two identical red fabrics under two different types of light reflect the light differently and therefore show two different colors. For example, heavy wool textures appear darker than sleek, satin fabrics that reflect rather than trap the light. In the absence of bold, bright colors or interesting color combinations, texture plays a critical role in bringing human interest to a space.

Understanding how people perceive and associate color assists the interior designer in selecting client colors for three-dimensional spaces. Realizing how the interaction of colors impacts the size, shape, and volume of interior places helps the designer determine where to put selected colors. Here are a few things to remember about color.

- Reds, oranges, and yellows grab attention.
- Green and brown combinations suggest tradition, elegance, and comfort.
- Complementary colors make a strong statement because they accentuate each other.
- Neutrals can be light or dark and warm or cool in a space.
- White interiors can appear to be sterile, harsh, and uninteresting. The warmth of wood brings an added human element to the space, **Figure 8-17**.
- Red increases the perception of time spent in a room, while blue decreases this perception.
- Bright colors against a neutral background appear brighter.
- Dark colors on a ceiling cause it to seem visually lower.
- Color can link unlike objects and furnishings to each other, unifying them.

The Global and Cultural Impact on Color Usage

As an interior designer, it is important to appreciate and be sensitive to different cultural meanings of color. Many designers practice overseas. As they present suggested color palettes to a client, they do not want to offend or risk communicating their designs inaccurately. In addition, in the U.S. there are people of many different cultures who retain their unique color meanings and associations. Cultural sensitivity during the planning of design projects, especially for public spaces, is critical. Therefore, there are two major reasons to study the cultural aspects of color from an interior designer's point of view.

- **Enhance client sensitivity**—showing appreciation and respect of differences and design accordingly and to avoid giving offense.

Photographer: Chris Little Photography/Interior design: Rabaut Design Associates

Figure 8-17 This wood floor adds warmth to this white interior.

- **Communication clarity**—knowing that a color may have a totally different meaning in another country than it does in the U.S.

In addition to different meanings, a specific color may have symbolic and historical importance in different parts of the world. For example, yellow had religious significance in early China while purple was the ancient, imperial color for royalty in the country at the same time.

Color preferences and associations hold different meanings in different countries and cultures. In general, those who live in climates with a lot of sunlight prefer warm, bright colors. Those from climates with less sunlight prefer cooler, less-saturated colors. For example, Native Alaskans actually use 17 different words for *white* as it applies to different snow conditions.

According to research, cultures also differ in their aesthetic expressions as colors represent different meanings and aesthetic appeal. Examples of disparate perception and response to color include

- **White.** In East Asia and Italy, white symbolizes mourning or death, but in Australia and New Zealand it represents happiness, purity, and birth. In the United States, white often represents marriage, while in many African and Middle Eastern countries it means holiness, peace, and goodness.
- **Black.** In China, black is the color for trust and high quality. In contrast, in the U.S., Peru, and Iran it is a color for death and mourning. Evil and bad luck are the connotations of black in Thailand.
- **Brown.** In Australia and the U.S., brown is the color of land and earth. Brown is often a successful color for food packaging in the U.S., while in India it symbolizes mourning.
- **Red.** In Nigeria, red is unlucky, but in China, Denmark, and Argentina it is the color of good luck and celebration, **Figure 8-18**. In North American countries, red can mean danger, love, or excitement. In India, red means purity and is often a bridal color. Red represents life in Japan, while in Celtic countries it represents death and the afterlife.
- **Orange.** In the U.S., orange is the color of the autumn harvest and Halloween, while in the Ukraine it means strength, and in Japan it is the color of courage and love. In Egypt, orange is the color of mourning.
- **Yellow.** In the U.S., yellow can represent warmth, hope, and happiness, but also cowardice and weakness. It is associated with jealousy in Russia, but represents pleasantness, happiness, good taste, and royalty in China. In Mexico and Egypt, yellow is the color of mourning. In Japan it means courage, but strength and reliability in Saudi Arabia.
- **Green.** In many countries and cultures, green represents environmental awareness and the color of military uniforms. However, it represents danger or disease in Malaysia, envy in Belgium, corruption in North Africa, and love in Japan. In Egypt and China, green is not a good color for packaging.
- **Blue.** In East Asia, blue is perceived as cold and evil. In Sweden it represents cold, but warmth in the Netherlands. Blue is associated with boys and pink with girls in the U.S., but in Belgium, the association is reversed—pink for boys and blue for girls. Other associations include trust in the U.S., cleanliness in Scandinavia, happiness in Africa, holiness in Israel, and heaven and spirituality in Iran.
- **Purple.** In China and South Korea, purple is the color of love, while in Egypt it means virtue. It represents anger and envy in Mexico, but sin and fear in Japan. In Brazil and Thailand, it is the color of mourning, while purple also relates to nobility and wealth in China.

wong yu liang/Shutterstock.com

Figure 8-18 In various cultures, color meanings and associations differ. For instance, red is the color of celebration in China. *What does red mean in other cultures?*

Designer Profile

Maryam S. E. Taylor—Architectural Lighting Design

Maryam has been in the lighting industry for six years. Read more about Maryam's mission with lighting design.

"As an architectural lighting designer, my mission is to explore innovative lighting solutions to complement the art, architecture, and interior design of a space, while balancing aesthetics and function. With every project, I have the end goal in mind to enhance every space with inspiring, yet efficient, lighting designs. People are attracted to good lighting. As a designer, I strive to generate good lighting that enhances the mood and desirability of a space, which increases the well-being of all occupants."

You can read more about Maryam's experience in Appendix B.

The Importance of Light in Interiors

Without light, color cannot and does not exist. The ability to see is one of the most noticeable and remarkable benefits of light. When you are working on homework, do you have enough light to see the textbook page? When you are trying on clothes in a retail store, is the lighting shadowy or bright enough to make a purchase decision?

People notice natural light in their homes as it streams through the windows. They appreciate its abundance and seek ways to bring more into spaces when it is lacking, **Figure 8-19**.

Without the appropriate quantity of light, people cannot see, use, or enjoy their interiors. It does not matter how much money a person spends on expensive interior finishes, dramatic architectural details, or innovative custom details—if a person cannot see it, all the planning and design is for nothing. Without proper lighting, people will perceive the most beautiful space in the world as ugly or not see it at all.

Similar to color, light manipulates mood, defines spaces, enhances function, and encourages movement

Ron Ruscio Photography/Interior Design: JJ Interiors

Figure 8-19 Appropriate lighting allows people to function better and enjoy their interiors.

within a space. It also adds drama and creates sparkle or certain radiance. Other than color, light is the most powerful element in shaping the interior.

Light is both a science and an art. Lighting engineers have monopolized this career for good reason. Their work involves the quantity of light. They calculate the amount of light—or *quantity of light*—in the footcandles needed to be safe and to function in the space, **Figure 8-20**.

Quality of light, however, is still a relatively new concept. Subjective in nature, *quality of light* allows users to function comfortably in an interior, feel safe in it, and appreciate its design aesthetics. Achievement of quality of light requires a comprehensive plan that includes a balance of both natural and electric light. The lighting industry strongly encourages interior designers to become more involved in aesthetically shaping the interior space with light.

Achieving a quality lighting environment necessitates skillful placement and layering light. Light is additive, and therefore **layering light** attracts attention, highlights the focal point of the space, and provides zest or sparkle, adding interest or excitement to the space. For example, in a retail store, to draw attention, a designer may use more light in wall displays to invite your exploration. Similarly, in a residence, a bright light over a fireplace draws attention to that focal point. It is important to layer electric light in interior spaces. Layered lighting gives occupants a variety of shade and shadow in an interior space, similar to what is found in nature, **Figure 8-21.**

Daylight

Natural light should always be a consideration when developing a lighting design for a client. This is one of the first steps when layering light in an interior.

Daylight is free but requires control to avoid glare and discomfort to the occupant. Successful daylighting is more than simply adding large windows or skylights.

Lighting Vocabulary

- **Efficacy.** A measurement of how efficient the light source is in converting electrical energy to *lumens* of visible light. Efficacy is expressed in *lumens-per-watt (LPW).*
- **Fixture.** A housing or apparatus that holds the lamp in place. Fixture examples include a track and track head or a recessed can. (See lamp.)
- **Footcandle.** A unit of illuminance or light that falls on a surface. It represents the light level on a surface one foot from a standard candle. One footcandle is equal to one lumen per square foot. (See Lux.)
- **Lamp.** A glass envelope from which light is emitted, commonly referred to as a *lightbulb.*
- **Layering light.** This term relates to visual hierarchy of light—where there is more or less light in a space to draw your attention when you first enter the room. The process of layering light is as follows. Electric light is layered into a lighting plan or reflected ceiling plan in three steps: first, indicate where general illumination lighting fixtures will be located. Second, indicate where task lighting fixtures need to be located. Lastly, insert the accent lighting fixture. Overlapping beams of light will create different levels of illumination in the space; or layers.
- **Line voltage.** Line voltage, 120 volts, is the common type coming into the home or building.
- **Low voltage.** Incorporating the use of a transformer, line voltage of 120 volts is reduced to 12 volts; thus using less energy to produce light. Commonly used for track lighting.
- **Lumen.** A measurement of the quantity and brightness of light emitted by a light source. For example, a dinner candle provides about 12 lumens. A 60-watt Soft White incandescent lamp provides about 840 lumens. Visible light is measured in lumens.
- **Lux.** Lux (lx). A unit of illuminance or light that falls on a surface. One lux is equal to one lumen per square meter. Ten lux approximately equals one footcandle. This measurement of light is often used outside the U.S. (See footcandle.)
- **Volt.** A unit of electric potential that relates to the force of electricity in the power line.
- **Watt.** A unit of electrical power. Lamps are rated in watts to indicate the amount of energy the lamp uses.

Figure 8-20 Knowing the vocabulary of lighting helps you make appropriate selections for the client.

photosphobos/Shutterstock.com

Figure 8-21 Layering light helps attract attention in interiors.

It involves thoughtful integration of design strategies that address heat gain, glare, light availability, and direct-beam penetration into a building. For a career, you could become an expert in *daylighting strategies*. These strategies are particularly important for commercial interiors and buildings because they relate to the amount of energy—such as air conditioning in summer months—needed to achieve human comfort.

There are a multitude of benefits for incorporating daylight into an interior. Daylight

- increases human well-being
- increases productivity
- increases morale and, therefore, attendance at work
- increases the amount of time consumers shop in a store
- enhances the perception of control over the environment through natural ventilation
- produces considerable energy savings—which means money savings
- brings nature into the interior space—people partake and experience nature rather than only look at it

This latter benefit is really the biggest advantage of daylighting. The use of windows to obtain natural light and a view to the outdoors develops a human connection to nature. It has a physical impact because gazing out a window provides relief for eye muscles. Humans also like to see seasons change and time pass. The constantly changing nature of daylight satisfies the biological and psychological needs for change—respite, relief of monotony, and stimulus.

Daylight has two components. They include

- **Sunlight**—directional light beams emitted by the sun. Direct sunlight is usually an impractical source for interiors unless it has shielding. It leads to visual fatigue without shielding.
- **Skylight**—diffused reflection of light from particles in the atmosphere. It is a useful light source without shielding. Skylight is particularly good for corridors, stairwells, and seating areas.

When developing a lighting plan with the use of daylighting strategies, it is important to incorporate special design considerations to control light. These include

- **Orientation of building to site**—direction of the building in relation to movement of sun
- **Glazing**—quality and finish of the windows, including thickness of glass
- **Location and size of windows**—locate most windows on north and south sides of building (for instance, clerestory window placement allows natural light to enter and fall into the interior)
- **Light shelves**—horizontal units on an interior or exterior wall help reflect daylight into a space
- **Light pipes**—these light tubes transport light into an interior space
- **Skylights**—shapes cut into roof, covered with glass or translucent material that allow light into interior
- **Photovoltaic cells**—panels that convert solar energy into electrical energy

Other strategies include shading devices, window size and spacing, and the color and texture of interior finishes. Strategies such as these are used to acquire LEED certification through USGBC. See the following Case Study on Fossil Ridge High School.

CASE STUDY

Lighting at Fossil Ridge High School, LEED Silver

For their new high school in Fort Collins, Colorado, the *Poudre School District's* primary goal was to provide students with the healthiest, most comfortable, and effective learning environment. Designed from the classroom out, learning was of primary importance. A school-within-a-school concept was utilized, which divides the building into three smaller teaching *houses*.

Many studies show that natural lighting improves students' reading and math scores. Therefore, the goal of the design team for *RB+B Architects, Inc.* was to focus on such daylighting strategies as placing windows on multiple sides of classrooms, roof monitors, and light tubes to bring light into interiors. While acquiring their education, each student also learns that their environmentally responsible, healthy building is saving the school district money.

Stepped roofline at the front entry captures natural light

Shade devices used at the auditorium entry

The gym entry canopy uses photovoltaic cells

Close-up of the photovoltaic cells

Clerestory window orientation to views and sun

Interior view of clerestory windows

Roofline windows fill the ceiling cavity with daylight

Clerestory windows fill the media center with light

RB+B Architects/David Patterson Photography

Facts about Fossil Ridge High School include

- **Building capacity**—290,000 square feet with capacity for 1,800 students
- **LEED certification**—the first high school in Colorado with this distinction and the second in the United States
- **Building cost**—$179 per square foot (with no extra cost to acquire LEED certification)
- **Lower energy costs**—about one-third less than newest high school in a district of the same size

Investigate and Reflect

Use the Internet to investigate another school in the United States that also has LEED certification. What characteristics make the school unique? How was lighting used in the school? Why was the school able to achieve LEED certification? How is the school similar to Fossil Ridge High school in its mission for education? Discuss your findings with the class.

Psychological Aspects of Lighting

Lighting a space requires you to understand psychological aspects related to light. For example, lighting in a space can influence the perception of safety. The greater amount of light in a place, the more there is a feeling of safety particularly in unfamiliar surroundings. The amount of light in an interior space impacts peoples' sense of spaciousness. Research indicates that light along the boundaries of a space, such as corners and walls of room, increases perception of the space as being larger. Lighting impacts sense of privacy. Too much light creates a feeling of being "in the spotlight."

People desire both differing levels and layers of light in a space to mimic the light in nature. Overall general, bright light in a supermarket is fatiguing to the human eye because there are no varying levels of light to offer respite to the eye muscle. Everything is the same brightness. Research indicates shoppers leave a store more quickly in this lighting environment.

Layers of light, similar to nature, offer a method of directing your attention in a space; serving as a type of visual hierarchy. Knowing what to look at first is reassuring as the human brain strives to quickly gather knowledge of the new place. It assists the brain in understanding where to look first to comprehend the information in the place.

There are psychological aspects related to light and dark—a presence or lack of light. A latitude-related winter depression, commonly called *seasonal affective disorder (SAD)*, occurs in people that need more light to stave off depression that often begins in the month of November. Research indicates 25 percent of people in Alaska and only two percent of people in Florida suffer from SAD. Symptoms of SAD can include

- decreased physical activity
- sadness, irritability, and anxiety
- changes in appetite, carbohydrate craving, and body weight
- changes in sleep patterns

Experts believe SAD occurs because of the disruption of the *circadian rhythms*—or biological activities or functions occurring about every 24 hours in the human body, **Figure 8-22**. Exercise during daylight hours and exposure to sun often resets these rhythms. In extreme cases, doctors prescribe artificial light therapy or exposure to bright, sustained amounts of natural light that has similar results to a visit to southern climates.

As interior designers specify and develop lighting designs, it is important to consider the psychological aspects of light. Critical attention to placement, amount, layers, color, and location of fixtures and lamps can help people feel their best in a space year round.

How People See Light

Electric light meets two basic human needs—safety and beauty. Properly lit areas help prevent accidents. Dramatic or focal light invites beauty and visual interest.

As a reminder, the study of light is both a *science* and an *art*. It is important to examine the science part of lighting first. Once you understand more about the visible spectrum and how the human eye works, you can understand how to develop lighting solutions that create beautiful spaces, enhance human function, and prevent accidents.

The vision process begins when light enters the *pupil*—the opening of the iris of the eye. During this process, the human eye takes in light and the image of an object. The *lens* of the eye adjusts the perception of light for near and far vision, and the *cornea* focuses light on the *retina* of the eye by refraction. This function is known as **accommodation**.

luxorphoto/Shutterstock.com

Figure 8-22 The lack of light or changes in light greatly impact people with seasonal affective disorder.

Rods and *cones* are detector cells located at the back of the retina. The cones of the eye perceive color, bright light, and detail. If the cones are damaged, the colors the eye perceives are not accurate. The rods, used for night vision, perceive low levels of illumination.

The *iris* is a membrane that dilates, opening to allow more light to enter the eye during darkness. This process of **adaptation** is similar to the way a camera lens works, the pupil constricts in bright light and expands in the dark. It happens when you go to the movies and the lights dim and then come up after the show. Your eyes require more time to adjust from bright to dark light than the reverse, **Figure 8-23**.

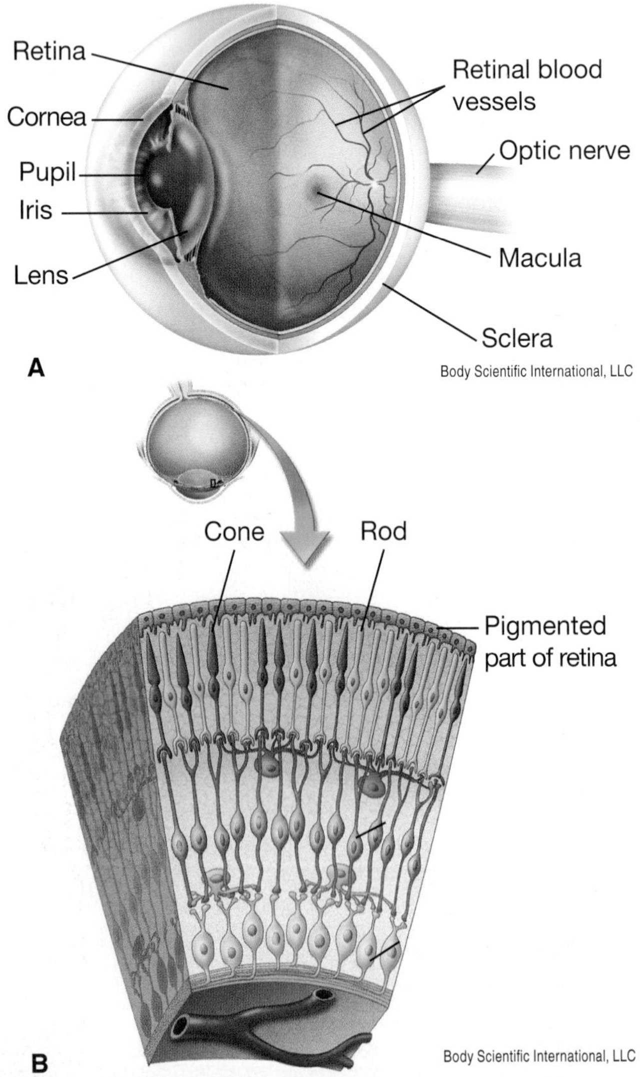

Figure 8-23 Understanding the anatomy of the eye and how it perceives color and light is important when making appropriate color choices (A). *What type of light activates the cones (B)? rods?*

To understand light, you also need to understand the *visible spectrum*. As you know, light is technically a form of energy that is part of the electromagnetic spectrum. The **electromagnetic spectrum** contains many wavelengths, such as microwaves, gamma waves, and radio waves. Within this spectrum is the visible spectrum that contains the wavelengths people perceive as light. As you know, light is the visible spectrum—the visible light (color) people can see that is a series of wavelengths measured in nanometers. A *nanometer* is one billionth of a meter. At one end of the visible spectrum is the red wavelength found in light. It is the longest at about 700 nanometers. At the other end of the spectrum is the purple wavelength. It is the shortest at 380 nanometers. When all light wavelengths are present at one time, white light occurs, **Figure 8-24**.

As lighting manufacturers develop each electric lightbulb (or *lamp*), they test it to determine what color wavelengths are present when the light is on. Some lamps have strong blue wavelengths, such as some fluorescent lights. Others provide primarily yellow wavelengths, such as incandescent lamps.

The Impact of Light on Color

Knowing that color and light, as two elements of design, affect each other significantly, it is important to study what influences your client's perception of color. Perception of color begins as a signal passing along the optic nerve. The brain translates this signal into a visual sensation. It then develops into an emotional, social,

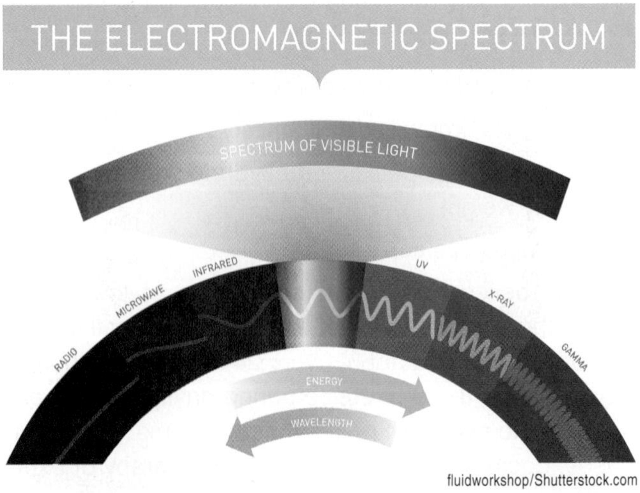

Figure 8-24 Visible light is part of the electromagnetic spectrum.

and spiritual phenomenon that carries many layers of vivid meaning. As you know, people view light with a wavelength of 700 nanometers as red. People may experience it, however, as warmth or danger, romance or revolution, heroism or evil depending on the cultural meanings.

Three factors influence the perception of a color. They include the

- light source and color temperature (color of light source)
- object itself (absorption quality of a surface)
- observer (health and age of human eye)

Light Source and Color Temperature

The color of electric light can change the color of an object or interior. Most electric light sources cast a white, yellow, or blue color tint on surrounding objects. As an interior designer, it is important to know *how* the color from the electric light affects the interior finishes you specify. For example, if you design a warm color scheme into a space and the light has a blue cast, the warm color scheme will have a blue cast to it. To understand what color will come from a light source, an interior designer often talks with a lighting company representative. Understanding how to talk about the lamp's color properties is an important task. The representative will address the light's color in three different ways. See **Figure 8-25**.

- **Kelvin temperature (K).** Every lamp has a Kelvin temperature rating provided by the manufacturer. Kelvin temperature (K) is a measurement scale used to determine the warmth of coolness of a lamp. The lower the Kelvin temperature is, the warmer the color will typically be. Incandescent lamps generally have a 3800 degrees Kelvin temperature. The bluer the light appears, the

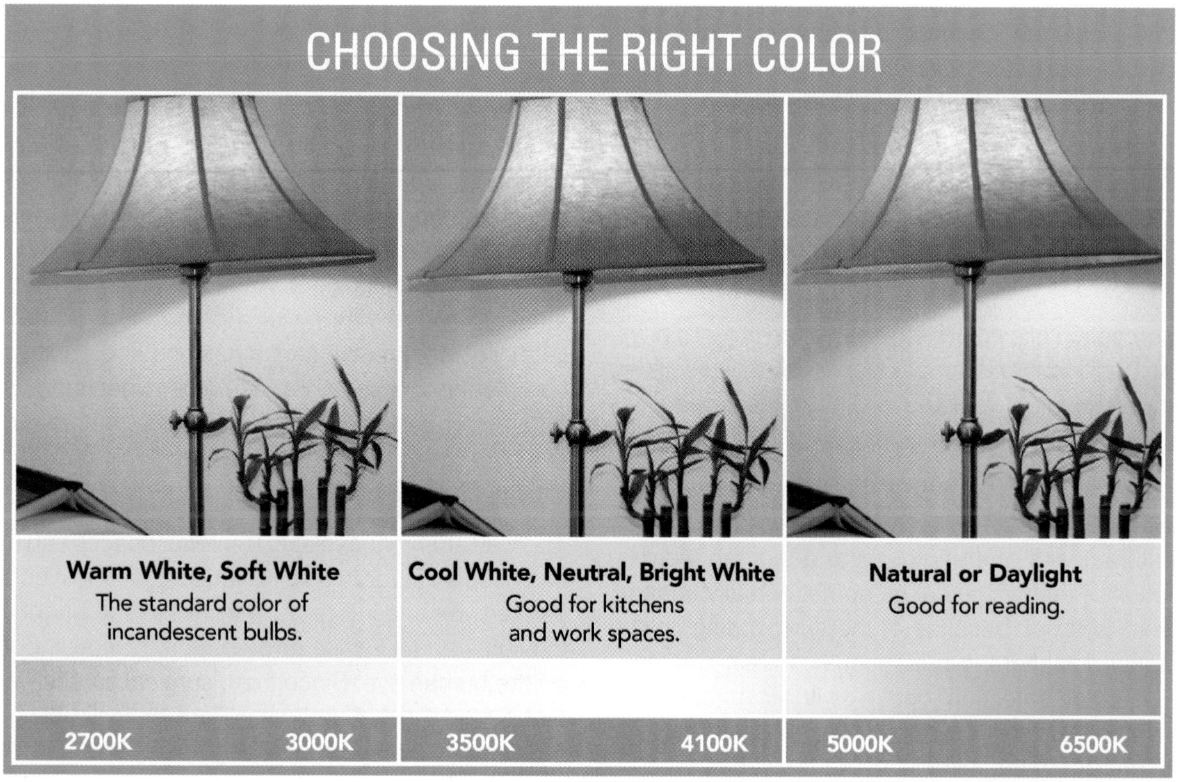

U. S. Environmental Protection Agency (EPA)

Figure 8-25 Understanding how the color of electric light influences color can impact the interior finishes you choose for clients. *How do CRI, Kelvin temperature, and SPD help in understanding the influence of light on color?*

higher the Kelvin temperature. For instance, most fluorescent lamps have a Kelvin temperature of 4100 degrees. Consumers can view the temperatures on a lamp package.

- **Color rendering index (CRI).** The color rendering index (CRI) is an international system of measurement. It is used to evaluate light sources (any lightbulbs) based on how well they indicate the true color of an object relative to a standard light source—typically an incandescent. The scale ranges from 1–100. A CRI of 85 or higher is good; a CRI of above 90 is excellent. The red of a red delicious apple looks a true red at this CRI.
- **Spectral power distribution charts (SPD).** Used to indicate the color characteristics emitting from a light source in specific wavelengths at each wavelength over the visible spectrum, these charts indicate to the designer the strongest colors that will emerge from a particular lamp. Note that some resources may call these spectral color distribution charts.

Metamerism can occur in interiors. **Metamerism** (muh-TAH-muh-rih-zuhm) happens when two colors appear to be the same under one light source, but not under another. For example, a blue upholstery fabric may appear one color in the store under fluorescent light and a different blue in natural daylight. For this reason, designers select client materials and finishes in natural daylight *and* in the interior electric lighting where the installation of the finish occurs. Even a professional can be fooled at times.

The Object

Your perception of a color depends on the object's physical composition. For example, transparent glass allows transmission of light while a dark, nubby-textured glass traps light and darkens the color.

Your perception also involves *simultaneous contrast.* As you recall, this occurs when two colors, placed side by side, interact with one another and affect the viewer's perception of them. The colors do not actually change, but seem to do so because of the surrounding colors. For interior designers, simultaneous contrast is a *major* issue. If color selection occurs without understanding this concept, wall colors can visually change even though physically the color is the same.

The Observer

The perception of a color may change if the human eye is aging, damaged, or is color deficient. If the eye is aging, the cornea of the eye takes on a yellow tinge. To understand the color an aging client may see, put on yellow sunglasses and view the world around you. This view is similar to how the aging person sees his or her world—and colors—through a yellow film. Selecting colors for healthcare interiors, retirement facilities, and planned-retirement communities necessitates more use of blue-tinged colors rather than yellow-tinged to compensate for this aging phenomenon.

With eye damage—through an accident—a person may no longer be able to perceive color accurately. A red apple may not appear red to this person. Similarly, if the human eye has a *color deficiency*, as an inherited genetic trait, then the client may not accurately perceive a color selection. According to the American Optometric Association, **color vision deficiency,** or color blindness, is the inability to distinguish certain shades of color or even colors at all, **Figure 8-26.** There are three different kinds of color deficiencies. The first is a lack of the ability to perceive particular shades of reds and greens (common). The second is inability to perceive blues and yellows (less common). The third is a complete lack of color vision (uncommon). Males have more color deficiencies than females, although the percentage is quite low for both.

Another way your perception of a color can temporarily change is known as *afterimage.* **Afterimage** is an optical illusion that occurs when a person looks at a lightbulb too long and the shape momentarily imprints on other objects in sight. An afterimage can also occur after prolonged viewing of a patch of color. When the latter occurs, the eye seeks balance and generates the complementary color. For example, when staring at red for a prolonged period, the afterimage the brain creates is a blue-green color if you turn and look at a white wall. Closing the eye helps it adapt more quickly.

The way afterimage relates to interior spaces can be seen in a hospital surgery unit. Historically, surgical units were painted white to indicate cleanliness. The bright operating lights and all-white environment, however, put strain on the human eye. Since then, surgical scrubs—clothes that surgical personnel wear—are typically blue-green. This assists the eye in adapting as the doctor looks from

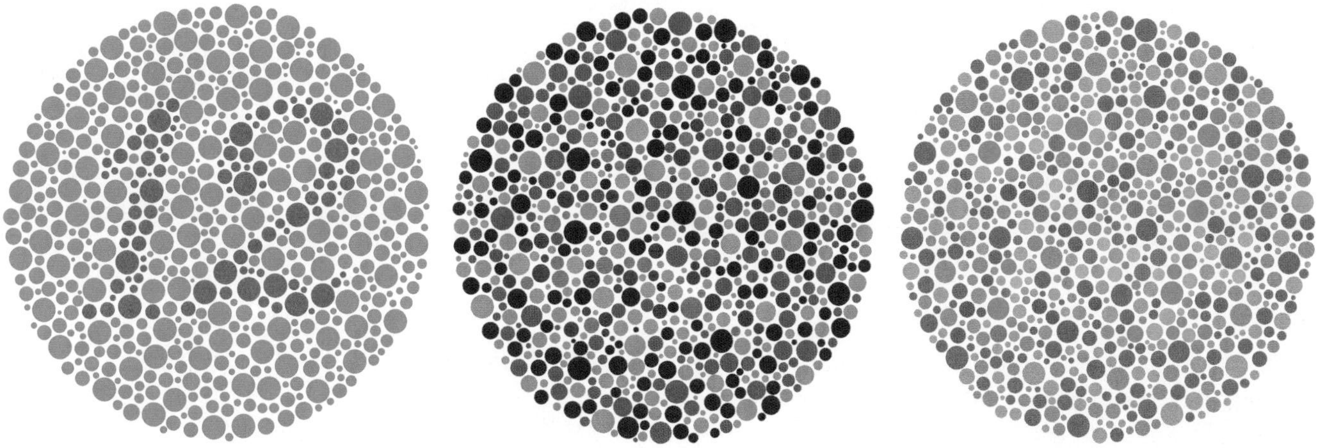

Portokalis/Shutterstock.com

Figure 8-26 The Ishihara color test helps doctors identify color vision deficiency. *How can color vision deficiency affect interior design?*

the red of a surgery to team members. Because the afterimage of red is blue-green, the doctor's eyes do not need to adjust because he or she looks up and sees the same color. This strategy averts the afterimage causing prolonged focus problems.

- minimizes or eliminates shadows
- minimizes form
- reduces the importance of things and people
- fills people with a sense of freedom of space
- suggests a lack of boundaries

Three Categories of Light

As you layer with light, you will use three categories—general, task, and accent light. Begin with general; then move to task before adding the accent light.

Ambient Lighting

With proper design and installation, **ambient lighting**—or general lighting—provides uniform, overall light for the space. Ambient light ensures people can walk safely through a space and offers a comfortable level of brightness. It should support the mood or character of the interior. On a sunny day, ambient natural light can fill elementary school spaces, but at night electric light still offers safe use of the interiors. Today, most people prefer ambient lighting fixtures that provide **indirect illumination**, meaning light that bounces off a ceiling or wall before it falls into the space. Ambient light fixtures can be the central light in a bedroom, fluorescent lights in a large office area, or dropped fixtures in a school corridor, **Figure 8-27**. Ambient light

Task Lighting

The more time it takes to complete a job or task, the more light is needed. This is because the eye fatigues over time with use. **Task lighting** is a direct form of light and usually provides three times the level of light as ambient lighting. Therefore, this light helps you perform a specific task accurately and efficiently. Due to the age of the eye muscle, people with aging eyes require more light to complete the same tasks as younger individuals.

A client's tasks that might require additional light include reading, accounting, performing surgery, or preparing meals. With the use of a dimmer switch—a type of lighting control—it is easy to control task lights. This offers flexibility if the amount of light needs to be increased as the day passes. A task-lighting fixture can be recessed or track lighting, pendant lighting over a dining table or kitchen island, and under-cabinet lighting in a kitchen or office area, **Figure 8-28**.

If a lighting fixture reflects a pool of light onto a task surface—such as a desk or at a favorite reading chair—it is considered a veiling reflection. A **veiling reflection**

Architectural Workshop, Mark Bowers, AIA/RM Ruwart Design, Rosalie M. Ruwart, ASID

Figure 8-27 The ambient light in this space ensures people can move safely within this bank at a comfortable level of brightness. *How is indirect illumination used in this space?*

involves glare and shadows that make it difficult to see when performing a task. To improve visibility, a designer might change the color of the work surface or reposition the furniture. Task lights

- are directive and create a bright center
- focus the viewer's eyes on the task
- offer additional light to alleviate eye strain

Warren Diggles Photography/Jon Rentfrow, Rentfrow Designs, LLC

Figure 8-28 Task lighting helps people perform specific tasks with efficiency and safety.

Accent Lighting

The purpose of **accent lighting** is to bring attention to an object, area, or element within a space. Accent lighting creates drama, variety, and excitement in an interior. When planning accent lighting, it is important for the designer to identify areas that need highlighting. Accent lighting can spotlight artwork, highlight a set of columns, or up-light landscaping. The details of a space are easily lost without the use of accent lighting. When effectively using accent lighting, it is easy to create interesting patterns and shadows. Creating enough contrast for accenting an object requires a minimum ratio of 3 to 1 respectively—at least three times as much light on the focal point as the general lighting surrounding it, **Figure 8-29**.

©Judy Davis/Hoachlander Davis Photography/Designed by ForrestPerkins

Figure 8-29 Adding interest, excitement, and drama are characteristic of accent lighting.

Accent lights

- stimulate interest
- create feelings of aliveness
- alert the mind—awakening curiosity
- offer sparkle or glitter to any space
- can be distracting or entertaining

Types of Lamp Families

There are four **lamp** (lightbulb) families of electric light—incandescent, fluorescent, high-intensity discharge (HID), and light-emitting diodes (LED). There are three major lamp manufacturers: General Electric, Osram/Sylvania, and Philips.

When comparing lamp or lightbulb types, it is important to understand the general characteristics of lamps. Characteristics to compare include the

- amount of produced light (light output)
- efficiency (recall *efficacy*—a ratio of lumens per watt)
- color rendering index (CRI)
- heat output
- energy efficiency
- maintenance of the lamp
- length of lamp life
- extra equipment the lamp requires
- size of the lamp

Understanding the advantages and disadvantages of each lamp family as well as basic lamp types is important, too. *Note*: The lighting industry is moving as fast as the technology industries in developing new products.

Incandescent Lamps

Incandescent lamps, developed around 1879, are the oldest electrical light source. These lamps provide a warm glow, flexibility of use, and are preferable in many residences today. They are an inexpensive light source. Incandescent lamps function by heating a filament inside the glass envelope to such a high temperature that it emits light. It is a very inefficient source of light because only 10 percent of the energy the lamp consumes creates light. The remaining 90 percent is lost to heat. These lamps come in a variety of shapes, wattages, sizes, and colors, **Figure 8-30**.

Halogen lamps are part of the incandescent lamp family. Halogen is a crisp, white light. It comes in both *line voltage* and *low voltage*. Halogen lamps with line voltage use the typical 120 volts of house or building electricity to produce light. Low-voltage halogen lamps require a transformer to reduce the incoming 120 volts down to 12 volts. Although the initial cost is higher, low-voltage lamps are popular today because of the energy savings.

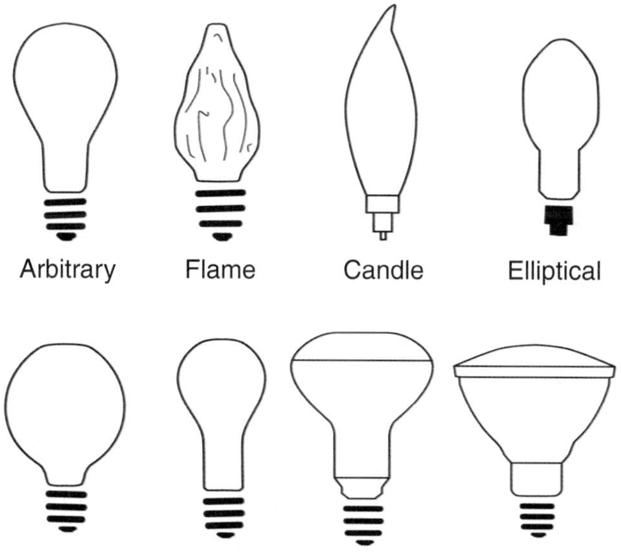

Goodheart-Willcox Publisher

Figure 8-30 Incandescent lamps (lightbulbs) come in a variety of shapes to meet client needs.

Halogen lamps, either low voltage or line voltage, produce a great deal of heat and are therefore, very hot to the touch. They have a longer life than traditional incandescent lamps, and are a favorite for accent lighting due to their sparkle and crisp, clean rendering capabilities. Halogen lamps come in several sizes and shapes. The most popular are MR16 and *parabolic aluminized reflector (PAR)* lamps.

With the enactment of the *Energy Independence and Security Act of 2007*, the United States began the phased elimination of many common incandescent lamps that do not meet strict energy criteria (for example, 100-watt incandescent and reflector lamps). Many countries have passed similar laws. This law requires that screw-based lightbulbs use fewer watts per similar lumen output. For example, residential lightbulbs that used between 40 and 100 watts now use 27 percent less energy for operation.

The way to purchase lighting is changing, too. Instead of buying a lightbulb based on watts, you buy the bulb based on lumens. The greater the number of lumens, the brighter the light will be. For instance, if you previously purchased a 100-watt bulb, now you will look for a bulb with 1600 lumens. The *Lighting Facts* label on the packaging can help you make a decision regarding what bulb to purchase. The advantages of incandescent lamps include

- low initial cost
- inexpensive to dim
- high CRI
- adds glitter and sparkle
- enhances texture and luster

The disadvantages of incandescent lamps include

- lowest efficacy
- produce heat
- short life

Fluorescent Lamps

The *fluorescent lamp* (linear or compact) is an electric-discharge light, meaning it does not need a filament to produce light. Instead, it requires a ballast to start the lamp and control the electric current. As an electrical current passes from one end of the lamp (through a cathode) to the other end of the lamp, it produces light similar to a lightning-bolt fashion. A phosphorous coating on the inside of the glass tube allows you to see the light. It also determines the color of the fluorescent lamp.

Fluorescent lamps are energy efficient, offer a long life, do not produce heat, and have a low operating cost. These lamps use up to 80 percent less energy and can last thousands of hours longer than incandescent lamps. Fluorescent lamps are available in a variety of sizes, shapes, and wattages or lumens, **Figure 8-31**. The most popular ones today are the straight tubes—T8, T5, and most recently, the T2.

Compact fluorescent lamps (CFL) were developed to replace incandescent lamps. They can yield up to 75 percent energy savings and last approximately 10 times longer than incandescent lamps. Historically, residential consumers have been slow in adopting CFLs in place of incandescent lamps because of their poor color rendering capabilities, their use of mercury, and the flicker that sometimes occurs with fluorescent lamps. The advantages of CFLs include

- linear or compact sizes
- high efficiency
- cold light—no heat generation
- good CRI
- a ballast to start the current flowing through the lamp
- a long life

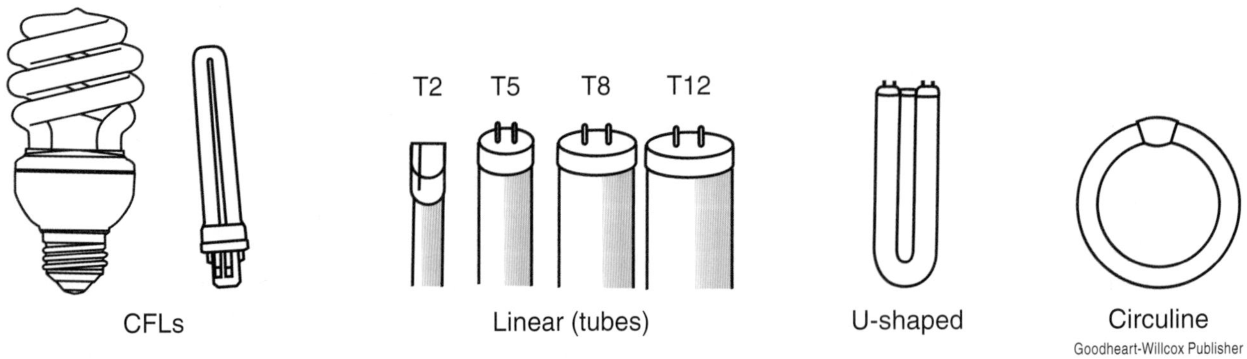

Figure 8-31 Compact fluorescent lamps and fluorescent lamps come in a variety of shapes and are energy efficient sources of light.

Compact fluorescent lamps have a higher initial cost than incandescent lamps. They are also inappropriate for outdoor use in cold temperatures. Because they contain mercury, CFLs require careful disposal rather than tossing them in the landfill. Many home improvement stores recycle them at no cost.

High Intensity Discharge (HID) Lamps

High-intensity discharge lamps (HID) offer higher efficacy, longer life, higher number of lumens per watt (lots of illumination per watt of energy), and can operate in a variety of exterior and interior temperatures. You often see them in large malls, on highways, and inside athletic stadiums. HIDs are constructed with an inner arc tube inside a large glass envelope. If the outer glass envelope breaks, the lamp must be recycled. It should not operate with only the arc tube because of the high amount of UV rays it produces.

HID lamps do not achieve full light output immediately after starting. Rather, they require a period of time—one to 15 minutes—to reach 90 percent of their full light output. Think of highway lights that come on partway as they warm up to full output. Therefore, these lamps require an emergency backup system (typically fluorescent) in interior spaces.

Once the HID lamps shut off, the inner arc tube needs to cool down before the lamp can restart. This period of time is the *restrike time* and lasts anywhere from two to 10 minutes for the light to come back on to full light output. The issue of restrike is particularly problematic in applications where safety and security are critical. For example, if you are at a baseball game and the lights turn off due to an earthquake, as happened years ago in California, backup lighting is a requirement to help people safely exit the stadium.

HID lamps operate similarly to fluorescent lamps. An electrical charge causes an arc to strike between two electrodes within the lamp. That arc, along with unique gasses inside the glass envelope, cause light to appear. All HID lamps require a ballast to start the lamp and regulate the electrical current into the glass envelope. No HID lamp can be used interchangeably with another lamp because the ballasts are designed for each specific lamp type. In addition, variations of color between lamps of the same type are problematic.

Three categories of HID lamps include

- mercury vapor (MV)—used primarily outdoors
- metal halide (MH)—often used indoors due to good CRI
- high-pressure sodium (HPS)—used primarily outdoors

Each HID lamp category was developed at a different time, has different advantages and disadvantages, and is used in different lighting situations, **Figure 8-32**.

Mercury Vapor (MV) Lamps

Mercury vapor (MV) lamps were the first HID lamps developed. They use radiation from mercury vapor to provide illumination. MV lamps cast a blue light, which is particularly good for landscaping applications (lighting a blue spruce tree). However, because of their inefficiency and the improvements of other lamps, the phase-out of MV lamps is happening over time.

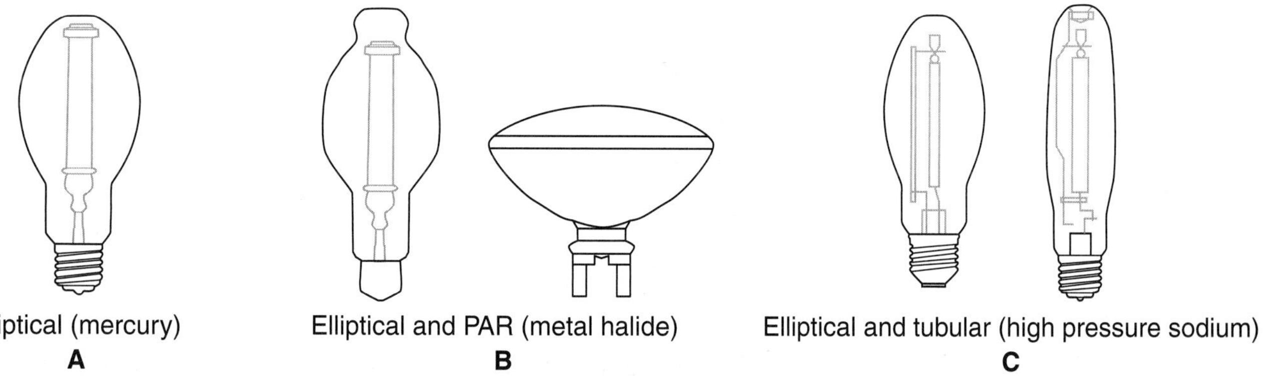

Figure 8-32 High intensity discharge lamps offer a higher level of illumination and have a longer life. Here are some common examples (A, B, and C).

Metal Halide (MH) Lamps

Metal halide lamps use chemical compounds of metal halides and metallic vapors to illuminate the lamp. They are the most popular HID lamps on the market with many indoor and outdoor applications. They have high efficacy, good color rendition, long life, and a wide range of colors and wattages. They are the number one HID lamp to use if people are present in or using the space. Common applications include gymnasiums, indoor arenas, malls, car lots, and hotels.

New technologies are making MH lamps compact and available in lower wattages. This makes them a better solution for display and track systems, such as in retail stores. In addition, the development of Ceramic MH lamps (CMH) is an improvement over standard MH lamps. They have the best performance characteristics, reduced restrike times, and better CRIs.

High-Pressure Sodium (HPS) Lamps

High-pressure sodium (HPS) lamps use sodium vapor for illumination. They have the best lumens per watt (LPW) rating because they can last 40,000 hours. You often find HPS lamps in car headlights—especially in Europe, in street lamps on highways, and in manufacturing facilities. HPS lamps have poor color rendering because the sodium gas in the glass envelope is orange, causing the emerging light to have an orange cast.

If you need a long-lasting lamp life, select an HID. If you need the longest lasting HID lamp, choose HPS. The best color rendering is MH (or CMH).

LED Lamps

The hottest trend in lighting is LEDs. *Light-emitting diodes (LEDs)*, first developed in the 1960s, operate via an interaction between an electrical field and a phosphor—a luminescent substance that emits light with exposure to electricity. A driver, or power source, is a requirement to produce LED light.

LEDs are the first *solid-state light (SSL)* source for general lighting. SSL refers to a type of lighting that uses light-emitting diodes as a source of illumination rather than filaments or gas.

LEDs involve forming a semiconductor (a material with varying ability to conduct electrical current) into a chemical chip that is embedded in a plastic capsule. A volt of direct electrical current energizes the chip, making visible light. The chip contains a chemical that determines the color of the light. Initially, LEDs produced only red, green, and amber light. With the development of blue LEDs in the 1990s, lamp manufacturers were able to produce white light. This development paved the way for use of LEDs in general lighting applications.

LEDs emit light in only one direction. Therefore, lenses or scattered diffusers help focus LED light. Alone, an LED lamp does not produce much light. Therefore, each lamp often contains multiple LEDs in the glass envelope.

LED lamps are durable, small, have a long life, use minimal electrical power, and have the ability to direct its light. They do not emit ultraviolet or infrared radiation. Their efficacy is better than incandescent, halogen, and some CFL lamps.

Smaller size, energy efficiency, and longer life are the major advantages of LEDs. They do not produce infrared or ultraviolet radiation, which makes them excellent for indoor and outdoor use. The major disadvantage of LEDs is that consistent color is still problematic. After manufacturing, some LEDs may be warm yellow and others cool blue. Lamp manufacturers believe they can address this problem. According to the U. S. Department of Energy, LEDs offer significant potential to save energy and enhance the quality of the built environment. The success of LEDs will radically reduce energy demands, **Figure 8-33.**

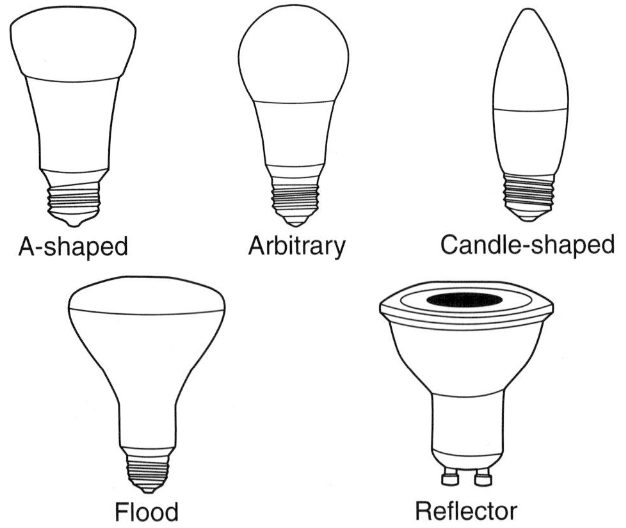

Goodheart-Willcox Publisher

Figure 8-33 Light-emitting diode (LED) lamps come in a variety of shapes and are extremely energy efficient. *Use Internet resources to compare incandescent lamps to LEDs.*

Types of Lighting Fixtures

Lighting fixtures, or **luminaires**, serve many purposes in addition to being functional and aesthetically pleasing. They hold the lamp in place, as well as control, shape, and reflect or refract the emerging light. The fixture can also modify the color of the light of the lamp. Each type of lamp has specific fixtures that hold the lamp in place for interior use. Some fixtures offer **direct light** in which 100 percent of the light shines downward, such as a recessed can light. Other fixtures provide **indirect light** in which a portion of light shines up and a portion shines down into the space.

Interchangeability between lamps and fixtures may be limited depending on the type of lamp as well as the base used to position the lamp in the fixture. There are literally thousands of light fixtures to hold incandescent, fluorescent, HID, and LED lamps. See **Figure 8-34** for a description of different types of luminaires. See **Figure 8-35** for examples of various luminaires.

Choosing Lighting Effectively

Now that you have some lighting vocabulary and you understand how people see light, it is important to understand the types of electric light to specify for the interior space.

When developing a lighting design for a client, the selection of the lamps and corresponding fixtures can be overwhelming. There are a myriad of choices. To narrow the selection, you may want to ask the following questions:

- What spaces are being lit?
- Who will use this space?
- What ages are the occupants or users?
- What activities will occur in this space?
- What type of focal point should you enhance?
- What architectural elements (columns or archways) should you highlight?
- Will the color scheme be warm or cool?
- What is the style and mood of the space?
- Are there places in the space that need to be lit to prevent accidents?
- How long do you want a lamp to burn before replacement (maintenance issue)?
- What do the codes require for light function and placement?

These questions can help you sift through the multitude of lamps and fixtures available. You will develop confidence once you understand the process.

Communicating Lighting Design

As an interior designer, it is important to communicate your lighting design in a manner recognizable by such team members as the architect, engineer, electrician, code official, and construction trades. If you hire or work with a lighting designer, it is important to understand the various construction documents that relate to the lighting design.

Effective lighting design installation requires proper explanation. The more complex the lighting design, the more detailed the lighting documents should be.

There are three common ways to communicate a lighting design to the client or colleague. All include a **legend**—an explanatory chart that clearly communicates with symbols the type of task or fixture that is to be included in the plan.

- **Electrical plan.** This plan, usually developed by the electrician, includes general electrical equipment (receptacles and outlets), electrical distribution plan (distribution of electrical lighting and wiring throughout the space), and lighting system (fixtures and controls). Electrical plans are usually a separate document within a set of building plans.
- **Lighting plan (interior).** Less technical and typical for smaller projects such as a house, this plan depicts the location of fixtures, wiring and switching, and lighting controls. Often, a furniture arrangement is layered under the drawing of the lighting plan to understand placement of fixtures.
- **Reflected ceiling plan (RCP).** Often used in large commercial spaces, this plan most often depicts location of fixtures on the ceiling. The drawing is a mirror-view of the ceiling as if it was a reflection from the floor, **Figure 8-36**. This way the reflected ceiling plan has the same orientation as the floor plan with which it is associated. An RCP also includes any architectural ceiling details, such as beams and equipment associated with the

Major Categories of Luminaires	
Surface Mounted Lighting—Ceilings and walls are typical locations of surface mounted fixtures. Installation can occur directly on the ceiling, against the wall, or under a shelf or cabinet. These luminaires offer direct, indirect, semi-direct, and diffused lighting. Sconces are favorite surface-mount fixtures.	
Ceiling Mount	■ **Suspended pendant light**—(chandeliers, fluorescent fixtures). These fixtures are mounted to the ceiling by a cord, cable, chain, or metal rod. The main fixture usually hangs from 6 inches to several feet below the ceiling. Pendant lights are often used in multiples and can be found over an island, in a classroom, or over a conference table. ■ **Track light**—Mounted on electrical raceways or tracks, these fixtures have multiple heads. The tracks are available in various lengths. They can be suspended from a ceiling by cables or surface-mounted on a ceiling or wall. Track lighting fixtures are very versatile. The track heads come in a variety of styles, colors, sizes, lamp types, and materials. Cable lighting often fits into this category.
Wall Mount	■ **Vanity or strip lights**—These are wall-mounted luminaires located adjacent to or above a mirror. ■ **Sconces**—These ornamental wall fixtures may hold a single or multiple lamps.
Floor Mount	■ **Uplighting**—As the reverse of downlighting, uplighting is very versatile. You can use uplights on the floor behind sofas or plants, under glass shelves, or in corners. They give a beautiful, dramatic accent to the room.
Shelf Mount	■ **Uplighting**—You can use uplights under glass shelves for a beautiful, dramatic accent to the room.
Recessed Lighting—These lighting fixtures are put into spaces cut in the ceiling. The spaces are then covered with screens or louvers to shield the light source from view and eliminate glare. This type of lighting may be in slots running vertically or horizontally, and in circular, rectangular, or square shapes.	
	■ **Recessed cans**—With this type of light, the fixture or can is built into the ceiling. Light is evident, but the can is not. ■ **Spotlights**—Limited to one area, this type of *downlighting* is used more for decoration and is an excellent method for emphasizing works of art.
Structural Lighting—These fixtures are part of an architectural element. They include cove, valance, cornice, soffit, wall-slot, and wall brackets. Many custom structural lighting fixtures are designed. In addition, they can be purchased from a fixture manufacturer.	
	■ **Cove lighting**—A form of indirect lighting in which the source of light is concealed from view by a trough-like structure. The light is directed upward on a reflecting surface such as the ceiling or upper walls. ■ **Cornice or valance lighting**—With this type of lighting, fluorescent tubes are placed behind the cornice or valance at a window. These fixtures throw the light up to the ceiling and down for direct window lighting. ■ **Soffit lighting**—Soffit lighting is a type of recessed lighting that is built into a soffit. A soffit is the trim applied to a roof eave or a hollow, box-like projection above a kitchen sink. Soffits can be used to cover unsightly features of a home or to add decorative architectural detail. ■ **Wall-slot lighting**—This lighting results from slots in the drywall. Generally, a fluorescent tube and fixture is mounted behind the slot in the wall and generates light through the slot. ■ **Wall washers**—Wall washing provides a smooth, even illumination for vertical, flat, non-textured surfaces such as marble, where there is no surface texture to highlight or imperfections of drywall installation. Wall washing is perfect for art galleries where framed art is constantly changing. When installed the correct distance away from a wall in the ceiling, these light fixtures will light the wall evenly from top to bottom without spilling light away from the wall into the room. ■ **Wall grazers**—Wall grazing provides dramatic illumination that reveals the texture of special materials such as brick, stone, stucco, glass block, or fabric panels.
Portable—This type includes table and floor fixtures that are primarily used in residences, hotels, retirement homes, restaurants, and private offices. They are easy to install, provide instant light, and are relatively inexpensive.	
	■ **Table and floor fixtures**—These luminaires are plugged into a wall, are easily moved, and bring aesthetics and character to the space.

Figure 8-34 There are many types of luminaires that meet client needs for function and beauty.

A Suspended pendant

Photographer: Emily Minton Redfield/Interior Designer: Andrea Schumacher Interiors

B Track lighting

hemu75/istock/Thinkstock

C Cove lighting

Damon Searles Photography/Aneka Jensen Interiors, Inc.

D Wall-slot lighting

Eric Laignel Photography/Design by Clanton & Associates, Inc.

E Soffit lighting

Damon Searles Photography/Aneka Jensen Interiors, Inc.

F Pendant and track lighting

Interior Design: Senger Design Group/Photographer: Paul Kohlman Photography

Figure 8-35 These images show a number of ways to utilize the variety of luminaires available to enhance an interior design.

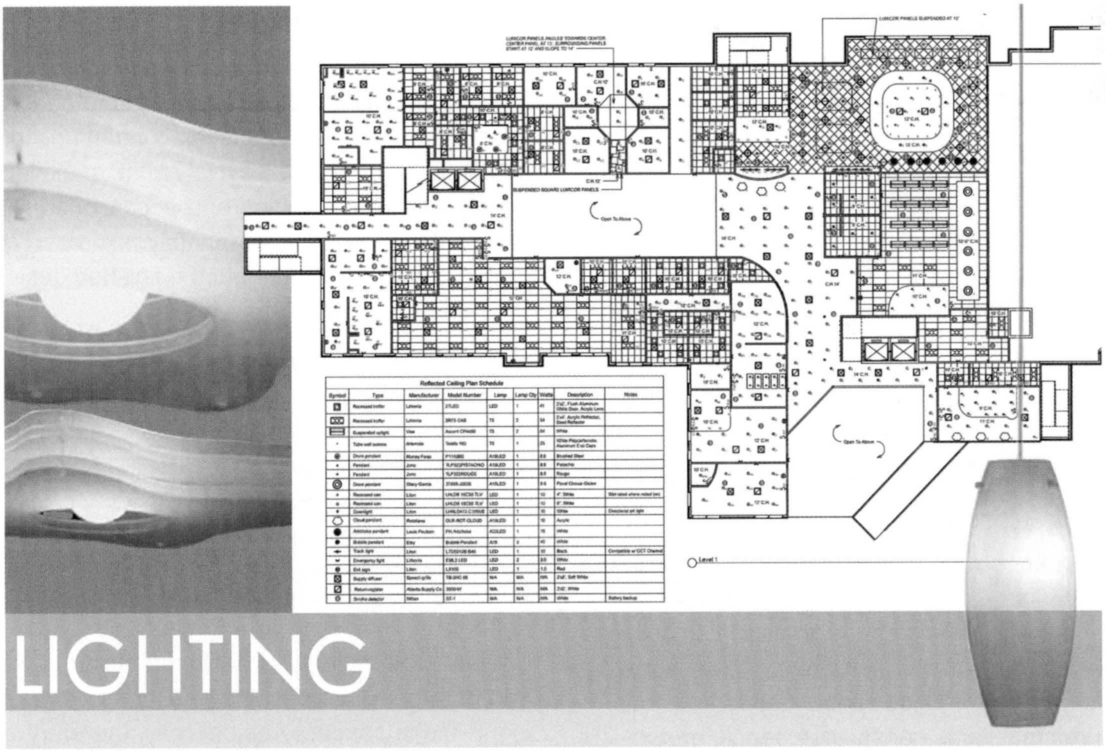

Courtesy of Anne Skrobacz, Interior Design Student/Colorado State University

Figure 8-36 This reflected ceiling plan has the same orientation as the floor plan and shows the location of lighting in the space.

heating, ventilation, and air conditioning (HVAC) located in the ceiling—such as air diffusers or duct work that might impact location of lighting fixture. It also shows sprinkler heads common to the type of structure.

In addition to the above plans, a lighting design also includes lighting sketches, a lighting schedule, detail drawings, a narrative, and written specifications. The most important goal is to communicate the lighting design clearly using symbols and terminology common with the industry.

Lighting Controls

Lighting controls meet two goals: reducing lighting energy costs and setting the mood of the space leading to client satisfaction and enhanced well-being. Proper lighting controls increase human productivity in the workplace. It also offers a psychological advantage resulting from the perception of having *control* over the physical environment. Lighting controls also offer the opportunity to develop moods and drama within a space by dimming lights or turning lights on or off.

Most high-end residential and commercial projects use some type of lighting control system. Local control gives you the ability to control the space or a zone—a combination of several spaces. Whole-building control systems give the ability to control light from a single location.

Light switches and controls work to deliver power to the luminaire, thus producing light. There are several different types of light controls, including

- **Light switches**. When on, light switches pass electricity on to the fixtures, or when off, stop delivery of electricity to the fixtures, **Figure 8-37**.
- **Dimmers.** Often combined with an on/off switch, dimmers control the brightness of an electric light source. The most popular light control, they allow the occupant to reduce or increase light emitting from a lamp. Just stepping down the amount of light one increment can increase the life of the lamp by 50 percent.
- **Motion sensors.** These sensors detect heat, motion, sound, or obstruction, and respond by automatically turning on the lights. It is possible to replace an ordinary switch with a motion sensor switch, making lighting control hands-free. This assures that lights go off when people are no longer present in a room.

lucato/iStock/Thinkstock

Figure 8-37 Light switches and dimmers help control the amount of electric light in a space.

Lighting for Residential and Commercial Interiors

When developing a lighting design for either a commercial or residential interior, the first priority is occupant safety related to codes. After addressing this priority, the interior designer can begin to layer in ambient, task, and accent lighting depending on the functions that occur in each space. Simultaneously, the designer uses creative artistry to capture the lighting concept of the space. If the lighting in spaces is both functionally and aesthetically poor, it takes away from, or diminishes, the quality of the furnishings and accessories. Therefore, the designer must appropriately express mood and drama creatively throughout the finished design.

Following are a few tips to consider when developing a lighting design for either a residential or commercial space. Some relate to function and others to the aesthetics of the space.

Residential

Functionally, a residential design should prevent accidents from occurring at any stairwells and entrances. Because the majority of accidents occur in the kitchen and bathroom, the designer must plan for proper lighting in these spaces. Aesthetically, the entry offers the first impression of the home. In addition, sparkle and drama are inviting to include in living and dining rooms, family rooms, and master suites. Media/theater rooms require specialized lighting and dimmers to raise and lower levels of light.

Commercial

Each practice specialty for commercial interior design has unique requirements for lighting design. These include

- **Healthcare.** Lighting considerations for healthcare include the needs of the occupants, performance of visual tasks, desired appearance of the space, energy constraints, and ages of patients and caregivers, **Figure 8-38**. Task lighting is very important. Excellent CRI is critical to accurately assess patients. Elimination of glare and control of light are key factors. Designers focus on three primary areas: physical and emotional comfort of patients, staff well-being and motivation, and visitor hospitality.
- **Hotels.** Lighting goals for hotels include differentiated guest experiences ranging from business meetings to spa activities, lounges and restaurants, and sustainability. Lighting helps set the mood for a variety of settings and activities. For instance, lobby lighting must create a first and lasting impression. As day turns into night, it is important to adjust the lighting mood—similar to a restaurant.
- **Movie theaters.** Designers must avoid a spill of light on the screen. For safety, aisles and stairs require specialty lighting, such as handrail lights.
- **Museums.** Lighting in museums and art galleries play an important role in the visitor's ability to perceive and enjoy both the artifacts in a museum as well as the building itself. Lighting in such buildings requires careful consideration of the conservation of the art and artifacts. This goal, at times, conflicts with need to offer an effective display. Designers must also take care to avoid lighting with ultraviolet rays that can damage the art.
- **Offices.** Office lighting influences people's energy levels and performance and enhances their sense of well-being. Lighting solutions should improve the visual quality of business premises, enhance employee efficiency and productivity, and help achieve energy reduction goals.
- **Restaurants.** Does the lighting design reflect the restaurant image and/or branding of the place? Is the lighting unique? Does it highlight the served food? Lighting should not be so dark that the client cannot view the menu. If shattered, will the lamp be deflected away from food? Indirect light is very popular in restaurants.
- **Retail stores.** Goals of lighting for a retail store include: attracting the customer, helping initiate the purchase, and helping complete the sale. The owner's goals are to increase customer traffic, improve store sales, and reduce energy costs. Store displays should be three to five times brighter than general illumination.
- **Schools.** Goals for schools require using a combination of natural light, indirect electric light, glare prevention, and energy-efficient light to enhance learning.

Lighting consumes 19 percent of all energy worldwide. Long lamp life is essential in commercial buildings to prevent constant replacement and maintenance of lamps. Also, code requirements dictate use of exit lights for all commercial spaces, including emergency exit lights with battery backups.

Interior Designer: SCI Design Group/Photographer: Michael McLane

Figure 8-38 Lighting in healthcare facilities must provide effective task lighting and lighting for wayfinding.

DESIGNER MATH SKILLS

Calculating Amounts of Residential Lighting

Calculating and selecting adequate lighting needed in an area is easier today than ever before. Here are a few tips to remember as you calculate lighting amounts.

- Lumen = brightness of a lamp
- Watt = amount of energy a lamp uses
- Footcandle = one lumen per square foot

Lighting engineers determine the number of *footcandles (FC)* needed for residential or commercial spaces. They create footcandle charts similar to the one shown here. Footcandle charts are also available online. Lumen and watt information can be located on lightbulb (lamp) packaging.

Footcandle Recommendations	
Room or Area	**Approximate Number of Footcandles (FC)**
Kitchen, overall	30–40
Range, kitchen	50–60
Dining room	30–40
Bedrooms	10–20
Bathroom	70–80
Hallways	5–10
Casual reading area	20–50
Study area	70–80
Detailed work area	200
Workshop/craft area	55–110

A simple method for determining the amount of lighting needed is to multiple the area of a room or space by the number of recommended footcandles. This calculation results in the approximate lumens an area requires for adequate illumination.

Area (width x length) x FC (chart above) = Lumens needed

Here are some examples.

- **Example 1:** A bedroom measuring 10 feet by 12 feet has an area of 120 square feet.
  120 sq. ft. (Area) × 20 (FC) = 2400 Lumens needed
- **Example 2:** A hallway measuring 6 feet by 12 feet has an area of 72 square feet.
  72 sq. ft. (Area) × 10 (FC) = 720 Lumens needed
- **Example 3:** A study area measuring 3 feet by 7 feet has an area of 21 square feet.
  21 sq. ft. (Area) × 70 (FC) = 1470 Lumens needed
- **Example 4:** A kitchen/eating area measuring 20 feet by 12 feet has an area of 240 square feet.
  240 sq. ft. (Area) × 40 (FC) = 9600 Lumens needed

When designing the lighting for the kitchen in Example 4, you as the designer, would develop a lighting plan by layering light using a variety of light fixtures. For example, you could use

- recessed cans to provide general ambient lighting
- pendant fixtures to provide task lighting over the island, sink, and table
- accent lighting above the upper cabinets to add a touch of visual interest

To insure the space is adequately lighted, total the number of lumens for all of the bulbs you will use in the space with the goal of reaching approximately 9600 lumens.

Today, with numerous energy-saving options available, there are new ways to select lightbulbs. Lighting Facts labeling began appearing on lightbulb packages in 2012. In the past, people commonly chose bulbs by the number of *watts* not realizing wattage had little to do with *brightness.* When selecting lightbulbs for a client's space, first choose the number of lumens you need for a certain level of brightness. Then look at the wattage to determine energy savings.

Watts to Lumens	
Watts (Energy) If you used to choose...	**Lumens (Brightness)** Choose...
40 watts	450 lumens
60 watts	800 lumens
75 watts	1100 lumens
100 watts	1600 lumens
150 watts	2600 lumens

Chapter 8

Review and Assess

Summary

- Color is a powerful design element that impacts the mood and physical appearance of a space.
- Color is very difficult to accurately describe to another person with words.
- Knowledge of the theory and use of color in interior design gives designers a common reference point and vocabulary to discuss and utilize color.
- The visible color spectrum is the portion of colored light the eye can see.
- Color wheels and color systems help people communicate about color.
- Basic color scheme combinations always produce beauty and harmonious relationships.
- Color psychology involves studying how color impacts peoples' moods, feelings, productivity, behavior, and functions within a space.
- Culture, life experiences, and gender shape color preferences.
- Color-forecasting organizations monitor industry trends and predict colors accordingly.
- Certain colors have historical significance.
- Developing sensitivity to color preferences of others is critical in design.
- Color has different cultural meanings, associations, and aesthetic appeal.
- Light influences and can modify the appearance of color.
- CRI is a measurement used to evaluate a light source based on how well it indicates the true color of an object relative to a standard light source.
- The biology of the human eye and the psychology of the brain play roles in understanding light and color.
- Knowing types of lamp families and lighting fixtures helps designers make effective client choices.
- Although the functions of lighting in residential and commercial spaces may differ, the designer's first lighting-design priority for both relates to occupant safety and codes.

Chapter Vocabulary

Working in teams, locate an image online that visually describes or explains each of the following terms.

accent lighting
accommodation
achromatic
adaptation
additive color theory
afterimage
ambient lighting
analogous
chroma
color psychology
color vision deficiency
color wheel
complementary
cool color
direct light
electromagnetic spectrum
hue
indirect illumination
indirect light
lamp
layering light
legend
luminaire
metamerism
monochromatic
pigments
primary color
refract
secondary color
shade
split-complementary
subtractive color theory
task lighting
tertiary color
tetrad
tint
tone
triadic
value
veiling reflection
warm color

Review and Study

1. Name six factors indicating why color is exciting and powerful.
2. What are three reasons why communicating color accurately can be challenging?
3. Explain the differences among hue, value, and chroma.
4. Contrast warm and cool colors.
5. What is the visible spectrum?
6. Name the primary, secondary, and tertiary colors on the color wheel. How are secondary and tertiary colors formed?
7. What is simultaneous contrast?
8. Name three color scheme harmonies. Give examples showing how you might use each for interior design.
9. What is color psychology?
10. What are six factors that can affect color trends?
11. Give an example showing how color impacts human behavior.
12. What are two major reasons why interior designers should study cultural aspects of color?
13. Contrast quantity of light with quality of light.
14. Name seven benefits for effectively incorporating daylight into an interior.
15. What are the three categories of light? What is one way each is used?
16. What are the general characteristics of lamps?
17. Name four major types of lamp families.
18. Contrast the pros and cons of incandescent and compact fluorescent lamps.
19. What are the three categories of high-intensity discharge lamps and where is each used?
20. What are luminaires and what are their purposes?

Critical Analysis

21. **Analyze variables.** How does reference point determine whether a client can visualize the color you want to use in his or her space? Analyze and discuss the variables that impact communication about color.
22. **Draw conclusions.** According to the text, no two people perceive color in exactly the same way. Some are unable to distinguish between colors at all. How could these factors be an obstacle to an interior designer's presentation to a committee in charge of final selections for a corporate office renovation? Discuss conclusions about what techniques the designer could use to overcome such obstacles.
23. **Infer meaning.** In the text the author states, "Without light, color cannot and does not exist." What does the author mean by this statement? Write an essay and cite the text and other resources to support your inferences.
24. **Generate solutions.** Analyze the lighting designs of two of the same type of commercial interiors (for example, two restaurants). Consider the mood, location of fixtures, color of lamps, color rendering, quality of lighting, lighting controls, well-being of occupants, and energy efficiencies. Share your suggestions for changes that would enhance the lighting for each space.

Think like a Designer

25. **Writing.** Analyze the *Design Insight* quote at the beginning of the chapter. How do designers shape space, communicate meaning, support human behavior, and create significant first impressions of a space with color? Locate evidence that supports this information for room design. Why is what the author says about color true? Write a summary.
26. **Writing.** Suppose you are working with a client in San Diego, but you are located in Houston. You have three color selections you want to use with your client's project. Write a description of each color selection.
27. **Speaking.** Reread text pages 231–233 about color and space. Then use Internet or magazine resources to locate photos of interior spaces that show how color can be used to change the feeling and volume of space. Discuss your photo display in class.

28. **Color trends.** Study your use of color in the clothes you wear for ten days. Take a picture of yourself each morning as you leave for work or school. Did you choose the colors for a reason? At the end of ten days, line up the photos of your clothing choices and study the clothing color palette. How does the color palette describe you? How does it relate to current trends? Write a summary of your findings. How influential do you think client trends are to planning an interior design?
29. **Speaking.** Choose two countries and research the color meanings and associations in both. How are they similar to and different from those in the United States? How would the differences impact the designs you might create for people in those countries? Create an illustrated digital report showing the color meanings and associations in these countries. Discuss your thoughts about designs with the class.
30. **Reading/writing.** Research *spectral power distribution charts* for various types of light, including incandescent, CFL, HID, and LED (solid-state lighting). What do these charts show you about the color of light? Specifically describe the color differences between the lamps. How is this information useful to an interior designer when planning the lighting for a space? Write a summary of your findings.
31. **Lighting categories.** Locate digital photographs showing effective use of the three categories of light: *ambient, task,* and *accent.* Use a school-approved web-based application to create a digital poster of your examples. Write a caption for each image indicating why it is a good example. Upload your poster to the class website for discussion with your classmates, citing the sources of your images.
32. **Math practice.** Identify the type of lamp used for ambient (general) illumination in your classroom. Research how many lumens and footcandles the lamp type provides. Count the number of fixtures in the classroom. Multiply this number by the number of footcandles and lumens the lamp provides to determine how much light is in the classroom space. Choose another space in your school, such as the media center or cafeteria, and repeat your calculations.

Design Application

33. **Creating color boards.** Develop a new color scheme and palette for your school using the following guidelines.
    A. Create a color board that shows the *current colors* used in your school. Locate paint-chip samples that look like those currently used in different parts of the school such as the entry, cafeteria, gym, classrooms, library, and reception office. Arrange them on the board by room. Add photographs of each space to your board showing color usage. Pair the room photos with the paint chips.
    B. Create a second color board in which you choose a *new* color palette for the school. Locate paint-chip samples for the color palette and arrange them on the board according to the space in which they will be used (with photos, if possible).
    C. Present your color boards to the class. Justify your choices convincingly for the new color palette based on details of color psychology discussed in the text.
34. **Evaluating the impact of light.** The goal of the following activities is to observe the impact of color and how it changes in different light.
    A. Clip a color photo of the face of a newborn from a magazine. Hold the photo under different color lamps—incandescent, CFL, and LED. How did the colors shift in the photo when you put it under each type of lamp? Why would a nurse need to accurately see a baby's facial color? Discuss your findings in class.
    B. Take digital pictures of an outdoor location at different times of the day, such as early morning, noon, and early evening. How do the shadows shift as the light changes? Show your pictures to the class and describe how the shifting shadows impact color in the location.
39. **Portfolio Builder.** Save copies of your digital products for items 28, 32, 33, and 34 in your portfolio.

Influences of Design Through the Ages

©Stirling Elmendorf Photography/Designed by ForrestPerkins

Chapter 9

Design Insight

"The study of history is critical to the practice of interior design for many reasons. History is a vast laboratory of opportunities and challenges, successes and failures. Learning from these past experiences across countless cultures helps designers make informed decisions with the intent of producing evermore inspiring and functional spaces."

John C. Turpin, Ph.D., FIDEC

Learning Targets

After studying this chapter, you will be able to

- identify various historic interior and furniture periods and styles that may also be used in interiors and furnishings today.
- summarize key exterior architectural styles and features.
- differentiate between various styles of today's interiors.

Introduction

Influences from decades past shape the interiors, architecture, and furnishings that surround you today. Without knowing it, you may find a piece of furniture in your home of historic-design origin. Furnishings were shaped by such factors as culture, travel, politics, religion, wealth (or poverty), ruling kings and monarchs, geography, migrations, advances in technologies, clothing apparel, weapons, art, and local materials. As these factors changed, so did the designs of the interiors and furnishings to reflect the place and time of the people.

Historical Link to Today

The study of historic interiors reveals fascinating stories of those who came before you. For example, the seven-drawer *rent table* was developed to organize the collection of rent from tenant farmers in England. Likewise, a tall English chair back reflects the common need to rest the head from the weight of heavy headdresses. How people lived their lives and the clothing they wore are reflected in historic furnishings that can be found in homes and public buildings today. To begin your study of historical interiors, visit well-known furniture websites, **Figure 9-1 A, B, and C**. A vast majority of these furnishings have historical roots in specific periods of design.

Becoming an expert on historic interiors and furnishings helps develop your credibility as a designer with your clients. By the end of this chapter, you will be able to identify styles and periods of furniture and answer questions about historic interiors and furnishings that clients often ask. You will know more about your personal style preferences and be able to identify key historical design details.

Historic Interiors and Furnishings

The changing design styles for the twenty-first century are difficult to predict. Inspiration for these design styles often come from those designs of the past. Although this chapter does not begin to capture the volumes of rigorous, historical information related to the history of interiors, you will develop appreciation for ancient to modern

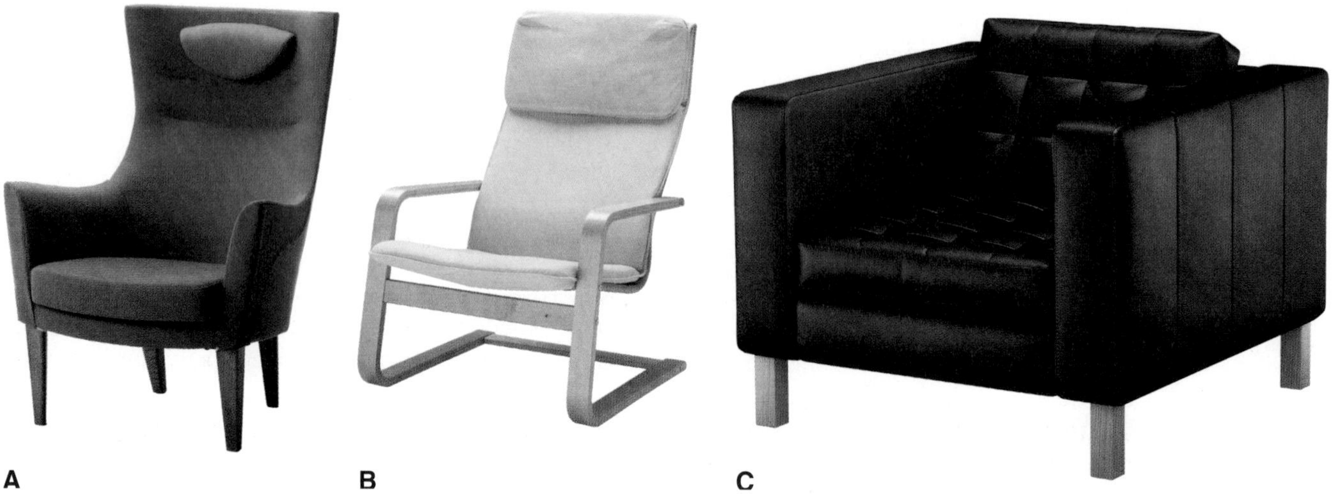

A B C

Used with permission of Inter IKEA Systems B.V.

Figure 9-1 Modern or contemporary designs often have their roots in history as do the Stockholm (A), Pello (B), and Karlstad chairs from IKEA.

to contemporary design periods and styles by learning stories and facts about the people who came before. Therefore, this chapter offers a cursory survey of the container of their lives: their interiors and furnishings.

Period versus Style

As you study the periods and styles that shape interiors today, it is important to define several terms. An **historic period** is an interval of time, often depicted as a fixed time frame with a beginning and an end. Periods always overlap other periods—similar to today. Historic scholars often debate exact chronological periods.

A **style** refers to designs reflective of an *individual* (Thomas Chippendale), *group* (the Shakers), or *philosophy of design* (Germany's Bauhaus School of Design) within a certain time period. Styles often appear in chronological order, although they tend to overlap with many frequently appearing within the same period.

Understanding the history of furnishings is a type of detective work. When you study classic furnishings, the clues for each style are in the details, **Figure 9-2**. Look at the following:

- wood type and color
- chair-back styles
- carvings of **motifs** (repeated elements in an ornamental design)
- leg and foot styles

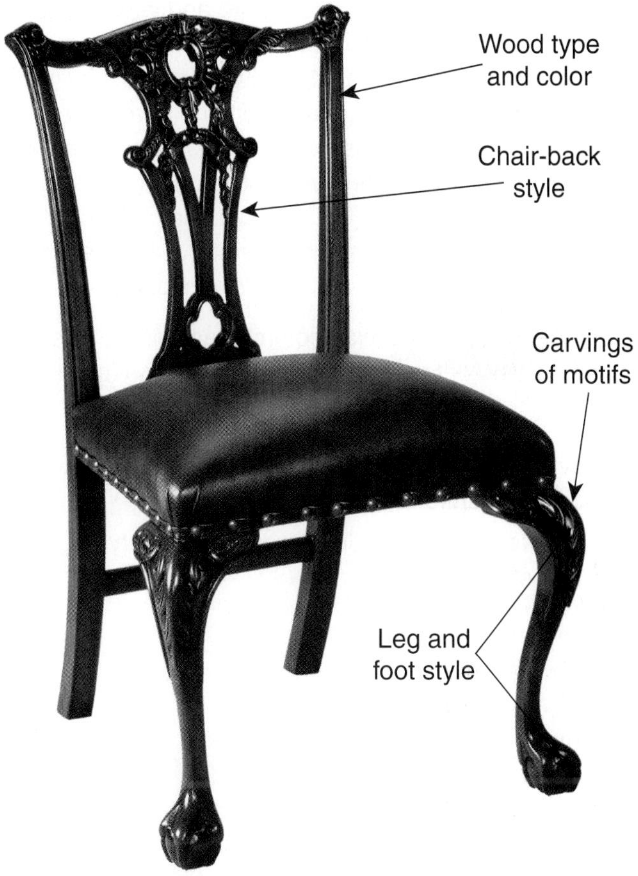

Alaettin YILDIRM/Shutterstock.com

Figure 9-2 Paying close attention to details can help you identify historic periods and styles. *Examine a piece of furniture at home or school. What details may relate to one or more historic periods? What evidence can you give?*

Also remember that with the introduction of new styles, old ones still remained popular for quite some time. It was not uncommon for rooms to be decorated with a variety of different styles because new furniture was (and is) expensive to purchase.

When studying the different periods and styles—both Western and non-Western—realize that residences were often used as locations for business transactions. For example, in many cultures, living quarters were located above the first-floor family business. Therefore, the text discussion may simultaneously address both residential and commercial design when discussing features of the residence and business.

Western developments in design are often viewed sequentially from ancient to modern. With non-Western design, developments began in separate geographical locations and progressed through many centuries without connection to Western events. The study of non-Western design history is complicated by a lack of many visual examples dating from early times. Therefore, while of equal importance, non-Western furnishings and interiors are mentioned here only briefly after the Western design developments.

Ancient Period—Egyptian (4500–330 B.C.)

Due to a lack of records, it is difficult to learn much about early humans that existed more than 35,000 years ago during the Stone Age. This discussion of ancient interiors begins with 4000 B.C. with the development of advanced settlements in the areas of Mesopotamia and Egypt. Although much of ancient life was lived outdoors, this text gives attention to the interiors of these people.

During ancient times, the architecture and interiors were influenced by a climate of minimal rainfall, intense sunlight, and little temperature variation. Egyptian society was highly *stratified* (divided by class) with the Pharaoh at the top. The middle class consisted of priests, mayors, governors, and officials. Houses were located in towns based on rank and social class. For example, merchant classes lived in the center of town in single-story, attached, row houses that later became multilevel dwellings.

The plan of the house was common among all classes and consisted of three parts that included the following:

- reception area off the front entrance
- living areas—living room or central hall—located near the entrance
- private areas—cooking, bedrooms, courtyard areas—in the rear

If the house was a single level, the ceiling of the central hall was higher than adjacent rooms and **clerestory windows**—those placed high in the wall—allowed light and ventilation to penetrate the innermost spaces. If houses were multilevel, bedrooms were on the second floor with terraces on top. Columns were used to support the structure, **Figure 9-3**.

Soil in the Nile Valley provided raw material for *plaster*—a form of gypsum combining the mineral calcium and mud—applied to brick or mud, and was used in residences in all socioeconomic levels. Walls were often decorated with colorful murals. Floors were mud, plaster, or brick.

Worker dwellings were built from sun-dried mud bricks with mud taken from the Nile. This material was economical and easy to use without advanced tools. Floors were made of dirt and at times, covered with straw.

Courtesy of Lydia M. Brown

Figure 9-3 This room is characteristic of an Egyptian design. *What motifs can you identify?*

Few pieces of furniture were used. Egyptians, from both upper and lower classes, had only utilitarian pieces—typically stools, chairs, chests, beds, and tables. The most basic furniture item was the stool, generally a folding type used primarily by men. The most universal piece of furniture was the chest. Chests contained such valuables as jewelry, clothing, cosmetics, and linens. Beds or reclining couches were rare because most people could not afford such luxuries. Wood was scarce in Egypt, but if used, most furnishings were made out of sycamore or palm. Accessories included vases, pottery or ceramic jars, baskets, and rugs. Common motifs, symbolic in meaning, included the following **(Figure 9-4)**:

- the lotus—a waterborne lily
- reeds and papyrus—both slender, tall grasses
- spiral—a curve beginning from a central point and slowly winding out
- rosette—a decorative disk in a foliage or floral design
- chevron—a V-shaped pattern
- griffin—a mythical animal with the head, forepart, and wings of an eagle and the body, hind legs, and tail of a lion
- sphinx—mythical creature with the body of a lion and a human head

Classical Period

This section includes both Greek and Roman periods. Geographically, Greece was a mountainous country surrounded by three seas—Aegean, Mediterranean, and Ionian. The landscape was dominated by mountains, small valleys, and islands. This isolation fostered great independence among the city-states.

Greek settlements expanded into southern Italy and the coast of Sicily. Northern Italy was inhabited by the Etruscan tribe. The Greek city-states fell to Roman rule in 146 B.C. Thus two races were instrumental in initially shaping the arts of the Romans of the Italian peninsula: Greeks and Etruscans. The Etruscans brought cultural influences from the Orient. Romans adopted much of the Greek way of life, including its religious practices, architectural styles, and artistic skill.

Greek (3000 B.C.–A.D. 150)

There were four distinct Greek style periods: Geometric, Archaic, Classical, and Hellenistic. Three classical orders of architecture were developed by the Greeks—Doric, Ionic, and Corinthian. The *Doric order* is simple in design, has no base, and has a saucer-shaped capital. The *Ionic order* is more elaborate than Doric and has a capital with two *volutes*—spiral-shaped scrolls. The *Corinthian order*

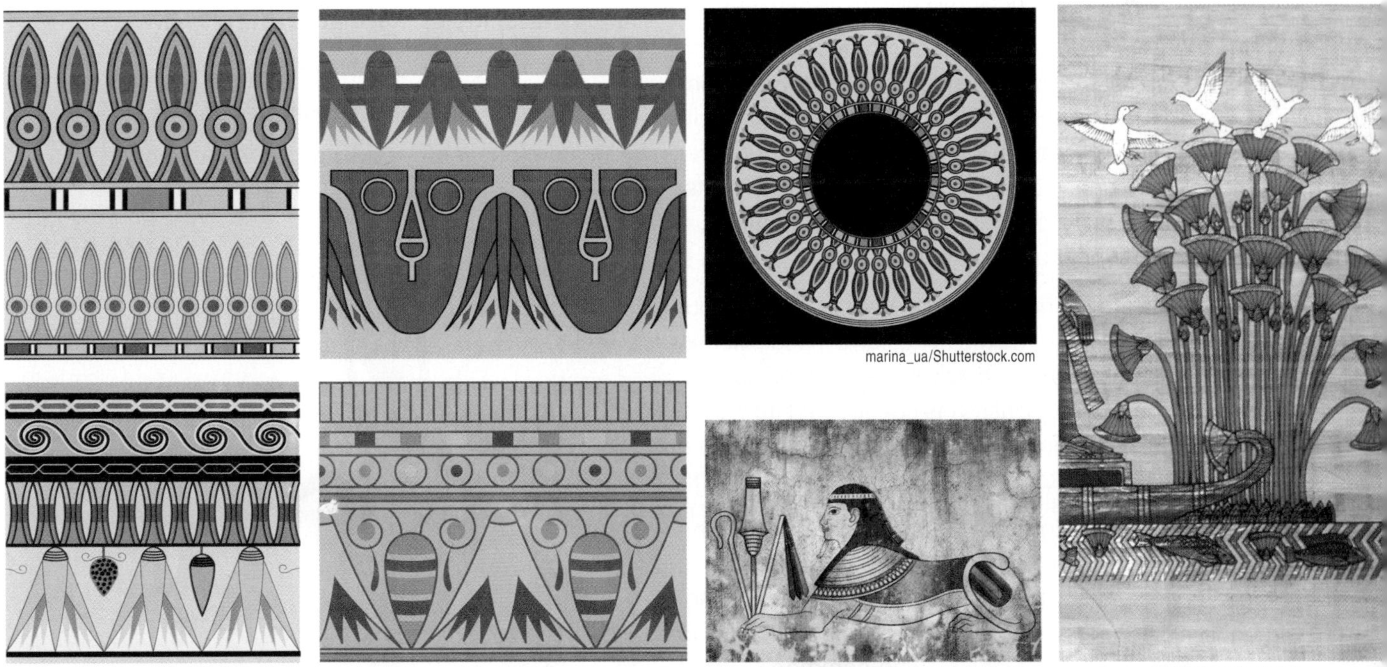

marina_ua/Shutterstock.com marina_ua/Shutterstock.com siloto/Shutterstock.com kilukilu/iStock/Thinkstock

Figure 9-4 These motifs are in the style of ancient Egyptian design.

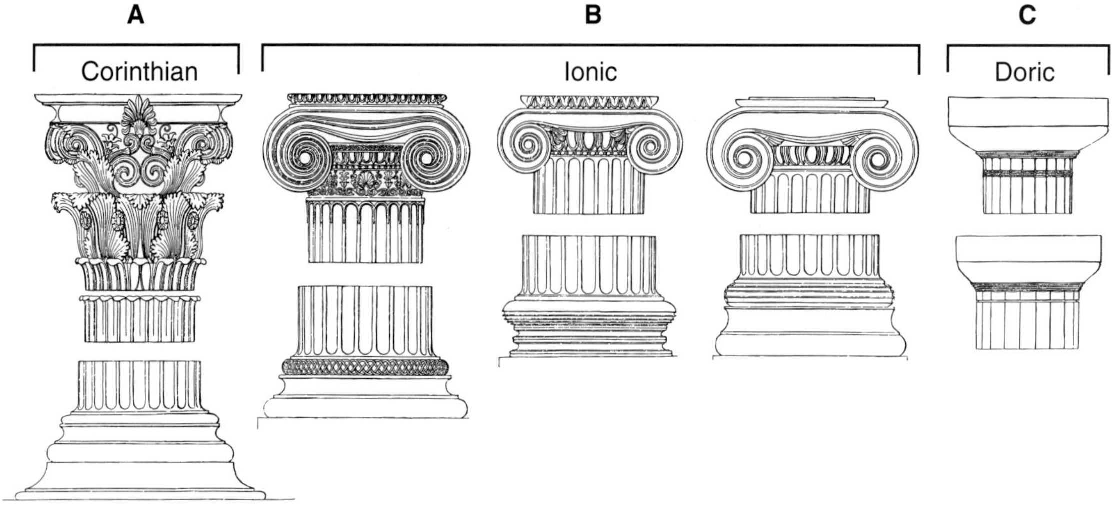

Hein Nouwens/Shutterstock.com

Figure 9-5 These columns represent three orders of Greek architecture—Corinthian (A), Ionic (B), and Doric (C).

has an ornate bell-shaped capital with acanthus leaves. Note: The *capital* is the top part of the column. All three orders have fluted columns, **Figure 9-5**.

One of the most well-known collection of Greek classical orders of architecture is a grouping of buildings located on the *Acropolis*—a site for a collection of temples honoring the Greek gods and goddesses in Athens. During the Classical period, the Doric and Ionic orders of architecture were used for exterior columns while the more delicate acanthus leaf capitals of the Corinthian order were used for the interior. Known for their use of proportion and columns, Greek design is still mimicked today.

Climate in Greece was well-suited to outdoor living and had a great impact on both public and private buildings. Civic rituals and debates were extremely important. Therefore, public buildings provided space for market centers, public assemblies, and cultural events. These buildings were often constructed from marble, a material in abundant supply in Greece.

Common Greek townhouses were usually two to four stories high with interior wall paintings and mosaic floors. A favorite floor design was a black, white, and red pattern. Housing for the working-class was constructed from mud bricks. If possible, housing was two to four stories with a central courtyard to take advantage of the southern sun.

More delicate than Egyptian furnishings, Greek furniture included stools, chairs, chests, reclining couches or beds, and tables. The **klismos chair**—an ancient armchair with saber-shaped legs spreading outward to the front and back of the chair—was common in most households, **Figure 9-6 A**. It was used for unofficial and official activities—such as box seats at a stadium. The stool was the most common piece of furniture due to its portability and was owned by all classes of society. The bed was considered the most important piece of Greek furniture. Either the bed or a reclining couch was used when the Greeks ate their meals. Small tables were placed nearby for use when serving meals. Chests of cedar were commonly used to store valuables and clothing. Functional accessories included pottery vessels such as the **kylix**—a two-handled drinking cup, **Figure 9-6 B**. Pottery surfaces and decorative accessories were lavishly decorated with motifs of architectural details. Motifs included **(Figure 9-7).**

- vine patterns—usually grape vines
- palmette—a leaf suggestive of palm
- acanthus leaf—a prickly perennial herb

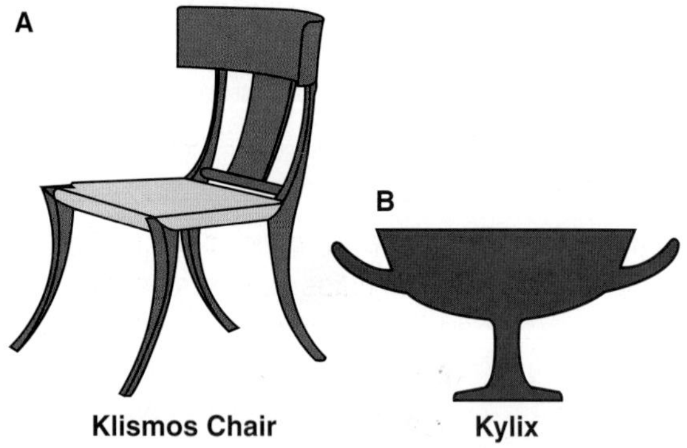

Goodheart-Willcox Publisher

Figure 9-6 Beauty and good function were typical characteristics of Greek design. *What makes each of these items functional?*

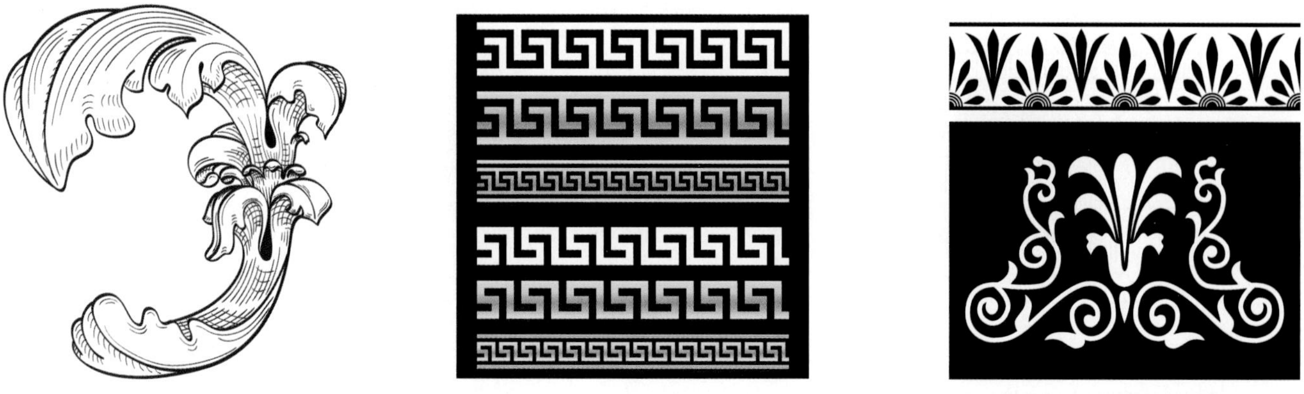

A Buravtsoff/Shutterstock.com B Techlogica/Shutterstock.com C marina_ua/Shutterstock.com

Figure 9-7 The acanthus leaf (A), fret border (B), and the palmette and antheminon (C) were common motifs in Greek design.

- honeysuckle—a fragrant, tubular flower
- fret border—small, straight bars intersecting at right angles
- griffin—legendary creature with the head, beak, and wings of an eagle
- anthemion—a floral motif inspired by Egyptian palmette flower

Classical Greek and Roman architecture had significant influence both structurally and decoratively in subsequent periods beginning with the Renaissance in Italy.

Roman (750 B.C.–A.D. 400)

Considered one of the greatest political nations in the Western world, the Roman Empire has three distinctive periods: Republic, Imperial, and Late Imperial. Well-known for engineering expertise in constructing roads and aqueducts (and causing the fall of Greece), Rome is known for adding two new orders to architectural design: The *Tuscan* and *Composite*. The Tuscan order was based on Etruscan examples, in ways similar to the Greek Doric order. The Composite order's capital combined both volutes (scroll-shaped forms) and acanthus leaves. Romans are also credited for architectural developments such as the barrel vault, arch, dome, and pilasters, **Figure 9-8 A and B**.

Romans built temples and civic buildings throughout their empire. Larger cities had residential districts with townhouses and private villas. Villas, owned by wealthy families, often had surrounding land. The Roman working class lived in town, rented an apartment or owned a town house ranging in height from two to five stories. The entry led to a reception room with an open-air atrium allowing in sun and rain with smaller rooms surrounding the atrium. A large, open-air courtyard was found in the back of the structure. Windows were located street-side only. To expand the sense of space, artists painted realistic perspective murals of landscape scenes known as **trompe l'oeil**—a French word roughly translated to mean "to fool the eye."

Romans greatly admired Greek design. Therefore, much of their furniture followed Greek examples including stools, small tables, and reclining couches. A wicker tub chair, made out of easy-to-obtain reeds and therefore economical to make, was also used. Easy to transport from room to room, practical and comfortable, this chair was often used by women. Accessories included lamps, vases and bowls, glassware, textiles, and weavings. Design motifs were taken directly from Greek artisans with additions of the dolphin, eagle, and ribbons, **Figure 9-9**.

The Middle Ages (A.D. 325–1500)

The Middle Ages, or Medieval or Dark Ages, are commonly known as the period between the fall of the Roman Empire and the European Renaissance. This time period is divided into four eras—early Christian, Byzantine, Romanesque, and Gothic. When Constantine the Great became the emperor of Rome, he legalized Christianity and the first Christian church was built. Churches and large-walled castles for rulers dominated new building construction during this period.

Constantine also divided the Roman Empire into eastern and western territories. After the Roman Empire lost its political influence in Western Europe, territories were divided and run by lords and ladies of the land. These lords later became kings over small kingdoms, which became strong, unifying forces for the people of this period.

A Morphart Creation/Shutterstock.com B Alchena/Shutterstock.com

Figure 9-8 The Romans added the Tuscan and Composite orders of architecture (A). Barrel vaults (B) such as these were also attributed to Roman design.

A B C D

Courtesy of Lydia M. Brown

Figure 9-9 The Four Periods of Roman Style include *Incrustation* (A), *Architectonic* (B), *Ornate* (C), and *Intricate* (D).

Due to the influence of the Roman Catholic Church, massive churches and cathedrals were built of local stone. The development of the *Romanesque style* of architecture was an adaptation from the Roman basilica. External buttresses—wood or masonry supporting members—were attached to exterior walls to distribute the weight of the building into the foundation. As a refinement, gothic-style cathedrals were built with tall spires, large arched windows, and decorative details carved from stone. A series of **flying buttresses**—masonry structures that typically consist of straight inclined bars carried on arches and solid piers or buttresses against which they abut—were used to support the vaulting systems in the interior.

The castle, made for wealthy rulers and gentry, dominated cities across Europe. Made of stone and timber, they revolved around the *great hall* where a fire was made directly on the stone floor to warm the area. To avoid fire damage, ceilings were often 20 feet high. The lord and lady of the castle greeted up to 100 guests while seated in large-scaled chairs placed at one end of the great hall. Tapestries decorated the walls and added additional warmth. The great hall served as the dining room, bedroom, and gathering room for all medieval life.

Townspeople and local parishes were taxed to pay for the construction of their public buildings. This left little money to build anything but modest cottages outside the protective city walls. The general population lived in mud, stone, or timber structures with thatched roofs and earth floors. These buildings often had a loft for additional sleeping space. Merchants lived inside the city walls in detached homes or townhouses made of stucco and timber. Family businesses were located on the first floor with living quarters above.

Private residences had furniture that was scaled proportionately to the building in which it was used—large, massive pieces for castles and smaller pieces for merchant or worker homes. Large trestle tables were used in the castles. Massive side chairs and armchairs with high, straight backs were made in limited quantities. Stools were the most practical and often used pieces of furniture. Due to their light weight, it was a common practice for guests to bring their own stools when invited to dinner. The chest was the most important piece of furniture in the castle and other medieval homes. Accessories included pottery bowls and jars, glassware, metalwork—including wrought iron for lanterns—and textiles. Plant (grape vine) and animal motifs were common as well as the (see **Figure 9-10**)

- trefoil pattern—a symbol with three leaflets
- quatrefoil pattern—representation of a flower with four petals
- linenfold—a type of relief carving imitating windows
- Gothic arches—pointed arches

The Renaissance (A.D. 1400—1660)

The Renaissance, meaning *rebirth* in French, stretched throughout Europe. Emerging from the dominance of competing religions, interest in the arts and sciences flourished after being suppressed since ancient times. In Italy, villas boasted high ceilings and intricately woven tapestries hung against brick, plaster, or stone walls. Also common was trompe l'oeil and elaborate **frescoes**—paintings done on freshly spread moist plaster with water-based pigments.

The Spanish *casa* (dwelling) was designed around a central patio created with wrought iron grille. Interior walls and floors displayed ceramic tiles of geometric patterns. French *chateaus* (large country houses or mansions) were transformed into Italian-inspired palaces. English country houses and medieval castles became refined estate houses.

A new middle class allowed people to possess finer household items, such as upholstered chairs, and such **case goods** as bookcases, bureaus, and dining and bedroom furniture. The Italian *Savonarola chair* and the *French Directoire-style armchair* are credited to this period of time, **Figure 9-11**. As furniture was more plentiful in this period, the need to move pieces from room to room or building to building decreased. Chairs were designed for specific purposes and locations. Chests continued to commonly be located in houses to store valuables and personal items. Accessories included pottery, glass, mirrors—including handheld ones—and metalworking. Lighting was expensive and was provided by candles and lanterns. Only the very wealthy could afford a chandelier or candlestick.

The Spanish, French, and English artists adopted classical motifs over time. Spanish designs emphasized Moorish geometric patterns. The French and English often selected motifs reflecting the aesthetics of Roman and Greek classical designs or reinvented Medieval designs including the

- arabesque (a-ruh-BESK)—an ornament that uses flower, foliage, or fruit, and sometimes animal outlines to produce an intricate pattern of interlaced lines
- rosette—a decorative disk in a foliage or floral design
- festoon—a carved, molded, or painted ornament representing a decorative chain
- fleur de lis (fluhr-duh-LEE)—a conventionalized iris in artistic design

The Baroque Period (A.D. 1600—1715)

Baroque, meaning *irregular*, was a period of extreme ornamentation in architecture, patterns, textures, and design. It was influenced primarily by Italy and France

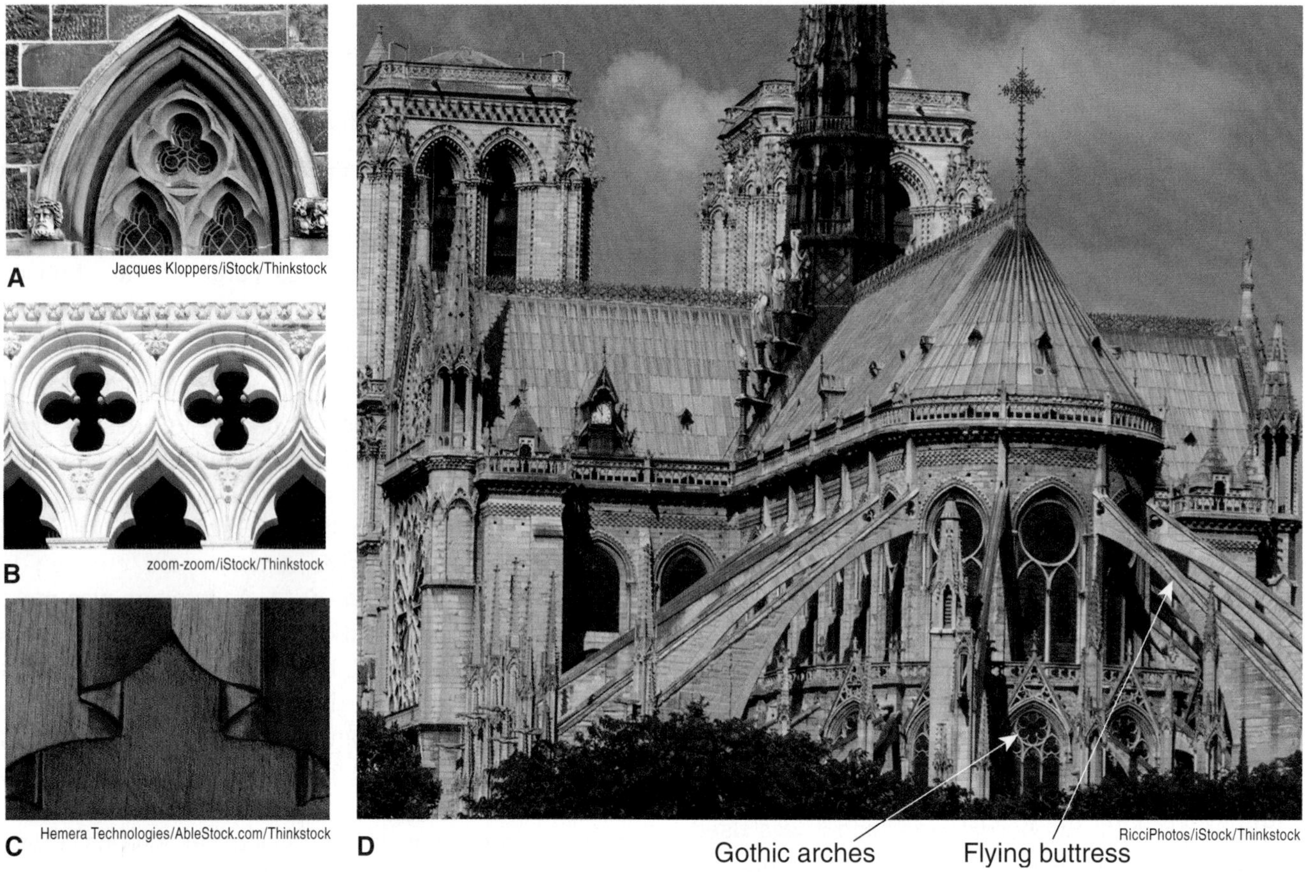

Figure 9-10 Medieval motifs and structures include the *trefoil* (A), *quatrefoil* (B), *linenfold* carvings, and *flying buttresses* and *gothic arches* (D).

Figure 9-11 The Italian *Savonarola chair* is an example of case goods from the Renaissance period. *What other case goods are common to this period?*

and featured such celebrated architects as Bernini who completed St. Peter's Cathedral in Rome. The architectural style was grand and symmetrical such as seen in the *Palace of Versailles*—the home of Louis XIV that is located outside of Paris.

Baroque's grandeur was tactfully developed to show the differences between commoners and royalty. Thus the architecture and interiors of this period were designed to impress rather than be enjoyed. Baroque interiors were considered extensions of the overall architecture with little thought given to how furniture would impact the overall impression.

The lavish Baroque style was translated into private residences as **pilasters**—a slightly projecting column applied to the wall—with gilded Corinthian capitals, wall niches, and classical moldings with walls and ceilings covered with trompe l'oeil paintings, **Figure 9-12**. England was not immediately influenced by the Baroque style because it still had not fully accepted the acclaimed Renaissance style.

Emya/iStock/Thinkstock

Figure 9-12 The pilasters on the front of the *Trevi Fountain* in Italy include Corinthian capitals.

After the Great Fire in 1666 destroyed most of London, Christopher Wren—a surveyor in King James' court—was commissioned to spearhead the design of new buildings. Wren's well-known architecture was influenced by both the Italian Renaissance architecture and the Baroque style.

During this time, the style of seventeenth-century architecture in America was much different. After sailing to the new land, priorities were to build shelter from the cold and to plant crops for food. Rather than grand houses, these people—English, Dutch, Spanish, and French—were building dwellings of one or two rooms out of wood planks from felled local wood.

Chairs were thought of more as a status and wealth symbol than a place of comfort. Unique furniture pieces of this period included the Baroque armchair or *fauteuil* (foh-TOEY)—an upholstered armchair with open arms (see **Figure 9-13**), the *bergere* (buhr-ZHER)—an upholstered armchair with an exposed wood frame, and the highly decorated *commode*—a low chest of drawers. Many tables were used for playing games, dining, and serving food. Furniture usually lined the walls, leaving the center of the room open. The gold or gilt furniture of Louis XIV contrasts sharply with the domestic village homes that contained tables, chairs, stools, beds, and chests.

Accessories included pottery, glass, mirrors, metalworking, and textiles, including lace. The practice of cover-

lynea/Shutterstock.com

Figure 9-13 The *fauteuil* is an example of a Baroque armchair.

CASE STUDY

The Jefferson Hotel—Washington, D.C.

The transformation of the interior of the historic *Jefferson Hotel* took three years through an extensive redesign and renovation process by the design firm of ForrestPerkins. This 99-room, Beaux Arts hotel reflects the designs of Thomas Jefferson's legacy as an architect, inventor, intellectual, and diplomat.

ForrestPerkins conducted extensive research to capture the exquisite, historic design details featured throughout the interiors. For example, the display of historic maps of France and custom fabrics reflect Jefferson's travels through Europe and depict a collection of his most distinctive architectural works.

Designers and principals involved in this project knew that the Jefferson Hotel had frequently been the setting for private discussions that eased the wheels of government, including the organization of a new President's Cabinet in the 1980s.

The hotel was replanned to represent a grand residential place reminiscent of a fine Parisian residence. The effect is to enter a grand city home furnished with an eclectic mix of antiques, historic reproductions, Jeffersonian artifacts, and a private art collection worthy of a European estate.

Investigate and Reflect

Use online or print resources to research a local historic hotel in your area. What historic design factors did the designers consider in the redesign and renovation of the hotel? Which time period does the hotel design reflect? Capture images to use in a report (be sure to properly credit the images). Create an illustrated digital report to share in class or on the class website showing key features of the hotel design and how the designer uses the elements and principles of design.

A

B

C

D

©Stirling Elmendorf Photography/Designed by ForrestPerkins

The designers and principals at ForrestPerkins carefully crafted the redesign of the Jefferson Hotel to reflect Thomas Jefferson's original work. Note the use of the elements and principles of design in architectural details of the ceiling (A), the arrival hall and concierge design (B), a premier suite (C), and the spa (D).

ing walls with fine cloth began during the Italian Renaissance period. Wallpaper appeared in homes before the seventeenth century and was hand painted or printed using wooden blocks on small pieces of paper. Each European country adopted individual Baroque motifs including the acanthus leaf, shells, griffins, pilasters, classical arabesques, garlands, and cupid-like figures.

French Styles

The eighteenth century saw wars and revolutions in Europe and in America. In England, an Act of Union between Scotland and England formed Great Britain, combining two parliaments into one government. France entered into wars with England over control of territories in North America and India. Settled by treaty—the Treaty of Paris—after Austria, Russia, Sweden, and Prussia became involved, the imperial control in North America was reorganized. As a result, Britain gained Canada, and France gained Florida and the territory east of the Mississippi. Spain acquired Louisiana with territory west of the Mississippi River.

By the end of the century, France was in its own revolution. At this point in the text, a few well-known styles are broken down into various areas of the world to allow you to study them in more detail, beginning with France in the eighteenth century.

Rococo (Louis XV, A.D. 1715–1774)

Meaning *shell*, the Rococo (roh-kuh-KOH) period began in Paris, France in the early part of the eighteenth century and extended through the reign of Louis XV of France. It is also referred to as *late Baroque*. Rather than the symmetry of Baroque, the work of Rococo artists and designers reflected a jubilant celebration of life. Designers opted for ornate asymmetrical designs with pastel colors and gold details.

Rococo rooms were elegant with ornate furniture, small sculptures, ornamental mirrors, and tapestries. Gentle curves and ornamentation based on natural forms were depicted in shells, scrolls, delicate bouquets tied with ribbons, and exquisite ceiling frescoes of mythological figures. Walls with **wainscoting**—paneling on the lower three or four feet of a wall—were painted creamy white with gold accents and framed the interior. Mirrors hanging over fireplaces reflected the hanging chandeliers.

A porcelain factory supplied cabinetmakers with decorative details that adorned furniture items. Pastel paintings of pastoral or idyllic scenes of goddesses in gardens appeared on interior walls. **Aubusson rugs**—durable, handmade wool rugs with a flat weave originally woven in the town of Aubusson in central France—were used on the floors.

Classic architectural details included columns, pilasters, and niches. The scale of furniture catered to the smaller living quarters of Louis XV in Paris' apartment or hotel, **Figure 9-14**. It emphasized graceful proportions and comfort over pretentiousness. Chairs were designed with shorter backs and arm supports set back from the front seat rail to accommodate the full skirts worn by ladies of the period. Furniture was often upholstered with velvet, brocade, and satin that matched the same fabrics worn by the wealthy. The portable stool was still popular along with the *bergere* (a type of upholstered easy chair), chaise lounge, commode (a chest of drawers on legs), and a variety of tables. Motifs included oriental influences as well as shells, garlands, **ormolu** (a gold, brass, or bronze decoration fastened to furniture), and festoons (garlands of fruit or flowers), **Figure 9-15**.

Neoclassical Period (A.D. 1760–1830)

The Neoclassical period coincided with the reign of Louis XVI and Marie Antoinette. It reflected a renewed fascination with Roman classical design that emerged with the excavation of Pompeii in 1748. The fascination with the artifacts discovered after 1800 years of burial were documented in precise line drawings and used for inspiration during this period. Architecture revived the use of the three orders of architecture—Doric, Ionic, and Corinthian. It was a return to rectilinear forms and a rejection of the serpentine curves typical of previous periods.

The Petit Trianon in France built by Gabriel exemplifies the Neoclassical elements in the interior and on the exterior. Interiors were designed with geometrical shapes—arcs, rectangles, and circles. They were used on wall panels, mirror frames, and in floor patterns. Roman architectural elements inspired designs of ceilings, door frames, and mantles. Walls were in white, gray, or soft pastels.

Greece, Rome, and Egypt had great influence on furniture design of the Neoclassical period. Chairs featured the lyre-back, medallion-back, and square-back. Tables and commodes were common. Robert Adam's

Courtesy of Lydia M. Brown

Figure 9-14 Roccoco rooms were ornate with pastel colors and gold.

Olivieri Le Queinec/Shutterstock.com

Figure 9-15 Ormolu was a gold, brass, or bronze ornamentation fastened to furnishings and accessories in the Louis XV period in France.

work in England and Thomas Jefferson's Monticello were examples of Neoclassical design. Motifs included gilt swags, urns, laurel wreaths, *paterae*—a circular ornament resembling a dish, wheat, and egg and dart, **Figure 9-16**.

Empire Style (A.D. 1800–1815)

The French Revolution and execution of King Louis XVI marked the beginning of the Empire (AHM-pihr) style. Under the reign of Napoleon Bonaparte, the style was developed to communicate the grandeur France achieved from military conquests including Egypt.

In the private dwellings, the central entry area—or *vestibule*—was often circular with a central staircase to the upper levels. Walls were decorated with frescoes, stretched fabric, paintings, and wallpaper. Draped textiles were used—sometimes in the impression of a tent as seen in the bedroom of the Empress Josephine

Courtesy of Lydia M. Brown

Figure 9-16 The Neoclassical period reflects Roman classical design. *What are some of the classic shapes and forms found in Neoclassical interiors?*

in her Chateau de la Malmaison near Paris. Semi-detached columns or pilasters were used as well as a **dado**—the part of a pedestal of a column above the base. Floors were wood using parquet or plain planks. Marble was used for more important rooms.

Furniture was more simple or unadorned than previous periods due to the country's financial austerity. Less use of **marquetry**—elaborate patterns formed by inserting pieces of wood, shell, or ivory into a wood veneer and applying it to furniture—and decoration was used with beech wood replacing mahogany. The scale of the furniture again grew larger to communicate importance to the observer. It was placed against the wall rather than within the room proper. Stateliness was communicated through rectilinear form and severe sharp corners.

Furniture pieces included the *lit bateau*—a bed that looks like a small boat (**Figure 9-17**), the chaise lounge, and a variety of tables and chairs. It was decorated with metal motifs, often influenced by Egypt, such as winged lions, falcons, or a sphinx. The chair legs were often carved to resemble an animal's legs. Motifs included the bee, the letter N (for Napoleon), laurel wreath, stars, the eagle, and exotic hieroglyphic motifs from Egypt. Empress Josephine also selected swans to decorate chair arms, curtains, carpets, and porcelain in the state rooms of her home at Malmaison. This period corresponds to the *Biedermeier style* in Germany, *Federal style* in America, and *Regency style* in Britain.

English Styles

The effects of the Renaissance spread slowly into England by way of the low countries along the coastal regions of northwest Europe—Belgium, the Netherlands, and Luxemburg. Its influence was retitled as *Elizabethan* in England and extended from sometime before Elizabeth's birth until sometime after her death. There are two major English furniture styles that emerged during the seventeenth century: *Jacobean* and *William and Mary*.

In the eighteenth century, there were the Early, Middle, and Late Georgian periods—spanning the reigns of

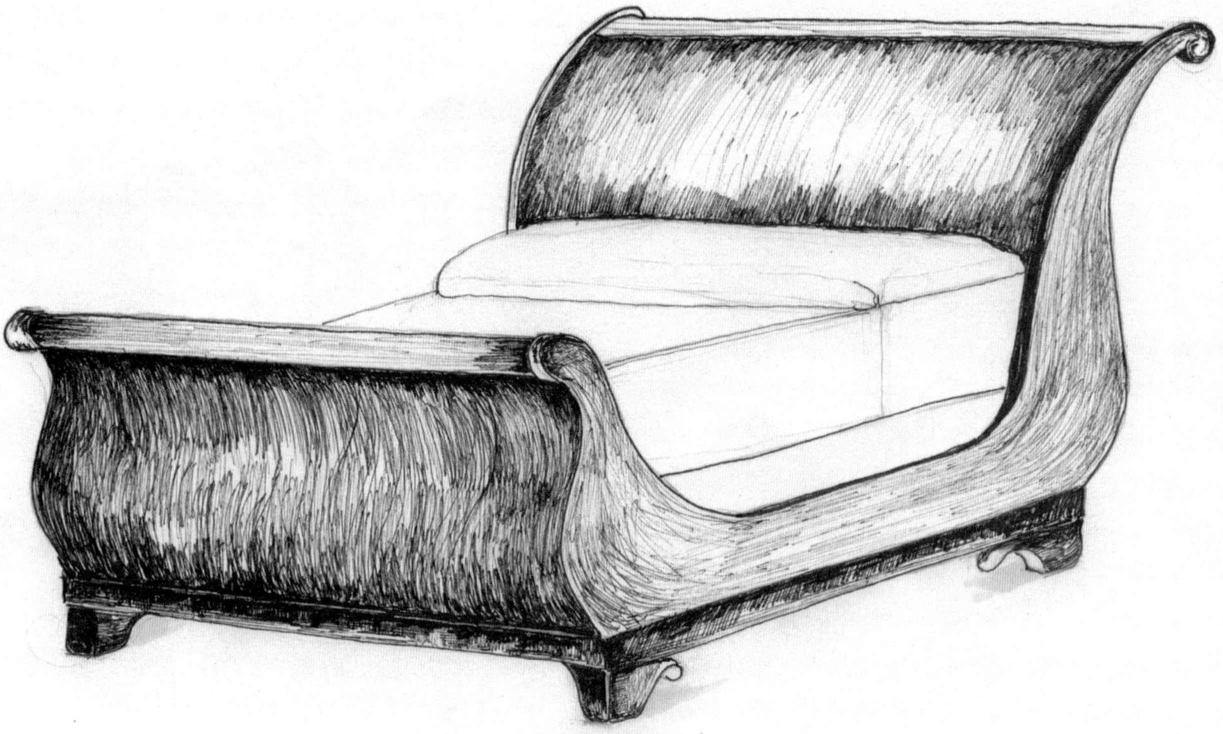
Susan R Casebeer

Figure 9-17 The lit bateau was a common style during the French Empire period.

four kings of England all named *George* (for example, George I and George II). This period roughly covers from 1714 to 1830 and was a time of British expansion throughout the world. Several styles of furniture emerged—many of which are seen in homes today—such as Chippendale. Finally, Queen Victoria reigned in England. She is the namesake of the next historical era—the Victorian period.

Jacobean (A.D. 1600–1690)

Medieval in appearance, these interiors and furnishings had straight lines, rigid designs, sturdy construction, ornate carvings, and dark finishes. The furniture was heavy; therefore, stretchers were required. A **stretcher** was a horizontal brace extending between the legs of a table or chair that provided additional support to prevent it from collapsing under its own weight, **Figure 9-18**.

Square chair seats were constructed of various types of wood or woven rush (a sturdy plant with cylindrical, hollow stems). If material was used on chair backs, it would be leather or velvet. The legs ended in a block, bun, or tapered shape. Motifs included acanthus leaf, acorns, carved heads, diamonds, and simple geometric shapes such as squares, circles, and triangles.

William and Mary (A.D. 1690–1725)

Still considered early Georgian, this period was named after rulers William and Mary of England. Interiors and furnishings had Dutch and Chinese influences. Chair backs were cane, upholstered, or wood. Chair seats were constructed of cane or woven rush, or padded with leather or fabric. If chair backs were wood, shapes were typically banister or stile and panel. Leg shapes were round or straight and often had elaborate **turnings**—decorations formed by using a lathe. The **cabriole leg** was a curved leg shaped like an animal leg with an ornamental foot, **Figure 9-19 A and B**. Oriental lacquer-work was occasionally used in furnishings. Motifs included acanthus leaf, floral, scroll, and shell.

Queen Anne (A.D. 1700–1755)

Another Early Georgian period—named after Queen Anne of England—showcased a graceful, elegant refinement of the William and Mary style. Furniture was based on the *S*-curve. Fiddle-back or splat-back chairs with padded seats and cabriole legs ending in pad or club feet were common, **Figure 9-20**. Later chairs had *claw and ball feet* as well. Fabrics for padded seats included

Susan R Casebeer

Figure 9-18 Ornate stretchers were common details in chairs and tables of the Jacobean period.

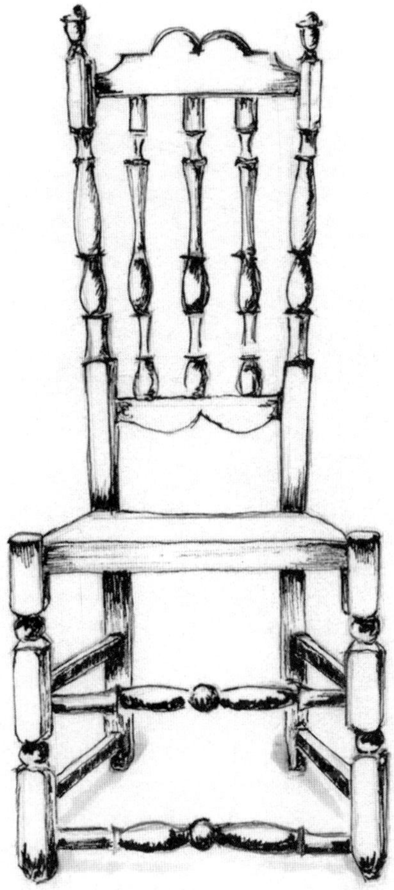

Susan R Casebeer

Figure 9-19 The stile and panel back chair was a characteristic trait of the William and Mary style.

damask, tapestry, velvet, and needlepoint. Motifs included acanthus leaf and the shell.

Chippendale (A.D. 1750–1790)

From the Middle Georgian period, these furnishings were named after cabinet maker Thomas Chippendale. They were classified into three types and influences: French, Chinese, and Gothic. Graceful and refined chairs had upholstered fabric seats made from brocade, silk, velvet, or tapestry. The Chinese-style yoke back was often a distinguishing characteristic of chair backs. Chair backs may also have been shaped as ladder-backs or slat-backs with a lattice or pierced central splat, **Figure 9-21**.

Cabriole legs were common. Chair legs also ended in ball and claw, bracket, or paw and claw feet. Motifs included acanthus leaf, lattice, Oriental patterns, scroll, shell, and urn. Ornamentation included fretwork often Oriental in style, chinoiserie, and finials. To give you a sense of time, the Middle Georgian period coincided with French Neoclassic style and discovery of Pompeii in Italy.

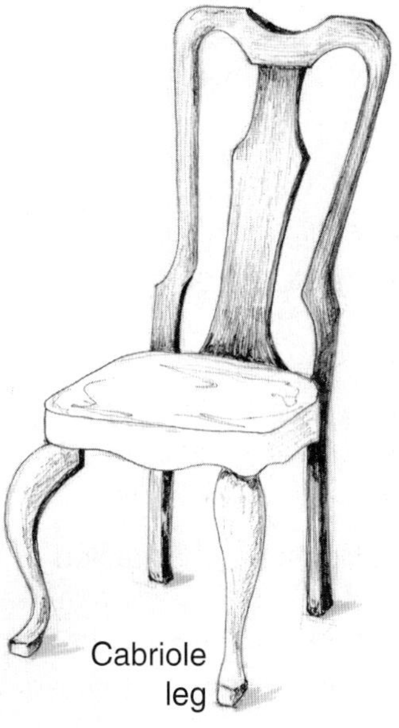

Susan R Casebeer

Figure 9-20 The Queen Anne fiddle-back chair includes the characteristic S-curve and cabriole leg.

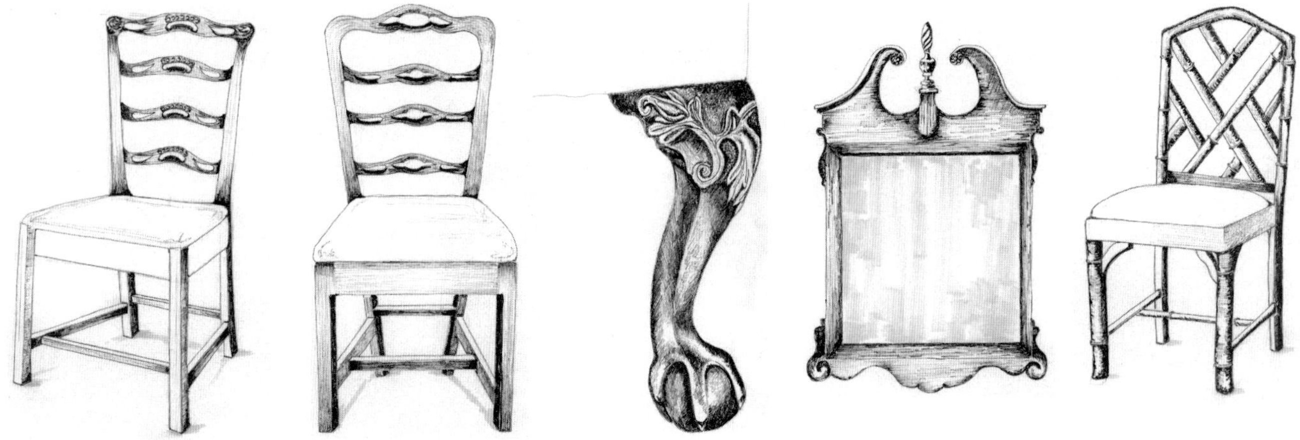

Susan R Casebeer

Figure 9-21 French, Gothic, and Chinese influences are evident in Chippendale furniture.

Adam (A.D. 1760–1795)

Furnishings and interiors from this Middle Georgian period were named after architect Robert Adam, who studied ancient Italian architecture. Robert Adam and his four sons all designed interiors and furnishings with classical motifs. Oval- or shield-shaped chair backs graced this elegant style of furniture, **Figure 9-22**. Chair seats were commonly upholstered in such fabrics as brocade, damask, or satin. Chair legs were tapered and ended in block or **spade feet**—a tapered, rectangular furniture foot resembling the blade of a garden shovel or spade. Motifs included drapery swag, honeysuckle, lyre, medallion, rams head, urn, or wheat.

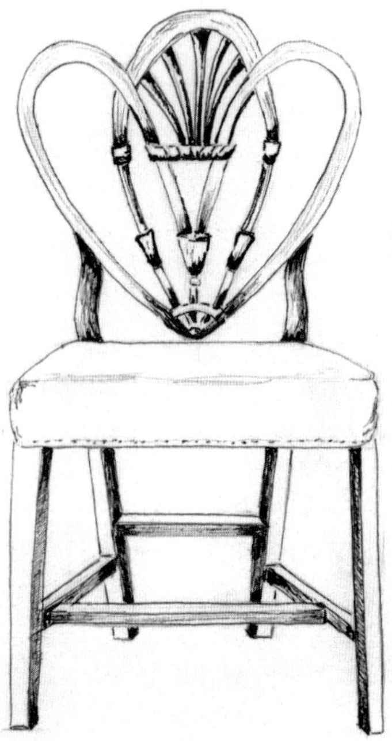

Susan R Casebeer

Figure 9-22 The graceful shield-back chair is characteristic of the Adam period.

Hepplewhite (A.D. 1765–1800)

Also from the Middle Georgian period, this style was named after cabinetmaker, George Hepplewhite. Neoclassic in style, the appearance of these furnishings was delicate and graceful. Characteristic chair backs were shaped in hearts, ovals, or shields. Reed-tapered legs commonly ended in spade feet. The horseshoe or horseshoe arch with a serpentine front were unusually shaped chair seats, **Figure 9-23 A**. They were typically covered in such fabrics as brocade, damask, or satin. Motifs included the conch shell, drapery swag, honeysuckle, palmetto, plume, urn, or wheat.

Sheraton (A.D. 1780–1820)

From the Middle Georgian period, this Neoclassical style was named after designer Thomas Sheraton. His style was characterized by delicate straight lines, light construction, use of **veneers** (thin overlays of wood), and use of Neoclassical motifs. Chair-back shapes included banister, lattice, rectangular or square, and urn, **Figure 9-23 B**. The most common chair back recognized today is the rectangle or square. Chair seats were fabric, and their shapes were curved or round or horseshoe. Delicate chair legs ended in tapered, paw or claw, and spade feet. Motifs included acanthus leaf,

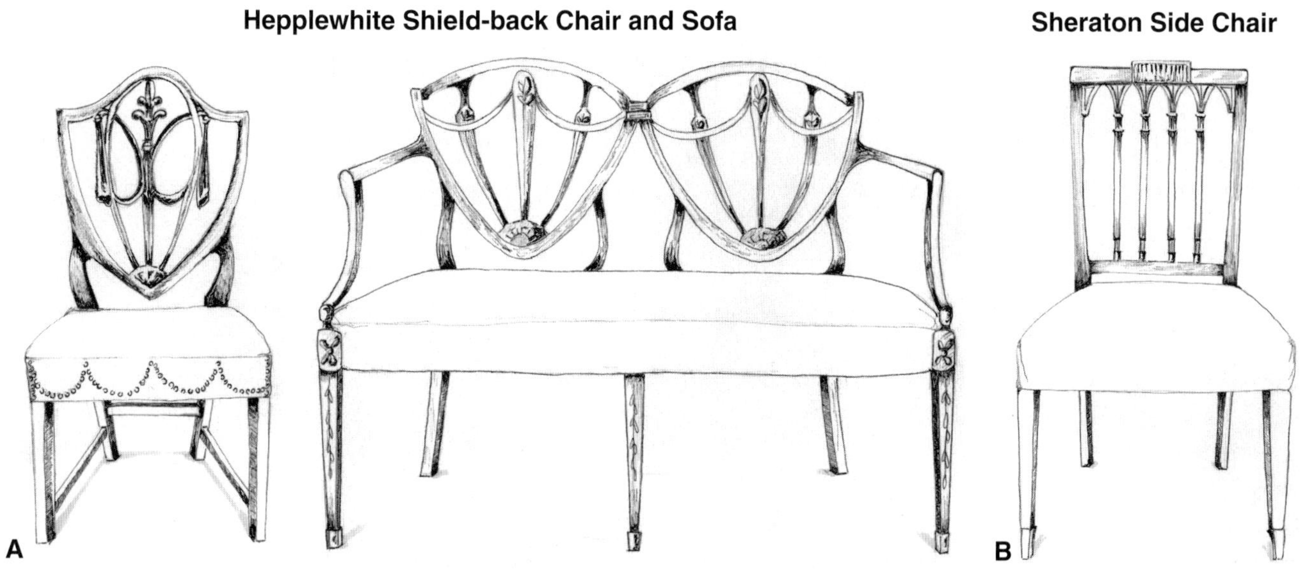

Susan R Casebeer

Figure 9-23 Although both are Neoclassic and delicate in style, Hepplewhite furnishings include hearts, ovals, and shields (A) while straight lines are characteristic of Sheraton furnishings (B).

drapery swag, festoons, floral, foliage, honeysuckle, lattice, lyre, plume, scroll, and urn.

American Styles

American styles are often refined or adapted from styles of other countries. Why? In the American colonies, the first concern was to build shelter and plant crops to create a food supply. Furniture was crudely designed and developed out of necessity and function rather than comfort, aesthetics, or luxury. Typically, the chest was the main piece of furniture brought from a homeland. Immigrant joiners or cabinetmakers brought with them furniture expertise and styles from their homelands. These styles were reflective of the small European peasant villages where they lived rather than the sophisticated designs found in the courts or wealthy homes.

Colonial or Early American (A.D. 1620–1700)

Throughout most of the seventeenth century, houses remained small, of one or two rooms, and constructed of local materials. Most Early American interiors included furnishings made from local hardwoods—oak,

Designer Profile

Deborah Lloyd Forrest—Historic Furnishings and Decorative Arts

Deborah Lloyd Forrest, FASID, has achieved distinction as an industry leader in hospitality design throughout her career, which spans more than 30 years. Ms. Forrest is president and sole owner of ForrestPerkins.

FORREST PERKINS
defining luxury®

Courtesy of ForrestPerkins

"As a designer of luxury hotels, I use my knowledge of historic and period furniture, window coverings, and decorative arts virtually every day. The best period furnishings incorporated detail, scale, proportion, and decoration to convey a unified and seamless aesthetic within the room for which they were designed. At the time, there was no separation between interior design and architecture, thus each room was fully conceived as a complete idea with each component complementing the whole. This is actually how I approach the spaces within the hotels I design. I consider the entire envelope and then design each component to complement the overall design concept, whether for a historic or traditional interior or a modern one."

You can read more about Deborah Lloyd Forrest in Appendix B.

maple, and pine—and modeled after European styles from England, France, Germany, the Netherlands, Scandinavian countries, and Spain. These furnishings were simple, with straight lines and little ornamentation. Chair-back designs included banister, ladder-back, slat-back, and spindle. Square chair seats were constructed of wood or woven rush. Legs ended in block, bracket, bun, or tapered shapes.

Furniture was designed to serve multiple functions. For example, the *table-settle*—a settle with a hinged back that can be let down on the arms as a table—is easily converted into seating after a meal. A drawer was provided in the same unit for the storage of linens or utensils.

Other furniture was designed to be portable. For example, a small, gateleg table or butterfly table could be folded up. Storage was still an issue. Therefore, the chest was still used to hold valuables or other items. It could also be used as a small table or bench. Beds were constructed of a wood frame with ropes that supported the straw mattress. If a loft was built into the house rafters, the beds might be located there. Very few accessories were found in early American homes. Furniture motifs included circles, diamonds, roses, scrolls, and tulips.

In southwest America, the *Santa Fe Style* incorporated bold colors and geometric forms. Local wood, leather, rush seats, and turned spindles were incorporated into chair designs. This period typically includes Jacobean and Spanish-Mission and Colonial-style influences, **Figure 9-24**.

Colonial Georgian (A.D. 1700–1780)

The word *colonial* refers to the political and economic system as well as a style of furniture, interiors, and

Courtesy of Lydia M. Brown

Figure 9-24 Most Early American or Colonial furnishings were simple with little ornamentation. *What interior features relate to previous periods?*

architecture. In the United States, colonial usually refers to English colonial—although much of America was settled by immigrants from the Netherlands, France, Portugal, and Spain.

As America flourished, a better lifestyle was established. By the end of the seventeenth century, tobacco, rice, and sugar created a prosperity reflected in the architecture. The Georgian style of architecture emerged at the beginning of the eighteenth century with such subtle classical details as pilasters. Symmetrical facades, two stories, lower ceilings, wood floors, and fireplaces were common. Paint was used on the outside of the homes and very occasionally inside.

This period of American furnishings was influenced by such English Georgian styles as William and Mary, Queen Anne, and Chippendale. Chair-back materials were cane, woven rattan, upholstery fabric, or wood. Chair-back shapes included fiddle-back (central splat), ladder-back or slat-back, solid, or spindles. Chair legs included cabriole, turned, round, and straight styles. Chair-seat shapes included the horseshoe and square. Motifs included acanthus leaf, floral, oriental patterns, seaweed, and shell.

Duncan Phyfe (A.D. 1795–1848)

The Neoclassical period typically includes *Federal, Greek Revival, Duncan Phyfe,* and *American Empire* styles. Furnishings from this period were named after cabinetmaker Duncan Phyfe, an immigrant from Scotland who moved to New York City. The style was adapted from Adam, Sheraton, Hepplewhite, and Empire. Chair-back shapes included crossbar (X-shaped splat), lyre, and scroll back. Chair-leg types included *curule* (KYOOR-ool)—a base used during Roman times—and X-shaped curved legs, reeded, round, splayed, or tapered shapes that ended with brass paw or claw, knob, or paw feet, **Figure 9-25**. Chair-seat shapes included horseshoe and square, and used such Neoclassical motifs as acanthus leaf, drapery swag, lyre, and plum. Other ornamentation included carvings, fluting, and fretwork.

Shaker (A.D. 1820–1860)

This style was named after a religious sect—the United Society of Believers in Christ's Second Appearing (called

Phyfe Lyre-back Chair

Phyfe Crossbar Chair

Susan R Casebeer

Figure 9-25 Curved legs with reeded, round, splayed, or tapered shapes ending with brass paw, claw, or knob feet were customary features of Duncan Phyfe furniture. *What other styles were common to this period?*

Shakers)—that settled in the northeastern area of America. Their furnishings were characterized by elegant simplicity, quality craftsmanship, and functional design. Chair backs included the ladder-back or slat-back. Chair legs were straight and tapered with woven seats that were square in shape. Seat materials included cane, rush, wood, and woven fabrics. Woods commonly used were maple and cherry. Because the Shakers considered surface decorations as excess, the furnishings used no motifs. Many Shaker principles of utilitarian design offered inspiration for Modern furniture designers.

Introduction to Modern Design

The historical eras end in the 1830s with the onset of the *Industrial Revolution*. The fine art of custom cabinetry and fine furnishings disappear with the development of mass-produced furniture. The evolution of Modern design began with rebellion against the elaborate motifs and materialism of the Victorian period. Modern design moved to an appreciation of clean, simple forms that introduced new classic designs.

The roots of Modernism can be traced to the Industrial Revolution (1880s to the early 1900s), an era in which furniture was manufactured along with other modern conveniences such as automobiles. Technological advancements and new materials—such as plastics and steel—led to architectural innovations, which moved into furniture.

One of the most important forward-thinking designers was Austrian-born Michael Thonet. He is considered to have produced the first modern furniture in the middle of the nineteenth century. He perfected a steam process for bending hardwood using a machine—a mass-production method. His classic Model No. 14 chair sold for 75 cents at the turn of the century. *De Stijl* designers and educators from the *Bauhaus School of Design* in Weimar, Germany also had significant impact on the movement. The Bauhaus is perhaps the design movement most associated with classic modern furniture.

Early modern architecture included such prominent American architects as

- Frank Lloyd Wright—architect and designer of the Prairie-style house
- Henry Hobson Richardson—developer of the Romanesque style of architecture
- Louis Sullivan—known as the "Father of the skyscraper" and credited with the expression "form follows function"

Victorian (A.D. 1840–1910)

Named after Queen Victoria of England and characterized by an ostentatious display of material wealth, Victorian-style furniture was the first mass-produced furniture in the United States. The furnishings—heavy in proportion—were elaborate in carving and applied ornamentation. The style was influenced by the French Rococo, Gothic, Renaissance, Oriental, and Jacobean periods. Chairs had a dark finish and chair backs were either wood (with horizontal or vertical slats) or upholstered. A balloon-shaped chair back was common. Chair-seat shapes were curved, horseshoe, and horseshoe arch with serpentine front. Chair feet were ball and claw and tapered, **Figure 9-26**. Motifs commonly used were foliage or scroll. Due to their size and weight, stretchers were used to support the legs.

The design intent of Victorian interiors was to display wealth to visitors. These interiors were commonly dark, formal, heavily draped, decorated with patterned wallpaper, and accessorized with area rugs and shelves to display trinkets collected during travels. Gilt (a gold surface finish), velvets, and mosaics were common in

Tom Grundy/Shutterstock.com

Figure 9-26 Furnishings of the Victorian era were elaborate with applied carvings. *What styles heavily influenced the Victorian style of furniture?*

interiors. Houses were multistoried with ornate details less numerous as each floor was ascended. Closets were nonexistent because they were taxed. Hidden rooms were often located behind fireplaces.

Arts and Crafts (A.D. 1860–1920)

As part of the Early Modernism period, these furnishings are also referred to as *Mission* or *Craftsman* style. Designers of this style include William Morris, Charles Eastlake, and Gustav Stickley. Morris and Eastlake were English, while Stickley was American. In a revolt against machine-made products, their design statement focused on returning to traditional craftsmanship. Unnecessary decoration was stripped away. Therefore, this furniture style was and is sturdily built and characterized by simple, straight lines, little ornamentation, and a heavy appearance. Chair-back shapes were ladder-back, slat-back, or spindle. **Dovetail joinery**—characterized by a flaring tenon and a mortise into which the tenon fits snuggly—was common. This interlocking joint was noticeable and a statement of furniture quality. Because of its simplicity, the Arts and Crafts style includes no motifs.

Arts and Crafts interiors were characterized by aesthetic simplicity, functional design, and quality craftsmanship. Wood was used heavily, usually with joints and handwork exposed, **Figure 9-27**. Wood floors, ceiling beams (which visually lower the ceiling), and area rugs with nature-inspired designs were common. Patterned textiles were handwoven in rich, nature-based colors. Draperies were made of linen or cotton. Many built-ins—shelving, seating, sideboards, and bookshelves—were used and generally constructed of oak, **Figure 9-28 A, B, C, and D.**

robcocquyt/Shutterstock.com

Figure 9-27 Arts and Crafts interiors and furnishings used many types of wood joints, especially dovetail joints such as this.

Art Nouveau (A.D. 1890–1915)

As part of Early Modernism, this style was short in duration but significant because of its dramatic use of naturalistic, organically flowing forms (lines that might be found in nature, rather than in a regular, mechanical shape). It was most prominent in France but widely recognized in America with its intricately detailed patterns and sinuous, curving lines. Perceived as an urban style, it was commonly used to decorate streets, such as the Paris Metro Stations, architecture, such as the work of Antoni Gaudi, and interiors, such as those designed by Victor Horta, in modern industrial cities.

Chair backs were upholstered or wood, with chair-back shapes including balloon and bentwood. Chair seats were cane or woven rattan, upholstered, or wood. Fabrics used included brocades, damask, linen, tapestry, and velvets. Motifs focused on such elements of nature as florals, foliage, and tulips. Prominent designers of this period included

- Charles Rennie MacIntosh (Scottish architect and furniture maker)
- Louis Comfort Tiffany (American lighting designer)
- Victor Horta (Belgian architect)
- Henri van de Velde (Belgian Flemish painter/architect)

Interiors commonly consisted of furniture, ironwork, and wallpaper. Accents used elongated, sinuous lines that curved and wandered throughout the space resembling growing plants. Vertical lines were a feature with distinctive use of a *whiplash* line. Natural elements such as butterflies, spiderwebs, dragonflies, birds, peacock feathers, and vines were common. Furniture was not

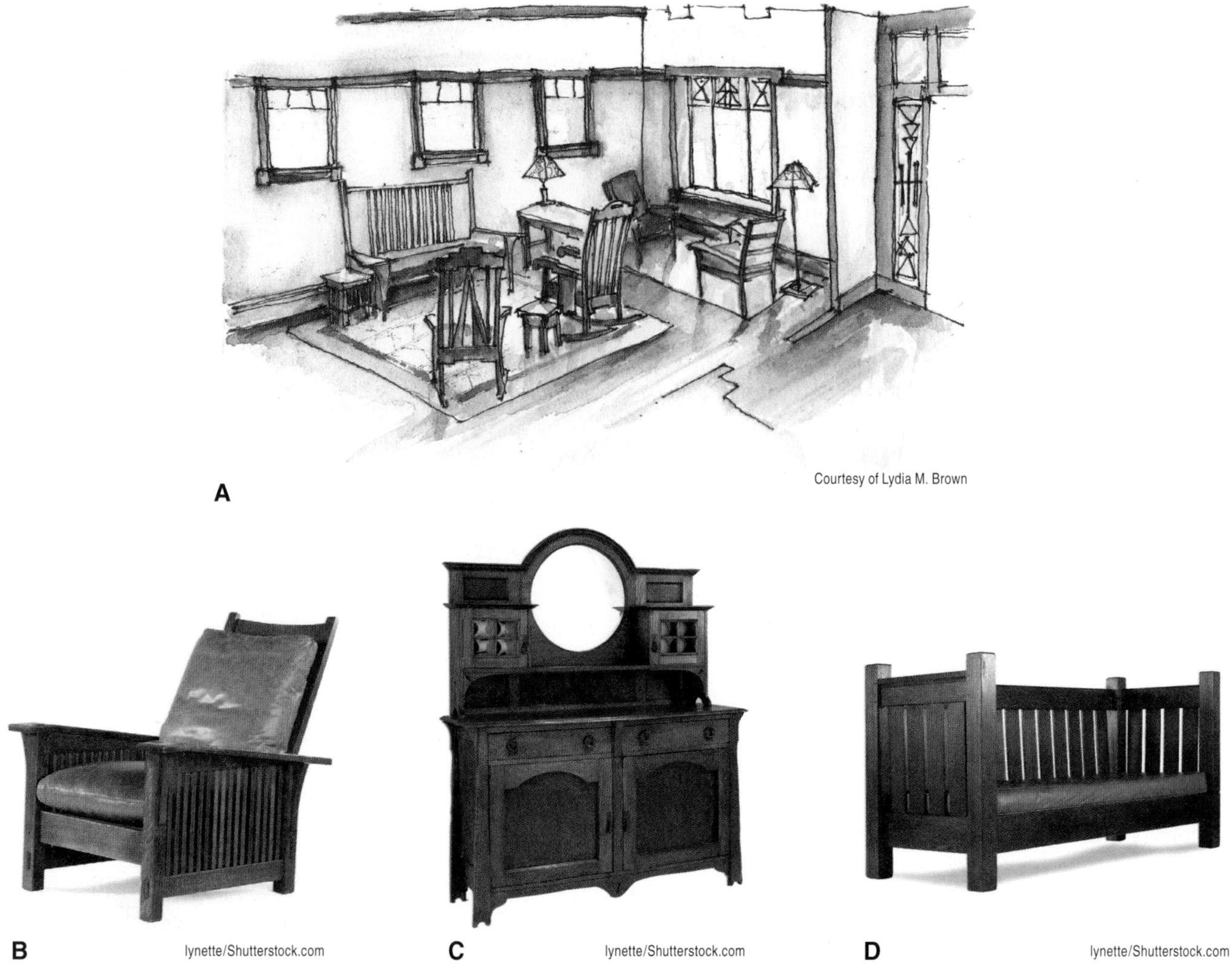

Figure 9-28 Interiors and furnishings of the Arts and Crafts era were simple, well-made, with no ornamentation as evident in this room (A), the Morris chair (B), the sideboard (C), and the settle (D).

a big element in an Art Nouveau interior, **Figure 9-29**. Instead, accents such as art glass were typical. Tiffany lamps emerged during this time. Colors were elegant and subtle in such combinations as mustard, sage, olive, brown, and gold, teamed with lilac and violet or peacock blue.

The Modern Movement

Essentially, modernism is associated with modern thinking. The twentieth century opens with European designers studying a purely geometric approach to design. Instead of relying on historical references, such as Victorian, designers introduced a rational approach to design that captured the international and cultural borders discovered during the war.

World War I brought a globalization to the world. A new look to architecture—the *International Style*—emerged and dominated much of European design during the years between the two world wars. Utilizing new construction techniques and materials, buildings of the International style were starkly different than those of previous eras. Flat roofed, asymmetrical, and with bands of windows set into a rectangular form, International style buildings were a dramatic departure from past eras. The interiors and furnishings of this style reflected this dramatic change.

Art Deco (A.D. 1925–1940)

Unlike Bauhaus and International style, Art Deco did not exploit the functional furniture characteristics for

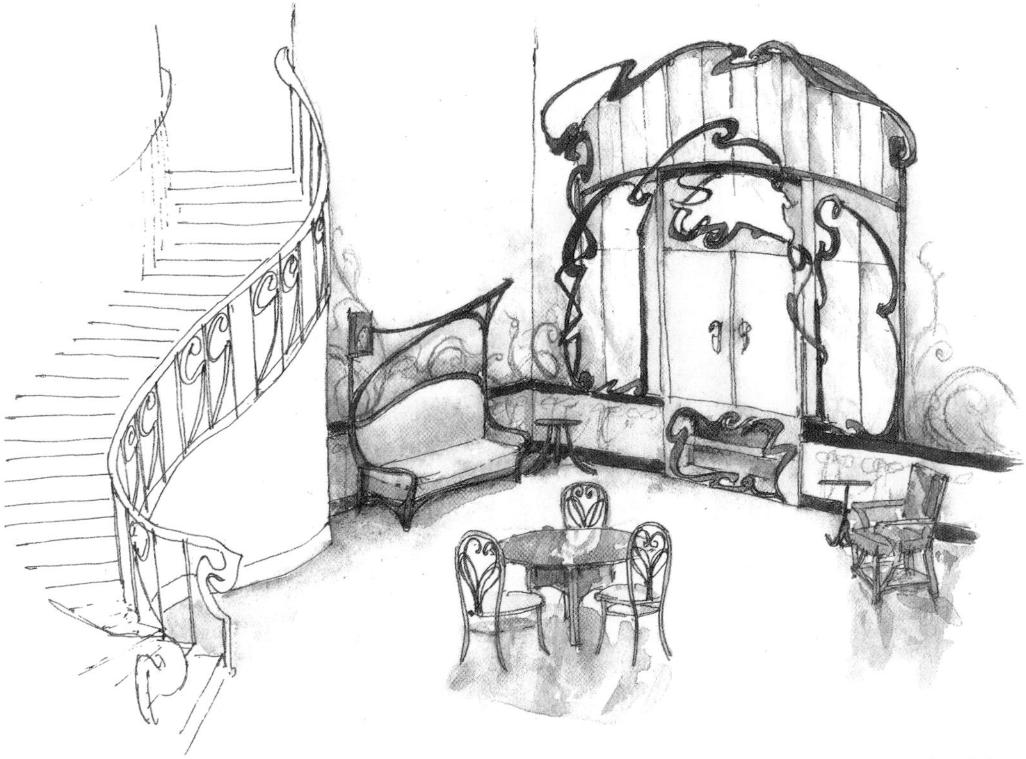

Courtesy of Lydia M. Brown

Figure 9-29 The Art Nouveau period used naturalistic, organically flowing forms in interiors and furnishings. *Use Internet resources to locate other examples of Art Nouveau furnishings and design.*

design themes. Sleek and streamlined with an attention to geometry were important features of Art Deco. Art Deco had an international appeal, and like Art Nouveau, was an international success.

Inspired by the Jazz Age of the 1920s, Art Deco design is characterized by smooth lines, geometric shapes such as triangles and circles, and use of such industrial materials as plastic, aluminum, stainless steel, and chrome. Design inspirations were drawn from products of the machine age—including skyscrapers, cars, planes, and ships as well as those of ancient Egypt inspired by the opening of the tomb of Tutankhamen in 1922, **Figure 9-30**. Deco motifs emphasized such geometric forms as spheres, polygons, rectangles, trapezoids, zigzags, chevrons, and sunburst motifs. Design elements were often arranged in symmetrical patterns.

Mid-Century Modern (1933-1965)

Modernism spread at different paces to different places around the world. Although typically attributed to occurring after World War II, modernism was spreading across the globe as early as the 1920s and 1930s. The 1930s brought the Great Depression, which caused unemployment for many. In Europe, economic instability was accompanied by political change—such as the Nazis coming to power in Germany. Many architects and designers were repressed with several forced to immigrate. Most styles of furniture design—including the International and Art Deco styles—were stifled.

While the United States struggled as well, there were also some great designers emerging from educational institutions—shaping architecture, interiors, and furniture styles. One such partnership was that of Charles and Ray Eames, who met at Cranbrook Academy in Michigan. Eames invented a technique for bending plywood into complex curves.

Another designer/architect—Eero Saarinen—was determined to get rid of the "slum of legs" under tables and developed new models of one-legged designs that revolutionized the furniture industry, **Figure 9-31**. As a result, pedestal chairs and tables were first designed and manufactured. Florence and Hans Knoll, also trained at Cranbrook Academy, founded Knoll International. They employed Harry Bertoia to develop a series of chairs using welded steel rods.

Courtesy of Lydia M. Brown

Figure 9-30 Smooth lines and geometric shapes are characteristic of the Art Deco period.

Courtesy of Lydia M. Brown

Figure 9-31 Mid-Century Modern design included bent-wood furnishings and chairs with pedestal legs. *Locate additional examples of the designs of Charles and Ray Eames and Eero Saarinen.*

Commercial design—particularly in offices—was being reconfigured using modular furniture. Frank Lloyd Wright is well-known for breaking down office cubicles while Robert Propst designed a system of components that could be arranged and rearranged into office settings. Many of these designs are classics today.

Postmodern Design

The Postmodern-design movement began in America around the 1960s and 1970s before moving to Europe and the rest of the world. Postmodernism emerged as a reaction to modernism. Modernism was perceived to be too functional and too minimalistic in its use of design. To many, the *glass box* architecture was lacking the human feel.

Postmodern architects and designers felt that ornamentation, color, decoration, and human scale were necessary. Where some felt modern architecture was graceful in its simplicity, others felt it failed to meet the human need for comfort both for the body and the eye. It was perceived that Modernism did not address the need for beauty. In response, architects sought to reintroduce ornament, color, decoration, and human scale to buildings. Form was no longer to be defined solely by its functional requirements or minimal appearance.

By the 1980s, the advanced use of new techniques and materials—with a renewed interest in craftsmanship—was popular in the United States. By using the latest materials and technology, high-tech designers achieved a clean, metallic, and utilitarian yet elegant look. Conversely, others went back to the natural materials of the arts and crafts movement. A diversity of design characteristics resulted.

By the 1990s, Target® department stores were showcasing Michael Graves—Postmodern architect—in a campaign called *Design for All*. Their marketing was based on the belief that good design was affordable by all and therefore, should be easily available.

Non-Western Historic Designs and Furnishings

The brief descriptions of the non-Western design styles that follow do not begin to capture their individual and collective historic design contributions to this world. Short summaries are offered in an attempt to illustrate their rich contribution to design throughout the ages. There is little published history on the interiors and furnishings of these countries.

Design in Mexico

Mexico had three major, native civilizations—Mayan, Toltec, and Aztec. The Mayan civilization commonly dates from A.D. 300–900. The Mayans occupied areas that can be located today in Southern Mexico, the Yucatan Peninsula, and Guatemala. They are considered to be pre-Columbian and the America's most brilliant civilization. The Mayans built cities that functioned as hubs for the surrounding farming towns. The ceremonial center of Mayan cities featured plazas surrounded by tall temple pyramids and lower buildings called *palaces*. Dominant buildings were religious temples on top of pyramids. The nobles and religious leaders lived in the stone palaces.

The Toltec civilization also influenced Mexico's cultural history. Their people appeared in central Mexico around the tenth century and built the city of Tula. Little is known about their architecture and interiors.

The Aztecs, the last of the pre-Columbian great native civilizations, rose to prominence in the central valley of Mexico around 1427 by partnering with the Toltecs and Mayans. The Aztec capital was Tenochtitlán, which today is Mexico City. The center of the city was located on an island in the middle of a lake with causeways connecting the island to shore. At its center, stood a large courtyard with a great double pyramid. In terms of scale and age, the most imposing ancient buildings in North America are found at Teotihuacan (100 B.C.–A.D. 200)—which is just north of Mexico City, **Figure 9-32**.

gary yim/Shutterstock.com

Figure 9-32 This ancient building of Teotihuacan, the *Pyramid of the Sun*, is found just north of Mexico City. *What types of artifacts representing ancient Mexican design exist yet today?*

As a center of agriculture and commerce, Teotihuacan was a major hub with a population of approximately 200,000. Residential quarters in the palaces were comprised of several rooms that adjoined a central courtyard. The less-wealthy and important lived in apartments built on a grid plan. They were multifamily units with central patios. Interior rooms were dark because they had no windows. Apartment complexes were surrounded by high walls and accessed from a single entrance. Tenochtitlan had a large number of craftsmen, such as painters and stone carvers. Wood was used for furniture.

The middle history era of Mexico involves the conquest by the Spaniards. Hernán Cortés arrived in the early sixteenth century. Believing Cortés might be a god, the Aztec King Moctezuma II invited the conquistador to Tenochtitlán. This gesture proved disastrous as only two years later Cortés and his followers attacked and conquered the Aztecs and colonized the area. Soon missionaries built monasteries and converted millions to Catholicism. In one generation after the conquest, people spoke Spanish. The Spanish conquest marked the beginning of a colonial period that would last 300 years. New cities were built on top of the old. For example, Mexico City was built directly on top of the ruins of Tenochtitlán.

As churches and monasteries were constructed, craftsmen were recruited from the old world to decorate and furnish the new buildings. At first, the style of furniture they produced was a replica of European décor. Once the colonial government was established, craft guilds were quickly formed to regulate the quality and style of Mexican furniture, as well as the requirements for membership into the guild. The regulations imposed on furniture craftsmen were generally limited to urban areas and religious institutions. Here, the accepted style usually included detailed carvings and designs for tables, chairs, armoires, and chests. Carpenters also enjoyed the luxury of choosing from a variety of woods such as mesquite, walnut, cedar, and cypress when carving lyre-leg refectory tables (a long table with heavy, lyre-shaped legs) and lavish altars for churches.

In provincial towns throughout rural Mexico, guild laws were more difficult to enforce. The formal, artistic furnishings produced in colonial cities needed to be more utilitarian in the countryside. Ornate furniture styles often proved too impractical in this rugged environment, and craftsmen frequently lacked the sophisticated tools and wood varieties to produce traditional Spanish-style furniture. Due to these limitations, Mexican furniture produced in rural settings became considerably more rustic than the furniture produced in urban settings. Elaborately carved armoire panels were converted to classic flat-panels, lyre-leg tables were replaced by A-frame legs, and the use of pine instead of more expensive woods steadily increased.

Restrictions and regulations imposed by the furniture guilds were lifted altogether when Mexico achieved independence in 1821. Although the traditional colonial furniture designs remained, craftsmen were now free to implement more creativity and variety into their work. Because of this, the production of Mexican furniture became less labor intensive, more rustic, and, consequently, more affordable to the public. Lighter wood such as Mexican cypress, white pine, and heart pine were increasingly used, allowing for easier transportation and lower costs. With these new innovations, the furniture that was once reserved for statesmen, landowners, and the church became staples of the Mexican home.

Inhabitants of the Mexican home were comprised of several generations living under one roof. The family was and is of paramount importance to the people of Mexico.

Design details and furnishings associated with Mexico include varieties of colored marble, geometric patterns, tiled walls, wrought iron, carved wood, panel doors, window shutters, ladder-back chairs, vargueno (vahr-GAYN-yoh)—a decorative writing cabinet, the Spanish foot on chairs, and the trestle table.

North African and Asian Countries

Although many designs found in North African and Asian countries parallel the time periods of Western design, notable design differences exist. As you read about designs of North Africa, the Middle East, and Asian countries evaluate the key features of the designs of these areas. Think about ways the designs are similar to and different from designs of today.

Islamic Design

With its design roots dating as early as the eighth century A.D., Islamic design has been influential in Spain, North Africa, the Middle East, and many other areas of the world. Islamic design, similar to Romanesque or Gothic design, is centered on religion.

A marked difference from Western design is that Islamic design—based on Islamic art and teachings of the Koran—avoids any depiction of human, animal, or plant forms as elements of design or decoration, as required by religious teachings. Therefore, surface ornamentation was purely geometric in style combined with calligraphy from the text of the Koran or other religious works.

The key structure in any Islamic community was the mosque. It served as a prayer hall where the faithful assembled (and still assemble today) facing Mecca to pray and to hear readings from the Koran. The enclosed portion of the mosque was an open space with long, columned aisles, **Figure 9-33**. The tower of the mosque was and is known as a **minaret**—a tall, slender tower with one or more balconies from which a call to prayer can be made to summon worshipers to the mosque several times each day. The Great Mosque at Damascus was begun in A.D. 707. Secular buildings such as palaces, baths, and markets were also influenced by Islamic design elements.

Vladimir Melnik/Shutterstock.com

Figure 9-33 The Mosque of Hassan II in Casablanca, Morocco is one of the largest mosques in the world and the only one open to non-Muslims in Morocco.

In Islamic design, arches were often built in a form that continued the curve of the arch below and beyond the semicircle to as much as 60–65 percent of a full circle. Furniture was minimally used in Islamic interiors. Low benches or couches were generally covered by textiles, carpets, and rugs. The development of weaving techniques in the Near East generated rug designs that were different from region to region and of great beauty and variety. Rugs were often used by kneeling worshippers. Such prayer rugs were of appropriate size and exhibited designs that pointed toward Mecca when in use.

Design in India

Ancient India covered a vast territory, including present-day Burma, Persia, and Central Asian empires. Located in South Asia, India experienced many invasions with many diverse peoples, cultures, kingdoms, empires, and republics. As a result, India's design traditions reflect cultural, social, and religious beliefs of these diverse groups. India has also been known by many other names including *Hindu*, which then became *India* in English.

Ancient people lived in very simple material conditions with a social structure based on *kutumb*, or family. The caste system (a form of social organization based on socially ranked occupations), was and is, the backbone of Indian society.

Religious traditions of the people of India had great impact on the architecture and interiors of the country. Buddhist design traditions include the *stupa*—a funerary mound representative of Buddha, **Figure 9-34**. The stupa is the earliest surviving form of religious architecture in India.

saiko3p/Shutterstock.com

Figure 9-34 The stupa is a funerary mound of the Buddhist design tradition.

Hindu designs include the sacred places of religious rites—the temples. Hindu temples are considered the home of gods; each god receiving its own home. The *Jain religion* is the doctrine of nonviolence, requiring that no harm be inflicted on any living creature. Jain temples borrowed many design elements from Hindu temples. Islamic design traditions revolve around the mosque with its traditional architectural element—the dome.

India's **vernacular architecture**—indigenous dwellings created using native materials without the influence of architects—begins with circular dwellings or huts made out of mud, branches, and stones. These residential dwellings were often rebuilt every couple of years due to weather conditions. In other areas of India, family dwellings were built to last longer and included the use of stones, bricks, and metals.

Wattle (a fabrication of poles interwoven with branches or reeds) and timber houses became common in still other regions. These dwellings employed the framing of light timber with walls of wattles and mud. The roof would be constructed of rough timber rafters and covered with thatch, bamboo, or ceramic tiles. Brick houses followed and were particularly common during their Colonial period when England occupied India.

Family compounds were developed. One such style of vernacular architecture used in the family compounds included the *bhunga*—a single cell, circular hut. As the need for the family grew—due to marriages in which the young woman joined the husband's family—one or more bhunga were built near the other and the open space among the bhungas formed a central courtyard. The interior of the home was considered female domain and the exterior, male domain. Interiors were decorated with embossed mud forms and mirror work. Furniture consisted of the *char pai*—a handmade four-post wooden cot, built-in shelves, and metal or wooden trunks.

Other tribal communities built rectangular dwellings of burnt bricks and wood. Rectangular rooms, used as bedrooms, were designed side by side with a shared verandah (a type of covered porch) known as a *parsal.* Two smaller, rectangular rooms—one used for grains and the other used for tasks associated with a kitchen—were placed at the opposite ends of the parsal.

Urban living spaces were also created. One of the most well-known styles of town living is the *pol house.* These multistory, wooden houses were divided into sectors by caste. Each caste built its houses in a row and in a cluster configuration. Pol houses were originally made as a protection measure when communal riots necessitated greater security. These rectangular, narrow structures were highly decorated, carved, and supported by many narrow balconies.

Pol houses were organized around a private open courtyard that offered a great deal of privacy. Due to age-old traditions, walls were not aligned completely, resulting in smaller fronts and larger backs. The front of the house was often used for a place of business, with the kitchens on the left side of the house. Pols are well-known for their wood carvings representative of naturalistic design, mythological stories, and religious beliefs. Entrance doors, windows, beams, and balconies, lintels, and columns were all carved with geometric, floral, human, and animal figures. Furniture was sparse; people sat on thin, floor-mounted mattresses, known as **gadi,** covered with hand-embroidered sheets. Today, pol houses are used by families across caste systems.

Overall, furniture does not play a major role in historic Indian interiors. People often sat on low cushions and would sleep on pads on the floor. Small, low wooden tables or stools were placed nearby. Thrones—such as the Peacock Throne of Shah Jahan—illustrate the richness of the imperial style. With the beginning of Muslim influence around A.D. 1000, larger beds, chests, and low tables were used. Carpets and textiles supplemented the minimal furnishings. Ivory, stone, or metals were used in some furnishings to avoid the use of wood because it deteriorated quickly in the Indian climate. In addition to India's reputation for exceptional textiles, carpets of varied designs are characteristic of different regions and valued highly throughout the world.

One of the most well-known buildings in the world is found in India. The Taj Mahal (A.D. 1632–1656) in Agra was commissioned as a mausoleum for Shah Jahan's favorite wife, **Figure 9-35**. It consists of numerous arches, galleries, pavilions, terraces, and gardens. The plan is a square that is symmetrical along two axes, with entrances on all four sides. An onion-shaped dome of white marble rises two hundred feet above the structure. Four tower minarets surround the main structure. Inside, screens of marble inlaid with jewels are geometrically patterned.

Chinese Design

China is located in the eastern part of Asia. The Chinese civilization is one of the world's most ancient. Chinese traditional culture has remained reasonably stable over

saiko3p/Shutterstock.com

Figure 9-35 Located in Agra, India, the magnificent *Taj Mahal* is the mausoleum of the favorite wife of Shah Jahan. Note the four minarets common to Islamic design.

time. Religion was never regarded higher than imperial power. Therefore, no religious building could replace the imperial palaces and official buildings located in the capital and cities.

There are several common values and philosophies evident in the architecture and interiors of China. These include the following:

- **Harmony with nature.** The inseparable relationship of man and nature is a basic tenet on which Chinese architecture is designed. Nature was valued and introduced often into interiors through ponds, gardens, light, and views.
- **Representation of the universe.** The design of buildings—for example, the Temple of Heaven from the Ming and Qing Dynasties—integrates symbols representing the universe in almost every design detail. This belief is seen in the circular structures reflecting ancient belief that the cosmos is round.
- **Yin and yang.** The concept of duality of heaven and earth, sun and moon, day and night, or fire and water—emerged through natural observations.

  The theory of yin and yang was developed into the Theory of the Five Elements—wood, fire, earth, metal, and water. This theory can be seen in a variety of practices including *feng shui*.
- **Etiquette.** In ancient China, etiquette was fundamental to the management of state and family affairs. It provided standards of behavior and moral values. Confucian beliefs indicate that order and harmony are the core of the patriarchal clan system and its hierarchy.

  To reflect this belief, formal documents were developed concerning the placement of altars, temples, palaces, official buildings, homes, gates, yards, platforms, roofs, building widths, doornails, and ornamental colors. Etiquette in design—its formality, rules and structure—ensured the architecture paid respect to ancestors and conventions, but provided little opportunity for innovation.

Temples, palaces, and houses all shared a basic system of construction using wooden columns that supported richly carved bracketed beams. Outside walls were masonry, but not used for structural support. Buildings were one-story with sloping roofs covered with tiles. The projecting exterior overhang with its upward curve gave architecture a unique profile, **Figure 9-36**. Interior walls were actually partitions, fitted between structural columns and attached with brackets. This construction resisted earthquake damage because the wooden elements and joints flexed without breaking.

Interiors of typical buildings had fully exposed structural elements that were colorfully painted. A favorite color was scarlet red with imperial-yellow roofs. A single door led through the outside rooms to a central courtyard that opened to porches, which then led to private rooms. The floor plan was symmetrically planned with **feng shui**—a Chinese art and philosophy influencing the orientation and arrangement of a space to achieve harmony. This form of planning was adopted for modest houses as well as for the planning of an entire city.

Before the second century A.D., furnishings were not used. Instead people sat on mats or sacks of fabric on the floor. After that period, stools, chairs, and chests were skillfully made out of wood, with fine joinery using no glue or nails. Palaces and houses of the wealthy also had couches, beds, cabinets, and tables. Lacquer finishes in red and other colors were used. Most traditional Chinese furniture uses minimal ornamentation. Lacquer was also used on screens and panels. Chinese wallpaper displayed landscapes, animals, and human figure motifs. Motifs of monkeys, pagodas, and mandarins (public officials) also appeared. Silk textiles and Chinese rugs woven in silk were also used in interiors.

Western influence on design was carried into the country by Chinese architects trained at Western universities. Chinese architects have embraced the International Style Modernism as seen in the Beijing, Fragrant Hill Hotel, by the American architect, I.M. Pei.

Korean Design

The construction system of China was introduced into Korea as early as 57 B.C. Houses were constructed of wood with painted or gilded details and tiled roofs. Well-preserved palaces can be found in Seoul with halls and pavilions dating back to the fifteenth century. The **loggia**, a type of roofed outdoor living space often

Hung Chung Chih/Shutterstock.com

Figure 9-36 Lijiang is the largest ancient old town in China. Note the sloping roofs and upwardly curved overhangs. *What other characteristics are common to ancient Chinese architecture and interiors?*

overlooking an open court from an upper story, was also included in palaces.

Traditional Korean interiors did not use chairs, elevated beds, or tables. Seating was on pads on the floor. Shelves, tables, and storage units were low. Furnishings were simple, even austere, for the men. Women's furniture was more colorful with the use of woods, lacquer finishes, and more decorative details. Metal hardware, hinges, knobs, and catches were partly ornamental.

Japanese Design

Historic Japanese architecture used supporting wooden columns located on a grid, based on the *tatami floor mats*. The modular **tatami floor mat** (3 feet by 6 feet) controlled the proportional planning of interior spaces. Some fixed walls and many movable **shoji screens**—wood and rice paper screens serving as walls, partitions, or sliding doors—divided space as required for living arrangements, **Figure 9-37**. Verandas overlooked gardens or courtyards.

In Kyoto, the famous Detached Villa (A.D. 1620–1647) was constructed of timber using plans based on the tatami mat. Rooms could be opened, separated, and reshaped by moving the sliding-screen wall panels (shoji). Interiors were of utmost simplicity, without furniture or any ornamentation. The design encouraged simple, peaceful living. A few built-in cabinets and shelves provided storage. Seating would be movable floor pads and beds made of futon pads, placed where needed.

Isabella Pfenninger/Shutterstock.com

Figure 9-37 Shoji screens are wood and rice paper screens that form movable walls in Japanese design.

The traditional house of Japan not only used those elements described earlier on a modest scale, but also included the kitchen. This was comprised of a cooking area on a low stove with low tables nearby for work. A sunken wooden tub was used for bathing. A box-like hearth set into the floor was used for charcoal burning. A mat or blanket could be used to cover the hearth and people could group around it. The portable stove, or *hibachi*, was a common convenience in the somewhat cold and damp Japanese climate. A toilet was a simple wooden box containing earth or sand, placed to provide privacy. The Japanese garden was an important part of the built environment and was accessed by a broad wooden porch, the **engawa**, protected by eaves.

Japanese furnishings were not important in traditional interiors. Simple mats on the floor served for seating and sleeping. A few chests or cabinets were used for storage and movable screens were common. A low table centered in the room, invited family and guests to be seated on flat, square zabuton cushions.

The Japanese concept of **Shibui** dictated color usage according to nature's guidelines—neutral colors that were closely blended with accents of bright hues. Wall colors were lighter above and darker below. Motifs included subtle patterns, either abstract (masculine) with clean angular lines, or (feminine) figurative lines and shapes. These included diamonds, tortoise shells, cherry blossoms, branches, simple floral designs, and women in Japanese costume.

In the twentieth century, travel and communications encouraged Japanese designers to receive their education in Western countries. American architects were commissioned to design various structures such as the Tokyo Imperial Hotel completed by Frank Lloyd Wright, **Figure 9-38**.

African Styles

Africa is the most diverse continent on Earth. As the second largest continent, almost all styles and time periods are present in Africa (note that Egypt, part of Africa, has already been discussed). Periods and styles, such as African Art Nouveau, Art Deco, Modernism, and Postmodernism are also part of the cultural design heritage.

During colonialism, the people of England, the Netherlands, Portugal, and Germany did bring their architectural and design styles to the continent and impacted architectural and interior design.

sangaku/Shutterstock.com

Figure 9-38 Built in 1923, the old Tokyo Imperial Hotel was designed by Frank Lloyd Wright. In 1968 when declared structurally unsafe, the grand entrance and lobby along with the reflecting pool were relocated to the Meiji-Mura Museum in Inuyama, Japan.

The iconic African round house was used in many regional areas of the continent. While the house was considered the *center of the world*, it was not the interior but the exterior space that was most important. This house was not a vessel for the family to live in, but was a part of the compound that included family, domestic animals, hunting dogs, goats, cattle, or horses. Reed mats were common to sit on.

A great variety of freestanding and movable furniture was used in Africa and reflects hundreds of ethnic groups. Ancient stools, as well as more recently, chairs were common. Backrests for reclining and thrones for sitting were found in interiors. Baskets and gourds were used to store clothes or other smaller items. Often crossed or checkered weaving dominated West African baskets. Beds, often out of wood, were raised platforms to enhance circulation of cooler air.

Native American Dwellings

Native Americans include those indigenous people of the continental United States—including Alaska and Hawaii. Many Native American people lived along the East Coast of the North American continent. Most of these groups developed agriculture and fixed established settlements. Some native groups built dwellings from wood with roofs of natural materials such as grass, leaves, bark, or thatch. Round structures, known as *wigwams*, were common. Rectangular structured dwellings, or *longhouses,* were also used, **Figure 9-39**. Interiors were simple spaces with woven rugs and blankets.

The *tepee* of the American plains had a frame of long poles tied together at the top. Its outer walls were skins arranged to permit a flap doorway and a top flap that could be adjusted to control air circulation, allow penetration of daylight, and act as a smoke outlet. The portable tepee was easy to deconstruct, pack, and transport when hunting required frequent moves to follow food supplies.

In the southwest region of the United States, remarkable towns containing as many as 200 rooms were created in mountainous cliffs. The Anasazi left these locations around A.D. 1300, leaving ruins such as those at Mesa Verde, Colorado. *Pueblos* were constructed by the Hopi, Taos, and Zuni tribes. Pueblo walls were of adobe brick with roofs of wooden poles. Navajos built round structures with walls of stone supporting a tepee-like roof. Like other Native American dwellings, furnishings were nonexistent

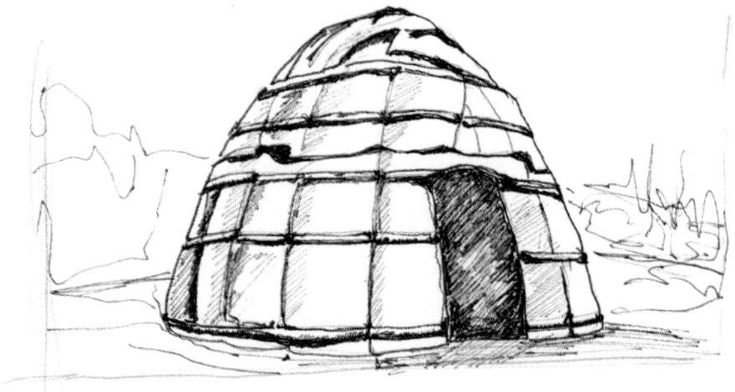

Wigwam

Longhouse

Pueblo

Teepee

Susan R Casebeer

Figure 9-39 Native American groups built their dwellings of materials common to the areas in which they lived. Some dwellings were portable and could easily be moved from place to place.

with baskets, pottery, and woven materials providing both color and warmth to these functional dwellings.

Key American Exterior Architectural Styles

An architectural style is developed with identifiable design characteristics, methods of construction, and regional features. Some styles have been developed by a specific architect, such as Frank Lloyd Wright. Other styles evolved over a period of time, having originated in another country, such as the Georgian style of architecture. Some architectural styles gain new popularity with the reinvention of an old theme such as the *Spanish Colonial Revival*, previously known as *Spanish Mission style*.

Knowing a few historical architectural styles enhances your design vocabulary and allows you to speak knowledgably about design in your community and in your country. The following list includes just a few styles you might find in the area in which you live.

Bungalow

Usually one to one and one-half stories, this style offers a low-pitched roof, a central entrance with a large porch, and a central staircase. The front door often opens directly into the living room. Other characteristics include an open floor plan with few hallways, and wood or stucco construction, **Figure 9-40**. This style is also known as *American Craftsman*.

Artazum and Iriana Shiyan/Shutterstock.com

Figure 9-40 The bungalow, or American Craftsman, is typically one and one-half stories. *Take a walking tour in your community to locate examples of the bungalow style.*

English/Colonial

Adapted from English-style homes and appearing often along the Northeastern seaboard, this category of architecture has four different styles: Cape Cod, saltbox, garrison, and gambrel. Each style evolved from the previous style based on the need and function of the colonists settling that territory. Common features include steeply pitched roofs with side **gables**—the vertical triangular ends of a building, wood construction, symmetrical front façades, central front doors, multipaned windows, and a central fireplace for efficient heating, **Figure 9-41**. These homes have no porches and minimal exterior ornamentation. The characteristics of each style are as follows:

- **Cape Cod.** This small home features one to one-and-one-half stories with a central-hall floor plan and a rectangular shape. A twentieth century Cape Cod offers **dormer windows** (those set vertically in the structure projecting through a sloping roof) and a chimney that is often placed at the side of the house. Shutters are also commonly added to accent the windows.

Cape Cod

rSnapshotPhotos/Shutterstock.com

Garrison

mtcurado/iStock/Thinkstock

Gambrel

Susan Law Cain/Shutterstock.com

Saltbox

Jody LaFerriere/Shutterstock.com

Figure 9-41 These English-style homes all feature steeply pitched roofs and gables.

- **Gambrel.** Characterized by a two-sided roof with two slopes on either side, this style allowed extra headroom in the second floor. This two-story house is sometimes compared to the design of an old-fashioned barn. (It is sometimes called *Cape Ann* or *Dutch Colonial* or *Dutch Gambrel.*)
- **Garrison.** With an overhanging second story, this style uses a timber-framed construction with four carved brackets below the overhang.
- **Saltbox.** Named after the wood boxes used to store salt (a precious commodity in colonial times), this style is characterized by a lean-to shape that tapers from two stories to one. The single story is in the back of the house, while two stories are in the front.

French Normandy

This architectural style, brought to America by the French, is one and one-half to two and one-half stories and constructed of brick, stone, or stucco. The distinguishing feature of this style is the front turret initially used for grain storage, **Figure 9-42A**. Multipaned windows are typical.

French Normandy

A Jeff Cowan/iStock/Thinkstock

Greek Revival

B Anne Power/Shutterstock.com

Georgian

C Jorge Salcedo/Shutterstock.com

Figure 9-42 Multipaned windows are common to the French Normandy (A), Greek Revival (B), and Georgian (C) styles of architecture. *What other common features do you see?*

Georgian

As the American colonies were established, prosperity followed. The Georgian style, transported from England by architect immigrants, was characterized by two and one-half or three stories, a hip or gable roof with dormers, a central door and staircase, a formal facade, two large chimneys at either end of the building, and brick or wood siding. Multipaned windows appeared on all stories, **Figure 9-42B**.

Greek Revival

Often seen in public buildings such as state capitols, this architectural style is characterized with a front facade of stately columns, symmetrical windows, and a long, shallow staircase. This style is also known as *Colonial Revival*, **Figure 9-42C**.

Modern

This architectural style, sometimes referred to as a movement, emerged in the United States and continues to evolve. It is characterized by clean lines and simplicity of form. The "form follows function" dictum is evident in both public (*Salk Institute* in La Jolla, California by Louis Kahn) and private (*Falling Water* by Frank Lloyd Wright) buildings. It often incorporates the topography of the land and offers no ornamentation, **Figure 9-43A**. It is sometimes called the *International Style* or *Expressionist Modern*.

Postmodern

This style is a combination of traditional forms with new ideas. It is a complex contradiction that incorporates symbols as a statement or as a delightful innovation.

Prairie Style

Touted as the first original American architectural style as developed by Frank Lloyd Wright, this design mimicked the line of the prairie horizon line—low and long, **Figure 9-43B**. Characteristic features include strong horizontal lines, use of indigenous materials, and one or two stories with cantilevered low-pitched roofs, ribbons of (typically) casement windows, a prominent central fireplace, built-in cabinetry, and an open flow between interior spaces rather than compartmentalized rooms.

Pueblo

This regional architectural style is prevalent in New Mexico and typical of southwestern areas of the United States. Inspiration is derived from Pueblos and Spanish

Modern

stocker1970/Shutterstock.com

A

Prairie

Thomas Barrat/Shutterstock.com

B

Figure 9-43 Both Modern (A) and Prairie (B) styles mimic the topography of the land. *What are the similarities and differences between these two styles?*

missions, and is characterized by stucco walls painted in earth tones, flat roofs, and wood roof beams (called *vigas*) that project from walls with no structural purpose, **Figure 9-44A**. This style is also known as *Adobe* or *Pueblo Revival*.

Ranch Style

As a low, one-story building inspired by ranchers' houses in Southwest, this architectural style is characterized by a lack of interior stairs, low-pitched gable roof, and over-hanging eaves. Often rectangular in shape, this style can also be seen in L, T, U, and H shapes. This style is generically referred to today as any style with a single story, **Figure 9-44B**.

Spanish Colonial Revival

Primarily located in the southern part of America, this architectural style is characterized by white or tinted stucco walls and low, red-barrel tiled roofs. Roofs have

Pueblo

mtcurado/iStock/Thinkstock

A

Ranch

Steve Holderfield/Shutterstock.com

B

Spanish Colonial

José Antonio Sánchez Poy/iStock/Thinkstock

C

Split Level

onepony/iStock/Thinkstock

D

Figure 9-44 Exterior stucco walls are common to the Pueblo (A) and Spanish Colonial (C) styles while use of rectangular shapes are common to the Ranch (B) and Split-level (D) styles.

a large overhang, windows and doors are arched, and *colonnades* (a series of columns set at regular intervals, usually supporting the roof structure) showcase iron grillwork, **Figure 9-44C**. Wide porches, roof beams, and balconies are typical. This style was previously referred to as *Mission Revival* and *Spanish Mission.*

Split Level

This architectural style is designed for maximizing a sloped hillside. It typically includes four levels—basement level, intermediate level, living level, and the sleeping level, **Figure 9-44D**. The split-entry is commonly located on the intermediate level.

Tudor

This English style of architecture is easily identified by its evident *half-timber* construction. Usually of two or three stories with a second-story overhang, the style is characterized by several gables, a side chimney, and decorative stucco-type masonry filling the spaces between the exposed half-timbers, **Figure 9-45A**.

Victorian—Queen Anne

Fanciful and flamboyant, this Victorian style of architecture commonly has a steep roof, a veranda that extends around two sides of the building, round towers, bay windows, ornamental brackets, and a generous amount of ornamental trim called *gingerbread,* **Figure 9-45B**. These houses were often painted in complex color schemes.

High-Tech

Influenced by technological breakthroughs in steel frame and structural design, this style proudly displays, rather than hides, the cutting-edge technologies evident in this industrial look—a type of skeleton-as-

Tudor

Ingram Publishing/Ingram Publishing/Thinkstock

A

Victorian—Queen Anne

Jesus Jauregui/iStock/Thinkstock

B

Figure 9-45 While the Tudor (A) style uses half-timber construction, the Victorian—Queen Anne (B) style is rather whimsical and uses much ornamentation.

exterior look, **Figure 9-46A**. This style is also known as *Structural Expression* or *Late Modernism*.

Expressionist

The Expressionist style is characterized by novel materials, innovation, and often forms from nature. Emotion is expressed in abstract assembly of curvaceous forms. See Frank Gehry's Weisman Art Museum, Minneapolis, MN, **Figure 9-46B**.

What Is Your Style?

Life is about style! Style reflects you, your mood, and your lifestyle. At times, a style can be different from room to room. At other times, a style is threaded throughout the home or workplace.

Clients react to style just like color—they like it or they do not. It reflects their preferences or their heritage or it does not. Clients often describe the style they want in their interiors by using such sentences as "I want this restaurant to have a *modern*, upbeat feel." Or "I like a family room to have a *country*, cozy mood." Or "I want a *postmodern*, industrial feel in this corporate office." Knowing how *Modern*, *Country*, and *Postmodern* styles look demonstrates your credibility to your client. Do you know how these styles look and from what period they originated?

Historic periods and various styles of furnishings are often grouped together and given a *new style* label—such as Hollywood Regency Style—to reflect people's preferences of today. Sometimes, historical styles have inspired modern designs such as the Egyptian X-form folding stool in comparison to the X-form stool designed by Mies van der Rohe for the 1929 World Exposition. Also consider the Greek klismos chair—with its curved back rails and splayed legs—and how it compares to such Neoclassical styles as the British Adam style, or the French and American Empire styles.

As you select your style, examine the historic design details. Look at such popular furniture websites as Ethan Allen®, Thomasville®, or Drexel Heritage® for modern-day furnishings with historic features. For example, examine how the Hepplewhite chair-back style compares to the Ethan Allen heart-back chair. The intricate design of the ribband-back Chippendale chair is similar to those used in many dining and living rooms today, **Figure 9-47**.

High Tech

sl-f/iStock/Thinkstock

A

Expressionist

nikitsin.smugmug.com/Shutterstock.com

B

Figure 9-46 The industrial, skeleton-like exterior of the High Tech (A) style is a stark contrast to the wildly abstract forms of the Expressionist (B) style found in the Frederick Weisman Art Museum designed by Frank Gehry. *What features do you find engaging about each style?*

Ambient Ideas/Shutterstock.com

Figure 9-47 When examining furniture designs of today, look to the past to identify features that remain classic through the ages.

What is your favorite style of furniture, interior, or architecture? Do you like contemporary designs or do you prefer country? How do designers use the past to create today's ever-changing design styles? How do these styles look and what are their historic roots? Take a walking tour of your community. What examples of historic buildings do you see? Do modern structures utilize design features from past eras?

Following are 20 *styles* of today that you or your client might prefer. Notice the differences both in mood and design details. Each is distinctive. Each is also timely and many will be reinvented throughout decades to come.

Art Deco Style

The streamlined, geometric style of furnishings popular from the 1920s and 1930s is characterized by this style. These pieces are detailed with rounded fronts, mirrored accents, and sleek lines. Painted wood furniture with chrome hardware and glass tops is common. This style sets a bright, sophisticated mood that screams *design.*

Arts and Crafts Style

This style is built around the Arts and Crafts movement, which emerged in the early 1900s as a reaction to the Industrial Revolution. It celebrates handcrafted pieces over machine-made products. This style features wood furniture, moldings, and accent pieces, along with rich paint colors such as deep browns, greens, and coppers. The focus of this style is on simple forms, use of local materials, no decoration, with revealed joinery (the joints with which the furniture was constructed). *Truth in materials* was a mantra of the original design period.

Asian (Oriental) Style

Rooms designed around an Asian theme—Japanese, Korean, Chinese, and Thai—are serene and calming. This style uses such materials as bamboo, natural fibers, and stone, as well as colors that evoke the great outdoors, especially browns and greens. Furniture is low to the ground and kept to a minimum. It may be lacquered or hand-painted. The spaces are clutter-free with a few strategic accessories of mythical creatures or statutes of animals. Textures are introduced through rice-paper accessories or grass wallcoverings.

Contemporary Style

Contemporary rooms feature such neutral color schemes as browns, creams, and whites. Architectural details include clean, smooth lines. Furniture is sleek, lower to the ground, and lightweight in appearance. At times, furniture may use metal frames or straight legs. Pale woods and modern materials such as glass and steel are standard. Pillows, rugs, or artwork sometimes introduce a splash of bold color in an otherwise neutral color palette.

Cottage Style

This is a relaxed, comfortable, sometimes whimsical, style that uses the soft blues, greens, yellows, and beiges of the seaside or lakeside for its color palette. Designers often pair floral fabrics with stripes and checks, and bring in textures with wicker furniture, baskets, and natural fibers. Iron furniture and metal or ceramic accent pieces that are weather-worn are also common. Window treatments often include light, airy fabrics. The look is crisp and clean with an ever-present feel of spring or summer. It resonates with a Caribbean, New England, or Southern California feel. Sea, sand, balmy breezes, and ever-present sunshine are characteristics of this style, **Figure 9-48**. This style is also called *Coastal* or *Caribbean.*

Alena Ozerova/Shutterstock.com

Figure 9-48 These soft hues and creatures of the sea represent cottage style interior design. *What other features might you add to create this design style for a client?*

Country or Country-Casual Style

A country-style space is built around time-worn pine or painted furniture, typically found in antique shops or flea markets. Wall treatments sometimes include white-wood paneling. Fabrics in checks, stripes, and soft floral patterns are typical, as are such handmade accessories as wooden bowls, toys, and clay vases. Sometimes designers will use items such as old milk jugs, baskets, hand-forged metals, or cookie jars in the shapes of barnyard animals to inject a bit of fun into these informal, easygoing spaces. Fresh daisies often appear on the window sill and throw pillows encourage comfort and informal living. This is a great style for a bed and breakfast, or a Cape Cod home.

Eclectic Style

Eclectic design brings together a variety of styles and historical periods. In an eclectic bedroom, for example, designers may pair a modern, streamlined bed with Art Deco travel posters and a vintage alarm clock from the 1930s. The key to eclectic design is to contrast styles, textures, and finishes, but also to use color or the lines of the furniture pieces to link them together. In other words, this style relies heavily on the appropriate use of design elements—line, shape, form, color, and pattern—to link disparate styles together. This style was developed for those who like a lot of different styles in the same space. It encourages a sense of imagination and adventure through unexpected contrasts in features—both for the owner and the guest.

English Cottage Style

This style is slightly more formal than standard country design. It features finely carved furniture and overstuffed sofas. Tufting and skirted furniture mixed with antiques and many small-scale accessories are characteristic of the style. It features floral fabrics, chintz, and fancy tassels and trim. The color palette focuses on the soft blues, greens, and pinks of an English garden. Framed prints of plants and flowers often adorn papered or stenciled walls. This style is also known as *Traditional English* or *English Country.*

Exotic Style

The inspiration for this style includes many diverse cultures such as Indian, Moroccan, and Chinese. Perhaps safari features from South Africa will appear on the walls and in shelving units, while textiles from a rural place in India will grace the living room. This style is about showcasing experiences rather than an observance of formality and symmetry. It is dramatic and exciting in its diversity.

French Formal Style

This style is characterized by ornate, formal, polished designs found throughout historic Paris. This style includes rich details with extensive use of crystal, gold, bronze, and gilt. Fine antique or heirloom furniture with dark woods contrasts with painted- or gilded-wood architectural details in a room. Dramatic window treatments of heavy, formal fabrics and abundant fresh flowers fill a French-styled space. Brocades, damasks, and silk fabrics are common and repeated throughout the room. The color palette—similar to Louis XV—is soft, understated, and rich. (Note: This is *not* Country French).

Hispanic Style

The primary characteristic of the Hispanic-style interior is the use of dramatic color contrasts. The rusty earth tones of adobe and clay offer a backdrop for such strong colors as bright yellows, deep indigos, and sunset shades of crimson and burnt orange. After color, strong patterns are a typical characteristic. Furniture is heavier in appearance, ceramic tiles are common, and elaborately painted sinks are evident. If weather permits, inner courtyards encourage outdoor living, and may include long porches under tiled roofs, and small, walled gardens. Accents often include hammered tin, wrought iron, colored glass, and large-scale pottery. Niches hold knickknacks, mementos, and shrines. This style is also known as *Latino* or *Mexican* style.

Mediterranean Style

This style uses strong, bright blues, whites, and yellows to evoke the essence of the countries bordering the Mediterranean Sea, especially Greece, Italy, and Southern France, **Figure 9-49**. Lightly textured plaster walls and tiled floors are common features along with arched doorways. The color palette may include terra-cotta (brownish-orange) and lavender. Furniture is short with turned legs and if needed, trimmed with heavy hardware. Fabrics include velvets, linens, and textured fabrics. Tapestries and candlesticks are common accessories. Plants and flowers bring the outdoors in.

LI CHAOSHU/Shutterstock.com

Figure 9-49 The features of this room design evoke the essence of countries that border the Mediterranean Sea.

Modern Style

Historically, this clean, streamlined style is characterized by smooth surfaces, strong lines, and a lack of ornamentation. Black, white, and gray are the colors of the stark modernist palette of the 1930s. Such industrial materials as steel, glass, and concrete are the building blocks of this style. However, the Modern style is always evolving. Today's Modern style has two different appearances—a sleek, urban look that incorporates the metals, glass, light-colored woods and the black-and-white color scheme of the bygone era. A second Modern look is warmer with clean, simple lines, natural finishes, minimal furnishings and details, and *green design* considerations. It is a chic, fresh, uncluttered style.

Mountain Retreat Style

Often found in the Northwest, Colorado, Minnesota, Wisconsin, and the Carolinas, the Mountain Retreat style begins with a central lodge-style fireplace, warm woods, large outside views, and sometimes natural materials. Typically, a vaulted ceiling enhances the feeling of volume. Decks or slate patios enhance this design. Beamed ceilings, wood floors, and rock or paneled walls are often evident. Colors are neutral and warm with bright accent colors of red, yellow, or green in a variety of naturalistic patterns. Rustic accessories urge relaxation—a casual atmosphere in which to enjoy the scenery.

Scandinavian Style

Long, dreary winters with a lack of natural light are the inspiration for this style of design. The goal is to bring the lightness indoors. This style is functional, minimal, and refined with a strong visual effect. Walls are stark white, cream, or softly tinted. Floors are wood with area rugs. Furnishings feature elegant, simple lines, low-backed sofas, medium- to light-colored wood tables and chairs with gently tapered legs.

Woods are often bleached or painted—and stained with white or pale colors. Local woods typically include birch, white pine, and alder. The color palette is pale, light, and airy. Blue is often the accent color of choice. Fabrics are simple, woven-textured white linen or cotton. Fabrics typically have a white background with patterned print. Textures, stripes, and checks are used in fabrics for accents. It is a calm and functional type of design. It is also known as *Swedish style*.

Shabby-Chic Style

This style, identified in 1980 by Rachel Ashwell, is characterized by weathered painted furniture, predominately white or light slipcovered sofas, and vintage accessories. A variety of textures adds interest to the neutral color palette. Time-worn, faded accents common to this style include linen pillows, vintage chandeliers, and anything with roses on it, **Figure 9-50**.

Gordana Sermek/Shutterstock.com

Figure 9-50 Combining painted furniture, vintage accessories, and an abundance of roses is characteristic of the shabby-chic design style.

Southwestern Style

A southwestern interior is designed around the colors of Arizona, New Mexico, and Texas—the states of the American Southwest. It features handcrafted accessories, warm earth tones, rough textures, and hand-painted tiles. Furniture most often has leather or suede upholstery, which is frequently draped with brightly colored woven-wool blankets.

Southern Style

This design style reflects Southern hospitality. Rooms are warm and inviting with painted walls accented with white trim. White painted woodwork is found in deep chair rails, crown moldings, and baseboards. **Palladian windows**—large windows divided into three parts with a larger arched center section flanked by two flat-topped sections—are found in built-in units and in architecture. Floors are wood and often covered with traditionally designed or one-of-a-kind rugs. Furnishings are often of dark woods and are overstuffed to encourage comfortable conversation. Fabrics are patterned with traditional motifs (such as an acanthus leaf), stripes, and checks and then framed in fringes or trims. Antiques are *character pieces* in the room. Other interior characteristics include use of French lace, glass and crystal chandeliers, and antique lamps with unique shades. Accents include wall plaques and wall plates, distressed white-wood pieces, wreaths and swags, greenery and topiary, family portraits, and books on tables.

Traditional Style

This style is a catch-all term for a formal, classic look that incorporates furniture styles from historic Europe, such as eighteenth-century English, nineteenth-century Neoclassic, and British Colonial revival. Symmetry creates a calm décor, but there are no real rules about this style. Both dark and light woods can be used. Walls are typically painted in muted tones and sometimes wallpapered. Color palettes are usually neutral and include formal fabric textures and patterns such as simple florals, solids, stripes, and *moirés* (maw-RAYS)—fabrics with irregular wavy finishes.

Tuscan Style

Interiors featuring this style have hand-painted murals or trompe l'oeil that illustrates a Tuscan landscape, **Figure 9-51**. The walls are typically rough plaster and are capped by a beamed ceiling. Windows are simple and left bare or have light coverings. Mosaics, worn wood floors covered with antique rugs, and elegant iron accents follow an earthy color palette. Outside living spaces will include terra-cotta tiles and stone patios.

Western-American Style

This style is indicative of the *real west* in that it is a potpourri of styles. Not formal, it features rough-hewn, stained or natural woods, cowboy-themed accessories, and worn leathers. The furniture is heavier in physical weight and shows the hard wear-and-tear of an active lifestyle. Wood-burning fireplaces or stoves are common with natural elements and color palette—such as those found in nature. Accessories in these spaces are often developed from such found objects as antlers, horsehair-braided materials, and enchanting twisted tree roots. Weathered wood floors are commonly covered with woven or braided area rugs to soften the harshness of colder weather.

Sir Armstrong/Shutterstock.com

Figure 9-51 The earthy colors mixed with the rustic elegance of the furnishings and fixtures reflect the Tuscan style of design.

Chapter 9 Review and Assess

Summary

- Historic periods and styles shape the interiors, architecture, and furnishings of today.
- Knowledge of historic interiors and furnishings establishes your credibility as a designer.
- Climate greatly influenced Egyptian architecture, with the house plan common among all classes of people.
- Classical Greek and Roman periods share many similarities including climate.
- The four eras of the Middle Ages include early Christian, Byzantine, Romanesque, and Gothic.
- With the Renaissance, the arts and sciences flourished after suppression during the Middle Ages.
- The Baroque period was a time of extreme ornamentation in architecture and design, reflecting the differences between commoners and royalty.
- French styles include Rococo, Neoclassical, and Empire.
- English styles include Jacobean, William and Mary, Queen Anne, Chippendale, Adam, Hepplewhite, and Sheraton.
- American styles include Colonial or Early American, Colonial Georgian, Duncan Phyfe, and Shaker.
- Onset of the Industrial Revolution led to the evolution of design in Early Modernism: Victorian, Arts and Crafts, and Art Nouveau.
- Modernism introduced dramatic changes in the approach to architecture and design. Art Deco, Mid-Century Modern, and Postmodern styles reflect modern thinking.
- Non-Western design styles offered a rich contribution to global historic design.
- Knowing key architectural styles enhances your design vocabulary when communicating with clients.
- Knowledge of design and furniture styles and the periods from which they originate gives you a better feel for the ways clients react to style.

Chapter Vocabulary

Use the Internet to locate pictures that represent each of the following terms. Then use school-approved presentation software to create a digital collage of these terms. Label and define each of the pictures with the appropriate term and share with the class.

Aubusson rug
cabriole leg
case goods
clerestory window
dado
dormer window
dovetail joinery
engawa
feng shui
flying buttress
frescoe
gable
gadi
historic period
klismos chair
kylix
loggia
marquetry
minaret
motif
ormolu
Palladian window
pilaster
Shibui
shoji screen
spade feet
stretcher
style
tatami floor mat
trompe l'oeil
turnings
veneer
vernacular architecture
wainscoting

Review and Study

1. What is the difference between an historic period and a style?
2. In ancient Egypt, what three parts of the house plan were common to all classes?
3. Name three pieces of furniture and three motifs common in ancient Egypt.
4. What are the three orders of Greek architecture and the characteristics of each?
5. Name five motifs common in Greek and Roman architecture.
6. During the Middle Ages, how were the furnishings in private residences similar for the rulers and gentry and merchants and workers?
7. How did the motifs of the Spanish, French, and English differ during the Renaissance? List three common motifs.
8. What was unique about Baroque architecture? What was its intent?
9. What three styles of design dominated eighteenth century and early nineteenth century France?
10. Name the seven English styles of design and a motif common to each.
11. List four American styles of design and a common chair-back design for each.
12. What are three styles of design that were included in the introduction to Modern design? Name an article of furniture common to each.
13. Name three styles of the Modern Movement and give a characteristic of each.
14. How did design details vary between urban and rural Mexico in the middle history era? How did craft guilds of this era influence furnishings?
15. What is the key difference between Western and Islamic design?
16. Contrast the bhunga with the pol house of India.
17. Name three common values and philosophies evident in Chinese architecture and interiors.
18. What types of furnishings were used in traditional Korean interiors?
19. What are shoji screens and how did they influence historic Japanese design?
20. What are four types of Native American dwellings? What furnishings were common to these dwellings?
21. List six key American exterior architectural styles and a characteristic of each.
22. As a designer, why is it important to understand historic periods and styles?

Critical Analysis

23. **Determine point of view.** Reread the *Design Insight* quote at the beginning of the chapter. What is the Speaker's point of view regarding the value of studying historical and cultural design for making informed decisions? Write a short essay explaining or justifying whether the writer's point of view applies to design today.
24. **Analyze evidence.** Research the Egyptian motifs the author lists in the chapter. Analyze evidence about the symbolic meaning of the motifs and how they were used in design. Discuss your findings in class.
25. **Deconstruct evidence.** Select a piece of furniture from a magazine picture of an interior. Use the text and other reliable resources to *deconstruct* (break apart) information about the historical roots of this furniture piece. To what period or style does this furniture relate? From this evidence, describe how people of this time may have used the furniture. What were their lives and material culture like at the time? Write a summary of your findings.
26. **Draw conclusions.** Draw conclusions about the value of preserving heritage and restoring historic structures. What are the benefits of preserving designs of the past to modern culture? Discuss your conclusions in class.

Think like a Designer

27. **Writing.** In teams, use text information to write 10 or more questions and answers about key design details of the historic periods and styles including ancient to Postmodern, non-Western, and key architectural styles for a group exam. Submit your questions and answers to your instructor. Then, in teams, complete the exam.
28. **Reading.** Choose one of the historic periods or styles that appeals to you. Use the library and reliable web resources to further read about your chosen period or style. How did materials, technology, and culture of the time influence the designs? Summarize the details for the class.
29. **Reading and writing.** Reread the Case Study on the Jefferson Hotel on text page 270. Examine images A, B, C, and D. With a partner, write a description for each image showing how the designers used the elements and principles of design in each space.
30. **Digital time line.** Use pictures or sketches from online magazines or other Internet sources to create a digital collage of historic interiors and furnishings of each period and style. Creatively arrange your time line from earliest to latest. Ask your classmates to identify the periods and styles you tried to represent.
31. **Speaking.** Select one or more pictures of historic pieces of furniture. Then locate pictures of today's furnishings that match or have similar features to your historic selections. Use websites for today's merchants for examples. Give an illustrated oral report pointing out the key similarities between historic furnishings and those of today.
32. **Virtual architecture tour.** Use the Internet to take a virtual architecture tour of structures in your community or a nearby community. List the key architectural styles you identify. What features of each structure helped you identify its style? To extend this activity, use a school-approved web application to create a digital poster of your findings to share on the class web page.
33. **Writing.** Review the text information on the 20 styles of today. Write an essay explaining and justifying which style you think is most influential today. What evidence supports your thinking?

Design Application

34. **Design your style.** Often a person puts many different styles in his or her interior. This style is known as "eclectic." What is your personal design style? Use the following steps to design your own style.
    A. To begin, find 15 to 20 images of interior spaces that appeal to you and reflect your personality and sense of design aesthetic.
    B. Based on your image selection, choose adjectives that describe the "mood" of your design style.
    C. List some key characteristics and features of your design style.
    D. Identify photos of specific furniture styles, wall treatments, flooring, color palette(s), and accessories your style includes.
    E. Use a school-approved web-based application to create a web page based on your design style and post it to the class blog or web page.
35. **Custom furniture design.** Based on your knowledge of historic interiors and furnishings, create a custom storage chest for usage in your bedroom. Be as creative as you want with adding features you like best. Your storage chest can include seating, drawers, or shelves or any combination. Hand draw or create a digital sketch of your design to share with the class. Ask your classmates to identify the historic features you added to your custom design.
36. **Portfolio builder.** Save the best examples of your work for items 24, 26, 30, 34, and 35 in your traditional or digital portfolio that express your analytical thinking and creativity for potential college or employers.

The Human Impact of Interior Design

Photography courtesy of Fred Fuhrmeister/Design by RB+B Architects

Chapter

10

Design Insight

"The responsibility of interior designers and interior architects is to advance the profession and advocate for social well-being. In addition, the confluence of environmental psychology and the science of anthropometrics are critical to the quantitative and qualitative knowledge that form the practice of interior design and interior architecture."

IFI Declaration

Learning Targets

After studying this chapter, you will be able to

- summarize theories that impact human behavior.
- demonstrate strategies to enhance human comfort including use of anthropometrics, ergonomics, and proxemics.
- understand issues related to social and environmental responsibility and how to apply strategies to resolve the issues.

Introduction

Knowledge of how clients experience space is essential for any practicing interior designer. Poor acoustics in a classroom negatively impact student learning. Chaos in an airport concourse, coupled with poor signage, often raises a traveler's blood pressure and stress levels. Gazing on something profoundly beautiful elicits pleasure and psychological release. Therefore, *how* interior spaces are designed significantly impacts the well-being of people physically, behaviorally, and emotionally.

The study of humans and their behavior in interior spaces is fascinating. While elements and principles of design shape the composition and details of a space, *theories* predict or explain how people perceive a space and behave within it. Successful practitioners of design need knowledge of the elements, principles, and theories of design.

Theories Impacting Human Behavior

Theories explain why and how an interior space produces a certain human response. To design interior spaces well, designers must understand what motivates or predicts a human behavior within a space. They must also understand how people react to the aesthetics of a place. To develop this knowledge, designers study theories not only from their field but also from such fields as environmental psychology, architecture, and art.

Theories offer designers a framework with which to understand the human environment experience. Theories also provide designers with a language to discuss human behavior and responses with clients and team members. When you can explain why you are designing an interior a certain way—based on theories—you become more credible as a designer.

The design of interiors should never be completed in a vacuum. Instead, theories should inform and shape your design decisions. In many ways, this chapter gets to the essence of what designers do.

The following includes a sampling of theories interior designers may use as they shape a space to encourage certain human behaviors. Take time to learn others. You will be amazed at how complex and varied human perceptions and behaviors are during the lifespan.

Fun Theory

This novel theory is so new, and therefore still under investigation, but is grabbing attention in a variety of countries. One big motivator of positive human behavior is fun. The **fun theory** is about changing human behavior for the better by making a tedious task fun to do.

Volkswagen introduced this theory when they marketed their environmental car as *fun* to drive, **Figure 10-1**. This theory was then expanded to raise conscious awareness of driving safety, the importance of picking up litter, the need to obey the speed limit, and the suggestion to use more stairs to increase physical activity. Some countries give rewards for shaping behavior for good by using innovation and fun to encourage behavior modification.

Red Bird 2009/Shutterstock.com

Figure 10-1 Although it is new, the fun theory focuses on making less-than-fun tasks more engaging and fun to do.

What are some applications of the fun theory to interior design? The world is struggling with an obesity issue. How could the office workplace be redesigned to encourage more physical activity through fun experiences while maintaining productivity? The U.S. and many countries are experiencing an energy crisis. How could citizens be encouraged to use less electricity in their interiors? What factors might make the choice of a smaller home (thus using less electricity) more appealing to families? How could designers make living in smaller spaces more fun?

Environmental Psychology Theories

Environmental psychologists study humans and their surroundings. A broad definition of *surrounding* or *environment* includes natural and physical places as well as social and learning settings.

Environmental psychology theories predict emotional and physical reactions to environmental stimuli and characteristics. They can explain why humans engage in certain behaviors within their interior environments.

There are major theories that guide research about the human and environment relationship. These theories relate to behavior setting, control, and stimulation.

Behavior-Setting Theory

The **behavior-setting theory** is about social events or public places in which people use routine, and often repeated, actions within a given time and place. For example, children often learn specific, socially acceptable behaviors at an early age—such as to move quietly or whisper in a library. They often repeat these behaviors either as a child or an adult in a similar environment.

Other similar public settings include schools, fine-dining restaurants, supermarkets, theaters, places of worship, and graduation ceremonies. The design of public spaces encourages and supports socially and culturally accepted behaviors. These behaviors may include how to move quietly to a seat in a library or interpret design cues indicating a fancy restaurant, **Figure 10-2**. The behavior-setting theory guides the designer's decisions when shaping such rooms, when selecting and placing furnishings, or when choosing interior finishes for an interior environment.

Photography courtesy of Fred Furhmeister/Design by RB+B Architects, Inc.

arek_malang/Shutterstock.com

Figure 10-2 The behavior-setting theory guides designers' decisions for public spaces that impact certain socially or culturally accepted behaviors. *For what places in your community might this theory have been used to guide design decisions?*

Control Theory

The **control theory**, a critical one for interior design, is the sense of control a person desires over his or her world and specifically, the physical environment. Three types of control are preferred. These include

- **Behavioral**—the ability to change an environmental event.
- **Cognitive**—the ability to change how you think of an environment.
- **Decisional**—the ability to choose your own actions, behavior, and response to an environment.

You can observe the control theory in many interior spaces such as a work environment. In their offices, people enjoy placing family photos. This personalizes their spaces, making them feel more *at home*—a location where they often feel more in control of their lives, **Figure 10-3**.

People also like to exert control in their environments to enhance their physical comfort. For example, they desire the control to change the amount of light around their desks (darken or lighten) and raise or lower the temperature to ensure they are not too cold or too warm. Therefore, employers often give employees access to individual light switches and the ability to open and shut their windows.

Haworth, Inc.

Figure 10-3 The control theory helps designers make design decisions that offer people control over their environments, and therefore increasing their comfort levels. *What design features in this office indicate behavioral, cognitive, or decisional control?*

Individual control over interior spaces—particularly personal places—is critical in all types of spaces. If desired, a teen likes to be able to close a door for privacy. Likewise, a patient in a hospital wants to be able to raise and lower his or her bed to achieve comfort. A restaurant guest may want to move his or her chair closer to or farther from the table rather than have it secured to the floor. Theoretically, offering control to people increases their comfort level in their environments.

Stimulation Theory

The **stimulation theory** explains the environment as a source of sensory information gathered through sight, sound, touch, taste, and smell. Each of the five senses can be overstimulated or understimulated.

The stimulation theory typically applies to interior spaces through the sense of sight. For example, vibrant, contrasting colors in an elementary or early childhood classroom may overstimulate children, causing increased, frenetic, and undesirable activity. Changing to a less-intense color palette in the same space may serve as a way to calm activity and create a sense of order.

For adults, usage of intense, bright colors or overly intense light in a conference room (where you sit for a long period of time) or in a small bathroom (in which the room is too small for the color palette) causes overstimulation to occur. People often express their reactions in a need to flee.

When the paint in a patient room of a healthcare facility is too bold or bright, anxiety or stress can result. Therefore, an accent wall behind the patient is often painted. Similarly, too much pattern in an already active room, such as a kitchen, can be difficult for the brain to process. People express such overstimulation as discomfort.

People who are overstimulated at their workplaces often desire reduced environmental stimuli at home. They prefer a place to rest and rejuvenate. Rather than bold, striking colors, they may require the use of calm, warm, grayed tones in their homes with views to the outside, **Figure 10-4**.

At times, people need stimulating interiors to get a jumpstart into increased, desirable activity. One such place might be a fitness center. Another might be a physical therapy room in a healthcare facility. Selection of color, pattern, and light are just a few ways designers apply this theory in interior spaces.

ERC: LaCasse Photography

Figure 10-4 Interior designers apply the stimulation theory primarily through sight. *How does creating the color feature wall behind the patient increase or decrease discomfort from over- or understimulation?*

Sense-of-Self Theory

Human comfort relates to people expressing their identities in their personal interior spaces. The **sense-of-self theory** involves the selection of objects and symbols to communicate personal identity to others. In the same way body tattoos communicate self-expression and apparel worn communicates identity, interiors communicate messages about *self*. For example, when a new friend walks into your dwelling, what clues does the space communicate about you as an individual through the objects and symbols you selected to put in the space? People see clues of who you are in

- how organized the room is compared to the rest of the house
- what colors your room is painted
- accessories you placed around the space
- artwork or posters hanging on the wall
- what type of window treatments—such as draperies—are used on the windows
- what objects are placed in a nearby bookcase or on top of a desk or end table
- types of patterns used in conjunction with each other

What you surround yourself with in your interior environment communicates a great deal about who you are and what you value in life. Therefore, when hired to complete a residential design project, an interior designer studies the symbols and objects placed in the client's current home to gather information about who they are, their preferences, and their living habits. The designer then strategically uses these symbols and objects in the future home.

Theories of Place

There are several theories related to place and place-making. Because *place* is such a critical part of a physical environment, several will be discussed.

Sense-of-Place Theory

Sense-of-place theory describes your relationship, which you express through feelings or perceptions, to a particular place or setting. It is a sense of belonging and authentic human attachment to a specific location. Usually, such places have unique characteristics that a person feels only in that one location.

A person may feel this sense of belonging in such a natural setting as the top of a favorite mountain mesa with a beautiful vista, **Figure 10-5**. A sense of belonging may

jeff Metzger/Shutterstock.com

Figure 10-5 Sense-of-place theory reflects a person's sense of belonging or attachment to a location.

also occur in a favorite culture-centric town such as Santa Fe, or in a family horse barn, a personal art studio, or a favorite gymnasium. Regardless of where you feel a sense of belonging, in these locations, the feeling you experience as you walk into it or toward it is often expressed in the thought: "I am home. This is where I belong."

Closely related to sense-of-place is **place attachment**—an emotion that evolves over time and involves positive bonds to a particular place. These person-place bonds often elicit a memory or feeling of security, or other such positive emotions as happiness, joy, and playfulness. The bonds you have with a place often begin at a young age. For example, you often form bonds with your childhood home. Visiting your childhood home as an adult may revive childhood memories and again evoke feelings of attachment to the place.

In addition to a childhood home, place attachment can also involve personal experiences with another place that elicits positive emotions about the place. When interior designers design the interior of a theme park hotel, they will use the concept of place attachment. For example, a designer may craft a hotel lobby to look like the Grand Canyon as a reminder to people of a favorite vacation. Alternatively, the designer might use images and interior finishes—such as a tree sculpture—that evoke childhood memories of climbing a favorite tree or swinging on a swing.

Frank Lloyd Wright, a well-known American architect, demonstrated the understanding of place attachment when he designed *Fallingwater*, a home for the Kaufman family in the woods of Pennsylvania. This family was attached to a favorite place on their property, a view from a rock overhang that allowed them to see a rushing waterfall. In honor of their place attachment, Frank Lloyd Wright designed their home directly over the exact location of their favorite perching rock—incorporating it into the family room floor. The house does not view the place, but participates in nature's drama. Mr. Wright honored the family's attachment to a specific place, **Figure 10-6 A and B**.

On a smaller scale, the design of space consciously and subconsciously communicates *personalization*—a factor of both sense-of-place and sense-of-self. **Personalization** is the stamp of your personality and a reflection of your values, preferences, or territory on a place or space. It establishes and communicates your unique identity, which is important to the overall expression of self. Examples of personalization include using accessories or items to decorate the college residence hall room or the placement of favorite objects around your workspace.

Research indicates that personalization is critical for elderly people as they move into a retirement or nursing home. They need objects and artifacts around them that symbolize memories and a sense-of-place about where they have been or where they are living. If they do not feel a sense-of-place, these older adults may give up on life, not feeling an identity with a place. Knowing of the need to personalize a space, an interior designer will incorporate horizontal and vertical surfaces—such as shelving—that can hold or showcase items of meaning for the individual using or living in the space, **Figure 10-7**.

The concept of *placemaking* originated in the 1960s when city planners focused on designing communities that catered to people rather than cars and shopping centers. The goal of **placemaking** was to make each community a unique place that showcased the community's assets, and offered to its citizens, public spaces that promoted health, happiness, and well-being.

Architects and landscape designers supported this concept when creating public squares, parks, and waterfronts to attract more people to a community by making it more attractive, pleasurable, and inspiring. Placemaking became an economic benefit to the town, city, or community.

A

Robert Crow/Shutterstock.com

B

Library of Congress Prints and Photographs Division, Washington, D.C.

Figure 10-6 Frank Lloyd Wright designed Fallingwater to incorporate views of a rushing waterfall (A). *How does the interior of Fallingwater reflect place attachment (B)?*

MNStudio/Shutterstock.com

Figure 10-7 Personalization of an interior space helps people feel a sense-of-place.

Likewise, interior designers use the placemaking theory when they want to evoke a feeling of pleasure and well-being in public interiors in locations around the world. For example, rather than designing a hotel chain to look similar in every location, the design of the hotel chain would capture the feeling of each location (city or community) so the traveler experiences the place even as he or she walks into the lobby. The goal is to capture the flavor or mood of each specific location in the interior. For example, if designing a hotel interior near an ocean, the designer will use space, lighting, color, and textures to capture that specific ocean location. If successful, the hotel interior should look much different than if it was located in Mumbai, India or Rome, Italy.

Third Place Theory

Coined by Ray Oldenburg, a **third place** is a location that is neither your home—*first place*—nor your place of work or school—*second place*—but a place where you relax on a regular basis and that you visit to get away. This third place is a setting that meets your social needs and allows you to develop a sense of community with others—even if they are familiar strangers.

A third place for a college student may be a favorite restaurant where he or she meets friends to laugh, talk, and relieve stress. It may be a favorite coffee shop where you begin your morning on the way to work, **Figure 10-8**.

Third places are convenient and supportive of human interaction. They often provide such comforts as food, beverages, and Internet access. As you use the place, you will see the same people frequenting it. These are *familiar strangers*.

When designing third places, interior designers use such research as that conducted by Lisa Waxman, Ph.D., Department Head, Interior Design, at Florida State University. This research indicates that third places commonly offer access to a view, comfortable seating, and background noise that encourages conversation. Examples of such places include bookstores, cafés, gyms, restaurants, and swimming pools. Their appropriate designs can generate more business and provide an outlet for community building.

Privacy and Privacy Theory

Rather than related to a place or environment, many theories interior designers use often relate to the human need for privacy—both in the home and in the workplace. Privacy meets multiple human needs such as survival, and physical and psychological health. Privacy facilitates development of self-identity, human comfort, and thereby encourages emotional release.

Importance of Privacy

All humans need time and a place to get away from daily life stresses. Time for relaxation is a difficult commodity to carve out of technology-driven, crowded lifestyles. People need spaces and places that allow them to choose their preferred amount of social interaction, visual and acoustical privacy, and types of stimulus.

The need for privacy is neither new nor a luxury; it is a basic human need. Benefits of privacy include the ability to rejuvenate, self-evaluate, and contemplate. Privacy allows emotional release and at times, concealment from surrounding negative effects. It is a dynamic condition that can lead to imbalance in people's lives. Too much privacy, for example, can lead to social isolation. Too little privacy, such as crowding, can create serious stress.

Across cultures, the need for privacy is universal. Its expression, however, may differ depending on personality, society, age, gender, stage of life, and environment. For example, young children need less privacy than adolescents. Interior designers must understand the cultural and societal norms or age differences that

Wutthichai/Shutterstock.com smoxx/Shutterstock.com

Figure 10-8 Third-place settings help meet social and relaxation needs. *What are some third places in your community? How does the design of these places promote socialization and relaxation?*

define and regulate the privacy of their clients in home environments.

People need privacy when they are stressed, ill, tired, sad, grieving, or angry. For example, if designing the interior of a mortuary, design professionals must consider feelings of mourning or stress that often result with the loss of a loved one. Such interiors must support various amounts of privacy.

Interior designers address the complex human need for privacy in many ways. For example, they may design a place of contemplation into a workplace setting to assist employees in achieving balance and greater productivity. Interior designers can also design spaces into the home environment for parents and children to be alone or together depending on their preference, **Figure 10-9**. Privacy settings support family interactions away from private spaces.

Privacy Regulation Theory and Territoriality

One well-known theory related to privacy was developed by environmental psychologist Irwin Altman. **Privacy regulation theory** explains why people prefer staying alone sometimes and at other times appreciate the opportunity for social interactions. This is a type of boundary regulation—the definition of your ever-changing preferences for personal boundaries.

Rather than an excluding process, Altman views privacy as a "...need for responsive environments that can accommodate individual needs for togetherness and separateness." He advocates that the key to supporting individuals is to allow them control over how much interaction they desire with others. Altman views *privacy* as the central motivational force driving people's needs for personal space and territorial behavior, as well as their responses to crowding.

Common to all animal species, *territoriality* for humans is the possession and defense of physical space. To indicate possession, occupants will use, mark, and personalize their spaces. Having their own territory makes people feel more secure and safe; and therefore, they relax. People want and need space to call their own.

Vasilyev Alexandr/Shutterstock.com

Figure 10-9 All people, including children, prefer to have some time alone. *How do you think this image expresses the need for privacy regulation?*

Territories are usually larger than personal spaces. People demarcate and defend their territories in a variety of ways including

- physical presence—such as sitting in a chair at your desk
- touching—such as putting a hand on a plate in a restaurant
- surveillance—posting "keep out" signs around a property boundary
- marking of territory—leaving a coat over a movie theater chair when going for popcorn

People often personalize their private territories, thus indicating their identity to others. Adding a family photo to a workplace desk or covering a cell phone with a colorful protective device are examples of ways people personalize their private territories. This type of territoriality links to the sense-of-place and sense-of-self theories described earlier.

As people age, part of their socialization is to note and respect another's territories. As resources diminish, territoriality and competition increase. There are three basic types of territories.

- **Primary.** Controlled on a relatively permanent basis, individuals or occupants own these spaces. Examples include a private bedroom or home.
- **Secondary.** Not owned by the occupants, these spaces or places do not allow exclusive ownership. These territories have only moderate significance to the occupants. Examples include corridors or workplaces.
- **Public.** These are places available to anyone on a temporary basis. Occupants have little control in these spaces because they are available to anyone in good standing within that society. Examples include movie theaters or hotel lobbies.

Territoriality plays a major role in the design of home, workplace, and place of recreation. Allocating enough space for each person and designing shared or common areas with space and amenities for each user offers the person an opportunity to personalize a space and establish territoriality. This results in human comfort. If space is not designed with territoriality in mind, competition for space occurs and conflict can arise.

Crowding and Density

When it is difficult for a person to define boundaries for privacy, a resulting negative condition is crowding. **Crowding** is the psychological response to overstimulation caused by too much interaction with others in a limited space. Think about the inner tension people feel when everyone wants to get through the gym door at the same time after a school assembly. **Density** relates to the number of inhabitants per unit of territory. The higher the density (more people in the space) the greater the *environmental load*—the amount of environmental stimuli people can handle, **Figure 10-10**. Uncertainty and unpredictability result from the invasion of personal space (territory) and stress results.

Many people regard crowds as negative. However, the excitement of a crowd can be infectious and serve as a release to inner stress. Think about the energizing response of the crowd at a royal wedding, a presidential inauguration, or a rock concert.

In interior spaces, designers must shape space to diffuse physical crowding. For example, they may

- design multiple entry and exit points for users of the space
- perceptually make the space appear larger with increased electric or natural light, incorporation of higher ceilings, and use of unobstructed outdoor views (a visual escape)
- create rectangular rooms because they generate less crowding than square rooms
- arrange furnishings less centrally rather than grouping them in the center of a space to make it perceptually less crowded

Thomas La Mela/Shutterstock.com

Figure 10-10 People may regard crowds as positive or negative. *How does this image reflect crowding and density? Why is crowding and density a concern for interior designers?*

- set a cooler temperature in a space to lessen the feeling of crowding

Higher-density environments are likely in the future with an increasing population. Designers must understand how to make the effects of crowding in interiors perceptually and physically less severe to achieve human comfort.

Attention Restoration Theory

Other theories interior designers use when shaping spaces relate to the human need for nature and natural surroundings. Natural environments are restorative. For example, solitude in a natural environment serves as a place of retreat that restores creativity and renews the spirit. Other benefits people receive from affiliating with nature include

- reduced mental fatigue and lowered stress levels
- enhanced productivity
- enhanced psychological recovery
- increased intelligence—the brain works better and becomes sharper
- improved cognitive functioning on higher-order tasks
- lower blood pressure and reduced muscle tension

Rachel and Stephen Kaplan developed the *Attention Restoration Theory (ART)*. This theory claims that people concentrate better after exposure to nature of any type—whether spending time looking at clouds move across the sky or looking at a photograph of a natural setting. The Kaplans also determined that restorative natural environments are aesthetically pleasing, **Figure 10-11**.

photobank.ch/Shutterstock.com

Figure 10-11 Views of nature can have restorative effects on health and well-being.

According to Stephen R. Kellert, Professor Emeritus of Social Ecology and Research Scholar at Yale University School of Forestry and Environmental Studies, without some connection to nature, people feel both emotionally and spiritually diminished. Kellert believes that humans have a genetic inclination to attach physical, emotional, and intellectual meaning with nature—something he calls **biophilia**—a human appreciation of and an association with other forms of life and the living world.

People need to see seasons change and time pass. Therefore, interior designers sensitively create interior environments that link people to nature through views to the outside in both residential and commercial settings.

For example, in a home a designer can include alcoves, window seats, and perches into the house to allow people to stay inside while looking out. Likewise, natural light comes from many sources and directions in a commercial environment. Rather than using uniform, artificial light, office spaces can incorporate natural light into the spaces (with appropriate filters to avoid glare) through the use of such strategies as solar tubes and skylights.

Designing for Human Comfort

Understanding theories and how they apply to human behavior and their physical environment is very important. Likewise, to design for human comfort, designers must have an understanding of how to position a person in relation to others. They must also understand the relationships of human body measurements within a volume of space. Average human dimensions are the standard used for the measurement and design of interiors.

People need to be comfortable, both physically and psychologically, in relation to the scale and proportion of their interiors. Scale of furniture and circulation paths are just a few human dimensions a designer must know and understand when planning an interior space.

Anthropometrics

Anthropometry is the study of human body measurements as compared to space. Gaining visibility in the nineteenth century, anthropometrics used measurement data, such as the length of a person's arm, and compare it to other people. In the mid-1900s, the military discovered the value of anthropometry for figuring out sizes of supplies used by soldiers, such as uniforms and helmets. With a captive audience, they performed large-scale anthropometric studies.

Today, anthropometric studies collect data to determine typical heights, widths, and sizes of people in various postures (sitting, standing, or reaching). In addition, such data collection includes necessary space needs, mobility, and physical strength data for those who are physically healthy and those who have disabilities or other challenges.

Anthropometric data are divided into categories for three different populations: males, females, and children. Measurement data is available in both metric and U.S. conventional measures. One outcome of this data is a list of standard clearances designers use when space planning or rearranging furniture. The use of some military anthropometric data is still common in kitchen design today. Anthropometry is a sub-discipline of *ergonomics,* **Figure 10-12**.

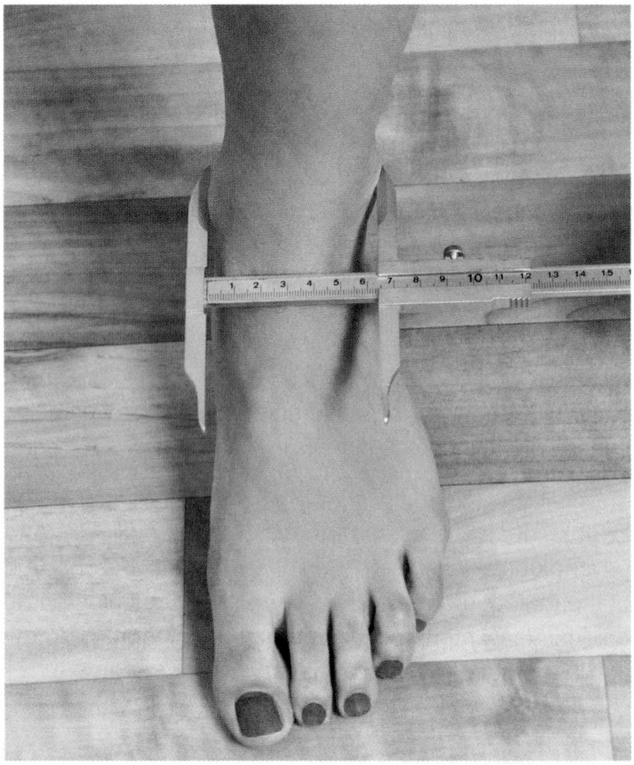

cirkoglu/Shutterstock.com

Figure 10-12 Anthropometric measurements provide data for meeting human space needs in environments. *For what spaces do you think anthropometric data is most important? Why? Justify your thinking with evidence from the text and other reliable resources.*

Ergonomics

Ergonomics—also known as *human factors* or *human engineering*—concerns the design and arrangement of things people use so that the people and things interact efficiently and safely. Human measurements (anthropometric data) include not only height and weight, but also hearing, tactile sense, and visual and auditory acuity (ability to see and hear well). Designers then use these ergonomic measurements to make design decisions. For instance, a designer must know how much width a child's car seat requires for a child between two and 18 months of age, or the best height of a kitchen counter for most people.

Ergonomic data helps determine the scale of furniture for sitting comfort and the proper arrangement for task completion, **Figure 10-13**. This data also indicates how to position the height and angle of equipment to make it easy to use and operate such as in an office setting. For example, such data influences the design of desks and desk chairs for the appropriate height to support the user and achieve human comfort.

Often, students recline, or lean back, on their beds to study for exams or homework. This posture or position is ergonomically poor. According to Humanscale, Inc.—an organization devoted to developing high-performance office tools—this posture can cause stress to the body and encourages injury risk and poor performance.

Proxemics

To design for human comfort, design practitioners must understand personal, interpersonal, and public space interactions. People tolerate closer interpersonal distance when they feel strong, secure, or safe. Conversely, they require more interpersonal space when they feel weak, insecure, or at risk.

Personal space is the physical distance between two or more people, or from an object. It is an important factor in design. It determines how comfortable people are in a particular setting. For example, in a public setting, three people rarely sit together on a sofa. The middle seat is always the last to be taken or avoided at all cost. If a person sits in the middle, he or she often strictly avoids personal contact and has minimal eye contact. Due to the discomfort, many people will quickly leave and sit on the floor to ensure they can face the people to whom they are talking.

Proxemics, a term developed by anthropologist Edward T. Hall, is the study of how humans use space and how it relates to environmental and cultural factors.

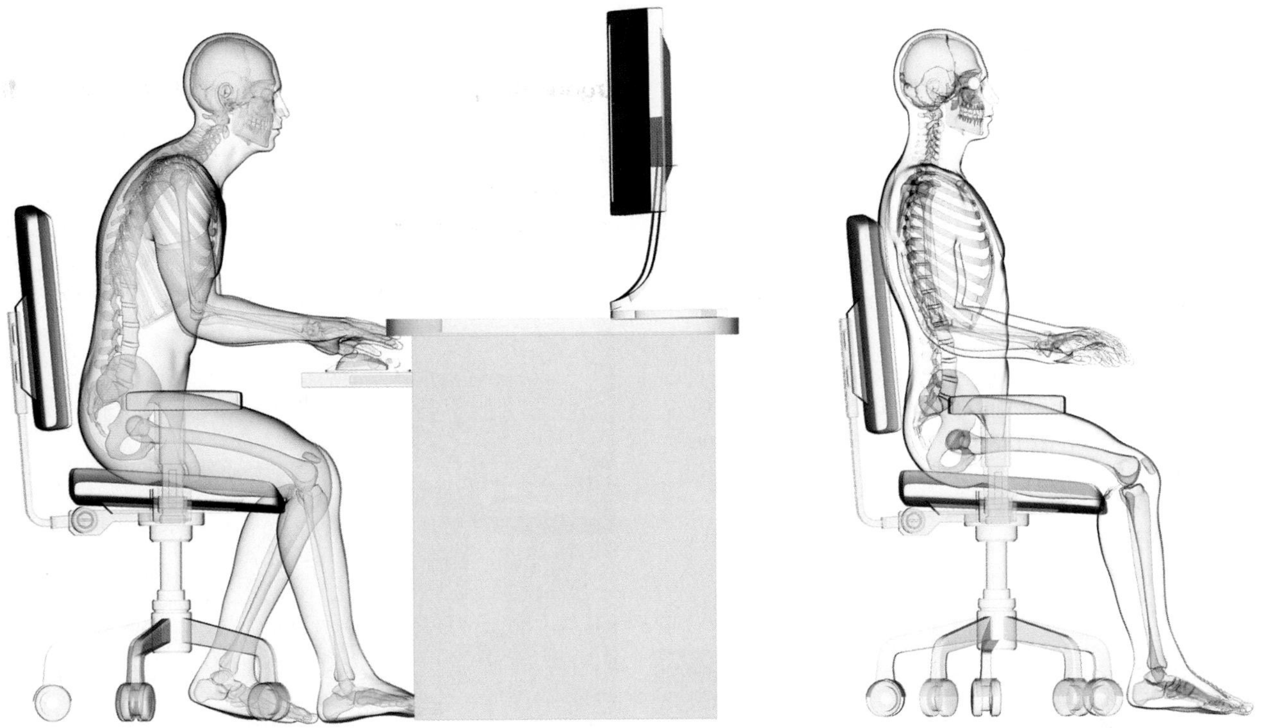

Sebastian Kaulitzki/Shutterstock.com Sebastian Kaulitzki/Shutterstock.com

Figure 10-13 Ergonomics in an office setting requires the proper equipment set-up and the correct sitting posture. *What are the effects of poor ergonomics?*

Hall's study identifies four distances or zones relevant to North Americans. They include

- **Intimate distance.** Ranging from zero physical contact to 18 inches, vision is minimal within intimate distance because people rely on touch and smell more than sight. To feel safe, people reserve this distance for displays of affection, comfort, or protection.

  This distance is often apparent between parents and infants or young children. Some people, however, use intimate distance to display physical aggression, creating a violation of personal space. Intrusion into an intimate zone can be unpleasant and offensive.

- **Personal distance.** Extending 18 inches to four feet from the body, personal distance is akin to "keeping a person at arm's length." Known commonly as the *physical bubble*, people typically reserve this distance for friends. It is the measurement people use to separate themselves from others—physically and psychologically.

  At this distance, touch is minimal except when shaking hands—vision and hearing become more important. It is possible to see subtle communications through eye contact and body language such as angling the body away from the other person. Within this distance, normal conversations easily take place. In other cultures where it is customary to touch or embrace, this bubble is much smaller.

- **Social distance.** A zone that is four feet to 12 feet from the body, social distance reflects *casual acquaintance*. You can observe this distance at such social events as parties, reunions, and sports events, or in other public spaces in which there are customer-merchant interactions. It is easy to flee at this distance if safety is threatened or undesirable behavior occurs.

  People who maintain this distance know *of* each other, but do not know each other well, such as friends of friends or casual acquaintances. Designers often use this zone to place furniture in offices or in public settings.

- **Public distance.** A zone that is 12 feet to 25 feet from the body is public distance and involves people with whom you have no acquaintance. This distance is similar to walking near a person in a hotel lobby. The only common

CASE STUDY

Herman Miller, Aeron Desk Chair

According to Herman Miller, "The Aeron chair did not end up in the Museum of Modern Art's permanent collection just because it looks cool. Although it does, its looks are only the beginning. Aeron accommodates both the sitter and the environment. It adapts naturally to virtually every body, and it is 94 percent recyclable. Even if it's black, it is *green*."

Fast-forward ergonomics and a look so distinctive is probably the reason the Aeron office chair is the only chair people can identify by name. The chair is adaptable to all sizes and shapes, and all the motions a person goes through every day while seated. Aeron provides healthy comfort and balanced body support with its innovative suspension and easy-to-use adjustment controls.

Investigate and Reflect ....
Go to the Herman Miller website and read the design story behind the Aeron chair. What was the designer's design philosophy in regard to this chair? What human factors did the designer consider? Give a clear, concise, and effective oral summary of your findings that explain and justify the designer's actions in creating the Aeron chair to the class.

Courtesy of Herman Miller, Inc.

The Aeron chair was designed with ergonomics in mind by Bill Stumpf and Don Chadwick.

association between the two people is that they are relatively near each other for some period of time.

Another place you can observe this distance is between the teacher and the student in a college lecture hall. Communication is one way (for instance, the teacher lecturing in a large college hall). If there is a violation of this public distance, a sense of crowding occurs, **Figure 10-14**.

Research indicates that children have smaller personal space bubbles than teens or adults. Within the Western culture, the perception of personal space may also differ between genders. Males need more personal space than females, and all individuals typically maintain more distance from males, too.

Western and Eastern cultures define and measure the need for personal space differently. For instance, eye contact may be more important in one culture than physical distance.

In his study of proxemics, Hall speculates that people may belong to a *contact* or *noncontact* culture. People in contact cultures—such as Middle Eastern, Asian, and Latin—prefer having objects within their personal spaces closer to them than people in such noncontact cultures as those of Northern Europe and North America. Different norms are important for designers to know, particularly if their firms are designing a workplace or lodging facility in another country.

Violation of personal space does not only occur on a physical level. Eavesdropping, staring, or watching without permission can also be an invasion of privacy. Likewise, so can making loud noises or playing loud music.

Proxemics also directly impacts how people judge an environment. For example, in a movie theater, if seats are too close together, a group of men will typically sit in every other seat.

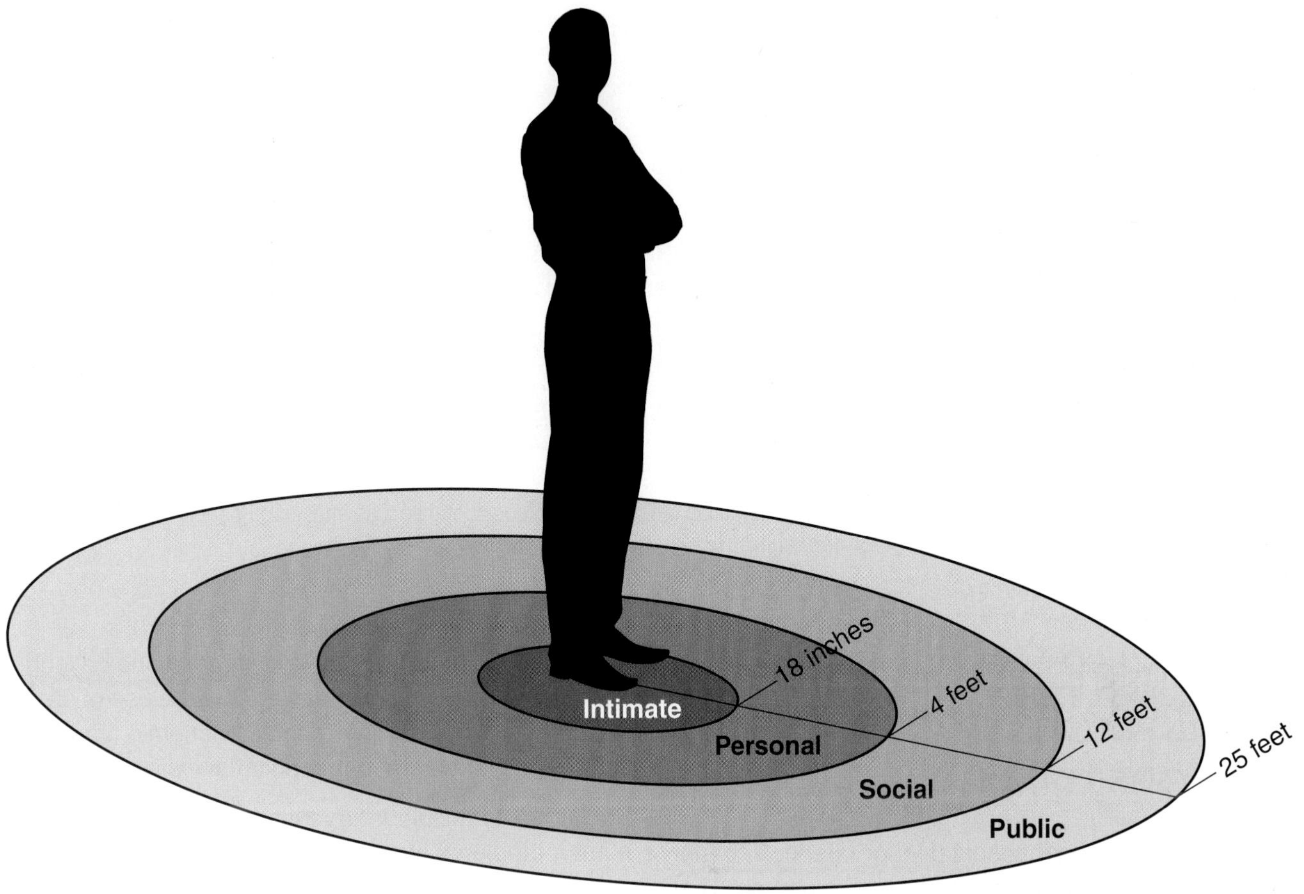

Galushko Sergey/Shutterstock.com; Goodheart-Willcox Publisher

Figure 10-14 Proxemics is the study of how humans use space and how it relates to environmental and cultural factors and human comfort in a space.

Architectural details can help individuals maintain a sense of personal space or public distance. For example, walls, windows, columns, and varying floor heights are strategies for managing personal and social distances. In both residential and commercial interiors, end tables, chairs with armrests, and potted plants also offer boundaries.

Grid-like theater seating creates a **sociofugal** space to discourage interaction and communication with others. In contrast, chairs tightly grouped in a radial fashion in a coffee shop or café encourages people to mingle and interact. These **sociopetal** spaces encourage interaction and communication with others, **Figure 10-15 A and B**.

If a boundary does not exist, people will physically move until they achieve a certain level of comfort. For example, when in a standing position, if someone is too close or too far from another person, he or she will compensate by taking a step backward or forward. If a person responds by taking a step closer, the subliminal message this conveys is the person views himself or herself as the other's equal. If your boss is nearby, a person may take a step back to indicate increased status. If there is no choice, such as on an elevator, the social norm is to: ignore others, stand rigid, stare up or down, or pretend you are alone.

Often increased personal space serves as a reward or an indicator of status within the group. You can observe this fact in a large private office in the workplace, a private bedroom in a home, and a first-class seat on a plane.

Observing distances between clients and others will help you as the designer determine the kind of relationship that exists. Designers use proxemics to create environments where furniture and room planning can meet human needs for comfort and safety—in residential and commercial places.

A Apples Eyes Studio/Shutterstock.com

B Lucky Business/Shutterstock.com

Figure 10-15 Sociofugal spaces discourage human interaction (A). In contrast, sociopetal spaces encourage people to interact (B). *How do these spaces increase or decrease human comfort?*

Human Impact: Social and Environmental Responsibility

Interior designers are accountable for offering a better human experience in the interior environment. That experience should not be at the expense of future generations and future use of the planet.

Good design is socially, ethically, and environmentally responsible—also known as *Environmentally Responsible Interior Design (ERID)*. Earlier in the text, you learned about the ethics part of this definition in relationship to professional practice. Following are some thoughts concerning socially and environmentally responsible design.

> *“A small group of thoughtful people could change the world. Indeed, it's the only thing that ever has.”*
>
> *Margaret Mead*

Socially Responsible Design

Socially responsible design (SRD) is an approach to design rather than a specific set of standards. It concerns the immediate as well as the long-term impact of design on society and the world. It is designing well for the present, future, and many generations beyond—a reference to sustainable design. It is the use of design to address social, environmental, economic, and political issues that embrace humanitarian values.

Socially responsible interventions use design to solve human problems, whether focused on the individual or wider society. These projects have national and international attention as they are taking place throughout the world. They have received national awards from the U.S. president and recognition from the *Cooper Hewitt Museum*, a Smithsonian Institute. Examples of socially responsible interventions include

- solutions for global housing crises, such as providing shelter in South Africa constructed with sandbags and timber framing
- suggestions to address the needs of those with limited access to clean water, electricity, and proper sanitation
- employment of two youths to paint brightly colored murals on buildings and staircases to reinvigorate city slums
- creation of community identity by mounting of enormous photographic prints of local residents on walls, rooftops, stairways, and train cars

Social responsibility is reshaping another's world side-by-side with design professionals, **Figure 10-16**. It is changing situations from an existing to a preferred state, and involves decision making on a global level. Socially responsible design offers the opportunity to leave a legacy for future generations that speaks of the current priorities, values, and choices.

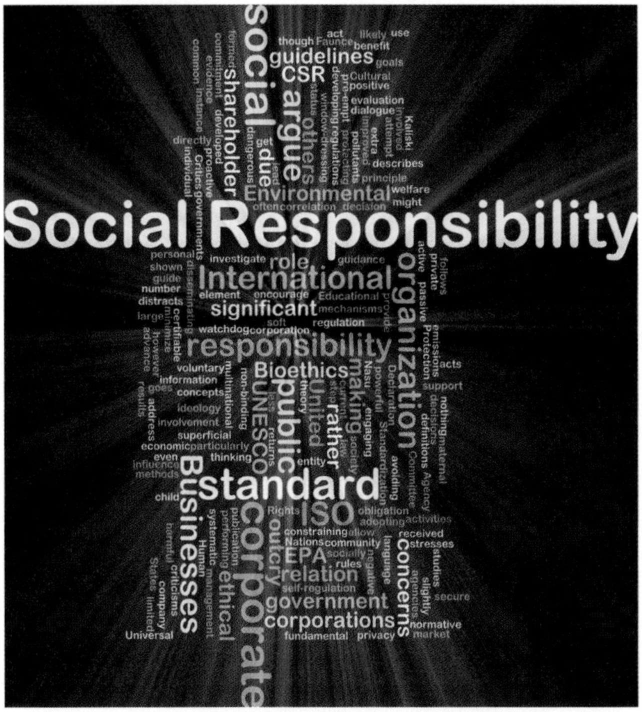

Kheng Guan Toh/Shutterstock.com

Figure 10-16 Social responsibility in interior design involves sensitivity to economic, social, and environmental impact on local and global levels.

Many architectural and interior design firms are involved in identifying *Social Responsibility Initiatives (SRI)* in which their employees participate. These firms strive to be sensitive to how they manage their economic, social, and environmental impact. They desire to give back to society by selecting a community or national project in which their members or employees can participate. The work on such projects is generally *pro-bono work*—or voluntary professional work done for the good of the public without a fee.

Nationally, socially responsible design involves everything from sustainable design and adaptive reuse of buildings to wise use of limited energy resources. It may also involve the use of the *integrated design process (IDP)* to create better designs for all people in a global environment. Inclusive design—or universal design—and design against crime fall into this category, too. All of these and more influence the human impact of design in society and the world. The following section discusses a few of these areas of socially responsible design.

Designer Profile

Rachelle Schoessler Lynn—Sustainable Design

Rachelle Schoessler Lynn, FASID, CID, LEED AP BD+C, is a senior associate with MSR in Minneapolis, MN. She has devoted her life to design excellence and sustainable design.

Designed by Studio 2030, Inc.—Design Principals David A. Loehr, AIA, AICP, LEED AP BD+C and Rachelle Schoessler Lynn, FASID, CID, LEED AP BD+C.

"Interior designers impact the human experience within buildings as well as both the physical transitional experience from inside to outside and the direct visual experience between inside and nature.

"Interior designers can design spaces that improve human health and well-being. I believe that interior designers have an ethical responsibility to design spaces that are building-code compliant, meet or exceed the requirement of ADA, and reduce toxic emissions from materials, finishes, and furnishings. Interior designers have the knowledge required to design for appropriate acoustics and ergonomic needs. They are experienced in understanding the positive health impacts of design solutions because they have considered the impacts of every design decision on human health.

"By its very meaning, design excellence is original, high performance, and sublimely beautiful. Good solutions are as satisfying to the soul as they are kind to the environment.

"Most people know when they are in a well-designed space but they are not always able to articulate what it is that makes the space so wonderful. This is the result of the work of an interior designer—someone who creates the space that functions as needed and improves the well-being of people using the space."

You can read more about Rachelle's design experience in Appendix B.

Sustainable and Green Design

As you recall, *sustainability* is a practice or way of using materials that has minimal long-term effect on the environment. It gives people the ability to grow, endure, and prosper now and in future generations. This concept applies to many entities such as businesses, economies, and even countries. *Sustainable design* addresses the health and well-being of the global ecosystems that support life now and in the future.

The American Society of Interior Designers (ASID) believes that sustainability is a critical part of the interior designer's professional responsibilities. ASID suggests that sustainable interior design embraces such goals as the following:

- integrated building design developed by interdisciplinary teams
- design of indoor environments that encourage occupant well-being
- consideration and specification of products that are energy efficient
- protection of the natural environment, **Figure 10-17**

Currently, humans are creating an unsustainable situation by using up natural resources faster than nature can replenish them. To sustain natural resources for future generations, designers and their clients can

- Limit the use of finite materials, such as granite, for countertops. Stone that took millennia to form

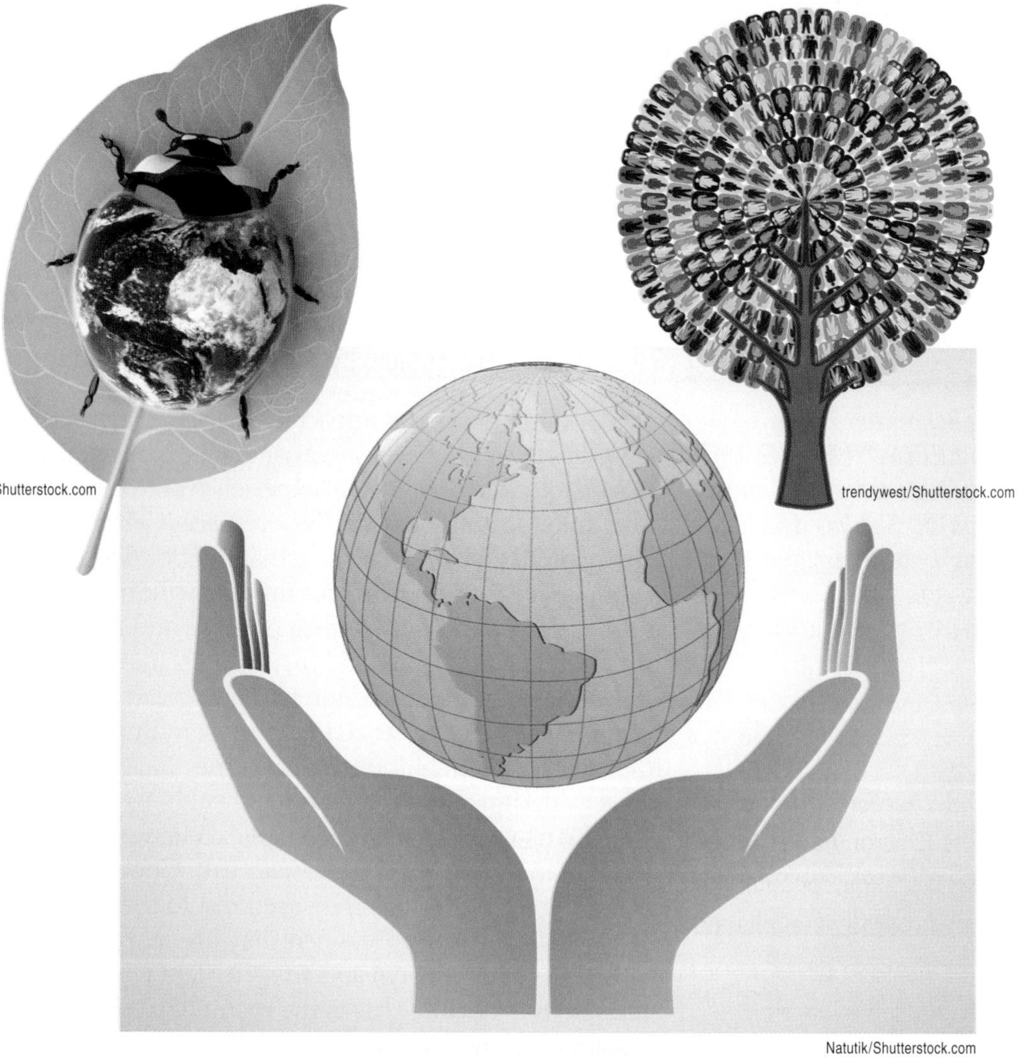

Konstantin Solodkov/Shutterstock.com

trendywest/Shutterstock.com

Natutik/Shutterstock.com

Figure 10-17 Symbols of sustainability serve as reminders to designers to use materials that have little or no long-term environmental impact. *What are some strategies interior designers can use to protect the environment and the health, safety, and well-being of their clients?*

in the earth is difficult to replace or renew as a natural resource. Instead designers can use reclaimed wood, resin, or glass countertops. Solid-surface counters are also available.

- Make an ecological choice of wood from a supplier who can verify through a chain of custody that the original trees came from an ecologically sustainable forest. Such forests are managed under guidelines of the international *Forest Stewardship Council (FSC)*.
- Specify products free of urea formaldehyde, a known carcinogen.
- Specify *green* paint and other finishing materials that have documented low levels of *volatile organic compounds (VOCs)*, or chemical-emitting materials that are the lowest possible levels. **Volatile organic compounds (VOCs)** are chemical-emitting gases or solids from interior products and materials that can cause short-term or long-term adverse health effects.
- Specify sustainable fabrics that support the use of materials from rapidly renewable or from post-consumer sources.
- Design around standard product sizes to reduce material waste.
- Consider the recyclability of all materials used to redirect them away from landfills, **Figure 10-18**. For example, reupholster or refurbish furniture rather than discard it.

As designers work in and with the construction industry, they are in a prime position to influence members of design and construction teams to protect and sustain the environment. Sustainable design strategies require human energy, thoughtful and earnest debate, and collaborative decision making. The payoff is well worth the effort. Designers can play a significant role in reducing the construction industry's impact on environmental problems.

Avoid Waste

Designers need to evaluate the effects of producing a particular interior. To do this, they must understand a product's journey from raw materials to installation. Design concepts should mimic nature—there is no waste in the natural world. It operates in balanced, continuous cycles.

Designing for longevity rather than annual fashion trends is the goal of good design. This involves specifying and purchasing materials in quantities closer to true need to help eliminate waste. At the beginning of any project, designers should ask the right questions. These include

- What is the purpose of this project?
- What materials are appropriate?
- What will happen to the design or structure when it is no longer useful?

Design Smarter

Evolving through generations of change are countless thriving animals, plants, and microbes—nature's ultimate engineers. To design smarter, interior designers can imitate nature's best ideas to create designs and processes to solve human problems. As you know, according to biologist Janine Benyus, this process is *biomimicry*.

With the use of biomimicry, a designer may study a leaf to invent a better solar cell or examine rain hitting the leaf to develop a new type of exterior house paint. Likewise, the study of microscopic-patterned sharkskin—a surface that

Environmental Impact of Buildings

According to the Environmental Protection Agency (EPA), buildings account for the following:

- 39 percent of energy consumption
- 68 percent of electrical consumption
- 38 percent of carbon-dioxide emissions (20.6 percent residential)
- 12 percent of water consumption (74 percent residential)
- 136 million tons of construction and demolition debris (43 percent residential)

Figure 10-18 By making informed choices, interior designers can help reduce the environmental impact of interior materials on the environment.

resists bacterial growth—led to the creation of bacteria-repellent coatings for light switches and door handles. These coatings dramatically reduce the transfer of bacteria among people in healthcare facilities.

Biomimicry is about viewing nature based *not* on what people can extract but what they can learn from its collective genius. Interior designers, as innate problem solvers, can design smarter by using nature as a model, measure, and mentor.

Exert Influence

Interior designers can influence behavior. Educate your clients on sustainable-design philosophies and green-design strategies. Help them know these strategies need not cost more over a life cycle. Ways to exert influence with team members is to use a checklist of green strategies such as

- **Low-energy design.** Reduce energy demands through passive design strategies (passive solar), specify energy-efficient products (electric light, appliances, electronics), and ensure the remaining energy demand is from a renewable source.
- **Water conservation.** Encourage team members to reduce water consumption both in the building and landscape. Specify plumbing fixtures, faucets, and appliances for water efficiency, **Figure 10-19**. These can include water-conserving showers (saving 75 percent water compared to ordinary showers), dual-flush toilets, and low-volume baths. Install an interior water meter to educate clients on usage.
- **Energy-efficient lighting and light controls.** Include fluorescent light fixtures or LED lighting. Unify automation of light controls such as occupancy/motion sensors, dimming controls, and automatic daylight dimming controls.

Specify Sustainable Materials

Designers must understand the life cycle of materials, minimize their environmental impact, and assess material merits. All materials have an environmental impact when obtained, processed, manufactured, transported, installed, maintained, and demolished.

To minimize environmental effects, designers can specify materials from renewable resources that avoid harmful by-products during the manufacturing process. This is a key area of influence for an interior designer. Questions to ask when choosing sustainable materials include

- Is the material needed?
- Is it reused or reclaimed?
- Is it sourced and processed near the building site?
- Does it have recycled content?
- Is it nontoxic during installation and use?
- Does it improve building performance?
- Does it require little maintenance or cleaning?
- Can it be reused or recycled?

Designers should be aware of unethical practices than can deceive clients. There are many manufacturers who market their products as green, but in reality some of these products are not. Be careful of **greenwashing**—the unethical practice of indicating a product is *green* when it is not. See the websites for *One Planet Living* and *The Green Guide* to view product assessment.

- **Check for pollutants and toxins.** Many interior materials that may be used in spaces produce fumes (such as new carpet), known as **off-gassing**. Such fumes can have a negative impact on occupant health.
- **Evaluate longevity and reuse.** After construction is underway and interior materials are specified, consider trading, restoring, or reusing a client's furnishings and accessories. During the Depression, this was called *making due*. During the 1980s, this was called *being cheap*. Today, we call it *being sustainable*. If new furnishings,

Marco Richter/Shutterstock.com

Figure 10-19 Contemporary faucets and showerheads can be aesthetically pleasing and water efficient.

CASE STUDY

Sick Building Syndrome

In 1989, five people died in a fire in Atlanta's 1720 Peachtree Street Building due to toxic-smoke inhalation rather than flames. One impact of toxins is *sick building syndrome* that affects human health. This relates to acute health conditions and discomfort effects that result from poor indoor-air conditions inside sealed buildings. Such buildings do not take in enough fresh air, resulting in off-gassing, smoke, and dust mites. Sick building syndrome strongly influences worker absenteeism, illness, and fatigue.

Investigate and Reflect

Use Internet or print resources to further investigate the problem of sick building syndrome. How prevalent is sick building syndrome? What examples exist near you? How can interior designers help prevent sick building syndrome? Give an oral report of your findings to the class.

fixtures, and equipment (FF & E) need to be purchased, select those that have a more timeless design and wear well.

- **Continue the discussion.** If questions arise during the design process, go back to rudimentary questions related to environmental ethics. What is the ethical relationship between people and the natural environment? How can designers minimize impact to the environment and maximize quality of design? There are also great resources to access during designbuild discussions. For example, if building or renovating a home, see the REGREEN website, codeveloped by USGBC and ASID.

Sustainable and Green Resources for Interior Designers

Interior designers continue to work with their team members in the built environment to produce energy efficient buildings without ignoring the people. They bring to sustainable- and green-design discussions the person-centered focus that is sometimes lacking. Penny Bonda, prominent writer, lecturer, and founding chairperson of *USGBC LEED for Commercial Interiors* was instrumental in bringing this person-centered focus to the LEED rating system.

Four green assessment methods used for buildings, representing four countries, include

- *Building Research Establishment Environmental Assessment Method (BREEAM)* from the United Kingdom
- *Green Star* from Australia
- *Comprehensive Assessment System for Built Environment Efficiency (CASBEE)* from Japan
- *LEED* in North America

LEED Certification—Commercial and Residential

The United States Green Building Council (USGBC) is an international organization that offers a LEED rating to those who are remodeling or building new projects. Currently, USGBC has certified 10 billion square feet of building space using the LEED rating. USGBC certifies about 1.7 million square feet per day around the world.

LEED is changing the way built environments are designed, constructed, and operated—from homes to commercial buildings to entire communities. USGBC certifies existing construction (renovations) and new construction. Initially geared to commercial buildings, there is now a LEED rating system for homes.

LEED certification is an independent, third-party verification that ensures buildings achieve high performance in human and environmental health. USGBC offers four ratings levels: *certified, silver, gold,* and *platinum.*

To gain the LEED rating, projects must satisfactorily meet the requirements under each of the environmental assessment categories and earn points. The number of points a project earns determines which of the four LEED ratings the project will receive. See **Figure 10-20** for the LEED environmental assessment credit categories.

Many interior designers become LEED Green Associates or at a more advanced level, LEED-accredited professionals (LEED-APs). They do so not only for the enhanced credibility but for the knowledge base it offers

LEED Environmental Credit Categories
Main Credit Categories
■ **Sustainable sites credits** encourage strategies that minimize the impact on ecosystems and water resources.
■ **Water efficiency credits** promote smarter use of water, inside and out, to reduce potable water consumption.
■ **Energy and atmosphere credits** promote better building energy performance through innovative strategies.
■ **Materials and resources credits** encourage using sustainable building materials and reducing waste.
■ **Indoor environmental quality credits** promote better indoor air quality and access to daylight and views.
Additional LEED for Neighborhood Development Credit Categories
■ **Smart location and linkage credits** promote walkable neighborhoods with efficient transportation options and open space.
■ **Neighborhood pattern and design credits** emphasize compact, walkable, vibrant, mixed-use neighborhoods with good connections to nearby communities.
■ **Green infrastructure and buildings credits** reduce the environmental consequences of the construction and operation of buildings and infrastructure.
Additional LEED for Homes Credit Categories
■ **Location and linkage credits** encourage construction on previously developed or infill sites and promotes walkable neighborhoods with access to efficient transportation options and open space.
■ **Awareness and education credits** encourage home builders and real estate professionals to provide homeowners, tenants, and building managers with the education and tools they need to understand and make the most of the green building features of their home.
Two Bonus Credit Categories
■ **Innovation in design or innovation in operations credits** address sustainable building expertise as well as design measures not covered under the five LEED credit categories. Six bonus points are available in this category.
■ **Regional priority credits** address regional environmental priorities for buildings in different geographic regions. Four bonus points are available in this category.

Figure 10-20 Gaining the LEED rating requires that projects meet the requirements under each of the environmental assessment categories.

when educating others. You can learn more about LEED on the U.S. Green Building Council's website.

NAHB—Residential and Multi-Family

In recent years, the National Association of Home Builders (NAHB) felt there was a need for a nationally recognizable standard for residential construction. The *National Green Building Standard (NGBS)* covers new construction, renovations and additions, site development, and multi-unit construction. The NAHB environmental categories include

- lot design, preparation, and development
- resource efficiency
- energy efficiency
- water efficiency
- indoor air quality
- operation, maintenance, and homeowner education

An interior designer may desire to become a *Certified Green Professional (CGP)* particularly if he or she is working in the residential construction industry. You can learn more about this certification on the NAHB website.

REGREEN—Residential Remodeling

REGREEN, launched in 2008 as a national residential remodeling program, is a partnership between the American Society of Interior Designers (ASID) and the USGBC. REGREEN professionals can assist with retrofit decisions that improve home performance, indoor air quality, and preserve the environment. The REGREEN website offers a multitude of case studies that list the green design strategies used for each project. In addition, it offers visuals showing before and after pictures. It is a great tool for interior designers to use when educating their clients.

REGREEN Remodeling Guidelines, a free booklet available on the REGREEN website, addresses major elements of green renovation projects such as the site of the home, water efficiency, energy and atmosphere, material and resources, and indoor environmental quality. Interior designers can apply these guidelines to all home projects such as a kitchen addition to an existing home or major additions to the house. Designers are now participating in the *REGREEN Trained Professional Certificate* program around the nation.

EPA Environmentally Preferable Products and Services

The *Environmental Protection Agency (EPA)* offers an *Environmentally Preferable Purchasing Program* which is a clearinghouse of information to guide federal agencies in purchasing environmentally preferable products and services. This program is not limited to federal agencies, but can also be used by businesses, nonprofit organizations, and state and local government agencies to provide purchasing guidance.

The standards and guidelines for products and services are written by national government agencies and third-party organizations from around the world. Environmentally preferable products and services offer a reduced-negative effect on human health and the environment. See the EPA website for more information.

Adaptive Reuse of Buildings

The best sustainable strategy is to, if appropriate, reuse existing buildings. This involves updating their energy efficiency and functionality for human habitation. It is a wasteful activity to just demolish older buildings as a standard procedure.

Adaptive reuse is the repurposing and redesign of an existing building for a new function and client, **Figure 10-21**. Most such buildings were designed decades ago for a specific purpose and then abandoned when they outlived their usefulness. By selecting an existing building, many firms discover that they can save money and help communities save natural sites that would otherwise be used, and thereby reducing *urban sprawl* (the spreading of urban housing and shopping centers on undeveloped land near a city). A good example of this practice is Google. They have many buildings, but only one building was new construction. All others have been recycled buildings.

Sean Pavone/Shutterstock.com

Figure 10-21 The Google building in New York City is an example of adaptive reuse. *Use the Internet to research more about the interior design of Google New York. Describe the key features of the interior design. Who are the other building tenants, and how does the building's redesign benefit them?*

Adaptive reuse, as a practice, often includes the revitalization of historic buildings. Although space alterations may occur inside, these structures offer period character with beautiful architectural details. Many times, historic buildings are also located in prime locations for future businesses.

Interior designers can specialize in adaptive reuse. They can retain historic desirable details, understand the new clients' needs, and creatively replan the interior. They can also inventory existing furnishings, fixtures, and equipment, and assist in planning the installation in a timely manner. Decisions on what to restore, replace, or keep depend on evaluation of the interior's condition, client's budget limitations, and practical needs.

Living Building Challenge

The *Living Building Challenge* is the built environment's most rigorous performance standard. It calls for the creation of building projects at all scales that operate as cleanly, beautifully, and efficiently as nature's architecture. To receive certification under the Challenge, projects must meet a series of ambitious performance requirements, including net-zero energy, waste and water, and over a minimum of 12 months of continuous occupancy. There are seven performance areas: site, water, energy, health, materials, equity, and beauty. See the Living Building Challenge website for more details and view case studies of projects that have met the challenge for green design.

> *“Everything designed disables or empowers!”*
>
> *Cynthia Leibrock, MA, ASID, Honorable IIDA*

Sutter Children's Hospital: Boulder Associates

Figure 10-22 Graphic symbols help children with wayfinding when they do not yet have the ability to read.

Design for All

As interior designers, the social and environmental responsibilities extend to all people. Specific populations of people—including children, older adults, the homeless, and those with mental, physical, or emotional disabilities—often require design features that enhance quality of life. With proper design, functional features and aesthetic designs for specific populations can be better for all people. Examples of design suggestions for two specific populations of people include children and elderly adults.

- **Children.** Designs that emphasize child safety benefit all users of a space. Because of their limited experiences, children may be unable to read signs, so they rely on graphic symbols, **Figure 10-22**. Placing windows at eye level can increase connections to nature or surrounding areas.

  Alcoves and small spaces encourage individual or small group play that enhances creativity and imagination. Scaling furniture to child-size increases self-sufficiency. Storage units can organize children's activities and develop sense of responsibility. Easy-to-clean surfaces not only prevent exchange of germs, but also allow the children to maintain their spaces.
- **Elderly adults.** As people grow older, they may become less active and move more slowly. In contrast, many older people live as they please and are both physically and intellectually active well into their eighties and nineties.

  Interior spaces that are accessible and efficient allow older adults to retain their independence. For instance, the ability to cook in an L-shaped kitchen offers a corner to lean against for a rest break. Countertops with a railed edge provide added support. Base cabinets with drawers and rollout shelves reduce the need to bend down, **Figure 10-23**. Deeper countertops help people with visual limitations spill less, while people who use wheelchairs prefer shallower counters. Shallow-depth cabinets and pantries facilitate reaching. Ranges and cooktops with front controls are easier to see and reach. Visual contrast is important in judging space and distance. In some public spaces, way finding is important. Color coding areas or floors are also helpful.

In the 1990s, when the *Americans with Disabilities Act (ADA)* became law, the number of people with disabilities was 48.9 million (U.S. Census Bureau, 2010). The ADA ensures equality for people with disabilities and allows them the same access that others enjoy, including employment, building access, and communication options.

Damon Searles Photography/Aneka Jensen Interiors

Figure 10-23 Pullout shelves are not only convenient to use but also eliminate the need to bend for those who have mobility challenges.

Barrier-free design provides a level of accessibility for people with disabilities. These designs, however, often result in separate and stigmatizing solutions such as a ramp that enters from a different entry other than the main one.

While ADA guidelines are useful for people with different abilities, design suggestions for people with temporary or permanent physical disabilities include

- **Motion disability.** Needs for those individuals with motion disabilities usually relate to addressing such physical barriers as curbs, stairwells and steps, and flooring materials of varying thicknesses. Doors also form barriers, particularly if they are too narrow or too wide.

  Where possible, include handrails, sliding doors, slide-out shelves, windowsills at maximum of 36 inches, hall space wide enough to allow a turning radius for wheelchair users, lever-type door handles for easier operation, floors that are flat with nonskid surfaces, and lighting sufficient to see areas of possible danger, **Figure 10-24**.
- **Hearing disability.** Over 20 million people in the United States have some type of hearing loss. Noise along with noise transmission, or reverberation, are issues to address. In addition, adequate light for communicating through sign language and lip reading is important.

ariadna de raadt/Shutterstock.com

Figure 10-24 Nonslip flooring helps eliminate slipping hazards. *Why should interior designers give attention to type of flooring materials especially for older adults and those who have mobility disabilities?*

Carpet and fabric wall coverings help reduce noise. Good lighting offers ability to see those who sign and psychological well-being. Facing furniture arrangements and round tables provide clear sight lines. Visual signals such as flashing lights can provide important cues for those with low or no hearing.

- **Visual disability.** People who are legally blind or who have low vision or vision loss rely on their senses of hearing and touch. Be aware of designing protruding objects that extend into the path of a person with a visual disability.

  Choose furniture with rounded corners and edges. Keep the grade of flooring level from space to space. Braille signage is critical with small groups of letters and numbers that can be easily read with the fingers.

Following are several movements that relate to designing better for all.

Universal Design

Universal design, a phrase coined by architect-trained Ronald Mace in the 1990s in the United States, is a process and approach to design. In Europe, similar concepts are known as *better design for all* and in the United Kingdom as *inclusive design.*

Universal design is a practice that is built on the premise that all people have changing needs throughout their lives and that as many people as possible should have access to good design. Private and public places should not be emblems of disability. Neither should they be places of segregation. Instead, the design of these spaces should be better functionally and aesthetically for anyone who uses the spaces.

For example, a wider entry area makes it easier to greet guests or to move furniture into the building. It also functions well for someone who uses a wheelchair. Horizontal door levers make it easier to open doors—for someone with a bag of groceries, a mother who has two toddlers in tow, and someone with arthritis who can no longer turn a knob. A thirty-inch-high rocker light switch helps a small child maintain independence by making it low enough to reach and accommodates a person who uses a wheelchair who may have difficulty lifting his or her arms.

You would think that if universal design is better for all, that it would be an easy sell to the client. Unfortunately, there is a perception that such solutions are only for those with disabilities. Many clients refuse to discuss universal design to avoid the thought of aging and disability when, in reality, it can help them in all phases of their lives.

To counteract this thinking, the designer shifts the client discussion to the advantages of universal design by using such terms as multi-level counters, easy-to-use equipment, large storage areas, and wide circulation areas. The designer also makes the point that every family or individual has relatives or friends who have some disability—even if temporary. Why not include a first-floor bedroom and bathroom for those who visit? Interestingly, although clients might not accept universal design strategies for themselves, they will for others.

Incorporating universal design typically does not cost more during building construction. It does require thoughtful, forward-thinking design solutions. With proper design, the interior spaces can reflect a functional, aesthetically pleasing design that allows people of all ages to live more comfortably, **Figure 10-25**.

Universal design is just good design! Its strategies make it fun to stay healthy. It considers function, appearance, and aesthetics—it is beautiful, seamless design that rejuvenates and regenerates. It supports the client and the caregivers. It supports the family and the business associate. Its appeal is for everyone—for their needs now and in the future.

There are seven principles of universal design published by the *Center for Universal Design (CUD),* North Carolina State University. See **Figure 10-26**.

Fred Fuhrmeister Photography/RB+B Architects, Inc.

Figure 10-25 Universal design in this school restroom offers equitable use for all people.

The Principles of Universal Design	
Principle	**Guidelines**
Principle One—Equitable Use: The design is useful and marketable to people with diverse abilities.	**1a.** Provide the same means of use for all users: identical whenever possible; equivalent when not. **1b.** Avoid segregating or stigmatizing any users. **1c.** Provisions for privacy, security, and safety should be equally available to all users.
Principle Two—Flexibility in Use: The design accommodates a wide range of individual preferences and abilities.	**2a.** Provide choice in methods of use. **2b.** Accommodate right- or left-handed access and use. **2c.** Facilitate the user's accuracy and precision. **2d.** Provide adaptability to the user's pace.
Principle Three—Simple and Intuitive Use: Use of the design is easy to understand, regardless of the user's experience, knowledge, language skills, or current concentration level.	**3a.** Eliminate unnecessary complexity. **3b.** Be consistent with user expectations and intuition. **3c.** Accommodate a wide range of literacy and language skills. **3d.** Arrange information consistent with its importance. **3e.** Provide effective prompting and feedback during and after task completion.
Principle Four—Perceptible Information: The design communicates necessary information effectively to the user, regardless of ambient conditions or the user's sensory abilities.	**4a.** Use different modes (pictorial, verbal, tactile) for redundant presentation of essential information. **4b.** Provide adequate contrast between essential information and its surroundings. **4c.** Maximize "legibility" of essential information. **4d.** Differentiate elements in ways that can be described (i.e., make it easy to give instructions or directions). **4e.** Provide compatibility with a variety of techniques or devices used by people with sensory limitations.
Principle Five—Tolerance for Error: The design minimizes hazards and the adverse consequences of accidental or unintended actions.	**5a.** Arrange elements to minimize hazards and errors: most used elements, most accessible; hazardous elements eliminated, isolated, or shielded. **5b.** Provide warnings of hazards and errors. **5c.** Provide fail-safe features. **5d.** Discourage unconscious action in tasks that require vigilance.
Principle Six—Low Physical Effort: The design can be used efficiently and comfortably and with a minimum of fatigue.	**6a.** Allow user to maintain a neutral body position. **6b.** Use reasonable operating forces. **6c.** Minimize repetitive actions. **6d.** Minimize sustained physical effort.
Principle Seven—Size and Space for Approach and Use: Appropriate size and space is provided for approach, reach, manipulation, and use regardless of user's body size, posture, or mobility.	**7a.** Provide a clear line of sight to important elements for any seated or standing user. **7b.** Make reach to all components comfortable for any seated or standing user. **7c.** Accommodate variations in hand and grip size. **7d.** Provide adequate space for the use of assistive devices or personal assistance.

Compiled by advocates of universal design, listed in alphabetical order: Bettye Rose Connell, Mike Jones, Ron Mace, Jim Mueller, Abir Mullick, Elaine Ostroff, Jon Sanford, Ed Steinfeld, Molly Story, and Gregg Vanderheiden. Major funding provided by: The National Institute on Disability and Rehabilitation Research, U.S. Department of Education. Copyright © 1997 NC State University, The Center for Universal Design.

Figure 10-26 The Principles of Universal Design provide a foundation for interior designers in meeting the health, safety, and well-being of all people.

Inclusive Design

Similar to universal design, *inclusive design*, originating in the United Kingdom, is now a popular phrase in Europe and Canada, too. It is a way of designing products and environments to make them usable and appealing to all regardless of age, ability, or circumstance.

According to the English Partnership (2008), the goal of inclusive design is to help users to remove barriers in the social, technical, political, and economic processes underpinning building and design. The Commission for Architecture and the Built Environment (CABE) indicates inclusive design is the process of developing places—planned, designed and built, managed and used—that offer ease of use, dignity, and a sense of belonging.

Both universal and inclusive design offer better and demand thoughtful design for people of all ethnicities—to move, see, hear, and communicate effectively. This includes older adults, children, people who are obese, people with temporary disabilities, and individuals who use wheelchairs.

Design for Aging-in-Place

Aging-in-place is the ability of people to remain in their current homes rather than relocate. It is a philosophy that promotes independence and livability in all living environments no matter the ages of the occupants or their level of abilities. Its principles allow an individual to remain in an environment of choice—often a house in a familiar neighborhood—for many years.

Priorities for aging-in-place include physical convenience, well-being, security, and comfort. This philosophy incorporates aspects of universal and barrier-free design, adaptability, visit-ability, and accessibility.

Designing for the aging population is a complex issue that will continue to gain more visibility as the U.S. population watches the baby boomers move to and through retirement. By 2025, baby boomers will comprise about 25 percent of the total U.S. population. Interior designers are in an influential position to assist this population through this phase of their lives with dignity and answers on how to remain independent.

The aging process can diminish physical and mental capabilities. Growing older often impacts mobility, agility, and how the senses of sight, hearing, touch, and balance diminish over time. Factors about aging for some older adults may also include denial, depression, loss of long-standing social connections, and dread of dependency on others.

How can designers help? There are many simple, low- or no-cost design adaptations and modifications to make to an existing bathroom, kitchen, or entry. These changes can make an older adult's daily routine flexible, easy to accomplish, and economical. The goal is to enhance access, mobility, and ease-of-use without detracting from the aesthetics of the place. Here are a few ideas from the ASID report on *Aging-in-Place* to consider:

- locate the master bedroom and bathroom on the ground floor
- increase ambient lighting levels; use rocker light switches
- select furniture with rounded corners that is easy to move as well as easy to get in and out of
- eliminate soft padding under carpet
- install an elevator or stair lift
- use color contrast as an aid to visual acuity

One of the greatest problems an interior designer faces when working with the aging population is that no one likes to perceive themselves as *old*. Because of this, clients may not want to consider aging-in-place features when they are building or renovating their homes. Building a relationship of trust is critical to providing thoughtful, long-term, design-savvy solutions rather than short-term, immediate fixes.

Interior designers with a special interest in aging-in-place may choose to obtain the *Certified Aging-in-Place Specialist (CAPS)* credential through the National Association of Home Builders (NAHB). To obtain this credential, interior designers (along with other industry professionals) are required to take a series of courses through NAHB. Once certified, professionals must complete 12 hours of continuing education every three years and pay a renewal fee to maintain certification. Review the NAHB website for more information about the Certified Aging-in-Place credential.

DESIGNER MATH SKILLS

Using Anthropometrics in Preschool Restroom Design

Designing space with anthropometric measurements in mind creates an environment that allows people to move easily and complete tasks without restriction. Anthropometric measurements guide design decisions. For instance, a designer considers the height of human sight lines when developing museum exhibits or recommends a dining table based on the space size, whether there are arms on the chairs, and the average width of adult shoulders. Thoughtful design considers body dimensions *and* how the user utilizes the space.

It is only when space or an object makes the user uncomfortable that awareness of its design becomes apparent. For instance, a parent who sits in a child-size chair quickly remembers the comfort, convenience, and even safety of furnishings ergonomically designed for an adult. How do you think children feel when they must use fixtures and furnishings designed for adults?

Toddler–Preschool Restroom Guidelines

Here are some general guidelines to use when planning restroom facilities for toddlers and preschoolers. *Note that facility requirements and group sizes may vary by state.*

- Restroom facilities are co-ed for children under age five.
- Adult guidance encourages independent self-care such as toileting.
- Partitions with no doors allow for supervision by adults.
- A separate adult restroom should be in or near the classroom.
- Toilet and sink areas should be in or near the classroom and can be shared between two classrooms.
- The typical facility ratios for determining the number of child-size fixtures include
  - One toilet and one hand-washing sink for 10 or fewer children
  - Two toilets and two hand-washing sinks for 10 to 16 children
  - If included, urinal fixtures should be no greater than 30 percent of toilet fixtures

Consider the design of a toddler-preschool facility. Using anthropometric measurements is important when designing such a facility for the most important users—small children. This learning environment includes smaller-scale furnishings, play areas, eating areas, and toileting areas that differ from those of a kindergarten learning environment. The average human dimensions of a two-year-old or four-year-old are quite different from those of a five-year-old.

Anthropometric Measurements of Average Human Dimensions

Toddlers and Preschoolers		Average Adult	
Body width (shoulder-to-shoulder)	12"–14"	Shoulder width	18"
Height	35"–39"	Height	5'–9"
Sight line AFF* (toddler)	26"–28"	Sight line AFF	5'–6"
Sight line AFF (preschooler)	30"–32"		

Toddler–Preschool Child-Size Fixtures	
Height of toilet seat AFF	10"–12"
Height of sink/countertop AFF, maximum	18"–22"
Partition height	36"
Mirror height, minimum	18"–22"

(*AFF=above finished floor)

(Continued)

DESIGNER MATH SKILLS *(Continued)*

State regulations dictate maximum group sizes and preschool staffing requirements based on the child/adult ratio. The younger the children, the higher the staffing needs.

The activities, group sizes, and staffing needs all impact the facility design, including restrooms. Designers must identify and incorporate relevant anthropometric measurements into the facility design.

The following shows an example of a floor plan and elevation of a toddler-preschool restroom.

Floor Plan View

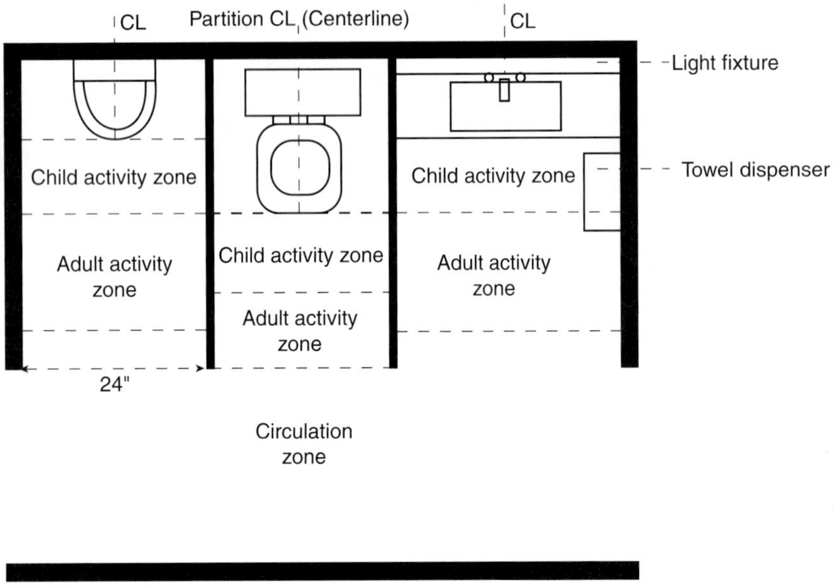

Toilet Measurements

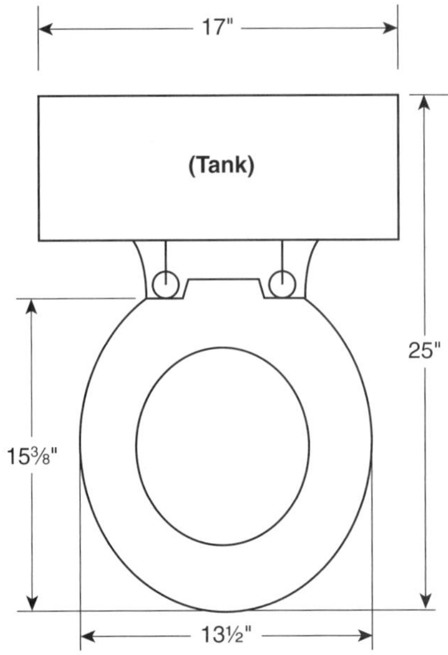

Elevation—Urinal, Toilet, and Sink Areas

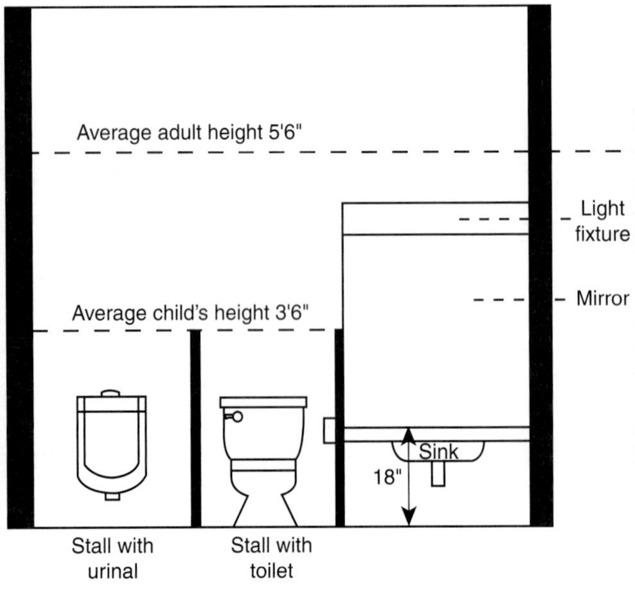

Elevation—Circulation and Activity Zones

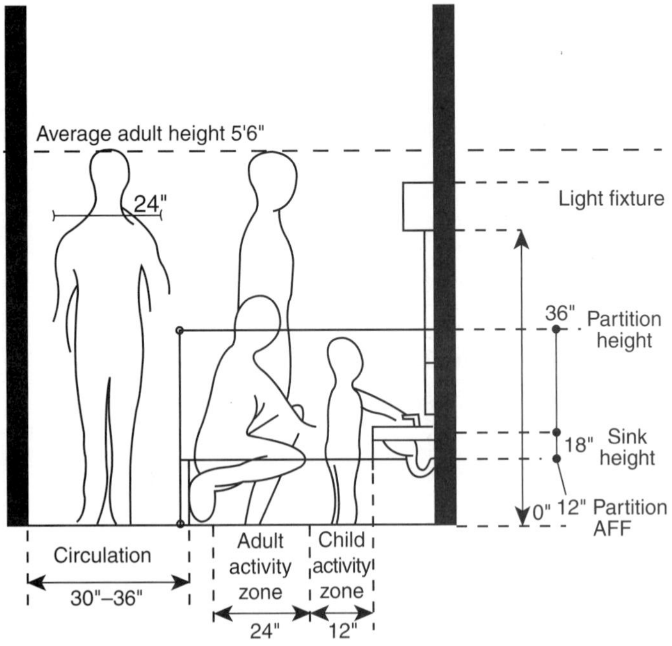

Goodheart-Willcox Publisher

Chapter 10

Review and Assess

Summary

- Theories on human behavior help designers explain how people perceive a space and behave within it.
- Privacy is a major contributor to a sense of control in people's environments.
- Designing for human comfort involves understanding how to position people in relation to others and the relationship of human body measurements to a volume of space.
- Knowledge of anthropometrics, ergonomics, and proxemics helps designers create spaces that meet human comfort needs.
- Interior designers scale interior spaces and arrange furnishings to meet proportions of users or clients.
- Designers develop spaces that provide safety and comfort to others.
- Socially responsible design considers the needs of future generations through preserving environmental resources, conserving energy, and using sustainable resources and materials.
- Socially responsible design involves avoiding waste, designing smarter, and exerting influence with clients and team members.
- USGBC, NAHB, ASID, and the EPA offer certifications and resources designers can use for socially responsible design.
- Designing for all people is a social and environmental responsibility of interior designers.
- Universal design, inclusive design, and designing for aging-in-place offer strategies to produce designs with proper functional features and aesthetics to meet the needs of specific populations and all people.

Chapter Vocabulary

Work with a partner to locate a small image online that visually describes or explains the following terms. Then share your images and explanations with the class.

adaptive reuse
anthropometry
barrier-free design
behavior-setting theory
biophilia
control theory
crowding
density
ergonomics
fun theory
greenwashing
off-gassing
personal space
personalization
place attachment
placemaking
privacy regulation theory
proxemics
sense-of-self theory
socially responsible design (SRD)
sociofugal
sociopetal
stimulation theory
third place
volatile organic compound (VOC)

Review and Study

1. What is the goal of the fun theory? Give an example of how this may be used in interior design.
2. How do the environmental psychology theories—behavior-setting, control, and stimulation—influence the design of interiors?
3. How does an interior designer use the sense-of-self theory when planning residential interior spaces? List three clues an interior designer might examine.
4. What is a *third place* location? Name three characteristics of third places.
5. What is privacy regulation theory?
6. What role does territoriality play in interior design and the promotion of human comfort?
7. Name three ways interior designers can shape space to diffuse physical crowding.
8. What benefits do people receive from affiliating with nature?
9. Identify one way that interior designers might use the Attention Restoration Theory to create interiors.
10. Contrast anthropometry, ergonomics, and proxemics.
11. Describe the difference between *sociofugal* space and *sociopetal* space. Give an example of each.
12. What is socially responsible design (SRD)?
13. What are four things interior designers and their clients do to sustain natural resources for future generations?
14. What is greenwashing and how can interior designers protect themselves and their clients against it?
15. List four sustainable and green resources for interior designers.
16. Name one design feature for children and one design feature for elderly adults that will enhance quality of life.
17. What are the seven Principles of Universal Design?
18. According to the ASID report on Aging-in-Place, what are four ideas for enhancing access, mobility, and ease-of-use for older adults to remain in their homes?

Critical Analysis

19. **Draw conclusions.** Think about a place to which you have *place attachment.* What qualities about the place caused you to form a positive person-place bond? How did it impact you as a person? Draw conclusions about how you can use your personal experience to help create place attachment for others with interior places.
20. **Identify evidence.** The author states that "People need to be comfortable, both physically and psychologically, in relation to the scale and proportion of their interiors." Use the text and other sources to discuss ways that anthropometry, ergonomics, and proxemics help the designer to meet these human needs. Show examples of these concepts in well-designed interiors.
21. **Assess and analyze.** Visit the *gbNYC* real estate group website—focusing on green building for commercial real estate in New York City—and read two or more articles on green building. Write a summary about the articles identifying green building strategies. Assess and analyze the articles for reliability of facts and objectivity of the author(s).
22. **Compare and contrast.** Research *CABE (Commission for Architecture and the Built Environment)* on the United Kingdom's Design Council website and review the *Principles of Inclusive Design.* Compare and contrast the CABE principles with the *Principles of Universal Design* used in the United States. Discuss how these principles are similar and different.

Think like a Designer

23. **Writing.** After reading the chapter, reread the *Design Insight* quote at the beginning. In your own words, summarize how environmental psychology and anthropometrics are critical knowledge a designer needs to promote the profession and advocate for social well-being.
24. **Writing.** Go to the *Fun Theory* website and review one or more videos to see how people used their creativity in a fun way to positively change behavior. Write a summary goal and outcome of the creative idea shown in the video(s) you watched.

25. **Writing.** Complete two field observations related to territoriality—one in a public place and one in a private place. Create a three-column chart to use during your observations. Label the columns from left to right as follows: *Primary Territories*, *Secondary Territories*, and *Public Territories*. During your observations, note key characteristics about territoriality in each place. How do people mark and defend their territories? Write a summary.
26. **Speaking/listening.** Choose one of the environmental psychology theories: behavior-setting, control, or stimulation. Review the theory and create a design concept for a room using it. Prepare a visual, oral report to share your concept with the class. Compare your design with those of your classmates. How are the designs similar and different? Why?
27. **Reading/writing.** Conduct research and capture data and illustrations about your "third place" using third place theory. Produce a booklet on your third place related to sense-of-self. Share your booklet with the class.
28. **Proxemics in action.** Evaluate how a person reacts when another invades his or her intimate or personal space. To test this reaction, half the class should leave the room for a minute while the remaining students spread out and find a location in the room. Have the students outside the room re-enter and randomly pick someone to tell what happened to him or her that day and get within the other's personal space. Assess and discuss the reactions of each team when someone impacts their personal space.
29. **Writing.** Go to the site map on the Humanscale website. Under "Form and Function," choose the link to "Ergonomics of Work." Watch the video called *The Four Pillars of Ergonomics*. Describe the four pillars and the characteristics of each in writing. Why is each pillar important to human functioning and health?
30. **Digital report.** Review the REGREEN program website, a partnership between ASID and USGBC. Read one of the Case Studies or REGREEN Projects. What was the problem focus of the Case Study or project? As you dig deeper in your reading, create a mind map to identifying the *who, what, when, where, why,* and *how* of the remodel project. Use a school-approved web application to write a blog about your findings for the class.
31. **Math practice.** Design a toddler-preschool restroom area to be shared by two classrooms of toddlers (24–36 months old). Total enrollment of the two toddler classrooms is 32 children. Create a list of relevant anthropometric measurements you will draw to scale in the floor plan. Draw and label the fixtures and partitions as well as circulation and activity zones using a scale of ½" = 1'-0". Use the *Designer Math Skills* feature on pages 337–338 as a guide.
32. **Math practice.** With a team member, measure a restroom facility in your school. Be sure to take measurements of the following dimensions: room size; stall size; partition height, depth, and thickness; sink; and counters. Include the measurements of an accessible stall and note the differences between stall and fixture size. Use your measurements to create an accurate floor plan view depicting your school restroom using a scale of ½" = 1'-0". Also draw an elevation view showing the outline of a person at the sink in the restroom. Identify circulation areas and activity zones.

Design Application

33. **Sustainability scavenger hunt.** To build your design resources for sustainability and green design, survey various design product and service company websites. You can start your search with local resources and expand to national and international resources. Then do the following:
    A. From your survey, choose five websites to review in depth.
    B. For each company's website, read the company history and its vision and mission statements related to sustainability, green design practices, and policies.
    C. Locate several images from each company that showcase its sustainable or green design practice, if possible.
    D. Create an illustrated, digital summary of each website, highlighting the history, vision, and mission of each related to sustainable and green design. If possible, use a school-approved web-based application to post and share your summary to the class web page.
34. **Portfolio Builder.** Save your room design from activities 27, 31, and 32 to your digital or hard-copy portfolio for future reference.

UNIT 3 Putting Knowledge into Practice

Image courtesy of Cathers Home Interior Architecture and Design Firm, Basalt, Colorado/Photographer: Michael Hefferon

Interior Materials and Finishes

Photography by Ben Tremper/Interiors by Associates III Interior Design

Chapter 11

Design Insight

"Materials and surfaces personalize interior spaces and influence how one experiences place. Interior finishes stimulate interaction, add character, express history, shape the physical appearance, communicate personal style, and encourage efficiency. Responsible selection impacts the environment."

Stephanie A. Clemons, Ph.D.

Learning Targets

After studying this chapter, you will be able to

- understand the role of the interior designer in selecting materials and interior finishes to protect the health, safety, and well-being (HSW) of clients.
- summarize key characteristics regarding the selection of interior finishes—including sustainable and green materials—to create the desired look for walls, floors, windows, and ceilings.
- differentiate between types of windows and types of window treatments.
- identify different textiles and finishes, their characteristic properties, and uses in interior design.

Introduction

Interior finishes are exciting and dynamic elements a designer selects once space planning is complete. Designers select them according to their client's personal preferences and echo them in other interior spaces.

Interior finishes are those materials applied to any exposed interior surface such as a wall, floor, or ceiling that connect rooms and styles together. Similar to the decision about what car to buy, the designer makes the selection of interior finishes consciously and purposely. If done well, interior finishes give users of a space the sense that they belong. Creativity is all it takes to transform any interior space into a true expression of individuality.

The Importance of Finishes

Often the first to attract attention when walking into a space, interior finishes on walls, ceilings, and floors should capture the style and mood of the client's concept. They express trends, evoke feelings of warmth and comfort, and humanize the space through the use of varying textures. Finishes reveal information about place as well as the traditions or culture of the people in both residential and commercial design (for example, in hotels and restaurants).

Appropriate selection of finishes is crucial. The factors that influence designer selections include visual characteristics—such as tactile qualities or pattern and color—and such performance characteristics as maintenance, life-cycle evaluation, and acoustical properties. For example, interior designers use the type and positioning of certain interior materials to enhance sound control. They also carefully select client's floor coverings based on function, durability, sustainability, and maintenance factors. They specify color based on differing occupant needs such as for an Alzheimer unit versus a children's daycare center.

What Are Interior Materials and Finishes?

Those interior finishes that cover walls, floors, and ceilings include such products as paint, carpet, wallcoverings, flooring, and countertops, **Figure 11-1**. Interior designers stay abreast of trends—global, technological, and environmental—that relate to these materials through

Photographer: Don Riley/Interior Designer: Andrea Schumacher Interiors

Figure 11-1 Interior finishes such as these bring a design to life. *What are the unique finishes in this space? What characteristics help bring this design together?*

such sources as their industry product representatives. The manufacture and use of interior finishes each have different properties and specifications for an interior. Continuous professional education ensures the designer is knowledgeable about specifying products accurately and appropriately for the application or occupant.

Interior designers often look forward to this phase of the design process. Interior finishes bring the concept to life. The application and placement of the finishes side-by-side in the space offer an opportunity to be creative.

Finishes are very visible to the client. Therefore, much discussion goes into their selection and reflection of the design. Finishes are difficult for the client to picture in a three-dimensional space. In recent years, many technologies, such as photorealistic software and interactive websites, have become available to designers and consumers. The manipulation of such technologies can assist the designer in illustrating how the interior will look with the selection of specific interior materials.

In addition to impacting the visual appearance of a space through the creative selection and application of interior materials, designers also impact the health, safety and welfare (HSW) of the public through their selection. The *inappropriate* selection of interior materials can

- promote flame spread if a fire begins
- result in toxic fumes that impact the occupant's health
- enhance the spread of bacteria that relates to illness and disease

Both state and federal codes and standards contain stringent requirements regarding fire, **Figure 11-2**. The intentions of such codes is to either inhibit the ignition of interior materials—such as draperies—or control the speed with which flames travel across surfaces, such as a ceiling. The purpose of such codes and standards is to provide time for staff or occupants to safely evacuate if fire erupts. The bottom line is that interior designers must consider the code and standard requirements for interior finishes in a specific type of interior *prior to* specifying them for that space.

There is also a growing awareness that poor *indoor air quality (IAQ)* and *sick building syndrome (SBS)*—which result from the combination of sealed buildings and pollutants—impact the occupant's comfort, health, and well-being. The Environmental Protection Agency (EPA) states that indoor air often contains more pollutants than outdoor air.

Standards Organizations and Codes

Interior designers often refer to the following standards organizations and codes during the design process:

- **American National Standard Institute (ANSI)**
- **ASTM International**
- **International Code Council (ICC)** (publishes the following codes)
  - International Building Code (IBC)
  - International Residential Code (IRC)
- **National Fire Protection Association (NFPA)** (publishes the following code)
  - International Fire Code

Figure 11-2 Interior designers often refer to codes and standards when specifying products and finishes.

Some individuals have allergic reactions when toxins are emitted from new carpet or paint used during the remodel or new construction of an interior, **Figure 11-3**. To promote efficiency of heating, ventilation, and air conditioning (HVAC) systems, many contemporary buildings are *sealed* environments. With the application of new interior finishes to walls or floors in a sealed building, the toxins do not easily dissipate. This may cause illnesses and allergies in employees and occupants. In the workplace, these issues impact employee productivity and can increase absenteeism, which affects an employer's profitability.

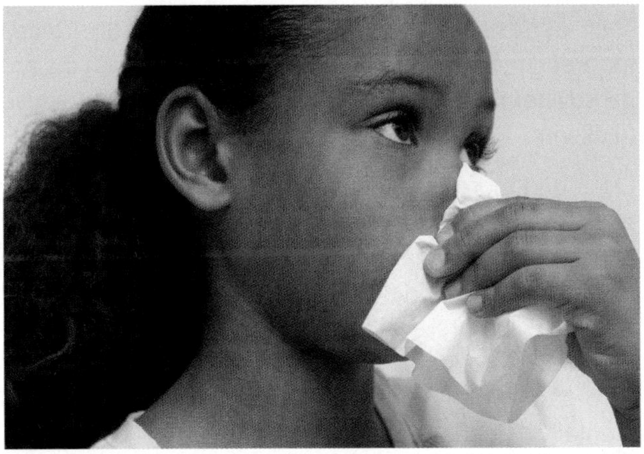

bikeriderlondon/Shutterstock.com

Figure 11-3 Allergic reactions can result from a combination of sealed buildings and gases and toxins emitted from new interior finishes. *What can interior designers do to help eliminate allergic reactions for their clients?*

One strategy to avoid interior pollutants is to refrain from specifying materials that trail pollutants with them. If that is not an option, then the designer must recommend filtering and cleaning the air before occupants move into the building or space. Once the air is clean, it is important to keep it clean with proper HVAC filters and indoor plants (a sustainable strategy) that cleanse the air of any harmful pollutant emissions that may remain.

Wherever possible, interior designers have the responsibility to protect the occupant's health. Recently, the U.S. Green Building Council (USGBC) LEED revised the Indoor Environmental Quality (IEQ) credit (4.3—Low-Emitting Materials) that addresses the need to use low-emitting interior products to ensure indoor air quality (IAQ). USGBC also offers indoor-air-quality credits for IEQ management during construction and before occupancy. IEQ credits involve specification of low-emitting materials such as adhesives, paints and coatings, and carpet systems as well as indoor chemical and pollutant source controls, daylight, and views. Other areas, such as LEED CI (commercial interiors), require project credits for

- materials and resources
- resource reuse of furniture and furnishings
- recycled content of materials
- use of regional materials
- rapidly renewable materials
- certifiable wood

Healthier interior spaces are becoming more probable as interior designers educate clients about the importance of purchasing of green, eco-friendly products. These products not only alleviate harmful side effects such as toxins but are also kind to the Earth. Prices for green products are decreasing and the products are improving; therefore, they are becoming more attractive to clients.

More and more businesses are seeking to incorporate environmental conscientiousness in the production of their sustainable materials. There is less river pollution in the manufacturing of interior materials. Resources and websites are available that identify credible, certified green products. To avoid *green washing,* reliable third-party organizations help designers identify environmentally friendly interior materials and processes, **Figure 11-4**.

There are a variety of ways to verify that the products you specify for interiors are healthy and safe for your client and the environment. The most obvious place is the product's label or its **Material Safety Data Sheet (MSDS)**—a document that contains important information about the characteristics of and actual or potential hazards of a substance, **Figure 11-5**. While MSDS sheets provide basic information, they often lack transparency because the information comes directly from the manufacturer.

A more rigorous source of information about a product's material health and environmental impact is an **ecolabel**—a second- or third-party verification of sustainability claims. The GREENGUARD® mark on a product represents third-party verification that it is low-emitting which contributes to healthy indoor air quality (IAQ). It is an example of a third-party certification program that is well-respected in the industry.

Walls

As you recall, there are two types of interior walls: load-bearing and non-load bearing. *Load-bearing walls* support the roof and structure of the building. *Non-load-bearing walls* are interior partitions used to shape space. To frame a wall, steel studs are common in commercial buildings, while wood is typical in residential applications.

Once the structure framing is complete, installation of the plumbing, insulation, and electrical wiring in the walls occurs before covering them with gypsum board. *Gypsum board* is a mixture of gypsum (calcium sulfate), additives (often starch, paper pulp, and emulsifiers), and water that forms a thick paste or slurry. The paste or slurry is spread between two layers of paper in thicknesses of 3/8 inch to 3/4 inch, pressed together, and then heat dried before ready to use in wall applications.

Some gypsum board has a third-party fire-resistant rating. This gypsum board has glass fibers imbedded in the gypsum paste. The product is not fireproof, but does slow fire spread to allow building occupants to escape. In parts of the United States, other names for gypsum board include drywall, wallboard, or *sheetrock®*. In addition to walls, builders use gypsum board to create archways, rounded corners, fireplace surrounds, stairway enclosures, and columns.

Functionally, walls establish visual and acoustical privacy. The wall-treatment application on gypsum board can either diminish or increase acoustical sound. Aesthetically, walls are the largest surface on which to place interior finishes and materials that establish

Independent *Green* Certification Organizations	
Cradle to Cradle[CM] Certified Products Program	This third-party certification system, administered by McDonough Braungart Design Chemistry (MBDC), reviews materials for overall life-cycle impact. This comprehensive approach starts with a baseline of environmentally benign ingredients that ends with a full life-cycle evaluation of the product. Cradle to Cradle encourages the use of closed-loop materials or those easily composted, or those that may provide fuel for other systems when a material's original use ends.
Forest Stewardship Council® (FSC)	The Forest Stewardship Council (FSC) is an independent nonprofit group that promotes third-party certification of sustainably managed forests. Its certification rating system is based on management practices in three areas: harvesting practices, ecosystem health, and community benefits. FSC verifies the chain of custody from the original forest through the supply chain.
GREENGUARD® Underwriters Laboratory (UL)	GREENGUARD Certification is a part of the Underwriters Laboratories (UL) Environment that helps manufacturers create—and consumers identify—interior products (such as flooring) and materials that have low chemical emissions, improving the air quality in areas in which the products are used. GREENGUARD certifies performance of the healthy aspects of a material.
Green Seal™	As a U.S.-based, non-profit environmental organization, Green Seal offers third-party certification for those companies, services, and products that meet specific sustainability criteria. It is also an ANSI-accredited standards developer. Green Seal is used as a tool to help designers and consumers find truly green projects.
Healthy Building Network (HBN)	The Healthy Building Network (HBN) is a nonprofit organization that strives to advance the best environmental, health, and social practices. HBN's goal is to introduce new, healthier building materials to the market. This organization has played a major role in developing green building guidelines for healthcare facilities. HBN was also the first to develop an online evaluation tool for building materials.
Pharos Project, Inc.	As a project of the Healthy Building Network (HBN), Pharos created a tool that cuts through prolific greenwashing. The project's foundation pairs those who use building materials with those who study the products' impacts on health and the environment. It offers information concerning carpets, paints, resilient flooring, and wood flooring as well as building materials such as thermal insulation and adhesives. HBN's goal for Pharos is to become the leading evaluation tool for the building industry.
Rainforest Alliance™	As an international nonprofit organization, The Rainforest Alliance is dedicated to the conservation of tropical forests by transforming land-use practices, business practices, and consumer behaviors.
SCS Global Services	Based on Federal Trade Commission (FTC) guidelines and ISO standards (*International Organization for Standardization*), the suite of SCS's material content certification programs validate claims for pre- and post-consumer recycled content as biodegradable, no added formaldehyde, and no added urea formaldehyde content.
Smart Certified©	Sustainable Materials Rating Technology (SMaRT) evaluates life-cycle and supply-chain attributes to create a comprehensive market definition of a sustainable product. Incorporating standards from FSC, LEED, Green Seal, and other programs, it measures the triple bottom line: social, environmental, and economic equity performance.

Figure 11-4 Independent, third-party certifying organizations help interior designers and their clients choose green interior finishes with low chemical emissions.

Travis Klein/Shutterstock.com

Figure 11-5 Material Safety Data Sheets contain important information about characteristics and potential hazards of various substances.

a certain visual style or mood in the space. There are many issues to consider when specifying or selecting wall finishes. A few of these include

- maintenance (for example, grass cloth wallcovering is not easy to clean)
- texture desired, and location and type of interior
- budget
- style preference for the space
- room size
- awkward areas to minimize
- length of time occupants spend in a space (an office, for example)
- objects to hang on wall surfaces
- moisture and humidity of the region
- color and pattern preferences

The purposeful selection of a wall-surface treatment enhances both function and aesthetics of the space. Walls and partitions are finished in one of three ways: paint, wallcoverings, or **cladding**—an overlay of masonry products such as brick or stone. The following describes some of each of these interior materials applied to wall surfaces.

Paint

Applying paint to walls is human nature as noted by cave paintings in Europe and Southwest Asia that date back about 32,000 or more years. One of the first civilizations was developed in Egypt. There, to ensure the soul would continue to exist, artists painted scenes of the dead person's life in the pyramid burial chambers. Paint was only for royalty due to the costly process.

Evidence from a few thousand years later shows **frescoed walls**—or paintings done rapidly in water color on wet plaster—on the walls of the Roman resort city of Pompeii. Now, a few thousand more years later, you find a people who really enjoy color on their walls. With paint today, you can easily choose a perfect palette, decorate with bold colors, or use it to add interest to a typically uninteresting wall. As the most inexpensive and easy way of changing an interior environment, paint

- protects the wall surface
- comes in a multitude of colors
- can imitate many other interior materials such as stone and wood when applied with a technique known as **faux painting** (Many historic buildings have examples of columns or walls painted to simulate marble.)

Selecting a paint color, or a palette of colors, is a very difficult task for most clients. To judge how a paint color will look in an interior from a small paint chip is unwise. To solve this issue, many paint companies now sell small samples of premixed paint to physically test the color in the room. Lighting (both natural and electric) as well as adjoining colored walls and materials significantly impact paint color. Paint manufacturer websites offer simulations of interior spaces with selected paint colors. This is a good opportunity to determine personal color preferences. However, once a client chooses a color, it is best to physically test the color in the client's interior, **Figure 11-6**.

Artazum and Iriana Shiyan/Shutterstock.com

Figure 11-6 Paint is a low-cost interior finish that can have a dramatic effect on a space. *Why do you think it is a good idea to physically test a paint color in a client's interior before application to the entire space?*

Paint is available in several reflectance levels, including

- **Flat.** This finish offers a rich, soft-looking surface with little reflectance that produces less glare. It washes poorly and, therefore, is not a good choice for kitchens and bathrooms.
- **Eggshell or satin.** With a slightly higher light reflection, this finish can handle light maintenance, such as scrubbing.
- **Semi-gloss.** These products provide midrange sheen with good scrubbing durability. It is one of the best choices for kitchens and bathrooms.
- **High gloss.** With a very shiny surface and easy washability, this finish shows wall surface imperfections, such as a poor texture job.
- **Suede.** This paint has a textured, fabric-like finish that creates a suede effect.

Specialty paints are also available on the market. Paints used for specific purposes include magnetic and chalkboard paints. Magnetic paint contains child-safe magnetic ingredients that allow actual magnets to adhere to the surface, which allows ease in hanging children's artwork. Chalkboard paint is erasable and safe to use with chalk in children's areas.

When applied in normal thicknesses, flame-retardant paints provide a *Class A* flame-spread rating over noncombustible wall material. Interior designers specify flame-retardant paints for many public installations such as schools, hospitals, offices, factories, and warehouses.

Mold-resistant paints are available for use in specific regions of the United States. Mold and mildew thrive in warm, damp, or humid areas that receive little air circulation and direct daylight, such as bathrooms, kitchens, and basements. Mold-resistant paints contain additives that help prevent mildew growth on the paint's surface. Before using mold-resistant paint, it is important to properly prime the surface.

Some tips about using and specifying paint include

- **Not all paints are created equal.** Paint with a higher price point is more likely to require fewer coats to cover the surface. Choose the best quality possible to meet client needs.
- **A good paint job requires a good prep job.** Scrutinize the subcontractor's preparation of the surface. Make sure the surface is clean, cracks and holes are filled, and the texture is consistent before paint application.
- **Keep touch-up paint on hand.** No matter how careful a client is, wear and tear is common on walls. Remind clients to keep some of the same paint on hand for occasional touchups. Also, remind them that daylight can fade paint just as it will fade a textile product.

DESIGNER MATH SKILLS

Calculating Paint Quantities

Paint is an inexpensive and quick way to change the appearance of a space. Select the colors and type of paint for each area and then determine the amount of paint you need. Choose the paint type by function and durability of the reflectance level (see page 351). A gallon of paint covers approximately 400 square feet while a quart of paint covers approximately 100 square feet. Purchasing paint by the gallon is generally more cost effective.

When painting a space, the focus is often on the walls with little thought given to baseboards, trim, doors, windows, ceiling, and other architectural details. In reality, paint requirements for these other architectural details must be accurately calculated, too, in order to remain on target with a client's budget.

Calculating Paint for Wall Areas

Example 1: To calculate the wall area, first add together the width measurements for all walls. Then multiply the total wall-width measurement by the ceiling height. To determine the number of gallons of paint, divide the square footage of wall space by 400 square feet. Here are the calculations for a room that measures 12 feet by 15 feet.

12 ft. + 12 ft. + 15 ft. + 15 ft. = 54 ft.
54 ft. × 9 ft. = 486 sq. ft. wall space
486 sq. ft. ÷ 400 sq. ft. = 1.22 gal.
(round up to 1 gal. + 1 qt.)

Designers typically do not deduct window or door openings from the wall calculations unless they fill the majority of the wall. For example, if a room has windows that measure 12 feet by 9 feet totaling 72 sq. ft., this leaves only 36 sq. ft. of wall area to paint. In such cases, it would be well worth the time and money to calculate the difference.

Calculating Paint for Baseboards and Trim

When calculating a straight line of trim for baseboards, crown molding, stair rails, banisters, balusters, windows, or doors, measure the linear feet and the width (or depth) of the trim. Then convert the total to square feet to make your paint calculation.

Example 2: Suppose your client wants to add crown molding to a room that measures 12 feet by 15 feet. To determine the linear feet of crown molding, add together the width of each wall. For example, for a room that measures 12 feet by 15 feet, you would add

12 ft. + 12 ft. + 15 ft. + 15 ft. = 54 linear ft.

Then convert the linear feet to square feet based on the width of the molding to determine the amount of paint needed for the crown molding (linear ft. × width = sq. ft.). Because the molding is 6 inches wide, or half a foot (½ or 0.5 ft.), multiply the linear feet by 0.5.

54 linear ft. × 0.5 ft. = 27 sq. ft.

Repeat the same steps for calculating paint for baseboards. Trim width up to 3 inches wide should be calculated as a quarter of a foot (¼ or 0.25). This means you should multiply the linear feet by 0.25 ft. to determine square feet as follows:

12 ft. + 12 ft. + 15 ft. + 15 ft. = 54 linear ft.
54 linear ft. × 0.25 ft. = 13.5 sq. ft.

Here is how a designer might organize paint specifications for some of the spaces described above.

Type of Paint/Color	Area to Paint	Total Square Feet	Amount to Purchase
Eggshell finish, Color #812	Walls	486 sq. ft.	1 gallon + 1 quart
Flat finish, Color #812	Ceiling	180 sq. ft.	2 quarts
Semi-gloss finish, Color #1077	Baseboards, 13.5 sq. ft. Crown molding, 26 sq. ft. Door and trim, 27 sq. ft. Window sill trim, 3 sq. ft.	69.5 sq. ft.	1 quart

- **Be smart when storing paint.** Remind clients to keep unused paint in airtight containers and store them in a cool, dry place.
- **Discard unused paint properly.** Provide state and community guidelines for proper paint handling and disposal to your clients. Never pour paint down the drain.

Paints are not only potentially hazardous to the environment, but also to your client's health. Paints can release hazardous chemicals, or *volatile organic chemicals (VOCs)*, into the air people breathe. Do you know that *new house smell*? This smell results from VOCs. Although not all VOCs are toxic, many of them have short- and long-term health consequences that include asthma, headache, nausea, and eye irritation. Asthma is the fastest-growing, chronic, incurable childhood disease that is responsible for more than 14 million missed school days each year according to the Asthma and Allergy Foundation of America. Therefore, use proper air filtration or open windows when applying paint to a surface. As a commitment to healthy interiors, paint companies now offer interior paints that do not emit VOCs.

Brick

The use of brick is a great way to pull the outside and inside together. Brick is a lasting material. Combining brick with other materials often gives rooms a warm and comfortable feeling, **Figure 11-7**.

Brick was one of the first building materials. Mud deposits along river beds—particularly after a flood—could be formed into cakes and used in the construction of huts. Ancient ruins of mud-brick homes can be found in Turkey, Greece, Scotland, Rome, Africa, Spain, Mexico, and colonial America. Well-known as both a structural material and a finish material, the process of brickmaking has changed little since the production of the first fired bricks thousands of years ago.

Clay is one of the most abundant natural mineral materials on earth. Brick's physical properties include compressive strength and durability. The *American Society for Testing and Materials (ASTM)* specification assigns a grade of severe, moderate, or negligible weathering to accommodate varying climates and applications of brick. The strength of brick construction depends on both its material durability and the layout pattern.

Typically rectangular and made of clay, shale, and water, bricks often have both interior and exterior applications. Brick surface textures can create interesting wall designs and shadows that replicate the variety of designs you see in nature. Bricks require little maintenance and are available in a variety of earth-friendly colors. Brick color is determined by raw materials and firing temperatures. Many manufacturers produce more

ifoto/Shutterstock.com

Figure 11-7 Brick is a natural material that adds casual warmth to interiors.

than 100 colors. Brick installation can be in a variety of patterns. Textures of brick include smooth, brushed, wire-cut, stippled, and bark. Many interior applications today utilize recycled bricks from demolished buildings.

Interior applications for brick include fireplaces, flooring, and walls. Interior walls commonly use *thin* brick for coverings that are ½ inch to 1 inch thick. Although thin brick has less fire and sound resistance, structural strength, and fewer insulation properties, its usage can include complex wall shapes, soffits, or arches. Paint can increase light reflection on interior brick walls.

Brick manufacturers use raw materials typically close to their location. Clay depletion is usually not an environmental concern. As a masonry material, brick has been largely ignored by modern designers. However, brick is reused more than most materials and is appropriate for today's designs. Massive quantities of antique bricks are often reclaimed from commercial buildings that have outlived their original purpose, such as abandoned warehouses. The durability and maintenance-free characteristics of brick make it a good material to consider.

victor zastol'skiy/iStock/Thinkstock

Figure 11-8 This polished concrete floor easily reflects light. *What is the benefit of high albedo in concrete floors?*

Concrete

People often use the words *concrete* and *cement* interchangeably. These materials are in fact different. *Cement* is a binder, a substance that holds other materials together. *Concrete* is a mixture of cement and various mineral aggregates, such as gravel, with water. When mixed with water, the cement hardens and binds the concrete mass. Concrete is inherently strong when compressed.

As a very affordable and malleable material, concrete gains strength over time. Moisture, mold, or pests do not weaken it. Due to its nonporous characteristics, it requires little maintenance. It is naturally fire-resistant and forms a highly effective barrier to fire spread. Concrete walls and floors slow the passage of heat; therefore, they reduce temperature swings and decrease the need for heating or air-conditioning. The high *albedo*, or reflective power, means concrete reflects more light and absorbs less heat, **Figure 11-8**. This also results in cooler temperatures.

Walls in commercial, industrial, or educational facilities such as elementary schools often use exposed, raw concrete. This durable surface handles a lot of abuse, yet requires little maintenance. If desirable, a concrete surface can be plain or have a pattern. Application of patterns occurs through acid etching or staining, sandblasting, or *bush hammering*—a textural finish a mason creates with a bush hammer, which has a grid of pyramid-like points. Acid staining colors include black, brown, blue-green, light tans, greens, browns, tans, and terra-cottas. At installation, concrete can also be steel-troweled for a smooth, hard, dense surface. It is difficult, but not impossible, to hang objects on concrete walls.

Concrete is one of those raw, industrial finishes designers like to use for a contemporary, edgy look. Commonly, designers use concrete in floors, fireplaces, counters, sinks, and water features. Although there are many positive reasons for using concrete, there are some negatives designers should consider. Usage of concrete for floors or counters requires sealing of the concrete. Standing on concrete or other hard-surface floors can cause human fatigue. As a surface for counters, concrete requires periodic resealing and may be subject to surface cracks over time.

Concrete is generally a local material and can be recycled as an aggregate for new concrete. Water pollution from washout water is the main environmental issue with concrete.

Glass Block

Glass offers both functional and aesthetic qualities. While glass is hard and rigid, it is also malleable when heated. Sand is the primary material in glass and is readily available. Glass is highly transparent, transmitting most of the light that falls on it. While glass does transmit heat through thermal conduction, it also adds sparkle and reflection to any interior.

Glass block, or glass brick, is composed of two halves of pressed glass. Designers often use it in non-load-bearing walls and in such applications as curved or three-quarter high walls. The beauty of glass block is that it permits light penetration into adjoining interior spaces and offers good insulation.

Use of glass block is common in commercial and residential applications where *some* visual privacy is a requirement, **Figure 11-9**. Such interiors can be bathrooms and offices. It is also useful as window openings and as dividers. Manufacturers can make glass block with a clear, textured, or patterned face.

Another popular interior glass application is the use of patterned or textured glass. During production, manufacturers press the glass with patterns such as flutes, grids, and random designs. Patterned glass can be sandblasted, or color coatings can be applied. Designers use patterned glass for decorative purposes as well as indoor and outdoor furniture, windows, and panels. Glass tiles in kitchens and bathrooms add a shimmer and contemporary look to the space. Maintenance of glass is minimal. Glass is a nonpolluting material.

Plaster

Used since ancient times, the earliest plaster consisted of lime, sand, animal hair, and water. Egyptian tombs feature paintings on the plaster walls lining the pyramid interiors. Fresco artwork adorned the walls of ancient Roman homes. Plaster is a very old material, traditionally used for walls and ceilings. It is used today to match existing finishes in older buildings.

Plaster is a combination of lime, sand, and water that forms a paste and hardens to a solid after it dries. Historically a time-intensive process, plaster was troweled on wood lath strips in three different coats and then sealed. Lath was the foundation of a plaster wall—hence the phrase **lath and plaster** is sometimes used to describe a wall type. Today, application of plaster may be over gypsum board or concrete block. Plaster finishes still require great skill and take time to apply.

Plaster is ideal for walls, ceilings, and partitions because it can be straight or curved. As needed, plaster can be textured, molded, cast, stamped, stenciled, colored, and

Warren Diggles Photography/Jon Rentfrow, Rentfrow Design, LLC

Figure 11-9 Glass block allows light penetration while offering visual privacy.

carved, or given applied textural designs to create interesting shadows in interiors. Usage of plaster with wood beams in interiors gives an *old world* feel. It can be applied directly to brick, clay tile, or concrete masonry. It is also a great surface for the application of other surface finishes such as paint.

Ornamental decoration is another application of plaster. **Ceiling coffers** (plaster panels between ceiling beams), **cornices** (horizontal building elements that crown walls and furnishings), egg and dart moldings, medallions for lighting fixtures, or columns can be cast in molds at a workshop and installed onsite.

Once hard, plaster can chip, crack, or peel. To repair simple hairline cracks in plaster surfaces, the plasterer opens and cleans out the cracks, dampens the cracks, and fills them with a thin application of plaster-crack filler. Repair of ornamental plaster takes expertise and time. Plaster is popular in both residential and commercial applications.

Plaster is nontoxic and safe. It can serve as a protection to buildings and their occupants as it offers passive fire resistance. Formerly, plaster's fire resistance was increased with asbestos, which is now a banned substance. Removal of asbestos-containing plaster materials is widespread and requires professional labor.

Stone

Historically, stone was a structural material that became an interior material with the application of paint and decorative elements. Egyptians painted hieroglyphics on stone. Interiors of stone churches and cathedrals were embellished with decorative tile, marble, and glass. Other great, ancient stone buildings can be found in England, Spain, North Africa, Peru, Italy, and India.

Stone is classified as igneous, sedimentary, or metamorphic rock that comes from a quarry. Because it contains embedded fossils and objects, stone often captures the time and place of an era, people, and location. Designers appreciate the imperfection and variability of stone as it brings character, texture, and aspects of nature into the interior. No two pieces of natural stone look the same. Aesthetically, stone communicates permanence and stability as it seemingly is immovable and gives the perception of lasting forever. Many man-made materials look like natural stones.

After removal from the quarry, experts cut, saw, or split the stone. The composition of materials determines the hardness of stone. For example, granite is hard, marble is softer, and sandstone is softer yet. Some of the most popular natural stone wall applications today use granite, limestone, marble, and terrazzo. Due to the weight of stone, its installation is typically as a **stone veneer**—a thin ornamental facing.

Use of stone is common in both commercial and residential settings for such items as fireplace surrounds, focal walls, and special features in rustic lodges, lofts, and restaurants, **Figure 11-10**. Medium to large applications of

Photography by Audrey Hall/Interiors by Associates III Interior Design

Figure 11-10 This natural stone fireplace communicates rustic stability in this interior space.

stone include flooring, furniture, toilet partitions, countertops, and columns. Smaller applications of stone include tiles (for example, tumbled-stone tiles are a favorite design feature for a counter backsplash), *stone mats* such as inlaid pebble river rock in a floor, sinks, pedestals, stacked stone accent walls, and the back wall of a shower. Some stones are translucent, such as onyx. If backlit, its design can be a textural accent in any space.

Stone adds a pleasing natural texture and beauty to any interior. It is easy to maintain with clean water and a brush. Avoid installing stone in areas where grease may stain it.

Stone works well as a passive solar material. It collects the sun's heat and then releases it as cooler air hits the surface. A simple stone ledge next to a window can collect heat in this manner. In its more natural state, stone can save energy. To reduce transportation and fuel costs and enhance sustainability, use rock and stone from local quarry sources.

Tile

Wall tile comes in ceramic, quarry, porcelain, and glass. As a popular choice, glass tile adds sparkle, shimmer, and depth of color as light reflects through the material, **Figure 11-11**.

All tiles create a hard surface; come in many shapes, colors, and patterns; and are quite durable unless chipped or broken. Square tiles come in an infinite range of sizes, although trends affect tile size. Although the 4-inch by 4-inch tile size is most common, current trends show that smaller and larger sizes are popular, too. Rectangular tiles are gaining popularity and range up to 24 inches by 48 inches, offering a slab-like look similar to natural stone. Common layouts include rectangular tiles set in a traditional brick (or running bond) pattern or plank-like pattern.

Many tiles come in preset sheets, ready to be set with adhesive. After the adhesive dries for 24 hours, grout application can occur. *Grout* is a thin mortar that fills the spaces between the tiles. The width and color of the grout joints impact the final design and appearance of the tile wall or floor. Tight grout lines are best to use on floors to prevent dirt or sharp rock from chipping the grout.

All tiles are abrasion resistant and offer a high degree of moisture resistance. Along with slip resistance, these properties make tile a good choice for areas exposed to

Interior Designer—JJ Interiors/Ron Ruscio Photography

Figure 11-11 Wall tiles come in a wealth of shapes, colors, and patterns and are extremely durable. *Describe the visual effects of the tiles in this bathroom.*

water. Designers use tiles extensively in both commercial and residential applications for accent walls, backsplashes in kitchens and bathrooms, flooring, and fireplace surrounds. Mosaics, comprised of tiles, are popular as accents in walls, fountains, and floors. Glass tiles are particularly popular because the material sparkles and reflects light. Tips for using tiles include the following:

- Ensure natural stone tiles such as travertine or marble are sealed properly.
- Always purchase an additional five to 10 percent more tile than needed. This allows replacement of broken tiles or selection of preferred tiles for natural materials.
- Choose a grout color that complements tiles to blend the grout lines.
- Consider using a border tile on a wall or backsplash to add a three dimensional quality to the application.

Wallcoverings

Every decade, trends and new styles introduce new wallcoverings. The available volume of patterns and colors make wallcoverings a popular choice. A wallcovering is no longer exclusively paper. It may be cork, vinyl, fabric, grass cloth, metal, leather, or a combination of materials. Depending on the material and/or backing, wallcoverings may be washable, scrubbable, stain resistant, strippable, and pre-pasted for easy application. Usage of flexible wallcoverings improves the durability and appearance of a wall. They are attached with wet or dry adhesives, **Figure 11-12**.

There are several types of common wallcoverings today, including vinyl, paper, and textiles. Vinyl wallcoverings are affordable, extremely strong, durable, lightfast, colorfast, scratchproof, impact-resistant, and are easy to care for. They can last 10 to 15 years in high-traffic commercial spaces such as hotel hallways or healthcare lobbies.

When durability or hygiene is important, vinyl wallcoverings may be the answer. They can be antibacterial, hygienic, and treated to stop the development of microorganisms and the growth of bacteria, mold, and mildew. Unfortunately, vinyl wallcoverings emit vinyl chloride and other VOCs. You can smell the off-gassing after hanging them in place. This makes vinyl wallcoverings environmentally problematic.

Photographer: Kimberly Gavin/Interior Design: Andrea Schumacher Interiors

Figure 11-12 Flexible wallcoverings are made from a variety of materials that enhance the aesthetics and durability of walls.

The use of wallpaper dates back to dwellings found from 200 BC in China. During the Industrial Revolution, wallpaper became a less-expensive option for people in the U.S. Similar to vinyl wallcoverings, wallpapers come in many patterns, textures, and **colorways**—arrangements of colors for various patterns and textures of wallcoverings or textiles. Of primary use in residential interiors, the designer and client view samples in large books in various colorways.

For residential applications, wallcovering rolls range from 20.5 to 28 inches in width and come in single or double rolls. Because wallcovering is hung in strips, it is important to align any pattern repeat on each strip where the two edges meet. This is called a **pattern match**. To ensure wall protection and a smooth surface on which to attach the wallcovering, use a good quality primer. Priming the walls before hanging wallcovering ensures proper adhesion to the surface.

Fibers for textile wallcoverings are often cotton, linen, silk, or manufactured fibers. Backings provide dimensional stability. Textile wallcoverings bring great texture and beauty to a space. Although many colors and designs are available for both residential and business environments, designers rarely specify textile wallcoverings in areas for which wear and maintenance is a concern. Tips for selecting and using wallcoverings include the following:

- Determine the pattern match before ordering (see the label on the pattern) because this impacts the amount you order.
- Order the correct amount of wallcovering at time of purchase to ensure your client has the correct number of rolls with the same **dye lot number**—a number that indicates the rolls of wallcovering were printed during the same print run to ensure color match.

Manufacturers make specific wallcoverings for such commercial facilities as hotels, apartments, offices, schools, and hospitals. These wallcoverings must pass specific performance standards related to flammability, tear strength, abrasion resistance, washability, scrubbability, and stain resistance. They are often solid vinyl or have vinyl coatings to enhance durability and cleanability. Commercial wallcoverings are typically 54 inches wide.

Many websites and manufacturers use software to illustrate how wallcoverings may look in an interior space. With the abundance of wallcoverings available today, this type of tool makes it easier to picture what the pattern or texture may look like after installation.

Wood

Historically, wood was used in ancient days of Egypt, Greece, and Rome. Britain, parts of Europe through Italy and Spain, and many Asian countries used wood both functionally and decoratively.

Wood as a natural insulator is used for walls as a solid board or as a sheet of plywood. Wood boards come in 2½-inch and 4-inch to 12-inch widths. Lumber is identified by its rough dimension before it is trimmed to its finished size at the lumber mill. Actual sizes are approximate lumber dimensions after trimming. For instance, a 2-inch by 4-inch stud is actually 1 ½ inches by 3 ½ inches.

As a natural material, wood is eco-friendly and multifunctional. Wood can be used effectively and decoratively on all surfaces of the interior: ceilings, walls, and floors, and in most any room of a residential space. However, there are restrictions where wood can be specified. For example, fire and building codes restrict the use of solid wood as a wall surface application in commercial interiors.

Either stock or custom, **millwork** is the common name for wood used on walls as built-in units, cabinetry, baseboards and crown molding, and paneling. If not used in standard measurements, millwork often requires custom detail drawings to communicate the design to the builder or subcontractor, **Figure 11-13**.

Link to History

Use of Wood Flooring Throughout the Ages

From ancient through modern times, wood was and is a common and popular flooring material for commercial and residential interiors. In colonial America, local white pine wood was cut into planks and held in place with pegs. Later, floors were stained and covered with Oriental rugs in homes of the wealthy. In the early nineteenth century, stenciling was done directly on wood floors to mimic rugs, parquet floors, tile, and marble. About 1885, machine-made tongue-and-groove wood floors became available. In the Victorian era, intricate *inlaid-border patterns* were used of light and dark woods. Later, strip oak became the common flooring rather than planks. This continued into the mid-1950s. It was at this time that mortgage approval of carpet caused the replacement of wood floors with carpet. Wood became a specialty flooring application.

Analyze It!

Research the top trends in wood flooring. Analyze the websites for such flooring manufacturers as Armstrong, Bruce, and Shaw, or organizations such as the World Floor Covering Association. What are recent trends in wood flooring? How are these trends similar to or different from trends throughout history?

A Photographer: Emily Minton Redfield/Interior Design: Andrea Schumacher Interiors

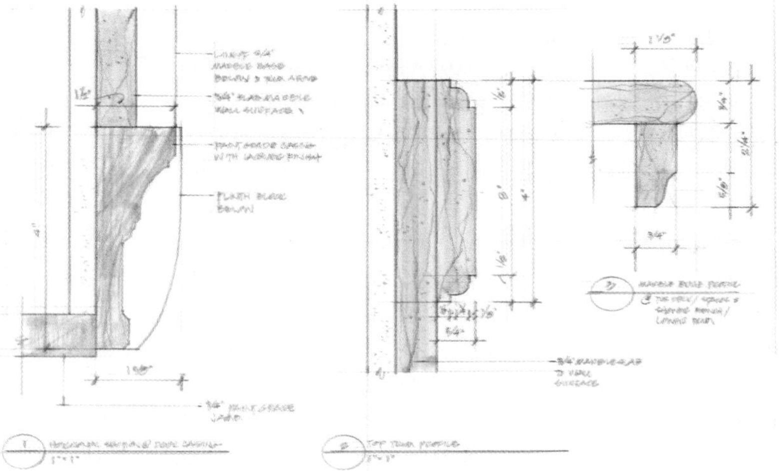

B Image by Jacqui McFarland

Figure 11-13 Wood is an eco-friendly material that adds warmth and texture to interiors (A). Some millwork requires the interior designer to create custom millwork detail drawings (B).

Today, there are many residential styles, from informal rustic and cottage style to minimalistic modern, that incorporate wood paneling in interiors. Sometimes the wood is run horizontally and other times vertically. The width of the wood panel and whether it is sanded or stained makes a difference in appearance. Natural or stained wood adds the feeling of warmth and texture to any space. Wood paneling may also be painted or antiqued.

Sustainably, you would want to specify local woods rather than tropical woods that are not renewable. Paneled wood walls are also made from reclaimed wood or wood that is from a beetle kill forest.

Floors and Floor Coverings

Today, clients have a myriad of choices within the categories of soft and hard flooring materials. Soft flooring materials include carpet, cork, and resilient flooring. They provide warmth and insulation. Hard surface floor coverings include wood and tile. They are smooth and easy to maintain. Because flooring materials usually account for more surface area than anything else in an interior except walls, they have a greater impact on indoor air quality. As people walk, play, and sit on floors, flooring materials wear down and people breathe anything these materials emit for many years.

When considering sustainability factors related to flooring, there is no correct answer. All types have a set of trade-offs. Safety, renewability, durability, off-gassing, and recyclability are issues that come up regularly when choosing flooring. Designers should weigh the following factors when making flooring decisions with clients:

- desired flooring type—soft or hard
- room function
- room occupants
- cleaning and maintenance issues
- aesthetic requirements (color, pattern, and texture)
- acoustical properties
- installation time and cost of materials
- location of installation
- tasks or activities taking place in the space
- client or occupant allergies
- personal preference
- potential hazards for people with physical or visual limitations

CASE STUDY

Interface, Inc.

"We're going for zero. Mission Zero. Zero emissions. Zero waste. Zero oil."

Historically, carpet companies have produced a lot of toxins and by-products that are harmful to the environment. This is why it was quite revolutionary when, in 1994, *Interface* founder Ray Anderson challenged his company, *Interface, Inc.* to pursue a bold new vision. The challenge was: "To be the first company that, by its deeds, shows the entire industrial world what sustainability is in all its dimensions—people, process, product, place, and profits—and in doing so, become restorative through the power of influence."

As a result, Interface's challenge, *Mission Zero,* was articulated and set in place. The goal of Mission Zero is to eliminate all environmental impacts by 2020. Its current goal is *ZERO oil*. It is a tough challenge since much carpet is made from oil, but the company is more than halfway in meeting its goal. By using less energy and material, making products that last, and recycling old carpet into new, they are making progress toward their goal. However, the company cannot make it to zero alone, and it does not want to. Interface works with its nylon suppliers to get pre- and post-consumer recycled content materials for their products by sending them the fiber from reclaimed carpet. They are also sharing what they have learned with other companies to help them make oil a part of their past as well.

Interface, Inc. is the world's largest designer and maker of carpet tile. Their products are purchased and installed in the Americas, Europe, Asia Pacific, Middle East, and Africa.

Investigate and Reflect . . . .
To learn more about the success of Interface, Inc. on reaching their goal, see the *Mission Zero* website. Write a summary regarding additional information you learned about the Mission Zero accomplishments. In what ways might other companies learn from the Mission Zero successes?

Soft Floor Coverings

Soft floor coverings typically consist of fibers—either natural or manufactured. These fibers then form carpets and rugs during manufacturing.

Carpet

Nomadic tribes in Asia (Turkey or Iran) are believed to be some of the first carpet weavers using wool from local sheep. In colonial America, the first floor coverings were herbs, rushes, or sand. Later, colonists created rugs from strips of old clothing that were braided into mats. It was not until the arrival of wealthy immigrants that Oriental rugs made an appearance in the United States.

Historically, carpets were generally for the wealthy. According to the *Carpet and Rug Institute (CRI)*, the carpet industry began in the United States in 1791 when William Sprague started the first woven carpet mill in Philadelphia. In 1839, Erastus Bigelow invented the power loom for weaving carpets. As a result, carpet production doubled in the first year and tripled by 1850. Today, carpet bought in large amounts is often less costly than a hard-surface flooring material.

Carpet comes in many colors, patterns, and styles that reflect trends of the furnishings industry, **Figure 11-14**. It can be *sculpted,* which means it has a three-dimensional appearance, typically with higher loops cut and lower loops uncut. It is available in different heights, densities, and weights. It also comes in different fibers, such as wool or nylon, that impact the look, feel, durability, and maintenance of the carpet. Different carpet grades reflect differences in consumer price points.

Carpet can enhance the quality of any interior—a special consideration in the hospitality (lodging) industry. Its degrees of softness make it comfortable and inviting for residential applications. For hospitals, carpet can have antimicrobial properties needed for germ resistance and maintenance. It absorbs 10 times more noise than any other flooring material, making it ideal in office settings and bedrooms. Carpet provides a coziness that tends to humanize otherwise sterile settings.

GWImages/Shutterstock.com

Figure 11-14 Designers and their clients may physically examine carpet options. *What factors might the designer and client consider when evaluating carpet?*

Its thermal insulation properties make carpet attractive in cold regions. Its cushioning capabilities reduce fatigue related to standing for long periods of time, making it attractive for medical, institutional, retail, and restaurant installations.

The *Carpet and Rug Institute (CRI)* is a trade association that represents the carpet and rug industry. CRI provides information on carpet construction, daily maintenance and long-term care, and technical information. Performance of carpet is evaluated by its

- flammability rating
- ease of maintenance
- stain resistance
- sound absorption
- static electricity control
- appearance
- resistance to sunlight
- resistance to wear and abrasion

For residential interiors, the most important carpet factors are the colors available, the physical comfort and tactile feel of the carpet fibers, quality, and the cost per square yard. Depending on the type of interior, priorities for selecting carpet in commercial settings often relate to the carpet's durability in regard to foot traffic, maintenance, and cost.

Carpet typically comes in **broadloom**—a term describing roll-goods woven on a wide loom of more than 54 inches. Generally, broadloom carpet widths are 12 feet, 13.6 feet, and 15 feet. Installers roll out carpet into an interior, measure, cut, seam, and install it.

Carpet also comes in modular carpet tiles that measure 12 inches by 12 inches, 18 inches by 18 inches, and 24 inches by 24 inches. Use of carpet tiles in commercial interiors is common where access to the subfloor for technology needs, such as computer cabling, is important. Such tiles are also easier to replace in commercial settings with high-traffic areas. Some carpet manufacturers, such as Milliken, offer online design features to custom design the carpet tile, **Figure 11-15**.

According to Interface, Inc., "even the most beautiful floor covering can harbor bio-contaminants." Bio-contaminants such as fungus, mold, mildew, and bacteria are commonly brought on to any carpet surface during use. These contaminants have a negative impact on indoor environmental quality. Therefore, Interface, Inc. developed *Intersept*, a preservative that is registered with the EPA as a protectant for carpet tile. It prohibits the growth of such contaminants and offers microbial growth control, which is critical particularly in healthcare and education environments.

Interface also introduced a new *Net Effect* collection of modular carpet that supports the benefits of sustainable product manufacturing. Net Effect contains up to 81 percent recycled content with 100 percent recycled content yarn. It is part of Interface's Mission Zero promise to eliminate negative environmental impacts by 2020.

Ninety percent of all carpet manufacture uses the tufting method. According to the Carpet and Rug Institute, **tufting** is the manufacture of carpet by inserting tufts of yarn through a carpet-backing fabric. The surface finish can have cut and/or loop ends. Production of *woven* carpet, another common carpet type, occurs on a weaving loom by interlacing the *warp* (length) yarns and *weft* or *filling* (width) yarns.

Dyes set the color in the carpet fiber. Just like wallcoverings, each run of carpet has a dye lot number. When ordering carpet, proper interior measurements are critical to ensure ordering the correct yardage amount of the same carpet dye lot. Otherwise, on installation, the carpet color may not match.

Maintenance and durability of a carpet relates directly to the type of fiber used in the carpet.

Photo Courtesy of Milliken/www.millikencarpet.com

Figure 11-15 Some manufacturers offer online custom design services for creating custom designs.

Common carpet fibers include

- **Nylon.** This is a manufactured fiber used in almost 90 percent of all carpet sold today. Nylon carpet is produced in a large variety of colors, has a luxurious soft feel, and excellent resiliency. It absorbs little water or liquids, therefore, stains remain on the surface, making them easy to remove.

  This fiber has excellent *abrasion resistance*—the ability to resist wear from continual rubbing that relates directly to durability. Its use minimizes wear and tear in heavily-used circulation paths.
- **Wool.** This high-quality natural fiber is from sheep. It is inherently flame resistant, has good soil resistance, and has excellent **colorfastness**—having color that retains its original hue without fading or running. Wool's beautiful, true colors relate to the dye-absorption properties of a natural fiber.

  Wool is naturally resilient—it bounces back quickly from foot traffic. Although wool carpet can cause static, special fiber treatments can significantly reduce static. Wool carpet is high in cost and some people may be allergic to this fiber.
- **Acrylic.** This manufactured fiber feels like wool. It is easy to maintain and is static resistant. Acrylic has excellent abrasion resistance and colorfastness. This fiber is not as resilient as nylon.
- **Polyester.** Also a manufactured fiber, polyester comes in excellent colors, is resistant to water-soluble stains, has good fade resistance, and is noted for a luxurious feel underfoot.

  Residential settings are the primary use for polyester carpet. It has good soil- and wear-resistance. On the negative side, polyester carpet can crush with wear and is not desirable in heavy-traffic areas, such as in commercial installations.

In addition to choices of carpet fiber, you also have choices in the type of carpet pile. The **pile** is the surface face yarns that form loops during tufting or weaving. The greater the number of loops in the pile, the more dense and durable the carpet will be. Carpet with a lower-density pile is less durable. The density of the pile impacts the carpet appearance, feel, and wear or abrasion resistance. See **Figure 11-16** for common carpet piles.

In commercial settings, the Americans with Disabilities Act (ADA) requires carpet pile to be ½ inch or less in height to allow wheelchairs to roll easily over its surface. In addition, carpet edges must be fastened to floor surfaces. These standards ensure accessibility for all people in commercial interiors.

Interior designers often design creative, custom area rugs for residential and commercial clients. Many also design

Common Carpet Piles	
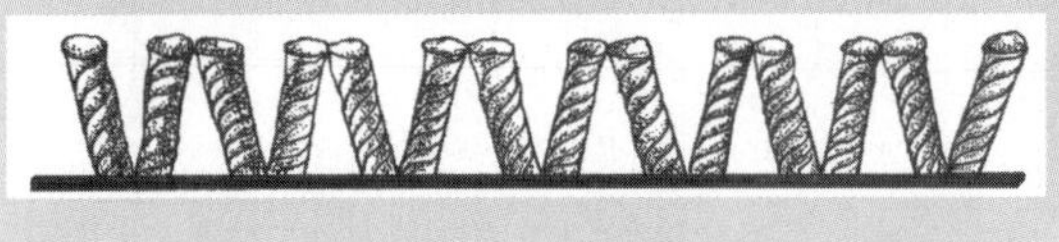	**Cut pile.** As the most popular carpet pile, the top surface of carpet is made of cut fibers. It offers a soft feel and can be sculpted to create an embossed design. Feet tracks and furniture indentations will show in this carpet. Cut-pile carpets with highly twisted yarns hold their shape longer, making them a smart choice for high-traffic areas.
	**Berber.** A loop-pile carpet style tufted with thick yarn, such as wool or nylon, is berber. It often has random specks of color in contrast to a base hue. This carpet style has a full, comfortable feel with an informal, casual look.
	**Shag.** This carpet has long cut-pile yarns. You can use a carpet rake to refresh the appearance between vacuum cleanings.
	**Loop.** The carpet surface has uncut loops. It is also available in multilevel loops and highly twisted yarns. Loop carpet wears very well.
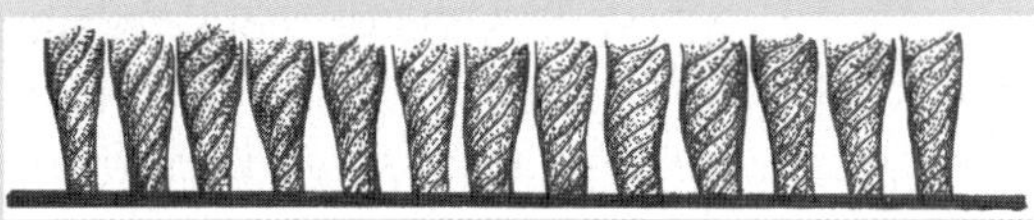	**Plush.** A dense cut-pile carpet in which the cut ends blend together. It offers a smooth, uniform texture and appearance. It hides footprints and vacuum marks, and is therefore desirable for busy households. It adds casual beauty to a room.
	**Tip-sheared.** This carpet is a loop-pile carpet with some loops sheared on the surface to create areas of cut pile and loops.
	**Frieze (free-ZAY).** These carpets are made from hard-twisted yarns in a cut pile. The cut yarns have a curly, textured surface because the yarns are extremely twisted. The density of these carpets minimizes footprint marks.

Sherilyn (Lixue) Yin, International transfer design student, CSU, ECNU

Figure 11-16 Familiarity with various carpet piles helps the designer make better recommendations to meet client needs.

custom carpet or broadloom patterns for commercial clients who order a large amount of carpet such as for an airport terminal. Custom broadloom usually comes in 12-foot widths, but may also be 13'-6" or 15' wide. Creation of **custom runs**—runs of carpet the manufacturer produces separately to client specifications—occurs through a partnership between the designer and the carpet manufacturer. To create such products, designers use the following process:

- Develop and draw designs using a computer and CAD software.
- Examine the set of construction drawings to do a **take-off**—the process of estimating how much product to order.
- Produce the design in a carpet sample—called a **memo sample**—for the client to view and approve.
- Manufacture the carpet through the partnership with the carpet manufacturer.
- Order the amount needed for the client's spaces.

Through this process, the interior designer can achieve a very custom *design* look for the client. These custom patterns must take into consideration the age and physical capabilities of the users. It is important to avoid carpet designs that create visual tripping hazards for those using the space.

Commercial interiors may require certain carpet treatments to address specific client needs. For instance, an antimicrobial treatment on carpet inhibits the growth of microorganisms and controls bacteria and fungi that are a major source of indoor-air-quality contamination. Healthcare facilities often require use of such carpet treatments. Another treatment offers protection from static electricity. Friction with carpet can produce an electrical shock. This static shock can cause a piece of equipment to malfunction. Use of this antistatic carpet finish is common in office settings.

Because flammability is a life-safety issue, carpets also have flammability ratings for interior spaces. For designers, there are legal consequences if carpet does not meet flammability standards for a specific type of interior. Failure to comply with flammability standards can result in property damage and liability lawsuits. Carpet representatives and manufacturers supply written documentation of the fire-code compliance for their products.

There are many brands of carpet for both commercial and residential spaces. For a client, selecting a carpet brand, fiber, and color can be an overwhelming task. For a designer, your carpet manufacturer representatives can help pare down the choices because of their product knowledge. With knowledge of client needs, such representatives can help you select a product suitable for the task. Manufacturer representatives are often an excellent resource for the designer because they can ensure the timely order and delivery of the product.

There are many green- or sustainable-design strategies for use with carpet. These include

- **Closed loop recycling.** In this process, carpet fibers are chemically renewed and reused in remanufacturing first-quality carpet.
- **Downcycling.** In this process, recycling of nylon carpet fibers occurs by melting them for use in low-value, plastic applications such as a park bench or speed bump.
- **Carpet reclamation.** This process involves heavy-duty cleaning and repair of used carpet for reinstallation.
- **Carpet recycling.** This process involves recycling various carpet parts. Photographs of carpet recycling can be found on the American Plastics Council website.

With the market for sustainable flooring growing at a steady pace, it is important for designers to keep up with the changes. New sustainable product standards are in development and under adoption consideration, and updates to green codes are underway. In addition, various organizations are introducing innovative product-evaluation tools. The following is an overview of flooring standards and certifications, **Figure 11-17**.

Flooring Standards and Certifications

- **CA Section 01350.** This is an emissions test method developed by the State of California that is applicable to all flooring types. Its full name is "Standard Method for the Testing and Evaluation of Volatile Organic Chemical Emissions from Indoor Sources Using Environmental Chambers Version 1.1." It limits a total of 35 VOCs that are known to off-gas from products. This is considered a product emissions baseline.
- **ECOLOGO Product Certification.** This lifecycle-based, multi-attribute sustainability standard for flooring was developed by ECOLOGO to help purchasers identify holistically greener products. Flooring products from bamboo to resilient flooring to modular carpet have been certified using this standard. ECOLOGO is part of Underwriters Laboratory (UL).
- **FloorScore® Program.** This program was jointly developed by the Resilient Floor Covering Institute (RFCI) and SCS Global Services and focuses on product emissions. Products that have this label meet indoor air quality emissions criteria of CA 01350, LEED ratings of the U.S. Green Building Council, Collaborative for High Performance Schools (CHPS) in conjunction with California, and the Green Guide for Health Care.
- **GREENGUARD Children and Schools Certification Program.** GREENGUARD is a third-party, health-based certification created and run by the Underwriters Laboratory (UL). More than 1300 flooring products have been certified to their standard of stringent emissions that limits total VOCs and certain chemical usage.
- **Green Label Plus.** The Carpet and Rug Institute's ecolabeling program focuses on product emissions and ensures that certified products meet CA Section 01350.
- **NSF/ANSI 140 Sustainability Assessment for Carpet.** NSF/ANSI 140 and NSF/ANSI 332 are based on life-cycle assessment principles. These assessments cover areas such as supply chain feedstock, manufacturing emissions, and energy use. Underwriters Laboratory (UL) certifies hundreds of carpet products to this standard.

Figure 11-17 Flooring standards and certifications help interior designers inform their clients about sustainable flooring choices.

DESIGNER MATH SKILLS

Calculating Wall-to-Wall Flooring

Interior designers must know how to accurately calculate materials. In her book, *Estimating for Interior Designers*, Carol A. Sampson says that "strong estimating skills will enable you to work better with clients, prepare accurate, comprehensive estimates, figure accurate completion dates, and verify subcontractors' figures." Accurate use of industry-standard calculations is important to timely completion of projects on budget. Inaccurate calculations may indicate the estimator's lack of knowledge, experience, or accuracy. Mistakes are costly!

When determining the quantity of materials you need, standard industry formulas help you complete calculations to compensate for challenges. Such challenges may include minor product irregularities, matching fabric repeats, or designing decorative flooring patterns. Be mindful that random upward rounding of quantities can result in wasteful quantities and increased costs. Excess materials quickly drive up project costs. Industry-standard calculations determine the general material amounts. Sales representatives can make recommendations to help you adjust calculations when ordering materials that require additional amounts.

Wall-to-Wall Flooring Calculations

When determining the amount of wall-to-wall flooring to purchase, calculate the area of the room (width × length = area) then add 10 percent of that amount to the total. This amount permits installation with a few leftover remnants to replace stained or damaged areas. Divide the square footage of the room by 9 square feet (a square yard) to determine how many square yards of flooring you need (Figure A).

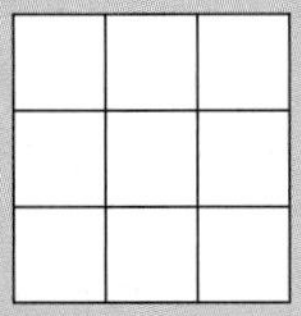

9 sq. ft. = 1 sq. yd.

Figure A

Width × Length = Area
Area × 0.10% = Sq. ft. overage
Area + sq. ft. coverage = Total sq. ft.
Total sq. ft. ÷ 9 sq. ft. = Total sq. yd.

Example 1: To determine wall-to-wall flooring for a room measuring 14 feet by 12 feet:

14 ft. × 12 ft. = 168 sq. ft.
168 sq. ft. × 0.10% = 16.8 sq. ft. overage
168 sq. ft. + 16.8 sq. ft. = 184.8 sq. ft. (rounded to 185 sq. ft.)
185 sq. ft. ÷ 9 sq. ft. = 20.55 total sq. yd.

Example 2: To determine the square yards of wall-to-wall flooring in multiple areas or rooms, do the following:

Master bedroom: 14 ft. × 14 ft. = 196 sq. ft.
Master bath: 5 ft. × 12 ft. = 60 sq. ft.
Walk-in closet: 10 ft. × 10 ft. = 100 sq. ft.
Total square feet of areas: 356 sq. ft.
356 sq. ft. × 0.10% = 35.6 sq. ft. overage
356 sq. ft. + 35.6 sq. ft. = 391.6 sq. ft. (rounded to 392 sq. ft.)
392 sq. ft. ÷ 9 sq. ft. = 43.55 total sq. yd. (rounded to 43.6 sq. yd.)

For an L-shaped room, divide the room into two sections, calculating the area of each space first. Then add the sections together to determine the total area of the room.

To ensure carpet wears better, is more comfortable, and lasts longer, install a quality carpet pad with the carpet. To determine the pad size, use the above formulas, omitting the additional 10 percent. Carpet padding comes in rolls of specific amounts. If purchasing padding that comes in 270-square-foot rolls, one roll would suffice for the room that is 14 feet by 12 feet, but two rolls would be necessary for the master bedroom carpet.

Linoleum

Invented in the mid-1800s by an English manufacturer of rubber materials, and first manufactured in Scotland, *linoleum* has been a standard flooring material for more than 100 years due to its quiet comfort, desirable price point, and many available patterns.

Made primarily of natural raw materials, **linoleum** consists of linseed oils, rosins (an amber-colored sap from pine trees), and wood flour (salvaged from sawdust) placed on a natural jute backing. Linoleum comes in rolls of sheet goods that require delivery and professional installation. It also comes in solid color, 13-inch-square tiles with borders for easy do-it-yourself projects.

Highly resistant to heavy-rolling loads and foot traffic, linoleum is durable, resistant to acid, grease, oil, solvents, and cigarette burns. Interestingly, its performance improves over time as exposure to air hardens it and increases its durability.

Linoleum is naturally antibacterial. The antibacterial properties halt the spread of microorganisms. It is VOC-free and its natural antistatic properties repel dust and dirt. Linoleum is easy to clean and hypoallergenic.

Linoleum is making a comeback in interiors. As a practical, quietly comfortable, eco-friendly flooring, designers can specify it in a variety of colors, with borders, specialty design insets, and unique tile designs. For the residential sector, it is *pet-friendly* in that it is resistant to scratches and allergens typical with pet dander. In addition, interior designers still consider linoleum an ideal flooring material for many healthcare and foodservice facilities.

Linoleum requires less energy to manufacture than most popular floor coverings and is biodegradable. One hundred percent of its postproduction waste can be recycled. Its installation uses one hundred percent solvent-free adhesive.

Vinyl Composition Tile

Vinyl was accidently created by Waldo Semon in the 1920s when trying to make a synthetic adhesive. The first vinyl flooring tile was not a solid vinyl product but rather a vinyl composition tile called *Vinylite* made by Carbide and Carbon Chemicals Corporation.

Invented in the 1930s, **vinyl composition tile (VCT)** was first shown in the Vinylite House at Chicago's 1933 Century of Progress Exhibition. It became widely used by the late 1940s in high-traffic areas in commercial interiors and later in the 1960s when it was popular in residential interiors.

Large manufacturers advertise VCT as composed of 85 percent limestone filler, which is a common material in great supply. It also contains polyvinyl chloride (PVC) resins, stabilizers, and pigments. Under heat and pressure, the component materials form thin sheets and are then cut into 12-inch square tiles. They are available from 1⁄16 to 1⁄8 inch thick. Vinyl composition tiles—like other vinyl products, cork, and rubber—are **resilient flooring**—or flooring that is flexible and provides impact absorption, **Figure 11-18**.

VCT is inexpensive; easy to install and maintain; and resists acids, alkalis, and strong cleaning compounds. It has improved slip-resistance, and resists staining, scratches, gouges, and tearing. VCT has low impact resistance, poor noise absorption, and is semi-porous compared with solid vinyl and solid rubber. VCT is a solid material tile. If you break a tile in half, you will see that the color is consistent throughout the material.

Today, the most common use of VCT is in high-traffic commercial applications and public spaces, such as retail stores and schools. It is highly durable and easy to maintain for less cost than most other material alternatives. These tiles are easy to install and can be laid in any orientation, from checkerboard to diagonal. Some vinyl tile can be grouted for a more realistic appearance. *Solid vinyl tile (SVT)* and *luxury vinyl tile (LVT)* contain more vinyl for a better performance and more realistic appearance.

Zoonar RF/Zooner/Thinkstock

Figure 11-18 Because of its durability, vinyl composition tile (VCT) is especially appropriate in high-traffic commercial applications. *As a designer, where would you specify its use?*

Vinyl Sheets, Tiles, and Planks

As the most popular type of resilient flooring, vinyl is durable, low maintenance, and relatively inexpensive. In residential settings, its use is common in the high-traffic areas such as kitchens, laundry rooms, and bathrooms. Vinyl often mimics patterns of natural materials such as stone, wood, marble, and slate. It also comes in a variety of colors and patterns and is warmer to the touch and softer underfoot than hard flooring surfaces.

Vinyl comes in various levels of gloss so you can get a range of looks. Some vinyl comes with extra foam cushioning to offer additional comfort for standing and noise reduction. Often, vinyl flooring is manufactured with antimicrobial protection to resist bacteria, mold, and mildew. It also does not require waxing and polishing as it did in the past.

Vinyl flooring has four layers—a protective urethane top coat, a protective clear vinyl layer, a printed design layer, and a felt or fiberglass backing. It is available in sheets, tiles, and planks. Vinyl planks closely resemble the look of hardwood and come in the same size as wood planks. They boast realistic features such as texturing and beveled edges. Vinyl sheets generally come in 6- or 12-foot-wide rolls. The installation of sheet vinyl can often be seamless, making it ideal in rooms with moisture.

Multilevel embossed sheet vinyl is increasingly popular for areas exposed to excessive dirt and moisture. The raised portions of this sheet vinyl cause dirt and water to drop down below the wear surface, thereby reducing abrasion or slippery surfaces. Heavy items can permanently dent and mar a vinyl surface. It is necessary to protect vinyl flooring from heavy office equipment and the legs of furniture and large appliances.

Some vinyl floors contain recycled content, and many manufacturers are moving toward greener practices, such as using low-VOC inks. Similar to VCT, sheet vinyl also contains the toxic chemicals polyvinyl chloride (PVC) and the plasticizer phthalate (THA-layt), which give vinyl products flexibility, but also raise health and environmental problems during manufacture, installation, and disposal. Adhesives for installation with low VOCs, which are generally water-based, are available.

Cork

First introduced in 1904, cork is the bark of the cork oak tree, which is native to Spain and Portugal. This bark, or cork, is a wood product that has a honeycomb, porous structure containing between 30–50 million cells.

Cork is resilient, impermeable (to both liquids and gasses), durable, wear resistant, and provides thermal and acoustical insulation, **Figure 11-19**. It is naturally resistant to mold, mildew, and termites. Cork is also hypoallergenic and antimicrobial, and resistant to fire and stains. Its resilience makes it comfortable to stand on. If dropped on cork flooring, fragile objects such as dishes will not break.

Cork can fade over time, particularly when exposed to direct sunlight. It can also be dented, punctured, and scratched fairly easily, allowing moisture to permeate it. However, due to its resilient nature, cork flooring bounces back. Therefore, furniture indentations will not be permanent. With proper maintenance, cork flooring can last 40 or more years.

From a design standpoint, designers use cork in residential and commercial applications. Because many consider cork a *green* product, it is gaining new popularity. Cork can be left a natural color, stained, or painted. It is available in tiles or planks in a variety of colors and sizes. It is important to know that no two cork tiles are identical in color or pattern.

Joe Ferrer/Shutterstock.com

Figure 11-19 Because cork is resilient, hypoallergenic, and antimicrobial, it is especially appropriate for kitchen areas.

DESIGNER MATH SKILLS

Calculating Linear Feet of Millwork

As you know, to determine the amount of hard flooring for a room, the designer calculates the area of the room. Finishing off the flooring for a room with baseboard trim requires another calculation. The measurement for baseboard trim and other millwork, such as crown molding, is taken in *linear feet,* or running feet.

To calculate the number of linear feet of baseboard needed for a bathroom that measures 6 feet by 8 feet, the designer adds together the length of each wall. Here is the formula.

width + width + length + length = linear feet

Example: For the 6 foot by 8 foot bathroom noted above, the designer calculation is

6 ft. + 6 ft. + 8 ft. + 8 ft. = 28 linear ft.

The designer needs to order 28 linear feet of the specified baseboard trim.

Although not recommended for bathrooms where floors routinely get wet, installation of cork floors can be in any other room in a residential setting. Commercially, designers often specify cork for public transportation areas, such as airports and train stations. Cork is a natural, nontoxic, and renewable material. Cork requires sealing with a natural wax or low-VOC polyurethane to prevent spotting.

Cork is renewable, recyclable, and biodegradable. Its harvest minimally impacts the environment and manufacturing produces very little waste.

Hard Floorings

Designers and their clients choose hard floor coverings for their aesthetic appearance, durability, and ease of maintenance. They are a desirable material in residential settings if the clients have allergies; however, sound absorption is minimal or nonexistent. Hard floorings can become slippery if wet, and can cause fatigue when standing on them for long periods of time.

Wood

There are two categories of wood that are used for flooring. The first is *hardwood,* which comes from deciduous trees, or those that drop their leaves in fall. The harder the wood, the more durable it is for flooring. Examples include oak (white and red), maple, walnut, cherry, poplar, birch, and ash. In the U.S., the most popular hardwood floors include oak, ash, and maple. The second type of wood is *softwood,* which comes from conifers, or evergreens. Examples include pine, balsam, beech, cedar, spruce, and fir. Floors consisting of soft woods scratch and dent more easily and are less durable.

The factors a designer must consider when choosing a wood-flooring material include durability, color, texture, and whether the product comes from a renewable source. Because wood tends to warp, twist, and bend when drying, *kiln-dried wood* is the designer's choice over naturally dried wood. In addition, the designer must consider the following when making wood-floor choices:

- **Location and climate.** Like any natural material, wood has quirks. Wood absorbs or releases moisture depending on exposure to or lack of humidity. Therefore designers must think about room location and climate when deciding whether to choose wood flooring for an interior. Wood from different climates must sit and adjust to the new location prior to installation.

  Depending on the season of the year, wood floors can shrink or swell in some climates. They also fade in natural daylight. Therefore, color changes in wood flooring will be obvious where area rugs or furnishings remain for extended periods of time.
- **Types of wood flooring.** There are three types of solid-wood flooring: *strip*, *plank*, and *parquet*. Wood strip floors come in strips that are 1½, 2, and 2¼ inches wide and 5⁄16 to ¾ inch thick. Wood plank floors range from 3 to 8 inches wide and ½ to ¾ inch thick. Both come in a variety of lengths. Parquet floors come in various sizes and patterns.

  Each type of flooring comes *unfinished* (and must be finished on-site after installation) or *prefinished* (sanded and finished at the factory—ready for installation). The look the client wants to achieve impacts the designer's choice in type of wood flooring, **Figure 11-20 A, B, and C**.

A Stockbyte/Stockbyte/Thinkstock
B Breadmaker/Shutterstock.com
C HoleInTheBucket/iStock/Thinkstock

Figure 11-20 Types of wood flooring come in (A) *strip*, (B) *plank*, and (C) *parquet*.

- **Quality.** The *grade* of wood indicates wood quality. Appearance alone determines wood grade. Labels for the best quality woods are *Clear* and *Select*. These grades have fewer knots and other defects. For some designers and clients, the *defects* are what add the character to the material for interior use.

Solid-wood strips and planks are cut out of a tree and processed with *tongue-and-groove* edges. **Tongue and groove** refers to a wood joint with a tongue on one edge that fits into the corresponding groove on another edge.

Also available on today's market is *engineered hardwood flooring,* which is factory-made from layers of wood. It is natural wood, but more stable than solid wood and is less susceptible to shrinking and expanding with changes in temperatures and humidity. The use of multiple wood layers increases durability. Since the face of the flooring uses only a thin veneer, the wood of other tree varieties forms the other layers.

Most engineered wood floors are prefinished at the factory and have tongue-and-groove joints. This eliminates VOCs, job-site mess, and saves installation time. Engineered hardwood flooring comes in many types of wood including birch, cherry, hickory, maple, oak, and pecan. Manufacturers can also give it a distressed or hand-scraped look to add character and individuality.

To keep wood floors looking good, suggest clients use **walk-off mats**—portable mats at entrance points to remove and collect dirt from shoes before stepping onto soft- or hard-surface flooring. Walk-off mats are generally rubber-backed carpets or rugs. It takes a minimum of eight steps for dirt removal from shoes. Reducing exposure to grit, shoe heels, pet nails, and furniture wheels or legs helps prolong the attractive appearance of wood floors.

The chemicals in wood oxidize in light and cause color changes in the floor. Remind clients to periodically move area rugs and furnishings to eliminate dark and light areas and mop up water spills immediately to avoid warping. Refinishing worn or damaged floors can often make them appear almost new.

Wood can be salvaged from many sources including old bowling alleys, barns, and industrial buildings. The distinctive patina of these woods adds character to any space. If specifying new wood (as opposed to salvaged), make sure the woods come from a sustainable source.

An organization that works with certifying sustainable forests is the Forest Stewardship Council™ (FSC®), **Figure 11-21**. Organized in 1992 by a group of businesses, environmentalists, and community leaders, the FSC mission is to stop deforestation and "promote environmentally sound, socially beneficial, and economically prosperous management of the world's forests." FSC is an independent, nonprofit group that promotes third-party certification for sustainably managed forests.

The FSC *Principles and Criteria* provides a foundation for all forest management standards globally. The FSC chain-of-custody certification traces the path of products from forests through the supply chain. According to FSC, a "*chain-of-custody* is the path taken by raw materials harvested from an FSC-certified source through processing, manufacturing, distribution, and printing until the final product is ready for sale to the end consumer." Oversight of the chain-of-custody ensures deforestation does not take place. FSC operates in more than 80 countries, wherever forests are present.

FSC®

Image courtesy of the FSC® Forest Stewardship Council™, the mark of responsible forestry.

Figure 11-21 When specifying wood products for clients, choosing products with the *Forest Stewardship Council*™ logo ensures the products come from sustainably managed forests.

Laminates

In the mid-1970s, laminates began replacing many hardwood floors due to cost and maintenance. Today, there are many laminate floor products on the market. Laminate floors have three layers, including a

- decorative surface for design and abrasion resistance

Designer Profile

Jo Rabaut, ASID, IIDA—Commercial Design

Jo was recently named Atlanta Decorative Arts Center—Southeast Contract Designer of the Year.

Photographer: Chris Little Photography/Rabaut Design Associates

"I launched Rabaut Design Associates in 1989 after working in my hometown of Detroit, Michigan, and then as an Associate at one of Atlanta's premier architectural interior firms. Twenty-five years after establishing Rabaut Design Associates, I am honored to have an award-winning portfolio as expressive and diverse as our brand, a leadership presence in our industry, and a genuine philanthropic role in our city.

"I owe a lot of my success to a thorough understanding of architecture that has continually informed and enhanced our body of work. As varied as our project types are, I am consistent in my belief that light and dimension are the most powerful tools for shaping a space. I try to sincerely nurture the unique goals and preferences of each client. As a result, no two Rabaut Design interiors look alike, and we love that about our brand."

You can read more about Jo in Appendix B.

- core board, usually of fiberboard or particle board, for stability and protection from moisture
- balancing backer board to prevent warping

Laminate is tough, easy to clean, and gives the look of hardwood floors without the cost. Laminate floors are easy to maintain. Simply vacuum the floors to remove dirt and clean occasionally with a damp, not wet, mop. For protection, use floor mats at entry points and felt protectors on the bottom of furniture—such as tables and chairs.

Laminate flooring comes in many plank widths and square tile sizes with finishes that realistically resemble hardwood, stone, or tile. They come in a variety of choices from maple and cherry to walnut. Laminate flooring is used in both residential and small scale commercial projects, **Figure 11-22**.

Bamboo

The use of bamboo dates back more than 5,000 years to ancient China. China's dominant use of bamboo is not unexpected since more bamboo grows in China than in any other area of the world. Bamboo made its appearance as a floor covering on the international market in the early 1990s to a relatively uninterested audience. In just over two decades, however, bamboo has become a very popular choice in flooring today due to its appeal as a sustainable product.

Manufactured from timber bamboo, these trees grow to 40 feet in height and mature in only five years while hardwood trees—like oak, ash, and maple—reach maturity in 40 to 50 years. Many consider bamboo a satisfying substitute for hardwood flooring.

Bamboo is dried and laminated in layers to produce bamboo plywood. The bamboo plywood is then cut into tongue-and-groove strips or planks similar to solid wood. Bamboo's durability varies.

- Natural bamboo, which is light in color, offers twice the stability of red oak (America's most popular flooring).
- Carbonized bamboo, which is darker and softer, is a less resilient material and therefore may dent or scratch with use.
- Solid bamboo is stronger than engineered bamboo.

Bamboo flooring from China may contain high levels of urea formaldehyde, a toxic chemical. Therefore, ensure the flooring you specify is certified by the Forest Stewardship Council (FSC).

A range of design options for bamboo are available, from edge-grain planks to exotic, striped *tiger* designs. In addition, bamboo can be painted during the manufacturing process to look like various hardwoods. Bamboo flooring lends a clean, contemporary appearance to any room. Designers may suggest clients use bamboo in such residential spaces as living rooms and dining rooms. They may also specify it for use in commercial spaces such as offices and restaurants.

The growing bamboo flooring industry may produce environmental benefits. In addition to relieving some

Adriano Castelli/Shutterstock.com

Figure 11-22 Laminate floorings are durable and easy to maintain.

of the demand for hardwoods, which helps preserve old-growth forests from illegal logging practices, bamboo itself is a remarkably efficient oxygen producer, especially during its early growth years. Adding a high-volume product like flooring to the list of uses for this amazing plant may address some pressing concerns for the future of the planet. See **Figure 11-23**.

Lorraine Kourafas/Shutterstock.com

Figure 11-23 Because it grows quickly and harvesting does not damage the plants, many designers specify bamboo as a *green* flooring alternative.

Marble

Historically, marble is the most ancient of all finished interior materials in use today. Used as part of the Taj Mahal in India and the Parthenon in Athens, marble was a preferred choice in building, furniture, and flooring materials.

Marble, a type of metamorphic rock, forms by submitting limestone to high temperatures and pressures over thousands of years. Minerals from impurities give marble its wide variety of colors and patterns. Marble usually has gray, brown, or pink streaks. This marbling effect can be subtle or very prominent. It is advisable to look at samples of the marble before deciding on a variety to specify for the client. *Terrazzo floors* consist of marble chips or other stones and cement as a binder.

Marble is elegant and durable. It is useful in high-traffic areas such as staircases and hallways. Although initially expensive, marble will last a lifetime with the proper care. Marble is watertight and easy to maintain. It is stain resistant, and any scratches are easy to polish out. Marble is generally cool to the touch. It is possible to install a type of radiant heat system under the floor to offer warmth if clients desire this feature.

Application of marble tiles can occur over almost any surface. For residential use, marble works well in kitchens, bathrooms, and staircases. In commercial interiors, use of marble is frequent in lobbies, reception areas, offices, hallways, and staircases. Often marble is used to form beautifully complex tile mosaics by combining stones of different classes and colors. Marble flooring lends a sophisticated and elegant look to any room.

Due to their heavy weight, marble floors require substantial subflooring. When marble floors are polished, they reflect light. Polishing can also make them slippery when wet. *Honed marble* has a matte finish (free of shine), which is desirable in areas with heavy foot traffic. It provides slip resistance and will not show scratches as readily as polished marble. Marble floors also lack cushion—causing people to tire easily when standing on them for long periods.

As a natural product, marble is inherently earth-friendly. Although available in a finite supply, marble has an enduring life cycle, durability, and recyclability. It is non-toxic and lasts a lifetime. No chemicals go into its quarrying or fabricating. It has a good *thermal mass*, which is the ability of a material to store heat and slowly release it. This positively impacts indoor ambient air temperature and thus is energy efficient.

Slate

Popular for use on floors for centuries, slate brings the colors and texture of nature to interiors. Natural stone comes out of the earth. Therefore, there can be extreme variations in its color and quality. Slate is a metamorphic rock that forms from shale and clay. It differs in color depending on geographical region. The shale and clay meld into sheets from heat and pressure deep below the Earth's surface. These sheets can be cut and made into tile.

Vermont slate is typically smoother, denser, and one color—red, green, black, or blue. Slate from India or China is softer and comes in many colors—some of which are variegated in color. Brazilian slate is typically dense and hard, and has interesting colors and patterns of color. Slate is also found in Wales, Germany, France, and Italy.

Slate is a popular choice for flooring today. Although its primary use is in residential settings, slate is gaining popularity in commercial interiors such as shopping malls, hotels, and restaurants. See **Figure 11-24**.

Slate has a distinctive, natural beauty, and requires little maintenance. Slate is naturally slip resistant, stain-resistant, and non-absorbent. It is antibacterial, chemical free, and non-combustible. It is available in distinctive rich colors and textures. Use slate color variations to your client's advantage when laying out the design of them.

Slate is available in many shapes and sizes such as large or small square tiles, rectangular tiles to use with staggered joints, and irregular shaped slabs. Sealers darken slate and give it a glossy appearance. Slate's sustainability characteristics are similar to marble.

Photography by Ben Tremper/Interiors by Associates III Interior Design

Figure 11-24 The rich colors and textures of slate add a distinctive, natural beauty to this rustic kitchen. *For what other projects might you specify slate?*

Travertine

Travertine is commonly found in Italy, Croatia, China, Guatemala, and Turkey. Similar to slate and marble, travertine is a natural stone of fine crystalline sedimentary rock. It often forms near hot, bubbly, mineral-rich springs. A combination of dissolved limestone and carbon dioxide gas that escapes during formation creates the unique pitted surface on the stone. One of the largest quarries and producers of travertine is in New Mexico.

Travertine is cut from the earth in huge blocks and then cut into tiles or pavers. If the client desires, the installer can fill the surface pits with epoxy or dust resin and to match the rest of the stone. Leaving travertine in its natural state offers a weathered look.

As with any stone, travertine is durable. Within the scope of stone, travertine is a limestone which has some limitations—it is fairly soft and prone to chipping and scratching. As flooring, travertine is porous. Although it has excellent traction, use of unsealed and unpolished travertine in an area such as a kitchen is not the best idea. While heat resistant, travertine does require sealing. Once polished, travertine is very slippery. Travertine also has a tendency to scratch and stain. These characteristics make travertine flooring difficult to finish and maintain.

Travertine stone is soft and delicate to look at. It signals a feeling of luxury, relaxation, tranquility, and serenity. It suggests a casual formalness. A polished or honed travertine becomes a bit more formal, yet is still inviting. The earthy colors of travertine range from the softest of ivories to deep mocha browns. Travertine never appears as one solid color. No two stones or tiles are alike.

In interiors, travertine is available in the following finishes: honed and filled, brushed and chiseled, or tumbled and polished. Rectangular or square tile patterns are most common. Tiles range in size from small mosaics to 36-inch by 36-inch tiles to huge slabs. In residences, tumbled travertine—a weathered, aged look—is a popular backsplash and it is often used in showers. See **Figure 11-25**.

Travertine is a natural product mined from the earth. With no manufactured additions or attributes, chemicals, or additives, it is eco-friendly and recyclable. It can be reused in other applications after the initial installation.

Granite

Used in the ancient Red Pyramid of Egypt, granite forms by the slow cooling and crystallization of *magma*, or molten rock. It is second only to diamonds for hardness. It resists blistering, scratching, cracking, and scorching. Granite is cut from a quarry in huge blocks and then cut into slices or slabs. Today, granite comes from India, China, Brazil, and Scotland, as well as the U.S. Granite is hard, durable, strong, and resists weather, chemicals, and staining.

Granite offers a luxurious look to any interior. It comes in slabs, tiles, stone bricks, circles, or medallions in many colors and patterns. The colors include white, gray, buff, beige, pink, red, blue, green, and black. Red and blue granites often have higher prices because they are rarer.

Every piece of granite is very individual. Small samples cannot give a good overall picture of the granite design. When placing it in a visible location—such as a hotel lobby or a kitchen bar—clients may want to hand-pick their granite slabs. Granite has the following three finishes:

- **Polished.** By moving the granite slab through a series of wheels with varying abrasive pads, the slab is ground and buffed to a high sheen that is very reflective.
- **Honed.** The slab of granite moves through a similar process as for polishing, but is not buffed. The honing process forms a smooth finish with dull sheen.
- **Flamed.** This finish results from applying a high-intensity flame to the slab, leaving behind a rough texture that does not shine.

Granite stands up well against heavy foot traffic, making it preferable for commercial lobbies and walkways. True granite is the hardest of the polished stones commercially available. Polished granite should not be used for floors because it will not hold up to scuffing feet and is slippery when wet. If water may be present, use the flamed finish to create a slip-resistant surface. Banking institutions often use granite to communicate a feeling of permanence and stability.

LaCasse Photography, Ed LaCasse/R M Ruwart Design, Rosalie M. Ruwart, ASID

Figure 11-25 The earthy colors of this polished travertine floor are warm and inviting.

Granite is a natural stone and *not* a renewable material. It can be recycled and reused in other applications. Granite has similar characteristics to marble. See **Figure 11-26.**

Ceramic Tile

There are two basic types of ceramic tiles: ceramic (or non-porcelain) and porcelain. Ceramic tile was used by ancient civilizations because of its beauty and durability. It comes in two forms: glazed and unglazed. Unglazed tile is known as *quarry tile.*

Glazed Ceramic Tile

Glazed ceramic tile is the most common tile in U.S. offices, stores, and residences. The raw materials used in making glazed ceramic tile include clay, sand, and glass. After forming the clay tiles, they are kiln-fired to dry them. Once dry, manufacturers spray or pour liquid glass onto the tiles which are again kiln-fired at high temperatures to produce a hard, nonporous glaze. The glazing process allows any number of color combinations. Shiny glazes scratch easily and can be more slippery than matte surfaces.

The benefits of ceramic tiles are numerous. They are easy to maintain, cost effective, easily repairable with

Figure 11-26 Cut from quarries, granite is the hardest of the natural stones and comes in a variety of colors.

another tile, scratch resistant, moisture resistant, as well as resistant to fire and fading. They do not retain odors, allergens, or bacteria, and do not emit toxic fumes. Their thickness often determines quality and durability.

Ceramic tiles come in a variety of colors. There are also hundreds of patterns to choose from including ones that mimic natural stone. In a residential setting, ceramic tiles are ideal for kitchens, bathrooms, basements, porches, and laundry rooms that are prone to moisture problems.

Tiles come in a wide range of sizes (for example, ½-inch square mosaics to 24 inches square and larger) and shapes. The square tiles come in a variety of sizes. Tiles larger than 12 inches by 12 inches are very popular with today's clients. Although all tiles require grout, bigger tiles require less grout and less maintenance. Sealing the grout makes it less prone to stains and dirt. If a tile is broken, smaller tiles are easier to replace.

Quarry Tile

Quarry tile is typically unglazed and consists of carefully graded shale and fine clays. The range of colors is not as wide as glazed ceramic tiles, but there are several shades of red, orange, brown, gray, and beige. The face of quarry tiles can be solid, variegated, and *flashed*—in which the edges of the tile are darker than the middle. Through an extrusion process, the quarry-tile material passes through the machinery in a ½-inch-thick ribbon and is cut to size. The extrusion process creates tiles that are very dense and durable. The tiles are dried and then kiln-fired at extremely high temperatures. An attractive patina emerges when stain-resistant quarry tiles remain in a rugged, unglazed state.

Quarry tiles are inexpensive and durable for commercial and residential applications. This unglazed tile surface has more traction and is therefore more slip-resistant. Because they are so durable, quarry tiles are also common in industrial settings. Due to the porous nature of the material, heavy water exposure can damage unglazed tiles. A great deal of water exposure can lead to mold growth in the grout. Quarry tiles can be sealed with a water-based, penetrating sealer (not a surface sealer) that does not impact the slip-resistance of the tile.

Porcelain Tile

The *Tile Council of North America (TCNA)* created a certification standard for porcelain tile to differentiate it from ceramic (non-porcelain) tile. Porcelain tile is a type of ceramic tile that has a water-absorption rate of less than 0.5 percent. In other words, if you were to weigh a porcelain tile, and then put it in a bucket of water for 24 hours, and then weigh it again, it would only weigh 0.5 percent more. Standard ceramic tiles absorb more than 0.5 percent water.

Porcelain tiles consist of special porcelain clays. Manufacturers fire them at a higher temperature, making them more dense and moisture resistant, **Figure 11-27**. Porcelain tiles are also less porous, making them more resistant to stains, bacteria, odors, and damage by most cleaning products. Similar to non-porcelain tiles, they come in a large variety of patterns and colors.

Because they absorb little water, most porcelain tiles are not susceptible to breakage as a result of rapid freezing and thawing and are therefore suitable for outside use, too. A general rule of thumb is that non-porcelain tiles are great on walls and light-use countertops, while porcelain tiles are suitable for use everywhere in residential and high-traffic commercial applications.

Ceramic tiles are one of the most cost-effective and environmentally friendly flooring choices consisting of natural clay and other recycled materials. Tile manufacturing does not necessitate the use of heavy chemicals or other harmful substances typical for other flooring types. There are no trees cut down as with hardwood floors and the best part is that tiles are durable and have a long lifespan. Tiles last can for centuries, whether in a building or landfill. They are also recyclable and useful for decorative purposes.

Concrete

Due to its incredible versatility and color range, concrete flooring is popular both in residential and commercial installations. Concrete is a paste mixture of aggregates (sand and gravel), portland cement, and water that hardens. Inexpensive, durable, and versatile, concrete requires treatment with a floor sealer for interior installations.

Concrete colors come in every hue, with dark colors most useful in passive-solar homes to absorb rays of the sun. Stamping concrete into stone, brick, and other designs, and painting it with epoxy or acrylic paint gives a unique finish. Texturing the surface or buffing it until glossy are other alternatives. For these reasons, interior designers still consider concrete a stylish choice for floors. See **Figure 11-28**.

Concrete floors are extremely durable and easy to clean. They resist water with proper sealing. Concrete is good for indoor air quality because it inhibits mold, mildew, and odors. Concrete works well with radiant heat because the surface absorbs heat, which can result in lower energy bills. Because cured concrete can absorb harmful chemicals, design professionals must consider the floor location and use.

Fragile items break easily when dropped on hard concrete surfaces. Standing for long periods can be uncomfortable. Sound absorption is minimal and hairline cracks can appear over time.

Using concrete avoids depletion of natural resources, requires less energy than other floor types to produce, and is locally made. It is recyclable and VOC-free.

©Ed LaCasse, Courtesy of Boulder Associates

Figure 11-27 Porcelain tiles come in a variety of colors, patterns, and textures. *What characteristics make porcelain tile different from glazed ceramic tile and quarry tile?*

©Ed LaCasse, Courtesy of RNL

Figure 11-28 Concrete floors give an edgy, contemporary feel to a space design. *For what areas do you think it is appropriate to specify concrete for floors?*

Brick

Historically, some bricks used in ancient Babylonia withstood the weather elements and still exist today. Sun-dried brick dates from 5000 BC. The Chinese used brick as part of the Great Wall of China. The Aztecs of Mexico and Central America used adobe bricks for building purposes, too. Bricks are considered humanity's oldest manufactured building material.

Bricks are typically rectangular shapes with solid or hollow cores. A mixture of clays and shale with water is pressed, cut, and kiln-fired at high temperatures. This process results in thin-brick flooring tiles that have the durability and beauty of brick with the convenience of tile flooring.

Brick floors vary widely in hardness, depending on the combinations of materials that go into their production. Brick floor tiles made from coarse-ground materials are more porous and soft, and more likely to chip and crack. Higher-quality brick tiles are comparable in hardness to some ceramic tiles. The denser the brick, the easier it is to maintain. For example, factories use very dense bricks to withstand the heavy use of machinery. For other applications, designers may specify thin brick pavers to reduce floor weight.

Bricks are durable, strong, fade-resistant, fireproof, and offer an anti-slip surface. They resist wear and tear, are weather-resistant, and offer a great texture to any interior. Installation in high-traffic areas is a common application, **Figure 11-29**.

Brick floors provide a unique, rustic flooring option. In contrast, use of brick flooring in elegant and contemporary interiors offers a perception of elegant stability. Bricks come in many colors and textures. The color of brick depends on the chemical composition of the clay, the method of firing bricks, and the kiln temperature. A number of patterns exist for laying down brick flooring, including herringbone or basket-weave styles.

Bricks consist of natural raw materials that are plentiful. In addition, they are VOC-free, making them a healthy option. When bricks come from a local source or are salvaged from another location, eco-friendliness increases. Reclaimed bricks have a patina that creates an interesting look.

Dr. Cloud/Shutterstock.com

Figure 11-29 The herringbone pattern in this brick floor adds interest and movement to a space. *Discuss residential and commercial areas for which you would specify a brick floor.*

Ceilings

Historically, ceilings were given a great deal of attention. During Greek and Roman times, intricate details were shaped with stucco and applied to the ceiling. In England, Tudor arch-shaped trusses or delicate decorative plasterwork was applied to the ceiling structure. More recently, during the Victorian era in the United States, stamped metal ceilings were popular as a decorative motif.

One of the most ignored yet critical areas of any interior space is the ceiling (designers might want to think of this space as a "fifth wall" in regard to importance). Ceilings are not just part of the roof structure, but are an integral component of the living space. With installation of lighting on or in it, light and shadow interact on the ceiling surface. Ceilings help shape space. Using different ways to construct or pitch a ceiling can add volume to a room. Vertical windows rise up to a ceiling, often drawing your eyes to it. Horizontal lines across the ceiling give an illusion of a low, cozy, human-scaled space.

The structure with one level, such as a ranch house or a small business in a detached building, will use the ceiling as a type of interior finish. For multilevel structures, such as an apartment complex or a high-rise office building, the ceiling is actually part of the floor system from above that serves as the ceiling of the space below.

A ceiling is a flat plane—typically eight-feet high for many residential applications. To add interest to a flat ceiling, many designers use crown molding around the perimeter to add a custom detail. If the budget allows, flat ceilings may also include one of the following ceiling structures:

- **Beamed.** Painted or natural, a wood beam, rafter, or truss offers a horizontal line across a space that directs the attention of the viewer from one side of the room to the other. In rustic applications, the wood remains in its natural state without finishing. These features can be carved or painted, **Figure 11-30**.
- **Coved.** In this ceiling structure, the wall meets the ceiling with a curve instead of a 90-degree angle. The cove softens the edge of the ceiling and creates a flow from the wall plane into the ceiling. Designers use this structure in formal and informal applications.
- **Coffered.** Waffle-like in shape, coffered ceilings consist of beams and cross beams that form honeycomb-shaped boxes attached to a flat ceiling. The beams can be painted or left as natural wood, **Figure 11-31.**

pics721/Shutterstock.com

Figure 11-31 This coffered ceiling offers a feeling of elegance to the space. *What role do you think ceiling height plays when specifying a ceiling such as this for a client?*

- **Dropped.** For this ceiling type, a portion of the ceiling is lower than the main ceiling height. Designers may use this technique to define such spaces as a dining room or a hotel lobby check-in area. Installation of recessed or indirect lighting is common in these structures.

Designer: Aneka Jensen/Damon Searles Photography

Figure 11-30 Wood beams draw your attention across this space, adding character and interest.

- **Plastered.** A designer may choose to have these ceilings textured with plaster, medallions, or raised patterns. The features can be painted the same as the ceiling or in contrasting colors.

In addition to flat ceilings, designers use angles and curves to create additional volume in an interior. These ceiling types include

- **Domed.** Spherical or inverted bowl-shaped in nature, a domed ceiling offers a feeling of grandeur to a space.
- **Cathedral.** A cathedral ceiling consists of two angled planes with equal sloping sides that meet in the middle of a room at a ridge. It also has the same pitch as the roof structure.
- **Tray.** With this ceiling type, the middle portion of the ceiling is usually six to eight inches higher than the remainder. At times, lighting is hidden in the perimeter. Tray ceilings are a more subtle design.
- **Vaulted.** A vaulted ceiling can have unequal sloping sides, a single sloping side, or a curved or arched slope, **Figure 11-32.** Vaulted ceilings are not typically constructed using the same pitch as the roof. A ceiling with a continuous semi-circle is a barrel vault ceiling. This feature creates great drama and interest in the ceiling space.

Commercial interiors not only use the above ceiling types, but many flat ceilings utilize acoustical tiles (sizes include 2 feet by 2 feet or 2 feet by 4 feet) that are inset into a suspended metal grid, **Figure 11-33**. Other popular commercial ceiling treatments include a *baffle ceiling* (with vertical elements hung from the ceiling), exposed ceiling, and unique assemblies of dropped acoustical tiles, and stretched ceiling systems.

Windows

A view to the outdoors is one of the most beneficial elements a designer incorporates into an interior space. The ability to see seasons change and time pass is a vital human need.

In both residential and commercial spaces, windows offer daylight, add architectural detail, and provide ventilation. Security and energy efficiency (for instance, solar heat gain) are factors that impact window choice for a building. Part of the interior design vocabulary is to know basic types of windows and window treatments. The term **glazing** refers to the use of glass as a construction material or the construction process a tradesperson uses to fit glass into frames.

©Ron Pollard, Courtesy of RNL

Figure 11-32 The vaulted ceiling in this space has a single, sloping side.

©Ed LaCasse, Courtesy of Boulder Associates

Figure 11-33 Many commercial interiors utilize suspended acoustical tile.

Window Types

Manufacturers use a variety of methods to construct windows. Common window materials include metal, wood, and vinyl. Other than stationary windows (fixed), all require some physical effort to operate. Therefore, when specifying them, consider the age and abilities of users. Also consider views to be captured with the location, size, and shape of windows, **Figure 11-34**. Popular window types include

- **Awning.** These windows are hinged at the top and swing outward. Usually multiple windows open with a crank handle or push bar.
- **Bay.** This is usually a multipaned window with angled sides that project out. Bay windows provide an architectural element to a building's exterior and create additional space in the interior.
- **Bow.** Bow windows feature vertical panes aligned in a curve that extends out. Such windows add interest and additional volume to an interior space.
- **Casement.** With a crank handle at the base of the window, casement windows swing open with an outward motion. They offer good airflow, but allow dirt to collect in window treatments.
- **Cathedral.** These angled, A-frame windows follow a vaulted roof line. They can capture large, natural views, but often take up the majority of one wall.
- **Clerestory.** Located above an architectural element, such as a door or another window, clerestory windows are usually rectangular in shape. They may be fixed or operable for ventilation. A big benefit is that clerestory windows provide light yet ensure privacy.
- **Double hung.** As the most common type of window, a double-hung window typically opens from bottom to top with a sliding motion. Readily available, these windows come in a variety of standard sizes. Because they do not project inside or outside, they do not interfere with window treatments or foot traffic.
- **Fixed glazing.** Flat windows that do not open, they often extend from floor to ceiling and can be quite small, too. Common shapes of fixed-glazing windows include circular, hexagonal, square, or triangular shapes.
- **Horizontal slider.** These windows open from side to side along tracks at the bottom and top of the window.

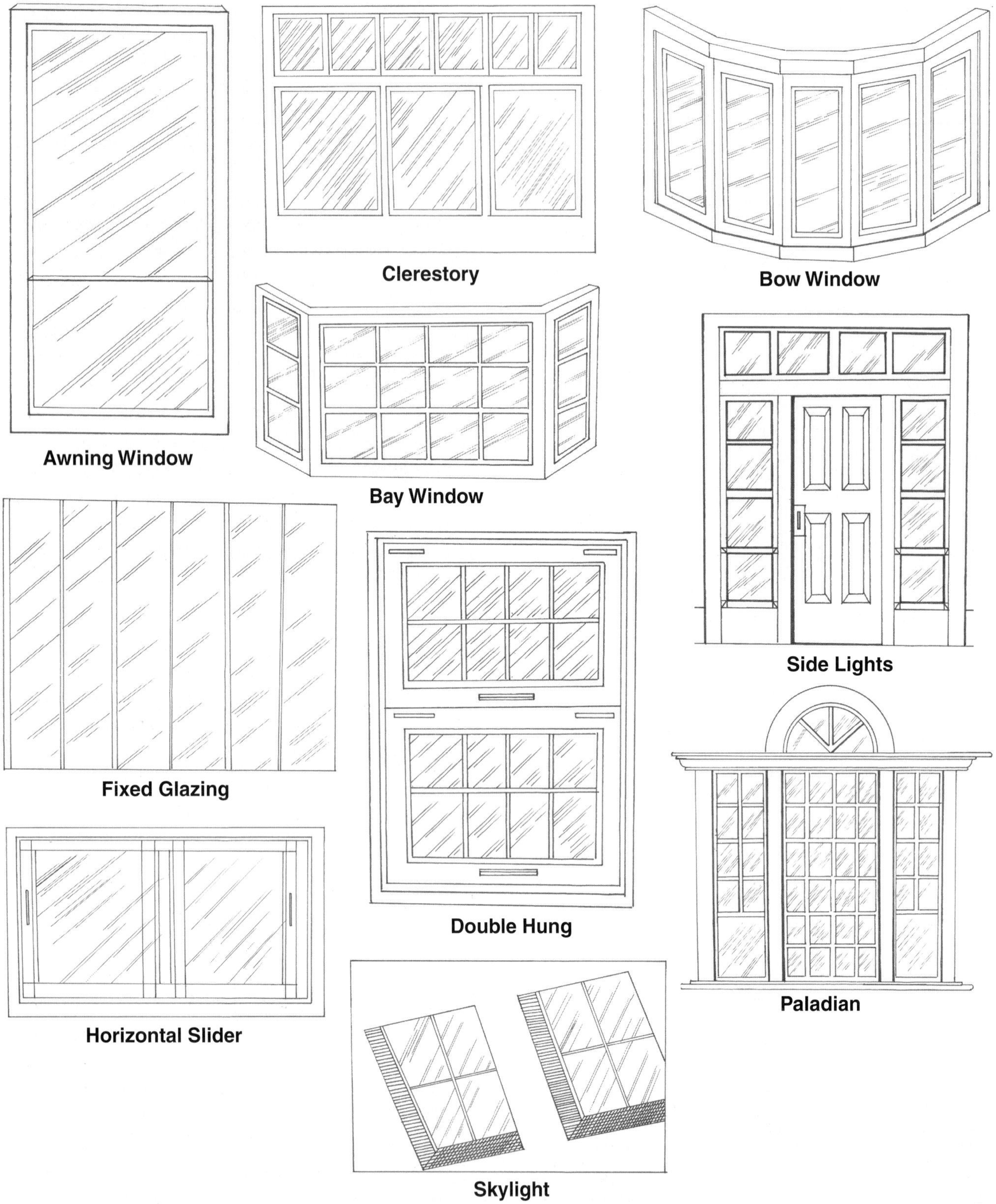

Sherilyn (Lixue) Yin, International transfer design student, CSU, ECNU

Figure 11-34 Windows bring in daylight and add architectural details. *Why should you consider the size and location of windows for client projects?*

- **Palladian.** Consisting of an arched window over multi-paned windows, pilasters or moldings are common additions to create the classical look of Palladian windows.
- **Sidelight.** These are narrow, vertical fixed windows located on one or both sides of an interior or front door.
- **Skylight.** Such windows are made of Plexiglas®, plastic, or glass and are mounted in the roof. This is a good way to bring natural light into interior spaces that do not connect with an exterior wall having a window.

Window Treatments

Window treatments can be functional or decorative. They provide thermal comfort, sound control, energy savings, aesthetic appeal, and privacy to an interior space. They range in transparency from sheer to room-darkening, which are ideal for people who want a glare-free television or who work nightshifts and sleep during the day. In a commercial setting, certain window treatments are ideal for showing technology presentations. Two categories of window treatments include *hard* and *soft*. Many times a designer will use a combination of both on the same window.

Hard window treatments include (see **Figure 11-35**)

- **Blinds.** Types of blinds include *venetian* blinds with wider horizontal slats, mini-blinds, micro-miniblinds, vertical, and woven wood or bamboo. The advantage of blinds is they roll or collapse into a small space, capturing more of a view through the window.
- **Shutters.** Two popular types of shutters include *louvered* and *plantation*. Louvered shutters can be designed with small louvers, shirred fabric, or raised panels. Plantation shutters have larger slats with 3-inch and 4-inch slats being highly popular. Although louvers and slats typically move within the shutters, the shutters do not collapse into a smaller space.
- **Specialty glass.** Rather than cover the window, the glass is modified to create a semi-private effect. The glass may be etched, art glass—such as blown glass created by an individual artist, stained glass, sand blasted, or beveled. Natural elements such as weeds or leaves pressed into matte-finish (low-luster) glass are also popular specialty glasses that designers use today as partitions in commercial settings or in the shower stall of a residence.

  This category also features two other specialty glass installations: glass block that can be glass or acrylic and liquid crystal, which is a fun technology that can change architectural glass from transparent to translucent with an electrical switch.

Soft window treatments include (see **Figure 11-36**)

- **Curtains.** These are panels of unlined lightweight fabric that can be window length or floor length. The top heading is sometimes *shirred*—a decorative gathering created by sewing a rod-pocket casing in the heading and sliding the rod through the casing.

  Curtains can be placed above a piece of furniture or fixture such as a sink. They can be ruffled or tied back. Café-style curtains cover the lower part of windows only. *Sheer curtains* are lightweight, translucent fabric curtains that diffuse harsh

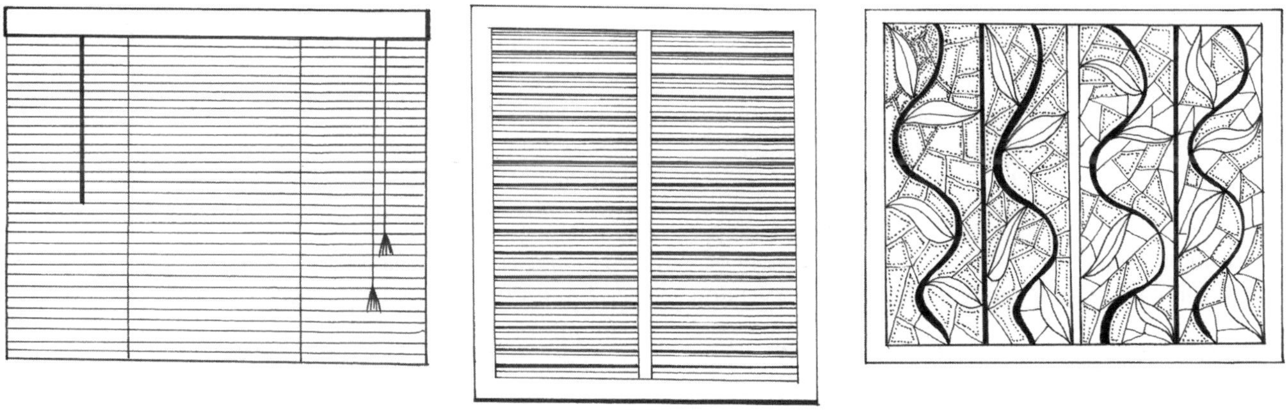

A B C

Sherilyn (Lixue) Yin, International transfer design student, CSU, ECNU

Figure 11-35 Venetian blinds (A), plantation shutters (B), and specialty glass (C) are examples of hard window treatments.

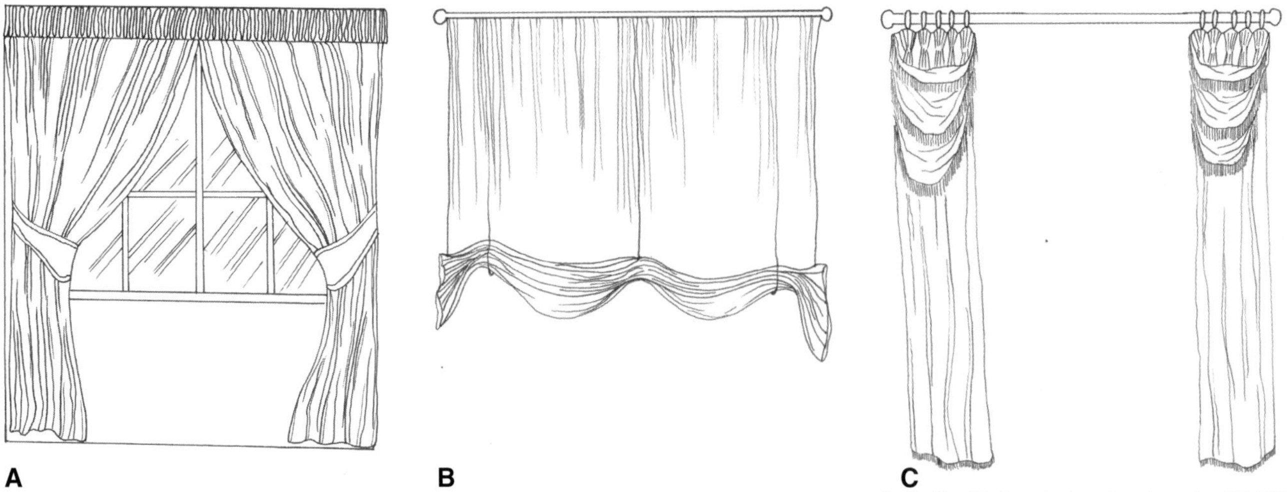

Figure 11-36 Soft window treatments include curtains (A), textile shades (B), and drapery (C).

daylight and provide daytime privacy. Decorative lace curtain panels come under this category.

- **Draperies.** Long panels of heavier pleated fabric that hang straight to frame a window, draperies can be opened from the center or side. They completely cover the window. Draperies are typically lined to protect the decorative fabric, and provide insulation, light control, and privacy.

  Designers may use draperies alone or in combination with such other window treatments as sheers. To offer a luxurious appearance, designers often *puddle* draperies on the floor, which requires extra length.
- **Shades.** There are many types of shades including Roman, Austrian, pleated, balloon, accordion, and roller. Operated by cords, shades come in many textures, colors, and patterns. Their key function is to block out daylight.

  Insulated shades offer thermal protection from heat or cold. Pleated shades are the most popular shade type and come in single- and double-pleated construction. The double pleat offers additional insulation because of the dead air space between the two pleats.
- **Stationary panels.** Similar to draperies, these are long panels of fabric that do not offer privacy or thermal comfort by closing. They frame a window with color, texture, or pattern, but use much less fabric.

Top treatments hide rods or add additional detail to the total look of the window. Choices of top treatments include the following:

- **Cornice.** Typically consisting of wood, fabric covered wood, or resin, a cornice is a decorative structure mounted above the window.
- **Jabots.** Fabrics with pleats, gathers, or folds, typically form jabots (zah-BOHs), which descend vertically on one or both sides of the window. Jabots are often cut on an angle.
- **Swags.** Half-round in shape, swags consist of fabric draped over the top of a window and sometimes inserted between jabots.
- **Valances.** Shorter pieces of fabric that cover the uppermost part of the window, hang valances alone or with such other treatments as pleated or balloon valances.

Understanding Textiles

To a designer, selecting textile products is one of the most enjoyable tasks he or she completes for the client. When selecting patterns, colors, and textures, designers visually and physically examine textile products to effectively meet client needs for a piece of furniture, an office acoustical panel, or a window covering.

At the same time, designers also study trends regarding colors and patterns that impact textile look and design. Colors and color combinations are ever changing. Patterns of textiles might include timeless Asian influences, bold geometric blacks and whites, or sophisticated monochromatic looks. Textile choices are exciting, dramatic, and virtually limitless.

Similarly, clients respond very strongly to the *material boards*—or interior finish, sample, or color boards—that designers produce to communicate the interior finishes for a space design, **Figure 11-37**. Clients may have difficulty reading a floor plan, but they respond very strongly to textile colors and textures they can envision in their spaces.

While the aesthetic appeal is fun, designers take the selection of textile products very seriously. After purchase and installation, clients use these products for years. In many states, codes that relate to occupant health and safety make the interior designer legally responsible for the specification of the interior materials and products installed in the space. Therefore, the designer weighs many textile considerations, including

- appearance and tactile quality (touch or *hand*—the feel)
- performance, or functional properties, that affect wear-life and durability
- safety factors such as flammability
- installation and maintenance
- quality
- cost—initial and lifecycle
- client budget

Textile Fibers

The basic building blocks of textile fabric products are fibers. Fibers are usually long, thin materials that have a length of at least one hundred times their diameter. To be useful in textile products, fibers must have some desirable properties including

- strength
- abrasion resistance
- flexibility
- moisture absorption

Designers need to know basic textile fibers and their properties to evaluate textile fabric performance for a client. There are two categories of fibers: natural and manufactured. **Natural fibers** are those that come from plant (*cellulosic*) and animal (*protein*) sources. **Manufactured fibers** consist of a combination of such materials as wood cellulose, coal, gas, oil, and chemicals.

Manufactured fibers can be categorized as *cellulosic*—those consisting of cellulose or plant fibers—and *noncellulosic*—those fibers that do not come from plant sources. Cellulosic manufactured fibers often have properties that are similar to cotton, flax, hemp, and jute. See **Figure 11-38** for more information about textile fibers and their properties.

Fabrics and Finishes

When choosing textile products and fabrics for clients, it is important to understand textile characteristics that impact durability and performance under various applications. Such characteristics include

- **Colorfastness**. As you know, the ability of fabrics to retain color properties with exposure to water and light is called colorfastness. The *Xenon Test* measures a fabric's resistance to color fading by reproducing a full-sun or rain or dew environment.
- **Flammability resistance.** The ability of a fabric or fiber to reduce fire spread or extinguish a fire is **flammability resistance**. The *Tunnel Test* rates a textile's response to heat and flame, testing its flammability.

SCI Design Group

Figure 11-37 Material boards help clients visualize the finishes for their interiors.

Natural and Manufactured Fibers			
Natural Fibers			
Natural Cellulosic Fibers			
Fiber	**Source**	**Characteristics**	**Uses**
Cotton	***Cotton plant seeds*** *Note:* Cotton is the most important natural fiber throughout the world. In the U.S., fourteen major cotton growing states.	*Advantages:* strong, soft feel, excellent moisture absorption, stronger wet than dry, dries quickly; flame-retardant finishes help reduce flammability *Disadvantages:* wrinkles, mildews, and fades; decomposes with prolonged sunlight exposure	Curtains, draperies, upholstery fabric
Flax	***Flax plant*** *Note:* Flax fiber is used to make linen fabric. It is the oldest of all domestically produced fibers and grown in three states in the U.S. Considered a luxury fiber so a limited quantity made.	*Advantages*: more luxurious than cotton, holds dye well, pliable, stronger when wet, excellent absorbency, highly resistant to UV damage, insects, and mildew *Disadvantages*: limited production, high cost, poor abrasion resistance, burns easily	Upholstery and drapery fabrics; wallcoverings
Hemp	***Hemp plant*** *Note:* Use of hemp dates back to the Stone Age. Gaining in popularity today as it is a rapidly renewable resource, maturing in about 100 days.	*Advantages*: can be grown organically; prevents erosion, removes toxins and aerates soil; highly resistant to insects; entire plant can be used; naturally resists mold, bacteria, and insects; high luster, durable, and strong with insulating properties; absorbs dyes readily and is less prone to fading *Disadvantages*: due to high processing costs, very expensive compared to cotton	Window coverings, draperies, wall and floor coverings
Jute	***Jute plant*** *Note:* One of the most popular and least expensive fibers in the world. It is grown only outside the U.S.	*Advantages*: less expensive than other fibers; excellent absorbency; antistatic; offers UV protection *Disadvantages*: low elastic recovery, strength, colorfastness, and sound and heat insulation	Curtains, draperies, wallcoverings; area rugs for residential and commercial applications
Bamboo	***Bamboo tree*** *Note:* Bamboo fiber resembles cotton in its unspun form.	*Advantages*: fast growing on almost all continents; grows without use of pesticides, herbicides, or fertilizers; fibers are smooth, strong, durable, highly absorbent, excellent wicking ability, softer than cotton, and long-lasting *Disadvantages*: cost, can allow UV light to penetrate the cloth; does not offer great protection from sun	Window shades, window coverings, and wallcoverings

(Continued)

Figure 11-38 Natural and manufactured fibers are used for many products and furnishings.

Natural and Manufactured Fibers *(Continued)*			
Natural Protein Fibers			
Wool	***Sheep hair*** (Can be organic. Other types of wool come from alpacas, Cashmere goats, and Angora goats.) *Note:* Sheep live in all 50 states. Major wool producers are outside of the U.S.	*Advantages*: flame resistant; resilient; durable, and water repellent; dyes well; thermal retention and sound absorption properties *Disadvantages*: yellows with age, shrinks, susceptible to insect damage	Upholstery, draperies, wallcoverings, and carpet
Silk	***Cocoon of silk worm*** *Note:* Discovery of silk occurred in China. Silkworms produce silk fiber.	*Advantages*: strongest of all natural fibers; soft and comfortable, has good luster, and absorbs dye readily; drapes beautifully; biodegrades in landfills *Disadvantages*: may require dry cleaning; sensitive to light; susceptible to insect damage and deterioration from soil	Window treatments, upholstery, and wallcoverings
Manufactured Fibers			
Fiber	**Type**	**Characteristics**	**Uses**
Acetate	***Cellulosic*** *Note:* First developed in Switzerland, manufacture of acetate utilizes plant fibers.	*Advantages:* has the look and feel of silk for lower cost; is smooth, silky, and drapes well; absorbent and dries quickly, cleans easily; holds shape well *Disadvantages:* heat sensitive; releases gases if not solution dyed	Drapery and upholstery fabrics
Acrylic	***Noncellulosic*** *Note:* Acrylic consists of elements from natural gas, air, water, and petroleum.	*Advantages:* similar to wool, but less costly; can be laundered; fibers are soft, warm, and have rich colors; resistant to insects and outdoor elements including sunlight *Disadvantages:* pills easily	Curtains, draperies, and outdoor upholstery fabrics
Nylon	***Noncellulosic*** *Note:* Introduced in the U.S. just before WWII.	*Advantages:* strong, silky, stable, resilient, natural luster, dyes well, drapes well, repels water, and is abrasion resistant; easy to launder *Disadvantages:* static electricity	Drapery and upholstery fabrics
Olefin (polypropylene)	***Noncellulosic*** *Note:* First developed in Italy, olefin is environmentally friendly.	*Advantages:* resistant to chemicals, moisture, abrasion, and stains; colorfast and extremely lightweight; low cost and durable *Disadvantages:* heat sensitive, nonabsorbent	Draperies and wallcoverings
Polyester	***Noncellulosic*** *Note:* Polyester was first introduced in the U.S.	*Advantages:* strong, abrasion resistant, and resilient; dyes easily; drapes well, and retains shape; resists wrinkles, stretching, moths, and mildew *Disadvantages:* nonabsorbent; creates static electricity; uses petroleum products	Curtain and drapery fabrics; wallcoverings
Rayon	***Cellulosic*** *Note:* Made from wood pulp, rayon fibers are sometimes blended with silk or wool to decrease price of these natural fibers.	*Advantages:* soft, highly absorbent fibers; resistant to shrinkage; dyes easily, less likely to fade, and drapes well; luster and sheen similar to silk, but less costly *Disadvantages:* low strength, poor dimensional stability; fades easily and deteriorates with continuous exposure to sun; low abrasion resistance	Curtains, draperies, and upholstery fabrics

Figure 11-38 *(Continued)*

- **Abrasion resistance.** This describes the ability of fabric or textile product to resist wear caused by people or objects rubbing against it. Abrasion tests can help predict how well fibers and fabrics stand up to wear. The *Wyzenbeek Test* evaluates abrasion resistance in terms of **double rubs**—back-and-forth motions rubbing over the length and width of a fabric to simulate wear. In contrast, the *Martindale Test* involves mounting fabric on a machine in a figure-eight pattern which also performs rubbing motions to test wear.
- **Physical properties.** The ability of fabrics to retain their shape, flexibility, and original fiber characteristics is also important to durability.

When evaluating fabric performance, textile fabric finishes are also key to certain applications—especially for commercial design. Many are applied after the textile product is created. Textile suppliers can help interior designers identify the performance finishes for specific applications. For instance, if a fabric is to be used in a hospital setting, a requirement would be to meet ASTM standards for antimicrobial finishes. Typical finishes applied to fabrics can be

- antibacterial or antimicrobial
- flame-resistant or flame-retardant
- moth-resistant or mothproof
- soil- and stain-resistant
- water-repellent, water-resistant, or waterproof

Textiles, particularly in the commercial market, often undergo treatment with flame-retardant and soil- and stain-resistant agents. The first is for the protection of the occupants; the other is for the protection of the fabric. These chemical agents can leave faint residues that emit toxic fumes, reducing indoor air quality (IAQ).

The VOCs new materials and finishes generate often go through the *off-gassing process*—the evaporation of volatile chemicals from nonmetal objects. If items receive chemical treatment to make them flame-retardant or stain-resistant, they are going to off-gas. The Environmental Protection Agency (EPA) ranks IAQ as one of the top five environmental concerns because of the amount of time people spend indoors. The EPA also reports that the amount of volatile material in indoor VOCs can be ten times higher than that found outdoors.

Environmental impact is another critical aspect of manufacturing textile products. The textile industry continues to implement environmental-protection strategies, redefining every aspect of production and processing. For instance, researchers are experimenting with growing organic cotton exhibiting soft earth tones, thereby requiring no dyes.

Commercial textile manufacturers are developing fabrics that are nontoxic, yet durable, attractive, and in compliance with the *Association for Contract Textiles (ACT)* and *ASTM* standards. Conversion of recycled plastic bottles into fibers and woven into fabrics has great success. Recycled polyester fiber is particularly appealing to the hospitality market because it is extremely durable and conserves nonrenewable resources. To attract environmentally conscious designers and clients, the textile industry is offering better consumer information about green textile products.

Accurately specifying textiles necessitates that designers stay abreast of new textile trends—both fiber types and design.

CASE STUDY

Designtex®—A Company that Strives for Sustainability

SCS Global Services is an organization that sets the standard for sustainability. It issued the first gold-level certification to *Designtex*, a Steelcase Company under the *facts™ ecolabel* developed by the Association for Contract Textiles (ACT). After companies demonstrate their products meet eight key *parameters* (rules or limits that control what something is or how something is done), issuing of the facts ecolabel occurs. These parameters include product lifecycle—fiber sourcing, safety of material, water conservation, water quality, energy, recycling practices, air quality in manufacturing, and social accountability. The basis for these requirements is the NSF/ANSI 336 standard. This is the principal standard used in the U.S. to evaluate and certify the sustainability of commercial furnishings. In particular, they recognized the Designtex textiles collection—including its *Concept, Precision,* and *Pop Art* styles.

Investigate and Reflect

Go to the NSF website and search for the NSF/ANSI 336 standard. Why is meeting these standards a benefit for textile producers and designers? How do clients benefit? What are the consequences to clients, designers, and the environment if manufacturers do not strive to meet such standards?

Chapter 11

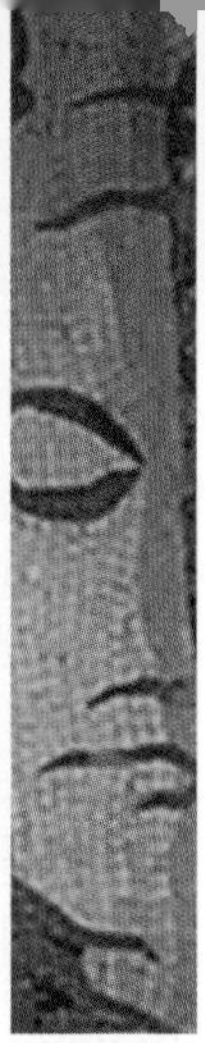

Review and Assess

Summary

- Interior materials and finishes reflect the client's personal preferences and reveal information about place as well as the traditions or culture of people.
- Interior materials and finishes cover walls, floors, ceilings, windows, and furnishings.
- By selecting green, eco-friendly materials and finishes, interior designers help create healthier client environments.
- MSDS and ecolabels help ensure material selections are safe for clients.
- Designers specify finishes that enhance the aesthetics and functionality of walls.
- Paint, brick, concrete, glass block, plaster, stone, tile, wallcoverings, and wood are all effective wall treatments.
- Soft floor coverings are resilient and consist of natural or manufactured materials.
- Hard floors and floor coverings have an aesthetic appearance, are durable, and are easy to maintain.
- Ceilings help shape space through their type of construction, use of lighting, and acoustical qualities.
- Windows provide daylight, architectural detail, and ventilation in both residential and commercial interior design.
- Hard and soft window treatments have functional and aesthetic qualities.
- Textiles offer aesthetic and functional properties in an array of colors and textures to enhance interiors and meet client needs.
- Textile fibers come from both natural and manufactured sources.

Chapter Vocabulary

With a partner, write the definitions of the following terms based on your current understanding before reading the chapter. Then pair up with another pair to discuss your definitions and any discrepancies. Ask your instructor for necessary clarification.

broadloom
ceiling coffer
cladding
colorfastness
colorways
cornice
custom run
double rubs
dye lot number
ecolabel
faux painting
flammability resistance
frescoed wall
glazing
lath and plaster
linoleum
manufactured fibers
Material Safety Data Sheet (MSDS)
memo sample
millwork
natural fibers
pattern match
pile
resilient flooring
stone veneer
take-off
tongue-and-groove
tufting
vinyl composition tile (VCT)
walk-off mat

Review and Study

1. What is the intention and purpose of fire codes in relation to interior materials and finishes?
2. Name three reliable third-party organizations that help designers select environmentally friendly interior materials.
3. What is the difference between an MSDS and an ecolabel?
4. Contrast a load-bearing wall with a non-load-bearing wall.
5. List at least five issues a designer must consider when specifying and selecting wall treatments.
6. Why should a designer test a paint color on a client's wall once the client selects the color?
7. What types of stone do designers use in wall applications today?
8. What characteristics make tile a good choice for use in areas exposed to water?
9. Contrast colorways, pattern match, and dye lot number.
10. Name six factors interior designers should consider when making a flooring choice with clients.
11. By what performance characteristics is carpet evaluated?
12. What are four green or sustainable design strategies used with carpet?
13. Contrast linoleum with resilient vinyl flooring.
14. What components are used to make glazed ceramic tile, quarry tile, and porcelain tile? Name a residential area for which you might specify each.
15. Name five types of flat ceiling treatments and four types of ceilings that use angles and curves.
16. List eight popular types of windows.
17. How do window blinds and shutters differ?
18. Name six considerations a designer weighs before specifying textiles for a client project.
19. Contrast natural fibers and manufactured fibers.
20. List five finishes that can be applied to textiles.

Critical Analysis

21. **Infer**. Suppose a local school district has hired you to specify durable paint finishes for the preschool classrooms, gymnasium, cafeteria and kitchen, and hallway areas. Infer which finishes, properties, and reflectance levels to recommend for each area. Write a summary of your recommendations.
22. **Analyze evidence.** The text cites that the bamboo flooring industry *may* produce environmental benefits. Use the text and other reliable resources (GREENGUARD, American Hardwood Information Center, USGBC, etc.) to further research whether bamboo is always a sustainable product. How do bamboo growth, harvest, and production methods contribute to whether the product is green? How does shipping distance impact whether the product is green? Analyze and discuss your findings in class.
23. **Identify central issues.** Suppose the principal designer at your firm wants you to research flooring options for a new commercial client. The client *does not* want wood, bamboo, natural stone, or tile flooring. Generate a creative list of questions to ask your client to identify central issues regarding flooring for the structure.

Think like a Designer

24. **Reading and writing.** Go to the websites for the International Code Council (ICC), International Building Code (IBC), American National Standards Institute (ANSI), and ASTM International. Read the "About" or "Overview" sections on each website to learn about their functions and services. Write a summary of each and note why an interior designer might refer to such codes when protecting the health, safety, and well-being (HSW) of the public.
25. **Color evaluation.** Experiment with choosing paint colors by utilizing one or more of the paint-visualizing tools on paint manufacturer websites. How can these evaluation tools help you and your clients select paint colors? Why is it still necessary to try client color choices on walls in your client's space?

26. **Materials disposal research.** Research the guidelines in your state for proper handling and disposal of environmentally hazardous materials used in the field of interior design, including paint and other finishes. Create a digital poster of your findings and post it to the class web page.
27. **Math practice.** Working in teams of four, select an office, lobby, bathroom, or classroom to be painted.
    A. Create a chart (see the example on page 352) to accurately determine the paint type and quantity needed for this project.
    B. Draw a quick sketch of the area, including all architectural details to be painted (baseboards, built-in bookcases, window and door trim, ceiling, etc.). List the areas on the chart.
    C. Determine suitable types of paints for the project and list them on the chart. Use colored pencils to highlight where each paint type will be used on the quick sketch. Create a legend in the lower right corner noting the color that represents each paint type.
    D. Take appropriate measurements to calculate the total square feet for each paint type. Record the results on the chart.
    E. Determine the quantity of paint to purchase.
28. **Digital poster.** Use the text and additional resources to create a digital poster that identifies the various types and properties of woods used for interiors. When complete, share your poster on the class web page.
29. **Math practice.** Presume you and your partner have been hired to replace the floor coverings in your classroom and an adjacent room. The school wants carpet in your room and linoleum in the other. Obtain the square-yard pricing from the website of a local flooring supplier. (Use the formulas on page 366.) Then do the following:
    A. Measure and calculate the area of each room. Make a quick sketch of the rooms and show your area measurements and calculations.
    B. Calculate the total square footage of carpet for one room and linoleum for the other. Calculate the 10-percent overage for each and the total cost of materials.
30. **Writing**. Presume you have a residential client who really likes the look of quarry tile and e-mails you about wanting to use it in a bathroom remodel. Write an e-mail reply to your client explaining why quarry tile may not be appropriate. Make recommendations that offer the desired look with more durability for the bathroom. Include photos of some possibilities.
31. **Research and writing.** Use reliable resources to identify different fabrics and finishes, materials, and their characteristics. Then create a fiber and fabric sample resource file to use as a reference for design projects.

Design Application

32. **Custom wallcovering or textile design.** Create a custom wallcovering or textile design for use in your own home. Use the following steps.
    A. Research the past four generations of your family heritage and history. Identify common symbols, colors, and design elements that capture the culture. Then create a family tree and record any relevant family stories.
    B. Use a CAD program to draw and combine the common symbols, colors, and design elements you found in different arts and artifacts into the design of your custom wallcovering or textile.
    C. Print at least 10 examples of your thinking process at different stages of the design. Save each example of your process drawings in your computer folder.
    D. Print a rendered copy of the final drawing. *Note:* You can render the print in Photoshop or Illustrator, or you can hand render it.
    E. Mount your rendered design to the front of your final design board.
    F. Write a summary of the following and attach it to the *back* of your final design board: yarn content of the textile or material content of the wallcovering; the scale of the design (for example, ½"=1'-0"); your source of inspiration; and your name.
    G. Deliverables to your instructor: the mounted final textile or wallcovering design and a *binder* containing your family history/heritage, documentation of research of design symbols/elements, and CAD drawings showing your thinking process and exploration of a design solution.
33. **Portfolio builder.** Select your best work from items 26, 28, 29, 31, 33, and 36 and save them in your traditional and/or digital portfolios for later use.

Furnishings and Accessories

Chris Little Photography/Rabaut Design Associates

Chapter 12

Design Insight

"The details are not the details. They make the design."

Charles Eames

Learning Targets

After studying this chapter, you will be able to

- analyze modern iconic chair designs and their influence on furnishings.
- distinguish among relevant features of common furniture types.
- evaluate quality, construction, and good design characteristics of common furniture types.
- identify types of accessories and common methods for using them in interior spaces.

Introduction

Furniture is often a design statement for the home or workplace that reflects a distinctive style and personality. Furniture may have a specific function, or it can make an artistic statement. It may have clean lines and right angles, swooping contours, and dainty details, or masculine hues, and a cultural emphasis. Furniture should also meet the scale of the user. Similar to finishes, furniture should reflect the concept of the space.

Designers select furniture based not only on function and style, but also on historical precedents (such as the influence of modern iconic chairs), quality and durability, ergonomic needs, and age of the occupant.

Interior designers generally select accessories together with their clients. Accessories complete and enhance interior spaces.

The Influence of Modern Iconic Chair Design

Chairs reflect the periods and styles throughout history. Like all material examples of culture, chairs are thoughts in intangible form—they mirror a record of people's lives, attitudes, and ideas. They enhance the understanding of people in the past and present.

As an object of constant experimentation, the chair has fascinated designers for centuries. It is one of the few pieces of furniture that has evolved across cultures over hundreds of years. A chair is not just a place to sit—it is a product and reflection of the age in which it was designed, **Figure 12-1**.

WHITE RABBIT83/Shutterstock.com

Figure 12-1 The chair has been a constant source of experimentation for designers over the years. *What do you think was the design inspiration for the rocking chair? Investigate the transformation of rocking chairs throughout history.*

The storyline of modern furniture begins in the middle of the nineteenth century at the end of the *Industrial Revolution*. This revolution encouraged the shift from hand-crafted, one-of-a-kind furnishings to mass-produced furniture.

Modern Iconic Chairs

The study of modern iconic design begins by using the most common piece of furniture in any home or office: *the chair*. Chairs express both aesthetic sculptural beauty as well as the functional needs of the user. Following are 34 modern *iconic* chair designs that have emerged as classic chair designs. Classic chairs transform an ordinary room into something stylish and memorable. Learning these designs will guarantee you have both an instant historical and everyday point of reference as you recognize these designs in your community. Studying the current helps affirm your knowledge of the past and will help you make better furnishings and accessories choices for your clients, **Figure 12-2**.

Ant Chair

Marko Tomicic/Shutterstock.com

Argyle Chair

Michael Ransburg/Shutterstock.com

Ball Chair

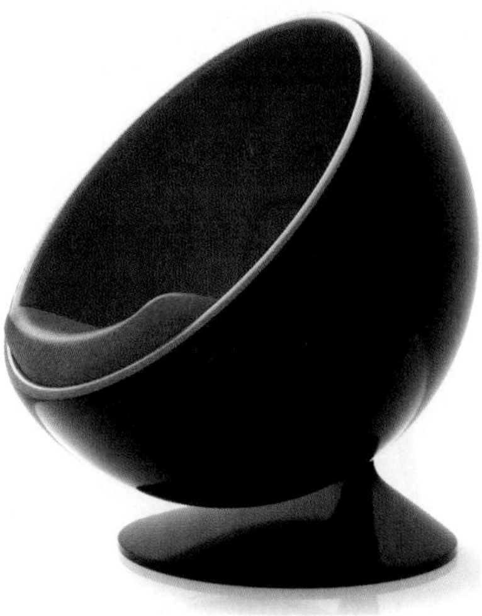

Your Design/Shutterstock.com

Barcelona Chair

Maksym Bondarchuk/Shutterstock.com

Bubble Chair

ZanyZeus/Shutterstock.com

Cantilever Cane Chair

Thomas Hernandez/Shutterstock.com

Ant Chair, *Arne Jacobsen.* Designed in Scandinavia in 1952, the shell of this stackable chair is molded plywood with a smooth lacquer finish. The legs are tubular steel.

Argyle Chair, *Charles Rennie Mackintosh.* As an Art Nouveau designer, Mackintosh used his chairs as a study of light and shadow in space. In his perpendicular style, this chair (circa 1890) has a stylized, flying-swallow cutout and a seat that narrows toward the back. It was designed for *Miss Cranston's Argyle Street Tea Rooms* in Glasgow, Scotland.

Ball Chair, *Eero Aarnio.* A futuristic looking chair, this 1960s design captures the whimsical feeling of sitting inside a sphere. It used fiberglass for the seating shell and Dacron polyester for the original orange-colored upholstery. Reproductions appear worldwide.

Barcelona Chair, *Mies van der Rohe.* One of the most famous pieces of furniture—the Barcelona Chair—was designed in the 1920s for the German Pavilion at the International Exposition in Barcelona, Spain. Made of welded steel and leather, once it is placed, it is rarely moved. Van der Rohe's mantra "Less is more" is evident in this design.

Bubble Chair, *Eero Aarnio.* Designed in the 1960s, this chair was made of clear fiberglass to encourage light to filter through the chair from all angles, achieving a visual weightlessness in interior spaces.

Cantilever Cane Chair, *Mies van der Rohe.* First displayed in 1927 at the renowned Weisshof in Germany, this cantilever chair was designed for the Bauhaus—a German design school. (The *cantilever* is a supporting member that projects from only one side of the chair.) It is functional simplicity at its best and reflects Mies's careful detailing and constructional clarity.

(Continued)

Figure 12-2 The designs of modern iconic chairs offer the interior designer both an instant historical and everyday point of reference when creating client designs. *Observe furniture designs in various commercial and residential places in your community. Which of these modern iconic chair designs appear to influence most of the furnishings you observed?*

Chair No. 14

Margo Harrison/Shutterstock.com

Cesca Chair

frotos/Shutterstock.com

Coconut Chair

Courtesy of Herman Miller, Inc.

Diamond Chair

Knoll, Inc.

Eames Lounge Chair

Courtesy of Herman Miller, Inc.

Eames Molded Plywood Dining Chair

nakamasa/Shutterstock.com

Chair No. 14, *Michael Thonet.* Perfecting a process of mass-producing bentwood furniture in the 1860s, Thonet used only 6 parts and 10 screws for this all-time classic chair.

Cesca Chair, *Marcel Breuer.* Labeled popularly as the *Breuer Chair*, this cantilever chair was named for Breuer's daughter. Inspired from turning one of his stools on its side, it was constructed of a single length of steel tubing.

Coconut Chair, *George Nelson.* Inspired by a cracked coconut, this chair was introduced in the 1950s. It is highly comfortable.

Diamond Chair, *Harry Bertoia.* Made in the 1950s, Bertoia experimented with welded metal to develop a chair that represents practical art. Bertoia is quoted as saying, "If you look at these chairs, they are mainly of air, like sculpture. Space passes right through them."

Eames Lounge Chair, *Charles and Ray Eames.* The Eames lounge chair was constructed in the mid-1950s with a plywood frame and leather cushioning. It is a modern design often seen in today's interiors.

Eames Molded Plywood Dining Chair, *Charles and Ray Eames.* Constructed in the late 1940's of molded plywood, the comfort and enduring design of the chair earned the *Time Magazine* honor of "The Best Design of the 20th Century" award.

Figure 12-2 *(Contined)*

Egg Chair

Ralf Juergen Kraft/Shutterstock.com

Eiffel Base Shell Chair

Courtesy of Herman Miller, Inc.

Hill House Chair

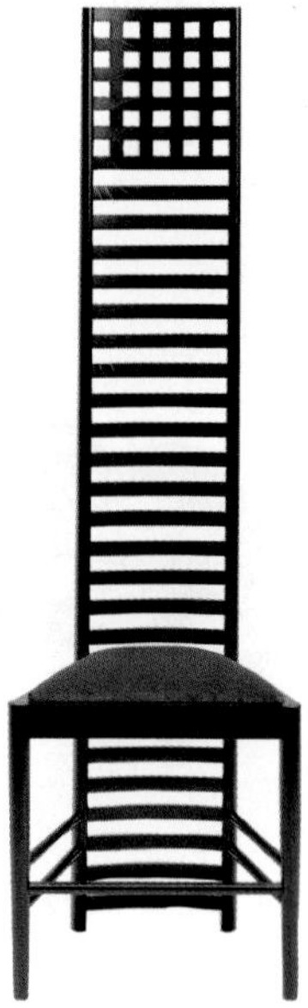

MATRIX INTERNATIONAL SRL
www.matrixinternational.it | www.matrix20.it

Jam Chair

Courtesy of Caligaris, Italian Smart Design since 1923

La Chaise Chair

plavevski/Shutterstock.com

LC2 Petit Arm Chair

3dimentii/Shutterstock.com

Egg Chair, *Arne Jacobsen.* Designed in the late 1950s for the interior of the Radisson Blue Royal Hotel in Germany, the chair reflects a design movement to adapt forms from nature into interior spaces.

Eiffel Base Shell Chair, *Charles and Ray Eames.* Designed in the late 1940s, the inspiration for this chair was the Eiffel Tower in Paris. The legs resemble the ironwork of the Eiffel Tower, and the seat mimics the curves of a turtle shell. It was designed to serve as a side chair.

Hill House Chair, *Charles Rennie Mackintosh.* Rather than a functional piece of furniture, this chair was designed to be decorative. The chair still sits at the Hill House in Helensburgh, Scotland.

Jam Chair, *Caligaris.* Timeless and unconventional, this Italian-designed chair is seen both in public and private interior spaces.

La Chaise Chair, *Charles Eames.* Designed circa 1940, this chair was entered into the Museum of Modern Art's International Competition for Low-Cost Furniture Design. The fiberglass seat is designed to hug the human body.

LC2 Petit Arm Chair, *Le Corbusier.* This cube-shaped chair body was designed in the late 1920s. It reflects a modernist response to the traditional club chair and reverses the physical structure of a chair by placing the supporting frame in an external location.

Figure 12-2 ***(Continued)***

LC-4 (Pony) Chaise Lounge

Baloncici/Shutterstock.com

Louis Ghost Chair

tony740607/Shutterstock.com

Mae West Lips

Victoria Andreas/Shutterstock.com

Model 3107

pio3/Shutterstock.com

Office Arm Chair

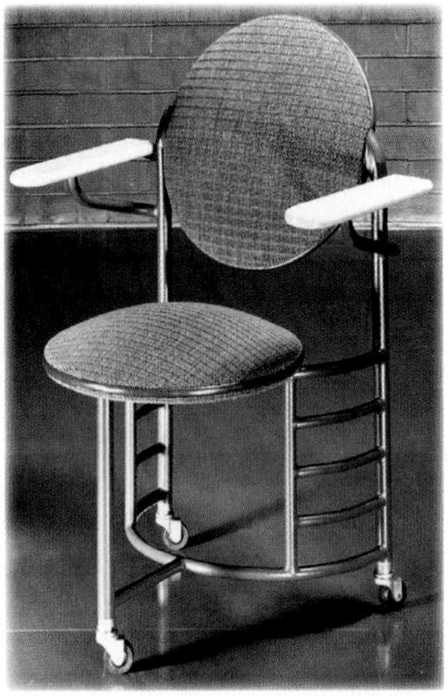

Courtesy of SC Johnson

Ondine Armchair

Jill Buckner Photography/As seen in the *Haute Living* showroom in Chicago.

LC-4 (Pony) Chaise Lounge, *Le Corbusier.* Also designed in the late 1920s, this modern lounge chair, also referred to as the *resting machine*, encourages only relaxation and respite. It is a piece of art in any space and is part of the permanent collection at the Modern Museum of Art in New York City. It was originally manufactured by Thonet Industries.

Louis Ghost Chair, *Philippe Starck.* The Louis Ghost chair is the best example of a modern take on an old classic Baroque-inspired chair. It is extravagant, yet subtle and elegant.

Mae West Lips, *Salvador Dali.* Salvador Dali created the appearance of this chair (circa 1930) in a painting of the 1930s movie queen—Mae West. French designer Jean-Michel Frank had it made into a piece of furniture. In the 1970s it was renamed for Marilyn Monroe.

Model 3107, *Arne Jacobsen.* This chair stirred the design world with its curves. This regular plywood coffee-shop chair is seen everywhere. The chair was and is heralded as a great Danish design.

Office Arm Chair, *Frank Lloyd Wright.* Developed in 1936, this office chair was designed for the Great Workroom in the Frank Lloyd Wright-designed SC Johnson Administration Building in Racine, Wisconsin. Wright designed for function as well as for the production of furniture by machines.

Ondine Armchair, *Bladamir Kagan.* With wing-like arms, curved back, and headrest, this chair illustrates comfort and elegance. It sits on a sculptured, oil-finished wooden base.

Figure 12-2 ***(Continued)***

Paimio Chair

Thomas Hernandez/Shutterstock.com

Panton Chair

Mostphotos/Shutterstock.com

Platner Chair

Knoll, Inc.

Red/Blue Chair

pentothal/Shutterstock.com

Risom Lounge Chair

Knoll, Inc.

Swan Chair

CHAIWATPHOTOS/Shutterstock.com

Paimio Chair, *Alvar Aalto.* This circa 1930 armchair was designed while Aalto was working on the tuberculosis sanatorium in Paimio, Finland. It was not, however, designed for use there. Molded plywood in sinuous inverted scrolls makes the chair memorable—particularly the striking profile of it. (*Note:* Aalto in Finnish means *wave*, a characteristic signature of his designs.)

Panton Chair, *Verner Panton.* Designed in 1960, this comfortable, Swiss-manufactured cantilever, strikingly sculptural stacking chair is made of a single piece of flexible polypropylene.

Platner Chair, *Warren Platner.* Created in the mid-1960s, this is a nickel-plated steel wire chair.

Red/Blue Chair, *Gerrit Rietveld.* Reflective of *De Stijl* (de-STUHL) movement (a design movement based on *functionalism*), this chair was designed circa 1920. The original chair had a natural wood finish, but later was painted with red, blue, and yellow lacquer. It is an abstract piece of sculpture and a seminal modern design.

Risom Lounge Chair, *Jens Risom.* Designed circa 1940, this casual lounge chair was inspired by Scandinavian design. It exemplifies a modern, casual style.

Swan Chair, *Arne Jacobsen.* As the Egg Chair's cousin, this commissioned design was for a hotel. It exhibits seamless curvature and defines the *Retro style* of today (a style fashionably nostalgic of the past).

Figure 12-2 ***(Continued)***

Tulip Chair

Knoll, Inc.

Wassily Chair

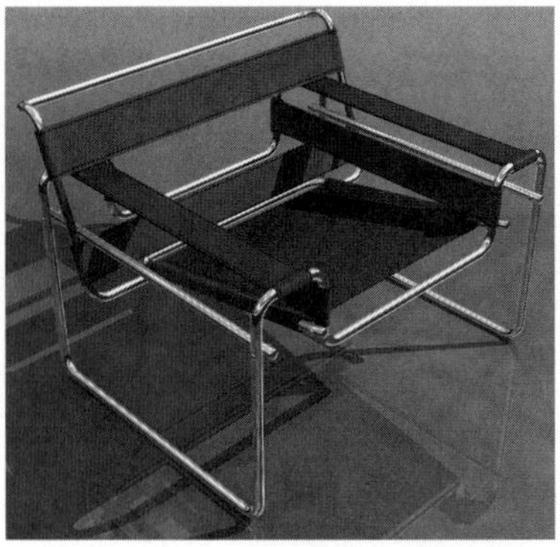

Neo Edmund/Shutterstock.com

Wishbone Chair

Marko Bradic/Shutterstock.com

Womb Chair

luckypic/Shutterstock.com

Tulip Chair, *Eero Saarinen.* The Tulip Chair, designed in the mid-1950s, made history with its pedestal base as the first one-legged chair. It was considered futuristic and an expression of pure modernism when it first appeared on the market. Now you can buy it with chair pads in different shades. It remains a popular chair today.

Wassily Chair, *Marcel Breuer.* This chair design of the 1920s was inspired by bicycle handlebars. The chair is boxy, but has a complex arrangement of planes. It was named after the German Expressionist painter Wassily Kandinsky.

Wishbone Chair, *Hans Wagner.* Designed circa 1950, this chair was inspired by a wishbone. Note the woven seat in this Scandinavian design.

Womb Chair, *Eero Saarinen.* Made in the late 1940s, this chair design was requested by Florence Knoll—an architect/interior designer who was a pioneer in workspace planning and design. Florence requested it to be something she could curl up in—like a basket full of pillows. The design offers a comforting sense of security; hence the name.

Figure 12-2 ***(Continued)***

STUDENT SPOTLIGHT

The Influence of Chair Design

Michael N. Bent. "The Barcelona chair is an iconic modern chair that was first displayed at the World Fair in 1929. Ludwig Mies van der Rohe also designed the Barcelona Pavilion, which showcased his modern designs. The principle of this chair is why it is my favorite; a mixture of cool black leather, chrome accents, and minimalism at this time must have been incredibly innovative. Now they are staples in design used often today, nearly 100 years later!"

Christine Nicolayason. "The LC4 Chaise Lounge by Le Corbusier is a favorite of mine because its shape is interesting and aesthetically intriguing, which also results in a very comfortable laying position. I also love how it combines shiny metallic metal with natural cowhide. The juxtaposition is unexpected and interesting."

Courtney Honigsberg. "The *Louis Ghost Chair* by Philippe Starck is a groundbreaking addition to the world of furniture design. By molding polycarbonate, this chair's transparency helps to enhance interiors without detracting from their aesthetics. With that in mind, the ghost chair is not only a harmonious addition within any interior but also a durable and functional piece!"

Courtney Sikora. "I love the *Lounge Chair* mainly because of the history behind the designers, Charles and Ray Eames. Their romance was like none other of the time. As a woman during this time period, I think it is incredibly fascinating how much input Ray had in the business and the design of their chairs. I think the lounge chair is a classic that will remain in homes for many years to come because it is comfortable as well as functional. Its classy, sleek lines look wonderfully inviting—a comfortable chair in which to relax and read a good book."

Selecting Furniture

Selecting furniture and placing it in an interior is another way that designers shape space. For both residential and commercial clients, furniture should meet the aesthetic and functional needs of the occupants, **Figure 12-3**. Furniture should also "fit" the size and scale of the people. As you know, *ergonomics* is the study of human relationships to the furniture and products that fill interior environments. The shape of the human form, its dimensions, and its need for movement are the basis for functional and comfortable furniture.

In interior spaces, furnishings communicate taste, style, and design preferences. Purchasing residential furnishings may happen on a whim or be added with deliberate planning over a period of time. For a commercial interior, the selection of furniture, fixtures, and equipment (FF&E) often occurs through a bid process. A bid process outlines specific details and standards for the furnishings to ensure whatever is purchased will handle the wear and tear of a commercial space.

Rabaut Design Associates/Photographer: VENVISIO, LLC.

Figure 12-3 Furniture should meet the aesthetic and functional needs of the users. *Predict the needs of the clients who use this furniture.*

Case Goods and Upholstered Furniture

Furniture falls into two general categories: case goods or upholstered furniture. **Case goods** are free-standing furniture pieces that are *not* upholstered. Examples of case goods include bookcases, wood desks, or sofa tables. It is relatively easy to determine the quality of case goods through the study of their materials, construction, and joinery used in the manufacturing or hand-production process, **Figure 12-4**. The quality of construction plays a role in the quality of the furniture piece. Construction techniques determine how the manufacturer joins pieces together to form a design that holds its integrity for the duration of use. Several such factors include drawers that glide easily, joinery, and the quality of sanding and finishing. **Casework** refers to built-ins or a piece of furniture attached to the wall such as a banquette.

Upholstered furniture often uses a frame, cushioning material, and covering. Examples are sofas and chairs. Construction of upholstered furniture is more difficult to assess in comparison to case goods. A solidly built frame and the selection of quality upholstery fabric are important to ensure proper wear for the client or occupant. After application to the furniture, upholstery fabrics range from cotton with a one-year warranty to synthetic fabrics with a five-year warranty.

Through client interviews, you can determine what factors, such as durability, to consider when specifying new furniture for their home or commercial setting. For example, in a residential setting, you might ask the client to indicate the number of family members and pets that inhabit the home. In a commercial setting, you might ask about typical use of space, volume, and frequency of use by the projected number of occupants. Determining the type of fabric to use on the furniture requires evaluation of performance standards. As you recall from your study of textiles, performance standards of the upholstery consider colorfastness, flammability, abrasion resistance, and the ability of fabrics to retain their physical characteristics such as shape and strength.

In addition to performance standards, designers also evaluate upholstery materials on the following:

- **Aesthetic appeal.** Is the color and pattern appropriate to capture desired style? There are a great number of patterns in upholstery fabrics. These include florals, paisleys, geometrics, stripes, plaids, and ethnic patterns.
- **Durability and construction.** How durable is the fabric? The type of fiber and the type and tightness of the weave determine durability of fabric.
- **Comfort.** How will the textile product impact human comfort? The geographical area and location of use (such as an outdoor patio) influence human comfort (for example, wool is rarely used poolside).

Shutterwolf/Shutterstock.com

Figure 12-4 Detail joints like the dovetail are a sign of quality in furniture.

- **Maintenance.** Easy maintenance is important to all clients. For instance, application of stain repellant makes it easy for clients to wipe away stain-causing dirt or grime.
- **Appropriateness.** Is the fabric or textile product appropriate for the application (for example, because silk often requires dry cleaning, using it on a kitchen stool is inappropriate)?

Designers often work with a client to order or specify furniture that is standard and in stock. See **Figure 12-5** for standard furniture dimensions. Furniture companies typically allow a customer to not only order from their standard upholstery fabric line, but also offer an option known as a **customer's own material (COM)**. This term is used by manufacturers to inform designers and clients that they will accept nearly any fabric you send to them, and they will apply it to any of their furniture pieces for you. "COL" stands for *Customer's Own Leather.* With COM or COL, the designer sends the fabric or leather to the furniture manufacturer to match at time of construction.

In other instances, a client may require the selection of custom furniture. Custom furniture offers the luxury of adjusting sizes and altering measurements beyond the standard range. Such furniture comes with upgrades and options. One such option is the use of COM.

Standard Furniture Dimensions (In Inches)			
Tables and Case Goods			
Tables	**Height**	**Depth**	**Width**
Buffet	34–38	24	60
Coffee	19	18	36–48
Conference	30	36	96
Dining	29	40	64
End	20	17	28
Hall	27	15	55
Sofa	26	14	72
Case Goods	**Height**	**Depth**	**Width**
Lowboy	36	38	18
Bookcase	50	36	10
Buffet	34	50	20
Chest of Drawers (three drawer)	Varies	18	30
Armoire	Varies	17	60
Seating and Upholstered			
Chairs	**Seat Height**	**Seat Depth**	**Seat Width**
Barstool	30 or 42	17	17
Dining, side	18 or 36	19	19
Upholstered armchair	16	26	30
	Seat Length	**Seat Depth**	**Seat Height**
Sofa (3 seat)	85	35	16–18
Loveseat	60	35	16–18

Figure 12-5 Although furniture can be manufactured in any size, standard sizes exist for convenience of the customer.

The fabric of an upholstered piece is the most visible sign of quality and style. To offer choice, a textile manufacturer will make the same fabric pattern in multiple color ways. Knowing that textile dye lots can vary slightly, the client or designer can request a **cutting for approval (CFA)**—a small sample cut from the same bolt of fabric from which the client's yardage will be cut. If the client has concern about the pattern repeat of the fabric, he or she can request a *memo sample*—a larger sample that shows the majority of the pattern repeat and colors of a specific material. Memo samples are only on loan; the client must return them to the manufacturer.

In addition to ordering new furniture, it is important to consider recycling and repurposing the client's existing furniture. Recycling furniture is a big design trend in the residential sector. Repainting furniture, faux finishing, and reupholstering give a new life to old or worn furniture in unexpected ways.

Repurposed furniture includes those pieces whose initial use has evolved into something different. Examples of repurposing furniture may include converting a dining table with missing legs into a foyer console table, or adding an old wooden door to the back of a bench to create a new, high-back bench style.

Similarly, but on a different scale and in a different volume, commercial furniture is recycled, too. For example, in the redesign of a large corporate office division, the designer may replace the fabric on the panel systems to create a new, fresh look. There are also specialty companies that facilitate the recycle of furniture for such uses as hotels and restaurants. For example, think of the number of dressers that a hotel recycles when retrofitting rooms with new product lines.

Influence of Design Centers and Trade Shows

New furniture styles and designs roll out annually at large trade shows. A *trade show* is an exhibition of new products and services—typically to tradespeople only rather than open to the public. The largest commercial-furniture trade show is *NEOCON—the National Exposition of Contract Furniture*. NEOCON debuted in 1969 with 750 exhibitors that filled 222,000 square feet of space in the Merchandise Mart, in Chicago. Today, it is considered the largest tradeshow of its kind in North America. It offers a unique combination of residential and commercial furnishings in one location.

For residential furnishings, the dominate tradeshow is High Point Market. Started as the Southern Furniture Market in 1909, High Point Market in North Carolina is the largest home-furnishings trade show in the world. It measures over 10 million square feet in approximately 180 buildings. This event draws over 70,000 people from 100 countries.

Common Furniture Types

As an interior designer, there are many general furniture types you need to know and recognize as part of your design vocabulary. The following includes a few descriptions that illustrate some common furniture pieces that designers use today. These pieces are used in both commercial and residential settings. Some furnishings unique to commercial design are also discussed.

Chair Types

Chairs are used in wildly different ways in residential settings. They can be iconic, such as a Mies van der Rohe leather chair, or small, side chairs that perch in a corner or alongside a period desk. Chairs add character and style to an interior. Here are a few chair types, **Figure 12-6**.

- **Rocking chair.** This chair is mounted on curved slats, called rockers, that permit it to be tipped forward and back. There are many types of rocking chairs available.
- **Side chair.** Small chair without arms, the side chair is intended to be placed against a wall when not in use.
- **Slat back or ladder back.** This is a wood chair whose back resembles a ladder.
- **Windsor chair.** Different varieties of the Windsor chair are distinguished by the design of their backs, including the scroll-back, comb-back, and bow-back. These wooden chairs are spindled back and have turned legs.
- **Wingback chair.** This high-backed, upholstered chair has side panels that are shaped like wings. It is designed to protect a person who is sitting in the chair from drafts.
- **Tub chair.** This is an upholstered, low-back chair with rounded back.
- **Club chair.** This is a cushy, upholstered chair with arms; usually upholstered in leather. The term comes from nineteenth century English Gentlemens' Clubs that used this type of chair.
- **Chaise lounge.** A French word meaning "long chair," this is a type of daybed or elongated armchair. The chaise has a long history from ancient Egypt to present time, **Figure 12-7**.

Figure 12-6 Common chair types allow for variety and add character and style to interiors. *As a designer, how and where might you use each type of chair?*

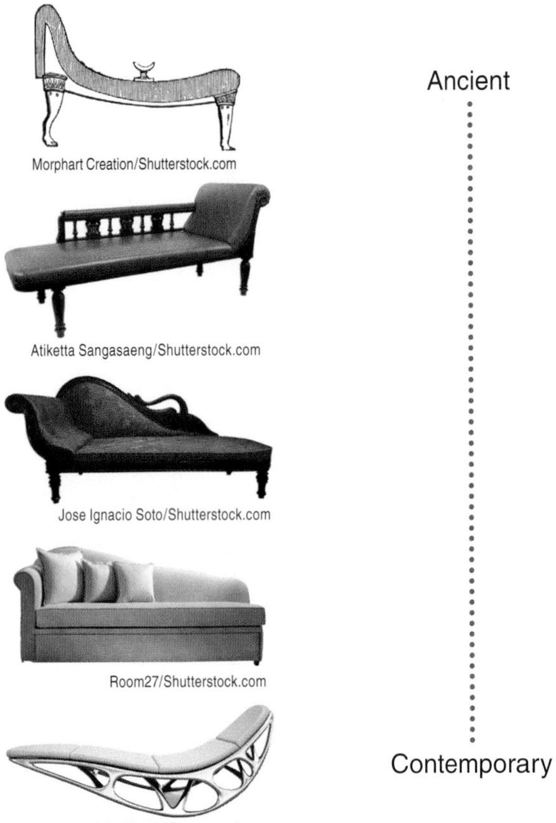

Morphart Creation/Shutterstock.com

Atiketta Sangasaeng/Shutterstock.com

Jose Ignacio Soto/Shutterstock.com

Room27/Shutterstock.com

Dim Dimich/Shutterstock.com

Figure 12-7 The chaise has a long history of use. *Choose your favorite chaise and investigate its history.*

Sofa Types

Sofas provide an anchor in any room—whether it is a hotel lobby or a living area in a residence. They are typically the largest piece of upholstered furniture and often support the focal point in a space. A sofa typically seats three people, while a loveseat seats two. Three features typically determine the style of a sofa: the arms, the back, and the legs or skirt. Certain arms and backs suggest modern or traditional styles, but the way a sofa is upholstered and trimmed can also have great influence on its look **Figure 12-8**.

Unique period pieces include

- **Camel-back sofa.** A sofa with a serpentine top originally design by Thomas Chippendale in the eighteenth century, this sofa is shaped metaphorically like the back of a camel. It is also available in double camel-back style.
- **Tuxedo.** This sofa has arms as high as the back. It usually has fairly clean lines with straight or slightly flared arms.
- **Lawson.** This sofa has a low, somewhat square back, with arms lower than back. It can come with square or rolled arms.

Ryan McVay/Photodisc/Thinkstock

Hofpils/Shutterstock.com

anekoho/Shutterstock.com

Petinov Sergey Mihilovich/Shutterstock.com

Figure 12-8 The arms, back, and legs or skirt of a sofa generally suggests a modern or traditional style.

- **Chesterfield.** With a tufted back, high rolled arms, and sometimes tufted seat, this sofa is often upholstered in leather and conjures up visions of English libraries.

Table Types

Tables are used for a focal point in a dining space. They may also hold favorite items in front of a sofa, or offer a surface to work on at all times of the day. When guests arrive, they often hold refreshments during social gatherings. Tables are versatile and often bring character to a room—similar to chairs, **Figure 12-9**. A few well-known period tables include

- **Drop-leaf table.** This is a generic term used to indicate a table with leaves that are hinged to the tabletop on either end. These leaves hang vertically when not in use. Supported in a variety of ways, the leaves enlarge the usable surface of the table.

Figure 12-9 Tables can serve many purposes and add versatility and character to any space.

- **Pie-crust table.** This is a circular table with scalloped rim, usually molded. The scallop looks similar to the crust of a pie.
- **Sofa table.** A higher table often placed behind a sofa, or in a hallway against a wall, it is characterized by a variety of elaborate leg designs.
- **Pedestal table.** A central or pair of columns is used to support this flattop table. Dining tables and end tables commonly use pedestals.
- **End table.** These tables add definition to a room. Place a side table between two chairs for conversation, at the end of sofa, or next to a bed.
- **Standing-height table.** For those who prefer to elevate their work or stand in a recreation room, they can lean on standing-height tables. Use them on their own or with stools for working or casual dining.

Case Goods

Case goods are free-standing furniture pieces that are not upholstered. Often case goods serve as portable storage in an interior, **Figure 12-10**.

- **Armoire.** This is a large, upright cupboard—sometimes with drawers—that is completely

Figure 12-10 Case goods offer clients unique, portable storage. *Investigate the unique history behind the lowboy and highboy chests of drawers.*

enclosed by a door or doors across the front. It is also known as a French wardrobe.

- **Chest of drawers (or bureau or dresser).** With a table-like base topped by drawers, historically, the dresser was used in the kitchen to prepare food. It is now often seen in bedrooms and topped by a mirror.
- **Lowboy.** A lowboy is a chest that is about three feet high with drawers.
- **Highboy.** A highboy is a chest with four or five drawers that sits on top of a lowboy.
- **Sideboard.** Often used against a dining room wall for serving food and drink and storing tableware, this furniture piece often has a shallow central drawer flanked by deeper drawers or cupboards on either side.

Desk Types

Desks are the most used work surface in the home and on the job. They keep people organized, and often store supplies and keepsakes. The height of the desk is critical to the comfort level of the user. If too low, it can cause back strain or shoulder fatigue. If too high, it causes strain in the forearm and wrists. Many styles of desks have been designed—from antique to modern, **Figure 12-11**.

Rolltop Desk

beautygut/iStock/Thinkstock

Secretary

sagir/Shutterstock.com

Kneehole Desk

sagir/Shutterstock.com

Figure 12-11 Desks are one of the most used work surfaces in residential and commercial interiors.

- **Rolltop desk.** A desk with a rolltop—which is a convex, **tambour shutter** of narrow strips of wood glued on canvas—that slides over the working surface.
- **Secretary.** This is a slant-top desk often with a chest of drawers below. At times, above the slant-top is a bookcase with doors. The user can open the slant-top and use it as a writing surface.
- **Kneehole desk.** This is a flattop desk with two sets of drawers that are located on either side of the unit.

Bed Types

There are many different types and sizes of beds in today's market, **Figure 12-12**. For example, in the hospitality sector, one of the most important pieces of furniture in the hotel is the bed. Comfort of the traveler is important. In the residential sector, a great variety of bed sizes and styles exist. Bed sizes range from king to crib. Bed types include those that are made to save space such as Murphy, platform, trundle, and bunk beds. In addition, there are those with historical precedent such as the

- **Sleigh bed.** This is a bed with high headboard and footboard; each with a scrolled top. It resembles a horse-drawn sleigh and was originally called a "French" bed.
- **Four-poster bed.** Four-posters were originally designed to hold hangings to insulate sleepers from drafts. The soaring posts make a dramatic style statement.
- **Tester bed.** Also known as a *canopy bed*, the tester bed is a four-poster with crossbeams that connect the posts and support a straight or arched canopy (or tester) above the bed. Today, loosely draped fabric is sometimes used to suggest a romantic atmosphere.
- **Platform.** The oldest style of bed, it is one of today's most modern choices. It is low to the ground, and sometimes does not even have a head- or foot-board. It offers a clean, uncluttered look in the bedroom.

Sleigh Bed

Melissa King/Shutterstock.com

Four-poster Bed

John Wollwerth/Shutterstock.com

Tester Bed

PlusONE/Shutterstock.com

Tester Bed

John Wollwerth/Shutterstock.com

Platform Bed

PlusONE/Shutterstock.com

Figure 12-12 Beds exist for human comfort and exist in a range of sizes. *When and where might you specify these historic bed types?*

- **Daybed.** These beds have two purposes. They can be dressed for use as a sofa by day, but include a twin-size mattress for sleeping at night. Daybeds work well in public spaces or private. Sometimes underneath they conceal a trundle with an extra mattress.

Commercial Furniture

There are many specialty pieces of furniture for every type of commercial space. Office furnishings are the most commonly used because the majority of commercial establishments have at least one office. The following includes several standard office pieces (**Figure 12-13**):

- **Conference table.** The design of a conference room should support the decision-making processes that take place in a corporate office. The main piece of furniture—and focal point of the room—is the conference table. The design and configuration of the conference table supports efficiencies and decision making when conducting company business. For instance, today's conference tables are equipped to support technology for conference calls, webinars, board meetings via Internet access, brainstorming sessions, as well as regular meetings.
- **Systems furniture or workstations**. Modular furniture allows for assembly and reassembly in different configurations to meet the work-space needs. Office modules consist of full- or partial-height panels, filing cabinets, bookcases, storage bins, writing surfaces, work surfaces, and drawer units. Wiring for technology and task lighting is integrated.

Conference Table

AptTone/Shutterstock.com

Workstation

zhu difeng/Shutterstock.com

Ergonomic Chair

Lydeke Bosch/Shutterstock.com

Reception Desk

Peter Rymwid Architectural Photography/Lita Dirks & Co., LLC

Credenza

Senger Design Group/Photographer: Paul Kohlman Photography

Figure 12-13 These standard office furniture pieces are common in many commercial settings.

- **Ergonomic chair.** The design of self-adjusting, individual office chairs sustains, supports, and accommodates the human body, which shifts and moves throughout the workday.
- **Reception desk.** This furniture piece is the first element of design and style that a customer or client sees on entering the business establishment. It communicates the company or corporate brand. The receptionist serves as the gatekeeper for the company. Often there are security and communication needs connected with the desk. Technology is an important component to the design of this piece of furniture. In addition, its functional design allows the receptionist to perform duties in a practical manner. The universal design of this piece of furniture accommodates all visitors.
- **Credenza.** Similar in function to a sideboard in a residence, commercial businesses may use a credenza in offices, workstations, and conference rooms. Today's credenza designs often include mini-refrigerators, room to store utensils, and shelving for additional supplies.

Green Furniture

When selecting furnishings for a commercial or residential interior, it is important to consider the source of the materials used to make or manufacture the product. With some research and help from the furniture representatives who provide you with specification sheets, you should be able to locate furnishings with quality construction and finishes that minimize environmental impact, **Figure 12-14**. Here are some questions to ask of furniture representatives:

- What furniture manufacturing processes were used to produce the furniture? Some can harm the environment.
- Was the wood for case goods locally harvested from FSC-certified forests rather than threatened or endangered species of trees? Oak and maple are better to use than mahogany or rosewood because they are more plentiful and often grow locally.
- Have safe, environmentally friendly finishes been used? Were VOCs released into the air when applying paint or other finishes?
- Are upholstery fabrics from rapidly renewable textile fibers such as cotton?
- What types of finishes were used in the fabrics? Were they low- or no-VOC products?
- What distance did the material or furniture travel to reach its final destination? For example, bamboo is a green product, but it is frequently harvested in another country. A great deal of fuel can be used to bring it to your client's office.

Designer Profile

Jill Salisbury—Environmentally Friendly Furniture

Jill Salisbury—founder and chief designer of el Environmental Language, now el Furniture—is a pioneer in green design.

el Furniture, LLC. designed by Jill Salisbury/ Michael McCafrey, McCafrey Photography

"As a design professional in support of sustainability, I struggled to find aesthetically stylish furnishings that were environmentally friendly. Inspired by the Cradle-to-Cradle philosophy of crafting design solutions that meet with life cycle and ecological goals, I began to seek ways in which I could offer alternatives for the interior design industry. I created *el Environmental Language* in 2001 after seeing this opportunity in the market place.

"My goal is to constantly apply nature's wisdom into my designs, resulting in stylish and sophisticated offerings that remain true to the promise of a better environment and healthier interiors. My passion and commitment to el's mission has cultivated a strong luxury brand that is recognized worldwide."

You can read more about Jill's design experience in Appendix B.

urbangreenfurniture.com:Made in NYC

Figure 12-14 The goal of interior designers is to specify furnishings that have minimal environmental impact. *What environmental factors should designers consider?*

- Do the furnishings utilize recycled materials? If so, what percentage of recycled material is used?

Be smart about asking the furniture manufacturers and their representatives to provide specifications and information relating to compliance with the *Clean Air Act* and use of sustainable forestry strategies before placing an order for your client.

Accessorizing the Space

Accessories—whether functional or decorative—are those objects that add beauty, style, and character to the space. Once space planning and the selection and specification of interior materials and furniture are complete, it is time to evaluate accessories to enhance the interiors.

CASE STUDY

Sustainable Furniture

The *Crescendo Console Table* is an elegantly sculpted piece, inspired by movement. Visually lightweight, the design of the curved side detail creates a sense of motion, providing mutable compositions, depending on the angle from which it is viewed. The design fuses classic elements with modern lines, juxtaposes light and dark, and integrates sophistication with sustainability, thus presenting an elegantly sculpted design that celebrates natural movement.

From design to fabrication, the ASID–Illinois Design Excellence award-winning Crescendo Console Table was developed with 100-percent sustainable materials. The frame is FSC-certified core material with a sustainably harvested walnut veneer and bamboo inlay. Bamboo is considered to be a rapidly renewable resource because it grows back quickly and is classified as a grass. The finish is a nontoxic natural lacquer derived from tree sap.

The Crescendo Console Table integrates style with sustainability, proving that luxurious living and environmental responsibility are not mutually exclusive.

el Furniture, LLC. designed by Jill Salisbury/Michael McCafrey, McCafrey Photography

Investigate and Reflect

Use the Internet to further investigate the Crescendo Console Table and design professional Jill Salisbury and her philosophy regarding sustainable furniture design. How can Ms. Salisbury's design philosophy influence your own developing philosophy about sustainable furniture design?

Without accessories, a space often feels empty or unfinished. Often the designer works with residential clients to select or rediscover accessories to personalize and beautify their spaces. The client may also need assistance strategically placing them once they get them home. With commercial clients, accessories usually receive a percentage of the project budget. With the budget in mind, the designer makes accessory selections in relation to location for viewing, type, size, and color. If the commercial project budget is large enough, the designer and client may **commission** (to place a special order) custom artwork for installation.

Accessories bring the important human touch to any interior and may include throw pillows, sculptures, keepsakes, or collectibles. They provide color and texture that, if placed properly in the space, unites the design elements and principles into a cohesive composition. For example, placing accessories in a grouping can support a fireplace focal point.

Accessories can also reinforce the client's concept developed at the beginning of the project by emphasizing a particular style, period, or design statement, **Figure 12-15**. For example, using accessories that support a country cottage style in a minimalist, contemporary setting may be out of place.

With residential clients, select objects that represent the family or individual's personality. These objects should reflect a *sense-of-self* for the family or individual. You should also consider scale, texture, and colors. Placement of accessories can be anywhere in the dwelling, including shelves, fireplace mantles, sofas, tables, countertops, and window ledges.

In public spaces, accessories often reflect the corporate brand and add warmth to an otherwise institutional feel. It is important to determine the maintenance and security of the accessories.

In private settings within the corporate interior, the corporation sometimes sets the standard for appropriate accessories that sit in view of visitors (such as family photos). While it is important for employee morale to have personal accessories nearby that mark their *place* or *territory*, it is also important for the corporation to limit size and number of accessories to communicate a business-like brand.

Gow27/Shutterstock.com PlusONE/Shutterstock.com

Figure 12-15 Accessories add a human touch and help reinforce the client's concept. *Review the images. What do you think the client's concept is? How do you think the accessories supported the concept?*

Accessories can serve different purposes in a space. They can be

- **Functional.** Examples of functional accessories include lamps, clocks, or mirrors.
- **Educational.** Accessories that serve an educational function may include an arrangement of alphabet letters or colorful geometric shapes in a pediatric hospital unit.
- **Decorative.** Sculptures and paintings are examples of decorative accessories.

Occupants view accessories from many directions and angles, and appreciate—particularly in residential interiors—the memories such accessories generate. They should delight and be delightful, meaningful, and enjoyable.

An unusual phenomenon often occurs after placing and arranging accessories. Once occupants walk past the accessories several times, they become almost *invisible*. To prevent this from happening, suggest your clients move accessories periodically. They will delight in them once again if located in a different place.

General tips for accessorizing include

- support for the period or historic style of the space
- an inventory of what the designer could or will use in the spaces
- placing accessories to support the focal point of the space
- considering balance of color, texture, form, and shape in the space
- considering the scale of objects in relationship to space and furniture
- determining how and where you want the eye to look or travel around the space (For instance, if you take the eye up to the ceiling through an art grouping placed on a diagonal, how will you, figuratively, bring the eye back down?)
- determining how accessories can move the viewer's eye away from an awkward corner in a space
- placing of large accessories before smaller ones (Experiment with a large accessory that is totally out of scale for the space. It may have unexpected, engaging results.)
- using the unexpected once in a while to combine different objects together, adding adventure and zest to the space
- using plants and fresh flowers to invite natural beauty to the space
- looking for *found objects* to reuse—they bring character and texture to a space that is difficult to find with new accessories

Common Accessories

There are many different types of accessories, **Figure 12-16**. Review this abbreviated list to see what you could use in the next design project. Remember that some of

nikitabuida/Shutterstock.com

Alena Ozerova/Shutterstock.com

Alena Ozerova/Shutterstock.com

Digital Vision/Photodisc/Thinkstock

VTT Studio/Shutterstock.com

Figure 12-16 Accessories help mark place or territory. Many of the best are "found objects" or a client's favorite things.

the best accessories are natural, free, recycled, refurbished, and rediscovered.

- clocks
- books
- baskets
- bowls
- photographs
- crystal
- plates
- sculpture
- ceramics
- earthenware

Wall Art

Wall art ranges from commissioned original work to a child's finger-painted print. A professional **curator**—a person who has the responsibility for the care and superintendence of objects such as art—commonly selects corporate art collections. Tips for choosing wall art include the following:

- Determine if natural or electric light can damage the art and place accordingly.
- Assess where light will focus on the art to best highlight it.
- Determine how wall color will impact the display of artwork.
- Hang art in relationship to furniture. For instance, if art is hung too high above a sofa or case good, it will appear to float and lack a relationship with the furniture.
- Group a number of small pieces of art into one composition rather than scattering them around the room, **Figure 12-17**.
- Leave appropriate negative space between groupings and around art. This *resting space* is important to avoid a chaotic look.
- Determine if the perspective viewpoint in the art will create an illusion of space on a particular wall.
- Make appropriate selections of the matt and frame based on the artwork. Color and size of the matt can conflict or focus attention away from the artwork.
- Carefully place wall mirrors. Place them only in locations where the view is important or pleasurable enough to see twice.

PlusONE/Shutterstock.com

Figure 12-17 Grouping smaller pieces of artwork into a larger composition gives a cohesive look.

- Consider finding a common element, such as a same color matt or frame, to unite them if using nonrelated pieces of artwork in a grouping.

Area Rugs

Area rugs are popular accessories today due to the mobility of the American family. Since movers can roll them up and transport them to the next home with relative ease, area rugs can bring familiarity in an otherwise new place. Area rugs are also popular in commercial settings where the designer uses them to anchor furniture groupings in areas such as a hotel lobby. While area rugs can pose a tripping hazard to some occupants or in some high traffic areas, they are versatile and have many uses in a variety of locations including

- accents for indoor and outdoor living areas
- wall accents
- accessories over existing carpet
- highlights on wood floors
- enhancement of a focal point in the lobby of an office building

With the popularity of wood or engineered floors in both commercial and residential settings, use of area rugs is more popular today, **Figure 12-18**.

Breadmaker/Shutterstock.com

Figure 12-18 Area rugs are popular in residential and commercial settings and help anchor furnishings in a space.

Sometimes an area rug is a source of inspiration for the colors and textures the designer uses in a space. Other times, an area rug is the last purchase for the location. Questions to ask a client might include

- Should the rug draw attention to some part of the space or create a new theme?
- Do you want a rug that will last for decades or for that location only?
- Will the location of the rug be in an area where there is moisture such as in a shower room?
- What shape do you want the area rug—square, rectangle, hexagonal, oval, or round?
- What type of fiber or pile height is preferred?

Before selecting and purchasing an area rug, gather some information. First, measure the area the rug is to cover. Dining room rugs should extend at least 18 inches beyond the edge of the table to accommodate chairs. To cover a living room area, choose a rug that is two feet shorter than the smallest wall in the room.

Consider whether the client prefers a traditional or contemporary design. There are many different styles and colors from which to select, **Figure 12-19**. Decide whether it will be a custom design or one already made—either by a machine or an adult artisan. Determine the preferred quality of rug. To assess rug quality, examine the following:

- **Knots per square inch.** Rugs are available in a myriad of densities, typically ranging from 30 knots per inch (very coarse) to 290 knots per inch (very fine). Finely knotted or finely woven rugs are most desirable. Curved lines in a rug's design appear smoother with more knots per square inch similar to pixels in a television screen. Density of the rug surface is also more attractive.
- **Construction.** Will you choose hand-knotted, hand-tufted, or flat-weave? *Hand-knotted* rugs tend to be higher quality because of the intensive labor required to make them. *Hand-tufted* rugs, which involve stenciling a pattern on the backing of the rug and then threading yarns into the design, are less expensive. *Flat-weave* rugs are less expensive because they require less labor.
- **Dye type.** In antique rugs, natural dyes are more desirable than synthetic. Natural dyes add charm and value, and they require more care and maintenance. Synthetic dyes are available today in an infinite array of colors that hold their color well over time.
- **Pile height.** Inexperienced rug buyers often mistake a thick pile for quality. In fact, the finest rugs are often the thinnest.
- **Appearance.** While some irregularity is part of the beauty of a handmade rug, all good rugs lie flat and straight on the floor and are reasonably regular in shape. The colors are in balance, without fading or bleeding of colors.

Common Types of Area Rugs

Rug Type	Key Characteristics
Oriental Rugs 	Recognized for centuries for their warmth and intricate design, Oriental area rugs are handmade and are ■ durable ■ often made from natural fibers such as wool, silk, or cotton, and *never* synthetic blends ■ considered works of art Each one is unique and playful—with the pattern often changing direction without warning. An ancient weaver took 900 days to complete an Oriental rug. They come from India, western China, central Asia, Iran, and Turkey.
Chinese Rugs 	Unlike most Oriental rugs, Chinese designs are very literal rather than decorative. Their simple, classic motifs have very exact meanings. The motifs do not unite to create one design, but stand alone and will stand out in any interior location. They often feature ■ a central, circular medallion ■ familiar objects in nature such as animals, flowers, and clouds ■ simple, wide borders and contrasting colors Usually high quality and extremely durable, by law, all modern Chinese rugs have the same number of knots per square inch.
Caucasian or Turkish Rugs 	For those with very geometric tastes, *Caucasian rugs* woven by tribal weavers in the region near the Caucasus Mountains may be a good choice. This region was the former Soviet Republic. Turkish rugs originated in Turkey, though many are produced in Afghanistan, Pakistan, and India today. These rugs ■ are generally coarser with simpler designs ■ include such designs as stripes, crosses, squares, diamonds, hexagons, triangles, and S-shapes ■ include geometric animal figures, such as crabs and tarantulas ■ have bright color palettes including blue, red, purple, yellow, green, navy, black, and beige—often all combined in one rug
Tibetan Rugs 	Tibetan rugs, woven exclusively with Nepalese coarse wool yarns, provide subtle variations of color and texture. They look rather primitive and are often a perfect complement to technology features in contemporary interiors. The distinguishing characteristics of Tibetan rugs include ■ vivid colors ■ huge and few motifs—such as medallions, flowers and rosettes, mythological animals and birds, and geometrical designs—woven in red, orange, pink, yellow, beige, blue, green, and white ■ relatively plain and dominant background colors of blue, black, red, orange, and less frequently, yellow or ivory

(Continued)

Figure 12-19 Whether traditional, contemporary, or historic, area rugs offer many styles and colors to meet client preferences.

Common Types of Area Rugs *(Continued)*

Rug Type	Key Characteristics
Kilims 	*Kilims* (kee-LEHMs) are flat-woven, reversible textiles made by nomadic people in Turkey, Iran, Iraq, Russia, China, Pakistan, India, and Morocco. No two kilims are alike. The kilim is a major part of a bride's dowry. The females weave each rug. Each piece contains symbols of family traditions and tribal identity. ■ Turkish kilims feature Mediterranean colors of gold, orange, and turquoise. ■ Iranian kilims are grounded in burgundy, rust, heavy blues, and greens. In addition to their use as prayer rugs, others uses for kilims may include coverings for the doors and windows of dwellings.
Persian Rugs 	Persian-style rugs are the most diverse worldwide. There are over 50 different Persian styles woven in Iran and other countries such as India, Pakistan, China, and some European countries. A *true* Persian rug is hand-knotted in Iran—formerly Persia—and features a border to emphasize the main pattern. Several other narrower borders may be part of the design. Persian prayer rugs are unique in that they contain a Moorish arch similarly found in mosques. Consisting of wool or silk, Persian rugs are very finely woven with complex designs. They may serve as wall hangings of accent rugs.
Native American Rugs 	Of the Native-American rugs, Navajo is the chief example. The original styles consisted of stripes and simple geometric shapes mainly associated with Navajo wool blankets.
Braided Rugs 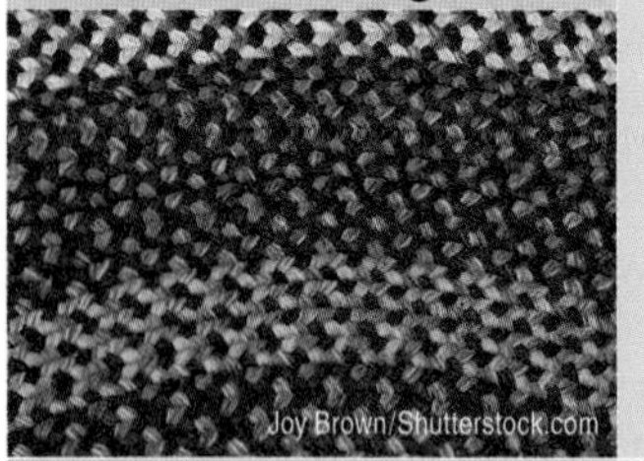	Practical and beautiful, braided rugs are constructed traditionally from wool but can be made from nylon, chenille, and olefin or polyester. Made from heavy strips of yarn or fabric that have been braided into thick ropes and then sewn side-to-side in spirals, ovals, round, or oblong shapes. They are very durable and hard wearing.
Sea Grass Rugs 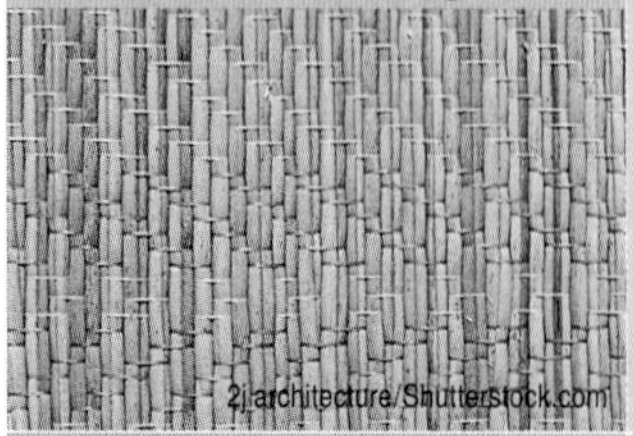	A product of the paddy fields of China and India, sea grass rugs are a popular choice among designers for their natural beauty and strength. Sea grass area rugs ■ are durable and stain resistant ■ come in warm, beige tones with undertones of green ■ include such different patterns as herringbone and basket weave
Bamboo Rugs 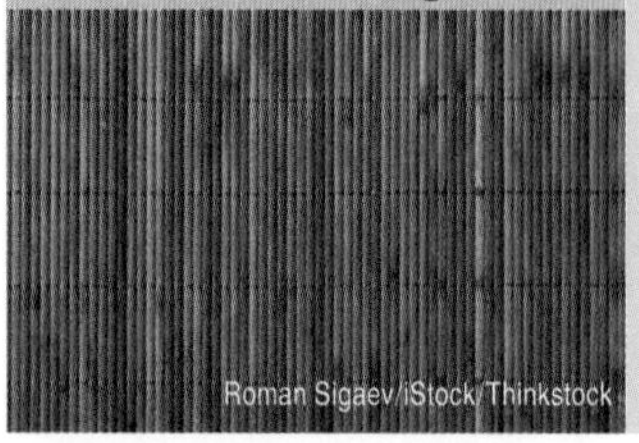	One of the fastest growing plants on the planet, bamboo is plentiful in supply and makes strong, beautiful area rugs. Woven from bamboo fibers, and featuring natural variations in color, these rugs offer texture and style to a room in a simple, understated way.

Chapter 12 Review and Assess

Summary

- Modern iconic chairs reflect periods and styles throughout history.
- Understanding iconic chair design gives the interior designer a reference point in making better furnishing and accessory choices for clients.
- Furniture should meet the functional and aesthetic needs of building occupants, both residential and commercial.
- Designers consider performance standards along with aesthetic appeal when specifying case goods or upholstered furniture.
- Designers and their clients may select standard in-stock furniture, furniture that utilizes the customer's own material, or custom furniture that allows for size modifications beyond the standard range.
- Recycling and repurposing a client's existing furniture is a trend in both residential and commercial sectors.
- Common types of furniture include a range of chairs, sofas, tables, case goods, and beds.
- Standard commercial furnishings for offices include conference tables, workstations, reception furnishings, and credenzas.
- Green furniture utilizes materials, finishes, and quality construction that minimize environmental impact.
- Accessories add beauty, style, and character to a client's space, and can serve different purposes.
- A designer often uses area rugs to anchor a furniture grouping in an area.

Chapter Vocabulary

For each of the following terms, identify a word or group of words describing a quality of the term—an attribute. Pair up with a classmate and discuss your list of attributes. Then discuss your list of attributes with the whole class to increase understanding.

case good
casework
upholstered furniture
customer's own material (COM)
cutting for approval (CFA)
tambour shutter
accessories
commission
curator

Review and Study

1. List five criteria on which interior designers base furniture selection for clients.
2. Why does the study of modern iconic design often begin with a common piece of furniture—the chair?
3. What is the basis for functional and comfortable furniture?
4. Contrast the process for purchasing residential furniture with that of furniture for a commercial interior.
5. In addition to performance standards, name five criteria designers also use to evaluate upholstery materials.
6. What is a *cutting for approval*? How does it differ from a memo sample?
7. Name the two largest furniture trade shows in North America.
8. List four questions a designer should ask of furniture representatives when selecting green furniture.
9. What are three reasons why accessories are important to the character of a space?
10. Name five general tips for accessorizing a space.

Critical Analysis

11. **Analyze reasoning.** The author makes the following statement in the chapter: "Like all material examples of culture, chairs are thoughts in intangible form—they mirror a record of people's lives, attitudes, and ideas." Analyze the reasoning behind the author's statement. Do you agree? Discuss your analysis with the class.
12. **Make inferences.** The text states that it is important to consider the source of materials used to manufacture furniture products and choose products that minimize environmental impact. Make inferences about other factors the designer should consider when selecting furniture products for clients.
13. **Draw conclusions.** Why should accessories for a client's project reflect sense-of-self? How does the concept of sense-of-self impact accessories in the commercial sector? Discuss your conclusions with the class.

Think like a Designer

14. **Writing.** Review the *Design Insight* quote at the beginning of the chapter. Write a one-page essay expressing your interpretation of the Eames' quote.
15. **Reading, writing, and speaking.** Investigate the *Zig Zag Chair* by Garrit Thomas Rietveld and the *Midway Chair* by Frank Lloyd Wright. Use Internet or print resources to locate images of the chairs. Read about the history of the chairs, including their used and unique design features. Use a school-approved web application to create an illustrated report to share with the class. Be sure to credit the source of any illustrations you use.
16. **Field trip.** Take an actual or virtual field trip to a design center showroom in your area. What products and services does the showroom offer to consumers, designers, and students? What designers and manufacturers exhibit at the showroom? If possible, obtain a map of the showroom and identify your key areas of interest. Write a summary of your findings including how this information will be important to you as a future interior designer.
17. **Research, writing, and speaking.** Select one piece of furniture to research from each of the following categories: chairs, sofas, tables, case goods, desks, beds, and commercial furnishings. Research the historical background story for each piece. How does the background story

impact the design of the piece? What are the key characteristics of each piece? How does the piece influence design today? Create a digital poster to put on your school-approved class website, blog, or discussion board. Include an image and brief summary about each piece.

18. ***Green* checklist.** Research the websites for at least five companies that are sources of green, sustainable furniture. Read the materials each company publishes regarding the sustainability features of its products. What organizations support the sustainability of their products? From your research, create a checklist or rubric you can use when evaluating the sustainability aspects of furniture for clients.

19. **Sense-of-self collage.** Create a collage of furniture and accessories that reflects your personality and *sense-of-self.* Label each item. Include a brief description of each and why it reflects your sense-of-self. Share your collage with a classmate. Does the classmate feel your collage accurately reflects your sense-of-self? Why or why not? To extend this activity, create a collage for someone you know as a potential client. What questions would you ask to determine the client's personality and sense-of-self? Present the collage with an overall summary of how the choices reflect the client's sense-of-self.

Design Application

20. **Custom rug design.** Design a custom rug for your own home. As a reminder, *symmetrical*, or traditional, area rugs or runners typically have a border, a centerpiece or medallion, and other symbols used in the background. *Asymmetrical*, or contemporary, rugs use cultural symbols in a simplistic way. Use the following steps to complete your design.
    A. Use the family heritage research/binder you completed in item 41 of Chapter 11 to complete the design of your rug.
    B. Use a CAD program to draw and combine the common symbols, colors, and design elements you found in different arts and artifacts into your custom rug design.
    C. As your design evolves, *print* at least 10 examples of your thinking process at different stages of the design. Save each example of your process drawings in your computer folder.
    D. Select yarn samples in representative fibers and colors for your rug design.
    E. Render a copy of the final drawing.
    F. Mount your rendered design and your yarn samples to the front of your final design board.
    G. Write a summary of the following and attach it to the *back* of your final design board: yarn content of the rug; the scale of the design (for example, ½"=1'-0"); your source of inspiration; and your name.
    H. Deliverables to your instructor: the mounted final rug design and the CAD drawings showing your thinking process and exploration of the rug design solution added to your family history binder.

21. **Portfolio builder.** Add the projects you completed for items 17, 18, 19, and 20 to your hard-copy portfolio or your e-portfolio for future reference. Be sure to include the best examples of your work.

Visual Communication: Drawings, Renderings, and Models

Chapter 13

Design Insight

"Drawings express the interaction of our minds, eyes, and hands."

Michael Graves

Learning Targets

After studying this chapter, you will be able to

- summarize the need for good visual communication and communication techniques.
- identify manual and digital visual communication tools.
- apply techniques for various presentation drawings.
- demonstrate sketching techniques and types.
- utilize various drawing systems, including orthographic, paraline, and perspective.
- summarize communication, techniques, and drawing conventions used in construction drawings.
- utilize architectural lettering techniques.
- demonstrate basic rendering techniques.
- create a basic model.
- summarize the BIM modeling system.
- produce interior drawings using both one-point and two-point perspective.

Introduction

The interior design profession relies heavily on the expression of ideas and solutions. The client cannot view the design ideas until the designer produces them in some format. Historically, hand-drawn illustrations and hand-built models were developed to assist clients in understanding proposed designs. Today, designers have their pick of many presentation techniques to help clients, team members, and even themselves visualize design proposals for a space that may yet require installation or building.

Interior designers use common communication tools also used by people in architecture, engineering, and the construction industries. They all work within the built environment and need to communicate clearly to each other.

In the past, a design student's innovative idea may have been lost because he or she did not possess adequate manual-drawing skills to clearly communicate it. With technologies today, students of all different skill sets—both manual and computer—can communicate their designs to others. The quality of the idea, however, is still most important.

Interior designers use three different methods to express design ideas: oral, graphic, and written. This chapter discusses both manual and digital ways designers visually communicate their ideas.

Importance of Good Visual Communication

Communication is a two-way street. *Visual presentations* are those that communicate design ideas to the client in two or three dimensions. Communication requires *visual literacy*—an ability to interpret and derive meaning from information presented in an image.

Graphic communication is the art and science of explaining ideas in picture form. A designer uses visual drawings, diagrams, models, and documents—all types of graphic communication—for ideation, construction, and presentation purposes. During the development of the design, interior designers use the following as they work through design process:

- **Ideation drawings.** Based on the client's needs, designers use **ideation drawings** to generate and explore ideas and design concepts. These drawings include bubble and block diagrams, concept drawings, and sketches and are generally used during Phase 2—Schematic design.
- **Presentation drawings.** Then designers use **presentation drawings**—also conceptual in nature—to illustrate design ideas and solutions in hopes of selling the design proposal to the client. They are also often conceptual in nature and include *sketches, elevations, perspectives,* and *renderings*. The designer generally uses these drawings during Phase 2—Schematic design and Phase 3—Design development. You will learn more about presentation drawings later in the chapter.
- **Construction drawings.** Once the client approves the design, **construction drawings**—or working drawings—offer precise, technical information to enable building or remodeling of the space. Construction drawings include *floor plans, elevations, sections,* and *detail drawings*. These drawings are generally prepared during Phase 4—Contract documents.

How well you communicate determines how the client perceives your skills as designer. Good design ideas deserve quality visual presentation. How clients perceive your professionalism depends on how good your visual presentation looks and what you communicate about it.

The more accurately the client understands the design, the fewer misunderstandings arise, resulting in a happier client at the project's completion. The bottom line—effective, professional communication makes money, helps eliminate problems, and develops satisfied clients who refer you to their colleagues and friends, **Figure 13-1.**

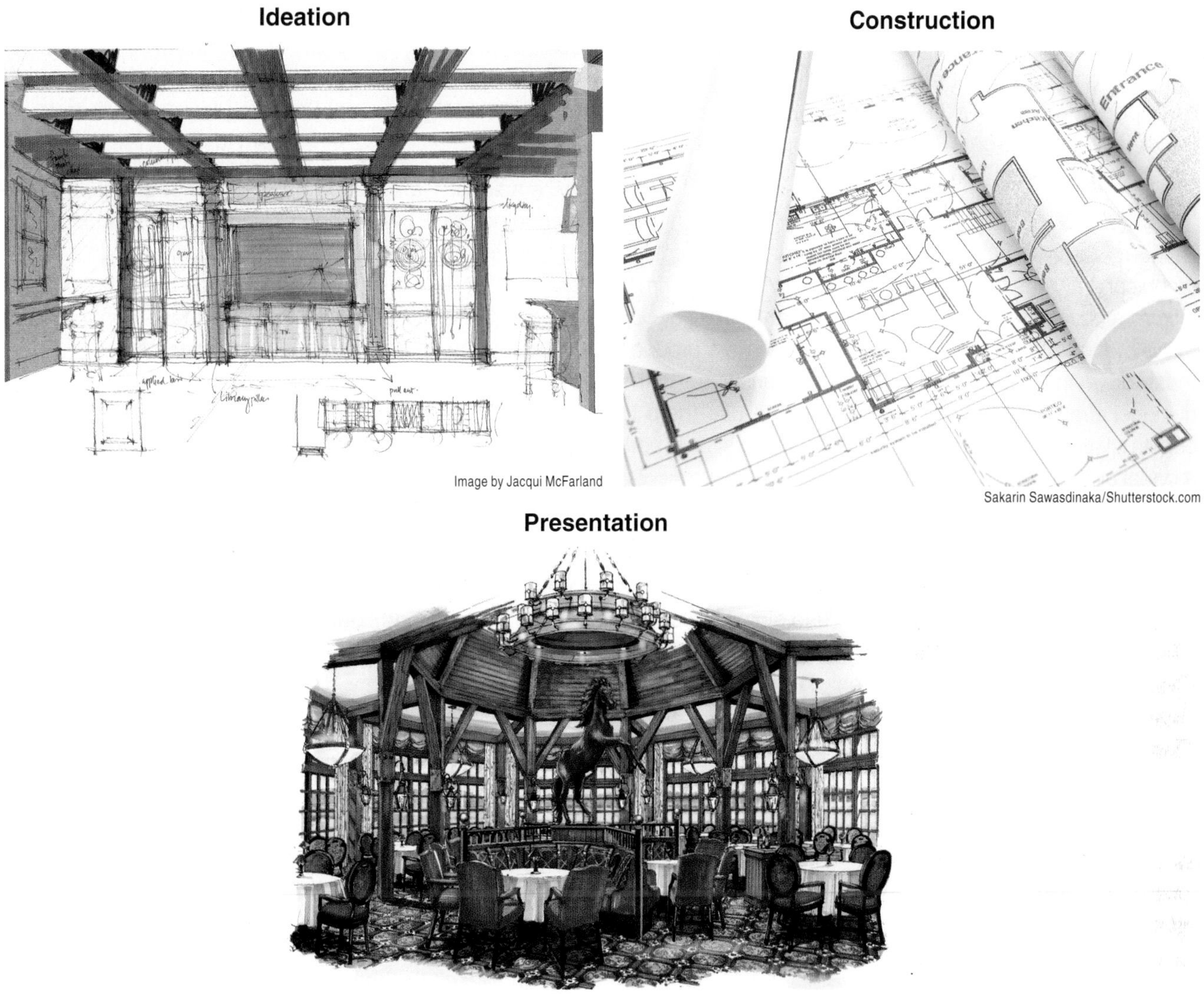

Figure 13-1 Using a variety of types of drawings helps ensure the client understands the design and eliminates problems.

The purposes of visual presentations are to

- translate the design concepts into a representative image or form
- sell the design idea to the client
- communicate the design to team members
- market yourself and your brand

Accurate communication is necessary with the client and also with team members. While a client may understand your idea for a hotel lobby niche in a conceptual three-dimensional sketch, your subcontractor may need a scaled, two-dimensional drawing to know how to actually build the niche. Therefore, an interior designer must have skills in a variety of communication media, particularly for today's technology-driven world.

Which visual presentation strategy you use depends not only on your communication skills, but also on the project's budget. A professionally developed hand-constructed model is expensive to build based on the number of hours required. If a quick, freehand sketch will communicate the idea or detail clearly, that is what a designer will use.

The four basic visual communication techniques commonly used today include sketching, drafting, rendering, and model building. **Sketching** is the use of fluid, loose lines to communicate an idea, concept, object, or space. Using only approximate measurements, these quick freehand drawings capture the main features of the idea or interior. Because the designer does not draw sketches to scale, you cannot build or construct from them. Freehand sketching is popular not only because of the client value, but also because the designer can perform it anywhere simply using a piece of paper and felt-tip pen—very inexpensive, portable tools. Designers create these drawings by either hand or on a computer using *CADD*—or computer-aided design and drafting software.

Drafting (architectural) is the development of hard-line technical drawings that systematically and visually communicate architectural structures—interior and exterior. By using precise standard measurements, designers produce these drawings in both two and three dimensions. As the designer draws them to scale, builders can use them to construct the project, **Figure 13-2**. Designers use both manual and digital drafting skills yet today.

Rendering is the process of adding color, values, texture, and pattern to an object or interior or exterior space using such manual tools as marker, pencil, pen and/or paint. The designer can also use digital tools. The goal is to communicate what and how the space will look like prior to building or installation. The use of implied shade and shadow in the "imaginary place" can convert a two-dimensional drawing into the appearance of a three-dimensional space.

A **model** is the scaled representation of a structure or interior space. An *interior model* shows interior space planning, millwork, doors, windows, and if needed, representative furniture. An *architecture model* is the scaled structure and often shows the proposed building on the site with representative landscaping. Both manual and digital model building is popular today.

Stocklite/Shutterstock.com

Figure 13-2 Designers use digital and manual drafting techniques to create precise drawings. *Predict the benefit of each type of drafting technique.*

Today, the most sought-after visual communication skills by employers are freehand sketching and computer-technology skills. Freehand sketching is popular because clients enjoy watching the process of an idea taking shape in front of their eyes. They appreciate the immediate feedback of observing the designer's communicate an idea to them and watching the idea evolve.

Computer-technology skills are popular because employers know the speed at which designers can accomplish their work using a computer. You will learn more about preferred digital tools later in the chapter. Often, the designer uses a combination of both freehand and digital technology tools to quickly and effectively present a design. A designer can use a combination of sketches, model building, and computer-generated imagery in every phase of the design process.

Basic Tools

The designer uses both manual and digital tools commonly and interchangeably in the development of professional visual presentations. There is also an intrinsic tool that designers need for developing visual presentations: *ethics*. Ideas and designs are what designers sell to their clients. Therefore, designs must always be original work.

Choosing Manual Tools

It is important to learn manual-presentation skills before learning such skills using a computer. The process of hand drawing helps you understand depth, proportion, and scale. This results in better work with computer drawing and rendering software. By understanding the principles of manually developing and constructing a drawing, you can more clearly direct the computer.

There are standard manual tools you can use to begin your manual visual presentation. The choice depends on client needs, your skills, the project's timeline, and client's budget. It also depends on your preference. Designers often develop strong preferences for favorite visual communication tools, **Figure 13-3**.

DESIGNER MATH SKILLS

Reading and Using an Architectural Scale

The tool of the trade used by designers to accurately and quickly determine scale is the *architect scale*. Similar to a ruler in length, this scale has a triangular shape with eleven different scales on three sides. It will be labeled *architect*. An engineer or designer uses a similar triangular scale for engineering projects such as site plans and maps. It is identical in appearance and size; however, its increments are different and are appropriate for engineering projects. It is labeled *engineer*. A designer can use both to accurately measure and create linear distance in proportional increments, but the ratios are different.

As you look at the architect scale, each side has scales in varying increments. Take a minute to become familiar with it. A twelve-inch ruler can be found on one side in addition to ten other scales. The number on each end of the tool indicates various proportional increments in 3/32, 3/16, 1/8, 1/4, 3/8, 3/4, 1/2, 1, 1/2, and 3 (Figure A).

To use the tool correctly for a 1/4″ scale drawing, locate the 1/4 label at the end of the scale. The 1/4 marking indicates the scale for measuring 1/4″ = 1′-0″. On the opposite end of the same scale, the 1/8″ scale can be found for measuring or creating drawings with a 1/8″ scale (1/8″ = 1′-0″). The two scales overlap and are read in opposite directions (read the 1/4″ scale from right to left and the 1/8″ scale from left to right).

- To read the 1/4″ scale, start with zero. Read the feet in increments of 2, 4, 6, and 8 from *left* to *right* ignoring the numbers increasing from right to left. Note that each of the marks to the right of zero on the 1/4″ scale represents 1″ (Figure B).
- To read the 1/8″ scale, start on the opposite end with zero and read the feet in increments of 4, 8, 12, and 16 from *right* to *left* ignoring the numbers increasing from left to right. Note that each of the marks to the left of zero on the 1/8″ scale represents 2″.

Below the zero mark, notice that there is a scale used to measure inches. For example, if you are checking clearances on a commercial construction plan (1/8″ scale) that reads 7′-8″, using the 1/8″align the 0 on the scale at *point A* and measure to 7′, placing a tick mark at that point. Then use the scale to the left of zero to accurately measure the remaining 8″ (Figure C). If a designer is creating a space, he or she uses the increments in feet on the scale to mark the footage and then uses the scale to the right or left of zero to measure the remaining inches.

Using an architect's scale, a designer can quickly check the accuracy of construction or presentation drawings and also create scaled drawings anytime, anywhere. With a little practice, the scale is more convenient and accurate than graph paper. To make sure those viewing the design documents know the general scale of the drawing, the scale should be written below each drawing even if there are several drawings on one page. When indicating the scale it can appear as 1/4″ = 1′-0″ or as a ratio of 1/4″:1′-0″.

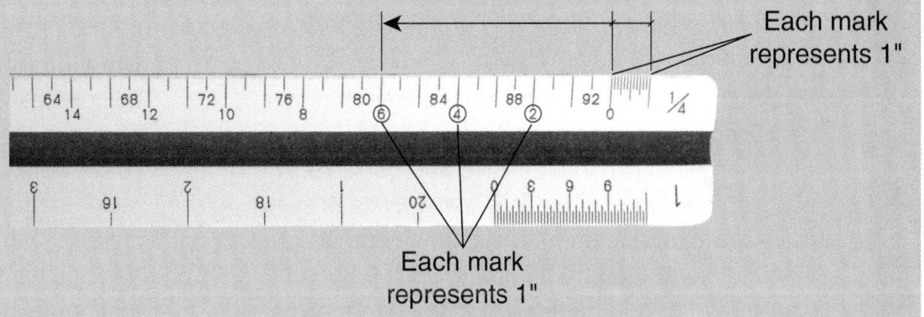

Figure B

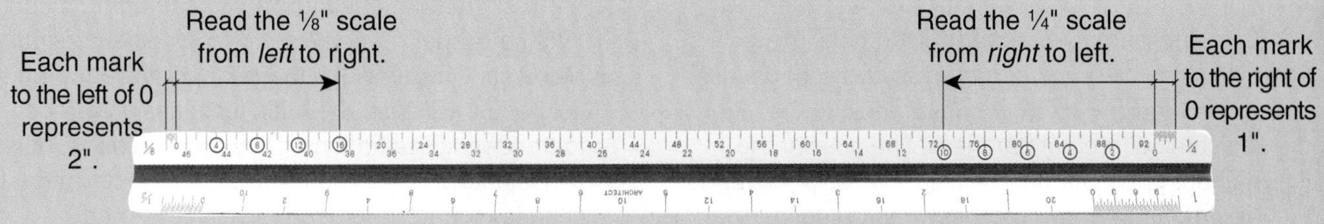

Figure A

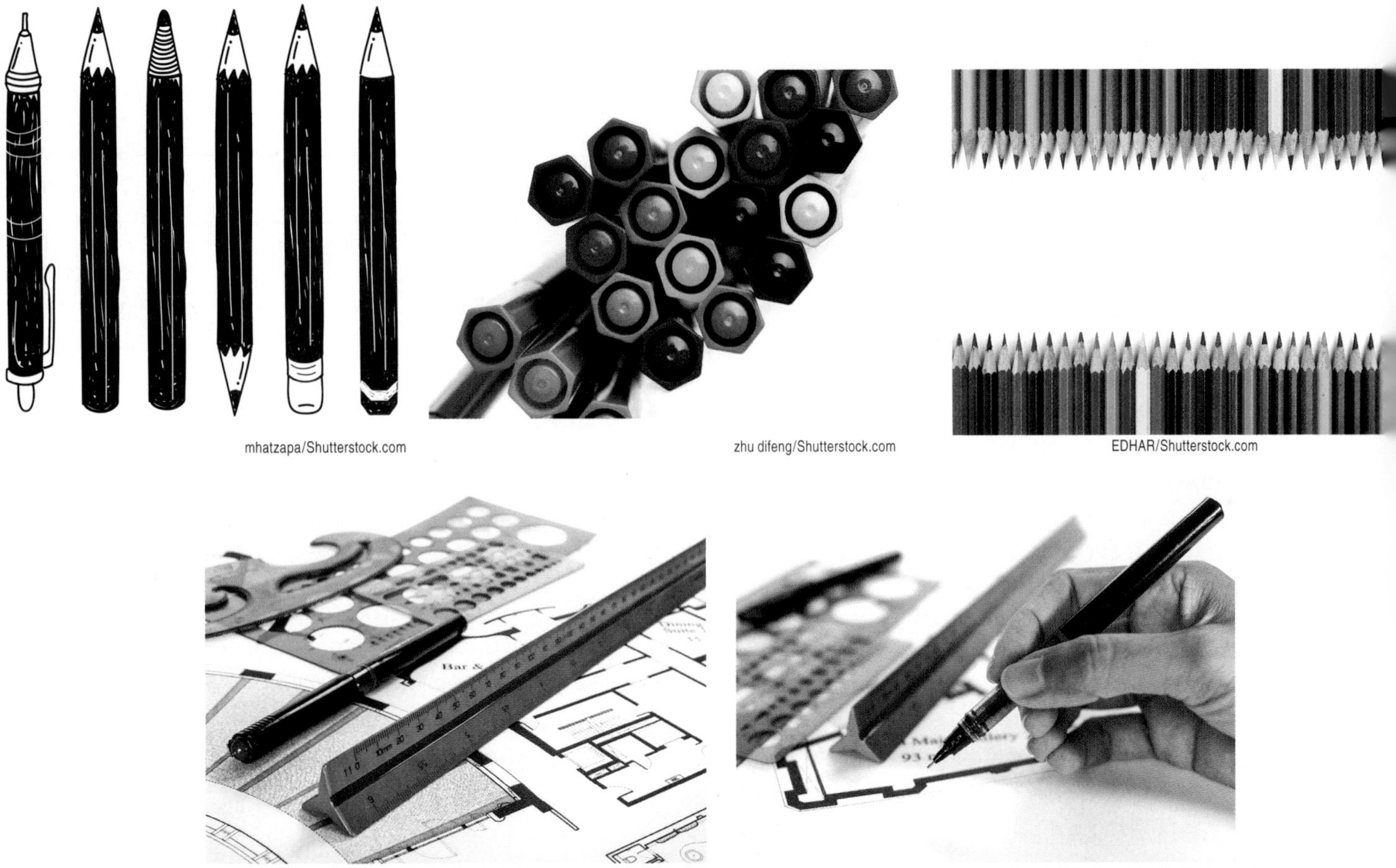

mhatzapa/Shutterstock.com zhu difeng/Shutterstock.com EDHAR/Shutterstock.com

Naphat Rojanarangsiman/Shutterstock.com Naphat Rojanarangsiman/Shutterstock.com

Figure 13-3 Depending on client factors, designers use a variety of manual tools to create their visual presentations.

- **Drawing surface.** A drawing surface can be flat or angled. Historically, drafting tables served this purpose. Today, a drawing surface can be anywhere—a pull-out surface on a plane or a stand-up counter in an office.
- **Paper.** Tracing paper is the most common paper used because of its transparency and layering capability. It is also inexpensive and portable. A step up from tracing paper is *Vellum*. It is thicker, more durable, and offers a rich finish and good stability. Nontransparent papers, such as bond, watercolor, or grid papers are also commonly used. *Mylar*, a sheet of plastic, also works well with ink pens.
- **Drawing pencil.** *Graphite* or lead pencils are available in a range of hardness and coded as *H* = *hard* and *B* = *black*. A number next to the letter indicates degree of hardness. The smaller the number is, the harder the lead. For instance, 2B is harder than 4B. You can get wood or mechanical lead pencils. To keep your pencils sharp, add a lead sharpener to your tool kit. Non-photo blue leads are used to draw guidelines and will not appear when drawings are photocopied. Colored pencils are often used for rendering a drawing.
- **Drawing pens (disposable).** Felt-tip or rolling ball pens are the most common drawing pens. They are low in cost and available with different point widths. Black is a favorite choice and most commonly used in the field. In fact, it is an industry-standard piece of equipment a designer has at all times. Technical pens work well on Mylar and come in a variety of tips sizes (commonly called *nibs*). They are costly and need extra care to maintain, but they work well for precisely inked drawings.
- **Markers.** Quality felt-tip markers, combined with colored pencils, are the main tools designers use for rendering illustrations. They are expensive, but can last for years. The basic colors include various shades of gray, green, red, blue, yellow, and brown.

- **Architectural scale.** This is a 12-inch triangular plastic ruler with standard measurements on every side. There are eleven scales in total. Each scale indicates a relationship to one foot. For example, 1/4" = 1'-0" indicates that 1/4 inch on the scale equates to one foot on a floor plan. Architectural scales are also available in metric for designs created for clients outside the U.S. When using the scale, take great care to record accurate dimensions. What looks like a small measurement on a scale translates to feet and yards on a site. Avoid using this for a straightedge as it damages the ruler and does not give you a very good line.
- **Straightedge.** Previously, the primary straight edge for manual drafting was the T-square. Today, a straightedge can be a metal or plastic yard stick, a triangle, or even a piece of hard cardboard. Designers use them to create casual guidelines or precise hand-generated drawings.
- **Miscellaneous tools.** Drafting tape or precut drafting dots, erasers and eraser shield, pencil sharpener, templates, sketch pad, compass, protractor, adjustable triangle, flexible or French curves, and drafting brushes are additional tools you might need. You may also need a good light source.
- **Portfolio case.** At least large enough to hold a 24- x 36-inch project, paper or canvas portfolios protect your manually-generated drawings during travel. Designers use digital portfolios and disposable portfolio samples the vast majority of the time.

Choosing Digital Technology Tools

Many disciplines, including interior design, rely on digital tools in today's competitive market. For designers, these tools speed up the process of creating a construction document or design drawing. In addition, designers use computer-technology tools for any drawing or design document that needs a revision—and clients often request revisions.

The challenge in using digital tools is the need to remain current with software and hardware updates. For those born in a digital world, this is a relatively easy task. For those professionals who have been away from design- or document-generating software for a number of years, it is difficult to rationalize time to remain current instead of generating new business. Therefore, many architecture and design firms count on emerging design professionals—*you*—to know the newest and most recent software and hardware.

Hardware

Technology driven hardware is powerful, transportable, and intuitive to use. Many colleges require students to enter with laptops. Digital tablets, however, are common in design studios, too, **Figure 13-4**. Often students use both for different purposes.

Digital tablets offer students and design professionals access to ever-evolving applications (apps), easy access to design inspiration sources, and e-mail connection to team members and clients—rapidly increasing the speed of communication. For example, with a digital tablet, the designer can

- take a photo
- sketch a revised drawing over the photo
- write a note on the photo
- link a source for a new cabinet detail to an e-mail
- upload both photo and link to the client and subcontractor for approval before ever leaving the site

Quick, easy, and effective communication—all with a digital tablet—enhances the designer-client relationship. This digital process helps omit numerous errors and saves time that favorably reflects on a client's bill.

Computers are becoming smaller, lighter weight, and more powerful. Some look and feel similar to a digital tablet. The advantages of the computer are still the processing speed and memory needed to run large software programs commonly used in the construction and design industries.

Computers also offer the client an opportunity to view design revisions in "real time." For example, if a designer is illustrating a *walk-through* of an interior space using a computer model, the client can view it and suggest "what if" scenarios. If the designer can make suggestions instantaneously using the software capabilities, the client can see the design modified. As a result, the designer and client can make the final decision quickly. Again, this type of communication enables the design process to move forward more rapidly, minimizing potential errors. When purchasing a computer, buy as much memory as you can afford. Visual presentations use a great deal of computer memory.

vovan/Shutterstock.com

jannoon028/Shutterstock.com

Figure 13-4 Interior designers use a variety of technology hardware in creating effective client designs. *What are the pros and cons of using a digital tablet versus a laptop?*

Software

There are many different types of software used in the architectural, construction and design fields. Some produce visuals that are construction related; others are for presentation purposes.

Software used for construction purposes includes computer-aided drafting (CAD) software which is a powerful tool in many industries besides design (for example engineers and landscape architects) on a global basis. Examples of such software include AutoCAD® and AutoCAD® Architecture by Autodesk®, Inc. These are **vector-based** drawing applications—they use mathematical formulas to create lines the designer can combine into shapes—that produce two-dimensional and three-dimensional documents. Vector-based software draws each object and then stores it in a numerical database. This ensures that the lines, shapes, and forms will be very accurate at any scale or zoom-in magnification. CAD is customizable to different industry needs.

The software used to develop construction documents for large, new construction, commercial projects is related to a *building information modeling* system. Along with use in design of the building and its interior, designers also use BIM in the planning, design, construction, and management of a building during its lifecycle. Using the same virtual information model, facility-management professionals maintain the building once the new occupants move into it. *All* information about the building—from design through construction to the time it is demolished and recycled—is integrated into the same building information modeling system.

To begin the BIM process, the designer virtually builds a computer-generated information model using vector-based software. A great deal of data about the building construction becomes part of the virtual model. Construction-drawing software creates large files and requires computers with the heavy-duty processors.

While construction drawings explain ideas precisely enough to build a design, presentation drawings explain ideas. They serve primarily as a sales or marketing tool and should be attractive and descriptive. Often a client understands presentation drawings much easier than construction drawings. Designers use various Adobe®

products (*Photoshop®, Illustrator®,* and *InDesign®*) for the different types of visual presentations.

Photoshop is the most popular and widely used image-editing software because it offers designers many tools to create and edit photographs, logos, and websites exactly the way they want. It is **raster-based**—meaning the image is made of pixels similar to a television. As pixels increase in size, raster-based images begin to degrade. In contrast, Illustrator is vector-based. Instead of painting with a brush as with Photoshop, you use shapes such as a box and text to create images on the screen with Illustrator. InDesign differs from both Photoshop and Illustrator. Designers use it to layout images and text to develop client book presentations and portfolio pages. All three software products work together.

There are licensed, student versions of all software needed for the study of interior design. Software companies want students to become proficient with their products and then use them in the architecture and design field. Student versions are less expensive. Ethically, once you graduate you should no longer use student versions. The use of pirated copies is a federal offense.

Peripherals, Cloud Computing, and File Sharing

Peripherals are technology-related items you need in addition to software and hardware. These may include a scanner, digital or phone camera, external hard drive, and USB drives.

Cloud computing—or web-based software, workspace, and digital storage—greatly impacts digital work in the design office. If you use web-based e-mail services such as Hotmail, Yahoo! Mail, or Gmail, you are using cloud computing. With cloud computing, you remotely log into your account using interface software such as a web browser. The software and digital storage for your account is on the service's computer cloud—not on your computer, **Figure 13-5**.

A great deal of digital storage today is free, particularly through the use of *cloud technology.* Designers use cloud technology for sharing and collaboration. It is important to make sure such storage is secure, but accessible to other team members. Cloud computing offers many benefits to the design process and design teams.

nmedia/Shutterstock.com

Figure 13-5 Because designers often communicate with clients around the globe, using cloud technology for digital storage enhances file sharing and collaboration.

- First, team members can remain part of the workflow by connecting to projects uploaded to the cloud.
- Second, virtually infinite computer power is available. This alleviates the problem with the time and storage requirements to process and store large files often resulting from CAD, BIM, or rendering work.
- Third, team members can work almost anytime and anywhere in a secure environment.

Online-file sharing helps meet increasing demands of both designers and clients for more services. More design services result in greater file size, making files difficult to send via e-mail. A decade ago, a simple CAD drawing was quite large. Today, with BIM and rendering software capabilities, file size has exponentially increased. You can send audio, video, and presentation files quickly and securely without requiring customers to download any extra software.

Online-file sharing is easy to learn, reliable, offers more freedom in the size of files sent, offers increased tracking and reliability, and keeps your files secure through password protection. Popular file-sharing companies include *YouSendIt* and *Dropbox*.

Visual Presentation Drawings

Visuals serve both construction and presentation purposes. As you know, construction drawings explain ideas precisely enough to build a structure or an item. Presentation drawings also explain ideas, but they are primarily sales or display tools and must be attractive as well as accurate.

A designer may use a visual presentation technique such as sketching in all phases of the design process. He or she may use others, such as construction documents, only in the Design Development and Contract Administration phases. A designer can complete presentation-drawing techniques manually or with computer technology, **Figure 13-6**.

As a design student, you can learn all of the following visual presentation skills. Sketching and learning CAD are not abilities only few possess. There are a variety of methods with which to communicate your ideas. Be persistent and confident. You will master all these skills.

Sketching Techniques

Professional designers use sketching for two reasons: to communicate and to visualize. Sketching is a useful communication tool for you, your team members, and your clients. As a visualization tool, sketching explores ideas from different angles. In order to take shape or form, the designer must sketch design ideas.

Dimitar Sotirov/Shutterstock.com

Figure 13-6 The designer typically uses construction documents during the Design Development and Contract Administration phases of the design process.

Sketching enables interior designers to "design think" through their fingers. Some refer to it as a type of *eye-hand coordination*. This is the translation of an idea or thought from the brain through the eye to the hand which is coordinated to perform the task. As a design student, your idea may be good. The challenge is to coordinate your hand.

Sketching is an effective tool a designer may use throughout all phases of the design process. The most extensive use is during the Schematic design phase when brainstorming and idea generation (*design thinking*) take place.

Sketching is not a neat or tidy process. Individually, as an idea forms and is sketched it can branch to other ideas that cascade out to collide with each other. When working in a team, the designer may modify a sketch again and again as team members give input until a final sketch emerges.

Freehand sketching is a desirable skill because sketches are not final or fixed in stone. Clients and team members both prefer to have input into a design. Sketches promise the opportunity for an exchange of ideas. In addition, the ability to create quick perspective sketches in client conferences and in team meetings is a highly useful skill.

Sketching tools are many and varied. Interior designers often joke that they *still* draw on napkins—a readily available, inexpensive surface during a luncheon meeting. At the simplest level, manual tools might be bond paper and a pencil or disposable black felt-tip pen. Digital tablets with a stylus also work well.

When and Where to Sketch

Designers and design students, if comfortable with sketching, sketch often and anywhere. With enrollment in a sketching class, instructors require design students to carry a sketchbook with them wherever they go. The goal is to practice frequently and sketch everywhere. As ideas come to students, they are to sketch them. If they are waiting for a class to begin, students are to sketch the architecture or interior detail near them. Research indicates that the frequency of sketching is an important part of improving comfort level and skill. Your confidence in sketching is visible as your skill progresses.

STUDENT SPOTLIGHT

Design Perspectives

Ajay Li. "As a design student, I have found that having access to technology programs like Revit, 3DS Max, and AutoCAD plays a vital role in the success of anyone who aspires to be a great interior designer.

"Design programs are poetically programmed to showcase designers' thoughts and ideas so that viewers can see exactly what the designer is visualizing. Every design program is unique and just as important as the other. I have found, however, that no other program can be as user friendly and customizable as AutoCAD. Although very basic, AutoCAD has the ability to create beautiful, custom, and even inspiring pieces that no other program can offer. AutoCAD allows the designer to tailor his or her ideas and even grow them into more intriguing pieces. I want to *inspire* viewers with my designs, and AutoCAD inspires me to be a better designer".

Sherilyn Yin. "As an international transfer student from Shanghai, China, I have a unique academic and life experience to share. Currently, I am participating in a double-degree undergraduate transfer program between East China Normal University (ECNU) and Colorado State University (CSU).

"Before I transferred to CSU's Interior Design program, I had been studying at ECNU for two years in Environmental Art Design (a field related to Interior Design). I am a quick learner, a dedicated starter, and a passionate challenger; and I excel in responsibility, achievement, positivity, and fairness.

"I also worked as a summer intern at Gensler, Shanghai, for three months in 2014. During that time, my unique academic background and desire for knowledge encouraged me to not only strengthen my skills and develop my design, but also to become a creative designer in the future."

Sketching Types

There are several different types of sketches. They all require the need to perceive edges of forms, negative and positive space, light and shadows, proportion, and spatial relationships. Types of sketches include **(Figure 13-7 A-H)**

- **Doodle.** A rough drawing made casually and in a matter of minutes, a *doodle* allows a person to visually think and work through ideas. A doodle is not sophisticated or fully developed. Designers doodle when capturing an intriguing detail or a new thought. See **Figure 13-7 A**.
- **Contour.** Originating in the art field, a *contour* drawing or sketch is one that follows the visible edges of a shape. The contour is the outermost edges of a form as well as changes of plane within the form. It is not about detail, but about the mass of the object. When finished, it looks like a silhouette of the object. Shading is not needed in a contour sketch, **Figure 13-7 B**.
- **Thumbnail.** These rapidly executed tiny sketches are about the size of an adult's thumbnail. Rather than spending time creating finished drawings, these doodle-like sketches serve to get the creative juices flowing. Designers often use them during the Schematic design process or to capture an idea or an inspirational detail. These sketches are not finished, formal, or typically used in professional design presentations. See **Figure 13-7 C**.
- **Value study.** The translation of an object or space to values of light to dark through the use of shade and shadow techniques is a *value study*. Light casts shade and shadows on or around objects and spaces. A value study makes a two-dimensional sketch appear three dimensional through the use of shade and shadow. These studies offer realism, depth, and distance. Designers use value studies in a variety of sketches and typically in Schematic Design or Design Development phases, **Figure 13-7 D**.

- **Concept.** A simplified sketch—or concept sketch (sometimes called an ideation sketch)—illustrates a concept often with arrows leading to labels or short phrases that explain the concept. A designer uses concept sketches in the ideation process during Schematic Design phase. See **Figure 13-7 E**.
- **Storyboard**. A storyboard is a series of square- or rectangular-thumbnail sketches that tell a story through sequential development. Designers sometimes use them to illustrate an idea or develop a presentation sequence for use with a client, **Figure 13-7 F**.

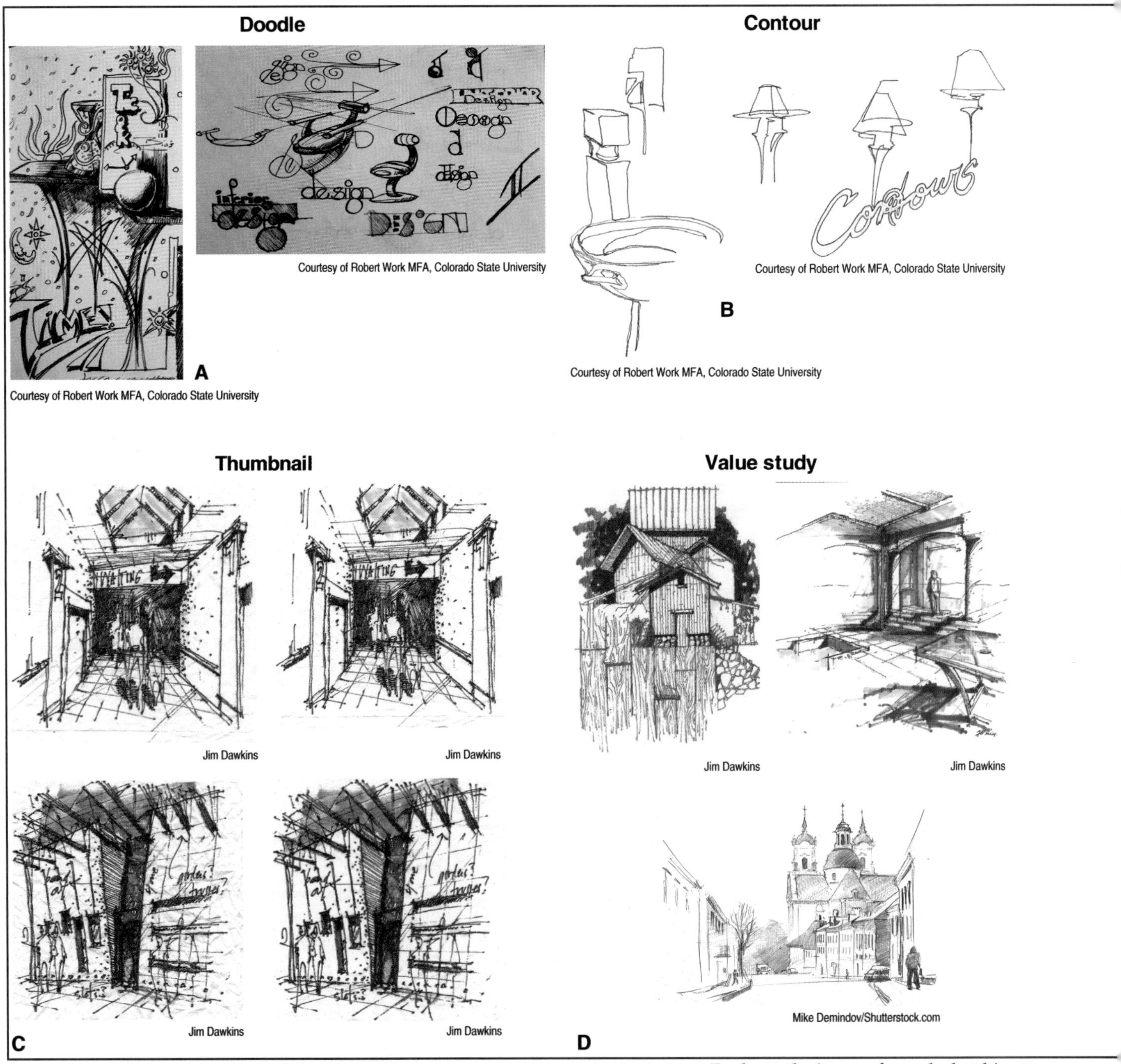

Figure 13-7 Ability to communicate well through sketching is an important skill for the interior designer. *Evaluate the images for each sketching technique. What do the images communicate to the viewer?*

- **Presentation.** Persuasive in nature, presentation sketches influence the audience and sell the design concept. For any space, designers create these sketches in varying degrees of refinement and sophistication to captivate the viewer's interest and visually explain the space. With primary use in Design development, use of presentation sketches in Schematic design is also common. Rendering these drawings adds color, texture, light, shade, and shadow, **Figure 13-7 G.**
- **Technical.** Explanatory in nature, technical sketches show the object or detail of the design in multiple views. Designers create them to explain function, structure, and form primarily in the Design development phase. Technical sketches

Concept

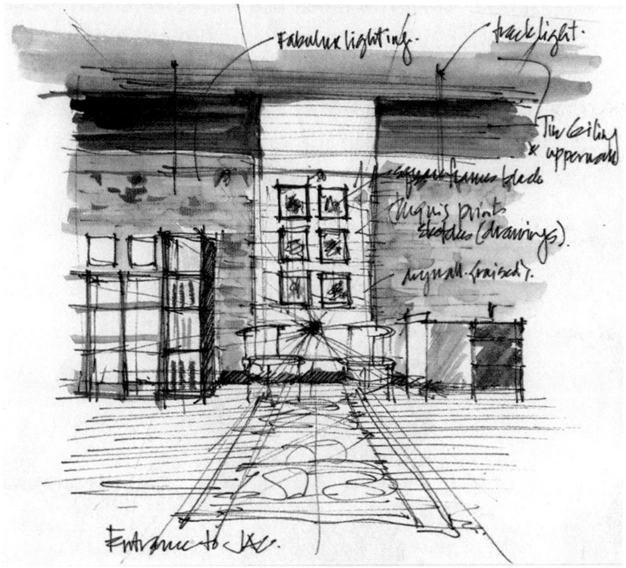

Image by Jacqui McFarl

E

Storyboard

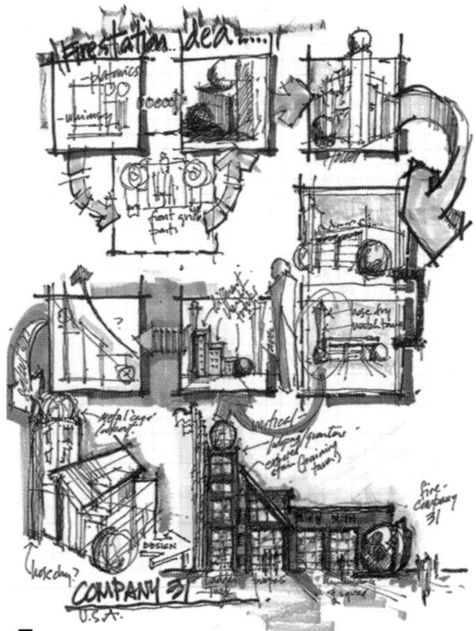

F

Jim Dawkins

Presentation

G

Robert Work MFA, Colorado State University

Technical

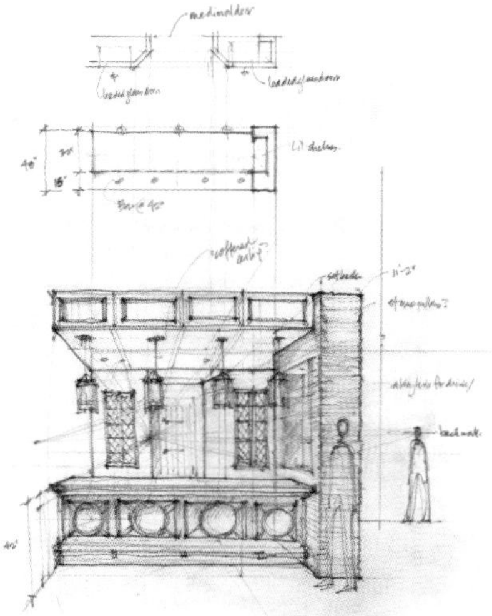

H

Image by Jacqui McFarland

communicate a design in a clear and neutral manner, focusing more on explaining the idea rather than selling it. They must be readable to others outside the design process, **Figure 13-7 H**.

Potential employers like to see different types of freehand sketches in student portfolios. They show the applicant's ability to see and think three-dimensionally. They also exhibit the process and progression of idea generation, rather than just a final product or finished design.

Preparing to Sketch

If you can write your name in cursive, you have made a sketching line. Sketching is easy. How well you sketch something you see in the world—such as a landscape scene—rests entirely on your ability to sketch what you see. To sketch what you see, you have to *see* first.

As you prepare to sketch, gather your sketchbook, several pencils, and black roller-ball or felt-tip pens. Your sketchbook is a type of journal or diary of images and places. Keep it with you at all times. Begin a collection of interior and exterior pictures from design magazines or books. Take pictures of some of your favorite spaces at different times of the day and print them to add to your collection. Begin to pay attention to the presentation of a space through lines, colors, and shadows.

Before you begin to sketch, first, loosen up! Drawing, like athletic activities, requires a *warm-up* phase. To loosen up, simple movements of the arms, wrists, and fingers can be effective. Then use your pencil or pen to sketch different types of lines in a variety of movements across the page, **Figure 13-8 A**. Complete these exercises at a fast pace with no judgment and only as a warm-up. If you wish, turn on relaxing music.

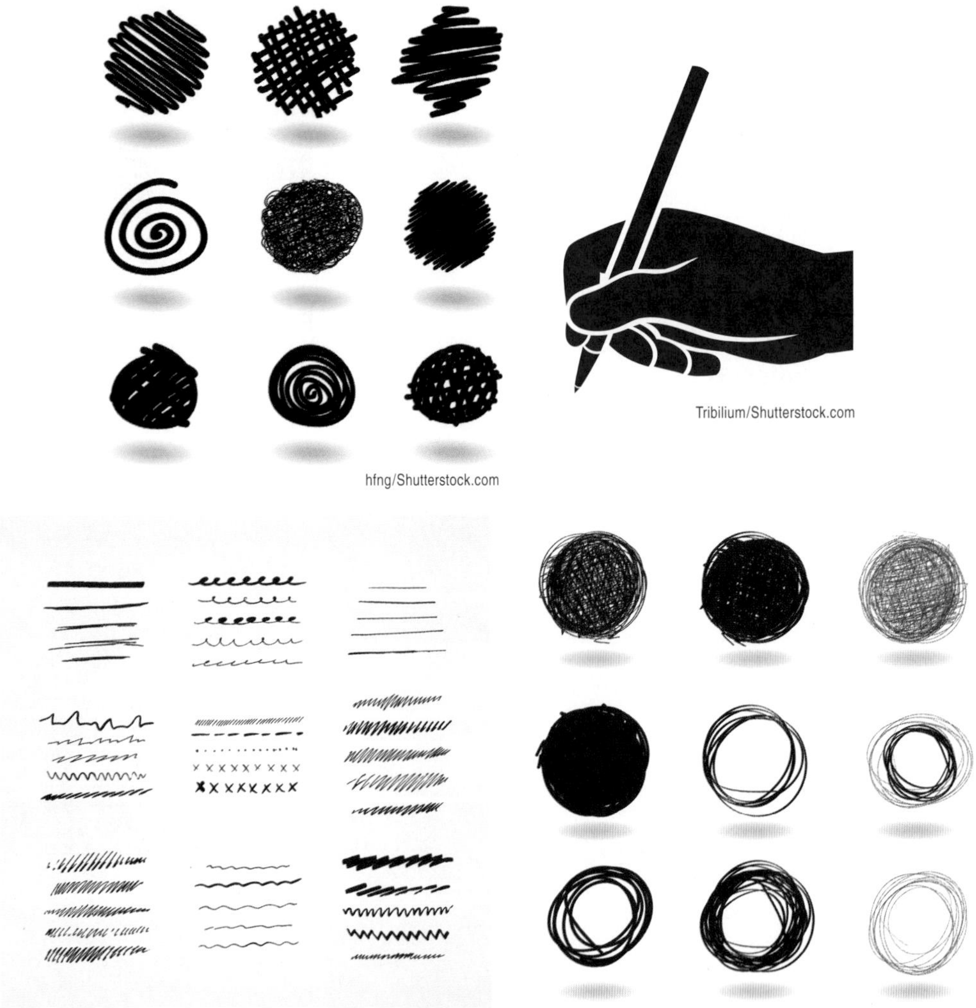

hfng/Shutterstock.com

Tribilium/Shutterstock.com

lliveinoctober/Shutterstock.com

hfng/Shutterstock.com

Figure 13-8 Relaxed, loose movements are important for sketching. Think about warm-ups for sketching in the same way you think of warm-ups for athletic activities.

Next, draw a variety of vertical, horizontal, and diagonal lines in a series of boxes. See **Figure 13-8 B**. Vary the spacing while keeping the line type consistent. Control is important as you complete this warm-up exercise.

Third, draw loops or swirls in consistent implied boxes. Use your imagination to develop different fluid lines. **Figure 13-8 C**.

When you are learning how to sketch in a studio setting, your instructor will begin by teaching you how to *look* at an object or setting. The first drawing or sketching skill is to learn how to perceive the edges of objects. Your instructor may ask you to sketch a single object, a piece of furniture, an accessory, or a space. Often, your instructor will place a group of objects in front of you and ask you to sketch or draw it.

There are two scenes to typically capture with sketching: those you physically see in front of you and those in your brain that are not yet built. The latter is the most difficult to sketch. As you practice sketching, draw things that already exist and that you can clearly see rather than using your imagination. Select things you want to improve and concentrate on them exclusively. Learning how to sketch what you see before you is an important skill.

Sketching Exercises for Eye-Hand Coordination

There are several simple, common eye-hand coordination exercises to begin with as you learn to sketch. Try the following.

Exercise One

Choose a 5- by 7-inch or 8- by 10-inch photo of a friend, family member, or famous person. Place the photo upside down in front of you. Keep your wrist loose and use a pencil to draw the portrait. Start anywhere you wish. Do not try to figure out what you are drawing. Do not try to identify parts of the portrait. Do not let yourself erase any lines. Instead, if you put a line where you do not want it, just continue to draw over it. The objective of this exercise is to truly see the lines of the portrait. Once you finish, avoid the temptation to turn your drawing right side up. Instead turn it 180 degrees and view it. See **Figure 13-9.**

Exercise Two

Use the same technique as in exercise one, but choose an 8 1/2- by 11-inch picture of an interior space from a design or architecture magazine or from a design-related website. Select one with relatively little detail. Once you make your choice, turn the image upside down. Use your pencil to draw the room. Avoid looking for recognizable shapes or forms. Do not worry about the perspective of the room. Simply draw what you see. After you finish, compare your drawing with the photo. See **Figure 13-10.**

Sherilyn (Lixue) Yin, International transfer design student, CSU, ECNU/ Shidong Yin 殷世东, Senior Photographer

Figure 13-9 Creating a sketch of a photo upside down forces you to look at the lines of the portrait.

Sherilyn (Lixue) Yin, International transfer design student, CSU, ECNU/ Shidong Yin 殷世东, Senior Photographer

Figure 13-10 Contour drawings follow the visible edges of a form.

Exercise Three

This exercise is often the first drawing skill taught in a sketching class. The goal is to perceive the edges of objects through drawing contour lines. Contour drawing follows the visible edges of a form. You will not put any shading on a contour drawing. Different line weights will make the contour of the object pop out on the paper. Strong, dark lines make that part of the contour visually advance and light, thin lines will appear to recede.

To begin, set an everyday object on the table in front of you. For instance, you might use a set of keys or one of your shoes. Then use the following instructions for each exercise. See **Figure 13-11**.

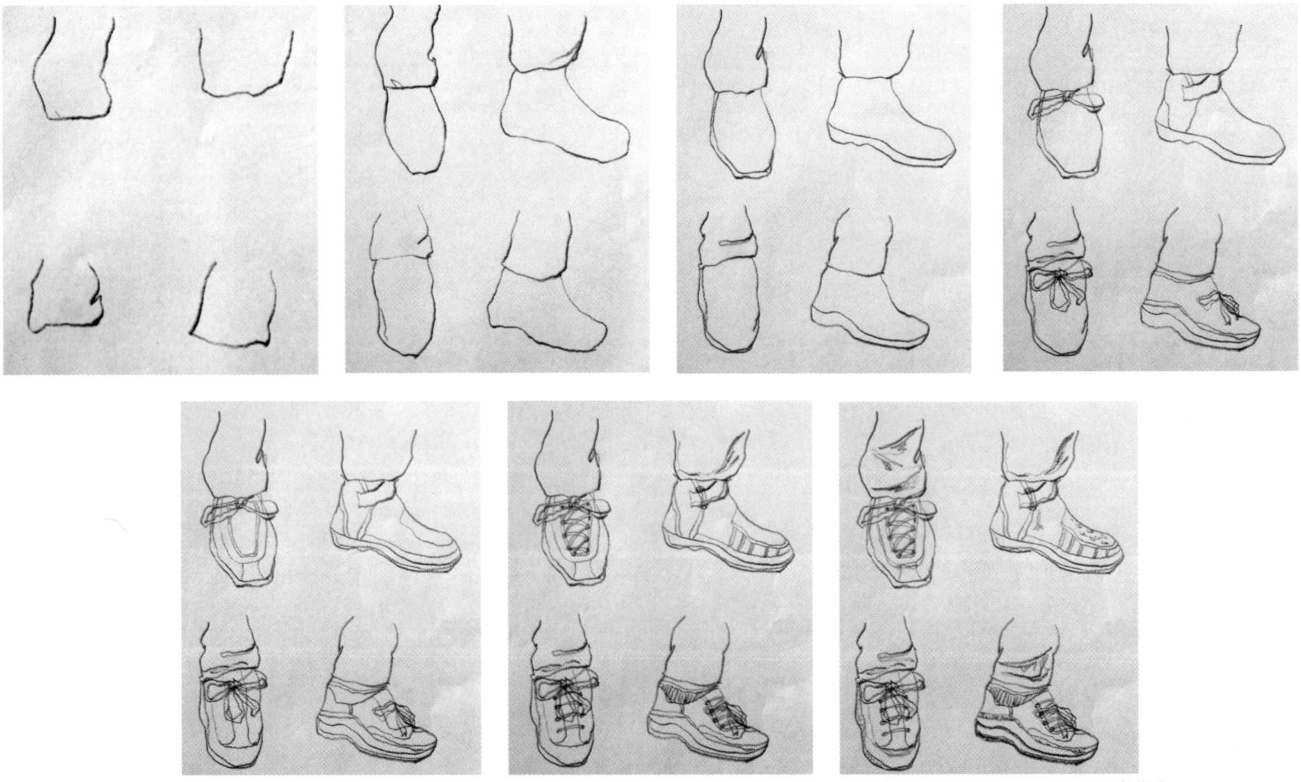

Sherilyn (Lixue) Yin, International transfer design student, CSU, ECNU/ Shidong Yin 殷世东, Senior Photographer

Figure 13-11 The "no lift" and "no look" contour sketching exercises helps you learn to look for the details in the objects you are sketching.

- **No lift.** The objective of this exercise is to learn that every line is important and that there are more details in the object than previously thought. To begin, look at the object you will draw. Set your pencil or roller pen down on the paper and begin drawing the object(s) without lifting up your tool. Use line only. You can look between the object(s) and the paper, but cannot lift your tool. Alter the pressure to change line weight, but keep the line continuous from start to finish. Use about 1 to 5 minutes for this sketch, but do not hurry.
- **No look.** Your objective is to learn to look at all details of an object. Select a new object or use your non-drawing hand for this sketch. Place the object in front of you. As you look at it, set your pencil or pen on the paper and begin drawing. Do not look at your paper at any time during this exercise. You can lift your drawing tool off the paper, however, and reset it down where you want. If the results are similar at all, you have been successful. This exercise can sometimes be frustrating. Use about 1 to 5 minutes for this sketch, but do not hurry.

Contour drawings help you develop the skill of truly seeing what you are drawing. Do this exercise several times with different objects. To create variety, place three or five objects on top of each other.

Exercise Four

Complete a contour-line drawing using a piece of furniture as a model. If possible, choose a curvy historic chair. If necessary, complete warm-up exercises to make sure your hand is relaxed and loose. Look at the furniture piece while keeping your pencil on the paper. Starting with the longest lines or edges, try to trace the edges and folds of the furniture. Move your pencil slowly to capture the furniture details, recording just what you see. When the edge of the furniture piece changes direction, so should your pencil.

After completing this contour drawing, put a piece of tracing paper over it. Then use a black, felt-tip pen to trace the pencil drawing. See **Figure 13-12**.

Exercise Five

Shift from drawing one piece of furniture to capturing an architectural detail in an interior space. Select a photograph of a fireplace detail that has accessories on or around it. Make sure it has something hanging over the fireplace, such as a picture or mirror. Place the photo in front of you and loosen up your wrist and hand. Position your drawing paper any way that is comfortable for you. Then begin by drawing the contours of the fireplace. Start with the longer lines and move to the details later. After completing the drawing, place tracing paper on top of it and use a felt-tip pen to make a new drawing. See **Figure 13-13**.

Exercise Six

Complete another contour drawing, but this time of an interior space. Select an 8 1/2- by 11-inch photo of a classical interior space such as a Gothic cathedral. Make sure the photo is from a viewpoint from which you can see the roof and ceiling details. These photos commonly have arches, vaults, columns, and windows. Before you begin, loosen up your wrist again. Then look at the major architectural components of the space—such as the columns with their capitals—and draw them. Do not worry about spacing. If the objects appear too complex and you are getting lost in the detail, turn the image upside down to make the forms less recognizable. Simple, geometric shapes should emerge. Darken certain lines that appear more dominant in the space. Use lighter, delicate lines for simple details. Once you complete the drawing, place tracing paper over the drawing and trace it with a felt-tip pen. Continue to keep your wrist loose to encourage fluid lines. See **Figure 13-14**.

Exercise Seven

Many times designers will use manual tools to complete a freehand sketch. Once they finish, however, they may transfer it to a digital format to modify. Drawing software easily captures the human imperfection of hand sketching, such as wandering lines.

For exercise seven, take one of your contour drawings and move it to a digital format. To do so, scan and save it to a computer. Upload it to the drawing software and use the *fill* feature to fill your drawing's contour lines with color. Use different tints and shades of the same color to add perceived depth to different parts of the drawing. Save it and print it out. See **Figure 13-15**.

Sketching Tips

Contour sketches are only a beginning drawing technique. You will learn many tips for adding texture, shade, and shadow later in this chapter.

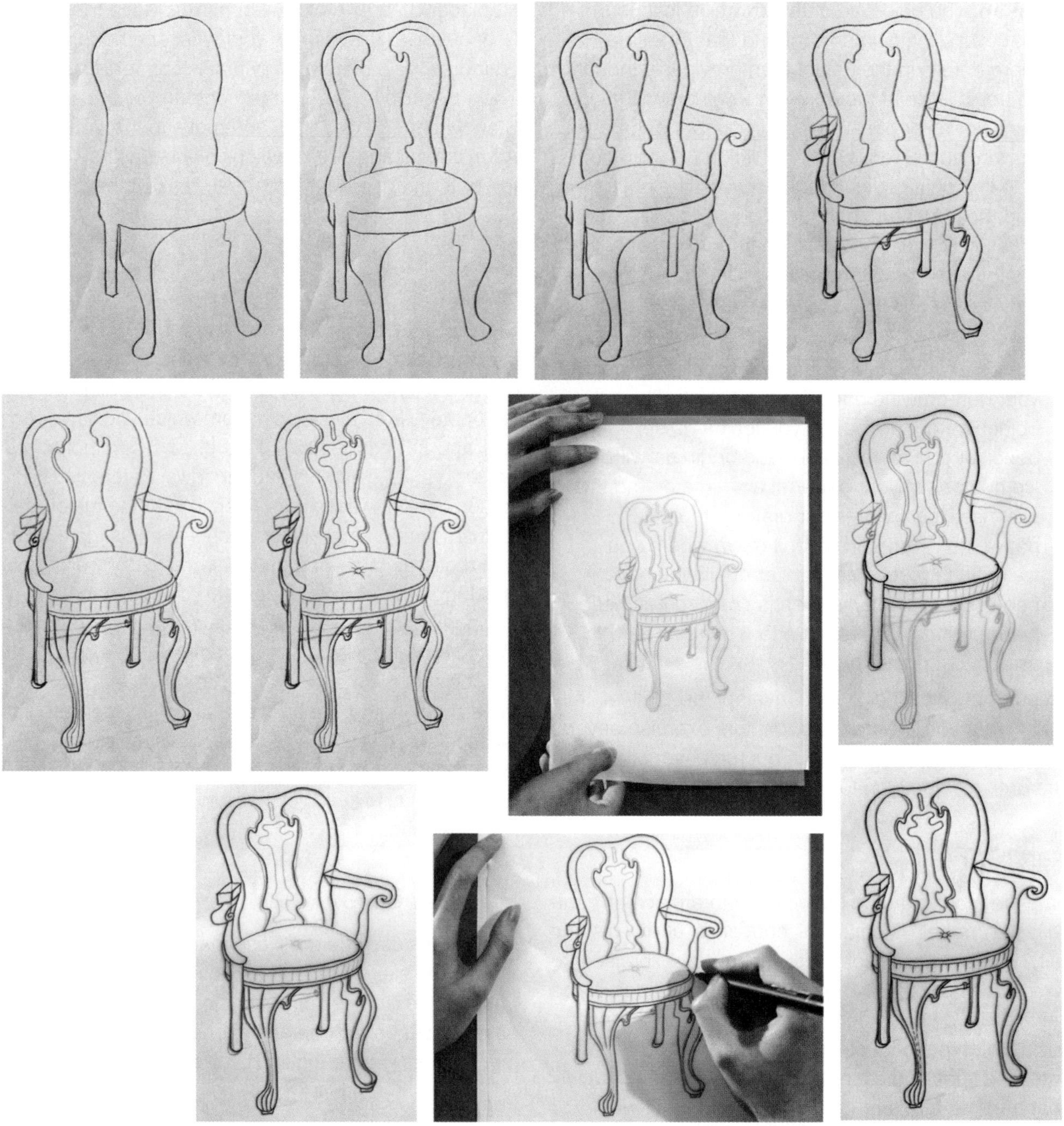

Sherilyn (Lixue) Yin, International transfer design student, CSU, ECNU/ Shidong Yin 殷世东, Senior Photographer

Figure 13-12 Extending your practice of contour sketching to furniture helps you to capture the details you see.

There are also many suggestions for improving your sketching technique. Many great books are devoted just to the details of *how* to sketch. Pick several to study the techniques suggested by different professionals. All books will encourage you to practice often and feel confident in what you are learning, practicing, and doing. Other tips include

- Draw every line deliberately. Begin a line with a point and end the line with a point. You can achieve a certain quality of line with this type of conscious, deliberate effort.
- Redraw over poor lines or just keep going, but do not erase. Erasing interrupts the process of learning to draw confidently. A few stray lines may only add interest and indication of process.
- Sketch anything that appeals to you. While what you are sketching may not work for your current assignment, it is a resource for a future one.

Sherilyn (Lixue) Yin, International transfer design student, CSU, ECNU/ Shidong Yin 殷世东, Senior Photographer

Figure 13-13 Learning to capture precise architectural details in your drawings enhances design communication with clients.

Sherilyn (Lixue) Yin, International transfer design student, CSU, ECNU/ Shidong Yin 殷世东, Senior Photographer

Figure 13-14 As you sketch the architectural details of a Gothic cathedral, you should begin to see simple geometric shapes emerge.

Sherilyn (Lixue) Yin, International transfer design student, CSU, ECNU/ Shidong Yin 殷世东, Senior Photographer

Figure 13-15 Moving freehand sketches to digital format allows you to fill in the contour lines with color to enhance understanding of the drawing.

- Sketch for different lengths of time. You will have different results from a 10-minute timed sketch than one that is 45 minutes in length.
- Move to a different position in the room if you do not like a scene's viewpoint from where you are sketching. Find one that offers interest and variety to your sketch.
- Use tracing paper to develop the beginnings of a sketch and then layer another piece of paper over it to refine and move forward. Layering is important to both sketching and rendering. Continue this process until your sketch is final.
- Remember that positive and negative space within a sketch is important for the total composition.
- Keep your sketches loose and easy. It indicates you are relaxed and confident.
- Add the image of a person or group of people to the scene to indicate approximate scale within the imaginary space when you complete a sketch of an interior. The image can just be a contour of a person inserted into the scene. Human dimension is always interesting in an interior.
- Sketch the exterior of buildings as well as interior spaces. Both offer different opportunities for capturing design details for use later.
- Keep your sketchbook with you at all times.
- Sketch often! Sketch everywhere! Sketch everything!

Sketching Techniques

Every design student develops his or her own sketching style. It is a type of signature. Some are more precise while others are carefree in nature. Some are bold and others are delicate. Do not worry if your sketches do not look exactly like those of another, even if you are looking at the same scene. Every designer's sketching style reflects his or her personality through freehand lines, marks, and strokes.

There are two different types of sketching techniques used in the design field. One is more artistic in its use of lines, shapes, and forms. The other is more technical and architectural in nature, **Figure 13-16**.

Digital Sketching

There are a number of digital tools to use for sketching. A favorite that designers frequently use is *SketchUp*. SketchUp is a three-dimensional modeling program that can produce digital sketches or digital models. A designer can create conceptual sketches and revise them, adding shading, shadowing, and lighting effects. *SketchUp Make* (for non-commercial home, personal, and educational use) is free to use and easy to learn. *SketchUp Pro* has additional features for professional use and has an annual licensing fee. If you need a few pointers, video clips are available on the web, **Figure 13-17**.

Drawing Systems

The way to represent a three-dimensional reality on a two-dimensional surface has been a struggle for designers for many years. This struggle led to the development of *drawing systems*—or methods of projection. According to renown architectural graphics author, Francis Ching, a **projection** is "…the technique of representing a three-dimensional object by extending all its points by straight lines, called projectors, to a picture plane, an imaginary transparent plane." This plane is the *plane of projection*.

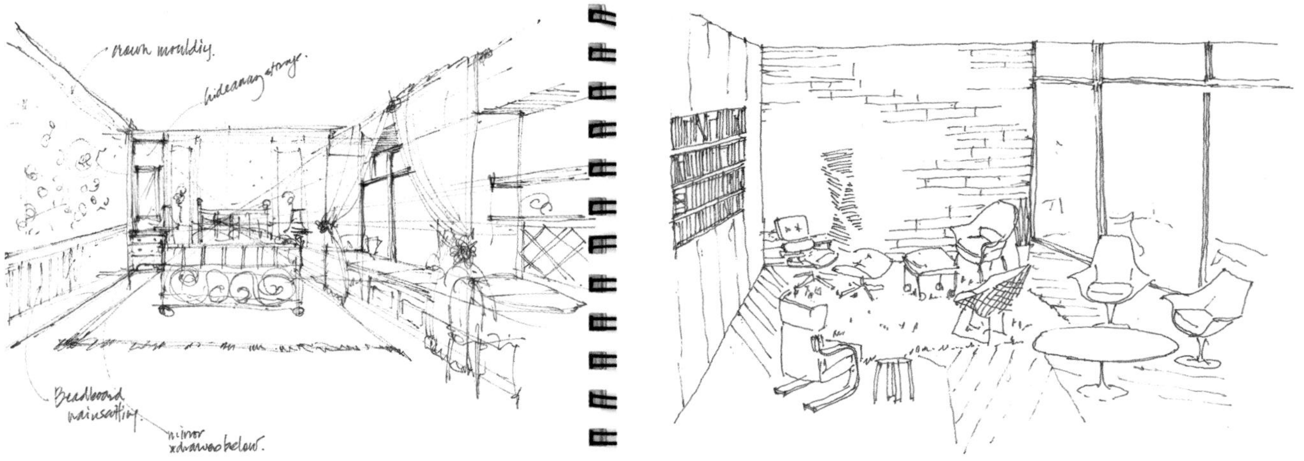

Image by Jacqui McFarland

Courtesy of Lydia Brown

Figure 13-16 Every designer develops his or her own style of sketching. *Which of the following images is more artistic in nature and which is more technical and precise? How do you know?*

Designer: Kia Weatherspoon/Firm: Carlyn & Company

Figure 13-17 Many designers create conceptual hand sketches and then digitally revise them by adding shading, shadowing, and lighting effects with such digital tools as *SketchUp*.

Learning how to use draw certain systems teaches you how to think spatially in three dimensions—a critical skill for interior designers. This skill helps a designer to visualize what a space will look like prior to construction and envision what issues might arise if not designed properly.

There are three major types of projection systems: *orthographic, paraline,* and *perspective*. You can develop each type of drawing using a straight-edge, such as a ruler, or by using a sketching technique. Each drawing system has different strengths in communicating the interior or space to the client and designer. Choosing which type of drawing to use depends on what you are trying to communicate to the client and what is *not* important.

Orthographic Drawings

Orthographic drawings include floor plans, elevations, and sections. Designers most commonly use these drawings to communicate interior environments in scale. Typically, the designer drafts orthographic drawings either by hand or on a computer. If drawn by hand, the designer completes each drawing separately. If using CAD software, he or she can draw the floor plan once and the computer program will generate the elevations and sections on command. If the building is multi-level, the software can easily generate a second floor plan using the first as a template. The designer then modifies the second floor as necessary.

Construction documents always include orthographic drawings. Once the designer establishes a drawing scale, he or she can determine less critical dimensions with an architectural scale. Residential projects are typically drafted using the scale of 1/4" = 1'-0". Commercial projects are typically drafted using 1/8" = 1'-0".

Floor Plans

Also called *plans,* designers develop **floor plans** from a bird's-eye view. See **Figure 13-18 A.** To determine what to draw, imagine a horizontal cut-through of the building at four feet above floor level with the ceiling or roof removed. You can then hypothetically peer inside and look down on the plan. The floor plan communicates the wall locations; door and window locations; means of vertical circulation through building, such as stairs or elevator; scale; and measurements and spatial relationships. In addition to scale, the plan always uses an arrow to indicate the *North* direction. This helps the designer to orient the building to the site and the path of the sun.

The designer or design team can analyze a floor plan to determine

- the advantages of room adjacencies
- whether door and window locations make sense
- the proportion of spaces related to each other
- circulation flow—or the way in which people move throughout the building from entrance to egress

In multi-level buildings, designers can also analyze a vertical stack, such as a common elevator core that pierces through each level. Unfortunately, clients typically struggle to understand a floor plan. As a two-dimensional drawing it can be difficult to perceive in three dimensions. With the addition of furniture to the floor plan, it becomes a *furniture plan*, **Figure 13-18 B**. A floor plan is the most common orthographic drawing used by architects and interior designers.

Elevations

If a floor plan is a two-dimensional drawing of the floor, an **elevation** is a two-dimensional vertical slice through the same space that shows a front or side or side view, **Figure 13-18 C**. If there are four walls to the room, then you may need to draw four elevations. An elevation indicates the height and width of each wall. Horizontal lines at the top and base of the drawing indicate ceiling and floor heights.

The goal is to communicate details you cannot see on the floor plan and to depict only the interior space. Elevations show window placement, wall details such as built-in cabinets, and such architectural details as columns or crown molding. Elevations also illustrate the heights of doors, windows, and other openings. The designer must clearly *key* the elevation (such as identifying the north wall), scale, and reference the elevation to the floor plan. With the inclusion of furnishings, the elevation becomes an *interior elevation*.

Sections

While an elevation is a single wall within a room, a **section** is series of multiple walls from different rooms along a consecutive plane, **Figure 13-18D**. They are a vertical slice cut through an entire length or width of building. The designer uses different line weights—thicker lines for outside walls and thinner lines for interior walls—to differentiate exterior or interior walls, three-quarter walls, and half-walls. A designer draws a section to indicate

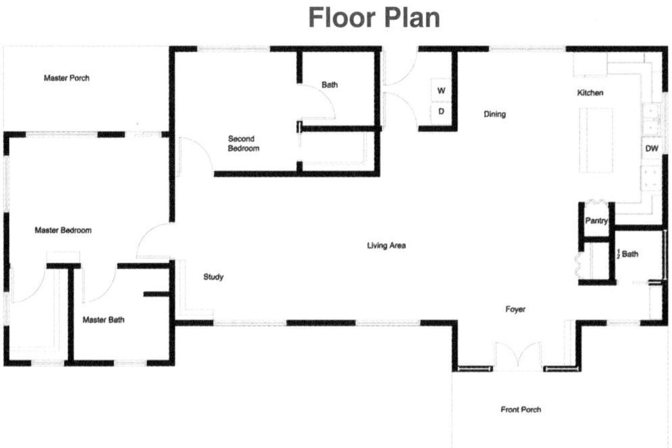

A Chase Margaux Robbins, Colorado State University

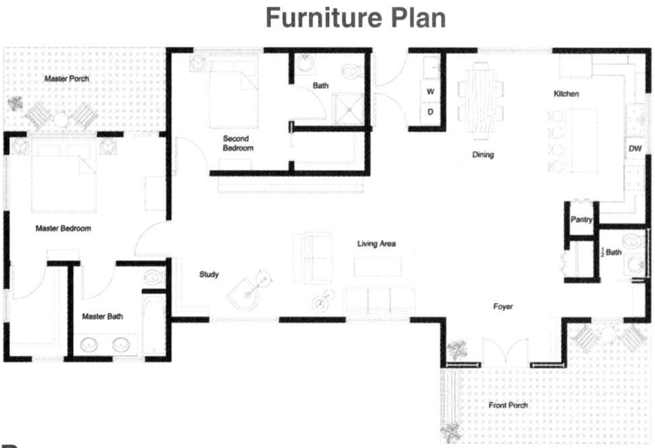

B Chase Margaux Robbins, Colorado State University

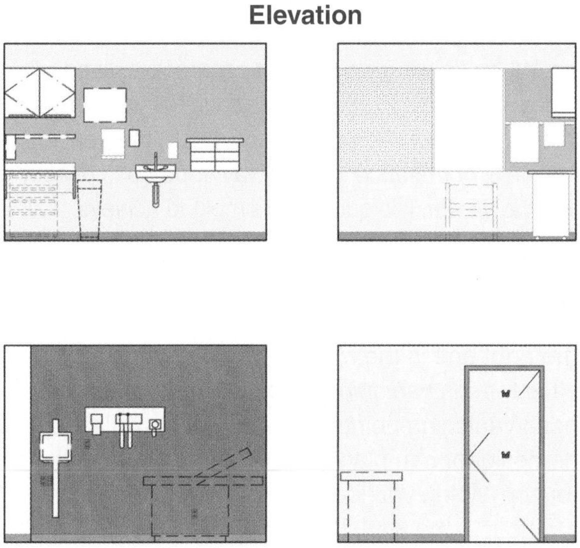

Interior Designer: SCI Design Group/Photographer: Michael McLane

C

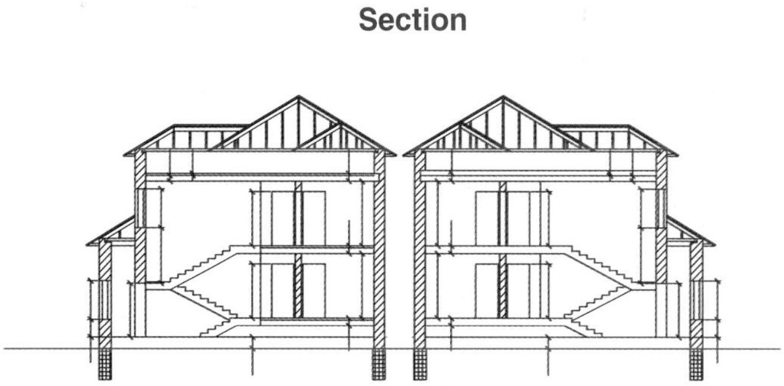

marina_us/Shutterstock.com

D

Figure 13-18 Floor plans, furniture plans, elevations, and sections are all types of orthographic drawings.

interior relationships, details such as doors and windows, changes in floor levels, and ceiling heights.

There are both construction sections and interior sections. *Construction sections* show materials and critical dimensions necessary for building walls, floor, and ceilings. *Interior sections* indicate forms and finish materials in the adjoining spaces. It is important to clearly key and reference all sections to the floor plan. The designer must also indicate scale on both types of sections.

Paraline Drawings

Clients understand three-dimensional drawings much better than two dimensional drawings, such as floor plans. Perhaps that is because since infancy, their view of the world has been three-dimensional.

Paraline drawings are simple, easy, and accurate three-dimensional drawings that allow the viewer to see multiple surfaces of an interior. Paraline drawings typically represent an aerial view of the interior. Another name for a paraline drawing is an *axonometric (ak-suh-noh-MEH-trik) projection* or *axon.* Paralines are constructed by the simple rotation and projection of the floor plan. The length and width of the paraline drawing is the same as the floor plan. In addition, the floor-plan scale is the same for the paraline. All vertical lines, drawn up from the floor plan, are parallel to each other. Height of vertical lines should mimic the intended height of the walls, architectural elements, and furniture (if desired).

The most common paraline is the isometric drawing. Less distorted than other paralines, the **isometric drawing** is a three-dimensional drawing with three axes, each at a 30-degree angle, **Figure 13-19**. An isometric drawing communicates how one space or form relates to another. This is very helpful for a client to see. The disadvantage of isometric drawings is that humans view *real life* spaces in perspective and the isometric drawing does not take into account adjustments needed from a perspective viewpoint.

Common usage for isometric drawings is in construction drawings. Because the basis of isometric drawings is the floor plan, a designer can create one using CAD with the push of a button. They are also relatively easy to hand draw because the floor plan determines many of the measurements.

Two other paraline drawings are *diametric* and *trimetric*. Interior designers rarely, if ever, use them.

Perspective Drawings

Interior designers use perspective drawings more often than paralines. **Perspectives drawings** describe three-dimensional volumes and relationships of space in a two-dimensional realm. They allow a single, more realistic looking image of an interior space. The viewer gains a sense of perspective as drawn lines converge as they recede into the depth of the drawing—similar to looking down a set of railroad tracks. The object appears smaller as the distance from the viewer increases. The designer always draws vertical lines vertically. Horizontal lines above eye level will slope up, and all horizontal lines below eye level will slope down. The designer can manually draw perspective drawings, technically drafting them using a straightedge—such as a ruler, and generate them digitally.

There are three different types of perspectives—all of which use a vanishing point(s). A **vanishing point** is the point at which all parallel lines merge on the horizon line. The designer can place the vanishing point anywhere along the horizon line, thereby controlling the view, **Figure 13-20**.

- **One-point perspective.** A one-point perspective has one *vanishing point* that typically sits on the horizon line. The designer places a **horizon line** at the viewer's eye level, typically 5'-0" off the floor line. When drawing a one-point perspective, lines appear to converge at the center point of vision—the vanishing point. When drawn accurately, the front of a building or entrance to a hallway appears to directly face the viewer. It is quick and simple to achieve.
- **Two-point perspective.** At eye level, there are two vanishing points sitting anywhere on the horizon line in a two-point perspective drawing. The right one is the *right vanishing point* and the left is the *left vanishing point*. In an illustration, these vanishing points represent each wall and the designer can place them arbitrarily along the horizon. When you look straight on at the corner of a house, the wall on your right disappears into the distance *and* the wall on your left disappears into the distance. This is an example of two

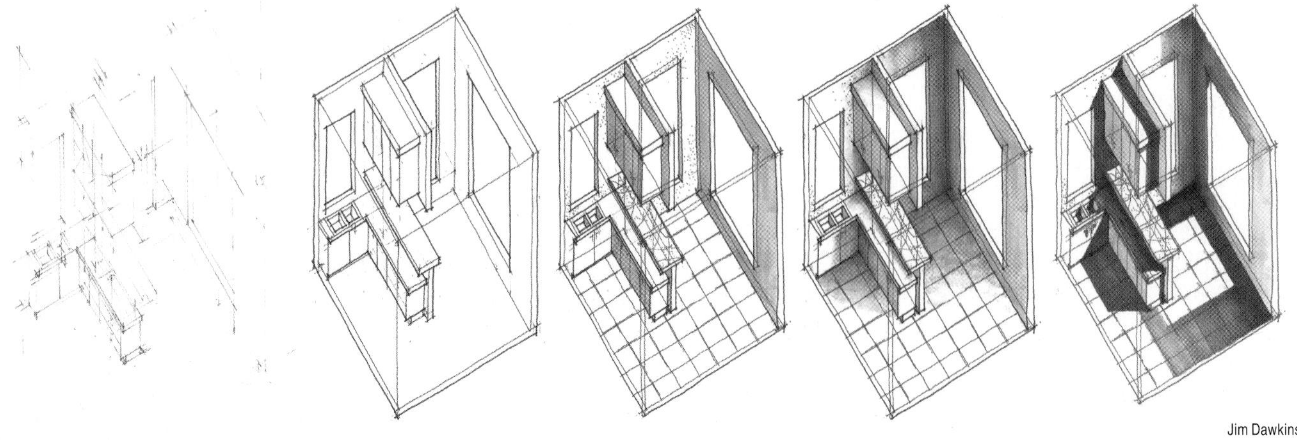

Jim Dawkins

Figure 13-19 The most common paraline (axon) drawing is the three-dimensional isometric drawing with each of the three axes at a 30-degree angle.

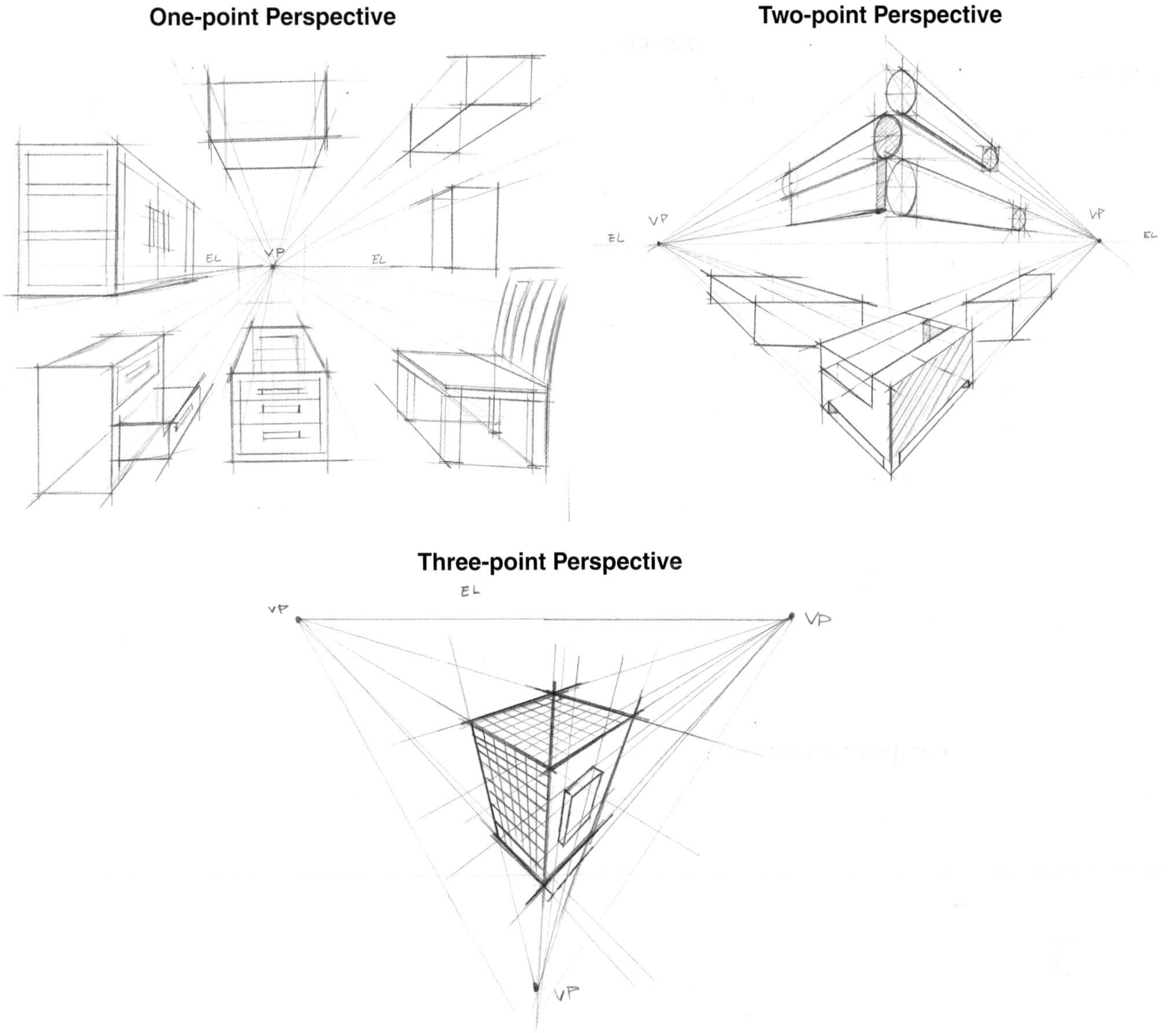

Courtesy of Robert Work MFA, Colorado State University

Figure 13-20 Perspective drawings show three-dimensional volumes and relationships of space in a two-dimensional realm. *Why do you think designers use perspective drawings more often than paraline drawings?*

vanishing points. This is the most common type of perspective an interior designer uses.

- **Three-point perspective.** In addition to the two vanishing points—one for each wall, the three-point perspective has a third vanishing point that shows how those walls recede into the ground. This third vanishing point is below the ground or high in space. Designers typically use this perspective when showing the view of buildings or interior spaces from high above.

Drawing Perspectives

When a client or team member requires clearer communication, the interior designer creates a perspective drawing. The objects or spaces that the client does not already understand determine the type of perspective drawing you create.

If manually drawn, the designer can create the perspective by beginning with a floor plan and determining the perspective view he or she wants to illustrate. Beginning with a square, the designer adds a horizon line and then a vanishing point. He or she then draws perspective lines

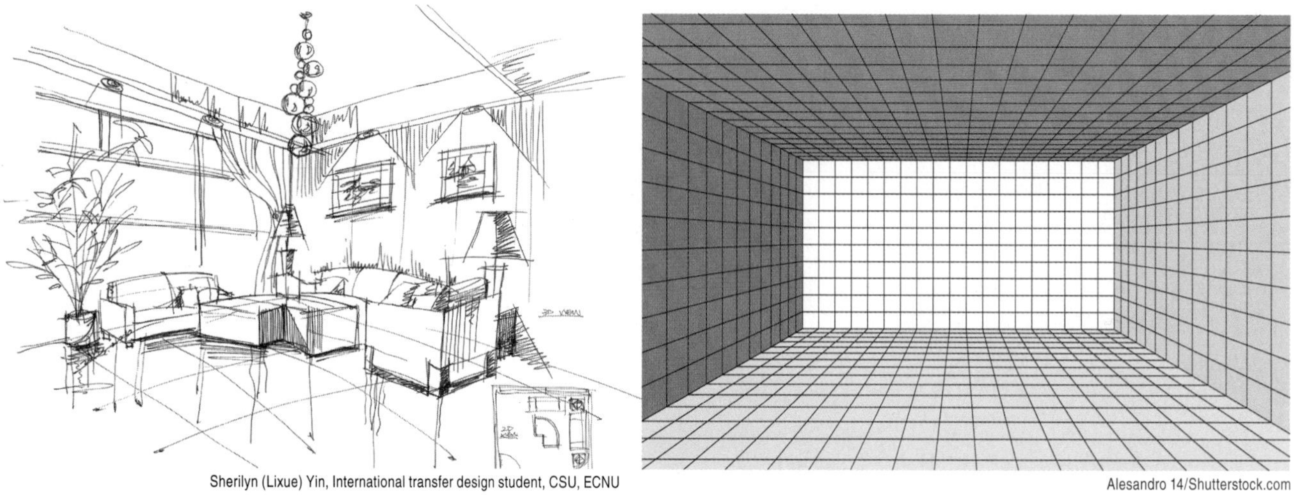

Sherilyn (Lixue) Yin, International transfer design student, CSU, ECNU Alesandro 14/Shutterstock.com

Figure 13-21 Using the perspective grid method—either manually or digitally— can assist you as you first learn how to draw a perspective.

through the vanishing point, creating a grid on the walls. Using another piece of tracing paper, the designer can create a clean line drawing. See **Figure 13-21**.

To speed up the process of completing a perspective, a design practitioner may sometimes use the *prepared grid method.* This method can be manual or digital. For the manual perspective drawing, the designer can purchase a grid template. For the digital prepared grid method, the computer can generate the grid template from a quick computer-generated drawing. Simplistically, the process begins with drawing the room in three dimensions in CAD, placing basic three-dimensional geometric forms where desired in the space to represent furniture location, and then printing the drawing. Laying tracing paper over the grid, the designer has a template to use under the perspective drawing.

When drawing a perspective, the interior designer may begin with four basic three-dimensional forms commonly used to depict space. They are the *cube, sphere, cone,* and *cylinder.* The designer can draw all interior furnishings inside the perspective space from these simple geometric forms. For example, he or she can modify the cube to become a table or chair, and modify a sphere to appear to be a vase or table lamp. If the perspective will not include color, it is important to add more lines and textures in strategic places to create shade, shadows, and interest in the interior illustration. Adding scaled *people* to the space, along with key accessories, generates a more realistic perspective for the client to view and understand.

If a client has an existing interior that needs modification, the designer can use a second technique, known as **photo tracing**. A photo of the client's interior serves as the grid template for the one- or two-point perspective, and then the designer draws over the image.

Interior designers commonly use perspectives in client presentations and often render them to indicate color and textures in the space. Quick perspective drawings are useful both for the designer to generate ideas, and to communicate a mood or feel of the space to the client.

Digital Perspectives

There are several software programs, such as *Revit* and *ArchiCAD* that can produce digital perspectives. After completing the floor plan in the software, it is possible to import free, three-dimensional (3-D) symbols from furniture manufacturers into the computer-generated interior. The symbols are quite detailed and represent furniture currently available on the market. Once you insert symbols into the room or building, you can

- indicate the location of the viewer
- select that hidden lines should be invisible on the screen
- view the perspective in one-point or two-point perspective

The beauty of software-generated perspectives is that they are easy to create and modify, **Figure 13-22**. The disadvantage is that they often appear mechanical with a hard edge to them once printed. The perspective can also appear distorted. To make digital perspectives look more realistic, many designers create a hybrid perspective that combines digital- and hand-drawing skills. To do this, they will generate the full perspective in the computer,

Samantha Wilson, Senior Interior Design Student, Colorado State University

Figure 13-22 In these sketches for the design of a homeless shelter facility, the designer used a software program to produce the digital floor plan and perspectives, and then imported 3-D symbols into the rooms.

print the perspective, and then lay tracing paper over it to re-sketch it by hand. This technique allows the designer to use the speed of the computer, and yet their manual skills to draw in the client's exact furniture details that may not be available in the software. This can be an effective, time-saving combination of skills.

Construction Drawings

Contract documents consist of the contracts (agreements), construction drawings, and specifications requirements for a new construction or a remodel project. *Contracts* are the legal documents outlining the responsibilities of each party, scope of project, the project timeline, and the parties involved in the agreement. The full set of contract documents indicate that you will deliver, for a certain sum of money, the project as outlined. If you do not follow the contract, there could be legal or financial consequences.

Specifications (or "specs") are documents in written format that clearly describe the requirements for type and quality of materials, work-quality expectations, and the conditions and details for executing the work. If the client's project is small, the designer can record the specifications directly on the construction drawings. If the projects are large, the specifications are included in a *job book* or *project manual*. Specifications should not duplicate the construction drawings, but complement them. The three major types of specifications are proprietary, descriptive, and performance.

- **Proprietary.** Proprietary specifications indicate a specific manufacturer's products by name, model, or part number, as well as color and finish. They are restrictive to those who wish to bid a job, but allow control over what is installed for the client's project.

- **Descriptive.** These specifications provide details about the materials, finishes, fabrication methods, acceptable workmanship, and installation methods to use for the project. They do not specify a manufacturer or trade name but do set a standard of quality.
- **Performance.** When describing the expected performance of the item(s) specified, designers often use performance specifications for custom components installed in the interior.

Construction drawings, or working drawings, are part of the contract document package and are highly technical in detail. The designer or design team creates them during the Design Development and Contract Administration phases of the design process. For design success, it is important to learn how to accurately decipher or read construction drawings and how to create them, **Figure 13-23**.

Organization

Construction drawings communicate how and where to construct the building. They indicate where to lay the foundation, how to finish the interior spaces, where to install the cabinets and add the built-in furniture, what type of window/door styles to use, and the exact materials with which to complete the specified project. For large commercial projects, a set of construction drawings may be over 100 pages long. For a small residential-remodel project, a set of construction drawings may total 10 pages.

Dimitar Sotirov/Shutterstock.com

Figure 13-23 Construction drawings are highly technical and details. They help the builders and contractors execute the design accurately.

Because construction drawings are a communication tool, you need to know your audience. While the intent of a perspective drawing is to enhance the client's understanding of a design proposal, construction drawings are for the contractor and subcontractors who are completing the work. Using their standard language—called *architectural drawing conventions*—ensures they and you obtain the desired result.

Construction drawings include pages about demolition, floor plans, sections, elevations, interiors, and electrical plans. In addition, they include *engineering drawings* which define exact structural components such as size and space of steel reinforcements in a wall. There are legal consequences connected with construction documents. For example, if installation of a perimeter drain around the house foundation does not properly follow the construction drawings, the house can heave up—destroying parts of the building. The liability for this error returns to the builder and possibly subcontractor.

The designer sequentially labels and numbers each page of the construction drawings set to show the order in which to construct the building—from location of the building on-site to the interiors. The designer uses prefixes to label each section. For example, *A-1* is the prefix for the first page of the *Architecture* section and *ID-3* is the prefix for the third page of the *Interior Design* section. Other section prefixes include

- **D**—Demolition
- **S**—Structural
- **M**—Mechanical
- **E**—Electrical
- **P**—Plumbing
- **FP**—Fire protection plan
- **FF**—Finishes and furniture
- **Q**—Equipment

Each page communicates to the expert the details he or she is responsible for as part of the project. This allows a subcontractor—such as an electrician—to turn directly to the page of the construction documents he or she needs to complete the work. See **Figure 13-24**.

The sheet size (page size) can vary among firms. Common sizes are 18 by 24 inches or 36 by 48 inches. *Mini-sets* of construction drawings—typically 11 by 17 inches—to easily transport to job sites. Typically, the designer produces sheets in horizontal format, and binds them on the left side.

Typical Sections: Construction Drawing Set			
Sheet Number	**Section Prefixes**	**Sheet Name**	**Components of Sheet**
1		**Cover Sheet**	Includes client, project name, location of project, architecture and designer contact information, professional stamp(s)
2		**Index of Sheets**	Identifies lists of pages and page numbers
3	A	**Standard Architectural Symbols and Codes**	Shows architectural symbols and abbreviations, applicable codes
4	A	**Site Plan**	Identifies location of building on site
5	D	**Demolition Plan** (if demolition is taking place)	Includes type of demolition—mechanical or implosion; factors to consider—adjacency to other buildings, historic significance, dangerous conditions or hazardous materials, salvage and/or reuse
6	FP	**Fire and Life Safety Plan** (may appear elsewhere in set of drawings)	Includes exits, firewalls, square footages, other code compliances
7	S	**Footing and Foundation Plan** (may be part of structural or engineering plans)	Identifies concrete footings, foundation walls, piers, posts, columns, basement
8	A	**Floor Plan(s)**	Begins with first floor and includes separate plan for each floor of the building
9	A	**Reflected Ceiling Plan**	Includes legend, coordinated with electrical and mechanical plans
10	A	**Exterior Elevations**	Shows style of building, doors, windows, siding, trim, chimneys; may also show underground building features
11	A	**Interior Elevations**	Shows vertical surfaces of interior walls, complex details, or special construction (kitchen cabinets, bathroom layouts, etc.)
12	A	**Building Sections**	Shows imaginary "cut" through entire building structure to show details
13	A	**Wall Sections and Stair Sections**	Shows imaginary "cut" through shows entire wall from floor to floor to roof
14	A	**Details**	Includes large-scale illustrations to provide necessary details for construction
15	FF	**Finish Schedule/ Furniture Plan**	Includes legend, specific finishes; door, window, room finish schedules and special treatments; furniture placement
16	M	**Mechanical Plan** (includes plumbing)	Includes heating, ventilating, and air-conditioning system (HVAC), sometimes piping systems
17	E	**Electrical Plan**	Includes legend, fixtures, wiring, switching
18	E	**Power/Communication Plan** (if needed, typically commercial)	Includes locations of data, electrical, and phone jacks
19	P	**Plumbing Plan**	Shows heating/circulating equipment, supply and waste systems, plumbing fixtures, and locations where water pipes enter
20	A	**Specifications** (if not in separate book)	*Nontechnical aspects* (contract agreement, responsibilities, permits, inspections, insurance) and *technical aspects* (building codes, materials standards, testing procedures, quality of work to be done, inspection and testing criteria)

Figure 13-24 The typical sections of the construction drawing set follow a certain organization so that subcontractors can easily find the documents needed to complete their work.

Construction drawings are scaled documents that use standard **drawing conventions**—such as line weights, types of lines, and symbols—to clearly communicate the design to team members. Each page of the working drawings is numbered and lettered to indicate the subcontractor's responsibility in the project. Interior designers most often reference the section illustrating floor plans, interior elevations, sections, and reflected ceiling plans.

Sherilyn (Lixue) Yin, International transfer design student, CSU, ECNU/ Shidong Yin 殷世东, Senior Photographer

Figure 13-26 Readability and consistency are important when hand lettering.

Title Block

Each construction drawing, and every page of a drawing set, has a title block along the bottom or extreme right side of the page, **Figure 13-25**. The **title block** is typically a rectangular box that contains key project information such as the

- design-firm name
- design-firm contact information with logo
- name of the client
- professional seal(s)
- sheet title and number
- job number and completion date

Lettering Techniques and Font Types

Legibility and professional appearance is critical in the selection of hand-lettering skills and digital fonts. Manual drawings look best with hand lettering. Digital drawings look best with appropriate computer fonts. The most important aspect of lettering is its readability. Consistency in style is important. When a large set of documents is created, the same font type should be used by all creating the set, **Figure 13-26.**

Hand lettering is an art. The more professional your hand lettering looks, the better others perceive you as a professional. Sloppy hand lettering can destroy a good impression of a great design. Use the following tips as you hand letter:

- Make your lettering legible and readable. This is very important to avoid misunderstandings.
- Create hand lettering that is consistent. It communicates confidence.
- Keep the lettering size proportional to the size of the completed drawing. For construction drawings, sheet-size numbers are 1/2 inch in height and main titles are 3/16 to 1/4 inches in height.
- Use a straightedge so your hand lettering does not slope vertically down the page.
- Use block-style lettering with uppercase letters that are square in shape.
- Create consistent space between letters for ease in viewing and reading. Measure the space between lines of the lettering with a ruler.
- Study samples of lettering styles. Then practice every chance possible.

Designers typically use hand lettering on schematic drawings, freehand sketching, and for informal, written client communications. Present yourself well.

Digital drawings should use font styles that are in scale to the drawing, easy to read, and reflective of the document type. Interior design is a business. Avoid unusual fonts. They trivialize the business product you are developing. Clean, crisp fonts are generally best. If you are completing a historical drawing, use fonts appropriate to the period.

Charles E. Smith, Areté 3 Ltd.

Figure 13-25 A title block appears on every page of a construction drawing set. *Why is it essential for the title block to be on every page?*

DESIGNER MATH SKILLS

Writing Measurements Accurately

As a project moves through the design process, the designer develops various design drawings. The rough draft sketches, the preliminary floor plan, and the furniture plan are all important steps leading up to the final detailed architectural plan. The goal of each stage is to troubleshoot the details, eliminating costly errors and disappointment later.

When the designer sketches ideas on paper, the client's dreams start to become a reality. Even though the sketch can be as simple as a drawing on a napkin, the rough draft develops over time to reflect specific details for a pantry, front coat closet, and the locations of the stairwell and doors. The sketches go through numerous changes as the designer focuses on function, storage, existing furnishings, and circulation.

To determine whether the plan will actually work, the rough draft must progress forward to a scaled floor plan which focuses on the actual square footage. The common scale for a residential drawing is 1/4″ = 1′-0″ which the designer writes below the drawing. The client's wish list for the dream home greatly determines the size of the structure as does the lot size and budget. Once the floor plan is final, the outside shape of the home, or the footprint, becomes clarified.

The use of *outside dimensions* reflects the overall measurement of the floor plan. These horizontal and vertical lines always have arrows (or *tick marks*) placed precisely where the dimension begins and ends. The designer draws dimensional lines indicating

- width of a structure outside the footprint which are readable from the bottom of the plan
- height of the structure vertically outside the footprint which are readable from the right side of the plan

Designers always write measurements *above* the dimensional line as 59′-6″ with a dash between the feet and inches.

The *middle dimensions* indicate measurements of a space or an object. For example, each room is labeled and underlined with the dimensions written *below* the line. Directional lines or arrows are excluded.

<u>DINING ROOM</u>
11′-10″ × 15′-3″

While developing floor plans, the designer also creates a scaled furniture plan document. Unlike floor plans, dimensions *are not* included on a furniture plan because this makes it cluttered and difficult to read. Since the furnishings are drawn to scale, the person reading the furniture plan can easily measure to determine if the clearances are adequate. It is critical to draw furnishings on the furniture plan to scale of the actual size of the furnishings specified. There are unfortunate tales of furniture that would not fit through the door or could not make the turn on a stair landing on delivery because measurements were inaccurate.

Standardized sizing for furnishings on electronic or plastic templates are only a general measurement. They are not accurate depictions of all furnishings. Again, it is imperative to use actual furniture measurements when creating a furniture plan.

Many people have a difficult time visualizing space and furnishings. Creating scaled templates for each specific piece of furniture allows the designer to experiment with furniture arrangements. For example, suppose your client owns a grand piano. Taking accurate measurements of the piano and creating a scaled template, allows you to put the piano in different locations in the room before actually moving the piano.

Today, many furniture manufacturers and design centers offer interactive space planning on their websites. You can select scaled furnishings from the website and paste them onto a custom-made 1/4″ grid to check the fit.

A furniture plan does not appear on the final detailed design documents the builder or contractor uses.

Drafting Standards

When developing a set of construction drawings, designers use specific drafting standards to enhance communication. These include appropriate line weights, abbreviations, and symbols that are uniformly acceptable in the building industry.

Line Types

Lines communicate information about objects, hidden conditions, and important relationships within the drawing. A line has both direction and weight. It can be continuous or dashed; straight, curved, or diagonal.

Continuous lines indicate objects and major architectural elements such as structural walls or columns. *Dashed lines* indicate objects hidden from view above the cutting plane of a floor plan such as wall cabinets or beams. Dashed lines can also indicate wheelchair-turning radius and ceiling height changes on a floor plan. *Dimension lines* indicate the physical distances of objects.

Line Weights

Designers use various *line weights*—intensity of blackness and width of line—to indicate the hierarchy of objects. Interior projects generally use three line widths: thick (dark), medium, and thin (light). The blackest and boldest lines should be the first you notice when looking at the drawing. This signifies that they are closest to the viewer and usually represent outer boundaries of an object. For example, in a floor-plan view, the designer draws wall lines the darkest to clearly define the spaces.

Each design or architectural firm identifies standards for line weights for the projects it manages. The *American Institute of Architects (AIA)* offers a list of national standards. If using CAD, line weights often have a layer assignment, too. Then, if the designer wants to see a particular part of the construction drawing, he or she can turn the rest of the layers off.

The following identifies general standards for different line weights. See **Figure 13-27**.

- **Border lines.** These lines have the boldest line weight that designers use to outline the elements that are cut through and are closest to the viewer (full-height wall lines).
- **Object lines.** Medium-weight lines, or object lines, lie below the plane of the cut but above floor plane and outline such objects as fixtures, built-ins, and furnishings.
- **Light lines.** The designer uses light line weights to outline the surface treatment of floors such as wood grain or tile. Light lines recede into background so they look lighter than other lines.
- **Hidden lines.** Objects that are not visible in specific views, such as shelving, are dashed lines.

Scale

Drawing scale is important for team member understanding. The typical scale a designer uses for residential projects is 1/4" = 1'-0". For commercial projects the typical scale is 1/8" = 1'-0". Usage of larger scales, such as 1/2", depicts details of an elevation or section. The designer must indicate the scale on each drawing, even if there are many drawings on the same page. To indicate the drawing scale, use the following method: scale 1/4":1'-0".

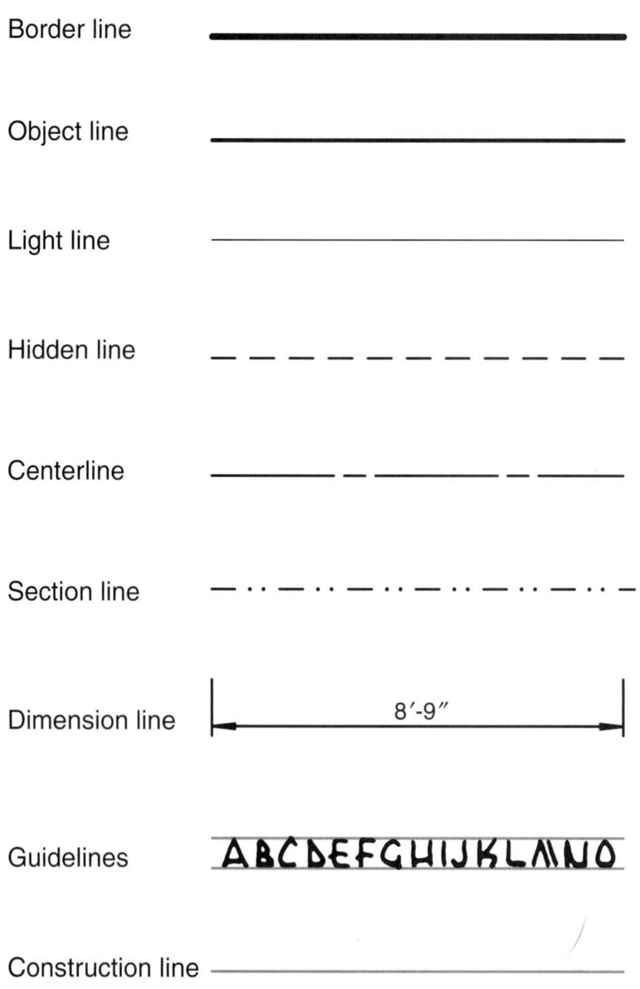

Goodheart-Willcox Publisher

Figure 13-27 These line types are typically used with interior design and architectural plans.

Drawing Conventions

Drawing conventions are industry standards designers use to reduce drawing time and space needs to convey information. Abbreviations, graphic symbols, keys, and legends convey important information. *Dimensions* are another convention that ensures exact communication about sizes and placement of objects.

Abbreviations

Construction drawings often use *abbreviations*—shorter forms of words and phrases that replace the whole forms. They can vary among different trades. As you learn to read a set of construction drawings, look for standard abbreviations. If they are not familiar to you, ask about them. You often find a list of abbreviations used in the construction drawings in the first few pages of the document. See **Figure 13-28** for some common abbreviations.

Symbols

Symbols are a type of pictorial shorthand language that reduces drawing time and coordinates separate drawings. Just as every page of the construction drawings has a title block, other pages that illustrate symbols include a **legend**—a combination of graphic symbols and notes—to indicate what the symbols represent. There are many types of legends in a set of drawings such as lighting, electrical, construction materials, and furniture plans. For example, a reflected ceiling plan uses lighting symbols and a demolition plan uses symbols indicating what is to be demolished as well as the placement of new construction. Legends should be concise and readable.

Symbols are divided into several types: material, line, and graphic. *Material symbols* represent types of construction materials. *Line symbols* relate to line weights and line types. *Graphic symbols* help index part of one drawing to another part on a different drawing sheet.

Designers use common symbols that are universal throughout the industry. For example, standard doors are drawn open at 90 degrees to the wall, with arc of door swing indicated. Likewise, universal symbols outline door frames, wall systems, and windowsills. Symbols may also show window frames and sheets of glass. Symbols for stairs generally show four or five steps with a cut-off—a broken, angled line. The symbols "UP" or "DN" are adjacent to stairs with a directional arrow. See **Figure 13-29**.

Common Abbreviations for Construction Drawings

A/C	air conditioning	**Dwr**	drawer	**Min**	minimum
AFF	above finished floor	**Elec**	electrical	**Nts**	not to scale
BR	bedroom	**Elev**	elevator	**Oc**	on center
Bldg	building	**Ext**	exterior	**Plas**	plastic
Bsmt	basement	**Flur**	fluorescent	**Pnt**	paint
Cab	cabinet	**Ftg**	footing	**Rad**	radius
Cem	cement	**Flr**	floor	**Refr**	refrigerator
Clg	ceiling	**Gyp**	gypsum	**Sch**	schedule
Clo	closet	**Hdr**	header	**Shr**	shower
Col	column	**Hvac**	heating, ventilation, and air conditioning	**Spec**	specification
Conc	concrete			**Std**	standard
Contr	contractor	**Incl**	include	**Stl**	steel
Cpt	carpet	**Int**	interior	**Str**	structure
Ctr	center	**Jst**	joist	**Thk**	thickness
Dem	demolish	**Kit**	kitchen	**Typ**	typical
Dia	diameter	**Laund**	laundry	**Util**	utility
Dim	dimension	**Loc**	locate/location	**Wc**	water closet (toilet)
Din Rm	dining room	**Mech**	mechanical	**Wd**	wood
Dn	down	**Mfr**	manufacturer	**w/d**	washer/dryer
DW	dishwasher	**Milwk**	millwork	**wh**	water heater

Figure 13-28 Using common abbreviations consistently in construction drawings helps all team members understand the design plans.

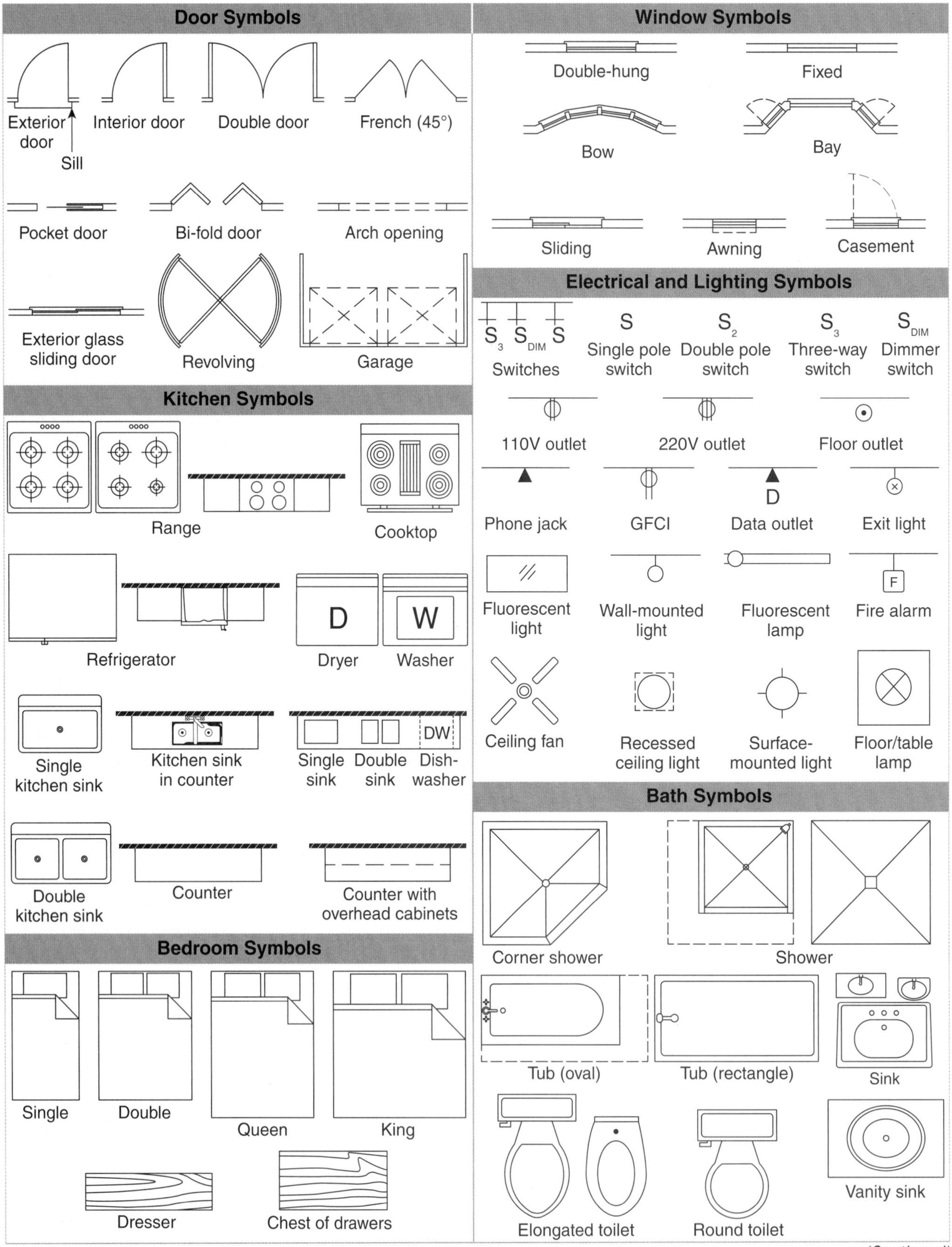

(Continued)

Goodheart-Willcox Publisher

Figure 13-29 Common floor plan symbols help express the details in the design plan and ensure understanding by all who use the plan.

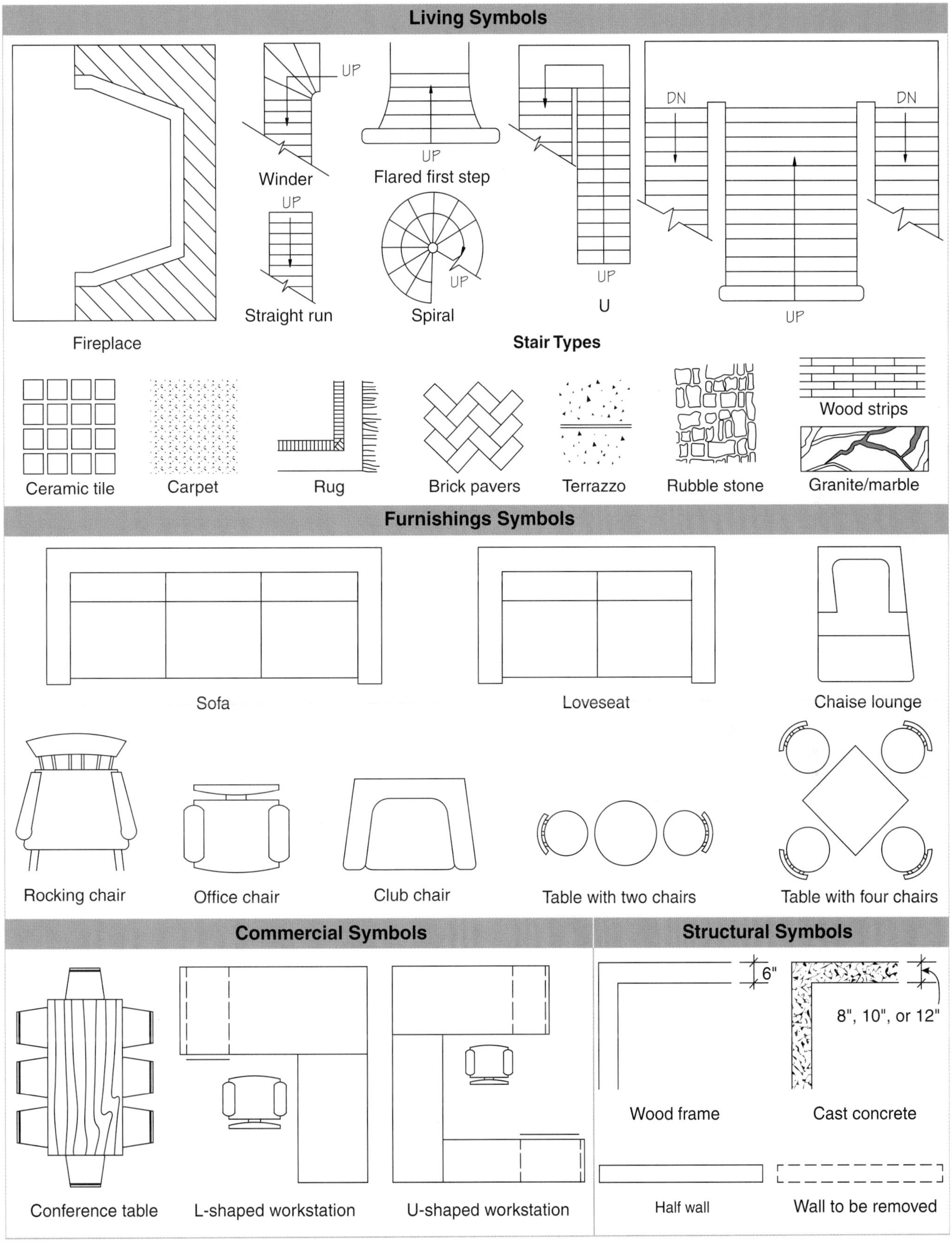

Goodheart-Willcox Publisher

Figure 13-29 *(Continued)*

Dimensions

Dimensions are important on any construction drawing. They indicate the plan's length, width, and components, as well as the distance of those components from each other. Dimensions include dimension lines with terminators such as *arrows* (or *tick marks*) that indicate where the dimension begins and ends. They must be accurate, complete, easily readable, and following certain standards.

Designers group and order dimensions in a hierarchical manner. There are two standards for dimensioning a floor plan: *The American Institute of Architects (AIA)* and the *National Kitchen and Bath Association (NKBA)*.

- The AIA standard for general design drawings of floor plans uses the 1/4" = 1'-0" or 1/8" = 1'-0" scale.
- The NKBA standard dimensions for specialized millwork drawings, which the designer draws to a larger scale, is typically 1/2" = 1'-0".

Generally, the designer specifies dimensions of 12 inches or above in feet and inches with a dash between the feet and inches as in the following: 2'-6" or 2'-0". The outside dimension is the overall measurement. The middle measurement is the dimension of a space or object. The smaller dimensions usually relate to details within the drawing. Horizontal dimensions should read across the page from left to right.

CAD software offers easy dimensioning capabilities with many styles and fonts from which to choose. Stick with one style throughout a set of drawings.

Digital Construction Drawings

One constant challenge of builders and designers is the delivery of successful projects to the client despite tight budgets, labor force limitations, and schedule accelerations. The clearer and more accurate the construction drawings, the better and faster the project proceeds.

Due to the amount of technical detail, designers complete the vast majority of construction drawings using AutoCAD® and Revit®. AutoCAD is an industry standard throughout the world. This is an important advantage because many other countries hire design firms to complete projects in their countries. AutoCAD runs on both MAC and PC platforms. As you know, Revit is modeling software that is quickly moving into the designbuild fields. See **Figure 13-30**.

There are many advantages for digitally creating the construction drawings. The designer can complete revisions common to any client's project more easily with a computer than by hand. The computer also allows drawings to "reference" each other. If a designer makes a change to a wall on the floor plan, the computer updates all other drawings linked to the part of the project with the same change. For example, the floor plan is often the *base* drawing for the electrical and furniture plans. When the designer makes a change to the floor plan, the computer software automatically updates the configuration of the electrical and furniture plans by using a cross-referencing command. This capability alone contributes to a significant decrease in the number of construction errors.

CAD programs allow the designer to designate lines and objects to their own layers. Each layer is like a separate drawing. The designer can make different line weight and line type assignments on each layer. Then, for the layers (or sheets) the designer needs, he or she can *turn off* layers unneeded in a particular drawing and print (or plot).

Additional benefits for using CAD programs include

- rapid reproduction—if you need more than one set of documents, you do not have to redraft them, just simply print (plot) them
- time and money savings
- increased value to clients by delivering more design alternatives in less time

Ionia/Shutterstock.com

Figure 13-30 Construction drawings prepared using AutoCAD or Revit consistently run on MAC and PC platforms and are easily understood across cultures.

- faster completion of projects and thereby reducing possible coordination errors
- enhanced perception of you as an up-to-date designer by the client

Other issues with CAD work is file sharing and file management. As the design project increases in size, the number of team members also increases. Effective management of the drawings and construction documents is a critical part of the design process. Clients and team members change their minds, requiring revisions to the design.

To ensure you are working off the most recent document file, you should use a system of file management. **File management** is a list of guidelines to indicate such things as the file name for the most recent version of the client's drawing. In addition, designers must outline and communicate methods of *file sharing*. File sharing through cloud technology has become easier and more secure.

Another advantage of completing construction drawings in CAD is their link to specifications. Construction drawings show the builder or subcontractor how to put together different parts of the exterior and interior. The specifications indicate the type and quality of products and the craftsmanship the project requires. The specifications and the construction drawings work hand-in-hand to give the builder a more complete understanding of the design installation.

Rendering

A rendering brings an image to life—it is the visual enhancement of any drawing through the application of color, value, and texture. It is a common visual presentation technique all design disciplines use. Rendering brings a three-dimensional human quality to otherwise two-dimensional images.

From an interior view, the goal is to render the space in a realistic way. This enhances the client's ability to visualize the space before building or installation begins. The designer often uses colors and textures that represent the client's interior when rendering. This helps clients visualize what the space will look like on completion. See **Figure 13-31.**

A rendering can be extremely refined and detailed or very loose and quickly completed. Quality differences depend on time. If you are making quick sketches during the Schematic design phase, a few marker and colored pencil strokes quickly communicates an idea to a team member or client. If more time is available, the client may be willing to pay for a more sophisticated rendering. A client typically incurs this type of expense for a very large project that requires communication to different constituents. For example, a town hall project for a nearby community requires a different level of refinement and sophistication.

Jim Dawkins

Jeff Curcio, Point of View, LLC/Designed by ForrestPerkins.

Figure 13-31 Every designer has a unique style of rendering. Whether a rendering is extremely refined or very loose may also depend on time and the client's budget for rendering.

Importance of Light

To be good at rendering, you must pay attention to light—where it lands, shifts, or falls off a surface. Both natural and electric light create shade, shadow, and textural effects. They both offer different colors that impact visual perceptions relating to time of day and mood of space. Therefore, the type of light, location of light source, and the material covering an object all impact the actual lighting of the object.

Objects have *shade* in areas that receive light indirectly. Where something blocks light from hitting a surface of an object, *shadows* develop. To understand how light strikes or enhances pieces of furniture, you have to look at *where* and *how* the light is naturally achieved in interiors around you. Hence, you learn to *see* spaces in a different way.

What to Render

A designer can render just about every type of two- and three-dimensional drawing. Floor plans are a favorite because they assist the client in understanding types and color of flooring proposed for the space(s). Shade and shadow can be added to give it a three-dimensional quality. The designer can easily develop elevations and sections from a floor plan and enhance them with color, texture, and shadow.

All orthographic projections require shadow during rendering. The designer should consider the location of shadows prior to rendering, and then render shadows in colored pencil, ink, or marker. The designer can also enhance paraline and perspective drawings with rendering. Manual drawings impress the client—especially if the designer renders them.

Rendering Media

There are many types of art media the interior designer can use to render an image. No one item does everything well. Therefore, most renderings require the use of several types of media. Following are some basic items that are successful in rendering beautiful images.

Pencil

Non-colored renderings can be developed using graphite pencils. While they create subtle and beautiful drawings, they do not reproduce as well as ink. See **Figure 13-32**.

Wax-based colored pencils are easiest to use when rendering. To work well, the designer needs to layer or manipulate color pencils. Without layering, colored pencils look grainy because the color is connecting only with the top surface of the paper. *Color-pencil blenders* are colorless but work magic! They blend color pencil lines and smooth the layers.

Colored-pencil renderings vary greatly based on type and texture of paper used. In addition, the way the designer holds the pencil and the type of stroke he or she uses produces different effects.

One of the best ways to use colored pencils is over marker renderings. Pencils enhance marker color and define shape better. A sharp white or light-colored pencil works well to clean up edges of marker renderings.

Ink

Ink comes in refillable or disposable pens. Both pen types create excellent line work that reproduces well. Disposable technical pens are useful in creating line drawings. Felt-tip ink pens work well on colored renderings to define edges. See **Figure 13-33.**

psynovec/Shutterstock.com

Figure 13-32 Pencil renderings are subtle and interesting drawings.

Jim Dawkins

Figure 13-33 Ink renderings look great and reproduce well. *What details do you see that ink captures readily? How could an ink rendering be helpful for client understanding of the design?*

Markers

Today, markers are a favorite rendering medium in the design field. They do not require a great deal of setup or cleaning time and they come in an incredible range of colors. Tips vary from blunt to very fine. Some markers have multiple tips in one unit.

The use of markers when rendering takes some skill. Without careful technique, application of marker color can give an image a "coloring book" look. Instead, apply marker color in layers. For instance, to create value—light and dark—contrast, apply a single marker color in layers. Layering gray marker under an appropriate color creates value or enriches color. When possible, apply marker strokes against a straightedge. Do not use metal or plastic edges as they can cause wet markers to smear. The best straightedge is a strip of mat board or illustration board that absorbs the excess marker as you run it along the edge. To also create value contrast or intensify a color, designers can also layer colored pencil and pastel media over marker color. See **Figure 13-34**.

Blender markers look like other markers but contain a colorless solvent that breaks down pigment. To use a blender marker, rub it over a darker marker color—such as deep blue—to *pick up* the color and then dab it in a nearby location. This technique creates a lighter blue color without having to purchase another marker and also looks more like watercolor.

olkapooh/Shutterstock.com

Image by Jacqui McFarland

Figure 13-34 With marker renderings, it is important to add the color in layers. *What are the pros and cons of marker rendering?*

The disadvantage of markers is that they dry up rather quickly. Keep caps on the markers when not in use. Because some markers can give off toxic fumes, use them in a well-ventilated area.

Watercolor

Watercolor is transparent, water-based pigment available in tubes or cakes. Watercolors create beautiful renderings; however, their use is difficult to master and time-consuming. Mix watercolor tube colors with water to use them in liquid form. The designer needs a watercolor brush to apply this liquid. Brushes are available in different sizes and tip types such as pointed, flat, and round. In addition, use of watercolor requires special watercolor paper to handle the moisture created by the paint. Due to the time commitment, designers rarely use watercolor in the Schematic design phase. Instead, they use watercolor renderings as final presentation drawings, **Figure 13-35**.

olkapooh/Shutterstock.com

Figure 13-35 Because watercolor renderings require much skill and are often time-consuming, interior designers typically use them for final presentation drawings.

Mixed Media

Again, no one media does everything well. Many architects and designers use a variety of media to take advantage of each tool they have. The prevalence of digital has largely replaced hand-rendering techniques because digital renderings make it possible to develop multiple views quickly and easily. Many proficient professionals who render perspectives, however, use multiple media techniques. With minimal effort, they can take a flat, uninspiring export image created with a computer and create a drawing with more depth, texture, and human detail than is always possible using strictly digital means, **Figure 13-36**. The overall goal is to sell the design and tell a story.

Rendering Papers

The way paper takes the media impacts how the rendering appears. Matching the paper with the correct media guarantees a certain success. Following are several types of paper used for different media.

- **Bond paper.** This paper is inexpensive, readily available, strong, and durable. You can use it for pencil, colored pencil, and marker—or a combination. Marker can soak the paper if you are not careful. Rendering directly on bond photocopies of illustrations has become popular in design offices. Designers also use bond paper for printing and plotting CAD work. Bond paper also comes in colors and creates an effective rendering if used with colored pencil.
- **Bristol paper.** A highly absorbent paper, Bristol comes in variety of weights, can go through a photocopy machine, and takes marker well. Many professional illustrators prefer this paper or Bristol board.
- **Kraft paper.** Inexpensive, brown paper found in rolls or on paper bags, this paper offers a rough, earthy quality to the design presentation. It is highly absorbent. Ink pen and colored pencil work well on it.
- **Watercolor paper.** Used for working with wet media such as watercolor paint, watercolor paper is a heavier-weight paper. It consists of 100 percent cotton rag paper that comes in different textures, colors, and weights.

Jim Dawkins

Figure 13-36 Using specialized software, designers may combine various media to add appeal to their visual presentations. *How did the designer use this photo to inspire visual appeal?*

Rendering Tips

Many resources are available to illustrate different rendering techniques you can mimic until you develop your own style. Be curious and experiment with different media. As with sketching, practice is important.

Manual rendering tips are many. Here are just a few.

- Collect a clip file of magazine pictures and digital images of marker/pencil rendering techniques as examples to follow in your renderings.
- Draw small sketches first and then use a copier to enlarge the drawings for rendering. Small drawings (2 inch by 2 inch or 2 inch by 4 inch) are easier to sketch than large ones.
- Photocopy any drawings you make as line work only. Make the photocopy on paper you plan to use for final drawing. Experiment with color on the copies before working on the original drawing.
- Begin by rendering areas that you know to be standard colors. For example, render wood floors, other flooring, and plants. Along with building confidence, this helps you in composing the rendering.
- Use marker media first to avoid removing ink and colored marker during application. Apply ink or colored pencil second.
- Purchase a colorless *marker blender* to smooth edges between various media you use.
- Use a straightedge to apply marker in wide strokes to plans, elevations, and sections.
- Use a marker and pastel pencil combination when rendering a floor plan. They mix well and enhance each other's rendering capabilities. If the image depicts carpet or wood flooring, use a straightedge and the lightest colored marker possible. When using a Prismacolor ® pencil, use a straightedge when drawing wood plank lines to keep them crisp looking. After the rendering is complete, use a fine-tip marker to sharpen the lines again in the floor plan.
- Apply colored pencil over markers to add highlights (for instance, white pencil), intensify dark areas, and intensify color.
- Soften and subdue marker color with colored pencil. Marker color alone is often too intense for use in interior renderings. When using Prisma colored pencils, remember to sharpen them to keep lines crisp. Prismacolor pencils have soft tips.
- Vary marker color slightly when rendering natural materials such as wood and stone. This requires going over particular areas with a second application of marker.

- Start with a medium olive green when rendering plants. Add a dark green in the middle of plants (dense part of the plant) and add light green on the perimeter to show where the light hits.
- Add a silhouette or image of a person to a drawing or sketch. There are many sketches online of different people. Print them and lay them under your drawing to trace the image. Verify that the posture is at the correct angle before adding the silhouette to your sketch. You could even add a client into your rendering.
- Decide where the natural light is coming from before casting shadows and highlights. Create shadows with gray marker *before* applying pencil. Learning how to apply such media effectively moves a rendering from good to great.
- Scale patterns on chairs and sofas to the floor plan.
- Avoid overworking a rendering. Simplest is best.
- Use a medium, darker, and lighter shade of the same color when rendering. Nothing you render is a single color. Even varying the pressure on a Prismacolor pencil allows you to get different tones.
- Keep your hands clean at all times. Wash them periodically to avoid smudging your finished product.
- Set a time limit for your rendering work. Sometimes rendering more quickly results in a better image.
- Look online, purchase books, and gather resources as you learn to render. Place them around you as you begin. Do not be afraid to mimic technique, but do avoid plagiarism.

Digital Rendering—Two-Dimensional

In recent years, digital renderings received much criticism for producing images with lack of charm, character, or the overall appeal of a high-quality hand-drawn illustration. Many thought such images were too *cold* or computerized.

Today, designers often want to enhance their hand-drawn illustrations—such as a perspective of a restaurant—with specialized software. Conversely, many designers also want to take digital photographs and add hand-drawn appeal to them—such as the interior photograph of a client's remodel project.

With a continuous stream of new software and updates, the new word in digital rendering—especially in the two-dimensional realm—is *experimentation*. Designers often use manual and digital tools purposefully and frequently. The goal is to deliver the most professional, accurate visual presentation in the shortest amount of time.

Photorealism (or *photoreal*) is a rendering style that looks like photography, **Figure 13-37**. It realistically shows spaces, textiles, materials, and furniture as they are to appear after building or installation. By scanning

Architectural Workshop, Mark Bowers, AIA/R M Ruwart Design, Rosalie M. Ruwart, ASID

Figure 13-37 With photorealism, designers can realistically show clients how materials and finishes will look in their spaces, enhancing client understanding of the design solution.

and importing images of exact materials selections for a client's project into specialized software, the designer can accurately show changes to the space. As with manual rendering, the goal of digital rendering is to help the client understand the design proposal before approving the design solution.

As you know, the most popular digital-editing software is Photoshop by Adobe. It offers the designer the use of layers, colors, brushes, and transparency adjustments when rendering images. Brushes can be set to any size or shape. The software can mimic different art media. With the software, the designer can manipulate colors, brightness, and contrast.

Architects and interior designers use Photoshop for graphics editing when digitally rendering drawings. For example, they may import a manually-drawn perspective into Photoshop with a scanner into the computer. Then the designer can manipulate the perspective with various tools to add shades and shadows that result in a more three-dimensional appearance.

Photoshop is also a photograph enhancing tool. Designers can also take digital photographs of a client's interior spaces and import them into Photoshop to manipulate and enhance. This is a powerful tool when selling the design to a client. For example, suppose a car dealership decides to remodel. After taking a photograph of the interior, the designer imports the photo into Photoshop and begins changing the space. The designer can crop out parts of the space, create additional walls, and add more windows. With little effort, the designer can display different color choices. Once the space revisions are complete, a *fill* layer creates a hand-painted look to the new rendering.

Photoshop is a companion to Adobe Illustrator. Image files can be imported and exported between the two software products to create a professional rendering. For example, the designer can prepare a digital photograph in Photoshop before importing it into Illustrator for hand tracing. Designers can also use Photoshop with digital modeling software such as SketchUp, and Autodesk products such as AutoCAD, Revit®, and Autodesk 3ds Max.

Digital rendering is popular, quick, easy to revise, and professional in appearance. Once the rendering is complete, you can plot it (print it) to different papers.

Similar to manual rendering, there are many tips for digital rendering. Here are a few.

- Scale the materials to the correct proportion before inserting them into the drawing.
- Plot (print) from Illustrator rather than Photoshop to enhance the image quality.
- Mix photos and hand drawings for dramatic effects.

Designer Profile

Joshua Brewinski, Designer, on Successful Design

As a designer for the company, Stantec ViBE, of Boulder, Colorado, Joshua's current portfolio of design work spans seven years, nine countries, and includes several million square feet of completed space.

"It sounds so simple: a good, clear idea is the hallmark of any successful design. More often than not, though, those ideas cannot stand on words alone. How we communicate as designers requires a multi-sensory approach, depending in large part on our audience. It is up to us to cultivate and exercise, not only the verbal, but the *visual* tools most effective in reflecting the desired outcomes of our clients, the aspirations of their stakeholders, and the vision of our design teams. From the napkin sketch, to the 3-D rendered animation, and to the final construction documents from which spaces are built, every line has meaning and every image has the potential to tell a story when words fall short."

You can read more about Joshua's background in Appendix B.

Models

A designer can use models for a simple study of form, such as a presentation model in scale, or to develop as a museum quality replica. Their main purpose is they allow designers and clients to study the volume of a certain space. Often the level of sophistication of the model reflects the state of the design process in which it is constructed. For example, a designer would use a rip and tear model in the Schematic design phase to explore concepts. Once the designer and client determine the concept and many design details, he or she typically creates a presentation model in the Design development phase.

Depending on the stage of the design process, client needs, and perceived advantages, a model may be worth the additional time to enhance client understanding. Many firms hire professional model-makers to assist with this type of visual communication.

The construction of any model begins with deciding its purpose and audience. For example, design projects that receive public funding often require use of presentation models to gain public approval. Project funding by investors also uses presentation models. Models are also helpful as a means of study for students of design. Interior designers build models to

- conceptualize and explore ideas and look for flaws
- study elements and principles of design—specifically proportion, volume, and light
- analyze spatial relationships—between spaces and within one space
- examine a design from different angles and perspectives
- communicate a design that is difficult to understand

There are two general types of models: hand or computer generated. Both assist the client in visualizing the proposed spaces. A designer can visually or verbally do a walk-through during a client presentation. You may find you have more skill with manual than computer-generated images or vice versa. Again, experiment.

Handheld Models

There are a number of different types of handheld models. See the following. Depending on the type of firm or client, you may use one type more than another. See **Figure 13-38** for some of the following types of models.

- **Concept model.** A concept model, or *study model*, represents a concept or idea for the client's space or project. It is a three-dimensional equivalent of a concept sketch. To develop a concept model, a designer can use almost any material to communicate the design. The more refined concept models present simplified or abstracted versions of finishes, materials, and colors but in accurate scale.
- **Construction model.** This is a scaled model indicating construction details or building components.
- **Presentation model.** Also called a *finish or working model,* this is a rough, scaled replication of what the final space or building will look like once built.
- **Daylighting model.** This model helps the designer study the shift of daylight across and through an interior during different years and seasons. These models can also be computer generated.
- **Parti model.** A type of conceptual model, a *parti model* is an abstract study of geometric shapes or series of lines and forms. A designer uses it to develop a floor plan.
- **Rip and tear model.** These informal models help capture the ideation process. Materials used to make them may be old boxes, paper, plastic, wood, and sheet metal—often scraps of materials the designer does not purchase.
- **Site model.** This model places emphasis on architecture to site rather than the interior.

Materials and tools for handheld models vary in construction capabilities, composition, and expense. Some are very flimsy, such as cardstock paper, while others are quite rigid, such as balsa wood. Designers can use them in combination, but they are often of pristine, monochromatic colors to encourage investigation of the spaces and shapes. The materials come in sheets and can be cut to specific shapes and measurements. Professional-looking models (whether concept or presentation) also require the right adhesives to properly hold them together. Adhesives include glue, tape, straight pins, knives (both artist and utility), and pliers.

Concept Model, Waterfall Chair

Lisa Taylor, Senior Design Student, Colorado State University

Lisa Taylor, Senior Design Student, Colorado State University

Concept Model, Foam Core Fountain

Maddie Roberts, Freshman Design Student, Colorado State University/ Damon Searles Photography

Maddie Roberts, Freshman Design Student, Colorado State University/ Damon Searles Photography

Concept Model, Chair Design

Lydia Brown, Senior Design Student, Colorado State University

Construction Model

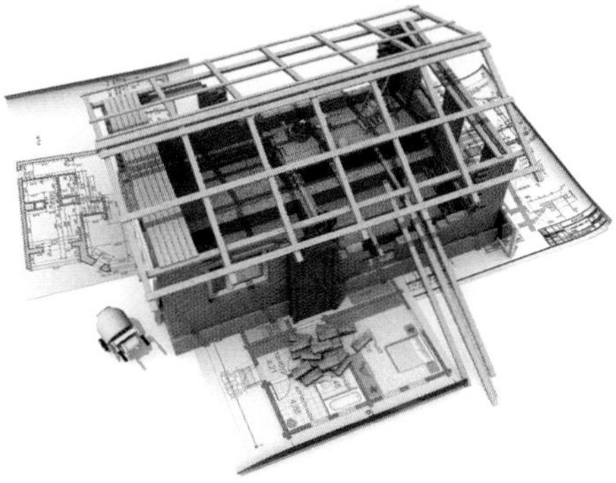

iurii/Shutterstock.com

Presentation Model, Commercial

Franck Boston/Shutterstock.com

Presentation Model, Residential

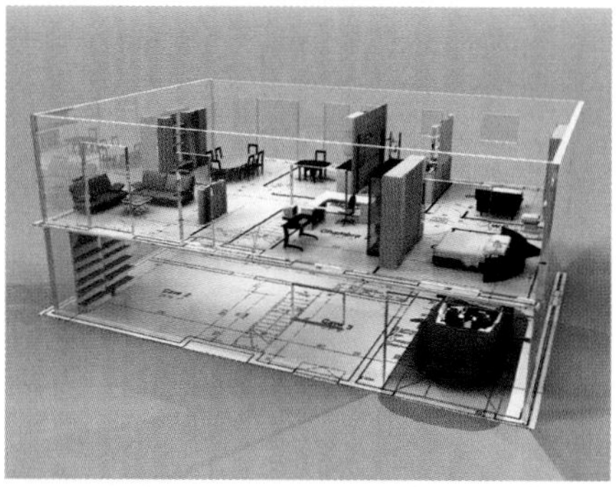

njaj/Shutterstock.com

Daylighting Model, Foam Core

Hannah Mahoney and Heidi Newlin, Junior Design Students, Colorado State University/Damon Searles Photography

Hannah Mahoney and Heidi Newlin, Junior Design Students, Colorado State University/Damon Searles Photography

Site Model, Foam Core

Miranda Wigner /Damon Searles Photography

Figure 13-38 Interior designers use models of many different types to enhance client understanding. As a designer in progress, building models can also help you analyze spatial relationships and conceptualize ideas.

When building presentation models, a few common construction materials include

- **Balsa wood.** Strong and lightweight with a tight grain, balsa wood is easy to cut and available in many thicknesses, **Figure 13-39.**
- **Cardboard.** Easy to cut and inexpensive to purchase, cardboard is paper layers glued together.
- **Chipboard.** Semi-rigid paperboard comprised of pressed and glued wood chips, chipboard is low in cost and easy to cut.
- **Foam core.** Available in many colors and widths, foam core (or foam board) is rigid polystyrene foam that is sandwiched between two pieces of paper. It is easy to cut, but must be scored with a new knife blade several times to achieve a clean cut.
- **Matte board.** Available in many colors, mat board (or presentation board) is paperboard with a pulp core. The cut edges look best when the mat board's core matches the surface paper color.
- **Museum board.** Expensive paperboard of high archival (acid-free) quality, museum board is available in neutral colors of white, beige, and black, and comes in several thicknesses. Handle museum board with disposable, white-cotton gloves to prevent hand oils from adhering to the surface.
- **Poster board.** Easy to cut, poster board is a thin cardboard.

To create a simple presentation model, use the following steps:

1. Print or draft a floor plan of your choice. (Optional: include the surrounding landscape.)
2. Add flooring textures with black pen or by using CAD. Rendering the floor plan is optional.

Balsa Wood Models

Lisa Taylor, Senior Design Student, Colorado State University

Figure 13-39 Balsa wood is a lightweight material that can be used to create handheld models.

3. Cut the finished floor plan out and mount it on a foam core or cardboard base.
4. Measure and cut all foam core pieces for the walls to the determined scale.
5. Add the elevation details. (Optional: render the elevation details.)
6. Cut out or draw the doors and windows into the elevations. (Optional: use transparency film to create the illusion of glass in doors and windows.)
7. Mount the walls to the base, one wall at a time, using the appropriate adhesive.
8. Use white tape to hide the exposed edges of the model.
9. Label the plan with the *North* arrow, logo, scale, and firm's name.
10. Add doors of either foam core or balsa wood.

Three-Dimensional (3-D) Digital Modeling and Rendering

Architects and interior designers use a variety of software programs to create three-dimensional digital models. A software model can be built as a wireframe model, surface model, or solid model.

- **Wireframe model.** Used in CAD, a **wireframe model** is a technique for representing three-dimensional objects in which all surfaces are visibly outlined in lines, including the opposite sides and all internal components that are normally hidden from view. Wireframe modeling is the least complex method for representing three-dimensional images. See **Figure 13-40**.
- **Surface model.** Widely used in CAD for 3-D illustrations and architectural renderings, **surface modeling** is a mathematical technique for representing objects that appear solid but in reality are not. Surface models do not have mass or volume (meaning they are not solid forms). A surface model is basically a wireframe model with a "thin skin" or outer covering. Although surface models are easier to visualize than wireframes, the designer cannot slice them open to examine the interior volume and mass. In addition, with surface modeling the object or area can be geometrically inaccurate. See **Figure 13-41.**

A computer model is a *true* three-dimensional environment. Therefore, you can select viewpoints from anywhere you want to figuratively stand within the model. You simply press a button to select the view, and the rendered image appears on the screen. *Three-dimensional rendering* is the process of producing an image based on three-dimensional data stored within a computer. The designer often renders the digital models to convey the client's interior materials and finishes. In addition, the designer can make changes as the client or team members suggest while viewing the model. This makes the design outcome a truly interactive process. Computer speed and client interaction allows the design process to progress more quickly—eliminating the tedious back-and-forth communications common with construction or remodeling projects.

Alexey Kashin/Shutterstock.com

Figure 13-40 Wireframe models are one method used to digitally represent three-dimensional objects and spaces. Designers and clients can easily see through these models to view interior details.

Chase Margaux Robbins, Sophomore Design Student, Colorado State University

Figure 13-41 Designers use digital surface models to help clients easily visualize the design. *Examine the images. Describe the differences between the initial drawings and how the drawings appear once the designer adds color and details. How might you use surface models when working with clients?*

Photoreal-rendered digital models produce lifelike walk-throughs—simulated tours of interiors, fly-by animations, and light and shadow renderings. To produce them, the designer must set up *scenes*. The process is somewhat like taking a photograph or filming a scene after finishing the setup in real life. Once the designer identifies the scenes, materials, and lighting, each scene is rendered. Rendering, the last step in an animation process, gives the final appearance to the models and animation with such visual effects as shading, texture-mapping, shadows, reflections, and motion blurs. The designer can easily modify the animation speed and views to achieve maximum understanding for the client.

Walk-throughs are very helpful when clients or team members want to understand relationships between spaces or proportional volumes within a space. Rendering an animation takes time, and computer processing speed and memory. Cloud technologies greatly reduce time and costs by enabling users to produce compelling, photorealistic visualizations without tying up the desktop or using specialized rendering hardware. In some cases, designers will *outsource*—hire the services of a specialized firm—to complete their models and renderings for efficiency and cost-related reasons.

Popular software products to use for building digital models include

- **AutoCAD (Autodesk).** Industry standard for CAD, it can produce three-dimensional models. It can generate perspectives, paraline, and orthographic drawings.
- **Revit (Autodesk).** Revit® is the industry standard BIM software program for construction drawings. The designer draws the building in three dimensions using icons of walls, floors, roofs, structure, and windows. A central file stores a master copy of the model. The designer can import the work created in AutoCAD and SketchUp into in the model.
- **3ds Max (Autodesk).** This software is standard for many design-related industries that use models, animation, and photorealism. Animation for motion graphics, visual effects, and design visualization are its strengths. Where Revit® can be used to construct and maintain a building, 3ds Max is software a designer uses for hypothetical or conceptual work. It is effective software for creating a walk-through of an interior. It is compatible with AutoCAD, which means you can import a three-dimensional interior from AutoCAD, render it, add lights for shade and shadow, and animate the model. Such models make great sales tools.
- **Form-Z (AutoDesSys).** Developed as CAD software, Form-Z is a three-dimensional modeler used by architects, interior designers, illustrators, and product designers. It is very good at developing photorealistic images and models. It is not used as frequently as 3ds Max; therefore, it is not an industry standard.

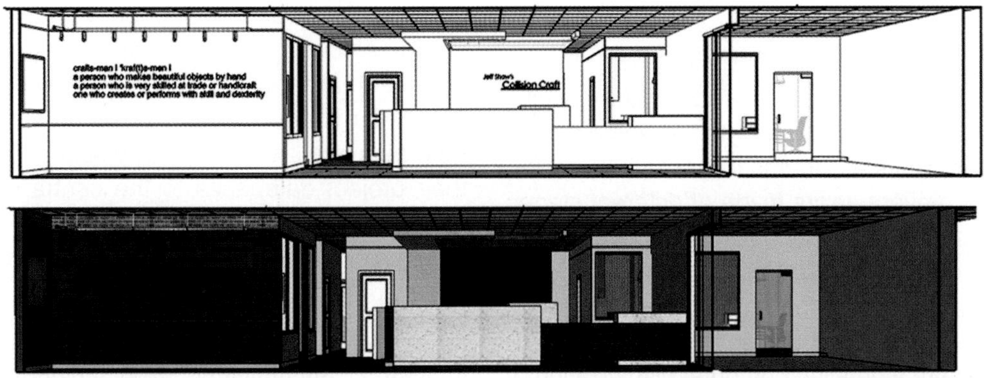

Kia Weatherspoon, Allied ASID/Determined by Design

Figure 13-42 An interior designer can import hand or CAD drawings into SketchUp to create quick three-dimensional models to use during ideation.

- **SketchUp.** This software is a modeling program that creates drawings resembling hand-drawn sketches. Owing to its quick learning curve and quickly generated three-dimensional models, SketchUp is an effective tool to use during the ideation. However, its rendering capabilities are somewhat limited. *SketchUp Make* is the free version of the software and is intuitive—easy to learn and use. Designers can share work through SketchUp's *3D Warehouse*, a website for storing the artists' SketchUp work. A designer can import two-dimensional drawings done by hand or CAD files into SketchUp. See **Figure 13-42**.

The benefits of digital modeling are many. Clients and team members appreciate the ability to explore, experiment, and view different interior configurations. Viewing an interior from different angles—from the air, ground, or in between—is helpful to understand spatial relationships, adjacencies, and proportion or scale. In some cases, a computer model can mathematically calculate how to construct a building or space.

Frank Gehry, a well-known architect, mentioned in an interview that sometimes he can see the design of the building, but he and his team of experts cannot figure out how to build it. Computer modeling helps take innovative ideas to reality, **Figure 13-43**. Three-dimensional views offer architects and designers the opportunity to see the construction and interiors before laying a single brick. This eliminates changes at the construction stage, resulting in dramatically lower costs. Building-project clients can also view what projects may look like before investing in them. This is a big selling tool. The designer can easily change materials, colors, and textures, too. A 3-D visualization says a thousand words. Designers can publish 3-D renderings online, making them available to a wide audience across the world.

You can view digital models and animations online or on a computer screen. You can also make individual scenes into still images and print them using photoreal technology such as a 3-D printer which uses rapid prototyping technology.

anderm/Shutterstock.com

Figure 13-43 Computer modeling allows interior designers and architects an opportunity to examine a structure prior to building it. Examine this image of the Walt Disney Concert Hall designed by Frank Gehry. *How can the ability to examine every aspect of design and construction via computer modeling be a benefit prior to building such an innovative structure?*

BIM Modeling System

The **building information modeling (BIM)** system is far more complex than 3-D CAD modeling. BIM, and the software with which it interfaces, offers rich information and a process for communication. The BIM process moves the building (the virtual-information model) through three different groups including the

- design team—architects, interior designers, surveyors, consulting engineers, and others

- contractors and subcontractors
- owner(s)—including facility managers

Each group adds its own additional discipline-specific knowledge and tracking of changes to the single model. The result greatly reduces information losses in transfer. BIM also helps prevent errors made at different stages of design development and construction. To prevent errors, BIM and the software interface use a conflict-detection feature in which the model actually informs the team about parts of the building in conflict or clashing. BIM also offers a detailed computer visualization of each building part in relation to the total building, including maintenance over its full life cycle.

There are several BIM-software programs used in the design industry. Several common to the industry are Revit® by AutoDesk and ArchiCAD® by Graphisoft. To begin the process, the design team builds the virtual model and then creates a central file to store a master copy of the model on a file server. All team members work on their own copy stored on their computers. Users save their changes to the central file and receive changes from other users, **Figure 13-44**. Once modeling structures and linking them to a database is complete, BIM can visually share information with an owner. With the push of a button, completion of a fly-through of the model makes the design visually meaningful to the client.

BIM allows experimentation and quantifiable feedback. Once the designers build the model in Revit, the design team can assess building performance, such as its energy-efficiency when building is complete. When a member makes a change in one view of the model, the software updates all other views automatically. If team members are from different disciplines, they can link their project databases to the central file and master copy of the model. Users report that the BIM process is more productive, more profitable, and produces a better quality project.

Managing building information using BIM can lead to substantial cost savings, from design and construction through to maintenance. The model saves time and waste onsite, and makes extra coordination checks largely unnecessary. The information the model generates leads to fewer errors on site caused by inaccurate and uncoordinated information. When all team members work on the same model from early design through construction completion, changes are automatically coordinated across the project. The information generated is therefore of higher quality.

BIM provides a powerful tool for design, construction, and long-term facility management. There is, however, still much confusion about what exactly it is and how design teams should utilize and implement it. BIM is a developing technology in an industry typically slow to adopt change. Many early adopters, however, are confident that BIM will grow to play an even more crucial role in building documentation.

Peter Bernik/Shutterstock.com gwycech/Shutterstock.com Goodluz/Shutterstock.com

Figure 13-44 Building information modeling allows all team members to communicate easily on all aspects of a project—from early design development through long-term managment of a facility.

Chapter 13

Review and Assess

Summary

- The ability to graphically communicate ideas clearly, quickly, and with impact is the most important and often most difficult skill for interior design students to learn.
- Four basic visual communication techniques include sketching, drafting, rendering, and modeling.
- Learning to draw by hand well helps you to understand depth, proportion, and scale, resulting in better work with drawing and rendering software.
- Digital tools include hardware—such as a computer, tablet, or peripherals—software, and cloud computing.
- Types of drawings designers use in various phases of the design process include ideation, presentation, and construction.
- Sketching and freehand sketching are tools designers use throughout the design process.
- Three types of drawing systems include orthographic, paraline, and perspective.
- Interior designers use perspective drawings to give clients and team members a more realistic view of an interior space.
- Construction documents consist of contracts, working drawings, and specifications requirements for design projects.
- Designers sequentially label and number the pages of a set of construction drawings using a standard language called *architectural drawing conventions*.
- A set of construction drawings includes a title block on each page and follows specific lettering and drafting standards.
- Digitally creating construction drawings allows the designer to work more quickly and efficiently.
- Rendering brings a drawing to life—adding a three-dimensional human quality to a two-dimensional image.
- Models allow interior designers and clients to study the volume of a space.
- Rendered digital models offer lifelike simulations of a space, giving the clients maximum understanding.
- Building information modeling (BIM) is a process that interfaces with certain software to help the design team and client evaluate all aspects of a project from design through construction and lifespan of the structure.

Chapter Vocabulary

Work in teams to locate a small image online that visually describes or explains each of the following terms. To create flashcards, write each term on a note card and paste the image that describes or explains the term on the opposite side.

building information modeling (BIM)
cloud computing
construction drawing
contract document
drafting
drawing convention
elevation
file management
floor plan
ideation drawing
isometric drawing
legend
model
orthographic drawing
paraline drawing
peripherals
perspective drawing
photo tracing
photorealism
presentation drawing
projection
raster-based
rendering
section
sketching
surface modeling
symbols
title block
vanishing point
vector-based
wireframe model

Review and Study

1. Why is good visual communication important?
2. Name four purposes for visual presentations.
3. Contrast sketching with rendering.
4. List at least 10 standard manual tools a designer uses for manual drawings.
5. What digital tools does an interior designer typically use?
6. How do construction drawings and presentation drawings differ?
7. List and describe eight sketching techniques an interior designer might use.
8. What are three types of projection or drawing systems interior designers commonly use?
9. What is a vanishing point and how does the designer use it?
10. Name the three major types of specifications and briefly describe each.
11. Why is it important to sequentially label and number the sections and sheets of the construction documents package?
12. What is a title block and what information does it contain?
13. What do line types and line weights communicate about a design project?
14. What are drawing conventions? Give an example.
15. What are three benefits of using CAD programs to create digital drawings?
16. How does rendering enhance a client's understanding of a space?
17. Name at least five art media a designer can use to render a drawing.
18. Contrast Bristol paper with watercolor paper.
19. List at least 10 rendering tips.
20. What is photorealism and how does it function?
21. Name seven types of handheld models.
22. Name three benefits of digital modeling.
23. What are three benefits of BIM and the software with which it interfaces?

Critical Analysis

24. **Draw conclusions.** Review the *Design Insight* quote by Michael Graves at the beginning of the chapter. Draw conclusions about ways that drawings "express the interaction of our minds, eyes, and hands." Cite text and personal examples.
25. **Analyze progress.** The author states that your sketchbook is "a type of journal or diary of images and places." Obtain a sketchbook and several pencils and felt-tip pens. Begin your journal of sketches by sketching everything you see during every available minute. After two or three weeks of sketching, analyze your sketches and describe the improvements you see.
26. **Distinguish effects.** Use a digital or phone camera to take a series of photographs of an object at home or school at different times of the day. Be sure to capture the effects of natural and electric light on the object. How does the shift in light throughout the day impact your visual perception of the object? How does the light create shade, shadow, and textural effects?

Think like a Designer

27. **Speaking.** Pull out a drawing or drafting tool from the mystery bag of tools on your instructor's desk. Name the tool and describe how to use it to the class.
28. **Math practice.** Presume a client is renovating a home built from a kit purchased from Sears, Roebuck and Co. in 1915. The *Hillrose House, plan #C189* was part of the Sears Modern Homes mail-order program (you can find the plan online using the plan's name and number). The client has the original floor plans and hopes to maintain its original design. The client is concerned whether the original bedrooms will accommodate today's bed sizes. The bedrooms measure: 13'-6" × 8'-0"; 12'-8" × 8'-0"; 13'-6" × 11'-6"; 12'-8" × 11'-6".

    Using an architectural scale (1/4" scale)—and the standard measurements for *twin, double, queen, king,* and *California king* beds that you find online—create templates for each of the bed sizes. Then create a document that shows the client your templates and a written rationale for the maximum bed size with clearances for each of the four bedrooms.

29. **Sketching practice.** To develop your sketching technique, follow the instructions for *Exercises One* through *Seven* on pages 439–444. Complete the exercises until you and your instructor are satisfied with the results. Save your best sketches for your portfolio.
30. **Floor plan practice.** Suppose you have a residential client who wants to remodel a small guest bathroom. The room is 6'-0" by 10'-0". Access to this bathroom is from the guest bedroom (12'-0" by 14'-5"). Your client wants to remove the bathtub and install a walk-in tiled shower. Draw a single-line floor plan of the bedroom and guest bathroom using a scale of 1/4" = 1'-0". Determine the size and placement of the bathroom fixtures—shower, vanity and sink, toilet, lighting, and heated towel bar.
31. **Drawing elevations and sections.** For the floor plan in item 30, draw an elevation of one wall. Then create a section drawing of the vanity and sink. Use a scale of 1/4" = 1'-0". Practice until you and your instructor are satisfied with the results.
32. **Math practice.** To practice using the architect's scale, draw a 28" × 7'-0" door using three different scales: 1/8", 1/4", and 1/2" on a sheet of paper. Accurately label the dimensions and scale on the drawing of each door.
33. **Manual rendering practice.** Draw and freehand render an elevation of one of the bathroom walls for the bathroom in item 30. Use your rendering media of choice—colored pencils, markers, or watercolors. Limit your colors to three or four.
34. **Isometric drawing practice.** Using the floor plan created for item 30, create an isometric floor plan showing the relationship of the guest bathroom to the bedroom. Remember, each axis is at a 30-degree angle.
35. **Interior perspective practice.** Produce interior drawings using both one-point and two-point perspective. Use the text and online videos to guide your drawings. Practice the techniques until you and your instructor are satisfied with the results.
36. **Manual lettering practice.** Following text directions on page 454, use a *2H* pencil to practice your manual lettering by writing the alphabet. First create lettering guidelines that are 1/4 inch high (main title size). Then create block-style uppercase letters. Practice your architectural lettering technique until you and your instructor are satisfied with the results.
37. **Manual rendering practice.** Locate online a simple lined perspective for a commercial or residential interior design working drawing and print a copy. Use two different colored pencils or markers to freehand render the space following text directions. Repeat until you and your instructor are satisfied with the results.
38. **Digital rendering practice.** Locate a simple lined perspective online to digitally render. Using the rendering tools in your software, practice rendering the image until you and your instructor are satisfied with the results.
39. **Manual modeling practice.** Create a simple model presentation following the text instructions on pages 470-471.

Design Application

41. **Design a 3-D model.** Three-dimensional models allow the designer and client to explore design ideas. and can be made with everyday materials. In teams, choose a phrase from the Dr. Seuss book, *Oh the Places You'll Go!,* on which to base your team model. Then do the following:
    A. Collect the following to put in your "kit of parts:" toilet paper tube; 3" × 5" card, plastic straw, plastic utensil, aluminum foil (12" × 5"), letter-size envelope, pencil, string, soda can, plastic sandwich bag, chop sticks, piece of fabric; a round object, a rough-surfaced object, a 12-inch object, a piece of wood, a red object, a white object. (***Note:*** The scale of all objects must fit in a brown paper lunch sack. You can only use these objects.)
    B. Locate a 16" × 16" platform for your team's model. It can be foam core, matte board, or brown cardboard.
    C. As a team, build the model using the items in your bag and the 16-inch platform. Your model must be based on the phrase from Dr. Seuss and must stick together for at least one week.
42. **Portfolio builder.** Save all satisfactory sketches, drawings, perspectives, renderings, and models in both your physical and digital portfolios. You will need to take photographs of some items for your digital portfolio.

Commercial Interior Design Applications

Rabaut Design Associates/©Jim Roof Creative, Inc.

Chapter 14

Design Insight

"People ignore design that ignores people."

Frank Chimero

Learning Targets

After studying this chapter, you will be able to

- analyze issues and needs related to commercial interior design projects.
- differentiate aspects of various sectors of commercial interior design, including healthcare, hospitality, retail, and educational design.
- analyze issues related to design of corporate offices and ways interior designers develop concepts for the design of corporate offices.
- examine the *Programming*, *Schematic Design*, and *Design Development* phases of the design process for corporate office design.
- generate a design concept for a commercial project based on identified text guidelines.

Introduction

Commercial interior design is the process of creating and overseeing the construction or renovation of commercial spaces. Individuals and groups enter and use public spaces almost every day. These places include restaurants, doctor offices, schools, stores, and libraries. As many commercial facilities are under construction, there are opportunities for designers to incorporate sustainable practices into their design for the health of the people and planet.

Issues for Commercial Design Projects

Commercial design projects are larger than residential projects and encompass all building types other than residential-related dwellings, **Figure 14-1**. The design of commercial spaces is often more complex due to their size and the need to consider various populations of people using the space.

Commercial interior designers address such issues as the layout and placement of interior walls, plumbing and power systems, and coordinating communications with construction teams, developers, owners, and service providers.

According to a recent *ASID Environmental Scanning Report*, the top five areas of commercial specialization as a percent of business are

- office (81 percent)
- hospitality (49 percent)
- healthcare (41 percent)

©Judy Dave, Hoachlander Davis Photography/Designed by ForrestPerkins

Figure 14-1 The design of commercial facilities is very complex as shown in this image of ForrestPerkins' adaptive reuse of Washington, DC's WestEnd 25 apartments. *View the details on the ForrestPerkins website. How did the designers go about transforming this space?*

- retail (39 percent)
- institutional (education) (30 percent)

Based on the above information, this chapter focuses on general functions and design issues related to these commercial design specialties. In addition, this chapter discusses details about the most commonly practiced specialty in the United States, corporate office design, within the context of the design process.

Note that many specialty areas of commercial design overlap, causing blurred boundaries. Interior designers may use similar design features in both hospitality design and heathcare design. For example, resort or spa-like amenities often appear in hospital lobbies and suites. Another example is the link between hospitality design and office design. According to the *ASID 2014 Industry Report*, there is a trend toward blending workplace and residential spaces.

Hotels are responding to, and taking advantage of, the changing work habits of people in today's workforce—those people who are deciding more and more *where* and *how* they are going to work. Hotels are making special efforts to engage travelers in their 20s and 30s—*Millennials* and a number of *Generation Xers*—who have a unique working style. Therefore, hotels are renting offices to traveling workers—or even local business people—who are looking for places to work. Like pop-up hotels and restaurants before them, *pop-up offices* are more commonplace in the hospitality industry.

There are many issues a design practitioner must address in the practice of commercial design. While some are specific to the specialty area, such as hospitality design, there are common issues, too.

Design Process

Commercial interior designers use the same design process as residential designers. However, some of the actions within each phase, the pace with which the design process is completed, and the number of times the designer revisits each phase due to client redesigns may differ.

The design process often begins with either a referral or a bid-process to acquire the client. Once the designer obtains the client and both parties agree on the scope of the project, comprehensive programming is critical. *Phase 2—Programming* requires understanding the detailed and often very specific needs of the **occupant**—defined by code books to be a person—and **end user**—the consumer who uses the finished space—requires a great deal of precision.

During *Phase 3—Schematic Design (SD)*, concept development is just as critical as it is with a residential project. Due to the size, scope, and scale of the project, if a concept is lacking it is often much more evident at the project's completion. If the common design thread does not tie all parts of the project together, the interior lacks a cohesive design, **Figure 14-2**.

©Ron Pollard, Courtesy of RNL

Figure 14-2 Concept development for commercial design is critical. *Review RNL's website to find out more about how the design concept for the Research Support Facility of the National Renewable Energy Laboratory (NERL) complements the original structure.*

Phase 4—Design Development (DD) has changed due to three-dimensional modeling systems and building management information systems (BIM). Accurately constructing digital models requires making many more design decisions during this phase rather than as traditionally done onsite.

The consequence of a longer DD phase is that the *Phase 5—Contract Documents (CD)* is completed faster because the design is thought out more thoroughly in the previous phase. As a result, during *Phase 6—Contract Administration (CA)*, the design team also completes the building schedule in a compressed time frame. Because costs relate to the project timeline, the faster the project is completed, the better the cost savings.

During *Phase7: Move-In and Post-Occupancy Evaluation*, the client moves into or takes possession of the space. The post-occupancy evaluation (POE) may take place once the client has "lived" with the space for a time. The POE may take the form of a questionnaire or a walk-through with the client. At this time, the client addresses how well the concept functions for the space.

Commercial design clients may have a single location (café) or multiple project locations such as a chain (hotel) or branch (bank) facility. Each client, however, focuses on the same bottom line: profit and productivity. What does this mean to the designer? It means the

- design features must support the client's ability to achieve profit and productivity
- rationale the designer uses to sell the design solution must support achieving these goals

These goals radically differ from a residential design project in which personal preferences and function shape the final design.

Meeting Needs of Multiple Groups

Commercial interior designers address the needs of multiple groups when designing public spaces. The first individual or group is the *owner* of the property or company. An owner may be a single individual such as a young entrepreneur developing a first restaurant, or a coalition of people representing a city that is building a new elementary school. Whoever they are, the owner(s) sets the budget, the direction of the commercial design project, and makes the decisions.

The second group involves the client employees who use the commercial space. Their satisfaction with the work environment leads to good morale, high productivity, and

Designer Profile

Tama Duffy Day, Healthcare Designer

Currently Tama is a Director and a firm-wide leader of the Health & Wellness Practice Area at Gensler, a research-driven global design and architecture firm. Her practice probes the healing capabilities of interior design and its capacity to influence well-being.

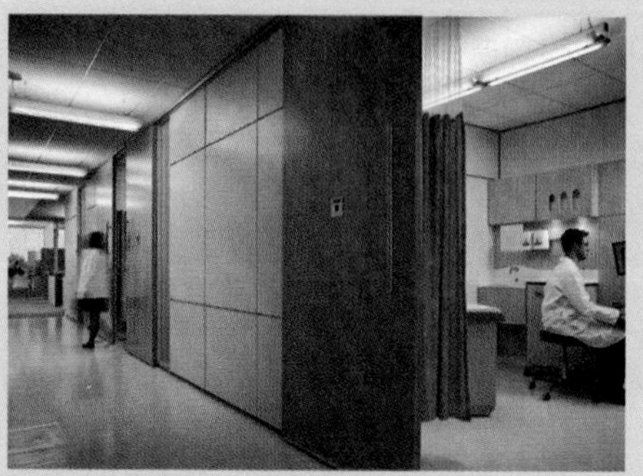

Tulsa Cancer Institute/Image courtesy of Gensler/Photographer: Nick Merrick

"My first memory of a healthcare environment was at the age of 12 when my mother and I visited my father in the hospital after he had a heart attack. It was a confusing and scary place. I drew pictures of the room and had bad dreams afterward. I decided in high school that I wanted to be an interior designer, mainly to improve other young children's experiences of hospitals by creating better places.

"For over 30 years, I have been leading teams in designing places for health and well-being that reduce fear and stress, places that provide positive measurable impacts on productivity, efficiency, and innovation. I entered the design profession before healthcare design really existed. Now, the profession fully embraces concepts of evidence-based design and generative place-making. Interior design has become front and center in the creation of places that align the physical space with social space, growing healthy communities and supporting healthy life styles."

You can read more about Tama's background in Appendix B.

low absenteeism. Employee wages are typically three-fourths or more of the cost of doing business. Designing a commercial space to enhance employee satisfaction is a critical consideration when developing the final design solution.

A third group includes the customer or guest using the space. This group generates the revenue to keep the business open. A poorly designed supermarket will not remain open if it is not functional for those using it. Therefore, how and when the space is used is critically analyzed during the design process.

Health, Safety, and Accessibility of Public

When designing and building a commercial facility, the health and safety of the public is the most critical issue. Commercial interior designers are knowledgeable about many codes that regulate the construction or remodel of the building. **Building codes** are laws created by federal, state, and local jurisdictions to ensure the safety of the public.

Commercial interior designers are also aware of *occupancy* classifications for the building type before designing the client's space. **Building occupancy classifications** refer to categorizing structures based on their usage. These classifications relate to the design of interior spaces because they guide egress practices due to *National Fire Protection Association (NFPA)* fire code standards. For example, a residence classified under Group R specifies that hallways can be as narrow as 36 inches. This dimension supports the belief that a family can safely exit a burning building using those hallway widths. Conversely, Group B, for businesses, specifies that hallways must be a minimum of 44 inches wide because many strangers exiting a larger building will need more space.

Commercial interior designers are also knowledgeable about accessibility codes such as the *American with Disabilities Act (ADA)*. These codes, set by the Department of Justice, include a set of federal rules and regulations that ensure architectural barriers are removed to make every building and structure accessible and usable by all persons, including those persons with any type of disability.

Knowledge of Systems

A commercial designer has to consider multiple *systems* when designing a client's space. Each system impacts how employees perform their work. These systems relate to the building as well as the comfort and safety of the people using the space. Due to the complexity of these systems, specialists are hired by the design and construction team to design and install them. Building systems include

- **Heating, ventilation and air conditioning (HVAC).** Factors that influence HVAC systems include sun paths into building, building structure generated heat, and internal heat loads from lights, people, and equipment.
- **Lighting and electrical systems.** Designer concerns include electrical supply and demand, lighting systems such as controls for fluorescent lighting, occupancy sensors, and emergency backup lighting systems.
- **Security systems.** These are systems— such as alarms and lights— that protect the occupants and end users.
- **Communications systems.** Designers must be concerned about technologies related to data and telecommunications.
- **People systems.** People-related systems are those that allow the flow of occupants from one space to another. This includes sources of vertical transportation, such as stairs and elevators, as well as pathways to spaces and equipment—both in and out of the building, **Figure 14-3**.

Technical information does not end with understanding building systems. There are also new technologies *within* each specialty area, such as high-tech equipment used in hospitals. There are also new technologies across all commercial design facilities such as factors that impact the acquisition of LEED certification or and lighting design advances and updates.

Commercial designers may juggle five to fifteen different design projects at various stages of the design process. You can understand why commercial design is a fast-paced, demanding but satisfying career.

©Judy Davis, Hoachlander Davis Photography/Designed by ForrestPerkins

Gensler Project Team: Charrisse Johnston, Danielle Gharst, Has Herst, Jenny Ogasawara, Phillipe Pare, Shawn Shin/Photography: Benny Chan, Fotoworks/Los Angeles Community Museum of Art

Figure 14-3 Vertical transportation such as elevators and stairs are important to moving building occupants from one part of a structure to another.

Specialty Commercial Design Space Needs

Commercial design responds to many different types and sizes of occupants and users of the space, while considering ages and abilities. Following are some of the more common commercial design specialties with a few basic design considerations listed for each. They are outlined here to give you an idea of how each specialty is a little, or a lot, different from each other.

Healthcare Facility Design

The healthcare field is constantly bombarded with cutting-edge technology and evolving healthcare practices and regulations. There are many specialized fields within the profession with highly educated individuals that grapple daily with demanding schedules and life-and-death situations. Interior design and architectural firms specialize specifically in the design of hospitals or other healthcare facilities due to their complex and life safety issues. Typically large in scale, these commercial projects generally take several years to complete and involve many diverse team members. Today, a guiding process used in the design of them is evidence-based design (EBD), which emerged from the healthcare profession.

When designing healthcare facilities, there are common issues to consider. Some of these include

- efficient and welcoming reception areas that direct traffic and guests to the proper locations
- convenient locations for nursing staff and stations in relationship to patient rooms
- high levels of cleanliness and sanitization throughout all areas
- separation of clean supply areas from soiled utility rooms
- space to prepare planned meals for those staying overnight
- design of patient rooms to support patient, family, and caregivers plus access to and from patient rooms (for instance, movement of patient beds from one area to another requires doorways that are a minimum of 48 inches wide)
- easy-access storage for lifesaving equipment in the patient room
- respite corners for family and staff off the nursing unit
- planned privacy for working with confidential issues related to patient records and private conversations
- planned wayfinding systems such as signage, color schemes, and positioning of staff and landmarks

Link to History

Influences on Healthcare Design

Florence Nightingale (1820–1910) was very influential in recognizing that hospital cleanliness correlated to patient survival. During the Crimean War, she was able to decrease the death rate of wounded soldiers from 60 percent to two percent in six months. Florence focused on providing patients with access to natural light, healthful food, and a sanitary environment. Of particular importance was her emphasis on fresh air and outdoor views of inviting landscapes. These recommendations are very similar to sustainable design strategies in use today.

Analyze It!

Read and analyze two or more reliable articles that present concepts and information about healthcare design today. How does this information relate to the early influence of Florence Nightingale? Write an informative summary effectively analyzing the content of the articles.

According to Roz Cama, Principal, Cama, Inc., an expert in healthcare design, stress is at the core of most individuals' healthcare experiences. Commercial designers who specialize in healthcare design have a real opportunity to improve experiences in these public facilities by reducing occupant stress. An occupant may be a patient, the staff, or the family. Designing spaces that allow a caregiver to relax helps him or her stay engaged and focused on helping patients heal. The staff retreat needs to be a quiet environment with pleasing views, natural light, comfortable seating, and distractions from daily work.

A designer typically works with the following common spaces when designing a healthcare facility:

- reception area, **Figure 14-4**
- waiting areas
- public restrooms
- checkout area
- records department; file storage/retrieval, insurance processing, billing
- exam rooms for patients
- lab spaces and X-ray areas
- private doctors' offices
- break rooms

If the healthcare facility is a hospital, its design needs to include specialty floors for surgery, pediatrics, obstetrics, and oncology. In addition to emergency room facilities, a kitchen and cafeteria, lobby, pharmacy, chapel, and administrative offices may also be requirements.

Formerly, the interiors of healthcare facilities were quite sterile in appearance. Today, many are visually stimulating to inspire an upbeat, encouraging attitude—especially in the pediatrics wing. Bathrooms and restrooms for patients have become more spa-like, and patient rooms have more comfortable amenities similar to those of a nice hotel room.

Wayfinding, the way to orient and navigate within a public space, is critical in healthcare facilities. The ability to find your way to and through a public facility is important to enhance personal control.

Patient Rooms

The patient room is very important to achieving a positive healing experience, **Figure 14-5**. Infection-control strategies shape patient room design. No issue has affected the design of inpatient rooms and units more over the past few years than the increased emphasis on controlling **nosocomial** (nah-suh-KOH-mee-uhl), or hospital-acquired infections. With current understanding that infection spreads by physical contact more frequently than airborne transmission, there is more emphasis on hand sanitation and contact isolation for patients. For example, it is now evidence-based practice to provide lavatories or hand sanitizers at the entries to patient rooms and in prominent locations throughout the hospital unit.

Since supplies and linens are considered contaminated once a patient leaves a room, hospitals are now greatly reducing the amount of supplies stored in the room. Most recent patient-room designs have minimal to zero storage in the room, substituted by either supply carts or built-in nurse servers directly outside the room.

Photo courtesy of Boulder Associates Architects

Interior Designer: SCI Design Group/Photographer: Michael McLane

©Judy Davis—Hoachlander Davis Photography/Designed by ForrestPerkins

Figure 14-4 Careful design of the reception area is critical in healthcare design. *Evaluate the images. What features help improve patient experience, provide comfort, and reduce stress?*

©Ed LaCasse, Courtesy of Boulder Associates

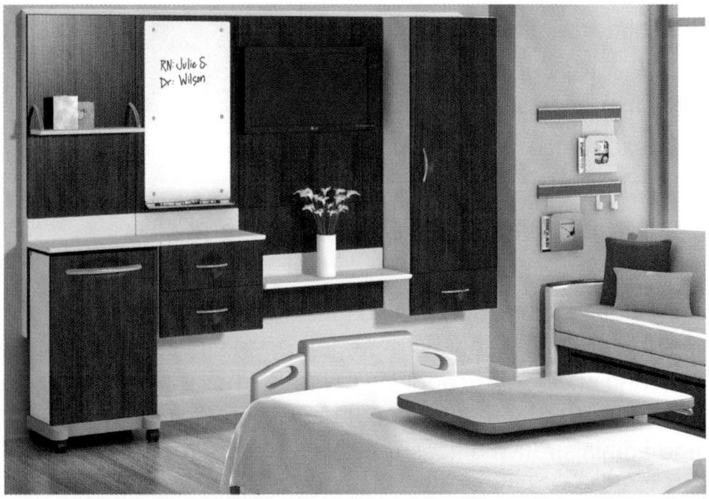

Courtesy of Herman Miller, Inc./Compass System, Patient Care/Designer: Gianfranco Zaccai

Figure 14-5 Patient comfort is important to a positive, healing experience. *What features in these patient rooms contribute to comfort?*

Hospitals are reevaluating what needs to remain in the patient room. Even the use of cubicle curtains for patient privacy is falling out of favor, since numerous people touch them when passing by. New designs of specially treated fabrics or disposable curtains may mitigate this problem. Because they harbor infection, hospitals are also reducing the number of horizontal surfaces in patient rooms. Manufacturers are taking a fresh look at infection-resistant computer keyboards and monitor controls for the same reason.

The creation of patient rooms that bridge care levels from medical/surgical (acute) to intermediate (step-down) to critical (intensive) care continues to be a strong need. This allows for the universal design of patient units for use with multiple levels of care at the same time, or changes from one level to the next over time. Many hospitals allow patients to remain in their rooms when their conditions change for better or worse, with according adjustments to staffing levels. The key elements of design for adaptable patient rooms continue to include

- **Toilet rooms.** Most facilities opt to include enclosed toilet rooms with showers in all patient rooms, including critical care. This allows patients to remain in their rooms as they gain mobility. It also allows families to remain with their loved ones in the higher care-level settings.
- **Visibility versus privacy.** The debate continues regarding how much visibility healthcare staff require of patients, especially in the critical care setting. All agree that there must be visualization of critical care and intermediate care patients in certain situations. To avoid moving patients to visualize them, this requires glass windows and/or doors in all rooms.
- **Flexible headwall configurations.** A headwall is the wall unit at the top of the patient's bed that contains electronics and access to life-saving equipment for the patient. New headwall products from several major manufacturers allow more flexible installation and reconfiguration of medical gases, power, and low-voltage systems than ever before.
- **Space relationships.** Effective use of universal design in decreasing the distance between the patient bed and the toilet helps patients remain more self-sufficient and makes it easier for staff to help those patients who require assistance in transferring from the bed to toilet.

Waiting Rooms

As you may know, spending time waiting is in healthcare settings. You may wait to hear the staff call your name for a doctor appointment, or you wait for a friend or loved one during his or her visit. Often highly emotional, waiting can seem to last a long time. For those who are anxious in healthcare settings, waiting time may seem even longer. What are some things to include when designing a waiting room that helps promote a positive experience for people who use the space?

First consider the seating. There is a wide variety of people who use waiting rooms—ranging from those of differing ages and genders to those with varying illnesses and concerns. Each person has distinct needs. Since people like to congregate in groups of different sizes, consider using movable furniture that can be repositioned to fit the needs of each group. In addition, using different sizes of seating helps people find what best meets their needs. A variety of seating adds to the interest of the space more so than the same style row after row. By mixing lounge chairs, extra-wide heavy-duty seating (bariatric), recliners, and tables with chairs, and children's seating that all share similar design elements (usually from the same vendor/product line), you can offer expanded options for users.

Be mindful of the continual use of these areas, too. Specifying materials and finishes that will weather high levels of use and abuse enhances durability.

It is also wise to provide a number of areas that can accommodate a wide variety of activities. When there are options and choices for using a space, users feel a greater sense of control over what they want to do and when and where they do it. Time seems to pass faster when there are activities to help pass the time. For instance, while waiting in a healthcare facility, some people enjoy watching television and like to be more active and noisy. Some like time to be quiet and read, **Figure 14-6**. Others enjoy a cup of coffee, watch people, or talk with people who are also waiting. Others, still, spend time checking their e-mail or play games. When designing a space, try to carve out specific areas to accommodate various activities.

How does a stunning outdoor view lift your spirits and change the way you feel? How do windows help decrease feelings of isolation? To truly support a healing environment, consider providing a connection to nature. For instance, an interior or exterior water feature may have a calming effect and can help people relax.

Photos courtesy of Boulder Associates Architects

Figure 14-6 The materials and finishes on walls, ceilings, and floors contribute to a comfortable and appealing waiting area. *Why is it important to consider the well-being and needs of those who spend time in healthcare waiting areas?*

The walls, ceilings, and floors can impact peoples' comfort level in a space, too. For instance, using materials and finishes that effectively control sound, add acoustical value. Including a fun wallcovering on an accent wall creates interest in a space. Consider painting an accent color in the ceiling bulkheads. In addition, with today's abundant flooring choices—including modular carpet, vinyl wood planks, and luxury vinyl tile—your choices are limitless. In the design plans, locate toilet rooms, refreshments, and drinking fountains near the waiting areas. Although very basic, these amenities are extremely essential for those who spend hours waiting in a space.

Because people like to have things to look at while they wait, including interesting displays adds to a positive experience. Incorporate into the plan a display for printed brochures and informational materials. Such information can spark a conversation between strangers and lead to ways to support each other in their healthcare journeys. Making connections with others can be a wonderful benefit of waiting.

Consider lighting in the design plan, too. Whether direct or indirect, lighting can significantly influence and improve the space. Remember that although people consume products, they experience environments. Choose daylighting and electric light that add to comfort of the space, avoiding the some types of overhead lighting that tend to be harsh. Careful planning and improving the environment that patients and visitors spend time in, helps ensure that they leave a healthcare facility with a favorable reaction and a generally positive experience.

Nurse Areas

It is widely recognized that nurses have some of the highest rates of work-related injuries in the United States. While the physical toll can be high, there is also an emotional toll. Recent studies of various healthcare professions show that emotional exhaustion and job burnout are common problems affiliated with increasing patient caseloads and close interaction with patients. The repercussions of this can be serious and far reaching. Perhaps the main concern regarding staff rest in healthcare is the impact on patient safety and errors that may occur due to stress and exhaustion. A staff retreat area should be separate from such support areas as staff lounges or staff conference rooms. The purpose of a staff retreat area is to provide respite for caregivers to relax and recharge from the stressful healthcare environment, **Figure 14-7**.

Family and Visitor Areas

Family and visitor accommodations play an important part in patient healing and overall satisfaction. Introducing a family retreat into the design of the nursing unit can contribute to improving the patient experience.

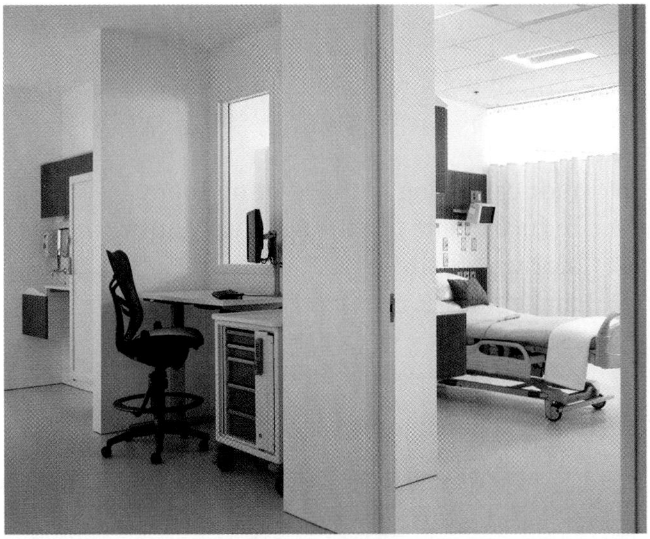

Courtesy of Herman Miller, Inc./Compass System, Caregiver Alcove Application/Designer Gianfranco Zaccai

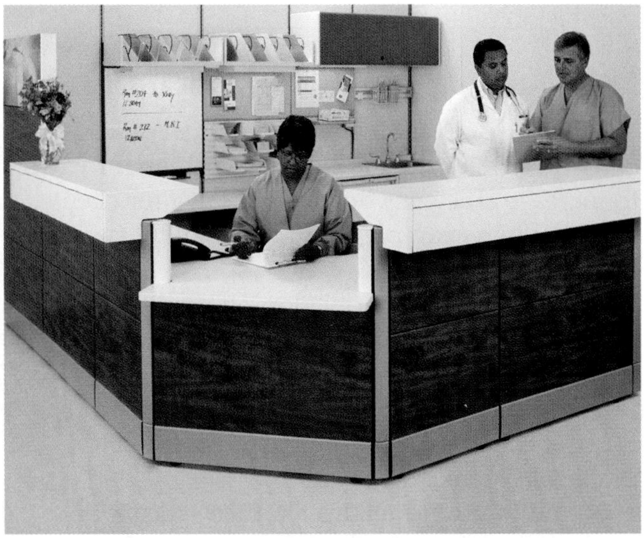

Courtesy of Herman Miller, Inc./Ethospace Nurses Station/Designer: Jack Kelly

Figure 14-7 Caregivers require quiet places away from lounges and conference rooms for concentrated work and respite along with spaces for collaboration.

Over the years, designer contributions to family and visitor satisfaction focus on improving the family zone environment in the patient room. Family zones may include overnight sleeping areas with privacy, Internet access, personal televisions, expanded seating options, and bathing facilities.

A second family retreat space is an improved visitor lounge that increases privacy by giving the family an area they can essentially “take over.” A retreat space with views to the outdoors and plenty of natural light helps link the interior and exterior environments of the facility. Other provisions, such as a kitchenette for beverages and food, a seating area with Internet access, a child’s play area, and background music all contribute to a soothing and satisfying family experience. Designing spaces specifically for families and visitors contributes to satisfying patients and making the healing environment as comfortable as possible.

The integration of family areas into the medical/surgical/intermediate care patient room is now a standard. This makes centralized family waiting rooms almost obsolete except on specialty units, such as oncology. Designers are creating smaller niches for families to find respite.

Most hospitals are also integrating family areas into critical-care rooms, although with some staff resistance. Family waiting rooms in critical-care areas are still a requirement for additional family members and children. Hospitals consistently include family sleeper sofas, many with blanket/pillow storage in the patient rooms. Also, additional folding chairs or ottomans are helpful to accommodate multiple visitors. Post-occupancy evaluations show less use for a desk surface—movable tables have far more utility for laptops and family dining.

Computer web access is increasing for patients and family. Hospitals are integrating both television and Internet access into flat screen monitors for patient and family use. This can include medical education programming, movies on demand, and music services. Because family members also bring their own electronic devices, including areas to charge these devices are also a concern.

Safety and Security

If an emergency arises, patients often have limits on their ability to leave the building on their own. Therefore, the facility design must include an area for the protection of occupants within the facility itself. In an emergency, staff members quickly move patients to an adjacent, smoke-resistant compartment until fire personnel arrive on the scene.

CASE STUDY

Money-Saving Trends in Healthcare Design

Because of the higher costs of real estate and construction, designers continually look for ways to increase efficiency and save money for clients. Here are two examples of money-saving trends in healthcare design.

Design teams are developing model patient rooms and model operating room *prior* to construction. This allows the teams to test the function and comfort level of the rooms for users before specifying the construction of multiples of same room type.

Another trend relates to office space for medical practitioners. In order to maintain profitability, it is increasingly important for medical office space to be efficient. Real estate costs, whether in the form of monthly rent or a mortgage payment, are one of the highest single expenses for medical practitioners. How can designers help make medical office space more efficient, thereby reducing the space requirements and real estate costs? Some possible solutions include

- reduce seating in the waiting room
- reduce onsite file storage by scanning or storing off-site
- make patient room sizes smaller and more efficient
- eliminate or reduce the break room size
- eliminate separate practitioner offices

Investigate and Reflect Use the Internet to research additional trends in the design of healthcare facilities. Use the key words "trends in healthcare facility design." Identify at least three additional trends, summarizing the purpose and approach to meeting the various design needs. Discuss your findings with the class.

Hospitality Establishment Design

The business of the hospitality industry is to transform the hectic lives of guests into a state of tranquility, relaxation, and enjoyment. This design sector includes the design of hotels, convention centers, spas, casinos, restaurants, cafés, and coffee shops. Hospitality occurs in any public facility that invites relaxation, offers entertainment, serves as a vacation destination, encourages recreation, and provides refreshment. It is an area of practice that incorporates a great many aspects of residential design into public spaces and is one of the most creative areas of commercial practice.

Today's fast-paced, global market demands much of travelers, as work/life balance often hinges on a satisfying experience. Whether traveling for business or pleasure, a consumer's perception of the experience can run the gamut from exciting and exhilarating to agonizing and downright exhausting. While it can be invigorating to experience different places and cultures, it also can be uniquely challenging for travelers, making the design of hospitality environments all the more important.

International business, global trends, technology and cross-cultural indicators all greatly influence the hospitality indurstry. Satisfying experiences and initiatives that build brand loyalty are the basis for positioning in this industry. These issues force designers to think beyond their own expectations, as spaces and facilities designs now need to focus on people from all cultural, social, and global backgrounds.

Working in this sector requires understanding of the impact of the global economy, shifts in consumer preferences, travel experiences, and how technology impacts nearly every aspect of the built environment. One such trend is the way in which consumers are taking direct control of their experiences through technology, and instant data sharing. Apps that offer ratings and customer feedback greatly affect industry bookings.

Thanks to shifts in business and consumer habits, the hospitality sector represents an exciting area of opportunity for designers. They can apply creativity not only to traditional hotel spaces like guestrooms and lobbies, but also to spas, restaurants, and entertainment areas—each unique to its location, customer base, and genre.

Hotels, Convention Centers, and Spas

Hotels offer accommodations for sleeping, dining, and entertainment. Convention centers and spas often link to hotels. With increased international travel, hotels have become more than a location to rest, but also a destination to gather with family and friends.

Hotels

Hotels vary in size from personable bed-and-breakfast inns, and clever boutique hotels to large, all-inclusive destination resorts. A **boutique hotel** is a small, stylish and unique hotel often located in trendy city centers which often includes one-of-a-kind features and the incorporation of distinctive and significant artwork along with an array of accessories, **Figure 14-8**.

Many hotels have unique attractions nearby such as rustic national parks and ocean-side theme parks. The designer of these hotels strives to capture the rustic, romantic, or trendy atmosphere of the hotel location.

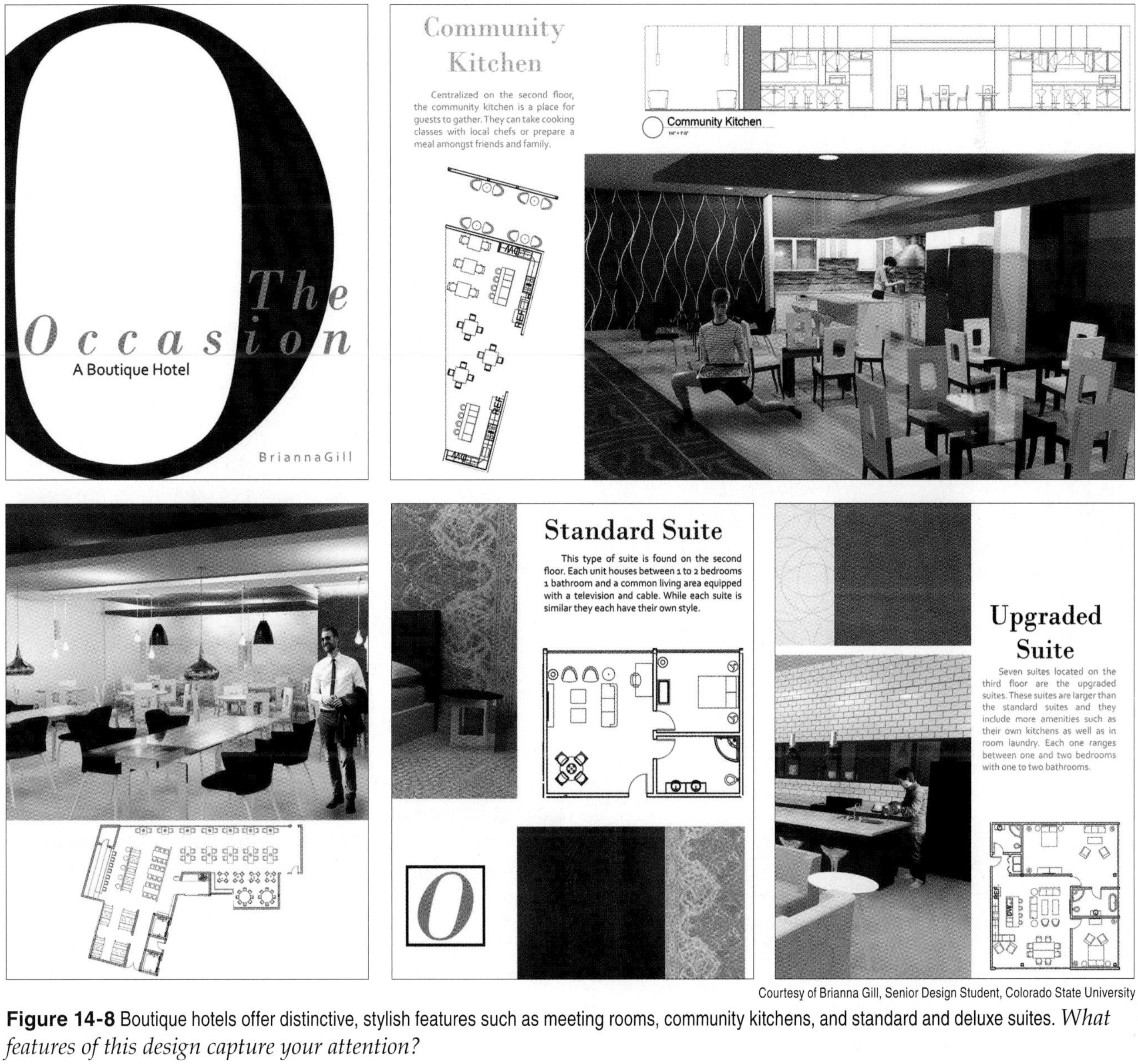

Courtesy of Brianna Gill, Senior Design Student, Colorado State University

Figure 14-8 Boutique hotels offer distinctive, stylish features such as meeting rooms, community kitchens, and standard and deluxe suites. *What features of this design capture your attention?*

For the hotel design to be successful, the designer must develop a good understanding of who the guests are. For instance, if your target market includes families on vacation, think about adding an ice cream shop or a play area in the lobby. If vacationing couples are the target, consider a romantic lounge within the space. The goal is to offer guests a delightful, welcoming area beyond their wildest imagination—and one they cannot envision missing on their trip.

Issues to consider in the design of a hotel include convenience, unique design, sustainable/eco-design, creativity, price point, amenities, and noise. Areas within a hotel include

- lobby/check-in/check-out area
- waiting/lounge
- luggage/concierge/bellhop areas
- coffee shops/cafés
- business center
- gift shop
- meeting rooms
- guest rooms with multiple prototypes
- banquet rooms
- fitness centers

The design of a hotel lobby is all about creating the first impression—similar to the impression you get from shaking the hand of someone you just met. A lobby can be aloof and intimidating or unbelievably marvelous and welcoming. The owner of the hotel cannot be standing by the front door to greet each guest, although the design of the initial experience can be exceptional and give the impression of such a greeting. Ideally, the lobby should feel like an oasis—a place of rest, relaxation, and revitalization. The best lobbies offer a haven for the tourist, the business traveler, and for the vacationing couple alike.

As a blend of the best of form and function—hotel lobbies foresee the needs of the guests and introduce the hotel style. Upon entering the hotel, guests will brand it as trendy, chic, cheap, or luxurious, **Figure 14-9**.

Allegria Spa at the Hyatt Beaver Creek/Photography by Don Riddle/Interiors by Associates III Interior Design

romakoma/Shutterstock.com

Photography: Kenneth M Wyner/Designed by ForrestPerkins

Figure 14-9 Hotel lobbies are functional yet serve as a social gathering place for hotel guests. Evaluate these hotel lobbies. *What features would cause you to brand the lobby as trendy, chic, cheap, or luxurious?*

Lobbies also serve as a place for social encounters. With new trends in business travel, hotel lobbies must offer multiuse spaces for casual and formal conversations, and spaces for working with and plugging in various electronic devices. Simple arrangements of sofas, chairs, and coffee tables are no longer enough. Ideas for lobby design include

- **Make a unique impression.** The lobby should be more than a passageway from the outdoors to the guest rooms. Create an environment that entices guests to stop and look around. For instance, offering a view of inspirational art along with well-designed and mood-appropriate lighting creates an environment that invites guests to linger, contemplate, and unwind.
- **Connect the experience with function.** A lobby accommodates the check-in desk, waiting area, and concierge stand, and it also serves as a social gathering place with supplementary seating and tables.
- **Incorporate revenue streams.** Design a lobby that offers guests a variety of shops and services. Convenient amenities right in the lobby eliminates the need for guests to shop elsewhere and provide other opportunities to increase revenue, too. For instance, even a boutique hotel can serve coffee, stock a snack bar, and sell gifts, toiletries, or sundries. Guests appreciate the convenience of such offerings.
- **Analyze the layout and architecture.** Closely analyze the structure of the hotel lobby. A large structure may appear uninviting, while a small, tight space dissuades lingering and relaxing. Because lobbies are generally wide-open areas, creatively utilize these spaces to shape zones that smoothly flow together, creating a cohesive guest experience.

  When designing a space, match the hotel era with the lobby—playing with the style while introducing furniture and accessories. Keep in mind a luxurious hotel requires a lavish lobby. In contrast, the lobby of a family resort might feature child-size tables, chairs, and activities along with comfortable seating for adults. Whether lavish or family friendly, the lobby must have adequate circulation to accommodate guests and their luggage during check-in and check-out periods.

Guest rooms occupy about 50 to 80 percent of a hotel's guest area. The design of guest rooms is changing, too. The traditional bed-table-chair-television combination is not enough to make a hotel room inviting or appealing. A trendy hotel room may include a creative office space for business travelers and an extra sofa next to a king-sized bed, **Figure 14-10**.

Where appropriate, there is also a blurring between the indoor-outdoor boundaries. For instance, large decks and terraces help expand hotel rooms to the outdoors while the designer seeks every possible way to bring nature inside. To help hotel guests relax and relieve tension, designers employ such elements as wood paneling, stone decorations, lush plants and flowers, and indoor water features. Most importantly, however, hotel rooms should offer comfort and that "home-away-from-home" feeling for every hotel guest. Regardless of how luxurious, tech-friendly, or unusual the room theme, comfort and warmth are major factors to consider in room design.

Guest bathrooms are taking on a spa-like design. Bathrooms are no longer spaces to minimize to expand living space in the guest room. Modern tourists expect more than they have at home when traveling. A resort bathroom encompassing spa-like features is an open invitation to refreshment and relaxation—surefire way to encourage people to stay at that specific hotel. Spa-like features may include en suite bedrooms, waterfall showers, oversized bathtubs, two sinks, giant towels, and plenty of space.

Photograph: Kenneth M Wyner/Designed by ForrestPerkins

Figure 14-10 Guest rooms, like hotel lobbies, are changing to accommodate guest expectations. *Review the description about the Presidential Suite at the Renaissance Arlington Capitol View Hotel on the ForrestPerkins website. What features enhance the guest experience?*

The hotel restaurant is also becoming a destination of its own. Cooking is an art and so should be the *exhibition space*. Increasingly, hotel restaurants are becoming memorable spaces through design. Experiential, sense of place, local, and comfortable—from fine dining to casual dining—these continue to be the key words for design success. Some restaurants are even outside the building. Beachside food trucks ensure convenience and an additional revenue stream. Using themes is highly recommended in restaurant design to reach new peaks of creativity. Overall, the new generation of diners wants an experience when dining out. These diners want a place where casual comfort reigns, and where fine dining encompasses more than just white tablecloths and servers in tuxedos, **Figure 14-11**.

The design of hotel meeting rooms is changing, too, blurring the line between the *office* and personal *social time*. Multiple hotel chains are transforming sterile meeting rooms into more comfortable lounges to encourage conversation, mingling, and the flow of ideas. The design of such areas includes conversational seating areas and a food service area. In addition, the designer may include shelves of books and decorative objects of interest. The total effect is more residential and relaxed.

Convention Centers

Convention centers are often attached to hotels in major metropolitan or resort areas. Due to the size and scope of many conventions and the resulting revenue generation, communities desire to attract as many visitors as possible. Flexibility and comfort is essential to convention center design. These centers must be flexible enough to accommodate various group sizes, whether larger crowds or smaller gathering. They also must accommodate various size meetings. Therefore, meeting rooms often use retractable walls, allowing ease of reconfiguration between conference events.

In the recent past, conferences were a means for communicating important information difficult to acquire in other ways. Because attendees can get most of a meeting's content via website, simulcast, or online videos, the on-site face-to-face networking can become the most important element of the meeting. To encourage conversations, the design offers small alcoves in larger spaces to provide areas for small groups of conference attendees to have private conversations. The design of mini-meeting spots and pod-seating areas fosters collaboration and a deeper connection in the community. The aim of convention center design is to offer a warm, stylish, and welcoming social experience for guests along with efficient space to learn and collaborate.

The main lobby of a convention center establishes branding of the place and offers signage for wayfinding, **Figure 14-12**. Permanent facilities in the convention center may include food courts, cafés, restrooms, and registration locations. Guests, staff, and maintenance workers require separate circulation paths. As with other commercial facility designs, the designer is responsible for specifying furniture, carpeting, draperies, tables, and chairs.

Convention centers offer many activities on-site or access to the activities and attractions in the community. On-site activities may include access to

Photographs: Kenneth M Wyner/Designed by ForrestPerkins

Figure 14-11 The unique design of hotel restaurants makes these spaces memorable in the minds of guests.

Photograph: Kenneth M Wyner/Designed by ForrestPerkins

Figure 14-12 The design of this LEED Gold certified hotel and conference center connects the spaces in intriguing ways, reflecting the evidence of motion. *What design features of this conference center encourage visitors to explore?*

©Stirling Elemendorf Photography/Designed by ForrestPerkins

Figure 14-13 Lavish spa facilities complement the therapeutic services offered by many luxury hotels and resorts.

recreational equipment, indoor water parks, and ice-skating rinks. Therefore, much thought goes into the design of these specialty spaces. In addition, all convention centers must all offer, as one of their amenities, technology equipment to support the meetings or evening events. These technologies include special lighting, sound equipment, video-capture capabilities, and large screens. With the popularity of teleconferencing, new technologies must also offer conferencing with participants in other parts of the world.

Spas

In the recent past, wellness retreats and destination spas did not encompass luxurious furnishings, gourmet health foods, or free locker-room amenities. Their key focus was on health and lifestyle programs for participants. With the advent luxury hotels and resorts getting in the spa game, changes are occurring. In fact, some hotels are converting current guest rooms into additional spa facilities because of the generated revenue. When designing a spa space, designers must consider private treatment villas, and high-tech facilities to complement the therapeutic services. These needs require different storage units, unique furniture, areas of privacy, and flexible lighting to enhance the concept and mood of the experience, **Figure 14-13**.

Restaurants and Dining Areas

Successful restaurants offer good food, good service, and good ambience. The first thing people love about a favorite restaurant is its food. Likewise, the first thing a patron notices about a restaurant is the quality of its interior. If the interior ambience is not welcoming, the patron may not enter or ever return.

Restaurant design is not as comprehensive as the design of hotels. Restaurants are smaller and require fewer configurations and rearrangements. They do, however, require great designs—perhaps even more so than hotels. An important goal of restaurants is to attract new customers, whether business travelers or vacationing tourists.

As they choose hotels, people place more emphasis on referrals and the hotel's reputation. They examine the daily rates and service charges. Food becomes a secondary priority. In contrast, when choosing restaurants, people often enter a restaurant on impulse without a clear-cut reason for their choice. Sometimes merely a glance inside encourages potential patrons to venture in. A unique interior design may be the key element that motivates a person to choose one restaurant instead of another.

The restaurant business is highly competitive, with over 50 percent going out of business the first year. Restaurants have demanding functions and require a creative design

Link to History

Emergence of the Restaurant

Eating has always been a sociable event. The restaurant as an institution, however, did not fully emerge until the seventeenth century. The word *restaurant* initially appeared in the sixteenth century, meaning a restorative broth. By 1771, the term evolved to reference an "establishment specializing in the sale of restorative foods," too.

It was the aspiring middle classes of post-revolutionary France that began using the term *restaurant* as it is used today. The first restaurant proprietor is believed to have been A. Boulanger, a soup vendor, who opened his business in Paris in 1765.

In the United States, by the 1930s some movement was seen toward simplifying restaurant design from something grandiose, to the paradigm of *dining out* in the 1960s. With a diversity of eating venues and socially mobile patrons hungry for new experiences, design became a powerful tool to distinguish between the new bistros, brasseries, cafés, diners, and casual dining chains that emerged then and still emerge today.

Analyze It!

Interview several older adults you know about the availability and design of restaurants in their youth. What aspects of restaurant design have evolved since this time? Predict how restaurant design may change in the future based on human need.

to remain competitive. The design concept must be very strong and reflect the food served. For example, a newer restaurant trend is a menu touting organically grown food that is harvested, prepped, and cooked on-site. The dining facility should reflect the essence of this trendy *farm-to-table* menu. It may include a healthy indoor/outdoor interior concept that would appeal to this diner profile. While the design concept should not mimic the food served, it must be easily identifiable and fit the location.

Perhaps the most common ambience mistake in a restaurant is poor acoustics. Conversations drowned out by loud noise can ruin even the most handsomely appointed restaurant. For example, a recent study in New York City indicated that city restaurants are too loud. The excessive noise in many places is actually more damaging to hearing than car horns and jackhammers.

Of a random sampling of nearly 40 restaurants, bars, stores, and gyms in NYC, nearly one- third exceeded healthy noise levels. Bars and restaurants were the worst offenders, some registering noise levels of up to 105 *decibels*, levels that cause headaches and hearing loss. (*Note:* A **decibel** is unit for expressing the relative intensity of sounds on a scale from zero for the least-perceptible sound to about 130.). For comparison, a subway train pulling into a station typically registers at 84 decibels, while the sound of normal conversation is 60 decibels. Designing for auditory comfort should be a priority.

For a restaurant, interior designers usually work on the *front of the house*, or dining area, including signage and menu graphics. The *back of the house,* or kitchen, is a critical functional area and typically designed by independent specialists, **Figure 14-14**.

Here are some areas of the restaurant facility on which designers typically work, with more details about dining room design.

- hostess station
- reception/waiting area
- payment/checkout area
- patron seating—include multiple types such as banquette, bench, and table and chair configurations
- outdoor seating
- private rooms
- bar area
- take-out/delivery station
- optional buffet
- public restrooms
- back of the house areas—kitchen/food prep, delivery/receiving dock, storage, office, and liquor storage

The dining area refers to spaces ranging from an informal café to an elegant five-star restaurant. Fire code regulations guide the safe[illegible] patrons.

The dining area should accommodate as many guests as possible without compromising the patron's comfort or safety. Leave enough space for servers to circulate around the table and guests. Make sure the table height is not so high that the diners cannot see the food.

zhu difeng/Shutterstock.com Pavel L Photo and Video/Shutterstock.com Alexander Chaikin/Shutterstock.com

Figure 14-14 Patron seating and eating areas—both indoor and outdoor—are part of restaurant facility design. *How do these facilities comfortably accommodate guests without compromising safety? How do the circulation patterns benefit patrons and staff?*

Link to History

The Evolution of Retail Shopping

Prior to the late eighteenth century, store owners took little care in the appearance of their stores or the presentation of merchandise. Actually, very little merchandise was displayed within the store. Rather, a customer would enter the store and speak with the retailer, who would then present merchandise that was kept in a back room. *Sales talk* and an ability to persuade were very important in convincing a customer of the quality of a product and making a sale. The evolution in store design brought about a new process of shopping. It was no longer a verbal engagement between retailers and customers, but now a *sensory experience*. The first step in the evolution of store design occurred when small stores began to display their merchandise openly to the public, instead of keeping it in back storerooms. Eventually, the deliberate display of goods became an important tool for retailers. The once unattractive stores that were not meant to visually appeal to consumers slowly became exciting shopping venues.

Today, shopping can be done completely online or from a telephone to save time and money. Whether it is in a brick-and-mortar store, pop-up, or online, it is important that retail establishments offer a hassle-free and enjoyable experience for the consumer.

Analyze It!

Analyze the shopping habits of your class with a quick survey. Do your classmates shop more 1) online, 2) in a mall, or 3) at independent stores? Tally the results of your survey. Have you or your peers ever shopped at a pop-up store? Draw conclusions about why one shopping experience is more attractive today than another. How do these conclusions influence the design of retail interiors today?

Configuring the tables, chairs, and banquettes in the dining area is a strategic exercise. The designer's goal is for guests to be comfortable and focus on the dining experience. **Circulation patterns**—the routes people follow as they move from one place to another within a space—for the diners, waitstaff, and busing staff must be thoughtfully integrated into the design solution. Diners prefer privacy and often look for corners, booths, and tables against the wall, preferably near a window.

Lighting is an important aspect of establishing restaurant mood. Most designs demand individual lights at each booth or dining area to create a sense of intimacy and privacy. Natural light is also important. Set light into scenes that can change as day turns to evening.

Retail Space Design

The shopping experience has changed. The growth in online shopping reflects how fast people are filling their virtual shopping carts. According to a recent forecast from Forrester Research, online retailers expect sales to jump in the United States from $262 billion in 2013 to an estimated $370 billion in 2017. While some perceive these numbers as a threat to the brick-and-mortar retail model, many leading retailers suggest this is an opportunity to collapse the walls that stand between the digital and physical sides of their businesses. Shrewd placement of technology within a store or a new experience online can encourage sales and develop a unique experience for the shopper.

Pop-up retail stores began to show their "faces" around 2000 and continue to develop in urban areas of the country. A pop-up retail store is typically a temporary structure that pops up unannounced, quickly draws in crowds to purchase items in a spontaneous manner, and creates a fun environment that engages passersby. This interactivity gives retail a relevant, fresh feel, **Figure 14-15**.

Shopping is a national pastime in some countries. Even toddlers indicate preference for certain products and a desire to take them home. With that knowledge,

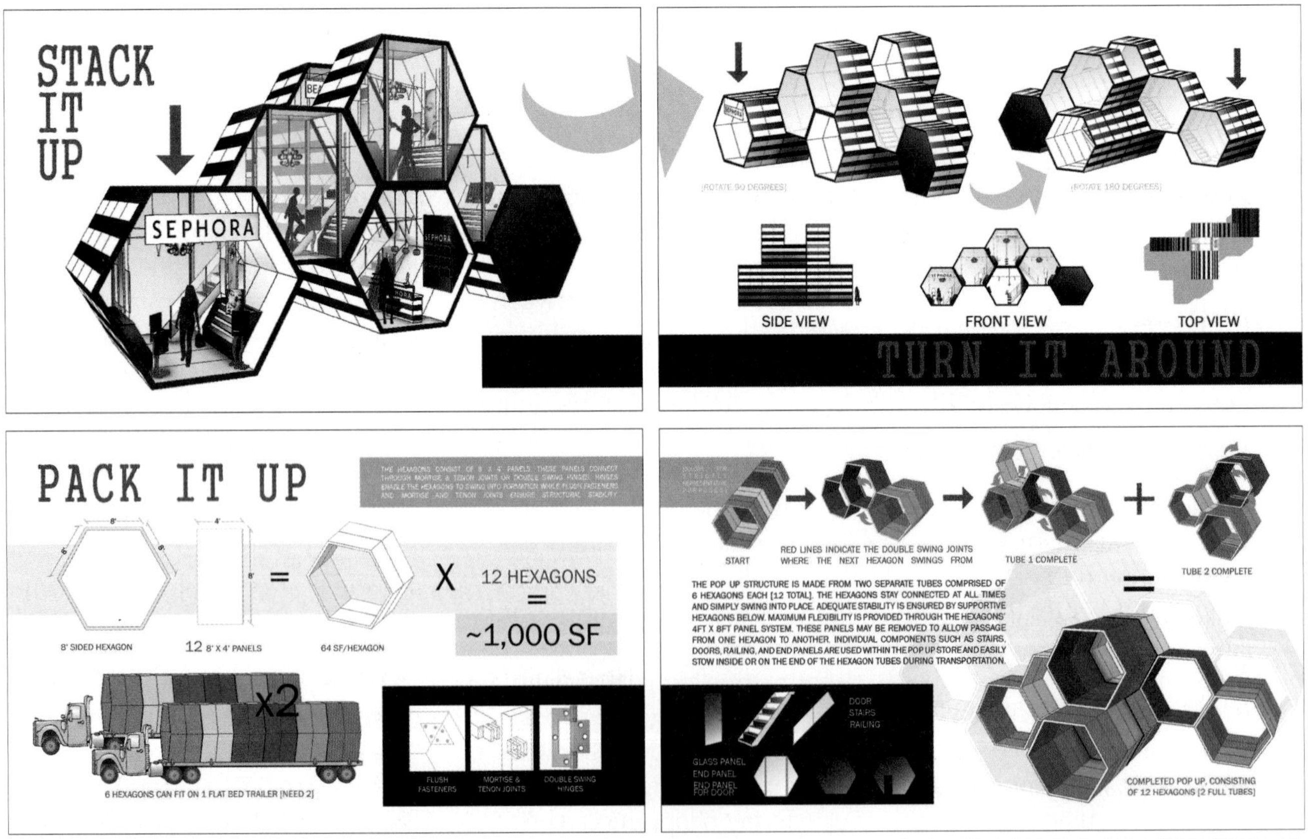

Courtesy of Carrie Zwisler/Design Student, Colorado State University

Figure 14-15 Pop-up retail stores are typically temporary structures that are moved from one location to another. *Examine the design of this pop-up retail store. What features about the design make it easy to move? What features capture customers?*

the primary design goal for retail space is to enhance retail sales. To achieve this goal, the designer's role is to plan the store layout based on consumer-driven research, know the consumer profile, include appropriate display and storage space, and make the products *pop*! The store manager will know the merchandise and the designer will know how to present the product in a creative way.

When developing the retail shopping experience, designers consider the

- store size
- continual movement of the product from delivery and storage to purchase
- congestion shoppers create at peak times
- lighting that creates a hierarchy of what is most important to look at first
- circulation patterns that move consumers through the store
- attraction of window displays
- signage and store branding

The design should become a planned series of sensations designed to entice consumers and make them want to be part of the brand narrative and experience. The most successful retail designs get consumers to simultaneously experience the product by experiencing the space. For example, Apple products are well-designed and minimal in design aesthetics. Apple's store design reflects the brand—elegant simplicity with a glass-curtain wall or floating glass stairs.

When space planning the store, areas the designer needs to consider include

- entrance and orientation to location
- traffic and circulation patterns
- merchandise fixtures and planning
- point-of-purchase
- customer service area
- changing rooms
- delivery and receiving areas
- storage and *back-of-the-house*
- restrooms—private and public
- lighting, color, furniture, and accessories
- store security and loss prevention

Store Layout

There is much research about retail consumer behavior that is helpful when designing a retail facility. For example, some key items designers should know include

- It takes a passerby about eight seconds to walk past a typical storefront. Once past the door, the potential customer will not turn around. The design must grab consumer attention within four seconds of approaching the store.
- Almost immediately upon entering a store, 75 percent of people know whether or not they will make a purchase. To grab consumer attention, stores use simple window displays and conveniently located entry tables to clearly and quickly express the latest hot commodity. Most train their staff members to welcome customers immediately as they enter the facility.
- An open retail door creates about 35 percent more business than one that is closed. Doors that meet the sidewalk are more inviting than doors that are recessed. What might a designer do to make recessed doors more inviting to capture customer interest?
- People like to walk in a loop. Over 90 percent turn right as they enter the store and loop through the store exiting on the left.
- Most shopping is completed in evenings and on weekends. About 75 percent of Americans do their shopping after 5:30 p.m. on weekdays and on Sunday.
- The typical American shopper is not fond of shopping. Usually a single mom, this shopper is often pressed for time. Getting in and out of a store quickly, with good savings on the items she purchases, is the main goal of this consumer.

Retail is a highly competitive arena. Each store requires a different layout. For example, a furniture store and a hardware store display their merchandise very differently, **Figure 14-16**.

Revealing products to shoppers in an efficient way is the goal of all store layouts, as is an effective way to control the traffic through the facility. The shape, size, and volume of business influence the variety of store layouts. For instance, supermarkets typically use a **grid layout** system which steers shoppers in a zigzag pattern through parallel rows of aisles. In contrast, a **loop layout** uses a circular pathway around a central

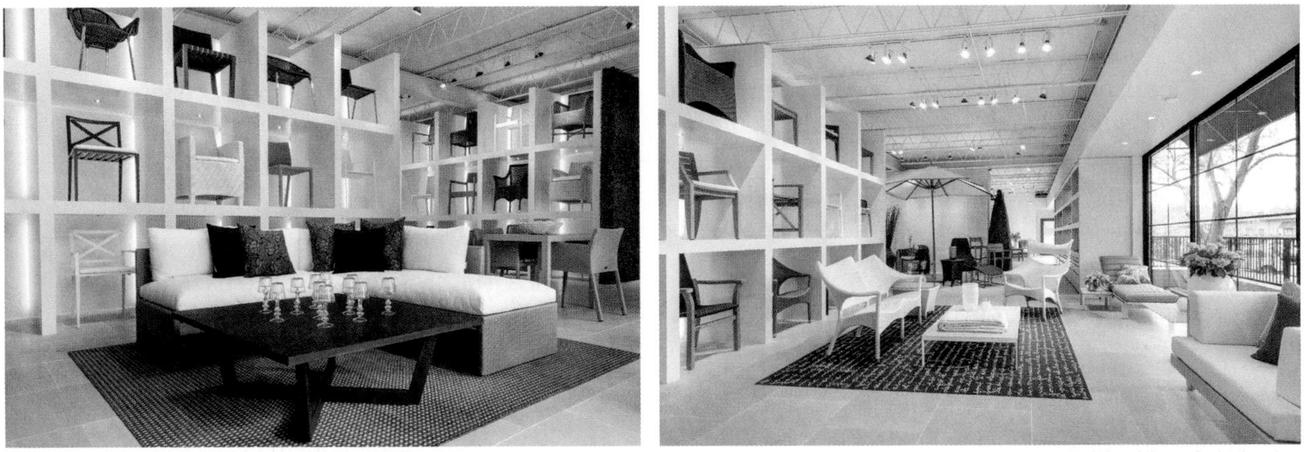

Photographs: VENVISIO, LLC/Rabaut Design Associates

Figure 14-16 Due to the nature of retail, each facility requires a unique design. What features of this furniture retail facility draw customers in to browse?

display. A **free-flowing layout** does not have set aisles. This layout allows shoppers to move about freely, increasing the probability of impulse buying. Designers need to work with store managers to create a captivating journey for customers to travel throughout their facilities.

Brand or image is a key element to a store's success which should be incorporated in the customer's profile. Remember that first impressions count. Because there is only one chance to excite the customer and create enthusiasm, it is essential to convey the store's message clearly through use of appropriate visual props, graphics, and merchandise displays. Therefore, the entrance makes the key first impression! The storefront design must capture customer attention, be appealing, and clearly show customers what they can find inside. Within 15 feet of the store entry, there is a **decompression zone** at which shoppers do not notice products. A cohesive design ensures that walls, colors, flooring, lighting, and signage tell a single, captivating story.

Designers must consider traffic flow and circulation patterns. As people enter a store, they typically turn right and browse through the store in a counter-clockwise direction, exiting the store after checkout. By setting up focal points, the designer has the power to stop and redirect customers to where the business owner wants them to go. Visual displays are useful for redirection, but must feel natural and make sense with no direction changes for customers. Depending on the store size, aisles should be a minimum of 2.5 feet to 4 feet wide. The design of main aisles and areas of two-way traffic must be wider, allowing two people to pass comfortably.

Appreciate the influence of a *power wall*—the area to the right where customers look first on entering a store. Retailers use power walls to display featured and seasonal items.

Fixtures are the movable units that hold store products. The strategic placement of fixtures makes store products visually enticing—encouraging customers to make impulse purchases. The designer can use fixtures to create stopping points in the midst of long aisles, giving customers a visual break. Most store managers are keenly aware that the arrangement of product displays, counters, and aisles impacts shopper behavior. In any of these areas, crowding will likely lead to lost sales and lost revenue.

Strategically design display locations and sizes. Customers continually critique window designs and displays—consciously or unconsciously. Color and light can add drama and interest. Unique and out-of-character display techniques need flexible space. For example, something that is larger-than-life, smaller-than-life, dramatically repetitive, or humorous and fun can attract customer attention. Therefore, space needs to be changeable. When thinking through the overall look of a store, be mindful that customers connect fewer displays and fewer items on display with higher prices.

Checkout counters must easily accommodate merchandise and have ample space for the staff to comfortably complete transactions. Including a display wall behind the checkout counter is an ideal spot to display unique products and additional gift item. An enticing layout should encourage shoppers to make additional impulse purchases as they finish their shopping journey.

Tell a story with the design plan of the store. Is there a logical progression from one product to the next? Are there options to have accessories next to big-ticket items for add-on sales? For instance, bicycle stores typically have bikes in one area, and display road bikes and mountain bikes separately. Next to the bike displays, store staff places shoes and pedals that go with each type of bike.

Creating the right interior store plan does not follow hard and fast rules. The bottom line is that shoppers often want to make their selections and purchases with ease. It is up to the designer to set the stage for an enjoyable experience, **Figure 14-17**.

Malls

Shopping malls are the most successful sites of sales, although online sales are quickly gaining a larger market share of the profits. Malls house both specialty shops and chain stores. Mall design includes considerations such as layout, directional signage (wayfinding), security, and variety. Some malls have an open-air design while others are enclosed spaces. The design of public areas in shopping malls should entice the visitor to stay longer and purchase more.

Goncharuk Maksim/Shutterstock.com

Figure 14-17 Creating an enjoyable shopping experience is an essential goal for the interior designer.

In terms of sales, the highest-performing malls and shopping districts have clear lines of sight from one storefront to another. Shoppers enjoy seeing the fronts of other stores from multiple locations. They are more likely to browse through high volume of stores when the windows are within sight from multiple places.

Malls accommodate basic services such as restrooms, first aid, seating, meeting points (such as fountain areas), food courts, and offices for mall staff. The space between the mall and the parking lot offers opportunities for parks, play areas, and entertainment venues. Be sure to plan for mall security features, such as appropriate lighting at the end of day.

Boutique Shops

Specialty retail or boutique stores often hire designers to develop a unique design with emphasis on window displays, attention-getting interior finishes, and dramatic lighting. Boutiques have very specific clientele who are looking for individual attention, customer service, and items not found in the big-box stores. They are often located near other shopping areas, but are totally separate. Boutique shops target customers who seek their inventory of specialty items, price range, and shopping experience.

Products carried by boutique stores are often *one-of-a-kind* items. They might sell original art, internationally acquired furniture, or handcrafted items. Therefore, the displays need to be adaptable to new products the store buyer locates.

The success of boutique shops is based as much on customer relations as the products. The designer must create space for comfortable furnishings, gift wrapping areas, beverage and snack services, and even guest artists or speakers.

Educational Facility Design

The planning and design of educational facilities—whether elementary, secondary or college levels—should begin with the learner. Learning is changing in the twenty-first century and so are the learning spaces, **Figure 14-18**. Technologies used for learning are altering the experiences and expectations of today's student. Current technologies include

- interactive whiteboards
- Internet service and high-quality digital learning resources
- wireless networks and mobile devices, including the ability to access many of these from home
- electrical systems, seating requirements, and acoustics that support those who bring their own devices
- flexible classroom space that easily accommodates different groupings

To address student needs, the physical design of educational facilities is also changing. Due to the investment of learning technologies and the need for more cost-effective space utilization, it is ever more important for decision-makers to keep up-to-date on new thinking about the design of technology-rich learning environments.

For the designer, understanding the features that make learning experiences effective is important. The best interiors inspire students to learn, producing confident, adaptable, and capable independent learners. The design of physical learning spaces must embody the institution's vision and strategy for learning and should be responsive, inclusive, and supportive of achievement by all.

An educational facility is a costly, long-term investment and resource. Because many projects utilize funds from taxpayers, budgets are generally tight and include a large number of people in the decision-making process. Materials must be durable, vandal-proof, easy to maintain, and cost-effective. The design of individual educational spaces should

- be flexible and suitable for current and evolving learning strategies
- be creative to energize and inspire learners and tutors
- support development of potential in all learners
- motivate and promote the activity of learning
- support collaborative work between students
- include technology that is effective, updateable, and invisible to students and teachers

Entrances

Entering any school or college facility should generate a sense of excitement about and passion for learning. As the first point of connection between the learning institution and its clients/students, the entrance sets the

A GameDesk Playmaker School, Santa Monica, CA/Gensler Project Team: Charrisse Johnston, David Herjeczki, Shawn Gehle, Ursula Marques/Photography: Ryan Gobuty, Gensler

B Loyola Marymount University, School of Film & Television Animation Department, Los Angeles, CA/Gensler Project Team: Charrisse Johnston, Nathan Kim, Peter Barsuk, Shawn Gehle/Photography: Ryan Gobuty, Gensler

Figure 14-18 Supported by the Bill and Melinda Gates Foundation and AT&T, the design of the GameDesk Playmaker School is to engage students in learning through a playful problem-solving process (A). The classroom design and small class sizes in the animation department at Loyola Marymount University encourage a high degree of student-faculty interaction (B).

cultural tone for visitors. An entrance area should establish a welcoming, secure environment, and must impart the capability of the institution to meet the educational needs of its learners. Designers should incorporate daylight, comfortable furniture, wireless technology, and security systems into the entrance.

Services

Visiting staff or faculty offices and areas of service—such as counseling, careers, and academic or financial advice—should generate a calming effect on those visiting with a need or passing through after an informal discussion. Wireless connectivity and varied arrangements of gathering areas with comfortable, maintenance-free furniture should be available.

Classrooms

At the collegiate level, classrooms are moving from large lecture halls to *flipped classroom* spaces that mimic elementary and secondary collaborative learning environments. The creation of fluid and flexibly designed environments include movable walls, tables, chairs, lighting, and technology. Effective interior design supports multiple forms of learning with areas designed to promote collaboration, individual study, small group discussions, and large group dialogues. Quieter spaces within the classroom space are available for individual reflective study. Larger spaces may include a nearby café for collaborative projects and social learning.

Furniture, fixtures, and equipment (FF&E) are designed lightweight and with casters. Rather than using fastened-down furniture—as in older schools—designers are specifying mobile furniture, including storage elements, for the interiors. Additions to the space also include student and teacher presentation reading stands, easel-marker boards, flexible screens, and partial-height walls that help absorb sound, along with display and presentation surfaces. Students and teachers alike can access and rearrange the FF&E daily—allowing more control over the learning environment. Interior designers also develop classroom configurations that encourage cross-discipline interaction.

Acoustical challenges are a key issue because noise levels interfere with student hearing and therefore, learning. Designers can address this issue with special sound systems installed in the classroom settings. Other suggestions for classroom design include

- daylighting appropriate to learning spaces
- viewing windows (with minimum 50 feet views) to outdoor areas or activities
- viewing windows in scale with student ages and sizes
- operable windows to control ventilation and fresh air intake
- quality electrical lighting that is adjustable
- room darkening ability
- adequate storage
- access to food and beverages throughout the day
- comfortable seating and spaces for reflection
- maintenance requirements to support the design

Gaining in popularity are outdoor learning environments with adjustable sun-filtering coverings, rain protection, exterior storage, and an electrical power source. Results of a recent research study show increasing improvement in student morale (from 17 to 80 percent) when students move from individual classrooms to the new arrangements. Teacher effectiveness jumped dramatically, too, as did their connections with peers from about 20 percent to more than 85 percent. The bottom line of such research shows that such renovations deeply impact learning with measurable outcomes.

Residence Halls and Academic Villages

The old *dorms* are gone; residence halls are in! When combined with other facilities, residence halls are known as *academic villages* or *living and learning villages*. **Academic villages** are clusters of buildings that consist of classrooms, dining facilities, and retail areas just minutes from student residence halls. These facilities also include faculty offices, tutoring centers, and spaces for workshops and small study groups, **Figure 14-19**.

The design and planning of academic villages are based on the concept that learning happens 24 hours per day, seven days per week. The concept also dictates that the total learning environment should be an all-in-one inclusive experience. Students who live on campus, especially the first two years, are more likely to

- feel a part of the university community
- persist with their studies
- graduate

Figure 14-19 Mixed-use residential villages provide a unique mix of student housing and academic and student amenity spaces designed for an all-inclusive learning experience. Such facilities are designed to attract the best and brightest students to colleges and universities.

The residence hall itself generally includes four-bed and two-bed suites, with shared study areas and a bathroom for each suite. The buildings are multistory with lounge spaces, a kitchen, and access to an exterior courtyard for each community. Dining halls are available in each building as well as cafés or food emporiums.

According to the *Wall Street Journal*, resident hall rooms average roughly 180 square feet in size with no expectations to grow any larger. This small space is the greatest challenge for designers. In addition, each living space must allow for individuality, offering incentive to students who might be comfortable living at home.

Because residence hall rooms are short on space, it is imperative that the design be multifunctional. There should be space for student studying, sleeping, entertaining, and even cooking. While the design task is weighty, a focus on lighting, zoning, acoustics, and maximizing storage solutions can make these multifunctional spaces a reality. With high-stress and pressure-packed lifestyles, especially during exam periods, it is important that the design of their personal spaces improve student quality of life. Residence hall spaces must help reduce stress and allow for personal growth by enabling creative freedom over the space. Also important is the ability of students to meet others through normal daily routines, and ability to feel safe, secure, and in control at all times.

Libraries

Barnes and Noble Bookstores were inspirational regarding changes to public, university, and school libraries. Their cafés and soft, informal seating areas promote conversation among customers and engage inquisitive minds to sit, read, and learn. Formal quiet areas that once demanded students to be quiet, libraries are transforming into places of inquiry and teamwork.

Differing qualities of light, acoustically hard/soft spaces, orientation to vistas, and openings to landscaped areas help distinguish one library space from another. Cafés and small, social-group learning areas are planned into the design of these spaces. Due to online resources, libraries had to reinvent themselves to ensure their existence on learning campuses of today.

Pop-Up Schools

School buildings are popping up in places around the world. Questions educators are raising include: Should we be constructing huge buildings called schools? Will the Internet and lack of public money combined lead to other kinds of learning places? (Note: The Internet has enabled everyone to learn anytime, anywhere.) Will schools become more like events than buildings? Why would students choose to come into school if they can learn on their own, at home, online, and at any time? Are schools always the best places to learn something?

In response to these issues and other questions, pop-up schools are springing up overnight in different pockets of the world such as Kenya and India. The design of these facilities is a new opportunity for designers interested in social responsibility and social justice.

Impact of Culture and Learning Needs

Educational institutions are changing their physical environments to reflect the culture and learning needs of their students. Additionally, educational facilities are including such areas as bookstores, supply centers, cafeterias, grading centers, fitness areas, study areas, and residence halls, **Figure 14-20**.

Courtesy of 4240 Architecture Inc./Photographs: Copyright Raul Garcia

Figure 14-20 The physical environments of educational institutions are changing to meet the cultural, learning, and social needs of students. *How does the design of these facilities support collaboration in learning?*

Using design principles that make buildings function better, last longer, cost less to renovate and maintain, and inspire and adapt to changing needs ensures the existence of collaborative, interdisciplinary educational centers of excellence. Part of the design excellence of these facilities includes sustainable design practices.

Corporate Office Design

As the world of work continues to change, so does the workplace. While a workplace can range from a factory floor to a penthouse radio station, one of the most common workplaces is the corporate office. How do you design a great office workplace environment?

The work processes of today are different from work processes during the industrial revolution. Historically, the white-collar office reflected the mind-set of a factory with work developed into a linear series of individual tasks. Today's products (knowledge and creativity) demand different environments in which they can be nurtured, shared, and produced. Today's work requires collaborative and nonlinear designs, as fewer workers create physical "things" and more workers analyze, create, collaborate, and act on information.

Corporate office design is the number one specialty area for interior designer practitioners in the United States. Today, the *office* can be located anywhere and accessed anytime. Employees are no longer tethered to a desk or workstation. With wireless technology, an office may consist simply of Internet access, a digital tablet, and an employee. Brick-and-mortar structures with walls and file cabinets may no longer be a need.

The rise of the mobile workforce is allowing companies to get work done faster and more efficiently (there are about 119.7 million mobile workers in the U.S. according to a study done by Cisco). For most companies, a corporate office serves as a recruitment tool, a place to be with friends, an inspirational place, and a place that launches the next billion-dollar company. To build a lasting company, the office is a key element.

Principles used when designing offices and workplaces include conversations about: "What are our work patterns?" "How do we work differently?" "How do we design spaces to enhance teamwork and collaboration?" "What are the basic psychological and human needs that need to be met and enhanced?"

Tenant improvement work (TI) is a related specialty area within the office design sector. Businesses, such as a set of law offices, often lease building space in which to conduct their work rather than owning the building. As different tenants, or businesses, move into the space, they sign a lease and the relocation of interior walls or partitions occurs to reflect the new tenant's brand and business. In addition to a new space plan, TI addresses all existing and new furniture, fixture, and equipment (FF&E) needs, **Figure 14-21**.

Office Design Issues

There are many opportunities to consider in the remodel, reconfiguration, or new construction of a corporate office. They revolve around two primary factors: employee satisfaction and the bottom line of any business—revenue generation. Employee salaries account for 80 to 85 percent of the cost to do business. Keeping employees happy is critical to the success of a business or corporation.

Enhancing Corporate Culture

Today, the corporate culture of an office is a means of attracting the most talented employees and enhancing employee satisfaction. **Corporate culture** is the collective beliefs, value systems, traditions, and customs that make a company unique. For example, *Fortune* magazine ranks *Google* as the best place to work in the country. It attracts people with some of the most brilliant minds and earns close to one million dollars in revenue for every person it employs.

Really strong companies all have very strong cultures that they communicate through the physical environment of

©Ron Pollard, Courtesy of RNL

Figure 14-21 Interior designers often work with clients who are using leased tenant spaces for their corporate offices.

their offices. For instance, as a company known for creative, human-centered design-based solutions to business problems, IDEO has an office environment that mirrors its innovative culture. Bicycles and airplane wings hang from the ceiling, individual workspaces reflect each employee rather than the corporate brand, and central areas are large enough to hold large-team brainstorming sessions that center on research and unique solutions.

Likewise, Pixar—the animation company known for the development of *Toy Story* and *The Incredibles*—reflects its corporate culture in the creative work environment of their headquarters located in Emeryville, California. Their headquarters includes a 600-seat theater, two 40-seat screening rooms, a café, and a fitness center.

Pixar's office interiors have been designed for fun! The interiors include bright colors, life-sized statues of characters from Pixar movies, a *clubhouse* that serves as offices and a game area with ping-pong, foosball, and pool tables. In the center of Pixar headquarters, sits a huge atrium that acts as a central plaza for the

CASE STUDY

VF Corporation Headquarters

Imagine a kayak commute, or taking a break to try out the office climbing wall. At one San Francisco Bay Area office of VF Corporation, which includes *The North Face*, employees are kept happy by being kept active and outdoorsy. If you fantasize about bouldering on your lunch break, and appreciate working in a zero-waste, net zero-energy environment, look at the Alameda, California headquarters of VF Corporation. Their headquarters was designed with their employee wish list in mind. It is an office created for people who would rather be outside.

The VF Corporation culture is expressed through amenities such as a large onsite garden in which grows kale, tomatoes, and basil. Lots of natural light was designed into the majority of interior spaces. Ninety percent of employees have access to direct sunlight, and many of the overhead lights can be kept off. All the windows in the complex open. Opportunities for onsite fitness are available, including an indoor fitness area and yoga room, an outside training area for Boot Camp, an outside *bouldering* (a type of rock climbing performed without special equipment other than climbing shoes) space, and an outdoor gear rental and repair shop. A café serving the vegetables grown in the garden was incorporated. The ability to kayak out into the water just outside the complex is also under investigation. The office space is inside out—executive offices are in the middle of the room and other employees sit by the windows.

There is at least one big money-saving tactic built into the headquarters. It was created with energy and waste efficiency. "It's the right thing to do, but it also has to make business sense. It will save money," says Adam Mott, director of corporate sustainability at The North Face. VF is installing a series of solar systems (on the building roofs, on top of the carport, and on the building awnings) that will provide 100 percent of all energy needs. There is also a towering wind turbine that greets entrants to the site—a symbol of their commitment to sustainability. The complex, built to achieve LEED Gold certification, will eventually have a recycling center that goes far beyond your average office. In addition to the soda cans and office paper that are normally recycled, VF will have the ability to take e-waste (electronic products nearing the end of usefulness), lightbulbs, batteries, plastic bags, and even clothing (for recycling or donation). Their ultimate goal: a zero-waste facility.

The idea about a company keeping employees active, innovating, and considering the environment should not be a novel one—it should be a future norm. Other factors important to employee satisfaction that are not related to the physical environment include ability to use skills, the relationship with the immediate supervisor, compensation, and benefits.

Investigate and Reflect

Read more about the VF Corporation's views on sustainability on their website. In addition, review the sustainability policies of other well-known companies in regard to sustainability. After reviewing these policies, discuss reasons why interior designers must be informed about sustainability practices for their clients.

campus and as a meeting area for employees. The offices are open, with collaborative spaces and lounges in which coworkers can socialize and engage. Individual work and collaborative work can occur anywhere in the complex.

For the imaginative and artistic minds at Pixar, this is the kind of place they always dreamed of working. It is a place where work does not feel like work, which is a reflection of the company's office environment. In contrast, because employees have a different way of working in an accounting firm, the office design would look very different from the office designs for IDEO or Pixar employees.

Supporting Communication and Collaboration

Two significant issues that impact office design today are *communication* and *collaboration*. To determine how employees work individually and with each other, designers conduct surveys to gather details on communication preferences. For instance, do employees prefer e-mail versus face-to-face conversations, and how much collaboration do employees need to accomplish their work? The younger workforce today prefers more teamwork and collaboration than previous generations, **Figure 14-22**.

Gensler, one of the world's well-renowned architectural and design firms, developed a *Workplace Performance Index (WPI)* to understand how people work within organizations and how workplace planning and design can best support their activities. Gensler's WPI revealed that office work falls into four categories:

- learn
- collaborate
- focus
- socialize

In today's economy, workplace success is determined not just by what people know, but by how fast they can *learn*. Gensler data indicates that workers at top companies spend 80 percent more time learning than their peers in average companies.

Collaboration is a workplace activity characterized by sharing, connecting, and building on ideas through a group process resulting in innovation and productivity. Proximity to each other in the office and visual contact help people interact.

Focused work is free of distractions and interruptions. Designers can create an office design, or workplace environment, that supports the privacy employees need for focused work.

Social networks help organizations solve problems, learn, innovate, and adapt. The resulting sense of community creates pathways of information sharing and helps to align values, culture, and mission. According to Gensler researchers, at top-performing companies, workers socialize 16 percent more than peers at average companies. Workplace design can enhance socializing through the development of such collaborative work spaces as non-dedicated team areas. This type of space allocation, which may be as much as 35 percent of the new office model, reflects the practical realities of today's mobile, collaboration-intensive work style.

millann/Shutterstock.com Goodluz/Shutterstock.com

Figure 14-22 Greater collaboration and teamwork are characteristic needs of today's workforce.

Catering to Changing Work Styles

Like Gensler, Herman Miller Inc., a pioneer in modern-day office design, has also been researching the new ways employees conduct work in the office today. Herman Miller's research reveals a typical workstation, also called a cubicle, is unoccupied 60 percent of the day, while private offices on average are vacant 77 percent of the day. Conference rooms are rarely used to capacity, because people prefer less formal meeting spaces in the office.

What do these statistics mean for the design of corporate offices? Changing employee work styles mean the physical office environment must change, too. Herman Miller researchers found employees engaged in ten key behaviors in the workplace: three were labeled as *alone* tasks and seven as *together* tasks. They call it the "Living Office."

- Alone tasks included *process/responding* (on computer/phone/text—process then talk), *contemplation* (ponder issues or status), and *creation* (solve problems).
- Together tasks included *chatting* (impromptu interactions), *conversing* (purposeful planned meetings), *co-creating* (group development of new ideas), *divide/conquer* (teams in close proximity), *huddle* (anytime connections to solve urgent problems), *show/tell* (lecture format), and *warm up/cool down* (conference room connections).

Each task was defined. For example, *divide and conquer* refers to a team with a common goal that divides up the work into individual tasks with members who work parallel to each other in close proximity. The team shares developments and information as it reaches its goal.

Understanding evolving work styles, Herman Miller designed office settings that support the ten research-identified behaviors in the office. These include

- Haven (heads down/private time)
- Hive (workstations)
- Jump space (touch-down spaces for mobile workers)
- Clubhouse (team-based activity with mobile marker board; group work)
- Cove
- Meeting space
- Landing
- Workshop
- Forum
- Plaza

Each setting was defined. For example, *landing* spaces are those that are adjacent to meeting places where people gather, waiting for the meeting to begin. Many conversations and *work* can take place prior to a meeting in such landing spaces. To accommodate the many needs of people doing different work, *Living Office* suggests designers move from the specification of standardized workstations and meeting rooms to a diverse configuration of purposeful settings, **Figure 14-23**.

Supporting the Generational Shift with Flexibility

Not only is the design of the workplace changing, but so are the people in it. Baby boomers, Generation X'ers and Millennials are working alongside one another. Each generation brings its values, goals, and communication approaches to the workplace. Results of a study by the Business and Professional Women's Foundation indicate that by 2025 Millennials will account for 75 percent of the world's workforce.

Designers face the difficult task of creating workspaces that can accommodate all generations. To do so, they are paying close attention to the need for flexibility in supporting different work styles, individual habits, and social interactions between different generations.

Supporting Need for Privacy

While the designs of many offices today are innovative in supporting varying work styles, many employees still work in open-plan offices. A survey of 2000 workers commissioned by Ecophon, part of leading international materials company Saint-Gobain, reveals that a lack of acoustic treatment in these spaces has a negative impact on employee productivity. Almost 80 percent of those surveyed work in open-plan or shared offices.

When asked their opinions about the present acoustic environment in their offices, more than half of the responders said it is sometimes challenging to concentrate on the jobs when working in open-plan workspaces. About two-thirds replied they are also troubled by the lack of privacy in open-plan offices. Additionally, more than 40 percent claim they have *no* access to private areas or quiet rooms. Regular noise disturbances can negatively impact employee concentration resulting in lost hours of work and poor performance and productivity.

Hive

Layout Studio, Hive 1

Layout Studio, Jump Space

Haven

Workshop

Locale Clubhouse

Locale Landing

Public Office Landscape Landing

All images courtesy of Herman Miller, Inc.

Figure 14-23 Herman Millers' "Living Office" designs focus on key behaviors in which employees most engage in the workplace. *Search the Herman Miller website to learn more about the "Living Office."*

Traditional Office Design Issues

While the text earlier addresses several issues related to corporate office design, it is also necessary to discuss many traditional interior design issues. These have not disappeared as new workplace designs evolve. Issues designers need to address include

- creating efficient traffic patterns
- enhancing workflow between departments and key individuals
- integrating flexible technology
- developing effective signage and wayfinding to assist those finding their way through the building
- understanding territoriality and integrating confidentiality
- improving ergonomics, anthropometrics, and comfort
- considering privacy versus spatial efficiencies
- integrating democratic use of space
- creating a healthy work environment that reduces absenteeism

Of all the hundreds of things that impact productivity in the office on a daily basis—interruptions, last-minute meetings, and the Internet—rarely does the desk chair come under consideration. This is an unfortunate mistake. According to research, proper office ergonomics can result in a 400 percent increase in productivity and an average of $150,000 in company savings year over year. (For instance, people who are comfortable in their seats sit longer, increasing productivity. Those who are uncomfortable get up and move around more often to relieve discomfort.) Common ergonomic issues employees face include wrong table heights, banging their knees on the keyboard tray, cramped space, no back support, no elbow support, and having to cradle the phone between shoulder and ear while using the computer. These are all issues the interior designer can, and should, address.

Common Office Spaces

There are common office spaces in the workplace. They are designed to support an organization that wishes to conduct business, assess quality of work, engage with clients and customers, develop marketing strategies and sales, and increase productivity.

Reception Area

The design of the reception area creates the first impression of the organization to visitors. Therefore, the design is very individualized in communicating the personality of the firm. The reception area is where branding is important and where visitors receive an initial greeting, **Figure 14-24**. The lobby itself often meets two basic needs, including

- assistance for the visitor during arrival and departure
- access to a waiting area.

Areas next to the reception area include the entrance, public conference room, workroom, break room, and storage space for guest outerwear. The receptionist's work area is located in the lobby and requires access to a workroom for photocopying and resource materials. It should have a two-level transaction counter or desk to meet needs of all visitors. The waiting area design generally has a grouping of furniture or multiple groupings of guest or lounge seating. Small tables are set between guest chairs. Artwork, plants, and sculptures are common accessories. Keeping in mind proxemics (public) distances, waiting room furniture often includes single chairs with adjoining tables, **Figure 14-25**.

Conference Room

The conference room should be accessible from private offices and the reception area. It should be welcoming and communicate the organization's brand. It can range from a small meeting room that seats four to six people to a large, elaborate boardroom that seats 30 to 50 people. If the organization is large, there will be one main conference room and multiple smaller conference rooms, **Figure 14-26**.

Conference rooms are spaces that businesses use to conduct in-person, group meetings. At times, this may be where a business holds a teleconference. Therefore, this space needs to be a **smart space**—one equipped with a screen, speakerphone, projection device, sound, large computer screen, and controls to operate technology. If possible, it should have a view to the outside with operable window shades for room darkening capabilities. Some storage space is also a requirement.

Four types of furniture are common in conference rooms: a medium-to-large table, armchairs, *credenza*—a sideboard for books and materials, and another side

Haworth, Inc.

Haworth, Inc.

©Ron Pollard, Courtesy of RNL

©Ron Pollard, Courtesy of RNL

Figure 14-24 The reception area provides visitors with a first impression of a business and its brand. *What does the design of these reception areas communicate to you about the personality of these businesses?*

Haworth, Inc.

Haworth, Inc.

Figure 14-25 The design of waiting areas should provide comfortable guest seating—generally a combination of single chairs and small groupings of chairs and tables.

Photography: ©Jim Roof Creative, Inc./Rabaut Design Associates

Photography: ©Jim Roof Creative, Inc./Rabaut Design Associates

Chris Little Photography/Rabaut Design Associates

Haworth, Inc.

Figure 14-26 Businesses use conference rooms to conduct in-person business or business via teleconference. *What factors does the designer need to consider?*

surface for either storage or refreshments. There is typically some type of audio-visual or other communication equipment available along with a podium and easel.

Public Restrooms

Restrooms should be accessible off the lobby and be compliant with ADA standards. Either unisex or both-gender restrooms are appropriate. You can see standard configurations online. These spaces require accessibility to plumbing lines. The location of public restrooms should be central without being a focal point of the design. Interior designers must be aware of the specific numbers and types of plumbing fixtures the codes require for public buildings of varying sizes. The plumbing codes include privacy and minimum clearances. Restroom entrances must strike a balance between accessibility and privacy—easy to find and enter, yet private for users.

Private Zones

Private zones in an office design relate to the spaces where employees accomplish their primary work. These spaces include private or open offices, support staff offices, break room or cafeteria, storage and mailing facilities, and restrooms. These areas often use standard and sometimes custom office furniture. There are nine general product types of furnishings, including

- **Case goods.** These include desks, credenzas, bookcases, and storage units. The style of these furnishing communicate the overall style of the office design.
- **Filing.** These systems may include lateral files, vertical files, pedestals, and storage cabinets.
- **Panel systems.** Also called workstations, cubicles, systems furniture, open-office furniture, they consist of different parts. The parts include a work surface (similar to a desk top only), base storage units, panels, and overhead bins. These systems may also require special attention to mechanical and electrical systems for human comfort and functionality.
- **Tables.** The selection of tables may include conference, training, lunchroom, and informal occasional tables such as an end table, **Figure 14-27**.
- **Seating.** Desk chairs, conference room chairs, guest chairs, sofas, lounge chairs, stools, and stack chairs may all be part of the design. Ergonomic desk chairs are some of the most expensive pieces of furniture in today's office.
- **Shelving.** Shelving types can be open, closed, and movable.
- **Custom furniture.** Desks, tables, counters, workstations, and seating can all be custom designed
- **Accessories.** Used to enhance the space design, accessories may include desk lamps, letter trays, and planters.
- **Equipment.** Office equipment needs will vary, but often include printers, copiers, computers, and audio-visual equipment.

Private Offices

Private offices are a status symbol in many office environments. These offices have full-height walls and

Haworth, Inc.

Figure 14-27 Depending on business needs, the designer includes a variety of case goods, filing systems, and tables in private areas of an office where employees accomplish their work.

a door with acoustical control to ensure privacy of confidential matters. Similar to a home office, private offices are in quiet zones of the building next to support staff, if necessary.

Furnishings for private offices consist of a desk, desk chair, two side chairs, bookcases, credenza, and sometimes a small conference table. Technologies must be supported in the private office such as digital and communication devices. The designer often consults the professional who uses this office about his or her preferred furnishings and configuration of them.

Private office layouts require customization. They should be pleasing and acceptable for each individual occupant. Furniture is generally positioned off a sidewall facing the door opening and not directly in front of the door to allow door swing clearance. Accessories include a marker board, plants, and artwork, **Figure 14-28**.

Workstations

Workstations, also called *systems, workspaces,* or *panel systems*, are exactly as they sound—open to other nearby people via sight and sound. Such systems do not use full-height walls to frame the room, but instead use panels in a system format, **Figure 14-29**.

Workstations are popular because they require much less space than private offices. For instance, a designer can put two, 100-square-foot workstations in the same 225-square-foot private office. Workstations lower yearly rent costs, decrease construction and operating costs (such as lower utility bills due to fewer light fixtures), and improve tax write-offs and **life-cycle costs**—the costs of products from purchase through disposal. They are easy to transport if the organization moves to a new location or relocates within the same building.

To enhance communication, designers often group or zone workstations together with other team members in the same department. Workstation groupings should be away from noise and adjacent to necessary support staff. Panels that serve as walls for workstations are usually *powered.* This means that the panels are wired with electrical, telephone, and data hookups that are typically located in walls. In addition, they can offer acoustical privacy depending on the way they are constructed and finished.

Furnishings within workstation groupings include a work surface, ergonomic chair, side chair, storage—usually in the form of movable bins, and technology support. Panels often form separations between the workstations.

There is no typical industry-accepted standard size or layout for workstations. Many businesses select two or three layouts and sizes as typical workstations based on their average employee needs. Workstations are often eight feet by eight feet. The work surfaces can be configured in an L- or U-shape.

Haworth, Inc.

Figure 14-28 Because private offices require customization, it is important for the designer to consult with the professional who uses the office regarding configuration of furnishings.

Support Staff Offices

Staff support offices are for those who assist in meeting business needs as a company defines them. Support staff members often produce reports, retrieve data, connect employees to others, and handle duplication production. Acoustical privacy is not always a requirement but is preferable to enhance employee focus and concentration on work tasks. Furnishings for a support staff member include a desk or work surface, desk chair, and storage. Electrical, phone, and data hookups are also a requirement.

Additional Areas

Depending on the size of an organization and its values and goals, the designer may incorporate other areas into an office design that support business functions and employee health and well-being. These include

Haworth, Inc.

Figure 14-29 The use of panels in workstations require less space but allow the designer to zone workstations within a department to enhance communication among team members.

- **Receivables and deliveries.** All offices handle deliveries and may produce product materials that require mailing. Even with technologies today, many items still require manual delivery. In addition, the business organization and the designer need to determine storage needs and a storage process.
- **Fitness center.** Depending on the facility size of, the organization may desire an employee fitness center. These facilities encourage physical and mental health that translates to workplace productivity. The employer generally provides the exercise equipment and staff to operate the fitness center.
- **Break room.** Employees are entitled to breaks and a lunch period during the course of a work day. They often stay on-site during these breaks. A break room generally has small tables and side chairs (usually stackable), refrigeration and microwave equipment, a sink, and possibly a view outside. Because noise and food aromas are associated with the space, it should be separate from the public zone. This space also requires accessibility to plumbing lines, **Figure 14-30**.
- **Restrooms.** The location of employee restrooms is often near open, private, and staff offices. They should also be ADA compliant. These spaces also require accessibility to plumbing lines.

©Jim Room Creative, Inc./Rabaut Design Associates

Figure 14-30 Break rooms are public spaces that employees use during break and lunch periods. *What design features do you think are most important in such spaces? Why?*

The Design Process: An Exercise in Corporate Office

As you continue your study of interior design, learning how the design process flows in commercial design projects is essential. The intent of this section is to walk you through the process from the designer's perspective, using corporate office design as the focus of the scenario.

Phase 1: Pre-Design

Let's talk about the design phases as a designer would approach the design. Presume you have been hired by *Innovativ Entrepreneurs Corporation (IEC)* to design their new offices. In the Pre-design phase, you and the client came to an understanding about the scope of services you would perform. The client has signed a contract, completing the pre-design phase of the project.

Phase 2: Programming

The usual name of the document that contains the information and criterion you need to design the spaces is the client's *Program*. The Programming phase for IEC has two parts. First, you will gather information and compile a list of needs the client has for their new spaces. The gathering of data often includes a walk-through of existing spaces as well as their future spaces, personal interviews, focus-group sessions, and employee surveys, **Figure 14-31** and **14-32**.

The second step of the Programming phase is to use written summaries, spreadsheets, diagrams, and charts of the research to compile the collected data into a **Program Report** that presents an ideal scenario for the client's new space. Depending on the size of the project, this report may be the size of a spiral-bound book or may utilize several three-ring binders. During the Programming phase, the designer determines the client's existing furniture, fixtures, and equipment (FF&E) and spatial needs, gatherers data that informs the design, and develops a summary for client approval and signature. The designer may complete this phase without knowledge of the building the client intends to lease or use.

Helen Filatova/Shutterstock.com

Figure 14-31 Prior to beginning a design project, it is important for a designer to walk through a client's space.

Questions for Programming Data	
Survey Questions	**Questions for Personal Interviews and Focus Groups**
■ What type of work does this organization, department, or unit do? ■ What is the culture of the organization? What are the interior design goals to reflect this culture? ■ What is the philosophy of the business related to customers? Does a mission statement exist? ■ What is the client's vision for the business in five and ten years? Is there projected growth that should be considered? ■ How many employees work at this location? Are there satellite offices? ■ What are the employee demographics in regard to age, gender, and culture? ■ What are preferred employee work styles? ■ Will the furniture be new or repurposed? ■ What type of organizational branding should be visible in the client space? ■ What type of communication is preferred between administration and key individuals? ■ What sustainable and green design factors are to be encouraged? ■ What do the current spaces look like now? How do they reflect or not reflect the needs of the corporation? ■ Do employees prefer to work in traditional workstation configurations or flexible cafés?	■ What is your department? What is its function? ■ Do you have a department organization chart to understand who reports to whom? ■ What adjacency requirements does your department have? ■ Who are your personnel? Are you expecting additional personnel? ■ What type of tasks of [specific personnel] are completed in a common workday? ■ What is your preferred work style? ■ What, if any, are the security requirements for specific tasks or departments? ■ What tasks are hindered by the current work space(s)?

Figure 14-32 Formulating survey and interview questions is key to the designer's programming work. *What questions might you add to these?*

The Program Report serves two purposes. First, the designer and team need finite details of the client's needs and functions for space. Second, others need macro-information from which to pull economic information or specifics about the space (such as the total square footage of project). The Program Report is often divided into six sections that include

- **Preliminary information.** Cover sheet, title page, and table of contents.
- **Executive summary.** Generally two to six pages in length, the **executive summary** compiles information and quantities from other sections of the report into a summary of data outlined in the Program. It includes an opening statement, objectives of the report, methods for gathering data, and a summary of data findings.
- **Organizational charts.** These charts diagram corporate departments and their relationships to each other. Usually there is a hierarchy within a company even if it is relatively innovative in design.
- **Adjacency or relationship bubble diagrams.** These diagrams indicate both internal and departmental interactions and associations. The internal diagrams focus on individuals, units or groups, and the support functions within each group. The external diagrams focus on interactions across departments or divisions. Designers can create diagrams using the matrix style or bubble diagrams.
- **Typical layouts.** Copies of a typical office furniture arrangement and size, workstation, and support room layout are also part of the Program Report. The designer creates a list of furniture needs and calculates the average square-foot-totals per person. Commonly called **prototypical layouts,** or *typical*, the designer develops them based on the minimum square-footage requirement for the tasks people perform in a space. The quality of the furniture, fixtures, and equipment (FF&E) relates to the organizational philosophy and budget. *Typicals* are easy to develop in CAD software.
- **Additional materials.** These can include interview summaries, existing or future floor plans, and budgets.

Once the client reviews the Program Report and the designer or design team makes all changes, the client will sign and date the report as a legal document. For a commercial project, it is possible that two weeks to six months may pass before *space planning* begins. At that time, the Program Report becomes the source for every aspect of the planning process, **Figure 14-33**.

Once the designer identifies the programmatic requirements, the client may ask the designer to perform a test fit. A **test fit** is the process of using the client's square footage needs and testing it—or diagramming it—into different available building spaces the client may lease in the desired location. The goal is to see if there is enough space available both for the current client needs and any future needs.

If the client has already leased space, as with IEC, the commercial interior designer reads the lease agreement to review details that might impact a design solution. If your client signs a multi-year lease, it is a common practice for building landlords to pay for all or part of the structural remodeling costs. This specialty of interior design practice is called *tenant improvement (TI)*.

Phase 3: Schematic Design (SD)

The Schematic design phase involves identifying a concept, analyzing the client's needs using a matrix and bubble diagrams, and preliminary suggestions for furniture, fixtures, and equipment (FF&E). As the designer performs the analysis of client needs, it is important to consider the zones of the spaces and the building envelope. The **building envelope** consists of the walls, floors, and ceilings of the building footprint. Drawings during this phase can be manually or computer generated.

Concept Development

After brainstorming ideas and selecting three to present to the client, *Innovativ Entrepreneur Corp* chose an *urban rustic* concept. The existing building has rough-hewn woods, exposed brick walls, and wide-plank floors. This space looks raw and unpolished to attract start-up entrepreneurs.

These materials are a throwback to a time when Americans built physical products and things without the use of modern tools. Likewise, employees and clients want to feel they are part of building something from the ground up—wanting to feel part of something greater than themselves. People want a raw space in which hierarchy is nonexistent—making all feel they are part of something distinctive. Such environments change the thinking of employees and clients from hierarchy to collaborative team, **Figure 14-34**.

Innovativ Entrepreneur Corporation: Program

The following Program outlines the client functions and needs for the *Innovativ Entrepreneur Corporation* new corporate offices.

Executive Summary: IEC is a well-known company headquartered in Seattle, Washington. It is fast-growing and employs young experts (20-somethings) that are knowledgeable and educated in the development of start-up companies. Their leased spaces will occupy one large floor of a short, multilevel, warehouse building on the shores of Puget Sound.

IEC's employees are environmentally conscious, untethered to corporate offices, highly collaborative and interactive, tech-savvy, and conscious of community-driven social responsibilities.

Five divisions occupy the fifth floor: administrative core, business and legal, research, marketing, and education and training. In addition, the public or service areas to be designed into the space include reception/waiting, conference room(s), copy centers, storage rooms, and café. (Note: The café is to be designed as an alternate workspace because many employees like to wander as they work or collaborate near food.) Public restrooms currently exist as part of the building core.

To mimic the new way of start-up companies, IEC wants to move away from strict use of workstations and move toward more open floor plans, where collaboration is as simple as looking across the desk to talk with a coworker sitting five feet away. In addition, the company wants to include *tertiary spaces*—spaces that are not conference rooms nor are they personal desks. They are in-between spaces—such as cafés or alcoves—that are quiet and engaging, where technical people can focus and collaborate without being separated from others in a sterile environment. A space that is full of collaborative areas but has zero quiet space is just as unsuccessful as a space that is full of offices and without collaborative space.

Programmatic Requirements

Public/Service Core

- Reception/Waiting Area: 400 SF (includes waiting for 6 people)
- Two (2) small conference rooms: one private
- Two (2) Copy/print rooms: 600 SF
- One (1) Café/Alternate Work space: 800 SF with a view outside
- One (1) Conference/Training room: 600 SF; technology proficient
- Two (2) Storage rooms: 150 SF

Administrative Core

- Four (4) Workstations: 150 SF each; grouped together; semi-private; space on wall to hang bikes; teleconference capabilities

Education/Training Division

- Fifteen (15) Workstations; semi-private; 100 SF ea.
- Two (2) Perch and plug-in collaborative areas; semi-private; 150 SF each
- One (1) Storage room; 50 SF

Business/Legal Division

- Five (5) Workstations; semi-private; 100 SF ea.
- One (1) Conference room; seats six; 200 SF
- Twenty (20) lateral files, minimum

Marketing Division

- Five (5) Workstations; semi-private; 100 SF each
- One (1) Conference room; seats six; 180 SF

Research Division

- Three (3) Workstations; semi-private; 100 SF each
- Five (5) lateral files, minimum

Restrooms; existing

Figure 14-33 Read through the sample Program Report for the *Innovativ Entrepreneur Corporation*. *Give examples explaining how this report remains the source document for the designer throughout the planning process.*

melis/Shutterstock.com photobank.ch/Shutterstock.com RoyStudio.eu/Shutterstock.com ifoto/Shutterstock.com Horiyan/Shutterstock.com Franck Boston/Shutterstock.com imging/Shutterstock.com

Figure 14-34 The materials in these spaces offer the feel of the urban rustic design of the Innovative Entrepreneur corporation. *Examine the photos. How do these images capture the client's desire for its offices summarized in the Program Report?*

Matrixes and Bubble Diagrams

To analyze the client's programmatic needs, a matrix was developed and relational—also known as adjacency—bubble diagrams were drawn. Once the relationships between the administrative core, divisions and public/service areas were determined, another series of bubble diagrams were drawn within the building footprint. When the second set of bubble diagrams is placed in the building footprint, the designer considers such space planning issues as:

- views/daylight
- furniture, fixtures, and equipment (FF & E)
- employee and user health, safety, and well being

Next, bubbles are moved around as needed within the building footprint to address the above issues as well as the client's needs, such as relationships between divisions and specific square footage to be allocated to each space. Once the location of the bubbles placed appropriately, you can shape the bubbles into blocks and begin the blocking stage, **Figure 14-35**. Again, as you do so, you consider the following four issues: building and fire safety codes, ADA regulations, circulation patterns, and wayfinding.

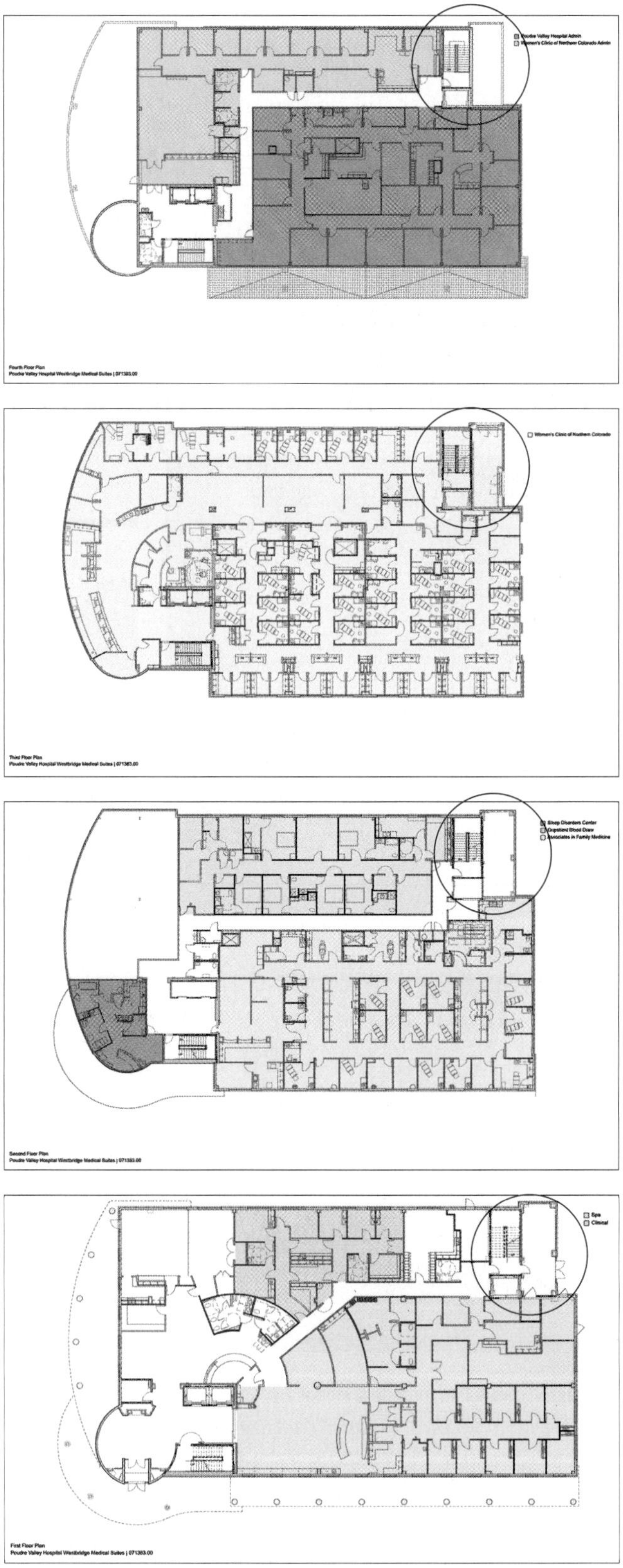

Drawings courtesy of Boulder Associates Architects

Figure 14-35 Block and stack diagrams are essential to evaluate alignment of building features such as stairways and elevators in all levels of a building. Note the circled areas on these drawings are a key area the designer must evaluate for egress and circulation.

Building Codes and ADA Requirements

In addition to the issues above, it is critical to incorporate appropriate building and fire safety codes. Building codes protect the health, safety, and well-being of the public by providing guidelines for constructing spaces under various conditions. The nationally recognized building code is the *International Building Code (IBC)*. The Americans with Disabilities Act (ADA) codes support and mandate accessibility to the workplace, regardless of physical ability. After working in commercial design, code requirements become second nature to the designer. It is the designer's responsibility, however, to verify codes relevant to the location of the project.

Circulation Patterns

As bubbles and blocking diagrams are used to allocate the client's space in a building footprint, the designer must consider circulation patterns. There are two types of circulation: primary pedestrian passageways—usually part of means of egress—and secondary passageways to facilitate the general flow of people. The designer addresses circulation in such areas as

- walking space
- standing space
- sitting space
- space to open doors and drawers
- space to move items such as furniture
- leftover or unusual space

As the design of paths occurs, one goal is to avoid dead-end corridors. These corridors do not lead to any means of egress. They may lead to an office or restroom, but not to a stairwell that building occupants can use to travel to safety. In buildings *without* sprinkler

DESIGNER MATH SKILLS

Codes, Occupancy, and Fire Exits

Daily people move in and out of supermarkets, hotels, malls, restaurants, medical facilities, entertainment venues, and even amusement parks with a sense of confidence, knowing that public spaces are regulated for health and safety by international building codes. Fire codes and safety regulations are the result of lessons learned from horrific commercial fires resulting in staggering numbers of fatalities. Causes for these fatalities include flammable materials, toxic fumes, inoperable doors, blocked hallways and exits, props, faulty wiring, inappropriate working conditions, and projects completed without permits or inspections.

Two critical design components when addressing safety to adequately serve the number of occupants in specific spaces include

1. establishing maximum occupancy limits
2. designing an appropriate emergency exit system—known as the means of egress

Maximum occupancy limits can be determined from the *International Building Codes (IBC)*. Its classification system categorizes spaces based on function (for example, airport terminals, bowling centers, courtrooms, day care, commercial kitchens, retail malls, warehouses and private residences). Using floor area allowances per occupant, known as *Occupant Load*, the IBC provides the following method for calculating maximum occupancy limits.

Size of Space	Function of Space	Occupant Load Factor*	Maximum Occupancy
1200 sq. ft.	Library reading rooms	50 net**	1200 sq. ft. ÷ 50 net load = 60 occupants
2000 sq. ft.	Assembly hall without fixed seats (standing space)	5 net	2000 ÷ 5 = 400 occupants
2000 sq. ft.	Airport terminal—baggage claim area	20 gross***	2000 ÷ 20 = 100 occupants
13,448 sq. ft.	Skating rinks, swimming pools (average public pool is 82 ft. × 164 ft. = 13,448 ft.)	50 gross	13,448 ÷ 50 gross = 692 occupants
512 sq. ft.	Stages and platforms	15 net	512 ÷ 15 = 39 people
644 sq. ft.	Assembly unconcentrated (with tables and chairs)	15 net	644 ÷ 15 = 43 people

**Occupant Load Factor is the net floor area per occupant (sq. ft.).*

***Net is the actual workable space i.e., a classroom, office, stage.*

****Gross is the outside dimensions of a building minus the exterior walls, atriums, mechanical closets providing a refinement in the occupant load determination.*

Once the designer calculates the maximum occupancy, the means of egress—the unobstructed exit system—must be addressed. For all portions of a building that can be occupied, design decisions are determined by the following *three* components of egress:

- ***Exit access*** is the area leading occupants of a building to exits (for example, a corridor, aisle, pathway, stairwell, or ramp). On a plane, travelers are asked to stow all items securely under their seats or in overhead bins to keep the exit access—the space under a passenger's feet and the aisle—free of interference. Elevators, escalators, and moving walks cannot be included in the egress system.
- ***Exits*** are exterior exit doors at ground level, exit passage ways, exterior exit stairs, and/or exit ramps.
- ***Exit discharge*** is the area that provides direct access to a lawn, courtyard, street, sidewalk, or open space, and must be large enough to accommodate the building occupants likely to use the exit route at any one time.

The three components of egress apply to all portions of a building that people can occupy including spaces such as boiler rooms, locker rooms, and meeting rooms. No building element or object can obstruct the means of egress at any time. For example, a piano cannot temporarily block a backstage fire exit. Likewise, stairwells cannot provide temporary storage for any reason. Proper maintenance of the egress system must occur for the life of the building.

(Continued)

DESIGNER MATH SKILLS

Codes, Occupancy, and Fire Exits *(Continued)*

According to the *Occupational Safety & Health Administration (OSHA)*, "…more than two exit routes must be available in a workplace if the number of employees, the size of the building, its occupancy, or the arrangement of the workplace is such that all employees would not be able to evacuate safely during an emergency."

When designing the means of egress, a designer requires additional information about a specific property to determine the exact number of exits. The designer considers the number of floors, seating (fixed seats, benches, and booths), door direction, travel distance to an exit, and the distance between exits. Posting the maximum occupancy of an assembly area is a requirement. This avoids overcrowding which would compromise an evacuation.

When designing a space with two or more exits, you must know the maximum distance of the space, and then calculate it based on whether a sprinkler system is present. To determine the maximum distance in a space (for example, in a cafeteria), you measure the furthest distance in the space (see diagram) then calculate it with or without a sprinkler system. If fire or smoke blocks one exit, the occupants can safely move away from the hazardous conditions evacuating through the second exit.

If there is *no* sprinkler system, divide the maximum distance of the space by two.

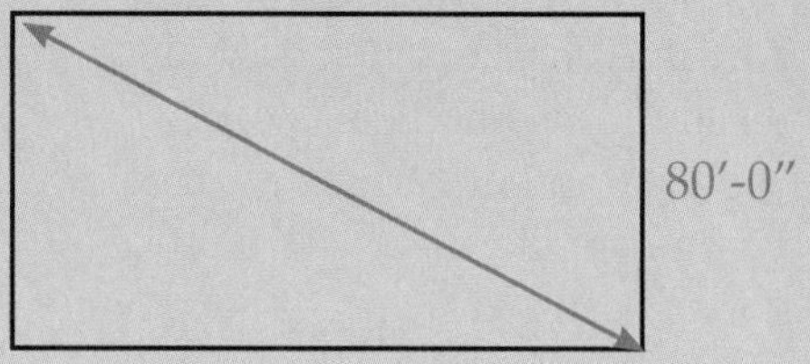

80′-0″ ÷ 2 = 40′-0″ distance between exits.

If there *is* a sprinkler system, divide the maximum distance by three.

80′-0″ ÷ 3 = 20′-7″ distance between exits

Additional detail information about the means of egress for specific commercial and residential buildings is available online by searching OSHA or the International Fire Code.

systems, dead-end corridors may not exceed 20 feet. In buildings *with* sprinkler systems, these corridors may not exceed 50 feet.

The designer plans large circulation paths around escalators, elevator banks, and stairwells. Security and emergency systems, ADA, and codes for fire safety must all factor into the design plan. Some of the issues that impact systems and circulation paths include

- **Number of end users.** The public can be several hundred or thousands.
- **Wayfinding strategies.** Upon entry of public building, the expectation is that a person can easily self-guide from point A to point B and back out again.
- **Safety and security.** Safely and securely moving occupants through the space and offering efficiency in customer service.
- **Health of end users.** Use a design approach that incorporates physical activity into the design plan for building and neighborhoods.

A designer must analyze the circulation needs and develop a design that enhances public safety and comfort of the end user. Some common strategies include

- Common paths of egress travel, including analysis of the distance people will travel before they have an option to take another path to safety.
- Egress corridors with a minimum of 44 inches and whether or not the space has sprinklers. For a commercial building with sprinklers, 44-inch wide corridors can serve floors up to 22,000 square feet. As square footage increases on each floor, wider corridor widths are a requirement. The higher the building, the wider the hallways must be at lower levels to address the volume of people exiting at the same time.
- Most organizations require at least two exit doors from its space, although office areas less than 3,000–5,000 square feet may provide only one exit door depending on code.

- Egress doors are double doors with **panic bars**—spring loaded metal bars on the inside of an outward-opening door used to push in emergencies.
- Lobby spaces appropriately sized to hold number of people moving through space and out of the building.
- **Airlock entries** which are small, enclosed spaces just inside a commercial building that keep bad weather out.
- Appropriate signage and wayfinding techniques related to fire exit.
- Compartmentalized spaces within the organization. Compartmentalization occurs when fire-rated walls are used to keep any fire contained in a specific location for a period of time—usually one hour—to allow safe public egress from the building.

Wayfinding

Wayfinding has been mentioned a number of times in this chapter. Helping people to find their way is the essence of effective wayfinding. Moving people from one space to another in large buildings (such as a 440,000 square foot hospital) is a challenge. **Signage**, the symbols and text used to visually communicate directions and locations of divisions must be well developed, **Figure 14-36**. Effective wayfinding includes

- **Spacing and location.** Sign placement can be best viewed when placed at consistent and strategic decision-making locations.
- **Legible signage design.** The ADA suggests options that have proven helpful when creating legible signage design.
- **Landmarks.** Those elements that help people remember a location as they find their way through a building (e.g. café, water feature)
- **Color.** Color visually connects one part or wing of a building to another.
- **Lighting.** This allows designers to accentuate areas within the building through light.

As blocking of spaces take place, the designer adds furniture and fixtures to determine if the allocation of square footage is appropriate and if shapes of proposed spaces require revisions. This is a fun part of space planning. It is like solving a jigsaw puzzle without a picture to look at!

In addition to space planning, the designer or design team also puts together suggested lighting plans, interior finishes and color palettes, signage and wayfinding strategies, as well as budget information. Sometimes, more than one space plan and interior material presentation board may be developed, although presenting too many options to the client is dangerously confusing. Your expertise guides the best design solution.

Photos courtesy of Boulder Associates Architects

Figure 14-36 Developing accurate and adequate signage symbols is important to visually communicate directions.

STUDENT SPOTLIGHT

Passion for Interior Design

Michael Bent. "I am interested in hospitality design specifically because I love the idea of third place and creating a home for people that is shared with their community. Whether it is restaurant café, a nightclub, or a hotel, these are places people go to relax and enjoy themselves while experiencing some unique and different that isn't offered anywhere else. I enjoy the flexibility and wide range of design concepts and creativity that can be expressed in hospitality design. I think society is moving toward smaller personal living spaces and more public spaces. These public spaces include restaurants, theaters, coffee shops, and more. I want to create a place that is someone's "spot."I want to design hotels that feel like home when you're thousands of miles away—or the favorite restaurant a person goes to every week because their favorite in the back is available every time.

"It is also my goal to get involved with projects internationally and eventually live abroad. After spending a semester in Paris, I am passionate about the idea of learning new cultures and ways of living. It adds a unique challenge as a designer to create a space for a client with a diverse background and differentiating values and habits. The world is shrinking everyday and it is the interior designer's duty to create spaces that understand various cultures and are as inclusive as possible."

Paul Vanderheiden. "I have a passion for family values and an intrigue for human relationships and behavior. Throughout my life, I have always been diligent and found happiness in the success of my creativity and hard work. I was the one always trying to draw the best portrait, or paint the best painting, or mold the best sculpture, and I was upset if my artwork didn't win the awards at the end of the year. I enjoyed pushing myself in analytical and creative ways with high school classes such as photography, studio art, architecture and engineering, as well as algebra, trig, and statistics. I was fortunate to receive some exposure to Autodesk Revit during my senior year, and I eventually won the award for Engineering Student of the Year partly because of my projects and work in the program. All of these things naturally led to my interest in interior design and architecture."

At the end of the Schematic Design phase, the designer presents the proposed design solution and preliminary budget to the client. Movement to Phase 4: Design Development requires a client signature on the design proposal and preliminary budget.

Phase 4: Design Development (DD)

During the Design Development phase, the designer refines the space plan and relevant design features developed in the Schematic Design phase. It is important to finalize the plan because all other features and subsequent construction and installation guidelines hinge on its successful completion. Typically, the designer develops the final drawings and FF & E specifications in this phase which become part of the contract documents that are signed prior to construction. The designer executes the drawings using CAD or REVIT software.

Guidelines for the refinement of the design and execution of final drawings include

- Evaluate the building footprint one more time. Verify accurate dimensions for the client's space.
- Determine the location of columns and **plumbing chases** (false walls—either horizontal or vertical—that conceal plumbing). The plumbing will guide the location of public restrooms and break rooms.
- Block out the public corridors, including locations and egress.

DESIGNER MATH SKILLS

ADA Standards for Wheelchair Accessibility

The Americans with Disability Act (ADA) *Standards for Accessible Design* of 1990 was established to ensure *equal access* to public facilities for people with disabilities. Structures built after the early 1990s are considered new construction and must meet all ADA standards. Buildings existing prior to 1990 are addressed as "alterations" or "exceptions" and are considered remodels, renovations, reconstruction, or historic preservation projects. Because of the construction and features of these buildings (for instance, a historic site) it may be impossible to comply with the standards and maintain the integrity of the building. ADA guidelines indicate these properties must comply with the "maximum extent feasible" or provide approved alternative methods of access.

A commercial property must provide access once an individual arrives on the property. The parking lot, unloading zone, or public transportation stop becomes the *site arrival point*. The *accessible route* (path of travel) includes curb ramps, sidewalks, ramps, entrances, elevators, hallways, and restrooms leading to the *primary function areas* where the major activities for which the facility is intended occur (for example, legal or financial services, sporting or concert events, theater productions, lecture halls, theme parks, courtrooms, ballrooms, hotels). ADA Standards for Accessible Design indicate the following:

1. At least one *accessible* route shall be provided within the site from accessible parking spaces and accessible passenger loading zones, public streets and sidewalks, and public transportation stops to the accessible building or facility entrance they serve. *Exceptions or alteration to the standards* for qualified historic buildings or facilities state that no more than one accessible route from a site arrival point to an accessible entrance is required.
2. The accessible route is to be readily accessible and usable by individuals with disabilities. If accommodations cannot be made for an individual with certain disabilities (for example, those requiring wheelchairs) the facility is expected to provide access to individuals with other types of disabilities (for example, those requiring crutches, or suffering from vision or hearing disabilities).
3. Any new additions to an existing older structure or additions made to affect the access must comply with the ADA accessibility standards.
4. If alterations are made to a primary function area (for example, a particular screening room in a movie theater), an accessible route must be provided to facilities servicing that area (restrooms, drinking fountains), as well as entrances, accessible routes, and site arrival points. The cost of the new accessible route and all that it includes cannot exceed 20 percent of the total cost of alterations to the primary function area.
5. If alterations are limited only to elements in a room or space (for example, the addition of restroom grab bars), then the accessibility standards apply only to the elements altered. If a room or space is completely altered, the entire room or space is fully subject to the accessibility standards.
6. The areas—such as supply storage rooms, employee lounges and locker rooms, janitorial closets, entrances, and corridors—are not areas containing a primary function.

When it is cost prohibitive to comply with accessibility standards, information or services must be offered in an alternative accessible manner or location. *Example:* When the location of a classroom, public meeting or courtroom is accessible only by stairs, someone in a wheelchair would not be able to participate. Other options would be to move the activity to a different location or provide audio access or teleconferencing.
Additional specific standards information is available from ADA Standards for Accessible Design or the United States Access Board.

- Insert the reception area into the space plan. It should be right off lobby or elevators. This space may fluctuate in size based on the room available and its location. It must also be an accessible, integral and unobtrusive design solution.
- Add private offices and then the large conference room. Determine the placement of offices as *window* or *interior* rooms.
- Insert workstations into the blocked space allocated to them.
- Add support rooms near appropriate offices. Continue to review your bubble and block plan analyses from the Schematic Design phase. Verify the adjacencies.
- Double-check the circulation including minimum widths for hallways and look for dead-end corridors.
- Use sound judgment to determine if there is any leftover space that could be incorporated into the space plan. If possible, allocate such space to additional storage units.
- Visually, walk your way through the client spaces from the point of entry to the exit. Complete this exercise several times as you look at circulation patterns that could impact different users of the space.

Once you complete the above process, look for good and poor **lines of sight**—views down a corridor or passage, either good or bad. For example, a good sight line is one by which you look down a corridor and see a view outside. A poor sight line is one in which a column blocks the receptionist's view of the entry in a reception area. Effective lines of site can also help direct guests to public spaces and keep them from private spaces. For instance, wide hallways invite passage while narrow hallways suggest a private passage.

Until the designer feels the space plan meets all program requirements in the best possible way, the plans should remain in work. Analysis of hallway widths and aisles between workstations, points of entry into an office, and workstation planning in a block diagram continues until the plan meets the program requirements. Although this seems like a standardized process, it actually necessitates creativity and technical expertise.

As refinement of the space plan continues the designer points out any changes in room size and/or workstations to the client. Depending on the scope of the project, the designer may hold ten or more update meetings throughout a year to inform the client about the design process. Each meeting involves a client presentation and often additional signatures to ensure everyone is up to date with the plans as the process moves forward. Once the basic plan is firm, the designer

- adds suggested furnishings to each space
- refines workstation configurations and specifications
- ensure outside views are maximized
- considers human factors such as ergonomics
- verifies all program requirements and circulation layouts are in a logical order
- puts critical rooms together or separates them per adjacency requests of the client
- ensures the design meets such code requirements as building, fire, and the barrier-free requirements of ADA
- verifies the incorporation of the creative concept
- confirms the design has some unique features that mirror the brand and philosophy of the client's business
- considers optional requirements such as universal design and sustainable design
- labels all areas clearly

The interior designer works with a lighting designer to determine how light will shape the newly designed spaces. Lighting enhances first impression of the space on the client as he or she walks through the front door. Specific lighting strategies are important for such other key areas as the large conference room, private offices, and workstation areas.

The designer then selects interior materials for upholstery, workstation panels, flooring, ceilings, walls, and window treatments. These materials must meet specific standards for commercial applications. Selecting *green* materials and products is important in this part of the design process.

Phase 5: Contract Documents (CD)

Eventually, everything comes together. Another client presentation takes place. Once the designer acquires client approval and the appropriate signatures, construction begins.

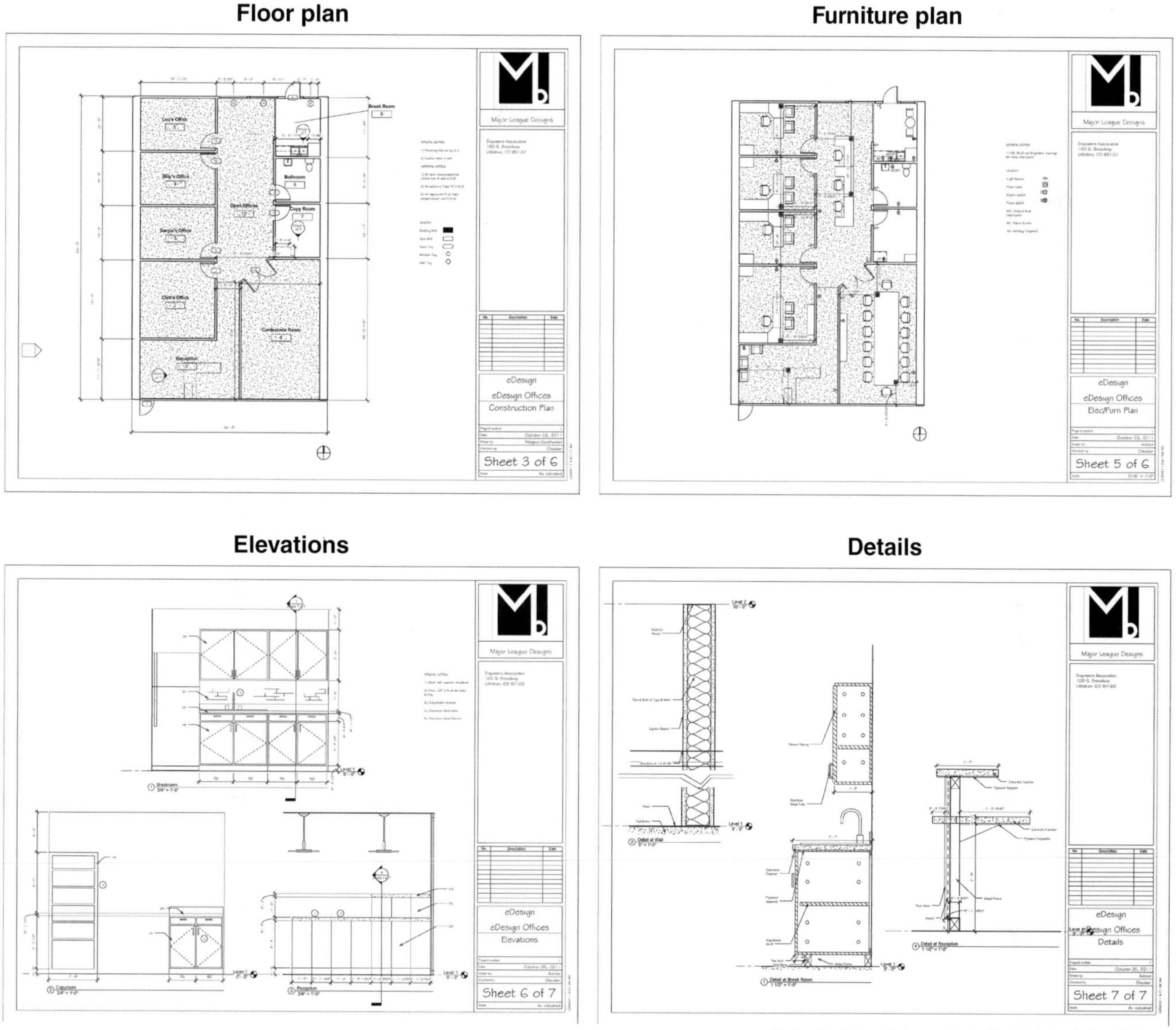

Meghan Bentheimer, Sophomore Design Student, Colorado State University

Figure 14-37 Contract documents contain the working drawings and specifications needed for construction.

Contract documents, or CDs, are the working drawings and specifications required to obtain a building permit and construct the finished space. CDs, by strict definition do not include the furniture plan, although it is often included to reference other details in the plan, **Figure 14-37**. CDs do include

- dimensioned plans
- reflected ceiling plans (RCP)
- power and communication data plans
- finish specifications
- elevations and sections
- mechanical, electrical, and plumbing (MEP) plans
- structural plans as needed

Another client presentation often takes place after the designer develops these documents.

Phase 6: Contract Administration (CA)

Contract administration involves managing your contracts to make sure you comply with and fulfill the contract conditions. Good contract administration ensures customer satisfaction and minimizes disputes. To successfully administer contracts, it is helpful to

- have significant experience with design and construction
- understand construction techniques and methods
- understand building codes and standards
- have the ability to communicate, negotiate, and resolve dispute
- review and understand drawings and product information
- have ability to organize and manage project records.

For commercial projects, tasks the designer must complete include the review, negotiation and finalization of subcontracts; management and tracking of project expenditures; administration of RFI's (requests for information) to clients, architects and consultants; and preparation of subcontractors' packages. If you are involved in contract administration, you need to be a detailed-oriented person with good communication skills.

Phase 7: Move-In and Post-Occupancy Evaluation

The design process ends with the construction of the space and the client move. Once the client moves in, the designer addresses **punch lists** along with the installation of the art and accessories. A punch list is a list of tasks the builder or subcontractor completes after construction. An example of an item on a punch list might be touching up wall paint that was nicked during the move-in process.

Many times, if the client is moving from one location to another, the client will hire a *move management* company to organize the move in the most efficient way, **Figure 14-38**. After a certain preset time period, a post-occupancy evaluation may take place in *Phase 7: Move-In and Post-Occupancy Evaluation (POE)*.

bikeriderlondon/Shutterstock.com

Figure 14-38 Often the most overlooked aspect of the design process, move-in and post-occupancy evaluation is essential to ensure client satisfaction.

Analyzing a Commercial Design

Designers often look at case studies and precedents to evaluate and analyze design work that has been installed to determine how the client's problem was solved. They are also interested in the impact of design on the end users.

Following is a case study of a growing, innovative organization known as OtterBox. Since water sports such as surfing and scuba diving were gaining in popularity, this waterproof product is an electronics case. His wife, Nancy, dubbed it the *OtterBox*, in reference , animal's waterproof fur.

The client problem was to take an existing building in a college town, and establish the headquarters for the organization using sustainable and green design features. While they had a projected growth planned into the design of the building, by the time the renovation was completed, the number of employees had increased so much that they had to purchase a second building shortly thereafter. Using points in the design process outlined above, and using their website online, analyze the design of the spaces.

CASE STUDY

Analyzing OtterBox Headquarters

OtterBox—located in Fort Collins, Colorado—is known particularly as an innovator in the development of protective covers and cases for cell phones. Created in 1998, these protective cases were designed "for all the klutzy, spontaneous, chaotic, graceless individuals who have broken a device … due to their active lifestyle, and like our customers, we've been there, too." Similar to an otter's fur, their original line of cases is waterproof. The company considers its organization cultural characteristics similar to the otter's—fun, creative, works hard, and plays hard.

OtterBox began as a start-up company. A small team began in the modest garage of the founder's private residence. In between developing product prototypes in the garage, meals were served in the residence's kitchen where additional product ideas were tossed around.

As OtterBox became a mainstream product manufacturer—a cell phone case, their first office headquarters was designed using an existing building and a new addition. In the interior spaces, the design team in charge of working on the project used many elements from the "beginnings" of OtterBox. For example, every floor has a full-sized kitchen to encourage employees to gather, munch on treats, and engage in brainstorming conversations that encourage the refinement or development of new ideas (**Figure A**).

As part of their public space, OtterBox headquarters has a unique, fun lobby that reflects its corporate philosophy. A unique, internationally designed "Otter" slide (accessible to employees) clearly communicates the OtterBox brand (**Figure B**). It doubles as a circulation path, moving people quickly from second floor to first floor. The unconventionally stylish café area is located right off the receptionist workspace.

OtterBox workplace has in-house departments such as sales, customer service, accounting, engineering, public relations, marketing, Web design, and graphics (**Figure C**). In addition, they have a gymnasium for their employees to use (**Figure D**), and bike storage areas to support the employees traveling from one OtterBox building to another in their downtown campus. Shapes such as the "O" for OtterBox and the square for "box" are used repeatedly throughout these departments to enhance the brand. In addition, garage doors are used on various floors in place of ordinary conference room doors. OtterBox has seven buildings as part of their corporate campus and have since branched into a number of countries where their design "brand" is still replicated throughout their facilities.

Figure A

(Continued)

CASE STUDY

Figure B

Figure C

Figure D

Investigate and Reflect . . . .
Go to the OtterBox website and read through the case studies under the "Media Center" tab. How did OtterBox help enhance the success of the companies featured in the case studies? Discuss your findings in class.

Chapter 14

Review and Assess

Summary

- Commercial design projects include offices, hospitals, healthcare facilities, educational institutions, and corporate offices. For these projects, interior designers must consider layout of interior walls, plumbing and power systems, and communications with other service providers.
- The design process for commercial design projects is similar to the process for residential design projects. In commercial design, however, interior designers must meet the needs of owners, employees, and customers or guests.
- Commercial interior designers need to be knowledgeable about building codes, including building occupancy classifications and accessibility codes.
- Commercial interior designers consider building systems and some specialty space needs during projects.
- Advances in science and technology (such as measures against nocosomial) affect current healthcare facility design. Current designs inspire an upbeat, encouraging attitude, but should always be sterile and safe.
- Hospitality establishment designs should transform the hectic lives of guests into a state of tranquility, relaxation, and enjoyment. Hospitality establishment interior designers design hotels, convention center, and spas; and restaurants and dining areas.
- When designing retail spaces, commercial interior designers must consider the types of retail layouts, incorporate a decompression zone, and strategically place fixtures.
- The design of educational facilities incorporates new technologies and promotes learning. Some educational facilities involve *academic villages*, or clusters of buildings.
- Corporate office design is concerned with enhancing corporate culture, supporting communication and collaboration, catering to changing work styles, supporting generational shifts with flexibility, and supporting the need for privacy.
- The process of designing commercial spaces is complex and involves Program Reports, the consideration of codes such as those established by the ADA, circulation patterns, and effective wayfinding.

Chapter Vocabulary

Write the definition of each of the following terms. Then write a sentence using each term in a design-related context.

academic village
airlock entries
boutique hotel
building codes
building envelope
building occupancy classification
circulation patterns
corporate culture
decibel
decompression zone
end user
executive summary
free-flowing layout
grid layout
lifecycle costs
lines of sight
loop layout
nosocomial
occupant
panic bars
plumbing chases
program report
prototypical layout
punch list
signage
smart space
test fit

Review and Study

1. Why are commercial design projects larger and more complex than residential design projects?
2. List the phases of the commercial design process.
3. Why do commercial interior designers need to be knowledgeable about building occupancy classifications?
4. Name four building systems commercial interior designers may need to consider.
5. Identify five common issues to consider during healthcare facility design projects.
6. What is *nocosomial* and how does it affect patient room design?
7. What are three issues to consider during the design of a hotel?
8. What are *circulation patterns* and how do they affect restaurant and dining area designs?
9. What is the difference between a *grid layout* and a *free-flowing layout*?
10. List four things that educational space designs should do.
11. Define and give an example of *corporate culture*.
12. What are the typical office spaces a commercial interior designer would design?
13. What are the six sections of a Program?
14. What issues impact emergency systems and circulation paths?
15. Name the five components of effective wayfinding.

Critical Analysis

16. **Analyze patterns.** Map a circulation pattern of your high school. How do students and staff get out of the building fast in case of a fire emergency?
17. **Make inferences.** The author states that "No issue has affected the design of inpatient rooms and units more over the past few years than increased emphasis on controlling nosocomial, or hospital-acquired infections." Make inferences about ways an interior designer can be most influential in creating designs and specifying materials to help control such infections.
18. **Analyze evidence.** Review the Design Insight quote by Frank Chimero at the beginning of the chapter. Then take a walking tour of various areas in your community. Cite evidence of design that either supports or does not support the quote. Discuss your findings in class.

Think like a Designer

19. **Speaking/listening.** Interview a fire chief in your community about the importance of circulation patterns related to life safety. Give an oral report of your finds to the class.
20. **Speaking/listening/writing.** Interview an older adult about his or her abilities or diminished abilities to navigate public and private spaces. What types of spaces (shopping, medical appointments, recreational facilities) does the older adult feel need to be redesigned to be more functional? After the interview, spend additional time observing the older adult navigate through a daily or weekly routine. What design features would make the spaces the older adult uses more functional and easy to navigate? Write a summary of your observations.
21. **Research/writing.** Use the text and reliable Internet resources to research the following types of healthcare facilities: birthing center, dental office, assisted-living facility, outpatient diagnostic center, rural health clinic, ambulatory surgery center, or hospital. Analyze the needs and design of each facility. Write a summary of your findings.
22. **Math practice.** Commercial buildings, including schools, have a means of egress and emergency evacuation systems. Using your school as an example:

A. Quick-sketch this commercial property—or a section of it—and show all fire exits, color-coding the three components of egress for each exit.
B. Select two assembly areas of the school (for example, a gym, library, cafeteria, or auditorium) and determine the maximum occupancy for the area.
C. Next determine the maximum distance in each area (see page 527) and calculate the distance between fire exits with and without a sprinkler system.
D. Document measurements on the drawings. (*Note:* Local codes may vary for structures that are historical, new, or remodels.

23. **Research/writing.** Use the text and reliable Internet resources to research the following a hospitality facility of your choice. Analyze the needs and design of the facility. Write a summary of your findings.

24. **Math practice.** Visit a community building that was built before 1990 or is a designated historic property. Make arrangements to meet with a building supervisor. Walk the property to determine the *site arrival point, accessible route* (path of travel), and specific *primary function area* (destination) accessible for a person who uses a wheelchair.
   A. Using an 11" x 17" or larger piece of paper, quick-sketch the site arrival point, accessible route, and primary function area. You do not need to draw the plan to scale but give attention to drawing proportionate distances.
   B. On the sketch, label and highlight the accessibility features the facility provides, for example, curb ramps, ramps, entrances with door controls with activation switches, handrails, accessible water fountains and restroom stalls, height of customer service areas and the three components of the means of egress (see *Designer Math Skills* feature on *Codes, Occupancy, and Exits*). The building supervisor can assist in identifying ADA accommodations.
   C. Use a colored pencil to mark the accessible path from the *site arrival point* to the *primary function area.*
   D. Estimate an approximate distance the person with a disability will travel from the *site arrival point* to the *primary function area* destination by doing the following:
      - measure and record the distances between each location including the parking lot to the entrance, the entrance to the restroom, the restroom to the destination
      - round the number of steps when walking up to the nearest 10th step and record them on the diagram
      - add all segments together and record the distance on the drawing
   E. Using the same technique in 24-D, estimate the approximate distance and mark the most common travel route someone *without* a disability would take from the site arrival point to the same primary function area. The paths of travel may not be the same for the two people.
   F. Share your findings of the similarities and differences in accessibility for each person, including restrooms. During bad weather, would the individuals have the same quality experience from the site arrival point to arriving inside the building (time, distance, covered entrances)?

Design Application

25. **Design a pop-up school.** Design a pop-up school for a different geographical location—national or international—based on information in chapter and additional Internet research. Locate case studies and characteristics of each. Do not be constrained with the design of schools today. Follow text guidelines for Programming and Schematic Design for your school design. Create the program documentation and schematic design plans.

26. **OtterBox revisited.** Suppose you and your design team have been asked to develop a design plan for an OtterBox satellite office. Develop the design concept and program for this satellite office. Present your design concept and program to your client (the class).

27. **Portfolio builder.** Place copies of the best examples of your work for items 21, 22, 24, 25, and 16 in your digital and hard copy portfolios.

Residential Interior Design Applications

Photography © Pat Sudmeier/Architecture by Poss Architecture + Planning/Interiors by Associates III Interior Design

Chapter 15

Design Insight

"There is a difference between a 'filled' space and a 'fulfilling' place that promotes thought and emotions about things that matter. Shun shallow design. Avoid the 'decorated box.' Design spaces and places that prompt contemplation and express meaning."

Jill Pable, Ph.D., Associate Professor, Florida State University

Learning Targets

After studying this chapter, you will be able to

- identify key factors of quality residential design including meeting human needs for sense of place and cultural sensitivity.
- describe public and social spaces and the functional and aesthetic factors of each.
- summarize key attributes of private spaces.
- identify key work areas and the functional attributes of each.
- describe how to add design details that add warmth and interest to a home.
- analyze floor plans to differentiate between those that are effective and those that are poorly designed.
- analyze furniture arrangements for effective circulation and groupings.
- create a simple, effective floor plan with furniture arrangements.
- identify trends impacting residential design, including smaller homes and intergenerational living.

Introduction

Quality interior design in the home is every bit as important as proper health and exercise. Both are important for physical and emotional *well-being*—a state of being comfortable, healthy, and happy especially in an age of profound change. The residence should be a safe haven and a retreat, a castle and cocoon; a place of solace and refuge for individuals or families inhabiting the space. Along with offering protection and security, it should be a place for creating meaningful memories.

The design of residential interiors is a complex task, perhaps more so than commercial design. Denise Guerin, Ph.D., Principal of InformeDesign and former Professor of Interior Design at the University of Minnesota wrote in *Interior & Sources*, "We need spaces that speak to the souls of the humans who inhabit and use the space. We must still create a space with artifacts, colors, furnishings, and finishes that reflect the needs of and create meaning for the users. And all of this must occur under the umbrella of universal design, in less square footage, with environmentally safe materials, and with identity and meaning for the human users."

Although a shelter meets a client's physical needs, is the home an expressive place to engage feelings, develop imagination, and stir a response from the individual or family? As you read this chapter, it is easy to understand space planning and furniture arrangement techniques. Also consider what a house with a soul—one that has meaning and memories for the inhabitants—can do for your clients and what you can do through design to achieve it.

Meeting Human Residential Needs

A residence serves as a home. The concept of *home* differs for every individual. There are many definitions of home including

- a shelter from a homeless environment, **Figure 15-1**
- a location where you live at a particular time
- a dwelling—a place someone lives in
- an institution where people are cared for
- a place where parent(s) or siblings live
- a home imbued with soul that arouses emotion and sentiment

Dr. Chad Gibbs defines *home* as a social environment that depends on time, or the impression of time, and is represented by a personalized, physical environment, such as a house, that nurtures the attachment of meaning. How can the design of a residence allow the occupants to quickly adapt and experience their sense of home longer? The meaning of home differs across cultures and among individuals. How can a dwelling reflect the diversity of the population?

The house serves as a physical and social setting that allows people a degree of control not found in other areas or places of their lives. There are many human

Gensler Project Team: Charrisse Johnston, Colin Thomson, Daphne Thiele, Hans Herst, Marc McManus, Parinaz Behbahani, Shaw Gehle, Stella Choi, Stephanie Lee/Photo Credit: Ryan Gobuty, Gensler

Figure 15-1 *Housing for Health* strives to end homelessness in Los Angeles County and improve health outcomes for vulnerable populations by providing permanent supportive housing, recuperative care, and specialized primary care for homeless people with complex health conditions. *If you were on a design team for a new homeless shelter, what questions might you ask the client regarding home and sense-of-place?*

needs to consider when designing a residence. For example, the need for privacy may impact the location of specific rooms. The need for nature may determine the size and location of windows and access to views. The need for a sense of spaciousness can affect architectural details designed into the place. Health needs, such as allergies, can impact the interior materials the designer selects for the spaces, **Figure 15-2.**

Human needs not only differ from one individual to another, but also between cultural groups. For example, certain cultures enjoy communal cooking traditions that impact kitchen size preferences. Other cultures invite extended family members to live in the home, creating a need for additional sleeping spaces. Still other cultures discourage male guests from viewing female family members in any rooms other than the living or dining spaces; therefore, enhancing privacy requires completely enclosing the entry away from nonpublic spaces. Residential space requires deliberate thought and planning. Sensitivity to cultural differences is necessary for success as an interior designer.

Inclusive design and visitability are accessibility issues an interior designer must consider when designing a residence. Barriers such as steps should not exclude those who use wheelchairs, walkers, or other mobility devices from entering a home. Some homeowners may have physical mobility limitations while others may have visual or hearing disabilities. Accommodating the needs of aging relatives who visit offers a welcoming feel. If the design of a home is inclusive, it accommodates the individual, family, friends, and guests of all ages and abilities.

This chapter walks you through residential spaces found in most homes beginning with the point of entry through service areas such as the kitchen and laundry to private spaces such as the fitness area or bedroom. Part of this discussion will also include outdoor living spaces. Each space includes questions you might pose when interviewing a residential client.

As you study each room, it is important to consider issues that impact the residence such as universal design, energy efficiency, and environmental concerns as well as the feature benefits. As you know, aesthetics—such as art and accessories, enrich the residence through complexity, novelty, and beauty.

The last section of this chapter discusses how to analyze residential space plans based on zones, conversation groupings, circulation patterns, and architectural features such as door placement and room relationships. A **zone** is two or more spaces that are a unit. To analyze the plans, you will need basic knowledge of how to place furnishings. Learning how to analyze the functional characteristics of floor plans helps you become a better space planner and designer for large or small residential interiors.

Photography by: Brian Gassel Photography/Design by: Lita Dirks & Co.

Figure 15-2 While privacy is important in a bathroom, there are key ways to link the outside and maintain privacy.

Factors in Residential Design

The residence meets basic human needs—*shelter, food, water, safety,* and *security.* As it becomes a *home*, the residence or house moves past basic needs to become a place of self-expression—a safe haven where people can lower their defenses and feel safe, **Figure 15-3**. Additionally and ideally, the residence provides a respite from chaos and a place to form relationships of trust.

If correctly designed, a residence offers a place for **personal autonomy**—or a place that allows individual freedom to separate self from others, to be alone with thoughts and feelings, to explore personal limitations, and strive for independence. Personal autonomy has a direct link to the need for *privacy*; a way to achieve selective distance from others.

Photograph: David O. Marlow/Interiors by Associates III Interior Design

Figure 15-3 As a residence becomes a home, it becomes a safe haven for the occupants. *What aspects of home offer a sense-of-place and sense of security?*

One of the most satisfying experiences of residential privacy is the feeling of safety—of being inside and looking out. Children delight in such places as playhouses, tree houses, and rock-boulder perches. The attraction of these temporary structures is the ability to observe the outer world from a position of relative safety. A home should capture and enhance this same feeling.

When considering the family unit of two or more people, the home may be a place of safety, interdependence, cooperation, learning, and mutual affection with spaces that support a sense of belonging, identity, teamwork, and shared values.

Today, technology gives people unexpected freedom in selecting a location for the residence. It makes it possible to have physical isolation while maintaining communications with others through telecommunication. It allows the residence to be remotely located from work.

During the residential design process, the designer prioritizes basic human needs and wants against time and money. He or she also considers *filled* versus *fulfilling spaces* as identified by Jill Pable of Florida State University, **Figure 15-4**. There is no perfect residential interior—every place is a set of priorities and trade-offs. Therefore, the client program shapes the residence often in dramatically different ways.

Public Zones

The house, or dwelling, is a functional series of spaces that offers both private and communal places. Public spaces should be inviting, lively centers for activity while private spaces should be personalized, discrete, and individually controlled. **Public zones** are social areas that include the

- entry
- living room
- great room
- dining room
- guest bathroom

Public or social spaces may also include the family room, library, guest bathroom, and outdoor living space. The more formal spaces such as the living room, dining room, and library are often separate from the kitchen and offer a

Characteristics of Filled versus Fulfilling Spaces	
Filled Spaces...	**Fulfilling Spaces...**
Offer instant gratification	Provide for contemplation
May provide superficial, unfocused complexity	Are usually delightfully simple
May include a potted plant in the corner	Develop the concept of inside and outside
Include more	Include less
Have objects placed around the perimeter of the space	Develop the concept from within, both mentally and physically
Communicate a fragmented message that produces only temporary satisfaction	Communicate deeper meaning and significance
Show a decorated box	Show integration with architecture
Offer an ignored ordinary place	Offer an extraordinary canvas of meaning and relevance

Jill Pable, Florida State University

Figure 15-4 When designing a residential space, the interior designer prioritizes basic human needs and wants against time and money to create fulfilling spaces that express meaning.

quieter place to study, listen to music, or hold more formal dinners. Given the more casual living style in many areas of the United States, formal areas—such as the formal dining room—are disappearing from the house plan.

Residential Circulation Patterns

There are three basic types of circulation patterns in the home—family, service, and guest. As you recall, *circulation patterns* utilize the entries, hallways, and stairways of the house and are a means of moving people *from* space to space. In contrast, **traffic patterns** refer to how the users move *within* a space (which is often evident by wear patterns on the flooring). You as the designer should identify and map each type of circulation as you evaluate a floor plan. Factors to consider for each type of circulation pattern include the following:

- **Family.** Primarily all family members use these circulation patterns that include travel between the kitchen, laundry, mudroom, bedrooms and bathroom. Questions to ask may include: Are the high frequency circulation routes short and simple? Are the related rooms positioned close to each other? Is there a bathroom located near the bedrooms? What traffic patterns do family members use within the spaces?
- **Service.** Key individuals in the residence use the service circulation patterns. These spaces may include the kitchen, laundry, garage, and mudroom. Questions to ask may include: Is the garage near the service entrance? Is the service entrance near the kitchen? Can the user remove kitchen trash without crossing another room? Is the circulation between the cooking and eating areas unbroken?
- **Guest.** The primary circulation patterns that guests use may include the entry, guest bathroom, great room, living room, dining room, and outdoor living area. Questions to ask may include: Is the coat closet near the main entry? Is the guest bathroom near the living room?

As you evaluate residential circulation patterns for your clients, observing and evaluating how the inhabitants move from space to space is essential.

Entries, Halls, and Stairwells

After a place of safety, there is nothing more critical to the residence than the impression it sets for both visitor and home owner. Both the action of arrival and then traveling around a house is a completely different way of knowing an interior than the more static feeling of simply being in a space.

This section discusses three important goals for this space include

- creating a welcoming entry
- rethinking passageways or halls
- understanding functional stairways

Entries

Before entering a residence, there should be some sense of arrival—a feeling of reaching a desired destination. A welcoming pathway and entrance to a residence is well-lit and devoid of obstructions. If possible, design a step-less (zero-step) entrance or one-half-inch maximum rise at the entrance threshold.

Once the door has opened and the guest or homeowner steps inside, a physical place (minimum 5'-0" x 7'-0") is necessary for orientation to the interior with a graceful transition to activities within the home. The entry includes easily accessible coat storage, a window to view the arrival of people, and electric light for security.

When shaping the entry, it is important to give careful attention to the volume of its space. A very tall space, such as a two-story entry, can make a person feel overwhelmed and insignificant. In contrast, a tiny space with barely room to stand can make the space feel cramped and awkward. Ideally, an entry should be large enough for two or three people to stand and talk comfortably and should offer interesting glimpses of other areas of the home, **Figure 15-5**.

To give an entry distinction, specify changes in flooring or wall finishes, add overhead beams, vault the space, add columns, or insert half-walls. An entry should be memorable as well as inviting. Using interior archways or openings can help by enclosing space but offering a view into adjacent spaces.

Space Planning Analysis

Entries

When analyzing entries, questions to ask about the space planning may include

- After entering a home, is there ample space for two or three people to stand, take off their coats, and be welcomed into the residence? (*space issue*)
- Can an occupant see a caller without opening the front door? (*security issue*)
- Does the entry have a hard-surfaced, easily cleaned floor covering? (*maintenance or accessibility issue*)
- Is there a coat closet near the entry for guest outerwear? (*storage issue*)
- Is there electric light overhead or next to the front door? (*visibility issue*)
- Does the occupant want a visual separation between the entry and the living area? (*privacy issue*)
- Does the occupant want a sitting space for people to use when removing footwear? (*functionality issue*)

Hallways

Hallways connect spaces, allowing users to move from one area to another. They serve the function of transporting people to their destinations and offer vantage points from which to view the other spaces within the home. Hallways can provide relief, encourage social contact, accentuate transitions and entrances, and create memorable spaces along the way, **Figure 15-6.**

Too often the design of a home focuses on the quality of rooms with the circulation routes superimposed after planning the layout. To a great extent, a person's impressions of the residence depend on his or her experience while moving from place to place within it.

pics721/Shutterstock.com.

Figure 15-5 A residential entry should be spacious enough for several people to hold a conversation while offering a view to other spaces in the home. *Think about a home you have visited that had a memorable entry. What features made it memorable and inviting?*

Jodie Johnson/Shutterstock.com

Figure 15-6 Hallways are circulation routes that connect spaces and should allow inhabitants to move efficiently from one space to another in a home. *What are some disadvantages of inefficient hallways? What can you as a designer do to avoid inefficiencies?*

Routes people follow as they move from one place to another are critical in establishing functionality and efficiency within the home. Paths are hierarchical. Not all paths move the same number of people or share the same degree of importance. For instance, because it is a primary service route used by multiple individuals, the hallway between the kitchen and garage is more important than the hall between two bedrooms.

Passageways with high-circulation frequency should be short and direct with the width typically ranging from three to four feet. If there is a need to accommodate an individual who uses a wheelchair or other mobility device within the home, the hallway width should be a minimum of 44 inches.

Rethinking passageways to make them more interesting and effective is easy. For example, adding windows along the hall or at the end of the hall create views to the outside. Designing an alcove with seating at a specific point of the hallway encourages people to rest a moment or read. Frame doorways with architectural elements such as a simple wood trim or a column that create presence for both the hall and room. Here are some questions to ask when planning hallways.

Space Planning Analysis

Hallways

Ask the following about space planning in regard to hallways:

- Are the hallways short and direct?
- Are they wide enough to accommodate a wheelchair or other mobility device, if necessary?
- Do any hallways dead-end into wasted space that could be reused for storage or a window?
- Is there a way to add interest (for example, accessories, architectural element, alcove, or view) to the passageway?

Stairways

Historically, stairs and stairwells were hidden between walls or in turrets (small towers). By the eighteenth century, the stairway became a dramatic focal point of many residences. Stairs can evoke strong responses and are a favorite backdrop for movie sets and homeowners desiring a dramatic entrance into the foyer. It is always an interesting experience to go from one level of the home to another.

Today stairways evoke many memories, such as sliding down the handrail or peeking unseen at events that were going on downstairs. How can stairways be designed to not only move people from one level to another safely, yet become a subject of fond memories between family members? See **Figures 15-7**.

The stairway, along with the hallway, is part of the circulation system through a residence. A stairway can be a dramatic focal point that acts as a functional sculpture or the designer can hide it within walls between rooms. Consider these guidelines for designing stairways.

- Locate a stairway close to the entry to add height and drama to the space if it is a focal point.
- Place a second stairway to the second floor off the kitchen if desired, with a connection between the two stairways half-way to the second floor.
- Locate a stairway going to the basement living areas near, but not in, the entry or off a central location in the garage.

Always strive to locate stairways to arrive in the midst of the rooms they serve. There are five basic stairway configurations: *L-shaped, U-shaped, curved, spiral,* and *straight*, **Figure 15-8.**

In addition to beauty and location, a designer must also consider safety issues and building codes when designing stairways. Building codes require stairways to have a handrail and a minimum and maximum dimension of stair width, tread width, and riser (step) height.

If possible, the stairway should be wide enough to accommodate a number of people passing or several people carrying items. Building codes require lighting at the top and bottom of the stairway. A trend today is to locate lighting along the side of the stairway or under the edge of stair treads, too. This is particularly helpful in the evening when daylight diminishes. Ramps sometimes replace stairs to accommodate people who use mobility devices such as crutches, wheelchairs, or walkers.

A few strategies for designing stairways include the following:

- Design a stairway to enhance the experience of a change in level. As people progress through the home, utilize interior windows that overlook activities in the residence or windows that capture outdoor views and changing elevations.

Warren Diggles Photography/Jon Rentfrow, Rentfrow Design, LLC

ShortPhotos/Shutterstock.com

Figure 15-7 Stairways, such as these spiral and curved stairways, add height and drama to a space.

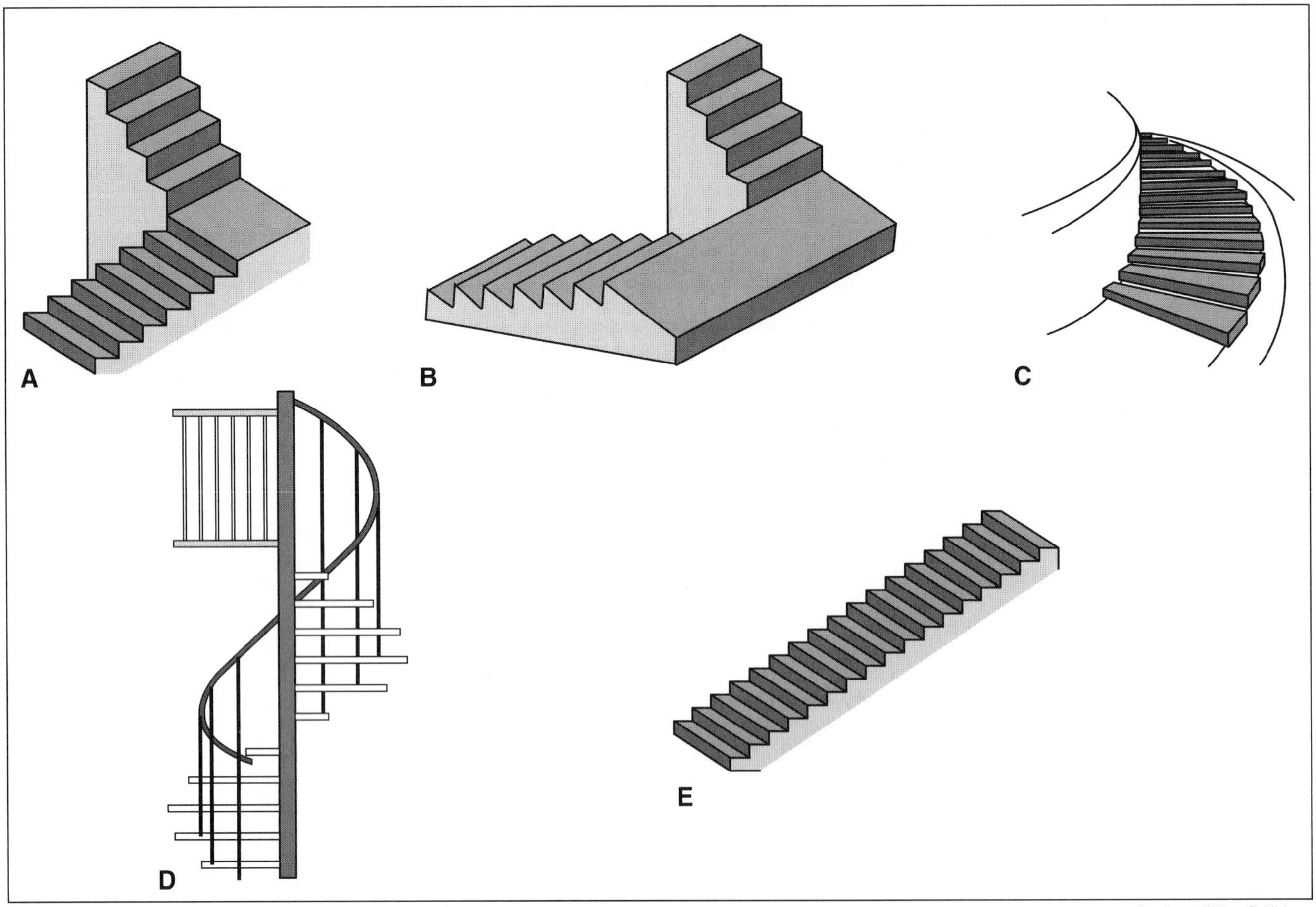

Goodheart-Willcox Publisher

Figure 15-8 Basic types of stairways include the L-shaped (A), U-shaped (B), curved (C), spiral (D), and straight (E).

DESIGNER MATH SKILLS

Residential Wheelchair Ramp—ADA Standards

Commercial facilities must comply with ADA standards for wheelchair accessibility, but compliance is not required for residential properties. Because the accessibility standards are designed for commercial compliance and a broad range of users, they are a reliable resource for construction of a wheelchair ramp at a person's home.

ADA specifications address the rise needed for a ramp which in turn dictates the length and space needed for installation. The *ADA Accessibility Wheelchair Ramp Standards* that are most useful to residential design require:

- ***A ratio of 1:12 which indicates 1 inch rise to every 12 inches of ramp length/run.*** The ADA 1:12 ratio creates an 8.3% grade or slope and is the recommended maximum steepness or slope for an unassisted wheelchair user. The disability, strength, and stamina of a particular person will determine the appropriateness of that slope and distance. The less slope (1:16, 1:20), the better.
- ***A minimum 5 feet by 5 feet flat, level unobstructed area at the top and bottom of the ramp.*** The unobstructed areas must be at least as wide as the ramp leading to them. *Note*: A wheelchair needs to be on a level surface when turning. It can become unstable turning on a sloped area.
- ***A minimum 36 inches in ramp width of unobstructed space.*** a. A width of 60 inches is necessary for wheelchairs to pass side-by-side on a ramp, a sidewalk, or in a hallway.
- ***A maximum run of 30 feet before a rest or turn platform.*** Rest or turn platforms must be least the width of the ramp leading to it and a minimum length of 60 inches. Ramps that change direction between runs at landings must be a minimum size of 5 feet x 5 feet. The length of a single ramp cannot exceed 30 feet. Therefore, the maximum rise of a ramp would be 30 inches before a landing or turn platform would be required.
- ***Handrails for adults are between 34 inches and 38 inches to the top of the gripping area on both sides of the ramp.*** If children are the primary users of a ramp, a second railing would be installed at a maximum height of 28 inches. A 9 inch minimum clearance between the railings helps prevent entrapment.
- ***Handrails shall extend horizontally 12 inches beyond the end of the ramp.*** They should either be rounded or return smoothly to the floor, wall, or post.

Calculating Ramp Ratio

To calculate ramp ratio, take two measurements including the *ramp rise* and the *ramp length*. Convert both numbers into a common unit such as inches and/or feet. Use the following formula to calculate ramp ratio:
ramp length (inches) ÷ ramp rise (inches) = ramp ratio

Example 1:
360″ (30′) ramp length ÷ 30″ ramp rise = 1:12 ramp ratio
(*Note*: every 1″ of ramp rise = 12″ of ramp length)

Example 2:
240″ (20′) ramp length ÷ 15″ ramp rise = 1:16 ramp ratio
(*Note*: every 1″ of ramp rise = 16″ of ramp length)

Calculating Slope Grade

To calculate the slope grade (steepness), use the ramp rise and ramp length and the following formula:
ramp rise (inches) ÷ ramp length (inches) × 100% = % slope grade

Example 1:
30″ rise ÷ 360″ ramp length × 100% = 8.33333% slope grade

Example 2:
15″ rise ÷ 240″ ramp length × 100% = 6.25% slope grade

The higher the percentage is, the steeper the slope. The lower the percentage, the less steep the slope.

Manufacturers now sell ADA-compliant ramps of many materials depending on the client's needs. It is important for designers to research the ramp best suited to the need of the individual and the property. You should be mindful of the age, health, and ability levels of the individuals, family members, and caretakers using the ramp.

Property and interior factors to consider include the *site arrival point* (for arrival to or departure from the property such as the garage, driveway, or curb), the path of travel to the entrances, entrance door widths, and accessibility once inside the home using this entrance.

Obstacles can include curbing, the distance from vehicles to the residence, the lack of sidewalks connecting the site arrival point and the ramp, the composition of sidewalk and driveway surfaces, and surface disturbances caused by tree roots, landscaping and drainage that can create puddles and icy areas. Attention to details increases the overall health, safety, and welfare of those using the ramp.

- Incorporate a window seat into a larger-than-typical landing to give people a resting point.
- Provide natural light. It enhances safety during the day and provides interest in the stairwell in the evening.
- Open a stairway, particularly at the lower level. To do this, remove part of the full-height wall and replace it with a handrail to increase the sense of volume in the space.
- Use the space below stairways to create play areas, nooks, a small home office, or useful storage.
- Add dramatic lighting to a stairway to enhance its sculptural design in the evening.

Space Planning Analysis

Stairways

Questions to ask about space planning for stairways include

- Is the stairway centrally located for efficient usage?
- Does the stairway comply with local building codes, including the use of a handrail?
- Is the stairway arriving into a central grouping of rooms?
- How can the stairway offer new architectural or design elements to the space?
- Is lighting located at the top and bottom of the stairway?
- How could a view to the outside and/or natural light be incorporated into the stairway?

Living Room

The formal living room, a minimum of 10 feet by 14 feet, is often located in the front of the house off the main entry. It can be small and intimate or quite large depending on the number of people who use it, how and when it is used, and the furniture the client and designer intend for placement in the space.

At times, a designer may include an adjacent patio, porch, deck, or balcony off the living room to convey a spacious feeling, **Figure 15-9**. A change in floor level can set the living room apart from other areas of the home, but may become a barrier for a person with a physical disability.

Three activity areas are commonly designed into a living room. They include

- **Primary grouping.** Designers often group furniture, such as chairs and sofas, in a **conversation grouping** to enhance a room's focal point. Comfortable seating enhances conversation when the grouping is no more than five feet apart.

  Culturally, people determine sincerity and honesty if they can look into the eyes of those with whom they are talking. Seating that is too far apart halts conversation, creating awkwardness for guests. Provide at least one arm chair with a firm seat. Older guests often need the arms to help get to their feet after visiting with you.
- **Secondary grouping.** A secondary furniture grouping supports the primary grouping and seats two or three people. If it is not a conversation grouping, it may contain a desk or reading chair.
- **Entertainment grouping.** Pianos or other instruments can be located in the living room. Placement of a piano away from outside walls is important for keeping the piano in tune. The temperature fluctuations near outside walls can easily cause a piano to get out of tune.

Photo by: Brian Gassel Photography/Design by: Lita Dirks & Co.

Figure 15-9 A living room is often located in the front of the home adjacent to the front entry. *Examine this image. Which activity groupings are designed into this space?*

Space Planning Analysis

Living Rooms

Questions to ask during space planning for living rooms include

- Where is the focal point in the room?
- What are the ages of those using the living room?
- Is it a formal or more informal space?
- Does the client prefer formal or informal seating arrangements?
- Can a bay window, large picture window, or French doors connect individuals to outside?
- Does the hallway go through the living room?
- Are doorways or entries grouped in the living room corner to avoid cross-circulation problems?
- Does the living room have semi-privacy?
- What types of storage are necessary to support activities in the space?
- What types of lighting enhance the space? Can the designer incorporate dimmers to add control of light levels for the occupants?

Family Rooms and Great Rooms

The family room is an American invention resulting after World War II to create a space for the televisions many families were acquiring. The *great room* or hearth room is an area that combines three spaces: kitchen, dining, and family room. Its typical location is directly off the mudroom or laundry room.

The great room can offer areas for family meals and a snack bar; comfortable seating for conversation, music, television, and homework; and such office tasks as bookkeeping or e-mail management. Due to the number of activities, the great room is larger than a formal living room and often boasts a high ceiling and views to the outside, **Figure 15-10**. Taller spaces can be difficult to bring down to a human scale. A few suggestions to use

Photo by: Fred Forbes Photogroupe/Design by: Lita Dirks & Co.

Figure 15-10 The great room is a space that combines three living areas—the kitchen, dining, and family rooms. *Can a great room have too much going on in it? Why or why not?*

when creating a more intimate living space in a great room include

- using furniture that looks visually heavier and solid looking
- adding area rugs to visually break up the floor space
- using large-scaled artwork
- creating multiple furniture groupings
- including horizontal architectural elements such as plant shelves

Space Planning Analysis

Great Room

Questions to ask during the space planning of a great room include

- Is the space location off the mudroom and laundry room?
- If included, can a kitchen table fit into the space with the chairs pulled out?
- Does the client desire the incorporation of a fireplace? How can the designer enhance this focal point?
- Is the kitchen island area large enough for preferred tasks and/or seating?
- Does the space require the addition of a small sitting area?
- Do circulation patterns dissect the room? In other words, is a *major traffic pattern* going through the center of the space?
- What are some ways to capture more views?
- Is a variety of light planned into the space to support all activities?

Dining

People eat everywhere—in the kitchen, family room, outdoors, and in bedrooms. To some, eating is a social event with friends and family. To others, it is an art form. Historically, middle-class families never ate in the kitchen—they ate in the parlor. Today, the residence may provide three dining areas—an informal table or island in the kitchen and a more formal place in the dining room. The formal area generally encourages formal behavior, **Figure 15-11**. With the advent

ShortPhotos/Shutterstock.com

Warren Diggles Photography/Jon Rentfrow, Rentfrow Design, LLC

romakoma/Shutterstock.com

Figure 15-11 The number of people to be served in the dining room impacts the room size and table size to be used in a space.

of low-to-mid priced housing, the formal dining room is starting to disappear. The trend today is for an open connection between the kitchen and dining room and between the dining room and living room.

The ideal size for a dining room is determined by the number of people to be served at one time, including necessary furniture. Here are a few guidelines to follow. Seating for

- four people requires a minimum room size of eight feet by 10 feet
- six people requires a minimum room size of 12 feet by 8 feet
- six people using a round table requires a minimum room size of 10 feet in diameter.
- eight people with a rectangular table requires a minimum room size of eight feet wide by 13 to 16 feet in length

Space Planning Analysis

Dining Rooms

Questions to ask about space planning for dining rooms include

- How many people does the client expect for a typical meal?
- How formal does the client want the space to feel?
- Is the dining room adjoining the kitchen and living room?
- Is there enough circulation space around the dining table and chairs?
- Do people have to go through a room to get to the dining room? (This is a pattern to avoid.)
- Does the client prefer the dining room close to the entry?
- What shape and what are the dimensions of the table?

Guest Bath

Typically available for guest use, a *half-bath*—or powder room—includes a sink and toilet but not a shower or bathtub. Many clients use this small, but critical space to express a strong mood or feeling different from other parts of the residence. Specialty sinks and toilets, dramatic lighting, and fun colors are commonly used.

Space Planning Analysis

Half Bath

Questions to ask about space planning for a half bath include

- Is the half bath accessible from the entry for guests? It should not be located in private areas of the residence.
- Is the toilet out of view if the door is open?
- Does the door open into a public room? If so, change location of doorway.
- Does the room offer privacy for the user?
- What type of mood does the client prefer for this space?

Outdoor Living Spaces

Today, the increasing and popular use of outdoor living spaces, outdoor rooms, courtyards, and atriums reflect the desire of people to spend more time outdoors. The popular phrase, "bring the outside in" has switched to "bring the inside out." Creating a relaxing, stylish outdoor living space enhances livability and comfort of those living in the residence.

Most people desire a connection to nature, so it is best to design doors, decks, porches, and terraces to take advantage of key exterior features. Natural surroundings help alleviate stress and can offer a restorative environment for all people. Many people derive visual pleasure from continual awareness of the changing sun, wind, sky, and landscape.

Outdoor living has become an extension of the indoors with many of the same amenities. Although outdoors, these spaces fit the definition of a room, with such necessities as floors, ceilings, and walls. Types of living spaces include the sleeping porch, outdoor family room, and the most popular—an outdoor kitchen. The outdoor kitchen often shares a wall with the indoor kitchen from which to pull water, gas, and electrical lines.

Outdoor living spaces are planned around geographical location and weather. Some residents live in tropical zones, so they can plan their outdoor living spaces with only one season in mind—summer. For other individuals, three to four seasons are a consideration in making the most of the outdoor investment. In addition to weather, there are several other considerations when planning this space, **Figure 15-12**. These include

Damon Searles Photography/Aneka Interiors, Inc.

bikeriderlondon/Shutterstock.com

zstock/Shutterstock.com

Figure 15-12 Outdoor living spaces offer a connection to nature and expand indoor living to the outdoors. *What factors should a designer consider when planning outdoor living spaces for their clients?*

- **Size.** What size outdoor living space does the client desire? Does the client want a large area in which to entertain or a small private refuge?
- **Lighting.** The right kind of lighting can enhance the space—both outside and inside—and can make a fun statement. Rust-resistant finishes on metal fixtures like chandeliers and sconces are attractive. Wood fixtures such as tiki torches offer flickering light while solar-powered LEDs offer drama and safety. Underwater lighting, playful party lights, and lighting in nearby trees also mimics nature's feeling of complexity and mystery in the space.
- **Enclosure.** Many clients want the space partially enclosed. How much enclosure and what type do the client desire? Draperies frame and give privacy to a deck or patio while gently filtering sunlight and the breeze. Retractable windows allow a space to be open when weather is mild. Many people desire walls around their outdoor space for privacy. Hedges, fencing, half walls, and columns serve as adequate obstructions.

Link to History

The Chinese Courtyard Residence

Courtyards are a type of outdoor living space. Historically, the population of early China had many clans in rivalry with each other. The ability of a clan to claim land enhanced its strength and power. To gain such power, a son and part of the family household was sent to an area with few people to build a city. In early China, building a new city was comparable to the building of a new family residence.

The family would build a Chinese courtyard residence, or the *siheyuan (suh-huh-ywaaan)*, meaning "court joined on four sides." The walls formed the courtyard boundaries on four sides. Within and adjoining these walls was a group of structures characterized by rectilinear lines in an organized, hierarchical format.

The son—serving as ruler—lived in the central dwelling of the structure. Extended family members, the ruler's subjects (who were socially subservient to the ruler), lived in structures located in a circular fashion around the ruler's central residence. Often, more than one courtyard was created by the placement of the structures.

Documents dating back to two thousand years B.C., illustrate an amazing consistency of this type of layout from city to city. For example, the *Forbidden City*, located in the center of modern-day Beijing, depicts this layout. Throughout China's long history, the pattern of the siheyuan is repeated multiple times in imperial city plans.

walkdragon/Shutterstock.com

Analyze It!

Use reliable Internet resources to further investigate and analyze how other cultures used a courtyard structure similar to siheyuan. Were these structures built in a hierarchical form as was the siheyuan? If possible, locate pictorial examples and discuss your findings with the class.

- **Egress.** Clients may desire varying types of egress to move to their outdoor spaces. Doors from indoor to outdoor living spaces include slider, accordion, and roller. Developing transparency from inside to outside is easy as walls completely disappear with the push of a button.
- **Shade.** Umbrellas, canopies, and awnings—whether fixed or retractable—can extend leisure time outdoors by adding much needed shade to a sun-drenched patio.
- **Garden feature.** Many clients desire to add flower gardens or areas for vegetable and fruit gardening.
- **Water feature.** Will the sound of water splashing be therapeutic or annoying? Water features add beauty to an exterior space and provide an extra level of comfort. Fountains, pools, and waterfalls are popular options. A trendy choice is a spa/pool, which can be a cooling pool in the heat and a soothing hot tub in the cold.
- **Fireplace.** Outdoor fireplaces allow for fun or relaxation to continue into the night or colder seasons of the year. They are available as permanent structures or portable models.

Space Planning Analysis

Outdoor Spaces

Questions to ask about outdoor space planning include

- Is the space accessible from the living room, kitchen, or family room?
- How close are the neighbors? Can the designer arrange adequate privacy with walls, curtains, or hedges?
- Do gas, electrical, or water lines need to be extended from the house?
- How large does the client want doorways to be from indoor spaces?
- How can furniture groupings relate to activities?
- Is shade needed or preferred?

Amenities for outdoor living spaces can also include durable, well-designed furniture, architectural features such as columns, roofed porches, pergolas, draped gazebos, arches, and fireplaces. According to a recent survey by the *American Society of Landscape Architects (ASLA)*, the following items are some of consumers' favorite outdoor amenities in order of preference:

- decorative water elements
- spas—including hot tubs, Jacuzzis, and indoor/outdoor saunas
- swimming pools
- utility storage
- stereo systems
- sinks
- refrigerators
- sports/recreational spaces, such as tennis and bocce ball courts
- wireless/Internet connectivity
- television/projection screens
- outdoor heaters
- showers/bathing
- outdoor cooling systems, including fans
- bedrooms/sleeping spaces

Private Zones

A residence offers an opportunity for restoration and renewal of energy. **Private zones** or spaces are those allocated to private living. People need privacy when ill, grieving, tired, anxious, and for rejuvenation. The two types of privacy most homes require are *solitude*, to enhance creativity and contemplation, and *familiarity* that contributes to recovery and respite. These types of privacy are often only available in the bedroom spaces.

Bedrooms

Today, the bedroom is a place of privacy and seclusion. It is used as a private retreat from the demands of everyday life—work, school, and family. Bedrooms serve two basic functions: sleeping and storage for private items. Privacy from sight and sound are also important bedroom preferences, **Figure 15-13**.

Bedrooms or sleeping areas can vary in size and physical layout. Other than the master suite, today's trends encourage smaller bedrooms. They are clustered and zoned in the same location within the residence or planned with the master bedroom separated from others for greater privacy. If possible, place a **flex room**—a room typically near the front entry or kitchen entry—on the first floor of the residence. This room can serve as a home office, child's playroom, music room, or with the addition of a closet can become a main-floor bedroom to conveniently care for a sick person or aging adult.

Although today's bedrooms serve as a retreat because of separation from the rest of the home, this is not the case with all cultures. Some Native American families use the living space as a communal sleeping area. Similarly, in Japan, some families roll out mats on the floor for communal sleeping and roll them up in the morning.

Photo by: Brian Gassel Photography/Design by: Lita Dirks & Co.

PlusONE/Shutterstock.com

Figure 15-13 Bedrooms serve as a retreat—a place of privacy and seclusion. *What factors should designers consider when making bedrooms functional for the users?*

Some U.S. dwellings have no formal bedrooms, but instead have designated sleeping areas, such as lofts. Smaller residences use convertible beds, such as **Murphy beds** that pull down for sleeping and later fold up into a closet for out-of-the-way storage. Bedrooms sometimes double as small offices, exercise rooms, craft and sewing spaces, spa areas, meditation areas, and guest rooms. **Figure 15-14** illustrates the minimum layout for basic bedrooms.

Inclusive Bedroom Details

Inclusive design in the bedroom impacts the circulation space, doors, closets, lighting, location of outlets, and walls. Here are a few suggestions to ensure your client's home is inclusive.

Starting at the interior walls, specify wall backing next to the bed (and elsewhere as preferred) for grab-bar or medical-device support. Reinforce the ceiling to allow for future installations of lifts or devices with 500–600 pound capacity.

Specify additional electrical outlets throughout the room to accommodate equipment needs. Provide a variety of light sources and controls. Offer adjustable shelving heights in closets or cabinets. Suggest walk-in or roll-in closets. Design in pocket doors if possible. Ensure there is at least 36 inches of clearance space on each side of the bed. To allow room for mobility devices, provide a five-foot (60 inch) turning radius in key areas of the bedroom such as in front or next to the closet.

Bedrooms for Children and Teens

One very creative, yet safe sanctuary of the house can be a child's bedroom. A child's curiosity and imaginative fantasy can be encouraged by designing safe yet enjoyable places in which to explore and learn.

Children's bedrooms do not need to be large. In fact, small, cozy spaces that relate to their human scale, such as an empty closet, a space under a stairwell, a window seat, or a storage room—with child-size scale and dimensions—is often preferred.

To accommodate a single bed, storage and chair or table, the minimum size bedroom can be as small as 10'-0" × 10'-0". If children share the space, it need only be slightly larger.

An increasing trend that impacts children's bedrooms is the presence of grandparents living in the home. Many are raising their grandchildren as one or both parents work outside the home. This trend affects design decisions since the designer is working with both the aging adult and young children.

Another trend that influences the design of children's bedrooms includes the needs of children in blended families. When possible, the designer should talk directly with the children to determine their needs and desires in this specialty area of design.

Basic needs that a child's bedroom should meet are safety, sleeping, storing, studying, and recovering from illness. The bedroom needs of children change as they grow. Designing with future needs in mind should be a consideration, **Figure 15-15.** Flexibility, creativity, and

mates/shutterstock.com

Figure 15-14 Basic bedroom configurations provide adequate space for functionality.

Rodenbery Photography/Shutterstock.com

Figure 15-15 Although children's bedrooms do not need to be large, interior designers must consider future needs when planning the space.

Space Planning Analysis

Bedrooms

Space planning questions for bedrooms include

- How many people will the private or joint bedroom accommodate? What are their ages?
- Is a bedroom for overnight guests or live-in relatives a need?
- Is the proximity of the bedroom close to a bathroom?
- Is the bedroom area in a quiet zone of the house to maintain acoustical privacy?
- In addition to sleeping, what other functions does the space need to accommodate?
- Are windows located to allow for cross-ventilation, if desired?
- Are clothes closets a minimum of two feet deep? Are they located right next to the bedroom door to avoid extra steps?
- Is there 15 inches of open space along the side of the bed closest to the wall for ease in bed-making?
- Where are infant or children bedrooms in relationship to the master bedroom? Are parent(s) close enough to hear an upset child?
- Is there an egress window for fire emergencies? Is the size to code?
- Is there a bedroom door that opens directly to the hallway? A person should not have to pass through one bedroom to reach another.
- Do bedroom doors swing into other doors? Is a pocket door a better option?
- Is there wall space for the bed(s) or are all walls taken up with closets and windows?

adjustability are keys to planning. Suggestions for a child's bedroom include

- a bed, or popular safe bunk-bed design to efficiently use space
- a bathroom access one room away, if possible
- a study/craft/computer area for learning and self-expression
- an abundant natural light and access to fresh air to sets child's biorhythms
- acoustical privacy to assist with enhanced sleeping patterns
- durable, easily maintained finishes
- ample storage with labeled or color coded areas designed into the space to encourage independence and organization
- clothes closets with repositioned clothing hooks and closet rods within children's reach allowing them to take care of their own clothing

As children evolve into teens, their bedrooms continue to serve as a sanctuary and place of self-expression. Whereas safety is a primary need in a young child's bedroom, *privacy* is the most critical need for a teen. Teen bedrooms are often a private place to study, reflect on life, and ponder personal values. It is important that teen spaces support organizational skills and academic skills, as well as decision-making skills and personal independence.

Teens like to choose how to decorate or rearrange their rooms to reflect their identities and personalities. Statistics indicate that they often watch design-related reality shows with cult-like passion. Teens have many ideas about what they want their spaces to look like.

Allowing teens to participate in making decisions about their rooms (or their part of a shared room), helps them develop a sense of pride, independence, and responsibility. To encourage a sense that the space is their own, enlist teens in the design of the space. Teen needs include

- study space
- grooming area
- bed
- table
- durable finishes
- soft surfaces
- a comfortable chair or beanbag, if possible
- privacy
- storage
- natural daylight

There is no one ideal method for designing spaces for children and teens. By considering the needs of each child and available resources, families can encourage desirable behaviors, foster learning, skill development, responsibility, and prevent potential conflicts.

The Master Suite

The master suite, especially for people with young children, is a private sanctuary and retreat. Similar to other bedrooms, it is a place for relaxation and sleep. The design of the master suite serves as a private oasis and one of the luxurious spaces of the home.

The master suite is one area in which to invest money with an assurance of a return on dollars spent if reselling the home. A bit of upscale luxury in the master suite is a major trend, perhaps because two-career couples feel they need a private place to unwind after a long day.

Sometimes the master suite is a type of mini-apartment. It will incorporate amenities such as the following:

- space for seating (for instance, a single chair/ottoman or chaise lounge), **Figure 15-16**
- an area for entertainment
- a small home office desk
- exercise equipment, spa facilities, or sauna area
- bookshelves for reading
- fireplace area
- window with a great view
- dual closets or double walk-in closets with built-in closet organization units
- access to the master bath suite

Rodenbery Photography/Shutterstock.com

Figure 15-16 The master suite is a private sanctuary and retreat as well as a place for sleeping and relaxation. *Why is the master suite often one area in which client's invest more money?*

Master suite closets are sometimes bigger than the bedroom itself. They can be linear or a walk-in space. Walk-in closets often include shelving, shoe racks, dressers, sitting stools, and drawers, **Figure 15-17**. In addition, such closets may include islands for folding

MR. INTERIOR/Shutterstock.com gualitiero boffi/Shutterstock.com

Figure 15-17 Closets in master suites vary in size and shape and often include shelving, shoe racks, and drawers.

clothes, cedar-lined areas, specialty jewelry drawers, mirrors, and a variety of hanging devices. Closets such as these require a minimum of 12 to 18 feet of space.

The master bathroom suite commonly called an **en suite bathroom**, adjoins the bedroom and has space that includes five functional pieces—dual sinks, shower stall, tub, and toilet room, **Figure 15-18**. The bathroom suite is often a dramatic space with a spa-like atmosphere which includes specialty lighting, luxurious materials, and design elements that evoke serenity and relaxation.

Hark back to ancient times when Roman baths were a popular aspect of daily life, the master bathroom can include massage tables, soaking tubs, steam-shower rooms or saunas, and tubs that utilize **chromatherapy**, or the use of colored light to create soothing effects. The master bath often has floor-to-ceiling tile work, wall-mounted fixtures, a freestanding tub, and a feeling of serenity. Master bathroom suites often include

- a whirlpool or spa tub
- a roomy shower stall with dual shower heads
- a toilet in a small room or closet with good lighting and ventilation fans
- closet or dressing areas adjoining the master bathroom
- double vanities at standing height with large mirrors and custom storage **Figure 15-19**
- a sit-down vanity area with drawers and cabinets
- drawers and cabinets for bathroom linens, supplies, and personal care items
- windows with a view (include window shades for privacy)
- a wet or dry sauna or massage area
- warming towel bars or flooring with radiant heat
- exercise equipment
- lounging furniture
- coffee and beverage center
- refrigeration space for makeup
- telephone, flat-screen television, and surround sound for music (waterproof electronics are widely available)

Tubs are frequently located in the center of the bathroom or along a window wall. They are available in all shapes, designs, and sizes. The design of soaker tubs is trending to smaller, shallower sizes to offer more water efficiency, although the large luxurious ones are still popular. A sunken tub is safer than stepping *up* to the tub, which is treacherous when stairs are wet. Candles, dimmable lighting, and a waterfall faucet are all part of the luxurious experience in today's master bathroom suites.

Most master bathroom showers offer controls near the door, an interior seat, storage shelving for soaps or other personal items, and fun shower heads with different spray options and shapes. Incorporating unique tile or stone designs into spaces helps add interest. Support bars on the outside of the shower stall are useful to prevent accidents.

Interior designer: JJ Interiors/Photography: Ron Ruscio Photography

Figure 15-18 Often a dramatic, spa-like space, the atmosphere of the en suite bathroom evokes a feeling of relaxation.

Damon Searles Photography/Aneka Interiors, Inc.

Photography by: Courtney Ebert, Choate Construction Company/Rabaut Design Associates

Figure 15-19 Double vanities and large mirrors enhance the functionality of the master bathroom.

Space Planning Analysis

Master Suite

Space planning questions for the master suite include

- What size do you want this space?
- Will you be using a king or queen size bed?
- Do you prefer end tables or do you want built-ins?
- Do you want to include a fitness area in the bedroom?
- Do you want a flat-screen or computer area included?
- What type of seating do you want in the bedroom? bench? chaise? two club chairs with ottomans?
- How much storage and what type of storage do you need in the bedroom and bathroom?
- Do you want separate closets or one larger closet?
- What type of lighting controls do you want in the room and near the bed?
- Where are the views?
- Are there any views? If so, on what wall?
- Do you want to include a tub or larger shower? If a shower, do you want a seat? Double shower heads?
- Would you prefer drawers or doors for the base cabinet in the master bath?
- Do you want the toilet to have a separate room?
- What type of finishes do you want on the floor in the bathroom?
- What type of technologies do you want to include in the bedroom and bathroom?
- Do you want a small beverage area in the bedroom for morning coffee or juice? How much counter space do you need in the bathroom?
- Do you want a center to apply makeup?

Bathrooms

At one time, a small, sterile room with three basic plumbing fixtures to meet basic hygiene needs has become a powder room, a dressing room, and sitting a room. Bathroom design revolves around the tub, toilet, and sink. In addition to function, the bathroom offers privacy and an opportunity for restful experiences such as soaking and meditation.

Many homes have more than one bathroom. Some may have half- or three-quarter baths. Activities include bathing, applying makeup, and dressing. The best placement of bathrooms is close to bedrooms. Here are common descriptions and diagrams of bathroom plans, **Figure 15-20**.

- **Half bath**—includes only a toilet and sink (also called *powder room* as discussed earlier); minimum dimensions are typically 5'-6" long × 3'-0" wide
- **Three-quarter bath**—includes a toilet, sink, and shower; minimum dimensions are 6'-0" × 6'-0"
- **Full bath**—includes all of the above plus a tub; minimum bathroom dimensions are 5'-0" wide × 8'-0" long

A **Jack and Jill bathroom** has two or more entrances. Typically, the entrances are from two bedrooms on either side of the bathroom, although there might be one entrance from a bedroom and one entrance from the corridor.

Other bathroom vocabulary terms and definitions to know include

- *Lavatory*—sink (individual or trough) or washbasin
- *Fixture*—an object firmly fixed in place; connected to existing plumbing system and include the bathtub, sink, toilet and shower
- *Toilet*—also called water closets (WC), loos (in Britain) or flush toilets
- *Bidet*—a low oval basin to wash an individual's private parts
- *Vanity*—a unit comprised of a bathroom sink surrounded by storage furniture

Designing a bathroom occurs in a series of steps and should take into consideration the client's hygiene, safety, ergonomics, and storage. The designer addresses the client's preferences for visual style as well as their functional goals. Code compliance is essential for bathrooms and kitchens.

Configurations of bedrooms often merge with bathroom design. Location of doors, vanities, and tub areas makes a difference in the efficiency for users especially on busy mornings. See **Figure 15-21** for standard dimensions for bathroom fixtures.

Space planning suggestions for bathrooms include the following:

- Compartmentalize the bathroom with a door between the sink and the remainder of bathroom.
- Place the toilet in a small room.
- Use double sinks. If this is undesirable, use a longer counter with single sink.
- Place a small bathroom between two bedrooms with an access door on each side.
- Put the bathtub and shower in separate areas.
- Plan doorways so that toilets are not in plain view.

Inclusive Bathroom Design

For aging individuals, people who are short in stature, or those who have disabilities, include lever-style door handles, slip-resistant flooring, and thermostatically controlled faucets to prevent scalding. For people who need an accessible bathroom, specify the following in the design plan:

- a clear, hard-surface flooring (such as slip-resistant tile) measuring at least 30 inches by 48 inches; in-floor heating
- turning radius of 60 inches of space to accommodate a wheelchair
- sink, toilet, and urinal mounting heights compliant with the local building code (toilet-seat heights 17 to 19 inches above the finished floor, flush controls on the open side of the toilet with clear floor space, and mounted no higher than 44 inches above the finished floor)
- clearance space of 40 inches to enter the bathroom
- pocket doors for greater clearance
- towel bars mounted at varying heights
- easy-to-operate controls for windows, lighting, and fixtures
- mirror placed at height for seated person
- grab bars near the toilet and roll-in shower
- knobs, levers, and push-buttons operable with one hand without twisting the wrist

Half Bath

Photography by Audrey Hall/Interiors by Associates III Interior Design

Three-quarter Bath

Image Courtesy of Cathers Home Interior Architecture Firm, Basalt, Colorado/Photographer: Michael Hefferon.

Full Bath

Image Courtesy of Cathers Home Interior Architecture Firm, Basalt, Colorado/Photographer: Michael Hefferon.

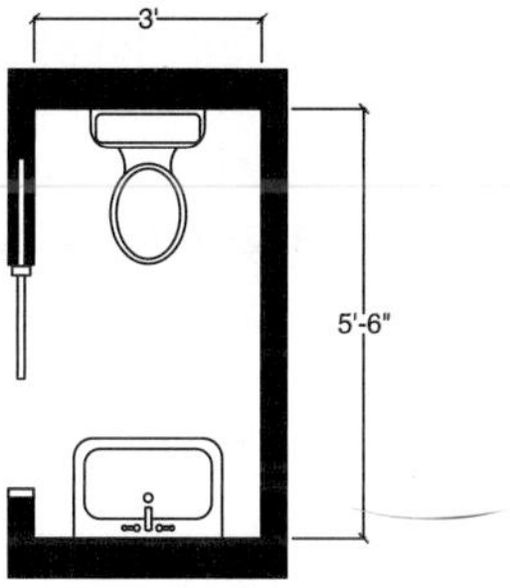

Half Bathroom
Julia Harmon, sophomore, Colorado State University

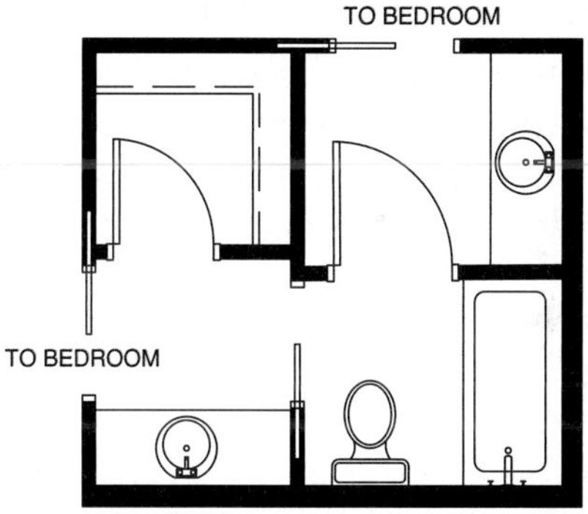

Jack and Jill Bath Christine Apple, senior, Colorado State University

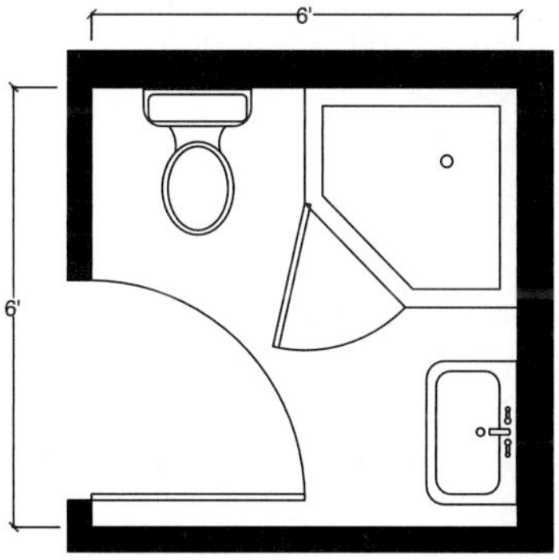

Three Quarter Bathroom
Christine Apple, senior, Colorado State University

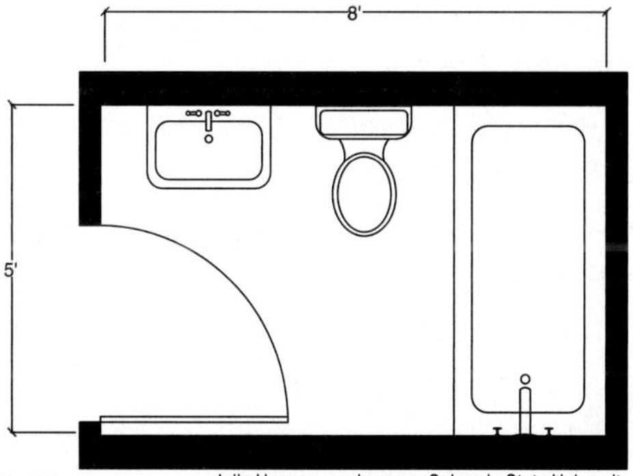

Full Bathroom Julia Harmon, sophomore, Colorado State University

Figure 15-20 With the exception of the half bath, bathrooms are typically located near the bedrooms in a residence. *What factors must the designer consider when planning client bathroom spaces?*

Standard Dimensions for Bathroom Fixtures

The *American National Standards Institute (ANSI)* published by the International Code Council provides technical standards and design guidelines for making buildings accessible to all people. ANSI A117.1 standards apply to the design and construction of new buildings and the remodeling or alteration of existing construction. Americans with Disabilities Act (ADA) guidelines fall within this realm. Here are a few ANSI standards for bathroom fixtures.

Bathroom Fixture	Standard Dimensions
Standard Single Vanity (single sink)	■ 24" deep ■ 30" to 43" high (*Note*: As a comparison, standard kitchen worktops are 36" high and 24" deep.)
Standard Double Vanity (double sinks)	■ 24" deep ■ 30" to 43" high ■ 76" wide (recommended) with 36" between the two washbasins (18" from each side of the center line to each basin)
Bathtub	■ 54" to 72" in length (standard length is 60" or 5') ■ 30" wide (standard width) (*Note*: The smallest standard bathtub is 5' feet long by 2.5' feet wide or 60" by 30".)
Standard Toilet	■ 16" deep from hinges to front edge; overall depth including toilet tank is 26" ■ 17" to 19" seat height from floor to seat
Elongated Toilet	■ 18" deep from hinges to front edge; overall depth including toilet tank is about 29" ■ 17" to 19" seat height from floor to seat
Shower	■ 36" by 36"—standard shower ■ 36" by 48"—rectangular shower (recommended dimensions) ■ 32" by 32"—smallest shower (*Note*: Shower door hinges face outward.)
Clearances for Fixtures	
Overall Clearances	■ 30" by 48" clear floor space at each fixture
Toilet, Bidet, Sink, Tub	■ 21" minimum in front of fixtures ■ 30" to 42" preferable in front of tub
Sink	■ 30" of clearance
Shower	■ 24" of clearance in front of shower entrance
Accessible Shower Compartment	■ 60" clearance next to shower opening, the length of the shower ■ 60" diameter, minimum turning radius for wheelchair

Universal Shower Features

- **Seating:** Include a stationary built-in shower bench or fold-down seat.
- **Grab bars:** For accessible showers, locate grab bars at the shower entry and install them horizontally at 33" to 36" above the floor on all three walls (do not put behind seat). Installation of support blocking in framed walls is essential to support weight placed on grab bar when used. For accessible toilets, provide grab bars on the rear wall and sidewall closest to the toilet *(NOTE: The sidewall grab bar should be at least 42" long and located between 12" and 54" from the rear wall.)*
- **Lighting:** Use overhead lighting.
- **Thermostatic faucet (water valve):** Use a valve that prevents scalding when in use.
- **Shower controls:** Install an adjustable handheld shower spray to offer maximum flexibility. Place the handheld shower within reach of the shower seat and outside the shower.

Figure 15-21 Standard guidelines for bathroom fixtures include standard dimensions.

Bathroom Trends

Bathroom trends include natural daylight, natural materials, free-standing furniture (chest or table), open walk-in frameless, clear-glass showers, unusual sink shapes, and a tranquil, spa-like influence. With day spas and spa hotels greatly influencing the desire for features that enhance relaxation and renewal, interior designers and architects are responding by incorporating such features as saunas, whirlpool baths, steam showers, and hot tubs into their designs. In addition, many bathrooms include a makeup vanity, toe-kick lighting, workout spaces linked with bathrooms, and toilet/bidet combinations.

Many high-end bathrooms are incorporating **hotel glam** which means incorporating glamorous hotel details such as a big, bright space that creates an illusion of extra space through large, back-lit cabinet mirrors, and zesty details like a zebra print on the bathtub.

Space Planning Analysis

Bathrooms

Questions to ask a client about space planning for bathrooms include

- How many people will use the bathroom? Who and when?
- Will the bathroom include facilities for laundry or sauna?
- Are plumbing fixtures arranged in an efficient manner? Could they be all placed along one plumbing wall, or is a centrally-placed tub desired?
- Is there an operable window (if possible) in each bathroom to offer views and fresh air?
- Is there need for a dual sink or a trough sink? See **Figure 15-22 A.**
- Is the toilet placed so it is not visible through an open door?
- Is there adequate storage located in convenient locations?
- Is there a preference for standard or tall vanity counters?
- Does the client prefer a pedestal sink?
- How is the shower or tub design going to incorporate into the space? See **Figure 15-22 B**.
- Do accessibility issues need to be addressed?
- Is there a place for soiled linens?
- Is there a place to hang a towel and bathrobe not more than one foot from the shower?

Fitness Areas

Continuing integration of private fitness or workout areas in the home is a reflection of peoples' health consciousness. The interior designer may gear the design of such spaces toward personal fitness regimens set by a casual recreational user, sport-related goals set by a serious athlete, or physical therapy needs.

Fitness areas in a condominium may be as simple as a treadmill and free weights. More extensive work-out areas include equipment based on personal interests such as spinning, yoga, martial arts, cardiovascular training, weight training, and swimming.

Other amenities may include flat-screen televisions, saunas, cool-down areas, lockers, steam rooms, and hot tubs. Mirrors, water coolers, towel storage, and mats are often part of fitness space designs. Many fitness companies are moving to wireless access for owner's access to computerized, interactive fitness programs.

Work Zones

Work zones, or areas, include the kitchen, laundry, mud or locker room, study, homework area, or home office. These spaces are highly functional areas that the designer needs to think through thoroughly in relation to tasks, location, and acoustics.

The Kitchen

Before refrigeration in colonial America, the kitchen was an outbuilding set apart from the main house. Today, the kitchen is anything but separate from individual and family activities. Most people view the kitchen as the center of household activity. While the main function is a place for food preparation, the kitchen also serves as an area for entertaining and conversation.

Many kitchens today are open and visible to other rooms of the residence. An island offers additional seating capacity along with preparation space, and pantries store more than just packaged foods. All household members and guests circulate around the kitchen and in it. It is the place where people cook, eat, and entertain. It is a location where children play and adults gather, although it is also more than this. The kitchen is also a place to complete homework, pay bills, and watch television. It is the most diverse space design in the residence, **Figure 15-23**.

Photography by Emily Minton Redfield/Design by Andrea Schumacher Interiors

A

Photography by Emily Minton Redfield/Design by Andrea Schumacher Interiors

B

Figure 15-22 When planning the bathroom space, the designer must consider how unique or trendy features the client desires will fit the space.

Photo by: Fred Forbes Photogroupe/Design by: Lita Dirks & Co.

Figure 15-23 Along with cooking, eating, and entertaining, the kitchen may also be a place to do homework, pay bills, or watch television. *How does the client's lifestyle influence kitchen design?*

Today's lifestyles focus on the kitchen as a gathering place for a wide and varied number of activities. Due to individual lifestyles, a kitchen layout for one person is not necessarily ideal for another. Some families are getting smaller while kitchens are growing in size.

Cutting-edge uses of technology have become a standard in many homes. Kitchens now incorporate nooks for laptops, gadget-charging stations, and appliances that interface with smartphones and televisions.

Before designing a kitchen, a designer needs to ask the client a series of questions including

- How many people in the household cook?
- Do several people clean up simultaneously or does one person?
- Do you enjoy preparing elaborate meals or is the kitchen considered misused space?
- Is an informal dining area needed within the kitchen space?
- Do you do a lot of baking? Will you need a lower surface for kneading and other tasks?
- Would you prefer a separate pantry or pull-out shelves?

Just as there are zones in the residence, kitchen subdivisions are activity zones, or *work areas.* These are food preparation, cooking, serving, and cleaning zones. Each zone has a worktop, appliance(s), and storage for its particular activity. Between appliances, worktops are necessary on which to set items.

Historically, the **work triangle** was shaped by three major work areas (sink, cooktop/oven, and refrigerator) and became the **work rectangle** with the addition of the microwave oven, **Figure 15-24**.

The work triangle is the distance between the three primary work centers—the sink area, cooktop/oven area, and refrigeration. The ideal total distance among work centers is 12 feet to 26 feet in length. Designing workspaces around the work triangle can reduce excess steps to perform each task. Because more than those who cook use the refrigerator, its location should be at the triangle's outer corner for easy access.

Standard kitchen layouts are the *U-shape, L-shape, island, galley,* and the *peninsula,* **Figure 15-25**. The result of designing additional tasks into the space is many other types of layouts.

- **U-shaped kitchen.** This kitchen layout has the most efficient work triangle. If the "U" is big enough, the designer can add an island workstation in the middle.

Damon Searles Photography/Aneka Interiors Inc.

Figure 15-24 The kitchen work rectangle includes the traditional major work areas with the addition of the microwave oven.

- **L-shaped kitchen.** Also popular, this arrangement works with two adjacent walls. It is less efficient than other layouts, although the work triangle is uninterrupted by traffic.
- **Island kitchen.** As the most popular layout today, this kitchen is a little longer than the U-shape with the island as a convenient place for serving food. This type often includes chairs along one side of the island for an informal eating area. A new popular trend is a double-island configuration.
- **Galley or corridor kitchen.** This kitchen layout is highly efficient, but is the least desirable of work triangles because it also serves as a traffic path through the kitchen. Counters and storage are limited.
- **Peninsula kitchen.** This open design incorporates the kitchen and dining area.

Here are some basic spatial requirements for kitchen seating, appliances, and counters.

- Rectangular table with seating for four to six— 2 ½ feet by 5 ½ feet of space (A round table takes up less space but can accommodate more people if necessary.)
- Dining area—3 feet of clearance around all chairs ensures adequate circulation
- Range width—30 inches of space
- Refrigerator width—36 inches of space
- Dishwasher—24 inches of space
- Countertop depth—20 inches to 35 inches

To help clients understand their kitchen design, it is common to use CAD software such as *2020 Design*. CAD software not only offers a plan view of the proposed space but also three-dimensional views to enhance client understanding of the space, **Figure 15-26**. In addition, client suggested changes to the space can be viewed as the designer makes the changes. This enhances communication and prevents misunderstandings.

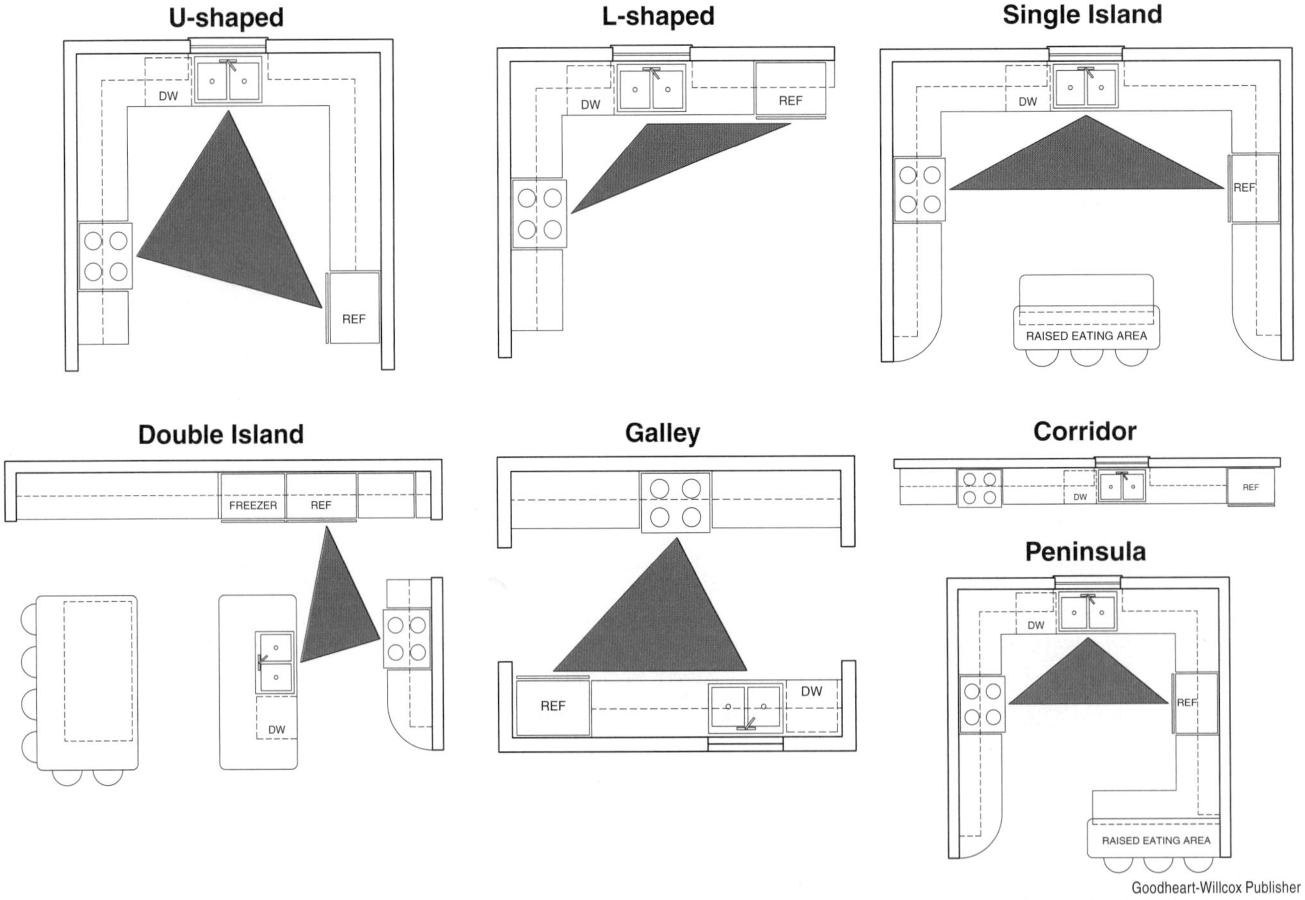

Figure 15-25 The standard kitchen layouts include a work triangle among the three primary work center areas—the sink, cooktop, and refrigeration.

RM Ruwart Design/Rosalie M. Ruwart, ASID/Architectural Workshop/Mark Bowers, AIA

Figure 15-26 Interior designers often use CAD software to show clients various dimensional views of their space.

Space Planning Analysis

Kitchens

Questions to ask regarding space planning for kitchens include

- How direct is the route from the garage to the kitchen?
- Do circulation paths cut through the work triangle?
- Is there a minimum of two feet of counter on either side of the sink?
- Is there two feet on either side of the range?
- Is there a minimum of 18 inches next to the handle side of the refrigerator?
- Is there sufficient counter space near the microwave to place a dish?
- Where is the three-foot long mixing counter?
- Is the dishwasher next to the sink? Can you load it without interference?
- Are dish and flatware storage close to the dishwasher?
- Are there storage areas adjoining every work area?
- Is there a three-foot clear passage through the kitchen?
- Are there views to the outside?
- How does the kitchen connect to existing outdoor living spaces?
- Is a window located over the kitchen sink?
- Is the pantry located away from direct sunlight?
- Can the refrigerator be opened without blocking a passageway?
- Should the plan incorporate an informal eating area?
- Will a great room or fireplace adjoin the kitchen?
- Is the kitchen oriented to the view and natural light?
- Is the kitchen open to adjacent spaces?
- Is the kitchen oriented to the social areas of the space?
- To what degree is the kitchen integrated with the rest of the house?

Inclusive Kitchen Design Details

A U- or L-shape layout is the best plan for easy movement with unobstructed work and traffic flow. For circulation in an inclusive kitchen, provide widths between 40 to 44 inches with a turning radius of five feet or 60 inches for those who use mobility devices and wheelchairs. For maneuvering at each workstation, provide a minimum clearance of 30 inches by 48 inches.

Flooring should be hard, non-slip, water-resistant, and easy to maintain. Base cabinets are much easier to access than upper cabinets for those who are short in stature or who use a wheelchair. In the kitchen design, plan for base cabinets of various heights such as 28, 30, 36, and 42 inches. This will benefit those who are tall, sitting, or standing.

Suggest roll-out carts or pull-out drawers to your client with strategic placement at work centers. Incorporate open storage shelves at the point of use. Raise the dishwasher by 8 to 10 inches above the finished floor with top racks aligned to countertop. This makes it more convenient to use from a sitting position, **Figure 15-27**.

Kitchen Design Trends

Today, a kitchen is becoming more than just a kitchen. Incorporating the kitchen with a dining room and sitting room creates a unified space, or great room. Consequently, kitchen cabinets look more like fine furniture, and counters and islands serve as dining tables. Banquette seating offers comfortable seating for people who gather in the kitchen for more than food. Formal dining rooms are becoming a thing of the past. A second family room may adjoin or be on the other side of a two-way fireplace. Yearly, trade shows and shelter magazines announce trends such as this along with many other kitchen trends, **Figure 15-28**. Additional trends to watch include

- stainless steel appliances; if preferred, fingerprint proof
- timeless white cabinetry
- eco-friendly products such as bamboo and wheatboard (made from straw and formaldehyde-free resin, similar to particle board)
- water-conserving faucets and energy rated appliances
- work zones such as specialty pizza centers
- enhanced technology usage—kitchens are going "wireless"
- trough sinks
- marble and stone countertops
- furniture feet and corbels designed into islands or base cabinetry
- ribbed, seeded, or beveled glass added to cabinet doors

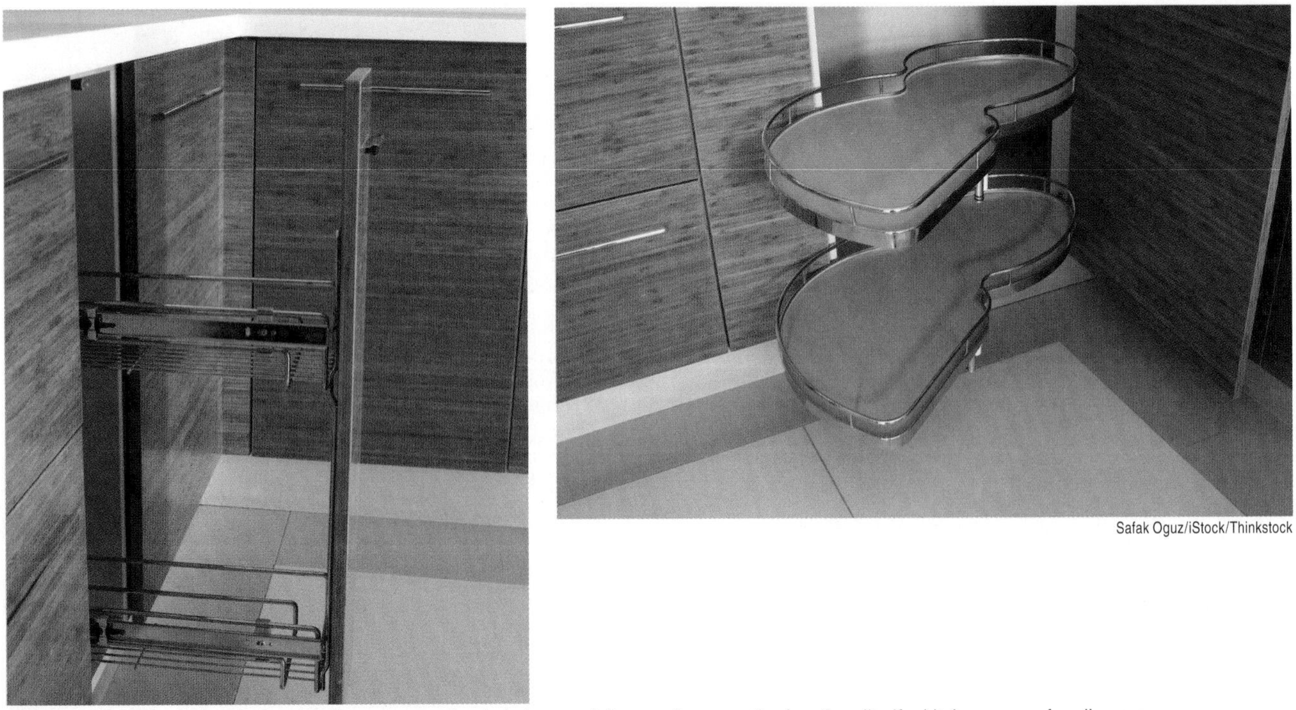

Safak Oguz/iStock/Thinkstock

Figure 15-27 Inclusive design details such as pull-out shelves and drawers increase the functionality if a kitchen space for all users.

Timeless White Cabinetry

Damon Searles Photography/Aneka Interiors Inc.

Contemporary Design

©Judy Davis/Hoachlander Davis Photography/Design by ForrestPerkins

Granite and Wood Countertops

Courtesy of Shirley Hammond

Etched Glass Details

Courtesy of Shirley Hammond

Rounded Dramatic Corners

Photography by Ben Tremper/Interiors by Associates III Interior Design

Double Ovens

Image courtesy of Cathers Home Interior Architecture and Design Firm, Basalt, Colorado. Photographer: Michael Hefferon.

Courtesy of Shirley Hammond

Figure 15-28 As client needs and wants change, so do trends in kitchen design. *What trends do you predict appearing in the next two to five years? What trends do you think may fade quickly? Why?*

- pull-out shelves
- narrow pull-out cabinets
- large islands that are longer, wider, and sometimes come in a pair
- rounded, dramatic bar counters
- fireplaces that enhance a *great room* feeling
- butler's pantry—a room for storage and food prep off the kitchen
- separate cooktop
- double ovens/commercial ovens or refrigerators
- walk-in pantry and cabinetry with rolling shelves
- universal design features, such as water temperature regulating devices
- recycling center
- cabinetry hidden appliances
- layered lighting
- drawers as warming ovens
- dual microwaves
- maximized storage
- increased automation, including faucets that start with the wave of a hand
- sensor-activated lights that illuminate the kitchen only when it is in use

Certified Kitchen Designers (CKD) are specialists in kitchen design. Kitchen design is very complex. Take advantage of the experts and available software in the field to help design this most critical space of the house. You can learn more about becoming a Certified Kitchen Designer on the National Kitchen and Bath Association website.

Laundry Areas and Closets

In the residence, the laundry room functions as the place to wash, dry, press, and maintain clothing. It often doubles as a mudroom and may contain closets or lockers for coats and sports equipment. As a space, the laundry area demands efficiency but rarely achieves it. Too often, the laundry area is tucked in a basement or crammed into a hallway or bathroom closet. Today, the laundry room is getting more attention as designers and clients plan them into the residence with spaces for hobbies such as sewing, art projects, or model-making.

Typical laundry room activities include sorting clothes, hand- or machine-washing clothes, drying and folding clothes, and ironing. When space planning, there are many locations to put the laundry room in a residence, **Figure 15-29**.

- **Near the kitchen.** Locating the laundry room off the kitchen provides the opportunity to multitask by simultaneously working in the kitchen and laundry room.
- **In the basement.** Although this location involves additional lifting and steps, it keeps the noise and functional mess from the main living spaces.
- **Off the bedroom area.** This convenient location eliminates carrying laundry up and down stairs in a two-story house.
- **In the bathroom of smaller homes or townhouses.** This location is near other plumbing needs and offers a hard surface in the event of water leaks.
- **In a mudroom or utility space near the garage or backdoor entrance.** This location encourages users to leave dirty clothing in the laundry area before tracking dirt through the residence. Less ideal places for laundry rooms are in hallways, between the kitchen and garage, and in the kitchen itself.

Space Planning Analysis

Laundry Rooms

There are many space planning questions to ask a client regarding the laundry room, including

- Where is the circulation pattern into and through the space?
- How does the work flow in an orderly fashion?
- Where do doors open and shut that might impede traffic or functional use of space?
- Is the dryer located on an outside wall for efficient venting?
- Are washer and dryer arrangements clustered together, preferably on the same wall?
- Is there a need for a sink? What about hooks or lockers?
- How much counter space do folding tasks require?
- Is high shelving for detergent adequate? Are drawers available?
- Is there a need for a bench seat?
- Is there a closet, in addition to lockers, for hanging clothes?
- Is there a need for an ironing board? Can it be folded into a space or collapsed into a drawer?
- Where are bins located for clothes sorting?
- Does a laundry chute come into the room?
- Is there daylight or a window in the laundry area? Natural light is good for color comparisons.

Iriana Shiyan/Shutterstock.com

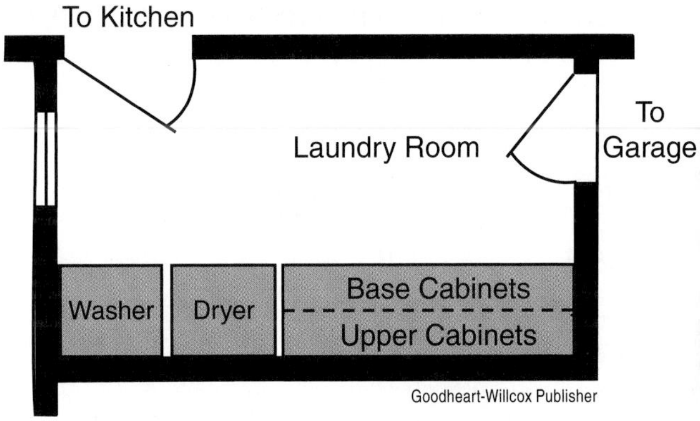

Goodheart-Willcox Publisher

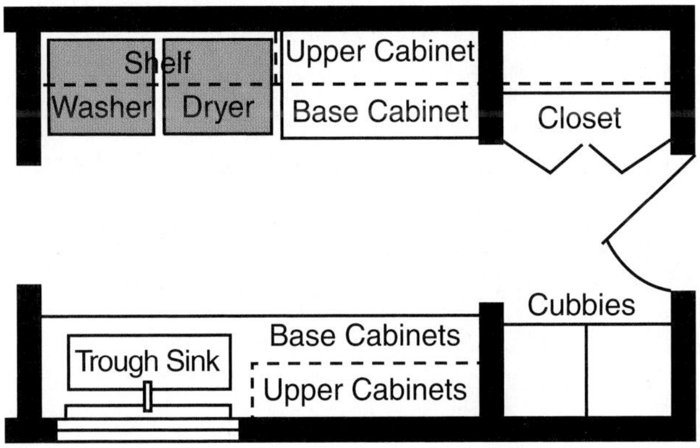

Goodheart-Willcox Publisher

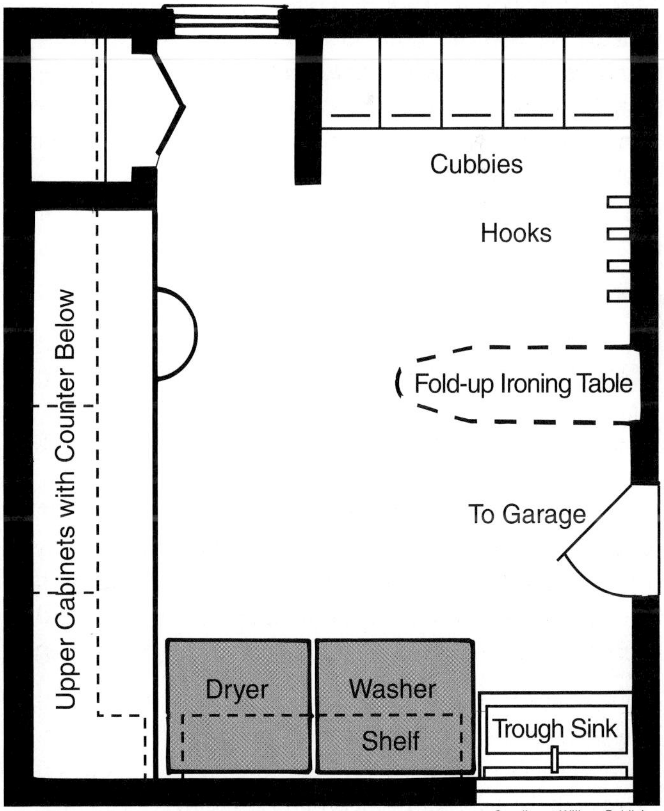

Goodheart-Willcox Publisher

Figure 15-29 The laundry room provides space for sorting, washing, drying, folding, and ironing clothes. Some offer space for other activities, too.

Laundry: Inclusive Design Details

The laundry area can be challenging for people of all ages and abilities. To make them user-friendly, consider using front-loading washers and dryers with front controls installed on pedestals 10 to 12 inches above the finished floor. This allows operation of the machines without bending or in a seated position. In addition, 36 inches of floor-space-width in front of the appliances that extends 18 inches beyond on either side provides easier access to machines from a seated position. Light sources with easy-to-reach adjustable controls are also a benefit of inclusive design.

Closets and Storage

With the fast-moving lives people lead, organization is critical in a residence. Proper organizational tools, such as well-designed and conveniently placed storage, modify behavior and increase efficiency. The design of closets is such a big trend in the United States that there are closet designers, closet organization systems, and software written just to design closets.

The first consideration in closet design is to always locate storage at point of use. To determine storage needs, conduct an inventory of how, what, and where your client uses various items. A closet can be more than a typical rod and shelf. A cabinet can be more than three, equidistant shelves. With some thought, even a small space can become highly efficient. Storage should be available in every space in the house, plus in areas in the garage and areas outside the residence. For more information on closets, view such websites as *Easy Closets* or *Easy Track™*.

Space Planning Analysis

Storage

Questions to ask regarding space planning for storage include

- Is storage located where it is used?
- Is it efficiently designed at its location?
- Do storage doors swing into hallways, blocking circulation patterns?

The Home Office

The location of today's office can be almost anywhere. Digital tablets, wireless Internet, and cell phones allow individuals to complete work and send it to and from just about any location in the nation and the world. On the home front, video conferencing and the virtual office is inclusive as well as a sustainable and practical method of doing business. Savings occur not only through lower fuel costs but also with the electronic exchange of files, saving paper and landfills.

The design world does not expect the evolution of the home office to become stagnant anytime soon. The home office continues to evolve around convenience and flexible lifestyles. Employees and employers are less willing to waste time with long commutes and travel hassles. With the interest in entrepreneurial activities, many people use their home offices to run a second business, **Figure 15-30**.

The location of the home office in the house is important. Although it can be anywhere, an office space in the front of the home off the entry is typically an unpractical location. To avoid distractions, choosing a space to dedicate to work is simplest, even if it is a little corner area adjoining the kitchen.

While it seems like a relatively simple task, designing a home office can be complex. Functional needs for a home office include a writing surface, storage, technology support, natural daylight, adequate electric light, an ergonomically designed chair, and shelving or drawers.

Rodenberg Photography/Shutterstock.com

Figure 15-30 The design of today's home office can take many forms. Connectivity to the digital world is essential for conducting business from home. *What design features do you think are most important for conducting business at home?*

Space Planning Analysis

Home Office

Questions to ask regarding space planning for the home office include

- How many people will use the space? If two, are they in the office at the same time?
- Is there sufficient privacy and acoustical control to avoid distractions?
- Is the work-surface area sufficient? Is there a lower work surface for keyboard comfort?
- Are outlets and data connections close to electronic equipment and hook-ups?
- Is there adequate storage for office supplies in drawers and on shelves?
- Is there sufficient storage for files?
- Does the office have an ergonomic desk chair with lumbar support that faces the door and natural light?
- Are upholstered side chairs available for extra seating?
- Does the office have both natural and electric light? Are there controls to raise the electric light level as daylight passes?

Adding Details

While the information in this chapter will assist you in developing a functional residence, it is the *design details* that shape it into a memorable design. Details enhance beauty and engage people's senses—adding elements of surprise and delight. The way the details are put together does not have to be costly but, more importantly, the details must be carefully thought out.

After designing the basic residence, take time to develop a layer of innovative detail that dramatically changes the living experience for the client. The following includes a few suggestions of places to interject detail into the residence. Take each idea, weave it into your design, and see how it comes to life!

- **Inviting places.** Add a thoughtful alcove, hidden window seat, unconventional or unique landing, or delightful side porch.
- **Ceilings.** Leave monotony behind. Mold and shape a ceiling plane with variety and interest. Surprise guests with a subtle ceiling detail or a variety of lowered and raised ceiling heights. Varying the height of a ceiling adds spatial interest, contrasting character, and room definition, **Figure 15-31**.
- **Light.** Drama, interplay of shade and shadow, and revealed texture can all result as lighting details that provide interest in strategic locations throughout public and private spaces.
- **Dropped soffits.** Soffits sculpt the space beneath and at the same time add height to a room. Use this element of human scale to create familiarity and interest.
- **Half wall with architectural details.** Break down boundaries and barriers with half walls that offer new sight lines and views of the outdoors.
- **Mysterious quirk.** Add elfin fun to a kitchen nook or great room. Take time to design one unique feature that someone will rarely notice unless looking for it. For example, a hidden, tiny door to leave Santa notes.
- **Connecting views.** Create a strong visual connection between two areas. Use wide doorways, openings with arches, or interior windows between spaces.
- **Artful nook.** Look for a small, unused space tucked into an odd corner of the residence to create a nook for displaying art.
- **Vistas and views.** Visually walk through spaces. Create a surprise view in an unexpected location.

pics721/Shutterstock.com

Figure 15-31 Ceiling details add interest and definition to a room. *As a designer, what other ceiling details might you include in a kitchen?*

Designer Profile

Annette K. Stelmack—Residential Designer

Interior Design Principal, Owner, Author, and Educator: Annette K. Stelmack, Inspirit-LLC, Louisville, CO—specializing in healthy, high performing, nurturing, and sustainable interiors for residential, multi-unit housing, hospitality and spa projects.

Photography by Ben Tremper/Interiors by Associates III Interior Design

"As a designer, I create *home*. Clients invite me into their life which brings a profound responsibility to serve them in one of the most personal expressions of who they are—where they live. It is an honor to genuinely listen to their needs, balance their dreams, provide potential solutions, and participate in long-term decisions. Aligning with my client's values is imperative to create a healthy, nurturing, high-performing, and vitalizing interior environment that reflects their personality and spirit along with supporting their health, safety, and well-being.

"Today, more than ever, the health, safety, and welfare of our clients is at the forefront of every design solution and decision we make. Our actions and choices have a dynamic impact on our clients, project teams, manufacturers, and the building industry. In my heart, I believe that we need to embrace restorative and regenerative design practices and solutions for the health of the planet and, ultimately, for our own health. With positive energy, passion, research, expertise, and a heartfelt commitment, we can succeed, being part of the change!"

You can read more about Annette's experience in Appendix B.

Encouraging Residential *Green* Design

What began as a call for eco-friendly products and materials in the home has moved into fully sustainable spaces that encourage healthy living by people who occupy the home. Key words of the sustainability movement include *reclaim, renew, repair, recreate, repurpose,* and *rethink.*

Ideally, designers can create and achieve a *green* residence with either new construction or remodel projects. As they do, it is important to note that there is still a gap between people who say they value sustainability and environmental protection and those who act on their values by making *green* purchases. According to recent studies, a large percentage of Americans have positive intentions in making green purchases, whereas a smaller number actually follow through with buying green products. Thankfully, as people become more knowledgeable about sustainability issues, the gap between positive intentions and actually making green purchases is getting smaller.

Although consumers are making the move toward more thoughtful purchases when it comes to the environment, interior designers must continue to be diligent in educating their clients about the win-win benefits of choosing green options. Such benefits include lower energy costs and healthier indoor environments by reducing allergens and toxins.

Checklist of Green-Design Strategies

The following lists a few ideas for incorporating green design strategies into residential projects:

- Choose energy-efficient appliances and equipment.
- Select energy-efficient lighting and light controls, such as fluorescents, LEDs, and window shade light sensors.
- Include recycled or salvaged doors, or domestic wood from reclaimed sources.
- Use natural-fiber carpet of 50 to 100 percent recycled content.
- Utilize domestic wood, cabinetry, and shelving from reclaimed sources or third-party-certified sustainably harvested wood.

- Choose bamboo or cork flooring or other rapidly renewable materials.
- Select paints with low- or no-VOCs or paints with recycled content.
- Choose countertops from reclaimed stone or recycled materials such as Richlite®, Icestone®, Paperstone®, or terrazzo.
- Use trim and millwork from reclaimed domestic wood sources or third-party-certified sustainably harvested wood.
- Create storage such as a built-in a recycling center with two or more bins.
- Select bathroom and kitchen faucets with flow-restricting aerators.
- Choose dual-flush toilets for all bathrooms.
- Use ceiling fans.
- Design spaces with passive solar heating.
- Make sure the residence meets or exceeds ENERGY STAR program requirements.
- Choose a smaller building footprint for a residence.

For additional information on *green* alternatives, visit the websites for the National Association of Home Builders (NAHB) or the U.S. Green Building Council (USGBC) *LEED for HOMES*. For ideas on remodeling projects and case studies, visit the website for the *REGREEN* Residential Remodeling Program—a partnership between ASID and USGBC.

Analyzing Floor Plans

There is no perfect residential plan. Each offers advantages and disadvantages. Poor plans—or no plans at all—often cause mundane and inefficient designs. Remember, residential design always has a set of trade-offs.

The following offers tips on how to evaluate a residential floor plan to ensure it is well-designed and efficient for the occupants. As you read, presume the client's concept and program have already been determined and are used to guide the plan. Analysis of a floor plan is based on the following:

- interior zones
- circulation patterns
- universal design
- door and window placement
- closet location
- egress and codes

Interior Zones

Similar to a commercial plan, residential spaces have zones. As you know, house zones are public or social, work, and private, **Figure 15-32**. When evaluating a floor plan, first analyze if the residence is broken into these zones. If desired, draw a bubble sketch around each zone and label it on the plan. Questions you might ask yourself during this evaluation include

- Are the spaces within each zone grouped together?
- Are the work areas near the service areas?
- What is the relationship of the kitchen to the rest of the residence?
- Should a family room be next to a living room? (*No.*)
- Should a guest bathroom be at the back of the residence? (*No.*)

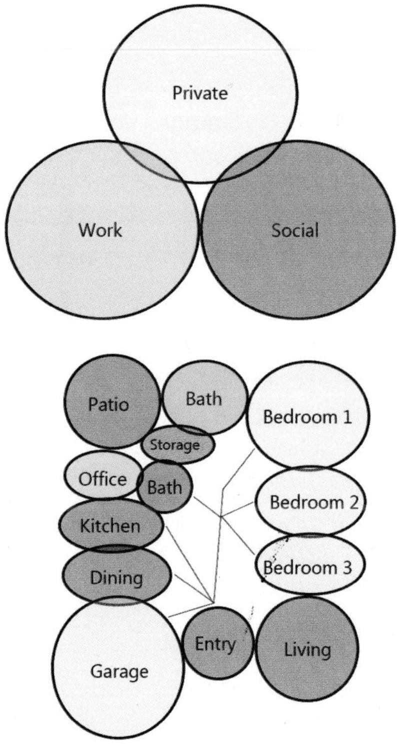

Julia Harmon, Colorado State University

Figure 15-32 During the Schematic Design phase, interior designers begin by using bubble diagrams to analyze the zones for a client's space. *How are bubble diagrams beneficial for both client and designer?*

Evaluating Circulation Patterns

Next look at circulation patterns in the house plan. Begin just outside the front door and visually walk yourself through the residence as if you are a guest. Then do the same thing presuming you are the owner or a family member. When moving from one place to another, a simple, direct route is most efficient and desirable. Lay a piece of tracing paper over the plan. Diagram each circulation pattern and color code it. Circulation patterns should not cross conversation groupings, television viewing, workspaces, and the kitchen preparation area, **Figure 15-33**. Knowing these tips, use the following questions to continue your analysis:

- Are the routes direct?
- Are rooms cut in half by any circulation route?
- Are related rooms positioned close together?
- Are the bathrooms close to the bedrooms?
- Can you easily move from the kitchen range to the sink and from the sink to the cooking or eating areas?
- Is the kitchen adjacent to the eating area(s)?
- Is the indoor living space accessible to the outdoor living area?
- Do furniture groupings obstruct movement?

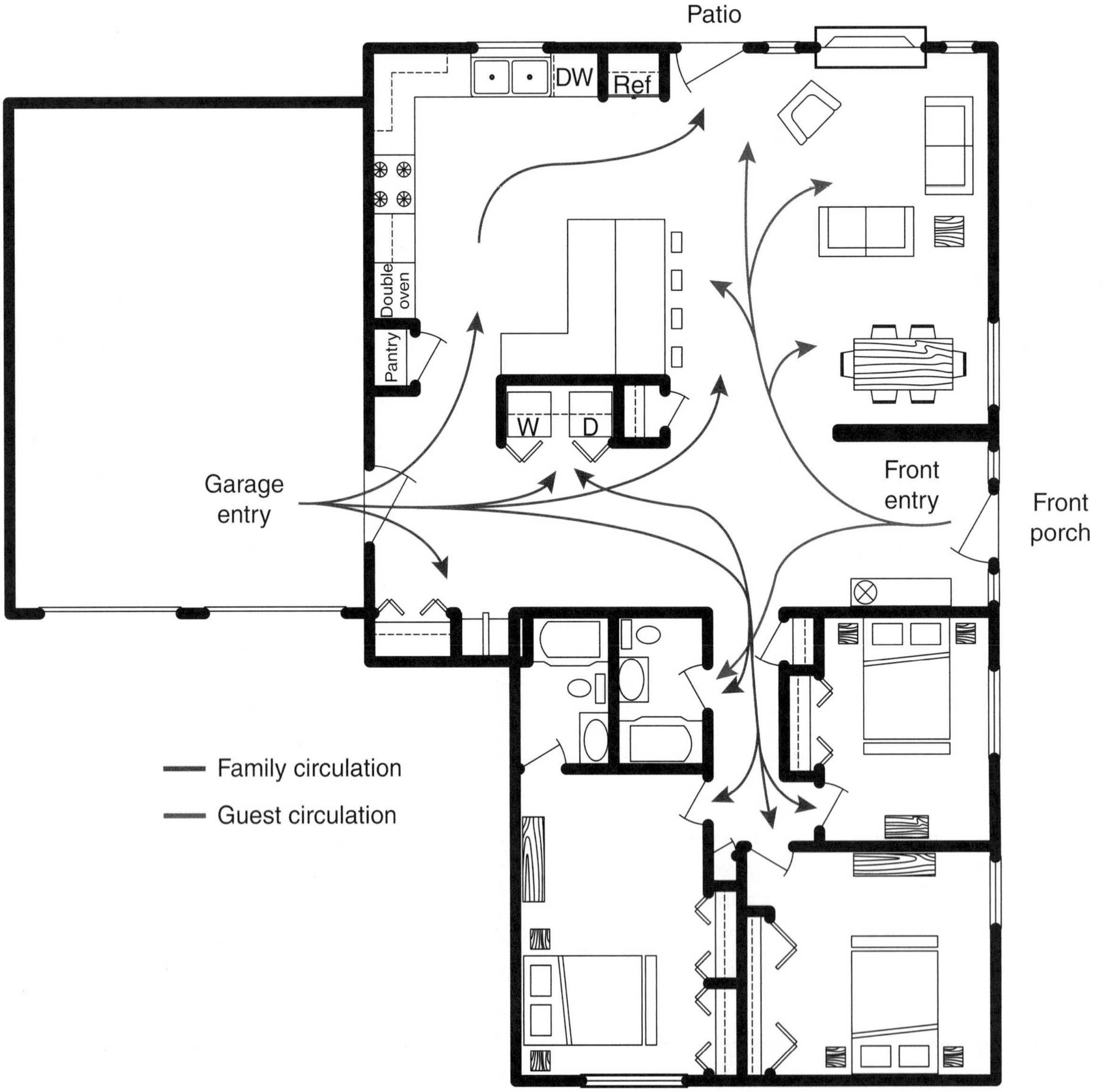

Goodheart-Willcox Publisher

Figure 15-33 The most desirable and functional circulation patterns are direct and efficient. *Locate a floor plan on the Internet. Then analyze and map the circulation patterns for the various interior zones.*

- Do occupants have to cross the kitchen to get to a basement?
- Can guests move from the entry to the living area without passing through other rooms?
- Can occupants get to the bedrooms without passing through the major public area?
- Can a guest get to a bathroom without passing through a bedroom?
- Are entrance areas large enough to hold two or three guests without having to move into the living area?
- Are hallways wide enough to permit passage of an individual in a wheelchair or movement of a piece of furniture?
- Are there too many hallways?
- Is the garage near the kitchen for ease in handling groceries?
- Is the kitchen close to work areas and entry areas?
- If preferred, is the laundry area near the bedrooms?
- Are areas large enough for movement of people and furniture?
- Does the traffic flow through work areas such as the kitchen sink or laundry area?
- Do occupants have to walk through the kitchen to get to a bedroom?
- Can you stand in a hallway or room and see the toilet in the guest bath?
- Are rooms too long and narrow, making furniture placement difficult?

After reviewing room relationships and circulation patterns, determine if you have used inclusive design strategies to ensure a welcoming place for all ages.

- Are major doors and hallways 44 inches wide?
- Does the design plan minimize various level changes such as a step?
- If present, is part of the kitchen bar at sitting height?

Door and Window Placement

The location of doors and windows significantly affects furniture placement, **Figure 15-34**. Door location in a room can be a hindrance, primarily due to the obstruction of the door swing, or due to the space needed to accommodate people entering through the door. Door placement should be located at corners of rooms rather than centrally located so all walls are available for furniture arrangement. The door should swing into the wall and allow you to walk into a room. Closets are grouped together to create a sound barrier between the rooms. A corridor may end with a wall, closet, or a focal point.

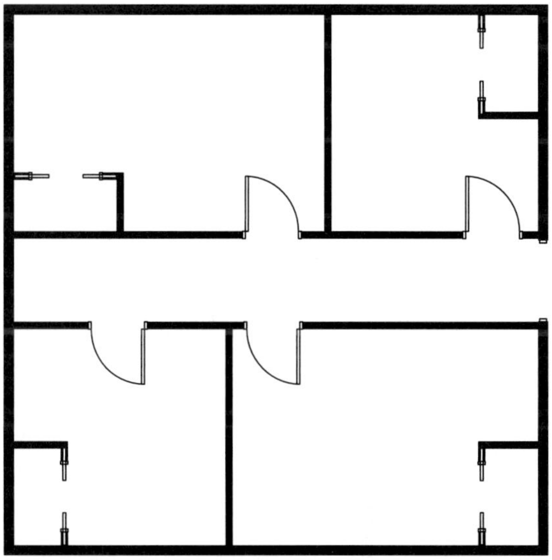
A

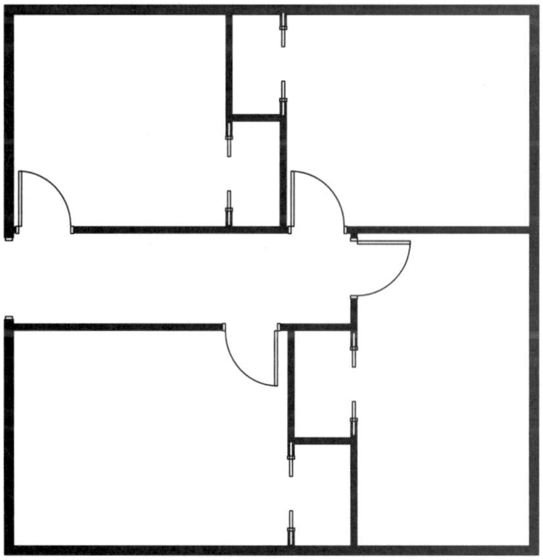
B

Julia Harmon, Sophomore Design Student, Colorado State University

Figure 15-34 The location of windows and doors can significantly impact circulation in a room. *Why is the door arrangement in sketch B better than sketch A?*

Window locations can impede placement of conversation groupings or furniture pieces such as a bed. Poor window locations can also interrupt wall space and greatly reduce usable space. A view to the outside is an important human need. Only storage rooms, closets, home movie theaters, and similar spaces should be without natural light.

Space Planning Analysis

Doors and Windows

When evaluating door and window placement, think about the following questions:

- Does the door swing into a pathway across a room?
- Are the doors located in corners of rooms where the door can swing into a wall rather than centered on a wall?
- Do the door locations force you to go through a conversation grouping?
- Does the front door lead to all areas of the house?
- Is there a view to the outside from every public and private room?
- Are windows located to allow furniture placement? Remember, you need to consider the height of the window off the floor as well as the width of the window.
- Could the window shape or size be adjusted to allow a better view?

Closet Location

Locate closets, particularly in bedrooms, close to the door. Occupants access closets often for clothing and other items. With continuous, constant use, a *traffic pattern*—sometimes very visible across carpet—can wear into the flooring. To save time as well as wear and tear on the flooring, place closets near doorways for easy access.

An advantage of closets is that the designer can place them back-to-back to serve as an acoustical barrier. Placement of closets between private and public spaces helps achieve a degree of privacy and acoustical control. As you evaluate the floor plan, ask the following questions:

- Do groups of closets deaden noise from one room to another?
- Does the location of the bedroom closet cause you to walk across the room?
- Are closets in strategic locations to meet storage needs?

Egress and Codes

As you continue to analyze a floor plan, it is important to determine if the plan addresses *codes*, including those relating to egress, **Figure 15-35**. Although there are national codes, your community—along with many cities and counties—may adopt and possibly revise the codes to meet community needs. Therefore, it is always important to talk with a code official in your location to determine applicable codes.

Space Planning Analysis

Egress and Codes

Some typical questions to ask when evaluating a floor plan in relation to egress and codes include

- Is the bedroom window large enough to exit through in case of fire?
- Are interior doorways the minimum width?
- Are there any tripping hazards designed into the plan?
- If there is a basement, is there a window opening large enough to allow an adult to exit?

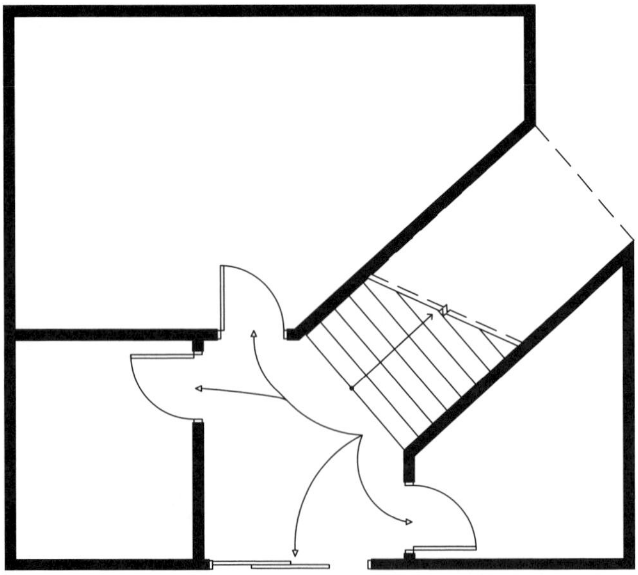

Julia Harmon, sophomore, Colorado State University

Figure 15-35 Stairways impact egress and circulation within a residence.

Kitchen Layout

As a highly functional place of the house, the designer should carefully evaluate the layout of the kitchen. Here are a few tips to use when assessing the design of the kitchen space.

- Avoid layouts that route traffic through the work area.
- Keep countertop surfaces among work areas continuous, if possible. Plan counter space next to the range, oven, refrigerator, and sink.
- Visualize appliance and cabinet doors in an open position to determine if they present traffic obstacles or safety hazards.
- Plan the number and location of electric outlets for small and major appliances.
- Plan lighting at task areas to ensure clients can see clearly.
- Place the largest countertop work area between the sink and the range, if possible.
- Place the refrigerator close to the sink to save steps.
- Assess whether windows are easy to open and have the optimal placement.

Well-Designed Plan

A well-designed plan offers efficiencies to the user. Conversely, a poorly designed plan can cause inefficiencies and even safety issues. A well-designed plan should include

- The dining room is adjacent to the living room and kitchen.
- The smaller eating area is located off the kitchen.
- The kitchen is easily accessible to the garage in a single dwelling.
- The living room is large enough to accommodate several people.
- A coat closet and bathroom are easily accessible by guests.
- All bedrooms are near a bath and a linen closet.
- The public and private spaces are well-defined.
- The floor plan shows a creative arrangement of space.
- The plan shows well-placed doorways and adequate space for furnishings.
- Rooms that require plumbing are grouped near one another or vertically stacked in different levels.
- The traffic patterns are well-arranged, allowing easy access to all spaces.

Poorly Designed Plan

When analyzing a floor plan, you can learn as much from one that is poorly designed as you can from one that is well-designed. See how many of the floor plan deficiencies from the following list you can find in **Figure 15-36**.

- The lack of an entranceway makes the living room a major traffic lane. For instance, having a front door that opens directly into the living room.

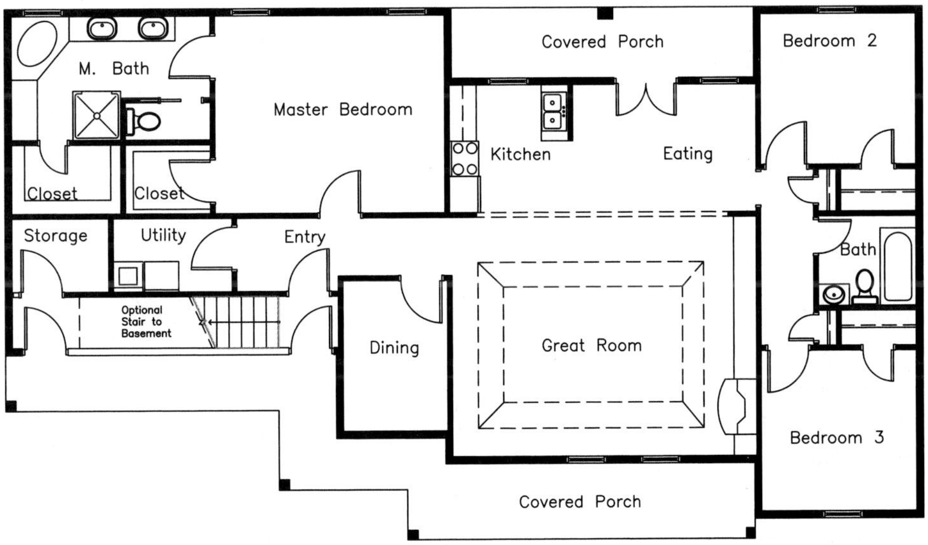

Julia Harmon, sophomore, Colorado State University

Figure 15-36 A well-designed floor plan is efficient, function, and meets the client's needs. *Evaluate this floor plan. Discuss the deficiencies that make this a poorly designed plan.*

- Lack of a front-hall closet.
- The poorly located front door causes traffic-pattern problems.
- There is no privacy in eating areas.
- The garage placement is inconvenient to the kitchen.
- No direct access from the front door to the kitchen, bathrooms, and bedrooms without passing through other rooms. For instance, to reach the three-quarter bath from the kitchen, it is necessary to cross through a bedroom. (Avoid plans that involve passage through one room to get to another.)
- Traffic patterns cross conversation groupings and television viewing, as well as the kitchen-preparation area.
- A dining room that is not easily reached from the kitchen.
- An outdoor view is not accessible from every major room or workspace.
- Walls interrupted by doors and windows, interfering with furniture placement around the room.
- Doorways are located at the end of corridors.
- Bathrooms that are visible from a public space.
- Inadequate storage available throughout the house. Storage that is available lacks a convenient location throughout the residence.

Furniture Arrangements

Evaluating the quality and efficiency of a floor plan is not complete without considering how furniture will fit into the space design. Many residential plans look good until visualization of furniture in the spaces occurs.

The proper arrangement of furniture can guide a person's movement through a space, enhance conversations, and encourage the use of specific rooms. It is important to understand which activities the client wants to occur in each space and then determine if the amount of space and furniture placement supports the activities.

Remember to consider desired movement around furniture as well as the strong natural focal points and window placement the plan depicts. In addition, consider the human factors that can impact the space: anthropometrics, privacy, and proxemics. All should influence the furniture layout.

Impact of Circulation on Furniture Arrangements

Circulation patterns impact furniture arrangements. Furniture can guide the way people move through as well as use the spaces, **Figure 15-37** show the natural traffic path and logical areas for furniture groupings in a living room. Controlling the flow of traffic at key locations with furniture placement forces traffic away from seating and conversation areas.

Balance and Form

Arrange furniture to provide a sense of balance within the space. Form, or mass, acts as a visual weight in the space and is a primary consideration in creating balance. A glass table, for example, appears lighter than a heavy oak table. Visual weight is more important than actual furniture dimensions when creating a well-balanced arrangement.

Furniture groupings create symmetrical and asymmetrical balance. Furniture can balance architectural elements such as a fireplace or large picture window. In rooms with slanted or vaulted ceilings, place large pieces of furniture against the taller wall. Placing large pieces of furniture tightly into room corners creates too much negative space in other areas. For instance,

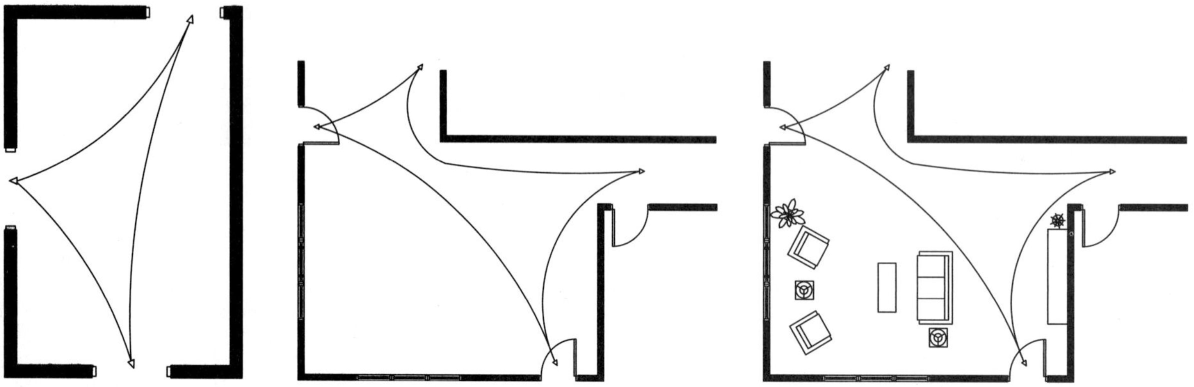

Julia Harmon, sophomore, Colorado State University

Figure 15-37 Understanding circulation patterns helps the designer control traffic flow around furniture groupings and conversation areas.

placing a desk perpendicular to a wall will be more interesting than pushing it against the wall.

Focal Point or Emphasis

Furniture arrangement enhances an area of focus within an interior. Because two focal points create conflict in a space, it is best for designers to avoid them. Natural focal points include fireplaces, windows, and unique architectural details such as archways. In rooms with a natural focal point, arrange furniture to emphasize it, **Figure 15-38**. Ignoring a natural focal point causes disharmony in a room or space. In rooms that lack natural focal points, a furniture grouping can become a focal point. Use some object, such as an area rug, to anchor and define the grouping.

Line and Harmony

Chairs in a grouping placed at a slight angle tend to make the arrangement feel less formal and rigid. They soften the solid feeling of a rectilinear composition in a room or space.

When introducing a new line into a space, it should relate harmoniously to the other existing lines. For example, a sofa or other large furniture piece placed diagonally across the corner of a room feels awkward unless other elements repeat and enhance the diagonal line of the piece.

Proportion

Carefully consider room proportions, long and narrow versus squat and square, when placing furniture. Rectangular rooms, if not too narrow, are the most flexible and easy to arrange. It is best to handle long spaces by dividing them into two groupings. Long, tall pieces can divide a room into smaller areas. Dropped ceilings and area rugs can delineate an area as a more intimate conversation space. To define a smaller area, place furniture perpendicular to a wall. Remember, the height of window off the finished floor impacts furniture arrangement, too.

Grouping Configurations

Furniture groupings may have different shapes. From your client, determine the preferred number of seats in a room or area. Remember, when counting the number of seats, do not include the middle seat of a sofa. No one will sit there because it is uncomfortable to carry on a conversation. Culturally, it is important to look others in the eye to see if they are genuine and honest.

Visually walk your way from the room entrance into a grouping. It is easy to forget the entrance point into a room or grouping.

Distances between four and six feet are most comfortable for normal conversation. See **Figure 15-39** for the following furniture groupings:

- **L-shaped.** Can offset large architectural element such as a window and provides an open, welcoming feeling.

Damon Searles Photography/Aneka Interiors Inc.

Figure 15-38 A fireplace is a natural focal point. *How would you as a designer use furniture groupings to enhance this room?*

- **U-shaped.** This shape provides additional seating and enhances the focal point. Remember to leave point of entry.
- **Rectangular-shaped.** This grouping serves as a focal point. Remember to leave point of entry.
- **Parallel grouping.** This grouping is symmetrical and is more difficult for conversations.
- **Circular grouping.** This grouping invites conversation and offers good eye contact.

Steps for Creating Furniture Arrangement

Creating a furniture arrangement is easy. The most difficult part is visualizing the space in three dimensions. If you can do that, you will understand that each piece of furniture impacts not only the plan but also the visual weight of the space. Following are a few easy steps to follow as you begin your furniture arrangement.

1. Draw the floor plan to scale. Indicate overall room dimensions. Determine sizes of major furniture pieces and write them on a piece of paper near your drawing.
2. Add any doorways, windows, or level changes to the room or space.
3. Locate focal point. Group your furniture around it beginning with the largest piece of furniture such as a sofa or large case goods.
4. Next, place smaller pieces next to large. These might be the end tables or upholstered chairs. Mix straight lines with round tables or curved chairs to create interest in an otherwise linear room. Include a balance of wood and upholstered furniture pieces.
5. When creating a conversation grouping, allow space for people to enter the arrangement. As people get to the seating, furniture should be close enough together to carry on a conversation.
6. Avoid having traffic pass directly through your well-planned seating areas. To interact comfortably, people generally prefer to sit opposite each other or at a slight angle. If there is too much distance between them, they then tend to sit side by side.
7. Place any secondary furniture groupings once you establish the primary grouping. For instance, add a reading nook in a bedroom or a place for playing games in a great room. Put a desk under a window to utilize the natural light and view. Soften a room corner with a curved item.
8. Avoid placing furnishings back-to-front as in a bus.
9. Avoid lining up furniture against walls because it is uninviting.
10. Avoid putting backs of large furniture pieces to the entrance of a room.
11. Angling furniture provides drama but may not follow the architectural footprint and requires more space.

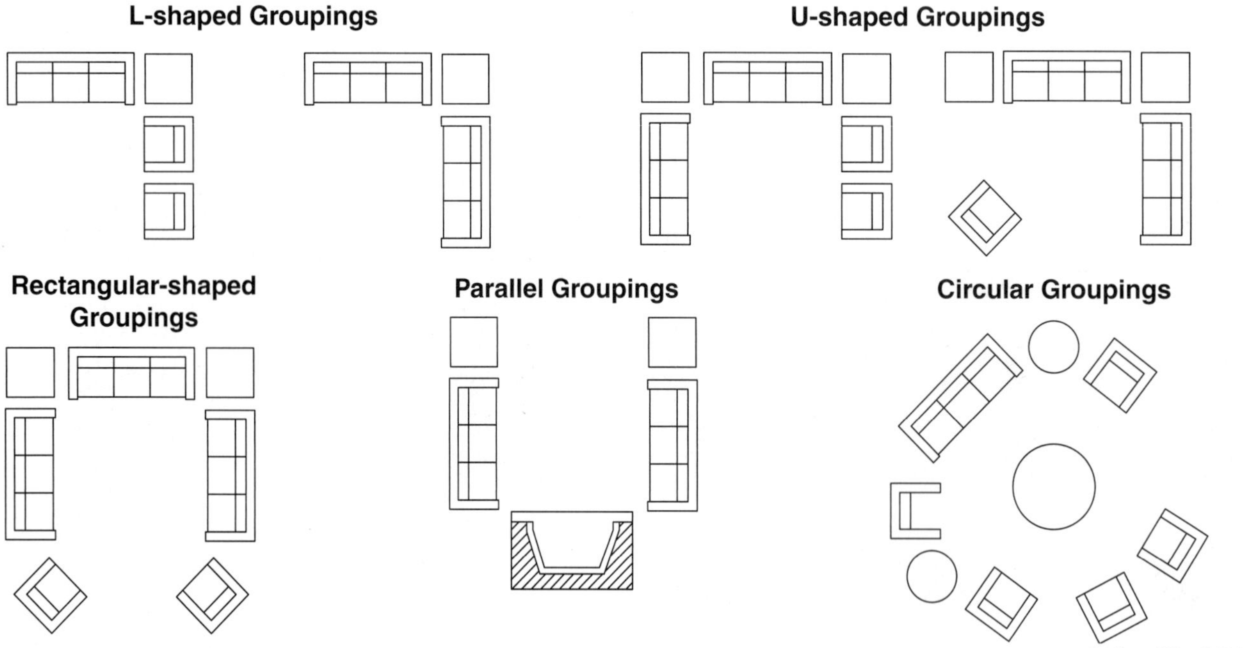

Goodheart-Willcox Publisher

Figure 15-39 Furniture groupings may have different shapes depending on the client's program and preferences.

12. Avoid placing a chair by itself. Incorporate it into a grouping or use it with a side table.
13. Bring furniture into the room to avoid the look of a doctor's waiting room. If you place a sofa against a wall, consider using a console or sofa table behind it.
14. Mix in taller pieces to break up the horizontal lines in a room.
15. Once done, reassess your traffic pattern. For walkways, allow a minimum of two and a half feet. Make sure traffic does not flow through conversation groupings. Be aware of flow from adjoining rooms.

Trends for the Future

As with commercial design, residential design continues to incorporate new trends into the public, private, and work zones of the residence. Here are just a few to watch over the upcoming years.

Multigenerational Households

As four separate generations now coexist in the workforce—interacting and influencing one another—career-minded adult children are asking their baby-boomer parents to move in and share not only the mortgage and other housing expenses, but child care, too. For instance, a mobile senior couple may move into a *granny flat* or *casita* on the same property as their adult children. An elderly grandparent may find it is safer and more economical to live under the same roof as his or her grown children or grandchildren than in an assisted-living facility. This trend is expected to increase. Together, families are changing the rules of what a home should be.

Smaller House Sizes

For many Americans today, house size does not equate to *dream house*. The latest *Design Trends Survey* from the American Institute of Architects notes an increasing demand for smaller homes, **Figure 15-40**. Many

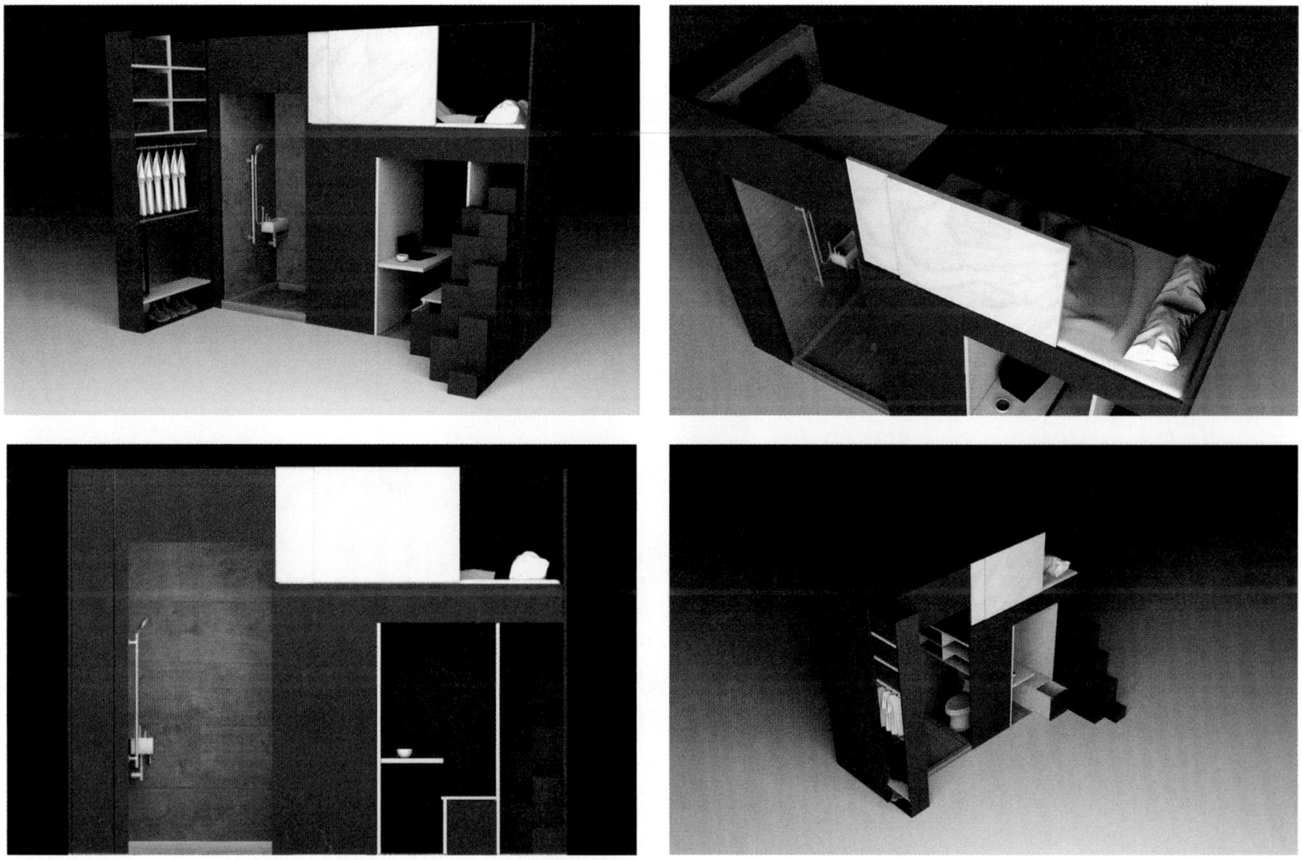

Tyler Myers, Colorado State University

Figure 15-40 As more and more people seek smaller homes, scale and functionality become the key goals of a space. *Examine these micro-apartment images. How is the space functional? Predict the lifestyle goals of the occupant.*

people continue to consider smaller as "better." Scale and function are the solution here, not sheer square footage. The following are two very different examples of the trend toward smaller homes.

Consider a 700 square-foot retreat loft in Bozeman, Montana that is feminine, pretty, and intentional—giving the owner just enough space to create and think. It may have one large living area, a small kitchen with an eat-in space, a full bath, and a bedroom/workroom combination. What is the goal of this design? To feel "found" and meaningful, not just purchased to fill the space. For the owner, favorite things and a grandmother's legacy received top placement in the home.

Compare the loft retreat with a home created outside Atlanta, Georgia for two transplants from New York City. As one of several residential units in a mixed-use structure, the building combines two levels of urban living with ground floor offices situated within two blocks of the town square. Comprised of 1,805 square feet, the residence incorporates contemporary and minimalist design details.

Both residences were designed small, but offer autonomy and personalization to the spaces. Baby boomers, empty nesters, and Gen Y groups express a desire for less maintenance and more private outdoor space, breaking away from the traditional public backyard. This design trend can be achieved by creating spaces that are private from the neighboring house by either positioning architecture around the outdoor space or by allowing the outdoor space to pierce the architecture, affording more interior living spaces to be exposed to the outdoor area.

Creative Use of Available Space

As more people share residences and houses become smaller, interior designers and their clients look for creative ways to make use of all available space and the technology that supports today's fast-paced lifestyles.

- **Smarter storage.** Always an important factor, smarter, well-designed storage is especially useful within smaller spaces. Consider space under a stairway for additional closet storage or tiny nooks of available kitchen space to keep kitchen tools within reach, **Figure 15-41**.
- **Functional garages.** Garages are more than housing for vehicles. In fact, the garage is one of the only places within a house that offers the consumer what designers call *idea space*. Creating a larger garage to accommodate more functions—such as a workshop, craft space, or home gym—becomes a value to the consumer.
- **Tech-savvy houses.** The constant use of technology products and handheld electronic devices creates a need for a new lifestyle. In the future, house designs may include small "server" rooms as smart technology continues to enter the home.

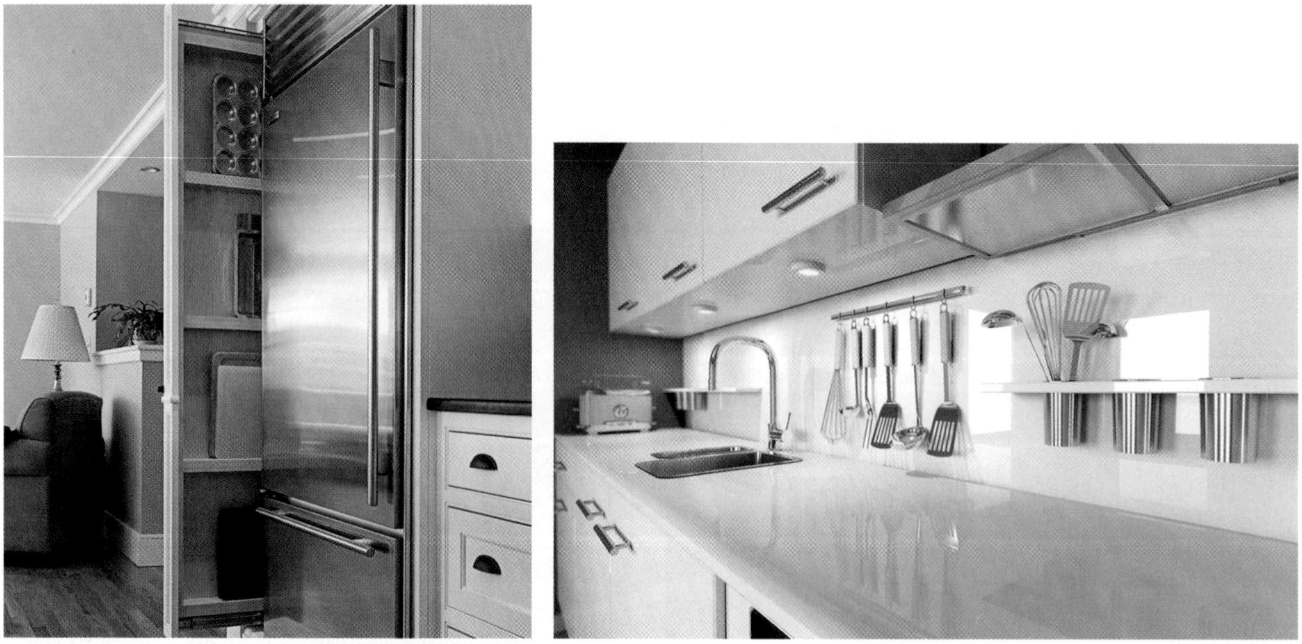

Lorraine Kournafas/Shutterstock.com

AnnalA/Shutterstock.com

Figure 15-41 As a designer, look for ways to creatively use smarter storage. *Think about houses of others you know. What additional spaces can you identify that could be designed with smarter storage in mind?*

Chapter 15

Review and Assess

Summary

- In addition to meeting the basic human needs of shelter, food, water, safety, and security, a residence needs to be a place of self-expression, where people feel safe and form relationships of trust.
- An effective residence encourages personal autonomy.
- Public zones should be inviting and lively, and should take into account traffic patterns (family, service, or guest) within the home.
- Even the most functional public zones, such as hallways and stairways, contribute to the feeling a guest or family member experiences while in a residence.
- Private zones serve residents' needs for solitude and familiarity. These zones may evolve as residents change, gain new preferences, and discover new outlets for contemplation and respite.
- Work areas include the kitchen, laundry, mudroom, office, and homework or study areas. These spaces are highly functional and should be designed to maximize productivity.
- While the functionality of a living space is important, design details enhance beauty and engage people's attention and senses.
- Elements of green design encourage healthy living by the people living in a residence.
- Every design includes a set of trade-offs which can be learned from. A well-designed plan offers efficiency to users. A poorly designed plan is inconvenient for users.
- Furniture arrangement should guide a user's path through a space, enhance communication, and encourage the use of specific rooms.
- Modern trends, such as multigenerational households, small house sizes, and the creative use of available space, affect residential design today.

Chapter Vocabulary

For each of the following terms, locate a photo that visually describes the meaning of the terms. Choose two terms and share your images and terms with the class. What attributes in the photos characterize the terms?

chromatherapy
conversation grouping
en suite bathroom
flex room
hotel glam
Jack and Jill bathroom
Murphy beds
personal autonomy
private zones
public zones
traffic patterns
work rectangle
work triangle
work zones

Review and Study

1. Give one example of how human needs differ between cultural groups.
2. Define and give an example of personal autonomy.
3. Compare and contrast the functions and movements of the three residential circulation patterns.
4. List the public zones described in this chapter.
5. What three activity areas are commonly designed into a living room?
6. Contrast the two types of privacy and how they might change across cultures and over a person's lifespan.

7. Describe the five kitchen work triangles and name a pro or con for each.
8. List three design details. Describe one way each could be effectively applied to a public, a private, and a work zone.
9. Describe five strategies for incorporating green design into residential projects.
10. Summarize the difference between a well-designed plan and a poorly designed plan and give two examples of each.
11. Name three residential design trends. Give one example for each, showing how each affects the ways that designers plan clients' residences.

Critical Analysis

12. **Identify.** In teams, acquire floor plans of favorite residential buildings and then identify the public, private, and work zones in each residence. Trade floor plans with another team. Identify the zones in the other team's floor plans and compare answers.
13. **Draw conclusions.** Presume you are an interior designer working with a client who has just moved to your region. Your client wants to have an extravagant outdoor kitchen and sleeping space and has not taken into account the reality of your region's weather patterns. What weather realities would you encourage your client to consider when planning the outdoor living space? What outdoor amenities would best fit with your region's seasonal changes?
14. **Cause and effect.** Use reliable online resources to research and locate examples of private zones that use chromatherapy to encourage relaxation. How do these lighting effects influence people's moods and mental states? How might you use the concept of chromatherapy in spaces other than master bathrooms? Write a summary about your ideas, including research examples.
15. **Evaluate.** Using the criteria for well-designed and poorly designed floor plans in this chapter, locate an example of a well-designed floor plan and of a poorly designed floor plan. Cite the sources for your floor plans and then create a presentation that evaluates the floor plans based on the criteria in this chapter. After your presentation, allow classmates to ask questions about your evaluation, and prepare answers to defend your assessments.

Think like a Designer

16. **Reading/writing.** Reread the *Design Insight* quote by Jill Pable and *Figure 15-4*. In teams, think specifically about those spaces that you have seen *filled* and those spaces that were designed as *fulfilling spaces* for you and others. Write a paragraph about an interior *filled space* in your life. Then, write a paragraph about a *fulfilling* interior space that you have experienced sometime in your life. What are the characteristics of each space? What makes one space *filled* and another space *fulfilling*? How does a *fulfilling* space shape your emotions and behavior? How have you seen others impacted by your *fulfilling* space?
17. **Speaking/listening.** Choose a residential building with furniture and visit that building. Walk through the rooms of the building and either photograph or sketch the furniture arrangement in each room. As you are walking, note how each room makes you feel. Does it make you feel welcomed? Does it feel cluttered? Collect your photographs or sketches and create a class pile. Do not indicate which residential building your photographs or sketches are from. Then, choose a set of sketches or photographs at random from the pile. Taking into account how your classmate felt when entering each room, describe how the furniture is arranged to achieve that effect. If you think you can improve the space, draw how you would rearrange the furniture in that room. Finally, present your analysis and drawings to the class.
18. **Research.** In teams, choose one culture you are unfamiliar with. Then, using reliable online or print resources, research how that culture defines *home*. What are the functions of a home? Who typically lives in a home and for how long? How is the typical home organized? Create a digital floor plan or model of a typical home in the culture you choose. Using a school-approved program, present your floor plan or model to the class, and explain how the residence you created aligns with the culture's definition of home. Afterward, ask the class for feedback on your model or floor plan. Take notes about their responses.

19. **Speaking/listening.** Review the space planning analysis boxes in this chapter and then, in teams, tour a residential building in your community. Individually, assess the building with each of the questions asked in the space planning analysis boxes. Write explanations for your answers to each question. Afterward, discuss your answers with your team. Listen to team members' responses about the building and its design. Is it well-designed or poorly designed? Why?
20. **Reading/writing.** Using online or print resources, research articles about what makes an effective entry, hallway, or stairway. If possible, read an article written by an interior designer. As you are reading, take notes about the article. Identify the article's audience and intent, and then briefly summarize its main points. Finally, compare the article you read with what you read in the chapter about entries, hallways, and stairways. Write a two- to three-page essay comparing and contrasting the information from both.
21. **Research and writing.** Choose a historical time period that interests you and then, using reliable online or print resources, research methods and trends in inclusive residential design during that time period. How inclusive were residential interiors? Why? How have current residential designs become more inclusive? less inclusive? Summarize your findings in a short essay and include photographs or sketches of inclusive designs from your chosen period of history.
22. **Speaking**. Research one of the kitchen design trends on pages 566–568. Use the *National Kitchen and Bath Association* website as one of your resources. What are the key characteristics of this trend? What factors encouraged the development of this trend? Locate several pictures showing this kitchen design trend and present your findings in an illustrated report to the class.
23. **Math practice.** Your clients are building their retirement home and want to connect the raised patio with the backyard using a ramp instead of stairs. A ramp is desirable for moving furniture, planting patio gardens, and for active grandchildren with tricycles. Because this is the gathering place for the extended family, whose ages and mobility vary (preschoolers, aging parents, and aging pets), they want the backyard design to be comfortable and accessible to all.
    A. Design a concrete ramp with a 1:12 ratio and a 45-inch rise using the ADA accessibility guidelines for a wheelchair ramp. The patio is centered on the back of the house. The garage is to the right of the patio and connects with the backyard by a sidewalk. At this time, there are no obstacles (curbs, slopes, landscaping, or utility boxes).
    B. Draw a scaled exterior plan view and elevation of the ramp and patio access to meet the ADA standards. Show and label all accessibility features and the site arrival point. Scale ¼" = 1'-0".

Design Application

24. **Develop a simple residential floor plan.** Design a small, functional and appealing residence for a family of four, incorporating the zones, circulation patterns, and furniture arrangements that you have learned in this chapter (Programming and Schematic Design phases only).
    A. Consider the needs of the residence. What needs must this residence meet? What is the primary function of this *home*? Write a concept statement for your residence that addresses these questions.
    B. Use relational and general bubble diagrams to evaluate space considerations. What spaces need to be adjacent to one another?
    C. Create a preliminary hand draft of a floor plan that meets all the space planning needs identified in your bubble diagrams. Add dimensions to your floor plan.
    D. Draft a preliminary furniture plan based on your floor plan. Lay a sheet of tracing paper over your floor plan to sketch your furniture plan. Identify the circulation patterns throughout your home. Do circulation patterns cross conversation areas or work zones?
    E. Choose interior furnishings and finishes for the residence interior. Create a material board to share your design plan with the family.
    F. Demonstrate your oral and written communication skills by writing an explanation of your design. How does your design reflect your concept statement? Give an oral presentation to family members, providing evidence for your choices along with your material boards.
    G. Revise your floor and furniture plans based on feedback from your family.
25. **Portfolio builder.** Create electronic files for your residential design plan from item 24. Save it to your e-portfolio for future reference.

You—The Beginning Designer

Sean Patrick Doran/Shutterstock.com

Chapter 16

Design Insight

"This is what we do, what we create, what we give. It is how we earn our place at the human table. It is why our work is important to our clients, to our societies, and to ourselves. It is the difference we make and why we choose this noble profession."

IFI Declaration

Learning Targets

After studying this chapter, you will be able to

- apply Pre-Design tasks which include drafting a letter of agreement and a first client interview.
- summarize how designers develop concept ideas.
- demonstrate effective verbal and written communication skills with individuals from varied cultures, including fellow workers, management, and customers.
- demonstrate proficiency with Programming tasks, including idenfifying client preferences and resources, gathering information, an inventory of FF&E, developing matrixes and relational bubble diagrams, writing the program, and client presentations.
- develop and complete Schematic Design drawings, including general bubble diagrams, block diagrams, floor plan refinements, and furniture plans.
- choose interior furnishings and finish materials.
- render freehand commercial or residential interior design working drawings.
- use industry accepted computer-aided drafting skills to complete various tasks during the design process.

Introduction

You are hired! The client picked *you*, so let's get started. In the professions of interior design, architecture, and construction managment, you will hear the design process described in several ways. For purposes of contractual organization, common project phases follow the process of design excluding the Pre-Design and Move-In/Post-Occupancy phases. These five basic project phases come from the *American Institute of Architects (AIA)* and the *American Society of Interior Designers (ASID)* Interior Design Services Agreement. Both of these agreements serve as contracts for design services and reflect project management in the United States.

Using the Process

As you read the chapter, it will walk you through the design of a small lakefront house, and provide you with a model to use later when you interview and work with your first client.

As you recall, the design process has seven phases: Pre-Design, Programming, Schematic Design (SD), Design Development (DD), Contract Documents (CD), Contract Administration (CA), and Move-In/Post-Occupancy Evaluation, **Figure 16-1**. This chapter covers tasks the designer completes in the first three phases of the design process: Pre-Design, Programming, and Schematic Design. Moving through these three phases offers you a taste of the excitement that comes from shaping space based on research and a client's preferences, needs, and requirements. It also teaches you not to be too overwhelmed by the amount of detail that can accompany a design project in the later phases. It is important to convert each client's problem into an organized, manageable project.

Pre-Design Phase

Begin with the Pre-Design phase which includes the retention of services. In this phase, you should draft a *letter of agreement* outlining your services. A letter of agreement is critical to reaching an agreement about the scope of the designer's services. The Pre-Design phase also includes your first client interview. During the first interview, you should ask questions such as the following:

- What is the client's design problem?
- What type of design project does your potential client need help with?
- What are the goals for this project?
- Where is the project located?
- What spaces are involved in this project?
- Who will be the users of the space—currently and in the future?
- What is the client's gender, age, ethnicity, and occupation?
- What is the time line and budget for this project?
- What is the scope of services the client needs from you and/or your firm?

These questions will help you learn valuable information about your client and their project. As you learned earlier in the text, effectively using your oral and written communication skills is essential in this phase and throughout the project.

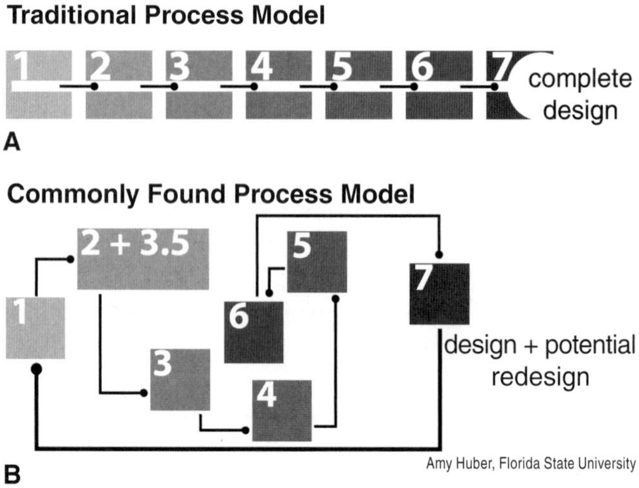

Amy Huber, Florida State University

Figure 16-1 The interior designer may circle back through several stages of the design process as he or she develops a design that solves a client's problem.

CASE STUDY

Introducing the Paul and Grace Emerick Family

Paul and Grace Emerick and their family are your new clients. The initial interview seems to go well, and you jot down the following notes about their answers to your questions.

- ***Who are the clients?*** Paul and Grace Emerick are a young couple in their early thirties. Grace is a physics teacher at a nearby high school and Paul is in his second career with a start-up company that works with cloud computing and technologies. Paul enjoys a variety of sports; Grace is an expert sculler and enjoys quiet, early-morning lake life. They have two children—Josh and Lily—whose respective ages are seven and five.
- ***What is the client's problem and what is the scope of the project?*** The client requires a remodel of a 1500-square-foot, ranch-style, lakefront cottage with a small beach. The existing building is weathered but is structurally sound. The client's design "problem" is to maximize the cottage's limited interior space and to take advantage of the views and natural daylight. They want to use sustainable and green strategies when remodeling the house.
- ***What is the scope of your (the designer's) services?*** The clients have hired me to complete their program, develop a design solution, and recommend a preliminary color palette. In addition, they want you to research daylight and green strategies for use within the existing house style. At this point, your contract indicates your are to complete work through the Schematic Design phase within a six-week period of time.
- ***Should you take on the project, and are you a good fit for these clients?*** Paul and Grace sought you and your firm via a referral from one of your previous clients. During the interview, they indicated that they were pleased with your qualifications, experience, references, and manner of doing business.
- ***Can you complete the project within the desired time frame and budget?*** After evaluating the status of other client projects you are working on, the fee offered, and the Emericks' needs/time frame, you feel it is a good fit to take on this project. The Emericks' time frame includes pulling the necessary building permits and beginning their remodel within the next six months. As a result of your evaluation, you should proceed to sign a contract.

Continued on page 591

Programming Phase

Once you have completed the Pre-Design phase, you can move on to the Programming phase. In this phase, you should prepare a Client Program. The *Client Program*, as you recall, is a written document that clearly and specifically outlines the client's project needs—its functions, issues, status of existing conditions, and spatial requirements. In addition, it involves detailed analysis of the client's budgetary factors and assets as well as analysis of architectural or site parameters and constraints. You complete the research and site observations as part of this phase. Your Client Program will serve as a type of checklist to ensure the client's project goals and objectives are ultimately met.

Residential projects generally require less intensive programming due to their scale and the number of people using the spaces. The relationships, adjacencies, and organization of the space are simple in comparison to large commercial, public spaces.

In the design world, the *client* may be more than one person. Make sure to include the decision makers in any interviews and, if the project is larger in scope, include representatives from any and all *end users*, or groups using the space.

The tasks you complete in the Programming phase include

- identifying client preferences and resources
- gathering information (discovery) by researching and collecting key facts and information related to the client project
- completing an inventory of the existing structure and existing furnishings, fixtures, and equipment (or *FF&E*) for potential reuse

- analyzing data collected
- summarizing and presenting information to the client

Identifying Client Preferences and Resources

The Programming phase begins with an in-depth client interview (sometimes with multiple end users) which is also known as a visioning session. A **visioning session** is a mental process in which you explore images of the desired future project. For commercial projects, you may also conduct interviews with different stakeholders or users of the space to ensure you meet their concerns and needs, too.

Arrive at the client interview with prepared questions and a way to document the answers clients give you. A professional appearance and demeanor is important, since you represent yourself and your firm. As your clients begin to respond to your questions—describing their project and preferences—expect your creativity and problem-solving skills to work overtime creating ideas and potential solutions that may address their problem.

Questions you might ask a client when conducting an in-depth interview include

- Why did you select this location, site, and house rather than others on the market?
- What are three priorities to consider when designing your house?
- Are there any issues to consider when working with the existing structure?
- What are three phrases to describe the feeling you want in your lake house?
- When you walk into the entry of the house, what type of mood would you like it to reflect?
- What resources do you have for remodeling this house?
- Once the house remodel is complete, what criteria will you use to determine if the design solution was successful?

Design preferences, space needs, and physical interrelationships (adjacencies) between distinct spaces should be at the root of your discussion points during the interview. The goal of this interview is to understand the Emerick client's viewpoint, preferences, needs, and issues in relationship to the project.

Designer Profile

Donna Vining, FASID, NCIDQ, RID, CAPS, REGREEN Trained—Residential Design

Donna Vining is President of Vining Design Associates, Inc., in Houston and has practiced interior design for almost 40 years.

Donna Vining, FASID/Miro Dvorscak Photography

"I have been blessed with fabulous clients and projects during my career. It didn't happen on day one, but after many years of hard work and continual learning. Residential design is not an easy path, but for me, it is the diversity and working with individuals to make their dreams a reality that makes this specialty most rewarding for me. Every decision an interior designer makes, whether residential, corporate, retail, etc., affects people's health, safety, and welfare. The wrong decision on flooring material for the elderly client could result in unsure footing and cause the client to lose his or her balance and a fall. Selecting the correct paint color and lighting for a child who has autism is crucial and should not be overstimulating.

"Universal and sustainable design is good for everyone and those two objectives are never far from my mind when I make recommendations to my clients. Once you have a successful relationship with a client, they normally include you in all their projects. I have clients that I have done 30 projects for and others 9 or 10. Second homes are one of their requests and can be so much fun and challenging, depending on the location. If you choose residential design, I truly believe you will make a difference in people's lives, and the smiles on their faces are extremely rewarding."

You can read more about Donna's experience in Appendix B.

CASE STUDY

In-Depth Interview with the Emerick Family

After signing a contract with the Emerick family, you perform an in-depth client interview and then conduct two site visits—one to the lake-house property and one to the Emericks' current home to observe their way of living and their design preferences. As you get to know Grace and Paul and ask more questions, you discover that they purchased the lake house due to its exceptional location and price point. Their three top design priorities include

- connecting the majority of the rooms to a lake view and all of the rooms to a quality outdoor space
- improving the overall energy efficiency and daylight quality throughout the house
- ensuring the interior materials are easy to maintain and offer a light, bright, comfortable feel for those living in or visiting this family sanctuary

racorn/Shutterstock.com

Continued on page 592

Discovery

The *discovery* task of the Programming phase is about gathering pertinent information that *informs* the design. Information gathering involves researching and gathering key facts and information related to the client project. There are two basic parts of discovery, including

- determining space needs, communication channels, and physical interrelationships (adjacencies) required within and between spaces
- gathering information, reviewing precedents or case studies, and researching pertinent project information

Space Planning, Communication, and Physical Interrelationships

As a designer, understanding how your clients work within spaces and whether the spaces require reshaping to meet their needs is vital. These discoveries are usually made through periodic client interviews and correspondence. Questions posed to clients should focus on "who needs to be next to whom" and the required size of specific spaces, the interrelationship of spaces, as well as communication needs between individuals. See **Figure 16-2** for sample client interview questions.

Planning the Space—Sample Client Interview Questions

Architecture and Site Questions

- How is the building oriented to the site?
- What is the architectural style of the building? What design elements can link interior to exterior?
- Where are entrances and exits to the building?
- On which side of the building are the best views located?

Physical Space Questions

- What types of spaces or rooms are needed? preferred?
- How are the spaces or rooms used and by whom? When?
- What are the present and future functions within the space?
- Do some of the spaces serve multiple functions?
- What views to the outside need to be captured with windows?
- Which areas need privacy or should address confidentiality issues?
- How can sustainable and inclusive design strategies be incorporated?
- What are the current circulation patterns? Where are there foot or pedestrian traffic issues?
- What are the structural elements that cannot be moved? Note load-bearing wall locations.
- How is natural light incorporated? Are electric light levels and their placements appropriate for use?
- What are the storage needs?

Figure 16-2 Interview questions are essential for gathering data to plan the design for a client's space. *What other questions might you ask?*

CASE STUDY

Emerick Lake House Description

The Emericks' lake house is a one-story structure with a crawl space and a shallow gable roof. It has an oddly charming, Palladian-style screened-in porch facing the lake with a different roofline from the main house. The dilapidated structure's meandering building footprint indicates it has had a number of additions over its lifetime. The house has a narrow profile facing the lake with a detached garage behind the house that faces the gravel road coming into the property.

Mikael Damkier/Hemera/Thinkstock.com

There are several issues with the house including the following:

- The window types and thick foliage around the house prevent daylight from penetrating too far into the interior spaces. Your clients desire more daylight with enhanced views of the lake.
- The master bedroom is small with limited closet space.
- A laundry area is currently located in the equally dilapidated garage. Moving it into the house is a high priority.
- The house location is 30 feet from the lakefront, limiting the dimensions of the outdoor living space.

Grace and Paul want three bedrooms—a master, one with bunk beds, and one guest room/office from which Paul will work remotely during the week. Due to the age of the children, the master bedroom does not need to be near the bunk room. They prefer a great room with a combination kitchen/dining/living area that opens lakeside onto a new outdoor living space. Two and one-half baths are a requirement as well as a small mudroom near the garage. Storage space is also a priority. The clients have a modest budget for completing the renovation.

Continued on page 593

Research and Gather Information

To gather information, you should also conduct formal and informal research, review similar completed projects (for example, case studies or precedents), and assess life-safety issues. These tasks will help you understand how others have solved similar client problems and review what research is available to ensure your design solution is strong and on target. This stage also includes gathering information about the structural needs of the building if it is not new construction.

Depending on the type of information you need, you may collect *quantitative data* (facts and numerical figures) or *qualitative data* (interviews). For the Emerick's design, quantitative data may include the family's budget figures. Qualitative data may involve an interview with each family member—including the children—to determine needs, uses, and priorities for the space. You can use both types of data to shape and support the final design solution.

Using Precedents

Often, as you gather information prior to developing the design for the client project, you will view or visit case studies or precedents online or in person. **Case studies**, or *precedents*, are examples of similarly completed interior design projects. (Note: *Precedents* is often used by architects with a similar meaning; however, interior designers who work in commercial design may also use the term precedents instead of case studies.) You can view case studies or precedents online by examining design-firm portfolios or by visiting a similar project in person as a *site observation*.

The goal of the information you are gathering is to answer the question, "How has a similar client problem been solved?" The information you gather can be very revealing and often prevent mistakes you might make on your client's project. Keep records of photos and observations during these visits or online searches. Then summarize the helpful information from each case study in the *Client Program*.

CASE STUDY

Researching Design Ideas for the Emerick Lake House

When reviewing case studies for Paul and Grace's lakefront house, your search takes you to similar lake homes in the same upper-Michigan region. You also pull design ideas from other case studies that might work for the Emerick family. As you review your research, you ask yourself the following Emerick questions:

- How are lakefront and outdoor views captured in this case study?
- What shapes are the windows? Could I enlarge the client's existing windows without compromising the building?
- In the case studies, how do the outdoor living spaces link to the indoor living spaces? What design elements link the outside to the inside and vice versa?
- Where are the access points to the outdoor living areas?
- What sustainable or green strategies could I reasonably incorporate into the Emericks' project?
- Are there any daylighting case studies that might help me solve my client's problem?
- What clever storage ideas could I use in Paul and Grace's home?

Continued below

While gathering information, you may also perform evidence-based design research. Remember, *evidence-based design (EBD)* is an approach to design that uses facts and professional judgment to develop informed design solutions for clients. Once you know the type of project you are designing, you can discover relevant facts and information about client or design issues and the resources available to address them. The more complex the project, the more numerous and complex the issues will be.

Gathering information on *life-safety codes* is also important at this time. You can visit your local building code official to learn what the codes are and how they might impact your client's project. Code officials offer suggestions and resources to help you remain compliant with all national and local codes.

Information-gathering tasks are significant. They enable you to design based on research and gathered data. When you present potential design solutions to your client, you establish significant credibility if you can cite research studies, precedents, statistics, or consumer interviews that support *why you designed the way you did.* Remember, you are weaving a design storyline that should be easy to communicate and justify to your client

CASE STUDY

Client Issues for Evidence-Based Design Research

After talking with Paul and Grace, you decide that using evidence-based design would help you complete this project. You decide to conduct evidence-based design research by asking the following questions:

- What type of glazing (on windows) will keep heat out during summer months but allow views during the cooler spring and fall months?
- Do any of the family members have *seasonal affective disorder (SAD)* that requires certain design features related to natural light?
- Will the Emericks' parents require installation of a ramp to address accessibility issues?
- How can I address energy-efficiency needs?
- What green materials can I use to address the Emericks' sustainability needs?
- What materials are easy to clean, yet stylish, bright, and light?
- What type of solar tubes can be used to bring daylight into the darker parts of the house?
- Would light shelves work without disturbing the architectural style of the house?

Continued on page 594

and others who may have involvement in the project. Your design should be *defensible*.

After gathering information about your client's needs and viewing case studies, your next task is to identify each space and its subsequent functions. Listing spaces in an organized manner allows you to clearly see what spaces to include and what each room requires.

For the Emerick residential design project, you would develop a list of spaces for eating, sleeping, playing, and working. Under the name of each room, such as the kitchen, list additional details with associated functions. Also list cultural needs such as a place for worship or the need for extra closets to store items needed only when a large family gathering takes place. For commercial clients, you might list the types of spaces needed, how the facility will function, and the major issues the clients need to address, such as privacy, security, sustainability, or confidentiality.

Completing an Inventory

After gathering information, your next step is to complete an inventory. Understanding the condition of the client's existing structure or location is essential for inventory. Be sure to document existing conditions such as the existing floor plan, site location, furnishings to reuse, and other information pertinent to the current condition.

Sometimes your client can provide existing drawings of the building and interior for your use. Regardless, be sure to take field measurements to verify accuracy of the drawings. Many times, the plans on file with the building department differ from actuality on-site. Typical field measurements include those you take of windows, doors, placement of outlets and switches, HVAC locations, as well as wall and flooring finishes. You may sketch plans and details on-site as well as photograph existing conditions.

If a building is a new construction, you may be part of the design team that determines circulation patterns, universal design elements, door and window placement, and site orientation to gather daylight and views. Depending on the project, you may be brought in at the end of the project to complete the furniture and finishes package.

CASE STUDY

Emerick Lake Home Needs and Preferences

After gathering information about relevant case studies or precedents and researching appropriate codes, you feel ready to list the types of spaces needed for the Emericks' lakefront house. During an interview, you ask the Emericks' about their needs and preferences for each space and take note of the following needs for each space:

- ***Entry.*** Sense of arrival. Small closet.
- ***Living room/dining combination.*** The living room may include lake views, a flat-screen television (hidden), comfortable seating for four, and a sound system for music. This area requires a breakfast nook off the kitchen with lake views.
- ***Kitchen.*** Client needs include ceiling-height cupboards, appliances (including a microwave oven), counter bar with chairs, under-cabinet lighting, windows with possible views of the lake, two drawer stacks in the base cupboards, natural ventilation, extra deep sink, tile backsplash, easy access to the breakfast nook, and green features as appropriate. The breakfast nook includes seating for four and could include a banquette.
- ***Master bedroom with master bath.*** Include lake views and king-size bed in the master bedroom. Master bath requires a shower, but no tub.
- ***Bunk room for Josh and Lily.*** Include two bunks with a nearby bathroom. The bathroom requires a tub/shower combination.
- ***Optional third bedroom.*** Serves as guest room and office and includes a Murphy bed, desk area, desk chair, storage, and Internet hook-up.
- ***Additional needs.*** Include a half-bath for guests and a mudroom with cubby storage and coat hooks.
- ***Outdoor living area.*** The outdoor living area should be on the lakeside.

Continued on page 595

CASE STUDY

Site Visit and Assessment of the Existing Emerick Lake House

With your list of spaces completed, you get ready to take an inventory of the existing structure and features of the Emericks' lake house. First, you find an old blueprint of the original structure at the local building department. After reviewing the blueprint, you make a site visit to verify dimensions and view modifications that were made to the structure over time. When a structural engineer assesses the existing building, she verifies it is safe and sound.

The overall structure is in better shape than you anticipated. The existing doors are quaint and can be refinished and reused. You take interior dimensions of each room and create on-site sketches and plans of the space. The Emerick family has several pieces of furniture to reuse in their remodel including a king-size bed, a small kitchen table and four chairs, a small desk, and one overstuffed, upholstered chair.

FLariviere/Shutterstock.com

Pushish Images/Shutterstock.com

TaraPatta/Shutterstock.com

Baloncici/Shutterstock.com

Continued on page 596

Analyzing Data

The analysis task of the Programming phase involves reviewing the project's functions and needs broken down by room (if residential) or division (if commercial). Using the client's needs, you can understand and analyze the data to determine the following:

- functions that can be grouped together to increase efficiency
- spaces that need to be located near other spaces
- spaces that need to be near a window or located near an exit
- offices that require acoustical or visual privacy
- departments or divisions that need to be within close proximity to enhance communication

Analyzing data is a methodical process that allows you to accurately understand the functions, end users, and tasks of each space and adjoining spaces. The process also refines and prioritizes client issues based on their feedback. Design is a series of trade- offs. The client often cannot have everything, so part of your job is to help establish priorities. This is where the client's previously identified priorities help guide decisions.

Two tools are useful for analysis of the client's problem: matrixes and bubble diagrams. Both offer opportunities for analyzing and prioritizing client needs.

Matrixes

Matrixes are extremely useful tools because they incorporate a wealth of information into a visual that is easy to comprehend. A complete matrix visually organizes and illustrates voluminous amounts of information from the Client Program to further enhance client understanding. It is revealing to see such a concise summary of the client's needs. Reviewing and analyzing the matrix helps you perceive how client priorities impact the design solution.

As you recall, designers use two types of matrixes—an *adjacency matrix* and a *criteria matrix.* If the project is small enough, you can combine these matrixes into one matrix. For instance, for the Emerick family, one matrix should be enough.

An *adjacency matrix* is a diagram or table that lists each room or space. It helps you look broadly at connections between different spaces in the project. Your goal is to determine, based on the Program, which spaces need to be next to each other or directly adjacent to each other.

For a residential client, this analysis may result in placing a bathroom next to a bedroom. For a commercial office client, this analysis may result in placing an administrative assistant's workstation adjacent to the office of the department head.

A *criteria matrix* lists each room or space of the client's project in the left-hand column. It lists each issue, prioritized by the client, as column headings. The goal is to determine the client's specific needs and in what order they occur *within each space.*

Priorities the criteria matrix might include are square footage needs, daylight or views, acoustical or visual privacy, and security. For a residential client, this may

CASE STUDY

Identifying Emerick Priorities—Creating a Sample Matrix

To analyze your data, you develop a matrix and share it with Paul and Grace. After reviewing your notes from the client interview, you learn the following about the Emericks' priorities:

- The kitchen/dining/living area as well as the master bedroom should be prioritized to have lake views. Any additional living areas with lake views are a bonus.
- The mudroom—with laundry facilities—should face away from the lake and be near the two-car, detached garage as well as located just off the kitchen.
- The third bedroom also functions as Paul's office when guests are not using it. This room requires some acoustical privacy to enhance Paul's work environment.
- Retaining some foliage on the south and west sides of the house without obscuring views remains important.

Using these priorities, as well as the spaces included in the house, you create a matrix to present your information to the Emerick family.

To begin your matrix, start with the public spaces: kitchen, dining, living room combination. Split them into three separate spaces on the matrix even though they will be connected in their open floor plan.

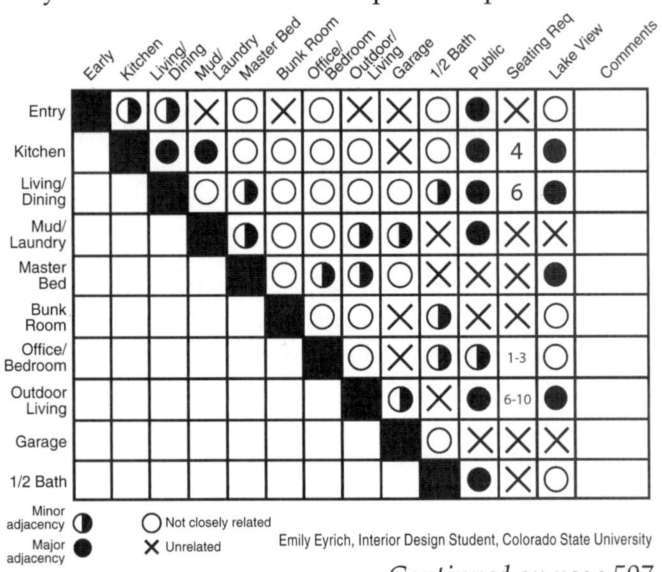

Emily Eyrich, Interior Design Student, Colorado State University

Continued on page 597

CASE STUDY

Creating Relational Bubble Diagrams

To analyze the data you have gathered and help Grace and Paul visualize your plan so far, you decide to create the relational bubble diagram for Paul and Grace's lake house. In creating the diagram, you use the following steps:

1. Begin drawing ovals or circles on tracing paper with a dark felt-tip pen. Start with the Emericks' largest, public spaces: kitchen, dining, and living area. Make three different colored circles and group them together. On the paper, label where the lake is located based on the circles. This tells you where to locate the views when looking at your bubbles. Who or what area needs to be next to that space and/or person? What area needs to be next to both spaces? (Figures A and B)
2. Add the entry and mudroom. Inside the mudroom, draw a smaller circle for the laundry area. Use connecting lines as you draw each space to make your diagram. Then indicate the paths of travel between spaces with heavier or multiple lines to indicate a primary relationship. Avoid crossing lines. Add notes and arrows if needed to remember and record the thought process as creative ideas begin to spark.
3. Add the master bedroom and bath to your drawing. Make sure it is near the back of the house for that requested lake view. The master bath should adjoin the master bedroom.
4. Add the other two bedrooms and two and one-half baths as well. The second full bath should be between the second and third bedrooms for ease of access. Remember that relational bubble diagrams are a type of visual literacy. Draw multiple relational bubble diagrams to help you understand who and what needs to be next to each other. If done manually, consider layering tracing paper. Add a key or legend that explains lines and what they communicate such as the need for proximity.
5. Stop now and evaluate your diagram. How well does the plan work? What advantages and disadvantages exist with what you drew?
6. List the pros and cons on the side of the relational bubble diagram you just finished. This step is important. Your critical analysis of the most and least effective parts of the plan will ensure you draw the next bubble diagram for your client with better locations.

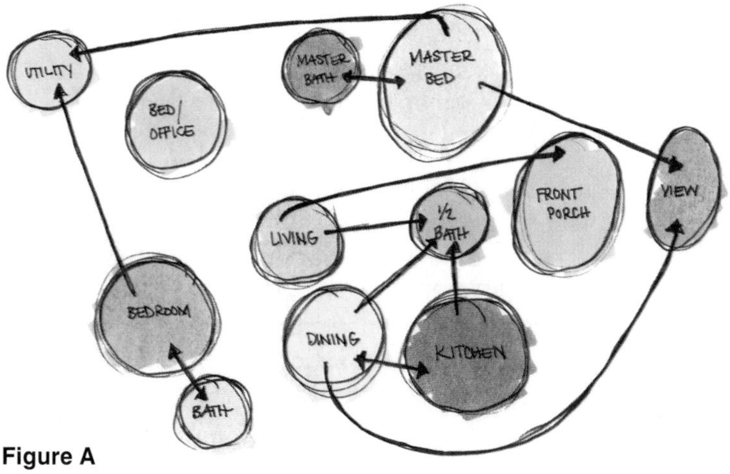

Figure A

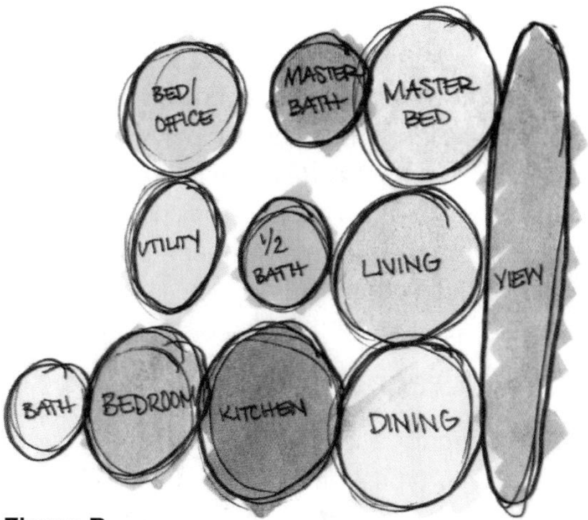

Figure B

Emily Eyrich, Interior Design Student, Colorado State University

(Continued)

CASE STUDY *(Continued)*

7. Look at a peer's set of relational bubbles for the same client. Note that using the same spatial requirements can result in different diagrams. Exploring multiple design solutions is part of the creative design process and results in a better final design solution for your client. (Figure C)

8. Create a general bubble diagram inside the boundary of the building footprint. Figuratively speaking, you pick up your relational bubble diagram and set it down as best you can inside the building structure. Through your analysis of relationships, you now have an understanding of what space needs to be next to another.

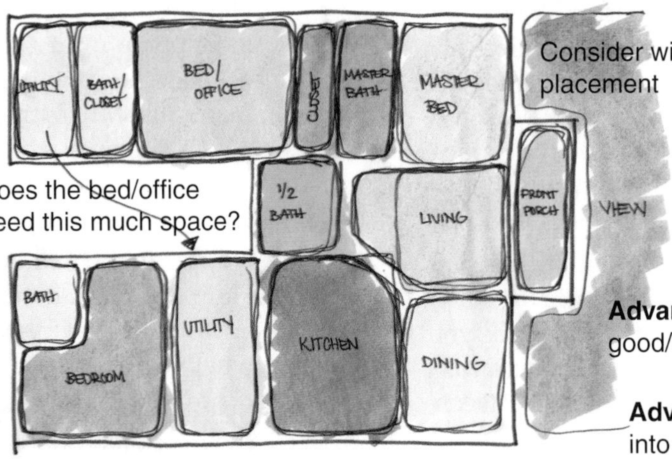

Emily Eyrich, Interior Design Student, Colorado State University

Figure C

Continued on page 600

result in the design of the master bedroom giving a mountain view with acoustical privacy. For a commercial office client, this may result in a receptionist space having 120 square feet, no visual or acoustical privacy, but with access to the business center. Answers resulting from matrixes directly impact the client's floor plan within a given structure.

Bubble Diagrams

As you recall, a second analysis tool is the bubble diagram—a type of mind map. These diagrams depict overall zones, areas of space according to activity, relationships to other spaces, and sometimes potential locations. Bubble diagrams allow the designer to quickly and creatively assess potential associations between spaces without the need to invest time in a complex plan that may not work. Your goal is to explore as many options as possible in a short period of time. If the plan becomes too finite, too quickly, the floor plan will be weak.

Draw bubble diagrams loosely as ovals or circles in representation of a room. The bubbles are often drawn and colored using different-colored markers, assigning each bubble a unique color. No square footage should be assigned to the bubbles; however, you might use larger bubbles for larger spaces. There are two types of bubble diagrams: *relational* and *general.*

Relational bubble diagrams are completed first, generally during Programming. Develop them on paper or on a digital tablet without any boundaries or building structure to guide the placement of the series of bubbles. Using the adjacency matrix, your goal is to capture in a two-dimensional plan the relationship of each space to another.

General bubble diagrams place the client spaces within the available square feet. While creating general bubble diagrams, group spaces together according to activity, relationships to other spaces, and locations. If need be, relocate a space or two to make all areas fit. Again, attempt to keep the spaces in similar locations. Similar to a chess game, as one space figuratively is moved to a new location, all other spaces are impacted, too. As the project and plan become larger, analyzing the client's needs becomes more complex.

Relational and general bubble diagrams incorporate matrix information, are drawn freely, and are analyzed when complete. The designer should not impose predetermined ideas into the plan to enhance the evolution of creative solutions. Instead, let the process unfold naturally.

Summarizing and Presenting to the Client

Once you finish the previous tasks, organize the Program data and analysis documents into a written report for the client. By compiling this data, you and the client can see the entire picture of the project, including both existing and future needs. The three goals of this step is to inform the client of what you have compiled about their project and verify accuracy, ensure the client's understanding about the project, and then receive their approval before moving forward on their project. Any misunderstandings are easier to clarify at this point of the project than later in the design process.

Write the Client Program

The Program should include photos, site observation sketches or diagrams, and field measurements. If the information is abundant, as is with many commercial projects, it is your job to distill the information into a manageable, understandable report.

A basic template for the Client Program includes a

- program outline
- executive summary (short summary of Program information)
- client profile
- client project description
- community/locale
- client needs and issues
- existing conditions
- research conducted
- list of client spaces, room by room; square footage needed for each space
- list of existing and future FF&E needs for each room
- matrixes and bubble diagrams analyzing relationships
- appendices

Once the Client Program is complete, a client's approval and "sign-off" is helpful to document the client's agreement with the project Program. By the end of the Programming phase, the designer and the client should fully understand and agree on the scope of the project, budget, and the approved time line. The designer often makes a client presentation and answers client questions during that meeting.

Presentation to the Client

You can handle the presentation of the Program to the client in a variety of ways. Ultimately, you want the decision makers at the table to determine if the identified issues and gathered research address the client's goals, needs, and preferences within the identified budget.

You generally deliver the oral presentation in person. Although with today's technology, long distance, "face-to-face" presentations can take place via the Internet, too. Use the meeting time to share the data collected and answer client questions. This helps ensure understanding among all parties as the project rolls to the next phase. If the project is large, you may make multiple copies of the Client Program and give them to various stakeholders. After this task, the next design phase begins.

Read the following Client Program for Paul and Grace Emerick and their children.

CASE STUDY

Program for the Paul and Grace Emerick Family; Elk Rapids, Michigan

Having gathered and analyzed all of the information you need, you are now ready to present your Client Program to Paul and Grace Emerick. In writing the Program, you are sure to be concise and present the information in a way the family will understand. After much time drafting and revising, you prepare the following Program:

Executive Summary

Remodel an existing, 1500-square-foot lake house using sustainable and green design strategies for a family of four. The family includes two children: Josh (age 7) and Lily (age 5). The Emericks' remodel goals include 1) to maximize the cottage's limited interior space, 2) to take advantage of the views and natural daylight, and 3) to enhance the energy efficiency of the house and convert it into an all-season home. The interior spaces should reflect a sense of place and a light, bright, easily-maintained feel that invites relaxation and serenity by the lake.

Client Profile

- Paul: 36, priorities are family and career, sports-minded, extensive user of computer technologies, entrepreneurial
- Grace: 30, physicist, high school science teacher, enjoys entertaining and active lake life
- Josh: 7, enjoys robots, speed boats, swimming, beach life, discovery activities, and creative inventions
- Lily: 5, loves swimming, horses, fairy tales, science, BMX biking, and playing

Client Project Description

Remodel an existing structure for a family of four. *House and Site:* 1500 square feet, detached two-car garage, structurally sound, and needs new roof and windows to enhance energy efficiency. Lake views are a priority.

Community/Locale

The Emerick house is located on Elk Lake, near the quaint town of Elk Rapids and the larger community of Traverse City, Michigan. Elk Lake is located in the Grand Traverse and Antrim counties in Northern Michigan. Elk Rapids has a cultural, tourist vibe and is especially busy during the summer months. After Labor Day weekend, most of the lake life closes down for the winter. Elk Lake is about one and one-half miles wide and nine miles long. It is the second deepest lake in Michigan.

Located on lakefront property, the Emerick house has heavy foliage surrounding the exterior. Sandy soil abounds in the area, which is one of the reasons the lake is a deep, clear, Caribbean blue color.

SNEHIT/Shutterstock.com

Michael G. Smith/Shuttestock.com

Thomas Barrat/Shutterstock.com

LesPalenik/Shutterstock.com

Sean Patrick Doran/Shutterstock.com

Sean Patrick Doran/Shutterstock.com

Robert Gubbins/Shutterstock.com

Client Needs and Issues

- Maintain house at 1500 square feet.
- Remodel to enhance energy efficiency of the house.
- Capitalize on lake views for combined kitchen/dining/living spaces and master bedroom.
- Do not move load-bearing walls.
- Enhance daylighting strategies.
- Use sustainable and green strategies.
- Enlarge outdoor living space; add fireplace.
- If included, ensure third bedroom doubles as home office with acoustical privacy needs.
- Address local building codes.

Existing Conditions

- Small, dark house with high energy bills
- Small windows allowing little daylight into interior spaces
- Dated bathrooms and kitchen
- No window to lake in the kitchen, making it difficult to supervise children playing on the lake side
- Awkwardly placed interior spaces
- Minimal storage
- House overrun with foliage; side and back views obscured
- No outdoor living space other than screened-in porch
- Sagging garage structure
- Laundry located in garage; needs to move into main house
- No mudroom
- No real relationship to the land or landscape

Research Conducted

- Building structure
- Community
- Energy-efficient windows
- Solar tubes; light shelves
- Zero VOC paints
- Salvaged, local woods
- Bio-based fiber content carpets
- Outdoor living spaces

Client Spaces—Room by room

- Kitchen centrally located with visual access to dining/family room and lake. Convenient access to mudroom and laundry. Compact and efficient, accommodating to family/friend gatherings; preferably with an island or peninsula and stools for seating. Energy Star appliances.
- Public spaces require convenient access to outdoor living spaces and views.
- Living room requires seating for four. Comfortable chair (existing).
- Master bedroom needs lake views and access to outdoor living space. Include a king-size bed with end tables and separate closets, if possible.
- Master bathroom to include large shower with no tub, double sinks, low-flow toilet, storage, and good lighting.
- Children's bunk room with shared bathroom includes one set of bunk beds with possible guest bunk. Include built-in storage with bins for toys and clothes.
- Shared bathroom must incorporate tub, sink, toilet, storage.
- Mudroom with laundry facilities and easy access to garage. Hooks, storage, and counter for folding, if possible; good lighting.
- Two-car detached garage; make accessible to house, reinforce structure. Exterior door.
- Outdoor living space. Seating for six. Table and chairs. Grill and small refrigerator. Speakers for evening music. Finish materials should tolerate inclement weather and heavy sun and be easily maintained.
- House should regain charm of region. Consider natural light and breezes in remodel. Requires incorporation of cable and wireless Internet systems.

(Continued)

CASE STUDY *(Continued)*

Existing FF&E

- King-size bed, 76″ x 80″
- Small kitchen table—circular, 4′-0″ diameter, four kitchen chairs
- Small black desk, 52″ x 23″ x 30″
- One overstuffed, upholstered chair, 35.5″ w x 45″ d, 34″h

Matrixes and Bubble Diagrams

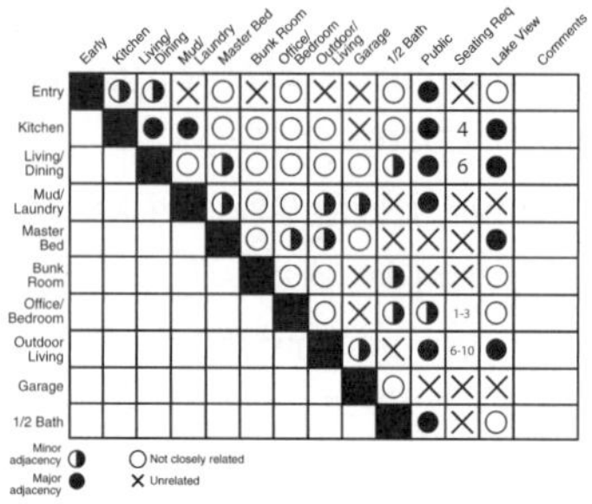

Emily Eyrich, Interior Design Student, Colorado State University

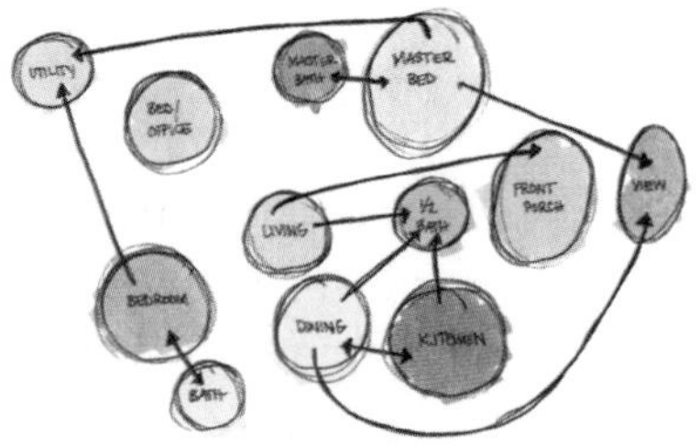

Emily Eyrich, Interior Design Student, Colorado State University

Appendix

- Sketches
- Photos
- Text containing case studies about other similar properties and their solutions

Mikael Damkier/Hemera/Thinkstock.com

Sean Patrick Doran/Shutterstock.com

Continued below

Schematic Design (SD) Phase

Once you have defined and critically analyzed the parameters of the client's problem, you can begin to develop a solution. The Schematic Design (SD) phase begins the problem-solving tasks of the design process. This phase includes the following major tasks:

- **Concept development**—process that guides future design decisions for the client's project
- **Preliminary space planning**—tasks to explore the layout of the physical space within the building shell
- **Drawings** (sketches and elevations)—to explore the client's three-dimensional space(s) and the designer's proposal ideas
- **Furniture, fixtures, and equipment (FF&E)**—proposed furnishings and equipment needed for spaces
- **Budget projection**—preliminary budget proposal

CASE STUDY

Presenting the Client Program

After much hard work, you present the Client Program to Grace and Paul at their home (see page 602 for more about presenting information to clients). The presentation is informal and you answer their questions. Small adjustments to the Program are made. During the presentation, the Emericks request that the kitchen/dining/living space be converted into a *great room* concept with a small kitchen nook. You receive their sign-off agreement after changes are made and then send them an electronic copy of their Program for future reference.

Continued on page 604

STUDENT SPOTLIGHT

Inspiration for Interior Design

Emily Eyrich (sophomore). "Growing up in Vail, Colorado, provides certain luxuries that are seldom seen elsewhere. One of these luxuries is gorgeous architecture. Seeing beautiful homes while I walked around town is one of the main reasons I chose to become a designer. Originally, architecture was my calling; however, I was rarely fortunate enough to see the interiors of these grand houses. When I grew older, I found that I was much more intrigued by how the inside of places shaped my experience. Ever since then, interior design has inspired me.

"After studying interior design at Colorado State University, I have learned about countless realms of design. Lighting design, space planning, custom home design, and sustainable design are only a fraction of the possibilities design has to offer. The idea that every place a person visits has been designed in some shape or form—whether good or bad—is fascinating to me. Design is endless. Design is ever changing. Design is impactful, and I want to impact people's lives for the better."

Kameron Stutzman (senior). "I grew up in Greeley, Colorado, and from an early age I loved the *decoration* aspect of interior design, especially in my room! When I went to college, however, I majored in *biology,* which is about as far away from interior design imaginable.

"After graduation, I worked in the healthcare industry for several years and decided to teach. I got a master's degree in education with a secondary science teaching credential, but decided to teach healthcare classes at a career college. Because the creative side of me was not engaged in my career, I attended an interior design class and thought, "these are my people." I couldn't believe my homework was 'homework' because I enjoyed it so much!

"I acquired my second bachelor's degree in interior design and I decided to join my two areas of expertise: *biology* and *interior design* to pursue healthcare design. Due to my previous experience in the medical industry, I have a working knowledge of what works and what doesn't in a healthcare facility. I am excited to bring research-based techniques to my design work that will enhance a patient's experience, reduce pain, and the time needed to heal.

"As interior designers, we have the ability to make a house a better functioning home, and create an *experience* for people at a restaurant, resort, or sports venue. We cultivate environments where people can learn in a creative space and be made more comfortable in a healthcare facility. I am passionate about being able to impact people in these ways with the 'behind the scenes' considerations and planning, and I look forward to making life better for my community, and world."

Julia Harmon (sophomore). "When growing up in Minneapolis, Minnesota, there were only two different seasons during the year—winter and *not* winter. Because of this, I spent a lot of time inside playing in my house. I truly believe that my desire to create spaces came from the countless hours I spent changing my room as a child. At one point, my parents ended up hiring a designer to work with me in changing my room just so I would stop making them help every other weekend. Though it started as a way to fight boredom, interior design soon became a true passion in my life.

"Interior design is so thrilling to me because, as a designer, you are helping a client create a vision that to them is just something of a fantasy. It can be difficult for some people to explain in words what they want to see or create in their spaces, which is why designing can be so interesting. While working with a client, you might find that something you are so sure will fit their wants is nothing they are expecting. As soon as you find that perfect match with your client, however, you have this moment of triumph that comes from creating something that another person loves so much."

The main way you communicate to the client during the conceptual tasks of the Schematic Design phase is with drawings and diagrams. A client presentation often takes place at the end of this phase (and sometimes during each task of the phase) to assess if your understanding and proposed ideas are appropriate and reflective of client needs and goals. It is not until the phase is complete and you receive the client's sign-off that the Design Development (DD) phase begins.

Concept Development

The first task of the Schematic Design phase is one of the most creative and innovative of the design process: *concept development.* As you know, a *concept* is an abstract idea or image formed in the brain that guides every decision you make throughout the design process to the final design solution. Evoking mood is the basis for some concepts, while the basis for others is functional aspects of the design goals.

Theory suggests that there are advantages to having a strongly identified design concept. For example, if you form a general image of the ideas supporting the design of the space or the series of spaces before engaging in the design and planning processes, you will be more creative with your ideas about an interior space.

A successful concept

- should appeal to a client's point of reference
- can be envisioned and understood by the client
- is strong and will guide the design from conception to installation
- can be communicated using written, oral, and visual methods
- addresses programming needs, is abstract, and is unique
- gives coherence and identity to a design
- becomes part of the design vocabulary for the client project

Developing and Using Concepts

You often conceive a concept during one or more brainstorming sessions. This concept should act like a homing device throughout the design process and should be incorporated into every decision (such as the floor plan, furniture, and finishes) that you make about the client's design. For example, if you need to make a decision about a furniture style, the question you ask yourself should be, *Will the style reflect and support the approved concept?*

A concept not only keeps you on track but it also keeps the client on course when other design ideas pop up during the project's design development and completion. It is reassuring to a client to have something that narrows the myriad of possibilities in the market.

Developing the concept—as a creative statement or image (or both)—is a very important step to finish before moving on through the rest of the design process. Without a concept, every other design decision lacks a target and measurement to determine the project's success.

The concept is the primary element that *sells* your design solution to the client and gives you a competitive edge over other design firms. Clients feel reassurance if they can visualize the mood or feeling of the overarching design.

Using Sources for Concept Ideas

What sources of inspiration can you use when developing a client's concept? The answer is, "Just about everything." Nature and views, geographic anomalies such as mountain ranges, architectural details in the

CASE STUDY

The Emericks' Concept Development

To establish a concept for this design project, you plan a brainstorming session. During the brainstorming session, you ask Grace and Paul what words and phrases they would use to describe the vision for their lake house. Paul and Grace provide you with the following words and phrases:

- Bright and serene
- Unexpectedly earthy, unsophisticated style
- Labor-saving, incredibly functional
- Transparency between the inside and outdoors
- Unpredictable charm; simply modern
- Inviting, flexible, and accommodating
- Lake-centric; family oriented

Continued on page 606

surrounding community, functional requirements, and cultural issues may all offer reference points to the client's project and therefore serve as inspiration for the client's project solution. A concept should communicate the design intent of the project. It should link the place and function of the space with the aesthetics and evoked mood. Consider where you look for concept ideas and what sources you find inspiring.

Writing Problem Statements versus Concept Statements

After developing a concept, you will need to distill that concept into a problem or concept statement. A **problem statement** is a description of issues you need to address during the design process. It is usually a sentence or series of paragraphs that describe the client's issues and needs that need to be addressed by the time the design process is complete. The **concept statement** is the vision of where to focus the design solution, **Figure 16-3**.

Communicating Concepts

Typically, you will write, verbally deliver, or visually present the concept once it has been developed. Communicating concept may involve written communication, oral communication, or visual communication. Because some concepts are hard to grasp without multiple communication strategies, you may often use all three techniques to communicate the concept to the design team or the client.

Written Communication

If using the written word, communicate a concept through a word pair, phrase, or sentence. It is important to carefully select imagery-evoking words and avoid using common, everyday terminology that does not offer a unique image for the client to envision.

When developing imagery-evoking words or phrases, remember the client needs a reference point to envision the concept or image. Reference points may include places clients have been, periods of art they viewed, a mood they have felt, or a movie they have seen. If clients do not have a reference point, you will need to explain the source of inspiration for the concept. If clients are unable to visualize the concept for their project, they may not approve it. Conversely, the concept should not be too general in nature, such as "warm and cozy." If the concept is too general, it could fit too many spaces and places.

Along with offering the client a written phrase, you may also supply a supporting paragraph that communicates additional details about the concept. For example, think about the following concept statement a design student developed for a restaurant project: "Laid-back, intimate, and artsy like an abstract sunrise." The supporting statement was, "This restaurant is a contemporary yet comfortable breakfast/brunch café near a college campus in the mountains. A place to escape from everyday stress, its atmosphere is laid-back, intimate, and artsy." What do you envision when you think about these statements?

Oral Communication

In professional practice, you as an interior designer will often give oral presentations to the client to communicate the intended concept for the project. From a design point of view, this is much like weaving a story for the client.

Visual Communication

In addition to the written or oral communication, you can use conceptual illustrations, sketches, or presentation boards to communicate the concept to the client. One popular method of developing an abstract, conceptual design is a *concept square*.

Characteristics of Concept and Problem Statements	
Concept Statements	**Problem Statements**
■ A word, metaphor, or phrase descriptive of a mental image ■ Something conceived in the mind; an abstract idea; a thought or notion ■ An idea that is measurable against the success of the final project ■ An idea based on visual aesthetics or functional needs ■ An image	■ Describes the function of the Client Program ■ Describes the character of the program and space ■ Describes the aesthetics of the space

Figure 16-3 Problem statements help the designer describe the client's issues that require solution while concept statements provide vision for focusing the design solution.

CASE STUDY

Concept Words and Concept Squares

After the brainstorming session with Grace and Paul, you continue the search of words and phrases that support Grace and Paul's vision for their lake house. You turn to the dictionary and thesaurus to look for words that other people typically do not use. There are many great words to use that can fully describe your concept. You started by looking up words like *lake*, *water*, *rustic*, and *retreat*, and their synonyms, and then look for less common words that are descriptive, inspiring, and memorable. You begin to jot down concept words which eventually lead you to a concept statement.

Another resource you use is your favorite Internet search engine. When searching for "lake" terms, you come across the word, *epilimnion* (eh-puh-LIHM-nee-uhn) which describes the warmer, well-lit surface waters of a lake when stratified. This term seems to capture the feeling Grace and Paul are going for with the design of their lake home. As you continue your personal brainstorming session, you decide to add *eclectic* to epilimnion not only for the alliteration it creates but also because it relates to the inclusion of things (and ideas) taken from many sources.

Concept Words: historic, charm, bright, sunny, cottage, cozy, lake, sun-kissed, tranquil, relaxing, haven, lake front, port, starboard, buoyant, epilimnion, lightsome, blithesome, eclectic, activity, float, retreat

Buoyant: Able to float, able to cause things to float, happy and confident

***Eclectic:** Including things taken from many sources

***Epilimnion:** The warmer, well-lit surface waters of a lake when it is stratified (thermally separated from the colder water at the lake bottom)

Kameron K. Stutzman, Interior Design Student, Colorado State University

As your creativity continues to flow, you begin drawing a series of concept squares, ending with one you think captures the essence of the Emericks' feeling for their design.

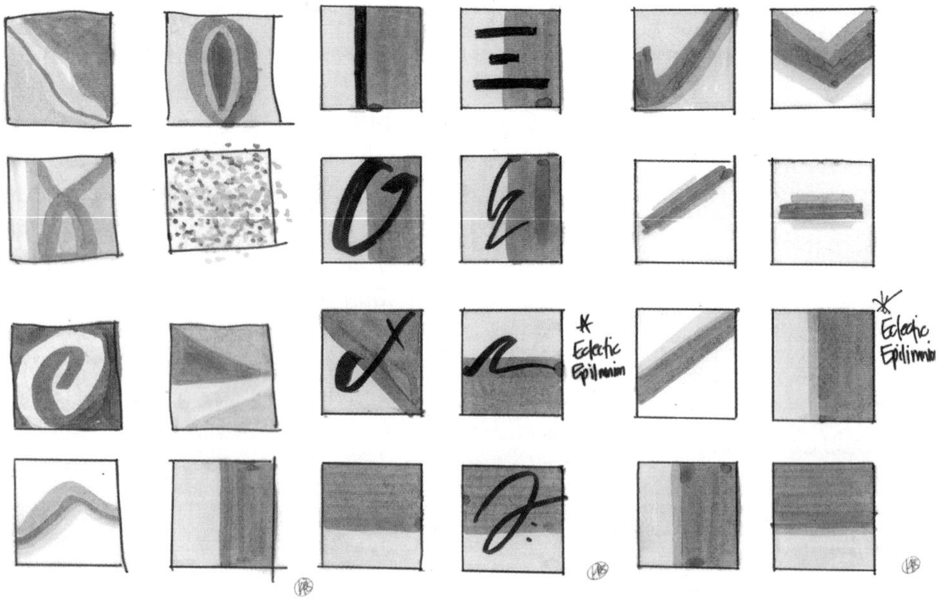

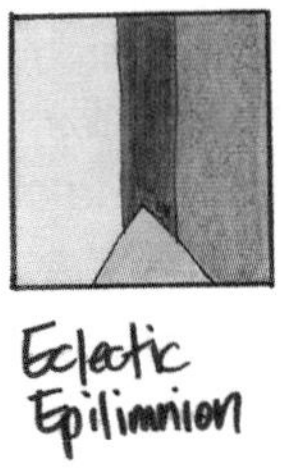

Concept Statement: To incorporate light, warmth, and furniture the family owns with modern, energy-efficient upgrades into this charming lake-front cottage while maintaining the historical and retreat-like atmosphere.

Kameron K. Stutzman, Interior Design Student, Colorado State University

Continued on page 608

The **concept square** is usually a three-inch by three-inch square containing abstract lines and shapes that can influence the design decisions for a client. Often, photo-realistic images—such as from a photograph—help jumpstart the abstract-thinking process. For example, you might use an aerial photo of a client's acreage to inspire an abstract concept design. The client can see his or her house in the design, but others may not understand the symbolism until they receive an explanation.

A **conceptual sketch** is a drawing or diagram that captures your vision for the project. For example, you may conceptually sketch a series of umbrellas to represent an atrium idea in a small office complex. A bald eagle's wingspan may conceptually convey a sense of flight for a start-up airline company. Whether a conceptual sketch or abstract design, illustrations always communicate lines, shapes, and colors that can contribute to a client's understanding.

There are other ways to visually communicate a concept to a client, including a three-dimensional model, a poem, or a piece of music. Depending on the client, use different methods to communicate the concept—keeping in mind that using more than one media to express the concept assists client understanding.

Using Inspiration Boards

Rather than using abstract designs to visually communicate a concept to the client, you may prefer to use an *inspiration board*. Today, it is easy to generate inspiration boards with the use of a computer, giving them a very professional appearance. Inspiration boards—similar to concepts—are instrumental in helping the client envision the design direction for the project. They also serve as a sales tool when communicating the design intention and direction with the client.

As you recall, an inspiration board often combines inspiring images—typically photos—of wildlife, nature, textiles and colors, textures, abstract art, models, or cultural colors. Inspiration for client solutions often come from places visited, architectural details in the client's *place*, trade publications, people visited, art studied, a song, an animal, or something from the natural environment.

To continue to generate inspiring concepts, keep learning, observing, traveling, listening, and developing sensitivity to culture- and design-trend changes. Absorb all you can from reading travel and style magazines. You, like many designers, will be influenced by what you see; whom you talk with; how people live, react, and respond; and what spaces or forms—whether an architectural relic or a magnificent garden—you experience. Respond to new materials, philosophies, and information so that, by nature, your designs will be fresh, new, and relevant. Whether using a concept drawing or an inspiration board to communicate the design direction to a client, always share the concept with the client and receive their agreement. Be sure to set up a client meeting and discuss or present the concept to the client. You do not want to proceed until you are sure your client is in agreement, and that the design concept reflects the vision, needs, and preferences of your client.

Preliminary Floor Plans

Once you outline and analyze the client's program and develop the client's concept, the design process continues through space-planning tasks. The goal of these tasks is to move from general bubble diagrams to a finished floor plan complete with furniture.

As you know, space planning includes potentially four types of drawings: block plans, block-and-stack plans, preliminary floor plans, and the preliminary furniture (FF&E) plans. Based on these plans, the designer develops a preliminary budget and suggestions for the interior finishes palette. These tasks culminate in a client presentation to acquire approval before moving to the Design Development (DD) phase.

General and Relational Bubble Diagrams

You will develop the block plan from general bubble diagrams. Remember, *relational bubble diagrams* are not constrained by walls or the building footprint; whereas, *general bubble diagrams* include the placement of spaces within the physical boundaries of the building—or the building footprint—in a two-dimensional plan view.

As you study and analyze bubble drawings—representing the spaces that fit into the building—consider the three-dimensional aspects of the spaces, such as views to the outside. Make sure your general bubble diagram includes the entries, windows, structural elements (such as columns), and **chases**—enclosed spaces within the walls of a structure that accommodate plumbing or ductwork for the HVAC system. At this point, the square footage for each space is often unknown. You can overcome this issue by placing the largest bubbles in the larger, open spaces with the smaller ones surrounding them. While doing this, keep in mind which spaces need to be next to others.

CASE STUDY

Inspiration Board for the Emerick Lake House

In addition to other communication methods you decide to present the project's concept using an inspiration board. For the lake house, you gather inspiration from a beautiful turtle shell, a turned piece of wood, a nearby garden, the colors of the lake, history of the area, a loon landing on the water, and the mist on a cloudy morning. You create two inspiration boards that highlight these objects and ideas.

(A) Irina_QQQ/Shutterstock.com (B) Elena Schweitzer/Shutterstock.com (C) KellyNelson/Shutterstock.com (D) More Images/Shutterstock.com (E) Thomas Barrat/Shutterstock.com (F) Ansis Klucis/Shutterstock.com (G) Judy Kennamer/Shutterstock.com (H) RaGaly/Shutterstock.com (I) Preto Perola/Shutterstock.com (J) MilarArt/Shutterstock.com (K) Cindy Hughes/Shutterstock.com (L) jadimages/Shutterstock.com (M) Klagyi/Shutterstock.com (N) ArTDi101/Shutterstock.com (O) Boris Ryaposov/Shutterstock.com (P) Mertsaloff/Shutterstock.com (Q) aldegonde/Shutterstock.com (R) Cousin_Avi/Shutterstock.com (S) nikkytak/Shutterstock.com (T) Otha Rohulya/Shutterstock.com (U) Attitude/Shutterstock.com (V) Konstanttin/Shutterstock.com

(A) Elena Shashkina/Shutterstock.com (B) Sarah Jessup/Shutterstock.com (C) Monkey Business Images/Shutterstock.com (D) Kharlanov Evgeny/Shutterstock.com (E) LesPalenik/Shutterstock.com

Continued on page 610

It is important not to use your first layout as the final solution. Instead, continue to explore other layouts. One technique to use when developing a different design solution is to change where you place the largest bubble. Put it in an opposite corner and see how that reshapes the plan. A second approach is to layer in different circulation patterns that may shape the way the bubbles relate to each other. For example, create a circulation path like a tree with branches. Start with the base of the tree at the main entry and draw in the branches. Then, place the bubbles (representing rooms or spaces) around them.

Similar to the relational bubble diagrams discussed earlier in this chapter, take time to analyze your general bubble diagrams, listing advantages and disadvantages of each diagram on the side of each plan. No one plan will be the best; each will have strengths and weaknesses to compare to client priorities.

After analyzing the general bubble diagrams, you will develop *block plans*. It is important to have three to four good sets of bubble diagrams to ensure you are looking at several possible design solutions for your client.

Block Plans and Block-and-Stack Plans

A *block plan* is a refinement of the best general bubble diagram from the previous step in Schematic Design. Block plans are particularly helpful in large residential or commercial projects. The square feet needed for a space is calculated and used in this phase. Bubbles from bubble diagrams are reshaped into blocks—typically rectangles—of space within the building footprint. Add corridors or hallways, making sure the additional width and space allocated equals the correct amount of square footage. (*Note:* If the square footage is not known, books such as *Architectural Graphics Standards*, offer standard dimensions and square-footage requirements for different types of spaces.) Be sure to review the Emerick Client Program and consider and plan for the activities of each room or space.

Use *block-and-stack plans* for residential or commercial projects with multiple floors. While a block plan is a horizontal assessment and allocation of space, block-and-stack plans are viewed and analyzed both horizontally *and* vertically.

To begin a block-and-stack plan, first draw the vertical architectural elements such as elevator shafts, stairwells, columns or piers, chases, multistory spaces that span two or more levels, common entry points, and window placement. Once you record those on paper, it is easy to see the remaining volume of area available for space planning your interior. Use block diagrams to indicate room locations and corridors. Using color will help you stay conscious of where specific rooms or departments move as you develop multiple design solutions.

Often, a group critique is helpful for analyzing proposed plans. Discussions often reveal stronger recommendations for the refinement of one or two plans in the next step.

Refinement of Floor Plans

Once the blocking task is complete, you will have refined the spaces into rooms for a residential project or into departments or units for a commercial project. You now need to add interior walls and partition widths, half walls, and doorways. At this point, you should also identify components such as windows, bathrooms (or restrooms), and other elements. If there are key dimensions, note the distances between them or from center-to-center of the walls, the width of openings for windows and doors, and changes in floor elevations if the floor is multilevel. You should notice the available interior space continues to shrink as you add wall widths to your plan.

To begin refining a floor plan, make sure your architectural and structural elements and plumbing are in place. Then, add wall widths around the blocks. Typically, interior walls should be 4 inches wide, and doorways should be 32 inches to 36 inches wide (the wider the better to create an accessible space).

Interestingly, where you place the door(s) in a plan significantly impacts the way circulation functions throughout the structure. Doors and walls shape human behavior and habits. You are radically shaping space and human behavior in this step of the design process.

Once you finish adding walls, doors, and partitions, critically analyze your plan again. If a full-height wall is too confining, offer a half- or three-quarter-height wall to allow daylight to enter an interior space. Can you insert an interior window to capture additional views to the outside? Although not complete in this task, ponder hypothetical furniture placement in these spaces. This evaluation may cause you to change your door or window placement. Remember, a good plan avoids excessive use of hallways. Try to minimize their use so you can allocate the square footage to other rooms or spaces.

CASE STUDY

Lake House Block Drawings

Because it is important to explore multiple solutions rather than just one, you return to your bubble diagrams and create multiple block plans that are very different from each other for the Emerick lake house. After the initial creation, you analyze the plans based on the relationships of spaces to the building, views, and daylight. You indicate zones within the space as public, private, or service and continue to refine the drawings until you have a floor plan of rooms blocked into the building footprint. As you work, you note advantages and disadvantages of each plan in the margins of the drawing. See the following illustrations.

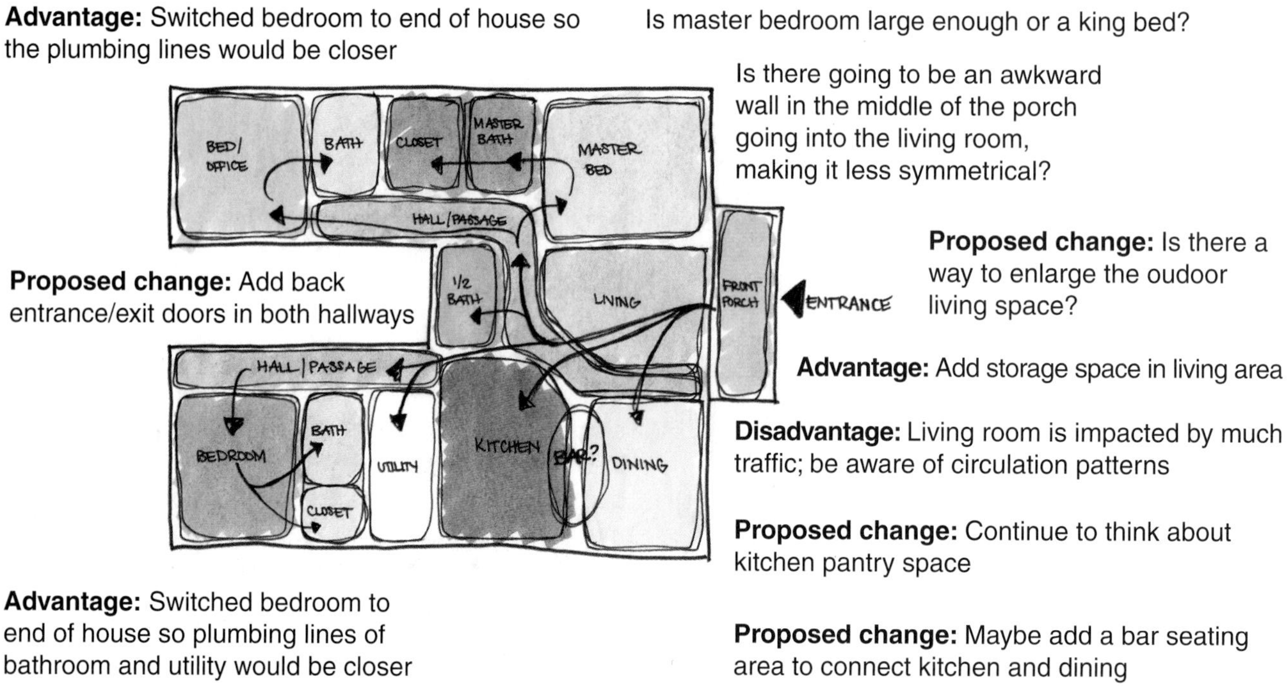

Emily Eyrich, Interior Design Student, Colorado State University

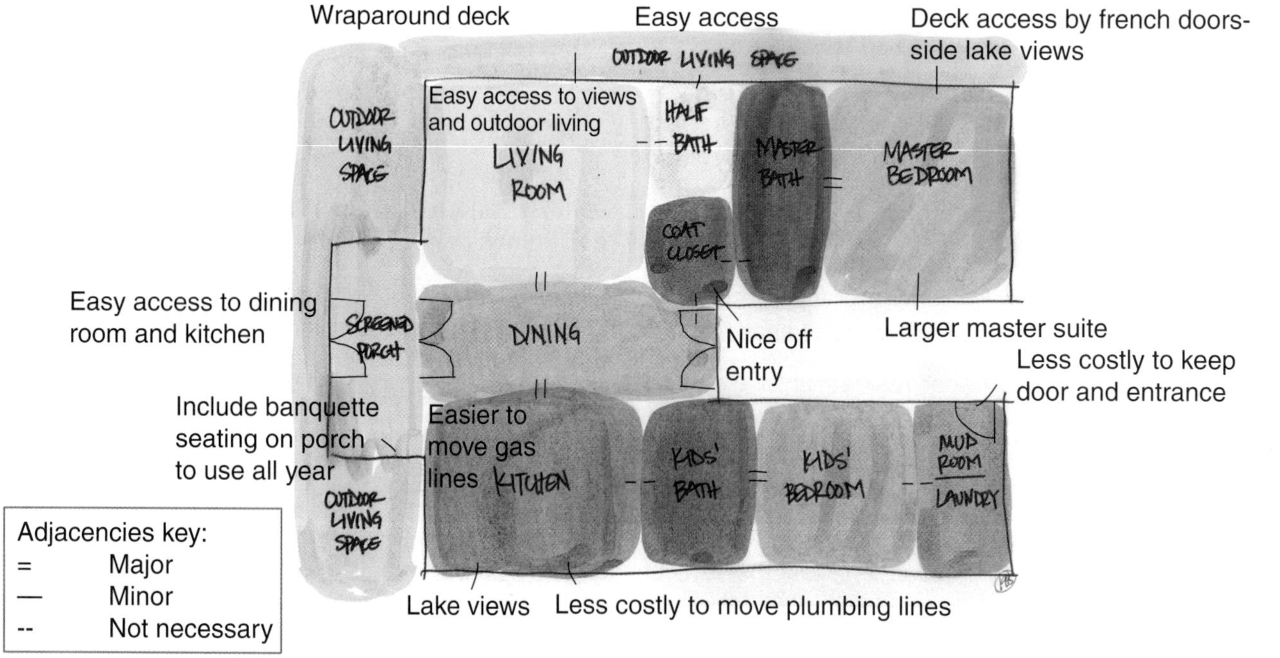

Kameron K. Stutzman, Interior Design Student, Colorado State University

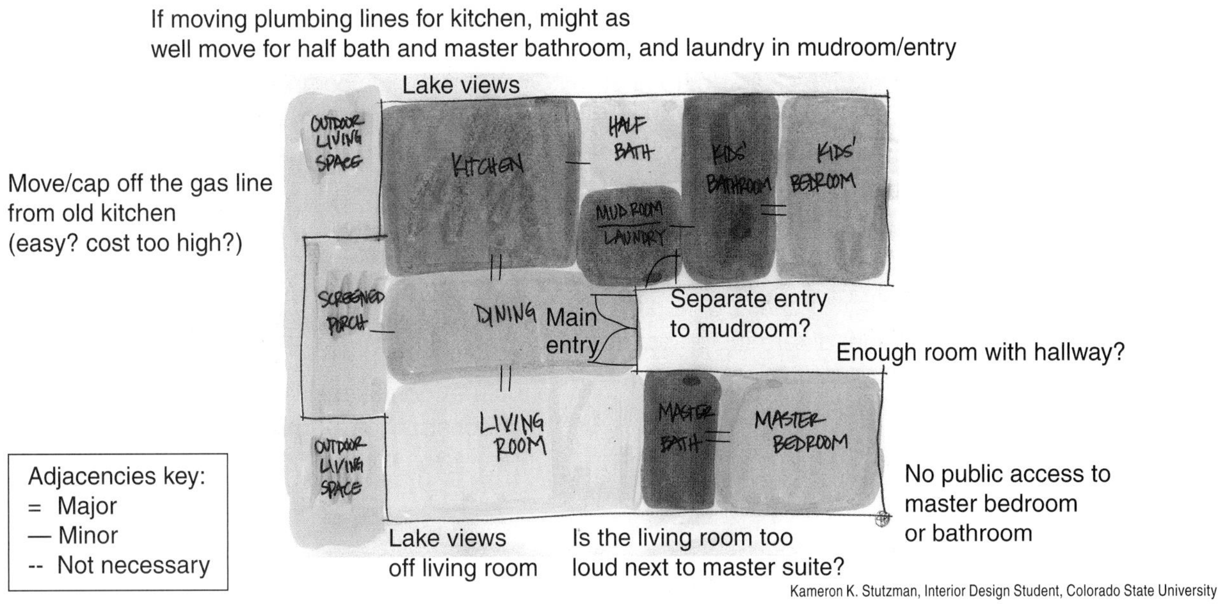

Kameron K. Stutzman, Interior Design Student, Colorado State University

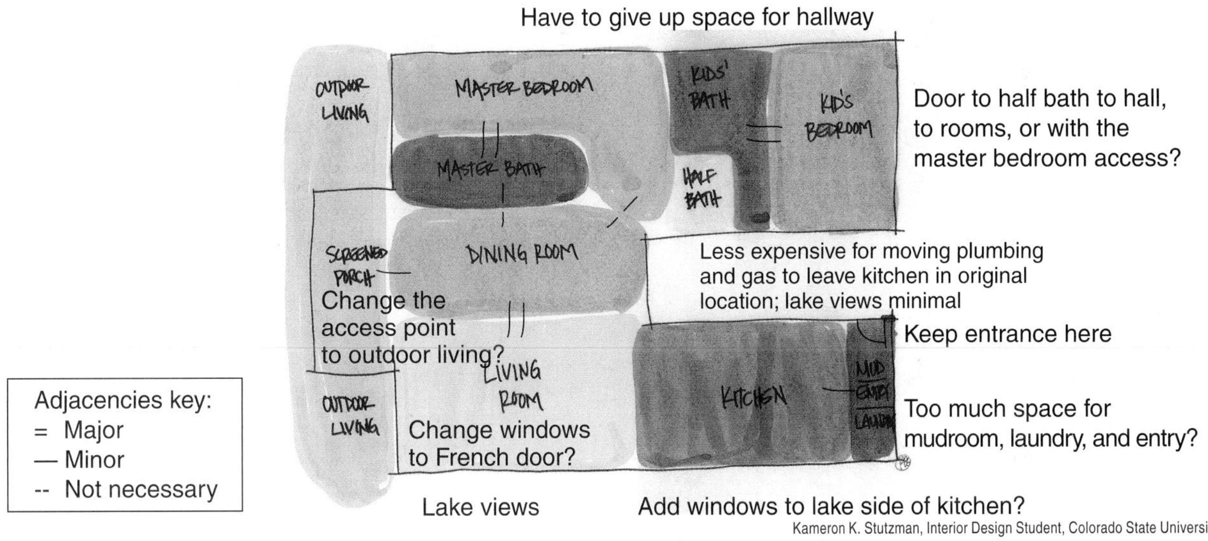

Kameron K. Stutzman, Interior Design Student, Colorado State University

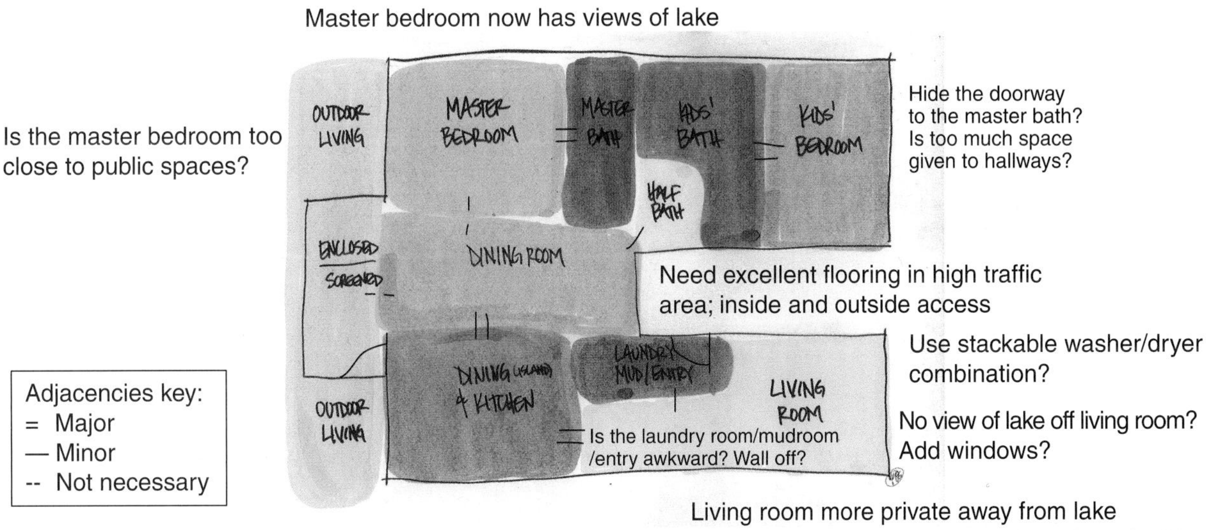

Kameron K. Stutzman, Interior Design Student, Colorado State University

Continued on page 612

During this phase, incorporate universal design or ADA principles and requirements. Also consider the proxemics, privacy needs, and territorial issues that impact an interior. Does your client have unique requirements that you should design into the space? What types of equipment does the plan require? How do codes impact how people egress the building in an emergency or exit a residence in case of fire?

Space planning is similar to playing chess. The pieces are all the same as you consider different plan options for your client, but how and where you move the pieces makes all the difference in the final outcome. Highly creative solutions develop because the designer views the client's problem from a variety of perspectives. Once this task is complete, you can move to visualizing the space in three dimensions.

Preliminary Demolition (Demo) Plan

Since the Emerick family is remodeling a structure rather than developing a house from new construction, you must complete a **demolition plan**—or a "demo" plan—which provides details of the current existing structural conditions to be demolished prior to beginning construction, **Figure 16-4**. A demolition plan is a

CASE STUDY

Emerick Preliminary Floor Plans

The following hand-drawn and digital floor plans show the designer's thinking in preparing the preliminary floor plans. Look carefully at both plans. What changes do you see between the two plans? What suggestions might you have for improving the plans to make them more functional for the Emerick family?

Hand-Drawn Floor Plan

Back Entry

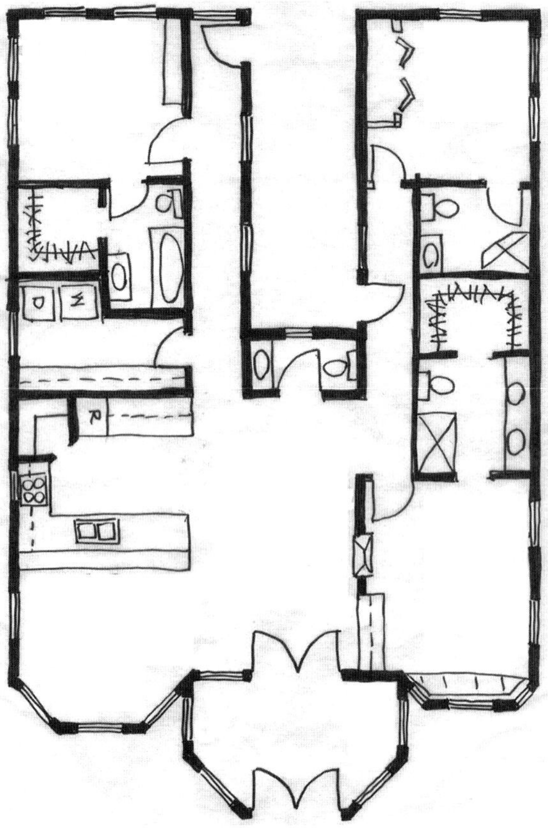

Lake View

Emily Eyrich, Interior Design Student, Colorado State University

Digital Floor Plan

Back Entrance

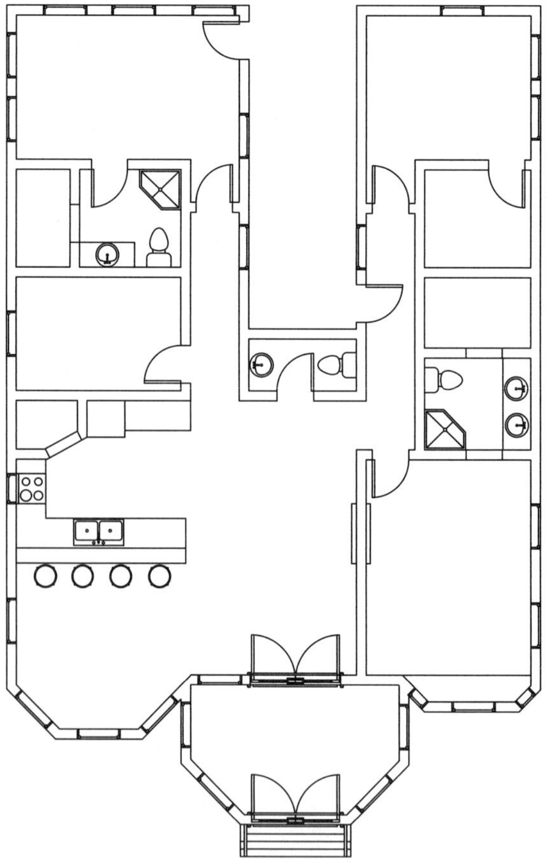

Lake View

Emily Eyrich, Interior Design Student, Colorado State University

Continued on page 614

Creating a Demolition Plan

Using a dashed line, draw a demo plan to indicate on the floor plan the location of existing walls for removal in relation to the proposal for new walls. The designer indicates new structural or architectural additions on a demo plan, including half walls, columns, windows, or other details. Here is one way to draw a preliminary demo plan.

1. Begin with the existing floor plan and lay a piece of tracing paper over the floor plan.
2. View your floor plan proposal through the tracing paper.
3. Use a red felt-tip pen and dashed lines to draw the new walls, windows, and doors on the tracing paper over the existing plan.

If you are creating all your preliminary plans using a computer, you can use a different layer in your CAD program rather than tracing paper to create your demo plan. CAD allows you to create a more professional-looking demo plan from your preliminary plan.

A demo plan is not only helpful for the building department or the subcontractors using it to complete the client's remodel, but it is also a good communication tool to use with the client. By viewing a demo plan, a client can see both existing and proposed structural components that comprise the final project plan.

Note: A structural engineer *must* analyze and approve all changes that impact load-bearing walls during the demolition phase of the project.

Figure 16-4 Demolition plans are necessary to pull building permits before construction begins on a project. *What are the possible consequences of failure to create demolition plans and pull building permits for a project?*

requirement to pull building permits before the construction phase begins. A **permit** is an official document or certificate issued by the authority—a city/county building department having jurisdiction—which authorizes performance of a specific activity. It is a requirement for any alterations to a building or structure. Alterations include not only architectural components, but also electrical, mechanical, gas, and plumbing systems.

Preliminary Furniture Plans

After redesigning the space according to the client's concept and program, it is time to add the furniture. Effective furniture placement is the biggest test of a good floor plan. While creating a furniture plan is often the last part of this phase, it is one of the most important. It is not until after you analyze furniture placement that you can determine if the spaces you have planned will function well for the client—both in the square-feet allocation and in the placement of doors and windows. Analysis is a key part of preliminary furniture plans. If construction or renovation of a structure moves forward without such analysis, it is likely the interior spaces will not function as you and the client intend. Taking time to analyze the furniture plan helps avoid this problem.

Creating the preliminary furniture plan only requires rudimentary placement of furniture in the plan, although it should include the largest or most critical pieces. The goal is not to determine furnishing styles but to determine if the plan will function once the furniture is in place in the space. You want to avoid selling your client on a design that will not function the intended way after installation.

For a residential project, place large furniture pieces such as dining tables, beds, sofas, and stools. Check clearances to ensure proper use and function of furniture pieces for users of the space. For a commercial design project, furniture placement and clearances depend on the type of project. For example, in an office, you will want to place prototypical office configurations in the spaces or check to see if the receptionist desk actually fits in the lobby. In a retail space, place the check-out station, basic product fixtures, and determine if storage shelving fits the space.

A good furniture plan does not result from the first attempt. Be sure to explore multiple furniture configurations for the space. Envision the space in three dimensions as you place hypothetical furniture pieces. This visualization exercise helps you avoid placing tall dressers or vertical file cabinets over a window.

Remember to leave space for people to walk into a conversation grouping of furniture, whether in a living room or in a hotel lobby. Also, include any fixtures and equipment in the spaces. For a residence, these might include the water heater in the furnace room and the refrigerator in the kitchen.

CASE STUDY

Paul and Grace's Furniture Plan

The following illustrations show the progression in the designer's thinking for Paul and Grace's furniture plan. Closely evaluate each illustration. What changes can you see from the preliminary furniture plan to the final plan?

First Furniture Plan

Advantage: Good closet space for two kids in one room

Back Entrance

Proposed change: Start adding windows

Good entrance/exit on both sides of the house

Proposed change: Think of better arrangement for bunk beds to better use space

Proposed change: Add pantry into kitchen corner
Disadvantage: Rearrange bath for more space

Disadvantage: Awkward wall lineup with kitchen and bath Move kitchen wall to line up

Proposed change: Provide higher bar seating to better use space of dining room

Proposed change: Maybe include one side with bench seating

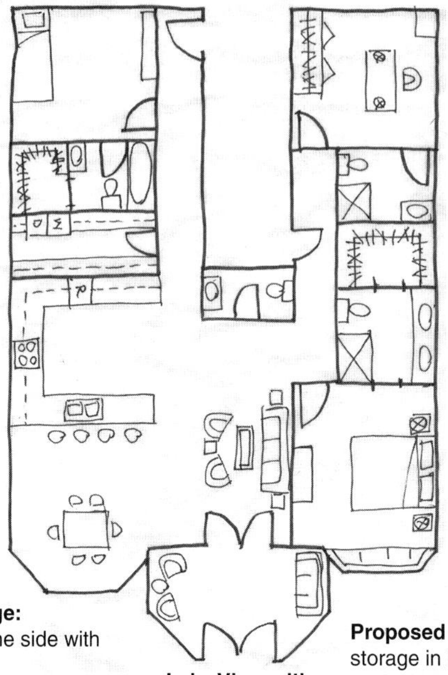

Disadvantage: Desk should either be facing the door or window for better view and flow

Disadvantage: Not enough space for toilet; move around for better spacing

Advantage: Open passageways through path and closet

Advantage: Cozy seating in master?

Advantage: Angled walls at front of house allow more space in the house a more interesting front façade

Proposed change: Think of how to add storage in living area—maybe putting built-in or double-wall fireplace

Lake View with Entrance to Porch

Emily Eyrich, Interior Design Student, Colorado State University

Second Furniture Plan

Back Entrance

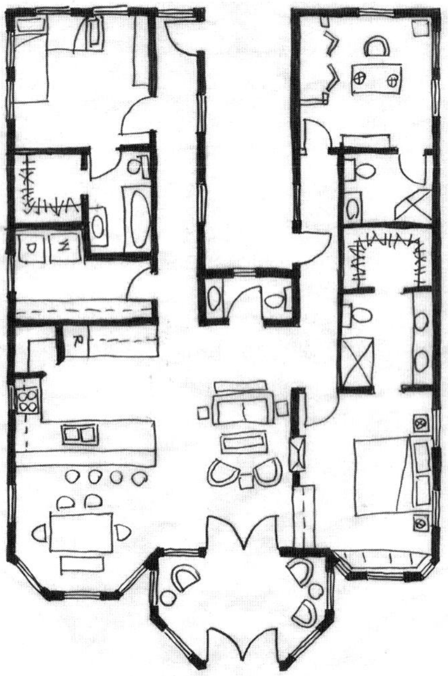

Lake View with Entrance to Porch

Emily Eyrich, Interior Design Student, Colorado State University

Final Furniture Plan—Digital

Back Entrance

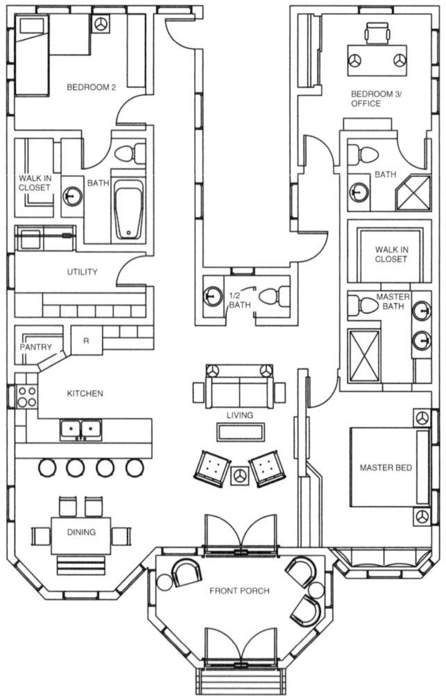

Lake View with Entrance to Porch

Emily Eyrich, Interior Design Student, Colorado State University

Continued on page 616

Drawings

Once preliminary furniture plans have been created, clients may ask for drawings. These drawings may include initial sketches of custom architectural details and drawings of sections and elevations.

Custom Architectural Details—Initial Sketches

Often a client hires an interior designer to complete custom details in their spaces. For an office design, this may be a drawing of a niche in the lawyer's lobby. In a residence, this may be the base of an island in a kitchen or custom crown molding, **Figure 16-5.**

Custom details offer you an opportunity to use the *elements of design* (for example, line or color) and *principles of design* (for example, proportion or scale) to communicate the project concept in a very visual manner. For example, you could communicate the inspiration drawn from an ocean wave by creating a custom design for a wooden hostess station with carved and painted curved lines. This detail visually communicates the restaurant's concept of movement or motion. Similarly, you could use the wave and motion concept as a custom detail for an aquatic museum or aquarium. For this structure, a custom ceiling detail might include a series of fabric-constructed, organically shaped mobiles that flutter across a 14-foot ceiling—rising and falling with the movement of air throughout the day. Although the concepts are similar, each should still be original and applicable to the client's needs and design intent.

It is the interpretation of the concept through custom details that differentiate a great interior from a good interior. Remember, design is in the details. Clients truly appreciate the original work you create just for their spaces.

Initial Elevations, Sections, and Perspectives

During the Schematic Design phase, you create preliminary drawings not only of the plan, but also those that show what the proposed spaces may look like. You may use **thumbnail sketches**—small sketches—to draw what a hypothetical space may look like prior to making a recommendation to the client. You may also draw simple sections or elevations to study the relationships of windows to ceiling heights or how a piece of furniture may look against a specific wall.

For commercial projects, you may draw sections to not only analyze the spatial relationships but also to communicate graphic-design ideas relating to a company's branding needs.

Interior FF & E and Preliminary Budget

Prior to presenting your proposed design solution to the client, it is helpful for the client to envision the space through your suggestions for interior finishes and major pieces of furniture. For this reason, it is important to prepare some FF & E for the client to review. Choose a palette of colors, textures, and materials based on the

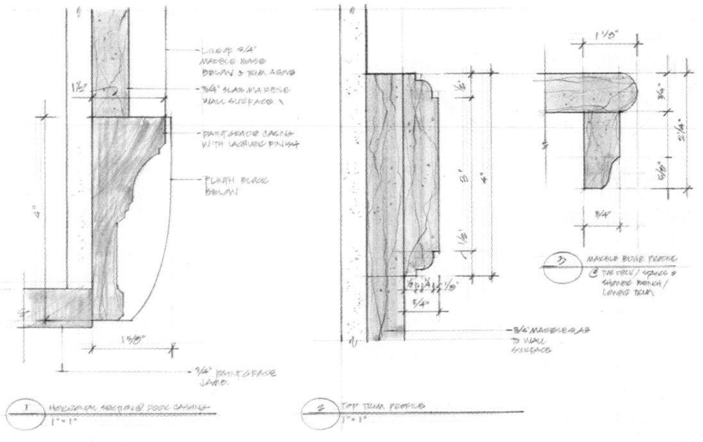

Image by Jacqui McFarland

Figure 16-5 Some clients want the designer to create designs for custom details to enhance the aesthetics of their space.

CASE STUDY

Lake House Perspective Drawings

Initial drawings such as elevations, sections, and perspectives are critical client communication tools. While clients may not understand a two-dimensional plan or elevation, they can often appreciate their proposed designs in a perspective drawing or model.

Evaluate the following perspectives drawings of the Emerick lake house. How do these drawings give you a better visual picture of what the lake house may look like after renovation?

Kameron K. Stutzman, Senior, Colorado State University

Continued on page 617

client's concept, program, and floor and furniture plans. Then, provide some time for the clients to review your choices.

Allow clients to respond to the interior finishes and furnishings and the proposed project budget. Respect for a client's budget is one of the surest ways to achieve client loyalty, satisfaction, and future referrals.

If you are working with team members in a large design firm, estimating the cost of a building construction is a specialized skill that experts complete. As an interior designer, a frequent client expectation is that you will develop the budgets for interior construction, lighting, and FF & E. There are standard software programs available that give pricing information for interior construction.

You will typically present the FF & E as a finish or *material board* to the client. The proposed budget may be set up in a variety of ways depending on the method a designer chooses to charge for design services, including hourly fee, daily rate, flat or fixed fee, percentage fee, or consulting fee. In most cases, the client has a specific amount of money dedicated to the project budget. It is up to the designer to create a design that meets the Client Program and budget requirements. The budget should guide the interior designer when specifying materials and furnishings, fixtures, and equipment, as well as any fees required for contractors and subcontractors. Typical budget categories include

- **Designer services.** Compensation the designer receives for developing the design and working on the project.
- **Products/material costs.** Budgetary items to include with products and materials include a description of the item, the quantity or size, color and style, estimated costs (acquired from vendors/manufacturers the designer works with), fabrication costs, delivery services and fees, and installation fees. Typical costs the designer estimates include furniture, wall treatments, floor treatments, and window treatments. These items are direct costs and the estimates must be accurate. When building a budget, do not overestimate costs.
- **Subcontractors.** Budget items may include materials and labor costs. Note that your client may obtain several *bids* for services provided by subcontractors.
- **Indirect costs.** These costs may include sales taxes, delivery fees, and costs due to delays on the project.

CASE STUDY

The Emericks' Finishes and Furniture

Before you present your entire design proposal to the Emericks, you decide to show them two different materials boards to help them capture the vision for their lake house remodel. The color palette, textures, materials, and furniture support the Emericks' concept and program. You explain how these selections embrace the design concept and inspiration for the lake house.

Board 1—Accessory and Furniture Options

Accessories

(A) Iveta Angelova/Shutterstock.com (B) cdrin/Shutterstock.com (C) Fotosenmeer/Shutterstock.com (D) Banana Republic Images/Shutterstock.com (E) Blinka/Shutterstock.com (F) Alena Ozerova/Shutterstock.com (G) Nielsklim/Shutterstock.com (H) GoodMood Photo/Shutterstock.com (I) Africa Studio/Shutterstock.com (J) Alena Ozerova/Shutterstock.com (K) Enfant Terrible/Shutterstock.com (L) Enfant Terrible/Shutterstock.com (M) arturasker/Shutterstock.com (N) Dasha Minaieva/Shutterstock.com

Furnishings

Kids' Bedroom & Bath

Kitchen

Outdoor Living

Living Room

Master Bedroom & Bath

(A) Petr Jilek/Shutterstock.com (B) Avanne Troar/Shutterstock.com (C) rj lerich/Shutterstock.com (D) pics721/Shutterstock.com (E) Iriana Shiyan/Shutterstock.com (F) Elena Elisseeva/Shutterstock.com (G) Constantine Pankin/Shutterstock.com (H) Brian McEntire/Shutterstock.com (I) Photobac/Shutterstock.com (J) MR. INTERIOR/Shutterstock.com (K) Ambient Ideas/Shutterstock.com

(Continued)

CASE STUDY *(Continued)*

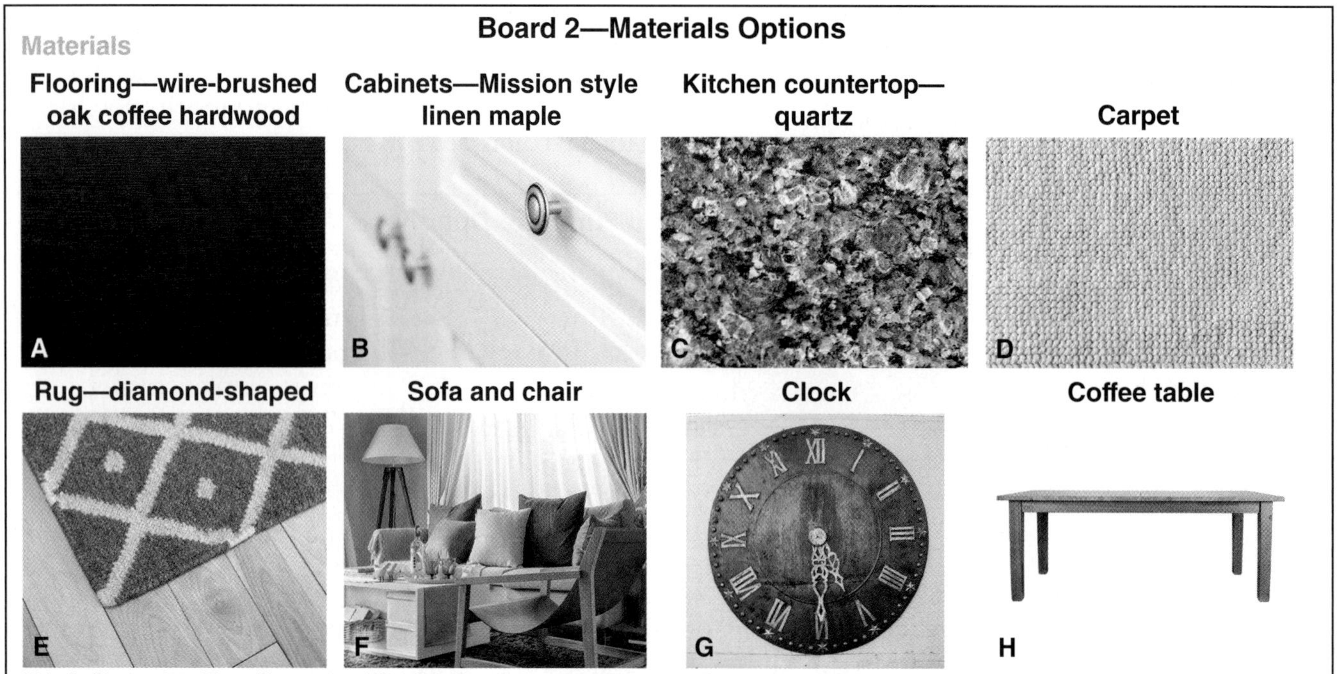

(A) Art_Zav/Shutterstock.com (B) serav/Shutterstock.com (C) Luis Carlos Torres/Shutterstock.com (D) Venus Angel/Shutterstock.com (E) GoodMood Photo/Shutterstock.com (F) Khongkit Wiriyachan/Shutterstock.com (G) Orhan Cam/Shutterstock.com (H) photka/Shutterstock.com

Continued on page 622

Client Presentation

Depending on the project, your client may give you input throughout the Schematic Design phase. With other clients, you may develop one or two solid design solutions and request client input at the end of the phase. Regardless, the client presentation determines whether your design solution accurately addresses their problems and if they are willing to proceed to the Design Development phase and ultimately through installation of the project.

The designer offers the client presentations at this point in a written, graphic, and verbal format. Mastering presentation techniques builds your self-confidence and your design abilities. Here are a few tips as you prepare to give professional client presentation with poise.

Written Presentation

Even if you orally and visually present a large part of your client presentation, your presentation will include written components. A professional presentation includes properly spelled words, grammatically correct phrases or sentences, and coherent, clear sentence structure. Avoid **colloquial**—or unacceptably informal—words and phrases. Keep language formal and clear. With current technology tools, clients know there is no reason to have poorly written materials.

Written parts of your client presentation include the concept statement, labels on boards and plans, matrices, and budgetary information. Use an appropriate font type and size to ensure that your clients can read the written components from a distance during the presentation. Select words carefully to create excitement for the design.

At times, clients request permission to keep material boards and documents for a period of time. In such situations, your written documentation needs to be concise, but clearly describe the design for future reference.

Graphic Presentation

The graphic presentation of your client's proposed design often includes the concept, proposed plan, elevations or sections as needed, perspectives, suggestions for interior materials, and possibly a model and lighting plan. Together these materials make a client package.

DESIGNER MATH SKILLS

Creating Invoices—Billing the Client

As you learned in Chapter 4, there are many aspects of starting an interior design business. Running a business has its complexities whether you are self-employed or running a firm. Therefore, it is important in the early stages of business development to identify business advisors in the areas of law, finance, accounting, and taxes.

A designer has a responsibility to keep careful records for clients, vendors, the company, and the Internal Revenue Service (IRS). Numerous business software programs are available to simplify financial tasks but a designer must still understand the ins-and-outs of running a business.

Important conversations to have with an accountant are about the business' budget and how to manage *cash flow*. An accountant can provide regular financial statements reflecting *profit and loss*. Business taxes can be complex, and a knowledgeable tax advisor can help the designer make business decisions that take advantage of tax opportunities and avoid expensive IRS audits.

Creating systems that manage, organize, and track a designer's decisions are critical to the integrity and profitability of the business. Each financial transaction throughout the year is important at tax time. Careful records of financial activity greatly reduce the stress of the year-end tax-preparation process.

Once a project begins, designers incur expenses which they ultimately bill to their clients. *Accounts payable* (bills the designer owes) are different than *accounts receivable* (money clients owe to the designer). Each project has unique variables that impact billing, so it is important to agree with the client on the frequency of bills. When sending an invoice, the goal is to provide the client with information they need to pay the designer promptly. Here are a few invoicing tips:

- Create an invoice with a professional appearance reflecting the designer's name, company address, and contact information.
- Give each invoice an individual invoice number to assist tracking.
- Verify the spelling of the client's name, address, and e-mail address. Delays will occur if the invoice is undeliverable.
- Address the account and invoice to a specific person rather than just to the company for *commercial projects*. The invoice often moves through several offices before approval and making payment. The more organized the information, the quicker the designer receives payment.
- Provide clients with a description of charges along with appropriate details for an opportunity to cross-check the invoice items with their records.
- Make the total amount owed and the date due payment obvious at a glance on the invoice.
- State payment terms clearly (for example, payment is due in 30 days).
- State on the invoice to whom the client should make payment (the designer's name or a company name) and any payment options.
- Let your clients know you appreciate their business with the simple phrase, "Thank you for your business!" Manners matter.
- Never accept personal payment information via e-mail.
- End the project on a positive and upbeat note! Send a thank-you note once you receive final payment.

Not getting paid is inevitable, so prepare for such an event. In such situations, communication is the first step. The client may have an explanation; perhaps an invoice did not arrive or it has been misplaced. Often a phone call or an e-mail reminder will resolve any problems. If a client is always late with bill payment, be flexible and courteous, and attempt to identify a mutually acceptable solution. Perhaps changing the billing date works better for prompt payment. If a delay occurs due to an invoicing error, send a corrected invoice immediately.

See the following sample invoice.

(Continued)

DESIGNER MATH SKILLS *(Continued)*

Stratton & Evans Interiors
1234 Union Blvd.
Chicago IL 60657
800.123.4321

Invoice #: ______________
Date: ____________

Client: ________________________________ Project Address: ________________________________

Address: ________________________________ ________________________________

____

Item & Description	Quantity	Unit Price	Total Price
Item: Window treatment, pinch-pleated panels, custom **Room:** Living room **Item Number:** 0000000 **Description:** Raw silk, pinch-pleated panels **Fabric/Color:** Raw silk, C-145/Autumn Ginger (Stripe) @ $43.00/yd. Tassel fringe (Autumn multicolored) @ $29.00/yd. **Installation Date:** TBD	2	$614.50	$1229.00
Item: Window treatment hardware **Room:** Living room **Item Number:** 0000000 **Description:** Wrought Iron/Iron Oxide finish—(2) Poles, (4) Brackets, (2) pr. birdcage finials **Color:** Black iron oxide **Installation Date:** 00/00/00	2	$165.50	$331.00
Item: Bench seat cushion with tufting **Room:** Living room **Item Number:** 0000000 **Description:** Custom cushion with zipper **Fabric/Color:** HC134/Autumn @ $41/yd.; 3" block foam $116.59 **Delivery Date:** 00/00/00	1	$573.00	$573.00
Item: Light fixture **Room:** Living room Item Number: 0000000 **Description:** Lightweight galvanized steel sconces **Color:** Weathered zinc finish **Shipping Date:** Backordered **Installation:** not included	4	$129.00	$516.00
Item: Accessory pillows **Room:** Living room **Item Number:** 0000000 **Description:** (5) Couch pillow covers—(3) Knitted pillow covers; (2) Basket-weave pillow covers;	5	$99.00	$495.00
(5) Pillow inserts **Fabric/Color:** (3) Knit fabric, latte color; (2) Basket-weave fabric, mocha color **Shipping Date:** 4 weeks	5	$14.00	$70.00
Item: Furniture **Room:** Living room **Item Number:** 0000000 **Description:** (2) Leather wingback chairs, button-tufted, nail head trim, solid wood frame **Fabric/Color:** Leather/Cognac **Shipping:** 12 weeks	2	$1119.00	$2238.00
Subtotal:			$5452.00
Tax: State and local @ 6.2%			$338.02
Invoice Total:			$5,790.02
Shipping and handling may apply.			

Please make payment to Stratton + Evans Interiors.
Full payment due 30 days from invoice date.

The quality of a graphic presentation is typically evaluated on three criteria:

- quality and type of visual presentation drawings
- board layout and composition
- organization and clarity of boards to enhance client understanding

Drawings and renderings best communicate the design proposal to the client. You typically select drawings and renderings for board presentation on the drawings' abilities to enhance client understanding. For example, if a floor plan view poorly communicates a critical element of the design proposal, then a perspective of the space may help enhance client understanding. How well you present your drawings and renderings is an automatic reflection on your professionalism and design skills.

Board composition and layout send a message to the client. Keep the message clear and clean to enhance client understanding. Do not let the details overpower the message. If boards have poor organization and design, then the client presumes that your design skills may also be lacking. In addition, be aware of your audience and how age and gender may influence your design approach. Here are a few tips to use when developing your client's boards, **Figure 16-6**.

Creating Effective Design Boards

Board Layout and Composition

- Draw or sketch your board composition before you begin to cut and adhere items to the board. Draw several ways to "compose" the board and message and then evaluate the best one to use.
- Design your board with a focal point just as you design a room with one. What do you want your client to look at first? text? color? Avoid multiple focal points because your client will not know what to look at first.
- Think about the design elements: line, shape, color. Use them effectively to move the client's eye and interest around the board.
- Make sure your boards have actual or implied borders. You can do this as you mount your materials by adding a piece of paper under the materials, drawing a line around them, or by using mounting tape.
- Use a straightedge (such as a ruler) to ensure items do not slant. The human eye picks up a slanted line very easily. A slight slant will make a board appear sloppy.
- If you want to place items on a diagonal (different than a slant), use a straightedge to ensure consistency. Realize that a diagonal attracts the client's eye faster than any other line type. The human eye will follow the diagonal right off the board (which you do not want) unless you have something that stops the eye at that point. Avoid using a diagonal unless you want a strong-impact message.
- Use board colors and backgrounds that *do not* compete with your finishes. It is best to use a neutral or subtle coordinating color. You are trying to sell the materials/finishes/furniture, not the board.
- Mount samples or finishes only to the front of the board. Clients will not turn the board over for additional information.
- Label or code your materials clearly. Be sure to include a key when you code the materials and finishes. Use a professional method of labeling (for example, a computer) and use a straightedge when you mount labels. Even a single letter ("A") can look slanted and ruin the professional look.
- Select a simple font type for clear communication. Avoid using multiple, hard-to-read fonts. Determine a proportional font size based on your board size (for example, a 14-point font or larger is typical). Remember that clients will be looking at your board from roughly 10 feet away. Also, avoid font colors that blend too much with the board. Use some contrast so the words are visible.

Multiple Board Presentations

- Format all boards the same direction, either horizontal *or* vertical. Do not format one board horizontal and the other board vertical.
- Use the same background and color for multiple boards.
- Use the same brand/logo in the same location on each board.

Source: Stephanie Clemons, Ph.D., FIDEC, FASID, ©2011

Figure 16-6 Effective board composition and layout enhance client understanding of the design concept and project.

CASE STUDY

The Emericks' Design Solution

The design solution for the Emerick family addresses their vision, needs, and design preferences. The remodel design solution took this small, dark, dilapidated house with high energy bills and made it into a light, airy, sustainable, and serenely welcoming residence. By removing nonload bearing walls and using larger, high-performance windows, light now streams into the charming cottage.

The spaces in need of the most remodeling were the kitchen, dining area, and living room. The result of this transformation is a new kitchen/dining/great room combination.

Kitchen

The new kitchen with efficiency improvements is actually smaller. Here are some of the changes:

- The interior west wall was moved about three feet into the original kitchen. The existing kitchen base cabinets were reused.
- New full-height upper cabinets were added (of a different wood and color from the base cabinets)—along with a small kitchen bar with two stools.
- New, larger, high-performance windows pull in more light, increasing the connection to the new outdoor living space.
- The backdoor was moved out of the kitchen and into the mudroom, adding wall space and managing dirt accumulation efficiently.
- New electrical wiring and insulation add to the efficiency of the kitchen.

zstock/Shutterstock.com

Dining Area

A small family eating nook in the kitchen replaces the separate dining room. With the addition of high-performance French doors, the Emericks have a better connection to the exterior garden and small deck. The family and their guests can now move easily from the eating nook to the deck for an outside meal.

Living Area

In keeping with the family's design preferences, the changes to the living room are simple in nature and meet the priority for a lake view. In the living space, new two-ganged high-performance operable windows replace the single-paned fixed window. The new windows align with a new porch skylight.

Bedrooms

The remodel of the third bedroom (also Paul's office) now includes a closet and new windows allowing views and light to permeate the space. The new doors between the office and living area offer better separation of the two rooms and ensure privacy for guests who use the room for sleeping.

(Continued)

Oral Presentation

Your proposed design is well developed and ready to present. Your solution is innovative and on target. You are excited about presenting to your client. Feel confident! You are ready.

The goals of your oral presentation are to

- establish your credibility and professionalism
- clearly outline the proposed design solution
- offer research that supports design features
- communicate enthusiasm both for the project and for working with the client
- determine client understanding
- sell the design

Begin your oral presentation by introducing yourself and possibly your design team. Prepare an exciting opening statement to grab your client's attention. Explain the client's concept and the source of inspiration behind it. Help the client envision the concept and how it reflects the Program and the client's needs and issues.

By increasing the room size and adding a larger, energy-efficient window, the designer was able to transform the master bedroom into a lighter space and include a small, organized, walk-in closet. The new wall holds the king-size bed. Achieving a view of the lake was a top priority, offering the space a better sense of *space* and *place*.

Bathrooms

By *truncating* (shortening) the kitchen space, the designer was able to reconfigure the two small, dark, and dysfunctional bathrooms into light, functional spaces. Larger, energy-efficient windows provide light while reducing energy costs.

Entries

The redesign created a backdoor entry with a quaint porch area. Movement of the laundry from the garage to the mudroom was a priority for the Emericks. Adding coat hooks, a counter for folding laundry, and additional storage enhance the functionality of the space.

Alfred Wekelo/Shutterstock.com

Iriana Shiyan/Shutterstock.com

Exterior Changes

Too many times a great home has no relationship to the land or landscape. The priority of this remodel was all about connecting interior and exterior spaces. The lake became the focus of the house redesign.

Cutting away some foliage to allow light to stream into the house increased views of the lake. Adding a deck on the lakeside of the house and an area for a large family garden reflected the family's desire for outdoor living and activity space.

Energy Efficiency and Green Design

Energy details included wood frame; double-hung windows; R-38 cellulose attic insulation; air-tight recessed lighting; all exterior walls insulated and air sealed; and an Energy Star dishwasher. Other environment-conscious decisions included low-flow toilets, rain barrels, and 1.5 gallons-per-minute (gpm) showerheads. Indoor air quality included low-VOC paints, soy-based glue plywood, reuse of porch posts, FSC-certified trim and interior doors, refinished existing pine floors, bio-based fiber carpet, bamboo flooring, salvaged sink and cabinet (mudroom), reuse of kitchen base cabinets, and double-paned windows.

As you move through the presentation, check in with your client. Ask for confirmation that the client understands each section of the design you are presenting. Responding to questions throughout the presentation enhances client understanding. Reference your research during the presentation to establish a solid rationale for your design. Also, develop a strong conclusion that easily leads to the request for approval to move to the Design Development phase.

Clients often have questions at the end of the presentation. Avoid defensive responses—this is the client's design. Be open to changes if needed. Here are some additional ideas for developing a strong oral presentation and evaluating your presentation, **Figure 16-7**.

Developing a Strong Oral Presentation	
Know Your Project	■ Determine the most important points for the oral presentation, whether residential or commercial. ■ Offer the *significant* points regarding the quality design solution without giving the client too much information. ■ Possess thorough knowledge of the project to professionally and completely respond to the client's follow-up questions. Thorough preparation also helps prevent any anxiety you may feel.
Know the Location and Process of Presentation	■ Arrive early to set up your presentation, if possible. ■ Understand the room layout, how the technology works, and identify where you will place your boards for best visibility. ■ Test all equipment before your presentation, including the computer, projection system, and lighting controls.
Develop a Presentation with a Beginning, Middle, and End	■ Begin your presentation with something "memorable" about the design to capture client attention. ■ Introduce the concept or source of inspiration to give the client a vision of where the design solution is heading or how you arrived at the concept. You may interweave a brief summary of the client's program as you present the concept and design solution. ■ Explain how the design solution meets the client's vision, goals, needs, and preferences. Highlight key points of your design without overwhelming the client with too much information. ■ Conclude your presentation by circling back to the memorable item you used to capture the client's attention. This helps the client understand the links among the *why* (their needs) and *how* (design concept and inspiration), to *what, when*, and *how much* (the cost).
Rehearse	■ Develop a script to organize how you will verbally "walk" the client through the proposed design. ■ Use only lay terms rather than "design speak." Use "their" or "your" when referring to the client's project (not "my") to enhance client ownership. ■ Rehearse your presentation several times in front of someone who has not been a part of the process. This helps you to spot and fix weak parts of the presentation before meeting with the client. If you have team members, develop subtle ways to shift the presentation no more than twice from one person to another. ■ Time your presentation during rehearsal to determine if you need to make adjustments in length. ■ Build your mental preparation and emotional confidence through rehearsal.
Dress Professionally	■ Wear professional and modest clothing, avoiding revealing or trendy outfits. ■ Shave (if male) and keep make-up minimal (if female). Some designers like to keep their clothing neutral in color to focus the client on the visual presentation. ■ Dress to sell your product, not yourself.
Engage the Audience	■ Speak clearly, emphasizing key points about the design and the visuals. Rarely does an audience remember all you say, but they will remember visuals and key points. ■ Strategically and very occasionally move to a different part of your boards. Avoid standing in one place. ■ Project your voice as appropriate to the size of the audience. ■ Converse with your audience rather than lecturing to them. Know the client's major concerns and address them. ■ Use language appropriate to audience knowledge and experience. Avoid jargon and acronyms they may not know.
Be Enthusiastic	■ Show your excitement and passion for the project. If you are not excited about it, why should your client be excited? ■ Understand there will likely be client changes to the design proposal. ■ Be prepared for questions and constructive criticism.
Be Aware of Your Body Language	■ Be mindful of your body language and posture—stand straight. Body language is a nonverbal form of communication. Make sure your stance, gestures, facial expressions, and movements are expressing the same message as your words. ■ Face the audience, not your drawings.

Figure 16-7 Ability to give a strong oral presentation helps strengthen your credibility as a designer.

Chapter 16

Review and Assess

Summary

- Shaping space is an exciting process that requires converting a client's problem into an organized, manageable project.
- The Pre-Design phase includes the first client interview and involves creating a letter of agreement for the retention of services.
- During the Programming phase, you as the designer prepare the Client Program which involves further client interviews, evaluating and outlining the project needs, analyzing spatial requirements including site parameters and constraints, and analyzing the client's budget factors.
- Effective communication, both written and oral, are vitally important during all phases.
- Research involves gathering information and using case studies and precedents in developing the Program.
- Completing an inventory helps you document details about existing conditions, floor plan, site location, and furnishings to reuse.
- The Programming phase ends with analyzing data, creating matrixes, and bubble diagrams, writing the Program, and making an initial presentation to the client about your research.
- Concept development is a key task of Schematic Design that guides decision making on the client's project.
- Concept development involves exploring a variety of sources for concept ideas and clearly communicating the concept to the client in writing, orally, and visually.
- After analyzing the client program and creating the concept, the design process continues with space-planning tasks including the development of relational and general bubble diagrams, block plans, and floor plans.
- Effective furniture placement is the test of an effective floor plan.
- The goal of a preliminary furniture plan is rudimentary placement of the largest and most critical furniture pieces.
- Clients often request the designer complete sketches of custom architectural details such as crown molding.
- Simple drawings of initial elevations, sections, and perspectives show what the proposed space may look like and allow the designer to analyze relationships among different areas of the design such as windows to ceiling heights before making a client presentation.
- Clients may offer feedback throughout the Schematic Design phase or you may develop several solid design solutions and request client input at the end of the phase.
- Client presentations involve written, graphic, and oral communication.

Chapter Vocabulary

For each of the following terms, identify a word or group of words describing a quality of the term—an attribute. Pair up with a classmate and discuss your list of attributes. Then, discuss your list of attributes with the whole class to increase understanding.

case study
chase
colloquial
concept square
concept statement
conceptual sketch
demolition plan
permit
problem statement
thumbnail sketch
visioning session

Review and Study

1. List three questions you might ask as client during the first client interview.
2. What tasks does the designer complete during the Programming phase?
3. What are the two basic parts of *discovery*?
4. What are case studies or precedents and how does the designer use them?
5. What does analyzing data help the designer understand?
6. Name three goals of summarizing the Program data.
7. What information is included in a basic client program?
8. List five major tasks of the Schematic Design phase.
9. What are the characteristics of a successful concept?
10. Contrast a problem statement with a concept statement.
11. What items might a designer use to visually explain a design concept to a client?
12. What types of drawings does space planning include? What does the designer develop based on these plans?
13. What are quality characteristics of the written and graphic parts of the client presentation?
14. What are the goals of an oral client presentation?

Critical Analysis

15. **Draw conclusions.** The author states that a *visioning session* is a mental process in which you explore images of the desired future project during the in-depth client interview. Examine the questions to use when conducting an in-depth interview on page 591. Then draw conclusions about how the designer identified the Emerick's top three design priorities for their lake house listed in the Case Study on page 592.
16. **Identify evidence.** Suppose you require further qualitative data to determine additional needs, uses, and priorities for the Emerick's lake-house space. You have not heard much from Josh and Lily, the Emericks' children. Although Grace's and Paul's interview answers will primarily help to shape the final design solution, you decide you need to find out more from Josh and Lily about their desires for the space. What are five questions you would ask the children to help identify evidence to support the design solution?
17. **Evaluate results.** Review the *Emericks' Design Solution* in the last part of the Case Study on pages 622–623. How does the design solution meet and support the Program for the Emericks found in the Case Study on pages 600–603 of the chapter? Why is this design solution effective? Write a summary to identify the key points of your evaluation.

Think like a Designer

18. **Writing.** Reread the *Design Insight* quote at the beginning of the chapter. Analyze the statement and write an essay explaining how this statement supports or does not support your view of yourself as a future interior designer.
19. **Speaking.** Present your concept for a client—as outlined in the chapter—to another group or individual as an *elevator speech.* You have 90 seconds before the elevator reaches the first floor to state the concept briefly, explain it, and determine if it was understood. The success of your presentation will depend on a strong concept that is easily explained, envisioned, and understood.
20. **Researching/writing.** Suppose you are the designer of the Emerick's lake house. Part of your research involves examining case studies or precedents—looking at designs of other lake houses, renovations, and the ways other designers solved similar design problems. Use the Internet to gather data regarding how other lake houses have been designed and find out about ways designers solved problems similar to the Emerick's. Write a detailed summary of your findings.

22. **Design concept development.** Before moving to the next step of the Schematic Design phase, develop a different concept for your lakeside client. Avoid immediately creating it from your head. Instead, review the client interviews, the program, and look through a variety of sources and images. The stronger your research, the more unique your concept will be. Once you have identified it, develop a design that captures it. You will need to experiment many times before arriving at the best one. Use written, oral, and visual methods (concept square and inspiration board) to communicate your concept to a classmate and determine understanding. Refine if needed.
23. **Block-and-stack practice.** Paul and Grace's lakeside cottage is one story. Therefore, no block-and-stack drawings were completed for them. Suppose your client decides to "pop the top" of their lake cottage and include a second floor. Create a block-and-stack drawing that shows how the second floor design might work. Your plan must identify the areas that must directly stack, such as stairways and plumbing chases. Refine the drawing until you and your instructor are satisfied with the results. Save a copy for your portfolio.
24. **Furniture plan practice.** Create a furniture plan for the design concept you developed for the Emericks' in item 22. Create a number of plans until you achieve the results that satisfy you and your client (your instructor). Save a copy for your portfolio.
25. **Materials board.** Create a material board for furnishings and fixtures to support the design concept and furniture plan you created for items 22 and 24. Follow the text guidelines for creating effective design boards. Save a copy of your materials board (and a digital photo of it) for your portfolio.
26. **Create a budget.** For one room of your design plan for the Emericks' lake house, use spreadsheet software to create a budget using text guidelines. Identify the budget categories and estimate the costs for supplies, materials, and furnishings, fixtures, and equipment, and labor costs. Estimate taxes on products based on the sales tax rate in the state of Michigan.
27. **Speaking.** Suppose you are the designer of the Emericks' lake-house remodel. Create a design presentation for the Emericks using the Case Studies in the Schematic Design section of the chapter (pages 602–618) and the guidelines for developing a strong oral presentation. Develop a rubric evaluating your oral presentation based on the guidelines. Practice your presentation until you are comfortable with it. Give the presentation to the Emericks (your class) along with the rubric for evaluation.

Design Application

28. **Residential design.** Your potential new client, Tasha Papadakis, recently purchased a small, bungalow-style house in Chicago, Illinois that was built in the early 1900s. Most of the interior has been renovated and kept in the design style of the original home. Tasha wants to renovate the small, eat-in kitchen space that measures 12 by 14 feet and the powder room is five by six feet. Tasha desires that kitchen and bath are functional with modern furnishings, fixtures, and equipment, yet keeping with the original design style of the home. Her renovation budget is $11,500. Complete the Pre-Design, Programming, and Schematic Design phases for this kitchen remodel following text guidelines for the design tasks in each phase, ending with a client presentation. Consider making a video recording of your client presentation for your portfolio.
29. **Commercial design.** Create the design plan following text guidelines through the Schematic Design phase for the Emericks' favorite ice-cream shop in downtown Elk Rapids, Michigan. Users of the space are typically tourists that visit between May and September. The owner of this small, quaint shop wants to do a complete renovation and branding. The owner wants you to meet the following design needs for the renovation:
    - seating for 12 to 15 people at small café tables
    - about 12 lineal feet for display cases and serving counter areas with cash register for check checkout
    - a place for customers to sample ice cream
    - back-of-the-house space for deliveries an storage
    - break room/office area for four or five employees plus the owner
    - small outdoor table/seating area for eight customers and a counter area with stools for five customers
    - new marketing, branding, and graphics ideas
    - color schemes, finishes, space plans, furniture arrangements
30. **Portfolio builder.** Save the documents, sketches, drawings, and budgets you created for items 19 through 26 and 28 and 29 for your portfolio.

Career Skills for Interior Design

Corepics/Shutterstock.com

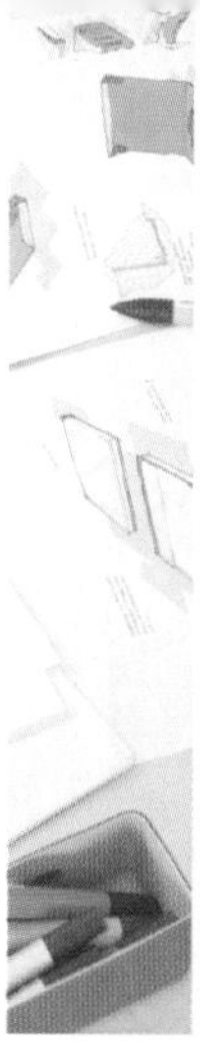

Chapter 17

Design Insight

"As design professionals, our knowledge enables us to form spaces that respond to human needs. These human spaces are the domain of our competence, our passion, and our work."

International Federation of Interior Architects/Designers (IFI)

Learning Targets

After studying this chapter, you will be able to

- analyze ways to prepare yourself for a career in interior design.
- identify employment opportunities, including entrepreneurship, for a career in interior design.
- create a personal brand and hone your skills in communication and social interaction.
- maintain a design portfolio that documents your interior design projects using a variety of multimedia techniques.
- investigate career resources for developing a professional résumé and a cover message for use in seeking meaningful employment.
- summarize the employability characteristics of a successful individual in the modern workplace.

Introduction

The actions you take now lay the foundation for your future career in interior design. Preparing for your career may seem overwhelming at first. Approaching this task one step at a time makes the process easier. If you have not started to think about your future, now is a good time to begin. Begin by asking yourself this question: "What can I do now, next semester, next year, and beyond to improve my chances of successfully entering the interior design career of my choice?"

Career Preparation

There are many goals you can set to prepare yourself for a career while in school. In school you can investigate job types, surround yourself with mentors, and develop connections within professional organizations. In addition, you can volunteer for community-service projects or accept leadership positions with various community or professional organizations.

In school, begin to *think* of yourself as a designer by acquiring valuable workplace skills rather than as a design student completing homework. As your perspective shifts, you will ask different questions in class, dress differently, and more readily accept opportunities to connect with designers on a professional level.

Here are some questions you will want to consider as you contemplate entering your interior design career.

- **What type of work would you like to do?** Do you like commercial, residential, or a mixture or both? Perhaps you prefer lighting design, facilities management, CAD work, or working as a manufacturer's representative.
- **What type of specialty would you like to practice?** Are the commercial design areas of hospitality, healthcare, institutional, or transportation of interest to you? Perhaps you are most interested in residential design.
- **What scope of work most appeals to you?** Do you want to work on a project from concept to installation or on a particular part of the client's project, such as lighting? Do you enjoy developing concepts, renderings, or working drawings and specifications? Perhaps you excel at research or client programming.
- **In what type of firm would you like to work?** Are you most interested in an interior design firm, architecture firm, construction management firm, designbuild firm (a multidisciplinary team with interior designers, architects, contractors, engineers, landscape designers), or a lighting design firm?
- **At what size of firm would you like to be employed?** A large firm is typically 20 to 50 employees (see the websites for ForrestPerkins, Gensler, or HOK, or see the *Top 100 Design Firms* annual rating), a medium-sized firm is typically 10 to 25 employees (see the Gallun Snow or Associates III websites), and a small-sized firm is typically 10 or fewer employees (see Krista Ninivaggi and the K&CO website).
- **What type of working environment most appeals to you?** Would you prefer to work in a department with a mid-size team or in a studio firm as an individual, **Figure 17-1**? Perhaps you prefer interaction with a computer—either behind the computer or in front of the client or both. Is telecommuting or freelancing in your future?
- **Where would you like to live?** Consider geographical, international, or national locations that appeal to you.
- **Do you want to practice interior design in a licensed state or another that does not have design-related legislation?** What are the advantages and disadvantages of such a decision?

Monkey Business Images/Shutterstock.com

Figure 17-1 Identifying the type of work you prefer to do can help you choose a work environment that suits your preferences and skills.

Inform Yourself

Information is power! As you prepare for the interior design profession, gather information about the field and trends taking place in this field. Determine what the most relevant and important qualifications for an *emerging professional* by viewing current job postings on various design career websites. Take advantage of opportunities to investigate the workplace, if only for a short time. These opportunities include

- design-practitioner interviews (with those working in the field)
- job-shadowing experiences
- internship opportunities
- work experiences

Experiences in the field help shape your thinking about *how* you should position yourself as you move into the interior design profession. Plan your steps and make conscious decisions about the direction you want your career to take. Develop your plan now with goals, timelines, and objectives. Then enjoy checking off the tasks you complete as you position yourself for the workplace.

Arm Yourself

The field of interior design values genuine, personal relationships and professional etiquette. As you position yourself to enter the design field, arm yourself with professional resources and a series of personal networks to ensure your transition from school to work is easy and enjoyable. Here are a few ways to achieve this goal.

Professional Memberships

Local, regional, and national chapters of design organizations such as ASID offer incredible and beneficial opportunities for leadership training, professional development and credentialing, connections across the country, and up-to-date product knowledge. Join one or two professional organizations and volunteer for committees of interest to you and to which you can contribute. The conversations you have with professionals will guide you to resources and new job opportunities in state, across the nation, or in other parts of the world. Professional organizations provide you with an established set of colleagues, contacts, and friends. Perhaps most importantly, they offer you an opportunity to shape the field of interior design and offer service to others in a meaningful way.

Effective Networking

The old adage "It is not *what* you know, but *who* you know" continues to hold true in the design field and the world today. Take this advice seriously. **Networking,** or the cultivation of productive relationships for employment or business, is one way to get to know other professionals, **Figure 17-2**. Develop strong, ongoing relationships by genuinely and professionally reaching out to others either in person or through social links. Although connections via various technologies are a *must*, come to meetings prepared with business cards. These cards are to be presented to others and serve as another way to share your personal brand. Networking tips include

- **Come prepared.** Create your brand by developing a business card and ensuring you are professionally dressed. The front of the business card should contain pertinent, but minimal contact information and should be professional looking with a clean, crisp business-like appearance. Your clothing should be modest and appropriate business attire.
- **Be brave.** When at an event, leave the security of your friends and colleagues to fulfill a pre-set personal goal of meeting five new people. Reach out with a handshake and introduce yourself.

baranq/Shutterstock.com

Figure 17-2 Meeting other interior designers at professional conferences is one way to network.

Professional designers are always impressed when a student extends his or her hand to them for an introduction. Search for similar interests with the professional designers and form new connections.

- **Give back.** Shape your network by introducing new professional contacts to your colleagues or peers. Design professionals are always interested in meeting talented design students as well as meeting colleagues.
- **Stay in contact.** Request a business card or a way to connect with new professional contacts after the event. Remember to use a more formal e-mail message or letter format than you would with a friend.
- **Follow up.** Use e-mail or a personal note to reconnect with people you encounter after the meeting. Make it a priority to follow up immediately after introduction to a new contact. A short e-mail message, or especially a handwritten note, can leave a positive impression. Offer assistance and resources as needed. If you are comfortable, join them through Internet communication channels such as LinkedIn.
- **Invite new connections.** The interior design field is very small. Ask your new contacts who they might know and try to make additional connections.

Be respectful and courteous at all times. By making a good impression, you will reap the rewards as you move into different career paths within the field. Strong professional networks are some of the most powerful tools at your disposal—in school and in the workplace. Use them. See **Figure 17-3** for more information about online networking.

Good Mentors

There is no substitute for several good mentors who can help you navigate the work world. Choose at least one in and out of the field of interior design who can teach you the cultural norms of the workplace and boost your confidence as you struggle with challenges. Select mentors who

- have a balanced perspective on the field
- are successful in the workplace culture
- care about your success on a personal level

Good References

As you make reputable and respected contacts in the field, approach these people to serve as one of your professional references. If these individuals accept, always give your contacts notice via e-mail if you are using their names when seeking employment. They can then prepare for any phone calls or e-mail messages they may receive on your behalf.

Passion for Design

Retain the wonder and excitement of meaningful, quality design in the world around you. Communicate it, revel in it, and celebrate it as you make professional connections. As you do, your passion will transfer to others who can easily identify with it. In job interviews, your excitement for design and positive demeanor will make you stand out among other candidates. Remember to always express yourself and your passion for design in a professional manner.

Mental Preparation and Design Preparation

Your design education will help you develop a good set of skills and a portfolio. Take advantage of additional professional workshops that keep you prepared and ahead of others in the field, such as becoming a USGBC Green Building Associate.

Mentally preparing yourself for your employment search is also important. Visualize yourself as confident, positive, and relaxed in a number of employment-seeking situations, including interviews. Your school will have done a good job preparing you for this time in your career.

Tips for Online Networking and Social Media Sites

Most design-related employers use social networking to research job candidates. They want to know about you before you enter the firm's door. The majority of jobs are also secured through referrals and networking. According to Bill George of the *Harvard Business Review*, "Social networking is the most significant business development..." *LinkedIn* and *Facebook* are the two largest social networking media.

Overall Tips

- Use clean, crisp, and professional digital images.
- Monitor what others say about you. Delete any unfavorable or unrequested content.
- Screen all pictures. Remove questionable images such as those showing drinking (even water) and inappropriate dress.

LinkedIn

- Maintain a complete profile.
- Join and start groups.
- Connect with industry leaders.
- Utilize hidden job boards. These do not appear with a typical website search.
- Add your LinkedIn "Public link" to your signature block.

Facebook

- Utilize a business photo. Maintain a clean image.
- Post your résumé, portfolio, and ask friends for referrals.
- Connect with previous coworkers and alumni.

Twitter

- Follow industry specific tweeters, such as ASID at NEOCON.
- Tweet between 12:00–3:00 EST—this seems to be the best time to hit the lunch-hour crowd.
- Link your portfolio to a tweet.
- Indicate what you are working on, if permissible. Be professional!

YouTube

(only if business appropriate)

- Post a video of design project you have completed.
- Discuss a hot, trendy topic.
- Give a video tour of a community service-learning project in which you participated.

Figure 17-3 Use of online networking sites can benefit your career, but make sure you use those tools that best suit your career needs. *What is the best way to use social networking? Is it possible to be over involved with technology? Why or why not?*

Seeking employment can be stressful, as can the workplace. Therefore, it is important to develop effective, healthful ways to deal with stress. See **Figure 17-4** for some useful tips.

Volunteer Yourself

One of the greatest ways to bring meaning into your design work is to offer it free of charge to someone in need within your community. In school, there are many opportunities for **service learning**—an educational experience that combines classroom instruction with meaningful community service—in which you select an *actual* client who is in need of design services. Both in and out of school, there are many opportunities for community service or **pro bono work**—professional work done for public good, generally without a fee.

After you select a favorite group or an individual in need, rally your friends to help out. This is one way you can demonstrate the principles of teamwork and your *leadership* skills as a citizen in a profound manner. Suggestions for community groups include Habitat for

Healthful Ways to Cope with Stress

- **Identify your stress triggers.** Knowing what causes you stress is the first step in coping.
- **Make a realistic "To Do" list.** Creating a realistic list of tasks and prioritizing them helps you maintain your focus. It also reduces the risk of forgetting something important.
- **Guard your time.** If you are working on something difficult, set aside time to work without interruptions. Then ignore distractions as you engage in the work.
- **Take periodic breaks.** Taking a minute or two to stand and stretch periodically throughout the day helps reduce stress and helps your productivity. If possible, take a quick walk outside. Fresh air can help you mentally relax.
- **Take care of your health.** Eat healthy meals and snacks, get plenty of regular sleep, and include physical activity in your daily routine. See your healthcare provider regularly to maintain your health.
- **Turn off your phone.** Make sure you control your time with your cell phone rather than having it control you. If you need time to focus on work or to spend concentrated time with friends and family, turn your phone off to avoid interruptions. To avoid sleep disturbances at night, charge your cell phone in another room.
- **Have some fun.** Take time everyday to do something you enjoy. Perhaps you like to spend time at the gym or working on your favorite hobby. Remember to relax with friends at a fun social evening event.

Figure 17-4 Develop healthful strategies to cope with stress and maintain physical and mental health for a lifetime.

Humanity, Rebuilding Together, abuse centers, or those impacted by natural disasters, **Figure 17-5**.

If working with local groups or agencies is not possible or you want to give back in a different way, develop a design for the national IDEC *Make a Difference Project* or engage with other social responsibility groups. The rewards from reaching out to others come back twofold—a reflection of the quality of your response to membership in a community, or your **citizenship**. In addition, a new group of friends or colleagues with similar interests to yours may result because of the service you provide to others.

Your Employment Path

Moving into your first employment position as an interior designer is exciting. Although there are several paths from which to choose, seeking your first professional job with an established design firm is highly recommended and has great merit and several benefits. When you work for others, you have the opportunity to learn from seasoned professionals, strengthen your skills, and build a positive reputation as a designer in the industry. The *Council for Interior Design Qualification (CIDQ)* recommends that you work for a minimum of two years in the design field. The decision to work for an established firm will generally arm you with the qualifications to take the NCIDQ exam. Documenting your work experiences, licenses, certifications, and credentials gives you further credibility with clients and your employer's firm. Setting professional goals early will build a strong employment path.

Habitat for Humanity International (HHI)/Will Crocker

Figure 17-5 Giving of your time and talents to meet a community need is one way to give back to your community and your profession. This group of volunteers is working on a *Habitat for Humanity* new-home build.

Some interior designers identify and choose entrepreneurship as an employment opportunity once they gain considerable on-the-job experience in an established firm. An **entrepreneur** is an individual who organizes, manages, and assumes the risks of a business. Recent information from the *U.S. Bureau of Labor Statistics* indicates that about 25 percent of interior designers are self-employed entrepreneurs.

It takes a number of years of work-related experiences to develop the necessary characteristics and skills to take on the role of entrepreneur in the field of interior design. Successful entrepreneurs are

- innovators who can envision a better way to deliver a task, product, or service to a client
- self-motivated, good planners, strategic thinkers, good record keepers, and willing to work hard
- knowledgeable about financial planning, have exceptional organizational and time-management skills, and know how to ask the right questions
- goal oriented, detail oriented, and responsible

The advantages and disadvantages of an entrepreneurial interior-design career are many. The advantages include independence, greater opportunity for personal recognition, and a chance to earn more money. You also have the ability to set the future vision for the firm, select your team members, and explore greater opportunities of self-directed design solutions. The disadvantages include risk and responsibility for making correct decisions, longer hours, limited employment benefits, fluctuating income, and greater tax burdens. While the freedom to design your business, its niche, and style may be personally satisfying, you need to seriously consider whether the disadvantages make this freedom worth the risk.

Sell Yourself

You are venturing into a great career with exciting and diverse opportunities. There are many traits you bring to the workplace that employers greatly value. Because the interior-design job market is *highly* competitive, do not wait until you are ready to start the job to identify your skills and traits. Begin six months or more in advance of your job search. Consciously determine how to promote your skills and traits. While employers appreciate humility in the design field, self-confidence is an expectation.

As you inventory your skills and traits, analyze how they might *fit* an interior design employer's expectations and their preferences for specific work habits. *Fit* in this instance is defined as matching your skills and interests with a design firm's needs.

ASID surveyed employers and found the top considerations when hiring a new designer in order of the most preferred include

- demonstrates strong technical design skills—in floor plans, elevations/sections, AutoCAD drawings, perspective sketches, reflected ceiling plans, lighting/electrical plans, and 3-D computer design
- displays sincerity and honesty, as well as ethical and moral character
- exhibits a good work ethic
- displays professional etiquette and good manners
- shows willingness to be a team player
- exhibits eagerness to grow and learn
- demonstrates effective time management skills
- relates well to others—is a good fit for the design firm
- exhibits a professional appearance and attire
- displays a positive, outgoing personality
- reveals strong passion and enthusiasm for design

You need these same skills whether you are job shadowing, serving an internship, entering your first career job, or moving into another position within the field. The workplace culture has some strict rules about professional language, behavior, dress, ethics, and image, **Figure 17-6**. As you sell yourself, consider your

- personal brand and image
- writing and speaking skills
- design skills

Dress for Success—Your Personal Brand

When you consider how to sell yourself, refresh your personal brand. As the former ASID National President Lisa Henry said, "If you do not design yourself well, why would you be trusted to design the world?" What do your outfits say—your accessories, belts, and ties? Do you work on your appearance as you do your design projects? Your appearance is a reflection on your future design firm and your colleagues. Employers may question your design skills if you dress inappropriately.

As you communicate your brand, your attire should be professional. Career websites offer professional suggestions about

Monkey Business Images/Shutterstock.com

Figure 17-6 The workplace has specific rules about how to dress. *What does the way these business people are dressed tell you about them and their confidence levels?*

professional and casual business attire, accessories, and proper footwear. Many discuss colors to wear, as well as appropriate grooming, makeup, and hairstyles. Similar to any design field, interior designers often dress in black. It is the accepted dress code for any event.

Your personal budget factors into your brand refresh. You want to look like a professional! Better-quality garments in a classic design are always the best wardrobe investment, **Figure 17-7**. Choose several key articles of clothing that you can mix and match with less costly accessories. Add to your work wardrobe as your personal budget allows.

Although designers appreciate the newest design trends in fashion and notice them as soon as you enter a room—male or female, be mindful that modest and professional attire is the expected norm in the workplace and with clients. Dress in a way that says "I'm a professional," rather than "Everyone look at me." The focus in the workplace should be on you and your design skills, not extremes in your attire, makeup, hairstyle, or grooming. In many formal workplace environments, employer dress codes require employees to cover visible tattoos and remove certain piercings. Making inappropriate choices about your personal brand is a quick way to lose a job offer or an actual job.

Personal Interactions

Personal interaction with others is another way to sell yourself and your design skills. As you open your mouth to speak, how will you represent yourself? The way you

Monkey Business Images/Shutterstock.com Samuel Borges Photography/Shutterstock.com Mark LaMoyne/Shutterstock.com

Figure 17-7 Your appearance—grooming, attire, and behavior—reflects your personal brand and impacts your career options. *How might you refresh your personal brand?*

demonstrate your effective verbal skills with individuals from varied cultures and fellow workers, management, and customers is a reflection on your personal brand and your design skills. Perception is reality. Be genuine and courteous and remember the five "B's":

- Be gracious.
- Be respectful.
- Be a good listener.
- Be honest.
- Be inclusive.

Develop an Elevator Speech

In addition to good manners, always have an elevator speech ready about what an interior designer offers. An **elevator speech** is short and to the point—it is a brief summary of who you are, what you do, and your career goals. For non-designers, develop a quick description of yourself and your work because many people do not understand the field of interior design. Interior design professionals are responsible for talking about their profession to others in ways that bring clarity about it to others and the world. For example say, "I shape human experiences through the design of interior spaces. What do you do?" While the first question may raise more questions than offer a complete answer, it serves as a good conversation starter and allows a dialogue about design to take place.

Introduce Yourself—Offer Your Name

As you meet someone for the first time, sell yourself as a designer by clearly offering your name when introducing yourself to others. Even if you are approaching someone you have met before, offer a handshake and reintroduce yourself. Designers meet hundreds of new people each week. They are very good at remembering faces, but less proficient with remembering names. Help them to connect with you. They will be grateful when you jog their memories and will actually remember you more because of the professional courtesy you offered by reminding them of your name.

Present Your Business Card

After making a good first impression with your professional dress and personal introduction, present your business card in a professional manner. Purchase a business-card case that holds a number of cards, not just one or two. Have your cards ready. Avoid trying to find them in the bottom of a purse or briefcase. Present your business card gracefully, **Figure 17-8**. Remember, you are presenting a little bit of yourself. Likewise, *look* at any business cards others present to you and treat them with respect.

Attend Social Events

As a design student, you will attend many social events. Be on time—it is a characteristic of a professional. If you can, arrive early so you are calm. Avoid arriving at the last minute. Visualize success. Instead of socializing with your companions, move to the center of the room and look for someone you do not know and introduce yourself.

As you offer a comment or two, include others in the conversation as it develops. It is part of your job to make other people feel comfortable in such social settings, and it is another way to demonstrate effective verbal skills. If you find starting a conversation difficult, plan ahead and develop a few *conversation starters* such as: "What do you think about (insert an interior design trend or topic of interest)?" "Tell me about the most meaningful piece of advice regarding an interior design career that someone ever gave you." "What trends do you see that are shaping the field of the built environment?"

AVAVA/Shutterstock.com

Figure 17-8 When networking with others, share the gift of your name and your business card with confidence and poise.

Keep your mind sharp and clear—avoid being distracted with refreshments or a ringing phone. Turn your phone off and focus on the people around you. Be present. Practice good listening skills and avoid talking too much about yourself. Ask questions of others and offer your knowledge about design and design trends. Help new contacts feel comfortable with you so that they in turn introduce you to others. When you are making introductions, follow business protocol by introducing men to women, young people to older people, and *less* important people to *more* important. Some additional tips for proper business etiquette include

- Be personable but professional.
- Be polite and respectful.
- Contribute to the conversation.
- Avoid slang or foul language.
- Avoid discussions of controversial topics, gossip, politics, or religion, and personal matters unrelated to design.
- For business events, research the event topic and venue location before arriving. This way you will know where you are going and will be able to speak with knowledge about the given topic.
- Thank the event host in person prior to leaving. Follow up by sending a thank-you note. Sending thank-you notes to the host indicates that you pay attention to details. It is a good reflection on you and your interaction with others. Send such notes within 48 hours of the event via traditional mail or e-mail.

Sell Your Designs

Your designs are part of your professional brand. You will likely present your portfolio in two formats—digital and in hard copy. It can also be *disposable*, meaning an 8½- by 11-inch sheet of paper folded as a brochure to tuck into an envelope or hand out during an employment interview. Portfolios can also be quite formal, such as a professionally bound portfolio.

Developing a focused portfolio that reflects you as a professional has many benefits. During development, it allows you to think analytically about your skill set and accomplishments and how they relate to potential employers. Technology today allows you to customize your portfolio and tailor it for specific, available positions. For example, if you are applying for a job in a large-scale commercial design firm, your portfolio should reflect the type of skills—such as with *Revit*—that are commonly used in a firm of this size. By doing so, you show employers you have done your *homework* and understand the unique characteristics they are seeking for the open position. A portfolio allows you to demonstrate your skills and experiences is a visual way. The design of your portfolio is just as important as the designs you place in it.

Your Portfolio

Remember, a portfolio is a collection of your design thinking, design solutions, and design interests. It serves as a visual presentation of your design competencies to be communicated in a variety of formats. It reflects your ability to conceptualize and analyze design. Because there are no specific standards, your portfolio serves as a unique, well-designed statement about you—a personal expression of your skills and personality. Employers view the way you develop your portfolio and how you graphically present it as a type of product design in and of itself, **Figure 17-9**. Your portfolio should convey creativity and spark employer interest. It should communicate, "I have creative design capabilities and up-to-date technology skills. I respect your firm. I am a good *fit* with your team. Hire me."

Your portfolio showcases examples of your best work across your educational experience and includes projects that demonstrate your readiness to enter the workforce. For example, your portfolio content might include a sampling of visual communication skills such as freehand sketching, CAD, or conceptual development of drawings such as floor plans, elevations, renderings, lighting and electrical plans, and reflected ceilings plans. These plans demonstrate knowledge of the built environment.

A portfolio is always a work in progress. You are either adding new designs or modifying existing items to present to a specific audience, such as a potential employer or a firm offering an internship. Tailor the contents of your portfolio to a firm's design specialty and those who will be viewing it.

The purpose of your design portfolio is not just to showcase and demonstrate your design skills, but to serve as a topic of conversation, or a storyline, during your interview. Your potential employer is curious to know how you

- present yourself while speaking
- convey confidence
- accurately use the vocabulary of design
- think through a design problem

Rebecca Hart/Senior Design Student

Figure 17-9 Craft your design portfolio carefully. Your creativity should spark employer interest in your skills and abilities.

Many students spend countless hours preparing a design portfolio and *never practice* how to orally present it. Be sure to develop a storyline for the portfolio, not just for individual projects. Knit the story together into a fluid presentation. Then practice your presentation—in front of a mirror or friends or family. You need to become comfortable with telling the story.

As you work in the design field, your portfolio will evolve and change. For career advancement or new clients, you will continue to present your portfolio to others. Tips for organizing and developing your portfolio include

- Develop a storyboard and storyline for your portfolio. Sketch the layout of each page on separate paper. Make notations to remember your thoughts as you create your portfolio product.
- Create a cover with little or no design on it. It should have minimal information, such as your name and brand. Make sure it has a clean, professional design look.
- Develop a table of contents for the second page. It identifies the organization of your portfolio and what can be found inside, **Figure 17-10**. Do not use page numbers—you will frequently reshape your portfolio.
- Organize the contents by either *project* (Holmes residence), by *theme* (sustainable design), by *skill set* (hand drawing and rendering, digital renderings, CAD/REVIT ability, construction or detail drawings, process drawings, models, finish boards, and other graphic skills such as photography, graphic design, or sculptures), or *design type* (commercial or residential).
- Include a team project if desired but clearly indicate your contribution to the project/work. Demonstrating your ability to work on team projects leaves a good impression with employers.
- Never use drawings or images that are not yours. Doing so is an infringement on copyright and, if perceived as such, could cost you the job.

Portfolio Suggestions
Items to Include
■ Résumé and contact information (if not sent separately)
■ Design philosophy (optional)
■ Minimum of one complete project
■ Process drawings to show your design thinking
■ Examples of
■ Manual sketching
■ Digital renderings
■ CAD/REVIT ability
■ Construction or detail drawings
■ Models
■ Finish boards
■ Other graphic skills: drawing, photography, graphic design, sculptures
■ Process drawings to show design thinking
Do Not Include
■ Any of your weak skills (for example, hand sketching) even if it is the only example you have
■ Poor examples of design or design solutions
■ Demographic information (race, religion, age, social security number)
■ Large amounts of text
■ Hand lettering, if poor
■ Design projects that are not your own work.

Figure 17-10 Choose the best examples of your work to include in your portfolio.

- Create effective, readable labels. Help the viewers understand the challenges or issues for various projects and how you solved them. Help them understand the significance of your design. Select words carefully to reflect purpose and personality. Avoid mundane phrases. Keep labels clear and concise. Spell correctly.
- Select a font type and size carefully for clear communication. The font type selected is very important. If need be, purchase specialty design fonts. Look at professional magazines for suggested layout and font types.
- Keep background page colors neutral: black, white, warm gray, or beige.
- Begin and end with your strongest work.
- Display the depth and variety of your skills. However, simplest is best. When in doubt, leave it out.
- Develop a brand and use similar design elements (such as line) that connect each portfolio page.

Although the preceding details focus on items to include in your portfolio, there are also items that you should exclude from your portfolio. Exclude demographic information about yourself including race, religion, age, and social security number.

The Traditional Portfolio

Many prospective design employers prefer to hold something in hand versus viewing it on a digital screen, thus the traditional portfolio is still popular. Employers know well that digital technologies can camouflage quality and depth of design. They also realize digital media cannot capture a tactile experience. Employers prefer not to struggle with difficulties related to opening files in unfamiliar formats or searching for portfolios on remote servers. Design employers want to meet you in person and discuss your design work.

Your traditional portfolio begins with the carrying case, **Figure 17-11**. Avoid the look of a photo album or scrapbook. Your portfolio is a business communication tool. Make the pages removable so you can add or delete projects or items not needed for upcoming interviews. Ensure you have a common brand that links each page, located in the same corner on each page—preferably the bottom right.

The disadvantages of traditional portfolios include the expense and the color which can shift when printing pages of your digitally constructed designs, changing their look. Select the quality of your paper carefully and print test sheets to determine if the color shift is acceptable before using the images in your portfolio.

The Digital Portfolio

For several reasons, the digital portfolio is more popular today than ever. First, the globalization of the interior design market is making the digital portfolio a necessity. You may need to send your portfolio across the nation or to another continent. Second, designers work in a highly technical, multimedia environment. To document your interior design projects you will use a variety of multimedia techniques. For instance, you can showcase digital skills, such as an interior walk-through or video clip—with sound—that you cannot capture in a traditional portfolio. Third, as mentioned earlier, you will want to update and tailor your portfolio to a variety of uses.

Due to the size of the computer design files, the two common ways to present a digital portfolio include a website and cloud server. A disadvantage of the digital portfolio is that distance separates you from the live presentation. While it can increase your visibility across state lines, it means the digital portfolio must answer all of the viewer's questions. Make sure your images are clean and crisp, and at the appropriate resolution to best showcase your skills, **Figure 17-12.**

yienkeat/Shutterstock.com

Figure 17-11 Use an appropriate, professional carrying case for your traditional portfolio.

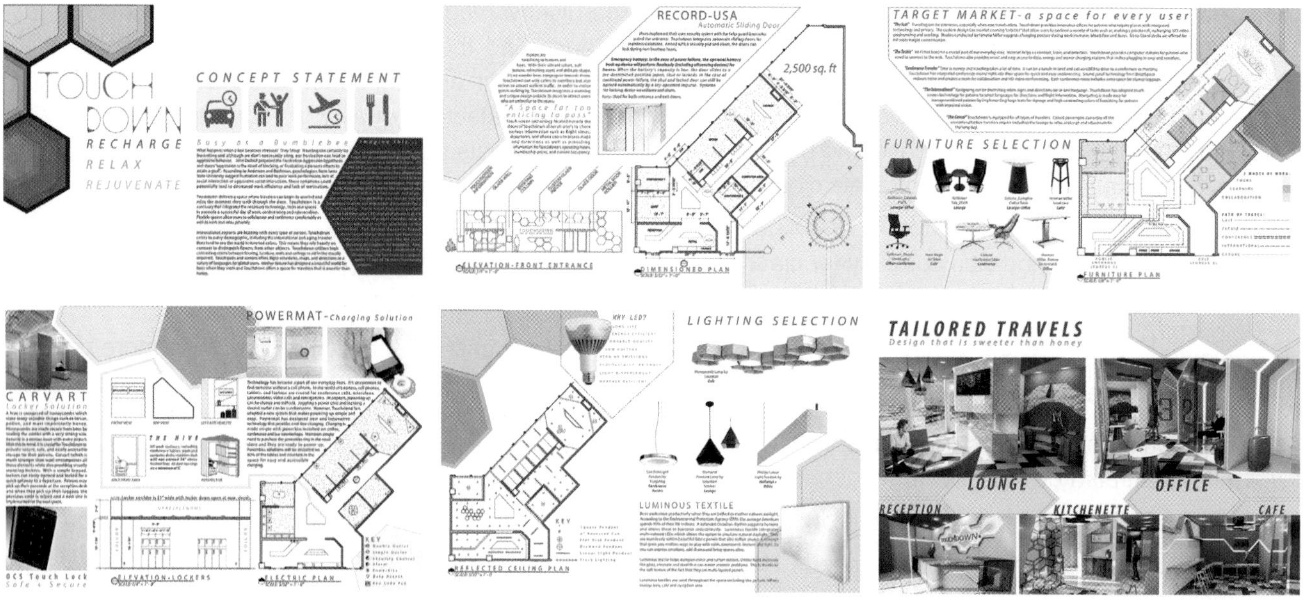

Ajay Chung Li/Interior Design Student

Figure 17-12 Your digital portfolio can be viewed by employers locally, across the nation, and overseas. Be sure to use a variety of multimedia techniques to clearly showcase your design skills.

Once your digital portfolio is complete, you can send it via e-mail, place it on a website, or rent space on a server. Often your school will provide some space for you on its server until you graduate. The size of your digital portfolio can be very large due to the images. Keep multiple backups of your files. If you need to send the digital portfolio to a potential employer or post-secondary educational institution, keep the following tips in mind:

- Utilize the correct file extensions when creating files.
- Avoid sending large portfolio files. Reduce the size of files without putting them in a zipped file. *Zipped files* are compressed files that require a compression utility on a computer to open the file.
- Upload your portfolio to a digital-portfolio hosting site if desired.

Sell Your Credentials

It is hard work to acquire an interior design degree. There is much competition to gain acceptance into a CIDA-accredited program. While in such a program, you work hard not only to pass your courses, but also to acquire additional credentials. You might participate in competitions—national, regional, and local.

As an interior design student, you may attend conferences, participate in study abroad, and serve in many design leadership capacities on campus and in the professional field. You will likely fulfill not one, but often two design internships or work experiences. These experiences, honors, and accomplishments shape who you are as a designer and prepare you to enter the design profession. It is important to showcase yourself, your work, and your credentials well.

Résumés and *cover messages* represent *you*! They showcase your graphic capabilities and written skills. Make them powerful, concise, and business-like with a design twist. For preparing a résumé and cover message that gets noticed, see the *Special Topics* later in the text.

As you approach drafting your résumé and cover messages, it is also important to examine your approach to locating your first design job. Since you will need to tailor your résumé and cover messages, it is important to review the background information on various types of firms and interior design positions.

Locate Your First Design Job

Stepping out to locate your first design job is an exciting, challenging adventure. Finding your first design job can depend on many things including the economy, your location, the design specialization you desire, how selective you are, your willingness to travel, your skill set, your internship, experience, and who you know!

Too often, students research design firms in their local areas, develop standard résumés, send their résumés electronically to all firms, and then wait for a job to arrive on their doorsteps. When no job offers come their way, they wonder why they worked so hard on their design degrees. What these students lack are the critical job-search skills this chapter outlines, especially the follow-up persistence necessary to inform employers of strong interest in the job! Assuming you have been networking, have a mentor, and are communicating a professional brand, your transition from school to work should have favorable results.

As you prepare for your first design position, display confidence, but also be humble and teachable. Experienced designers identify these traits as highly desirable in aspiring professionals. Your first job may not be ideal, but once you get into the field and make meaningful contributions, it is much easier to move to your next position.

One of your best resources is your network—both on campus and off. When it comes to potential employers, look beyond your local area. Here are some ways to increase your connections.

- Use your internship coordinator, mentors, professors, and peers to begin a list of potential firms to which you might apply, **Figure 17-13**.
- Use family, friends, and acquaintances to identify new leads.

auremar/Shutterstock.com

Figure 17-13 Consulting with your professors, internship coordinator, or peers can lead to connections with potential design employers.

- Contact the firm at which you completed an internship. The firm may have open positions or may connect you with firms that do.
- Consider people you have met at professional meetings or on-site visits. Ask them about job prospects.
- Expand your employer options beyond interior design and architectural firms. Consider construction and graphic design firms. Also, look at the availability of design positions for county and city planning departments.
- Review the list of the top 100 design firms that is published yearly. Contact those firms aligning with your skills and interests.
- Use online resources to find designers holding some of the same professional memberships as you have and contact them.
- Arrange an informational interview with a designer to learn more about his or her firm.
- Contact alumni of your school to discuss potential employer prospects.
- Review LinkedIn or Facebook to view contacts available through these sources.
- Attend a national conference and strategically place your business card where potential employers can see it.
- Visit with materials and furnishings industry representatives to learn if they know of any job openings.

Once you have gathered data about firms for which you may work, make a list of your top 10 to 20 firms. For each firm, create an electronic folder or prepare a traditional binder with a summary sheet for each firm. Include specific information you find for each firm such as the following:

- A cover sheet with a table showing the firm's name, contact person, when you contacted the firm, and when and how you followed up
- Research information about the firm, its design philosophy, the type of design work it performs, and project examples *(Note: Put one or two of their projects in your binder so you can reference them during a conversation on the phone or via e-mail.)*
- An analysis of how well your skills, interests, and abilities align with the firm
- A list of any alumni you could contact, if possible, for additional firm information

Look at the company website. The goal is to determine if there is a fit for you within that firm. Be objective but positive. It is a win-win situation if you find a great firm to work for and they find a great employee. Here are some questions to think about, **Figure 17-14**. Note these questions are not meant to persuade you to be too selective. Instead, they are provided to help you to be informed when you apply for available positions.

Make Connections

Once you complete your research and draft your résumé and cover message, it is time to connect with the design firms of choice. The time between the beginning of your job search to the time you begin employment generally averages three to six months. As you begin your employment search, present a very low-key, persistent, professional sales pitch about yourself. Double-check your voice mail to make sure it is professional. Keep it simple and just record your name and phone number.

Making Phone Calls

A phone call is the best way to request an interview if you cannot do so in person. Identify yourself promptly, thank the designer for granting you a few minutes of his or her time, and state the reason for the call. Make it easy for the designer to talk with you. Prepare a script for what you will say, but do not read it. Request 30 minutes of the designer's time to meet and discuss employment options at his or her convenience. Be personable. Smile—people can sense your enthusiasm and attitude without seeing your face, **Figure 17-15**.

If a job does not exist at the firm, ask if you can still submit a résumé and cover message to the designer. Then ask the important, often forgotten question: "Do you know of any other firms that might be looking for an entry-level designer?" Often, the designer can put you in contact with a colleague or two.

Using E-mail

If a design firm has posted a job opening on an online job board, in the newspaper, or with an employment agency,

Researching Design Firms

Here are some questions to think about when researching design firms as potential employers.

- Do your values align with the firm's?
- What is the firm's philosophy and mission? Is it compatible with yours?
- What is the firm's reputation?
- What size firm do you prefer? There are large firms (such as Gensler, HOK, and Perkins + Will), medium firms (such as OZ Architecture and Gallun Snow), and small one-person firms.
- Look at the projects on which the firms work—both commercial and residential. What are their specializations—tenant improvement, law offices, hospitality design, or high-end residential design?
- Do you know any of the team members and potential coworkers at the firm?
- What is the firm's sense of design? What does its brand convey? Just looking at the firm's website can provide answers.
- What is the company's history? Historical data can give you a feel for the company's design philosophy and where the firm is headed in the future.

kzenon/iStock/Thinkstock

Figure 17-14 As you research potential design firms as employers, answering these questions can help you determine whether various employers are a good fit for your skills and with what you value in design and life.

wavebreakmedia/Shutterstock.com

Figure 17-15 When you smile while talking on the phone, potential employers can sense your attitude and enthusiasm for the job.

the firm will provide a contact name and e-mail address to which potential candidates send their application materials. The job posting lists the application deadline and the method by which the employer wants potential candidates to submit their information. Here are some tips for communicating with potential employers via e-mail.

- Keep your message short. Make it succinct and professional, carefully crafting what you want to say.
- Use the subject line to indicate the purpose of your e-mail.
- Use the name of the employer contact in the salutation at the beginning of the message.
- Avoid using e-mail stationary and backgrounds. They tend not to be business-oriented.
- Indicate any attachments and their purpose.
- Watch your use of humor. It can be easily misinterpreted.
- Keep your e-mail signature (typed) short and precise.

Using Text Messaging

Many designers access their e-mail messages via cell phone. It is very likely they will respond to you by text messaging. When using text messaging, be sure to text sparingly. Do not use abbreviations (for instance, "R" for "are"). Always use professional language.

The Interview

Landing an interview is a great experience, regardless of the end results. Accept multiple interview opportunities. You want to keep all potential employment doors open. Each interview will help you narrow your decision about the type of firm for which you want to work and how well your skills and interests align with various types of firms. Sometimes the process has a real surprise ending.

Before you walk through a design firm's doors for an interview, there are a few items to double-check. These include your

- **Wardrobe.** Prepare your interview wardrobe. Dress in business attire that reflects your personal brand, **Figure 17-16**.
- **Portfolio.** Reassess your portfolio and refresh your memory on the storyline about your work. Practice your presentation several times—preferably in front of others. Do not expect to just hand your portfolio to the designer for review.
- **Research notes.** Review your research notes about the firm and be familiar with some of their recent design projects.
- **Skill fit.** Make a list showing how your skills are a good fit for the design firm. Memorize the key points to use in the interview.
- **Business cards and materials.** Bring extra copies of your business card, cover message, résumé, and disposable portfolio to leave with the employer as you leave the interview.

Employers expect you to know about their firms: who they are, what they do, and why they do it. To learn more about interview questions and following up after an interview, see the *Special Topics* later in the text.

Evaluate Job Offers

After interviewing and as you consider a job offer or compare two or more interior design positions, you need to examine the items that follow. You will not want to approach these points until after an employer offers you the position. Remember, you need to use

andresrimaging/iStock/Thinkstock

Figure 17-16 First impressions count! Your personal brand is reflected in your appearance. *What might be the consequences of failure to pay attention to designing yourself as you do to honing your design skills?*

considerable diplomacy when approaching these topics with any potential employer.

- **Work schedule.** Can you commit to the scheduled work hours and workdays? Is occasional overtime a work requirement?
- **Income and benefits.** Is the salary or wage proposal in line with reported averages? *(Note: Know the averages in your area before you begin the interview process.)* Will you receive benefits that are just as valuable as extra income, such as medical and life insurance, paid vacation time, and a retirement plan? Will the employer pay for professional development courses and programs related to the position such as taking the NCIDQ or LEED GA examinations? Does the employer pay for any professional development opportunities (continuing education courses)?
- **Job obligations.** Is membership in a professional organization a requirement? If so, what are the costs? Is there reimbursement for these costs? Will meetings occur after work hours?
- **Advancement potential.** Is there opportunity for advancement? How soon after demonstrating consistently good performance can you pursue additional responsibilities? How often are job reviews conducted? Does advancement require additional degrees or certifications? What training programs does the employer offer?

Workplace Success

Workplace success is the result of hard work, high motivation, and a diverse skill set. Whether your career path involves interior design or a related career, you will need to give your best effort on the job. Successful employees display energy, cooperation, and enthusiasm for their work, **Figure 17-17**.

As an employee, you have many responsibilities. Employers expect their employees to help the design business operate and make a profit. Employees are also expected to work to the best of their abilities, follow the rules and instructions put in place by the employer, take constructive criticism well, and finish projects in a timely manner. Along with following the dress code and having good grooming habits, your employer will expect you to be punctual, use good time-management and organizational skills, and interpersonal skills.

LDprod/Shutterstock.com

Figure 17-17 Cooperation and teamwork are just several of the qualities that lead to a successful career. *Discuss other employee traits that lead to career success and advancement.*

Punctuality

Punctuality means being on time. Being late is inconsiderate and is not tolerated in the working world. Coworkers will have to take on the work of employees who are late or absent. It is important to show up ready for work every day and on time.

Punctuality is a good sign of dependability. **Dependability** shows a person's ability to be reliable and trustworthy. Being dependable means others can count on you to do what needs to be done. Dependable people keep their word, are honest, and carry their share of the workload. Dependable employees tend to be given the important jobs in a company.

Positive Attitude

Your attitude is your outlook on life. Your response to events and people around you reflects in your attitude. Cheerfulness, cooperation, and courteous behaviors help pave the way to successful working relationships with coworkers, designers, and clients.

Enthusiasm and passion for the work you do spread quickly from one person to another. When you demonstrate enthusiasm for your work, it is a sign that you enjoy what you do. This leads to pride in your accomplishments and a desire to achieve greater goals.

Time Management and Organization

"Work smarter, not harder" is a phrase frequently quoted in business and industry. Employees who understand how to organize both their time and job responsibilities can meet or beat project deadlines. They are able to take on more responsibilities and eventually earn promotions to advance their careers.

Time management is the practice of organizing time and work assignments to increase personal efficiency. It is another very important skill in the workplace because work assignments may include a variety of tasks and projects. Like many designers, you will need to work on several tasks at the same time. You will need to prioritize those tasks by determining which ones to complete before others. When uncertain as to which tasks are the most important, always ask your direct supervisor. The difference between average and excellent workers is often not how *hard* they work, but how well they prioritize assignments.

Problem-Solving Skills

Your ability to make responsible decisions and use problem-solving skills applies to solving client problems through design, solving workplace problems, and all other aspects of life. Using these skills well demonstrates to your employer that you can handle additional work responsibilities. Effective use of problem-solving skills can also help strengthen team efforts.

As you may know, problem-solving skills can help you address many complex client problems in the built environment as well as answering tough questions and resolving difficult workplace situations. Problem solving generally involves adapting to a new way of doing things, or "thinking outside the box." Employers highly value employees who can solve problems effectively. Here is a summary of the steps in effective problem solving.

1. Identify the real problem.
2. List alternative courses of action for solving the problem.
3. Evaluate the consequences of each course of action.
4. Choose an alternative and implement the course of action.
5. Evaluate the outcome for reference when facing future problems.

Interpersonal Skills

Interpersonal skills are those skills that help people communicate and work well with each other. Your company or business will expect you to have good interpersonal skills. These skills are necessary to complete the job duties and ensure a positive working environment. The ability to communicate well, show respect for others, and teamwork are skills all employers want in their employees, **Figure 17-18**.

Communications

Giving and receiving information efficiently is the key to effective communications. Time is limited in the workplace and all employees have many duties and responsibilities. Others appreciate it when a person gets to the point quickly and in a positive manner. Being able to state your needs or intentions clearly to others can be learned through practice.

Careful listening and responding are also hallmarks of good communication. If you do not understand what someone

Stephen Coburn/Shutterstock.com

Figure 17-18 Effective interpersonal skills help ensure a positive work environment and cooperation among team members and coworkers.

wants, ask the person to clarify the request. Make sure to follow directions carefully. Always ask questions when you do not understand how to do a certain task. As in every part of life, communicating in a positive manner gets better results than negativity or a bad attitude.

Respect

Respect is the feeling that someone or something is good, valuable, and important. Be considerate of the feelings of coworkers. A smile and a few minutes of friendly conversation are good ways to promote good working relationships.

Work environments are usually diverse, including people of many different cultures, beliefs, and ages. Regardless of personal differences, show respect to your supervisors, coworkers, clients, and any other person you interact with on the job. Make sure to remember the golden rule: treat others as you would like to be treated.

Teamwork

Many employers consider teamwork skills to be necessary in the workplace. As work needs arise, employers may assign employees to work in different teams based on skills the employees bring to the teams. Participation as a team member of a design-firm work group is similar to playing on a sports team. Success is measured in terms of the success of the team, not each player. Teamwork involves putting the team goals ahead of personal goals.

Leadership

Employers want to know if you can function as a team leader. When you volunteer to lead others to achieve a goal, you demonstrate the principles of group participation and leadership. Leadership and problem-solving skills go hand-in-hand.

Although a number of leadership styles exist, most businesses favor a democratic style of leadership. This style encourages all team members to take initiative, work to carry out goals, and assume responsibility for team accomplishments in a timely manner. How can this leadership style benefit you in your interior design career? See **Figure 17-19**. In general, the traits of effective leaders include the ability to

- encourage individual team members to resolve problems and differences of opinion
- guide the team to overcome obstacles in reaching the team goals
- work through challenges with team members to make changes happen
- take responsibility for their actions and the actions of the team
- offer inspiration, flexibility, and creativity

Workplace Ethics

Ethics are guiding principles of conduct and character that govern the actions of individuals or groups in making

Dusit/Shutterstock.com

Figure 17-19 Inspiring leaders encourage team members to do their best work. *What are your leadership traits?*

Designer Profile

Krista Ninivaggi—Career Pathway

In 2014, Krista Ninivaggi launched her boutique firm K&CO, with focus on hospitality and large scale multifamily residential interiors. CONTRACT magazine named Krista Ninivaggi its 2014 Designer of the Year for her work as director of the interior design group at SHoP Architects in New York City.

Christine Han Photography

"My Grandpa Perry, a first generation Italian-American, was a sweet and charming man who built and designed the house where both my father and I grew up. My grandfather was well meaning in his ambitions—he was a great policeman and maybe an amateur carpenter—but *not* a designer. Even as a small child there were details about the house that baffled me: the interior plan, the room adjacencies, the exterior color, the entry sequence, to name a few. As a seven-year-old, I would often walk my parents through my grand plans to knock down walls, add bathrooms, expose the staircase, and incorporate new paint schemes!

"By the time I was a senior in high school and my eyes were exhausted from picking out the patterns in the grain of our birch slab bedroom doors, I found my way to art school. I had a clear interest in design but it wasn't until I turned 21 and my friends and I began to explore the hospitality and entertainment establishments on the edge of the Palisades that I understood its potential.

"I was extremely fortunate that David Rockwell gave me my first job as a designer when I graduated from school. The nearly four years I spent in his studio is where I truly received my education in hospitality design. It was also where I first met the partners of SHoP Architects who would later give me the biggest opportunity of my career.

"My relationship with SHoP did not start over heady discussions about design or shared material specs, but over softball. I'm not sure how it all came up, but somehow I ended up helping start the Rockwell softball team with SHoP as one of our opponents. Eight years later I found myself starting the Interiors Group at SHoP—receiving an invitation into the firm as a friend and design comrade. Up until this point I had tackled plenty of design challenges, but now I was faced with business challenges, proposals, staffing, hiring, billing… Without this experience I would have not had the confidence, or to be frank, the knowledge to strike out on my own.

"I am fortunate to have been a designer at three influential firms. Each experience has profoundly influenced my opinions and methodologies of design. Distilling the lessons learned at each firm created a road map for the founding of my own practice—but I'm still learning. There's always a next chapter and skills you can learn to fulfill your ambitions. You just have to look very carefully because curiosity may influence your next move, and not opportunity."

You can read more about Krista's background in Appendix B.

right decisions. *Workplace etiquette* is a set of guidelines for appropriate behavior on the job. An employer's employee handbook includes a code of conduct that outlines the manner in which employees should behave while at work and when representing the company or design firm, clients, or the profession. For instance, professional organizations, such as ASID, have guiding principles or **codes of ethics** by which members of a profession should conduct themselves (*see Appendix A—ASID Code of Ethics and Professional Conduct*). Companies may define specific issues as inappropriate, unethical, or illegal. For example, employers have rules for maintaining confidentiality, avoiding computer threats, using company equipment, and downloading software.

Company Equipment

Company equipment is designated for business-related functions, not for personal use. Office equipment includes desktop computers, digital tablets, phones, and photocopy machines. Employers provide this equipment to employees to improve efficiency. In many cases, it is impossible for an employee to perform his or her job without it.

Many codes of conduct also have guidelines for visiting websites and rules for downloading to company computers. These rules protect the business' computer system and its private information.

Company-owned mobile devices, such as smartphones or tablets, are also company property. Never use them for personal reasons. Follow the company policies for appropriate communication and workplace behavior.

Software Downloads

It is unethical and illegal for an employee to download software that has not been purchased and registered by the employer. Buying software involves purchasing a license to use the software. A *license* is the legal permission to use a software program. All software has terms of use that explain how and when to use the software.

Use of some software programs may only be lawful after purchase. Another name for these programs is *for-purchase software*. Demo, short for demonstration, software may be used without buying. However, demos may have either limits in functionality or time. If you decide to keep using the software, you must purchase it. *Piracy* is the illegal copying or downloading of software, files, or other protected material. This includes scanning or downloading images or music.

Intellectual Property

Intellectual property is something that comes from a person's mind, such as an idea, invention, or process. Intellectual property laws protect a person's or a company's inventions, artistic works, and other intellectual property. Any use of intellectual property without permission is called **infringement.**

A **copyright** acknowledges ownership of a work and specifies that only the owner has the right to sell the work, use it, or give permission for someone else to sell or use it. The laws cover all original work, whether it is in print, on the Internet, or in any other form or media. You cannot claim work as your own or use it without permission. **Plagiarism** is claiming another person's material your own**,** which is both unethical and illegal.

Proprietary information, or trade secrets, is any work employees of a company create on the job that the company owns. It is confidential information a company needs to keep private and protect from theft.

Proprietary information can include many things, such as product formulas, special design features or custom details, customer lists, or manufacturing processes. All employees must understand the importance of keeping company information confidential. The code of conduct should explain that sharing company information may only occur with permission from human resources. Employees who share proprietary information with outsiders are unethical and, possibly, breaking the law.

Netiquette

Netiquette is etiquette to use when communicating electronically. Netiquette includes accepted social and professional guidelines for Internet communications, **Figure 17-20**. It applies to e-mails, social networking, blogs, texting, and chatting. For example, it is generally unprofessional to use texting language in a business environment. Always proofread and spell-check e-mails before sending them. When communicating electronically, it is important to follow the same common courtesy you use in face-to-face discussions.

Use the Internet access the company or design firm provides only for business purposes. Checking personal e-mail or shopping online is not acceptable workplace behavior. When using the Internet, you are a representative of the design firm or business for which you work.

Kheng Guan Toh/Shutterstock.com

Figure 17-20 Appropriate netiquette is essential for both personal and professional electronic communication. *Discuss the consequences of failure to use appropriate netiquette.*

Chapter 17

Review and Assess

Summary

- When transitioning from school to the workplace, think of yourself as a designer by acquiring valuable workplace skills rather than as a student completing assignments.
- Interior design is a diverse profession with many opportunities.
- Arm yourself with information about cutting-edge qualifications for emerging design professionals through interviews with professionals, job-shadowing experiences, internships, and work experiences.
- The benefits of membership in a professional organization such as ASID include leadership training, professional development, credentialing, as well as connections with other professionals.
- Networking provides a way to get to know other professionals and cultivate relationships that can lead to employment opportunities.
- Choose mentors in and out of the interior design field that can boost your workplace confidence.
- Volunteer opportunities help you demonstrate your design skills through group participation and citizenship in career preparation.
- Entrepreneurs organize, manage, and assume the risks of a business.
- Identify and analyze your best skills and traits to determine how they fit an employer's expectations and ideas about appropriate work habits.
- Workplace attire and the way you present yourself represent your personal brand to potential employers and other professionals.
- As you sell yourself and your design skills, remember the "five B's" of genuine and courteous personal interactions.
- When attending social events, arrive early, remain calm, join in conversations and include others, and avoid distractions.
- The most common portfolio formats are digital and hard copy.
- Networking is one of your best resources when it comes to locating potential employers.
- When beginning your employment search, present a low-key, persistent, and professional sales pitch about yourself.
- Success in the workplace results from hard work, high motivation, and a diverse skill set while meeting employer expectations.
- Employers highly value employees who use problem-solving skills effectively to solve complex client and workplace problems.
- Designers are responsible for following ethical guidelines as established by their employers and professional organizations. This includes the workplace environment and working with clients.

Chapter Vocabulary

Write each of the following terms on a separate sheet of paper. For each term, quickly write a word you think relates to the terms. In teams, exchange papers. Have each person on the team explain a term on the list. Rotate turns until all terms have been explained.

citizenship
code of ethics
copyright
dependability
elevator speech
entrepreneur
ethics
infringement
intellectual property
interpersonal skills
networking
plagiarism
pro bono work
proprietary information
punctuality
respect
service learning
time management

Review and Study

1. What are four workplace opportunities you can use to gain experience and inform yourself as an emerging designer?
2. Name three beneficial opportunities of membership in a professional organization such as ASID.
3. List six tips for effective networking.
4. What are three characteristics of good mentors?
5. Name at least six of the top considerations of design firms when hiring a new interior designer.
6. What are the five "B's"?
7. What are five additional tips of business etiquette to remember?
8. What is a disposable portfolio?
9. Name three benefits of developing a well-crafted portfolio.
10. What does an employer seek to know about you through conversation about your portfolio during an interview?
11. Name at least eight tips for organizing and developing your portfolio.
12. List six ways to increase your connections with potential employers.
13. What information should you keep on file about your top 10 to 20 potential employers?
14. Name at least five tips for communicating with potential employers via e-mail.
15. What are the steps for effectively solving problems?
16. Contrast intellectual property with proprietary information.

Critical Analysis

17. **Analyze.** Use the author questions on page 630 to analyze the type of employer and design work you want to do as an aspiring professional. In your analysis, research additional career-guidance references such as the current edition of *What Color Is Your Parachute?* by Richard N. Bolles. Why is it important to analyze your career in relation to your passion for design? Write a summary of your analysis.
18. **Infer relationships.** In the chapter, the author quotes the previous ASID National President Lisa Henry as saying, "If you do not design yourself well, why would you be trusted to design the world?" Infer the relationship between this quote and your personal brand and appearance. What value is there in designing yourself and your personal brand as you pursue a career in interior design? How can failing to do so impact your career?
19. **Evaluate decisions.** The text states that when evaluating job offers you must approach certain topics and questions with employers with considerable diplomacy. Why is diplomacy important when evaluating whether to take a job position? How do the questions you ask an employer when evaluating whether to take a position relate to your answers to the questions on page 630?
20. **Evaluate actions.** Review *Appendix A—ASID Code of Ethics and Professional Conduct* item *3.0 Responsibility to the Client,* and then discuss your responses to the following situation. Suppose a designer is working on a complex residential project that involves specifying all interior finishes and materials, as well as furniture and accessories. The designer charges the client a 20 percent commission on all project services and products. The designer's furniture supplier gives the designer a 45 percent discount on all furniture orders. The designer does not tell the client about the discount and continues to charge the client the commission on furniture items, too. Is the designer acting ethically according to the ASID Code of Ethics? Is the designer telling the truth? How do the designer's actions hurt the client, the designer, and the profession?

Think like a Designer

21. **Writing.** Review the *Design Insight* quote at the beginning of the chapter. Write an essay explaining your views on how forming spaces that respond to human needs are the domain of the designer's competence, passion, and work.
22. **Volunteer.** Demonstrate the principles of team participation and leadership by organizing a group of peers in utilizing design skills and services for a community-service project. Contact groups such as Habitat for Humanity, Rebuilding Together, or other community agencies. Encourage others by sharing your experiences.

23. **Reading.** Use reliable Internet resources to read about top digital tools for entrepreneurs. Identify the tools and write a brief summary about each.
24. **Speaking.** Demonstrate effective verbal communication skills by developing an *elevator speech* about your interior design career that can be used in varied cultures and with fellow workers, management, and customers. Give your elevator speech to the class and ask about ways to improve it.
25. **Writing**. Write four or five conversation-starter questions you can use at social events during which you meet many new people. Memorize these questions as you prepare for such social events. Consider exchanging questions with your classmates on a class web page.
26. **Speaking**. Presume your class is at a potential employer's social event for prospective design employees. Practice introducing yourself to others with a firm, but professional and friendly handshake. Repeat until everyone in the class has had a turn. Then practice introducing one classmate to another as outlined in the chapter (one potential employee to another).
27. **Reading and writing.** Review digital portfolio hosting websites such as *Cloroflot, Behance,* or *Wix*. In the "about" section of each website, identify the important characteristics of the services these websites provide. Write a summary of features, advantages, and disadvantages for each website and save your summaries for future reference.
28. **Reading and writing.** Search the Internet for examples of professional portfolios from contemporary interior designers. You can often find them on the designers' web pages. Compare the portfolios. Write a list of items that are often included in interior design portfolios. Then write a short narrative describing the benefits of maintaining a professional portfolio.
29. **Investigate résumé websites.** Along with reading the *Special Topic* called *Preparing Résumés and Cover Messages* in the back of this text, read the *Résumé Advice* and *Letters* documents under *Résumés + Interviews* on the CareerOneStop website. Write a summary indicating how the advice in the text and CareerOneStop can help you develop a professional résumé to use in seeking meaningful employment.
30. **Writing.** When making phone calls to request an employment interview with an interior designer, the author indicates you should prepare a script for what you will say. Write your script. How will you: introduce yourself to the designer; thank the designer for his or her time; state the reason for your call and make it easy for the designer to talk with you; and align yourself and your skills to the needs of the firm.
31. **Speaking.** Research various core rules of *netiquette* for a variety of situations including the workplace and social media. Discuss the results that occur when people do not follow such core rules for communicating electronically. Why is it important to identify employer expectations for use of electronic media?

Design Application

32. **Traditional portfolio.** Many design employers prefer to review a traditional portfolio when interviewing potential job candidates. Do the following to prepare and maintain your traditional portfolio that documents your interior design projects with a professional résumé.
    A. Choose an appropriate carrying case.
    B. Identify which design examples to include in your portfolio. See *Figure 17-10*.
    C. Write the storyline for your portfolio.
    D. Follow the tips of pages 640–641 of the text to organize your portfolio.
33. **Digital portfolio.** Due to global options for some design positions, employers may need to remotely review digital portfolios when interviewing potential job candidates. Do the following to maintain a portfolio that documents your interior design projects using a variety of multimedia techniques with a professional résumé.
    A. Identify which digital design examples to include in your portfolio, including a virtual walk-through of one of your room designs.
    B. Write and record the storyline for your digital portfolio.
    C. Follow the tips of pages 640–641 of the text to organize your portfolio.
    D. Use the correct file extensions when creating files.
    E. Upload your portfolio to the class hosting site.
34. **Portfolio builder.** With a classmate, take turns practicing your portfolio presentation (traditional or digital). One classmate takes the role of interviewer and the other the role of job candidate. Share your storyline about your portfolio. Then switch roles until everyone has had an opportunity to present their portfolios.

Special Topics

Monkey Business Images/Shutterstock.com

Preparing Résumés and Cover Messages

The Interview Process

Workplace Safety and Health

Stop and Think

Before studying these special topics, consider the following questions.

- What should I know about developing and maintaining a professional résumé?
- How can I write a cover message that clearly expresses my design skills and interest in a job position?
- What should I know about sending résumés and cover messages electronically?
- How should I prepare for the interview process? What questions might be asked of me?
- How can I demonstrate knowledge of the concepts and skills related to health and safety in the workplace?
- What government regulations and agencies regulate health and safety in the workplace?

Vocabulary

résumé
cover message
headline and summary
career objective
chronological résumé
functional résumé
hypothetical questions
behavioral questions
musculoskeletal disorders
workers' compensation

Preparing Résumés and Cover Messages

Résumés and cover messages are both business and design communication tools. A **résumé** is a brief account of your career goals, education, work experience, and other employment qualifications. The purpose of the résumé is to acquire an opportunity for an interview and portfolio presentation. A **cover message** is a letter or e-mail message that accompanies a résumé. Its purpose is to invite potential employers to review your résumé.

Your résumé and cover message serve as your introduction to a potential employer. Employers want to see that you are serious about your work and passionate about design. They also want to observe that you pay attention to critical details such as

- skillful layout of your résumé
- competence in presenting information accurately

Writing skills are valued in the interior design profession. The focus of both the cover message and résumé is to communicate who you are and what you have to offer the design firm. In preparation for developing a professional résumé, it is important to maintain a record documenting all work experiences, licenses, certifications, education and training completion, and credentialing. Update this record regularly. See **Figure A.**

Preparing Your Résumé

Keep your résumé easy to review—use a bullet format, no full sentences, and clear bold headings. Many design firms use applicant-tracking systems that perform *key word searches.* Typically, when a firm needs a new employee it posts a job listing in various places including newspapers, employment agencies, and online job boards. Résumés and applications are searched for key skills or degrees. It is important to carefully select educational and work history highlights when creating a personal résumé. The words you use in your résumé have never been more important. You want your résumé to pop up if employers use this type of search. You also want your résumé to make a good first impression and capture employer interest. Here are the categories to include in your résumé.

Name and Personal Information

List your name (plus any acronyms that note a record of licenses or certifications, such as NCIDQ or LEED

Draft, Revise, Edit, and Proofread Your Résumé

- **Draft.** Choose the standard résumé parts or categories of information that best fit your situation. Follow chapter guidelines for writing your descriptions.
- **Revise.** Revise your résumé descriptions to fit the length of your résumé, usually one to two pages. Use one page if you have a shorter work history and two pages if you have more experience.
- **Edit.** Be sure to include the key words that the employer is looking for. Describe your work responsibilities and accomplishments in language that is currently used in the interior design field. Also, use words or phrases that appear in the job description in case an employer scans your résumé for these words. Delete extraneous words that do not clearly outline your education, skills, and interests.
- **Format.** Choose a format that best suits your information and the position for which you are applying.
- **Review.** Have someone else review your résumé. Enlist the opinion of someone who has good writing skills and experience with résumé writing.
- **Check spelling/grammar and proofread.** Make sure your résumé is error-free. Do not rely on computer spell checkers and grammar checkers. Conducting quality control on your résumé is essential if you want to make a good impression with an employer. Remember, the competition for jobs is great—there are many applicants for the same job. A design firm sifts through candidate résumés looking for reasons to eliminate those that are not outstanding.
- **Choose a style that is clean and businesslike, but also design-conscious.** The look of your résumé should communicate design through font types and spacing.

Figure A

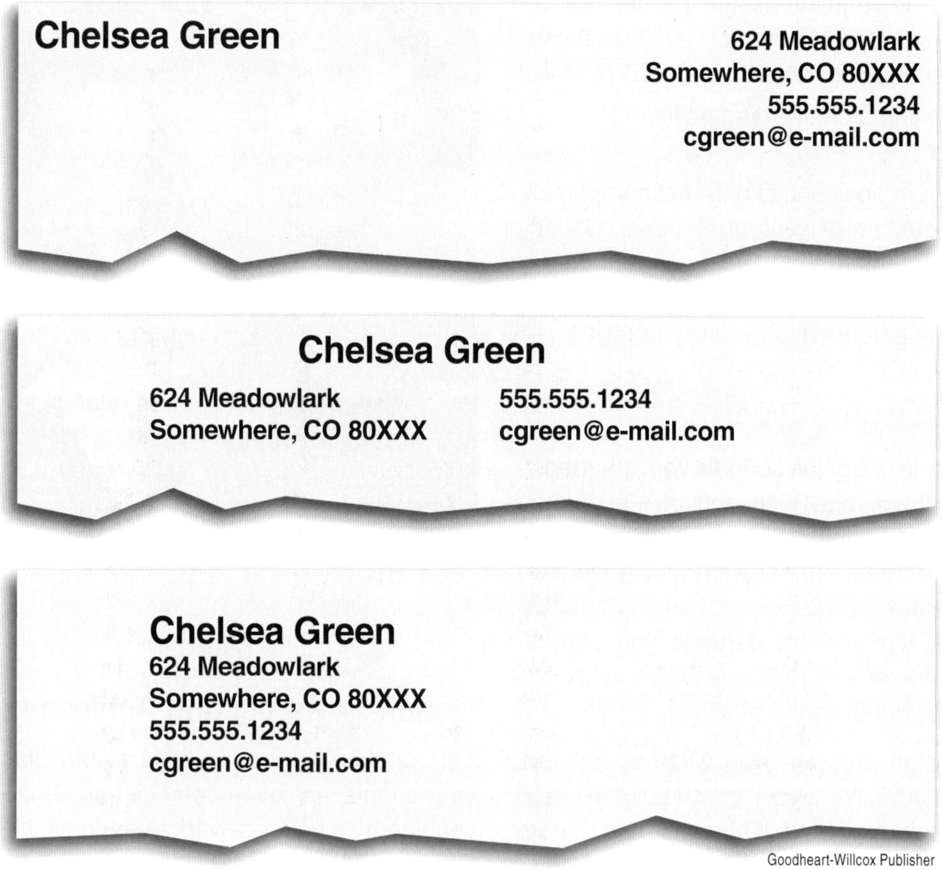

Goodheart-Willcox Publisher

Figure B

Green Associate), complete address—including city, state, and zip code, telephone number (cell phone, too), and e-mail and LinkedIn addresses on your résumé, **Figure B.** You want to be sure employers can reach you to set up interviews and make job offers. Put your design skills into practice by placing your personal information at the top of the résumé in an engaging way that balances the remaining information on the résumé.

Career Objective or the Headline and Summary

Follow the personal information on your résumé with your career objective or headline and summary. Using a **headline and summary** is beneficial for people who have much experience and expertise in the interior design field or those who want to highlight their qualifications for a specific position. A headline and summary for an experienced designer may read as follows:

Interior Designer—Project Coordinator

Technology-savvy professional with five years experience in supporting principal and senior interior designers with high-profile design projects. NCIDQ and LEED GA certified and proficient in:

- Project Management
- Contract Documents and Administration
- AutoCAD
- Revit
- Microsoft Products

In contrast to a headline and summary, a **career objective** is a one-sentence description that aligns you and your skills with a specific job at a particular design firm or company. It is often used by recent graduates or those with less work experience. Use the job listing as your guide and include key words the employer is looking for. State your career objective in clear, simple language. Here are two examples of career objectives—one specific and one general. Which do you think is most likely to capture an employer's attention?

- **Specific:** "Seeking a junior design position with a firm focusing on corporate interiors and healthcare design that uses *space planning* and *REVIT* skills."
- **General:** "Seeking a challenging position in interior design."

If you are interested in positions at different companies, you may need to customize several résumés. Usually they require adjustments to the wording of your career objective or your headline and summary to incorporate key words about the job for which you are applying.

Education and Degree Type

Under this heading, list all of the schools you attended—college, design school, and high school—in reverse chronological order, beginning with the most recent school first. List the name and location (city and state) of each school, dates of attendance, and graduation dates. Identify the diplomas or degrees you earned, such as an *Associate of Arts (AA)* or a *Bachelor of Arts (BA)*, and highlight your program of study.

If your interior design program was CIDA accredited, list this on your résumé. Note your grade point average (GPA) only if you achieved a 4.0. Otherwise, list honors you achieved as a result of your GPA such as *Dean's list* or *cum laude*. Highlight any overseas study (even if it was not design related) and foreign-language experience. If you participated in an internship, note the location and type of internship.

Work Experience

Employers are especially interested in the information that appears under this heading. It is important to document and maintain a record of all work experiences for your résumé. The best résumé describes your job functions in language that showcases your skills and achievements. List employers by date in reverse chronological order beginning with the most recent. Briefly describe the work and scope of services you provided. Use such phrases as *responsible for*, *coleader in*, or *responsibilities included* instead of just focusing on duties.

When describing your services and responsibilities, use distinctive words that communicate your achievement. Verbs that show action are always good choices. You want potential employers to view you positively—as a dynamic achiever who has something of value to contribute to the company and the world of design. Do not include school assignments as work experience.

Rawpixel/Shutterstock.com

Honors, Awards, and Achievements

This section of your résumé is the place to highlight your special achievements. List any honors, awards, or scholarships you received. In addition, highlight competition awards, such as winning first place in a *USGBC* contest. Note that employers are especially interested in activities or achievements outside of work or school. Be sure to mention any leadership positions you held. Relate the name of this section to the items you list in it.

Memberships and Professional Associations

Include a list of your memberships in design-related professional organizations, such as the *American Society of Interior Designers (ASID)*, the *U.S. Green Building Council (USGBC)*, or the *National Kitchen and Bath Association (NKBA)*. List your memberships in order of importance, putting the most relevant first. If you held a leadership position in any of these organizations, mention it here.

Skills and Interests

In this section, list any skills you have that you think enhance your job performance. Employers look for your ability with computer skills. Design firms especially show interest in your proficiency with AutoCAD, Microsoft Office Suite, as well as the Adobe Creative Suite. Larger design firms are now demanding skills with REVIT. If you can fluently communicate in a language in addition to English, mention it here.

References and Recommendations

In general, do not list your references on your résumé. Instead, write the phrase *References available on request.* A reference is a person who knows you well and will speak highly of your skills, abilities, work ethic, and your character. Have at least three *nonfamily* professional references ready to give to employers (note that some employers may view family references as biased). The list should include the names, titles, work addresses, phone numbers, fax numbers, and e-mail addresses of your references.

Be sure to contact and acquire each person's permission before adding his or her name to your reference list. This is not only a common courtesy but also helps you verify that certain individuals want to be on your reference list. This also gives your references time to prepare what they want to say about you. In addition, contact your professional references to acquire appropriate letters of recommendation. This will give you a feel for what your references are saying about you.

Potential employers who are seriously interested in you as a job candidate will ask for your references. Be prepared to give employers your reference list. Print your reference list on the same high-quality paper as your résumé in case an employer requests it during an interview.

Develop your standard résumé, but be prepared to modify it frequently to appeal to the broad range of firms to which you apply. Avoid sending the same standard résumé to each firm. In addition, pay careful attention to setting up electronic résumés, **Figure C.**

Choosing a Résumé Format

You need to think about two things when choosing a résumé format—how to organize and present your work history information and how to visually present your information in terms of layout and formatting to best capture interest of potential employers. Two basic résumé formats include

- **Chronological.** As the most popular résumé format, a **chronological résumé** focuses on your employers and your work experiences listing each in reverse chronological order with the most recent listed first. Potential employers expect to see company names, dates of employment, job titles, and a list of work responsibilities and achievements. See **Figure D.**
- **Functional.** In contrast, the **functional résumé** emphasizes your qualifications, skills, and achievements. The main advantage of this résumé format is to showcase your best skills even though you may not have used them in a previous position. The functional résumé is also useful for those who have much experience to showcase. By emphasizing the overall qualifications, the employer typically sees those pertinent details first in a headline and summary statement. See **Figure E.**

Whichever format you choose, make sure it is neat, readable, original, and creative while highlighting your accomplishments in the best possible manner. See the following examples of a typical interior design graduate résumé.

Using Electronic Résumés

Some employers request you to send an electronic résumé via e-mail or post it to the employer's website. You can also post your electronic résumé to a number of online job-search sites or job boards. Employers may use electronic résumés to scan for key terms that match their descriptions of ideal interior designer candidates. To create an electronic résumé

- Save your résumé as a *text only* document without any formatting.
- Review the text only résumé to make sure lines and headers break properly.
- Save your electronic résumé in a separate file from your formatted résumé.

Figure C

Chelsea Green, LEED GA

654 Meadowlark
Somewhere, CO 80XXX
(Cell) 555.555.1234
cgreen@e-mail.com

CAREER OBJECTIVE

Obtain a junior interior design position specializing in hospitality design with a team-focused design firm.

EDUCATION

20XX Graduate *Magna Cum Laude*	Colorado State University (CSU), Fort Collins, CO Bachelor of Science—Interior Design, CIDA Accredited Minor in Construction Management
Jan. 20XX–May 20XX	Florence University of the Arts Study Abroad—Interior and Sustainable Design
20XX Graduate GPA–4.0	Pikes Peak Community College, Colorado Springs, CO Associate of Arts—Business Administration

DESIGN EXPERIENCE

Jan. 20XX–May 20XX — Interior Design Intern—Facilities Management, Colorado State University (CSU)

- Assisted with client programming, research, conceptual design, master planning, branding and signage development
- Prepared space plans, sketches, elevations, 3D models, and renderings, construction detail drawings
- Met program requirements and applicable codes under senior designer's direction
- Created furniture specifications, material boards, and purchase orders for FF&E
- Worked with contractor and design team to ensure construction complied with building codes and client program

DESIGN and TECHNICAL SKILLS

- Autodesk 3DS Max Design
- Autodesk Revit
- AutoCAD & AutoCAD Architecture
- Adobe Creative Suite
- Microsoft Office Suite
- SketchUp
- Hand sketching & Rendering
- 3D Model Building
- Hand Drafting

PROFESSIONAL AFFILIATIONS and LEADERSHIP

American Society of Interior Designers—Colorado State University (CSU)—Student Chapter Board Member

- 20XX–20XX — Chair, Social Media
- 20XX–20XX — Chair, Community Service
- 20XX–20XX — Student Hospitality Design Network—CSU—Student Chapter Board Member
- Chair, Professional Development Activities
  Coordinated student chapter events/programs with professionals and organizations focused on hospitality design and educational seminars based on student interest

HONORS and ACHIEVEMENTS

20XX — ASID Foundation Legacy Scholarship

- National Portfolio Scholarship Award Recipient

20XX — Interior Design Educators Council (IDEC)— Regional Finalist

- Design Competition—Sustainable hospitality design focused on Eastern design practices, Fort Collins, CO

20XX — Brass Ring Awards

- Interior Design—Digital Rendering of Choice—Gold
- Interior Design—Commercial Design, less than 2500 sq. ft.—Gold

INTERESTS

- Interior design, landscape architecture and gardening, and furniture design
- Fine art, photography, and theater production

REFERENCES

Available on request

Figure D—Chronological résumé

Chelsea Green, ASID, NCIDQ, LEED AP

654 Meadowlark
Somewhere, CO 80XXX
(Cell) 555.555.1234
cgreen@e-mail.com

Interior Designer—Hospitality Design—Specializing in Boutique Hotels
Progressive, innovative, team-focused interior designer and project manager with five years experience in hospitality sector. Experienced in sustainable design practices. Current with design trends, products, building codes, and construction systems. Effective communication and interpersonal skills. Extensive background in oversight of the design concept through all phases of the design process. Proficient with...

- Autodesk 3DS Max
- Autodesk Revit Architecture
- AutoCAD & AutoCAD Architecture
- Adobe Creative Suite
- SketchUp
- Quick Sketch Ideation
- 3D Model Building
- Microsoft Office Suite

DESIGN EXPERIENCE
Aspen Design Architects, Somewhere, CO—Interior Designer, January 20XX–Present
- Experienced with project management from client consultations to final move-in phase
- Proficient with facilitating conceptual design direction in response to client's program and goals
- Developed and/or facilitated development of code- and program-compliant space plans, elevations, 3D models, sketches of architectural details—including materials and design intent, presentation boards, branding, and signage
- Executed Contract Administration duties through installation and post-occupancy evaluation

CL Design Group, Lake Forest, CA—Junior Interior Designer, June 20XX–December 20XX
- Assisted principal designer with hospitality client programming and conceptual design direction
- Assisted project manager in interface with clients, vendors, and team members to collect data and communicate design requirements
- Prepared space plans, sketches, elevations, 3D models, renderings, specifications, material boards, and purchase orders for FF&E meeting program requirements/codes as directed by assigned designer

Colorado State University (CSU) Facilities Management, Fort Collins, CO—Interior Designer and Architectural Assistant, January 20XX–June 20XX
- Responsible for programming and research, conceptual design, master planning, space planning, construction detail drawings, presentation renderings, and 3D computer models and branding and signage
- Prepared furniture specifications, material boards for client presentations, and purchase orders

PROFESSIONAL AFFILIATIONS and LEADERSHIP
American Society of Interior Designers (ASID), Professional Member Chair, Emerging Professionals Council

Network of Executive Women in Hospitality (NEWH), Professional Member; Rocky Mountain Region Publicity Chair

EDUCATION
Kansas State University, Logan, UT
Master of Fine Arts—Interior Design Specialization—GPA—4.0
Colorado State University (CSU), Fort Collins, CO
Bachelor of Science—Interior Design, CIDA Accredited—Magna Cum Laude
Concentrations in Sustainable Design and Construction Management
Florence University of the Arts, Florence, Italy
Study Abroad—Interior and Sustainable Design
Pikes Peak Community College, Colorado Springs, CO
Associate of Arts—Business Administration, GPA 4.0

HONORS and ACHIEVEMENTS
ASID, Colorado Chapter; Chapter Community Service Award Recipient
NEWH, Rocky Mountain Region, Designer of Distinction

INTERESTS
- Rock climbing, furniture design, photography
- Habitat for Humanity volunteer

REFERENCES
Available on request

Figure E—Functional résumé

Writing Your Cover Message

Your first contact with a potential employer should be through an associate or personal meeting. If not, you will need to develop a cover message. In your cover message, you will introduce yourself and summarize the reason you are applying for the position without repeating your attached résumé. Remember, its purpose is to capture the interest of the employer enough to arrange an interview with you.

Cover messages can make a lasting impression. Make sure your message is neat and follows standard business format. Use the same family of fonts and graphic design to link your cover message to your résumé and your portfolio. Be sure to check the spelling and punctuation. Consider having several people proofread your message and offer advice on improvements. If desired, include a *disposable* portfolio with your cover message and résumé to impress potential employers.

A good message or letter is brief, positive, and to the point. Send the message only to employers and design firms at which you are truly interested in working. When responding to online or newspaper ads, be sure to follow the specific instructions given. Review the following for items to include in your cover message, **Figure F**.

The Interview Process

A job interview is the employer's opportunity to get to know you and your communication skills as well as review your résumé and portfolio. This is your opportunity to sell yourself in person. Your answers to interview questions are important in the employer's decision-making process. See **Figure G.**

The first step in preparing for a job interview is to learn as much as you can about the job and the firm. There are several ways to do this. If the company has a website, thoroughly study the site. Pay special attention to the *About Us* section for an overview of the design firm. Look for a list of their design projects, press releases, annual reports, and information on products or services the company offers. Also look for community service projects they are engaged with and projects they have on the boards.

While a firm's website can be a valuable source of information, do not limit your research to just the company site. Use your network to find people who are familiar with the employer and get as much information as you can from them. Use your alumni network if possible.

Call any peers who currently work at the firm. Also, contact the company's human resources department. Indicate that you are interested in employment opportunities at the firm and would like to know more about working for the company. The human resources department often has materials designed specifically for potential employees.

Items to Include in a Cover Message

When writing a cover message, use the following guidelines:

- ***Contact information and salutation.*** List the date, your name, and contact information. If possible, address the message to a specific person or title, such as the Human Resources Director, Hiring Manager, or Principal Designer.
- ***Introduction.*** Explain who you are and the title of the position you are seeking. You may mention specific points about the design firm (or designer) that you appreciate and value. Note how you heard about the position. Create a good impression with the design firm with your thorough research and confidence.
- ***Body.*** Be sure to target the message to the employer or design firm. Identify your specific strengths, skills, and abilities, describing why you are qualified for the position and why you perceive there is a good fit between your skills and the firm's needs. Since you are attaching your résumé, do not repeat all of the facts in it. Provide enough facts to capture the employer's interest to look at your résumé for further facts about you. Also, refer to your résumé in the message.
- ***Conclusion and signature.*** In your closing paragraph, thank the reader for his or her time. Politely request an interview and state when you can begin working. Identify when and how the employer can reach you and indicate how you will recontact the reader. Then sign your message or letter. Use blue ink for your signature because it best shows the message is original and not a photocopy.

Figure F

The Interview	
What to Bring	**What Not to Bring**
While the design firm has a position available, feel confident about what you have to offer. You bring the following: ■ energy, fresh ideas, and fresh eyes ■ contact with your generation; team orientation ■ skill with the latest technology ■ upbeat attitude; smile	When you enter the room for an interview, you should not bring the following: ■ cell phone (unless it is off) ■ negative or defensive attitude ■ personal, school, or work problems ■ questions about salary or benefits (ask about these *after* a job offer)

Figure G

During the Interview

When you arrive for the interview, introduce yourself and thank the interviewer for his or her time. Be sure to indicate your pleasure and enthusiasm for the interview opportunity. Offer a strong professional first impression by making direct eye contact and offering a firm handshake. Let the interviewer lead the interview. Often you will be asked to discuss yourself, education, and skills. Of course, an interviewer can read about them on your résumé, but will want to see and hear how you present and *sell* yourself. Review **Figure H** that includes specific questions for interior designers. If there are any topics or contacts you have in common with the person interviewing you, weave that information into the interview. For example, you may have attended the same school or know some of the same people.

Interviewers may also ask several other types of questions: *hypothetical* and *behavioral questions.* **Hypothetical questions** are those that require you to imagine a situation and describe how you would act. Frequent topics of hypothetical questions relate to working relationships with clients and coworkers. Examples of hypothetical questions include: "How would you handle a disagreement with a coworker?" or "How would you handle a difficult client?" You cannot prepare specific answers to these questions, so must rely on your ability to think on your feet. Remaining poised and projecting confidence carries a lot of weight, even if you think your answer is not ideal.

Behavioral questions are those that draw on your previous experiences and decisions. Your answers to these types of questions indicate past behavior, which an employer may use to predict future behavior and

Interview Questions for Interior Designers
According to ASID surveys, following are common design employer questions during an interview. ■ What are your strengths and weaknesses? ■ Why do you want to work here? ■ What would you bring to our firm? ■ What are your professional goals? ■ What has been your biggest challenge and what did you learn from that experience? ■ Describe the design process. Where do you begin? ■ Why are you an interior designer? ■ Tell me about your business skills. ■ What were your least favorite design projects in school and why? ■ Describe your work ethic.

Figure H

FuzzBones/Shutterstock.com

Minerva Studio/Shutterstock.com

success in a position with a design firm. The following are some examples of behavioral questions.

- Tell me about a time when you needed to assume a leadership position on a team. What were the challenges and how did you help the team meet its goals?
- Describe a situation when you made a mistake. Tell me how you corrected the mistake and what measures you put in place to ensure it did not happen again.

Again, you cannot prepare specific answers to these questions. Remain poised, answer honestly, and keep your answers focused on the question.

Keep in mind that the portfolio you have worked so hard to put together may not be used during the interview. The employer will know your skill set by looking at the degree you have earned. Instead, they want to assess the type of "fit" you will have in the culture of the design firm. If you have a chance to present your portfolio, lay it out facing the designer. If the interviewer asks you to explain one of your portfolio projects, be brief but to the point. Concisely explain the client issues, concept, and solution. Avoid talking while the interviewer examines your work. If the interviewer wants additional information, he or she will ask for it.

When asked about yourself, always try to link your remarks to the firm and its goals, projects, or work. Outline the value you will be to the firm: your skills, integrity, and experience. Be honest and respectful. Realize that with larger design/architecture firms, there may be several interviews with different individuals rather than just one. Do not be afraid to accept the most entry-level of positions. If you are good, you will move up quickly. Be enthusiastic and indicate your willingness to work hard.

After the Interview

After an employment interview, follow up is important to keep your name in front of the employer. Immediately after the interview, write a short *thank-you message* to the person or persons with whom you interviewed. The purpose of this message is to thank the interviewer for his or her time and reinforce your interest in the design position. Either a handwritten letter or an e-mail to the interviewer is appropriate. By sending a personal, hand-written thank-you message, you will stand out as someone who has good manners and a genuine interest in the position.

Employment decisions can take a long time. Some companies notify all applicants after making an employment decision, but some do not. If you have not heard anything a week or two after the interview, it is appropriate to send an e-mail to follow up and inquire about an update on the position.

If you did not get the position, use your follow-up thank-you note to indicate your interest in the position and invite the employer to contact you if a future position becomes available. Also ask if it would be appropriate for you to stay in contact with the employer to determine if another designer is needed. As a design firm acquires additional projects, it will often hire another person six months or a year later. Remember, this field is built on relationships. Keep in touch. If a position does not become available at the firm where you are being interviewed, many times the prospective employer will pass your name onto a colleague who is looking for a designer.

Workplace Safety and Health

Employability characteristics of successful workers include having knowledge of concepts and skills related to workplace safety and health. Knowing how to maintain your health and follow safe practices as outlined by government regulations and employer guidelines for a safe and healthy workplace is imperative. Failure to maintain health and comply with safe practices at work has many costs—both personally and to the economy.

Interior designers are key assets to the design and construction teams with which they work by helping to ensure all team members follow safety and health codes and regulations. Following government regulations and knowing safe and healthy practices help protect workers. Here is a summary of some the laws that protect the workforce, **Figure I.**

Laws Relating to Employee Safety, Health, and Protection

- ***Americans with Disabilities Act.*** This act prohibits discrimination against people with disabilities within the United States. This legislation opens up employment and service opportunities to citizens with disabilities. The act requires employers to give reasonable accommodations to persons with disabilities during the hiring process. Employers must also make reasonable accommodations—such as physical changes to the workspace, time off for treatment, and so forth—to allow a person with a disability to successfully perform job duties.
- ***Equal Employment Opportunity Act.*** This act prohibits employers from discriminating against any employee or job applicant because of race, color, religion, national origin, sex, physical or mental disability, or age.
- ***Equal Pay Act.*** This act requires that men and women be paid the same amount for doing the same jobs under the same conditions.
- ***Fair Labor Standards Act.*** This act sets the national minimum wage and overtime practices that employers must follow. It also regulates the employment of minors.
- ***Occupational Safety and Health Act.*** This law requires employers to provide working conditions that are free of known hazards for their employees. It covers most employees in the private sector. As a result of this Act, the *Occupational Safety and Health Administration (OSHA)* was created. OSHA sets and enforces standards that protect worker safety and health in the workplace. This agency also provides information, training, and assistance to workers and employers.

Figure I

Safety in the Workplace

The government plays an important role in providing regulations that promote workplace safety. Because of government laws and regulations, workplace safety in the United States has continuously improved during the twentieth century and beyond. Gradually, injuries, deaths, and illnesses related to working conditions have declined. This is due to changes in the type of work people do today and in the safety precautions put in place to protect workers.

With the professional mandate to protect the health, safety, and welfare of the public, interior designers are keenly aware of appropriate government regulations and the body of knowledge that guides the best practices in designing and maintaining safe workplaces. The *Occupational Safety and Health Administration (OSHA)* sets and enforces standards that protect employees in the private-sector workplace. When designing various workplace environments, interior designers work with employers to ensure these facilities meet governmental regulations such as those set by OSHA, the EPA, and building and fire codes.

Under the *General Duty Clause* of the OSH Act, employers and employees both have certain responsibilities for knowing safety concepts and developing appropriate safety skills in the workplace. For instance, OSHA mandates that employers provide a workplace that is free of recognized safety and health hazards. In addition, employers must make certain that employees understand and follow OSHA rules and safety procedures. Likewise, employees have the responsibility to do the following:

- Read the OSHA poster at their workplace and know their responsibilities and rights.
- Follow OSHA safety standards and those set by the employer in an *employee handbook.*
- Wear personal protective equipment when necessary. For interior designers, personal protective equipment may include a hard hat, safety shoes, and eye protection when at a building or renovation site.
- Report any workplace injury or unsafe working conditions or practices, following OSHA and employer guidelines. If an employer does not correct unsafe working conditions or practices, the employee can contact OSHA and request an inspection.
- Participate in fire drills and other emergency-response activities. Awareness of emergency evacuation exits and safe places within a facility can help save a life or prevent injury.

The following offers some additional concepts and skills to prevent the most common workplace accidents—injuries from falls and improper lifting and materials storage.

Preventing Injuries from Falls

Falls are a consistent hazard and the most common of workplace accidents in all occupational settings. Falls can occur from simply walking and tripping or climbing a ladder to install a window treatment. Slippery or cluttered surfaces are common causes of falling incidents. Preventing workplace falls is relatively simple, including

- close drawers completely
- use a stepstool or ladder properly to reach high objects instead of standing on a chair or box
- wipe up liquid spills immediately
- secure cords, rugs, and mats
- use fall prevention equipment appropriately

Preventing Lifting Injuries

Lifting hazards are sources of potential injury from improperly lifting or carrying objects. For an interior designer, this may mean improperly lifting a box of accessories or sample books of wallcoverings or fabrics. Most back injuries result from improper lifting. To avoid injuries from lifting:

- make several trips with smaller loads of items rather than one trip with an overly heavy load of objects
- use handcarts or dollies whenever possible to move objects
- carry items that *do not* block vision
- position the feet a shoulder-width apart; bend the knees and lift with the legs, not the back
- keep the load close to the body and lift smoothly without sudden movements
- move the feet to turn the whole body and avoid twisting the back while lifting or holding a load

Preventing Injuries from Improper Material Storage

Material-storage hazards that come from improperly stored files, books, office equipment, building materials, and other items are a source of potential injury. A cluttered workplace is an unsafe workplace whether an office or a building site. Materials that are stacked too high can fall on employees. Paper, files, interior finish materials, or building materials improperly stored on the floor or in a hall are a fire risk. To prevent material-storage injuries:

- keep tops of tall cabinets or storage areas free of boxes, papers, files, or other objects
- store heavier objects and materials on lower shelves
- keep hallways and aisles clear of objects and materials

Health in the Workplace

As with safety in the workplace, the General Duty Clause of the OSH Act requires employers to keep the workplace free of recognized *health* hazards, too. Employers must also make certain that employees understand and follow health-related procedures to maintain workplace health such as those put in place by OSHA. Employee responsibilities also include reporting any workplace injury or health issue or unhealthful working conditions following OSHA and employer guidelines.

Possible health hazards will vary depending on the type of workplace. For most interior designers, the main workplace will be an office or design studio. Examples of health-related issues in an office or design studio environment may be poor indoor air quality (IAQ) and ergonomic issues that can cause **musculoskeletal disorders**—those relating to muscles, nerves, and tendons.

Workplace Indoor Air Quality

The quality of indoor air can impact the health, comfort, and productivity of workers. Good indoor air quality is important to a healthy indoor environment. According to OSHA, good indoor air quality includes comfortable temperature and humidity, an adequate supply of fresh outdoor air, and control of pollutants from inside and outside a building. With adequate air quality, worker productivity tends to increase.

Although OSHA does not have a *general* standard related to indoor air quality, it does provide guidance on how to prevent the most common indoor air quality issues relating to temperature, humidity, lack of outside air, and smoking. In addition, OSHA does have standards that address potential health hazards including specific air contaminants, ventilation systems, and the General Duty clause. OSHA also encourages employers and business owners to develop preventive IAQ programs following guidelines from the *EPA* and the *National Institute for Occupational Health and Safety (NIOSH)*. Read through **Figure J** to identify additional ways employers and employees can improve indoor air quality.

Workplace Ergonomics

As interior designers know well, *ergonomics* is the science concerned with designing and arranging the objects people use so they can interact efficiently and safely in the work environment. In the workplace, this often involves designing workstations to fit the unique

Improving Indoor Air Quality	
What Employees Can Do	**What Employers Can Do**
■ Do not block air vents or grilles. ■ Water and maintain plants properly. ■ Dispose of garbage promptly and properly. ■ Store food properly. ■ Avoid bringing products into the building that could release harmful or bothersome odors or contaminants. ■ Notify the building or facility manager immediately if an IAQ problem is suspected.	■ Place office furniture and equipment in locations based on adequate air circulation, temperature control, and pollutant removal functions of the HVAC system. ■ Avoid procedures and products that can cause indoor air quality problems. ■ Integrate indoor air quality concerns into purchasing decisions. ■ Ensure use of only necessary and appropriate pest-control practices, using nonchemical methods when possible. ■ Before starting to remodel or renovate, meet with building management and contractors to identify ways to minimize building-occupant exposure, and to ensure that the air-distribution system is not disrupted.

Figure J

Source: OSHA, Indoor Air Quality in Commercial and Institutional Buildings needs of the worker and the equipment he or she uses on the job. For the interior designer, this may mean setting up an effective computer workstation as well as space to complete other design tasks. By taking such actions, the employer can substantially reduce the risk of musculoskeletal disorders resulting from awkward body positions and carrying out certain repetitive tasks. The application of ergonomic principles results in a comfortable, efficient, and safe workplace.

There are many types of ergonomic equipment and accessories that may improve worker comfort at a computer workstation. These include specially designed chairs, wrist supports, keyboard trays and mouse supports, antiglare filters for monitors, footrests, and back supports. The following illustrates actions to take to create a comfortable computer environment to help prevent injury or strain to a worker's body, **Figure K.**

Workers' Compensation

Despite prevention efforts, in the event of workplace injuries or illnesses **workers' compensation** laws and programs exist in every state to protect workers and their employers. For work-related injuries and illnesses, these employer-paid programs provide compensation including

- wage replacement
- medical treatment
- vocational rehabilitation

Additionally, some programs require employers to provide job modifications or alternative assignments, which may also qualify as reasonable accommodation under the Americans with Disabilities Act (ADA). The *Office of Workers' Compensation Programs* at the U.S. Department of Labor provides contact information for each state's workers' compensation program.

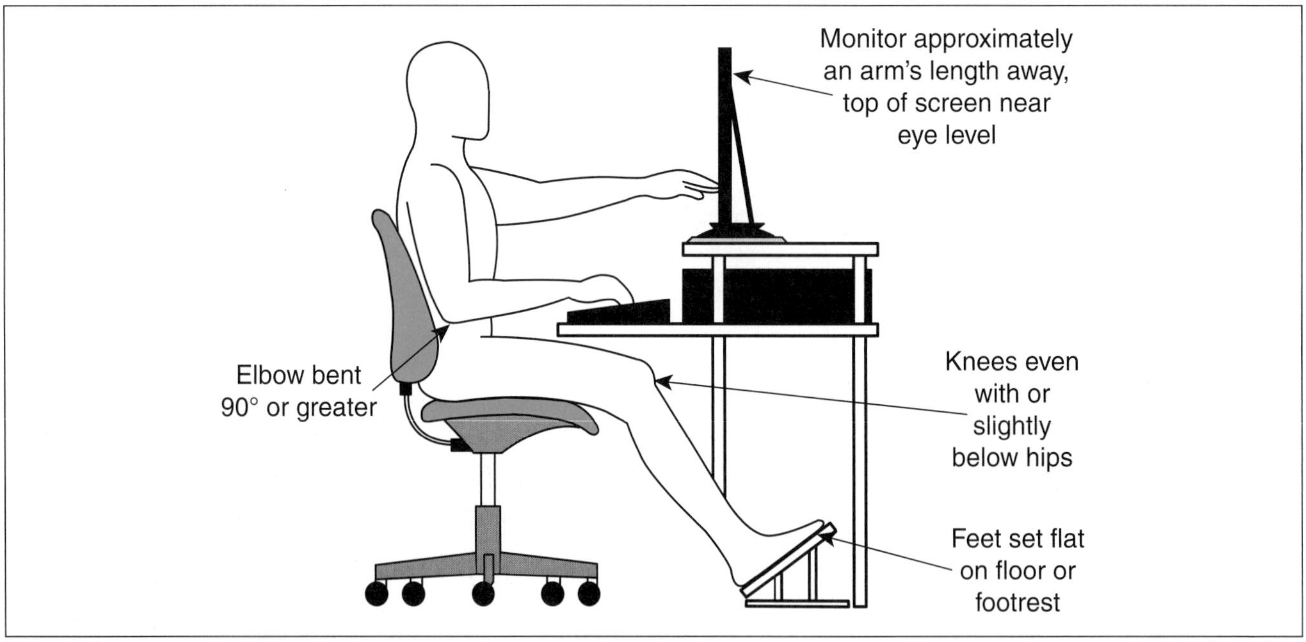

Figure K

Goodheart-Willcox Publisher

Special Topics Review

Preparing Résumés and Cover Messages

1. What are the categories to include in your résumé? Write a brief summary of each.
2. What are the differences between a chronological résumé and a functional résumé?
3. Why should you contact individuals on your reference list and ask for their permission to include them on the list?
4. What is the purpose of a cover message? Briefly describe the parts of a cover message.
5. **Prepare a résumé.** Draft your résumé including all categories described in the text. Select your educational and work history highlights carefully to include in a personal résumé. Write your professional résumé by using word-processing technology. Follow the guidelines on pages 656-661 of the text for drafting, revising, editing, and proofreading your résumé.
6. **Write a cover message.** Draft an adaptable cover message that will help capture an employer's interest in your résumé and in you as a potential interior design employee. Also draft a cover message to accompany your résumé that can help you get into the post-secondary interior design program of your choice. Follow the guidelines on page 662 of the text.

The Interview Process

7. What is the purpose of a job interview?
8. What can you do to prepare for an interview with a specific employer?
9. What should you bring with you to an interview and what should you leave behind?
10. Name six or more questions an employer may ask you during an interview. Write a brief summary of your response to each question.
11. What is the difference between a *hypothetical question* and a *behavioral question* during an employment interview?
12. **Interview practice.** Apply interview knowledge and techniques for interview practice. With a partner, conduct an interview role play. One partner takes the role of the interviewer and the other the role of the interior designer interviewing for the job. Then switch roles so each partner has an opportunity for interview practice.
13. **Write a follow-up message.** Suppose you have just had your first employment interview in the field of interior design. Write a follow-up thank-you message to the employer. If necessary, review the qualities of an effective thank-you note on the CareerOneStop website. Click on *Résumé and Interviews*, and then click on *Thank-You Notes.*

Workplace Safety and Health

14. List the employer and employee responsibilities for a safe workplace under OSHA's *General Duty Clause* to demonstrate your knowledge of concepts and skills related to workplace *safety* as specified by appropriate government regulations.
15. What is the cause of each of the following workplace hazards?
    A. Fall hazards
    B. Lifting hazards
    C. Material-storage hazards
16. List the ways to prevent each of the following workplace hazards:
    A. Fall hazards (list five)
    B. Lifting hazards (list six)
    C. Material-storage hazards (list three)
17. Identify employer and employee responsibilities for workplace *health* according to OSHA to demonstrate your knowledge of concepts and skills related to workplace safety as specified by appropriate government regulations.
18. What are the characteristics of good indoor air quality?
19. Why is good indoor air quality important?
20. OSHA does not have a *general* standard related to indoor air quality, but does provide guidance on preventing poor indoor air quality. To what government agencies does OSHA refer employers for additional information on developing preventive IAQ programs?
21. What are three specific types of standards that OSHA does have regarding indoor air quality?
22. What is ergonomics? How does this impact an interior design office or design studio?
23. **Speaking.** Create a design and presentation board for an interior designer's ergonomic workstation in an office or design studio. Include an image, floor plan, and furniture plan for the workstation. Also include images and materials samples for equipment and accessories that improve employee comfort at the workstation. Present your presentation board to the class, explaining how your design is ergonomic and supports employee health and safety.
24. **Writing and reading.** In writing, describe workers' compensation and how it benefits workers. Then locate the U.S. Department of Labor website. Use the search box to locate information on workers' compensation laws and programs. On the "Workers' Compensation" page, click on the link to "state workers' compensation board" and follow the links to workers' compensation information for your state. Then create a written summary identifying basic information about workers' compensation in your state.

Appendix A

american society of interior designers
american society of interior designers
american society of interior designers
american society of interior designers
american society of interior designers
american society of interior
american society of i
american

ASID CODE OF ETHICS AND PROFESSIONAL CONDUCT

Government & Public Affairs
www.asid.org/about/ethics

AMERICAN
SOCIETY OF
INTERIOR
DESIGNERS

Used with permission from the American Society of Interior Designers

ASID Code of Ethics and Professional Conduct

1.0 PREAMBLE

Members of the American Society of Interior Designers are required to conduct their professional practice in a manner that will inspire the respect of the general public, their clients, fellow professional designers, as well as suppliers of goods and services to the profession. It is the individual responsibility of every member of the Society to uphold this Code of Ethics and Professional Conduct and the Bylaws of the Society.

2.0 RESPONSIBILITY TO THE PUBLIC

2.1 Members shall comply with all federal, state and local laws, rules, regulations and codes governing business procedures and the practice of interior design in the jurisdictions in which they practice ("Applicable Laws").

2.2 Members shall not seal or sign drawings, specifications, or other interior design documents except where the member or the member's firm has prepared, supervised or professionally reviewed and approved such documents, as allowed by Applicable Laws.

2.3 Members shall at all times consider the

health, safety and welfare of the public in spaces they design. Members agree, whenever possible, to notify property managers, landlords, and/or public officials of conditions within a built environment that endanger the health, safety and/or welfare of occupants.

2.4 Members shall not engage in any form of false or misleading advertising or promotional activities.

2.5 Members shall neither offer, nor make any payments or gifts to any public official, nor take any other action, with the intent of unduly influencing the official's judgment in connection with an existing or prospective project in which the members are interested.

2.6 Members shall not assist or abet improper or illegal conduct of anyone in connection with a project.

3.0 RES PONSIBILITY TO THE CLIENT

3.1 Members' contracts with a client shall clearly set forth the scope and nature of the project involved, the services to be performed and the method of compensation for those services.

3.2 Members may offer professional services

to a client for any form of legal compensation.

3.3 Members shall not undertake any professional responsibility unless they are, by training and experience, competent to adequately perform the work required.

3.4 Members shall fully disclose to a client all compensation which the Member shall receive in connection with the project and shall not accept any form of undisclosed compensation from any person or firm with whom the member deals in connection with the project.

3.5 Members shall not divulge any confidential information about the client or the client's project, or utilize photographs of the project except as is expressly allowed by agreement between the Member and client.

3.6 Members shall be candid and truthful in all their professional communications.

3.7 Members shall act with fiscal responsibility in the best interest of their clients and shall maintain sound business relationships with suppliers, industry and trades.

4.0 RESPONSIBILITY TO OTHER INTERIOR DESIGNERS AND COLLEAGUES

4.1 Members shall abide by common law and statutory prohibitions against tortuous interference of contract and will not unlawfully interfere with another interior designer's existing contractual relationships.

4.2 Members shall avoid making any intentionally false communication, either written or spoken, that harms another interior designer's reputation or otherwise disparages his or her character.

4.3 Members may, when requested and it does not present a conflict of interest, render a second opinion to a client, or serve as an expert witness in a judicial or arbitration proceeding.

4.4 Members shall not endorse the application for ASID membership and/or certification, registration or licensing of an individual known to be unqualified with respect to education, training, experience or character, nor shall a Member knowingly misrepresent the experience, professional expertise or moral character of that individual.

4.5 Subject to the provisions of section six, members shall only take credit for work that has actually been created by that Member or the Member's firm, and under the Member's supervision.

4.6 Members shall respect the confidentiality

of sensitive information obtained in the course of their professional activities.

5.0 RESPONSIBILITY TO THE PROFESSION

5.1 Members agree to maintain standards of professional and personal conduct that will reflect in a responsible manner on the Society and the profession.

5.2 Members shall seek to continually upgrade their professional knowledge and competency with respect to the interior design profession.

5.3 Members agree, whenever possible, to encourage and contribute to the sharing of knowledge and information between interior designers and other allied professional disciplines, industry and the public.

6.0 RESPONSIBILITY TO THE EMPLOYER

6.1 Members leaving an employer's service shall not take drawings, designs, photographs, data, reports, notes, client lists, or other materials relating to work performed in the employer's service except with permission of the employer.

6.2 Members shall not divulge any

confidential information obtained during the course of their employment about the client or the client's project.

7.0 ENFORCEMENT

7.1 The Society shall follow standard procedures for the enforcement of this Code of Ethics and Professional Conduct as approved by the Society's Board of Directors.

7.2 Members having a reasonable belief, based upon substantial information, that another member has acted in violation of this Code of Ethics and Professional Conduct, shall report such information in accordance with accepted procedures.

7.3 Any deviation from this Code of Ethics and Professional Conduct, or any action taken by a Member which is detrimental to the Society and the profession as a whole shall be deemed unprofessional conduct subject to discipline by the Society's Board of Directors.

Appendix B Interior Designer Biographies

Marc Herndon

Interior designer and project manager Marc Herndon, of Gensler in the Washington, D.C. Metro area (formerly of RNL in Denver), has practiced interior design for the last 13 years. Some of Marc's clients have included the World Bank Group; Kaiser Permanente; Starwood Resorts; Prudential Financial; the Bureau of Alcohol, Tobacco, and Firearms; the United States Army Corps of Engineers; the University of Maryland; Metro State University; and the University of Colorado.

Christopher D. Martinez

Christopher D. Martinez practices design in the Greater New York area. He works for Poggenpohl USA, a German company specializing in high-end kitchens. His projects include Manhattan high-rises, New York condos, Hoboken lofts, and homes across New York and New Jersey.

Chelsea Lawrence

Chelsea Lawrence is an interior designer at Rowland + Broughton Architecture/Urban Design/ Interior Design in Denver, Colorado. Chelsea was formerly a junior designer at SCI Designs in Los Angeles, California, and an interior designer with Davis Partnership in Colorado. Primarily focused in healthcare, Chelsea worked on small-scale lobby remodels to large-scale new construction LEED-bound medical office buildings upward of 80,000 square feet.

Chelsea's accomplishments as a student directly impacted her success as a professional designer. Acquiring a number of honors and scholarships paved Chelsea's transition to the industry and inspired her former employer to pursue similar recognition for the firm. She feels involved, valued, and instrumental to the forward-thinking design progress in the interior design field.

Denise A. Guerin and Caren S. Martin

Denise A. Guerin, Ph.D., FIDEC, FASID, IIDA, is a principal at InformeDesign, a collective team of professionals throughout the interior design field that focuses on research-based design. Guerin's research specializes in post-occupancy evaluation in sustainable buildings and implementation of evidence-based design in practice. Denise was formerly a Morse-Alumni Distinguished Professor of Interior Design at the University of Minnesota. She taught undergraduate studios, ethics and professional practice, and interior design research methods. Dr. Guerin has also advised students for both masters and Ph.D. degrees. Guerin served as IDEC's 2010–2011 President. She is a recipient of IIDA's Michael Tatum Excellence in Education Award, CIDQ's Louis Tregre Award, ASID's Distinguished Educator, and ARIDO's award for Educational Leadership.

Caren S. Martin, Ph.D., CID, FASID, IFMA, is also a principal for InformeDesign. Caren was formerly an associate professor of interior design at the University of Minnesota in the College of Design. Dr. Martin practiced institutional, corporate, and healthcare interior design and project management for 17 years in Minneapolis and St. Paul. As a two-term appointee on Minnesota's professional licensing board, Martin's scholarship focused on opportunities and threats facing the interior design profession and evidence-based design. In 2012 she received the Louis Tregre Award from CIDQ for her commitment to the public's health, safety, and welfare. Inducted as an ASID Fellow in 2009, Dr. Martin has received presidential citations and awards from ASID and the Interior Design Educators Council (IDEC) for her scholarship and advocacy of the interior design profession. Martin serves as IDEC's representative to the National Academy of Environmental Design.

Rosalyn Cama

Rosalyn Cama, FASID, EDAC, is President and Principal Interior Designer at the evidence-based planning and design firm CAMA, Inc., located in New Haven, Connecticut. You can read more about Rosalyn on the company's website.

Cynthia Leibrock

Cynthia Leibrock, M.A., ASID, Hon. IIDA, is an award-winning author, international lecturer, and designer with over 30 years of experience. Her mission is to improve health, longevity, and life quality through universal design. She is the principal/founder of EASY ACCESS TO HEALTH, LLC. Prominent projects include The Betty Ford Center, the UCLA Medical Center, automotive interior design for Toyota, and a universal design exhibit for the Smithsonian (with Julia Child). In conjunction with Eva Maddox, she completed a showroom for the Kohler Company in which over one million consumers have learned about universal design. Cynthia and Eva also collaborated to create a living laboratory in Fort Collins, Colorado, researching the environmental needs of older people. Cynthia has written three books: *Beautiful Barrier Free*, *Beautiful Universal Design*, and *Design Details for Health,* which is now in its second edition.

Lisa Henry

Lisa Henry, FASID, is CEO of the Greenway Group in Colorado Springs, Colorado. As a leader in strategic workplace design, Lisa has been a consultant for Fortune 100 companies and other institutions. As a speaker on the economic and social impact of good design, she also served as a lecturer and program advisor for the Rocky Mountain College of Art and Design in Denver, Colorado. Lisa served as ASID national president from 2011–2012. She also worked as Knoll Director of Architecture and Design in the Southwest Region.

Charrisse Johnston

Charrisse Johnston—ASID, LEED AP, Associate AIA—is a principal at Steinberg Architects in Silicon Valley, California. She was formerly with Gensler, a global architecture, design, planning, and consulting firm. Charrisse initially worked corporate offices for such clients as Port of Long Beach and Nixon Pabody in California. More recently, her education projects have included University of Southern California (USC), Loyola Marymount University, Ventura College, Santa Monica College, GameDesk Playmaker School, and the New Community Jewish High School. Charrisse has also spearheaded pro bono/community-service projects on behalf of Gensler. These projects have included the Los Angeles Youth Network; the Ecole Nationale Jacob Martin Henriquez in Jacmel, Haiti; Inner City Law Center; Alpert JCC; the new LA County "Housing for Health" clinic; and offices in the Skid Row Housing Trust's Star Apartments.

Shirley E. Hammond

Shirley E. Hammond, Fellow of the American Society of Interior Designers, is a graduate of the University of Alabama with a B.S. and M.S. in interior design. She has 38 years of experience in residential and commercial projects in New Orleans, Louisiana, and northern Alabama. Her specialties are kitchen and bath, historic preservation, and corporate and professional offices. She has promoted professional licensure legislation for over 30 years and has served Alabama as a governor's appointee and board chairman of the Alabama State Board of Registration for Interior Design. Shirley is a past international president of the Council for Interior Design Qualification (CIDQ).

Penny Bonda

Popularly referred to as the "mother of green interiors," Penny Bonda is the founding chair of the US Green Building Council committee for LEED Commercial Interiors rating system. She has been an active participant in the green building industry since its early stages and has pioneered the development of many of the accepted practices and recognized standards that have defined the sustainability movement.

Kia Weatherspoon

In her role as principal of Determined by Design, Kia Weatherspoon focuses on an unconventional approach to hospitality and multifamily design. The approach starts with four key values which include the following:

- Practice safe design by starting with a strong concept. Determined by Design doesn't focus on the pretty picture at the end of a project, but instead the *process* that captures the moment and creates a unique space every time.
- Ensure motivation drives design, not the deliverables.
- Create spaces that transcend current design trends.
- Focus on crafting spaces that evoke a positive emotional connection to the interior environment.

One of Kia's and Determined by Design's most humbling projects to date was partnering with *Room to Rebloom*—a nonprofit organization. Room to Rebloom's mission is to create healing environments for women who are survivors of domestic violence. When Determined by Design had its initial client meeting, it started with the same question they ask all their clients: "How do you want the space to feel?" The responses of the women were: "Does it matter?" "We've never had a space that made us feel anything." Those answers took Determined by Design back to the essence of what interior design is about—creating an environment that enhances and heals the human experience.

Maryam S.E. Taylor

Maryam has been in the lighting industry for six years. Her lighting clients and projects include, but are not limited to, The Bellagio and the Monte Carlo for MGM casinos in Las Vegas; the Olympic Water Front Mall in China (Summer Olympics 2008); Government Buildings in Jakarta, Indonesia; the Qingdao Mall in Mumbai, India; the W Hotel and the Four Seasons Hotels in Beverley Hills, California; and the Lamb Hotel in New York City.

Deborah Lloyd Forrest

Deborah Lloyd Forrest has achieved distinction as an industry leader in hospitality design throughout her career, which spans more than 30 years. From work early in her career on such acclaimed hotels as The Empress Hotel in Victoria, British Columbia, and Canadian Pacific Hotels and Resorts (now Fairmont Hotels and Resorts), Ms. Forrest has focused on landmark and luxury hotels. In 1986, Ms. Forrest established Deborah Lloyd Forrest Associates. As she built a portfolio of exceptional projects, she became recognized for her extraordinary color sense and interpretation of timeless luxury for discerning hospitality clients. In 1998, Ms. Forrest teamed with architect and long-time collaborator, Stephen Perkins, AIA, ISHC, to establish ForrestPerkins as a dynamic design practice dedicated to providing exceptional, fully integrated design services to the owners and operators of luxury hotels and resorts worldwide. After a successful 14-year partnership, Ms. Forrest acquired Mr. Perkins' shares in the firm and became President and sole owner of ForrestPerkins in 2012.

Ms. Forrest leads the firm's projects worldwide, which include the St. Regis Amman in Amman, Jordan; The Jefferson Hotel in Washington, D.C.; and the New York Marriott Marquis at Times Square, among many other projects. Ms. Forrest, who has designed several collections of fabrics for Kravet, has also served on the board of directors of the American Society of Interior Designers (ASID) and on the Board of Trustees of the ASID Foundation. The ASID elected her a Fellow of the society in 2000, and in 2004 ASID designated Ms. Forrest as Designer of Distinction for the outstanding contribution her work has made to the profession of interior design. In 2004, *Hospitality Design* magazine elected her to its prestigious Platinum Circle to honor her design leadership. In 2012, *Boutique Design* featured Ms. Forrest and her outstanding career for its cover story.

Rachelle Schoessler Lynn

Rachelle Schoessler Lynn is a senior associate with MSR in Minneapolis, Minnesota. She has devoted her life to design excellence and sustainable design. She is a national leader in sustainable design solutions, and several of her projects garnered national and state design awards. For five years, Rachelle cofounded and led Studio 2030, an independent architecture and interior design studio focused on sustainable design. She also led the interior design and workplace practice for two major Minnesota design firms. Rachelle served as national president of ASID. Appointed by the Governor of Minnesota, Rachelle served two terms on the licensing board for the State of Minnesota. Rachelle is a frequent lecturer on workplace issues and sustainable design, and is an adjunct faculty member at the University of Minnesota. She was inducted into the ASID College of Fellows in 2009, awarded the 2011 Design Achievement Award from Iowa State University, and received the 2004 Designer of Distinction Award from the Minnesota Chapter of ASID. Rachelle is also a recipient of a Minneapolis/St. Paul Business Journal "40 Under 40" Award.

Jo Rabaut, ASID, IIDA

Jo Rabaut is the Principal Owner of Rabaut Design Associates in Atlanta, Georgia. She has been honored with the ASID Design Achievement Award and was recently named Atlanta Decorative Arts Center—Southeast Contract Designer of the Year. Rabaut Design Associates has received countless design excellence awards from both the International Interior Design Association and the American Society of Interior Designers.

Jo has practiced interior design for over 35 years. Some of her clients include AT&T, General Motors, Herman Miller, Janus et Cie, as well as numerous higher education, corporate office, and showroom projects.

Jill Salisbury

Jill Salisbury, founder and chief designer of *el: Environmental Language,* is a pioneer in green design. *el FURNITURE,* formerly known as *el: Environmental Language,* is an award-winning Chicago-area furniture and custom kitchen design firm that specializes in dovetailing environmentally sound materials and manufacturing practices with stylish design. This approach reflects *el*'s eco-chic design philosophy and promise of heirloom-quality craftsmanship.

el FURNITURE has been patronized by such clients as Celebrity Cruise and Four Seasons Hotels & Resorts, both nationally and internationally. Recent residential projects include the Healthy Home 2010 Showcase & Tour in Palatine, Illinois and the LEED Platinum Charityworks Green Home in 2009 located in McLean, Virginia. *el* has been featured in numerous publications, including *Interior Design* magazine, *Town & Country, Robb Report, Traditional Home, Natural Home, Chicago Magazine, Chicago Home & Garden,* and *Luxe Home.*

After serving for two years on the national ASID Sustainable Design Council, Ms. Salisbury was appointed as the chair of the Council and served from 2010–2011. Ms. Salisbury was also the cochair for the Healthy Home 2010 Showcase & Tour in Palatine, Illinois, which was featured in an eight-page spread in the July/August 2011 issue of *Traditional Home* magazine. This beautifully designed community model served as an educational platform for builders, interior designers, manufacturers, and the general public on how to build, design, and live in healthier homes.

Ms. Salisbury's goal is to constantly apply nature's wisdom to her designs. The result is stylish and sophisticated offerings that remain true to the promise of a better environment and healthier interiors. This passion and commitment to *el's* mission has cultivated a strong luxury brand that is recognized worldwide.

Joshua Brewinski

Joshua's current portfolio of design work spans seven years, nine countries, and includes several million square feet of completed space. With projects covering retail, restaurant, hospitality, entertainment, corporate office, education, and residential design, he has had the pleasure of collaborating with clients both locally and abroad. Joshua has worked across multiple disciplines of design, including interior, architecture, graphic, wayfinding, and placemaking.

Tama Duffy-Day

Tama's projects range from six million square-foot health campuses and one million square-foot academic medical centers in the Middle East to 2,000 square-foot, federally qualified health centers, each receiving the same focus—creating culturally supportive healing environments.

Annette K. Stelmack

Annette K. Stelmack brings over 30 years of experience in the building industry as a nationally recognized sustainable design leader, educator, and author. Stelmack innately guides project teams with her passion, knowledge, and strategies for sustainable interiors. A LEED® AP Building Design + Construction design professional, Stelmack excels in programming, planning, design, research, documentation, and specification and implementation of interior architectural finishes/details and furnishings. Annette has experience in multiunit housing, residential, hospitality, and spa projects.

Stelmack has received numerous awards and recognition as a designer and advocate for sustainability including USGBC 2014 Best in Building—Small Interior Design Firm. She was recently featured in *Green Economy Post* and *Innovative Home* magazine, which named her one of the "Top Ten Green Design Gurus."

As a founding member of the U.S. Green Building Council Colorado Chapter, Stelmack is honored to serve on the Chapter's board. In the Chapter's formative years, she served as steering committee chair 2002–2003, the Chapter's first president in 2003–2006, and coleader of the finance committee for Greenbuild 2006, hosted in Denver. Recently, USGBC Colorado honored Annette as Volunteer of the Year.

Donna Vining

Donna Vining, FASID, NCIDQ, RID, CAPS, REGREEN Trained™, is president of Vining Design Associates, Inc., of Houston, Texas. She has practiced interior design for almost 40 years. Her projects have been in the Houston area as well as in Florida, Maryland, Nevada, California, and Mexico. Donna also does retail and commercial design in Houston.

Krista Ninivaggi

In 2014, Krista Ninivaggi launched her boutique firm K&CO, with focus on hospitality and large scale multifamily residential interiors. Ninivaggi started her professional career at the Rockwell Group and later moved to the firm AvroKO before joining SHoP Architects as the Director of the Interior Design Group. During her tenure at SHoP, she completed interiors for projects such as the Barclay's Center in Brooklyn and the New York Corporate Office of Shopbop. Ninivaggi is a graduate of the Rhode Island School of Design. In 2013, Ninivaggi was honored with the title of "Young Gun" by *curbed.com*. Most recently, Ninivaggi was named "Designer of the Year" for 2014 by *Contract Design Magazine*.

References

Abercrombie, Nicholas, Stephen Hill, and Bryan S. Turner. *Dictionary of Sociology*. New York, NY: Penguin Books, 1984.

Altman, Irwin. *The Environment and Social Behavior: Privacy, Personal Space, Territory, and Crowding*. Monterey, CA: Brooks/Cole Publishing Company, 1975.

Asay, Nancy, and Marciann Patton. *Careers in Interior Design*. New York, NY: Fairchild Books, 2010.

Bakker, Mary Lou. *Space Planning for Commercial Office Interiors*. New York, NY: Fairchild Books, 2012.

Berens, Michael. "Environmental Scanning Report." *American Society of Interior Designers (ASID)* (2011): www.asid.org.

Berens, Michael. "Environmental Scanning Report." *American Society of Interior Designers (ASID)* (2012): www.asid.org.

Binggeli, Corky. *Interior Design: A Survey*. Hoboken, NJ: John Wiley & Sons, Inc., 2007.

Binggeli, Corky. *Materials for Interior Environments*. Hoboken, NJ: John Wiley & Sons, Inc., 2008.

Blair, Kevin. (2012). Retail 2020. New Ground. See www.newground.com. St. Louis.

Bureau of Labor Statistics, U.S. Department of Labor, *Occupational Outlook Handbook, 2014–15 Edition*, Interior Designers.

Cama, Rosalyn. *Evidence-Based Healthcare Design*. Hoboken, NJ: John Wiley & Sons, Inc., 2009.

Ching, Francis D. K. *Architectural Graphics*. Hoboken, NJ: John Wiley & Sons, Inc., 2015.

Colombo, Sarah, and Guy Ryecart. *The Chair: an Appreciation*. San Diego, CA: Laurel Glen, 1997.

Crochet, Treena M. *Designer's Guide to Furniture Styles*, 3rd ed. Prentice Hall, 2012.

D'Amelio, Joseph. *Perspective Drawing Handbook*. Dover Publications, 2013.

De Wolfe, Elsie. *The House in Good Taste*. New York: The Century Co., 1913.

Draper, Joan. "The Ecole des Beaux-Arts and the Architectural Profession in the United States: The Case of John Galen Howard" in *The Architect: Chapters in the History of the Profession*, edited by Spiro Kostof. New York: Oxford University Press, 1977.

Faimon, Peg, and John Weigand. *The Nature of Design*. Cincinnati, OH: HOW Design Books, 2004.

"Furniture Style Guide." *Connected Lines*. http://www.connectedlines.com/styleguide/.

Gandy, Charles D., and Susan Zimmerman-Stidham. *Contemporary Classics: Furniture of the Masters*. New York: McGraw-Hill Companies, 1981.

Guerin, Denise A., and Jo Ann Asher Thompson. "Interior Design Education in the 21st Century: An Educational Transformation." *Journal of Interior Design* 30, no. 2 (2004): 1–12.

Guthrie, Pat. *The Architect's Portable Handbook: First Step Rules of Thumb for Building Design*. New York: McGraw-Hill Companies, 1995.

Hanks, Kurt, Larry Belliston, and Dave Edwards. *Design Yourself!* Los Altos, CA: William Kaufmann, Inc., 1978.

Hinchman, Mark. *History of Furniture: A Global View*. New York, NY: Fairchild Books, 2009.

"IFI DFIE Interiors Declaration." International Federation of Interior Architects/Designers (IFI) (2011). www.ifiworld.org.

Jones, Louise. *Environmentally Responsible Design: Green and Sustainable Design for Interior Designers*. Hoboken, NJ: John Wiley & Sons, Inc., 2008.

Jones, Lynn M., and Phyllis Sloan Allen. *Beginnings of Interior Environments*, 10th ed. Prentice Hall, 2009.

Kaplan, Rachel, and Stephen Kaplan. *The Experience of Nature: A Psychological Perspective*. Cambridge, New York: Cambridge University Press, 1989.

Kellert, Stephen R. *The Value of Life: Biological Diversity and Human Society*. Washington, D. C.: Island Press, 1996.

Kelley, Tom, and Jonathan Littman. *The Ten Faces of Innovation: IDEO's Strategies for Defeating the Devil's Advocate and Driving Creativity Throughout Your Organization*. Doubleday, 2005.

Kilmer, W. Otie, and Rosemary Kilmer. *Construction Drawings and Details for Interiors*. New York: John Wiley & Sons, 2003.

Koenig, Peter A. *Design Graphics: Drawing Techniques for Design Professionals*. Upper Saddle River, NJ: Pearson Prentice Hall, 2006.

Kopec, Dak. *Environmental Psychology for Design*, 2nd ed. New York, NY: Fairchild Books, 2012.

Knackstead, Mary V. *The Interior Design Business Handbook*, 4th ed. Hoboken, NJ: John Wiley & Sons, Inc., 2005.

Knoll, Inc. 2015. http://www.knoll.com/.

Lauer, David, and Stephen Pentak. *Design Basics*, 9th ed. Cengage Learning, 2011.

Lawlor, Drue, and Michael A. Thomas. *Residential Design for Aging in Place*. Hoboken, NJ: John Wiley & Sons, Inc., 2008.

Martin, Caren S. "Rebuttal of the Report by the Institute of Justice Entitled *Designing Cartels: How Industry Insiders Cut Out Competition*." *Journal of Interior Design* 33, no. 3 (2008): 1–49.

Martin, Caren S., and Denise A. Guerin, eds. *The State of the Interior Design Profession*. New York, NY: Fairchild Books, 2010.

Mitton, Maureen. *Interior Design Visual Presentation: A Guide to Graphics, Models and Presentation Techniques*. Hoboken, NJ: John Wiley & Sons, Inc., 2012.

Mitton, Maureen, and Courtney Nystuen. *Residential Interior Design: A Guide to Planning Spaces*, 2nd ed. Hoboken, NJ: John Wiley & Sons, Inc., 2011.

Moxon, Siân. *Sustainability in Interior Design*. London: Laurence King Publishing, 2012.

Nielson, Karla J., and David A. Taylor. *Interiors: An Introduction*, 5th ed. New York: McGraw-Hill Education, 2011.

Nussbaumer, Linda L. *Evidence-Based Design for Interior Designers*. New York, NY: Fairchild Books, 2009.

Nussbaumer, Linda L. *Inclusive Design: A Universal Need*. New York, NY: Fairchild Books, 2012.

Pedersen, Darhl M. "Psychological Functions of Privacy. *Journal of Environmental Psychology* 17, no. 2 (1997): 147–156.

Pile, John F. *A History of Interior Design*, 2nd ed. London: Laurence King Publishing, 2005.

Piotrowski, Christine M. *Becoming an Interior Designer: A Guide to Careers in Design*. Hoboken, NJ: John Wiley & Sons, Inc., 2008.

Piotrowski, Christine M. *Professional Practice for Interior Designers*. Hoboken, NJ: John Wiley & Sons, Inc., 2008.

Portillo, Margaret. *Color Planning for Interiors: An Integrated Approach to Color in Designed Spaces*. Hoboken, NJ: John Wiley & Sons, Inc., 2010.

Reed, Ron. *Color+ Design: Transforming Interior Space*. New York, NY: Fairchild Books, 2010.

Rengel, Roberto J. *Shaping Interior Space*. New York, NY: Fairchild Publications, 2003.

Searing, E. "Perception of Sense of Place and Sense of Self Through the Design of the Home." Unpublished thesis, Colorado State University, 2000.

Seidler, Douglas R. *Digital Drawing for Designers: A Visual Guide to AutoCAD*. New York, NY: Fairchild Publications, 2007.

Slotkis, Susan J. *Foundations of Interior Design*, 2nd ed. New York, NY: Fairchild Books, 2013.

Sommer, Robert. *Personal Space: The Behavioral Basis of Design*. Englewood Cliffs, NJ: Prentice Hall, 1969.

Stewart-Pollack, Julie. "Biophilic Design for the Optimum Performance Home." *Ultimate Home Design, GreenBuild* 4 (July/August 2006): 36–41.

Stewart-Pollack, Julie, and Rosemary Menconi. *Designing for Privacy and Related Needs*. New York, NY: Fairchild Publications, 2005.

Stimpson, Miriam. *Modern Furniture Classics*. London: Architectural Press, 1987.

Tate, Allen, and C. Ray Smith. *Interior Design in the 20th Century*. New York: Harper & Row, 1986.

"The Interior Design Profession: Facts and Figures." *American Society of Interior Designers* (2012).

Tilley, Alvin R. *The Measure of Man and Woman*. New York: Whitney Library of Design, 1993.

Turpin, J. C., and N. Blossom. "Challenging the Metanarrative to Read Again the Mini-Narratives of the Field of Interior Design." Proceedings of the 2010 Annual Interior Design Educators Council Conference. Atlanta, GA, 2010.

"Tips for Interior Design Graduates: What Employers are Looking For." *American Society of Interior Designers* (2012).

Ulrich, Roger. "Biophilia, Biophobia, and Natural Landscapes" in *The Biophilia Hypothesis*, edited by Stephen R. Kellert and Edward O. Wilson. Washington, D. C.: Island Press, 1993.

Veitch, Ronald M., Dianne R. Jackman, and Mary K. Dixon. *Professional Practice: A Handbook for Interior Designers*. Winnipeg, Canada: Peguis Publishers, 1990.

Wang, David. "A Form of Affection: Sense of Place and Social Structure in the Chinese Courtyard Residence." *Journal of Interior Design* 32, no. 1 (2006): 28–39.

Wilkoff, William L., and Laura W. Abed. *Practicing Universal Design: An Interpretation of the ADA*. New York: Van Nostrand Reinhold, 1994.

Wilson, Edward O. *Biophilia: The Human Bond with Other Species*. Cambridge, MA: Harvard University Press, 1984.

Winchip, Susan M. *Fundamentals of Lighting*, 2nd ed. New York, NY: Fairchild Books, 2008.

Winchip, Susan M. *Sustainable Design for Interior Environments*, 2nd ed. New York, NY: Fairchild Books, 2011.

Yeager, Jan. *Textiles for Residential and Commercial Interiors*. New York: Harper & Row, 1988.

Zelanski, Paul, and Mary Pat Fisher. *Shaping Space: The Dynamics of Three-Dimensional Design*. Wadsworth Publishing Company, 2007.

Websites

American Society of Interior Designers (ASID)
CareersinInteriorDesign
Council for Interior Design Accreditation (CIDA)
Council for Interior Design Qualification (CIDQ)
Furniture Style Guide
Interior Design Educators Council (IDEC)
International Interior Design Association (IIDA)
InformeDesign
Haworth
Herman Miller
Knoll
National Association of Home Builders (NAHB)
National Kitchen & Bath Association (NKBA)
ReGreen
Steelcase
United States Green Building Council (USGBC)

Glossary

A

academic villages. These are clusters of buildings that consist of classrooms, dining facilities, and retail areas just minutes from student residence halls. (14)

accent lighting. Lighting that brings attention to an object, area, or element within a space. (8)

accessories. These are objects that add beauty, style, and character to the space. (12)

accommodation. A condition when the lens of the eye adjusts the perception of light for near and far vision. (8)

accreditation. When educational institutions conform and maintain the professional standards required that prepare students for interior design practice. (2)

achromatic color scheme. A neutral color scheme that possesses no hue; commonly comprised of such neutral colors as gray, ivory, beige, black, white, tan, and brown. (8)

adaptation. A process by which the iris of the eye dilates, opening to allow more light to enter the eye during darkness; similar to the way a camera lens works. (8)

adaptive reuse. A form of sustainability that involves the redesign and repurposing of an existing building for a new function and a new client. (10)

additive color. Color produced when electric light mimics natural light in replicating the visible spectrum of light; mixing color with light. (8)

adjacency matrix. A diagram or table which lists each room or space in a structure to determine which room or space needs to be adjacent to another. (6)

afterimage. An optical illusion that occurs when a person looks directly at a lightbulb too long and the shape of the bulb momentarily imprints on other objects in sight; also occurs after prolonged viewing of a patch of color. (8)

aging-in-place. A term describing the goal of older adults choosing to live longer and independently in their homes rather than moving to retirement facilities; design of such facilities. (2)

airlock entries. Small, enclosed spaces just inside a commercial building that keep bad weather out. (14)

albedo. Reflective power meaning concrete reflects more light and absorbs less heat. (11)

allied. Closely associate. (5)

ambient. A form of general lighting that provides uniform, overall light for a space. (8)

amenities. Attractive features that hold value to hotel guests. (3)

analogous color scheme. A color scheme that utilizes three to five adjacent hues, those that are next to each other, on the color wheel. (8)

anthropometry. The study of human body measurements in comparison to a space such as a room or building. (10)

Articles of Incorporation. The first act of incorporation, this legal document outlines the name of incorporation and original incorporators, the purpose and nature of business; place of business to be incorporated, board of directors' names, number of shares and the stakeholders' rights, and initial capital structure. (4)

articles of organization. A business document filed with the state that includes the business name, address, the name of the members, and possibly the name and address of the person who is authorized to accept legal documents for the business. (4)

asymmetrical balance. When objects on both sides of the central visual axis are dissimilar yet appear to have identical visual weight. (7)

Aubusson rugs. Durable, handmade wool rugs made with a flat weave; originally from the town of Aubusson in central France. (9)

B

balance. A term that describes the equilibrium of elements in a space. (7)

barrier-free design. A type of design that provides a level of accessibility for people who have disabilities. (10)

behavior-setting theory. A theory that relates to social events or public places in which people use routine, and often repeated, actions within a given time and place. (10)

best practice. A business strategy, or method, that shows superior results. (4)

bid process. A process in which a designer or architectural firm presents a packet with a conceptual design, a description of services offered, and a statement of fees in response to a request for proposal (RFP) from a potential client; generally for commercial projects. (4)

biophilia. A term describing an appreciation for life and the living world. (10)

block and stack diagram. Diagrams that show the vertical functions such as stairways and elevators the designer must consider and place in the same location on each floor; also called stacking diagrams. (6)

block diagram. Diagrams that refine the shapes of the bubbles into rooms and more clearly align the shapes and their locations within the building structure. (6)

body of knowledge. The foundation of any profession and includes the concepts, skills, and activities involved in carrying out such work. (2)

boutique bank. A small bank using 500–1000 square feet of space in such prime locations as coffee shops, library lobbies, retail stores, or post offices. (3)

boutique hotel. A small, stylish and unique hotel often located in trendy, city centers, and often including one-of-a-kind features and the incorporation of distinctive and significant artwork along with an array of accessories. (14)

brand. A company's identity enveloped in a communication device that sets it apart from competitors; a logo or graphic. (4)

branding. An advertising process for creating a unique name and image for a product or service; it attracts the public and loyal clients. (4)

brand position. The image a brand has in the mind of a client. (4)

brand strategy. A strategy that helps to precisely identify marketplace position and what is different about a company's services from others in the market. (4)

broadloom. A term describing rolled carpet goods that are woven on a wide loom of more than 54 inches. (11)

bubble diagram. A type of concept map that uses ovals and circles to represent rooms and their relationships within the diagram of a building footprint. (6)

building codes. Regulations adopted by a community to govern the construction of buildings; ensures structural integrity and safe evacuation in the event of fire Laws created by federal, state, and local jurisdictions to ensure the safety of the public. (6, 14)

building envelope. The walls, floors, and ceilings of a building footprint. (14)

building footprint. The area a building or structure takes up on a site as defined by its perimeter. (3)

building information modeling (BIM). A process designers use (that interfaces with software) in the planning, design, construction, and management of a building during its life cycle. (13)

building occupancy classifications. Categories for structures based on their usage. (14)

building permit. A term referring to written authorization from a government agency to construct a building in a specific location. (6)

building-related illness (BRI). A term used when symptoms of a diagnosable illness are identified and attributed directly to an airborne building contaminant. (4)

built environment. Man-made surroundings that provide the setting for human activity, from the largest civic buildings to the smallest personal space. (1)

C

C2C (cradle-to-cradle). A concept based on a simple theory that the planet has nonrenewable resources that cannot be consumed indefinitely. (2)

cabriole leg. A curved leg shaped like an animal leg with an ornamental foot. (9)

cantilever. A structure supported only on one end. (9)

case goods. Free-standing furniture items without upholstery; examples include bookcases, bureaus, and dining and bedroom furniture. (9, 12)

case study. A real-life situation to look at or study; an example of similarly completed interior design projects; also called *precedents*. (6, 16)

casework. Built-ins or a piece of furniture attached to the wall such as a banquette. (12)

ceiling coffers. Plaster panels between ceiling beams. (11)

change order. Written instructions that modify part of a project's design. (4)

chase. An enclosed space within the walls of a structure, a chase accommodates the plumbing or ductwork for the HVAC systems in the building. (16)

chroma. The saturation or intensity of a color, describes the brightness or dullness of a hue. (8)

chromatherapy. A type of light therapy that uses colored light to create soothing effects. (15)

circulation patterns. The routes people follow as they move from one place to another within a space. (14)

citizenship. Membership in a community. (17)

cladding. A term referring to an overlay of masonry products, such as brick or stone, on a structure. (11)

clerestory windows. Windows placed high in a wall. (9)
client program. A document that outlines the client project—functions, specific need requirements in each space, issues, and current status. (6)
closed corporation. A corporation in which shares of stock are privately held and are not traded on any public markets. (4)
cloud computing. Use of web-based software, workspace, and digital storage. (13)
cloud technology. A web-based method used to store data, software applications, and design information. (2)
code of ethics. A combination of best practices in business with moral principles to guide the interior design professional in simple, personal, or complex business relationships. (4)
codes of ethics. These are guiding principles of conduct and character that are established by and within professional organizations. (17)
collaborate. To work jointly as an interdisciplinary team to solve problems. (1, 4)
colloquial. Unacceptably informal words or phrases used in communication. (16)
color psychology. The study of how colors impact the moods, feelings, and behaviors of people. (8)
color rendering index (CRI). An international system of measurement used to evaluate light sources (any lightbulb) based on how well they indicate the true color of an object relative to a standard light source; scale ranges from 1–100 with a CRI of 85 or higher as good and above 90 as excellent. (8)
color vision deficiency. The condition in which a person is unable to distinguish among certain shades of colors or even colors at all; also called *color blindness*. (8)
color wheel. A diagram with an arrangement of the spectrum colors in a continuous circle. (8)
colorfastness. Having color that retains its original hue without fading or running. (11)
colorways. Arrangements of colors for various patterns and textures of wallcoverings or textiles; primary use is in residential interiors. (11)
commercial design. Nonresidential design that involves all other spaces. (2)
commission. To place a special order for custom artwork. (12)
compact fluorescent lamp (CFL). A type of fluorescent lamp that yields up to 75 percent energy savings, lasting approximately 10 times longer than an incandescent lamp.
competitive bid process. A process in which contractors (minimum of three) submit a sealed bid detailing the type of work to be completed, by whom, and at what cost based on a list of specifications for the client project. (6)
complementary color scheme. A color scheme that utilizes colors directly opposite each other on the color wheel for high contrast and visual interest. (8)
concept square. Usually a three-inch by three-inch square containing abstract lines and shapes that can influence the design decisions for a client. Often includes photorealistic images to help jumpstart the abstract-thinking process. (16)
concept statement. The vision of where to focus a design solution for a client. (16)
conceptual sketch. A drawing or diagram that captures the designer's vision for a project to help contribute to the client's understanding. (16)
congress. A formal meeting of delegates of a group such as a professional organization. (1)
conspicuous nonconsumption. The action of avoiding lavish or wasteful spending for social prestige. (3)
construction documents. The contracts, drawings, and specifications requirements for a new construction project or a remodel project. (13)
construction drawings. These working drawings offer precise, technical information for building or remodeling a space and include floor plans, elevations, sections, and detail drawings. They are generally prepared during the Contract documents phase. (13)
continuing education units (CEUs). Optional courses offered by design or industry professionals to keep the design practitioner informed about trends, theories, and skills to remain competitive in the workforce by taking courses in person, online, or at conferences. (5)
control theory. A theory that focuses on the sense of control a person desires over his or her world and specifically, the physical environment. Three types of control include: behavioral, cognitive, and decisional. (10)
convergent thinking. The ability to use logical and evaluative thinking to critique and narrow ideas to ones that best fit certain situations or set criteria. (6)
conversation grouping. An arrangement of furniture that fosters communication among users. (15)
cool colors. Those colors that perceptually recede in a space. (8)
copyright. An acknowledgement of the ownership of a work; specifies that only the owner has the right to sell the work, use it, or give permission for someone else to sell or use it. (17)
copyright. The document that protects the exclusive right to reproduce, publish, sell, or distribute the matter or form of something; protects a designer's designs, ideas, and drawings during the design process. (4)

cornice. A type of horizontal building element that crowns walls and furnishings. (11)
corporate culture. The collective beliefs, value systems, traditions, and customs that make a company unique. (14)
corporation. A type of business structure in which the legal entity consists of individuals known as shareholders or stockholders. The shareholders elect a board of directors to run the business. (4)
co-working. A work situation in which multiple individuals gather to work in a shared space and split overhead costs. They share values and enjoy working around others, but usually have different jobs, such as various young entrepreneurs. (3)
creativity. A mental activity performed in situations where there is no prior correct solution or answer; a complex process to develop and communicate a creative idea. (6)
criteria matrix. A table that lists each room or space of the client's project in the rows of the left column, and lists each issue—as prioritized by the client—as column headings to determine specific needs of each space and the order in which they occur. (6)
crowding. The psychological response to overstimulation caused by too much interaction with others in a limited space. (10)
curator. A person who has the responsibility for the care and superintendence of objects such as art. (12)
custom run. A run of carpet the manufacturer produces separately to client specifications and occurs through a partnership between the designer and the carpet manufacturer. (11)
customer's own material (COM). Term used by manufacturers to inform designers and clients that they will accept nearly any fabric you send to them and will apply it to any of their furniture pieces. (12)
cutting for approval (CFA). A small sample cut from the same bolt of fabric from which the client's yardage will be cut. (12)

D

dado. The part of the pedestal of a column that is above the base of the column. (9)
daylighting strategies. Those strategies that harvest natural light to minimize the use of artificial lighting during the day. (3)
De Stijl. A design movement that is based on *functionalism*. (12)
decibel. A unit of measurement for expressing the relative intensity of sound on a scale from zero (for the least-perceptible sound) to about 130. (14)
decompression zone. A space near the entry of a store in which shoppers do not notice products. (14)
demolition plan. A plan or drawing that provides details of the current existing structural conditions to be demolished prior to beginning construction. (16)
density. The number of inhabitants per unit of territory. (10)
dependability. The ability to be reliable and trustworthy. (17)
design concept. An abstract idea, thought, notion, or image that involves an imagery-evoking statement that describes the desired mood or feeling for the client's interior space. (6)
design philosophy. A set of beliefs and values related to how you design, made real and evident in clients' design solutions. (4)
design process. A method designers use for organizing work, guiding their actions, and finalizing decisions as they work with team members and clients; includes five phases. (6)
design thinking. An active thinking practice that develops in the proper environment and causes a person to look at the world with evolving potential and probable possibilities. It combines future thinking and analysis with creativity. (1)
desk audit. An evaluation of a commercial company's organizational structure, policies, and procedures that impact the design of the series of spaces. (6)
direct light. A type of light in which 100 percent of the light shines downward; example is a recessed light can. (8)
divergent thinking. A type of thinking that does not follow a linear path but instead branches out in all directions. (6)
dormer windows. Windows set vertically in a structure projecting through a sloping roof. (9)
double rubs. The back-and-forth motions rubbing over the length and width of a fabric to simulate wear characteristic of the *Wyzenbeek Test*.
dovetail joinery. Joinery characterized by a flaring tenon and a mortise into which the tenon fits snuggly. (9)
drafting. The development of technical drawings to systematically and visually communicate information about architectural structures, both interior and exterior. (13)
drawing conventions. Standard line weights, line types, and symbols that clearly communicate the design to team members. (13)
dye lot number. A number that indicates given rolls of wallcovering were printed during the same print run to ensure color match. (11)

E

ecolabel. A second- or third-party verification of sustainability claims. (11)

eco-resort. A resort facility that supports quality, natural, and local living. (3)

ecotourism. The practice of touring natural habitats in a manner meant to minimize ecological impact to enhance economic opportunities for the host areas. (3)

egress. A safe exit from a building or facility. (3)

electromagnetic spectrum. A form of energy that contains many wavelengths, such as microwaves, gamma waves, and radio waves; within this spectrum is the visible spectrum that contains the wavelengths people perceive as light (color). (8)

elements. The tools used to achieve the principles of design including line, shape, form, space (volume), texture, pattern, color, and light. (7)

elevation. A sketch that shows the vertical representation of a wall or space; a two-dimensional scale drawing that shows a vertical slice through a plan that shows window placement, wall details, and architectural details. (6, 13)

elevator speech. A brief verbal summary about who you are, what you do, and your career goals. (17)

en suite bathroom. Another term for a master bathroom suite. (15)

end user. The end user is a consumer who uses the finished space. (14)

engawa. A broad, wooden porch providing access to a Japanese garden. (9)

engineered hardwood flooring. A natural wood product which is factory-made from layers of wood; it is more stable than solid wood and is less susceptible to shrinking and expanding with changes in temperatures and humidity. (11)

entrepreneur. An individual who organizes, manages, and assumes the risks of a business. (17)

ergonomics. The design and arrangement of things people use so that the people and things interact efficiently and safely; also known as *human factors* or *human engineering*. (10)

ethics. The guiding principles of conduct and character that govern the actions of individuals or groups in making right decisions. (17)

evidenced-based design. An approach to design that uses facts (such as those in the previous paragraph), together with professional judgment, to develop informed design solutions for clients. (2)

executive summary. A statement compiling information from other sections of the report into a summary of data outlined in the Program. (14)

F

faux painting. A painting technique that imitates other interior materials such as stone or wood. (11)

feasibility study. An in-depth fact-finding analysis of the client problem and estimates of product and construction costs to solve the problem. (6)

feng shui. A Chinese art and philosophy that influences the orientation and arrangement of a space to achieve harmony. (9)

Fibonacci Series. The most commonly taught proportioning system developed by a thirteenth century mathematician named Leonardo of Pisa, who was called *Fibonacci*. This system is comprised of a series of numbers that include 0,1,1,2,3,5,8,13,21,34 with each new number being the sum of the previous two. The Fibonacci series is a closely linked mathematical cousin to golden mean, section, rectangle, and ratio. (7)

field measurements. Those on-site measurements a designer takes of room dimensions, windows, doors, placement of outlets and lighting, HVAC locations, and wall and flooring finishes; may include sketching plans and details on-site or photographing existing conditions. (6)

file management. A list of guidelines for effective file management that indicate such things as file names for the most recent versions of client projects. (13)

flammability resistance. The ability of a fabric or fiber to reduce fire spread or extinguish a fire. (11)

flex room. A room that is close to the front entry or kitchen entry that can serve many uses. (15)

floor plan. A drawing, or plan, that communicates wall locations, door and window locations, and spatial relationships in scale from a bird's-eye view. When furniture is included, this plan is called a *furniture plan*. (13)

fluorescent lamp. An electric-discharge light that requires a ballast to start the lamp and control the electric current; electric current passes from one end of the lamp to the other through a cathode, but does not produce heat. The phosphorous coating inside the glass tube allows you to see light. (8)

flying buttresses. Medieval masonry structures of straight inclined bars carried on arches and solid piers or buttresses; used to support vaulted interiors. (9)

focal point (emphasis). The dominant feature of a space or composition that is the first to demand someone's attention. (7)

focus group. A small group of people who study the response of a few people to something, such as a product, to determine the response of a larger population. (1)

form. The result from combining the elements of line, shape, and volume. (7)
free-flowing layout. A store-layout system that allows shoppers to move about freely, increasing the probability of impulse buying. (14)
frescoed wall. Paintings done rapidly with water color on wet plaster. (11)
frescoes. Paintings done on freshly spread moist plaster with water-based pigments. (9)
fun theory. A theory that focuses on a way of changing human behavior for the better by making a dreaded or tedious task fun to do. (10)
furniture plan. A plan that uses templates or furniture symbols to show the locations of furnishings and equipment once the spaces are identified in the building footprint and roughly drawn in proportion to actual size; helps identify whether more or less space is needed for furnishings and equipment. (6)
furniture, fixtures, and equipment (FF & E). The many objects used in residential and commercial interiors. (2)

G

gables. Vertical triangular ends of a building. (9)
gadi. Thin, floor-mounted mattresses for sitting. (9)
Gestalt theory. A theory related to visual perception and psychology that concerns how the human brain perceives and organizes visual information into categories or groups. (7)
glazing. The use of glass as a construction material or the construction process a tradesperson uses to fit glass into frames. (11)
golden rectangle. A rectangle with sides in the *golden ratio* of 1:1.618. (7)
golden section. A proportion in which the ratio of the whole to the larger part is the same as the ratio of the larger part to the smaller, moving in progressions of 3 to 5 to 8 to 13 to 21. (7)
graphic communication. Includes shapes, pictures, and lettering used in combination to allow both the client and designer to understand the purpose of the communication. (5)
green interiors. Those interiors that incorporate the use of products that are healthy for humans, save landfill space, and adhere to earth-friendly criteria of quality, sustainability, beauty, and time-tested performance. (2)
green-design practices. Those practices that protect peoples' health and welfare in the built environment. (3)
greenwashing. The unethical practice of indicating a product is *green* when it is not. (10)
grid layout. A store-layout system that steers shoppers in a zigzag pattern through parallel rows of aisles. (14)
Gross World Product (GWP). The sum value of all final products and services produced worldwide in a given year. (1)
gypsum board. A mixture of gypsum (calcium sulfate), additives (often starch, paper pulp, and emulsifiers) and water that forms a thick paste or slurry. (11)

H

halogen lamp. A type of incandescent lamp that provides crisp, white light; comes in both line voltage and low voltage and has a longer life that traditional incandescent. (8)
harmony. The combination of design elements and principles in an aesthetically pleasing or orderly whole; a planned balance of unity and variety in a space. (7)
health, safety, and well-being (HSW). A key responsibility and legal liability of the interior design profession to produce designs that do not adversely impact the public; also health, safety, and welfare when referring to legislation (1)
high-intensity discharge lamp (HID). Constructed with an inner arc tube inside a large, pressurized glass envelop; light occurs when an electrical arc passes between the cathodes in the pressurized tube, causing the metallic additives to vaporize; longer lamp life, much illumination per watt of energy, and can operate in a variety of indoor and outdoor temperatures. (8)
high-pressure sodium (HPS) lamp. A type of high-intensity discharge lamp that uses sodium vapor for illumination; HPS lamps have the best lumens per watt (LPW) rating. (8)
historic period. An interval of time, often depicted as a fixed time frame with a beginning and an end. (9)
hotel glam. Glamorous hotel details such as big, bright spaces, back-lit cabinet mirrors, and zesty details like a zebra print on the bathtub. (15)
hotelling. The ability for mobile employees to check into an office space at their employer's office—similar to checking into a hotel—to use the space to conduct necessary business without having exclusive ownership/assignment of the space. (3)
hue. The pure name of a color. (8)
human scale. The perception people experience within a space. (7)

I

ideation drawing. A drawing that generates and explores ideas and design concepts generally during the Schematic design phase, including bubble and block diagrams, concept drawings, and sketches. (13)

immersion. The use of logical design elements to showcase a location's unique materials, cultures, and traditions which provide visitors with memorable, flavorful experiences. (3)

incandescent lamp. The oldest form of electrical light; provides a warm glow and flexibility of use; highly inefficient. Produces light by heating a filament inside a glass envelope to such a high temperature that it emits light. (8)

inclusive design. More common in European countries, this type of design supports any individual by removing barriers and improving personal well-being (for example, increasing light levels to sharpen the vision of aging eyes). (2)

incorporation. The act of forming a corporation. (4)

indirect illumination. Light that bounces off a ceiling or wall before falling into a space. (8)

indirect light. Light that shines up and down into a space. (8)

infringement. Any use of intellectual property without permission. (17)

innovation. The process of introducing creative ideas to a firm or organization than can result in increasing product or service performance; involves extracting the value from a creative idea that has direct impact on company or organization performance. (6)

intangible. Something that is abstract and creative, such as an idea. (1)

integrated design process (IDP). The collaboration of all project team members early and often throughout the project's process of design to achieve a holistic design. Also known as the *whole building design approach.* (3)

intellectual property. Something (property) that comes from a person's mind, such as an idea, invention, or process and the rights to it. (17)

interior. A space enclosed by walls, ceilings, and floors with openings such as windows and doors. (1)

interior content. Anything in a building such as personal belongings, furniture, interior materials, and wall partitions. (4)

interior decoration. The art of accessorizing and color mixing. (2)

interior design. The creation of interior environments that support the function, aesthetics, and cultures of those who inhabit interior spaces by using technologies to protect and enhance the health, safety, and well-being of those who live, work, and play in these spaces. Also, the art and science of understanding people's behavior to create functional spaces within a building. (1, 2)

internship. An educational work experience for credit that allows the student to investigate different areas of the interior design field, learn the culture of various firms, and understand how academic preparation corresponds to the practice of design. Some firms offer a small wage for internships. (5)

interpersonal skills. Skills that help people communicate and work well with each other. (17)

inversion. A design-thinking technique that involves flipping something upside down or right-side out and interpreting it or looking at it in a different way. (5)

isometric drawing. A three-dimensional drawing with three axes, each at a 30-degree angle; communicates how one space or form relates to another. (13)

J

Jack and Jill bathroom. A bathroom with two or more entrances adjoining two bedrooms. (15)

job-shadowing. An educational experience that involves following a designer for a day or more while observing and recording what the job involves; may also involve interviewing the designer. (5)

K

Kelvin temperature (k). A measurement scale used to determine the warmth or coolness of a light source. The lower the Kelvin temperature, the warmer the light; the higher the Kelvin temperature, the cooler or bluer the light appears. (8)

klismos chair. An ancient armchair with saber-shaped legs spreading outward to the front and back of the chair; common in ancient Greek households. (9)

knowledge economy. An economic system based on investing in such intangible assets as leadership, management, and human skills—such as the ability to design. (1)

kylix. A two-handled drinking cup that was common in ancient Greek households. (9)

L

lamp. The technical name for a lightbulb. (8)

lath and plaster. Historically, plaster troweled on wood lath strips in three different coats and then sealed. Today, application of plaster may be over gypsum board or concrete block. (11)

layering light. Additive light that attracts attention, highlights the focal point of the space, and provides zest or sparkle to add interest or excitement to a space. (8)

Le Corbusier's Modulor. A complex measuring system using geometric rations based on proportions of the human body to determine patterns of and for architectural design; developed in the twentieth century. (7)

LEED rating system. A system that ensures built environments are designed and built using strategies aimed at achieving high performance in key areas of human and environmental health. (2)

legend. An explanatory chart that clearly communicates with symbols the type of task or fixture that is to be included in the lighting plan; a combination of graphic symbols and notes to indicate what the symbols represent. (8, 13)

letter of agreement. An initial written letter, or contract, outlining the expectations of each party—designer and client. (6)

levy. A tax assessment that often helps pay for new commercial designs for community buildings. (3)

licensing. An assurance to the public that the buildings they enter meet a standard of physical health, safety, and security; related to state regulations that determine if a designer has the education and qualifications necessary to perform a service in question. (4)

life-cycle costs. The costs of products from purchase through disposal. (14)

life-safety issues. Those issues related to the health and safety of building occupants, such as inclusion of safe egress, smoke detectors and fire alarm systems, backup power and light systems, and fire extinguishers. (6)

light-emitting diodes (LED). A semiconductor material imbedded in a plastic chip produces light when electrical current energizes the chip causing an interaction between the electrical field and phosphor inside the plastic capsule. LEDs are durable, strong, and long-lasting. (8)

limited liability company (LLC). A combination of a general partnership and a corporation—developed as a partnership but with limited liability protection of a corporation. (4)

line. An element of design that connects two points. (7)

lines of sight. The views down a corridor or passage. (14)

linoleum. A natural flooring material consisting of linseed oils, rosins (an amber-colored sap from pine trees), and wood flour (salvaged from sawdust) placed on a natural jute backing. (11)

load-bearing wall. A wall that holds up the roof and supports the building structure. (4)

lock-off unit. Self-contained living quarters consisting of an apartment with a separate entrance attached to the main home. (3)

loggia. A roofed outdoor living space overlooking an open court from an upper story. (9)

loop layout. A store-layout system that uses a circular pathway around a central display. (14)

luminaire. A lighting fixture. (8)

M

manufactured fibers. Those fibers that consist of a combination of such materials as wood cellulose, coal, gas, oil, and chemicals. (11)

market assessment. An assessment that identifies the perceived needs in the community or overseas, the competition, and the demand for services based on economy, geographical locale, and resources available. (4)

market niche. A specialized market. (4)

market segment. One or more potential customers that is more likely to utilize the services of a firm, thereby creating a market niche. (4)

marquetry. Elaborate patterns formed by inserting pieces of wood, shell, or ivory into a wood veneer and applying it to furniture. (9)

material board. A sample board prepared by the designer that contains swatches of interior materials as well as photographs of furniture proposed for the spaces based on the client's concept and program. (6)

Material Safety Data Sheet (MSDS). A document that contains important information about the characteristics of and actual or potential hazards of a substance. (11)

matrix. A concise visual summary that organizes the client's Program requirements. (6)

memo sample. The reproduction of the design in a carpet sample for the client to view and approve. (11)

mercury vapor (MV) lamp. A type of high-intensity discharge lamp that uses radiation from mercury vapor to provide illumination. (8)

metal halide lamp. A type of high-intensity discharge lamp that uses metal halides and metallic vapors to illuminate the lamp. (8)

metamerism. When two colors appear to be the same under one light source but not under another light source. (8)
millwork. The common name for wood used on walls as built-in units, cabinetry baseboards and crown molding, and paneling. (11)
minaret. A tall, slender tower with one or more balconies from which a call to prayer can be made. (9)
minimalist. Design characterized by extreme sparseness and simplicity. (5)
mixed-use design facilities. A phrase that describes those structures that combine elements of commercial and residential design spaces in the same facility. (3)
model. A scaled representation of a structure or interior space that shows space planning, millwork, doors, windows, and possibly furniture. (13)
monochromatic color scheme. A color scheme that utilizes one hue in multiple and different values and intensities. (8)
motif. Repeated elements in an ornamental design. (9)
Murphy bed. A convertible bed that pulls down for sleeping and later folds up into a closet for out-of-the-way storage. (15)

N

nanometer. One billionth of a meter. (8)
natural fibers. Those fibers that come from plant (cellulosic) or animal (protein) sources. (11)
networking. The cultivation of productive relationships for employment or business. (17)
nosocomial. A reference to hospital-acquired infections. (14)
nonload-bearing wall. A wall that helps shape a space but does not support the structure. (4)
nonverbal communication. Facial expressions, gestures, eye contact, posture, and tone of voice used in communication. (5)

O

occupant. A person who occupies a space. (14)
off-gassing. Fumes produced by interior materials used in spaces, such as new carpet. (10)
open-office planning. A type of office design that involves groupings and partitions to encourage more collaboration among workers. (2)
operating agreement. A document required by many states that identifies the percentage of each member's ownership; describes each member's responsibilities, duties, and powers; explains how the business will distribute profits and losses; describes how and when meetings are held; and identifies procedures for buying out or transferring interest when members leave. (4)
ormolu. A gold, brass, or bronze decoration fastened to furniture. (9)
orthographic drawing. A drawing that shows the height, width, and depth of a three-dimensional space on a two-dimensional drawing; includes floor plans, elevations, and sections. (13)

P

palladian windows. Large windows divided into three parts with a large arched center section flanked by two flat-topped sections. (9)
panic bars. Spring loaded metal bars on the inside of an outward-opening door used to push in emergencies. (14)
paraline drawing. An accurate three-dimensional drawing that allows the viewer to see multiple surfaces of an interior (typically from an aerial view); also known as an *axonometric* (ak-suh-noh-MEH-trik) *projection*. (13)
partnership. A business structure that involves two or more people who carry on business, sharing the vision, risks, workload, profits, losses, and stresses of the business. (4)
patent. A document that protects intellectual property—such as a unique, or novel design or invention—for a limited time. (4)
patina. A surface appearance that grows beautiful with age. (7)
pattern. The repetition of a specific motif (artistic design) in an orderly manner. (7)
pattern match. The alignment of a pattern repeat on strips of wallcovering where the two edges meet. (11)
peripherals. Technology-related items designers use in addition to hardware and software and may include a scanner, digital or phone camera, external hard drive, or USB drive. (13)
permit. An official document or certificate issued by the authority—such as a city/county building department having jurisdiction—which authorizes the performance of a specific activity. (16)
permitting statute. An amendment to an existing architecture law allowing interior design professionals who meet the education, experience, and examination requirements of the profession to submit plans for and acquire building permits within their scope of service. (4)

personal autonomy. The freedom to separate self from others, to be alone with thoughts and feelings, to explore personal limitations, and strive for independence. (15)

personal space. The physical distance between two or more people, or from an object. (10)

personalization. The stamp of personal personality and a reflection of values, preferences, or territory on a place or space. (10)

perspective drawing. A drawing technique designers use to show a three-dimensional space on a two-dimensional plane. (6)

perspective drawing. A three-dimensional drawing that shows volumes and relationships of space in a two-dimensional realm; allowing for a more realistic looking image of an interior space. (13)

photo tracing. A one- or two-point perspective the designer draws over a photo of a client's interior (the photo serves as a grid template). (13)

photorealism. A rendering style that looks like photography; also *photoreal.* (13)

pigments. Substances that impart black, white, or a color to other materials that absorb certain parts of the light wave and reflect others. (8)

pilasters. Slightly projecting columns applied to a wall; found in private residences during the Baroque period. (9)

pile. The surface face yarns of carpet that form loops during tufting or weaving. (11)

place attachment. An emotion that evolves over time and involves the positive bonds to a particular place, such as a childhood home. (10)

placemaking. A concept originating in the 1960s, the goal of which is to evoke feelings of pleasure, happiness, and well-being in public interiors. (10)

placemaking. The ability to transform a space from simple habitation to one that holds meaning, reflects self-identity, and evokes the history of the individual or culture. (2)

plagiarism. The act of claiming another person's material as your own. (17)

plumbing chases. False walls—either horizontal or vertical—that conceal plumbing. (14)

portfolio. Visual, fluid samples that showcase a person's design and communication abilities, and includes such items as photographs of finished interior spaces, floor-plan drawings, free-hand sketches, or conceptual models. (4)

positioning. Actions the designer takes to create a certain image, such as a recognizable brand of a service in the minds of their clients. (4)

post-occupancy evaluation (POE). A systematic evaluation of the user's opinion of the final design in which the designer analyzes the client's original goals, identifies the problem, and compares them to the final design solution. (6)

practice act. Legislation that requires individuals who practice interior design to be licensed in addition to regulating who can use the title *registered, certified,* or *licensed interior designer.* (4)

presentation drawing. A conceptual drawing designers use to illustrate design ideas and solutions in hopes of selling the proposal to the client. These drawings are generally used during the Schematic design and Design development phases. (13)

price point. Standard prices set by a designer or manufacturer. (3)

primary colors. The hues of yellow, red, and blue are primary colors. (8)

principles. Guidelines that govern the choices and actions designers take to achieve good design including creatively using the elements of design. (7)

privacy. A process that involves both seeking human interaction and controlling it. (1)

privacy regulation theory. A theory that explains why people prefer staying alone sometimes and at other times appreciate the opportunity for social interactions; a type of boundary regulation. (10)

private zones. Spaces allocated to private living. (15)

pro bono work. Professional work that is done for the public good, generally without charging a fee. (17)

problem statement. A description of issues the designer needs to address during the design process. It can be a sentence or a series of paragraphs that describe the client's issues and needs to address by the time the design process is complete. (16)

profession. An occupation that requires specialized knowledge and in-depth academic education and training. (2)

profitability. A business concept that shows the importance of making more money than is spent. (4)

Program. A written or visual document that presents an ideal scenario for the client's new space. (14)

projection. According to Francis Ching, a projection is "...the technique of representing a three-dimensional object by extending all its points by straight lines, called projectors, to a picture plane, an imaginary transparent plane." (13)

proportion. The relationship between a whole object and one of its parts. (7)

proprietary information. Any work that employees of a company create on the job and is owned by the company. (17)

prototype. An idea produced in three dimensions; an original model of a product or idea. (6)

prototypical layouts. Layouts based on the minimum square-footage requirement for the tasks people perform in a space. (14)

proxemics. The study of how humans use space and how it relates to environmental and cultural factors; developed by anthropologist Edward T. Hall. (10)

public zones. Social areas that include the entry, living room, great room, dining room, and guest bathroom. (15)

punch lists. Lists of tasks the builder or subcontractor completes—during and after construction—before the final building inspection and client occupation of a space. (6, 14)

punctuality. The quality of being on time. (17)

Q

qualitative research. A type of research,—such as personal observations that require a judgment and more than *yes* and *no* answers to questions—to determine how the existing structure and spaces shape human behavior. (6)

quality of light. Subjective in nature, quality of light allows users to function comfortably in an interior, feel safe in it, and appreciate its design aesthetics. (8)

quantitative research. A type of research that deals with facts and figures that can be numerically analyzed, such as diagrams of peak times consumers visit a store.

quantity of light. The amount of light in footcandles needed to be safe and to function in a space. (8)

R

radial balance. When all elements radiate out from one center point in a circular fashion similar to spokes on a wheel. (7)

raster-based. An image-editing application that uses pixels to form images rather than mathematical formulas. As pixels increase in size, raster-based images tend to degrade. (13)

reassembly. Splicing something into puzzle pieces and rearranging them into a new design or viewing them from a new perspective for a new purpose. (5)

refracts. When light splits apart as it travels through a prism and appears to the human eye as a rainbow. (8)

relational bubble diagram. Two-dimensional illustrations that capture the priority of relationships of spaces to each other as identified in the adjacency matrix. (6)

rendering. The process of adding color, values, textures, and patterns to a representative interior or exterior space using a variety of manual or digital tools. (13)

request for proposal (RFP). A design plan submitted by a designer or design firm to a government entity that requests it. The designer or design firm is not under contract with the government entity. (3)

re-scaling. Interpreting and envisioning a different scale (larger or smaller) for an object or situation. (6)

residential design. The process of designing the interiors for primary residences and secondary dwellings. (2)

resilient flooring. Flooring that is flexible and provides impact absorption. (11)

respect. The feeling that someone or something is good, valuable, and important. (17)

restrike time. A period of time (usually two to 10 minutes) in which the inner arc tube of an HID lamp needs to cool down before restarting the lamp. (8)

retention of services. A contract that both the designer and client sign when both agree the designer's skills match the client's needs. (6)

retro. A style that is fashionably nostalgic of the past. (12)

rhythm. A creative, repetitive blend of movement and visual form in a conscious, regular arrangement. (7)

S

scale. The size of an object or building relative to a known constant, such as the human body. (7)

schematics. Quick drawings the designer uses to help the client envision floor plans, circulation patterns, three-dimensional spaces, and more. (6)

scope creep. Project requirements a client adds to existing project demands that are not defined in the scope of work. (4)

scope of services. The type and extent of design services or tasks the designer completes for the client's design project which affects the associated fees. Also *scope of work.* (4)

sculpted. The three-dimensional appearance of carpet, typically with the higher loops cut and the lower loops uncut. (11)

secondary colors. Colors formed by mixing two primary colors together; green, orange, and purple. (8)

section. An elevation drawing that shows a series of multiple walls from different rooms along a consecutive plan; a vertical slice cut through a series of elevations along the entire length or width of a building. (6)

selective admissions process. A process a student goes through at the college level for getting into a major of choice. (5)

selective advancement process. A portfolio-review process a student goes through to move into sophomore, junior, or senior levels of a college program. (5)

sense-of-place. A personal experience in a place and how a person feels about it. (3)

sense-of-self. Your personal identity or who you are as a person. (3)

sense-of-self theory. A theory that involves the selection of objects or symbols to communicate personal identity to others, relating to human comfort. (10)

service learning. A method of learning that combines classroom instruction with meaningful community service. (17)

shade. Darker values that result from adding black to a hue. (8)

shape. The shape that is created when the beginning and ending points of any line meet. (7)

Shibui. A Japanese color concept in which neutral colors are closely blended with accents of bright hues. (9)

shirred. A decorative gathering created by sewing a rod-pocket casing in the heading and sliding the rod through the casing of a curtain. (11)

shoji screens. Wood and rice paper screens serving as walls, partitions, or sliding doors. (9)

shop drawings. A set of drawings the contractor produces that show understanding about the fabrication and installation of specific parts of the work on a project. (6)

sick building syndrome (SBS). A term used to identify acute health and discomfort effects that people experience after spending time in a building. (4)

sidewise. A design-thinking technique that involves twisting something 180 degrees to view it from a different angle. (5)

signage. The symbols and text used to visually communicate directions and locations of divisions. (14)

simultaneous contrast. The contrast that occurs when colors placed side by side appear to change; colors appear to vibrate or *sing*. (8)

site visit. Visiting the site of a project to gather information. (6)

sketch. A rough drawing with little detail that serves as a preliminary study of a space. (6)

sketching. The use of fluid, loose lines to communicate an idea, concept, object, or space. These quick drawings use approximate measurements to capture the main features of a space or interior. (13)

smart space. Space equipped with a screen, speakerphone, projection device, sound, large computer screen, and controls to operate technology. (14)

socially responsible design. An approach to design rather than a specific set of standards; the use of design to address social, environmental, economic, and political issues that embrace humanitarian values. (10)

sociofugal. Grid-like spaces that discourage interaction and communication with others. (10)

sociopetal. Spaces that encourage interaction and communication with others, such as tightly grouped chairs in a coffee shop. (10)

sole proprietorship. A type of business structure in which the company and owner is one entity. (4)

solid modeling. A mathematical technique for representing solid objects that ensures all surfaces meet properly and that the object is geometrically correct. A CAD technique. (13)

solid-state light (SSL). Refers to a type of lighting that uses light-emitting diodes as a source of illumination rather than filaments or gas. (8)

space. A volume within an enclosure. (1)

space planning. The analysis and design of interior spaces in response to occupancy needs. Moving forms, such as walls and partitions, within a space. (3, 7)

spade feet. Tapered, rectangular furniture feet resembling the blade of a garden shovel or spade. (9)

specifications. Precise, detailed information that builders and tradespeople use to describe the appearance, performance, and construction methods used for the building of a structure or interior. (6)

spectral power distribution. Charts indicating the color emitting from a light source in specific wavelengths at each wavelength over the visible spectrum. (8)

split-complementary color scheme. A color scheme that consists of three colors—one main hue plus two hues each adjacent to its complement. (8)

stimulation theory. A theory that explains the environment as a source of sensory information gathered through sight, sound, touch, taste, and smell. Each sense can be overstimulated or understimulated. This theory typically applies to interior spaces through the sense of sight. (10)

stippling. Small, soft touches of paint or ink that together produce an even or softly graded shadow to add a level of darkness to walls and planes. (13)

stone veneer. A thin ornamental facing of stone. (11)

stretcher. A horizontal brace extending between the legs of a table or chair to prevent furniture from collapsing under its own weight. (9)

style. Designs reflective of an *individual, group,* or *philosophy of design* within a certain time period. (9)

subcontractor. The individuals or firms—often specific tradespeople—who contract to perform all or part of a project's work. (3)

subtractive color. Color that results from the use of the pigments red (magenta), yellow, and blue; when all light rays are absorbed the viewer sees black. (8)

surface modeling. A mathematical technique for representing solid-appearing objects that cannot be sliced open to examine volume and mass; can be geometrically incorrect. A CAD technique. (13)

sustainability. A way of using resources that does not deplete them; involves a method or practice or way of using materials that has minimal long-term effect on the environment. (2)

sustainable design. An environmental responsibility that considers the protection of the health and welfare of global ecosystems for current and future generations. (3)

symbols. A type of pictorial shorthand. (13)

symmetrical balance. The arrangement of objects on both sides of a center point or line (either vertical axis or horizontal axis) that results in a mirror image. (7)

T

tactile texture. Surface textures that can be felt through simple human touch. (7)

tagline. A phrase that identifies a business. (4)

take-off. The process of estimating how much product to order by examining the set of construction drawings. (11)

tambour shutter. Narrow strips of wood glued on canvas. (12)

task lighting. A direct form of light that usually provides three times the level of light as ambient light. (8)

tatami floor mat. Modular floor mats that served as interior flooring material that controlled the proportional planning of Japanese interiors. (9)

telecommuter. A worker who conducts work from anyplace but his or her business office; also called *nomad workers.* (3)

tenant improvement work (TI). A process that involves design and construction upgrades to the interior design of a leased space. The lessor often pays for a small part of the upgrades to attract tenants; however, the tenant pays for the majority of changes to the interior space. (3)

territoriality. The need to control a fixed area by laying claim to it. (1)

tertiary colors. Intermediary colors formed by mixing a primary with a secondary color; yellow-green, blue-green, blue-violet, red-violet, red-orange, yellow-orange. (8)

test fit. The process of using the client's square footage needs and testing it—or diagramming it—into different available building spaces the client may lease in the desired location. (14)

tetrad color scheme. A color scheme consisting of four colors that are equally spaced along the color wheel. (8)

thermal mass. The ability of a material to store heat and slowly release it. (11)

third place. A setting—different from home, school, or work—that meets a person's social needs and where he or she can develop a sense of community with others. (10)

thumbnail sketch. Small sketches the designer uses to draw what a hypothetical space may look like prior to making recommendations to the client. (16)

time management. The practice of organizing time and work assignments to increase personal efficiency. (17)

tint. Lighter values that result from adding white to a hue. (8)

title act. Legislation that guarantees the right of an interior designer to use a certain title such as *licensed interior designer, registered interior designer,* or *certified interior designer.* (4)

title block. A rectangular box, typically in the lower-right corner of a page that includes key project information such as the design firm name, design firm contact information with logo, name of the client, professional seals, sheet title and number, and job number and completion date. (13)

tone. Addition of gray to a hue to lower its chroma or intensity. (8)

tongue-and-groove. A wood joint with a tongue on one edge that fits into the corresponding groove on another edge. (11)

trademark. A documented mark that protects such specific intellectual property as words, phrases, designs, or symbols—brand, logo, and taglines are examples. (4)

traffic patterns. The patterns in which users move *within* a space. (15)

transference. The application of an idea from one context to another. (6)

triadic color scheme. A color scheme consisting of three colors that are equally spaced along the color wheel. (8)
trompe l'oeil. A French word roughly translated to mean "to fool the eye." (9)
tufting. The manufacture of carpet by inserting tufts of yarn through a carpet-backing fabric. (11)
turnings. Decorations formed by using a lathe. (9)

U

unity. A set of conscious choices to tie the composition together, a sense of order, oneness, and uniformity. (7)
universal design. Developed by Ron Mace, universal design is the "...design of products and environments to be usable by all people, to the greatest extent possible, without adaptation or specialized design." (2)
upholstered furniture. Furniture that uses a frame, cushioning material, and covering. (12)

V

value. Describes the lightness or darkness of a color. (8)
vanishing point. The point at which all parallel lines merge on the horizon line. (13)
variety. The absence of monotony or sameness. (7)
vector-based. A drawing application that uses mathematical formulas to create lines the designer can combine into shapes to produce two- and three-dimensional documents. (13)
veiling reflection. Glare and shadows that make it difficult to see when performing a task. (8)
veneers. Thin overlays of wood. (9)
vernacular dwellings. Indigenous dwellings created using native materials without the influence of architects. (9)
vinyl composition tile (VCT). A flooring material composed of 85 percent limestone filler, polyvinyl chloride (PVC) resins, stabilizers, and pigments; thin sheets form under heat and pressure and are then cut into 12-inch squares. (11)
visible spectrum. The portion of colored light within the electromagnetic spectrum that is visible to the human eye. (8)
visioning session. A mental process in which you explore images of the desired future project; also called an in-depth client interview. (16)
visual literacy. The ability to interpret and derive meaning from the composition of images rather than words. (7)
visual scale. A comparison of one object to another as perceived with the eyes. (7)
visual texture. A perception or illusion of physical texture. (7)
volatile organic compounds (VOCs). Chemical-emitting gases or solids from interior products and materials that can cause short-term or long-term adverse health effects. (10)

W

wainscoting. Paneling on the lower three or four feet of a wall. (9)
walk-off mat. A portable mat at entrance points to remove and collect dirt from shoes before stepping onto soft- or hard-surface flooring. (11)
warm colors. Those colors that perceptually appear to advance toward you in a space. (8)
wayfinding. The use of signs and graphics to help individuals easily find their way when travelling through a building. (3)
wireframe mesh model. A CAD technique for representing three-dimensional objects in which all surfaces are visibly outlined in lines, including the opposite sides and all internal components that are normally hidden from view. (13)
work ethic. A set of values that promote hard work and diligence (for instance, team members work hard for the team). (3)
work rectangle. The four major work areas: sink, cooktop/oven, refrigerator, and microwave oven. (15)
work triangle. The historic three major work areas: sink, cooktop/oven, and refrigerator. (15)
work zones. Highly functional areas where any type of work occurs. (15)
working drawings. Construction documents, or drawings, that builders and tradespeople use to guide the building of a structure; historically called *blueprints*. (6)
woven. A type of carpet produced on a weaving loom by interlacing the warp (length) yarns and weft or filling (width) yarns. (11)

Z

zones. An organizational technique that groups together areas or spaces with similar activities or functions in a space. (6)

Index

B

D

E

F

G

H

I

J

K

L

M

N

O

P

S

T

U

V